Knowledge Solutions

Olivier Serrat

Knowledge Solutions

Tools, Methods, and Approaches to Drive
Organizational Performance

Olivier Serrat
Asian Development Bank
Mandaluyong
Philippines

Additional material to this book can be downloaded from http://extras.springer.com.

ISBN 978-981-10-0982-2   ISBN 978-981-10-0983-9   (eBook)
DOI 10.1007/978-981-10-0983-9

Library of Congress Control Number: 2016943039

Foreword

The Asian Development Bank strives to improve people's lives in a world of heightening interaction between globalization and advances in knowledge, technology, and innovation. To meet the increasingly complex challenges of a fast-transforming Asia and Pacific, and seize opportunities, it aims to offer "finance ++"—finance plus leverage plus knowledge—to raise the effectiveness of its operations.

Are we doing things right? Are we doing the right things? How do we decide what is right? If organizational and operational effectiveness is about getting results from purpose, processes, and people, we must all improve at reflecting *on* action and reflecting *in* action. To reflect unremittingly on content, process, and premise with self-knowledge, critical thinking, inquisitiveness, and emotional intelligence, our organizational development endeavors must encompass such subjects as change, structure, culture, strategy, systems, values, decision making, leadership, teamwork, alliances, human capital, learning, creativity and entrepreneurship, communications, incentives, engagement, networking, corporate reputation, technology, measurements and scorecards, and resilience, to name but a few. All through, the management of knowledge has a decidedly important role to play. Knowledge management is not an abstract matter: identifying, creating, storing, sharing, and using knowledge—both individual and collective—is a real-world imperative that can prime organizational performance.

A "signature" knowledge product of ADB, this compendium of *Knowledge Solutions* offers a healthy mix of ecological, organizational, and techno-centric perspectives on how organizations can ignite performance. Its wide-ranging and time-tested tools, methods, and approaches, arranged in a comprehensive framework for competence-building, will help facilitate decision making, build a learning organization, and stimulate creativity and innovation. I am certain these *Knowledge Solutions* will be heartily welcome and of immediate use in the public, private, and third sectors; they will be of interest in academia too, for instance in Master of Business Administration programs around the world.

Amy S.P. Leung
Deputy Director General concurrently Chief Thematic Officer
Sustainable Development and Climate Change Department
Asian Development Bank

Preface

In 2000, Jeffrey Pfeffer and Robert Sutton[1] argued that the gap between knowing and doing is greater than that between ignorance and knowing. To translate great ideas into everyday actions, organizations must close the knowing–doing gap, which arises when talk substitutes for action, memory replaces thinking, fear prevents acting on knowledge, measurement obstructs good judgment, and internal competition turns friends into enemies. These *Knowledge Solutions* offer organizations tools, methods, and approaches with which to bridge the gap.

If core insights are about "know why", the powerful motivator one must assume organizations have else they will not perdure, core competencies are about "know-how", the processes that will take them there and generate results. Competence is the state or quality of being adequately or well qualified to deliver a specific action, function, or task successfully; it is also what knowledge, skills, or behaviors improve performance. In organizations, core competencies are deep proficiencies that open access to markets and create and deliver unique value to clients, audiences, and partners there; the litmus test is that they differentiate an organization and are difficult to copy or imitate. Organizational and operational effectiveness derives from strenuous efforts to identify, cultivate, and exploit an organization's core competencies, the tangible fruits of which are composite packages of products, services, processes, and methods of delivery—or other elements of business models such as policy and strategy or system interaction—that anticipate and meet demand.

To improve people's lives, the Asian Development Bank partners with a myriad of stakeholders: they are government bodies, international organizations, multilateral development banks, humanitarian aid organizations, bilateral donors, the private sector, foundations, civil society, nongovernment organizations, community-based organizations, research institutes and think tanks, academia, and youth. Not to forget, ADB itself is both a source of knowledge and an audience

---

[1]Jeffrey Pfeffer and Robert Sutton. 2000. *The Knowing–Doing Gap: How Smart Companies Turn Knowledge into Action*. Harvard Business School Press.

ready to listen as *ADB: Reflections and Beyond*,[2] its seminal exercise in storytelling, demonstrated. Across the public, private, and third sectors, then, as well as ADB itself, this compendium of *Knowledge Solutions* can build competencies in the areas of strategy development, management techniques, collaboration mechanisms, knowledge sharing and learning, and knowledge capture and storage—all of which are essential to high-performance organizations. A bonus is that about half of the *Knowledge Solutions* are also arranged in 11 recurrent themes such as corporate creativity and innovation, creating teams with an edge, leading in organizations, making partnerships work, and nurturing knowledge ecologies.

Mandaluyong, Philippines   Olivier Serrat

---

[2]ADB. 2010. *ADB: Reflections and Beyond*. Manila.

Contents

Author and Contributors

About the Author

Olivier Serrat is a principal knowledge management specialist in the Asian Development Bank. A staunch advocate of learning, he has written numerous publications and developed multiple initiatives to prime and energize organization, people, knowledge, and technology for learning, and help ADB evolve into a learning organization that continuously improves its development effectiveness and is accountable to its stakeholders.

On his current agenda is the *ADB Sustainable Development Timeline* project, an anthology of videos he conceived to catalog landmarks in ADB's operations since 1966. From 2008–2012, Olivier served as Head of ADB's Knowledge Management Center. In that capacity, he was the focal point for implementing and monitoring the progress of ADB's knowledge management framework, and responsible for overseeing the development and delivery of ADB's knowledge management agenda. To guide ADB's transformation into a learning organization, Olivier formulated *Enhancing Knowledge Management under Strategy 2020*—that plan of action sharpened the knowledge focus in ADB's operations, empowered the communities of practice, strengthened external knowledge partnerships, and further enhanced staff learning and skills development. In 2010, Olivier produced *ADB: Reflections and Beyond*, an archive of the memories and experiences of senior and younger personnel of ADB, past and present, and the *Guidelines for Knowledge Partnerships*, which specified the essentials of designing such collaborative arrangements for performance, articulated building blocks, and underscored success factors and special considerations. In 2009, he wrote *Learning for Change in ADB* to give timely, practical guidance to support and energize learning. In 2008, he introduced the *Knowledge Solutions* series to offer handy, quick reference guides to tools, methods, and approaches to drive organizational performance. In 2008 also, he introduced the *Knowledge Showcases* series to highlight innovative ideas from ADB technical assistance and other knowledge products to promote further discussion and research. In 2006–2008, Olivier's brief in ADB's Operations

Evaluation Department was to leverage knowledge management to help ADB become a learning organization that continuously improves its development effectiveness and is accountable to its stakeholders. In 2007, he wrote *Independent Evaluation at the Asian Development Bank*, a retrospective that highlighted accomplishments since 1978 but looked to the future. That year, he also drafted *Learning Lessons in ADB* to set the strategic framework for knowledge management in operations evaluation. *Auditing the Lessons Architecture*, published in 2008, described a knowledge audit methodology developed to tie in with audiences for evaluation. With the addition of *Learning for Change in ADB* in 2009, these three short books were published in 2010 under the title of *Learning in Development*.

Olivier's specialties include environmental management, evaluation, knowledge management, project design, project implementation, public relations, and strategic planning. He obtained an undergraduate degree in economics from the University of Kent and a master's degree in agricultural economics from the University of London.

Contributors

Frances Marie Alcaraz is a freelance illustrator.

Philip Ash was formerly advisor (human resources), Asian Development Bank.

Albert Dean Atkinson is a principal human resource specialist, Asian Development Bank.

Haidy Ear-Dupuy is a social development specialist (civil society and participation), Asian Development Bank.

Norman Lu is a senior results management officer, Asian Development Bank.

Peter Malvicini is a management consultant.

Muriel Ordoñez is a communications specialist, Asian Development Bank.

Arnaldo Pellini is a research fellow, Overseas Development Institute.

Part I
Strategy Development

Proposition 1
Linking Research to Practice

In a Word The volume of research greatly exceeds its application in practice. Researchers must pay greater attention to the production of their research findings in a flexible range of formats in recognition of the varied needs of consumers.

Knowledge Increases by Diffusion and Grows by Dispersion

Research is about both generation and dissemination of findings. In spite of this, disseminating research findings has often been an afterthought in busy research agendas. When the funding of a research program is considered, insufficient time and money are set aside to link research to practice. And, if efforts have in truth been made to incorporate dissemination into the earliest stages of planning, experience reveals that matching the research design to the characteristics of intended users is not easy. No matter what, research findings will simply not be used if the latter are ignored. And so, willy-nilly, research institutions have come to agree that they must find ways to relate research findings to practical applications in planning, policy making, program administration, and delivery of services. There is evidence that they are becoming better at this: some pay attention to the production of research findings in a wide range of formats in recognition of the variety of users. Notwithstanding, while important initiatives undoubtedly exist, research findings

© Asian Development Bank 2017
O. Serrat, *Knowledge Solutions*, DOI 10.1007/978-981-10-0983-9_1

still do not inform practice to the extent that they should. For each research agenda, this calls for a dissemination policy, a dissemination plan, and a dissemination strategy. Dissemination tactics will then come into play.

Articulating a Dissemination Policy

A dissemination policy is the expression of a research institution's mission and values to its staff members and to the public. It establishes a common vision and the values and measures that will be engaged to achieve accessibility to information content. A dissemination policy can be an effective and economical instrument that links research to practice: rarely do research institutions explain how efforts at dissemination will be tied to utilization.

Drawing a Dissemination Plan

The most successful dissemination processes are usually designed before the start of a research agenda. Dissemination should produce a response—utilization of the research findings—on the part of users. In drawing a dissemination plan, researchers should consider at least the following major elements:

- **Impact and Outcomes** What is the desired impact of dissemination?[1] What outcomes does the dissemination plan aim to accomplish? In what ways will users benefit?
- **Users** Which users are most affected by the research? Which would be most interested in learning of the research findings? What are their scope and characteristics?
- **Information Content** Does the information content match the users' expressed informational needs? Does the comprehension level required to understand the information content match the characteristics of the users? Is the information content reviewed through a quality control mechanism to ensure accuracy and relevance?
- **Medium** What is the most effective dissemination method to reach each user group? What resources does each group typically access? What capabilities does each group have?

---

[1]The desired impact of dissemination is, simply, utilization. The basic reason to acquire and then disseminate new research-based information is to ensure that it is appropriately considered for use in making decisions, driving changes, or taking action designed to improve outcomes. The critical element of utilization is that the research finding must be thoroughly digested: the users must assimilate it in their understanding and experience.

Table. Characteristics of an effective dissemination plan

1	The plan orientates itself to the needs of the users. It relies on appropriate form, language, and information content levels
2	The plan incorporates various dissemination methods, such as written, graphical, electronic, and verbal media. The methods include research summary documents; press releases; media coverage; flyers, posters, and brochures; letters of thanks to study participants; newsletters to study participants; events and conferences; and seminars. Each method calls for its own format and means of dissemination and includes both proactive and reactive channels—that is, it includes information content that users have identified as important and information content that users may not know to request but are likely to need. The dissemination methods are more likely to succeed when their packaging and information content has been influenced by appropriate inputs from the users
3	The plan draws on existing resources, relationships, and networks to the maximum extent possible. It also builds the new resources, relationships, and networks needed by users
4	The plan includes effective quality control mechanisms to ensure that the information content is accurate, relevant, and representative
5	The plan establishes linkages to resources that may be required to implement the information content, e.g., technical assistance

Source Author

- **Execution** When should each aspect of the dissemination plan occur? Who should be responsible for dissemination activities?
- **Obstacles** What potential obstacles may interfere with access to or utilization of the research findings by each user group? What actions could be developed to overcome these obstacles?
- **Accomplishment** How will accomplishment be described and measured? If data is to be gathered, who will gather it?

Dissemination processes based on mechanical, one-way flow of written information have not been successful in encouraging adoption and implementation of research findings.

Developing a Dissemination Strategy

A dissemination plan outlines basic elements that must be implemented. A dissemination strategy can be understood in terms of how a research institution will address particular issues to ensure that dissemination leads to utilization. The most successful dissemination strategies will be broad based and formulated so that the unexpected does not cause the dissemination plan to fail. The major issues related to a dissemination strategy include:

- **Users** Is the readiness of the users to change limited? Are there needs for widely divergent formats and levels of information content? Is the number of trusted information sources limited?

- **Source** Is the credibility of experience limited? Is the level of perceived competence low? Is the motive suspect?
- **Information Content** Is confidence in the quality of research and its methodology low? Is the credibility of outcomes limited? Is the utility and relevance of the information content unclear? Are there cost implications to access to information content? Is the format of the information content nonuser friendly?
- **Context** Are there competing research findings? Does the general economic climate or circumstances favor adoption of research findings? Can the research findings find practical application in the field?
- **Medium** Is the information content clear and attractive? Is the dissemination method flexible and reliable? Is the dissemination method cost-effective? Are the time frames required to access the information content lengthy?

Applying Dissemination Tactics

Strategy is the overall effect one wishes to create; tactics are the method by which one wishes to achieve that effect. Dissemination tactics can be basic or advanced depending on the scale and complexity of the dissemination plan.

Proposition 2
Creating and Running Partnerships

In a Word Partnerships have a crucial role to play in the development agenda. To reach the critical mass required to reduce poverty, there must be more concerted effort, greater collaboration, alignment of inputs, and a leveraging of resources and effort. Understanding the drivers of success and the drivers of failure helps efforts to create and run them.

Enhancing Strategic Alliances

A partnership is a formal or informal agreement between two or more partners to work together to achieve common aims. For instance, multilateral and bilateral agencies can compensate for abilities and resources that fall far short of requirements by partnering with nongovernment organizations, both national and international. Such organizations are able to form close linkages and engender ownership and participation. Their consultative and participatory methods note and express stakeholder views that might otherwise not be entertained. This enables them to identify up-and-coming issues, respond rapidly to new circumstances, and experiment with innovative approaches. Therefore, partnering can improve the relevance, effectiveness, efficiency, and sustainability of operations. However, few would-be partners fully consider the opportunities and constraints that are

© Asian Development Bank 2017
O. Serrat, *Knowledge Solutions*, DOI 10.1007/978-981-10-0983-9_2

associated with the creation and running of partnerships. A frequent cliché relates to the need to avoid duplication and overlap. Habitually, extant memoranda of agreement are worded loosely.

Drivers of Success

The drivers of success include:

- Agreement that a partnership is necessary;
- Esteem and trust between different interests;
- The leadership of a respected individual (or individuals);
- The commitment of key interests developed through a clear and open process;
- The development of a shared vision of what might be achieved;
- Shared mandates or agendas;
- The development of compatible ways of working, which presupposes organizational flexibility;
- Good communication, perhaps with the help of facilitators;
- Collaborative decision-making, with a commitment to achieving consensus;
- Effective organizational management; and
- Time to build the partnership.

Drivers of Failure

In opposition, the drivers of failure include:

- A history of conflict among key interests;
- One partner manipulates or dominates;
- Unrealistic goals and objectives;
- Differences of philosophy and ways of working;
- Poor communication;
- An unequal and unacceptable balance of power and control;
- An absence of common interests;
- Hidden or irreconcilable agendas; and
- Financial and time commitments that outweigh potential benefits.

Guidelines for Managers

In general:

- Informal partnerships work best when a project is specific and achievable.
- Where the project is complex and spans several years, it may be necessary to create formal partnership structures for decision-making.

- It is not easy to tackle a wide range of issues through an informal partnership. It is better to address such matters through consultations.
- Simply setting up a partnership structure does not solve all problems. Partners still need to clarify the joint goal and objective, values, and interests, among others.
- Partnerships do not have to be equal but the partners do need to feel that they are involved to an appropriate degree.

Guidelines for Project Officers

The following suggests how project officers can make a start:

- Clarify the goal and objective behind forming a partnership.
- Identify the stakeholders and the key interests that can help or hinder the development of a project.
- Consider who one really needs as a partner and who would really want to be a partner: some stakeholders may only want to be consulted.
- Before approaching potential partners, make sure that you have support and agreement about working with others.
- Make informal contact with partners to understand their values and interests before formulating formal proposals.
- Communicate with your partners in a language they will understand, focusing on what they may want to achieve.
- Plan the partnership process over time.
- Use a range of methods to gather people in workshop sessions as well as in formal meetings.
- Encourage ideas from partners because ownership leads to commitment.
- Be trustworthy. One of the main barriers to creating and running successful partnerships lies in the attitudes that people bring to the process. To develop trust, it is necessary to draw out and deal with suspicions from past contacts; be open about what one is trying to achieve and about problems; be prepared to make mistakes and to admit to them; and deliver what one promises.

Creating and Running Partnerships

Since partnerships are formal or informal agreements to work together to achieve common aims, there can be no recipe for success. Whatever the working arrangements, and whatever phase of the partnership one is in, there will be problems: people will not read documents or come to meetings, colleagues will fail to deliver on promises, different interest groups will have conflicting aims, deadlines will be missed, and the champions behind the partnership may become scapegoats. Notwithstanding, the need to enhance strategic alliances calls on managers and project officers to:

- Advertise country strategies and programs and details of loan, grant, and technical assistance projects through media, such as the Internet, newsletters, and public meetings, and take care to give evidence of strategic integration.
- Map potential partners for strengths, weaknesses, opportunities, and threats.
- Understand the priorities and skills of potential partners.
- Develop a partnership structure based on a clear purpose, trust, and agreement on responsibilities and accountability.
- Identify champions and communicate with them frequently.
- Build partner confidence through early participation in project work.
- Accept that partnerships need long-term support and make abilities and resources available.
- Develop a forward strategy for partnerships.
- Ensure appropriate monitoring of progress by the partnership.

The existence of commonalities of interest and memoranda of understanding offers only the promise of partnership. The onus of enhancing strategic alliances is on managers and project officers to integrate partnerships in annual operating outputs in the myriad ways that the multifarious nature of such associations dictates.

Proposition 3
Reading the Future

In a Word Scenario building enables managers to invent and then consider in depth several varied stories of equally plausible futures. They can then make strategic decisions that will be sound for all plausible futures. No matter what future takes place, one is more likely to be ready for and influential in it if one has thought seriously about scenarios. Scenario planning challenges mental models about the world and lifts the blinders that limit our creativity and resourcefulness.

Rationale

The future will not happen just because one wishes hard. It requires action now. Because nothing lasts forever and no product or service sells itself for long, small businesses and large organizations (individuals too, for that matter) have no alternative but to forerun the future, endeavor to shape it, and balance short-term and long-term objectives. This means that the short term calls for strategic decisions just as much as the long term. And so, strategic planning stands for the unremitting process of making decisions systematically with the greatest intelligence of their futurity, organizing the resources and efforts needed to carry them out, and measuring outcomes against expectations with feedback and self-control. Only then can one avoid extending carelessly past and present trends.

© Asian Development Bank 2017
O. Serrat, *Knowledge Solutions*, DOI 10.1007/978-981-10-0983-9_3

Readjusting Mindsets

More often than not, however, strategic planning holds out only one scenario that underplays the unpredictability of the world. That future stands for the set of assumptions implicit to blind spots. Yet, the point is not to pick an ideal future, hope that it will come to pass, or even strive to create it. Nor is it to find the most probable future and bet the house on it. Rather, it is to make decisions that will be suitable for all plausible futures. That is why the challenge is to develop a small set of distinct scenarios covering the main areas of uncertainty—and in so doing define direction without confining it.

Thinking the Unthinkable

A scenario is an internally consistent view of the future. Scenario analysis is the process of generating and analyzing a small set of scenarios. This exercise stretches mental models, enhancing perception of events as part of a pattern, and leads to better thinking about the future. Scenario analysis involves discrete steps (explained by Peter Schwartz (1996) in *The Art of the Long View*).

- **Uncovering the Focal Issue** For small businesses and large organizations alike, "What should our business be?" is usually the first (and natural) question. If not, the focal issue should be what keeps one awake at night.
- **Making Out Key Factors** Once the focal issue has been decided on, the next step is to identify the key factors in one's environment. What will managers want to know when they have to make choices? What will be seen as success or failure?
- **Listing Driving Forces** Then, after the key factors have been identified, the third step involves listing candidates for prime movers (driving forces) that will impact the key factors. They lie in society, technology, economics, politics, and the natural environment. This is, without doubt, the most research-intensive stage of the process of generating and analyzing scenarios; it requires much information hunting and gathering.
- **Ranking Driving Forces** Next, comes the ranking of driving forces based on two main criteria—the degree of importance vis-à-vis the focal issue, and the degree of uncertainty surrounding each driving force. The outcome of such ranking will, effectively, draw the lines along which scenarios differ. However, if scenarios are to serve as learning Learning before doing tools, the lessons that they teach must be fundamental to the resolution of the focal issue. So, the driving forces must also be few to curtail generation of scenarios around every conceivable uncertainty.

- **Fleshing Out Scenarios** The scenario skeletons can then be fleshed out with regard to the key factors in one's environment and the driving forces identified. Every one of them should be given some attention in each scenario.
- **Drawing Implications** Once the scenarios have been fleshed out, it is time to return to the focal issue and examine how it comes across in each scenario. What vulnerabilities have been revealed? Is a strategy robust across all scenarios? And, if it looks robust in only one instance, then it qualifies as a gamble.
- **Selecting Indicators** Last, it is important to know quickly which of the several scenarios is closest to the course of history as it plays out. And so, one must identify indicators to monitor. Fortunately, the coherence built into the scenarios makes easy the selection of indicators.

Abandoning Stale Pursuits

The end result of building scenarios Scenario building is not an accurate picture of tomorrow but better thinking about the future. And, since scenarios provide a context for decisions, better thinking should lead to more robust decisions. Still, just as important as the permanent process of making decisions about what things to do is planned and systematic abandonment of the old that no longer fits purpose, conveys satisfaction, or makes a contribution. As events unfold, it is therefore necessary to continue to review existing products and services (as well as processes and distribution channels). Do they still fit the realities of society, technology, economics, politics, and the natural environment? And, if not, how can one discard them, or at least stop devoting more resources and efforts? Otherwise, the best definition of the focal issue will turn out to have been a thankless exercise: energy will be used up in defending yesterday.

Reference

Schwartz P (1996) The art of the long view: planning for the future in an uncertain world. Doubleday, New York

Proposition 4
Auditing Knowledge

In a Word Knowledge audits help organizations identify their knowledge-based assets and develop strategies to manage them.

Definition

Developing a knowledge-sharing culture is a change process on the way to better organizational performance. To achieve that change, an organization needs a vision of where it wants to be and an accurate picture of where it is now—that is, its current reality. A knowledge audit is one way of taking that picture.

What is a knowledge audit? The traditional concept of an audit is an evaluation of a person, business, system, process, project, or product by an independent third party. Financial audits are well understood. They examine the financial statements of a company to check performance against standards. A knowledge audit works differently, and some demystification is called for. It is by and large—granted differing objects, breadth of coverage, and levels of sophistication—a qualitative review (or inventory, survey, check) of an organization's knowledge health at both the macro and micro levels. The defining feature of a knowledge audit is that it

© Asian Development Bank 2017
O. Serrat, *Knowledge Solutions*, DOI 10.1007/978-981-10-0983-9_4

places people at the center of concerns: it purports to find out what people know, and what they do with the knowledge they have. It can be described as an investigation of the knowledge needs of an organization and the interconnectivity among leadership, organization, technology, and learning in meeting these. Put in a different way, a knowledge audit is an investigation of the strengths and weaknesses of an organization's knowledge, and of the opportunities and threats that face it.

Purpose

A knowledge audit can have multiple purposes, but the most common is to provide tangible evidence of what knowledge an organization needs, where that knowledge is, how it is being used, what problems and difficulties exist, and what improvements can be made. Although there can be no blueprint, a typical knowledge audit will—not necessarily at the same time or level of detail[1]—query the following:

- What are an organization's knowledge needs?
- What tacit and explicit knowledge assets does it have and where are they?
- How does knowledge flow within the organization, formally and informally, and to and from clients and relevant organizations?
- How is that knowledge identified, created, stored, shared, and used?
- What obstacles are there to knowledge flows, e.g., to what extent do its people, business processes, and technology currently support or hamper the effective movement of knowledge?
- What gaps and duplications exist in the organization's knowledge?

Deliverables

Deliverables from knowledge audits are multiple, and can impact organizational performance and the individuals and groups associated severally with it. Not all can be quantified. Regardless, to be of any use, benefits cannot just be shown; they must be realized. Specifically, depending on its thrust and coverage, a knowledge audit can be expected to:

---

[1]The audit could span the whole organization, but preferably cover constituent parts of it. For the same reason that opinion polls do not sample the entire population, marginal returns diminish as the scale of related exercises increases. The same consideration applies to the number of questions that might be posed.

- help the organization identify what knowledge is needed to reach its goals and support individual and group activities;
- recognize the knowledge created and help assess its value and contribution to organizational performance, thus making it more measurable and accountable;
- give tangible evidence of the extent to which knowledge is being effectively managed and indicate where changes for the better should be made;
- identify intellectual assets and facilitate the creation of an intellectual asset register;
- distinguish pockets of knowledge that are not being used to good advantage and therefore offer untapped potential;
- review the use of external knowledge and suggest ways in which it might be used to better effect;
- assess the use and effectiveness of knowledge products such as flagship publications, how valuable they are, and how they might be improved;
- circumscribe knowledge flows and current bottlenecks within those flows;
- make out present and future knowledge gaps;
- develop knowledge and social network maps of the organization;
- supply data and information for the development of knowledge management initiatives that are directly relevant to the organization's specific knowledge needs and current situation; and
- pinpoint quick wins that could be implemented easily to produce clear, tangible, and immediate benefits.[2]

Knowledge audits might be small and discreet. But they must all give a clear direction regarding what can be achieved and must engender a realistic expectation of what might then be done with requisite resources. They must also create active interest and highlight important facts to management. They will work best if their original purpose is discussed in some detail before the audit begins. Reporting may be done both through short written reports, presentations to managers—preferably one at the divisional level and another at the departmental level—and collation of detailed results for later use.

---

[2]Benefits can come in a range of forms and need not represent a radical overthrow of organizational structures and systems. They can include smoother induction of new employees; insights for coaching, mentoring, and training; more congenial working relationships between people across the organization; a more positive working environment; improved use of internal and external knowledge products and services; easier retrieval of data, information, and knowledge across the organization; enhanced quality and consistency of data, information, and knowledge; fewer obstacles to knowledge sharing; more efficient work processes; superior work flows; higher quality client service delivery; and better transfer of knowledge from departing employees to successors or replacements.

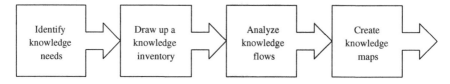

Fig. Knowledge audit constituents. *Source* Author

Constituents of Knowledge Audits

The typical constituents of knowledge audits, each of which can be conducted at different levels of complexity using a variety of tools,[3] are shown in the figure.[4] They are preferably, but not necessarily, in order: knowledge needs analysis, knowledge inventory analysis, knowledge flow analysis, and knowledge mapping. Throughout investigations, elements of knowledge, relationships, context, and external environment should be borne in mind, together with the fact that about 80% of an organization's knowledge is tacit—the greatest challenge lies in the audit of that.

- **Identify Knowledge Needs** The objective of knowledge needs analysis is to identify what tacit and explicit knowledge individuals, groups, and the organization possess; and what knowledge they might require in the future to perform better. The analysis can help an organization develop strategy. Besides shining light on bread-and-butter wants, it can also draw attention to staff skills and competency enhancement needs; opportunities for staff learning and development; organizational culture practices concerning leadership, collaboration, team work, and the performance management and rewards system; and staff relationship with management, peers, and subordinates.
- **Draw Up a Knowledge Inventory** Knowledge inventory analysis is stock-taking to identify, locate, and document existing knowledge assets. It involves, to the extent possible, counting, indexing, and categorizing tacit and explicit knowledge. For explicit knowledge, the analysis might cover numbers, types, and categories of documents, databases, libraries, intranets, hyperlinks, and subscriptions to external knowledge resources; knowledge locations in the organization and in its systems; the organization and access of knowledge; the

---

[3]The common tools used for knowledge audits are face-to-face and telephone interviews; structured, semi-structured, and unstructured questionnaires; workshops; focus group discussions; and online consultations. Other data and information can be gathered by referring to the documentation of the organization, conducting direct inspections, and examining the information and communications technology infrastructure, including the organization's website.

[4]Naturally, in a large and diverse organization, the dimensions and conduct of a knowledge audit will differ radically from that applicable to a small, less complex one.

purpose, relevance, and quality of knowledge; and use of knowledge. For tacit knowledge, the analysis might relate to staff directories and academic and professional qualifications, skills and core competency levels and experience, staff learning and development opportunities, and leadership potential in employees. An organization will be able to identify knowledge gaps and areas of duplication by comparing the results of the knowledge inventory analysis with those of the knowledge needs analysis.

- **Analyze Knowledge Flows** Knowledge flow analysis investigates how knowledge moves from where it is to where it is needed in an organization, revealing good and bad practices. The analysis determines how employees find the knowledge they must have, and how they share what knowledge they have. Knowledge flow analysis should examine people, business processes, and technology. Regarding people, this entails exploring attitudes toward—and experiences, beliefs, values, and skills in—knowledge sharing. In relation to business processes, one should look at how people go about their daily business and the extent to which identification, creation, storage, sharing, and use of knowledge forms part of that; policies and practices concerning knowledge flows, for instance, on data and information handling, management of records, or web publishing. For technology, there should be a focus on information and communications technology infrastructure, such as portals, content management, accessibility and ease of use, and current levels of usage.
- **Create Knowledge Maps** Knowledge maps—whether they are real, Yellow Pages, or specially constructed databases—are communication media designed to help visualize the sources, flows, constraints, and sinks (losses or stopping points) of knowledge within an organization. They can specify, for instance, creators, critics, collectors, connectors, and users of knowledge. They are useful navigational guides to tacit and explicit knowledge and underscore importance, relationships, and dynamics, for example, within social networks.[5] They can flip perspectives on knowledge from bottom-up to top-down, and focus knowledge management initiatives on the highest potential opportunities.

Further Reading

ADB (2008) Auditing the lessons architecture. Manila

---

[5]In contrast to organization charts, social network analysis maps show informal relationships. Who do people seek data, information, and knowledge from? Who do they share theirs with?

Proposition 5
The Sustainable Livelihoods Approach

In a Word The sustainable livelihoods approach improves understanding of the livelihoods of the poor. It organizes the factors that constrain or enhance livelihood opportunities, and shows how they relate. It can help plan development activities and assess the contribution that existing activities have made to sustaining livelihoods.

Livelihoods

A livelihood comprises the capabilities, assets, and activities required for a means of living. It is deemed sustainable when it can cope with and recover from stresses and shocks and maintain or enhance its capabilities, assets, and activities both now and in the future, while not undermining the natural resource base.

The Sustainable Livelihoods Approach

The sustainable livelihoods approach is a way of thinking about the objectives, scope, and priorities for development activities. It is based on evolving thinking about the way the poor and vulnerable live their lives and the importance of policies and institutions. It helps formulate development activities that are.

© Asian Development Bank 2017

O. Serrat, *Knowledge Solutions*, DOI 10.1007/978-981-10-0983-9_5

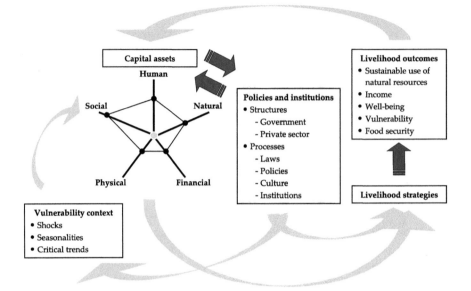

Fig. The sustainable livelihoods framework. *Source* Author

- People-centered
- Responsive and participatory
- Multilevel
- Conducted in partnership with the public and private sectors
- Dynamic
- Sustainable

The sustainable livelihoods approach facilitates the identification of practical priorities for actions that are based on the views and interests of those concerned but they are not a panacea. It does not replace other tools, such as participatory development, sector-wide approaches, or integrated rural development. However, it makes the connection between people and the overall enabling environment that influences the outcomes of livelihood strategies. It brings attention to bear on the inherent potential of people in terms of their skills, social networks, access to physical and financial resources, and ability to influence core institutions.

Appreciative inquiry—originally developed as a tool for industry to avoid negative approaches to problem solving—extends this constructive outlook. Appreciative inquiry is a highly inclusive process that maximizes the positive (as opposed to minimizing the negative) in which a community takes responsibility for generating and gathering information and then forms strategies based on the most positive experiences of the past.

Capital Assets

The sustainable livelihoods framework helps to organize the factors that constrain or enhance livelihood opportunities and shows how they relate to one another. A central notion is that different households have different access livelihood assets, which the sustainable livelihood approach aims to expand. The livelihood assets, which the poor must often make trade-offs and choices about, comprise:

- **Human capital**, e.g., health, nutrition, education, knowledge and skills, capacity to work, capacity to adapt
- **Social capital**, e.g., networks and connections (patronage, neighborhoods, kinship), relations of trust and mutual understanding and support, formal and informal groups, shared values and behaviors, common rules and sanctions, collective representation, mechanisms for participation in decision-making, leadership
- **Natural capital**, e.g., land and produce, water and aquatic resources, trees and forest products, wildlife, wild foods and fibers, biodiversity, environmental services
- **Physical capital**, e.g., infrastructure (transport, roads, vehicles, secure shelter and buildings, water supply and sanitation, energy, communications), tools and technology (tools and equipment for production, seed, fertilizer, pesticides, traditional technology)
- **Financial capital**,[1] e.g., savings, credit and debt (formal, informal), remittances, pensions, wages

Vulnerability Context

Vulnerability is characterized as insecurity in the well-being of individuals, households, and communities in the face of changes in their external environment. People move in and out of poverty and the concept of vulnerability captures the processes of change better than poverty line measurements. Vulnerability has two facets: an external side of shocks, seasonalities, and critical trends; and an internal side of defenselessness caused by lack of ability and means to cope with these. The vulnerability context includes

- shocks, e.g., conflict, illnesses, floods, storms, droughts, pests, diseases
- seasonalities, e.g., prices and employment opportunities
- critical trends, e.g., demographic, environmental, economic, governance, and technological trends

---

[1]Financial capital tends to be the least available livelihood asset of the poor. Indeed, it is because the poor lack it that the other types of capital are so important to them.

Policies and Institutions

Livelihood strategies and outcomes are not just dependent on access to capital assets or constrained by the vulnerability context; they are also transformed by the environment of structures and processes. Structures are the public and private sector organizations that set and implement policy and legislation; deliver services; and purchase, trade, and perform all manner of other functions that affect livelihoods.

Processes embrace the laws, regulations, policies, operational arrangements, agreements, societal norms, and practices that, in turn, determine the way in which structures operate. Policy-determining structures cannot be effective in the absence of appropriate institutions and processes through which policies can be implemented. Processes are important to every aspect of livelihoods. They provide incentives that stimulate people to make better choices. They grant or deny access to assets. They enable people to transform one type of asset into another through markets. They have a strong influence on interpersonal relations. One of the main problems the poor and vulnerable face is that the processes which frame their livelihoods may systematically restrict them unless the government adopts pro-poor policies that, in turn, filter down to legislation and even less formal processes.

Livelihood Strategies and Outcomes

Livelihood strategies aim to achieve livelihood outcomes. Decisions on livelihood strategies may invoke natural-resource-based activities, nonnatural resource-based and off-farm activities, migration and remittances, pensions and grants, intensification versus diversification, and short-term versus long-term outcomes, some of which may compete. (One of the many problems of development is that projects and programs, while favoring some, can disadvantage others.[2]) Potential livelihood outcomes can include more income, increased well-being, reduced vulnerability, improved food security, more sustainable use of the natural resource base, and recovered human dignity, between which there may again also be conflict.

Implications

The sustainable livelihoods approach encourages thinking out of the box. It frees development practitioners from conventional approaches that are often restricted to identifying problems and finding solutions. It invites them to look at contexts and

---

[2]There is no quick fix for this problem. Its existence underlines the need to give choice and opportunities to the poor and build their ability to take advantage of these, and extend safety nets for those who still cannot achieve their livelihood objectives in a competitive environment.

relationships so that development activities can become more process-oriented. It compels them to look for multiple entry points and to move beyond a homogenous "community" view and a narrow sectoral perspective. It represents an important shift away from the focus on project inputs and outputs and the assumed mechanical links between them. In particular, the sustainable livelihoods approach stresses the importance of understanding institutions by mapping the institutional framework and linking the micro to the macro and the formal to the informal Therefore, it calls for a new style of policy appraisal that moves from universal prescriptions to context-specific approaches that allow alternative, local perspectives to reveal themselves in the policy framework.

Caveat

The sustainable livelihoods approach is only one way of organizing the complex issues that surround poverty. It must also be made appropriate to local circumstances and local priorities.

Box: The Sustainable Livelihoods Framework—Strengths and Weaknesses

Strength	Weakness
Seeks to understand changing combinations of modes of livelihood in a dynamic and historical context	Underplays elements of the vulnerability context, such as macroeconomic trends and conflict
Explicitly advocates a creative tension between different levels of analysis and emphasizes the importance of macro- and microlinkages	Assumes that capital assets can be expanded in generalized and incremental fashion
Acknowledges the need to move beyond narrow sectoral perspectives and emphasizes seeing the linkages between sectors	Does not pay enough attention to inequalities of power
Calls for investigation of the relationships between different activities that constitute livelihoods and draws attention to social relations	Underplays the fact that enhancing the livelihoods of one group can undermine those of another

Source Author

Further Reading

ADB (2004) Future solutions now—the tonle sap initiative. December

Proposition 6
Outcome Mapping

In a Word Development is about people—it is about how they relate to one another and their environment, and how they learn in doing so. Outcome mapping puts people and learning first and accepts unexpected change as a source of innovation. It shifts the focus from changes in state, viz, reduced poverty, to changes in behaviors, relationships, actions, and activities.

Rationale

Development agencies must show that their activities make significant and lasting contributions to the welfare of intended beneficiaries. But they may well be trying to measure results that are beyond their reach: the impacts they cite as evidence are often the result of a confluence of events for which they cannot realistically get full credit. The questions that they cannot easily answer are

- How can assessment of impact move beyond attribution to documenting contributions to social change?
- How do you methodically and reasonably capture the richness of what is occurring in projects or programs?
- How do you effectively involve stakeholders in monitoring and evaluation of projects or programs?

© Asian Development Bank 2017

O. Serrat, *Knowledge Solutions*, DOI 10.1007/978-981-10-0983-9_6

- How do you effectively integrate monitoring and evaluation into projects or programs from the planningstage?
- How do you decide what to monitor and evaluate?
- How do you notice, explain, and respond to unexpected results?

Outcome mapping exposes myths about measuring impacts and helps to answer such questions. A project or program that uses the framework and vocabulary of outcome mapping does not claim the achievement of development impacts, nor does it belittle the importance of changes in state. Rather, it focuses on its contributions to outcomes (that may in turn enhance the possibility of development impacts—the relationship is not inevitably a direct one of cause and effect). More positively, because outcome mapping limits its concerns to those results that fall strictly within a project or program's sphere of influence, development agencies can become more specific about the actors they target, the changes they expect to see, and the strategies they employ.[1]

Definition

Outcome mapping is a (still evolving) method for planning, monitoring, and evaluating development activities that aim to bring about social change. It was developed in 2001 by the International Development Research Centre to clarify what human, social, and environmental betterment projects or programs hope to contribute and then focus monitoring and evaluation on factors and actors within their direct sphere of influence. The fundamental premise of outcome mapping is that for each change in state there are correlating changes in behavior that are best encouraged if continuing responsibility has been devolved to local people and local institutions.

The Stages of Outcome Mapping

The full process of putcome mapping involves three stages of thinking:

- **Intentional Design** This stage helps the project or program design team clarify and reach consensus on the macro-level changes it would like to support and to plan appropriate strategies. The design team should clearly express the long-term, downstream impacts that it is working toward, bearing in mind that

---

[1]Characteristically, for example, the evaluation of a water purification project focuses on whether water quality has improved. Outcome mapping also examines whether the beneficiaries maintaining the system now have and use the knowledge and skills, tools, and other resources needed to keep it running in the long term, for instance, by monitoring contaminant levels, changing filters, or bringing in experts when needed.

the project or program will not achieve them single-handedly. These desired impacts will provide reference points to guide strategy formulation and action plans, rather than serve as mere performance indicators. Progress markers, which will be used to track performance, should be developed for each boundary partner. They will identify the incremental—and often upstream—changes that the project or program sensibly hopes to influence, prompt behavioral change, and build the foundations of sustained social change. After clarifying what changes the project or program hopes to influence, the design team should select activities that maximize the likelihood of success. In short, the intentional design stage articulates answers to four questions: why, how, who, and what.

- **Outcome and Performance Monitoring** This stage provides a framework for monitoring actions and the progress of the boundary partners toward outcomes. The performance monitoring framework builds on the progress markers, strategy maps, and organizational practices developed at the intentional design stage. There are three data and information collection tools: an outcome journal to monitor boundary partner actions and relationships, a strategy journal to monitor strategies and activities, and a performance journal to monitor the organizational practices that keep the project or program relevant and viable. These tools will provide workspace and processes and help the design team reflect on the data and information that it has collected and how these can be used to improve performance.
- **Evaluation Planning** This stage helps the design team set priorities to target evaluation resources and activities where they will be most useful. Evaluation planning outlines the main elements of the evaluations to be conducted.

Benefits

People involved in national and local policymaking, staff and consultants of development agencies, and field personnel can use outcome mapping. Used prospectively, it can help

- Understand and influence more effectively human and ecological well-being.
- Plan and measure social change in projects or programs.
- Foster social and organizational learning.
- Identify individuals, groups, and organizations with whom one might work directly to influence behavioral change.
- Bring stakeholders into the planning and monitoring and evaluation processes.
- Strengthen partnerships and alliances.
- Plan and monitor behavioral change and the strategies to support those changes.
- Monitor the internal practices of projects or programs so that they remain effective.
- Design an evaluation plan to examine particular issues more precisely.

The Importance of Participation

Outcome mapping is based on principles of participation and iterative learning. It is usually initiated through a participatory workshop led by an internal or external facilitator who is familiar with the methodology. It purposefully includes those implementing the project or program in the design and in data and information collection to encourage ownership, use of findings, and adaptation. It is a consciousness-raising, consensus-building, and empowering methodology. The process for identifying the macro-level changes, selecting the monitoring priorities, and designing the evaluation plan is intended to be participatory: wherever feasible, it should involve the full range of stakeholders. Engagement means that stakeholders will derive benefit and be credited for fulfilling their development roles; projects and programs will be credited for their contributions to this process.

Further Reading

Earl S, Carden F, Smutylo T (2001) Outcome mapping: building learning and reflection into development programs. International Development Research Centre, Ottawa, Canada

Proposition 7
Culture Theory

In a Word Culture theory strengthens the expectation that markets work, not because they are comprised of autonomous individuals who are free of social sanctions but because they are powered by social beings and their distinctive ideas, beliefs, values, and knowledge. It can contribute to understanding and promoting development where group relationships predominate and individualism is tempered.

Rationale

Some needs are common to all people—at all times and in all places. They are the need to make a living, the need for social organization, the need for knowledge and learning, the need for normative and metaphysical expression, and the need for aesthetic manifestation. These nuts and bolts of everyday life work through the coevolving realms of environment, economy, society, polity, and technology to make up systems of mutual sustainability or (in opposition) mutual vulnerability.

Since people (not economies) are the main object and ultimate purpose of endeavors to progress, a society's culture is not just an instrument of development cooperation: it is its basis. The marriage of economy and environment was overdue

© Asian Development Bank 2017

O. Serrat, *Knowledge Solutions*, DOI 10.1007/978-981-10-0983-9_7

and has spawned a world agenda for that purpose. Likewise, the relationship between culture and development should be clarified and deepened in ways that are authentic, indigenous, self-reliant, sovereign, civilized, and creative.

Definition

Culture, defined in its broadest sense, is the totality of a society's distinctive ideas, beliefs, values, and knowledge. It exhibits the ways humans interpret their environments.

Applications

Culture theory is a branch of anthropology, semiotics, and other related social science disciplines such as political economy, in particular, but also sociology and communication (to name a few). It seeks to define heuristic concepts of culture. Hence, cultural studies often concentrate on how a particular phenomenon relates to matters of ideology, nationality, ethnicity, social class, and gender.[1] The potential for application is correspondingly vast—it follows that practitioners of culture theory draw from a diverse array of theories and associated practices and encompass many different approaches, methods, and academic perspectives.[2] And so, it remains relatively unstructured as an academic field that needs to move from "Let's" to "How". Taking culture into account should mean understanding how cultural dimensions enter utility and production functions of various kinds. In the case of development agencies and their partner countries, new processes of policy analysis and participatory management should surely be devised so that noneconomic social sciences become full partners in the decision-making concerning the policy and investment decisions that guide business processes. Much remains to be done.

Characteristics

Therefore, approaches to cultural studies are likely to range widely. However, Sardar (2004) sees that most tend to share the following characteristics:

---

[1]Increasingly, cultural studies also focus on the interface of information and communications technology and society.

[2]For instance, one branch of culture theory places a primary importance on the cultural institutions that are involved in the production, dissemination, and consumption of culture.

- They aim to examine their subject matter in terms of cultural practices and their relation to power.
- They aim to understand culture in all its complex forms and to analyze the social and political contexts in which it manifests itself.
- They consider culture as both the object of study and the location of political criticism and action.
- They expose and attempt to reconcile knowledge divides to overcome the split between tacit cultural knowledge and objective (so-called universal) forms of knowledge.
- They are committed to an ethical evaluation of society, and to political action.

Benefits

Culture theory's holistic perspective, englobing the needs common to all people, does not lend itself to easy action. But, culture theory alone pays simultaneous and even attention to these needs and makes possible a focus on the whole and the parts, on contexts and contents, on values and value systems, and on strategic relationships between key variables, countries, blocs of countries, and human beings and the natural environment. And so, it yields conceptual insights and practical benefits and allows informed choices and intelligent decisions to be made about the future. It enables us, for instance, to deal better with complexity and fragmentation—the emphasis is on systems rather than on parts of systems. And it helps to ensure that economies are contextualized properly and pointed in the right direction. For those reasons, among others, they can be constrained and enriched by the larger cultures in which they are located. Consequently, they stop functioning as self-governing entities. Also, by focusing on the totality and innate worth of a given society, culture theory can minimize the ethnocentric bias that results from one's cultural conditioning.

Reference

Sardar Z (2004) Introducing cultural studies. Icon Books Ltd, Cambridge

Further Reading

Eade D (ed) (2002) Development and culture: selected essays from development in practice. Oxfam GB in association with World Faiths Development Dialogue, Oxford
Harrison L, Huntington S (eds) (2001) Culture matters: how values shape human progress. Basic Books, New York

Proposition 8
The Most Significant Change Technique

In a Word The Most Significant Change technique helps monitor and evaluate the performance of projects and programs. It involves the collection and systematic participatory interpretation of stories of significant change emanating from the field level—stories about who did what, when, and why, and the reasons why the event was important. It does not employ quantitative indicators.

Rationale

Development (as so much of knowledge and learning) is about change—change that takes place in a variety of domains.[1] To move toward what is desirable and away from what is not, stakeholders must clarify what they are really trying to achieve, develop a better understanding of what is (and what is not) being achieved, and explore and share their various values and preferences about what they hold to be significant change. Evaluation has a role to play. However, in the alleged words of Albert Einstein, "Not everything that can be counted counts, and not everything that counts can be counted."

---

[1]For instance, the domains might relate to changes in the quality of people's lives, the nature of their participation in development activities, or the sustainability of organizations.

© Asian Development Bank 2017
O. Serrat, *Knowledge Solutions*, DOI 10.1007/978-981-10-0983-9_8

Definition

The Most Significant Change technique is a qualitative and participatory form of monitoring and evaluation[2] based on the collection and systematic selection of stories[3] of reported changes from development activities. The technique was developed by Rick Davies in the mid-1990s to meet the challenges associated with monitoring and evaluating a complex participatory rural development program in Bangladesh, which had diversity in both implementation and outcomes. The technique is becoming popular, and adaptations have already been made.

Benefits

The Most Significant Change technique facilitates project and program improvement by focusing the direction of work away from less-valued directions toward more fully shared visions and explicitly valued directions, e.g., what do we really want to achieve and how will we produce more of it?[4] It can also help uncover important, valued outcomes not initially specified. It delivers these benefits by creating space for stakeholders to reflect, and by facilitating dynamic dialogue. As a corollary, project and program committees often become better at conceptualizing impact (and hence become better at planning). The unusual methodology of the Most Significant Change technique and its outcomes are a foil for other monitoring and evaluation techniques, such as logic models (results frameworks), appreciative inquiry, and outcome mapping—especially where projects and programs have diverse, complex outcomes with multiple stakeholders groups and financing

---

[2]Qualitative monitoring and evaluation is about learning: it is dynamic and inductive and therefore focuses on questioning. The data is hard to aggregate. Goal displacement is not an issue. Quantitative monitoring and evaluation is about proving (accountability): it is static and deductive and therefore focuses on measurement. The data is easy to aggregate. Goal displacement can be a problem. The Most Significant Change technique is a form of monitoring because it occurs throughout the project cycle and provides information to help people manage that. Michael Quinn Patton has argued that evaluation findings serve three primary purposes: (i) to render judgments, (ii) to facilitate improvements, and/or (iii) to generate knowledge—the Most Significant Change technique contributes to evaluation because it provides data on outcomes that can be used to help assess the performance of a project or program as a whole.

[3]Ideally, the stories will be 1–2 pages long in proforma.

[4]The Most Significant Change technique differs from common monitoring and evaluation techniques in at least four respects: (i) the focus is on the unexpected (rather than predetermined quantitative indicators that do not tell stakeholders what they do not know they need to know), (ii) information about change is documented in text, not numbers, (iii) major attention is given to explicit value judgments, and (iv) information is analyzed through a structured social process.

agencies—to enrich summative evaluation with unexpected outcomes and very best success stories. What is more, the technique's reliance on participatory monitoring and evaluation can only enhance the chances that lessons will be learned and that recommendations will be acted upon.[5]

Process

The central process of the Most Significant Change technique is the collection and systematic selection of reported changes by means of purposive sampling with a bias in favor of success. This involves asking field staff to elicit anecdotes from stakeholders, focusing on what most significant change has occurred as the result of an initiative, and why they think that change occurred. These dozens, if not hundreds, of stories are passed up the chain and winnowed down to the most significant as determined by each management layer until only one story is selected—a story that describes a real experience, reviewed, defended, and selected by the people charged with the success of the project or program. Participants enjoy the process and usually bring to it a high level of enthusiasm—this owes mainly to the use of storytelling.[6]

Enablers

Four broad enabling contextual factors drive successful implementation of the Most Significant Change technique. They are

- Support from senior management.
- The commitment to the process of a leader.
- The development of trust between field staff and villagers.
- An organizational culture that prioritizes reflection and learning.
- Infrastructure that enables regular feedback of the results to stakeholders.
- Time to run several cycles of the technique.

---

[5]Some have suggested that the technique could be improved by adding a process to formally incorporate the lessons learned from the stories into short-term and long-term project or program planning. This might be accomplished by requesting those who report stories to make recommendations for action drawing from the stories they selected.

[6]The advantage of stories is that people tell them naturally (indigenously). Stories can also deal with complexity and context and can carry hard messages (undiscussables) that people remember. However, they are not known for accuracy (truth).

Caution

The Most Significant Change technique is still evolving. Suggestions for improvements have been made,[7] while others look to adapt it to different contexts or to combine it creatively with other approaches. Further, although it can address what follows, the Most Significant Change technique should not be used to

- Capture expected change.
- Prepare stories for public relations.
- Understand the average experience of stakeholders.
- Generate an evaluation report for accountability purposes.
- Conduct a quick evaluation.
- Conduct retrospective evaluation of a completed project or program.

Further Reading

Davies R, Dart J (2005) The "Most Significant Change" (MSC) technique: a guide to its use

---

[7]Some have suggested that the technique could be revised to (i) elicit and include the voices of critics and nonparticipants, (ii) conduct en masse participatory analysis of stories, (iii) improve the feedback process, and (iv) establish a formal process for incorporating the insights gained into both short- and long-term project and program planning.

Proposition 9
Social Network Analysis

In a Word Power no longer resides exclusively (if at all) in states, institutions, or large corporations. It is located in the networks that structure society. Social network analysis seeks to understand networks and their participants and has two main focuses: the actors and the relationships between them in a specific social context.

Rationale

The information revolution has given birth to new economies structured around flows of data, information, and knowledge. In parallel, social networks[1] have grown stronger as forms of organization of human activity.[2] Social networks are nodes of individuals, groups, organizations, and related systems that tie in one or more types of interdependencies: these include shared values, visions, and ideas; social contacts; kinship; conflict; financial exchanges; trade; joint membership in

---

[1]The term was coined by John Barnes in 1954.

[2]Information and communications technology explains much but not all. The other agents that have catalyzed social networks include globalization; the diversification of policy making to include more nongovernmental actors, e.g., civil and nongovernment organizations, under the banner of good governance; growing recognition of the importance of social capital; and practical applications in knowledge management and organizational learning.

O. Serrat, *Knowledge Solutions*, DOI 10.1007/978-981-10-0983-9_9

organizations; and group participation in events, among numerous other aspects of human relationships.[3] Indeed, it sometimes appears as though networked organizations outcompete all other forms of organization—[4]certainly, they outpace vertical, rigid, command-and-control bureaucracies. When they succeed, social networks influence larger social processes by accessing human, social, natural, physical, and financial capital, as well as the information and knowledge content of these. (In development work, they can impact policies, strategies, programs, and projects—including their design, implementation, and results—and the partnerships that often underpin these.) To date, however, we are still far from being able to construe their public and organizational power in ways that can harness their potential. Understanding when, why, and how they function best is important. Here, social network analysis can help.

Definition

The defining feature of social network analysis is its focus on the structure of relationships, ranging from casual acquaintance to close bonds.[5] Social network analysis assumes that relationships are important. It maps and measures formal and informal relationships to understand what facilitates or impedes the knowledge flows that bind interacting units, viz., who knows whom, and who shares what information and knowledge with whom by what communication media (e.g., data and information, voice, or video communications).[6] (Because these relationships

---

[3]"Social networks" is an umbrella term that covers many forms and functions, with each node having distinct relative worth. (Sometimes, nodes are used to represent events, ideas, or objects.) Communities of practice are an important form. Others include policy and advocacy networks that work on problem identification and agenda setting, policy formulation, policy implementation, and policy monitoring and evaluation; private–public policy networks; knowledge networks; etc. (Increasingly, social networks are social communities of the web, connected via electronic mail, websites and web logs, and networking applications such as Twitter, FaceBook, Lotus Quickr, or LinkedIn.) Functions differ too, with nodes behaving as filters, amplifiers, investors and providers, convenors, community builders, and/or facilitators.

[4]In such instances, their strengths arise among others from (i) a unifying purpose and clear coordination structure; (ii) multiple, interactive communications (spanning both horizontal and vertical dimensions) that encourage simultaneous action, (iii) dynamism and creativity (owing to multiple, interactive communications between members), (iv) consensus (born of like-minded actors who rally around shared interests or a common issue), (v) strength in numbers, (vi) the quality and packaging of evidence, (vii) sustainability, and (viii) representativeness.

[5]This is in contrast with other areas of the social sciences where the focus is often on the attributes of agents rather than on the relations between them.

[6]In contrast, an organization chart shows formal relationships only—who works where, and who reports to whom. Ten years ago, Mintzberg and van der Heyden (1999) therefore suggested the use of "organigraphs" to map an organization's functions and the ways people organize themselves in it.

are not usually readily discernible, social network analysis is somewhat akin to an "organizational X-ray".) Social network analysis is a method with increasing application in the social sciences and has been applied in areas as diverse as psychology, health, business organization, and electronic communications. More recently, interest has grown in analysis of leadership networks to sustain and strengthen their relationships within and across groups, organizations, and related systems.

Benefits

We use people to find content, but we also use content to find people. If they are understood better relationships and knowledge flows can be measured, monitored, and evaluated, perhaps (for instance) to enhance organizational performance. The results of a social network analysis might be used to:

- Identify the individuals, teams, and units who play central roles.
- Discern information breakdowns,[7] bottlenecks,[8] structural holes, as well as isolated individuals, teams, and units.
- Make out opportunities to accelerate knowledge flows across functional and organizational boundaries.
- Strengthen the efficiency and effectiveness of existing, formal communication channels.
- Raise awareness of and reflection on the importance of informal networks and ways to enhance their organizational performance.
- Leverage peer support.
- Improve innovation and learning.
- Refine strategies.

Development work, for one, is more often than not about social relationships. Hence, the social network representation of a development assistance project or program would enable attention to be quickly focused (to whatever level of complexity is required) on who is influencing whom (both directly and indirectly).

---

[7]Breakdowns in information occur most often at one or more of five common boundaries: (i) functional (i.e., breakdowns between individuals, teams, or units; (ii) geographic, i.e., breakdowns between geographically separated locations); (iii) hierarchical (i.e., breakdowns between personnel of different levels), (iv) tenure (i.e., breakdowns between long-time personnel and new personnel); and (v) organizational (i.e., breakdowns among leadership networks).

[8]Bottlenecks are central nodes that provide the only connection between different parts of a network.

(Outcome mapping is another method that attempts to shifts the focus from changes in state, viz., reduced poverty, to changes in behaviors, relationships, actions, and activities.) Since a social network perspective is, inherently, a multi-actor perspective, social network analysis can also offset the limitations of logic models (results frameworks).

Process

Typically, social network analysis relies on questionnaires and interviews to gather information about the relationships within a defined group. The responses gathered are then mapped. (Social network analysis software exists for the purpose.)[9] This data gathering and analysis process provides baseline information against which one can then prioritize and plan interventions to improve knowledge flows, which may entail recasting social connections.

Notwithstanding the more complex processes followed by some, which can entail sifting through surfeits of information with increasingly powerful social network analysis software, social network analysis encourages at heart participative and interpretative approaches to the description and analysis of social networks, preferably with a focus on the simplest and most useful basics. Key stages of the basic process will typically require practitioners to

- Identify the network of individuals, teams, and units to be analyzed.
- Gather background information, for example, by interviewing senior managers and key staff to understand specific needs and issues.
- Define the objective and clarify the scope of the analysis, and agree on the reporting required.
- Formulate hypotheses and questions.
- Develop the survey methodology
- Design the questionnaire, keeping questions short and straight to the point. (Both open-ended and closed questions can be used.)[10]

---

[9]Sociograms, or visual representations of social networks, are important to understand network data and convey the result of the analysis. Free and commercial social network analysis tools are at hand, each with different functionality. They include UCINET, Pajek, NetMiner, and Netdraw. In each case, the graphics generated are based on three types of data and information: (i) the nodes that represent the individuals, groups, or organizations being studied; (ii) the ties that represent the different relationships among the nodes (which may be insufficient, just right, or excessive); and (iii) the attributes that make up the different characteristics of the individuals, groups, or organizations being studied. Key measurements apply to the centrality of the social network analyzed; the makeup of its various subgroups (which can develop their own subcultures and negative attitudes toward other groups); and the nature of ties (viz., direction, distance, and density).

[10]Typical questions are: Who knows who and how well? How well do people know each other's knowledge and skills? Who or what gives people information about xyz? What resources do people use to find information about xyz? What resources do people use to share information about xyz?

- Survey the individuals, teams, and units in the network to identify the relationships and knowledge flows between them.
- Use a social network analysis tool to visually map out the network.
- Review the map and the problems and opportunities highlighted using interviews and/or workshops.
- Design and implement actions to bring about desired changes.
- Map the network again after a suitable period of time. (Social network analysis can also serve as an evaluation tool.)

With the rise of Facebook, Google+, LinkedIn, Twitter, etc., interest has grown in social network analysis of electronic communications. Most likely, social network analysis is set to emerge as a key technique in modern sociology.

Reference

Mintzberg H, Van der Heyden L (September–October, 1999) Organigraphs: drawing how companies really work. Harvard Business Review: 87–94

Proposition 10
Overcoming Roadblocks to Learning

In a Word The gulf between the ideal type of a learning organization and the state of affairs in typical bilateral and multilateral development agencies remains huge. Defining roadblocks, however numerous they may be, is half the battle to removing them—it might make them part of the solution instead of part of the problem.

Background

> *An organization belongs on the sick list when promotion becomes more important to its people than accomplishment in the job they are in. It is sick when it is more concerned with avoiding mistakes than with taking the right risks, with counteracting the weaknesses of its members rather than with building on their strength. But it is sick also when "good human relations" become more important than performance and achievement ... The moment people talk of "implementing" instead of "doing" and of "finalizing" instead of "finishing," the organization is running a fever.*
>
> —Peter Drucker

These *Knowledge Solutions* draw in part from Goold, L. 2006. *Working with Barriers to Organizational Learning*. Bond.

Organizational learning is collective learning by individuals, and the fundamental phenomena of individual learning apply to organizations. However, organizational learning has distinctive characteristics concerning what is learned, how it is learned, and the adjustments needed to enhance learning. These owe to the fact that an organization is, by general definition, a collective whose individual constituents work to achieve a common goal from discrete operating and supporting units. Practices bring different perspectives and cultures to bear and shape data, information, and knowledge flows.

Political considerations are the most serious impediment to becoming a learning organization. However, by understanding more fully what obstacles to learning can exist in a complex organization in a complex environment, one can circumscribe the problem space and create enabling environments for a more positive future. Such environments would facilitate self-organization, exploration of the space of possibilities, generative feedback, emergence, and coevolution. They would create an explanatory framework and facilitate action.

The Bias for Action

The organizational context[1] of nongovernment organizations seems to give more value to action than to reflection. An activist culture can lead to quick fixes that in the long term can exacerbate the problems faced if the second-order causes of the problems are not recognized and tackled. The forces that favor jumping into "solutions mode" include (i) time spent in inconclusive deliberations; (ii) the urgency of task; (iii) the felt need for action[2]; (iv) avoidance of reflective observation, unclear concepts, and uncertainty of outcomes; and (v) fear of failure leading to avoidance of decisions. Such pressures reinforce the bias for action instead of encouraging reflection and inquiry. Process and task must be seen as interdependent, as should reflection and action.

---

[1]Every organization has a discrete environment, defined by factors such as identity, values, culture, and worldview of the organization; strategic alignment; activities and processes; size; geographic spread; staff skills and experience; organizational history; available resources; and marketplace factors.

[2]The felt need for action may drown discordant information, i.e., learning that challenges organizational consensus or threatens short-term institutional interest, especially with regard to roles and responsibilities.

Undiscussables

Behind some pressures that reinforce the bias for action is inability to handle anxiety and fear, compounded by the defensive routines that are built in response. People faced with error, embarrassment, or threat will typically act to avoid these, make the avoidance undiscussable, and make its undiscussability undiscussable. They will do so because they assume that their actions will reduce the likelihood of a situation escalating further. Much energy can be wasted in avoiding controversy; however, it is not potential conflict but the avoidance of action to resolve conflict that causes problems. One approach to undiscussables is to invite speculation, perhaps with the help of a facilitator or with simple guidelines: What is the worst thing that might happen? What would happen if it did? The way to remain scared is to not find out what one is afraid of.

Commitment to the Cause

The individuals who are drawn to development work acknowledge a basic commitment to reducing poverty. From their perspective, they are altruistic and action-oriented. Yet their commitment can become compulsive—the cause is never ending, and if they were to pause and reflect, they may question what they have really been doing. Some keep "doing" and suffer from exhaustion, cynicism, or burnout. They may also allow an element of self-righteousness to creep in. Hard work, high energy, and dedication to poverty reduction are not per se negative or unhealthy at the individual or collective level, but their meaning and purpose and one's attachment to them must be questioned with an open mind.

Advocacy at the Expense of Inquiry

> *It is a strange trade that of advocacy. Your intellect, your highest heavenly gift is hung up in the shop window like a loaded pistol for sale.*
>
> —Thomas Carlyle

In much aid work, more value appears to be given to advocating a position than inquiring about the view of beneficiaries. This gives little opportunity for new insights and concepts to emerge. Many universal practices and behaviors of dialogue and inquiry can help, such as the ability to suspend assumptions, listen to one another earnestly, give voice to what one really thinks, and respect difference. To improve the quality of everyday conversations and make better use of collective spaces for learning, there is an urgent need to develop the art of talking and thinking differently together.

Cultural Bias

Western cultural assumptions have shaped development work, perhaps also the debates on organizational learning. They are apt to value outputs and outcomes over process, and show a predilection for linear, predictable causality (evidenced, for instance, by the design and monitoring framework, also known as logical framework analysis).[3] East Asian cultures place more emphasis on discussing the problem at hand, after which those present will know what is needed without feeling locked into a specific decision. The rigidity of fixed assumptions apparent in aid agencies should be tempered by insights and concepts such as nonlinearity, edge of chaos, self-organization, emergence, and coevolution (Ramalingam et al. 2008).[4] At the village level, tools that have been found useful include storytelling, community theater, and participatory approaches. *Learning Lessons in ADB* (2007) specifies other cultural roadblocks in the form of psychological and social factors.

Practicing What Is Preached

Some values and processes that development agencies promote, such as good governance and results-based management, are not practiced internally. At least this raises questions of integrity. If aid agencies reflected on the difficulty of learning in their organizations, they might promote it more sensitively and build absorptive capacity both in-house and elsewhere.

---

[3]Sponsors of organizational learning tend to flag learning as a process. However, how then should one balance the evaluation of process and that of outcome? If learning is emphasized as a process, the fact that an organization is learning at all is, in itself, highly desirable. Conversely, if priority is given to effectiveness in accomplishing outcomes, learning will be ascribed less importance. Rationally, the way forward can only be found in the right mix of emphasis in various situations. For a note on the design and monitoring framework that recognizes the limitations of this planning tool and proposes improvements, see the *Knowledge Solutions* on output accomplishment and the design and monitoring framework.

[4]For a note on cultural theory and coevolution, see ADB (2001).

The Funding Environment

Funding that is tied to particular programs or projects—ironically often to capture "lessons learned"—does not encourage creative thinking and innovation. Nor does it pave the way for intraorganizational and interorganizational learning, let alone partnerships in developing countries. Second-order forms of learning can be developed without tying funding to prespecified outcomes, such as looking at the qualities and approaches needed for better learning in programs and projects. Elsewhere, where funding is not tied, the constant pressure to demonstrate low overheads may also dissuade aid agencies from investing other resources necessary for effective organizational learning. Elsewhere still, competition for funding may induce fabrication of success stories and detract from constructive self-criticism and analysis, when it does not exacerbate the trend to "go cheap" and claim unrealistically low operating overheads.

Thinking Strategically About Learning

How responsibility for learning is structured reveals much about mind-sets and assumptions in an organization. Where efforts are made to mainstream it, responsibility will tend to be held by an individual postholder at the middle-management level. Although this can give organizational learning a profile, legislating for learning is dangerous. Learning may be seen as the responsibility of an individual rather than as core to organizational practice and central to the organization's identity, values, culture, and worldview. Staff members who are held responsible for organizational learning will also often carry some anxiety about conveying clear statements to others (including senior managers). This could restrict the self-organizing potential of learning. If work on organizational learning is to be structured by the circumstances in which the work is to be performed (i.e., if form were to follow function), an organization may find it more useful to tend existing relationships, create spaces for experimentation and for conversations between people to grow across departmental boundaries, support informal links between and across organizations, offer opportunities and support for peer learning, and go where the energy is for as long as that is needed.[5] (This entails offering incentives and rewards for learning.) Given the unpredictable nature of learning, any strategy should be flexible, that is, not bound to specific outcomes. Investigations should start with an inquiry into the existing practices of staff members, the roadblocks that they face in context, and their assumptions about learning. From this, calculated

---

[5]Interdependent inputs toward these would be a function of the nature of the task, the range of competencies required, the technology (to be) deployed, and the scale of operations.

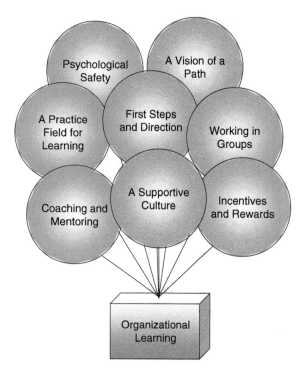

Fig. Overcoming learning anxiety. *Source* Author

responses might then be explored, experimented with, and learned from iteratively. This approach would shape strategic thinking. The below above makes out eight means to focus on and reduce learning anxiety, each of which requires dedicated attention.[6]

The Role of Leadership

> *Leadership is based on inspiration, not domination; on cooperation, not intimidation.*
>
> —William Arthur Wood

---

[6]Blaming it on biological determinism, John Cacioppo explains that very early the brain exhibits a "negativity bias," meaning that it reacts with far more electrical activity to the stimuli of bad news than to good, and that this is seen at the early stages of information processing. Thus, our attitudes are more heavily influenced by downbeat than good news (Ito et al. 2002).

More surprises occur as the result of a failure to act than as the result of a failure to see. Organizations have more to fear from not having strong leadership. It is the leader's responsibility to live the values the organization espouses, set the right tone, and lead truly by example. Much as they must visibly promote the right culture by rewarding those who lead by example, leaders must strengthen or challenge patterns and norms that limit learning. Their reactions will be amplified by the position they carry. If they encourage staff members to take on work and then question their judgment, or constantly check on them, they will undermine the staff members and reduce creative thinking, innovation, and risk taking. Leaders must be aware that much value exists in communication, which allows leadership skills— good or bad—to show through. It is important that they seek formal and informal feedback on the impact of their gestures and that they be aware that second-order learning, by its very nature, may work against the improvement initiatives they promote.[7] To recap, the principal role of leaders is to create the conditions within an organization through which staff members will first want to learn, then learn to learn, and finally internalize the habit of continuous learning. The motive, means, and opportunity for learning must also align.

Learning to Unlearn

Unlearning may be the real challenge of learning. It may be simply characterized as the process of letting go of what is known, with openness and freshness of mind, to create fresh space for new learning to take root. It involves habits one has carried for many years. Learning is intimately part of the elaboration of a system—indeed almost synonymous with it. However, in discovering what must change, the greatest difficulties are often found in its structures and patterns. Consciously reading, assessing, and unlearning these will become fundamental. Ultimately, one may have to concede that it is not policies, strategies, processes, tools, methods, and approaches that define the core and quality of development practice but the past, present, and future, and the openness, judgment, intuition, creativity, integrity, and strength that one can muster to face these that do. In large bureaucratic organizations, unlearning also involves risk and requires psychological safety and the trust on which that rests, and both may be in short supply.

---

[7]For a note on the importance of management education and training, see ADB (2000).

Organizational Structure

> *The quality of an organization can never exceed the quality of the minds that make it up.*
>
> —Harold R. McAlindon

Although Liz Goold never mentioned hierarchical, centralized, or control-oriented structures, by all accounts, such roadblocks to organizational learning are formidable in most bilateral and multilateral agencies. Arguments against strong hierarchies are about the division of labor, office politics, and interpersonal relations. Hierarchical, centralized, and control-oriented organizations are inclined to separate thinking and acting, and entrust strategy and policy making to particular departments, offices, and senior managers. Top-down flows are inimical to teamwork within and across units. What is more, the structure fires up office politics: the priority of staff members is not learning but protecting or advancing their position, unit, or budget. To these, mastery of the operating system is of greater consequence than appreciating the context and probing the quality of a policy or operation. Conformity—not local accountability, flexibility, innovation, or critical reflection—is rewarded. To boot, field staff members find themselves at the bottom of the hierarchy, their views and interpretations overlooked or overruled. Capacity to learn is interrelated with power and authority in the sense that opportunity (time, space, and priority) to learn depends on where one stands in the hierarchy.

Knowledge Inaction

Goold also omitted to mention the inadequacy of information systems. Information overload[8] is common in most aid agencies, but information and communications technology for collaboration mechanisms, knowledge sharing and learning, and knowledge capture and storage is underdeveloped, underresourced, or inefficient in all but a few.[9] There is a problem, then, with identifying, creating, storing, sharing, and using quality data and information—synonymous with poor knowledge management. Bottom-up, formal routine reporting in hierarchical organizations has

---

[8]The exception is baseline data and information, which are critical to track progress and make changes if necessary during implementation of an operation, and to monitor and report on its contributions to outcomes.

[9]*Auditing the Lessons Architecture* shows with a real-life example how a survey of perceptions conducted in 2007 provided entry points against which the Operations Evaluation Department (now the Independent Evaluation Department) in the Asian Development Bank (2008) can take measures to tie in with audiences in these areas.

limited learning value. The emphasis is on outputs; accomplishments, not problems, are brought to light; time frames are too short. Reporting is seen as an obligation rather than an opportunity for ongoing, collective, interactive, and inquisitive conversation and dialogue based on quality data and information. By poor knowledge management, hierarchical organizations create self-supporting systems of misinformation.

False Images

Moreover, development agencies may have fallen victim to the false portrayal of their work as quick and simple. Even now, the sometimes surreal expectations of taxpayers continue to be fueled by annual reports highlighting success stories. Despite the high level of uncertainty of development work, there is pressure to be able to predict, if not appear infallible. In opposition, critics argue that development agencies have failed profoundly. With better public education work, development agencies can generate a more insightful understanding of the complexity of the work with which they are tasked (or task themselves).

(Lack of) Penalties for Not Learning

Additionally, the absence of a market test for aid agencies removes the discipline that forces a business to change its ways or go bankrupt. They do not have profit margins, which ultimately depend on client interest and satisfaction. (In quite opposite ways, the beneficiaries of development programs and projects often have little voice and choice.) Therefore, aid agencies are tasked with measuring the larger part of their own performance (notwithstanding the small share of operations examined by independent evaluation) and, in so doing, downplay problems and failures. None of this, however, offers a good excuse for not learning; on the contrary, such arguments underscore learning as a necessity and priority. However, sadly, the judgment that an avoidable mistake in development work has been committed cannot always be argued beyond reasonable doubt—this does not ease the formulation of penalties for not learning, at least not immediately. Additionally, if indulgence for learning lessons were not granted and fair penalties for avoidable mistakes were formulated, how much time should one wait before witnessing improvements in performance at individual, team, cross-functional, operational, and strategic levels?

Multiplying Agendas

> *I do have a political agenda. It's to have as few regulations as possible.*
>
> —Dan Quayle

The combined efforts of shareholders and (advocacy) nongovernment organizations to make aid agencies do a better job of development (by their criteria) tie them down with procedural requirements and prompt them to expand agendas to build coalitions of support. The circle is vicious; promises are not met, and these parties ratchet up requirements with tighter audits of compliance and the instigation of penalties for noncompliant staff members. In situations of no budgetary growth, the broadening scope of work puts staff members in a bind and undermines (when it does not prevent) learning. Conversely, growing operating costs may reduce demand from borrowing governments.

Exclusion

> *I know that most men, including those at ease with problems of the greatest complexity, can seldom accept even the simplest and most obvious truth if it be such as would oblige them to admit the falsity of conclusions which they have delighted in explaining to colleagues, which they have proudly taught to others, and which they have woven, thread by thread, into the fabric of their lives.*
>
> —Leo Tolstoy

Development agencies recruit professional staff members from the international market and local staff members from applicants residing in duty station countries. It cannot be assumed that they share the same space for learning. In 2003, a study[10] of the humanitarian sector found that international staff members accessed about 10 times more explicit knowledge assets from their organizations than their national counterparts. International staff members also attended meetings at approximately 10 times the rate of national staff members. Thus, how national staff members learn and are assisted in their learning and development is of central importance to the effectiveness of their agencies. Conversely, their importance as sources of "real" knowledge (including history) and their ability to approach things the right way are

---

[10]Active Learning Network for Accountability and Performance (ALNAP) in Humanitarian Action (2004).

undervalued if not ignored. Only rarely are they seen as worthy of investment, supported, or given incentives. This waste of key knowledge assets is compounded by the fact that professional staff members characteristically move on when projects and programs end.

Complexity

Cultural bias suggests why development aid follows a linear approach to achieving outputs and outcomes. That approach is guided by business processes (and associated compliance standards) applied with limited and out-of-date insights on dynamic operational contexts. Any planning process is based on assumptions[11]—some will be predictable, others wishful. If the assumptions are based on invalid theories of change (including cause-and-effect relationships) and on inappropriate tools, methods, approaches, and procedures derived from those, development agencies will jeopardize the impacts that they seek to realize. Yet the cultural perspective draws insufficient conclusions about what complexity thinking should mean for development interventions. How might emerging insights from the complexity sciences and systems thinking, combined with field practice, systemically (rather than through a patchwork approach) reshape assumptions about the design of development assistance, improve reading of signals, and foster appropriate adapting of actions? What might be the implications of a shift from compliance with external standards to investing in capacities for navigating complexity?

References

ADB (September 2000) Where do we stand on bureaucratic performance? In: News from ERO. Manila

ADB (September 2001) Seeing the forest and the trees. In: News from ERO. Manila

ADB (2007) Learning lessons in ADB. Manila

ADB (2008) Auditing the lessons architecture. Manila

Humanitarian Action (2004) Learning by field level workers. In: ALNAP review of humanitarian action in 2003. London

Ito T, Larsen J, Smith K, Cacioppo J (2002) Negative information weighs more heavily on the brain: the negativity bias in evaluative categorizations. In: Cacioppo J et al (eds) Foundations in social neuroscience. MIT Press, Cambridge, Massachusetts

---

[11]Kurtz and Snowden (2003) identified three basic, universal assumptions prevalent in organizational decision support and strategy: assumptions of order, of rational choice, and of intent.

Kurtz C, Snowden D (2003) The new dynamics of strategy: sense-making in a complex and complicated world. IBM Systems Journal 42(3):462–483

Ramalingam B, Jones H, Reba T, Young J (2008) Exploring the science of complexity: ideas and implications for development and humanitarian efforts. In: Working Paper 285. Overseas Development Institute, London

Further Reading

ADB (2009) Learning for change in ADB. Manila

Proposition 11
Building a Learning Organization

In a Word Learning is the key to success—some would even say survival—in today's organizations. Knowledge should be continuously enriched through both internal and external learning. For this to happen, it is necessary to support and energize organization, people, knowledge, and technology for learning.

The Learning Organization Model

> *It is not the strongest of the species who survive, nor the most intelligent; rather it is those most responsive to change.*
>
> —Charles Darwin

For organizations wishing to remain relevant and thrive, learning better and faster is critically important. Many organizations apply quick and easy fixes often driven by technology. Most are futile attempts to create organizational change. However, organizational learning is neither possible nor sustainable without understanding what drives it. The below figure shows the subsystems of a learning organization: organization, people, knowledge, and technology. Each subsystem supports the others in magnifying the learning as it permeates across the system.

© Asian Development Bank 2017
O. Serrat, *Knowledge Solutions*, DOI 10.1007/978-981-10-0983-9_11

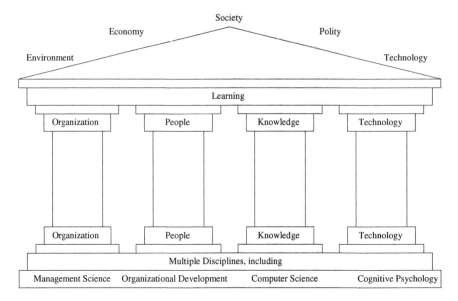

Fig. Building a learning organization. *Source* Author

Organization

The supreme accomplishment is to blur the line between work and play.

—Arnold Toynbee

A learning organization values the role that learning can play in the development of organizational effectiveness. It demonstrates this by having an inspiring vision for learning and a learning strategy that will support the organization in achieving its vision.

The leadership of a learning organization is committed to the importance of learning and clearly communicates that learning is critical to organizational success. The leadership recognizes the importance of providing the motive, means, and opportunity for learning: (i) the motive being the "why?"—the purpose and reason for learning; (ii) the means being the "how and what?"—the models, methods, and competencies required; and (iii) the opportunity being the "where and when?"—the spaces for learning. Leaders take an exemplary leading role in creating and sustaining a supportive learning culture.

The structure of a learning organization takes into account the common obstacles to learning so it is carefully aligned with strategy, avoiding the development of "silos" and minimizing unnecessary levels of hierarchy.

Communication systems are used to facilitate the lateral transfer of information and knowledge across formal structural boundaries. In decentralized and geographically spread organizations, particular care is taken to use communication to encourage lateral communication and to overcome the increased danger of the development of "silos".

Adequate resources are allocated for learning in terms of time, space, specialist support staff, and budgets for knowledge management and learning infrastructure, formal and informal communities of practice[1] and other value networks (both internal and external),[2] and learning and development programs. Support to communities of practice, for example, is extended in a structured manner throughout their life cycle.[3]

To stimulate creativity and generate new insights and innovative practices, a learning organization takes a balanced approach to the importance of both planned and emergent learning. Planned learning is addressed through the careful development of strategy, structure, systems, procedures, and plans. In a learning organization, planning is based on careful reflection through probing questions that draw on data and information from monitoring, review, and self- and independent evaluation.

Emergent learning is equally important but takes an inherently more speculative and opportunistic approach. It is dependent on encouraging a passion for learning and knowledge sharing among staff members, developing learning competencies, creating opportunities for informal sharing, and cultivating a supportive learning culture.

Failures and unintended outcomes are the focus of constructive discussions leading to new approaches. When such incidents involve clients, care is taken to protect their reputation.

---

[1]Communities of practice emerge in the social space between project teams and knowledge networks. They are groups of like-minded, interacting people who filter, analyze, invest and provide, convene, build, and learn and facilitate to ensure more effective creation and sharing of knowledge in their domain. What they know, who they are, and what they do define them.

[2]A value network is any web of relationships that generates both tangible and intangible value through complex dynamic exchanges. Value networks include communities of practice, knowledge networks, and networks of practice. Their growing importance requires that organizations pay more attention to their forms and functions, evolve principles of engagement, circumscribe and promote success factors, and monitor and evaluate performance with knowledge performance metrics.

[3]There are five stages of community development: (i) potential, (ii) coalescing, (iii) maturing, (iv) stewardship, and (v) transformation.

People

I have no special talents. I am only passionately curious.

—Albert Einstein

A learning organization needs people who are intellectually curious about their work, who actively reflect on their experience, who develop experience-based theories of change and continuously test these in practice with colleagues, and who use their understanding and initiative to contribute to knowledge development. In short, it needs people who are reflective practitioners. Reflective practitioners understand their strengths and limitations and have a range of tools, methods, and approaches for knowledge management and learning, individually and in collaboration with others.

Reflective practice flourishes when people experience a high level of psychological safety and trust, and it is undermined when people feel exposed to unfair negative criticism and when they believe that they cannot rely on colleagues. Teamwork is, therefore, a vital ingredient of a genuine learning organization. Indeed, one characteristic of teams in learning organizations is that they operate as learning communities in which sensitively expressed dissent, conflict, and debate are encouraged as positive sources of learning. Developing the safety and trust upon which reflective practice and positive teamwork depend requires careful attention to relationship building and the management of individual and collective performance.

To grow and protect the investment made in staff members, a learning organization pays careful attention to developing and retaining its people. Closely linked to development and retention of staff members are the importance of recognition and incentives for learning. Learning organizations ensure that time and effort spent on effective knowledge management and learning are recognized as core activities in the organization's time and performance management systems. Rewards for contributing to learning and knowledge development can be more conventional (e.g., career advancement, increased income, and greater formal status) or may be less conventional (e.g., informal peer status, time made available for study, or public acknowledgement for an innovative contribution made).

Learning organizations also provide a wide range of opportunities for individual and collective learning and development. Learning and development programs are available to ensure that individuals and teams develop the competencies of reflective practice and collaborative learning. While learning and development systems may focus on more formal programs, a learning organization is one where the maximum benefit is also leveraged from other learning opportunities such as day-to-day work experiences, team meetings, short-term secondments, and membership of task groups.

In a learning organization, an important source of individual learning and development is coaching and mentoring support from managers, specialists, and other experienced colleagues. High-quality coaching and mentoring can help reflective practice flourish. However, both involve skills that cannot be taken for granted and must be consciously developed in the organization. It cannot be assumed that good contract managers and technical specialists automatically make good coaches and mentors.

Learning organizations require and encourage the development of leadership competencies at all levels in the organizational hierarchy, not just at the top. Leadership is viewed as a valuable skill that is based on the possession of expertise and knowledge, not simply positional status.

Knowledge

Knowledge is the true organ of sight, not the eyes.

—The Panchatantra

Knowledge is a critical asset in every learning organization. Because learning is both a product of knowledge and its source, a learning organization recognizes that the two are inextricably linked and manages them accordingly.

The units of knowledge production are both the individual and the collective. Learning organizations understand that while knowledge is created in the minds of individuals, knowledge development thrives in a rich web of social contact among individuals, groups, and organizations. A learning organization provides creative opportunities for this knowledge to be developed and shared with others through interpersonal contact and access to documentation.

An organization's main repositories of knowledge are the design and delivery of its products and services and the strategies, systems, and procedures it has developed to guide its decision-making. Learning organizations know how best to take a learning approach to the development of this embedded knowledge by putting in place the necessary systems and infrastructure for knowledge management (ADB 2008–).

Feedback is the dynamic process of presenting and disseminating information to improve performance. Feedback mechanisms are increasingly being recognized as key elements of learning. Key (and often underutilized) sources of knowledge in organizations are the data and information that emerge from monitoring systems and the analyses, conclusions, and recommendations that arise from self- and independent evaluations. Learning organizations have sophisticated ways of designing evaluations with learning (as well as accountability) in mind. Methods such as after-action reviews and retrospects[4] are successfully adopted and generate lessons that are carefully targeted at specific audiences. Learning organizations have systems that ensure that the outputs of self- and independent evaluations are made widely available, used to question orthodox thinking, and trigger creativity and innovation. Most significant changes are collected, systematically selected, and interpreted.[5] Peer assists,[6] drawing on individuals' expertise and documented lessons learned, are used in planning new initiatives to reduce the likelihood of repeated unintended negative outcomes. Action learning is used to tackle more intractable challenges.[7]

A learning organization recognizes the importance of a resilient organizational memory. Learning organizations ensure that individuals and teams are encouraged to use a range of ways of surfacing their tacit knowledge and making it available to others through carefully targeted documentation and collaborative working practices. Recognizing that organizations change in the direction in which they inquire, they leverage the powers of appreciative inquiry.[8] Documentation is made accessible to others in the organization with a range of user-friendly information and communications technology.

Learning organizations are networked with the wider world. They know how to create and run partnerships.[9] Collaborative mutual learning arrangements with other organizations are common and fruitful.

---

[4]Organizational learning calls for nonstop assessment of performance—its successes and failures. This ensures that learning takes place and supports continuous improvement. After-action reviews and retrospects are tools that facilitate assessments by bringing together a team to discuss an activity or project openly and honestly.

[5]The most significant change technique helps monitor and evaluate the performance of projects and programs. It involves the collection and systematic participatory interpretation of stories of significant change emanating from the field—stories about who did what, when, and why, and the reasons the event was important. It does not employ quantitative indicators.

[6]Peer assists are events that bring individuals together to share their experiences, insights, and knowledge on an identified challenge or problem. They also promote collective learning and develop networks among those invited.

[7]Action learning is a structured method that enables small groups to work regularly and collectively on complicated problems, take action, and learn as individuals and as a team while doing so.

[8]Appreciative inquiry is the process of facilitating positive change in organizations. Its basic assumption is uncomplicated: every organization has something that works well. Appreciative inquiry is therefore an exciting generative approach to organizational development. At a higher level, it is also a way of being and seeing.

[9]In development work as elsewhere, partnerships have a crucial role to play. To reach the critical mass required to reduce poverty, there must be more concerted effort, greater collaboration, alignment of inputs, and a leveraging of resources and effort. Understanding the drivers of success and the drivers of failure helps efforts to create and run them.

Technology

> *This is perhaps the most beautiful time in human history; it is really pregnant with all kinds of creative possibilities made possible by science and technology which now constitute the slave of man—if man is not enslaved by it.*
>
> —Jonas Salk

Learning organizations know how to harness the power of information and communications technology—without the technology constraining knowledge management and learning. In a learning organization, information and communications technology is used, among other purposes, to strengthen organizational identity; build and sustain learning communities; keep staff members, clients, and others informed and aware of corporate developments; create unexpected, helpful connections between people and provide access to their knowledge and ideas; encourage innovation and creativity; share and learn from good practices[10] and unintended outcomes; strengthen relationships; develop and access organizational memory; share tools, methods, and approaches; celebrate successes; identify internal sources of expertise; and connect with the outside world.

The creative use of information and communications technology such as shared document drives, intranet pages, online communities and networks, wikis and other collaborative work spaces, blogging and online storytelling,[11] staff profile pages,[12] online webinars, podcasts, and social network analysis[13] indicates that an organization takes learning seriously.

Finally, in a learning organization, sufficient opportunities are provided for staff members to learn how to make use of available information and communications technology for knowledge management and learning. Box 2 offers a structured questionnaire with which to gauge perceptions of competencies to learn for change.

---

[10]Good practice is a process or methodology that has been shown to be effective in one part of the organization and might be effective in another.

[11]Storytelling is the use of stories or narratives as a communication tool to value, share, and capitalize on the knowledge of individuals.

[12]Staff profile pages are dynamic, adaptive electronic directories that store information about the knowledge, skills, experience, and interests of people. They are a cornerstone of successful knowledge management and learning initiatives.

[13]Power no longer resides exclusively (if at all) in states, institutions, or large corporations. It is located in the networks that structure society. Social network analysis seeks to understand networks and their participants and has two main focuses—the actors and their relationships in a specific social context.

Box: Seeking Feedback on Learning for Change[14]

Organization

(i) There is an inspiring vision for learning and an organizational learning strategy that clearly communicates that learning is critical to organizational success.

(ii) Leaders take an exemplary leading role in creating and sustaining a supportive learning culture.

(iii) The formal organizational structure facilitates learning, adaptation, and change.

(iv) Sanctioned informal organizational structures enable and encourage learning across formal structural boundaries.

(v) Good use is made of communication systems to facilitate the lateral transfer of information and knowledge and to minimize the development of "silos".

(vi) Adequate resources are allocated for learning in terms of time allocation, specialist support staff, budgets for knowledge management infrastructure, formal and informal communities of practice and other value networks, and learning and development programs.

(vii) A balanced approach to learning that recognizes the importance of both planned and emergent learning is taken.

(viii) Planned learning is addressed through the careful design of strategy, structure, systems, procedures, and plans.

(ix) Emergent learning is encouraged by creating opportunities for informal sharing of knowledge and experience.

(x) Failures and unintended outcomes are the focus of constructive discussions leading to new approaches. When such incidents involve clients, care is taken to protect their reputation.

People

(i) Staff members are required to be reflective practitioners to reflect on their experience, develop experience-based theories of change, continuously test these in practice with colleagues, and use their understanding and initiative to contribute to knowledge development.

(ii) All staff members make frequent use of a range of tools, methods, and approaches for learning and collaborating with others.

(iii) Staff members experience a high level of psychological safety and trust; they can rely on colleagues and are not exposed to unfair negative criticism.

(iv) Teams operate as learning communities in which success and unexpected outcomes are analyzed and in which sensitively expressed

---

[14]The use of a six-point scale from *Strongly Agree* to *Strongly Disagree* is recommended.

dissent, conflict, and debate are encouraged as positive sources of learning.

(v) Staff members are encouraged to look outside the organization for new ideas, trends, and practices and to share what they learn with colleagues.

(vi) Equal attention is paid to developing and retaining staff members at all levels.

(vii) Staff members successfully use a wide range of opportunities for individual and team-based learning and development.

(viii) Time and effort spent by staff members on learning and knowledge development are recognized as core activities in the organization's time and performance management systems.

(ix) A wide range of formal and informal rewards and incentives for contributing to organizational learning and knowledge development is used (e.g., career advancement, increased income, informal peer status, additional time provided for study, and public acknowledgment for innovative contributions made).

(x) Leadership (based on the possession of expertise and knowledge) is expected from staff members at all levels in the organizational hierarchy.

Knowledge

(i) There is a widespread recognition that while knowledge is created in the minds of individuals, knowledge development thrives in a rich web of professional networks among individuals.

(ii) Important knowledge is easily accessible to people who need and use it.

(iii) There are creative opportunities for knowledge to be developed and shared with others by facilitating networks between individuals.

(iv) The design and delivery of products and services demonstrate how effective the organization is at applying what it has learned about the nature of good practice.

(v) The necessary systems and infrastructure for knowledge management are in place, understood, and working effectively.

(vi) Evaluations are carefully designed with learning (as well as accountability) in mind. Systems ensure that the outputs of internal and independent evaluations are made widely available; carefully examined; and used to influence decision-making and planning, question orthodox thinking, and trigger creativity and innovation.

(vii) Peer assists, drawing on individuals' expertise and documented lessons learned, are used in planning new initiatives to reduce the likelihood of repeated and unintended negative outcomes.

(viii) The organization has a resilient organizational memory and is not vulnerable to the loss of important knowledge when staff members move to other jobs in the organization or leave.

(ix) Individuals and teams successfully use a range of methods for surfacing their tacit knowledge and making it available to others, for example, using carefully targeted documentation and collaborative working practices.

(x) Adoption of after-action reviews and retrospects to learn from experience has been successful.

Technology

(i) There is a thorough and shared understanding of the value of information and communications technology for knowledge management and learning.

(ii) Information and communications technology facilitates but does not drive or constrain knowledge management and learning in the organization.

(iii) Information and communications technology is successfully used to create and sustain learning communities.

(iv) Information and communications technology is successfully used to keep people informed and aware of corporate developments.

(v) Information and communications technology is successfully used to create unexpected, helpful connections between people and to provide access to their knowledge and ideas.

(vi) Information and communications technology is successfully used to encourage innovation and creativity.

(vii) Information and communications technology is successfully used to enable people to share and learn from good practices and unintended outcomes.

(viii) Information and communications technology is successfully used to enable people to identify internal sources of expertise.

(ix) Creative use of information and communications technology is high. At least five of the following have been successfully adopted: shared document drives, intranet pages, online communities and networks, wikis and other means of collaborative document production, blogging, online storytelling, lessons learned databases, staff profile pages, online webinars, podcasts, and social network mapping.

(x) Sufficient opportunities are provided for staff members to learn how to make use of available information and communications technology for learning and knowledge sharing.

Source ADB (2009).

References

ADB (2008–) Knowledge showcases. Manila
ADB (2009) Learning for change in ADB. Manila

Proposition 12
Building Institutional Capacity for Development

In a Word The conditions of economic and social progress include participation, democratic processes, and the location of necessarily diverse organizational setups at community, national, regional, and increasingly global levels. Access to and judicious use of information underpins all these.

Rationale

Every day, we are reminded of the changes needed for economic and social progress, but not that institutions are the channels through which such changes can happen. We would do well to consider what is meant by (and can be accomplished through) participation, how participation grows out of democratic processes, how these processes depend on the structure of institutions, and how institutions originate from (and are supported by) human resources. Only then will we understand better the processes of progress and picture more accurately the necessarily diverse levels of the organizational setups on which progress depends.

© Asian Development Bank 2017
O. Serrat, *Knowledge Solutions*, DOI 10.1007/978-981-10-0983-9_12

Participation

The rights and responsibilities of people are central to progress. Participation is essential since privileged minorities seldom approve of reforms and concentration of political, economic, or social power in their hands has retarded development. Therefore, five questions must be asked. Who initiates? Who participates? Who decides? Who controls? And who is benefitted? If it is the people, then development activities will most likely succeed (bearing in mind that the chance to take part hinges in turn on access to information, freedom of association to hold discussions, and arrangement of regular meetings at which officials and representatives can listen and respond to communities and be held accountable for delivering particular outputs).

Democratic Processes

But democracy is more than multi-partyism or the granting of concessions by authorities. Civil society needs to be fortified at all levels in agreement with the customary checks and balances of cultures. So one should also ask what manner of democratic processes and what kinds of institutions are necessary to release the productive energies of people, and what conditions are required to make these processes and institutions work. The answer is that democratic processes must start from where people are and that—for democratic processes to unfold—account-ability, transparency, predictability, and participation are essential.

Institutions

It follows that institutions should be located at three levels:

- **Community** At the community level, a viable institution reflects the ideas, interests, and needs of communities. It has their confidence and the strength to communicate their views to higher authorities. Naturally, this assumes a degree of decentralization of decision-making. It presupposes too a capacity to act on rights and responsibilities. Above all, perhaps, the right to organize must exist.
- **Nation** At the national level, a viable institution has competence in policy-making, in socioeconomic analysis, and in technical research. It has negotiating parity with international bilateral and multilateral agencies. It provides inputs to national policy-making without relying on external advice. And it assists in the identification of linkages between the national, regional, and community levels.

- **Region** At the regional level, a viable institution possesses a mix of technical, managerial, and information-handling skills. It has also the ability to interpret communities to the nation (and vice versa). Most of all, it has a reasonable measure of autonomy (including independent revenues).

A tall order? Yes. On which economic and social progress depends.

Further Reading

ADB (2012) Strengthening participation for development results: an asian development bank guide to participation. Manila

Proposition 13
Learning Lessons with Knowledge Audits

In a Word Knowledge from evaluations will not be used effectively if the specific organizational context, knowledge, and relationships of evaluation agencies, and the external environment they face, are not dealt with in an integrated and coherent manner. Knowledge management can shed light on this and related initiatives can catalyze and facilitate identification, creation, storage, sharing, and use of lessons.

Introduction

Most development agencies have committed to become learning organizations. But the use of evaluation for learning may be less important than that of other inputs, such as self-evaluation and training, and evaluation results may only marginally support policy, strategy, and operational changes. The Independent Evaluation Department of the Asian Development Bank (2006) determined to apply knowledge management to lesson learning. In 2007, it formulated a strategic framework to improve the organizational culture, management system, business processes, information technology solutions, community of practice, and external relations and

These *Knowledge Solutions* abridge a paper presented at the Malaysian Evaluation Society's Third International Evaluation Conference held from 31 March to 4 April 2008 in Kuala Lumpur, Malaysia.

© Asian Development Bank 2017
O. Serrat, *Knowledge Solutions*, DOI 10.1007/978-981-10-0983-9_13

networking for that. These *Knowledge Solutions* explain the strategic framework. They also describe the knowledge audit methodology developed to tie in with the department's audiences. The online, questionnaire-based survey of perceptions conducted as a first exercise that year provided ready and multiple entry points against which the department can take measures to that intent, as well as a comprehensive baseline assessment against which to judge progress. Fundamentally, these *Knowledge Solutions* contend that evaluation agencies should move from "make and sell," at the simplest level, to "sense and respond" in ways that are increasingly satisfying to stakeholders. Knowledge from evaluations will not be used effectively if the specific organizational context, knowledge, and relationships of evaluation agencies, and the external environment they face, are not dealt with in an integrated and coherent manner. Knowledge management can shed light on possible operating frameworks for this and knowledge management initiatives can be applied to catalyze and facilitate identification, creation, storage, sharing, and use of lessons. That would be knowledge utilization indeed.

Knowledge, Relationships, Context, and External Environment

Knowledge must not be seen as something supplied from one person to another or from better-off countries to developing countries, but as something that can flow back and forth and be continually improved, adapted, and refreshed using knowledge management tools. What is more, knowledge management tools are more effective where the specific knowledge, relationships, and context of organizations and the external environment they face are dealt with in an integrated and coherent manner.

Audiences

Evaluations are conducted to find out what results are being achieved, what improvements should be considered, and what is being learned. In ADB, this is done with systematic and impartial assessment of policies, strategies, partnerships, programs and projects, including their design, implementation, and results. Sharing lessons[1] also demonstrates good governance and advances understanding of what an organization aims to accomplish, thereby generating support for it. The principal audiences for evaluations, using ADB as an example, include the Board of

---

[1]Lessons are of two types: operational and developmental. Operational lessons relate, among others, to performance measurement, aid coordination, resource requirements, team building and coordination, procurement practices, delivery and reporting systems, and logistics. Developmental lessons pertain to realization of development results, improvement of developmental practice, and delivery on priorities.

Directors, Management, the operations departments, ADB's developing member countries, the international evaluation community, and of course ADB's Independent Evaluation Department itself.

Interfaces

In the case of ADB, inter- and intra-organizational relationships encompass ADB's Independent Evaluation Department, other departments,[2] developing member countries, and the international evaluation community. Figure 13.1 shows these

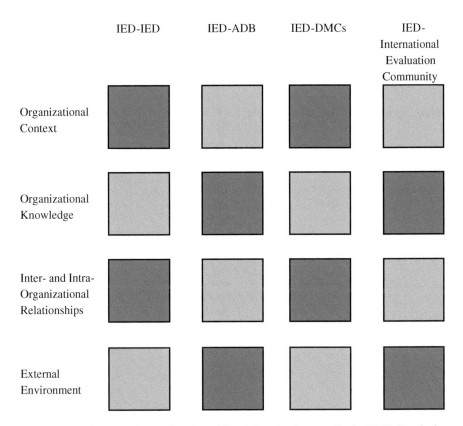

Fig. 13.1 Interfaces for lesson learning. *ADB* Asian development bank, *DMC* Developing member country, *IED* Independent evaluation department. *Source* ADB (2007)

---

[2]In large measure, these are operations departments. But ADB's Independent Evaluation Department also interacts with nonoperations departments and offices including the Asian Development Bank Institute, the (then) Economics and Research Department, the (then) Regional and Sustainable Development Department, and the Strategy and Policy Department.

primary interfaces with the specific organizational context, knowledge, and relationships of ADB's Independent Evaluation Department and the external environment it faces to structure entry points for lesson learning.

Architecture

Knowledge management must be embedded into an organization's business processes. It is not an activity delivered exclusively by a distinct business unit or a particular process. An architecture must be built to initiate and implement organization-wide knowledge management initiatives. Here, four pillars are critical to success. They are (i) leadership, (ii) organization, (iii) technology, and (iv) learning. The below table outlines the core functions, typical activities, and implementation elements of a stable architecture for lesson learning.

Table. Architecture for lesson learning

Pillar	Function	Typical activity	Illustrative implementation element
Leadership	Drive values for knowledge management	• Identify knowledge critical to learning lessons in ADB • Conduct work-centered analysis • Plan high-level strategic approach • Establish goal and prioritize objectives • Define requirements and develop measurement program • Promote values and norms. • Implement strategy	• Strategic planning • Vision sharing • Definition of goal and objectives • Executive commitment • Knowledge management programs tied to metrics • Formal knowledge management roles in existence • Tangible rewards for use of knowledge management • Encouragement, recognition, and reward for knowledge sharing • Communications

(continued)

(continued)

Pillar	Function	Typical activity	Illustrative implementation element
Organization	Organize to support values for knowledge management	• Identify critical knowledge gaps, opportunities, and risks • Develop business process model • Engage key audiences with incentives	• Organizational structure • Organizational culture • Business process workflows • Business process reengineering • Management by objectives • Total quality management • Operating procedures for knowledge sharing • Knowledge performance metrics • Communications
Technology	Collect and connect knowledge	• Enhance system integration and access • Deploy intelligent agents for people • Exploit semantic technologies • Reuse existing capabilities in new ways • Monitor, measure, and report knowledge performance metrics	• E-mail • Data warehousing • Data management software • Multimedia repositories • Groupware • Decision support systems • Intranet • Search engines • Business modeling systems • Intelligent agents • Neural networks • Lessons learned systems • Videoconferencing • Communications
Learning	Cultivate and use virtual teams and exchange forums for knowledge management	• Enliven collaboration • Facilitate communities of practice • Encourage storytelling	• Tacit and explicit knowledge • Capturing, organizing, and disseminating knowledge • Team learning

(continued)

(continued)

Pillar	Function	Typical activity	Illustrative implementation element
		• Recognize and reward knowledge sharing	• Management support for continuous learning • Virtual teams • Exchange forums • Communities of practice • Encouragement, recognition, and reward for innovation • Communications

Source ADB (2007)

Knowledge Management Tools

Learning lessons is contingent on improving organizational performance in five areas of competence. They are (i) strategy development, (ii) management techniques, (iii) collaboration mechanisms, (iv) knowledge sharing and learning, and (v) knowledge capture and storage (Collison and Parcell 2001).[3] Sundry knowledge management tools can support endeavors in each area, including, for example, knowledge audits, activity-based knowledge mapping, action learning sets, peer assists, and exit interviews. Conspicuously, the advent of the Internet has brought information technologies that complement and supplement the knowledge management tools at hand to make knowledge flow more effectively around and across organizations. The technologies include e-learning, web conferencing, collaborative software, content management systems, Yellow Pages, e-mail lists, wikis, and blogs. Where an organization might aim to be in specified time and the priority areas of competence that it might therefore decide to focus on can be investigated by means of such diagnostic tools.

Putting It All Together: The Strategic Framework

Drawing the elements of knowledge, relationships, context, and external environment; audiences; interfaces; architecture; and knowledge management tools in a conceptual structure generates the operating framework within which decisions on

---

[3]The Five Competencies Framework helps determine priorities for immediate action by selecting the area that will yield the greatest benefits if improved.

knowledge management initiatives can be taken and implemented. Figure 13.2 depicts the operating framework within which knowledge management tools were leveraged by ADB's Independent Evaluation Department for lesson learning in ADB.

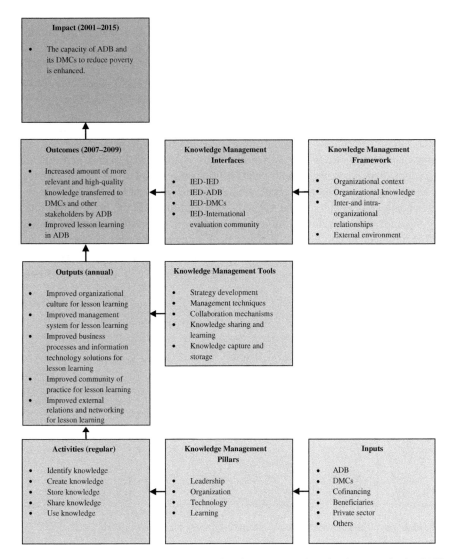

Fig. 13.2 Operating framework for lesson learning. *ADB* Asian development bank, *DMC* Developing member country, *IED* Independent evaluation department. *Source* ADB (2007)

Business Planning

Organizations looking to knowledge management develop business plans that are aligned with their goals and objectives. To raise knowledge vigilance to the point where attitudes are realistic and automatic, and tacit knowledge is internalized, such plans usually identify needs and issues within the organization and are couched against a framework for addressing these. Needs and issues, as well as the business processes associated with them, are typically determined by (i) the external environment; (ii) the mandate, vision, goal, and objectives of the organization; (iii) the overall strategic direction; (iv) the size and spread of the organization; (v) organizational history and culture; (vi) staff skills and experience; and (vii) available resources.

The elemental steps of business planning are (i) identify key staff groups in the organization; (ii) conduct comprehensive and holistic analyses with the key staff groups to identify needs and issues and barriers to organizational performance; (iii) supplement the analyses with inputs from managers and organizational strategy documents to determine an overall strategic focus; (iv) develop findings and recommendations to address the needs and issues and to tackle the barriers identified; and (v) implement a series of knowledge management pilots based on the findings and recommendations, leveraged by suitable knowledge management tools, and with concern for measuring the effectiveness of outreach. Figure 13.3 illustrates the process commonly followed to develop a business plan for knowledge management.

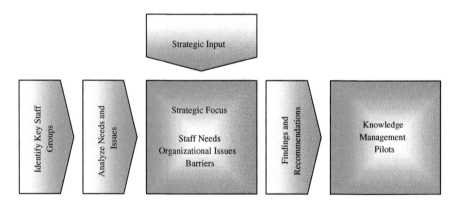

Fig. 13.3 Developing a knowledge management business plan. *Source* ADB (2007)

Learning is a process, not an attainment. Hence, in ADB, the Independent Evaluation Department's knowledge management business plans are aligned against ADB's to set in train the drive for continuous improvement that is at the heart of strategic frameworks. Moreover, the annual business planning process specifies that regular annual knowledge audits linked to annual business plans will deliver outputs steadily against each interface based on operational needs and priorities but also resources, with flexibility and adaptability.

Auditing Knowledge

Knowledge audits help organizations identify their knowledge-based assets and develop strategies to manage them.

- **Definition and Purpose** Developing a knowledge-sharing culture is a change process on the way to better organizational performance. To achieve that change, an organization needs a vision of where it wants to be and an accurate picture of where it is now—that is, its current reality. A knowledge audit is one way of taking that picture. What is a knowledge audit? The traditional concept of an audit is an evaluation of a person, business, system, process, project, or product by an independent third party. Financial audits are well understood. They examine the financial statements of a company to check performance against standards. A knowledge audit works differently, and some demystification is called for. It is by and large—granted differing objects, breadth of coverage, and levels of sophistication—a qualitative review (or inventory, survey, check) of an organization's knowledge health at both the macro and micro levels. The defining feature of a knowledge audit is that it places people at the center of concerns: it purports to find out what people know, and what they do with the knowledge they have. It can be described as an investigation of the knowledge needs of an organization and the interconnectivity among leadership, organization, technology, and learning in meeting these. Put in a different way, a knowledge audit is an investigation of the strengths and weaknesses of an organization's knowledge, and of the opportunities and threats that face it.

  A knowledge audit can have multiple purposes, but the most common is to provide tangible evidence of what knowledge an organization needs, where that knowledge is, how it is being used, what problems and difficulties exist, and what improvements can be made. Although there can be no blueprint, a typical knowledge audit will—not necessarily at the same time or level of detail[4]— query the following:

---

[4]The audit could span the whole organization, but preferably cover constituent parts of it. For the same reason that opinion polls do not sample the entire population, marginal returns diminish as the scale of related exercises increases. The same consideration applies to the number of questions that might be posed.

- – What are an organization's knowledge needs?
- – What tacit and explicit knowledge assets does it have and where are they?
- – How does knowledge flow within the organization, formally and informally, and to and from clients and relevant organizations?
- – How is that knowledge identified, created, stored, shared, and used?
- – What obstacles are there to knowledge flows, e.g., to what extent do its people, business processes, and technology currently support or hamper the effective movement of knowledge?
- – What gaps and duplications exist in the organization's knowledge?

- • **Constituents of Knowledge Audits** The typical constituents of knowledge audits, each of which can be conducted at different levels of complexity using various tools,[5] are shown in the Fig. 13.4.[6] They are preferably, but not necessarily, in the following order: (i) knowledge needs analysis, (ii) knowledge inventory analysis, (ii) knowledge flow analysis, and (iv) knowledge mapping. Throughout investigations, elements of knowledge, relationships, context, and external environment should be borne in mind, together with the fact that about 80% of an organization's knowledge is tacit—the greatest challenge lies in the audit of that.

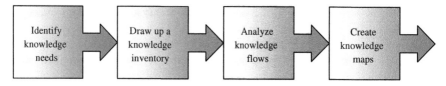

Fig. 13.4 Knowledge audit constituents. *Source* ADB (2008)

Knowledge Audit Methodology

In 2007, IED particularized a knowledge audit methodology, its principal means, and associated time frame, to be applied in four phases spanning about 5 months. The methodology draws on the elements of knowledge, relationships, context, and external environment; interfaces; and architecture deemed most relevant to the department. The four phases are (i) knowledge audit preparations, (ii) knowledge audit analysis, (iii) knowledge audit review, and (iv) business planning. Box 1 enumerates possible related steps and activities and Box 2 sketches an indicative

---

[5]The common tools used for knowledge audits are face-to-face and telephone interviews; structured, semi-structured, and unstructured questionnaires; workshops; focus group discussions; and online consultations. Other data and information can be gathered by referring to the documentation of the organization, conducting direct inspections, and examining the information and communications technology infrastructure, including the organization's website.

[6]Naturally, in a large and diverse organization, the dimensions and conduct of a knowledge audit will differ radically from that applicable to a small, less complex one.

time frame for implementation. Since knowledge management is a *process* for optimizing and leveraging the stores of knowledge in an organization, the accent placed (concurrently or in turn) on each constituent of a knowledge audit will depend on where an organization is and where it wants to be. Boxes 1 and 2 should be interpreted in view of that. A second important caveat is that the following section on the survey of perceptions conducted by IED in 2007, which emphasized identification of knowledge needs, should not be taken as all that a knowledge audit can be.

Box 1: Knowledge Audit Methodology—Suggested Steps and Activities

Phase 1	1. Plan Knowledge Audit • Identify objectives • Conduct background investigations • Hold preliminary discussions		2. Assimilate Core Knowledge Activities • Identify • Create • Store • Share • Use
	3. Delineate Interface Characteristics • IED–IED • IED–ADB • IED–developing member countries • IED–international evaluation community	4. Identify and Liaise with Key Audiences • Agree on interface representatives • Make initial contact	5. Select and Design Audit Forms • Consider interface characteristics • Formulate audit deliverables
Phase 2	6. Identify Knowledge Needs • Investigate what important knowledge the interfaces need to meet goals and objectives • Determine what important knowledge is available and what is missing • Consider, with attention to people, business processes, and technology, how faster access to important knowledge might be secured		7. Draw up Knowledge Inventory • Track down explicit knowledge products and services, their locations, purposes, relevance, and accessibility • Make out tacit knowledge about who the key audiences are, where they are, what they do, what they know, and what they learn • Identify gaps in tacit and explicit knowledge
	8. Analyze Knowledge Flows • Examine how knowledge products and services flow in IED, and to and from its interfaces, with attention to people, business processes, and technology		9. Create Knowledge Maps • Locate knowledge products and services and map out flows, constraints, and sinks • Map knowledge gaps • Analyze social networks

(continued)

(continued)

	• Characterize stock-based and flow-based knowledge, trends and patterns, and efficiency and effectiveness		
Phase 3	10. Assess Knowledge Audit Findings • Analyze evidence • Suggest courses and means of action • Devise improvements	11. Discuss Knowledge Audit • Carry out after-action reviews and retrospects • Conduct in-house workshops	12. Close Knowledge Audit • Incorporate suggestions for improvement • Identify matters for follow-up
Phase 4	13. Decide on Knowledge Management Initiatives • Prioritize knowledge management initiatives • Design knowledge management initiatives		14. Formulate Business Plans • Propose capital, operational, administrative, and recurrent expenditures • Submit annual budget document

Source ADB (2008)

Box 2: Indicative Knowledge Audit Time Frame

Phase	Activity	Month 1	Month 2	Month 3	Month 4	Month 5
1	Knowledge Audit Preparations	■	■			
	Plan knowledge audit		■			
	Assimilate core knowledge activities	■				
	Delineate interface characteristics	■				
	Identify and liaise with key audiences		■			
	Select and design aud it forms		■			
2	Knowledge Audit Analysis			■		
	Identify knowledge needs					
	Draw up knowledge inventory					
	Analyze knowledge flows					
	Create knowledge maps					
3	Knowledge Audit Review			■		
	Assess knowledge audit findings			■		
	Discuss kn owledge audit				■	
	Close knowledge audit					■
4	Business Planning					■
	Decide on knowledge management initiatives					■
	Formulate business plans					■

Source ADB (2008)

To underpin future knowledge audits, IED formulated in 2007 survey questionnaires that drew out perceptions of the performance of independent evaluation across the four interfaces. The questionnaires were designed against the Five Competencies Framework. The framework of organizational competence for knowledge management comprises (i) strategy development, (ii) management techniques, (iii) collaboration mechanisms, (iv) knowledge sharing and learning, and (v) knowledge capture and storage.[7] The questionnaires were comprehensive, organized, systematic, and inclusive; they provide the framework within which IED can search for continual opportunities to ameliorate the independent evaluation function and its feedback mechanisms. The responses to the questionnaires also revealed rich seams of "as-is," baseline information, which will be mined vigorously. Box 3 shows for each interface the area of competence on which the questionnaires centered.

Box 3: Perceptions Survey Questionnaires—Interface and Areas of Competence

Interface	Strategy development	Management techniques	Collaboration mechanisms	Knowledge sharing and learning	Knowledge capture and storage
IED–IED	✓	✓	✓	✓	✓
IED–ADB	✓		✓	✓	✓
IED–DMCs			✓	✓	✓
IED–IEC			✓	✓	✓

ADB Asian Development Bank, *DMC* Developing member country, *IEC* International evaluation community, *IED* Independent Evaluation Department
Source ADB (2008)

The Survey of Perceptions

Knowledge surveys The survey that opened IED's first knowledge audit aimed to gain insight into how people within the four interfaces perceive the department's knowledge management activities. From the results, IED measured awareness of and identified gaps in the department's knowledge products and services. The Five Competencies Framework was used to assess the department's organizational performance. This framework identifies these areas of organizational competence for knowledge management as (i) strategy development, wherein tools are used to help an organization achieve a particular goal in knowledge management through a long-term plan of action; (ii) management techniques, which cover a range of

---

[7]A competency approach befits organizational learning. It offers safeguards against drain of knowledge, inappropriate use of knowledge, and accumulation of poor knowledge.

practices from assessing the forces for and against desired organizational changes to assessing managerial approaches to mistakes, in order to do things right; (iii) collaboration mechanisms, which pertain to facilitating effective practices in working with others; (iv) knowledge learning and sharing, which means using techniques to learn from and improve future activities; and (v) knowledge capture and storage, wherein routines are applied to ensure that an organization retains essential knowledge. For each interface, survey questionnaires covered only the areas of competence deemed most relevant.

The survey adopted a variant of the Likert scale[8] to evaluate the perceived level of organizational performance per competence area, wherein respondents specify the extent of their agreement with a statement. Five choices were given per question to gauge perception of IED's competences: (i) never, (ii) seldom the case, (iii) sometimes the case, (iv) often the case, and (v) always the case. Two methods were used to determine overall perception of organizational performance in each area of competence. The first was based on the responses of the majority per question. The second established an objective measure by computing the weighted average score to account for the perception of the entire sample.

Survey Results

Box 4 gives a snapshot of the perception of the performance of IED in each area of competence by respondents from each interface.[9] Respondents from IED thought that the department is doing well in the areas of strategy development, collaboration mechanisms, and knowledge capture and storage. But the department is "on the fence" in knowledge sharing and learning, and its competence with management techniques must get better. Respondents from other departments felt that IED does well only in strategy development. They were ambivalent with regard to collaboration mechanisms. They recommended that the department should deploy more efforts in the areas of knowledge sharing and learning, and knowledge capture and storage. Respondents from the international evaluation community felt that the department is doing well in all three areas of competence regarding which their opinions were sought.

---

[8]A Likert scale is usually composed of an odd number of points measuring positive or negative responses to a statement.

[9]Sadly, no responses were received from evaluation agencies in developing member countries, with implications for the tools that can be applied to that interface in the future.

Box 4: Summary of Perceptions by Area of Competence

Interface	Strategy development	Management techniques	Collaboration mechanisms	Knowledge sharing and learning	Knowledge capture and storage
IED–IED	✓	X	✓	?	✓
IED–ADB	✓		?	X	X
IED–IEC			✓	✓	✓

ADB Asian Development Bank, *IEC* International evaluation community, *IED* Independent Evaluation Department
Note ✓ = More than half of the items in the questionnaire were rated as "often the case" to "always the case" by most of the respondents; ? Half of the items in the questionnaire were rated as "often the case" to "always the case" by most of the respondents, while the other half were rated as "sometimes the case" to "never;" X = More than half of the items in the questionnaire were rated as "sometimes the case" to "never" by most respondents
Source ADB (2008)

Associated Initiatives

The survey of perceptions substantiated the basis of the knowledge management initiatives that IED introduced from 2007. It clarified the need for others. Among the new knowledge products and services developed, *Learning Curves* are handy, two-paged quick references designed to feed findings and recommendations from evaluation to a broader range of clients. *Success Rates* present condensed information on successful ADB projects. The Evaluation Information System is an online database of lessons, recommendations, and ADB Management responses. The department hosts the secretariat of the Evaluation Cooperation Group.[10] It has also overhauled ECGnet, the group's communication tool. *Evaluation Alerts* are targeted information bytes delivered to personal mailboxes. Methods and guidelines for using plain English, disseminating findings and recommendations, and conducting exit interviews have been prepared. The evaluation pages were refurbished from top to bottom. They are updated daily and are now one of the most accessed first-level directories in adb.org. IED formulated regional technical assistance for capacity development for monitoring and evaluation, expected also to suggest a strategy for evaluation capacity development.[11] The department advertises its

---

[10]The Evaluation Cooperation Group was established by the heads of evaluation in multilateral development banks in 1996. Its membership comprises the African Development Bank, ADB, European Bank for Reconstruction and Development, European Investment Bank, Inter-American Development Bank, International Monetary Fund, and the World Bank Group. The United Nations Evaluation Group and the Evaluation Network of the Development Assistance Committee of the Organisation for Economic Co-operation and Development are observer members.

[11]Progressively more, evaluation ownership must move from ADB to its developing member countries.

knowledge products and services on *ADB Today*[12] and adb.org (and through other channels and at several venues) with one-time, near-term, and continuous efforts. The survey of perceptions suggested other opportunities. They included *Evaluation Chats*, a communication tool that would facilitate the establishment of an evaluation community of practice focused on the conduct and dissemination of strategic evaluations, harmonization of performance indicators and evaluation methodologies, and development of capacity in evaluation and evaluative thinking. *Evaluation News* and *Evaluation Presentations* were introduced too. They offer, respectively, reports on events in monitoring and evaluation and short photographic or PowerPoint displays on evaluation topics. IED's knowledge management initiatives are framed deliberately to increase value-added from operations evaluation, and are managed with knowledge performance metrics. Client feedback is sought regularly by various means.

Box 5 identifies the that might be leveraged to fill the remaining knowledge management gaps identified, and emphasizes with shading the areas of organizational competence found wanting at the time of the survey.

Box 5: Knowledge Management Tools Prioritized for Leverage

Interface	Strategy development	Management techniques	Collaboration mechanisms	Knowledge sharing and learning	Knowledge capture and storage
IED–IED	• Knowledge Audit • Most Significant Change • Outcome Mapping • Scenario Testing and Visioning	• Five Competencies Framework	• Communities of Practice • Action Learning Sets • Social Technologies	• Peer Assists • Challenge Sessions • After-Action Reviews and Retrospects • Intranet Strategies	• Taxonomies for Documents and Folders • Exit Interviews • Shared Network Drives
IED–ADB	• Scenario Testing and Visioning		• Communities of Practice • Social Technologies	• Peer Assists • Challenge Sessions • After-Action Reviews and Retrospects • Intranet Strategies	• Staff Profile Pages • Blogs
IED–IEC				• Stories • Peer Assists • After-Action Reviews and Retrospects	• Staff Profile Pages • Blogs

ADB Asian Development Bank, *IEC* International evaluation community, *IED* Independent Evaluation Department
Source ADB (2008)

---

[12]*ADB Today* is a daily e-information resource for all ADB staff in headquarters, resident missions, and representative offices. It is the main internal communication vehicle to keep ADB staff abreast of events and activities of ADB-wide interest. It is produced and edited each working day by the Department of External Relations with inputs from other departments.

References

ADB (2007) Learning lessons in ADB. Manila
ADB (2008) Auditing the lessons architecture. Manila
Collison C, Parcell G (2001) Learning to fly: practical knowledge management from leading and learning organizations. Capstone Publishing
Independent Evaluation Group—World Bank (2006) Annual report on operations evaluation. World Bank, Washington, DC

Further Reading

Ramalingam B (2005) Implementing knowledge strategies: lessons from international development agencies. Working Paper 244. Overseas Development Institute
Senge P (1990) The fifth discipline: the art and practice of the learning organization. Currency Double Day, New York

Proposition 14
Enhancing Knowledge Management Strategies

In a Word Despite worldwide attention to strategic planning, the notion of strategic practice is surprisingly new. To draw a strategy is relatively easy but to execute it is difficult—strategy is both a macro and a micro phenomenon that depends on synchronization. One should systematically review, evaluate, prioritize, sequence, manage, redirect, and if necessary even cancel strategic initiatives.[1]

Background

On 4 May 2009, at the 42nd Annual Meeting of the Board of Governors of ADB, Haruhiko Kuroda—ADB President and concurrent Chairperson of ADB's Board of Directors—stressed the importance of knowledge to that organization:

> To be fully effective, we must also consciously and actively blend knowledge with financing. We will focus on developing, capturing, and sharing knowledge in all our work, ensuring that ADB serves an intermediary role for both financing and knowledge.

---

[1]These *Knowledge Solutions* abridge *Enhancing Knowledge Management Under Strategy 2020*, the plan of action for 2009–2011 that the Asian Development Bank approved in July 2009.

Enhancing Knowledge Management Under ADB's Strategy 2020

These *Knowledge Solutions* showcase the set of actions/outputs that, on 31 July 2009, President Kuroda then approved to advance the knowledge management agenda under *Strategy 2020*, the long-term strategic framework of the Asian Development Bank (2008). Four pillars will support them: (i) sharpening the knowledge focus in all ADB operations, (ii) promoting and empowering communities of practice for knowledge capture and sharing, (iii) strengthening external knowledge partnerships to develop and disseminate knowledge, and (iv) scaling up staff development programs to improve technical skills and manage knowledge. The four pillars are closely related: the set of actions/outputs that make up the first focuses on adding value to ADB's operations in its developing member countries; the other three sets deal with how that might be achieved.

Articulating Actions/Outputs

Plans are only good intentions unless they immediately degenerate into hard work.

—Peter Drucker

ADB's plan of action for knowledge management connotes a pragmatic, step-by-step approach: the initial actions/outputs are for a 3-year time frame; measures for their implementation will be incorporated into ADB's Work Program and Budget Framework (2010–2012); and the progress will be monitored and reviewed at the time of ADB's annual budget review by the Regional and Sustainable Development Department in ADB, in consultation with ADB's Budget, Personnel, and Management Systems Department and Strategy and Policy Department.

Identifying Complementary Measures Contributing to Actions/Outputs

Half the failures of this world arise from pulling in one's horse as he is leaping.

—Julius Hare

ADB's plan of action does not discuss but flags aspects that support and facilitate knowledge management practices, viz., budgetary allocations, business process improvements, and information technology. Several measures are already under way; ADB's Budget, Personnel, and Management Systems Department, Office of Information Systems and Technology, and Strategy and Policy Department will address others separately, after consultations with relevant parties. These offices and departments were requested to ensure that complementary measures contribute to and fully support the implementation of the actions/outputs presented in the plan.

Box: Enhancing Knowledge Management Under Strategy 2020: Plan of Action for 2009–2011

Introduction

Knowledge management at ADB is evolving purposefully in the right direction, although more needs to be done. In 2001, *Moving the Poverty Reduction Agenda Forward in Asia and the Pacific: The Long-Term Strategic Framework of the Asian Development Bank (2001–2015)* stressed the role of knowledge management and committed ADB to becoming a "learning organization". In 2002, ADB established a Knowledge Management Committee, among other measures, to guide the implementation of the long-term strategic framework. In 2004, ADB issued a framework paper on *Knowledge Management in ADB* that set out five areas to prioritize ADB's knowledge management actions.[2] The progress made is highlighted below:

(i)   Enhanced appreciation for ADB's flagship knowledge products, such as the *Asian Development Outlook*, *Key Indicators for Asia and the Pacific*, and *Asia Economic Monitor*, among many others.

(ii) The launch of communities of practice and the establishment of regional knowledge hubs, both adding to ADB's growing array of knowledge partnerships.

(iii) Improved coordination mechanisms that govern cooperation between the knowledge and operations departments, and encouraged development of approaches such as the Technical Assistance Strategic Forum.[3]

---

[2]The framework sought (i) improved organizational culture for knowledge sharing, (ii) an improved management system, (iii) improved business processes and information technology solutions for knowledge capture, enrichment, storage, and retrieval, (iv) well-functioning communities of practice, and (v) expanded knowledge sharing, learning, and dissemination through external relations and networking.

[3]The Technical Assistance Strategic Forum was introduced in 2008 to provide direction for ADB-wide research and development technical assistance and knowledge products on topics of high relevance and impact to developing countries in Asia and the Pacific.

  (iv) Nomination of focal persons for knowledge management in the oper-
        ations departments, and establishment of knowledge management units
        in several departments.
   (v) New information technology solutions for improved knowledge shar-
        ing in ADB, such as C-Cube and e-Star.
  (vi) Corporate-level recognition of knowledge management and learning
        by inclusion of chapters on sector and thematic highlights, generating
        and sharing knowledge, and independent evaluation in ADB's annual
        reports.
 (vii) Transformation of the ADB Library into a knowledge hub to encourage
        knowledge networking. The Library hosts book launches and activities
        of the communities of practice, and provides kinesthetic informational
        resources such as a touch screen that allows staff to show project loca-
        tions. In addition to its self-service information resources, it provides
        timely information support to ADB staff engaged in project design and
        development. Demand for the Library's knowledge services is driven by
        the human need for connectivity, collaboration, and storytelling. The
        Library also created new staff positions to align its operations with the
        information requirements of *Strategy 2020: The Long-Term Strategic
        Framework of the Asian Development Bank (2008–2020)*.

To further accelerate progress, better institutionalize knowledge, and help
ADB change the way it conducts its core business, the Knowledge
Management Center in the Regional and Sustainable Development
Department conducted in 2008 a fundamental review of knowledge management practices in ADB, with support from the German Agency for
Technical Cooperation. The review involved ADB staff, including those in
resident missions, in surveys and focus group meetings. It confirmed the
progress made in the five areas of the Knowledge Management Framework,
and contributed the following strategic findings and recommendations:

   (i) While the main thrusts of *Knowledge Management in ADB* remain
        valid, ADB needs to make adjustments to strengthen its work on
        knowledge.[4]
  (ii) Adjustments must be practical, incremental, and forward-looking, and
        in particular be aligned progressively to the new corporate strategy
        (then) being finalized.

---

[4]Data from ADB's fourth Most Admired Knowledge Enterprise survey, conducted in 2008,
indicate that many staff remain unconvinced of ADB's commitment to knowledge management and learning. Notwithstanding the small number of questions on which it is based,
which suggests that ADB should develop additional mechanisms with which to assess
progress at distinct organizational levels, the survey invites action to guide more effectively
ADB's transformation into a knowledge-based institution.

(iii) Emphasis should be placed on improving ADB's ability to deliver more adequate and focused knowledge support to developing member countries.
(iv) A renewed effort in knowledge management is needed vis-à-vis the coordination mechanisms that drive internal and external knowledge partnerships.

The review conducted in 2008 emphasized also that knowledge management is not the sole responsibility of a department, office, or unit: it is an ADB-wide responsibility and all departments have important roles and accountability—the Knowledge Management Center serves as focal point to coordinate knowledge management practices across the institution.

Under Strategy 2020, knowledge solutions are one of five key drivers of change that underpin ADB's lending and technical advisory services to developing member countries. The generation—and application—of knowledge underpins development effectiveness. It increases the relevance of ADB to developing member countries but also to other development partners. The strategy states that "ADB will play a bigger part in putting the potential of knowledge solutions to work in the Asia and Pacific region". Recognizing the steadily increasing value that developing member countries attach to knowledge services and knowledge solutions, Strategy 2020 explains that ADB's knowledge management activities must be enriched through (i) internal learning from operational practice, and (ii) external learning from long-term strategic partnerships with other international finance institutions and world-class academic and research institutions. Strategy 2020 also calls for streamlining and enhancing institutional arrangements for knowledge management where appropriate.

Based on the findings of the 2008 review and in light of Strategy 2020, this paper presents a practical set of actions/outputs to further advance ADB's knowledge management agenda. The fundamental premise considered when drafting the paper was: "What does ADB need to know to achieve its goals?" The associated questions considered regarding knowledge in ADB were: "When do we need it?", "Where do we source it from?", and "How will we use it?" Knowledge is treated mainly in terms of flow, not stock, to emphasize the need to continue to develop insights and new practices and actively support knowledge intermediation through ADB's operations. Knowledge, if not replenished continuously, is likely to be the fastest depreciating resource in ADB over time and even across ADB's clients. The implication is that ADB must invest in knowledge very judiciously from realistic assessments of what value a particular knowledge product or service will provide to ADB and its clients with emphasis on "usability" and "use," that is, knowledge that can and will be used in clearly defined and intended ways. All this, in turn, has implications for human resources and recruitment of relatively "specialized" expertise against a range of "knowledge positions".

The action plan starts with emphasis on sharpening the knowledge focus in ADB's operations, to be supported by efforts to empower communities of practice for knowledge capture and sharing, since internal demand is important, with related knowledge demonstrating faster value to feed in at critical points of corporate planning and priority setting. The plan then aims to strengthen external knowledge partnerships for knowledge development and dissemination, and finally scale up staff development programs. Taken together, the action plan represents a pragmatic and step-by-step approach, and the actions/outputs are initial measures for a 3-year time frame beginning 2009. Measures for their implementation will be incorporated into the Work Program and Budget Framework (2010–2012). The progress of implementation will be monitored and reviewed as part of the annual budget review. The draft paper benefited from interdepartmental comments, which were incorporated as appropriate. This final paper reflects the comments from a Management briefing session on 4 June 2009 and from the Management Committee Meeting held on 21 July 2009.

The paper does not offer detailed discussions of aspects that facilitate knowledge management practices, such as budgetary allocations, business process improvements, and information technology. These are critical to implementation but must be addressed separately. For example, the involvement of the Office of Information Systems and Technology is essential to ensure that follow-up facilitative actions/outputs fully support the implementation of those presented in the paper.[5]

Proposed Actions/Outputs

The action plan rests on our pillars:

- **Sharpen the Knowledge Focus in ADB's Operations** ADB's unique abilities to generate, disseminate, and apply knowledge are based on three

---

[5]Advances in information technology can leverage knowledge solutions and knowledge services, and the Office of Information Systems and Technology has a significant role to play in helping deliver the increased effectiveness that Strategy 2020 seeks, both in ADB and outside it. Indeed, progress cannot be achieved in the absence of information technology. It can help ADB collect and connect knowledge (that often gets lost) more systematically. One such example is an ADB-wide, web-based repository of good practice notes capturing lessons learned throughout the program or project cycle. Information technology can also be deployed for staff profile pages that store and share information about the knowledge, skills, experience, and interests of staff, and for content-rich communications within ADB, and across resident missions. Improvements in information technology systems can also support web-based communications with external stakeholders, and thus store and share their know-how (and possibly even add value to it). It stands to reason that the Office of Information Systems and Technology should be a bigger part of ADB's knowledge agenda, in coordination with the knowledge and operations departments. The motive, the means, and the opportunities can be clarified when the Office of Information Systems and Technology formulates a follow-up to the Information System and Technology Strategy (2004–2009).

areas of comparative advantage: ADB's central position in identifying trends within and across the region; its capacity for interdisciplinary and integrated approaches; and its ability to then blend knowledge and insight with large, concessional financing. Knowledge enriches financing operations and, in combination with ADB's convening power, spurs development effectiveness. Effective knowledge management can—in fact, must— help identify and put potential knowledge services and knowledge solutions to work through regional and country partnership strategies, investment programs and projects, and technical assistance and policy dialogue. The following actions/outputs are proposed to sharpen the knowledge focus in ADB's operations at the regional, country, and project levels:

(i) At the regional level, ADB has made notable progress in undertaking and disseminating high impact regional studies. ADB is increasingly recognized as a lead policy advisor that actively contributes to regional forums on key challenges facing developing Asia. Regional strategic studies also support ADB's corporate operational planning. To better serve this function, ADB needs a focused and coordinated approach to identifying and organizing priority regional studies. The Technical Assistance Strategic Forum is one such mechanism to coordinate, over the medium term, research and sector work among knowledge and operations departments.

(ii) At the country level, the country partnership strategies are key documents that guide medium-term operational programming, in line with international good practices, with focus on results and development effectiveness. Measuring results and assessing development effectiveness call for attention to explicitly reflecting knowledge management as part of formulating and implementing country partnership strategies.[6] In particular, the results matrix in country partnership strategies should specify knowledge indicators. Knowledge management activities should also be properly resourced in the country operations budgets, including resources for economic and sector work, and country diagnostics to inform the country partnership strategy preparation and policy dialogue.

(iii) At the project level, there is ample room to sharpen the knowledge focus. Lending and technical assistance grants are among the primary

---

[6]This invites revision of the template for country partnership strategies. For instance, the new format for country strategic opportunities programs introduced by the International Fund for Agricultural Development in 2006 contains a section on knowledge management and communication that articulates the Fund's knowledge management strategy relative to country-level objectives. It aims to ensure that knowledge management processes are effectively mobilized in country-level policy dialogue, program development, and program implementation.

channels through which ADB brings value to its clients. Lending and technical assistance operations also represent unique opportunities for introducing innovation and promoting learning. Is a project relevant and responsive to the specific problem being considered? Does the design of interventions reflect the knowledge, lessons, and insights of similar situations? What innovative features characterize the project design and implementation? How can the project or program be designed to support rigorous impact evaluation, and to encourage learning and knowledge sharing? These are questions project teams are encouraged to emphasize when developing loan and technical assistance proposals and presenting them to the clients and the ADB Management for decision making.

Implementation of these actions/outputs, especially to sharpen the knowledge focus at the country and project levels, will be supported by the ongoing review of ADB's business processes. This will strengthen ADB's ability to provide innovative services to its clients—both to respond to new challenges and opportunities as they emerge and to implement tried and tested practices.

- **Empower the Communities of Practice** Communities of practice are a potential instrument with which to implement knowledge management within ADB, ultimately to the benefit of its clients. The communities of practice keep know-how of a domain alive by sharing what they know, building on that, and adapting knowledge to specific sector and project applications. ADB introduced the concept of communities of practice in 2002 at the time of ADB's reorganization, with adjustments in 2005. At present, ADB has 12 communities of practice in key sector and thematic areas. The performance of the communities of practice was reviewed in 2009. The exercise identified that (i) the communities of practice have limited outreach to all staff, especially those in resident missions and representative offices; (ii) the budget for staff development and knowledge sharing through the communities of practice is limited; and (iii) there is a need to realign the work and mandates of the communities of practice with the priorities of Strategy 2020. The following actions/outputs are proposed to empower the communities of practice to act as drivers of change, to promote exchange of ideas and good practices, and to upgrade technical skills among peers:

(i) Ensure that communities of practice become an integral part of ADB's business processes. Supervisors should fully support both professional and national staff (including those in resident missions and representative offices) to participate in the communities, with the staff's contributions recognized more vigorously in the performance and development planning exercise. Management will ensure provision of sufficient time for the chairs of the committees to perform their functions for the communities of practice.

(ii) Increase the budget of the communities of practice, based on a clear set of objectives and, most importantly, measurable "outcomes" of improved knowledge management. Increased budgets will be allocated clearly, directly, and explicitly in proportion to how practical and tangible knowledge management occurs. This will be a case of "output-based financing," rewarding those who generate and share useful and usable knowledge. Communities of practice with vague or input and/or process-focused proposals will not be funded. This will entail revising the current purpose and structure of the sector and thematic biannual reports.

(iii) Require the communities of practice to more purposefully engage in external partnerships including especially the regional knowledge hubs that ADB finances. (Engaging nonregional knowledge hubs is to be considered as well.)

(iv) The role of the knowledge management coordinators in ADB will be reviewed and ways to harness their knowledge, skills, experience, and interests in the form of a community of practice in knowledge management will be proposed.

- **Strengthen External Knowledge Partnerships** Knowledge networks facilitate information exchange toward practice-related goals. ADB will need to further augment internal knowledge sharing through communities of practice by strengthening its knowledge networking and partnerships with external institutions within and outside Asia and the Pacific. Through such external knowledge networking, ADB can share insights from its development financing practices with external partners and benefit from knowledge generated by others. Significantly, external knowledge networking enables ADB to serve one of its core roles as a multilateral development bank—to promote learning and innovation for the benefits of developing member countries.

ADB (2005) decided early to encourage research and networking on innovative knowledge products and services. This led it to establish seven regional knowledge hubs under regional technical assistance in 2005. These hubs are expected to facilitate learning and dissemination, exchange, and sharing of knowledge with and among developing member countries including South–South cooperation. It is important that ADB make them work effectively, including by tasking and using them itself. Other thematic and sector knowledge networking arrangements are through the Asian Development Bank Institute, Economics and Research Department, Office of Regional Economic Integration, and Regional and Sustainable Development

Department. The operations departments have also initiated strategic and policy research partnerships with institutes in and outside the region.

A framework for knowledge partnerships that focus on the region's future development needs must be established—based on Strategy 2020s overarching goal of an Asia and Pacific region that is free of poverty and to meet the Millennium Development Goals. The Regional and Sustainable Development Department reviewed the performance of the regional knowledge hubs in 2008. That review concluded that knowledge partnerships should be based on a better understanding of the forms and functions of networks, and clear definition of expected outputs and outcomes in response to needs. It should also be understood that networks that tie developing member countries to other developing member countries do exist: ADB needs to position itself to add value accordingly. Additionally, it is crucial to foster closer links between ADB's communities of practice, the knowledge and operations departments, and relevant external knowledge partners. Accordingly, the following actions/outputs are proposed:

(i) Develop criteria for the selection of external knowledge networks including nonregional institutions (from ADB's member countries). Key criteria include (a) the three strategic directions under Strategy 2020 (namely, inclusive socioeconomic growth, environmentally sustainable growth, and regional cooperation and integration); (b) the priority sectors and thematic areas; and (c) the research priorities established under the Technical Assistance Strategic Forum.

(ii) Ensure that expected outputs and outcomes are strategically aligned to ADB and developing member country priorities, specified during the selection process, and include requisite support from the relevant communities of practice. For hubs located in developing member countries, the active involvement of the resident missions is strongly recommended. Most importantly, highlight a few well-focused performance and "output and outcome" targets that knowledge hubs know they will be held accountable for delivering against.

(iii) Make sure that agreements with knowledge networks spell out the need to conduct proactive dissemination activities in ADB and its developing member countries, and encourage the networks to disseminate ADB's knowledge products too.

(iv) Consider knowledge partnerships when ADB enters into agreements with other institutions through documents such as letters of intent and memorandums of understanding.

- **Further Enhance Staff Learning and Skills Development** The ability of ADB and all staff to learn is a precondition to the success of Strategy 2020. Engaging all staff in knowledge management is crucial to generating and sharing knowledge. Yet mainstreaming knowledge management in ADB takes time and resources. Staff learning and development should be reflected in annual performance and development plan reviews. This is included in the Human Resources Action Plan (ADB 2009). Staff need not only update technical and professional skills but must also acquire and master methods and techniques specifically for knowledge management.[7] The Budget, Personnel, and Management Systems Department has already begun to review ADB's staff learning and development program. The following actions/outputs will complement the ongoing work:

(i) Design and implement a focused (and needs-based) knowledge management and learning program for all staff, including those in resident missions and representative offices. This program would be jointly developed by the Knowledge Management Center and the Budget, Personnel, and Management Systems Department and involve the communities of practice.

(ii) Introduce the concept of "sabbatical" in the current "Special Leave Without Pay" arrangement that is based on merits and focused on results, to encourage staff to compete for external learning and knowledge-sharing opportunities (and be recognized for their accomplishments).

(iii) Invite a number of senior and junior researchers to ADB for short-term assignments in forward-looking studies that are aligned with the priorities of Strategy 2020, with nominations subject to approval by the Vice-Presidency for Knowledge Management and Sustainable Development.

(iv) Increase the budget for external training for administration by the Vice-Presidents.

(v) Capture the knowledge and experience of departing staff, especially retiring members, through exit debriefings and participation in the induction program.

These actions/outputs are intended to incorporate knowledge management and learning into ADB's learning and development program, and to enhance knowledge sharing. The overall goal is to ensure that ADB's activities are henceforth based on more innovative and creative approaches that meet the changing needs of developing member countries.

---

[7]The Knowledge Management Center began to publicize knowledge management and learning tools in October 2008: the *Knowledge Solutions* series specify tools, methods, and approaches to propel development forward and enhance its effects; the *Knowledge Showcase* series offers an effective tool to disseminating innovative ideas and good practices from ADB operations; *Learning for Change in ADB* offers timely, practical guidance to support and energize ADB's organization, people, knowledge, and technology for learning.

Next Steps

The actions/outputs proposed above are practical, incremental, and supportive of Strategy 2020. Several of them are already under way. A critical next step to ensure continuing and effective implementation is to incorporate all firmly in ADB's Work Program and Budget Framework (2010–2012). As noted at the beginning of this paper, knowledge management is a bank-wide agenda, and all departments and offices are to be actively involved in implementing the actions/outputs proposed.

Another critical step is to set up a system that monitors and reports on the implementation progress, with a particular focus on "results" and what is actually happening that is different. As the corporate focal point, the Knowledge Management Center will serve this function in collaboration with other relevant departments and offices.[8] The center will facilitate and monitor action plan implementation and report annually through the Regional and Sustainable Development Department to the Vice-Presidency for Knowledge Management and Sustainable Development, and subsequently to the Senior Management Team. The annual report on implementation progress will highlight implementation issues and propose remedial measures and follow-up actions/outputs for Management endorsement. These will be incorporated into subsequent annual budgets and work plans for implementation and continuing monitoring.

Appendix: Results Framework for the Action Plan

Impact:[9] The capacity of ADB and its developing member countries to reduce poverty is enhanced.

Primary Outcomes:[10] (i) an improved management system; (ii) improved business processes and information technology solutions for knowledge capture, enrichment, storage, and retrieval; (iii) improved organizational culture for knowledge sharing; (iv) well-functioning communities of practice; and (v) expanded knowledge sharing, learning, and dissemination through external relations and networking

Responsibility Centers: All knowledge and operations departments; Asian Development Bank Institute; Budget, Personnel, and Management Systems

---

[8]Year-on-year monitoring of the progress toward the directions of change will be assessed. This will be effected through the annual budget planning exercise in consultation with the Budget, Personnel, and Management Systems Department and the Strategy and Policy Department.

[9]The impact targeted is that indicated in *Knowledge Management in ADB*.

[10]The primary outcomes supported are those listed in *Knowledge Management in ADB*.

Department; Community of Practice Committees; Economics and Research Department; Office of Co-financing Operations; Office of the General Counsel; Office of Regional Economic Integration; Regional and Sustainable Development Department; and Strategy and Policy Department

Outcome Indicator	Action/Output	Complementary Measures Contributing to Action/Output	Assumptions and Risks[a]
First pillar statement: the knowledge focus in ADB's operations is sharpened			
At the regional level, ADB is increasingly recognized as a lead policy advisor, notably through the knowledge agenda that its technical assistance for research and development advances	Coordination of the Technical Assistance Strategic Forum is improved	Business process improvements[b]	• Strong commitment by the Senior Management Team • ADB values adjust in support of knowledge management and learning • Close coordination among offices and departments • Availability of adequate resources
At the country level, country partnership strategies guide medium-term operational programming with a focus on results and development effectiveness	Country partnership strategies make explicit reference to knowledge management[c]	Business process improvements	
At the project level, key documents embody quality, knowledge, and innovation	Project processing documents for lending and technical assistance operations incorporate the knowledge, lessons, and insights of similar situations, display innovative features, and lend themselves to learning and knowledge sharing[d]	Business process improvements	
Second pillar statement: the communities of practice are empowered			
Communities of practice become an integral part of ADB's business processes	Participation in communities of practice is encouraged and recognized	Business process and information technology improvements	• Availability of staff capabilities (experience, competencies, and technical and professional skills)
Output-based financing rewards communities of	The budgets of communities of practice are increased	Budgetary allocation	

(continued)

(continued)

Outcome Indicator	Action/Output	Complementary Measures Contributing to Action/Output	Assumptions and Risks[a]
practice that generate and share useful and usable knowledge	based on a clear set of objectives and measurable outcomes of improved knowledge management		• Staff attitudes (values and beliefs about innovation, commitment, and flexibility) adjust in support of knowledge management and learning
The communities of practice engage more purposefully in external partnerships	Partnerships are struck between communities of practice and regional (and nonregional) knowledge hubs	Business process and information technology improvements, budgetary allocation	
The contributions of the knowledge management coordinators in ADB are enhanced	Terms of reference for knowledge management coordinators are drawn and a community of practice in knowledge management is proposed	Business process improvement, budgetary allocation	
Third pillar statement: external knowledge partnerships are strengthened			
The selection of external knowledge networks is improved	Criteria for the selection of external knowledge networks are developed[e]	Business process improvement, budgetary allocation	• Staff behaviors (performance, productivity, teamwork, and cooperation) adjust in support of knowledge management and learning
Outputs and outcomes of external knowledge networks are strategically aligned to ADB and developing member country priorities	Expected outputs and outcomes are specified with support from the communities of practice and resident missions	Business process improvement	
The external knowledge networks disseminate knowledge products proactively	Agreements spell out proactive dissemination activities	Business process improvement, budgetary allocation	
ADB's partnerships agreements encourage knowledge partnerships	Letters of intent and memorandums of understanding consider knowledge partnerships	Business process improvement	

(continued)

(continued)

Outcome Indicator	Action/Output	Complementary Measures Contributing to Action/Output	Assumptions and Risks[a]
Fourth pillar statement: staff learning and skills development are enhanced further			
Staff skills in knowledge management and learning are developed	A focused (and needs-based) knowledge management and learning program is designed	Business process improvement, budgetary allocation	
Staff are encouraged to pursue learning and knowledge sharing opportunities when on special leave	The concept of a results-based and competitive sabbatical is introduced	Business process improvement	
Research in priority areas of Strategy 2020 is boosted	Senior and junior researchers are invited to conduct short-term, forward-looking studies	Business process improvement, budgetary allocation	
Opportunities for external training are expanded	The budget for external training is increased	Budgetary allocation	
The tacit knowledge of departing staff is captured to drive organizational performance improvement	The knowledge and experience of departing staff are captured through exit debriefings and participation in the induction program	Business process improvement	

[a]The assumptions and risks identified apply across the four pillars. *Learning for Change in ADB* specifies roadblocks to learning and identifies 10 challenges that ADB can overcome to minimize the risks listed

[b]A business process is a collection of related, structured activities or tasks that produce a specific service or product for a particular client. In ADB, business processes are revised from time to time, typically to strengthen (i) the country ownership in ADB operations; (ii) the partnerships ADB develops with national and international development partners; (iii) ADB's capacity to more effectively engage with civil society; and (iv) ADB's capacity to provide a wider range of services, including knowledge products and services, to developing member countries. Examples of what business process improvements might be called for in relation to some actions/outputs are given in footnotes below. In most instances, their definition will require consultations between the Budget, Personnel, and Management Systems Department, the Regional and Sustainable Development Department, and the Strategy and Policy Department

[c]This will likely entail a revision of the Board document template for preparation of country partnership strategies

[d]This will likely entail a revision of the Board document template for preparation of reports and recommendations of the President, technical assistance reports, etc.

[e]This will likely entail preparation of guidelines on designing knowledge partnerships for collaborative advantage

References

ADB (2005) Technical assistance for establishment of regional knowledge hubs. Manila
ADB (2008) Strategy 2020: the long-term strategic framework of the asian development bank
    (2008–2020). Manila
ADB (2009) Human resources action plan. Manila

Proposition 15
From Strategy to Practice

In a Word Strategic reversals are quite commonly failures of execution. In many cases, a strategy is abandoned out of impatience or because of pressure for an instant payoff before it has had a chance to take root and yield results. Or its focal point is allowed to drift over time. To navigate a strategy, one must maintain a balance between strategizing and learning modes of thinking.

Preamble

Despite worldwide attention to strategic planning, the notion of strategic practice is surprisingly new. This owes to widespread perception that strategic reversals owe to strategic miscalculations—the strategy was not sufficiently perceptive, imaginative, or visionary. Alternatively, it was too much of a good thing. But the truth is that strategic reversals are quite commonly failures of execution. In many cases, a strategy is abandoned out of impatience or because of pressure for an instant payoff before it has had a chance to take root and yield results. Or, its focal point is allowed to drift over time.

To draw a strategy is relatively easy but to execute it is difficult. Strategy is both a macro and a micro phenomenon that depends on synchronization. For that reason,

© Asian Development Bank 2017
O. Serrat, *Knowledge Solutions*, DOI 10.1007/978-981-10-0983-9_15

it is worthwhile to examine a few elements of a disciplined process for systematically reviewing, evaluating, prioritizing, sequencing, managing, redirecting, and, if necessary, even canceling strategic initiatives.

Scenario Thinking

Strategic planning stands for the unrelenting process of making decisions systematically with the greatest intelligence of their futurity, organizing the efforts necessary to carry them out, and measuring outcomes against expectations with feedback and self-control. The short-term calls for strategic decisions as much as the long term. However, planning must take account of unpredictability and should not stake everything on one possible scenario. It must develop a small set of distinct scenarios covering the main areas of uncertainty and all plausible futures.

A scenario is an internally consistent view of the future. Scenario thinking is the process of generating and analyzing a small set of different futures. In discrete steps, it (i) reveals the focal issue, (ii) characterizes factors and players, (iii) lists driving forces, (iv) ranks driving forces, (v) fleshes out scenarios, (vi) draws implications, and (vii) selects indicators. The end-result of building scenarios is not an accurate prediction of tomorrow but better thinking about the future. Moreover, since scenarios provide a context for decisions, better thinking should lead to decisions that are more robust. As events unfold, it is necessary to continue to review whether plans fit the realities of environment, economy, society, polity, and technology. If they do not, how can one discard them, or at least stop devoting more resources to their perpetuation?

> Unless a variety of opinions are laid before us, we have no opportunity of selection, but are bound of necessity to adopt the particular view which may have been brought forward.
>
> —Herodotus

Navigating a Strategy

To navigate a strategy, one must maintain a balance between strategizing and learning modes of thinking. This is achieved by more skilful action within the environment, in which the aim to make sense of an environment one finds puzzling is balanced by adaptive learning.

> All this will not be finished in the first one hundred days. Nor will it be finished in the first one thousand days; nor in the life of this administration; nor even perhaps in our lifetime on this planet. But let us begin.
>
> —John F. Kennedy

Strategizing involves a vision, a goal, a blueprint for the future, and a plan on how to get there. In almost any field of human activity, the factors and players that interact to create both the present and the future are complex and numerous. They include market forces, globalization, regionalization, natural resources, information flows, media, culture, and governance. Theories call for abstractions; for that reason, they apply only in a few domains.

Learning adheres to the same principles as the process of evolution. The events that unfold suggest new hypotheses, based on which one decides on the next steps. In a state of uncertainty, there is little alternative to adaptation. Only through action can organizations and people participate and gather the experience that both sparks and is informed by the process of learning.

Strategy as Practice

Execution is a process. It is not an action or a step and it rests on more people than strategy formulation. Strategy as practice means treating earnestly the habits of practitioners. It reconciles the dichotomy between strategy and learning. Therefore, the practice perspective is concerned with managerial activity, that is to say, with how managers do strategy. There are exciting moments in this, such as the grasping of situations, the begetting of ideas, and the identification of opportunities. But there is also the daily fare, including the routine of planning and budgeting each year, the sitting in committees, the writing of official documents, and the making of presentations. Here, attention to detail and persistence counts as much as foresight: at all times, questions of suitability, feasibility, and acceptability must be asked and answered. It is best to factor in smaller steps, celebrate their achievement, and move sequentially. The practice perspective embodies concern for the effectiveness and efficiency of strategists and not just of organizations. It connects to structured thinking; building, organizing, and working teams; appraising options; creating support mechanisms; assigning and holding responsibilities and accountability; choosing the right metrics; planning delivery; monitoring results; evaluating performance; and managing stakeholders and communications. Strategies that are not deliverable are of no use.

Further Reading

ADB (2006) From strategy to practice: the tonle sap initiative. Manila

Proposition 16
Marketing in the Public Sector

In a Word Marketing in the public sector may be the final frontier. Agencies operating in the public domain can use a custom blend of the four Ps—product (or service), place, price, and promotion—as well as other marketing techniques to transform their communications with stakeholders, improve their performance, and demonstrate a positive return on the resources they are endowed with.

© Asian Development Bank 2017

O. Serrat, *Knowledge Solutions*, DOI 10.1007/978-981-10-0983-9_16

Transforming the Public Sector

The public sector is the part of economic life, not in private ownership, that deals
with the production, delivery, and allocation of basic public goods and services at
global,[1] regional, national,[2] or local levels. (Its processes and structures can take the
form of direct administration, public corporations, and partial outsourcing. Its
activities are funded through government expenditure financed by seigniorage,
taxes, and government borrowing, or through grants.)

The public sector is vast. From 1996 to 2006, for example, government spending
in the United States made up 35% of gross domestic product. (In numerous large
European economies, for many years, its range has been 45–55%.)[3] What happens
in the public sector has major implications for economies[4]: since the relevance,
efficiency, effectiveness, sustainability, and impact of a country's public sector is
vital to national welfare, its organizations, and their activities have come under
scrutiny.

---

[1]There is an international public sector. Multilateral cooperation was a feature of the second half of
the twentieth century, representing a historical reckoning of the nation state with the growing array
of social, political, economic, and environmental issues that affect us all. The composition of this
international public sector is varied and evolves; its institutions range from large organizations that
are household names, e.g., the United Nations, to smaller regional organizations comprising a few
member countries. Areas of broad-based international cooperative activity include (i) political and
administrative cooperation; (ii) international justice and law; (iii) international cooperation for
development; (iv) regional cooperation; (v) science, technology, and education; and (vi) human
rights and humanitarian affairs.

[2]At its most common level, namely, that of the country, the composition of the public sector varies.
Yet, public institutions typically deliver such critical services as national defense, police protection, public buildings, fire fighting, urban planning, modes of transport, public transit, corrections,
taxation, primary education, and various social programs. They might extend goods and services
that nonpayers cannot be excluded from such as street lighting; that benefit all of society, not just
individuals such as parks and recreation areas; or that encourage equal opportunity such as
subsidized rent. Sometimes, provision is moved from the public to the private sector. This is
known as privatization, which has from the early 1980s taken place on a large scale everywhere in
the world. (In other, less common instances, provision may shift from the private to the public
sector—health care is but one area where some public institutions now make available, or are
experimenting with, goods and services previously furnished by the private sector.) Elsewhere,
with differing extents even within countries, areas of overlap exist: this is most often seen in water
management, waste management, and security services, among others. To note, the public sector
routinely engages the private sector to provide goods and services on its behalf, a practice known
as outsourcing.

[3]From the twentieth century, growth in gross domestic product per head in Western Europe and
North America, and later in some Asian countries, was accompanied by a more-than-proportionate
growth in government expenditure. Some consider this the most important single influence on the
evolving structure of advanced economies.

[4]Government expenditure affects the structure of employment, the direction of private sector
efforts to conform to government policies and supply government needs, and the composition of
personal incomes (which increasingly depend on government expenditure).

Many consider public services reform the dominant political narrative of the age. Pioneering ideas of entrepreneurial government (Osborne and Gaebler 1992),[5] originating from the United States in the mid-1990s, have been influential, and the public sectors of that country and the United Kingdom,[6] to name early adopters, have each experienced continuing reforms to their structures, objectives, and approaches. (Canada, New Zealand, and others soon followed.)

Founded on a client-centric philosophy, reforms in government structures, civil service, and public finances have aimed to help public services become more flexible and cater better to individual needs. In particular, this shift toward a delivery-based philosophy has encouraged (i) changes that move the civil service from being a body giving policy advice to one that assures the availability of quality public goods and services; (ii) the discovery of new avenues to finance public sector activities and their servicing; and (iii) greater reliance on the private and not-for-profit sectors, away from a monopoly state provision model to that of a public service economy.[7]

Increasingly, the lines between private sector and public sector models are blurring; managers should not regard the private–public context as a dichotomy but rather as a continuum from "pure private" to "pure public". At one end of the

---

[5]The authors contended that government bureaucracy in the United States, appropriate to the industrial era and times of economic and military crises during which it was created, is not the best system of governance for the postindustrial information age. From the 1960s, the American public has increasingly desired quality and choice of goods and services and efficiency of production. Arguing that quality and choice are not what bureaucratic systems are designed to provide and that efficiency is not possible in a system of complex rules and drawn-out decision-making, David Osborne and Ted Gaebler introduced 10 principles of reinvention to guide the transformation of industrial-era public systems. The principles are (i) catalytic government (steering rather than rowing); (ii) community-owned government (empowering rather than serving); (iii) competitive government (injecting competition into service delivery); (iv) mission-driven government (transforming rule-driven organization); (v) result-oriented government (funding outcomes, not inputs); (vi) customer-driven government (meeting the needs of the customer, not the bureaucracy); (vii) enterprising government (earning rather than spending); (viii) anticipatory government (prevention rather than cure); (ix) decentralized government (from hierarchy to participation and teamwork); and (x) market-oriented government (leveraging change through the market).

[6]From 1988, the United Kingdom had made an early start with the Next Steps initiative to transforming the functions, organization, and traditions of the executive and its relations with Parliament. The reforms sought to separate service delivery functions from policy functions, and have the public sector provide services through markets or market-like arrangements, managed by people with the resources and authority to provide those services. The difficulties met by the Next Steps agencies were lack of clarity in the relationship between these agencies and their parent departments, uncertainty concerning who is accountable for performance, and complexity in developing and setting performance goals.

[7]On a par with the reforms, personnel in the public sector are being transformed from administrators and custodians of resources into accountable managers with greater delegated authority. The notion of delegated authority is important: it provides managers greater opportunities to match the provision of goods and services to the needs of clients, audiences, and partners in their area.

continuum, one might find transactional marketing, rooted in classical economics, and dealing with one transaction at a time. At the other would be relationship marketing, focused on building relationships. At the core of such relationship building would be trust.

Marketing and the Public Sector

Barring admittedly wide differences of opinion among socialist, liberal, and libertarian political philosophies[8] regarding the public sector's role (and scope), which vary further depending on specific economic circumstances such as recessions, it is generally accepted that the public sector is to make ensuring content and process decisions aimed at collective social improvement from which all human lives should gain. (Key among these are stabilizing functions justified in terms of the failure of markets or the presence of externalities, which require the provision of a regulatory framework that underpins law and order, provides the preconditions for the operations of the market, and promotes equity.)[9]

Marketing is the activity, set of institutions, and processes—always interconnected and interdependent—meant to identify, anticipate, create, communicate, deliver, and exchange valuable offerings that satisfy clients, audiences, partners, and society at large. In an era when public sector organizations must perform better to respond better to the public interest, irrespective of whether they govern the character of public provision as opposed to producing goods and services themselves,[10] marketing can help.

However, arrangements for governance or provision cannot be the same for different types of goods and services.[11] Hence, marketing in the public sector must be astutely informed by what its organizations do and the way in which they operate, that necessarily being the outcome of political decisions on the purpose and content of the public realm (which are almost always about balancing conflict over

---

[8]In summary, socialists favor a large public sector consisting of state projects and enterprises (while social democrats tend to favor a medium-sized public sector limited to the provision of universal programs and public services); liberals favor a small public sector; and libertarians favor no public sector, with government tasked primarily with safeguarding property rights, drafting and enforcing laws, and resolving disputes.

[9]In economics, a market failure exists when the production or use of goods and services by the market is not efficient. The externality (or spillover) of an economic transaction is an impact on a party that is not directly involved in the transaction.

[10]The uptake of notions of entrepreneurial government suggests that we may perhaps be moving toward public sector organizations that have extensive powers and responsibilities but, except in times of crisis, produce few public goods and services themselves.

[11]Naturally, marketing a service also differs from marketing a product. What is significant about services, as opposed to products, is the relative dominance of intangible attributes in their makeup.

values).[12] Therefore, marketing in the public sector can only become relevant when fundamental political decisions have been made on commitment to and responsibility for collective agency.

Marketing in the Public Sector

Once marketing as a language of discourse in the public sector has been agreed to and its distinctive purposes, conditions, and tasks are appreciated (since the public domain has different values), then marketing as an integrated set of ideas can be used.[13] (This need not mean that the civil service's traditional strengths of equity, accountability, impartiality, and a wide review of the public interest will thereby be forsaken.) Of course, the public sector has long had elements of marketing[14] but they have usually been marginal to the provision of core public goods and services. Detractors have argued that marketing approaches entailed little other than the use of specific tools, not the development and adoption of a marketing orientation.

> *There is more similarity in the marketing challenge of selling a precious painting by Degas and a frosted mug of root beer than you ever thought possible.*
>
> —A. Alfred Taubman

Still, over the last 20 years, considerable latent potential has opened on a par with the growth of consumerism,[15] the adoption of strategic marketing,[16] and the use of promotional techniques. Marketing must surely now be seen to be an essential part of public sector management. Private sector tools, methods, and approaches have already been adopted in the public sector. (Monitoring and evaluation figures

---

[12]Politics is the activity through which people make, preserve, and amend the general rules under which they live. It is inextricably linked to the existence of diversity and conflict and willingness (or lack thereof) to cooperate and act collectively.

[13]All the same, differences should not be exaggerated and used as an excuse for inefficiency, ineffectiveness, and waste.

[14]Examples include the promotion of local areas for tourism or economic development.

[15]Consumerism has both fuelled and been sped by decentralization, rising customer consciousness, improved communications, greater choice, and systems of redress.

[16]If the public sector must now abide more closely by the key market principles of transaction, price, and competition—which rest inter alia on encouraging end-user choice, internal markets, quality-based management systems, market testing, competitive tendering, and contracting out—it is de facto being placed in a similar position as the private sector, against which it may have to compete. Public sector organizations must therefore also become conversant with such notions as market segmentation, market positioning, and the marketing mix. (Even where there is no competition from the private sector, public sector organizations are often part of an internal market and are compelled in any event to compete against one another.)

prominently.) But many public sector organizations—especially not-for-profit—are realizing that strategic marketing can help address two challenges: the challenge of meeting mandates and satisfying stakeholder needs in the face of diminishing resources, and the challenge of meeting specified revenue or cost-recovery targets. With the shift of the public sector to more managerial, business-like approaches, the adoption of marketing and related managerial practices can also strengthen accountability in operations.

One of the greatest obstacles to using marketing in the public sector is lack of understanding of the different types of marketing in which it might engage and how each might help build relational capital.[17] According to Madill (1998), four major forms exist:

- **Marketing of Products and Services** Many public sector organizations offer products and services free of charge or for a fee (either on a cost recovery or for-profit basis to support core public good programs). Marketing in this context is not so dissimilar to that conducted in the private sector.[18] However, many public sector organizations are much more familiar with promotion than with the other Ps of the marketing mix—such as product (or service), place, and price—because many have developed communications plans outside of a marketing framework. The negative image of marketing in the public domain may well owe to the fact that many managers there equate marketing with advertising.[19] The understanding that all four elements of the marketing mix are aspects of a complete marketing strategy can be developed though marketing training.

---

[17]Notions of relational capital and relationship marketing can do much to offset resistance to the use of marketing in the public sector. First, they offer a conceptually valid framework with which to locate and articulate in public sector organizations a marketing function that emphasizes its strategic rather than operational significance. Second, they give practical insights into how marketing might help meet the challenges of the plural state, including suggestions as to intra- and interorganizational management and governance aspects of it.

[18]Advertising is a case in point: the same advertising techniques used to promote commercial goods and services can be used to inform, educate, and motivate the public about noncommercial issues, such as HIV/AIDS, political ideology, energy conservation, and deforestation. In its noncommercial guise, advertising in the public interest can be a powerful educational tool capable of reaching and motivating large audiences.

[19]Kotler and Lee (2007) agree: "Marketing is much more than advertising; it is about knowing your customers, partners, and competitors; segmenting targeting and positioning; communicating persuasively; innovation and launching new services and programs; developing effective delivery channels; forming partnerships and strategic alliances; performance management and pricing/cost recovery. Marketing turns out to be the best planning platform for a public agency that wants to meet citizens' needs and deliver real value. In the private sector, marketing's mantra is customer value and satisfaction. In the public sector, it is citizen value and satisfaction".

- **Social Marketing** According to Philip Kotler and Gerald Zaltman, social marketing is the design, implementation, and control of programs calculated to influence the acceptability of social ideas and involving considerations of product, planning, pricing, communication, distribution, and marketing research. It may involve campaigns to change attitudes and the behavior of target audiences.
- **Policy Marketing** This type of marketing entails campaigns to convince specific sectors of society to accept policies or new legislation.
- **Demarketing** "Don't Use Our Programs" marketing calls for campaigns that are launched by public sector organizations to advise or persuade targeted groups not to use programs that have been available to them in the past.

Well-designed marketing that takes into account the characteristics of the public sector can greatly assist public sector organizations in serving their stakeholders. Failure to take account of the differences in purposes, conditions, and tasks that distinguish them from the private sector will likely lead to inappropriate and ill-conceived marketing programs. That noted, the institutionalization of marketing (and associated behaviors) should proceed.

A Road Map for Improved Marketing Performance

Next to doing the right thing, the most important thing is to let people know you are doing the right thing.

—John D. Rockefeller

Usefully, in the book cited earlier, Philip Kotler and Nancy Lee identified eight ways to apply marketing tools to the public domain. Each tackles an accepted private marketing tenet and shows how to apply it as part of an agency's marketing effort.[20] The tenets are

- developing and enhancing popular products, programs, and services;
- setting motivating prices, incentives, and disincentives;
- optimizing distribution channels;
- creating and maintaining a desired brand identity;
- communicating effectively with key publics;
- improving client service and satisfaction;
- influencing positive public behaviors through social marketing; and
- forming strategic partnerships.

---

[20]The book ends with vital information on how to manage the marketing process by gathering data, input, and feedback; monitoring and evaluating performance; and developing a compelling marketing plan.

References

Kotler P, Lee N (2007) Marketing in the public sector: a roadmap for improved performance. Pearson Education, Inc
Kotler P, Zaltman G (1971) Social marketing: an approach to planned social change. Journal of Marketing 35:3–12
Madill J (1998) Marketing in government. Optimum 28(4):9–18
Osborne D, Gaebler T (1992) Reinventing government: how the entrepreneurial spirit is transforming the public sector. Addison-Wesley

Further Reading

Walsh K (1994) Marketing and public sector management. European Journal of Marketing 28 (3):63–71

Proposition 17
The Future of Social Marketing

In a Word Social marketing is the use of marketing principles and techniques to effect behavioral change. It is a concept, process, and application for understanding who people are, what they desire, and then organizing the creation, communication, and delivery of products and services to meet their desires as well as the needs of society, and solve serious social problems.

Introduction

Marketing is at a crossroads. Until 1960, when Levitt (1960) wrote *Marketing Myopia*, it had not been considered a serious function of strategic management. From there, the discipline developed at such pace that *Marketing Management* (Kotler and Keller 2008),[1] Philip Kotler's classic textbook, is in its 13th edition counting 816 pages.

---

[1]The topics covered brand equity, customer value analysis, database marketing, e-commerce, value networks, hybrid channels, supply chain management, segmentation, targeting, positioning, and integrated marketing communications.

© Asian Development Bank 2017

O. Serrat, *Knowledge Solutions*, DOI 10.1007/978-981-10-0983-9_17

Organizations have never had such powerful information and communications technology[2] with which to interact with clients, audiences, and partners; explore, find, capture, store, analyze, present, use, and exchange information data and information about them; and tailor products and services accordingly. Along with that, never before have end users expected to interface so closely with organizations and with one another to define and shape what they need. In its highest form, marketing is now considered a social process, composed of human behavior[3] patterns concerned with exchange of resources or values.[4] It is no longer a mere function used to increase business profits.

Tellingly, in the 2010s, the attention of public sector agencies, nongovernment organizations, and the private sector is increasingly drawn to the potential of social marketing. In an age of climate change, environmental destruction, natural resource shortages, fast population growth, hunger and poverty, as well as insufficient social services, what contributions might marketing make? Expressly, some ask whether the tools of marketing can be used to promote public goods in areas other than public health, the traditional arena of social marketing.[5] Might, for instance, its applications help encourage wider socially and environmentally beneficial behavioral changes, promote protective behaviors, prevent risky behavior, increase use of community services, or facilitate the formulation and adoption of new policies and standards? The behavior, that is, not just of individual citizens but also of public sector agencies, nongovernment organizations, and the private sector.

Definition

The term "social marketing" was coined by Kotler and Zaltman (1971). Drawing from bodies of knowledge such as psychology, sociology, anthropology, political science, and communication theory—with practical roots in advertising, public relations, and market research—it is the application of principles and techniques drawn from the commercial sector to influence a target audience to voluntarily

---

[2]They encompass radio, television, cellular phones, computer and network hardware and software, satellite systems and so on, as well as the various services and applications associated with them, such as videoconferencing and distance learning.

[3]Human behavior is the population of behaviors exhibited by human beings under specific conditions and influenced by culture, values, ethics, rapport, authority, persuasion, coercion, attitudes, emotions, hypnosis, and/or genetics.

[4]The motivation to become involved in an exchange is to satisfy needs.

[5]Famously, as long ago as 1952, research psychologist Wiebe (1952) posed the much-quoted question, "Why can't you sell brotherhood and rational thinking like you sell soap?" He then argued that the success of mass persuasion, in terms of motivating behavior, is a function of the audience member's experience with regard to five factors: (i) the force, (ii) the direction, (iii) the mechanism, (iv) the adequacy and compatibility, and (v) the distance.

accept, reject, modify, or abandon a behavior for the benefit[6] of individuals, groups, organizations, or society as a whole. Its intent is to create positive social change. It can be applied to promote merit products and services or to make a target audience avoid demerit products and services and thus promote its well-being.

The Dimensions of Social Marketing

Some consider social marketing to do little but use the principles and practices of generic marketing to achieve noncommercial goals. This is an oversimplification: social marketing involves changing seemingly intractable behaviors in composite environmental, economic, social, political, and technological circumstances with (more often than not) quite limited resources. If the basic objective of corporate marketers is to satisfy shareholders, the bottom line for social marketers is to meet society's desire to improve quality of life.[7] This requires a long-term planning approach that moves beyond the individual end user to groups, organizations, and society, characterized in the figure below. Hence, the desired outcomes of social marketing are usually ambitious: the products are more complex, demand is diverse, the target groups are challenging, the necessary involvement of end users is greater, and competition is more varied. However, like generic marketing, behaviors are always the focus: social marketing is also based on the voluntary (but more difficult)[8] exchange of costs and benefits between two or more parties. To this end, social marketing too proposes a useful framework for planning, a framework that social marketers can associate with other approaches at a time when global, regional, national, and local problems have become more critical. (The other approaches might include advocacy; mobilizing communities; building strategic alliances with public sector agencies, nongovernment organizations, and the private sector[9]; and influencing the media.) Unsurprisingly, besides public health,[10] social

---

[6]Behavior will change only if perceived benefits outweigh perceived costs.

[7]This does not mean that commercial marketers cannot contribute to achievement of social good.

[8]Social marketing asks target audiences to do something for which social marketers will not always be able to give immediate payback, or show them something in return, most importantly in the near term. In addition, they must usually concentrate on removing barriers to an activity while enhancing the benefits.

[9]Many social marketing issues are so complex that one organization cannot address them alone.

[10]Applications include cholesterol, tobacco prevention, safety, drug abuse, drinking and driving, seatbelt laws, nutrition, obesity, physical activity, HIV/AIDS, immunization, mental health, breast feeding, breast cancer screening, and family planning.

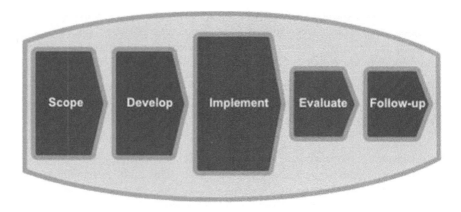

Fig. The social marketing process. *Source* Author

marketing is being applied in environmental,[11] economic,[12] and educational[13] fields, among others.

In the United Kingdom, the National Social Marketing Center has worked to clarify the salient features of social marketing. Building on work by Alan Andreasen in the United States, it has drawn social marketing benchmark criteria. They aim to ease understanding of the principles and techniques of social marketing, encourage consistency of approach leading to impact, uphold flexibility and creativity to tailor interventions to different needs, facilitate capture and sharing of transferable learning between interventions, and assist monitoring and evaluation of interventions. Other criteria, critical to successful interventions, might have been included, e.g., strategic planning, partnership and stakeholder engagement, monitoring and evaluation, etc. However, those that the National Social Marketing Center promotes are unique to social marketing. The criteria are

> *Always remember that you are absolutely unique. Just like everyone else.*
>
> —Margaret Mead

- **Orientation** This implies a strong client orientation, with importance attached to understanding where the customer is starting from, e.g., their values,

---

[11]Instances are pollution, energy conservation, clean air, safer water, recycling, and preservation of forests and national parks.

[12]Areas relate to attracting investors, revitalizing older cities, boosting job skills and training, and civic involvement.

[13]Cases in point are literacy and stay in school.

experiences, knowledge, beliefs, attitudes, and needs, and the social context in which they live and work.

- **Behavior** This refers to a clear focus on understanding existing behavior and key influences upon it, alongside developing clear behavioral goals. These can be divided into actionable and measurable stages, phased over time.
- **Theory** This connotes the use of behavioral theories to understand human behavior and to build programs around this understanding.
- **Insight** This calls for gaining a deep understanding and insight into what moves and motivates people.
- **Exchange** This rests on the use of the "exchange" concept—understanding what is being expected of people, and the real cost to them.
- **Competition** This hinges on the use of the "competition" concept. This means understanding factors that impact on people and compete for their time.
- **Segmentation** This demands that the audience be clarified using segmentation to target people effectively.
- **Methods Mix** This requires the use of a mix of different interventions or methods to achieve a behavioral goal. When used at the strategic level this is referred to as the intervention mix. When used operationally, it is described as the marketing mix.

The Importance of Process

The stages of the social marketing process will be familiar to anyone who has been involved in project or program development. However, the National Social Marketing Center highlights in particular the importance of the scoping stage—it drives the entire process. At the scoping stage, the primary concern is to establish clear, actionable, and measurable behavior goals to ensure focused development throughout the rest of the process. The effectiveness of social marketing rests on the demonstration of direct impact on behavior; it is this feature that sets social marketing distinctly apart from communication or awareness-raising approaches (where the main focus is on highlighting information and helping people understand it). The aim of the scoping part of the process is to define the objectives of the intervention and what the stakeholders want to achieve. This requires close engagement and much insight. At this stage, social marketers attempt to understand what moves and motivates the end users to determine how the behavioral goals might be reached. Referring to generic marketing, it might be useful to consider this stage as that when the product (or service) is defined.

The complexity of marketing a societal behavioral change requires that the process of social marketing be well structured. Yet, there may have been insufficient discussion of a step-by-step methodology for the social marketing process in the literature. The principal stages followed in public health applications in the United States are initial planning, formative research, strategy development, program development and pretesting of material and nonmaterial interventions, implementation, and monitoring and evaluation. The core marketing principles, the four Ps, are at the heart of this process because they are used at the initial planning stage.

Social Marketing for a Sustainable Future

Given the roots they share, both generic and social marketing have seen a move to relational capital and relationship marketing, away from transactional thinking. Somewhat belatedly, the private sector came to realize that it is easier, and more profitable, to retain clients than to continually attract new customers. Social marketing adopted that thinking earlier simply because it must embrace long-term strategic approaches. Indeed, the inescapable need for long-term thinking in social marketing and the related development of appropriate principles and techniques now position it advantageously in the quickening fight against global, regional, national, and local problems.

Box 1: Case Study: Tonle Sap Environmental Management—Formulating and Implementing a National Environmental Education and Awareness Campaign

Sustainable management and conservation of natural resources and biodiversity are a priority for Cambodia, which relies heavily on land, water, and biotic resources and is on the verge of rapid urban, industrial, and agricultural development. In such cases, environmental policies should be fitted to the conditions and traditions of the country. Implementation will not be successful without the active participation of all citizens, especially those who depend on natural resources.

When Cambodia nominated in 1996 the Tonle Sap for designation by the United Nations Educational, Scientific, and Cultural Organization as a biosphere reserve, the government recognized that the site should respond to the conservation, development, and logistic functions of a biosphere reserve and that education and public awareness should be given importance. At the national level, information on conservation and sustainable use, as practiced in biosphere reserves, should be included in school programs and teaching manuals and in media efforts. At the local level, involvement of local communities should be encouraged, information for visitors should be produced, and environmental education centers should be promoted.

Since its creation in 1993, the Ministry of Environment has worked toward such ends. As a result, an Interministerial Steering Committee for Environmental Education was established that year with assistance from the United Nations Development Programme's Environmental Technical Assistance Project. The United Nations Educational, Scientific, and Cultural Organization was associated with related environmental education activities, particularly with developing environmental education materials for school curricula and producing teacher guides for primary and secondary schools. A special program for educating monks was also put in place. However, many of these activities were interrupted when the Environmental Technical Assistance Project ended in 1998. Considering the importance of the Tonle Sap Biosphere Reserve and the severity of the threats against it, it is urgent that progress in environmental education and awareness continue and that a national campaign be mounted in support. This would also help Cambodia meet obligations under the 1992 Convention on Biological Diversity that stress the importance of education and public awareness on biodiversity.

The goal of the project is sustainable management and conservation of natural resources and biodiversity in the Tonle Sap basin. The objective that formulation and implementation of a national environmental education and awareness campaign will help accomplish is strengthened natural resource management coordination and planning for the Tonle Sap Biosphere Reserve, particularly by establishing a coordination framework and information dissemination mechanisms. The outputs needed to formulate and implement the campaign are as follows: (i) publicizing the Tonle Sap's environmental importance, (ii) integrating concern for natural resources, and (iii) developing formal and nonformal environmental education. These outputs will be defined by the target audience, i.e., the general public and the press, decision makers, schoolchildren (at primary and secondary levels), university students, and communities living in the Tonle Sap region.

Source Extracted from ADB (2002). See also Live & Learn Environmental Education (2005, 2006a, b, c).

Box 2: Case Study: Tonle Sap Sustainable Livelihoods—Educating for Protection of Natural Resources

In Cambodia, decentralization and deconcentration have boosted local autonomy and participation in national development. Accordingly, the structures supporting this effort—at central, provincial, district, and commune levels—have received considerable assistance. But, given their short history, the impact on improved livelihoods, though encouraging, has been modest: there remains a need to strengthen institutions and processes at all levels. This includes improving cross-sectoral linkages in development planning, building skills for community-driven development, and raising awareness of the need to protect natural resources. Component 3 of the Project plans to build skills and awareness for sustainable livelihoods.

Specifically, to help raise awareness of the need to protect natural resources, the Project will (i) assemble educational materials on natural resource management, including those developed under component 3 of the

ADB-assisted Tonle Sap Environmental Management Project; (ii) hold environmental awareness forums for staff of the Ministry of Agriculture, Forestry, and Fisheries, Ministry of Environment, Ministry of Rural Development, Ministry of Women's Affairs, their provincial departments, and commune leaders; (iii) prioritize villages according to their potential impact on resource extraction; (iv) assemble, train, and equip a mobile training team to extend environmental awareness in priority villages; (v) deliver the environmental awareness program; and (vi) conduct monitoring and evaluation. The activities will build on achievements under component 1 of the Tonle Sap Environmental Management Project, according to the principles developed under an ADB-assisted pilot and demonstration activity conducted in 2004.[a]

[a]See ADB (2004). See also Live & Learn Environmental Education (2004, 2006d, 2007).

Source Extracted from ADB (2005).

A small group of thoughtful people could change the world. Indeed, it's the only thing that ever has.

—Margaret Mead

Kotler and Lee (2009) contributed to expand the traditional scope of social marketing by considering global poverty, 90% of which is found in developing countries,[14] from the viewpoint of the marketer. They examined how marketing perspectives might drive poverty solutions that work by (i) segmenting the poverty marketplace (who are the potential market segments for our efforts?); (ii) evaluating and choosing target market priorities (who should we focus on first or most?); (iii) determining desired behavior changes (what do we want them to do?); (iv) understanding barriers, benefits, and the competition for change (what do they think of the idea?); and (v) developing a desired positioning and strategic marketing mix (what do they need to do this?). They stressed the need to ensure an integrated approach by developing a social marketing plan and elucidating the distinct roles of

---

[14]Applying social marketing principles and techniques in developing countries is not new. Poverty is affected by behavioral choices, and behavior is influenced by the creation, communication, and delivery of products and services that modulate it. Therefore, from the 1980s organizations such as the World Bank started to use the term "social marketing" and have continued to promote interest in it. However, Philip Kotler and Nancy Lee's book is a valuable addition to the toolbox of development aid. It describes and illustrates with actual cases the major steps in planning, implementing, monitoring, evaluating, and controlling social marketing programs for poverty reduction; this level of analysis had been missing in all the previous work on helping the poor.

the public sector, nongovernment organizations, and the private sector in poverty reduction.

References

ADB (2002) Report and recommendation of the president to the board of directors on a proposed loan and technical assistance grant to the kingdom of Cambodia for the Tonle Sap environmental management project. Manila

ADB (2004) Regional technical assistance for promoting effective water management policies and practices (phase 3). Manila. Pilot and demonstration activity in the Kingdom of Cambodia for developing and testing environmental education and awareness methodologies and tools

ADB (2005) Report and recommendation of the president to the board of directors on a proposed Asian development fund grant to the Kingdom of Cambodia for the Tonle Sap sustainable livelihoods project

Kotler P, Keller K (2008) Marketing management. Prentice Hall

Kotler P, Lee N (2009) Up and out of poverty. Pearson Education, Inc

Kotler P, Zaltman G (1971) Social marketing: an approach to planned social change. Journal of Marketing 35:3–12

Levitt T (July–August 1960) Marketing myopia. Harvard Business Review

Live & Learn Environmental Education (2004) Environmental issues in the Tonle Sap: a rapid assessment of perceptions; learning circle facilitators' guide to promote sustainable development in the Tonle Sap; Community theatre guide to the water awareness program

Live & Learn Environmental Education (2005) Building a sustainable future: a strategic approach to environmental education in the Tonle Sap region. Cambodia

Live & Learn Environmental Education (2006a) Community environmental awareness flipchart

Live & Learn Environmental Education (2006b) Community environmental awareness flipchart—facilitation guide

Live & Learn Environmental Education (2006c) Cambodia's environmental education status report 2005

Live & Learn Environmental Education (2006d) Practical tools for schools

Live & Learn Environmental Education (2007) Tonle Sap information guide

Wiebe G (1952) Merchandising commodities and citizenship on television. The Public Opinion Quarterly 15(4):679–691

Further Reading

Kotler P, Lee N (2007) Marketing in the public sector: a roadmap for improved performance. Pearson Education, Inc

Proposition 18
Design Thinking

In a Word The need for twenty-first century mindsets and protocols has sparked interest in design thinking. That is a human-centered, prototype-driven process for the exploration of new ideas that can be applied to operations, products, services, strategies, and even management.

A Design for Life

In a world of continuous flux, where markets mature faster and everyone is affected by information overload, organizations regard innovation, including management innovation, as the prime driver of sustainable competitive advantage. To unlock opportunities, some of them use mindsets and protocols from the field of design to make out unarticulated wants and deliberately imagine, envision, and spawn futures.

Design is more important when function is taken for granted and no longer helps stakeholders differentiate. In the last five years, design thinking has emerged as the quickest organizational path to innovation and high-performance, changing the way creativity and commerce interact.[1] In the past, design was a downstream step in the product development process, aiming to enhance the appeal of an existing product.

---

[1] In truth, companies such as Apple in particular, but also General Electric, Levi Strauss, Nike, and Procter & Gamble, to name a few, pioneered the notion some time ago.

© Asian Development Bank 2017

O. Serrat, *Knowledge Solutions*, DOI 10.1007/978-981-10-0983-9_18

Today, however, organizations ask designers to imagine solutions that meet explicit or latent needs and to build upstream entire systems that optimize customer experience and satisfaction.

Therefore, although the term "design" is commonly understood to describe an object (or end result), it is in its latest and most effective form a process, an action, and a verb, not a noun: essentially, it is a protocol to see, shape, and build. Lately, design approaches are also being applied to infuse insight into the heart of campaigns and address social and other concerns.[2]

> *The proper study of mankind is the science of design.*
>
> —Herbert Simon

Defining Design

Simon (1969)[3] defined design as the changing of existing conditions into preferred ones.[4] Design thinking, then, is about using the sensibilities and methodologies that characterize designers to create new ideas, new alternatives, new choices, and new viabilities that satisfy stakeholder desires. It is fundamentally abductive,[5] even if designers still induce patterns and deduce answers.

Stemming from abductive reasoning, design thinking is empathic, personal, subjective, interpretive, integrative, experimental, synthetic, pictorial, dialectical,

---

[2]See, for instance, Brown and Wyatt (2010). In 2007, Oxfam approached IDEO, a global design consultancy, with a brief. How might the charity better educate people to understand climate change? How might Oxfam translate that understanding into a better relationship with donors?

[3]Herbert Simon (1916–2001) was an American political scientist, economist, and psychologist whose research ranged across the fields of cognitive psychology, computer science, public administration, economics, management, philosophy of science, sociology, and political science.

[4]Herbert Simon saw that the rationality of individuals is limited by the information they have, the cognitive limitations of their minds, and the finite amount of time they have to make decisions. "Bounded rationality" leads them to "satisfice", that is, choose what might not be optimal but will make them sufficiently happy.

[5]Abduction is the process of inference to most likely, or best, explanations from accepted facts. Deduction means determining the conclusion. For example: "When it rains, the grass gets wet. It rains. Thus, the grass is wet." Induction means determining the rule. To illustrate: "The grass has been wet every time it has rained. Thus, when it rains, the grass gets wet." Abduction means determining the precondition. For instance: "When it rains, the grass gets wet. The grass is wet, it must have rained." Abductive thinking is very close to the concept of lateral thinking, for which numerous tools exist.

opportunistic, and optimistic. It is a frame of mind for problem solving that can balance legitimate needs for stability, efficiency, and predictability with the requirement for spontaneity, experimentation, and serendipity. In the conceptual age,[6] it is a "people first" approach to the full spectrum and minutiae of innovation activities that has applications in operations, products, services, strategies, and even management.[7]

> *If I'd asked my customers what they wanted, they'd have said "a faster horse".*
>
> —Henry Ford

Inside the Design Thinking Process

Design thinking revolves around three key phases: inspiration, ideation, and implementation.[8] During these phases, problems are framed, questions—also about questions—are asked, ideas are generated, and answers are obtained. The phases are not linear; they can take place concurrently and can also be repeated to build up ideas along the continuum of innovation. The design thinking process allows information and ideas to be organized, choices to be made, situations to be improved, and knowledge to be gained as depicted in Roger Martin's three-stage funnel.[9]

Design thinking is, inherently, a prototyping process powering deep understanding of what people want in their lives as well as what they like (or not) about the way that is made, packaged, marketed, sold, and supported. To this end,

---

[6]Pink (2005) has identified six high-concept, high-touch abilities that have become crucial in the conceptual age. (The term "conceptual economy" describes the contribution of creativity, innovation, and design skills to economic competitiveness, especially in the global context.) The six abilities are design, story, symphony, empathy, play, and meaning. By high-concept, he means the ability to detect patterns and opportunities, to shape artistic and emotional beauty, to craft satisfying narratives, to fuse apparently unrelated ideas into an invention. By high-touch, he connotes the ability to understand the subtleties of human interaction, empathize, and find happiness in the pursuit of purpose and meaning. Design is one profession that relies on all six abilities.

[7]It can, for instance, be used to develop and drive strategy, open new markets, fashion new offerings, formulate new business models, identify new applications for technology, articulate new ways of connecting to customers, and forge new partnerships.

[8]Some articulate these further into seven: define, research, ideate, prototype, choose, implement, and learn.

[9]The first stage of the knowledge funnel is the investigation of a mystery (that may have several forms). The second is the delineation of a heuristic, viz., an educated guess, intuitive judgment, rule of thumb, or simple common sense, that narrows the area of inquiry so that it may be managed. The third is the creation of an algorithm, viz., a formula. As one moves down the funnel, one creates efficiency but must necessarily leave things out (Martin 2009).

multidisciplinary teams of T-shaped individuals[10] are encouraged to fail often to succeed sooner through trial and error: innovations do not arise from incremental tweaks.

> *Design is not just what it looks like and feels like. Design is how it works.*
>
> —Steve Jobs

By the same token, design is never done: a market is always changing, least of all because good ideas are copied, and design must change with it. Design success is the integration of design thinking into an organization: at that level, it becomes a powerful tool to solve unpredictable problems.

Designing Business

To Heather Fraser, the greatest payout of design thinking lies in the design of strategies and business models for organizational performance that creates both economic and human value. Broadening the definition of design, she argues that it can be the path to understanding stakeholder needs, the tool for visualizing new solutions, and the process for translating cutting-edge ideas into effective strategies (Fraser 2009). Heather Fraser, from whose work the following draws, sees three iterative gears in business design. Anchored in the needs of stakeholders, they apply deep user understanding to stimulate high-value conceptual visualizations and extract from these the strategic intent needed to reform business models.

- **Gear One: Deep User Understanding** The first step is to turn the telescope around to reframe the organization and view its business entirely through the eyes of the customer (and, of course, other critical stakeholders). It is necessary to look beyond the direct use of an organization's products or services to the contexts in which they are located, in terms of the activities surrounding their utilization, to gain deeper insight and broader behavioral and psychographic perspectives. It is also critical to understand the "whole person" engaged in any given activity—not just what they do, but how they feel and how their needs surrounding their activities link to other parts of their life.

---

[10]T-shaped individuals possess deep knowledge in a core area of expertise as well as broad knowledge in disciplines such as management, finance, and business operations. Kelley (2008) of IDEO has also observed a number of roles that people can play in an organization to foster innovation and new ideas and offer an effective counterpoint to naysayers. They are the anthropologist, the experimenter, the cross-pollinator, the hurdler, the collaborator, the director, the experience architect, the set designer, the caregiver, and the storyteller.

- **Gear Two: Concept Visualization** With renewed empathy and a broader set of criteria for innovation serving as springboard, creativity can be unleashed and move through multiple-prototyping and concept enrichment, ideally with users. It is vital to look beyond what is to what could be, using imagination to generate altogether new-to-the-world solutions. At this stage, there are no constraints, only possibilities. Engaging all functions and disciplines on the team infuses ideas into the process, fortifies team alignment, and prepares the traction that will lock down strategies and activate them later.
- **Gear Three: Strategic Business Design** With well-defined, user-inspired solutions at hand the third gear aligns broad concepts with future reality. This entails prototyping business models to integrate their parts and assess the impact of the activity system as a whole. It is imperative to identify what will drive the success of the solutions; prioritize what activities an organization must undertake to deliver related strategies; define relationships strategically, operationally, and economically; and determine what net impacts the new business models will have.

References

Brown T, Wyatt T (2010) Design thinking for social Innovation. Stanford Social Innovation Review. Winter

Fraser H (2009) Designing business: new models for success. Design Manage Rev 20(2):55–65

Kelley T (2008) The ten faces of innovation. Profile Books Ltd

Martin R (2009) The design of business: why design thinking is the next competitive advantage. Harvard Business School Publishing

Pink D (2005) A whole new mind: why right-brainers will rule the future. Penguin Books Ltd

Simon H (1969) The sciences of the artificial. Massachusetts Institute of Technology Press

Further Reading

Dunne D, Martin R (2006) Design thinking and how it will change management education: an interview and discussion. Academy of Management Learning & Education 5(4):512–523

Proposition 19
Seeking Feedback on Learning for Change

In a Word Feedback underpins organizational learning. To find the highest level of success in learning for change, feedback should be invited, analyzed in the most positive manner possible, and used to impact decision making.

Learning to Change …

The rapidly changing—and, at times, excessively complex—nature of development work demands diverse competences from aid agencies such as the Asian Development Bank. In addition to technical knowledge and skills, they include no less than appreciating political economy; building relationships; reading and responding to complex organizational and social predicaments; and increasing capacity to contend with uncertainty, task-compromise, and deal with difference and diversity. The learning challenges that these demands present require the ability to work more reflectively in a turbulent practice environment. There is no alternative: to remain relevant and effective, an organization's rate of learning must be at least equal to—but preferably greater than—the rate of change in the environment.

Learning for Change in ADB (2009) was published to help deliver the increased development effectiveness that Strategy 2020, ADB's long-term strategic framework, seeks. It broadly defined a learning organization as a collective undertaking, rooted in action, that builds and improves its own practice by consciously and

© Asian Development Bank 2017
O. Serrat, *Knowledge Solutions*, DOI 10.1007/978-981-10-0983-9_19

continually devising and developing the means to draw learning from its own (and others') experience. Usefully, it assimilated the manifold dimensions of the learning organization and marked out generic roadblocks to learning. Notably, *Learning for Change in ADB* specified how action across organization, people, knowledge, and technology—the learning organization model it created—can energize and support individual, team, and cross-functional learning, and in return be enriched by learning.

> *Feedback is the breakfast of champions.*
>
> —Ken Blanchard

... With Feedback

Organizations that neither invite nor cherish feedback from personnel, clients, audiences, and partners are working in a vacuum. Feedback is the answer to their travails. These *Knowledge Solutions* showcase the details of the internal Learning for Change survey that ADB launched in 2010 to gauge perceptions of competencies to learn for change in ADB.

Box: 2010 Learning for Change Survey

Purpose and Design

The internal, electronic Learning for Change survey was introduced in 2010 to place an accent on organizational learning in ADB.[1] The questionnaire featured 10 positive statements depicting ideal levels of organizational competence across four "pillars" representing four sub-systems deemed necessary for organizational learning, namely (i) organization, (ii) people, (iii) knowledge, and (iv) technology (Sect. "Seeking Feedback on Learning for Change"). The perceptions of staff members were captured in absolute confidence using a six-point Likert scale: 1 = strongly agree, 2 = agree, 3 = neutral, 4 = disagree,

---

[1]The rationale for the learning organization model used in the survey is laid out in ADB (2009).

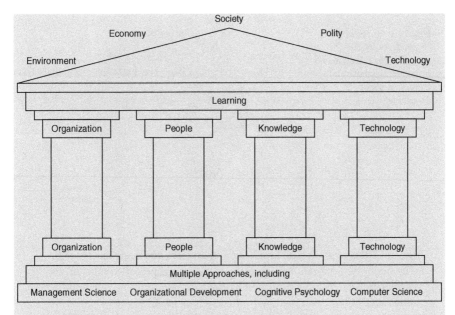

Fig. 19.1 Building a learning organization. *Source* ADB (2009)

5 = strongly disagree, and 6 = don't know. The results of the survey provide a baseline for subsequent rounds (Fig. 19.1).[2]

Respondents

A total of 256 staff members from a complement of 2,705 (as of 30 June, 2010) responded to the survey from 23 departments

---

[2]Since 2005, ADB has conducted annual electronic surveys to gauge staff perceptions of knowledge management. Survey findings are benchmarked against eight recognized MAKE (Most Admired Knowledge Enterprises) knowledge performance dimensions: (i) creating and sustaining an enterprise knowledge-driven culture, (ii) developing knowledge workers through senior management leadership, (iii) developing and delivering knowledge-based products/services/solutions, (iv) managing and maximizing the value of enterprise intellectual capital, (v) creating and sustaining an enterprise-wide collaborative knowledge-sharing environment, (vi) creating and sustaining a learning organization, (vii) managing client knowledge to create value and enterprise intellectual capital, and (viii) transforming ADB knowledge to reduce poverty and improve clients' standard of living. The results of the 2009 MAKE survey were the most positive to date. However, the number of dimensions the MAKE surveys benchmark is limited and their focus is on knowledge management: the 2010 Learning for Change survey was conducted to introduce a new diagnostic tool that examines organizational learning and deepens understanding of progress toward creating and sustaining a learning organization.

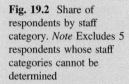

Fig. 19.2 Share of respondents by staff category. *Note* Excludes 5 respondents whose staff categories cannot be determined

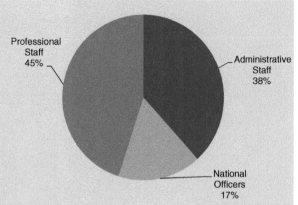

(Sect. "Number of Respondents by Department and Staff Category").[3] The majority (45%) of the respondents regrouped professional staff, the second-largest group comprised administrative staff (38%), and the remainder (17%) were national officers (Fig. 19.2).

Across departments, 47% of the respondents were from the regional departments,[4] 12% from the knowledge departments,[5] and 41% from other departments (Fig. 19.3). Departmental response rates varied considerably—from 2 to 75%, with 7 out of the 23 responding departments showing relatively high response rates of 20% or over.

Overall Results

Feedback from staff members on each statement deserves dedicated attention. However, overall, survey results (Sects. "The Organization Subsystem–The People Subsystem by Staff Category") indicate that, among the four subsystems, staff members perceived ADB to be most competent in relation to the technology subsystem; it needs most improvement in the people subsystem.

---

[3]This represents a response rate of 9%. The survey sample is considered statistically representative of the total target population.

[4]The regional departments are the Central and West Asia Department, East Asia Department, Pacific Department, South Asia Department, and Southeast Asia Department.

[5]The knowledge departments are the Asian Development Bank Institute, Economics and Research Department, Office of Regional Economic Integration, and Regional and Sustainable Development Department.

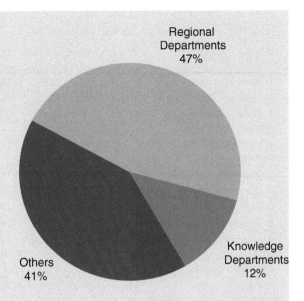

Fig. 19.3 Share of respondents by department. *Note* Excludes 5 respondents whose departments cannot be determined

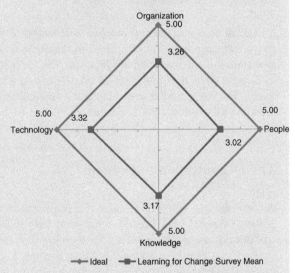

Fig. 19.4 Perceptions of staff on ADB as a learning organization

Dropping the "don't know" (or 6) responses and inverting the Likert scale, where 5 is equivalent to "strongly agree" (hence becoming the ideal score) and 1 represents "strongly disagree," the mean score for the responses for all 10 items under the technology subsystem is 3.32 while that for the people subsystem is 3.02 (Fig. 19.4). The organization and knowledge subsystems have mean scores of 3.26 and 3.17, respectively.

Table 19.1 Perceptions of the organization system (%)

Statement subject	Strongly agree	Agree	Neutral	Disagree	Strongly disagree	Don't know
1. Inspiring vision	13	46	18	16	5	2
2. Learning culture	12	39	23	16	7	2
3. Formal organizational structure	8	38	23	23	7	2
4. Informal organizational structure	4	43	29	14	3	7
5. Communication system	7	41	23	18	6	5
6. Resources	5	38	17	26	8	5
7. Approach to learning	4	35	34	18	5	4
8. Planned learning	7	42	25	16	7	4
9. Emergent learning	7	52	21	13	4	3
10. Failures and unintended outcomes	3	34	36	9	5	13
Average	7	41	25	17	6	5

Note Numbers may not total 100% because of rounding

Taking into account the average percentage of respondents who collectively "strongly agree" and "agree" to the 10 statements per subsystem, the rankings of the subsystems are retained. The technology and people subsystems are first and last at 53% (Table 19.4) and 38% (Table 19.2), respectively. The organization subsystem ranks second at 48% (Table 19.1) while the knowledge subsystem is positioned third at 43% (Table 19.3).

The Organization Subsystem

Among the 10 statements under the organization subsystem, respondents "strongly agree" and "agree" most with two statements (59% for each): (i) "there is an inspiring vision for learning and an organizational learning strategy that clearly communicates that learning is critical to organizational success" (statement 1), and (ii) "emergent learning is encouraged by creating opportunities for informal sharing of knowledge and experience" (statement 9). The majority (51%) also agrees that "leaders take an exemplary leading role in creating and sustaining a supportive learning culture" (statement 2). The highest rate of neutrality (36%) is toward the statement, "Failures and unintended outcomes are the focus of constructive discussions. When such incidents involve clients, care is taken to protect their reputation" (statement 10). This is also one of two statements for which the highest percentage of "don't know" responses overall (13%) is found (probably because many respondents would be unable to answer the second part of the statement regarding the protection of client reputation). Finally, there is highest rate of disagreement (34%) with the statement, "adequate resources are allocated for learning in terms of time, allocation, specialist support staff, budgets for knowledge management infrastructure, formal and informal communities of practice and other value networks, and learning and development programs" (statement 6). Table 19.1 presents the survey results for the organization subsystem.

The responses to statement 1 demonstrate a strong sense of communicated vision concerning the importance of learning for ADB's success. This is a critical issue and provides a strong platform for building ADB's organizational learning capacity. The responses to statement 2 concerning leadership's role in creating a supportive learning culture are encouraging. The fact that the number of respondents who "agree" with this statement outnumber those who "disagree" with it by over two to one, with a sizeable share being "neutral," suggests that many ADB leaders are successfully creating a supportive learning culture for their colleagues. It is also significant that statements 1 and 2 have the highest "strongly agree" responses (13 and 12%, respectively). This indicates a firm belief on the part of those respondents which suggests that there may be some examples of particularly good practice to disseminate and learn from. Statement 4 concerning sanctioned informal organizational structures reveals the widest gap in the organization subsystem between those who "strongly agree" (4%) and those who "agree" (43%). This suggests the need to examine current areas of good practice and make these examples more widely known within ADB. In statement 7, the noticeable clustering around "neutral" may be explained by a lack of understanding of the terms "planned" and "emergent" when applied to learning and a reluctance to admit to this in the "don't know" category. Statement 10 on "failures and unintended outcomes" reveals the highest level of "neutral" responses (36%). This may be explained by the limited awareness of many respondents concerning the second half of the statement on the protection of client reputations.

The People Subsystem

Regarding the 10 statements under this subsystem, respondents generally "strongly agree" and "agree" (52%) with the statement, "leadership (based on the possession of expertise and knowledge) is expected from staff members at all levels in the organizational hierarchy" (statement 10). ADB staff are mostly "neutral" (32%) about the proposition that "staff members successfully use a wide range of opportunities for individual and team-based learning and development" (statement 7). The highest percentage of respondents (44%)

Table 19.2 Perceptions of the people subsystem (%)

Statement subject	Strongly agree	Agree	Neutral	Disagree	Strongly disagree	Don't know
1. Reflective practitioners	6	44	22	20	7	2
2. Tools, methods, and approaches	1	33	27	27	6	5
3. Psychological safety and trust	3	31	29	28	6	3
4. Learning communities	3	35	30	22	6	5
5. New ideas, trends, and practices	9	38	27	15	9	2
6. Developing and retaining staff	3	23	29	28	12	5
7. Individual and team-based learning and development	1	35	32	23	5	4
8. Time and performance management systems	3	37	23	22	11	4
9. Rewards and incentives	2	24	25	29	15	6
10. Leadership	4	48	22	16	6	4
Average	3	35	27	23	8	4

Note Numbers may not total 100% because of rounding

"strongly disagree" and "disagree" that ADB "uses a wide range of formal and informal rewards and incentives for contributing to organizational learning and knowledge development (e.g., career advancement, increased income, informal peer status, additional time provided for study, and public acknowledgment for innovative contributions made)" (statement 9). Table 19.2 presents the survey results for the people subsystem.

In general, the statements in the people subsystem are likely to represent aspects of organizational learning with which respondents are most familiar. As a result, one would expect to see the highest prevalence of "strongly agree" and "strongly disagree" responses to these statements. What is interesting, however, is that 7 out of the 10 statements cluster noticeably around the "agree"–"neutral"–"disagree" responses with these three taking up 78% for statement 9, 80% for statement 6, 87% of responses for statements 2 and 4, and a peak of 88% of responses in statement 3. The broad balance between "agree"–"neutral"–"disagree" responses suggests a very varied perception of experiences and the potential for significant improvements in this dimension of organizational learning in ADB. Adopting a learning charter might help establish ground rules and common reference points.

Segregating responses by staff category—namely, local staff[6] and professional staff—it is evident that local staff feel more positively about the people subsystem, with a greater share of them agreeing to more statements than

---

[6]Local staff includes administrative staff and national officers.

professional staff (Sect. "The People Subsystem by Staff Category"). For example, over half of local staff "strongly agree" and "agree" collectively to five statements—namely, statements 1, 4, 5, 8, and 10—while the highest rate of agreement for professional staff is 44% for statement 10 only. Further, no professional staff "strongly agree" with statements 2, 6, 7, and 9. Finally, there is a difference of 25% points and above between the local and professional staff for those agreeing with statements 2, 4, 7, and 8. It would be interesting to inquire in depth why this is so.

The Knowledge Subsystem

In terms of the knowledge subsystem, the statement to which the highest percentage of respondents "strongly agree" and "agree" (64%) is "there is widespread recognition that while knowledge is created in the minds of individuals, knowledge development thrives in a rich web of professional networks among individuals" (statement 1). The good majority (59 and 51%, respectively) also " strongly agree" and "agree" that in ADB (i) "there are creative opportunities for knowledge to be developed and shared with others by facilitating networks between individuals" (statement 3), and (ii) "the design and delivery of products and services demonstrate how effective the organization is at applying what it has learned about the nature of good practice" (statement 4). ADB staff were found to be largely "neutral" (32%) to the statement, "adoption of after-action reviews and retrospects to learn from experience has been successful" (statement 10). Incidentally, this is the other statement (as mentioned in paragraph 6) to which the highest rate (13%) of "don't know" responses was recorded (explicable, perhaps, by lack of familiarity with the concepts used). On the other hand, respondents most "disagree" and "strongly disagree" (44%) that "the organization has a resilient organizational memory and is not vulnerable to the loss of important knowledge when staff members move to other jobs in the organization or leave" (statement 8). This reveals a significant concern about loss (or potential loss) of organizational memory. This should be of real concern to the Human Resources Division, which provides the "last resort" means of capturing knowledge and expertise from departing staff. However, better means of addressing this would be the introduction of exit interviews in offices and departments and a personal commitment from each staff to consider: "What knowledge and experience should I be passing on to colleagues so that they and ADB gain from my work in case I move on to another job?" Table 19.3 presents the survey results for the knowledge subsystem.

The balanced responses to statement 5 suggest that further investigation would be fruitful here to examine what systems and infrastructure for

Table 19.3 Perceptions of the knowledge subsystem (%)

Statement subject	Strongly agree	Agree	Neutral	Disagree	Strongly disagree	Don't know
1. Professional networks	9	55	17	9	5	5
2. Access	5	42	27	20	4	2
3. Opportunities for knowledge development and learning	4	55	23	14	3	2
4. Products and services	4	47	26	11	5	7
5. Systems and infrastructure	2	34	24	27	8	4
6. Evaluations	4	30	28	20	7	11
7. Peer assists	3	38	29	18	4	7
8. Organizational memory	3	27	21	32	12	5
9. Tacit knowledge	2	35	31	20	4	9
10. After-action reviews and retrospects	2	30	32	19	4	13
Average	4	39	26	19	6	7

Note Numbers may not total 100% because of rounding

knowledge management need to be developed, better understood, or made more effective. The responses to statement 6 reveal a very diverse range of views. It is a complex statement that would benefit from further investigation.

The Technology Subsystem

Under the technology subsystem, 74% "strongly agree" and "agree" that "information and communications technology is successfully used to keep people informed and aware of corporate developments" (statement 4). Further, more than half of the respondents believe in the following statements: (i) "There is a thorough and shared understanding of the value of information and communications technology for knowledge management and learning" (statement 1, 54%), (ii) "Information and communications technology facilitates but does not drive or constrain knowledge management and learning in the organization" (statement 2, 63%), (iii) "Information and communications technology is successfully used to create and sustain learning communities" (statement 3, 52%), and (iv) "Creative use of information and communications technology is high. At least five of the following have been successfully adopted: shared document drives, intranet pages, online communities and networks, wikis, and other means of collaborative document production, blogging, online storytelling, lessons learned databases, staff profile pages, online webinars, podcasts, and social network mapping" (statement 9, 54%).

Table 19.4 Perceptions of the technology subsystem (%)

Statement subject	Strongly agree	Agree	Neutral	Disagree	Strongly disagree	Don't know
1. ICT for knowledge management and learning	7	47	26	10	6	4
2. ICT as facilitator	6	57	24	9	2	3
3. Learning communities	4	47	25	17	4	3
4. Corporate developments	8	66	16	6	3	1
5. Connections	4	45	27	13	3	7
6. Innovation and creativity	4	38	29	18	6	5
7. Good practices	4	44	30	15	3	4
8. Internal sources of expertise	4	38	31	17	5	5
9. Creative use	7	46	21	17	3	4
10. Opportunities	5	43	23	19	7	3
Average	5	47	25	14	4	4

ICT Information and technology
Note Numbers may not total 100% because of rounding

The most "neutral" responses are found in the statement, "information and communications technology is successfully used to enable people to identify internal sources of expertise" (statement 8). The highest percentage of respondents (although only 26%) "strongly disagree" and "disagree" that "sufficient opportunities are provided for staff members to learn how to make use of available information and communications technology for learning and sharing" (statement 10). Table 19.4 presents the survey results for the technology subsystem.

The use of technology for knowledge management and organizational learning seems to emerge as a success story in most responses. It would be interesting to understand in depth why this is so. Positive perceptions may owe in part because the uptake and use of technology in ADB does not require the support of managers or the creation of a supportive learning environment in one's team—one can use the technology if it is there and one knows how. The responses to statement 3 represent a very positive assessment of the contribution of technology to learning communities. Statement 4 shows a very significant recognition by respondents of the value of technology in keeping them informed of corporate developments. While this may not in itself lead to improved organizational learning, personnel who are aware of their place in the wider organization are generally considered to be more likely to contribute their knowledge for its collective good. The responses to statement 8 suggest a need for greater use of technology for internal peer support. Peer assists require an understanding of where expertise resides (not only in terms of current roles and responsibilities but also in light of previous experience). Staff profile pages surely have a role to play.

Subsystem Comparison

The largest proportion of respondents (74%) "strongly agree" and "agree" that "ADB has made successful use of information and communications technology to keep people informed and aware of corporate developments" (technology subsystem, statement 4), while the highest rate of disagreement (44%) is with the statement that ADB has a "resilient organizational memory and is not vulnerable to the loss of important knowledge when staff members move to other jobs in the organization or leave" (knowledge subsystem, statement 8).

Three statements pertaining to actions taken by ADB ex-post (e.g., evaluations, adoption of after-action reviews and retrospects) consistently generated relatively high frequencies of "don't know" responses. To wit, these statements are (i) "Failures and unintended outcomes are the focus of constructive discussions leading to new approaches. When such incidents involve clients, care is taken to protect their reputation" (organization subsystem, statement 10, 13%); (ii) "Evaluations are carefully designed with learning (as well as accountability) in mind. Systems ensure that the outputs of internal and independent evaluations are made widely available; carefully examined; and used to influence decision making and planning, question orthodox thinking, and trigger creativity and innovation" (knowledge subsystem, statement 6, 11%); and (iii) "Adoption of after-action reviews and retrospects to learn from experience has been successful" (knowledge subsystem, statement 10, 13%). This reflects minimal awareness of existing policies or the lack thereof.

Concluding Remarks

The survey response rate of 9%, given likely survey fatigue in ADB, is acceptable if not robust and compares reasonably with what is usually considered good for an online survey (10%). What are very positive are the high response rates from some departments: these demonstrate what is possible when both participant interest and management encouragement are present. The survey mean scores per subsystem are all above 3 (the score that represents "neutral"), which indicates a somewhat favorable yet uncertain view of ADB's capacities, barring exceptions. It is worth remembering that, using a five-point Likert scale, to reach a mean score of 4 would require a significant number of "strongly agree" and "agree" responses to balance "neutral", "disagree", and "strongly disagree" feedback so any organization is highly unlikely to achieve a mean score of 4, let alone the ideal score of 5. This needs to be emphasized in any interpretation of results. In these circumstances, indicators such as the percentage of "strongly agree" and "strongly disagree" responses become significant. Moreover, one should bear in mind that mean scores can obscure significant differences in distributions of responses between statements.

Organizations do not change—the people in them change, and then change their organization. Surveys provide the starting point for effective interventions. On organizational learning, ADB now has a baseline against which to gauge perception of progress, noting that cultural change can take time to anchor. Since the value of any survey increases considerably when there are two or more data sets to compare, therefore, it is recommended that the survey be repeated, perhaps annually, primarily for purposes of organizational learning, not performance measurement. ADB should also ponder what is likely to encourage higher response rates: communicating key findings from the survey[7]; involving staff in office-and department-led improvements plans to secure buy-in and build lessons into systems, the principal recommendation from the meeting of 3 September, 2010 with ADB's knowledge management coordinators[8]; sharing evidence that the survey has led to actions being taken[9]; and requesting management to both take part and encourage personnel to participate in future surveys, thereby enabling deeper analysis at office and departmental levels.[10]

---

[7]On 3 September 2010, the Knowledge Management Center shared and discussed the key findings of the 2010 *Learning for Change Survey* at a meeting of ADB's knowledge management coordinators. (Three resident missions took part.) The meeting helped validate survey results and provided grassroots suggestions for next steps. These might include self-assessments, task analyses, desktop meetings, awareness raising, learning and development, and behavioral reinforcement.

[8]Even if each must be involved in knowledge sharing and learning, individual staff typically feel no responsibility and usually do not hold themselves accountable for that.

[9]Conducting a survey without intent to change sends the wrong message and can even do harm. The problems of the workplace are not created by what we do but by what we fail to do.

[10]To have credibility, leaders must "walk the talk" of organizational change. (Their failure to do so is one of the most common complaints of personnel.) The majority of staff will espouse the corporate values leaders propound if they perceive these to be what upper management truly wants. Importantly, one cannot overcommunicate vision and values. Culture is resilient and hard to change: people will revert to old habits if they are not steered by leadership. Its role is to create positive consequences for positive performance.

Appendix 1: Seeking Feedback on Learning for Change

Organization Subsystem

1. There is an inspiring vision for learning and an organizational learning strategy that clearly communicates that learning is critical to organizational success.
2. Leaders take an exemplary leading role in creating and sustaining a supportive learning culture.
3. The formal organizational structure facilitates learning, adaptation, and change.
4. Sanctioned informal organizational structures enable and encourage learning across formal structural boundaries.
5. Good use is made of communication systems to facilitate the lateral transfer of information and knowledge and to minimize the development of "silos".
6. Adequate resources are allocated for learning in terms of time, allocation, specialist support staff, budgets for knowledge management infrastructure, formal and informal communities of practice and other value networks, and learning and development programs.
7. A balanced approach to learning that recognizes the importance of both planned and emergent learning is taken.
8. Planned learning is addressed through the careful design of strategy, structure, systems, procedures, and plans.
9. Emergent learning is encouraged by creating opportunities for informal sharing of knowledge and experience.
10. Failures and unintended outcomes are the focus of constructive discussions leading to new approaches. When such incidents involve clients, care is taken to protect their reputation.

People

1. Staff members are required to be reflective practitioners to reflect on their experience, develop experience-based theories of change, continuously test these in practice with colleagues, and use their understanding and initiative to contribute to knowledge development.
2. All staff members make frequent use of a range of tools, methods, and approaches for learning and collaborating with others.
3. Staff members experience a high level of psychological safety and trust; they can rely on colleagues and are not exposed to unfair negative criticism.

4. Teams operate as learning communities in which success and unexpected outcomes are analyzed and in which sensitively expressed dissent, conflict, and debate are encouraged as positive sources of learning.
5. Staff members are encouraged to look outside the organization for new ideas, trends, and practices and to share what they learn with colleagues.
6. Equal attention is paid to developing and retaining staff members at all levels.
7. Staff members successfully use a wide range of opportunities for individual and team-based learning and development.
8. Time and effort spent by staff members on learning and knowledge development are recognized as core activities in the organization's time and performance management systems.
9. A wide range of formal and informal rewards and incentives for contributing to organizational learning and knowledge development is used (e.g., career advancement, increased income, informal peer status, additional time provided for study, and public acknowledgment for innovative contributions made).
10. Leadership (based on the possession of expertise and knowledge) is expected from staff members at all levels in the organizational hierarchy.

Knowledge

1. There is widespread recognition that while knowledge is created in the minds of individuals, knowledge development thrives in a rich web of professional networks among individuals.
2. Important knowledge is easily accessible to people who need and use it.
3. There are creative opportunities for knowledge to be developed and shared with others by facilitating networks between individuals.
4. The design and delivery of products and services demonstrate how effective the organization is at applying what it has learned about the nature of good practice.
5. The necessary systems and infrastructure for knowledge management are in place, understood, and working effectively.
6. Evaluations are carefully designed with learning (as well as accountability) in mind. Systems ensure that the outputs of internal and independent evaluations are made widely available; carefully examined; and used to influence decision making and planning, question orthodox thinking, and trigger creativity and innovation.
7. Peer assists, drawing on individuals' expertise and documented lessons learned, are used in planning new initiatives to reduce the likelihood of repeated and unintended negative outcomes.

8. The organization has a resilient organizational memory and is not vulnerable to the loss of important knowledge when staff members move to other jobs in the organization or leave.
9. Individuals and teams successfully use a range of methods for surfacing their tacit knowledge and making it available to others, for example, by using carefully targeted documentation and collaborative working practices.
10. Adoption of after-action reviews and retrospects to learn from experience has been successful.

Technology

1. There is a thorough and shared understanding of the value of information and communications technology for knowledge management and learning.
2. Information and communications technology facilitates but do not drive or constrain knowledge management and learning in the organization.
3. Information and communications technology is successfully used to create and sustain learning communities.
4. Information and communications technology is successfully used to keep people informed and aware of corporate developments.
5. Information and communications technology is successfully used to create unexpected, helpful connections between people and to provide access to their knowledge and ideas.
6. Information and communications technology is successfully used to encourage innovation and creativity.
7. Information and communications technology is successfully used to enable people to share and learn form good practices and unintended outcomes.
8. Information and communications technology is successfully used to enable people to identify internal sources of expertise.
9. Creative use of information and communications technology is high. At least five of the following have been successfully adopted: shared document drives, intranet pages, online communities and networks, wikis, and other means of collaborative document production, blogging, online storytelling, lessons learned databases, staff profile pages, online webinars, podcasts, and social network mapping.
10. Sufficient opportunities are provided for staff members to learn how to make use of available information and communications technology for learning and sharing.

Number of Respondents by Department and Staff Category

Department	Position not indicated	Administrative staff	National officers	Professional staff	No. of respondents	No. of staff	Response rate (%)
BPMSD	0	5	0	1	6	149	4
COSO	0	3	0	1	4	82	5
CTL	0	2	2	2	6	157	4
CWRD	0	2	0	4	6	267	2
DER	0	1	1	1	3	27	11
EARD	0	1	1	12	14	62	23
ERD	0	1	2	1	4	63	6
IED	0	4	1	4	9	48	19
OAS	0	3	12	3	18	147	12
OCO	0	0	1	2	3	37	8
OCRP	0	1	0	0	1	5	20
OGC	0	4	0	3	7	57	12
OIST	0	0	2	2	4	118	3
OSPF	0	1	1	1	3	4	75
PARD	0	2	0	2	4	89	4
PSOD	0	2	3	5	10	91	11
RSDD	0	8	5	14	27	126	21
SARD	0	18	0	12	30	314	10
SEC	0	5	2	5	12	33	36
SERD	0	26	4	32	62	128	48
SPD	0	5	3	5	13	51	25
TD	0	2	2	0	4	93	4
TRANS	0	0	0	1	1	36	3
Not indicated	5	0	0	0	5		
Total	5	96	42	113	256		

BPMSD Budget, Personnel, and Management Systems Department, *COSO* Central Operations Services Office, *CTL* Controller's Department, *CWRD* Central and West Asia Department, *DER* Department of External Relations, *EARD* East Asia Department, *ERD* Economics and Research Department, *IED* Independent Evaluation Department, *OAS* Office of Administrative Services, *OCO* Office of Cofinancing Operations, *OCRP* Office of the Compliance Review Panel, *OGC* Office of the General Counsel, *OIST* Office of Information Systems and Technology, *OSPF* Office of the Special Project Facilitator, *PARD* Pacific Department, *PSOD* Private Sector Operations Department, *RSDD* Regional and Sustainable Development Department, *SARD* South Asia Department, *SEC* Office of the Secretary, *SERD* Southeast Asia Department, *SPD* Strategy and Policy Department, *TD* Treasury Department, *TRANS* Transitory

Note Feedback from the Asian Development Bank Institute is incorporated in TRANS

The Organization Subsystem

1. There is an inspiring vision for learning and an organizational learning strategy that clearly communicates that learning is critical to organizational success

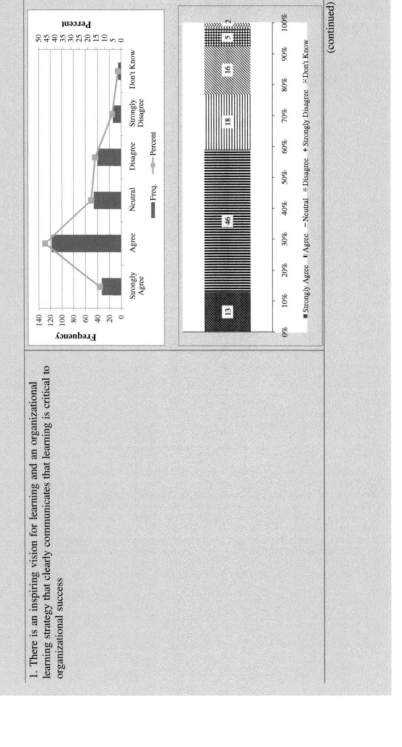

(continued)

(continued)

2. Leaders take an exemplary leading role in creating and sustaining a
supportive learning culture

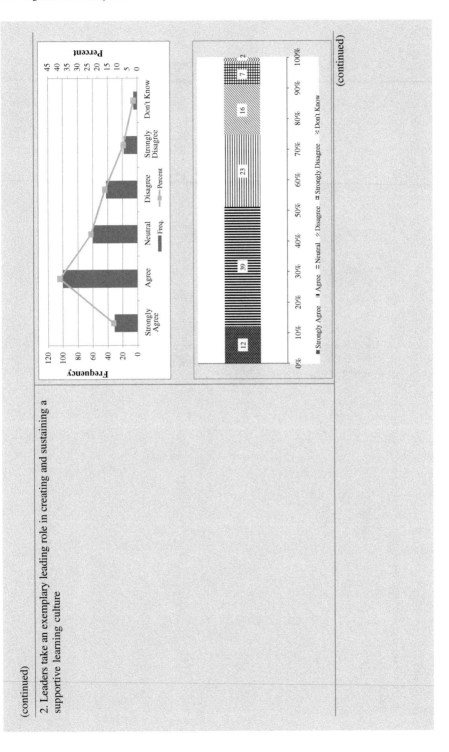

(continued)

(continued)

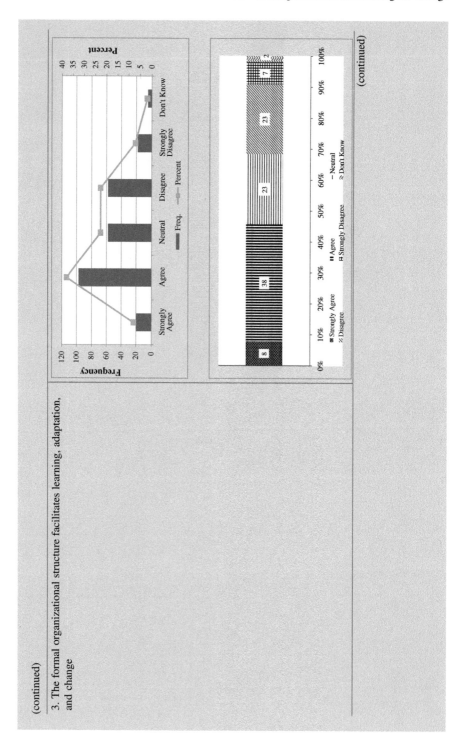

3. The formal organizational structure facilitates learning, adaptation, and change

(continued)

(continued)

4. Sanctioned informal organizational structures enable and
encourage learning across formal structural boundaries

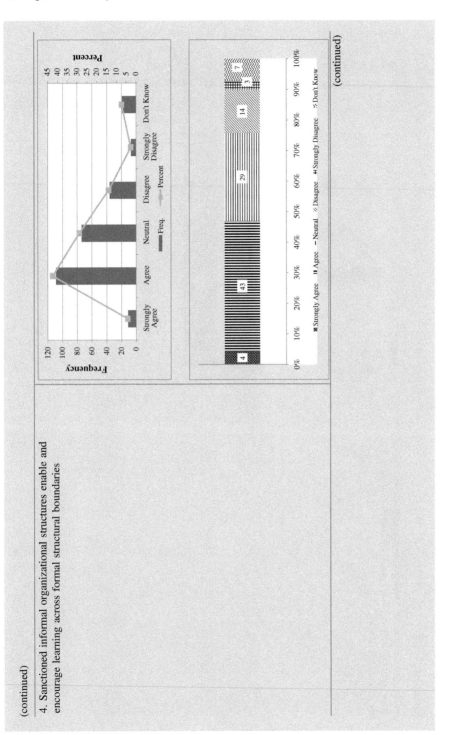

(continued)

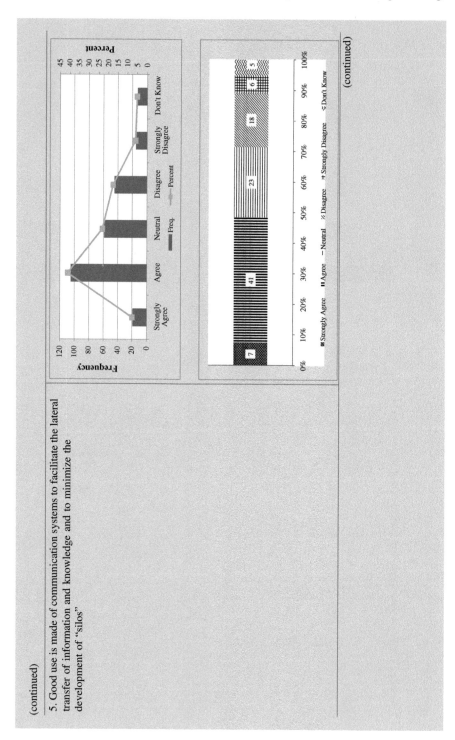

(continued)

5. Good use is made of communication systems to facilitate the lateral transfer of information and knowledge and to minimize the development of "silos"

(continued)

(continued)

6. Adequate resources are allocated for learning in terms of time, allocation, specialist support staff, budgets for knowledge management infrastructure, formal and informal communities of practice and other value networks, and learning and development programs

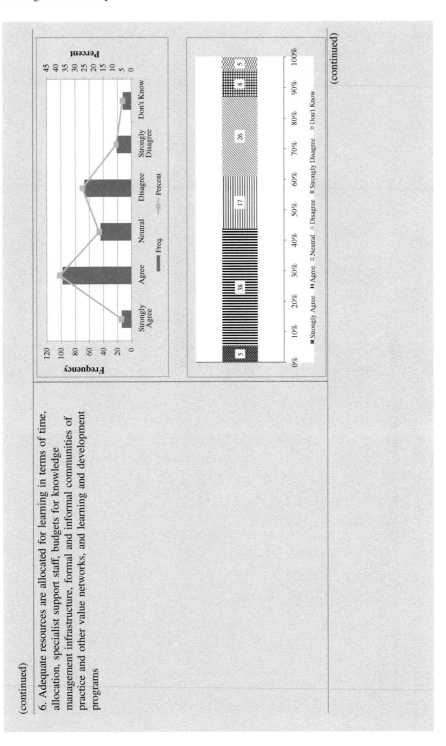

(continued)

(continued)

(continued)

7. A balanced approach to learning that recognizes the importance of both planned and emergent learning is taken

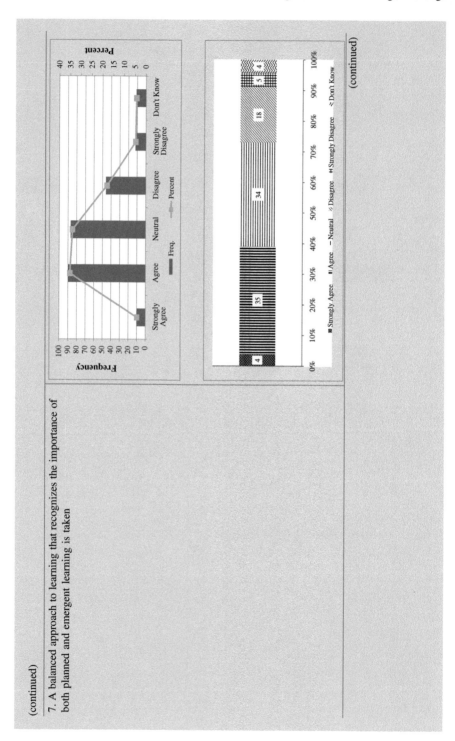

(continued)

(continued)

8. Planned learning is addressed through the careful design of strategy, structure, systems, procedures, and plans

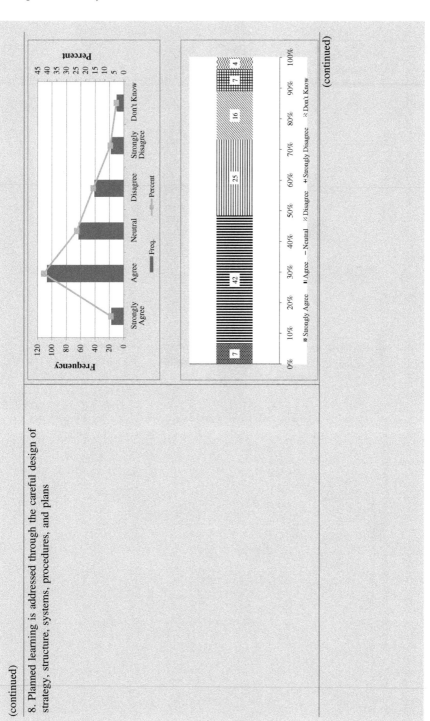

(continued)

(continued)

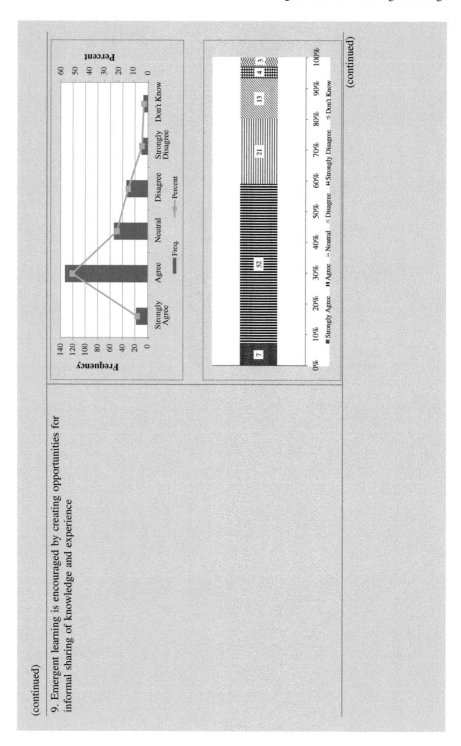

9. Emergent learning is encouraged by creating opportunities for informal sharing of knowledge and experience

(continued)

(continued)

10. Failures and unintended outcomes are the focus of constructive discussions leading to new approaches. When such incidents involve clients, care is taken to protect their reputation

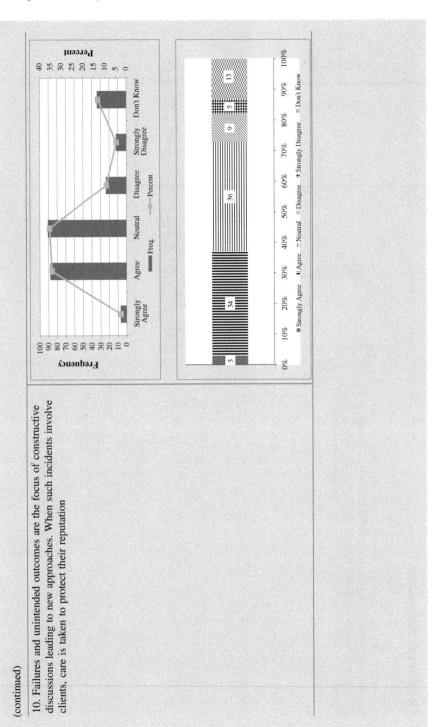

The People Subsystem

1. Staff members are required to be reflective practitioners to reflect on their experience, develop experience-based theories of change, continuously test these in practice with colleagues, and use their understanding and initiative to contribute to knowledge development

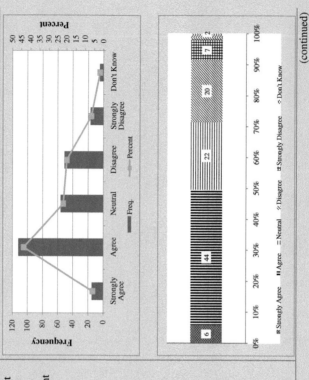

(continued)

(continued)

2. All staff members make frequent use of a range of tools, methods, and approaches for learning and collaborating with others

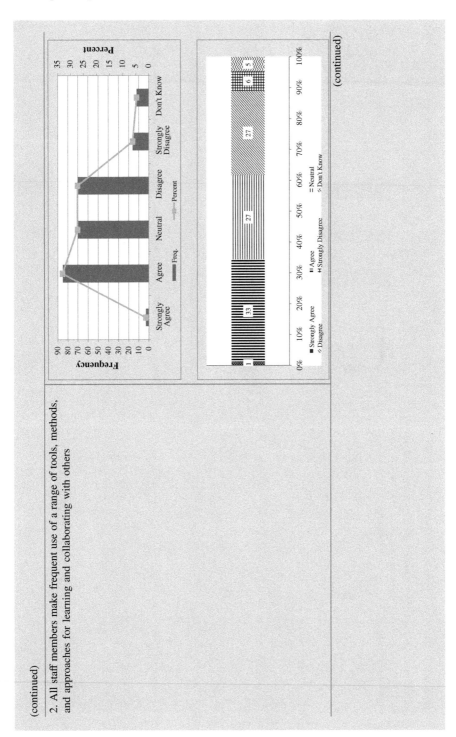

(continued)

(continued)

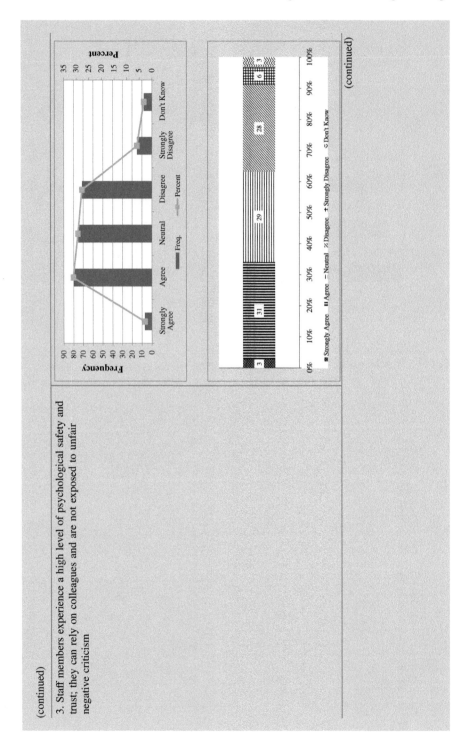

3. Staff members experience a high level of psychological safety and trust; they can rely on colleagues and are not exposed to unfair negative criticism

(continued)

(continued)

4. Teams operate as learning communities in which success and unexpected outcomes are analyzed and in which sensitively expressed dissent, conflict, and debate are encouraged as positive sources of learning

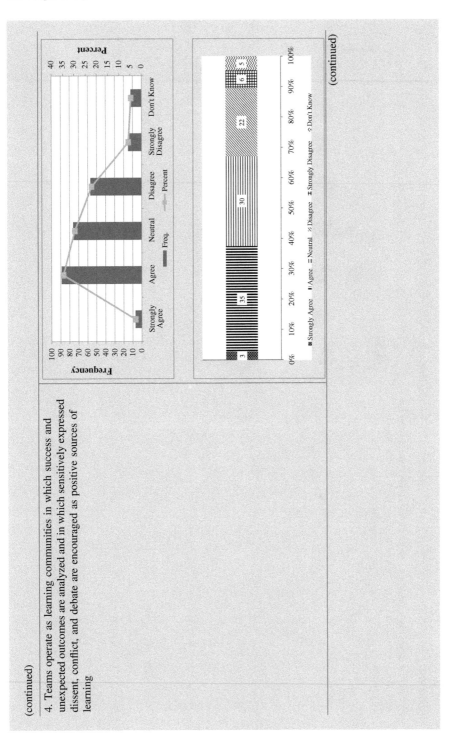

(continued)

(continued)

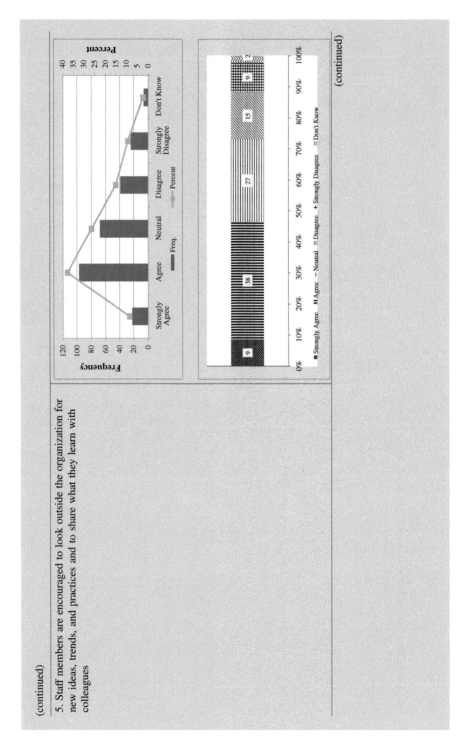

5. Staff members are encouraged to look outside the organization for new ideas, trends, and practices and to share what they learn with colleagues

(continued)

(continued)

6. Equal attention is paid to developing and retaining staff members at all levels

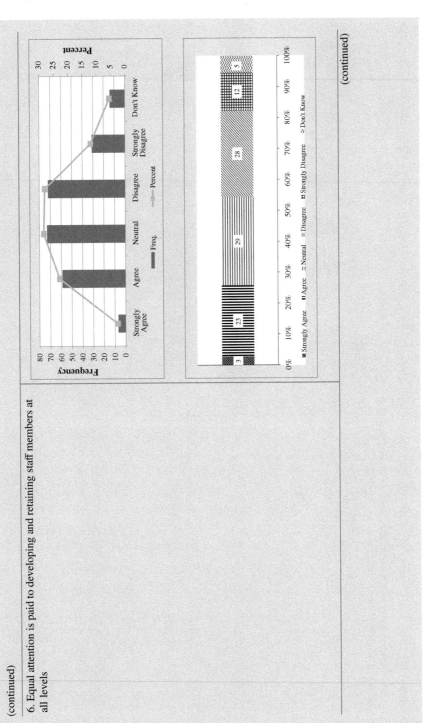

(continued)

(continued)

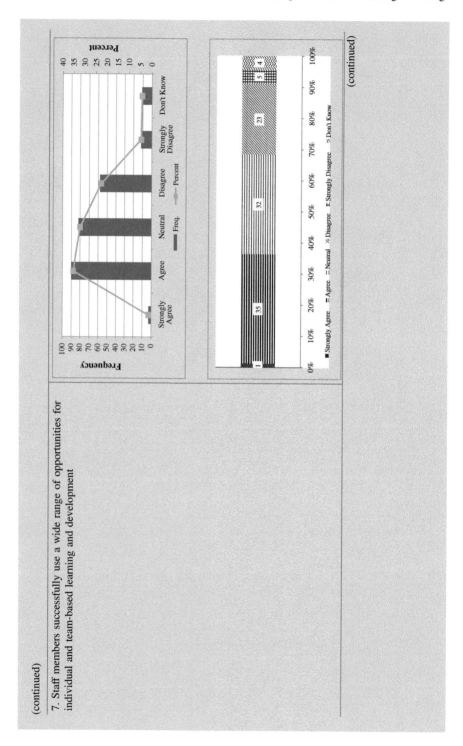

(continued)

7. Staff members successfully use a wide range of opportunities for individual and team-based learning and development

(continued)

8. Time and effort spent by staff members on learning and knowledge development are recognized as core activities in the organization's time and performance management systems

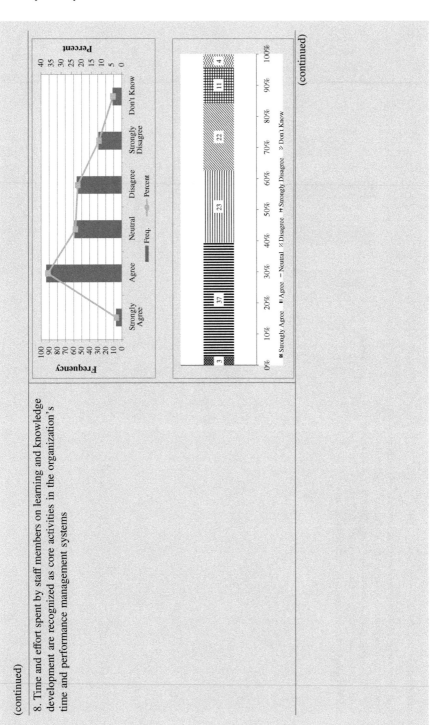

(continued)

(continued)

9. A wide range of formal and informal rewards and incentives for contributing to organizational learning and knowledge development is used (e.g., career advancement, increased income, informal peer status, additional time provided for study, and public acknowledgment for innovative contributions made)

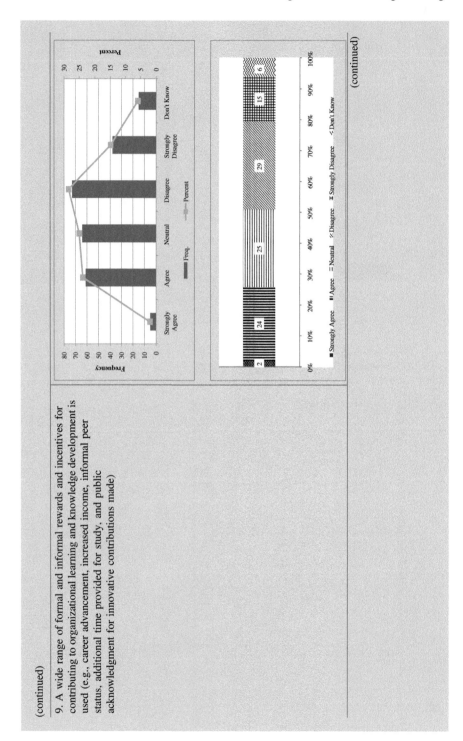

(continued)

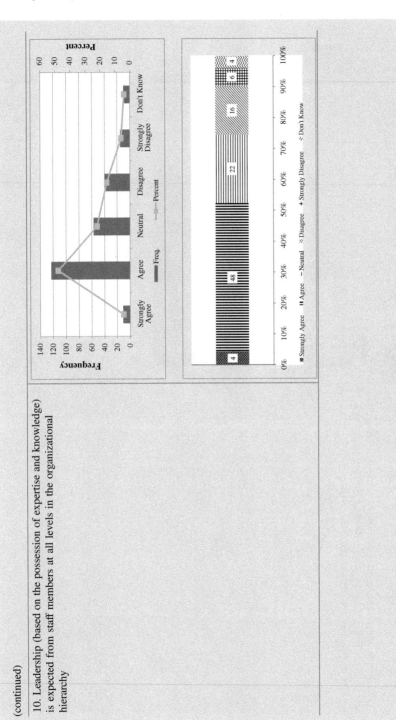

(continued)

10. Leadership (based on the possession of expertise and knowledge) is expected from staff members at all levels in the organizational hierarchy

The Knowledge Subsystem

1. There is widespread recognition that while knowledge is created in the minds of individuals, knowledge development thrives in a rich web of professional networks among individuals

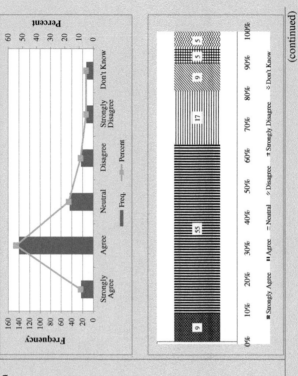

(continued)

(continued)

2. Important knowledge is easily accessible to people who need and use it

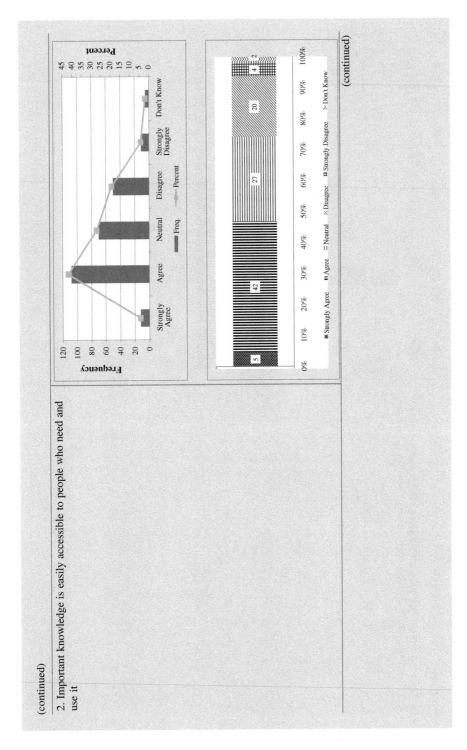

(continued)

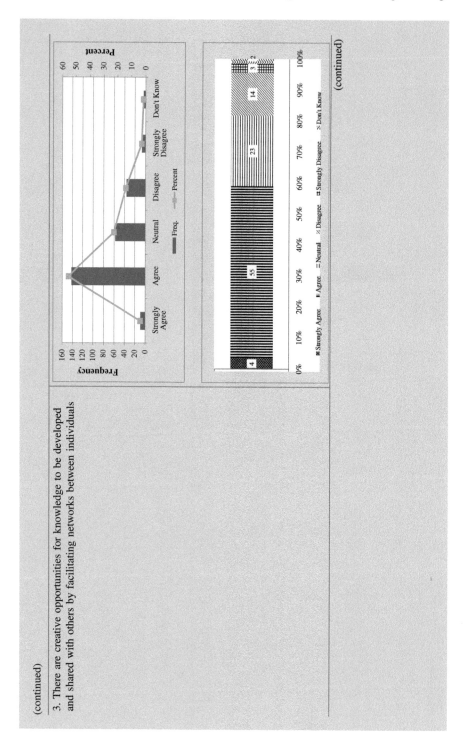

(continued)

3. There are creative opportunities for knowledge to be developed and shared with others by facilitating networks between individuals

(continued)

4. The design and delivery of products and services demonstrate how effective the organization is at applying what it has learned about the nature of good practice

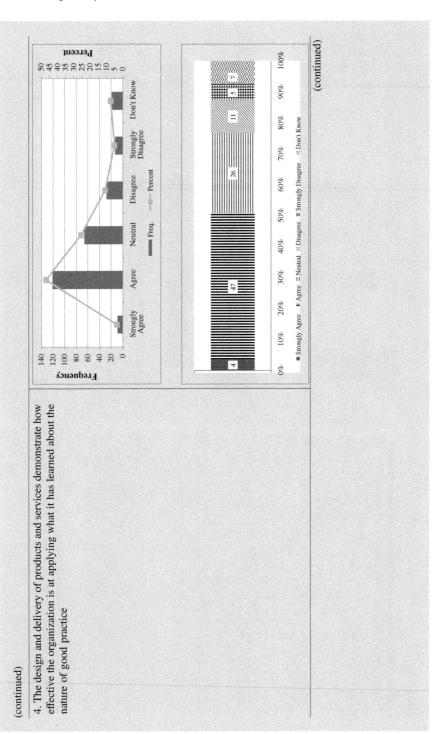

(continued)

(continued)

5. The necessary systems and infrastructure for knowledge management are in place, understood, and working effectively

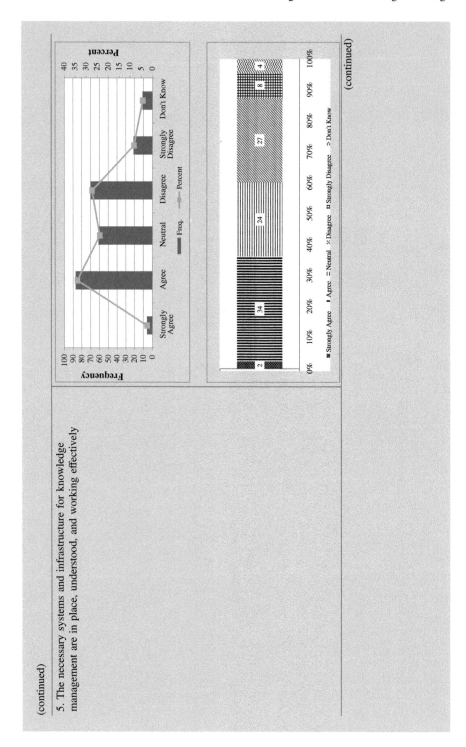

(continued)

(continued)

6. Evaluations are carefully designed with learning (as well as accountability) in mind. Systems ensure that the outputs of internal and independent evaluations are made widely available; carefully examined; and used to influence decision making and planning, question orthodox thinking, and trigger creativity and innovation

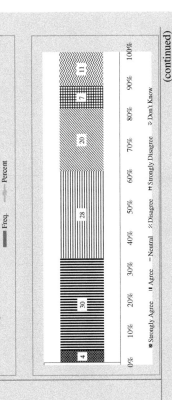

(continued)

(continued)

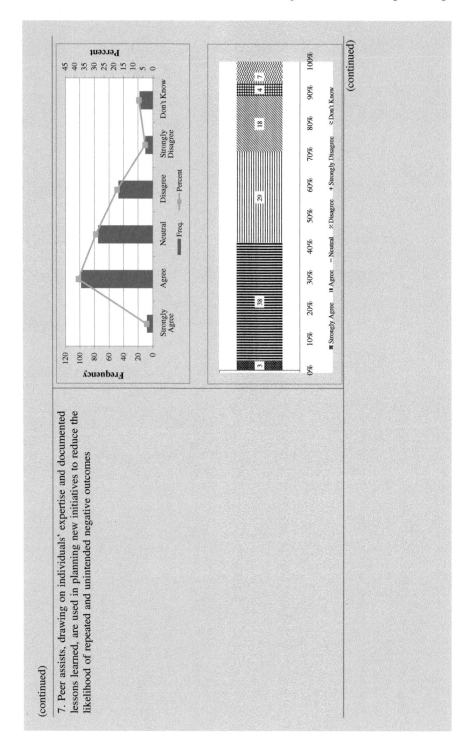

7. Peer assists, drawing on individuals' expertise and documented lessons learned, are used in planning new initiatives to reduce the likelihood of repeated and unintended negative outcomes

(continued)

(continued)

8. The organization has a resilient organizational memory and is not vulnerable to the loss of important knowledge when staff members move to other jobs in the organization or leave

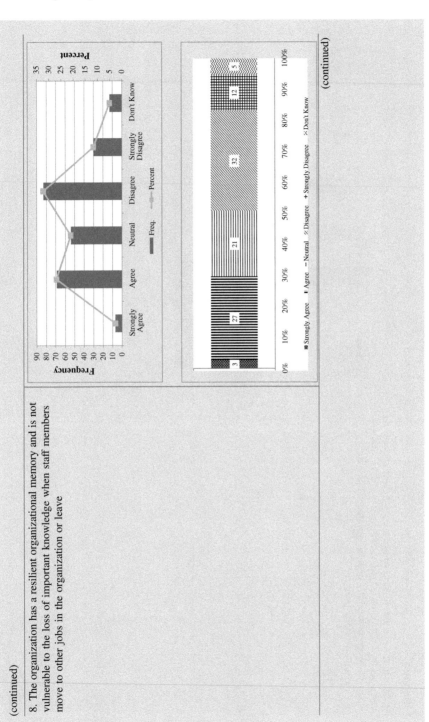

(continued)

(continued)

9. Individuals and teams successfully use a range of methods for surfacing their tacit knowledge and making it available to others, for example, by using carefully targeted documentation and collaborative working practices

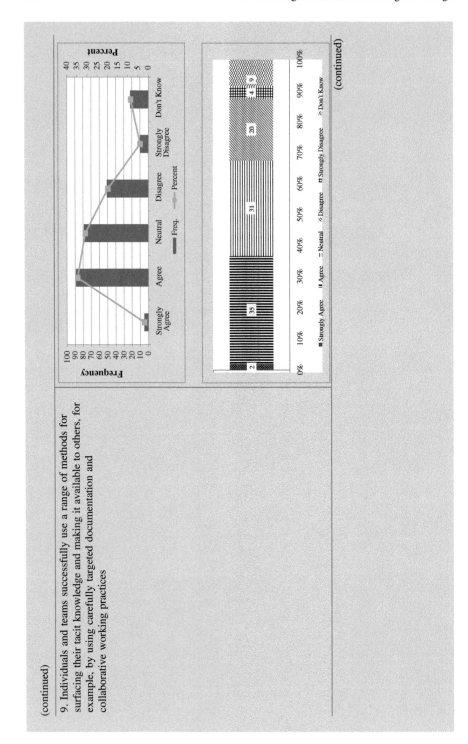

(continued)

(continued)

10. Adoption of after-action reviews and retrospects to learn from experience has been successful

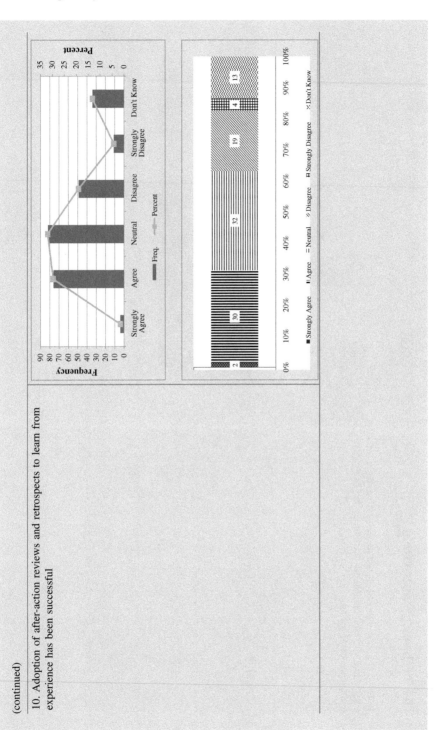

The Technology Subsystem

1. There is a thorough and shared understanding of the value of information and communications technology for knowledge management and learning

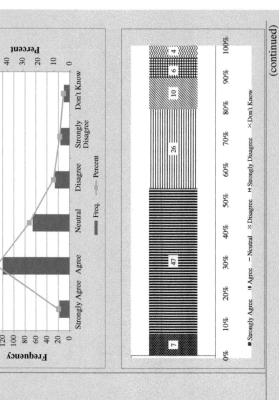

(continued)

(continued)

2. Information and communications technology facilitate but do not drive or constrain knowledge management and learning in the organization

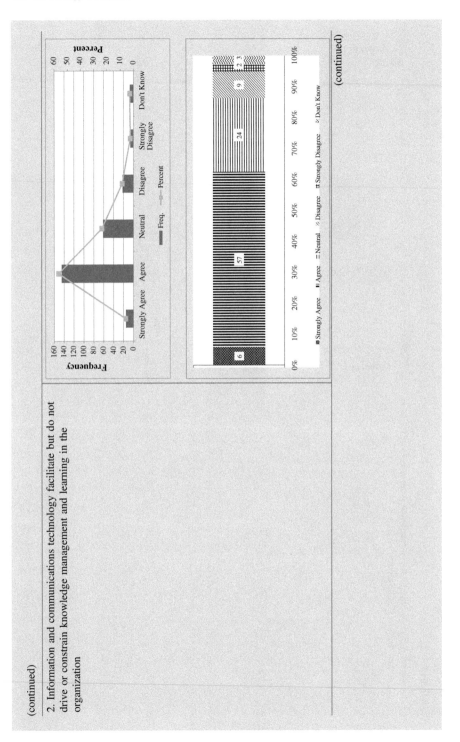

(continued)

(continued)

3. Information and communications technology are successfully used
to create and sustain learning communities

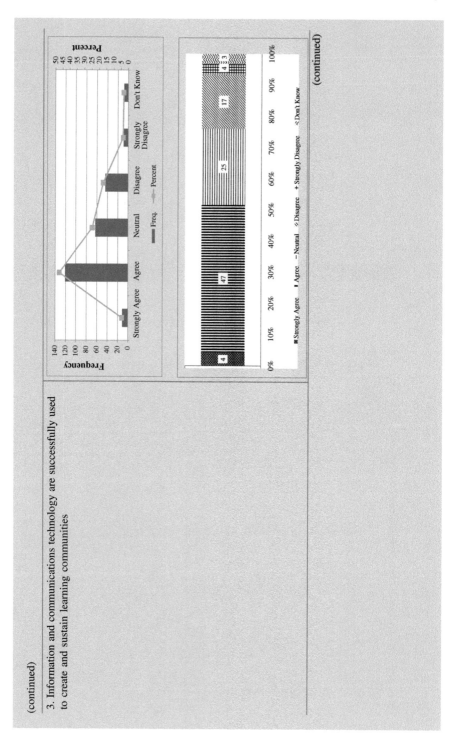

(continued)

(continued)

4. Information and communications technology are successfully used
to keep people informed and aware of corporate developments

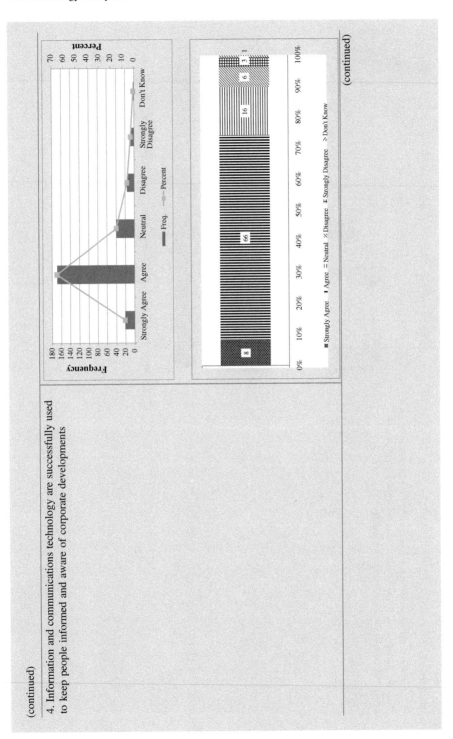

(continued)

(continued)

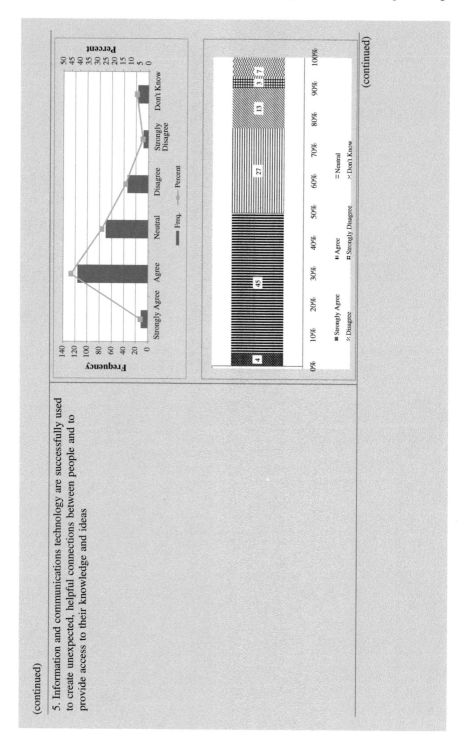

(continued)

5. Information and communications technology are successfully used to create unexpected, helpful connections between people and to provide access to their knowledge and ideas

(continued)

6. Information and communications technology are successfully used to encourage innovation and creativity

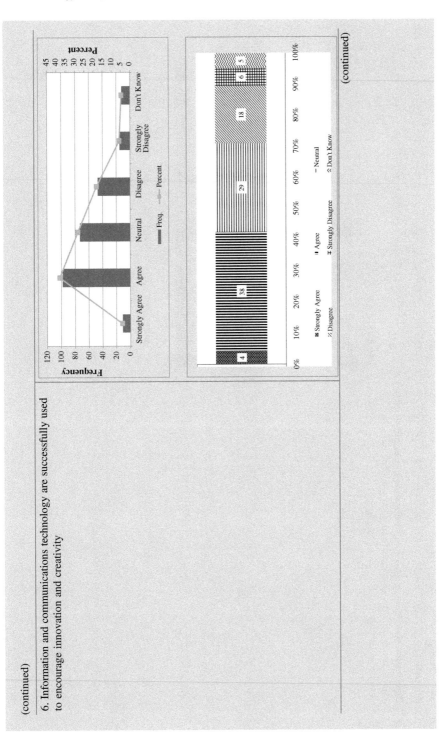

(continued)

(continued)

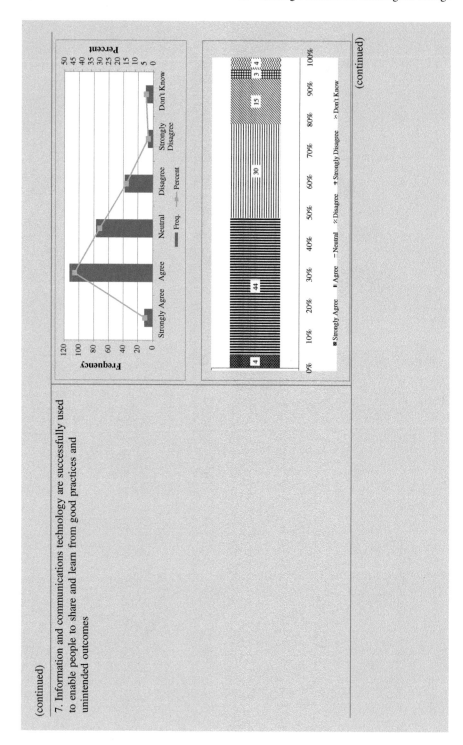

7. Information and communications technology are successfully used
to enable people to share and learn from good practices and
unintended outcomes

(continued)

(continued)

8. Information and communications technology are successfully used to enable people to identify internal sources of expertise

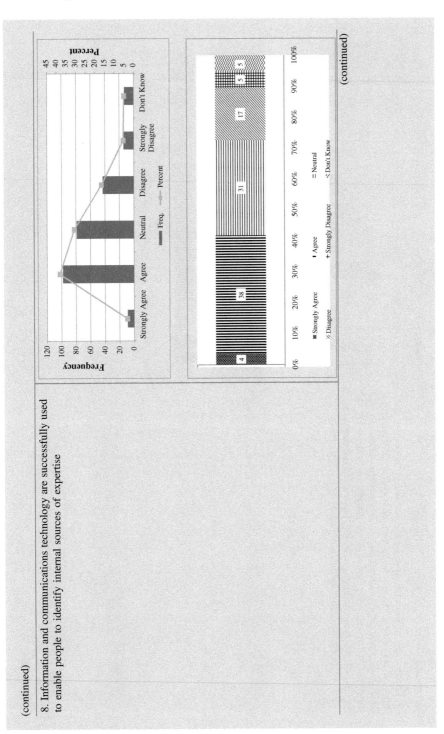

(continued)

(continued)

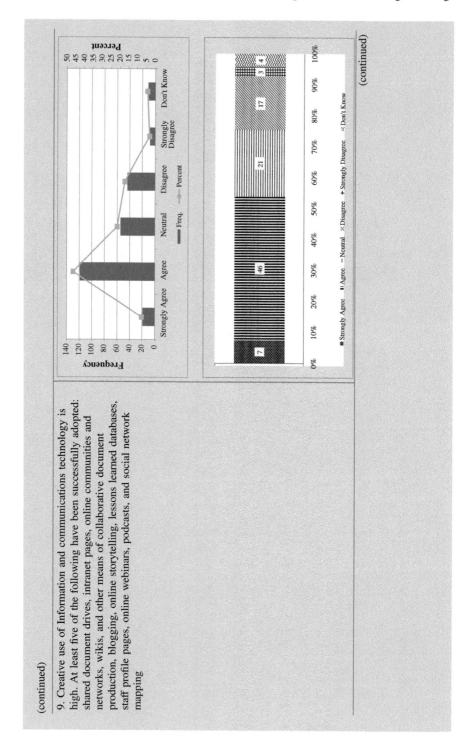

9. Creative use of Information and communications technology is high. At least five of the following have been successfully adopted: shared document drives, intranet pages, online communities and networks, wikis, and other means of collaborative document production, blogging, online storytelling, lessons learned databases, staff profile pages, online webinars, podcasts, and social network mapping

(continued)

(continued)

10. Sufficient opportunities are provided for staff members to learn how to make use of available Information and communications technology for learning and sharing

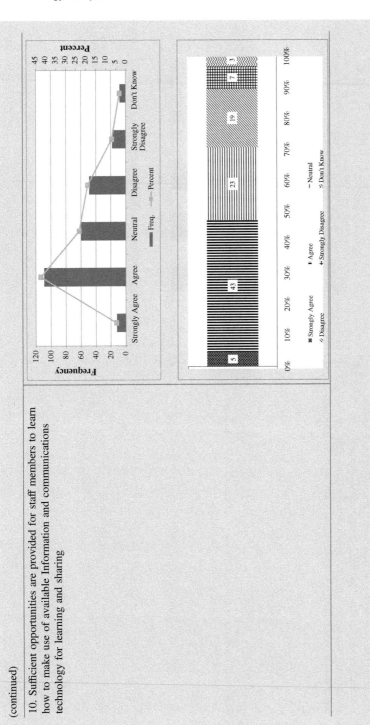

The People Subsystem by Staff Category

1. Staff members are required to be reflective practitioners to reflect on their experience, develop experience-based theories of change, continuously test these in practice with colleagues, and use their understanding and initiative to contribute to knowledge development

2. All staff members make frequent use of a range of tools, methods, and approaches for learning and collaborating with others

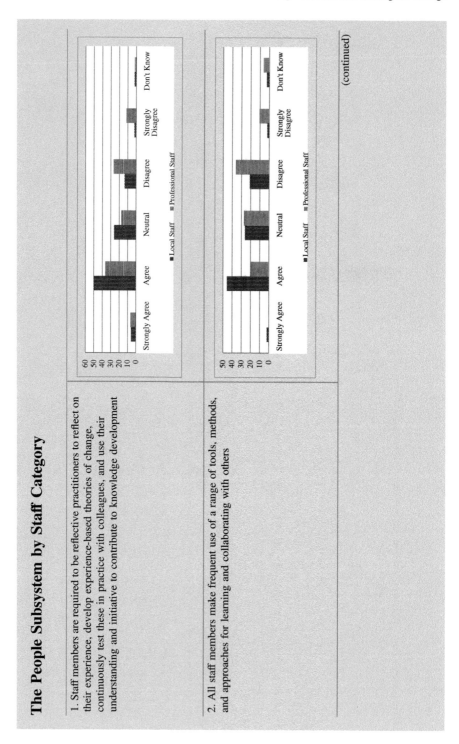

(continued)

(continued)

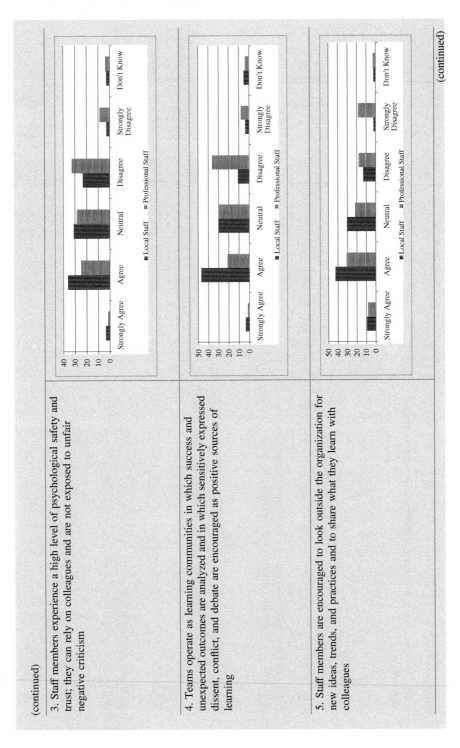

3. Staff members experience a high level of psychological safety and trust; they can rely on colleagues and are not exposed to unfair negative criticism

4. Teams operate as learning communities in which success and unexpected outcomes are analyzed and in which sensitively expressed dissent, conflict, and debate are encouraged as positive sources of learning

5. Staff members are encouraged to look outside the organization for new ideas, trends, and practices and to share what they learn with colleagues

(continued)

(continued)

6. Equal attention is paid to developing and retaining staff members at all levels

7. Staff members successfully use a wide range of opportunities for individual and team-based learning and development

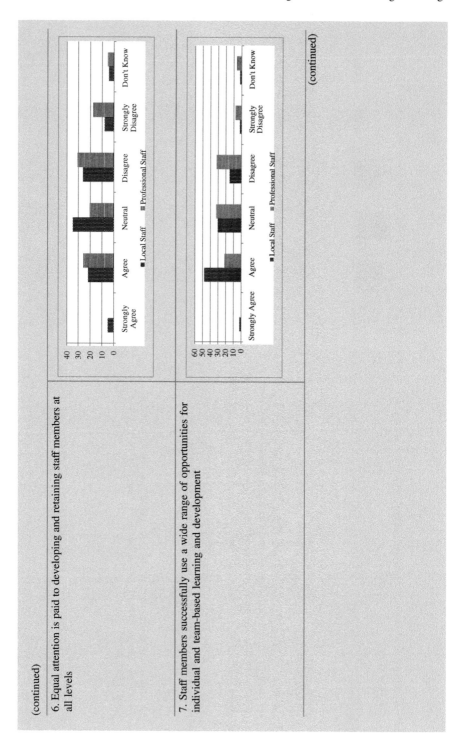

(continued)

(continued)

8. Time and effort spent by staff members on learning and knowledge development are recognized as core activities in the organization's time and performance management systems

9. A wide range of formal and informal rewards and incentives for contributing to organizational learning and knowledge development is used (e.g., career advancement, increased income, informal peer status, additional time provided for study, and public acknowledgment for innovative contributions made)

10. Leadership (based on the possession of expertise and knowledge) is expected from staff members at all levels in the organizational hierarchy

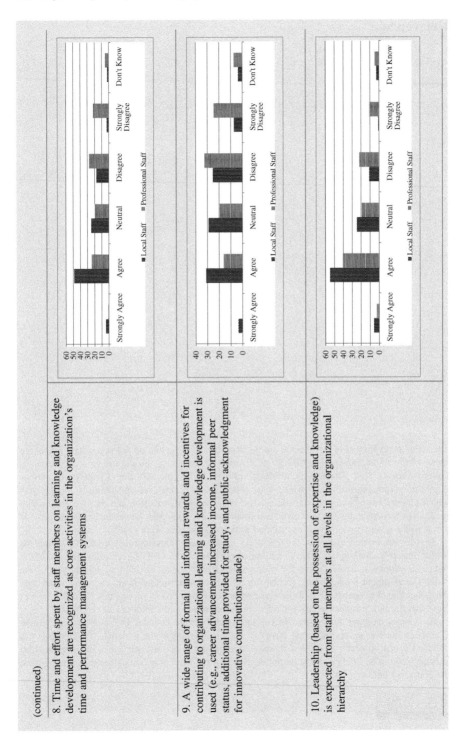

Reference

ADB (2009) Learning for change in ADB. Manila

Chapter 20
A Primer on Intellectual Capital

In a Word Intellectual capital has become the one indispensable asset of organizations. Managing its human, relational, and structural components is of the essence of modern business.

Karl Marx Redux

> *Karl Marx would be amused. He longed for the day when the workers would own the means of production. Now they do.*
>
> —Charles Handy

Following Smith (2010),[1] factors of production—the inputs or resources needed to turn out goods and services (and contribute to a nation's wealth)—were for long classified into (i) land (or natural resources); (ii) labor (or human effort); and

---

[1] Adam Smith (1723–1790), a Scottish political economist and social philosopher, laid the intellectual framework that explained the free market. The magnum opus he published in 1776, *The Wealth of Nations*, is considered the first modern work of economics.

© Asian Development Bank 2017
O. Serrat, *Knowledge Solutions*, DOI 10.1007/978-981-10-0983-9_20

(iii) capital stock (or machinery, tools, and buildings). (The classical economists did not include money since they did not think it was used to directly turn out goods and services.)[2] Although early interest can be traced to the seventeenth century, certainly in the work of William Petty, only in the last 50 years has been capital theory distinguished human capital[3] (the stock of knowledge in individuals) from labor. More recently still, starting in the early 1990s, knowledge has been recognized as a factor of production in its own right.

The Wealth of Knowledge

Stewart (1997),[4] for one, has come to believe that knowledge is the most important factor in the modern economy and the key to achieving competitive advantage in a globalizing world. (Obviously, conventional assets have not disappeared and will not.) If they know what they know,[5] the knowledge that individuals and organizations hold (and hopefully fructify) can advance their purposes by enhancing the

---

[2]To note, notwithstanding their agrarianist philosophy, the French physiocrats—such as François Quesnay (1694–1774) and Anne-Robert-Jacques Turgot (1727–1781)—who succeeded the mercantilists and immediately preceded the classical economists had identified entrepreneurship (or enterprise) to tally four factors. The prime advocate of a labor theory of value, Karl Marx (1818–1883), a German philosopher, sociologist, economic historian, journalist, and revolutionary, believed that all production belongs to labor because workers alone create value in society. Later schools, including the neoclassical economists, have continued to argue over which factor, including entrepreneurship, is the most important; proposed further distinctions of capital, e.g., fixed, working, and financial capital, as well as additions such as the state of technology and human capital; and, as we shall see, made intellectual capital the object of interest in sundry disciplines other than economics.

[3]Human capital refers to the stock of knowledge, skills, and experience embodied in labor. (Some bring in health, values, behaviors, and motivation.) It is the sum total of attributes, in general cultivated by a worker through education and experience, that determine his or her value in the marketplace.

[4]A brief account of the early days of the intellectual capital movement must cite the pioneering contribution of Hiroyuki Itami who brought out *Mobilizing Invisible Assets* in Japanese in 1980. In 1986, Karl-Erik Sveiby published the *Know-How Company* in Swedish. Chronologically, Brian Hall, David Teece, Leif Edvinsson, Hubert Saint-Onge, and Patrick Sullivan were other precursors of work on value creation, value extraction, and value reporting. The frequency and specificity of contributions to the field—theme might be a better word—have multiplied since its inception in the 1980s. (The dates suggest that managing intellectual capital was perhaps the first coherent theme that emerged under the discipline of knowledge management, even if collaboration between knowledge management and intellectual capital management researchers leaves something to be desired).

[5]Knowledge equates with the meaningful links that, through experience or association, people make in their minds between data and information and their application in action in specific situations. It only becomes an asset if some useful order is created so it may be formalized, captured, and leveraged in actionable value propositions that accomplish something that could not be done before.

value[6] of other factors of production. Certainly, however, this requires that the nature of knowledge assets be understood at something more than skin depth.

Define: Intellectual Capital

We make doors and windows for a room. But it is the spaces that make the room livable. While the tangible has advantages, it is the intangible that makes it useful.

—Lao Tzu

Born of the information revolution, knowledge management has arisen in response to the belated understanding that intellectual capital is a core asset of organizations and that it should be circumscribed better.[7] From this perspective, it is the growing body of tools, methods, and approaches, inevitably underpinned by values, by means of which organizations can bring about and maximize a return on knowledge assets, aka intellectual capital.[8] That, Thomas Stewart explained pithily (yet broadly) is organized knowledge that can be used to generate wealth.[9] (Conversely, it also helps to think of what intellectual capital is not, that is, monetary or physical resources.)

---

[6]Value is (i) a fair return or equivalent in goods, services, or money for something exchanged; (ii) the monetary worth of something: market price; (iii) relative worth, utility, or importance; (iv) a numerical quantity that is assigned or is determined by calculation or measurement; and/or (v) something (as a principle or quality) intrinsically valuable or desirable.

[7]The intangible (but, at the commonly cited rate of 80% of an organization's value, nonetheless very precious) assets that make up intellectual capital are not normally ascribed a value in an organization's balance sheet. (Put differently, they are roughly—but not exactly—the difference between the market and book value of its equity.) Yet, they are used to manufacture goods or provide services and are expected to create value (as well they do through, say, profit generation from products, services, or intellectual property; strategic positioning; acquiring the innovations of others when new personnel joins; customer loyalty; cost reductions; or improved productivity). The notion of intellectual capital provides a conceptual platform from which to view, analyze, and (hopefully) quantify them.

[8]The steps involved in capitalizing return might involve, say, acquiring, developing, utilizing, and exploiting knowledge assets.

[9]Although everyone agrees that intellectual capital underpins organizational performance, there is a regrettable—yet unavoidable—lack of consensus over definitions of it owing to the diversity of disciplinary and interdisciplinary views from which it is examined. Usefully, Marr (2005) elucidates economics, strategy, accounting, finance, reporting, marketing, human resource, information systems, legal, and intellectual property perspectives. The interdisciplinary views he brings to the subject are interfirm, public policy, knowledge-based, and epistemological.

More specifically, aggregated intellectual capital comprises[10]

- Human capital—the cumulative capabilities and engagement of an organization's personnel, rooted in tacit and explicit knowledge, that can be invested to serve the joint purpose.
- Relational (or customer) capital—the formal and informal external relationships, counting the information flows[11] across and knowledge partnerships in them, that an organization devises with clients, audiences, and partners to cocreate products and services, expressed in terms of width (coverage), channels (distribution), depth (penetration), and attachment (loyalty).
- Structural (or organizational) capital—the collective capabilities of an organization—many of them codified, packaged, and systematized, including its governance, values, culture, management philosophy, business processes, practices,[12] research and development, intellectual property,[13] performance metrics, and information systems, as well as, the systems for leveraging them.

---

[10]Most models of intellectual capital assume a three-way distinction. However, they differ in the names and levels of aggregation. Structural capital is sometimes segregated into according to what has been formalized, e.g., business processes, and what has not, e.g., organizational culture. Pell-mell, and unmanageably so hence the usefulness of discriminating between them, the constituents of intellectual capital include competencies, experience, know-how, knowledge, skills; creativity, innovation; computer programs, databases, information systems, technologies; business processes, methodologies; designs, documents, drawings, publications; intra-organization and inter-organizational relationships; brands, trademarks, etc.

[11]As you would expect, information flows and the perceptions they shape influence corporate reputation.

[12]Formal and informal practices determine how business processes are handled and how work flows through an organization. They comprise, for example, virtual networks, tacit rules of behavior or workflows, and process manuals that lay out codified procedures and rules.

[13]Intellectual property, very broadly, means the legal industrial property and copyright secured from the use of notable mental capacity in the artistic, industrial, literary, and scientific fields. To wit, creations of the mind such as inventions and scientific discoveries; literary and artistic works and their production, performance, and broadcast; and symbols, names, images, and designs can receive legal protection, for instance, by means of copyright and related rights, design rights, geographical indications, industrial designs and integrated circuits, patents, protection against unfair competition, trademarks, and trade secrets. It is no curiosity that explicit rights should be associated with intellectual property and not so readily with other forms of intellectual capital: the latter are frequently (though not always) a process, not an outcome, and are therefore more intangible. (In comparison, when patenting an intellectual property, the owner must make a full disclosure of characteristics by including a specification (description and claims), relevant drawings, prototypes, etc. that clearly define it.) For these reasons, intellectual property usually has a life, certainly in the case of patents, and can often be traded. (Then again, it does not necessarily provide competitive advantage.).

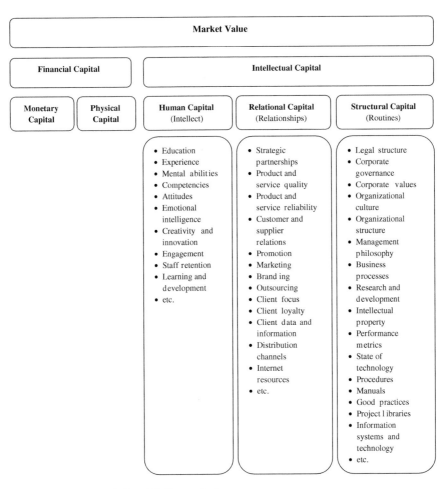

Fig. An intellectual capital model. *Source* Author

Managing Intellectual Capital

The greatest achievement of the human spirit is to live up to one's opportunities and make the most of one's resources.

—Marquis de Vauvenargues

Intellectual capital management is the active management of intellectual capital resources with multiplicative effects. The schemes that can be applied singly or across the three types relate to

- Value creation—the strategic generation of knowledge and its conversion into valuable forms.[14]
- Value extraction—the strategic conversion of created value into useful forms.[15]
- Value reporting—the accurate reflection of the value of intellectual capital— once the what, why, how, when, and where of qualitative and quantitative measurement, as well as its responsibility center, have been decided—for both analysis and decision making,[16] internally by senior management and externally by clients, audiences, and partners.[17]

Naturally, managing intellectual capital effectively rests on balancing value creation, extraction, and reporting to meet the goal of the organization.

Moving from First- to Third-Generation Thinking ...

The continuing rise of knowledge-based economies demands that organizations devise new—or at least parallel—systems for measuring qualitative, nonfinancial items of intellectual capital to supplement traditional, quantifiable, financial measures of their fitness for purpose. Intellectual capital and its hidden capabilities are now visualized and there is a discourse we can all engage in.[18] To date, however, the measurement of intellectual capital remains relatively new, with a smattering of

---

[14]*Knowledge Solutions* that promote tools, methods, and approaches to create value pertain to action learning, appreciative inquiry, asking effective questions, building communities of practice, building networks of practice, coaching and mentoring, creating and running partnerships, critical thinking, drawing mind maps, engaging staff in the workplace, the Five Whys technique, harnessing creativity and innovation, identifying and sharing good practices, learning and development for management, leading top talent in the workplace, learning in strategic alliances, managing corporate values, the reframing matrix, the SCAMPER technique, sparking innovations in management, sparking social innovation, social network analysis, and working in teams.

[15]*Knowledge Solutions* that advance tools, methods, and approaches to extract value have to do with conducting after-action reviews and retrospects, conducting exit interviews, conducting peer assists, enriching policy with research, harvesting knowledge, learning from evaluation, learning lessons with knowledge audits, linking research to practice, the Most Significant Change technique, picking investments in knowledge management, and staff profile pages.

[16]Without reporting systems, on what basis other than guesswork can one invest new capital into worthy, but intangibles-reliant, ventures?

[17]*Knowledge Solutions* that advertise tools, methods, and approaches to report value refer to auditing knowledge, disseminating knowledge products, focusing on project metrics, e-learning in the workplace, monthly progress notes, outcome mapping, output accomplishment and the design and monitoring framework, the perils of performance measurement, sector and thematic reporting, showcasing knowledge, social reminiscing, storytelling, and taxonomies for development.

[18]In the first phase, the bulk of effort was expended on raising awareness of the potential of intellectual capital in creating and managing sustainable competitive advantage.

organizations, more often than not in Scandinavian countries, actually using measurement systems since the mid-1990s. There are a dozen disclosure systems, of which three or four are popular.[19] The basic objectives are comparable but taxonomies are not aligned: therefore, a second body of work for unreported assets would concentrate on standardizing voluntary reporting frameworks, including their boundaries and associated vocabulary; shedding light on the why, what, and how of reporting on intellectual capital with performance metrics that serve both as a management and a communication tool[20]; and replacing rhetoric with actionable statements.[21] A third wave would broaden the context of measurement to move beyond simple causal maps and amplify efforts to build future capabilities.

---

[19]Robert Kaplan and David Norton introduced the Balanced Scorecard in 1992 to help organizations view themselves also from perspectives of learning and growth, business processes, and clients, in addition to finance, for each of which objectives, indicators, targets, and measures should be specified. (This said, the learning and growth perspective has been something of a black hole, with organizations plugging the gap with human resource-related measures, prompting Kaplan and Norton (2004) to posit in 2004 a new definition of intangible assets, viz., human capital, information capital, and organizational, that might have made more of existing classifications.) In 1995, Leif Edvinsson devised the Skandia Navigator, which embodies the same set of concerns as the scorecard but also considers what processes the organization has to nurture personnel. In 1997, Karl-Erik Sveiby devised the Intangible Assets Monitor, which invites application of growth, efficiency, and stability indicators across the accepted tripartite model; unlike the Balanced Scorecard, no financial targets are to be set. (At about the same time, Göran and Johan Roos advertised their proprietary Intellectual Capital Index providing a dynamic view of how intellectual stocks can change over time—by simplifying categories into indices, the index aims to predict returns as investment strategies shift).

[20]Measurement, a quantitatively expressed reduction of uncertainty based on one or more observations, is at the end of the day more about the process of measuring than it is about hard numbers. When designing measurement systems, a rule of thumb is that it is better to be roughly right than precisely wrong. At appropriate levels of control, the common criteria used to improve effectiveness are (i) time, (ii) cost, (iii) resources, (iv) scope, (v) quality, and (vi) actions. It is critical to understand an organization's context; epistemology; and value creation, -extraction, and -reporting pathways if they are to serve as benchmarks.

[21]In 2000 and 2003, the Ministry of Science, Technology, and Innovation in the Government of Denmark gave guidance on formulating intellectual capital statements to help organizations build up, develop, share, and anchor the knowledge that can make their products and services worth more. The four elements of the statements are (i) a knowledge narrative that expresses the ambition to increase the value a user receives from an organization's goods or services, (ii) a set of knowledge management challenges highlighting the knowledge resources that need to be strengthened through in-house development or by sourcing them externally, (iii) a set of initiatives that can be started to do something about the challenges, and (iv) a set of indicators that make it possible to follow up whether the initiatives have been launched or whether the challenges are being met (Danish Ministry of Science, Technology, and Innovation 2003). (The indicators suggested might measure effect, activities, and resource mix.).

... With Early Steps

> *A problem well stated is a problem half-solved.*
>
> —Charles Kettering

The five generic reasons why organizations (ought to) seek to measure intellectual capital are to (i) formulate strategy, (ii) assess strategy execution, (iii) make diversification and expansion decisions, (iv) broaden justification for compensation (and other benefits), and (v) communicate measures to internal and external stakeholders. The business case for managing intellectual capital is becoming stronger: in knowledge-based economies, investments that compound intangible assets have a better return than those in other factors of production.[22] In the final analysis, the only thing limiting progress is the willingness of organizations to define, measure, analyze, improve, and control.[23] Intellectual capital might then, on the word of Ulrich (1998), truly equal competence times commitment. Paraphrasing further, earnest responses to 10 effective questions will according to Petty and Guthrie (2000) help achieve visible benefits.

- What motivates the organization to want to measure its intellectual capital?
- What are the current and anticipated effects of reporting intellectual capital?
- Is generating information on intellectual capital feasible from a cost-benefit perspective?
- Within the organization, who is best positioned to measure and manage intellectual capital?
- How might current methods of measuring intellectual capital be improved?
- What is the extent of demand for intellectual capital reporting by stakeholders?
- Is information on intellectual capital transparent, robust, reliable, and verifiable?
- In what manner are current gaps in information a barrier to better management of intellectual capital and improved decision-making?

---

[22]This is so regardless of whether an organization is in the public or private sector.

[23]This can only take place after an organization's critical intellectual capital has been marked out, conceivably also by means of knowledge audits. Then, because many types of intellectual assets are difficult to gauge directly, proxy measures can be used. Consider, for example, the budgets needed to operate (i) human capital—such as the costs of finding and recruiting talent, learning and development, etc.; (ii) relational capital—such as the outlays for promotion, marketing, branding, outsourcing, acquiring product or quality certifications, etc.; and (iii) structural capital—such as the internal and external expenditures for building processes, hiring process development consultants, developing software applications for internal systems, running knowledge management systems, investing in research and development, acquiring and documenting intellectual property rights, etc.

- What specific difficulties are associated with the development of a reporting system on intellectual capital and how might they be overcome?
- Where should information on intellectual capital be presented?

References

Danish Ministry of Science, Technology, and Innovation (2003) Intellectual capital statements—the new guideline. Copenhagen

Kaplan R, Norton D (2004) Strategy maps: converting intangible assets into tangible outcomes. Harvard Business School Publishing

Marr A (ed) (2005) Perspectives on intellectual capital: multidisciplinary insights into management, measurement, and reporting. Butterworth-Heinemann

Petty R, Guthrie J (2000) Intellectual capital review: measurement, reporting, and management. Journal of Intellectual Capital 1(2):155–176

Smith A (2010) An inquiry into the nature and causes of the wealth of nations. General Books

Stewart T (1997) Intellectual capital: the new wealth of organizations. Currency Doubleday

Ulrich D (1998) Intellectual capital = competence × commitment. Sloan Management Review 39 (2):15–26

Further Reading

Ehin C (2000) Unleashing intellectual capital. Butterworth-Heinemann

Sullivan P (2000) Value-driven intellectual capital: how to convert intangible corporate assets into market value. Wiley, Inc

Proposition 21
Political Economy Analysis for Development Effectiveness

In a Word Political economy embraces the complex political nature of decision making to investigate how power and authority affect economic choices in a society. Political economy analysis offers no quick fixes but leads to smarter engagement.

Define: Political Economy

Economics—the social science that deals with the production, distribution, and consumption of material wealth and with the theory and management of economic systems or economies[1]—was once called political economy.[2] Anchored in moral

---

[1]There is no universally accepted definition of economics. Two other characterizations that both place an accent on scarcity consider it the study of (i) the forces of supply and demand in the allocation of scarce resources, and (ii) individual and social behavior for the attainment and use of the material requisites of economic well-being as a relationship between given ends and scarce means that have alternative uses. The field is subdivided into microeconomics—which characteristically examines the behavior of individual consumers, groups of consumers, and firms—and macroeconomics—which ordinarily looks at growth, inflation, unemployment, and the role of government.
[2]Antoine de Montchrestien (1575–1621), a French poet, dramatist, and economist, is credited with the first use of the term.

© Asian Development Bank 2017
O. Serrat, *Knowledge Solutions*, DOI 10.1007/978-981-10-0983-9_21

philosophy, thence the art and science of government, this articulated the belief in the eighteenth to nineteenth centuries that political considerations—and the interest groups that drive them—have primacy in determining influence and thus economic outcomes at (almost) any level of investigation. However, with the division of economics and political science into distinct disciplines from the 1890s, neoclassical economists turned from analyses of power and authority to models that, inherently, remove much complexity from the issues they look into.[3]

Today, political economists study interrelationships between political and economic institutions (or forces) and processes, which do not necessarily lead to optimal use of scarce resources.[4] Refusing to eschew complexity, they appreciate politics as the sum of activities—involving cooperation, conflict, and negotiation—that shape decisions touching the production, consumption, and transfer of scarce resources, irrespective of whether the activities are formal or informal, public or private, or a combination thereof.[5] (Lest this compass be thought beyond reach, it should be pointed out that politics are not normally random and therefore unpredictable.) In summary, they analyze and explain the ways in which governments affect the allocation of scarce resources in society through laws and policies and, by the same token, the ways in which the nature of economic systems and the behavior of people acting on their economic interests impact governments and the laws and policies they formulate. Depending on the outlook, they can thereby, for example, bring a focus to bear on outcomes—practices might be a better term—such as inequality or exclusion.

A Précis on Political Economy Analysis

It is only the novice in political economy who thinks it is the duty of government to make its citizens happy.—Government has no such office. To protect the weak and the minority from the impositions of the strong and the majority—to prevent anyone from positively working to render the people unhappy, (if we may so express it,) to

---

[3]Power refers to the ability of an individual or group to achieve outcomes reflecting objectives. (Some distinguish hard and soft power.) Authority exists whenever an individual or group is explicitly or tacitly permitted to control, command, or determine. (Some distinguish formal and informal authority.) At heart, politics is but the struggle for the acquisition and application of power and authority.

[4]If economics is the study of the optimal use of scarce resources, subject to well-defined constraints and a market environment, political economy embraces the complex political nature of decision making to investigate how power and authority affect economic choices in a society.

[5]The approach is impartial in that it neither presupposes nor favors a particular type of polity or mode of decision making, policy package or development strategy, structure of incentives, or scale of application. However, by explaining outcomes, it helps diagnose possible sources of positive change—or, conversely, opposition—as well as their dynamics.

> *do the labor not of an officious inter-meddler in the affairs of men, but of a prudent watchman who prevents outrage—these are rather the proper duties of a government.*
>
> —Walt Whitman

Obviously, questions of power and authority come to the fore when heterogeneity of interest leads to conflict[6] among actors in a society.[7] Political economy is founded on the predicament of economic choices in a society comprising heterogeneous agents. Its focus is different from that of welfare economics[8]: the issue is not the technical problem of what implications different welfare weights might have but the political problem of how weights are ascribed and the processes associated with that. (Simplifying, technical and informational approaches ask "what" questions; political economists ask "why" first, and then "how," taking political feasibility into account. This shifts attention from what is missing to what there is.)

In a nutshell, political economy analysis investigates the interaction of political and economic processes in a society; in the context of historical legacies, this entails comprehending.

---

[6]Conflict may be defined as a disagreement, contest, or struggle between people with opposing beliefs, concerns, goals, ideas, interests, needs, or values. Conflict often connotes with war or violence but it occurs more commonly at all levels of society in all sorts of situations. (Some think it is an unavoidable aspect of everyday life.) Surface conflict has shallow or no roots; it often owes to misunderstanding and can be addressed by improved communications and the conscious effort of opposing groups to understand one another. Latent conflict is conflict below the surface; it might have to be brought out into the open before it can be effectively addressed. Open conflict is very visible and has deep roots, sometimes spanning generations. Because it causes more physical, social, psychological, and environmental damage than the other types, both its causes and effects need to be addressed.

[7]This is where economics falls short: the optimal solutions it seeks, subject to technical and informational constraints, will not eventuate where conflict exists yet collective choices must nevertheless still be made.

[8]Welfare economics uses microeconomic techniques to evaluate, under conditions of competitive equilibrium and with due concern for economic efficiency and the income distribution associated with that, what economic policies will create the highest overall level of social good.

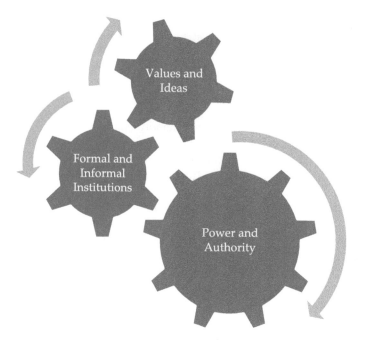

Fig. The wheels of political economy analysis. *Source* Author

- The power and authority of groups in society, counting the interests they hold and the incentives that drive them, in conducing particular outcomes;
- The role that formal and informal institutions play in allocating scarce resources;
- The influence that values and ideas, including culture, ideologies, and religion, have on shaping human relations and interaction.

Naturally, bilateral and multilateral development agencies seek to maximize the quality and impact of the assistance they extend.[9] For this, since development is not a technocratic process but fundamentally political, they must gain a "real-world" sense of what is achievable; only then can they with knowledge expand the feasible space for reform, engage, and help actors surmount what might otherwise be

---

[9]Quite simply, even if it is never easy to achieve it in practice, development effectiveness refers to the extent to which development interventions accomplish their objectives. The Paris Declaration on Aid Effectiveness of 2005 outlined five fundamental principles for making aid more effective: (i) ownership—developing countries set their own strategies for poverty reduction, improve their institutions, and tackle corruption; (ii) alignment—donor countries align behind these objectives and use local systems; (iii) harmonization—donor countries coordinate, simplify procedures, and share information to avoid duplication; (iv) managing for results—developing countries and donors shift focus to development results and results get measured; and (v) mutual accountability —developing countries and donors are accountable for development results.

impossible.[10] To this intent, problem driven, dynamic, and actionable political economy analysis can, for instance, (i) contribute to deeper understanding of political context and how it affects pro-poor development assistance; (ii) lead to more politically astute—and therefore more realistic and effective—country partnership strategies and related programming, including the selection of lending and nonlending modalities, through the identification of pragmatic solutions to challenges; (iii) support scenario planning and risk management by helping identify critical factors apt to drive or obstruct positive change; (iv) broaden the scope for quality dialogue among and engagement by clients, audiences, and partners around key political challenges and opportunities, for example, at country, sector or thematic, and policy or project levels[11]; (v) foster coherence across joint goals through a common analysis of the underlying political and economic processes shaping development; and (vi) build coalitions for innovative or "good enough" change. The boxes below illustrate how a political economy perspective might add value to development work by changing the way it is conducted.

Box 1: Caring for the Earth: A Marxist Critique

In 1980, the International Union for Conservation of Nature and Natural Resources, the United Nations Environment Programme, and the World Wildlife Fund published the *World Conservation Strategy: Living Resource Conservation for Sustainable Development.*[a] The document stressed the interdependence of conservation and development and greatly influenced thinking about the environment. Their new document, *Caring for the Earth:*

---

[10]The mandates of bilateral and multilateral development agencies usually—and explicitly—preclude them from engaging in politics. Notwithstanding, it is common sense that they must understand political economy contexts from a diagnostic—not prescriptive—perspective if they are to successfully help design and implement development policies and strategies.

[11]Of course, the different levels can be and often are combined. Broadly, country-level analysis would delve on interactions among structural variables, institutional variables, and agents (aka actors or stakeholders). Sector- or thematic-level analysis would scrutinize roles and responsibilities, ownership structure and financing, power relations, historical legacies, corruption and rent-seeking, service delivery, decision making, implementation issues, and potential for reform. Policy- or project-level analysis would identify the problem, issue, or vulnerability to be addressed; map out the institutional and governance weaknesses that cause it; and drill down to the specific issues that constrain or might support progressive change (Department for International Development 2009). In guidance to its offices, the department notes that several elements of the framework for political economy analysis cut across the three levels: they are (i) legitimacy; (ii) inputs in the form of influences, demands, and oppositions; (iii) inputs in the form of supports and withdrawals; (iv) modes of inputs, e.g., advice, conditionality, terms, threat, or treaties where inputs are external and discourse, ideas, petitions, or votes where they are internal; (v) gatekeepers; (vi) decision-making power maps; (vii) lobbying; (viii) decision making; (ix) outputs; (x) capacity and the politics of implementation; and (xi) feedback effects.

A Strategy for Sustainable Living,[b] conveys two important messages: care for the planet on which we live, and sustainability in the use of its resources.

Caring for the Earth represents a departure from the *World Conservation Strategy* in that conservation is now seen as a means to achieve genuine development and not vice versa. It is presented as both an analysis and a plan of action. Although the strategy is aimed at everybody, its particular targets are those who will decide on the next essential steps. It addresses leaders, ministers of government departments, heads of national agencies, and inter-governmental organizations.

Caring for the Earth

The stated purpose of *Caring for the Earth* is to help improve the condition of the world's people. The text has three parts. Part I, The Principles of Sustainable Living, begins with a chapter that defines principles to guide the way toward sustainable societies. Part II, Additional Actions for Sustainable Living, describes corresponding actions required in relation to the main areas of human activity, and some major components of the biosphere. Part III, Implementation and Follow-up, proposes guidelines to help users to adapt the strategy to their needs and capabilities and to implement it.

The principles to guide the way toward sustainable societies are the following:

- Respect and care for the community of life.
- Improve the quality of human life.
- Conserve the earth's vitality and diversity.
- Minimize the depletion of nonrenewable resources.
- Keep within the earth's carrying capacity.
- Change personal attitudes and practices.
- Enable communities to care for their own environments.
- Provide a national framework for integrating development and conservation.
- Create a global alliance.

Thank God men cannot fly, and lay waste the sky as well as the earth.

—Henry David Thoreau

The first part of *Caring for the Earth* elaborates on these nine principles for sustainable living. Respect and care for the community of life is an ethical principle reflecting the relationships between mankind and other forms of life. Improving the quality of human life requires short and long-term development. Conserving the earth's vitality and diversity raises issues of biodiversity and is related to minimizing the depletion of nonrenewable resources. These two principles, in turn, imply that the planet has a particular carrying capacity and that the human population should keep within that capacity. How to change personal attitudes and practices is not easy; education is important and might also help enable communities to care for their own environments. And so, suitable environmental and other education can provide in each nation or region a national framework for integrating development and conservation. But because "no nation today is self-sufficient," there is a need to create global alliance.

I think the environment should be put in the category of our national security. Defense of our resources is just as important as defense abroad. Otherwise what is there to defend?

—Robert Redford

These nine principles to guide the way toward sustainable societies are phrased as commands. The question, however, is whether it is sufficient to have concepts, principles, and targets. The answer is "no" because action is required to put the principles into practice and realize the targets identified. Paradoxically, however, it is perhaps at the action end that *Caring for the Earth* is weakest as a self-proclaimed strategy for sustainable living. Only one chapter is given over to this, listing 132 actions that would be required to pull off the strategy for sustainable development. It is, nonetheless, up to governments, nongovernment organizations, and people to consider which of these actions they can and should take. Judging *Caring for the Earth* by the standards called for by its avowed intentions, therefore, the reader may wonder what use to make of such directives as to

- Develop the world ethic for living sustainably.
- Prepare for climate change.
- Develop more effective local governments.
- Build up the global alliance.

Marx to the Rescue

We never know the worth of water till the well is dry.

—Thomas Fuller

Still, the faults of *Caring for the Earth* are more serious than its failure to present anything more than a potpourri of directives. Put bluntly, many conservationists now promoting conservation programs threaten merely to pay lip service to the social contexts within which they propose to operate their systems of management. Despite the superficially attractive approach of such initiatives as *Caring for the Earth* in seeking to enlist the integration of development goals with conservation objectives and the participation of local people, some of the assumptions that underlie these initiatives are disturbing.

At heart, *Caring for the Earth* intimates that the conservationists' utopian vision of society must predominate. Although the document appraises aspects of socioeconomic and political organization which have brought about environmental degradation and social deprivation, the strategy it advocates does not even begin to examine the social and political changes that would be necessary to meet the conservation goals set out in Part II of the document. As seen by Marxists, *Caring for the Earth* reflects the narrow academic or ideological preoccupations of the specialists who formulated it.

Environmental problems are rarely environmental in origin. A study of environmental destruction in southern Honduras by Susan Stonich[c] concludes that environmental degradation arises from social structure and is intricately connected to land tenure, unemployment, poverty, and demography. She identifies political and economic factors and export-promotion policies of international lending institutions and aid agencies as the key element of a development policy for the whole of Central America that is likely to lead to destruction of the remaining tropical forests, worsen poverty and malnutrition, and increase inequality and conflicts within and between nations. To those that subscribe to the political economy perspective, therefore, the biological explanation offered by conservationists and ecologists is simplistic and overlooks the social context of development and land distribution within which worldwide destruction of traditional agriculture and the rain forests is now occurring.

From a perspective that combines the concerns of political economy, then, the environmental management proposed in *Caring for the Earth* is ahistorical in the sense that it ignores the importance of modes of production. It presents environmental dilemmas in terms of fixed and unchanging limits upon human action. This means that the document deals primarily with symptoms, not causes, and that it places the environment above people despite recurring statements to the contrary. Such biological explanations are deterministic, conceal the choices that are open to people to change their society and their own destiny, and can lead to pessimism about man's ability to create harmony with nature through social reform.

At root, documents such as *Caring for the Earth* offer no structural changes to redress "underdevelopment," to use a once popular coinage, and their appeals on behalf of the planet are little more than calls for the survival of the industrial system. Changes are advocated without any analysis of how mismanagement came about that would in all likelihood lead to increased polarization in the economy and the society penalizing people for actions resulting from their own poverty. An alternative, political economy, perception would not have social, economic, or technical factors explain environmental dilemmas but rather depict the environmental situation examined as evidence of a social, economic, or political dilemma, laying emphasis on such factors as inequality in resources and power and structural "underdevelopment". David Pepper[d] contends that, as seen by Marxists, "This is politically reactionary, leading to repressive attitudes which are legitimated through the appeal to an 'objective' science and a pretence that environmental problems are 'above politics'." The environmental movement maintains a facade of technical objectivity which, a Marxist critique would argue, provides new techniques for members of the elite to gain professional status, notably through articles in specialized journals.

Indeed, "*Caring for the Earth* is intended to be used by those who shape policy and make decisions that affect the course of development and the condition of our environment". Almost as an afterthought, it is also considered to be of use to other citizens in communities and settlements everywhere. The approach, which corresponds to the appeal for an "objective" science, is dogmatic. Readers are directed to engage in certain activities and refrain from others.

We do not inherit the earth from our ancestors; we borrow it from our children.

—Anonymous

Societies, however, are neither mere population aggregates nor unified biotic communities. Rather, they are specified by their mode of production. Crisis tendencies and profit generation constitute the core of societal development, which is dominated by the capital accumulation process. Questions to be asked and answered are: What is the character of power and inequality? How do they relate to ecological patterns? How do production and reproduction processes of capital accumulation, as well as the processes of crisis adjustment, manifest themselves in sociospatial organization? *Caring for the Earth* does not raise such questions, let alone attempt to answer them, and its attempt to enthrone conservation as a means to sustainable development is, at best, awkward. Conservation, which can be defined as the management, protection, and preservation of the earth's natural resources and environment, has opportunity costs. These are the development benefits foregone. Yet, *Caring for the Earth* argues that its aim is sustainable development.

What Next?

And Man created the plastic bag and the tin and aluminum can and the cellophane wrapper and the paper plate, and this was good because Man could then take his automobile and buy all his food in one place and He could save that which was good to eat in the refrigerator and throw away that which had no further use. And soon the earth was covered with plastic bags and aluminum cans and paper plates and disposable bottles and there was nowhere to sit down or walk, and Man shook his head and cried: "Look at this Godawful mess".

—Art Buchwald

The dilemmas facing mankind are extreme but not new. Those living in affluence have often taken it for granted that the poor should pay the price of their wealth and comfort. From a Marxist perspective, one would say that class struggle, against which history is played out, continues unabated, and that in the struggle for survival some countries and some social classes will manage better than others. But sustainable development, if it is to find expression in reality, would require changes in modes of production and consumption as well as new social and political structures.

To make development sustainable, progress must be made to integrate the perspectives of three disciplines: (i) that of economists, whose methods seek to maximize human welfare within the constraints of existing capital stock and technologies; (ii) that of ecologists, who stress the preservation of ecological subsystems; and (iii) that of sociologists, who emphasize that the key actors are human beings, whose patterns of social organization are crucial for devising viable solutions.

Sadly, sociological approaches, even when application oriented, have been largely timid, inactive, or simply reactive. In the case of environmental sociology, an explanatory factor is the difficulty of adapting bioecological concepts to the human context, which can pose problems of inappropriate or illegitimate use. At a more fundamental level, harsher critics of the political economy approach to the environment remark that natural resources were never at the center stage of Marxist thinking and that the environment was in any case rarely looked upon as a distributive issue. Nevertheless, sociologists such as Edgar Borgatta[e] have sought to develop an important field called "proactive sociology" to close the gap between sociological theory and practice. Rather than wait to study the aftereffects of environmentally destructive activities or policies, when the problem is historically interesting but socially irrelevant, proactive sociology would concern itself with the dynamics out of which dilemmas arise, anticipating potential problem areas and their alternative solutions as the means to translate desired values into effective policy. This would involve identifying possible futures and the consequences of action or inaction for their attainment, a policy dimension that sociologists largely ignore.

Notwithstanding this critique of *Caring for the Earth*, therefore, it remains to be said that the document and its forerunner, the *World Conservation Strategy*, are successful documents in environmental education. *Caring for the Earth* significantly advances the framework established by the *World Conservation Strategy*. To be fair, the reason for setting out the utopian model toward which we should progress is stated clearly: "The world is running out of space and time."

[a]IUCN-UNEP-WWF (1980).
[b]IUCN-UNEP-WWF (1991).
[c]Stonich (1989).
[d]Pepper (1984).
[e]Borgatta (1989).

Source Author. 1994. Unpublished.

Box 2: Deforestation Benefits

Forests provide countless products of vital use and are a source of livelihood to millions. For those reasons, abuse of forest resources has intensified dramatically in the wake of improved methods of exploitation, processing and transport, growth of external markets, and rapidly expanding populations. Since forests also play a key role in the ecosystem, deforestation has led to desertification, soil erosion, flooding, loss of biodiversity, and poorer environments for the poor. If that were not enough, some contend too that deforestation changes the atmospheric oxygen and carbon dioxide balance— which alters the albedo and accelerates the greenhouse effect. So, with growing unease about the consequences of deforestation, attention is shifting from production to conservation. Sadly, an environmental management perspective that ignores the environmental conflicts at hand sways it.

The Beneficiaries of Deforestation

Deforestation happens because it is profitable. That is why the perspective of those who gain from it, in conflict with one another, is of interest. The beneficiaries are

- Governments, since pioneer settlements divert attention from pressing social problems;
- National treasuries, which derive foreign exchange earnings from forest products;
- Commercial loggers (legal and illegal);
- People employed in the logging and wood processing industries;
- Commercial interests that use deforested lands to grow a product for the market, speculate on land near roads and new settlements, and buy and sell charcoal or fuelwood;
- Local commercial businesses that benefit from frontier settlements;
- Urban consumers of charcoal and fuelwood, who pay a price that does not internalize the costs of deforestation;
- Consumers in industrialized countries, who also profit because the prices of tropical forest products do not reflect their true value;
- International corporations trading tropical forest products;
- Migrant farmers and shifting cultivators, who benefit from the removal of forest cover because it allows them to farm.[a]

A virgin forest is where the hand of man has never set foot.

—Anonymous

Clearly, the process of deforestation is not amenable to technical solutions. It does not hinge on the relative merits of different silvicultural practices or the choice of the discount rate. It is fueled by conflicting interests over the use of forest resources. So far, in many developing countries, the answer has been that the forests belong to loggers and their allies—the interests of communities and the many sectors that use or influence forests have never received much notice. Yet, to control the process of deforestation, it is necessary to identify all those who benefit from it. Only then will policy, market, and institutional instruments for sustainable development work.[b]

A Framework for Conflict Resolution

Man has been endowed with reason, with the power to create, so that he can add to what he's been given. But up to now he hasn't been a creator, only a destroyer. Forests keep disappearing, rivers dry up, wildlife's become extinct, the climate's ruined and the land grows poorer and uglier every day.

—Anton Chekhov

Demand for wood will rise by one third over the next 10 years. Worsening conflicts among forest users might be avoided if a cross-sectoral approach were adopted. Such an approach would identify all the sectors and groups that benefit from forests; define the benefits and establish objectives for sustaining and balancing them; and state how the objectives will be achieved. The intention would be to resolve conflicts by integrating compatible uses of forest resources or zoning where uses are incompatible. Solutions would permit the establishment of a stable forest continuum accommodating changing circumstances. Backed by (now) informed policy, market, and institutional instruments, the continuum would encompass protected forests in their natural state, managed natural forests, shifting cultivation, agroforestry, and plantations.

Toward Sustainable Forest Strategies
Deforestation will be addressed most suitably by a multidisciplinary approach that emphasizes the socioeconomic and political environment in which deforestation takes place, against a pragmatic realization that societies (and forests) are dynamic. The advantages of social ingenuity over technical ingenuity should not be overlooked. A stable system of markets, legal regimes (including property rights), financial agencies, and institutions is a prerequisite to any economic and social progress. But developing countries are ill endowed with this social capital. Their ability to create and maintain it is being eroded by the very environmental problems they are hoping to address.

[a]The benefits they derive are short-lived. The clearance process must be repeated elsewhere after a couple of years because of insect plagues, weeds, and soil impoverishment.

[b]Also, these instruments need to consider the motives of the agents of deforestation. The poor eke out a living and perform much of the expansion of agriculture into previously forested areas. But logging, some agriculture, and some charcoal making are carried out for commercial reasons.

Source Author. 2001. Unpublished.

Box 3: A Note on Floods in Bangladesh

Flood losses in Bangladesh grow despite large investments in flood control infrastructure. There are only two plausible explanations. They are a physically driven increase in the occurrence and importance of floods and a man-driven increase in vulnerability caused by denser floodplain occupancy. Deforestation is occurring in the Himalayan region. But, without evidence to support arguments that environmental degradation there is exacerbating floods in Bangladesh, it is generally accepted that human actions are on the whole responsible.

> *What is the appropriate behavior for a man or a woman in the midst of this world, where each person is clinging to his piece of debris? What's the proper salutation between people as they pass each other in this flood?*
>
> —Buddha

Even though floodplains are one of the more obvious hazard-prone environments, widespread invasion has occurred because of countless individual decisions based on the belief that locational benefits outweigh risks. Population pressures and general poverty have encouraged this expectation further. Once floodplains become urbanized, however, there follows an almost inevitable demand for flood protection from (now organized and vocal) local communities. This is because the construction of flood embankments or other physical controls is perceived to render part of the floodplains safe. Next, land values rise and the development of floodplains gathers steam (even though structural works cannot withstand the most powerful river flows and channel changes that threaten human life in disaster years). Development encourages further human encroachments and it becomes more and more difficult to shake off the massive structural legacy. Yet, in the meantime, flood embankments and other physical controls isolate fish farmers and jute farmers from the beneficial spread of monsoon floods in normal years.

International assistance may have advanced this trend. The Flood Action Plan prompted by heavy floods in 1987 and 1988 recommended greater reliance on embankments along the major rivers. This worked well at first. But some doubt the sustainability of the embankment program. It is long-term by nature and must be sustained to make sense, with the embankments raised every year to cope with the rising channel beds that result from deposition. And then again, history shows that the integrity of embankments is the exception rather than the rule.

Bangladesh may be in a no-win situation and failure to understand environmental management issues could have dire consequences. Experience confirms the need to develop more open systems of management permitting flexible attitudes to turbulent environments, where local community needs define the modi vivendi. Flood proofing—which entails going back to using floods as much as possible instead of trying to prevent or control them—may be a more appropriate behavioral approach preferable to structural responses. The latter usually aggravate the situation in many economic, social, ecological, and institutional ways and tend to impact the poorest most severely because they are not empowered to participate in making the decisions that shape their lives.

In Bangladesh, cost-benefit analysis of planned abandonment of the floodplain structures might show acceptable financial and economic returns that equal or surpass those from further investments in flood control infrastructure. Social analysis would reveal a complex of necessary concessions between winners and losers but the opportunities to avoid poverty and conflict would then be richer overall. Ecological analysis would undoubtedly indicate greater possibilities for a return to ecosystem health and vitality. Institutional analysis would show also the need for a more open society where public servants serve the people better and calm their engineering fervor to supply management services that encourage and sustain development outside the floodplains.

Source Author. 2001. Unpublished.

Box 4: A Note on Land Degradation

Land producing economically useful crops, trees, or livestock can be managed to sustain yields. Techniques that protect land even in fragile ecosystems exist. But, almost everywhere, land is being degraded through overgrazing, overcultivation, destruction of woodland and vegetation, or poor irrigation practices. Why? It is easy to blame ignorance, overpopulation, or short-term gain. But single explanations are always inadequate. Reasons lie in the social, political, and economic circumstances that put pressure on the land users to manage land in a non-sustainable way. So, understanding why land users degrade land means embracing the range of relations affecting land users and their intercourse with the world at large.

Most research projects just look at impacts on biodiversity and land degradation without integrating socioeconomic factors. Changes in social systems are all reflected in the environment. It is critical to link the two.

—Jennifer Olson

A Chain of Explanations ...

Land degradation occurs because of repeated land use decisions under specific conditions. Subtle (and not so subtle) incentives underpin each decision. Yet, they enter the picture somewhere along a chain of explanations. To begin, physical changes in soil and vegetation leading to land degradation become noticeable at a site—for example, sheet and gully erosion, or bush or weed encroachment. This leads to symptoms that impact the land user, such as falling or increasingly variable yields, or increased morbidity and mortality of livestock. And, sure enough, these symptoms are brought about by specific land use practices at the site (e.g., tree felling, short fallowing periods, overstocking, plowing down slope, or planting crops that provide no ground cover or protection for the soil when it rains). Why does the land user treat the land in this way? Causes are found in his immediate circumstances, an important level of explanation and knowledge that has to do with access to resources, skills, assets, and time horizons—to name a few—but also to the nature of agricultural society (including the distribution of rights to land, laws of inheritance, and the gender division of labor). Higher still, one can examine how the state affects land management through laws on tenure, prices, or agricultural extension. Finally, one can study important international forces that act through the state to affect land management. They relate to foreign debt, oil prices, or structural adjustment programs. To sum up, the chain of explanations pulls together

- recognized physical changes at a site;
- symptoms affecting the land user;
- specific land use practices at the site;
- the resources, skills, assets, time horizon, and technologies of the land user;
- the makeup of agricultural society;
- the makeup of the state;
- the global economy.

... And Logical Interventions

In view of that, understanding why land degradation takes place necessitates a political economy perspective locating analyses within specific social formations and explaining development processes in terms of the costs and benefits that they carry for different social classes. Interventions can then be made at all points along the chain. They would seek to address the policy, market, and institutional failures that break or pervert the necessary correlations between scarcity and prices, costs and benefits, rights and responsibilities, and actions and consequences.

Source Author. 2001. Unpublished.

Reference

Borgatta E (1989) Towards a proactive sociology. Paper Presented at the 29th International Congress of the International Institute of Sociology, Rome, Italy
Department for International Development (2009) Political economy analysis: how-to note
IUCN-UNEP-WWF (1980) World conservation strategy: living resource conservation for sustainable development. Gland, Switzerland
IUCN-UNEP-WWF (1991) Caring for the Earth: a strategy for sustainable living. Gland, Switzerland
Stonich S (1989) The dynamics of social processes and environmental destruction: a central American case study. Population and Development Review 15(5):269–296
Pepper D (1984) The roots of modern environmentalism. Croom Helm

Proposition 22
The Premortem Technique

In a Word Assumptions that do not associate with probabilities create a false sense of certainty. Working backward, considering alternatives that emerge from failed assumptions broadens the scope of scenarios examined. The Premortem technique raises awareness of possibilities, including their likely consequences, to enrich planning.

Why History Repeats Itself

An autopsy—aka a postmortem examination—is a specialized surgical procedure conducted by a pathologist to thoroughly assess a corpse to determine or confirm the exact cause and circumstances of death or the character and extent of changes produced by disease.

Knowledge is what you harvest from experience—be that your own or someone else's—through sense-making.[1] In sundry areas of human endeavor, it is common (but not common enough) to conduct the equivalent of a postmortem by means of formal completion or evaluation reports—after-action reviews, retrospects, and learning histories are rarer still—to try to understand why an initiative did or did not

---

[1]To engage in sense-making is to exploit information for awareness, understanding, and planning to make faster and better decisions.

© Asian Development Bank 2017

O. Serrat, *Knowledge Solutions*, DOI 10.1007/978-981-10-0983-9_22

succeed. And so, except in learning organizations, lessons (to be) learned mostly eventuate in the form of hindsight—that, by and large, focusing on accountability, not learning—at the (wrong) end of a plan.[2] Paraphrasing Karl Marx, this is why history repeats itself; the first time as tragedy and the second time as farce.

> *You got to be careful if you don't know where you're going, because you might not get there.*
>
> —Yogi Berra

On Safe Silence, Bias, and Dissent

> *To consult the statistician after an experiment is finished is often merely to ask him to conduct a postmortem examination. He can perhaps say what the experiment died of.*
>
> —Ronald Fisher

> *When personal judgment is inoperative (or forbidden), men's first concern is not how to choose, but how to justify their choice.*
>
> —Ayn Rand

Does the following development seem familiar? A proposal is drawn by a task force, endorsed by decision makers, approved by senior management, launched with fanfare, but leads nowhere. Why? There are two explanations. In bureaucratic organizations—and not only during planning but also across their operations—people are reluctant to express reservations about the workability of a plan: they keep mum because it can be dangerous to oppose what bosses—mark, not managers—command. Cognitive barriers play a role too: individuals and groups may be biased;

---

[2]Depending on the context, just-in-time opportunities to identify, create, store, share, and use knowledge can of course arise before and during a situation, not only after it has come to pass. To note, projects and programs, but also the policies, strategies, and partnerships that underpin them, are developed in response to the existence of a perceived opportunity or problem: they do not exist in a vacuum. (Therefore, the external environment—not to mention the specific organizational knowledge, inter- and intra-organizational relationships, and organizational context of the parties that formulate them—is very important because it will shape the kinds of actions considered.) However, because change is the only constant, ongoing monitoring and evaluation must be integrated into the implementation of projects, programs, etc. and coevolve with emergence. Otherwise, as so often happens, managers will find that their activities are judged ex-post by methods and associated data requirements that were never built into the original endeavor. The chance to learn powerful lessons before and during the activities will have been lost and the value of those promulgated after them will most likely be lesser.

when they have worked hard on a plan they can also become psychologically committed to the idea of success, be overconfident, and therefore blind to some of its risks. (Bias[3] is the inclination to present or hold a partial perspective at the expense of possibly equally valid alternatives. A related, prevalent phenomenon, groupthink, refers to the mode of thinking that happens when the desire for harmony in a decision-making group overrides a realistic appraisal of options.)

> *In the space of two days I had evolved two plans, wholly distinct, both of which were equally feasible. The point I am trying to bring out is that one does not plan and then try to make circumstances fit those plans. One tries to make plans fit the circumstances.*
>
> —George Patton

Analysis is an exercise in judgment under conditions of uncertainty, and the errors in judgment we make, singly or in groups, in a day or through life, are countless. In organizational settings, especially in complicated, complex, or, chaotic situations, a dependable measure might be—as Daniel Kahneman et al. intimate but do not underscore—to legitimize early dissent and quickly place creative, contrarian[4] objections and suggestions on the table to reinforce the decision-making process and thereby improve a plan's chances of success before it stalls, peters out, or backfires.

---

[3]Bias comes in many forms. Kahneman et al. (2011) recommend that the proponents of a plan should check for (i) self-interested biases; (ii) affect heuristic; (iii) groupthink; (iv) saliency bias; (v) confirmation bias; (vi) availability bias; (vii) anchoring bias; (viii) halo effect; and (ix) sunk-cost fallacy, endowment effect. The challenge questions associated with each bias that they helpfully pose are, respectively, as follows: (i) Is there any reason to suspect the team making the recommendation of errors motivated by self-interest? (ii) Has the team fallen in love with its proposal? (iii) Were there dissenting opinions within the team? Were they explored adequately? (iv) Could the diagnosis be overly influenced by an analogy to a memorable success? (v) Are credible alternatives included along with the recommendation? (vi) If you had to make this decision again in a year's time, what information would you want, and can you get more of it now? (vii) Do you know where the numbers came from? Can there be unsubstantiated numbers, extrapolation from history, or a motivation to use a certain anchor? (viii) Is the team assuming that a person, organization, or approach that is successful in one area will be just as successful in another? (ix) Are the recommenders overly attached to a history of past decisions?

[4]The Devil's advocate was a function and office introduced by the Roman Catholic Church in the 16th century to take a skeptical view of proposals for the canonization of a candidate. The canon lawyer appointed would oppose God's advocate, whose task was to make the argument in favor of canonization. In common parlance, a devil's advocate is someone who takes a position he or she does not necessarily agree with to test the quality of an argument and help improve or force the withdrawal of the original proposal.

There's No Risk of Accident for Someone Who Is Dead

> *Live as if you were to die tomorrow. Learn as if you were to live forever.*
>
> —Mohandas K. Gandhi

Enter, thanks to Klein (2007), the Premortem technique[5]: based on a process known as reframing,[6] this risk-mitigation planning tool attempts to identify threats at the outset. Specifically, it helps challenge key assumptions, generate multiple hypotheses, discover unknown unknowns, track alternative future trajectories, and anticipate the unanticipated. For sure, by testing, probing, and even attacking individual and collective mindsets, greater rigor in critical thinking can reduce the chance of (unpleasant) surprises.

A premortem is the imaginary converse of an autopsy; the hindsight this intelligence assessment offers is prospective. In sum, tasking a team to imagine that its plan has already been implemented and failed miserably increases the ability of its members to correctly identify reasons for negative future outcomes. This is because taking a team out of the context of defending its plan and shielding it from flaws opens new perspectives from which the team can actively search for faults.[7] Despite its original high level of confidence, a team can then candidly identify multiple explanations for failure, possibilities that were not mentioned let alone considered when the team initially proposed then developed the plan. The expected outcomes of such stress-testing are increased appreciation of the uncertainties inherent in any projection of the future and identification of markers that, if incorporated in the team's design and monitoring framework and subsequently tracked, would give early warning that progress is not being achieved as expected.

---

[5]The technique is reminiscent of Disaster Charting, a method that—itself in the vein of the Five Whys technique—endeavors through repeated questioning to map post hoc a fault tree of precursors that might have contributed to an accident.

[6]Reframing holds that insights can be gained simply by looking at a situation from a different perspective, or in a different context, than one is accustomed to. The Reframing Matrix and the Six Thinking Hats technique are two methods to achieve this.

[7]What might go wrong? What might be the cause? What might we do to prevent the problem from happening? What might we do if the problem does occur? These questions, which in real life beggar interest when they do not try our patience, have reached their sell-by date. Instead, we must assume that a compelling worst-case scenario detailing embarrassing organizational malfunction took place. Thus, by establishing the certainty that a fiasco has actually occurred—thus preempting equivocations of likelihood—the Premortem technique rectifies the predilection that individuals and groups have for scenario development by forcing a focus on scenario analysis.

The Premortem technique is low cost and high payoff. Its application is straightforward and need not take more than 1 or 2 hours, preferably with the help of a facilitator

- Settle on a period, in months or years, after which it might be known whether a plan was well formulated. Imagine the period has expired: the plan is a fiasco and has spawned dire consequences; what could have caused this?
- Request each team member to suggest 10 reasons for failure, particularly those that he or she would never bring up for fear of being impolite—sensitive issues might be divulged anonymously. Reasons can also be found in the external environment, not just the organizational context, organizational knowledge, and inter-and intra-organizational relationship to which priority attention is habitually given. Starting with the team leader, ask each team member to voice one reason from his or her list. Everyone should mention a reason in turn until all have been revealed and recorded.
- After the session is over, gather and prioritize the comprehensive list of reasons that grew out of collective knowledge.
- Look for ways to strengthen the plan by avoiding or mitigating essential drivers of failure, beginning with the two or three items deemed of greatest concern.

Some may worry the Premortem technique that could lead to situations where opposition so threatens a plan it must be abandoned. (The rejoinder to this is that a

Fig. Conducting a premortem. *Source* Author

plan should indeed be ditched if the objections to it are that strong.) However, common sense suggests that a plan would be modified for the better, not abandoned, in most instances.

References

Kahneman D, Lavalo D, Sibony O (June 2011) Before you make that big decision … Harvard Business Review: 51–60
Klein G (September 2007) Performing a project premortem. Harvard Business Review: 18–19

Further Reading

Klein G (1998) Sources of power: how people make decisions. MIT Press

Proposition 23
Future Search Conferencing

In a Word To enlist commitment, organizations depend on a clear and powerful image of the future. Future Search conferencing has emerged as a system-wide strategic planning tool enabling diverse and potentially conflicting groups to find common ground for constructive action.

On Politics by Other Means

Nine times out of ten, large-scale gatherings for exchange of ideas in (darkened) assembly rooms only dispense information; powerful individual or collective learning experiences rarely take place there. Why should this be the case if the raison d'être of a conference is to generate and share knowledge that impacts behavior and links to results? One explanation is that organizers do not shine a light on the conditions for learning outcomes.[1] Another is that learning may not, from the outset, be the real

---

[1]The shortcomings of assemblies are that: (i) conference programs are set by event planners and do not predict well what sessions are actually wanted; (ii) a distinction is made between presenters (teachers) and participants (learners); (iii) sessions are dominated by presenters—participants receive predetermined information passively; (iv) logistics revolve around general and breakout sessions; (v) content is broadcast in long, uninterrupted sessions; and (vi) chances to network are restricted to meals and social gatherings outside sessions.

© Asian Development Bank 2017
O. Serrat, *Knowledge Solutions*, DOI 10.1007/978-981-10-0983-9_23

intent: indeed, paraphrasing Carl von Clausewitz, it often seems conferencing is the continuation of politics by other means. And so, when the agenda is—unequivocally —to learn, the mode of operation is increasingly participant-driven meetings such as unconferences; Future Search conferencing bodes well too.

Back to the Future

> By the street of by-and-by, one arrives at the house of never.
>
> —Miguel de Cervantes

Futures studies—aka futurology—is a transdisciplinary field of social inquiry for systemic study of medium- to long-term futures.[2] With foresight, futurists aim to discover or invent, propose, examine, and evaluate probable, possible, preferable, and prospective futures.[3] Specifically, since the future depends on what one does today, futurists argue with good sense that exploring alternative futures can help people make out and create their preferred future. "In the fields of observation chance favors only the prepared mind," Louis Pasteur remarked. It stands to reason too that, where the stakes are communal, they might want to apply common sense for organizational change as a group.

The Flux Capacitator

> Life can only be understood backwards; but it must be lived forwards.
>
> —Søren Kierkegaard

Strategic planning is customarily the prerogative of a few—much as chefs de cuisine, senior staff task sous-chefs, chefs de parties, cuisiniers, commis, appentices, plongeurs, marmitons, and other members of the kitchen brigade with activities,

---

[2]Bertrand de Jouvenel (1903–1987), a French philosopher, political economist, and futurist, signposted the emergence of the modern futures movement. In the 1960s, de Jouvenel's (1967) work critiqued the deterministic and fatalistic view of the postwar period and stressed understanding of the past and present as a mechanism to gain insight to future possibilities.

[3]These futures are all subject to cultural, psychological, and sociological influences but cannot be explored in the same way: the first (one future) entails trend analysis; the second (many futures) calls for imagination and flexibility; the third (an "other" future) springs from value positions, both critical and ideological; the fourth (futuring) hinges on preparedness to act, rooted in self-reliance and solidarity. The research methods associated with each orientation differ too.

inputs, and outputs. Would they understand that strategic planning is not haute cuisine: in that field, not many can ever describe—even less understand, enter into, and actively support—what they have summarily been told to lend force to. "You can fool all the people some of the time, and some of the people all the time, but you can't fool all the people all the time," Abraham Lincoln is thought to have said: what with the time-honored predilection for top–down strategic planning, people by now know beyond doubt when they are merely asked to lend legitimacy to someone else's vision.

> *To change an organization, the more people you can involve, and the faster you can help them understand how the system works and how to take responsibility for making it work better, the faster will be the change. It doesn't happen through isolated pilots projects.*
>
> —Marvin Weisbord

Quite the opposite, Future Search conferencing is a democratic approach to real time, large group change planning from a systems perspective.[4] It was developed by Weisbord (1992) and Sandra Janoff in the late 1980s to help organizations (and communities) create shared visions of the future in complex situations, including those characterized by ambiguity and conflict, and plot organizational directions linked to results.[5] The process is anchored by three principles informed by behavioral science:

- Represent the system in one room.
- Explore the whole in context before seeking to act on its parts, focusing on common ground and desired futures and considering problems as information.
- Self-manage work and take responsibility for action.

---

[4]To note, Future Search conferencing is distinct from action learning. Action learning derives from the premise that there is no learning without action and no action without learning; assumptions must be tested against real consequences. In action learning, individuals present urgent, personal challenges to others in small teams and work collectively over a period of months to help one another resolve them in actual work conditions. In action learning, history offers no solutions: critical reflection leads to reframing and to just-in-time learning, unlearning, and relearning. Neither is Future Search conferencing like Appreciative Inquiry—another complementary (because participatory) form of action research that emerged in the mid-1980s—because that particular process concerns itself in smaller groups with what is already working well in an organization. (Notwithstanding, some have tried to marry the two—without conclusive effect in this writer's opinion.)

[5]Future Search conferencing has found applications in the arts and culture; business; community; congregations; economics; education; environment; government; health care; social services; technology; and youth sectors of private, public, and not-for-profit organizations.

In its most recurrent format, Future Search conferencing is a structured, 3-day event involving up to 64 participants[6] from the same organization. It requires a minimum lead time of 2 months, during which a steering committee of mixed stakeholders selects the Future Search topic, makes necessary preparations, and briefs participants in advance—participants must know what to expect. It benefits from having a facilitator[7] and cofacilitor/logistics manager. Last but not least, a working group must be set up before the conference to turn its outputs into a report and communicate that quickly.

> *We already have the statistics for the future: the growth percentages of pollution, overpopulation, desertification. The future is already in place.*
>
> —Günter Grass

Not a loose brainstorming exercise, Future Search conferencing is a carefully designed methodology linking inputs, activities, and outputs to result in a vision built on (i) appreciation of an organization's history; (ii) acknowledgment of present-day strengths and weaknesses; and (iii) considered opinion about major opportunities in the future. Toward these, in four or five sessions each lasting half a day, participants keep to the following in small groups or plenary sessions:

> *You don't need to predict the future. Just choose a future—a good future, a useful future—and make the kind of prediction that will alter human emotions and reactions in such a way that the future you predicted will be brought about. Better to make a good future than predict a bad one.*
>
> —Isaac Asimov

---

[6]Practical experience suggests eight round tables of eight persons in a broad cross-section of stakeholders. (Groups of 10 find it harder to manage themselves.) True diversity that represents the broadest range of viewpoints means including staff from all levels and functions as well as clients, audiences, and partners. They should have as features among them the authority, resources, expertise, information, and motivation to act if they choose.

[7]For facilitators, a windfall is that Future Search conferencing requires little rehearsing compared to traditional gatherings. It involves learning, not teaching: there are no keynote speeches, shows-and-tells, overheads, training exercises, or dry runs. The principal difficulty probably lies in energy management: for participants to remain attentive throughout the conference, and not lose momentum, requires stamina in the first instance and excellent facilitation in the next. However, Future Search conferencing's participative, inclusive, and open approach to discovery learning has compensations: people feel pulled by blank sheets of paper and whiteboards, hand-drawn charts, open questions, simple images, and uncertainty. (Moving so-called "experts" to the background appeals, too.)

- **Focus on the Past: Highlights and Milestones** In the first half-day, preferably after a warm up allowing participants to converse with one another, the Future Search gets underway with a look at the past. The eight groups contribute historical information and compose timelines of key events in the world, their personal lives, and the history of the Future Search topic. The groups tell stories about each timeline and what implications the stories have for the work they have come to do. No items are too silly or too small and no one dominates: forbearance on the beliefs and positions of others deepens comprehension and acceptance. This process creates a shared, global context for the Future Search.
- **Focus on the Present: External Trends** Later, the entire assembly draws a mind map and ranking of ongoing trends affecting the system the participants operate or exist in and identifies which are most important in relation to the topic. This process clarifies what is impacting the organization.
- **Focus on the Present: Responses to Trends** In the morning of the second day, the groups describe what they are doing about the key trends identified and explain what they plan to do in the future. This process helps assess current actions.
- **Focus on the Present: Owning Actions** Later, the groups report on what they are proud of and sorry about in the way they are dealing with the Future Search topic. This process surfaces strengths and weaknesses in the organization and affords psychological safety for admission of errors.
- **Focus on the Future: Ideal Scenarios** In the afternoon of the second day, the groups project themselves into the future and describe their preferred vision[8] of the future as though it had already come about. This process generates a clear and powerful image of a healthy organization—and its values—through which the participants would like to advance their joint purpose, to be made real over a 5–20-year horizon.[9]

> *Nothing is more terrible than activity without insight.*
>
> —Thomas Carlyle

---

[8]An effective vision is (i) imaginable—it conveys a picture of what the future may look like; (ii) desirable—it appeals to the long-term interest of all who have a stake in the organization; (iii) feasible—it is realistic and attainable; (iv) focused—it is sharp enough to guide decision making; (v) flexible—it allows individual and collective initiative in light of changing conditions; and (vi) communicable—it can be successfully explained in 5 min.

[9]Not all topics call for the same time span. The maximum horizon should lie beyond the normal planning vista, but not stretch so far away as to seem irrelevant; one should still be able to make an impression with today's decisions. The factors that help define the perspective of a Future Search exercise are (i) the inertia or volatility of the system; (ii) the schedule of decisions to be made, the authority to make them, and the means to be used; and (iii) the degree of rigidity or motivation of participants.

- **Discover Common Ground** Later, the groups post themes they believe hold common—but not necessarily easy—ground for all participants. Disagreements are acknowledged without further discussion. This process enables participants to locate springboards for action, having elucidated what assumptions—e.g., the nature of society, the means of social change, and the attributes and roles of knowledge—underpin each.
- **Confirm Common Ground** In the morning of the third day, the entire assembly dialogues to agree on common ground. This process helps participants conceptualize new behaviors for cooperative ventures.
- **Action Planning** In the afternoon of the third day, champions throughout the organization sign up to implement action plans. Of course, authority, resources, and arrangements for action are confirmed by reality checks.[10] Participants walk out of the assembly room committed and ready to accomplish the envisioned future based on a more cogent framework that connects values and actions in new relationships and real time. This process formulates mutually supportive, practicable sets of rapid undertakings for individuals, groups, and the organization they are members of, close follow-up on which will determine whether change has occurred.

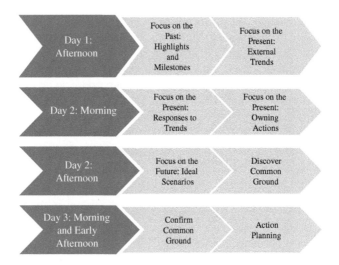

Fig. Typical future search agenda. *Source* Author

---

[10]Questions that would frame the process include the following: (i) who else must we include in action planning? (ii) how will we organize our roles and functions to deliver our undertakings? (iii) how will we communicate the vision to others? (iv) what will we selectively abandon so as to realize the vision? (v) how will we continue to self-manage? and (vi) what are the criteria for monitoring and evaluating progress?

To Infinity and Beyond

> *It is always wise to look ahead, but difficult to look further than you can see.*
> —Winston Churchill

Summoning up what we are prone to forget, the very existence of organizations and communities intuits they already have the resources they need to achieve their purpose. What they may be short of is access to key others and enough time—away from distractions—to discover or invent what else they are capable and willing to realize in multiparty cooperation. Future Search conferencing is predicated on meeting 10 conditions for successful, fast change: (i) senior management adopts a new model of leadership, (ii) the need for change is self-determined and the change process is self-managed, (iii) the change model is based on trust and cooperation, (iv) there is broad stakeholder involvement, (v) awareness of circumstances is comprehensive, (vi) the focus is on seeing and realizing future possibilities, (vii) the entire organization is involved in shaping the vision, (viii) systems thinking is employed, (ix) change is guided by and emerges from strategic conversations, and (x) planning and implementation are simultaneous.

In today's ever-more-interdependent yet polarized societies, building shared understanding of and achieving multiparty action on complex issues are certainly not straightforward. But it is harder to achieve it using conventional, problem-centered interventions. Future search conferencing can catalyze the transition from bureaucratic to learning organizations. It is a human process that takes decisive steps toward informed, democratic (meaning, noncoercive), and reflective enterprise. Even if not many evaluations of Future Search conferences are at hand,[11] its growing popularity gives an idea about what is possible when the right people are in the room, take time to grasp the whole system, and become able to act in creative and innovative ways. What is more, people tend to commit to plans they—not higher-ups—develop.

References

de Jouvenel B (1967) The art of conjecture. Basic Books
Weisbord M (1992) Discovering common ground: how future search conferences bring people together to achieve breakthrough innovation, empowerment, shared vision, and collaborative action. Berrett-Koehler Publishers.

---

[11]To be meaningful, common ground statements should be sufficiently fleshed out; they should also prioritize claims to the same resources. To enhance ownership of and identification with common ground statements, more time than the typical Future Search methodology allows may also need to be given to clarifying differences.

Proposition 24
Theories of Change

In a Word A theory of change is a purposeful model of how an initiative—such as a policy, a strategy, a program, or a project—contributes through a chain of early and intermediate outcomes to the intended result. Theories of change help navigate the complexity of social change.

The Complexity of Social Change Processes

Social change[1]—the process whereby individuals and communities adjust or abandon customs and associated leading ideas, values, and purposes to act differently in response to random (unique) or systemic factors—is no simple matter. It is

---

[1]Social change is any alteration in the social order of a society—reflected for instance in institutions or relations, brought about by modified thought processes. (Illustrative examples of social change that, chronologically, produced profound social consequences include the industrial revolution, the abolition of slavery, and the feminist movement.) Sociologists have proposed evolutionary, conflict, and functionalist theories of change to elucidate what triggers it. [The chief proponents of each theory of change were Auguste Comte (1798–1857), Herbert Spencer (1820–1903), and Emile Durkheim (1858–1917); Karl Marx (1818–1883); and Talcott Parsons (1902–1979), respectively.].

© Asian Development Bank 2017

O. Serrat, *Knowledge Solutions*, DOI 10.1007/978-981-10-0983-9_24

driven by a composite array of cultural, demographic, economic, environment, political, religious, scientific, and technological forces, singly but more often than not in coevolutionary combination, and almost always in the face of vested interests that favor the status quo. What is more, irrespective of evolutionary, conflict, or functional explanations, there are different forms, nay, intensities, of it:

> ...one cannot but wonder how an environment can make people despair and sit idle and then, by changing the conditions, one can transform the same people into matchless performers.
>
> —Muhammad Yunus

- Discursive—a change in the narrative(s) that actors hold about a concern, problem, or issue.
- Procedural—a change in the way the processes that manage a concern are carried out.
- Content-based—a change in the nature of a concern.
- Attitudinal—a change in the way actors think about a concern.
- Behavioral—a change in the way actors behave vis-à-vis a concern, in other words, act or interface with others, in consequence of formal and informal changes in discourse, procedure, content, or attitude.

Development aid, for one, is ever more sternly asked to demonstrate results, an ancillary of which is to clarify what works or does not work and under what circumstances.[2] If development aid is about human, social, and economic progress, which of course intuits change, it needs therefore to frame more clearly what concrete outcomes—from dedicated inputs, activities, and outputs—can augment well-being and better the quality of life. Specifically, development aid needs good theories of change that test and validate the assumptions, rationales, means, and ends of all who are involved in processes of development as academic and research institutions, communities, consultants, civil and nongovernment organizations,

---

[2]The bilateral and multilateral development agenda of the 2000s revealed (continuing) concern for effectiveness. In 2005, the signatories to the Paris Declaration on Aid Effectiveness adopted a concise framework for improving the quality of aid and its impact on development. It is now the norm for aid recipients to forge their own national development strategies with their parliaments and electorates (ownership); for donors to support these strategies (alignment) and work to streamline their efforts in country (harmonization); for development policies to be directed to achieving clear goals and for progress toward these goals to be monitored (results); and for donors and recipients alike to be jointly responsible for achieving these goals (mutual accountability). In 2008, the Accra Agenda for Action reaffirmed these commitments; it also invited greater collaboration among donors, recipients, governments, and civil society organizations. Evidence-based solutions, among others, form part of the emerging development agenda of the 2010s. Naturally, what theories of change they rest on are not static and call for diffusion, replication, critique, and modification so they may prove themselves valid (or not).

donors, implementing and executing agencies, individuals, private companies, etc. Unfortunately, *pace* the cause-and-effect structure of logic models, current project planning tools do not readily help them do so.

Explicating Assumptions ...

First say to yourself what you would be; and then do what you have to do.

—Epictetus

Marrying visioning, planning, and evaluation perspectives, leveraging also concepts of logic models, the Theory of Change method is an outcomes-based, participatory approach that applies critical thinking to the design, implementation, and evaluation of an initiative, e.g., a policy, a strategy, a program, or a project, planned to foster emergent, projectable, or transformative change.

Concisely, a theory of change explains how and why a sequence of logically linked events, aka pathways of change, should lead to an ultimate outcome. It does so by articulating assumptions[3] (or worldviews), and the beliefs and hypotheses they rest on, about how short-, medium-, and long-term change happens in a specific external context; and stipulating how early and intermediate outcomes (preconditions) toward the long-term change will be brought about and documented with indicators that suggest how much of, for whom, and when each outcome is to be realized.[4] In short, a theory of change explores and represents a "so that" chain.

Box: Logic Models and Theories of Change—Telling Them Apart

A logic model (results framework) is a tactical description of the process of delivering an outcome: it insists on, somewhat mechanistically, inputs and activities, the outputs they generate, and the connections between the outputs and the desired outcome. (A recurring weakness is that assumptions are poorly articulated and stakeholders are unsure about how the change process will unfold across components.)

In contrast, a theory of change is a strategic picture of multiple interventions required to produce early and intermediate outcomes that are

---

[3]In development aid, three standard assumptions must perforce be explored. Time and again, they relate to: (i) causality, (ii) implementation, and (iii) external factors.

[4]Some outcomes may eventuate in a domino effect; this means that achieving an early outcome may lead to an intermediate outcome without further intervention under the initiative.

preconditions to a long-term change. (A strength is that causal pathways specify what is needed for outcomes to be achieved: assumptions can be tested and measured. Hence, the Theory of Change method enables organizations to think about their work more deeply.) Once an outcome has been identified, a results framework can be drawn to explain how it will be reached; thus, a theory of change could be underpinned by several logic models.

In short, logic models and theories of change differ markedly in terms of the views and experiences each holds in store vis-à-vis explanation or exploration on the one hand and accountability versus learning on the other.

Source Author

> *Social advance depends as much upon the process through which it is secured as upon the result itself.*
>
> —Jane Addams

For sure, Reeler (2007) argues persuasively, development is a complex process; power both lives and is transformed in relationships; learning from experience is the basis of self-determination; and not all crises are failures. However, without seeking absolute truth or a definitive recipe to eliminate uncertainty, making theories of change more explicit from the onset helps ascertain just what needs to happen if, say, an initiative is to get the target population from here to there. A theory of change should answer six overlapping questions: (i) what concern, its underlying causes, and consequences, does one and others wish to ameliorate in the long term (external context)? (ii) who does one seek to benefit or influence (beneficiaries)? (iii) what benefits does one aim to deliver (results)? (iv) when will the benefits be realized (time span)? (v) how will one and others make that happen (interventions)? and (vi) why, and based on what evidence, does one believe the theory of change will bear out (assumptions)? (Figs. 24.1 and 24.2).

Between Intentions and Results Lies a Theory of Change

> *The society which scorns excellence in plumbing as a humble activity and tolerates shoddiness in philosophy because it is an exalted activity will have neither good plumbing nor good philosophy: neither its pipes nor its theories will hold water.*
>
> —John W. Gardner

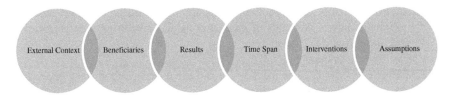

Fig. 24.1 Focusing and scoping a theory of change. *Source* Author

Fig. 24.2 Elements in a pathway of change. *Source* Author

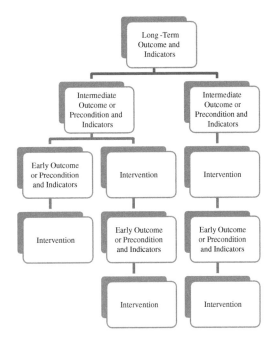

The Theory of Change method is a conscious and creative visualization exercise, preferably a habit, not a product. Where the initiative it purports to rationalize is ambitious, the thinking that underpins the theory must be given time to evolve with reflective analysis and practice; therefore, it should not be set in one single attempt. (Because assumptions can take time to firm up, an iterative, staged process—integrated with other approaches for continuous improvement, e.g., the Plan-Do-Check-Act cycle—can sharpen the outlook.) Some advantages of the Theory of Change approach are that it can help

- Develop joint understanding of an initiative and surface differences.
- Circumscribe and bridge the gaps between local- and national-level changes.
- Unearth assumptions.

- Strengthen the focus, clarity, and effectiveness of an initiative by better locating the rationale, means, and ends of interventions and measuring their success.
- Design strong plans of action.
- Clarify lines of responsibility.
- Empower people to become more active and involved in a multistakeholder and collaborative experiential learning exercise.
- Identify resources and check them for adequacy.
- Recognize the most appropriate clients, audiences, and partners a sponsor can work and hold open conversations with.
- Foster collaboration between donors and avoid duplication.
- Communicate work more succinctly with a common language.
- Support organizational development in line with the core focus and priorities.
- Build a fruitful framework for monitoring and evaluation.
- Point up ineffective interventions.

Of course, such advantages are contingent on a theory of change being

- Meaningful—the magnitude of the long-term outcome being pursued is worth the effort.
- Plausible—evidence and commonsense suggest that the interventions, if implemented, will lead to the long-term outcome.
- Doable—resources, e.g., financial, human, institutional, knowledge, political, skills, technical, and time, will be available and sufficient to execute the interventions.
- Testable—the theory of change is suitably specific and complete for an evaluator to track progress in credible and useful ways.

> *Facts do not speak for themselves. They speak for or against competing theories. Facts divorced from theories or visions are mere isolated curiosities.*
>
> —Thomas Sowell

What initiatives actors propose reflect the health of their theories of change and willingness to measure what accomplishments really matter. Needless to say, both hinge on their own stage of development. In the final analysis, therefore, the real benefit of the Theory of Change method is that it builds capacity for purposeful theory and its effective use.

Reference

Reeler (2007) A three-fold theory of social change and implications for practice, planning, monitoring, and evaluation. Community Development Resource Association

Further Reading

Funnell S, Rogers P (2011) Purposeful program theory: effective use of theories of change and logic models. Jossey-Bass

Proposition 25
On Resilient Organizations

In a Word Organizations must be resilient if they are to survive and thrive in turbulent times. Learning from experience, investments in leadership and culture, networks, and change readiness can help them move from denial and paralysis to acceptance and practical solutions.

Darwin Semper Vivens

Vulnerability has few friends. Naturally, the ability to cope with and recover readily from adversity is the preferred attribute of living organisms and their environments: in the face of shocks that threaten existence or viability, it enables them to bounce back to a previous state of normal functioning, or simply not show deleterious effects. Indeed, the ability of an entity or system to maintain and renew itself—or not—in the presence of stressors is of paramount significance to life on Earth.

> *Life is like a game of cards. The hand you are dealt is determinism; the way you play it is free will.*
>
> —Jawaharlal Nehru

© Asian Development Bank 2017
O. Serrat, *Knowledge Solutions*, DOI 10.1007/978-981-10-0983-9_25

As you would have thought, resilience has a long history in ecology and, when persons are the subject, psychology. Additionally, of late, it has been used in the context of communities, hence, organizations, where it is more and more defined in active, not passive, terms to connote deliberate efforts to deal with—perhaps even thrive on—hardship. For communities and organizations, resilience must surely stand for more than mere survival.

As a matter of fact, with an initial focus on tragedies in the wake of 9/11,[1] the notion of organizational resilience has burgeoned because of the need to manage uncertainty and ambiguity in modern societies and their economies, all of them complex and increasingly interconnected.[2] Where once-isolative system boundaries rupture or wear away, applying the concept of resilience to organizations—the fundamental building blocks of collective human endeavor—is vital to ensure enduring social well-being and economic prosperity in the twenty-first century. Because of its intimate, assimilitative, relationship with such fields as enterprise risk management and business continuity management,[3] organizational resilience is now considered an outcome—and a fundamental concern—of corporate governance.

The Case for Organizational Resilience

When, in an epoch of change, tomorrow is necessarily different from yesterday, and so new things need to be done, what are the questions to be asked before the solutions are sought? Action learning differs from normal training (education, development) in that its primary objective is to learn how to ask questions in conditions of risk, rather than to find the answers to questions that have already been precisely defined by others—and that do not allow ambiguous responses because the examiners have all the approved answers.

—Reginald Revans

---

[1] From that perspective, resilience was defined as the ability of organizations to deal with catastrophes such as a natural disaster, e.g., an earthquake, a tsunami, or a volcanic eruption; a power outage; a fire; a bomb; or similar event after they have become manifest. This led many governmental emergency response systems to adopt the "4Rs" approach to risk management—reduction, readiness, response, and recovery.

[2] The forces that drive structural transformations in the globalizing economy comprise, for example, shifting demographics; fast advances in science and technology; shrinking markets; the explosion of digital networks; the thinning out of accountability, governance, and power; the realignment of economic influence in a polycentric world; and rising concern for environmental sustainability.

[3] Other practices of organizations seeking to protect themselves are emergency management, crisis management, physical security, and cybersecurity.

Certainly, in the private sector, success has never been so fragile[4]: large organizations fail more often than in the past.[5] Every day, the sustainability of organizations is tested in a world that constantly changes and offers new challenges: in deference to the Red Queen hypothesis, depending of course on the environment they operate in, it is as if they must get better just to keep in the same place.[6] Therefore, with respect to organizational resilience, beyond unrewarding portrayals of maladaptive processes and on a par with concepts of the learning organization, emerging ideas evolve ways to accommodate environmental turbulence and effectively manage disruptive change[7] and its pace[8] to engage, adjust, adapt, and recover; capture or realize opportunity; and in some cases actually morph to become stronger on account of the experience.

Do I contradict myself?

Very well then I contradict myself,

(I am large, I contain multitudes).

—Walt Whitman

Every organization faces a unique risk landscape and resilience thinking must embrace learning. Achieving desirable outcomes amid strain requires creativity and innovation, aka, competencies borne of practiced skill at harnessing internal and external resources[9] and authority productively to address issues at the edge of chaos.[10]

---

[4]The average lifespan of a company listed in Standard & Poor's 500 index of leading companies in the United States has shrunk by more than 50 years over the last century, from 67 years in the 1920s to only 15 years of late.

[5]Irrespective of an organization's lifespan, dysfunctions in sectors such as business, disaster assistance, energy, environment, healthcare, humanitarian aid, international relations, or transport can beget terrible upshots.

[6]Organizational evolution would have it thus: faced with competition, an organization is likely to look for ways to raise its performance; when successful, generative learning boosts its competitive strength, which in turn triggers adaptive learning in resistant rivals and makes them more robust, thereby inciting the first organization to continue to learn more.

[7]Here, disruptive change is brought about by surprises that destabilize organizational performance and can even threaten viability.

[8]The pace of change is driven by variations in the kind, number, and recurrence of conditions an organization experiences.

[9]Here, the term "resource" is taken in its broadest sense, meaning, a financial, human, informational, and material resource, including a service, made available to a system so that it can function.

[10]Complexity thinking helps analyze what has become a key descriptor of our world. Eschewing reductionism, which interprets data and information in simple terms, it offers pointers where organizations find it difficult to predict, control, and influence because of self-organization and co-evolution. When a system risks decline or collapse—stagnation is not an option in a competitive world, double-loop and triple-loop learning can remedy inadequacies and leapfrog the (inexorably declining) curve of organizational performance over time.

Importantly, given the developmental properties of resilience, the capacity to constantly adapt, improvise, and even shape change can only spring from latent potential at individual, group, and organizational levels, nurtured over a history of prior experience.[11] As organizations build on the past to expand their behavioral repertoires across new competencies the range of possible actions they can take to meet hazards grows in breadth and depth. They are not error-free, yet errors do not disable them: they become high-reliability organizations that continuously focus on performance.

> *There exist some evils so terrible and some misfortunes so horrible that we dare not think of them, whilst their very aspect makes us shudder; but if they happen to fall on us, we find ourselves stronger than we imagined; we grapple with our ill luck, and behave better than we expected we should.*
>
> —Jean de La Bruyère

Responding without delay, thoroughly, and constructively with minimal stress to unexpected events and circumstances is now an organizational imperative, alongside client-orientation and agility.[12] In times of change, organicity[13] trumps the day

---

[11]To overcome the innate cognitive, ideological, political, and strategic barriers to organizational sustainability that crises expose, three basic questions would need answering after each experience: (i) what have we learned? (ii) how—or in what conditions—did we learn? and (iii) how can we integrate what we learned in individual and collective capabilities to understand complex, interdependent issues; engage in reflective, generative conversations; and cultivate personal and shared aspirations?

[12]Agility is the twin of resilience. It connotes with the means to move rapidly and flexibly to reap benefits from opportunities or adapt to threats arising from volatile environments. Fleetness of foot or, better, the ability to change the rules of the game typifies agility. For latitude, by and large, organizations need to develop: (i) financial agility—this means having liquidity with which to absorb downturns and buy the freedom to venture, (ii) operational agility—this equates with being lean and efficient, (iii) organizational agility—this entails having less hierarchical and more empowering structures that involve and engage personnel, and (iv) portfolio agility—this signifies being able to reallocate, reshape, or reinvent resources with all necessary speed. From such broad-based capability, they can then—as a matter of orchestrated routine—strategize dynamically, correctly perceive environmental transformations, test possible responses, and implement changes in, say, capabilities, methods of delivery, operations, policy, processes, products, services, strategy, structures, systems and their interactions, and technology.

[13]Burns and Stalker (1961) contrasted what they termed "organic" and "mechanistic" forms of organization more than 50 years ago. A mechanistic management system befits stable conditions; an organic form meets changing conditions. In a closed system design, the former exhibits low levels of uncertainty typified by centralized decision making, low integration of offices and departments and functional areas, standardization and formalization, and low differentiation of tasks; in an open system design, the latter exhibits higher levels of uncertainty characterized by decentralized decision making, high integration of offices and departments and functional areas, little standardization and formalization, and high differentiation of tasks. This said, there is no optimum way of organizing: configuration is conditioned by the efforts a venture deploys to achieve landscape fitness.

through structural flexibility, viz, relaxation of command and control; expansive processing of information; and opportunistic appropriation of redundancy, slack resources, and capabilities for improvisation.[14]

Dimensions of Organizational Resilience

Happiness is not the absence of problems but the ability to deal with them.

—H. Jackson Brown

Resilience is neither a series of principles nor an end state: it is a never-ending journey that, within a risk landscape, is conditioned as much else by organization, people, knowledge, and technology, as well as the interactions[15] among these. Notwithstanding, in the here and now of recurrent crises, resilience must be an act of mindful,[16] strategic anticipation and active waiting spanning day-to-day, exceptional, and emergency management.

Interest in organizational resilience grows daily but, sorry to say, the state of the art still leaves much to be desired—to date, most of the literature propounds generic traits. They include such recommendations as: avoid being overprotective; bounce back from adversity; build a culture of commitment and accountability; entertain the inconceivable; foster trust between leaders and teams; listen to complainers; make sure employees engage with the strategy of the business; move the goal posts every three years; put your motivators where your mouth is; refuse to rest on your laurels; self-correct; shore up your decision-making processes; show the courage of your convictions; think horizontally; use people to change people; etc.

Yes, certainly ... But, what specifically might it be that makes some organizations survive and thrive in turbulent times? Helpfully, Resilient Organizations suggest that the resilience of an organization is a function of three interdependent attributes: (i) leadership and culture—which define the adaptive capacity of the

---

[14]To improvise is to do something on the spur of the moment without preparation and with what resources are available.

[15]An aside on organizational silos is warranted. The *Knowledge Solutions* on bridging organizational silos explain that large organizations rely on teams to develop and deliver products and services. However, the defining characteristics of specialized units often hamper collaboration among different parts of an organization. Promoting intra-organizational resilience demands that an enabling environment be built for effective cross-functional teamwork.

[16]The *Knowledge Solutions* on knowledge behaviors showcase 16 habits of mind that attend to value, inclination, sensitivity, capability, and commitment—all defined toward behaving intelligently when confronted with problems.

organization; (ii) networks—which amount to the internal and external relationships fostered and developed for the organization to leverage when needed; and (iii) change readinesss—which signifies the planning undertaken and direction established to enable the organization to be change-ready.[17]

Reference

Burns T, Stalker G (1961) The management of innovation. Tavistock

---

[17]Resilient Organizations also provides a resilience benckmark tool and associated questionnaire to gauge the resilience of an organization, monitor progress over time, and compare resilience strengths and weaknesses against other organizations in the sector of interest or of a similar size.

Proposition 26
Past Visions of Rural Asia's Future

In a Word Strategic efforts to effect change are constantly challenged by emerging forces about which there is little advance knowledge. For constructive action, it is useful to look at the past to gain a perspective on the present; but, it is even more profitable to revisit past visions of the future from an interpretation of the present. The concepts of change over time, context, causality, contingency, and complexity help make sense.

Picturing the 2010s by Way of the 1960s

In 1967, ADB conducted a first Asian Agricultural Survey in recognition of the fact that the agricultural sector was the mainstay of the economies of most of the developing countries of Asia and the Pacific. In the wake of the Green Revolution,[1] the survey was planned as an economic and technical study of ADB's developing member

---

[1]The term "Green Revolution" refers to a series of research, development, and technology transfer initiatives that, beginning in Mexico in the 1940s, aimed to increase agricultural production worldwide, most markedly in the 1950s–1970s. Specifically, researchers developed high-yielding varieties of wheat, maize, and rice that produced a large output when combined with fertilizers and pesticides. (The yield of major plantation crops, e.g., rubber, oil palm, tea, and coconut, was also raised.)

© Asian Development Bank 2017
O. Serrat, *Knowledge Solutions*, DOI 10.1007/978-981-10-0983-9_26

countries and took as its focus of concern the issues surrounding the modernization of regional agriculture through the application of science and technology.

> *Optimism is a strategy for making a better future. Because unless you believe that the future can be better, you are unlikely to step up and take responsibility for making it so.*
>
> —Noam Chomsky

In 1976, ADB undertook a second Asian Agricultural Survey because agricultural development during the late 1960s and early 1970s was slower than had been anticipated and institutional constraints and shortages of resources and inputs had emerged as a barrier to faster development. That survey looked at social, economic, and institutional factors as well as the interrelationships between agriculture and other sectors of the economy. Its intellectual underpinnings were nevertheless akin to those of the first in that the survey team also believed that intensifying production would lead to agricultural development; the only difference was that it intended to pay more attention to the presumed obstacles to such development.

These *Knowledge Solutions* reproduce a memorandum the author drafted in 1996 to make the case for a third survey, 20 years after the second and in an altogether very different context. The objective was to catalyze attention and action to address rural development concerns over the following decade: food security still featured high on the agenda but the challenges were, increasingly, deemed to be socioeconomic and environmental. A new study of rural Asia was launched in 1998 (ADB 2000–2001).[2]

Box. Memorandum on the Working Group on Rural Asia Update—Themes and Arguments

Development Revisited

Over the last two decades, an economic transformation has occurred in much of rural Asia: large parts of the region have made remarkable progress with substantial gains in food security, per capita income, quality of life, and poverty reduction. Yet, rural Asia remains home to more than 700 million people living in poverty. What with continuing population growth and the damage being inflicted on the environment, it is necessary to adopt a more sensitive attitude that moves away from an agricultural commodity focus. Approaches are required that, among others, meet the nutritional needs of

---

[2]The six volumes that made up the study were *Beyond the Green Revolution—An Overview* (2000), *Transforming the Rural Asian Economy: The Unfinished Revolution* (2000), *Growth and Sustainability of Agriculture in Asia* (2000), *Rural Financial Markets in Asia: Policies Paradigms, and Performance* (2000), *The Quality of Life in Rural Asia* (2001), and *The Evolving Roles of the State, Private, and Local Actors in Rural Asia* (2001).

people qualitatively and quantitatively while providing other agricultural products; reduce the vulnerability of agriculture to adverse natural and socioeconomic factors; promote durable employment, sufficient income, and decent living and working conditions for rural communities; preserve, enhance, and develop rural amenities; enable communities to care for their own environments; and satisfy the demand for natural capital in keeping with the Earth's carrying capacity. Such approaches are best developed from an interdisciplinary perspective that embraces knowledge, values, social organization, technology, and the natural resource base.

Economy

... the ideas of economists and political philosophers, both when they are right and when they are wrong, are more powerful than is commonly understood. Indeed the world is ruled by little else. Practical men, who believe themselves to be quite exempt from any intellectual influences, are usually the slaves of some defunct economist.

—John Maynard Keynes

Like other policies, economic policy is shaped not only by events but also by the prevailing intellectual environment. Following the successful reconstruction of Western Europe after the Second World War, hopes for rapid development were extravagantly high and political leaders and professional development economists alike saw underdevelopment as a temporary and primarily material problem to be solved by increasing investment in capital goods to promote industrial development. An important factor in this endeavor was development assistance.

Until the late 1960s, therefore, economic growth was the sole aim of economic policy. It was also widely believed that the spread of welfare would automatically follow growth through the trickle-down effect and, accordingly, need not be considered in the formulation or implementation of economic policy. Although economic growth did improve the lot of the poor in many developing countries, however, it became apparent that the distribution of welfare in a society depends more on the structure of the economy, which does not necessarily change as a result of favorable growth rates.

Environmental degradation is an iatrogenic disease induced by economic physicians who treat the basic malady of unlimited wants by prescribing unlimited growth. We experience environmental degradation in the form of increased scarcity of clean air, pure water, relaxed moments, etc. But the only way the growthmania paradigm knows to deal with scarcity is to recommend growth. Yet one certainly does not cure a treatment-induced disease by increasing the treatment dosage.

—Herman Daly

Despite a mounting debt burden and the first oil crisis (1973–1974), which saw the price of raw materials fall, economic growth in developing countries was nevertheless still favorable throughout the 1970s. However, skepticism about growth as the sole measure of development mounted in developed countries because of growing poverty, unemployment, and income inequality. The growth objective was therefore joined by increased employment, redistribution of welfare, and the satisfaction of basic needs. These ideas, however, were not well received in developing countries because they threatened to divert attention from the perceived need to reduce inequalities between countries, and from the developed countries' joint responsibility in this enterprise. At the end of the decade, moreover, the second oil crisis (1979–1980) provoked a deep economic recession in developed countries and a further drop in the demand for raw materials, which had already been in structural decline as a result of technological advances, stemming from greater efficiency and recovery of used products, and the emergence of substitutes. Many countries experienced swingeing adjustment programs. More people than perhaps ever before suffered falling standards of living because of the forced reductions in government spending, elimination of food subsidies, devaluations, and privatizations.

The 1980s were overshadowed by the debt crisis and structural adjustments but also witnessed a reassessment of the market mechanism and the role of the private sector, and important steps towards the liberalization of the world economy. East and South-East Asian countries were the only developing countries able to achieve more rapid growth than that experienced in the 1960s, largely because they managed to stabilize their economies (low inflation, realistic exchange rates, control of government spending), implemented adjustment programs, and therefore attracted more development assistance. Because of the retreat of central planning in the 1980s and the apparent success of East Asian countries, there is now a desire for less government control, financial sector liberalization, more private enterprise, more autonomy for government-owned enterprises, and more reliance on competition.

The breaching of the Berlin Wall on 9 November 1989 symbolized the end of the Cold War. With the fading of the political dividing lines in the world, this current has changed the intellectual environment for economic policy. There are now signs of a world order geared to economic performance, and of a division splitting the South and the East into front runners, those of intermediate pace, and stragglers. The front runners are those countries whose economies feature high levels of technical innovation in products and production processes, and in methods of organizing production, distribution, and marketing. Those of intermediate pace are the countries whose economies will certainly not lead the field, but which will have sufficient comparative advantages in certain sectors to derive a measure of benefit from their activities. The stragglers are those countries whose economies do not have enough inherent vitality to stay the pace. With the end of the Cold War, the political relevance of the latter has waned and they are being left more to their own devices.

To complicate this problem, however, there is ample evidence to suggest that development does not work when attention is focused exclusively, or even primarily, on economies. Until the 1990s, the reigning worldview that economic growth deserves highest priority because it is connected with the provision of basic needs went almost entirely unchallenged. Not only was it assumed that the development of economies should be the central preoccupation of public policy, but most corporations, governments, and international institutions exerted all their efforts to this end: societal goals became synonymous with economic goals, e.g., material production and consumption, investment, productivity, growth, and profit. Those favoring societal goals now contend that culture, defined as the total way of life of a people or society, should be the focus of future developmental activity because it is concerned with the entire spectrum of human needs, as well as mankind's relationship with the environment.

Some of the less appealing consequences of the Western economic miracle are also condemned. They include pollution and destruction of the global ecosystem; exploitation and exhaustion of renewable and nonrenewable resources; and satisfaction of the materialistic demands of the few at the expense of the many. Not only is the environment increasingly polluted and incapable of generating the resources required to support a rapidly expanding population, but the economic system as a whole fosters the interests of a small group of countries to the detriment of others. Thus, despite the appreciable gains that have been achieved in industry, agriculture, commerce, health, education, and technology as a result of placing economics and economies at the center of public policy and decision-making, these accomplishments have been offset by the numerous inequalities, inequities, and injustices which exist in income distribution, as well as by the colossal damage being inflicted on the environment.

Society

Unlike plagues of the dark ages or contemporary diseases we do not understand, the modern plague of overpopulation is soluble by means we have discovered and with resources we possess. What is lacking is not sufficient knowledge of the solution but universal consciousness of the gravity of the problem and education of the billions who are its victim.

—Martin Luther King, Jr.

Mortality started to decline in Europe and North America about two hundred years ago. In the developing countries, enormous reductions in child mortality occurred between 1960 and 1990, mainly through the prevention of infectious diseases but also through improved nutrition. The factors that have been important in the decline of mortality are income growth, improvements in medical technology, and public health programs combined with the spread of knowledge about health. However, death control without birth control has sparked a population explosion.

Two hundred years ago, there were about one billion people on earth. The second billion was added over the next 130 years; the third in 35 years; the fourth in 15 years; and the fifth in just 10 years. The population of the world, now at 5.7 billion, is expected to reach 6.3 billion in 2000. Each year, it increases by almost 100 million. It was once forecast that the world population would settle at about 10.2 billion by 2100; this estimate has now been revised to 12 billion. More than 90% of this growth is occurring in developing countries, where death rates have been falling without commensurate declines in birth rates, and much of the population increase will be in cities, as it has been in the past.

The age structure of population in developing countries also gives ground for deep concern. This population contains more children who have yet to reproduce than it does adults (the mean proportion of the population under 16 years of age in developing countries ranges from 40 to 50%). With age structures so heavily skewed toward the young, the obvious conclusion would be that, when these children move up to reproductive age, the population will grow rapidly. Without birth control and with low death rates for children, this will be true. Moreover, the age structure of the population provides a measure of the economic impact of the population. The dependency ratio, the ratio of people over 65 and under 15 years of age to the rest of the population, indicates the proportion of the population that contributes little to the economy and must be supported. A high dependency ratio is a fearful burden on the economy. It is now increasing in most countries.

The worldwide economic slowdown experienced since the late 1970s and population growth mean that incomes have declined in many countries. More than one billion people, or one fifth of the world's population, live in poverty. Between 700 and 800 million are in Asia and about 500 million of them live in absolute poverty. It is now accepted that economic growth is by itself not enough for reducing poverty. Governments must also promote employment and offer poor people the opportunity to acquire skills, health, and the information they require to improve their lives. The proportion of people living in poverty can be reduced if there is, among others, broad-based economic growth; a firm government commitment to reduce poverty; an institutional capacity to design and follow through on appropriate policies and programs; good public sector management that minimizes unproductive expenditures; and a strengthening of essential services, e.g., primary education and vocational training, preventive health care, family planning, nutrition, clean water, sanitation, and rural infrastructure. None of these are easy to achieve.

Population growth adds to the need for employment and livelihoods, which exerts additional direct pressure on the environment. It also increases the demand for food, drinking water, and sewage and solid waste disposal, as well as for some energy-intensive products and services such as transportation. To the extent that per capita incomes rise and practices remain unchanged, such demand will be exacerbated. Excessive demand for natural resources from a rapidly increasing population leads directly to environmental degradation as economic, social, and political systems fail to keep pace with demands. In rural areas, inequitable land distribution obliges the poor to survive on marginal lands, causing erosion and other environmental problems. To survive, the poor tend to use the resource base to derive the quickest benefit: this is an action forced on them by poverty that can only be rationalized if our understanding is located in the concerns of the poor.

One way or another, population growth will slow down because many developing countries simply cannot sustain their escalating numbers. It will happen through family planning and development, or by famine, disease, and war brought about by collapsing economies. The risk to future generations would be less and the options would be greater if population growth were to cease sooner rather than later. The longer population growth continues, the more committed all countries become to a particular set of problems: more rapid depletion of resources; greater pressures on the environment; more dependence on continued rapid technological development to solve these problems; fewer options; and perhaps continued postponement of the resolution of other problems, including those resulting from past growth. The sooner population growth ceases, the more time humanity has to redress the mistakes of past growth, the more resources it has to implement solutions, and the more options it has to decide how it wants to live in the future.

Environment

Here is your country. Cherish these natural wonders, cherish the natural resources, cherish the history and romance as a sacred heritage, for your children and your children's children. Do not let selfish men or greedy interests skin your country of its beauty, its riches or its romance.

—Theodore Roosevelt

Until recently, it was thought that developing countries could postpone environmental improvements while awaiting economic growth. Better understanding of the complex linkages between the environment and economic growth now underscore the urgent need to devise new approaches for dealing with the former in order not to derail the latter. This need has been intensified by increasing environmental degradation in even the wealthiest of developing countries and by the realization that the well-being of developed countries can be significantly affected by activities in the developing world. The fear is that continued population growth and economic growth, along with the energy-intensive and materials-intensive consumption patterns they bring, will aggravate environmental degradation in developing countries.

	Rising Sea Level	Acid Rain	Waste Disposal a/	Marine and Coastal Resource Degradation b/	Industrial Pollution	Urban Congestion and Pollution	Pesticides and Fertilizers	Land and Soil Resource Problems c/	Water Resource Problems d/	Deforestation e/
South Asia										
Bangladesh	Medium			Low	Low	Medium	Medium	Low	High	Medium
People's Republic of China	Medium	High	Low	Low	High	High	Medium	Low	Low	High
India	Low	Medium	Low	Medium	High	High	Medium	High	High	High
Myanmar	Low						Low	Medium		Medium
Nepal	n.a.			n.a.		Low	Low	High	Low	High
Pakistan	Low		Low	Low	Low	High	Medium	High	Medium	Medium
Sri Lanka				High	Low	Low	Low	Medium	Medium	High
Southeast Asia										
Cambodia			Low	Medium	Low	Low		Medium	Low	High
Indonesia	Medium		Low	Medium	Medium	High	Medium	Medium	High	High
Lao People's Democratic Republic	n.a.			n.a.				Medium	Medium	High
Malaysia	Low			Medium	Medium	Medium	Low	Low	Low	High
Philippines	Medium		Low	Medium	Medium	High	Medium	High	Medium	High
Thailand	Medium	Low	Low	Medium	Medium	High	Medium	Medium	High	High
Viet Nam	Low		Low	Medium	Medium	Medium	Low	Medium	Medium	High
Pacific Islands	High		High	High	Low	Medium	Low	Medium	High	Medium

Legend: high priority; medium priority; low priority; n.a. not applicable

a/ includes dumping of industrial and toxic wastes.
b/ includes driftnet fishing, coral mining, and coastal development.
c/ includes desertification, salinization, soil erosion, and other forms of land degradation such as waterlogging.
d/ includes water shortage, groundwater depletion, flooding, and water pollution.
e/ includes industrial wood production, fuelwood collection, watershed degradation, and loss of biological diversity.

Source: ADB. 1990. *Asian Development Outlook*. Manila.

Fig. 26.1 Relative significance of resource and environmental issues in selected developing member countries of ADB

> *As a remedy to life in society I would suggest the big city. Nowadays, it is the only desert within our means.*
>
> —Albert Camus

There is a basis for such fear, although environmental problems should not be viewed solely through the lens of the developed countries' preoccupations. The Asian and Pacific region contains the world's fastest growing and most dynamic economies. The unprecedented growth of the region is expected to continue. However, growth rates though high are derived from low levels of per capita income, so that demand for goods and services will continue to grow, and the rapid industrialization of the region is said to be one of the dirtiest ever. Continuing high population growth rates are exerting great pressure on the environment. Poverty is rampant and more than two thirds of the world's 1.2 billion people living in poverty reside in the region. Urbanization and industrialization, resulting in high levels of pollution, also create other adverse environmental and social impacts. Policy and market failures are many. Institutions are weak and absorptive capacities uncertain. By the end of the twentieth century, the Asian and Pacific region will contain 12 of the world's 21 megacities.

The relative importance assigned to resource and environmental issues in selected developing member countries of the Bank is presented in Fig. 26.1. Although environmental problems were once considered to be limited to those resulting from urbanization and industrialization, the figure reveals they now include air and water pollution; land degradation; soil erosion; desertification; deforestation; loss of biological diversity; greenhouse gas emissions, which contribute to global warming; acid rain; urban pollution; and toxic and hazardous wastes.

Interactions between the environment, population growth, and economies have continual, complex, and multiple feedback mechanisms that are difficult to identify and understand. This has implications on the balance of actions to resolve problems. Uncertainty centers on how physical processes will respond to human intervention, how people will react, and how institutions will change in response to policy initiatives. Because the environment can no longer be looked upon as an area of marginal concern best addressed by the expertise of natural scientists, social scientists now find themselves called upon to provide both an analysis and prescriptions for environmental problems. Economics, once again, makes strong claims for its abilities to contribute to the environmental policy debate.

From an economic perspective, nature performs three main functions. First, the environment is a resource base comprising renewable and nonrenewable resources. It provides the economy with both raw materials, which are transformed into consumer products by the production process, and energy, which fuels this transformation. Ultimately, all these raw materials and energy are discharged into the environment as waste products. From this, it follows that the environment also acts as a waste sink, which refers to the environment's regulating or stabilizing function, including its capacity to process waste products. Last, the environment also serves as an amenity base whose services, e.g., recreational facilities, flow to individuals without the intermediation of productive activity.

We are being made aware that the organization of society on the principle of private profit, as well as public destruction, is leading both to the deformation of humanity by unregulated industrialism, and to the exhaustion of natural resources, and that a good deal of our material progress is a progress for which succeeding generations may have to pay dearly.

—T.S. Eliot

On the basis of this model, economics promises and often delivers predictions to policy-makers aimed at environmental management. However, it ignores the environment's primary function as a life support system; ascribes little or no value to the three economic functions it recognizes; allows substitution between natural and produced capital even though the former is multifunctional and sometimes irreplaceable; provides no guidelines for approaches to environmental uncertainty; and cannot answer questions regarding the equity of resource use across people and through time (intragenerational and intergenerational equity objectives). If, as generally agreed, sustainable development is economic development that endures over the long run; economics must resolve these issues before it can really help society to attain the goal of sustainability.

Economic frameworks and methods, however, are founded upon an a priori commitment to a particular model of human nature and social behavior. At the close of the twentieth century, the traditional growth ethos that inspired and sustained developed countries for several centuries, and which most developing countries have sought to emulate, has become counter-productive. The planet's physical endowment does not accommodate this expansionist worldview. Instead, it is experiencing negative growth, resource domination, environmental degradation, and species elimination. In short, society and the environment are experiencing forms of development that can no longer be sustained. It is therefore worth examining the underlying social commitments that determine the way we use the environment and the cumulative social impacts of individual choices.

Agriculture

During the 1950s and the 1960s, extreme interest in the development of industry naturally led to the neglect of agriculture. Although agriculture was the mainstay of the majority of developing countries, accounted for the major share of their national product, and employed the bulk of their labor force, rural areas were considered to be no more than sources of labor and a few primary products and markets for industrial goods. Investment in agriculture was low and government funds earmarked for the sector went primarily to the more modern farms producing for export and to parastatal enterprises. Foreign currency earnings from the export of agricultural products served to finance industrial investment in and around the towns. Excessive duties on exports of agricultural products did not lead to reinvestment in agriculture and overvalued exchange rates made the import of agricultural products financially attractive. Having once exported food, many developing countries became net importers. The low regard in which the agricultural sector was held was due, *inter alia*, to the urban bias of policy-makers and professionals in the developing countries and to an incorrect assessment of the opportunities for increasing agricultural production, which only began to emerge in the 1960s, initially through the Green Revolution. It was reinforced by the early concentration of development assistance on infrastructure and energy, and by the domination which engineers and economists exerted in multilateral development banks and aid agencies.

> *The word agriculture, after all, does not mean "agriscience," much less "agribusiness". It means "cultivation of land". And cultivation is at the root of the sense both of culture and of cult. The ideas of tillage and worship are thus joined in culture. And these words all come from an Indo-European root meaning both "to revolve" and "to dwell". To live, to survive on the earth, to care for the soil, and to worship, all are bound at the root to the idea of a cycle. It is only by understanding the cultural complexity and largeness of the concept of agriculture that we can see the threatening diminishments implied by the term "agribusiness".*

> —Wendell Berry

The paradigm underlying the Green Revolution held that the first step in agricultural development was intensification of agriculture; the resulting increased productivity would supply labor and capital for initiation of other industries. Two key components of the Green Revolution directly reflect the industrial model. They are (i) the priority given to increasing production; and (ii) a belief in the neutrality of technology. The dominant assumption underlying the first component was that increases in production are the best way to solve the problems of hunger. The second key component in the Green Revolution involved a belief that the high-yielding varieties developed for wheat, maize, and rice were economically, socially, and politically neutral. Hence, the Green Revolution had a strongly technocratic element and there never was any intention to modify the economic, social, and political structures that maintain inequality of incomes and access to resources.

The impact of the Green Revolution is well documented. Agriculture became increasingly productive in many developing countries with crop yields increasing as much as three-fold. These yield increases have been attained through the use of large amounts of inorganic fertilizers and pesticides. However, these dramatic increases in crop productivity have been accompanied in many instances by environmental degradation (soil erosion, pollution by pesticides, salinization), social problems (elimination of the family farm, concentration of land, resources and production, growth of agribusiness and its domination over farm production, change in rural/urban migration patterns) and by excessive use of natural resources. They have also led to a shrinking farm population, much larger farms and fields, and the production of a very restricted number of crops, often grown in monoculture or biculture. Moreover, the transfer-of-technology approach embodied in the Green Revolution has not worked well outside irrigated areas and is confined to about one fifth of all farmland in the Asian and Pacific region. The remaining areas are mainly rainfed, undulating areas found in hinterlands, mountains, hills, wetlands and the semi-arid, sub-humid, and humid tropics. In these areas, there has been a deepening crisis, with populations rising, land holdings becoming smaller, environments degrading, and per capita food production remaining static or declining. In the Asian and Pacific region, about 1 billion people depend on such agriculture.

To a large extent, rural life was also rearranged to suit the new technology. While the Green Revolution was underway, every aspect of agriculture and rural life was reassessed. Social institutions in rural areas were assessed in terms of their contribution, or presumed contribution since evidence was not always at hand, to agricultural productivity. At best, agricultural development occurred in spite of these social institutions; at worst, agricultural development required changes in these institutions since they were commonly thought to hold back development. A panoply of modern rural institutions was also created to provide technological packages; they were chiefly concerned with marketing, credit, the supply of agricultural inputs (seed and fertilizer), and extension advice. The small farmers who failed to take advantage of these institutions were characterized as resistant to agricultural change.

It is now finally realized, though, that one of the most important areas of difference between agriculture and the industrial model lies in the great contextual variability of agriculture (where climate, weather, soil, topography, resources, cultural, social, and institutional variations all profoundly affect its viability) as opposed to industry, where the universalism and rationalism of modern science and technology encourage blueprint approaches whereby local variation can be fitted, although not easily, to the design. It is, belatedly, accepted that the contemporary challenges of agriculture in developing countries are not technical since development projects emphasizing capital-intensive, high-input technologies (mechanization, agrochemicals, imported seeds) are in many instances proving ecologically unsound and

socially inequitable by mostly benefiting a small portion of the local populations. The challenges are, increasingly, socioeconomic and environmental.
Thus, in the 1990s, rural development includes two new but crucial dimensions: the ecological management of agricultural resources; and the
empowerment of rural communities into actors of their own development.

Intersectoral Constraints, Imperatives, and Linkages

*If you ask an economist what's driven economic growth, it's been major advances in
things that mattered—the mechanization of farming, mass manufacturing, things
like that. The problem is, our society is not organized around doing that.*

—Larry Page

Poor living conditions and impoverishment, the importance of a certain
level of food provision and of agriculture in general, the imperative of providing employment for growing numbers of people, and the need to stem the
exodus to the cities all explain why concern for rural areas needs to occupy a
central place in the theory and practice of development. For most of the
poorer developing member countries of the Bank, agriculture is the principal
means of livelihood for the majority of the population although its contribution to gross national product and exports is declining in importance. For
many small farmers, it is a way of life. It plays a crucial role in ensuring food
security and, if neglected, compromises the main natural resources upon
which these countries depend. Of all the economic sectors, agriculture alone
can simultaneously contribute to the achievement of all of the Bank's
strategic development objectives, e.g., reducing poverty, supporting human
development, protecting the environment, improving the status of women,
and promoting economic growth. To develop an effective strategy aimed at
overcoming obstacles to progress in its developing member countries, the
Bank must act more decidedly in the agricultural sector. However, the
background against which social, political, and economic action must be
based is extremely complex and transcends sectoral boundaries. It relates,
inter alia, to food production (including land resources), water resources, and
forest and energy resources. The Bank first needs to come to grips with such
intersectoral constraints, imperatives, and linkages in a coexistent and
mutually supporting manner. All the while, its understanding of interrelationships should also be founded on recognition that development is sustained
by economic ideology rather than resources.

Food Production

The total population in the Asian and Pacific region is projected to grow
from 2.6 billion in 1985 to 3.4 billion in 2000 and 4.4 billion by 2025. This

growth assumes that the current annual growth rate of about 2.1% will slow to 1.9% by 2000 and fall further to 1.1% by 2025. Despite lower population growth rates, however, an additional 350 million and 1.5 billion people will have to be fed by 2000 and 2025, respectively, bearing in mind that approximately 50% of the current population are still below the poverty line and more than 300 million are chronically malnourished. According to the Food and Agriculture Organization, food production is projected to increase at 3% per annum to 2000, slightly below demand, thus making the region a net importer of food. Import requirements will become more substantial or average food intake will decline if assumed food production increases are not realized.

The key constraint on the supply of food meeting demand is reduced availability of arable land. Cropping intensities already average 108% and there is little room for expansion, especially when losses of arable land to urbanization and degradation are taken into account. Sizable land reserves now exist only in Cambodia, Indonesia, the Lao People's Democratic Republic, Malaysia, and Myanmar. Apart from problems of land availability as such, much land in South and South-East Asia, estimated at 85%, is affected by shallow and poor soils, steep topography, low water holding capacity or impeded drainage, or seasonal drought and flooding. Moreover, land degradation continues and substantial parts of arable land in Bangladesh, the People's Republic of China, India, Nepal, Pakistan, and Thailand are affected by water and wind erosion, salinity, or flooding.

Irrigated areas are by far the most productive with an output several times higher than non-irrigated areas due to double or even triple cropping and higher yields per crop. This has been a major factor behind the Green Revolution together with high-yielding varieties and inputs of fertilizer and other chemicals. However, irrigation has not been without problems due to faulty design and management leading to waterlogging, salinity build-up, and decline in soil fertility. Moreover, even high-yielding varieties developed for favorable conditions appear to have reached a yield plateau and raising yield levels will require further strategic breeding.

Whether food requirements scenarios turn out to have been conservative or exaggerated, the additional output required will in any case be so large that a major part of the incremental requirements will have to be met from irrigated land and rainfed land under favorable production conditions. This can, hopefully, be done by closing the yield gap still available in the fields of inefficient farm operators and possibly through new plant types or hybrids with still higher yield potentials. There can be no doubt, however, that irrigation investment, through rehabilitation and improvement of existing schemes and new irrigation development, will have to play a major role.

Water Resources

Water has no taste, no color, no odor; it cannot be defined, art relished while ever mysterious. Not necessary to life, but rather life itself. It fills us with a gratification that exceeds the delight of the senses.

—Antoine de Saint-Exupéry

The capacity to control water supplies for human purposes has increased markedly. But as water development has expanded, the opportunities for adding to water supplies have declined, the economic and environmental costs of new supplies have risen sharply, and the threats to supplies from pollution and groundwater depletion have mounted. Demand for water has continued to grow with increases in population and incomes. Yet, despite this rising demand and the increasing scarcity of supplies, fresh water is commonly treated as a free resource.

By far the largest use is irrigation, which commonly accounts for about 70% of all water withdrawals. Generous subsidies and institutions that ignored some of the costs associated with agricultural water use fostered the growth of irrigation throughout the world until the 1980s. In the Asian and Pacific region, the area of land irrigated increased from about 85 million hectares in 1966 to about 137 million hectares in 1991, an overall increase of about 60%. However, rising water costs, high government debt burdens, loss of arable land to urbanization, increasing competition for scarce water supplies, and growing awareness of environmental problems are forcing some previously irrigated lands out of production. Many developing member countries of the Bank now experience water shortages.

The demands for water and the services it provides will continue to grow in the future. As water becomes increasingly scarce, however, pressures will mount to develop additional supplies, to improve management of existing water supplies, and to transfer water from agriculture to other uses. In the short term, this underscores the need to use prices as a mechanism to achieve appropriate water allocations and to ensure efficiency. However, since the provision of irrigation and drinking water also follows social inequalities, it will be important not to reinforce inequalities in distribution during the ensuing reallocation of water resources, and to strive to reduce them.

Forests and Energy Resources

What we are doing to the forests of the world is but a mirror reflection of what we are doing to ourselves and to one another.

—Mahatma Gandhi

Tropical deforestation is now a pressing environmental and developmental issue. Loss of tropical forests diminishes biological diversity, contributes to climate change by releasing stored carbon into the atmosphere, and often results in serious land degradation, sometimes rendering land unfit for future agriculture. Of the three tropical regions, Asia's rate of deforestation is the highest (1.2% per annum over the period 1981–1990), followed by Latin America (0.9%), and Africa (0.8%). Incentives to cut trees will remain strong.

Of special concern is the fuelwood crisis: fuelwood accounts for a large proportion of all energy consumption in many Asian countries. Even in countries with large industrial sectors, fuelwood dominates the life of rural inhabitants. For example, wood accounts for only a third of India's total energy consumption but, together with dung and crop wastes, meets over 90% of rural dwellers' energy requirements.

According to the United Nations, measures that need to be taken if the fuelwood crisis is to be resolved include a fivefold increase in current levels of tree planting, improvement of fuelwood distribution networks, and the adoption of better conversion technologies. At the same time, however, there must be a pragmatic realization that societies are dynamic. Remaining forests will not, therefore, remain intact. Attempts to solve forest problems cannot succeed if they remain confined to the simple trade-off between "deforestation" and "saving the forest", since forests can and should perform a variety of economic, social, and environmental functions. With some exceptions, forests must be used, not merely preserved or liquidated. Accordingly, decisions regarding which forests are to be used, by whom, how, and when will greatly influence forestry resources in the twenty-first century.

Building Blocks for a Strategy
There are distinct polarities between the traditional goals of modern, or economic, agriculture, and the new social and ecological goals to be set. The strategic development objectives of the Bank are relevant to the challenges of the 1990s and beyond but the Bank needs to equip itself with the conceptual framework necessary to redirect its interventions in agriculture. This requires a different perspective on the issues at hand, new objectives for agricultural development, and the elaboration of fresh approaches and instruments. It is also necessary to enrich our store of knowledge in several areas.

A Perspective
Culture
Six needs, common to all people at all times and in all places, can be identified. They are (i) the need to make a living; (ii) the need for social organization; (iii) the need for law and order; (iv) the need for knowledge and learning; (v) the need for aesthetic expression; and

Population and Migration
- Density
- Change
- Structure
- Households
- Communities

Social Well-Being and Equity
- Income
- Housing
- Education
- Health
- Safety

Economic Structure and Performance
- Labor Force
- Employment
- Sectoral Shares
- Productivity
- Investment

Environment and Sustainability
- Topography and Climate
- Land Use Change
- Habitat and Species
- Soil and Water
- Air Quality

Fig. 26.2 Rural indicators: a basic set. *Source* Author

(vi) the need for normative and metaphysical expression. These cultural segments can be correlated with five areas that together make up a system of mutual vulnerability or, conversely, can become one of mutual sustainability. They are (i) the environment; (ii) the economy; (iii) the society; (iv) the polity; and (v) the culture. Culture is defined to include science and technology, values, goals, religion and philosophy, aesthetics, and patterns of behavior. This holistic perspective, englobing all six needs, does not lend itself to easy action. But there is considerable value in using this kind of approach to view societies as systems, with all segments of the pattern interlinked and interacting. Also, by focusing on the totality and innate worth of a given society, we can minimize the ethnocentric bias that results from our own cultural conditioning, a bias to which those from Western countries have been all too prone.

Culture is the widening of the mind and of the spirit.

—Jawaharlal Nehru

By paying simultaneous attention to all six needs, cultural theory makes it possible to focus attention directly on the whole as well as the parts, contexts as well as contents, values and value systems, and especially strategic relationships between key variables, countries, blocs of countries, and human beings and the natural environment. It allows informed choices and intelligent decisions to be made about the future. Schafer (1994) has explained that shifting attention from economies to cultures in this holistic sense could yield a number of theoretical, conceptual, and practical benefits which should be seized and exploited in the future. According to him, it would to begin enable us to deal more effectively with complexity and fragmentation because the emphasis would be on systems rather than parts of systems. Second, it would confirm the fact that the principal object and ultimate purpose of all development is to build cultures, not economies. Third, it would also help to ensure that economies are properly contextualized, and pointed in the right direction. The reason for this is clear and unambiguous: rather than functioning as self-governing entities, economies would be constrained and enriched by the larger cultures and cultural contexts in which they are situated.

Rural Development

It follows that focusing attention on cultures can provide a useful perspective on rural development and can help to illuminate the codes, maps, values, value systems, and worldviews held by large percentages of the world population. Rural development is a complex, multisectoral concept. Partly because previous attempts were not properly contextualized and were simply aimed at the fulfillment of economic needs at the expense of non-economic needs, the experience of development assistance to rural development has often been disappointing, particularly in the case of integrated rural development projects. In many instances, the latter were divorced from the grass roots, or were too short-lived or complicated to be sustainable after project completion. On the whole, therefore, the main beneficiaries of integrated development projects have not been the poorest farmers, but those best able to exploit market opportunities. Benefits have also tended to be concentrated in provincial towns, rather than deprived rural areas, and confined to improvements in rural infrastructure which came about in uncoordinated fashion. However, integrated multisectoral programs are often the cheapest and most cost-effective approach for reaching a large number of low-income families. Recognition of the need to incorporate the macro components of culture into rural development projects can answer many of the criticisms leveled at integrated rural development projects if a decision is taken to extend political and economic support to the rural areas.

Rural conditions and trends can only be described by using a comprehensive set of rural indicators. Figure 26.2 presents a simplified set of rural indicators with which to gauge four main rural development concerns. These are demographic, economic, social, and environmental. Increasingly, Bank interventions for rural development will have to be based on detailed analyses of rural problems and perspectives to complement the information contained in basic sets of rural indicators, and to more fully reflect the many dimensions of development of significance to the developing member countries of the Bank. This will require an awareness of both the technical side of agriculture and cultural dimensions at various levels within rural society, e.g., the household, the village, and the regional levels. An approach which considers the system as a whole will provide the perspective required. It is, however, only the first step: it is also necessary to fully understand and actively promote sustainable agricultural systems since they are immediately concerned with livelihood.

From Agriculture to Sustainable Food Systems

The more clearly we can focus our attention on the wonders and realities of the universe about us, the less taste we shall have for destruction.

—Rachel Carson

Most of the successful breakthroughs in productivity since the Green Revolution have occurred in resource-rich areas and involve intensive use of irrigation water and modern inputs such as fertilizers, pesticides, and improved seeds. These areas are by far the most productive areas, with an output several times higher than non-irrigated areas due to double or even triple cropping and higher yields per crop. However, high-yielding varieties developed for favorable conditions appear to have reached a yield plateau and irrigation has not been without problems. On the other hand, a large share of the Asian and Pacific region's growing population lives in resource-poor areas with agricultural potential but limited and unreliable rainfall as well as fragile soils. The land in these areas is often degraded and deforested. Outmigration, where possible, will only transfer poverty and population pressures to already congested urban areas and rural areas with better natural resources and is not a long-term option. Failure to stabilize agricultural and natural ecosystems within resource-poor areas will accelerate degradation of natural resources and increase poverty, food insecurity, and malnutrition.

Promoting sustainable agricultural systems in these areas is therefore the only viable way of preserving livelihoods and requires a distinct set of policies, technologies, and investments embodied in the proper cultural setting.

Yet one need not be forced into the debilitating debate between agriculturalists and environmentalists over the meaning of sustainable agriculture in high and low potential areas. In some regions, agriculturalists are justified to argue for a higher use of modern inputs. In others, a lower use of modern inputs is required and it is more appropriate to preserve traditional farming techniques suited to the local environment and the circumstances of resource-poor farmers. In other regions still, neither group is entirely correct. The key to moving the argument forward is to recast it in a region-specific and politically aware form that emphasizes the vastly different circumstances of farmers in different parts of the Asian and Pacific region. Conceiving of different agroecological zones, each with a different sustainable potential, effectively removes the somewhat artificial and recent distinction between resource-rich and resource-poor areas.

To the extent possible, agriculture must conform to the principles of (i) ecological efficiency; (ii) use of complementary technology; (iii) no unnecessary use of animals; and (iv) embodiment in a proper cultural setting. Increasingly, it is recognized that indigenous systems of food (and fiber) production are not irrelevant or detrimental to development. They can provide workable models of how to achieve sustainability and a greater measure of equality without doing irreparable damage to the environment.

According to Dahlberg (1994), transition from modern agricultural production to sustainable food systems is a critical element of sustainability. He notes that most societies are now facing global limits and the resulting collisions threaten the life-supporting capabilities of the biosphere, which in turn threatens societies. The same applies to modern agricultural production, which endangers societies mainly through linkages between fossil fuel use and global climate change; the explosion of livestock populations; loss of cultural and biological diversity; and the growth of income inequality.

To move from modern agricultural production to sustainable food systems, we need to (i) restructure and decolonize agriculture, forestry, and fisheries; (ii) maintain and enhance indigenous and traditional food systems; and (iii) build regenerative, localized food systems. To restructure and decolonize agricultural regimes, it is necessary to internalize the social and environmental costs of modern agricultural production. It is also essential to rethink the nature of trade, restructure trade regimes, and broaden the types of negotiators involved in trade policy. Other measures include changes to social frameworks, including property rights and political and tax reforms. Indigenous and traditional food systems are also reservoirs of both cultural and biological diversity. Their maintenance depends on developing a greater appreciation of their values, and finding ways to institutionalize systems approaches to agriculture and natural resources research, and to policy making. However, work on indigenous and traditional food systems is still limited and more information must be gathered about their cultural, social, economic, and ecological dimensions. Greater self-reliance must also be built at all levels. This requires a shift from economic and production criteria and, *inter alia*, a move toward bioregionalism, landscape ecology, and urban agriculture.

An Approach

There is this hope, I cannot promise you whether or when it will be realized—that the mechanistic paradigm, with all its implications in science as well as in society and our own private life, will be replaced by an organismic or systems paradigm that will offer new pathways for our presently schizophrenic and self-destructive civilization.

—Ludwig von Bertalanffy

Increasingly, planning, development and management of water resources is decentralized to an appropriate level responding to basin boundaries. Similarly, there is a need to approach rural communities at an intermediate level between farm systems approaches and the macroeconomic analysis that now considers the world as a global village. Ecoregions may be considered as systems with well-defined boundaries within which farms and other elements and their interactions take place. They should form the basis of investigations under the third Asian Agricultural Survey (AAS-III). The intention, however, should not simply be to maximize agricultural production based on ecoregional studies that explore possibilities at the regional level. This is because agroecosystems are not strictly determined by biotic or environmental agents and social factors such as a collapse in market prices or a change in land tenure can disrupt agricultural systems as decisively as drought, pest outbreak or soil erosion. The perspective of AAS-III should therefore incorporate ideas about a more environmentally and socially sensitive approach to agriculture that moves away from an agricultural commodity focus and considers agricultural systems as human artifacts.

There is a need to approach rural communities at an intermediate level between farm systems approaches and macroeconomic analysis. Agroecological regions should form the basis of investigations under AAS-III to explore options for development and present a menu of strategic decisions. Attempts to enhance the sustainability of agriculture must move beyond simply addressing production constraints and must give careful attention to the underlying causes of unsustainability. This requires an understanding of the biophysical and socioeconomic interactions from a systems perspective in each major agroecological region. These comprise (i) drylands and areas of uncertain rainfall; (ii) hill and mountain areas; (iii) humid lands; and (iv) irrigated lands.

The studies carried out under AAS-III would assess the socioeconomic importance of each agroecological region, identify the main indicators of unsustainability, formulate strategic options and propose strategic objectives. The agricultural and natural ecosystems defined by each region include (i) pastoral systems; (ii) extractive systems, e.g., forestry; and (iii) exploitative systems, e.g., irrigated agriculture and cropping on marginal lands. The strategic options formulated and the strategic objectives proposed would relate to the agricultural systems relevant to each region.

The Challenge

Your corn is ripe today; mine will be so tomorrow. 'Tis profitable for us both, that I should labor with you today, and that you should aid me tomorrow. I have no kindness for you, and know you have as little for me. I will not, therefore, take any pains upon your account; and should I labor with you upon my own account, in expectation of a return, I know I should be disappointed, and that I should in vain depend upon your gratitude. Here then I leave you to labor alone; You treat me in the same manner. The seasons change; and both of us lose our harvests for want of mutual confidence and security.

—David Hume

Based on such an approach, the challenge would be to propose in each case interventions that (i) reduce the vulnerability of the agricultural sector to adverse natural and socioeconomic factors and other risks, and strengthen self-reliance; (ii) maintain and where possible enhance the productive capacity of renewable resources, without disrupting the functioning of basic ecological cycles and natural balances, destroying the sociocultural attributes of rural communities, or polluting the environment; (iii) meet the basic nutritional requirements of rural communities qualitatively and quantitatively while providing a number of other agricultural products; and (iv) promote durable employment, sufficient income, and decent living and working conditions for all those engaged in agricultural production.

After Conway (1985), these criteria suggest that agricultural systems should be assessed on the basis of four properties: (i) productivity (measured in terms of yield or net income); (ii) stability of yield or net income; (iii) sustainability of yield or net income; and (iv) equitability in terms of income distribution. The properties are applicable in any of the four major agroecological zones and relate to the propensity of an agricultural system to withstand collapse under stress. It should be noted, however, that the four properties per se do not suggest what trade-offs should be made between characteristics when a choice is available or who should make trade-off judgments. However, an ex-ante assessment of rural conditions and trends using a cultural perspective should facilitate this exercise.

Agriculture and Natural Resources Research

It has become appallingly obvious that our technology has exceeded our humanity.

—Albert Einstein

The lessons of the Green Revolution demonstrate that technology alone cannot ensure sustainable development but also that agriculture and natural resources research has a role to play. Future research on high potential areas should be aimed at higher yields per hectare, at less cost, and in such a way as to conserve and not degrade natural resources and the environment. Such research should also take into account the socioeconomic phenomena that attend the release of new technology. Future research on areas with relatively lower potential should be aimed at higher yields per hectare, at very low cost, while making maximal use of indigenous resources, e.g., physical, biological, and human, on a sustainable basis. In addition, there is also greater scope for research that specifically focuses on poverty reduction, as well as on natural resources and environmental protection.

Poverty Reduction

A substantial segment of the Asia and Pacific region's population remains in poverty and more than half is found in the rural areas. As such, an important focus of agriculture and natural resources research needs to be on rural development. Rural development projects have often failed in the past but new research and new participatory approaches give hope that appropriate technology and methods can be found to promote successful development.

Technical change can have a positive impact on the poor and greater efforts must be exerted to harness technical change in effective ways to reduce poverty. Accordingly, an agenda for agriculture and natural resources research that addresses poverty reduction in rural environments would, for instance, include (i) examining ways to attain each region's agroclimatic potential; (ii) redesigning crops and foods consumed by the poor to improve nutrients and dietary components; (iii) focusing major efforts on subsistence farmers, where most of the gains will be retained within the family; and (iv) targeting impacts by gender to ensure maximum effectiveness. While the targeting of agriculture and natural resources research carries risks, targeted research in the past has yielded positive outcomes. Moreover, the alternative of continuing growth-oriented agriculture and natural resources research of the more traditional variety has its own risks in that there is a growing concern that the resulting growth will not bring corresponding gains in the incomes of the poor.

In such research efforts, socioeconomic issues cannot be considered secondary to technical issues, and agriculture and natural resources research for poverty reduction would also include analyzing farming and natural resource exploitation systems in their complexity. In particular, research into the multidisciplinary social dimensions of these systems, whether crops, livestock, forestry and agroforestry, or fisheries, including gender-specific organization in different systems, provides scope for poverty reduction.

Natural Resources and Environmental Protection

But the sun itself, however beneficent, generally, was less kind to Coketown than hard frost, and rarely looked intently into any of its closer regions without engendering more death than life. So does the eye of Heaven itself become an evil eye, when incapable or sordid hands are interposed between it and the thing it looks upon to bless.

—Charles Dickens

The desire for food security has left its mark on the environment, sometimes permanently. Natural assets such as agricultural land, and surface and ground waters are being degraded. Degradation includes water and wind erosion, loss of soil nutrients, salinization, acidification, pollution, compaction, water logging, and subsidence. Most of these, but not all, result from inappropriate agricultural practices. Other natural assets which contribute to food security, such as forest lands and wildlife habitats, are being lost at unprecedented rates.

Given the present state of knowledge, the supplies of energy, land, water, climate, and genetic resources are insufficient to meet present and future demands at acceptable economic and environmental costs. The implication is that meeting demands must be achieved by increasing the productivity of natural assets and rationalizing their use. This calls for a substantial increase in the body of knowledge and agriculture and natural resources research will have to focus more on technologies and practices that are less dependent on irrigation and fossil fuels and more environmentally benign than those in use at present.

Gaps in fundamental knowledge which must be filled through agriculture and natural resources research include the scale and causes of land degradation; the potential of tropical forests for renewing themselves and supporting sustainable production; the potential effect of climate change; and technologies for renewable energy. Of certain interest to the Asian and Pacific region is research for agricultural intensification to reduce the pressure on forests. For example, opportunities for maintaining productivity on deforested land and so reducing pressures for additional forest conversion include continuous crop rotation, legume-based pastures, and agroforestry.

I would rather trust a woman's instinct than a man's reason.

—Stanley Baldwin

While there have been reservations concerning the effectiveness of targeting agriculture and natural resources research to contribute to rural development, such targeting can be effective within a relatively new framework of conceptual approaches that has been working in recent years. Some of the more important principles are:

(i) *Local Communities* Competing demands for the dwindling stock of natural resources call for a careful consideration of alternative uses and appropriate economic pricing of resources. The clarification of ownership rights is often a key prerequisite for effective resource management. Accordingly, efforts should be made to use designs and technologies that acknowledge the role of local communities as the de facto owners and the only potentially effective managers of the scarce resources.

(ii) *Indigenous Technical Knowledge* Farmers possess an accumulated and mostly unwritten fund of knowledge concerning, for example, plants, soils, climate, seasons, and pests. This knowledge remains largely untapped and is largely ignored by formal research systems and conventional approaches to research. It has been ignored to the detriment of more rapid progress in solving the problems of resource-poor farmers in difficult environments. Greater recognition of indigenous technical knowledge in adaptive, farmer first, and farming systems approaches to agriculture and natural resources research should be encouraged.

(iii) *Gender and Development* Agriculture and natural resources research to develop more effective farming systems in difficult resource environments should not be undertaken without the full involvement of farmers, who are the key to the adoption of new approaches. In this context, interaction with farmers involving steps such as on-farm trials and feedback between farmers and research stations should incorporate the role, needs, and objectives of women as full partners in finding solutions for farming systems. There is a strong need to take gender into account in research policy and to encourage research initiatives to improve farming systems that incorporate the role of women.

(iv) *Market Information* There is a need to promote agriculture and natural resources research that has a sound basis relative to market needs. Incorporation of up-to-date market information can reduce the failure rate of new technologies, and enhance the efficiency of the research process.

Other Areas for Investigation

Other important areas for research and investigation include (i) new approaches to alternative agriculture in low-income countries; (ii) rapid urbanization and rural-urban linkages; (iii) challenges for sustaining the natural resource base while meeting future food demand; (iv) degradation and depletion of natural resources; (v) technological options and requirements for sustainable agriculture and rural development; (vi) indigenous and traditional food systems; (vii) bioregionalism, landscape ecology, and urban agriculture; (viii) social frameworks, including property rights and the political and tax environment; and (ix) the future of public agricultural organizations. One output from AAS-III would be the definition of strategic options for sustainable agriculture and rural development in major agroecosystems.

Fiscal Constraints, Capital Markets, and the Need for Rationalization

The role of the Bank, however, needs to be seen in the broader context of fiscal constraints in the donor countries and the rapid development of capital markets. The relatively recent expansion of capital markets means that funds are increasingly available to borrowers from sources other than the multilateral development banks. For a long time, of course, sizable bilateral assistance in the form of grants and loans has been available from the aid agencies of such countries as the United States and Japan. Because of its bilateral nature, however, such assistance has been extended according to the distinctive frameworks drawn by each donor country. Nevertheless, although bilateral assistance should not be neglected, the general ease with which private sector capital can be mobilized by borrowers is such that funds available from capital markets now dwarf multilateral development bank lending.

In the face of capital market development and the fiscal constraints associated with aid fatigue, the multilateral development banks must come to terms with the fact that the leverage they once enjoyed is rapidly decreasing and that they cannot, if they ever did, intervene across the board. In a similar vein, it goes without saying that the effectiveness of policy dialog, which has become an important Bank tool as reflected in the importance of program and sector lending in the Bank's portfolio, is directly related to the volume of the Bank's lending to any country and its relative importance.

The greatest evil that fortune can bring to men is to endow them with feeble resources and yet to make them ambitious.

—Marquis de Vauvenargues

The trends outlined above have deep implications for all the multilateral development banks. To continue to play a significant role, the Bank needs to rationalize its activities in the Asian and Pacific region. It may be trying to do too many things without the resources necessary. It has not established a recognized expertise in any particular area, though it has qualified and experienced staff in many. It must, first of all, assess those areas where it can have a truly catalytic role. This calls for reexamination of the sectors in which it is active and limitation of Bank interventions in sectors or subsectors where its activities are not crucial.

Source Author. 1996. Unpublished.

References

ADB (2000–2001) A study of rural Asia. Manila

Conway G (1985) Agroecosystem analysis. Agricultural Administration 20(1):31–55

Dahlberg K (1994) A transition from agriculture to regenerative food systems. Futures 26(2):170–179

Schafer DP (October 1994) Cultures and economies: irresistible forces encounter immovable objects. Futures 26(8):830–845

Further Reading

ADB (2010) ADB: reflections and beyond. Manila

Part II
Management Techniques

Proposition 27
Output Accomplishment and the Design and Monitoring Framework

In a Word The design and monitoring framework is a logic model for objectives-oriented planning that structures the main elements in a project, highlighting linkages between intended inputs, planned activities, and expected results.

Logic models (results frameworks) neither guarantee a good project (or program) design nor replace other instruments of project management. But they help to analyze problems; identify desired outcomes; establish a logical hierarchy of means by which the desired outcomes will be reached; identify clusters of outputs; determine how accomplishments might be monitored and evaluated, and planned and actual results compared; flag the assumptions on which a project is based and the associated risks; summarize a project in a standard format; build consensus with stakeholders; and create ownership of the project (Table 27.1).

They also support creative analysis. It is a rare project that unfolds exactly according to plan. During project implementation, one must pay close attention to the cause-and-effect relationships between inputs, activities with milestones,

© Asian Development Bank 2017
O. Serrat, *Knowledge Solutions*, DOI 10.1007/978-981-10-0983-9_27

Table 27.1 The design and monitoring framework

Design summary	Performance targets and indicators	Data sources and reporting mechanisms	Assumptions and risks
Impact: The broader impact of the project at a sectoral and national level	Measures of the extent to which the project has contributed to the impact	Sources of information and ways to gather and report it	Assumptions and risks at the impact level are beyond the control of the project but essential to attainment of the impact
Outcome: The expected outcome at the end of the project	Conditions at the end of the project indicating that its outcome has been achieved	Sources of information and ways to gather and report it	Assumptions and risks at the outcome level are those that relate to attainment of outcome targets
Outputs: The direct results of the project (works, goods, and services)	Measures of the quantity and quality of outputs and the timing of their delivery	Sources of information and ways to gather and report it	Assumptions and risks at the output level are those that are external and beyond the control of the project implementers but essential for successful attainment of the outputs
Activities with Milestones: The tasks executed to deliver the outputs identified			**Inputs**: The various resource categories required to undertake the project should be identified

Source Author

outputs, outcome, and impact. Repeatedly, one must make certain that inputs for activities are deployed successfully. Or one must adjust the means of attaining the outcome, including the definition of outputs, the mix of activities, and the indicators needed to measure accomplishment of the newly defined performance targets. Administration can become complex and it helps to have structure. Because of this, it is useful to deepen and extend typical logic models, for example, using the tool depicted below. (It lists only two targets per output). For each output, one can examine methodically whether targets are being achieved, how the activities are being implemented, and how activities might be improved. One can then itemize individual action plans, which should be monitored constantly (Table 27.2).

Systematic analysis of output accomplishment leads to telling improvements in relevance, effectiveness, efficiency, and sustainability, thereby achieving impact. It clarifies materially the chain of causality in a design and monitoring framework.

Table 27.2 Analysis of output accomplishment and improvement of activities

Output			N°
Targets			N°
			N°
Is the output being accomplished?	Yes	Partially	No
Are the targets being achieved?			
N°			
N°			
How are the activities being implemented?			
Strength	**Weakness**		
N°	N°		
N°	N°		
How can the activities be improved?			
Proposed Change	**Justification**		
N°	N°		
N°	N°		
Action plan to improve the activities			
Action	**Target date**		
N°	N°		
N°	N°		

Source Author

Further Reading

ADB (2007) Guidelines for preparing a design and monitoring framework. Manila

Proposition 28
Managing Knowledge Workers

In a Word A knowledge worker is someone who is employed because of his or her knowledge of a subject matter, rather than ability to perform manual labor. They perform best when empowered to make the most of their deepest skills.

Rationale

Assumptions about people working in organizations are less and less tenable. One misleading notion is that they are subordinate employees retained around the clock; another is that they rely on their organization for livelihood and career. One hundred years ago, in the United States and Europe, the largest single group of workers labored in agriculture. Sixty years later, it consisted of technical, professional, and managerial people. Today, it is made up of knowledge workers who may practice at an organization but might not be its employees. And, if they are in full-time employment, fewer and fewer are subordinates.

What of it? Observers make out that working habits are shifting from lifetime employment in a single organization to portfolio work. Knowledge workers produce and distribute ideas and information rather than goods or services. They are individuals with different aspirations from the hierarchy-conscious personnel of the past; they are also mobile and they do leave. Hiring talented people is difficult. Keeping them is more difficult still. So, to plug the drain of human capital in a

© Asian Development Bank 2017
O. Serrat, *Knowledge Solutions*, DOI 10.1007/978-981-10-0983-9_28

competitive knowledge economy, knowledge workers should be treated as an asset rather than as a cost. Preferably, they should be managed as though they were partners (or at least volunteers).

Managing Talent

Making knowledgeable people perform is not a matter of making them work harder or more skillfully. Naturally, they are dedicated and such interventions are beside the point. Rather, the managerial task relates to removing obstacles to performance and then channeling efforts into areas that will contribute to the accomplishment of an organization's objective. For that reason, managing talented workers for performance is best understood as a process of influence. To begin, establish a framework in terms of culture, structure, and style of management in which the talent of knowledge workers can flourish. In exercising this process, accommodate these people's preferred ways of working. The result is that knowledge workers understand, identify with, and see how their own contribution can be enhanced. They put their best abilities to the test. They challenge and achieve. To build such a framework,

- Recognize outstanding talent wherever it is found.
- Establish clear task objectives and performance standards in consultation with each knowledge worker.
- Extend incentives, rewards, and reinforcements that meet the motivational patterns of each knowledge worker.
- Provide opportunities for improvement.

As organizations redesign in the knowledge economy, they will have to quickly address the elemental issue of motivation. Consider the major rewards typically provided to workers for effort (irrespective of the type of worker). Wages, for instance, cannot be consumed at work. Fringe benefits (such as leave, health and medical insurance, pay for overtime, or proceeds from stock purchase plans) yield satisfaction only when workers leave the organization. And, sadly, promotion often means little more than a bigger office, a resounding title, or a special parking place. Is it surprising then that so many workers perceive their job to be a form of punishment? The field of motivation is still wide open: but the organizations that thrive will have (more appetizing) menus of benefit options from which knowledge workers can choose.

… With Knowledge Managers

Certainly, knowledge workers require knowledge managers, not bosses. These new-era managers need to set and enforce on themselves exacting standards for their performance of those functions that determine ability to perform. Time and again, traditional managers exercise no leadership at all but only position power. Many reach the top by being tough and self-affirmative or by being the kind of person that others feel safe in following or promoting. Yet managing knowledge workers requires that managers themselves act as good follower and team player as well as leader and technologist. Since the process of influencing the performance of knowledge workers is mainly developmental, they need also to hone skills in appraising, coaching, mentoring, and providing feedback. One measure of their effectiveness will be by the quality of the (internal and external) relationships that they create.

The knowledge economy is pruning status, power, and upward mobility from the managerial role. From now on, would-be new-era managers will be asked to reply convincingly to a simple question: Why should a knowledge worker want to be managed by you?

Proposition 29
Focusing on Project Metrics

In a Word The need to ensure that scarce funding is applied to effective projects is a goal shared by all. Focusing on common parameters of project performance is a means to that end.

Six parameters are always given weight in methodologies for project management. They are:

- Time
- Cost
- Human Resources
- Scope
- Quality
- Actions

By gauging performance against these parameters, an image of the parts of a project that are in order and of those that are not can be formed. Is the activity on schedule? Is the activity within budget? How many human resources are being expended? Is the activity's scope in line with original expectations? Is project personnel analyzing and fixing problems with quality actions? Are actions outstanding? If all lights are green, performance will be highly satisfactory in all areas. If one or more are orange, the activity will have one or more potential problems. A red light will signal a parameter that requires urgent attention.

© Asian Development Bank 2017
O. Serrat, *Knowledge Solutions*, DOI 10.1007/978-981-10-0983-9_29

Based on project documents, such as the design and monitoring framework, indicative activities schedule, and cost tables, as well as participatory mechanisms, review missions can assess the attainment of (usually quantified) benchmarks for each parameter by means of project metrics using the activity dashboard depicted in the above figure.

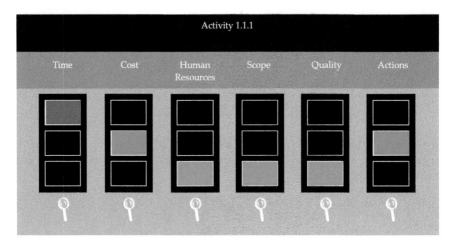

Fig. Activity dashboard. *Source* Author

Proposition 30
Notions of Knowledge Management

In a Word Knowledge management is getting the right knowledge to the right people at the right time, and helping them (with incentives) to apply it in ways that strive to improve organizational performance.

What Is Knowledge?

Data are facts, and information is interpreted data. Knowledge is created and organized by flows of information, shaped by their holder. It is tacit or explicit. Tacit knowledge is nonverbalized, intuitive, and unarticulated knowledge that people carry in their heads. It is hard to formalize and communicate because it is rooted in skills, experiences, insight, intuition, and judgment, but it can be shared in discussion, storytelling, and personal interactions. It has a technical dimension, which encompasses skills and capabilities referred to as know-how. It has a cognitive dimension, which consists of beliefs, ideals, values, schemata, or mental models. Explicit knowledge is codified knowledge that can be expressed in writing,

© Asian Development Bank 2017

O. Serrat, *Knowledge Solutions*, DOI 10.1007/978-981-10-0983-9_30

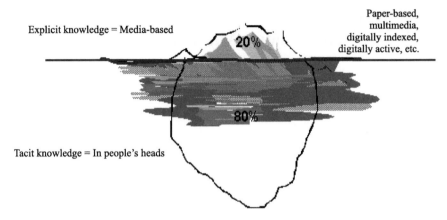

Fig. 30.1 Knowledge assets. *Source* Author

drawings, or computer programs, for example, and transmitted in various forms. Tacit knowledge and explicit knowledge are mutually complementary forms of meaning. Figure 30.1 exemplifies the iceberg metaphor used to describe the hidden nature of tacit knowledge.

Model of Learning Progression

Forms of meaning such as data and information are more rudimentary than knowledge. Knowledge is more rudimentary than wisdom. Data and information are associated with forms of knowing that are specific and limited. Knowledge is systemic and integrates reason, values, intellect, and intuition. The typical model of learning progression locates knowledge in relation to other forms of meaning. Figure 30.2 describes stages in human learning.

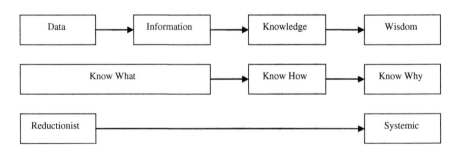

Fig. 30.2 Model of learning progression. *Source* Author

Knowledge Agents

Most models of knowledge management assume four agents of knowledge, namely the individual, the group, the organization, and the inter-organizational domain. They view knowledge and its creation as a spiral process from the individual to the group, the organization, and sometimes the inter-organizational domain. Figure 30.3 shows that each agent holds distinct forms of knowledge and performs work that the others cannot. Figure 30.4 reveals how knowledge is generated by interplay.

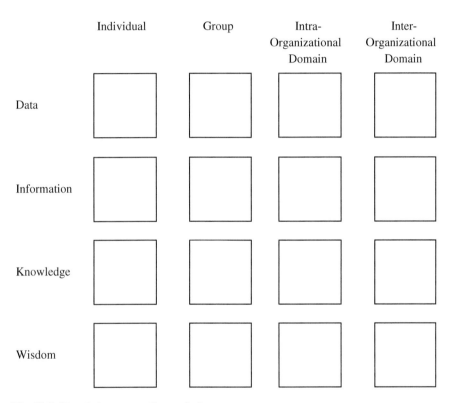

Fig. 30.3 Knowledge agents. *Source* Author

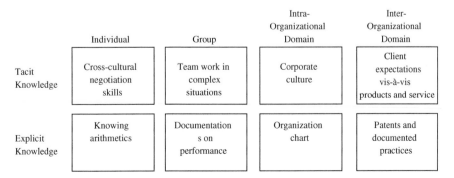

	Individual	Group	Intra-Organizational Domain	Inter-Organizational Domain
Tacit Knowledge	Cross-cultural negotiation skills	Team work in complex situations	Corporate culture	Client expectations vis-à-vis products and service
Explicit Knowledge	Knowing arithmetics	Documentations on performance	Organization chart	Patents and documented practices

Fig. 30.4 Knowledge management model. *Source* Author

Modes of Knowledge Creation

In large organizations, knowledge is created through continuous dialogue on tacit and explicit knowledge via four patterns of interactions: (i) socialization, (ii) externalization, (iii) combination, and (iv) internalization.

Figure 30.5 frames the process of knowledge creation. Socialization is the process of creating common tacit knowledge through interactions including observation, imitation, or apprenticeships. Externalization is the process of articulating tacit knowledge into explicit knowledge by means of metaphors, analogies, or sketches. Combination is the process of assembling new and existing explicit knowledge into systemic knowledge such as a set of specifications for the prototype of a new product. Combination involves combining explicit knowledge through meetings and conversations or using information systems. Internalization converts explicit knowledge into tacit knowledge. Externalization converts tacit knowledge into explicit knowledge.

There are five conditions to encouraging the process of knowledge creation: (i) intention, (ii) autonomy, (iii) creative chaos, (iv) redundancy, and (v) requisite variety. Managers must be committed to accumulating, exploiting, and renewing the knowledge base within the organization and be able to create management systems that will facilitate the process. New ideas usually develop at the individual level, rather than at the group or organization levels, and the individuals generating it must be given scope to follow their initiatives. This process of exploration can be encouraged by creative chaos, where flux and crisis cause people to reconsider precepts at a fundamental level. Incentives can then be given to exchange knowledge rather than ration or hoard it. The organization should be made to be conducive to this.

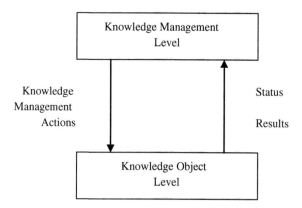

Fig. 30.5 Levels in knowledge management. *Source* Author

Knowledge Management Levels

Management implies a set of activities directed at an object. Figure 30.5 defines two aspects of knowledge management: a knowledge management level dealing with a knowledge object level.

If knowledge is an organizational asset, as resource-based views of organizations suggest, its management will need to live up to objectives that are common to all resources. Typically, these objectives endeavor to make sure that the resource is (i) delivered at the right time, (ii) available at the right place, (iii) present in the right shape, (iv) obtained at the lowest possible cost, and (v) of the required quality. Apart from the question of how to achieve this, it must be understood that knowledge does have properties that set it apart from other resources. It is intangible and difficult to measure, volatile, and embodied in agents with wills. It is not consumed in a process; conversely, it can increase with use. It cannot always be bought on the market; on the contrary, its development can require lead time. It is nonrival in that it can be used by different processes simultaneously. And, its use can have wide-ranging impacts.

Knowledge Management Architecture

The architecture of knowledge management must be strengthened in support of organization-wide initiatives. Stankosky (2000) has identified its four pillars to be leadership, organization, technology, and learning. Figure 30.6 exemplifies the need to seek balanced interconnectivity.

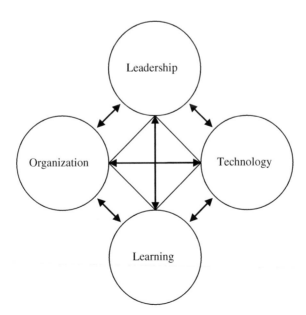

Fig. 30.6 Balanced knowledge management. *Source* Author

Leadership

Leadership develops the strategies necessary to position for success in an environment. Those strategies determine vision and must align knowledge management with business tactics to drive the values of knowledge management throughout the organization. Focus must be placed on building executive support. Successful implementation of a knowledge management strategy requires champions at or near the top of an organization.

Organization

Respect for knowledge must pervade an organization. Introducing knowledge management requires organizational change, and knowledge management inevitably acts as a catalyst to transform the organization's culture. The increasing value placed on capable people, rising job complexity, and the universal availability of information on the Internet are fundamental changes contributing to attempts to leverage knowledge management solutions. To begin to change an organization, knowledge management must be integrated into business processes and connected to changes in organizational culture.

Technology

Knowledge management tools are essential to achieving knowledge management strategies. However, any technical solution must add value to the process and achieve measurable improvements. Properly assessing and defining information technology capabilities is essential, as is identifying and deploying best-of-breed knowledge management tools to match and align with the organization's requirements. Ten processes that must be built collectively make up full-function knowledge management: (i) capture and store, (ii) search and retrieve, (iii) send critical information to individuals or groups, (iv) structure and navigate, (v) share and collaborate, (vi) synthesize, (vii) profile and personalize, (viii) solve or recommend, (ix) integrate, and (x) maintain.

Learning

People are responsible for using knowledge management tools in support of organizational performance. Organizational learning must be addressed with approaches such as increasing internal communications, promoting cross-functional teams, and creating a learning community. Learning is an integral part of knowledge management. In this context, learning can be described as the acquisition of knowledge or a skill through study, experience, or instruction. Organizations must recognize that people operate and communicate through learning that includes the social processes of collaborating, sharing knowledge, and building on each other's ideas. Managers must recognize that knowledge resides in people and that knowledge creation occurs through the process of social interaction.

Core Knowledge Activities

Knowledge management activities can be described in relation to many different disciplines and approaches but almost all focus on five basic activities: (i) identify, (ii) create, (iii) store, (iv) share, and (v) use. Figure 30.7 interprets the routine associated with core knowledge activities.

Knowledge Management Activities

Treating knowledge as a resource opens up promising opportunities for knowledge management activities. These can be split into four categories, each impacting a particular time segment of the knowledge management cycle. They relate to (i) reviewing, (ii) conceptualizing, (iii) reflecting, and (iv) acting.

Reviewing involves checking what has been achieved in the past and what the current state of affairs is. Conceptualizing entails sitting back, trying to grasp the state of knowledge in the organization, and analyzing the strong and weak points of

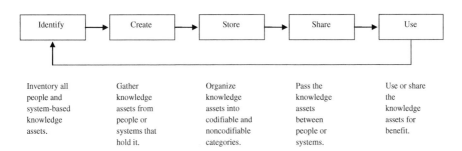

Fig. 30.7 Core knowledge activities. *Source* Author

its knowledge architecture. Reflecting calls for directing toward improvements by selecting the optimal plans for correcting bottlenecks and analyzing them for risks that might accompany their implementation. Acting is the actual effectuation of the plans selected.

Most of the time, the actions will be one or a combination of generic operations that involve (i) developing knowledge, i.e., buying knowledge, establishing learning programs; (ii) distributing knowledge, i.e., channeling knowledge to the points of action, preparing manuals, connecting networks; (iii) combining knowledge, i.e., finding synergies, reusing existing knowledge; and (iv) consolidating knowledge, i.e., preventing knowledge from disappearing, instituting tutoring programs, establishing knowledge transfer programs.

Cultural Roadblocks to Knowledge Management Success

Culture has been characterized as the glue that holds organizations together. It can, for instance, be a critical success factor in the execution of strategy. It can play a crucial role in determining the success or failure of operations. At the micro level, there are close relationships between organizational culture, employee satisfaction, and job commitment and turnover. As one might expect, organizational culture plays a pivotal role in knowledge management.

Organizational culture is shaped by many factors, some of which can be changed while others are intractable. Organizations adapt to their external environments by designing responsive structures and systems, adopting relevant technologies, and harvesting appropriate skills and qualities. Though constrained by their external environments, organizations make choices that, collectively, eventually define their cultures. These choices are influenced by the mission, values, and norms of each organization and the assumptions of its leaders. In due course, the choices will also define the success or failure of knowledge management initiatives. Thus, knowledge is inextricably bound to human cognition, and its management will occur within a structured psychological and social context. Figure 30.8 juxtaposes the psychological and social barriers that impact knowledge sharing.

Fig. 30.8 Barriers affecting knowledge sharing. *Source* Author

Psychological Factors

Knowledge represents a source of power to people. By sharing valuable knowledge with a colleague, one runs the risk of diminishing one's value in an organization; potentially, one is no longer indispensable. There are three conditions under which, as an employee, one will share knowledge: (i) reciprocity, (ii) repute, and (iii) altruism. One's time and energy are finite and one will more often than not take the time to help a colleague if one is likely to receive valuable knowledge in return, either now or in the future. In addition, it is in one's interest to be viewed as an expert in an organization; if one does not have a reputation for expertise, one's knowledge cannot represent a source of power. Likewise, before sharing, one needs to be certain that colleagues will acknowledge the source of knowledge and will not claim credit for it. But, in a process akin to self-gratification, there is also the need to talk to others about subjects that one finds fascinating and important.

Following resource-based views of organizations, which identify knowledge as potentially the primary source of sustainable competitive advantage, one can imagine that there are internal markets for knowledge within organizations. Knowledge is exchanged between buyers and sellers, with reciprocity, repute, and altruism functioning as payment mechanisms. Trust, however, is an essential condition to the smooth functioning of such a market. This trust can exist at an individual level, through close working relationships between colleagues, or at group and organization levels, by the creation of a cultural context that encourages and rewards knowledge sharing and discourages and penalizes knowledge hoarding.

Social Factors

Organizational culture, and the social networks that frame it, is the most frequently cited roadblock to knowledge management success. Based on understanding of psychological factors, the onus is on leadership to drive people-focused knowledge management and move from old to new knowledge management paradigms. People are more likely to understand and energetically support an initiative when they observe leadership behavior that is both credible and supportive. Box 1 summarizes the differences between what may be termed industrial and knowledge cultures.

Box 1: Industrial and Knowledge Culture Paradigms

<table>
<tr><td>

Industrial Culture

- Limited information distribution
- Many management levels
- Uneven responsibility
- Rules based
- Structured
- Risk averse
- Inward orientation
- Occasional training
- Financial focus
- Political

</td><td>

Knowledge Culture

- Wide information distribution
- Few management levels
- Shared responsibility
- Principles based
- Unstructured
- Able to take some risks
- Outward orientation
- Continuous learning
- Marketing focus
- Open

</td></tr>
</table>

Source Author

Table. Organization and culture

	Feudal culture	Industrial culture	Knowledge culture	Creativity culture
Organization	Territorial	Hierarchies	Networks	Flows
Focus	Land	Profit	Customer	Innovation
Culture	Domination Control	Control Responsibility	Responsibility Contribution	Contribution Creativity
Key measure	Quantity	Efficiency	Effectiveness	Quality of Life

Source Author

The above table makes observations on organization and culture, and suggests what might lie a little beyond the knowledge culture. One may appreciate that (i) cultures are not static (there is movement from left to right); (ii) individuals who are absorbed in a particular culture tend to find the culture to the right a little meaningless and the culture to the left almost valueless; (iii) transition from one culture to another is not smooth; and (iv) the concepts of control, responsibility, and contribution provide interesting analytical links between cultures.

Assessing the Behavior-Performance Continuum

Within any organization there may also be a variety of cultures—shaped by characteristic differences in professional orientation, status, power, visibility, and other factors. Understanding these cultures in terms of their expected behaviors helps to appreciate why organizational units can exhibit behaviors that are opposite to the organization's expressed mission, values, and norms. At a more pressing level, behaviors can also temper what cooperation is displayed in a group. Thus, cultures create behaviors, some of which can result in obstructive (or at least nonconstructive) interactions that limit knowledge sharing and, in the fullness of time, hold back knowledge management. Assessing the behavior-performance continuum of key stakeholders in knowledge management initiatives will spell the difference between success or failure. It transcends the notion of knowledge flows that is fundamental to knowledge management initiatives and has deep implications for fostering ownership among those involved in associated efforts.

Early Pathways to Progress

Figure 30.9 poses simple questions to locate an organization's progress toward knowledge management. Box 2 highlights early pathways to progress.

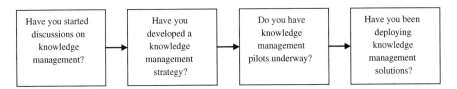

Fig. 30.9 Where are you in the journey? *Source* Author

Box 2: Early Signposts to Knowledge Management

- Knowledge products and services are strategic and must be accounted for and valued accordingly
- Knowledge management requires integration and balancing of leadership, organization, technology, and learning in an organization-wide setting
- Knowledge management requires integration and balancing of leadership, organization, technology, and learning in an organization-wide setting
- Knowledge management must both meet the requirements of and conditions for success and the desired benefits and expectations of the organization
- Organizational culture affects knowledge management, especially at the lower levels
- Streamlined organizations with strong organizational cultures have a higher chance of success in knowledge management
- An atmosphere of trust is a precondition to knowledge sharing
- Proposals for knowledge management should include both soft and hard measures if managers are to support knowledge management initiatives

- The success factors for knowledge management are dominated by management concerns for people, process, and outcome orientation. They are interspersed throughout the knowledge management architecture of leadership, organization, technology, and learning.

Source Author

Getting Results from Knowledge Management

First and foremost, knowledge management is about results. Figure 30.2 described the typical model of learning progression under which data are analyzed to generate information, information is placed in context to produce knowledge, and evaluated knowledge begets wisdom (or informed actions). However, there are limits to looking upstream and concentrating on the supply of knowledge. It can result in the creation of unfocused data and information whereby strategy is blindly driven by technology. It is also helpful to examine the desired results and deduce what knowledge will be required to accomplish them. Figure 30.10 demonstrates how awareness of the stages in human learning can be exercised to imbed the relationships between forms of meaning to focus on results. It reinforces the idea that knowledge management is primarily a matter of people, process, and outcome orientation.

Building Commitment

As part of an approach to managing change programs, it is helpful to observe the stages that people live through before committing to a new way of working. From simple awareness, they must first hear, then understand the change. Based on the actions of leaders and peers, they then opt to support the change and can be seen to

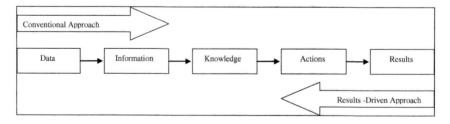

Fig. 30.10 A results-driven knowledge management model. *Source* Author

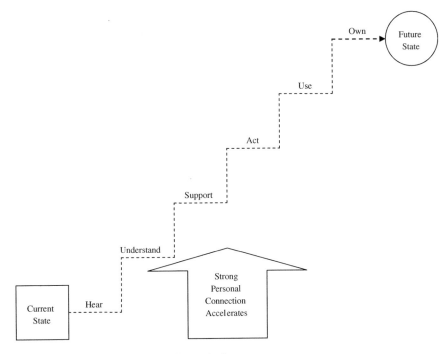

Fig. 30.11 Committing to change. *Source* Author

act in the desired manner. Commitment is built when they use the new way of working in regular activities and finally own the change in their environment. At every stage, commitment is fragile and invokes active sponsorship from leaders. Figure 30.11 illustrates the process of committing to change.

Reference

Stankosky M (2000) A theoretical framework. KM World, Special Millennium Issue

Further Reading

ADB (2007) Learning lessons in ADB. Manila
ADB (2008) Auditing the lessons architecture. Manila

Proposition 31
The Reframing Matrix

In a Word Everyone sees things differently—knowledge often lies in the eye of the beholder. The reframing matrix enables different perspectives to be generated and used in management processes. It expands the number of options for solving a problem.

Rationale

Perspective is a mental view, an ingrained way of perceiving the world. Different people have different experiences and see in different ways: understanding how they do expand the range of solutions that one might devise to address a question or problem.

Definition

The reframing matrix is a simple technique that helps examine problems from distinct viewpoints. In other words, individuals or groups place themselves in the mindsets of different people and imagine what solutions the latter might come up with. The reframing matrix was devised by Morgan (1993).

© Asian Development Bank 2017
O. Serrat, *Knowledge Solutions*, DOI 10.1007/978-981-10-0983-9_31

Process

The reframing matrix lays a question (or problem) in the middle of a four-box grid.
It is then examined from four typical business perspectives:

- **Program Perspective** Are there issues with the program (or product or service)
  we are delivering?
- **Planning Perspective** Is the business (or communications plan) appropriate?
- **Potential Perspective** Is the program replicable? Can it be scale up?
- **People Perspective** What do the people involved think?

Then again, the four-box grid can be used to consider a question (or problem) from
the perspectives of different groups of stakeholders, e.g., staff, clients, suppliers, and
partners, or specialists, e.g., engineers, lawyers, economists, or information technology specialists. How would each stakeholder perceive the question (or problem)?
What would each stakeholder see as benefits and drawbacks? What might each
stakeholder see as potential benefits and drawbacks? What solutions might each
stakeholder offer? How relevant is each stakeholder to the situation at hand?

Reference

Morgan M (1993) Creating workforce innovation: turning individual into organizational
    innovation. Allen & Unwin

Proposition 32
The Five Whys Technique

In a Word When confronted with a problem, have you ever stopped and asked "why" five times? The Five Whys technique is a simple but powerful way to troubleshoot problems by exploring cause-and-effect relationships.

Rationale

For every effect there is a cause. But the results chain between the two is fairly long and becomes finer as one moves from inputs to activities, outputs, outcome, and impact.[1] In results-based management,[2] the degree of control one enjoys decreases

---

[1]Inputs, activities, and outputs are within the direct control of an intervention's management. An outcome is what an intervention can be expected to achieve and be accountable for. An impact is what an intervention is expected to contribute to.

[2]Results-based management is a life-cycle management philosophy and approach that emphasizes results in integrated planning, implementing, monitoring, reporting, learning, and changing. Demonstrating results is important for credibility, accountability, and continuous learning, and to inform decision-making and resource allocation.

© Asian Development Bank 2017
O. Serrat, *Knowledge Solutions*, DOI 10.1007/978-981-10-0983-9_32

higher up the chain and the challenge of monitoring and evaluating correspondingly increases.

In due course, when a problem appears, the temptation is strong to blame others or external events. Yet, the root cause of problems often lies closer to home.

For Want of a Nail

For want of a nail the shoe is lost;
For want of a shoe the horse is lost;
For want of a horse the rider is lost;
For want of a rider the battle is lost;
For want of a battle the kingdom is lost;
And all for the want of a horseshoe nail.

—George Herbert

The Five Whys Technique

When looking to solve a problem, it helps to begin at the end result, reflect on what caused that, and question the answer five times.[3] This elementary and often effective approach to problem solving promotes deep thinking through questioning, and can be adapted quickly and applied to most problems.[4] Most obviously and directly, the Five Whys technique relates to the principle of systematic problem-solving: without the intent of the principle, the technique can only be a shell of the process. Hence, there are three key elements to effective use of the Five Whys technique: (i) accurate and complete statements of problems,[5] (ii) complete honesty in answering the questions, (iii) the determination to get to the bottom of problems and resolve them. The technique was developed by Sakichi Toyoda for the Toyota Industries Corporation.

---

[3]Five is a good rule of thumb. By asking "why" five times, one can usually peel away the layers of symptoms that hide the cause of a problem. But one may also find one needs to ask "why" fewer times, or conversely more.

[4]Root cause analysis is the generic name of problem-solving techniques. The basic elements of root causes are materials, equipment, the man-made or natural environment, information, measurement, methods and procedures, people, management, and management systems. Other tools can be used if the Five Whys technique does not intuitively direct attention to one of these. They include barrier analysis, change analysis, causal factor tree analysis, and the Ishikawa (or fishbone) diagram.

[5]By repeating "why" five times, the nature of the problem as well as its solution becomes clear.

Process

The Five-Whys exercise is vastly improved when applied by a team and there are five basic steps to conducting it:

- Gather a team and develop the problem statement in agreement. After this is done, decide whether or not additional individuals are needed to resolve the problem.
- Ask the first "why" of the team: why is this or that problem taking place? There will probably be three or four sensible answers: record them all on a flip chart or whiteboard, or use index cards taped to a wall.
- Ask four more successive "whys," repeating the process for every statement on the flip chart, whiteboard, or index cards. Post each answer near its "parent". Follow up on all plausible answers. You will have identified the root cause when asking "why" yields no further useful information. (If necessary, continue to ask questions beyond the arbitrary five layers to get to the root cause.)
- Among the dozen or so answers to the last asked "why" look for systemic causes of the problem. Discuss these and settle on the most likely systemic cause. Follow the team session with a debriefing and show the product to others to confirm that they see logic in the analysis.
- After settling on the most probable root cause of the problem and obtaining confirmation of the logic behind the analysis, develop appropriate corrective actions to remove the root cause from the system. The actions can (as the case demands) be undertaken by others but planning and implementation will benefit from team inputs.

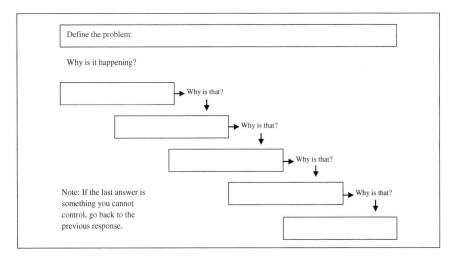

Fig. Five whys worksheet. *Source* Author

Caveat

The Five Whys technique has been criticized as too basic a tool to analyze root causes to the depth required to ensure that the causes are fixed. The reasons for this criticism include:

- The tendency of investigators to stop at symptoms, and not proceed to lower level root causes.
- The inability of investigators to cast their minds beyond current information and knowledge.
- Lack of facilitation and support to help investigators ask the right questions.
- The low repeat rate of results: different teams using the Five Whys technique have been known to come up with different causes for the same problem.

Clearly, the Five Whys technique will suffer if it is applied through deduction only. The process articulated earlier encourages on-the-spot verification of answers to the current "why" question before proceeding to the next, and should help avoid such issues.

Further Reading

ADB (2007) Guidelines for preparing a design and monitoring framework. Manila

Proposition 33
The SCAMPER Technique

In a Word Ideas are not often plucked out of thin air. The SCAMPER brainstorming technique uses a set of directed questions to resolve a problem (or meet an opportunity). It can also turn a tired idea into something new and different.

Rationale

A problem is a situation, condition, or issue that remains unresolved and makes it difficult to accomplish a desired objective. A problem is perceived when an individual, group, or organization becomes aware of a significant difference between what is desired and what actually is. Trying to find a solution to a problem is known as problem solving.

Problem solving is the process by which a situation is analyzed, a workable solution is determined, and corrective action is taken. The common milestones of problem solving are to:

- Define (or clarify) the problem.
- Analyze causes.
- Generate ideas (identify alternatives).
- Weigh up ideas (assess alternatives).

© Asian Development Bank 2017

O. Serrat, *Knowledge Solutions*, DOI 10.1007/978-981-10-0983-9_33

- Make a decision (select an alternative).
- Determine next steps to implement the solution.
- Evaluate whether the problem was solved or not.

The SCAMPER Technique

Every problem invites a solution and, needless to say, there are numerous problem-solving techniques.[1] The SCAMPER technique, for one, uses a set of directed, idea-spurring questions to suggest some addition to, or modification of, something that already exists.[2] It has also received much attention as a learning tool that fosters awareness, drive, fluency, flexibility, and originality. The stimulus comes from being asked to answer queries that one would not normally pose. The changes that SCAMPER stands for are:

- S—Substitute (e.g., components, materials, people)
- C—Combine (e.g., mix, combine with other assemblies or services, integrate)
- A—Adapt (e.g., alter, change function, use part of another element)
- M—Magnify/Modify (e.g., increase or reduce in scale, change shape, modify attributes)
- P—Put to other uses
- E—Eliminate (e.g., remove elements, simplify, reduce to core functionality)
- R—Rearrange/Reverse (e.g., turn inside out or upside down)

---

[1]They include Affinity Diagrams (organizing ideas into common themes); the Ansoff Matrix (understanding the different risks of different options); Appreciation (extracting maximum information from facts); Appreciative Inquiry (solving problems by looking at what is going right); the Boston Matrix (focusing effort to give the greatest returns); Brainstorming (generating a large number of ideas for the solution of a problem); Cause-and-Effect Diagrams (identifying the possible causes of problems); Core Competence Analysis (get ahead, stay ahead); Critical Success Factors (identifying the things that really matter for success); the Five Whys Technique (quickly getting to the root of a problem); Flow Charts (understanding how a process works); The Greiner Curve (surviving the crises that come with growth); Lateral Thinking (changing concepts and perception); the Marketing Mix and the 4 Ps (understanding how to position a market offering); the McKinsey 7Ss (making sure that all the parts of an organization work in harmony); PEST (Political, Economic, Sociocultural, and Technological) Analysis (understanding the big picture); Porter's Five Forces (understanding where power lies); the Reframing Matrix (examining problems from distinct viewpoints); Risk Analysis; Systems Diagrams (understanding the way factors affect one another); Root Cause Analysis (identifying the root causes of problems or events); SWOT Analysis (analyzing strengths, weaknesses, opportunities, and threats); and USP (Unique Selling Propositions) Analysis (crafting competitive edge).

[2]The principles of the SCAMPER technique were first formally suggested by Alex Osborn and later arranged by Bob Eberle as a mnemonic in 1991 to increase interest in the perceptive, imaginative, and creative abilities of children.

Table 33.1 Help guide to the SCAMPER technique

Substitute	Think about substituting part of the product or process for something else.
	Typical questions: What else instead? Who else instead? What other materials, ingredients, processes, power, sounds, approaches, or forces might I substitute? Which other place?
Combine	Think about combining two or more parts of the product or process to make something new or to enhance synergy.
	Typical questions: What mix, assortment, alloy, or ensemble might I blend? What ideas, purposes, units, or appeals might I combine?
Adapt	Think about which parts of the product or process could be adapted or how you might change the nature of the product or process.
	Typical questions: Does the past offer a parallel? What else is like this? What other idea does this suggest? What might I adapt for use as a solution? What might I copy? Who might I emulate?
Magnify, Modify	Think about changing part or all of the product or process, or distorting it in an unusual way.
	Typical questions: What other meaning, color, motion, sound, smell, form, or shape might I adopt? What might I add?
Put to Other Uses	Think of how you might put the product or process to another use or how you might reuse something from somewhere else.
	Typical questions: What new ways are there to use this? Might this be used in other places? Which other people might I reach? To what other uses might this be put if it is modified?
Eliminate	Think of what might happen if you eliminated parts of the product or process and consider what you might do in that situation.
	Typical questions: What might I understate? What might I eliminate? What might I streamline? What might I make smaller, lower, shorter, or lighter?
Rearrange, Reverse	Think of what you might do if parts of the product or process worked in reverse or were sequenced differently.
	Typical questions: What might be rearranged? What other pattern, layout, or sequence might I adopt? Can components be interchanged? Should I change pace or schedule? Can positives and negatives be swapped? Could roles be reversed?

Litemind's (2015) blog on *Creative Problem Solving with SCAMPER* suggests more than 60 questions that can be asked, along with almost 200 words and expressions one can create associations with
Source Author

Caveat

The SCAMPER Technique is used to produce original ideas. The creative process thrives on preparation, concentration, incubation, illumination, and verification (production testing). In organizations, its fruitful application depends on the existence of an enabling environment. There are, of course, personal blocks[3] to creativity but these can often be removed. Supervisors who do foster creativity listen, are willing to absorb the risks borne by their subordinates, are comfortable with half-developed ideas, do not dwell on past mistakes, expect subordinates to succeed, capitalize on the strengths of subordinates, enjoy their jobs, and can make quick decisions. They must then help sell ideas to senior management. This involves assessing the "sellability" of ideas[4] and developing persuasive arguments.[5]

Reference

Litemind (2015) Creative problem solving with SCAMPER

---

[3]I do not want to look foolish. I do not want to fail. I am not creative. This is not my area (e.g., skill, style, job, etc.). I am not paid to have fun!.

[4]Will the idea work? Will people accept it? Is it timely?

[5]This requires that the proponents relate the idea to a recognized need, appeal to positive values, anticipate objections, get others involved, and advertise their credibility.

Proposition 34
Conducting Effective Meetings

In a Word Meetings bring people together to discuss a predetermined topic. However, too many are poorly planned and managed, and therefore fail to satisfy objectives when they do not simply waste time. The operating expenses of time wasted include related meeting expenditures, salaries, and opportunity costs.

Rationale

When did you last join a work-related meeting[1] that was productive and fun from beginning to end? That is, a meeting that had lucid objectives[2] and a well-designed agenda; engaged all participants all the time; made them laugh; reached decisions; clarified follow-up actions; and secured commitment to achieve expected, positive, and constructive outcomes? Can you remember?

---

[1]This issue focuses only on programmed meetings of more than two persons.
[2]Possible aims might be to engage in joint consultation, develop support for action, and resolve problems.

© Asian Development Bank 2017
O. Serrat, *Knowledge Solutions*, DOI 10.1007/978-981-10-0983-9_34

Managing Meetings

Meetings are essential in any form of human enterprise. These days, they are so common that turning the resources they tie up into sustained results is a priority in high-performance organizations. This is because they are potential wasters: the other persons present may not respect their own time as much as you have come to respect yours, and it is therefore unlikely that they will mind wasting your time.[3] Generic actions before, during, and after can make meetings more effective.

Table. Generic tips for meeting management

Before	During	After
Make sure you need a meeting by asking what would happen if it were not held	Arrange skilled facilitation to smooth the process of the meeting and deal with conflict, start on schedule, and manage time to keep the meeting focused and moving	Publish within 24 hours, but preferably within the same working day, concise and definite minutes that record the items discussed, the decisions of the meeting, the actions agreed, and the owners of these. In some cases, the minutes may include the main arguments or steps leading to the decisions
Develop (and pre-publish) a strategic agenda (and related papers) with easily understood objectives listed in order of importance, articulate the process to reach these, and plan the meeting and its ground rules	Introduce the topics for discussion, use the prework delivered for the meeting, and keep debates relevant to the stated objectives	Arrange effective meeting follow-up, i.e., who will do what by when
Ensure appropriate participation at the meeting, with attention to good decision-makers and problem-solvers, for a maximum of 12 persons but if possible fewer	Ensure everyone's thoughts and ideas are heard to keep them interested and empowered, use humor to alleviate tension, gain consensus, and involve each participant in actions toward explicit outcomes	Agree on accountability for preparations toward the next meeting if one is necessary

(continued)

---

[3]Time is a precious asset. (Charles Darwin held that a man who dares to waste 1 hour has not discovered the value of life.) Therefore, it is important to develop a personal sense of time, both to save and spend it wisely. In organizations, the activities that consume time include committees, working groups, and taskforces; interviews; discussions; learning and development; telephone conversations; typing; reading; inspecting; traveling; and thinking. It is illuminating to keep a time log and find what a comparatively small percentage of one's time is actually absorbed by the top-priority tasks on one's "to-do" list.

(continued)

Before	During	After
Plan, assign, and distribute prework before the meeting	Recognize degrees of feelings and changes of opinion, check for quorum, summarize key points of agreement and disagreement, explain rulings, check understanding and acceptance, create an effective follow-up plan, state responsibilities, gain commitment, and close the meeting on time (or even before time) on a positive note and with a sense of gathering	Evaluate the meeting process for continuous improvement, for example regarding ground rules, timing and scheduling, agendas, and the drafting of minutes

Note Before calling a meeting, one should consider whether the matter might not be dealt better by telephone, electronic mail, or talks with individuals. Often, 10 min spent with six persons individually are more productive than gathering them in a room for 1 hour. If a meeting is to be held, the objectives should be clear, specific, measurable, attainable, realistic, and time-bound. Preferably, they should also be agreed, challenging, consistent, worthwhile, and participative. Time-honored rules are to raise hands (stay in order) except for points of clarification or process; refrain from interrupting the speaker; keep to the subject; be concise (and avoid repeating others); and be respectful and polite. These days, electronics are to be put on silent mode and no telephone calls are allowed unless one steps out. "Parking lots," i.e., posts on a wall, can be used for issues not on the agenda
Source Author

When I give a lecture, I accept that people look at their watches, but what I do not tolerate is when they look at it and raise it to their ear to find out if it stopped.

—Marcel Achard

He who knows most grieves most for wasted time.

—Dante

Success depends upon previous preparation, and without such preparation there is sure to be failure.

—Confucius

When the outcome of a meeting is to have another meeting, it has been a lousy meeting.

—Herbert Hoover

Time is the scarcest resource; and unless it is managed, nothing else can be managed.

—Peter Drucker

The Chairperson's Role

A good chairperson is essential to the conduct of effective meetings. In any order, expectations are that the chairperson will stimulate and inspire (not dictate), have the right answers, make decisions, and get things done. But what exactly are those skills and qualities that make someone a good chairperson? He or she must be authoritative yet flexible; impartial and impersonal; a quick thinker and an attentive listener; capable of succinct expression; ready to clarify views that have not been well expressed; mature and tolerant; equipped to handle disruption and inappropriate behavior; and courteous, but brisk and business-like. Humor can be a useful tool, if only to calm rising tempers. To manage difficult meetings, an essential characteristic of a good chairperson must surely be "helicopter vision".[4]

Different Kinds of Meetings

To practice with effect the generic tips for meeting management given above, a chairperson must also act on the knowledge that different kinds of meetings take place in working life. Each has its own nature and challenges (even though any one may have attributes of two or three of these). The kinds of meetings are

- **Briefings** A briefing is called to direct or instruct. Such meetings are used to give information and instruction to subordinates, clear up misunderstandings, and integrate ideas and views where appropriate.
- **Advisory meetings** An advisory meeting is called to share information. Such meetings are used to seek advice about a problem, inform participants about ideas, and listen to their views.
- **Committee meetings** A committee meeting gathers interest groups to decide on matters of common concern. Such meetings are characterized by a sense of authority, compromise, and the resolution of differences by voting.
- **Council meetings** A council meeting is held by persons of equal status to contribute to a matter at hand. Such meetings are typified by group accountability, the resolution of differences through discussion, and consensual decisions.
- **Negotiations** A negotiation also sees interest groups gather, but decisions are through bargaining, not voting. Such meetings are differentiated by quid pro quo decisions from sides having different but overlapping aims, with each seeking to achieve the best possible terms for itself.

---

[4]"Helicopter vision" is the ability and motivation to (i) examine problems from a different perspective with concurrent attention to their details, (ii) place problems within a broader context by detecting relationships with systems of wider scope, and (iii) formulate and deliver one's work accordingly, but based on a personal vision.

Further Reading

Adair J (1988) Effective time management. Pan Books

Proposition 35
Managing by Walking Around

In a Word Management by walking around emphasizes the importance of inter-personal contact, open appreciation, and recognition. It is one of the most important ways to build civility and performance in the workplace.

Background

The hallmarks of the modern organization are satellite offices, remote offices, home offices, virtual offices, hoteling facilities, and the electronic mail that underpins—and promotes—these. Today, knowledge workers receive few telephone calls and electronic mail is their communication vehicle of choice. (The use of videoconferencing is growing too.) After all, why should they walk around if they can type, point, and click? At the receiving end, managers are known to collect more than 150 messages each day. Yet, as knowledge workers on the rise tote up electronic status, they also distance themselves from colleagues.

Managing by walking around was popularized by Tom Peters[1] and Robert Waterman in the early 1980s because it was (already then) felt that managers were becoming isolated from their subordinates. At Hewlett-Packard, where the approach

---

[1]Peters saw managing by wandering around as the basis of leadership and excellence and called it the technology of the obvious.

© Asian Development Bank 2017

O. Serrat, *Knowledge Solutions*, DOI 10.1007/978-981-10-0983-9_35

was practiced from 1973, executives were encouraged to know their people, understand their work, and at the same time make themselves more visible and accessible. Hewlett and Packard's (1995) business philosophy, centered on deep respect for people and acknowledgment of their built-in desire to do a good job, had evolved into informal, decentralized management and relaxed, collegial communication styles. Theirs was the opposite of drive-by management.

Rationale

The basic principle is that command and control is ineffective in modern organizations. Nothing is more instructive than seeing what actually transpires in the real world and learning from that. Management by walking around is a leadership technique that has stood the test of time and can be used by any manager. Except for virtual organizations,[2] and most of us still do not work through these even if we interface variously with them, face-to-face interaction remains a sure way to receive and give feedback wherever managers see staff regularly. Why? Because it is staff, not managers, who create an organization's products and deliver its services, and appreciation of that can only come from knowing what happens on the ground. Because people live to be part of something, and being intimately in touch opens up more lines of informal communication[3] and produces stronger team dynamics and performance. The human touch still works best.

Approach

> If you wait for people to come to you, you'll only get small problems. You must go and find them. The big problems are where people don't realize they have one in the first place.
>
> —W. Edwards Deming
>
> A desk is a dangerous place from which to view the world.
>
> —John le Carré

---

[2]Virtual organizations are organized entities, whether corporate or charitable, that does not exist in any one central location but instead exist solely through the Internet. There are social, psychological, ethical, and technical implications to the nature and rise of these, better discussed elsewhere.

[3]In high-performance organizations the intensity of communications is unmistakable. It usually starts with an insistence on informality.

Managing by walking around requires personal involvement, good listening skills, and the recognition that most people in an organization want to contribute to its success. It should not be forced and cannot be a charade. It works if you display sincerity and civility and are genuinely interested in staff and their work. Try to

1. Wander about as often as you can, but recurrently and preferably daily.
2. Relax as you make your rounds.
3. Share and invite good news.
4. Talk about family, hobbies, vacations, and sports.
5. Watch and listen without judgment.
6. Invite ideas and opinions to improve operations, products, services, etc.
7. Be responsive to problems and concerns.
8. Look out for staff doing something right, and give them public recognition.
9. Project the image of a coach and mentor, not that an inspector.
10. Give staff on-the-spot help.
11. Use the opportunity to transmit the organization's values.
12. Swap value and legacy stories.
13. Share your dreams.
14. Have fun.

Benefits

Managing by walking around does not just cut through vertical lines of communication. It also

1. Builds trust and relationships.
2. Motivates staff by suggesting that management takes an active interest in people.
3. Encourages staff to achieve individual and collective goals.
4. Strengthens ability to drive cultural change for higher organizational performance.
5. Refreshes organizational values.
6. Makes work less formal.
7. Creates a healthy organization.

Reference

Packard D (1995) The HP way: how Bill Hewlett and I built our company. HarperCollins Publishers

Proposition 36
Growing Managers, not Bosses

In a Word In the twenty-first century, managers are responsible for the application and performance of knowledge at task, team, and individual levels. Their accountability is absolute and cannot be relinquished. In a changing world, successful organizations spend more time, integrity, and brainpower on selecting them than on anything else.

Imagine

Your organization has the right strategy. It also has the right structure (since that follows strategy). Are you happy? Not yet. You do not have enough of the right stuff.

The Right Stuff

The right stuff is inspiring, caring, infusing, and initiating managers who go about their business quietly, on the word of Henry Mintzberg. Warren Bennis, always keen on leaders, sees them as white knights who can somehow herd cats. Most people would be happy with either variety. Indeed, they would be happy with any

© Asian Development Bank 2017
O. Serrat, *Knowledge Solutions*, DOI 10.1007/978-981-10-0983-9_36

of the prototypical characters drawn in management textbooks. But the fact is that such high-caliber material is not available for nearly all organizations.

So it is important to make the most of what organizations do have. And to spend, therefore, more time, integrity, and brainpower on making people decisions than on anything else. There are good reasons for this: experience shows that one in three promotions end in failure, that one in three is just about effective, and that one in three comes to pass right. The quality of promotion and staffing decisions reveals the values and standards of management and whether it takes its duties seriously.

Managerial Responsibility

> *Ninety percent of what we call "management" consists of making it difficult for people to get things done.*
>
> —Peter Drucker

To whom do these decisions relate? Let us look at what is required. In the twenty-first century, managers are responsible for the application and performance of knowledge at task, team, and individual levels. This accountability is absolute and cannot be relinquished. Once upon a time, the standard tasks of managers were to set objectives, organize, motivate and communicate, measure accomplishments, and develop people. Excepting the smallest organizations, they must now also know how to integrate worldwide phenomena into strategic decisions, take greater risks more often over longer periods, visualize their organization as a whole and blend their function within it, manage by objective, inspire and motivate knowledge workers, build cohesive teams, and communicate information rapidly and succinctly. Some necessary generic attributes are enthusiasm, integrity, toughness, fairness, humanity, humility, and confidence. Without a doubt, management and its requirements are more complex and there is no room for safe mediocrity.

Manager Development

It follows, then, that managers must be groomed and developed for strategic, operational, and team leadership. (The long-standing, false dichotomy between managers and leaders is on its last legs: management is a role, leadership an attribute.) As luck would have it, however, the art of manager development is in its infancy. Mistaken beliefs abound: manager development is not about attending courses; it is not about finding potential; it is not about promotion or replacement planning; and it is definitely not a means to change personality. Its sole purpose is to make a person effective. For this reason, manager development must deal with the structure of management relations, with tasks, with the management skills that a person needs, and with the changes in behavior that are likely to sharpen existing skills and make them more operative. In sum, if managers are to be grown, the elements of identity that should be cultivated relate to quality (what a manager has to be), function (what a manager has to do), and situation (what a manager has to know).

Growing Managers

It follows further that human resource management needs to change. Too often, what passes for management of human resources has little to do with human resources and even less with management. Detractors say that most human resource divisions would be hard pressed to prove that they are making a real difference. As a minimum, it should be recognized that the majority of people want to work productively and that managing them is the responsibility of their manager, not that of a human resource specialist. But there are vital roles that are best carried out by human resource divisions. One of them is growing managers, not bosses. There are implications for training, selection, coaching and mentoring, giving people who merit it the chance to manage, education for management and leadership, and strategies for manager development.

Afterword

These days, people do not so readily accept as manager someone whose credentials they do not admire. If persons are promoted because they are politicians, others will deride management for forcing them to become politicians too. They will stop performing or they will quit. This should matter very much. When rewards and perquisites go to mere cleverness, obsequiousness, or nonperformance, an organization declines in tune with these attributes.

Further Reading

Adair J (2005) The John Adair handbook of management and leadership. Viva Books Private Limited

The opinions expressed in this chapter are those of the author(s) and do not necessarily reflect the views of the Asian Development Bank, its Board of Directors, or the countries they represent.

Proposition 37
Understanding and Developing Emotional Intelligence

In a Word Emotional intelligence describes ability, capacity, skill, or self-perceived ability to identify, assess, and manage the emotions of one's self, of others, and of groups. The theory is enjoying considerable support in the literature and has had successful applications in many domains.

Introduction

The intelligence quotient, or IQ, is a score derived from one of several different standardized tests to measure intelligence.[1] It has been used to assess giftedness and sometimes underpin recruitment. Many have argued that IQ, or conventional intelligence, is too narrow: some people are academically brilliant yet socially and

---

[1]When psychologists began to think about intelligence they focused attention on cognitive aspects such as memory and problem solving.

© Asian Development Bank 2017

O. Serrat, *Knowledge Solutions*, DOI 10.1007/978-981-10-0983-9_37

interpersonally inept.[2] We know that success does not automatically follow those who possess a high IQ rating.

> *If your emotional abilities aren't in hand, if you don't have self-awareness, if you are not able to manage your distressing emotions, if you can't have empathy and have effective relationships, then no matter how smart you are, you are not going to get very far.*
>
> —Daniel Goleman

Wider areas of intelligence enable or dictate how successful we are toughness, determination, and vision help. But emotional intelligence, often measured as an emotional intelligence quotient, or EQ, is more and more relevant to important work-related outcomes such as individual performance, organizational productivity, and developing people because its principles provide a new way to understand and assess the behaviors, management styles, attitudes, interpersonal skills, and potential of people. It is an increasingly important consideration in human resource planning, job profiling, recruitment interviewing and selection, learning and development, and client relations and customer service, among others.

Definition

Emotional intelligence describes the ability, capacity, skill, or self-perceived ability to identify, assess, and manage the emotions of one's self, of others, and of groups. People who possess a high degree of emotional intelligence know themselves very well and are also able to sense the emotions of others. They are affable, resilient, and optimistic. Surprisingly, emotional intelligence is a relatively recent behavioral model: it was not until the publication of *Emotional Intelligence: Why It Can Matter More Than IQ* by Goleman (1995) that the term became popular.[3]

---

[2]As early as 1920, Robert Thorndike used the term "social intelligence" to describe the skill of understanding and managing other people. In the 1940s, David Wechsler defined intelligence as the aggregate or global capacity of the individual to act purposefully, think rationally, and deal effectively with his (or her) environment. In 1943, he submitted that nonintellective abilities are essential for predicting one's ability to succeed in life. Later, in 1983, Howard Gardner wrote about multiple intelligences and proposed that intrapersonal and interpersonal intelligences are as important as the type of intelligence typically measured by IQ and related tests.

[3]Emotional intelligence draws from branches of behavioral, emotional, and communications theories. Goleman is the person most commonly associated with it. (But he is by no means the only researcher: the most distant roots of emotional intelligence can be traced to Charles Darwin's early work on the importance of emotional expression for survival and adaptation.) Wayne Leon Payne is credited with first using the term "emotional intelligence" in 1985. Soon after, in 1990, John Mayer and Peter Salovey described that as the ability to monitor one's own and others' feelings and emotions, to discriminate among them, and to use this information to guide one's thinking and

Benefits

> *Emotions have taught mankind to reason.*
>
> —Marquis de Vauvenargues

By developing their emotional intelligence individuals can become more productive and successful at what they do, and help others become more productive and successful too. The process and outcomes of emotional intelligence development also contain many elements known to reduce stress—for individuals and therefore organizations—by moderating conflict; promoting understanding and relationships; and fostering stability, continuity, and harmony. Last but not least, it links strongly with concepts of love and spirituality.[4]

The Model

Individuals have different personalities, wants, needs, and ways of showing their emotions. Navigating through this requires tact and shrewdness—especially if one hopes to succeed in life. This is where emotional intelligence theory helps. In the most generic framework, five domains of emotional intelligence cover together personal (self-awareness, self-regulation, and self-motivation) and social (social awareness and social skills) competences.[5] They are

- Self-Awareness

  (i)   Emotional awareness: Recognizing one's emotions and their effects.
  (ii) Accurate self-assessment: Knowing one's strengths and limits.
  (iii) Self-confidence: Sureness about one's self-worth and capabilities.

(Footnote 3 continued)

actions. In 1997, their four branch model defined emotional intelligence as involving the abilities to perceive, accurately, emotions in oneself and others; use emotions to facilitate thinking; understand the meaning of emotions; and manage emotions. They also tried to develop a way to scientifically measure differences between people's abilities in the area of emotions.

[4]Nor surprisingly, perhaps, Goleman (2006) published *Social Intelligence: The New Science of Social Relationships* to illuminate theories about attachment, bonding, and the making and remaking of memory as he examined how our brains are wired for altruism, compassion, concern, and rapport. Good relationships nourish us and support our health, while toxic relationships can poison us. He proposed that social intelligence is made up of social awareness (including empathy, attunement, empathic accuracy, and social cognition) and social facility (including synchrony, self-presentation, influence, and concern).

[5]The material that follows comes from the Consortium for Research on Emotional Intelligence in Organizations. 1998. *Emotional Competence Framework*.

- Self-Regulation

  (i)   Self-control: Managing disruptive emotions and impulses.
  (ii) Trustworthiness: Maintaining standards of honesty and integrity.
  (iii) Conscientiousness: Taking responsibility for personal performance.
  (iv) Adaptability: Flexibility in handling change.
  (v)   Innovativeness: Being comfortable with and open to novel ideas and new information.

- Self-Motivation

  (i)   Achievement drive: Striving to improve or meet a standard of excellence.
  (ii) Commitment: Aligning with the goals of the group or organization.
  (iii) Initiative: Readiness to act on opportunities.
  (iv) Optimism: Persistence in pursuing goals despite obstacles and setbacks.

- Social Awareness

  (i)   Empathy: Sensing others' feelings and perspective, and taking an active interest in their concerns.
  (ii) Service orientation: Anticipating, recognizing, and meeting customers' needs.
  (iii) Developing others: Sensing what others need in order to develop, and bolstering their abilities.
  (iv) Leveraging diversity: Cultivating opportunities through diverse people.
  (v)   Political awareness: Reading a group's emotional currents and power relationships.

- Social Skills

  (i)   Influence: Wielding effective tactics for persuasion.
  (ii)   Communication: Sending clear and convincing messages.
  (iii) Leadership: Inspiring and guiding groups and people.
  (iv)   Change catalyst: Initiating or managing change.
  (v)   Conflict management: Negotiating and resolving disagreements.
  (vi)   Building bonds: Nurturing instrumental relationships.
  (vii) Collaboration and cooperation: Working with others toward shared goals.
  (viii) Team capabilities: Creating group synergy in pursuing collective goals.

In brief, the five domains relate to knowing your emotions; managing your emotions; motivating yourself; recognizing and understanding other people's emotions; and managing relationships, i.e., managing the emotions of others.

Table. The personal and social attributes of emotional intelligence

Competence	Attribute
Self-awareness	
Emotional awareness	Individuals with this competence • Know which emotions they are feeling and why • Realize the links between their feelings and what they think, do, and say • Recognize how their feelings affect their performance; and • Have a guiding awareness of their values and goals
Accurate self-assessment	Individuals with this competence are • Aware of their strengths and weaknesses • Reflective, learning from experience • Open to candid feedback, new perspectives, continuous learning, and self-development; and • Able to show a sense of humor and perspective about themselves
Self-confidence	Individuals with this competence • Present themselves with self-assurance and have presence • Can voice views that are unpopular and go out on a limb for what is right; and • Are decisive and able to make sound decisions despite uncertainties and pressures
Self-regulation	
Self-control	Individuals with this competence • Manage their impulsive feelings and distressing emotions well • Stay composed, positive, and unflappable even in trying moments; and • Think clearly and stay focused under pressure
Trustworthiness	Individuals with this competence • Act ethically and are above reproach • Build trust through their reliability and authenticity • Admit their own mistakes and confront unethical actions in others; and • Take tough, principled stands even if they are unpopular
Conscientiousness	Individuals with this competence • Meet commitments and keep promises • Hold themselves accountable for meeting their objectives; and • Are organized and careful in their work
Adaptability	Individuals with this competence • Smoothly handle multiple demands, shifting priorities, and rapid change • Adapt their responses and tactics to fit fluid circumstances; and • Are flexible in how they see events
Innovativeness	Individuals with this competence • Seek out fresh ideas from a wide variety of sources • Entertain original solutions to problems • Generate new ideas; and • Take fresh perspectives and risks in their thinking

(continued)

(continued)

Competence	Attribute
Self-motivation	
Achievement drive	Individuals with this competence • Are results-oriented, with a high drive to meet their objectives and standards • Set challenging goals and take calculated risks • Pursue information to reduce uncertainty and find ways to do better; and • Learn how to improve their performance
Commitment	Individuals with this competence • Readily make personal or group sacrifices to meet a larger organizational goal • Find a sense of purpose in the larger mission • Use the group's core values in making decisions and clarifying choices; and • Actively seek out opportunities to fulfill the group's mission
Initiative	Individuals with this competence • Are ready to seize opportunities • Pursue goals beyond what is required or expected of them • Cut through red tape and bend the rules when necessary to get the job done; and • Mobilize others through unusual, enterprising efforts
Optimism	Individuals with this competence • Persist in seeking goals despite obstacles and setbacks • Operate from hope of success rather than fear of failure; and • See setbacks as due to manageable circumstance rather than a personal flaw
Social awareness	
Empathy	Individuals with this competence • Are attentive to emotional cues and listen well • Show sensitivity and understand others' perspectives; and • Help out based on understanding other people's needs and feelings
Service orientation	Individuals with this competence • Understand customers' needs and match them to services or products • Seek ways to increase customers' satisfaction and loyalty • Gladly offer appropriate assistance; and • Grasp a customer's perspective, acting as a trusted advisor
Developing others	Individuals with this competence • Acknowledge and reward people's strengths, accomplishments, and development • Offer useful feedback and identify people's needs for development; and • Mentor, give timely coaching, and offer assignments that challenge and grow a person's skills

(continued)

(continued)

Competence	Attribute
Leveraging diversity	Individuals with this competence • Respect and relate well to people from varied backgrounds • Understand diverse worldviews and are sensitive to group differences • See diversity as opportunity, creating an environment where diverse people can thrive; and • Challenge bias and intolerance
Political awareness	Individuals with this competence • Accurately read key power relationships; • Detect crucial social networks; • Understand the forces that shape views and actions of clients, customers, or competitors; and • Accurately read situations and organizational and external realities.
Social skills	
Influence	Individuals with this competence • Are skilled at persuasion • Fine-tune presentations to appeal to the listener • Use complex strategies like indirect influence to build consensus and support; and • Orchestrate dramatic events to effectively make a point
Communication	Individuals with this competence • Are effective in give-and-take, registering emotional cues in attuning their message • Deal with difficult issues straightforwardly • Listen well, seek mutual understanding, and welcome sharing of information fully; and • Foster open communication and stay receptive to bad news as well as good
Leadership	Individuals with this competence • Articulate and arouse enthusiasm for a shared vision and mission • Step forward to lead as needed, regardless of position • Guide the performance of others while holding them accountable; and • Lead by example
Change catalyst	Individuals with this competence • Recognize the need for change and remove barriers • Challenge the status quo to acknowledge the need for change • Champion the change and enlist others in its pursuit; and • Model the change expected of others
Conflict management	Individuals with this competence • Handle difficult people and tense situations with diplomacy and tact • Spot potential conflict, bring disagreements into the open, and help deescalate • Encourage debate and open discussion; and • Orchestrate win-win solutions

(continued)

(continued)

Competence	Attribute
Building bonds	Individuals with this competence • Cultivate and maintain extensive informal networks • Seek out relationships that are mutually beneficial • Build rapport and keep others in the loop; and • Make and maintain personal friendships among work associates
Collaboration and cooperation	Individuals with this competence • Balance a focus on task with attention to relationships • Collaborate, sharing plans, information, and resources • Promote a friendly and cooperative climate; and • Spot and nurture opportunities for collaboration
Team capabilities	Individuals with this competence • Model team qualities such as respect, helpfulness, and cooperation • Draw all members into active and enthusiastic participation • Build team identity, esprit de corps, and commitment; and • Protect the group and its reputation and share credit

Source Author

Can Emotional Intelligence Be Learned?

> *Nothing great was ever achieved without enthusiasm.*
>
> —Ralph Waldo Emerson

A common question relates to whether people are born with high EQ or whether it can be learned. The truth is that some will be more naturally gifted than others but the good news is that emotional intelligence skills can be learned. (This must be so because emotional intelligence is shown to increase with age.) However, for this to happen, people must be personally motivated, practice extensively what they learn, receive feedback, and reinforce their new skills.

Promoting Emotional Intelligence in the Workplace

> *Comfort in expressing your emotions will allow you to share the best of yourself with others, but not being able to control your emotions will reveal your worst.*
>
> —Bryant H. McGill

The work conducted in most organizations has changed dramatically in the last 20 years. Of course, there are now fewer levels of management and management styles are less autocratic. But there has also been a decided move toward knowledge and team-based, client-oriented jobs so that individuals generally have more autonomy, even at the lower levels of organizations. Since modern organizations always look to improve performance, they recognize that objective, measurable benefits can be derived from higher emotional intelligence. To name a few, these include increased sales, better recruitment and retention, and more effective leadership.

Naturally, the criteria for success at work are changing too. Staff is now judged by new yardsticks: not just by how smart they are, or by their training and expertise, but also by how well they handle themselves and one another, and that is strongly influenced by personal qualities such as perseverance, self-control, and skill in getting along with others. Increasingly, these new yardsticks are being applied to choose who will be hired and who will not, who will be let go and who will be retained, and who will be past over or promoted.

> *I respect the man who knows distinctly what he wishes. The greater part of all mischief in the world arises from the fact that men do not sufficiently understand their own aims. They have undertaken to build a tower, and spend no more labor on the foundation than would be necessary to erect a hut.*
>
> —Johann Wolfgang von Goethe

Emotional intelligence may be the (long sought) missing link that unites conventional "can do" ability determinants of job performance with "will do" dispositional determinants. Modern organizations now offer learning and development that is explicitly labeled as "emotional intelligence" or "emotional competence" training. In support, their leaders create and manage a working environment of flexibility, responsibility, standards, rewards, clarity, and commitment.[6]

---

[6]This climate determines how free staff feel to innovate unencumbered by red tape; perceptions of responsibility to the organization; the level of standards that are set; the sense of accuracy about performance feedback and the aptness of rewards; the clarity staff have about the organization's mission, vision, and values; and the level of commitment to a common purpose.

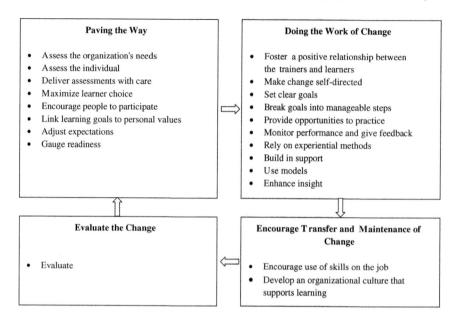

Fig. Good practices that cultivate emotional intelligence in the workplace. *Note* The four phases correspond to those of the development process, viz., preparation, training, transfer and maintenance, and evaluation. Each is important. *Source* Author

References

Goleman D (1995) Emotional intelligence: why it can matter more than IQ. Bantam Books
Goleman D (2006) Social intelligence: the new science of social relationships. Bantam Books

Further Reading

Ehin C (2000) Unleashing intellectual capital. Butterworth-Heinemann
Goleman D (1998) Working with emotional intelligence. Bantam Books

Proposition 38
The Roots of an Emerging Discipline

In a Word Organizations must become information-based: (i) knowledge workers are not amenable to command and control; (ii) in the face of unremitting competition, it is vital to systematize innovation and entrepreneurship; (iii) in a knowledge-based economy, it is imperative to decide what information one needs to conduct one's affairs.

Preamble

Knowledge is the result of learning and the process of identifying, creating, storing, sharing, and using it to enhance performance has always occupied man. The pursuit of any human activity leads to the acquisition by those involved of know-how about how that activity may be successfully conducted and, insofar as what is learned can be harnessed, subsequent practitioners—even later generations—can build on experience and avert costly rework. Even so, for much of history, applications of know-how were confined to farming and craftsmanship.

© Asian Development Bank 2017
O. Serrat, *Knowledge Solutions*, DOI 10.1007/978-981-10-0983-9_38

Background

The Industrial Revolution that took place in Britain in the late eighteenth century, spread to Western Europe and North America in the nineteenth century, and eventually affected the rest of the world replaced economies based on manual labor with economies dominated by machine tools. Beginning with the mechanization of textile manufacturing, fast-paced technological progress in other industries from the mid-nineteenth century continued into the early twentieth century and sparked unprecedented socioeconomic changes. The First World War spread new technology even wider and shaped the modern world. It also laid the seeds of the Second World War, another high point of technological escalation.

In post-industrial economies—a term associated from the 1970s with a phase when the relative importance of manufacturing decreases and that of services and information grows—those who possess knowledge—not land, labor, or capital goods—own the new means of production. Accepting great variations within and across countries, changes from industrial to knowledge economies have since been quickened by the complex series of economic, social, technological, cultural, environmental, and political changes that followed the Second World War. Their practical expression, referred to as globalization, is seen as increasing interdependence, integration, and interaction between people in far-flung locations.

Knowledge has always been transferred in one form or another. In varying forms of complexity, this has been accomplished by imitation; storytelling; written symbols and letters; apprenticeships; primary, secondary, and tertiary schooling; on-the-job discussions with peers; maintenance of corporate libraries; and professional training and coaching and mentoring programs, among others. However, from the early 1980s, expanding technologies for distribution of data and information opened opportunities for the development of a fertile environment enabling knowledge to be identified, created, stored, shared, and used for benefit.

Table. Organization and culture

	Feudal culture	Industrial culture	Knowledge culture	Creativity culture
Organization	Territorial	Hierarchies	Networks	Flows
Focus	Land	Profit	Customer	Innovation
Culture	Domination control	Control responsibility	Responsibility contribution	Contribution creativity
Key measure	Quantity	Efficiency	Effectiveness	Quality of life

Source Author

The Present

In the knowledge-based economies that emerged in the mid- to late 1990s, information moves everywhere and its effects are pervasive. Irrespective of their nature, actors must organize themselves around information. There are three reasons why large organizations—a form of social institution involved in business (or more recently nonprofit) activities that developed from the late 1860s and is now prevalent—must become information-based. The first is that knowledge workers, who increasingly make up workforces, are not amenable to the command and control methods of the past. (In a knowledge workforce, the system must serve the worker.) The second, in the face of unremitting competition, is the requirement to systematize innovation and entrepreneurship, this being quintessentially knowledge work. (The implementation of knowledge management processes, systems, and applications has been shown to improve efficiency, forestall knowledge loss, and stimulate knowledge growth and creation.) The third is the imperative to come to terms with information technology: in a knowledge-based economy, an organization must decide what information it needs to conduct its affairs; if not, it will drown in data. (Typically, staff spend about 30% of their time looking for information.)

> *An investment in knowledge pays the best interest.*
>
> —Benjamin Franklin

Prospects

The forces of technology, globalization, and the emerging knowledge-based economy are sparking yet another revolution that is forcing large numbers of people and their organizations to seek new ways to manage themselves. Those tasked with leading must operate under the principle that the unique knowledge that knowledge workers bring to work is the key competitive differentiator. Still, the transfer of knowledge is inherently difficult even with modern knowledge management tools. Those who possess knowledge are not necessarily aware of all the potential applications of what they know. Knowledge is also "sticky" and tends to remain in people's heads. And so, organizing for knowledge management requires new structures and managerial attitudes.

> *Knowing is not enough; we must apply. Willing is not enough; we must do.*
>
> —Johann Wolfgang von Goethe

Box: Old and New Knowledge Management Paradigms

Old Paradigm	New Paradigm
• Organizational discipline	• Organizational learning
• Vicious circles	• Virtuous circles
• Inflexible organizations	• Flexible organizations
• Management administrators	• Management leaders
• Distorted communication	• Open communication
• Strategic business units drive product development	• Core competencies drive product development
• Strategic learning occurs at the apex of the organization	• Strategic learning capacities are widespread
• Assumption that most employees are untrustworthy	• Assumption that most employees are trustworthy
• Most employees are disempowered	• Most employees are empowered
• Tacit knowledge of most employees must be disciplined by managerial prerogative	• Tacit knowledge of employees is the most important factor in success, and creativity creates its own prerogative

Source Author

Further Reading

ADB (2007) Learning lessons in ADB. Manila
ADB (2009) Learning for in ADB. Manila

Proposition 39
Understanding Complexity

In a Word In development agencies, paradigms of linear causality condition need much thinking and practice. They encourage command-and-control hierarchies, centralize decision-making, and dampen creativity and innovation. Globalization demands that organizations see our turbulent world as a collection of evolving ecosystems. To survive and flourish they must then be adaptable and fleet-footed. Notions of complexity offer a wealth of insights and guidance to twenty-first century organizations that strive to do so.

Introduction

Lord Kelvin (1824–1907), a Scottish physicist, mathematician, engineer, and one-time President of the Royal Society—the national academy of science of the United Kingdom and the Commonwealth—is alleged to have remarked in an address to the British Association for the Advancement of Science that "There is nothing new to be discovered in physics now. All that remains is more and more precise measurement."

© Asian Development Bank 2017
O. Serrat, *Knowledge Solutions*, DOI 10.1007/978-981-10-0983-9_39

Building on centuries of progress in human thought, sped by the Newtonian Revolution,[1] the early years of 1900s were characterized by such declarations in Europe and North America.[2] (In a word, with the birth of modern calculus in the seventeenth century owing to Newton and Gottfried Leibnitz,[3] the dominant philosophy had been one of integration: from reasoning one could sum up and draw global conclusions about a system.)

Soon enough, however—*pace* Lord Kelvin, Michelson, and others—multiple transformations in environment, economy, society, polity, and technology threw up fundamental challenges to linear conceptualizations (and mankind's desire to control the physical world). We do not stand outside the systems we study: rather, we are an increasingly essential part of the complex patterns in which we live: our perceptions, thoughts, beliefs, and ways impact the world profoundly.

The End of Certainty

As one would expect, development work is not immune to ordered and reductionist thinking. Karl Marx (1818–1883) and W.W. Rostow (1916–2003), among others, strove to force development into rigid, sequential patterns. Not to be outdone, from the Second World War, development economics fired silver bullets for food aid, free trade, foreign direct investment, import substitution, industrialization, human capital investment, basic human needs, poverty alleviation, structural adjustment, sustainable development, governance, gender and development, poverty reduction, debt relief, community-driven development, and partnerships—to name a few—in succession or volley according to the changing modernist ideological stances and foci of donors, all firmly based on conceptions of Western liberal democracy.

The reasons of a phenomenon defined at a high level might not explain that low-level properties can be several, ranging from mere ignorance of hidden relations to theoretical uncomputability. But whatever these causes may be, a consistent issue remains—that of emergence. Over the course of twentieth century, rapid

---

[1]Isaac Newton (1642–1727), an English physicist, Mathematician, Astronomer, Natural Philosopher, Alchemist, and Theologian, is generally regarded as the most original and influential theorist in the history of science. In addition to his invention of infinitesimal calculus and a new theory of light and color, Newton transformed physics with his three laws of motion and the law of universal gravitation. He was recognized in his lifetime for having created a revolution.

[2]In 1894 Albert Michelson (1852–1931), a German-American physicist and soon-to-be Nobel Laureate, had also quipped: "The more important fundamental laws and facts of physical science have all been discovered, and these are so firmly established that the possibility of their ever being supplanted in consequence of new discoveries is exceedingly remote. Many instances might be cited, but these will suffice to justify the statement that 'our future discoveries must be looked for in the sixth place of decimals'."

[3]Gottfried Leibniz (1646–1716), a German mathematician and philosopher, invented infinitesimal calculus independently of Newton—his notation has been in use since then. He also invented the binary numeral system, used by all modern computers since 1950s.

advances in fields such as physics and biology that highlight holism, uncertainty, and nonlinearity[4] (and de-emphasize reductionism, predictability, and linearity) forged related, interdisciplinary intuitions and concepts that attempt to explain complex phenomena, e.g., catastrophe theory, chaos theory, coevolution, dissipative systems, nonlinear dynamics, self-organized criticality theory, and systems thinking. In loosely bound form, they are often referred to as complexity theory (or the sciences of complexity, to emphasize their plural nature). Even though reductionist and mechanistic thinking persists in the face of now major global concerns,[5] interest in applying concrete and practical complexity approaches to social systems, such as how organizations strategize and change, is growing.

> *For my part I know nothing with any certainty, but the sight of the stars makes me dream.*
>
> —Vincent van Gogh

To date, however, the use of complexity thinking in aid and development, for instance, where it might collectively and in individual organizations help promote the Paris Declaration on Aid Effectiveness,[6] is still unusual and rarely older than about 10 years. Even so, complexity approaches may one day counterbalance the path dependence and "lock-in" management practices embodied in the near-universal (and all too often restrictive) use of the logical framework (and the evaluations based on these). When facing volatile, uncertain, complex, and ambiguous environments such as those that characterize development work, monocausal explanations founded on "rational choice," best specified top—down, are ever more recognized as inadequate or at least insufficient (Figs. 39.1 and 39.2).[7]

---

[4]A nonlinear system displays no simple proportional relation between cause-and-effect. The weather is famously nonlinear and, therefore, diverse and unpredictable: simple changes in one part of the system produce myriads of effects throughout.

[5]A non-exhaustive list of world problems includes (i) population growth; (ii) natural resource depletion or degradation; (iii) pollution; (iv) climate change; (v) unequal distribution of financial resources; (vi) rising expectations in developing countries; (vii) military approaches to resolving quarrels; (viii) nuclear weapons; (ix) genocides; (x) bigotry, racism, and sexism; (xi) terrorism; and (xii) the power of multinational corporations over elected governments.

[6]The Paris Declaration on Aid Effectiveness is an international agreement to intensify efforts for harmonization, alignment, and managing for development results.

[7]A typical logic model might progress thus (i) certain resources are needed to operate a program; (ii) if one has access to them, one can use the resources to accomplish planned activities; (iii) if one accomplishes the planned activities, one will hopefully deliver the products or services intended; (iv) if one accomplishes the planned activities to the extent intended, participants to the program will benefit in certain ways; and (v) if the benefits to participants are achieved, certain desired changes in organizations, communities, or systems might be expected to take place. More simply: (i) identify the problem, (ii) commission studies and investigations, (iii) analyze the results, (iv) select the best option, (v) agree on the change, (vi) implement the change, and (vii) monitor and evaluate the development intervention.

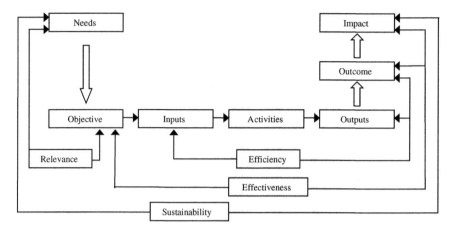

Fig. 39.1 The results chain explained. *Source* Author

Logic				Degree of Control	Challenge of Monitoring and Evaluation
Impact			What the development intervention is expected to contribute to		
Outcome		What the development intervention can be expected to achieve and be accountable for			
Outputs	What is within the direct control of the development intervention's management				
Activities					
Inputs					

In the "Degree of Control" column: *Decreasing Control*. In the "Challenge of Monitoring and Evaluation" column: *Increasing Difficulty*.

Fig. 39.2 Challenges and limits to management. *Source* Author

Defining Complexity

A complex system is one in which at least two parts interact dynamically to function as a whole. The parts are interconnected, and each is composed of sub-systems nested within a larger one. (For instance, a person is a member of a family, which is part of a community, institution, village, province, region, country, group of countries, the earth, the solar system, our galaxy, the observable universe, and the universe.) Complex systems exhibit properties that are not obvious from the properties of their individual parts. Typically, they are characterized by (i) a number of interconnected and interdependent elements (or dimensions); (ii) local rules that apply to each element; (iii) constant movement and responses from these elements; (iv) adaptiveness so that the system adjusts to guarantee continued operation; (v) self-organization, by which new settings in the system take form spontaneously; and (vi) progression in complexity so that the system becomes larger and more sophisticated over time. Although a wide variety of systems are complex, some more or less than others depending on the range of characteristics they possess, all exhibit emergence and self-organization. Other features of complex systems are that their characteristics change over time, frequently in nonlinear ways, and that they seldom (yet sometimes) reach long-term equilibrium.

Key Concepts of Complexity Theory

> *The theory of evolution by cumulative natural selection is the only theory we know of that is in principle capable of explaining the existence of organized complexity.*
>
> —Richard Dawkins

Complexity theory is the science of complex systems.[8] Its origins lie in biology, ecology, and evolution as a development of chaos theory.[9] It is the theory that random events, if left to happen without interference, will settle into a complicated pattern rather than a simple one. In common parlance, complexity is often used to mean difficult or convoluted, that is, a problem where the answer is not obvious. However, when referring to complexity theory a more appropriate word to use might be complicated.[10]

Usefully, Ramalingam (2008) and colleagues at the Overseas Development Institute have circumscribed 10 concepts of complexity, organized into the three domains of (i) complexity and systems, (ii) complexity and change, and (iii) complexity and agency. The following excerpts their paper:

---

[8]Like many other scientific explanations, complexity theory does not present a unified perspective. But all its variations begin with the notion of complexity, be that taken literally or as a metaphor.

[9]The first discoverer of chaos was Henri Poincaré (1854–1912), a French mathematician, physicist, and philosopher of science. The problem of finding the general solution to the motion of more than two orbiting bodies in the solar system, originally known as the three-body problem, had eluded mathematicians since Newton's time.

[10]For example, an iPod is a complicated system but making Annette Poulard's famously perfect omelets is complex. A space rocket is also a complicated system but the stock exchange is complex. Harking back to Poincaré, three planets interacting altogether are a complex system.

- **Complexity and Systems** These first three concepts relate to the features of systems that can be described as complex

  1. Systems characterized by *interconnected and interdependent elements and dimensions* are a key starting point for understanding complexity theory.
  2. *Feedback processes* crucially shape how change happens within a complex system.
  3. *Emergence* describes how the behavior of systems emerges—often unpredictably—from the interaction of the parts, such that the whole is different to the sum of the parts.

- **Complexity and Change** The next four concepts relate to phenomena through which complexity manifests itself:

  1. Within complex systems, relationships between dimensions are frequently *nonlinear*, i.e., when change happens, it is frequently disproportionate and unpredictable.
  2. *Sensitivity to initial conditions* highlights how small differences in the initial state of a system can lead to massive differences later; butterfly effects and bifurcations are two ways in which complex systems can change drastically over time.
  3. *Phase space* helps to build a picture of the dimensions of a system, and how they change over time. This enables understanding of how systems move and evolve over time.
  4. *Chaos and edge of chaos* describe the order underlying the seemingly random behaviors exhibited by certain complex systems.

- **Complexity and Agency** The final three concepts relate to the notion of adaptive agents, and how their behaviors are manifested in complex systems:

  1. *Adaptive agents* react to the system and to each other, leading to a number of phenomena.
  2. *Self-organization* characterizes a particular form of emergent property that can occur in systems of adaptive agents.
  3. *Coevolution* describes how, within a system of adaptive agents, coevolution occurs, such that the overall system and the agents within it evolve together, or cosevolve, over time.

Complexity Theory, Aid, and Development

Development is a complex, adaptive process but—with exceptions—development work has not been conducted as such. It was suggested earlier that development assistance often follows a linear approach to achieving outputs and outcomes, underpinned by economic consensus among Western liberal democracies. That approach is guided by processes (and associated compliance standards) applied with limited and out-of-date insights on dynamic operational contexts. Any planning process is based on assumptions[11]—some will be predictable, others wishful. If the assumptions are based on invalid theories of change (including cause-and-effect relationships) and on inappropriate tools, methods, approaches, and procedures derived from those, development agencies jeopardize the impacts they seek to realize.[12]

> *I know that most men, including those at ease with problems of the greatest complexity, can seldom accept even the simplest and most obvious truth if it be such as would oblige them to admit the falsity of conclusions which they have delighted in explaining to colleagues, which they have proudly taught to others, and which they have woven, thread by thread, into the fabric of their lives.*
>
> —Leo Tolstoy

Yet, even culture theory draws insufficient conclusions about what complexity thinking could mean for development interventions. Some hard questions remain. How might emerging intuitions from complexity approaches, combined with field practice, systemically (rather than through a patchwork approach) reshape assumptions about the design of development assistance, improve reading of signals, and foster appropriate adapting of actions? What might be the implications of a shift from compliance with external standards to investing in capacities for navigating complexity?

Exploring the Science of Complexity gives lenses with which to distinguish, study, and see differently, the deeper realities that development agencies must grapple with. (Some hold that the rise of complexity theory, which questions the concepts and assumptions of Newtonian science, represents a paradigm shift in thinking.) Complexity approaches can potentially enhance insight and innovation among development leaders and practitioners and facilitate navigation of dense webs of connections and relationships. Specifically, *Exploring the Science of Complexity* calls for rethinking five key areas of development assistance: (i) the tools, methods, and approaches for planning, monitoring, learning from, and

---

[11]Kurtz and Snowden (2003) identified three basic, universal assumptions prevalent in organizational decision support and strategy: assumptions of order, of rational choice, and of intent.

[12]The rhetoric of local ownership, participation, empowerment, institutional reform, and aid effectiveness, for example, should not be at odds with actual development assistance practices.

evaluating;[13] (ii) the nature of the processes utilized; (iii) the dynamics of the changes triggered; (iv) the role of beneficiaries and partner organizations; and (v) the wider contexts and the real influence. To this intent, it invites development agencies to (i) cultivate collective intellectual openness to ask new, potentially rich but challenging questions about their mission and work; (ii) exercise collective intellectual and methodological restraint to accept the limitations of complexity thinking as a fresh, potentially valuable set of ideas; (iii) be humble and honest about the scope of what can be achieved through "outsider" interventions, about the types of mistakes that are repeatedly made, and about the reasons such mistakes are made so often; and (iv) develop the individual, organizational, and political courage to face up to the implications of complexity approaches.

The potential benefits of complexity theory in development work are that, by understanding what it means for a system to be complex in a complex environment, stakeholders including policy makers can work with those concepts and not block them unintentionally. One may then use the logic of complexity to understand the problem space (better, the space of possibilities) when addressing seemingly intractable problems and create coevolving enabling environments and more positive futures. Thus, complexity theory can be used as an explanatory framework, as a different way of seeing and thinking, and as a different language and set of concepts.

> *Human beings, viewed as behaving systems, are quite simple. The apparent complexity of our behavior over time is largely a reflection of the complexity of the environment in which we find ourselves.*
>
> —Herbert Simon

Still, where complexity meets development, a framework that helps decision makers determine the prevailing operating context comes in handy. Building on the Cynefin framework[14] reproduced above, Snowden and Boone (2007) have shown how effective leaders can learn to shift decision-making styles in simple, complicated, complex, and chaotic environments.

---

[13]The tools, methods, and approaches that are supportive of complexity thinking include culture theory; alignment- interest and influence matrixes; learning partnerships, outcome mapping; scenario planning; social network analysis; and storytelling. Training in their use should be promulgated. Collections of others should be built.

[14]Cynefin is a Welsh word, commonly translated into English as habitat, place, or haunt. (Related adjectives are acquainted, accustomed, or familiar.) The Cynefin framework was developed by David Snowden and his collaborators to explore the relationship between man, experience, and context and propose new approaches to communication, decision-making, policy making, and knowledge management in complex social environments.

References

Kurtz C, Snowden D (2003) The new dynamics of strategy: sense-making in a complex and complicated world. IBM Systems Journal 42(3):462–483

Ramalingam B, Jones H, Reba T, Young J (2008) Exploring the science of complexity: ideas and implications for development and humanitarian efforts. Working Paper 285. Overseas Development Institute

Snowden D, Boone M (November 2007) A leader's framework for decision making. Harvard Business Review: 69–76

Proposition 40
A Primer on Organizational Culture

In a Word Culture guides the way individuals and groups in an organization interact with one another and with parties outside it. It is the premier competitive advantage of high-performance organizations. Sadly, for others, organizational culture is the most difficult attribute to change: it outlives founders, leaders, managers, products, services, and well-nigh the rest. It is best improved by organizational learning for change.

In Brief

The principal competitive advantage of successful organizations is their culture. Its study is a major constituent of organizational development—that is, the process through which an organization develops its internal capacity to be the most effective it can be in its work and to sustain itself over the long term.

Organizational culture may have been forged by the founder; it may emerge over time as the organization faces challenges and obstacles; or it may be created deliberately by management.

© Asian Development Bank 2017

O. Serrat, *Knowledge Solutions*, DOI 10.1007/978-981-10-0983-9_40

Organizational Culture Defined

Organizational culture comprises the attitudes, experiences, beliefs, and values of the organization, acquired through social learning, that control the way individuals and groups in the organization interact with one another and with parties outside it.

A standard typology refers to communal, networked, mercenary, and fragmented cultures. Numerous other typologies exist.[1] Nevertheless, the necessary notion to grasp is that organizational culture is determined by sundry factors that find expression in organizational structure, making structure itself an important culture-bearing mechanism.

> [Organizational culture is] *A pattern of shared basic assumptions that the group learned as it solved its problems of external adaptation and internal integration, that has worked well enough to be considered valid and, therefore, to be taught to new members as the correct way you perceive, think, and feel in relation to those problems.*
>
> —Edgar Schein

The figure below delineates 10 components that, together, influence organizational culture. Importantly, identifying discernible elements of culture allows organizations to determine features that can be managed to help implement and sustain constructive organizational change. But just as none of the 10 components in the figure shapes organizational culture on its own, none can individually support desired improvements.

---

[1]Numerous other typologies exist. One distinguishes coercive, utilitarian, and normative organizations. (To this, others add another dimension, namely, the professional or collegial organization.) Another focuses on how power and control are delegated, with organizations labeled as autocratic, paternalistic, consultative (else democratic), participative (else power sharing), delegative, or abdicative. A third classifies organizations according to their internal flexibility (viz., clans or hierarchies) and external outlook (viz., adhocracies or markets). The four cultures that Charles Handy popularized are power cultures (which concentrate power among a few), role cultures (which delegate authority within highly defined structures), task cultures (which form teams to solve particular problems), and people cultures (which allow individuals to think themselves superior to their organization).

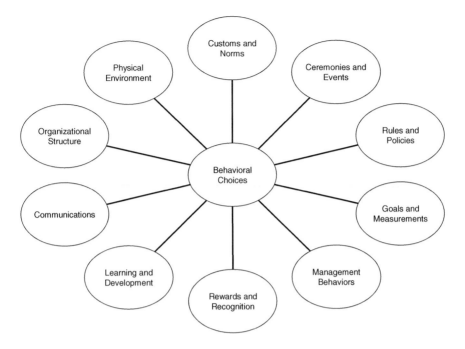

Fig. Components of organizational culture. *Source* Author

Strong and Weak Cultures

Organizational culture varies more than any other corporate asset, including large and tangible information and communications technology infrastructure. It is said to be strong where employees respond to stimuli because of their alignment with it. Conversely, it is said to be weak where there is little alignment, and control is exercised with administrative orders.

Organizational Culture and Change

The thing I have learned at IBM is that culture is everything.

—Lou Gerstner

Regardless, if an organization is to succeed and thrive, a knowledge culture must develop to help it deal with its external environment. But organizational culture is hard to change in the best circumstances. Employees need time to get used to new ways of organizing. Defensive routines pollute the system, more often than not unwittingly, and undermine it. The dynamics of culture change must be considered an evolutionary process at individual, group, organizational, and interorganizational levels, to be facilitated by psychologically attentive leaders who do not underestimate the value of selection, socialization, and leadership. People cannot share knowledge if they do not speak a common language. And so there is a serious, oft-ignored need to root learning in human resource policies and strategies.

Organizational Learning for Change

Observers recognize a correlation between the orientation of organizational culture and organizational learning. Indeed, the inability to change organizational behavior is repeatedly cited as the biggest hindrance to knowledge management. For this reason, even if the need to take a hard look at an organization's culture extends the time required to prepare knowledge management initiatives, the benefits from doing so are likely to tell.

Organizations that are more successful in implementing knowledge management initiatives embody both operations- and people-oriented attributes. Typically, a learning culture is an organizational environment that enables, encourages, values, rewards, and uses the learning of its members, both individually and collectively. But many cultural factors inhibit knowledge transfer. The table below lists the most common frictions and suggests ways to overcome them. Most importantly, when sharing knowledge, the method must always suit the culture as that affects how people think, feel, and act.

Further Reading

ADB (2008) Auditing the lessons architecture. Manila
ADB (2009) Learning for change in ADB. Manila
Schein E (1999) The corporate culture survival guide. Wiley, Inc.

Proposition 41
A Primer on Organizational Learning

In a Word Organizational learning is the ability of an organization to gain insight and understanding from experience through experimentation, observation, analysis, and a willingness to examine successes and failures. There are two key notions: organizations learn through individuals who act as agents for them; at the same time, individual learning in organizations is facilitated or constrained by its learning system.

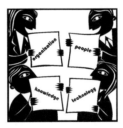

In Brief

A knowledge advantage is a sustainable advantage that provides increasing returns as it is used. However, building a knowledge position is a long-term enterprise that requires foresight and planning. To begin, one should grasp the fundamental, allied notions of organizational learning, and the learning organization, which some contrast in terms of process versus structure.

© Asian Development Bank 2017

O. Serrat, *Knowledge Solutions*, DOI 10.1007/978-981-10-0983-9_41

On Learning Organizations

In the knowledge-based economies that emerged in the mid- to late 1990s, the organizations with the best chance to succeed and thrive are learning organizations that generate, communicate, and leverage their intellectual assets. In *The Fifth Discipline*, Senge (1990) labels them "...organizations where people continually expand their capacity to create the results they truly desire, where new and expansive patterns of thinking are nurtured, where collective aspiration is set free, and where people are continually learning to see the whole together." He catalogues their attributes as personal mastery, shared vision, mental models, team learning, and systems thinking (the fifth discipline that integrates the other four).[1] Command of these lets organizations add generative learning to adaptive learning.[2] Thus, they seldom make the same mistake twice. Organizational learning promotes organizational health.[3] As a result, organizational performance is high.[4] Peter Senge has characterized the core learning capabilities of organizations as a three-legged stool—a stool that would not stand if any of its three legs were missing.

> *The most useful piece of learning for the uses of life is to unlearn what is untrue.*
>
> —Antisthenes

---

[1]According to Peter Senge, personal mastery hangs on clarifying personal vision, focusing energy, and seeing reality. Shared vision is built by transforming personal vision into common vision. Mental models are put together by unearthing internal pictures and understanding how they shape actions. Team learning grows from suspending judgments and fostering dialogue. Systems thinking fuse the first four disciplines to create a whole from distinct parts.

[2]Generative learning concentrates on transformational change that changes the status quo. This type of learning uses feedback from past actions to interrogate the assumptions underlying current views. At heart, generative learning is about creating. Adaptive learning focuses on incremental change. That type of learning solves problems but ignores the question of why the problem arose in the first place. Adaptive learning is about coping.

[3]The notion of organizational ill health is easily understood and needs no explanation. As long ago as 1962, Warren Bennis identified three dimensions of it: (i) adaptability, (ii) coherence of identity, and (iii) the ability to perceive the world correctly. The point here is that organizational learning can provide a necessary and valuable contribution to organizational health by advancing the shared values, clarity of purpose, institutionalized leadership, technical capability, open and honest channels of communications, and ability to deal constructively with conflict. All are qualities that employees expect from their work nowadays.

[4]Organizational performance comprises the actual outputs or results of an organization as measured against its intentions. It is commonly examined in terms of relevance, effectiveness, efficiency, and sustainability. The forces that drive these are organizational context, organizational knowledge, inter- and intra-organizational relationships, and the external environment.

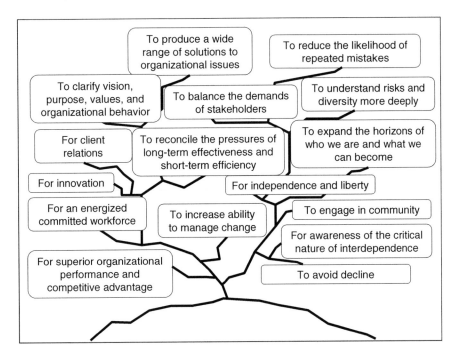

Fig. 41.1 Why create a learning organization? *Source* Author

Other authors[5] see learning organizations in different ways and the search for a single, all-encompassing definition of the learning organization is attractive but frustrating. In the final analysis, the most useful description is likely to be that which each organization develops for itself. That should be a well-grounded, easy-to-apply definition. An important feature to bear in mind is that, for associated benefits to arise, a learning organization must be organized at five, sometimes overlapping, levels: (i) individual learning,[6] (ii) team learning, (iii) cross-functional learning, (iv) operational learning, and (v) strategic learning (Fig. 41.1).

---

[5]Pedler et al. (1996) argue that a learning company is an organization that facilitates the learning of all its members and consciously transforms itself and its context.

[6]Individual learning is not covered in these *Knowledge Solutions*, even if it is the starting point of the learning organization and something that a learning organization should certainly encourage. Employees who are willing and able to learn new things are very important to an adapting organization. Without them, there will be no new products or services. There will be no growth. Specifically, learning organizations need skilled, enthusiastic, entrepreneurial, results-oriented, and improvement-minded individuals. To describe how individuals learn, David Kolb has framed a well-known experiential learning model: (i) doing, (ii) reflecting, (iii) connecting, and (iv) testing. Learning cycles can begin at any stage, depending on individual learning styles, but typically originate from doing. Reflective practitioners can choose to strengthen their ability at each stage to become all-round learners. Nevertheless, a learning organization is more than a collection of

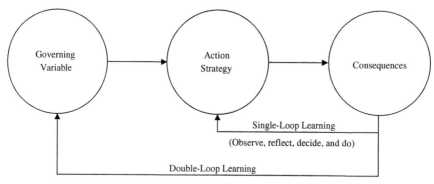

Fig. 41.2 Single-loop and double-loop learning. *Source* Author

... And Organizational Learning

In the final analysis, other definitions of learning organizations share more with Peter Senge's than they disagree with, but it should not be assumed that any type of organization can be a learning organization. In a time of great change, only those with the requisite attributes will excel. Every person has the capacity to learn, but the organizational structures and systems in which each functions are not automatically conducive to reflection and engagement. There may be psychological and social barriers to learning and change. Or people may lack the knowledge management tools with which to make sense of the circumstances they face. In this sense, the learning organization is an ideal toward which organizations must evolve by creating the motive, means, and opportunities (Fig. 41.2).[7]

The literature on learning organizations is oriented to action and geared to the use of strategies and tools to identify, promote, and evaluate the quality of learning processes. In contrast, that on organizational learning concentrates on the detached collection and analysis of the processes involved in individual and collective learning inside organizations. That is to say, organizational learning is the activity

---

(Footnote 6 continued)

individuals who are learning—individual learning is a necessary but not a sufficient condition for organizational learning.

[7]A motive is a reason for doing something. Here, the motive is to understand learning and why it is important. The means are models, methods, competences, and support. Opportunities are in the space made available for learning, with implications for prioritizing time.

and the process by which organizations eventually reach the ideal of a learning organization. The dividing line between the two is the extent to which proponents emphasize organizational learning as a technical or a social process.

> *Everybody who is incapable of learning has taken to teaching.*
> —Oscar Wilde

Jean Lave and Etienne Wenger think that learning is inherently a social process that cannot be separated from the context in which it takes place. They coined the term "community of practice" in 1991 based on their work on learning theory in the late 1980s and early 1990s (even if the phenomenon to which it refers is age old). Learning is in the relationships between people. Social learning occurs when persons who share an interest collaborate over time to exchange ideas, find solutions, and build innovations based on ability, not hierarchical position. Jean Lave and Etienne Wenger argue that communities of practice are everywhere and that we are generally involved in several of them—at work, school, or home, and even in our civic and leisure activities. We all are core members of some groups and at the margins of others. Naturally, the characteristics of communities of practice vary. But they can be defined along three dimensions: (i) what they are about (their domain), (ii) how they function (their community), and (iii) what capabilities they produce (their practice) (Wenger et al. 2002).

> *I never teach my pupils; I only attempt to provide the conditions in which they can learn.*
> —Albert Einstein

More recently, communities of practice have been associated with knowledge management as organizations recognize their potential contributions to human and social capital[8] as well as to organizational performance. Communities of practice can drive strategy, spawn new ideas for products and services, transfer good practice[9] and decrease the learning curve of new employees, respond more rapidly

---

[8]Human capital refers to the stock of productive skills and technical knowledge embodied in labor. Social capital refers to connections within and between social networks.

[9]A good practice is defined as anything that has been tried and shown to work in some way—whether fully or in part but with at least some evidence of effectiveness—and that may have implications for practice at any level elsewhere. Three possible levels of good practice flow from this: (i) promising practices, (ii) demonstrated practices, and (iii) replicated practices.

to specific client needs (requested or anticipated) for certain information, solve problems quickly, minimize organizational knowledge loss (both tacit and explicit), reduce rework and prevent "reinvention of the wheel," develop professional skills, and help engage and retain talented individuals. Even with the help of community-oriented technologies,[10] however, harnessing them in support of organizational development is not easy. Communities of practice benefit from cultivation, but their organic, spontaneous, and informal nature makes them resistant to supervision and interference. Importantly, knowledge and activity are intimately connected, and knowledge workers[11] have a strong need to feel that their work contributes to the whole. To get communities of practice going, leaders should (i) identify potential communities that will enhance the organization's core competencies, (ii) provide supportive infrastructure, and (iii) use nontraditional methods to measure their value. In a learning organization, leaders are designers, stewards, and teachers. Fundamentally, they should move from managing to enable knowledge creation. Communities of practice are voluntary, and what will make them successful over time is their ability, within an enabling environment, to generate enough excitement, relevance, and value to attract, engage, and retain members.

References

Pedler M, Burgoyne J, Boydell T (1996) The learning company: a strategy for sustainable development. McGraw-Hill, London

Senge P (1990) The fifth discipline: the art and practice of the learning organization. Currency Double Day, New York

Wenger E, McDermott R, Snyder W (2002) Cultivating communities of practice: a guide to managing klnowledge. Harvard Business School Press, Boston, Massachusetts

Further Reading

ADB (2008) Auditing the lessons architecture. Manila

ADB (2009) Learning for change in ADB. Manila

---

[10]In a fast-changing market, numerous community-oriented technologies have emerged. They include (i) the desktop, with portal-like applications for managing participation in several groups; (ii) online project spaces for joint work; (iii) website communities; (iv) discussion groups; (v) synchronous meeting facilities, online auditoriums, conference rooms, and chat rooms; (vi) e-learning systems; (vii) expert profiles; and (viii) knowledge repositories. The advantages of one over another have to do with time and space, participation, membership, value creation, connections, and community development.

[11]The knowledge worker, a term coined by Peter Drucker back in 1959, is anyone who works for a living at the tasks of developing or using knowledge.

Proposition 42
Fast and Effective Change Management

By Phillip Ash

In a Word When embarking on a change initiative, one should rapidly implement change that results in the higher levels of performance that were envisioned when the decision to make the changes was made. To make this happen, organizations must first overcome the resistance to change and then secure as much discretionary effort as possible.

Introduction

John Kotter remains one of the most respected experts on the subject of change management. He began writing about change management back in the mid-1990s, when he first declared that only one change initiative in three actually achieved its stated objectives.

After more than a decade of research by academics and practitioners, one would think that we are now doing a much better job of managing change. Actually, that does not seem to be the case. In 2008, McKinsey & Company conducted a global survey of change management and found just about the same results as Kotter had 12 years before—only a third of change management attempts are successful. What are we doing wrong?

© Asian Development Bank 2017

O. Serrat, *Knowledge Solutions*, DOI 10.1007/978-981-10-0983-9_42

Why We Resist Change

To be honest, many organizations do not make much of an effort to manage change. They simply announce what the changes will be and expect everyone to comply. There are two problems with this approach. First, the change sponsors have apparently failed to consider that we are creatures of habit, are generally satisfied with the status quo, and will tend to initially resist change. The second problem has to do with the fact that mere compliance behaviors do not make change initiatives successful—a large measure of discretionary effort is required.

There is initial resistance to organizational change for at least three reasons. First, people have had negative experiences as a result of previous organizational change efforts. However, this is not to suggest that most people have had generally bad experiences with the entire organizational change process; we are specifically referring to the "transition" part of change. In the change process, you do not just go from the old to the new—from the status quo to a new, better alternative. The transition period spans the time from when people first learn about the proposed changes to the time they are successfully implemented. It is within this transition period that change makers (those being asked to change) experience discomfort.

Implementing organizational change initiatives invariably involves people changing themselves. The change you want to make cannot happen until people decide to change. Bridges (1991) expressed this point quite well in his book *Managing Transitions: Making the Most of Change*, where he suggested that the transition, not the change, matters. Change is not the same as transition. Change is situational because of the new technology, the new boss, the new team roles, the new policy, etc. Transition is the psychological process people go through to come to terms with the new situation. Unless transition takes place, the planned change will simply not work.

> *Leaders establish the vision for the future and set the strategy for getting there; they cause change. They motivate and inspire others to go in the right direction and they, along with everyone else, sacrifice to get there.*
>
> —John Kotter

Some discomfort is inevitable, but organizations generally fail to minimize the negative consequences of transition. Workers fear they cannot conform and succeed in the postchange work environment. They are often confused about why organizations make the change, exactly what the scope of the change is, and how their jobs will be impacted. Most organizations do little to allay such fears and concerns. If they did, implementing organizational change can be much faster and done more effectively.

A second reason for the pain during the transition period is the "mourning" change makers feel from the "death" of their work status quo. To help change makers accept the need for change, change managers attempt to portray the status quo as unacceptable, undesirable, and no longer viable. In other words, the status quo must be "killed" so that we can progress with making changes and creating a better future.

Resistance to change is not often strongly expressed when the proposed changes are initially unveiled because there is widespread denial that they will be pushed through. Not long after denial (when people realize that change is inevitable), a period of depression will typically follow. Depression is the critical period which must be made as brief as possible to allow change makers to at least conditionally accept the changes and begin testing new behaviors.

In a sense, change managers need to "kill" the status quo in the minds of personnel before they can move on to the new vision the organization has for the future. However, we must understand that many staff members have a stake in the status quo. One of the best pieces of research that helps us understand what workers experience psychologically during the transition period is *On Death and Dying* by Kubler-Ross (1973). Psychologically speaking, many workers mourn the loss of the status quo much as if they would mourn the loss of a person. Several change researchers support Kubler-Ross' proposition that mourners (be they mourning the death of a person or the loss of the status quo at work) pass through five stages: denial and isolation, anger, bargaining, depression, trial, and acceptance. The depression phase is obviously painful, and often protracted.

The third reason many people initially resist change is the uncertainty created by the announcement of impending change. Conner (1993) described change as the disruption of expectations. He proposed that people resist change because it disrupts the certainty and order of their work lives. Combining these three sources, it is easy to understand why many change makers will initially resist change no matter how badly needed the changes may be.

> *Faced with the choice between changing one's mind and proving that there is no need to do so, almost everyone gets busy on the proof.*
>
> —John Kenneth Galbraith

Strategies for Overcoming Resistance

Our own experience confirms the truth about the importance of "unfreezing" the status quo. One "unfreezing" strategy is to portray the proposed changes as a much better alternative than maintaining the status quo. However, while explaining the benefits of planned changes is important, this will almost certainly not be sufficient to "unfreeze" the status quo.

To make change fast and effective, you need to convince change makers that the status quo is no longer acceptable and that change is unavoidable. A classic metaphor for the "unfreezing" process is the "burning platform". An oil platform caught fire in the North Sea trapping hundreds of workers between a blazing fire and the icy cold water below. Even though managers ordered workers to stay on the platform and wait for a rescue party, a few workers disobeyed and jumped more than a hundred feet into the freezing water that contained patches of blazing oil and debris. As it turned out, the only workers to survive the ordeal were those who jumped into the water. Once on shore, one survivor was asked how he found the courage to make that terrible jump. His response was, "My God man, I was standing on a burning platform—I had no choice but to jump". One way to get change makers to abandon the status quo is to create a burning platform for change. In other words, make it easy to let go of the status quo by making it impossible to maintain.

Getting Past the Valley of Despair

After you've done a thing the same way for two years, look it over carefully. After five years, look at it with suspicion. And after ten years, throw it away and start all over.

—Alfred Edward Perlman

As noted earlier, people do not strongly express resistance when the proposed changes are initially unveiled because there is widespread denial that the changes will be pushed through. But you will remember from the Kubler-Ross model that depression typically follows denial, anger, and bargaining. Depression is the critical period that must be made as brief as possible to allow the targets of change to at least conditionally accept the changes and begin testing new behaviors.

During the denial period, any thoughts that the organization might abandon the proposed changes should not be reinforced. In a sense, we need to "kill" the status quo in the minds of personnel before they can move on to the new vision the organization has for the future. However, we must understand that many staff members have a stake in the status quo.

During the anger period, we should remain as unemotional and rational as possible. Displays of compassion and understanding are appropriate; portraying the positive aspects of organizational life that one can expect once the change initiatives are completed is also important. Allow for some venting of frustration, but reinforce the absolute necessity for change.

The bargaining phase is a good time to express some flexibility in the details of implementation and invite change makers to participate in refining implementation plans. While expressing some willingness to adjust the change initiatives through participation, maintain your commitment to reject the status quo in favor of the change initiatives.

Often, the depression phase is the most difficult for change managers. During this phase, change makers need to have their "space" to "mourn the death" of the status quo; but this is characteristically a period of lowered productivity that is not good for anyone. One of the keys to moving change makers through this period quickly is to encourage discussions between change makers who have moved on to trial and acceptance and those who remain in the depression stage. Change agents can also play an important role in carefully prodding change makers into the trial phase from being in depression.

In both the depression and trial stages, you should look carefully for examples of "trial behaviors". Once spotted, you should positively reinforce these to produce more of the same type of behaviors. While you need to show compassion during depression, do not employ positive reinforcement since you will just be prolonging the length of time in the "valley of despair". The key to both the trial and acceptance phases is lots of positive reinforcement for appropriate behaviors.

It is necessary to recognize and accept the fact that little progress will be made toward implementing change, so long as change makers have not yet made it past the depression stage. Their effectiveness in the status quo environment will also deteriorate. Therefore, it is critical to focus on getting the change makers on to trial and acceptance as quickly as possible. It is also important to not get "ahead of the game" by focusing on other change management issues when large numbers of people are not yet ready for acceptance. You must finish the "unfreezing" job and move change makers through the depression stage before real change can happen.

The 3 C's Communication Strategy

The 3 C's communication strategy is the primary communication-planning tool used to address resistance to change. The 3 C's stand for the types of change issues that communication strategies should address:

- **Context**—Why make these changes? What is happening with our customers, competitors, stakeholders, and the like, that make these changes so important for us?
- **Content**—What exactly is it that we are changing? What are the scope, nature, and timing of the planned change initiatives?
- **Consequences**—What is in it for me personally, if I demonstrate defiance, compliance, or alliance with the proposed change initiatives?

The mistake that most companies make is simply announcing the content of the proposed change initiatives and soon thereafter treating any employee who does not exhibit a "positive, can do" attitude as disloyal. This ignores the psychological reality of change. We have seen companies making 80% of their communication effort on the content of change, and 10% each on context and consequences. Actually, we recommend about 20% on content issues and 40% each on context and consequences.

Discretionary Effort, Not Compliance

Performers can adopt one of three positions relative to proposed changes:

- **Defiance**—They adopt dysfunctional behaviors that are detrimental to the changes we want to occur.
- **Compliance**—Performers do not directly oppose the changes, neither do they exhibit much, if any, discretionary effort. Often, compliant performers will declare support for proposed changes but will not match their words with effort. What they say is not what they do.
- **Alliance**—Performers not only support the proposed changes with their words but they also exhibit strong discretionary efforts and their actions match their words.

The amount of discretionary effort is the difference between the least amount of effort required to just conform to a change request and the maximum possible effort. Behavioral research in workplace environments estimates that maximum discretionary effort can produce 100% greater results. Therefore, an important objective of a performance management program is to maximize discretionary effort.

Typically, few people are consistently defiant when confronted by change requests. The much more challenging problem is compliance. For one thing, it is hard to detect. Lack of discretionary effort is just one explanation among many for sub-par performance. It could be lack of training, poor coaching, lack of cooperation and support from others, etc. And so it is difficult to conclude with certainty that someone or a group is making little or no discretionary effort.

Ways to deal with lack of discretionary effort include communication, training, and consequences. A communication problem might exist if we have not thoroughly explained what behaviors we desire. Another explanation for the lack of discretionary effort is lack of competency. In other words, employees are not performing well because they simply are not able to. Perhaps training is needed to develop new competencies or strengthen existing ones. If we can be sure that performers know what is expected of them and they have the ability to perform, then we can reasonably conclude that applied behavior analysis principles can be used to improve discretionary effort and performance.

Fast and Effective Change Management

Slowly obtaining acceptance is not a reasonable objective for change management. At best, this approach will disrupt current operations and result in the same or lower levels of performance stemming from compliant behaviors only.

When thinking about a change initiative, one should seek to rapidly implement change that results in the higher levels of performance that were envisioned when the decision to make the changes was made. Key to making this happen is to first overcome the resistance to change and then secure as much discretionary effort as possible.

Most change initiatives are developed to improve performance. Yet, too often, the original objectives pertaining to better performance, improved quality, enhanced customer satisfaction, or whatever dimension of improvement was envisioned seem to be forgotten. Once the decision to introduce change is made, the attention of the sponsors of change tend to shift from the reasons for making the change and the promise of better performance to making sure the targets of change understand what the requested changes are and will comply. In reality, change management and performance management should be viewed as flip sides of the same coin. After all, why change if not to improve performance? Change for the sake of change makes little sense. Change managers should focus first on unfreezing the status quo and reinforcing trial behaviors as soon as they occur, then focus on driving performance higher by improving discretionary effort. That is fast and effective change management!

References

Bridges W (1991) Managing transitions: making the most of change. Addison-Wesley Publishing
Conner D (1993) Managing at the speed of change. Random House Publishing
Kubler-Ross E (1973) On death and dying. Routledge Publishing

Further Reading

Daniels A (1994) Bringing out the best in people. McGrawHill
Kotter J (1996) Leading change. Harvard Business School Press
Kotter J (2002) The heart of change. Harvard Business School Press

Proposition 43
New-Age Branding and the Public Sector

In a Word Branding is a means to identify a company's products or services, differentiate them from those of others, and create and maintain an image that encourages confidence among clients, audiences, and partners. Until the mid-1990s, brand management—based on the 4Ps of product (or service), place, price, and promotion—aimed to engineer additional value from single brands. The idea of organizational branding has since developed, with implications for behavior and behavioral change, and is making inroads into the public sector too.

Background

The core concept in marketing[1] has always been that of transaction, whereby an exchange of values takes place. However, in parallel with changes in cultures, lifestyles, and technologies, the emphasis in marketing has shifted from individual transactions: the new focus is on establishing long-term relationships.

---

[1]Marketing is the activity, set of institutions, and processes—always interconnected and interdependent—meant to identify, anticipate, create, communicate, deliver, and exchange valuable offerings that satisfy clients, customers, audiences, and society at large.

© Asian Development Bank 2017

O. Serrat, *Knowledge Solutions*, DOI 10.1007/978-981-10-0983-9_43

Marketing and branding are inextricably linked. To meet demand and facilitate transaction, the objectives that a good brand achieves are to deliver the message clearly, confirm credibility, connect emotionally to the targeted prospects, motivate the end users, and concretize user loyalty.

Having a strong brand is invaluable as competition intensifies. Brand management—that is, the art of creating and maintaining a brand—now requires that the whole organization support its brand with integrated marketing. The stronger the brand, the greater the loyalty of end users is. The stronger the brand, the more flexible an organization is. Higher staff morale leads to higher productivity and better results.

Definitions

A brand[2] is a distinguishing name, term, logo, slogan, sign, symbol, or design scheme—and a combination of these—intended to identify a product or service. Branding is the communication effort to promote brand identity,[3] aiming to help end users differentiate[4] the product or service from that of competitors[5]—and view it in a favorable way, often termed brand equity.[6] Branding is devoted to establishing and nurturing a relationship with end users. Indeed, some now define branding as nothing more or less than a relationship. Thus, it is very important to reflect on the fragility of brands: because trust is the basis of all value, organizations that own brands must work hard to retain and deepen it.

---

[2]In its English usage, the word is derived from the Old Norse *brandr*, meaning "to burn". It refers to the practice that producers had of burning their mark onto products. Although connected with the history of trademarks—of which Roman blacksmiths were the first users when they forged swords, brands were popularized from the nineteenth century with mass marketing of packaged goods. (Industrialization moved the production of many items from local communities to centralized factories that, when shipping them, would brand their insignia on the barrels used, thereby extending the meaning of brand to that of trademark).

[3]Brand identity embraces the attributes that a brand aspires to communicate. It is built by brand vision, brand culture, brand personality, positioning, relationships, and presentations. Examples of brand identity are youthfulness, seriousness, reliability, or luxury. The determinants of that include a technical innovation, superior performance, reliability and durability, convenience and ease of ordering, owner safety, and appealing design.

[4]An undifferentiated product or service is a commodity. A commodity is standard, cheap (and becoming cheaper), widely available, and of low status. However, differentiation matters only to the extent that the end users value the difference.

[5]From a marketing perspective, a competitor is a company (or organization) that satisfies, or intends to satisfy, the same clients that your organization satisfies.

[6]Brand equity is the intangible value-added aspect of any given good or service that is otherwise not considered unique.

A Primer on Branding

For a business not to advertise is like winking at a girl in the dark. You know what you are doing but no one else does.

— Stuart H. Britt

The six key concepts in branding are

- When considering a product or service, the targeted prospects hold thoughts and experience feelings.[7] Brand reputation, or brand perception, exists whether an organization considers it or not.
- A brand's reputation is the sum total of the experiences that clients, audiences, and partners have had with an organization's products and services—including features, quality, dependability, advertising campaigns, client interaction and service, public relations, presentations, websites, etc. Building a reputation takes time, authenticity, and consistency in words and actions. At the outset, a brand is always a seed that must be designed, positioned, and driven to grow.
- Marketers need a clear idea of the end users with whom the organization plans to build a relationship. Target groups should be tightly defined and well understood in terms of psychographics (covering self-image, self-identification, motives, needs, aspirations, and values) and their competitive sets, viz., the reference they use when thinking about how the product or service fits in their context.[8] Marketers should then conduct continual qualitative research—especially on feelings (rather than facts)—and seek answers severally, for example, by means of intrapersonal theories of psychology, social psychology, sociology, and anthropology.
- A branding strategy is about using certain tools, methods, and approaches to achieve strategic and operational goals.
- Myriads of decisions and tradeoffs are associated with developing a branding strategy. (The goal, marketing requirements, and value proposition of specific products or services may lead to a unique branding strategy for each.)
- An organization's branding strategy is a component of its overall corporate strategy.

---

[7]In other words, a brand is a person's gut feeling about an organization. It is an emotional, sensory understanding of what the organization is rather than an intellectual, rational memory of its tagline or logo.

[8]People make choices against a running list of priorities. They perceive a need, seek value, assess value, buy value, and find (or not) value in consumption or use. Naturally, a brand with a positive image makes the end user's choice easy. Therefore, for brand builders, the effective question should be: "What is the significance of this brand in the end user's life?".

Branding and Social Marketing

Brands are customarily associated with the private sector. Nonetheless, public sector organizations should also be aware of the ways they are portrayed and perceived by society, and endeavor to manage these to demonstrate improved responsiveness to public needs. (Their client orientation and the breadth of choice they offer to targeted prospects are routinely questioned). Logically, this can only involve changing their products or services or changing perceptions without changing the products or services.

> The purest treasure mortal times afford
> Is spotless reputation: that away,
> Men are but gilded loam or painted clay.
>
> —William Shakespeare

Either way, branding should help. public sector organizations have, essentially over the last 15 years, often been asked to bring about dramatic overhauls including process improvements[9] and organizational culture shifts. A strong brand personality can attract support for their missions, but also inform these. While public sector organizations typically do not see one another as competitors—and, unlike commercial entities, do not battle it out for clients and attention—it is still critical for them to better define and align vision, culture, and image, and harness the needs of their targeted prospects as commercial marketers do. In sum, brand logic would enable public sector organizations to be perceived as institutions that enable end users to achieve their goals, be relevant to and consistent with how end users view themselves and their lifestyles, help end users relate to others they aspire to be like or associate with,[10] and strengthen or nurture their identity[11] and sense of well-being.

> The mass market has split into ever-multiplying, ever-changing sets of micromarkets that demand a continually expanding range of options.
>
> — Alvin Toffler

---

[9]This includes, for example, shifting out of mass provision to efficient, personalized modes of service provision.

[10]Interestingly, although marketers target a particular group when building a brand, that frequently attracts others. Nonetheless, they must first target to develop the brand relationship before they can facilitate diffusion to a broader market.

[11]Identity relates to individual and collective identification with an organization's mission, values, corporate strategy, competitive advantage, and brand promise.

The notion that marketing tools, methods, and approaches might be used to promote social good developed in the late 1960s and early 1970s. Philip Kotler was the first to argue that marketing is relevant to all organizations having customer groups: in 1971, together with Gerald Zaltman (1971),[12] he proposed that social marketing is the design, implementation, and control of programs calculated to influence the acceptability of social ideas and involving considerations of product planning, pricing, communication, distribution, and marketing research. From there, arguing that marketing technologies can influence the voluntary behavior of end users to improve personal welfare and that of society was a short step. Branding would add new ways to think about the current behavior of end users and how to address that and, just as importantly, serve as a feedback mechanism. (Marketers should consider brands as learning opportunities.)

Notwithstanding, at the beginning of the twenty-first century, public sector organizations still do not make much use of marketing concepts and tools even though so many have been tested and are at hand. Conversely, attempts at branding in public organizations often arouse derision. Yet, there is considerable promise in well-defined areas: (i) stakeholder mapping, (ii) value chain analysis, (iii) competitive analysis,[13] (iv) positioning analysis,[14] (v) lifestyle segmentation, (vi) Unique Selling Propositions,[15] (vii) copy and concept tests,[16] (viii) experimentation,[17] (ix) customer satisfaction measures, (x) event marketing, (xi) integrated marketing communication, (xii) and niching, among others. In the age of globalization and the Internet, many argue that the next big thing in branding is social responsibility: and that surely is where public sector organizations have a niche.

---

[12]Typically, Kotler had earlier also broken new ground when he proposed that marketing had a role to play in nonprofit organizations (Kotler and Levy 1969). Kotler is widely regarded as the world's leading authority on marketing. Until he (and Theodore Levitt) turned their attention to the subject in the early 1960s, marketing had not been seen as a serious function of strategic management but as a tiresome occupation best left to sales departments. Importantly, Kotler's work carries the recurring theme that organizations compete for clients, customers, and audiences and that they cannot succeed by trying to satisfy all segments: they must select and focus on well-denied target groups whose needs they understand. Therefore, marketing must match an organization's capabilities to appropriate opportunities.

[13]Inexplicably, public sector organizations tend to think of themselves as unique. They would benefit from careful study of for-profit marketers.

[14]Public sector organizations are always pressured to follow the preferences and interests of their stakeholders, sometimes omitting to consider fully alternative positions or learning whether end users perceive their positions in the way the organization does.

[15]The Unique Selling Proposition refers to the unique benefits that an organization's products or services offer targeted prospects that differentiate them from those of competitors. (Instead of looking at the product or service from the organization's viewpoint, the Unique Perceived Benefit considers it from the perspective of the end user.).

[16]Public sector organizations frequently rush to impact, making strategic and tactical blunders that pretesting might have avoided.

[17]Too often, public sector organizations formulate only one "best" strategy, ignoring plausible alternatives that they might test and learn from at modest cost.

Box: International Organizations in the Globalized Economy

The information technology–savvy protestors who rocked Cologne, Seattle, Washington DC, Prague, Quebec City, and Davos before Nice, Gothenburg, Salzburg, and Genoa—the list grows—are multigenerational, multi-class, and multi-issue oriented. They are a motley crew of lobbyists, activists, pacifists, and extremists. Regardless, they share a distrust of what international organizations (or gatherings) have to say.

Geopolitical, economic, and demographic forces gave birth to anti-globalization about 2 years ago. The phenomenon is spreading and will continue to make headlines. All the same, not a lot is being said about how to cope with it, aside from retreating to mountaintops, fortresses, or islands. For sure, little conversation can be had with hooligans who hurl Molotov cocktails when they are not looting banks, shops, and cars. But international organizations ought to anticipate and respond to the demands of protestors who conduct their activities in peace and with legitimacy. Surveys report also that protestors command a greater level of trust than international organizations: predictably, respondents think that protestors are driven by morals and ethics. All the more reason, then, to act on the perception that there is a democratic deficit. So what can they do expressly?

Realigning Brands Of course, they can raise appeal. The monetary, trade, environmental, and development organizations that the protestors target in turn have never done work on branding. They need to align vision, culture, and image. And they must for this find out where these props are out of kilter.

• *Vision and Culture* Do they practice the values they hold up? Do their visions inspire their cultures?

• *Image and Vision* Who are their stakeholders? What do they expect? Do the organizations convey their visions to them effectively?

• *Image and Culture* What images do stakeholders associate with international organizations? How do staffs and stakeholders interact? Do staffs fuss about what stakeholders think?

Misalignment between vision and culture would reveal that the international organizations pursue strategic directions that staffs do not understand or support (or, worse still that the visions are too grand to implement). The gap would represent a rift between rhetoric and reality. Next, misalignment between image and vision would reveal discrepancies between the image that stakeholders have of international organizations and the vision promoted by the managers of these organizations. The gap would imply disregard for stakeholders. Finally, misalignment between image and culture would signify confusion among stakeholders as to what international organizations stand for. The gap would mean that international organizations do not put into effect what they preach.

Defusing Threats International organizations can also make potent threats less harmful by providing platforms from which protestors can express their opinions. (In this way, troublemakers would be shown up for what they are.) Many opportunities to do so exist. International organizations can readily grant website access, organize newsgroups, conduct live Internet debates, link their websites to those of prominent protestors, and stage press conferences or public debates with them.

Re-perceiving Social Responsibility More profoundly (and sustainably), international organizations can build up more inclusive relationships with members of civil society. How? In no particular order, the plethora of red-hot issues agitating protestors include global warming and climate change, biodiversity, genetically modified organisms, nuclear power, missile defense, disarmament, Third World debt, terms of trade, underdevelopment, corporate dishonesty, anti-capitalism, anti-Americanism, human rights, unfair labor practices, race and gender issues, health, and AIDS. To begin with, international organizations must think about these issues from the perspective of all stakeholders (not just shareholders) to take in changing expectations. Having decided to spend more time on stakeholder analysis—and that means identifying those participants who have the most direct interaction and examining their interests from their points of view—they would soon identify areas where new competencies are required. They would then need to investigate more facts, stretch internal and external networks, think in scenarios to draw out rigorous explorations of possible futures, build the new competencies required to deal with stakeholder concerns, integrate the new competencies into their operating systems, and support these initiatives with positive internal and external strategies safeguarded by independent verification mechanisms.

Global issues call for international organizations. But many people—the great majority of whom are peaceful—are so angered that they travel long distances to protest outside international gatherings. A spirit of inclusion would let their voices be heard in constructive ways. After all, who wants to take over a crisis when it is too late?

Source Author. 2001. Unpublished

Branding, Relationships, and Behavior

The traditional view of the exchange process presented above emphasizes voluntary transactions between parties who exchange something of value in return for satisfaction. However, bearing deep implications for both marketing and branding, a fundamental question is: "Who is exchanging what and with whom?"

> *Companies have to wake up to the fact that they are more than a product on a shelf.*
> *They're behavior as well.*
>
> — Robert Haas

Marketers have come to agree that the parties to a transaction are in fact exchanging one behavior with another as individuals or communities. They do not just transact. And so, if relationships—in other words, supply chains—are indeed crucial to marketing and marketing is not an act but a habit, both private and public organizations should.

- Think in terms of social capital and relationships, which requires that they plan for the long-term and build brand equity accordingly.
- Consider what deep-seated values relate to the behaviors of targeted prospects and ascertain better what value and motivational attributes their products and services have from the perspective of end users.[18]
- Focus, simplify, and organize products and services by emphasizing and facilitating understanding of their unique selling propositions: therefore, for all products and services marketers should look at the who, what, how, where, when, and why of end-user behaviors.
- Bring more and different partners together to initiate and deploy synergies.
- Constantly monitor and evaluate their efforts by surveying the perceptions of end users.
- Visualize marketing as change management, the success of which hinges on explicit consideration of relevant determinants of intraorganizational behaviors throughout marketing activities, institutions, and processes.
- Accept that organizational behavior is central to marketing and branding:[19] it is a management philosophy for organizational practice; a strategy that helps relate with end users; an organizational tool for structuring and infusing teams; a tactic with which to drive inputs; and a measurement of the relevance, efficiency, efficacy, sustainability, and impact of activities, outputs, and outcomes.[20]

Everybody can own a behavior: that starts with action, not images or words, because clients, audiences, and partners judge organizations by what they do, not

---

[18]There is an interesting aside to this: better educated, aware, and informed end users reduce the value of the product-or service-only brand.

[19]The entire organization, including its networks and information technology functions, must be involved in delivering the experience of the products and services that the organization promotes. Hence, marketing must exit functional silos to become a corporate passion—that is, the agile management of the organization's engagement with its external environment. This requires unity of purpose, a "one company" mentality with everyone pulling together. It requires new, integrated skills and tools for database marketing, multimedia and photography, publishing, communications through modern media, public relations, and end-user service, to name a few.

[20]Each behavior measures the health or ill-health of the organization.

what they say. From a marketing perspective, some components of behavior are transparency, authenticity, interactivity, applicability, and sustainability. The attributes of well-regarded brand-owning organizations are leadership, citizenship, pride, talent, innovation, transparency, and long-term view.

References

Kotler P, Levy S (1969) Broadening the concept of marketing. Journal of Marketing 33:10–15
Kotler P, Zaltman G (1971) Social marketing: an approach to planned social change. Journal of Marketing 35:3–12

Further Reading

Clifton R, Simmons J (eds) (2003) Brands and branding. The Economist Newspaper Ltd

Proposition 44
A Primer on Talent Management

In a Word Talent is not a rare commodity—people are talented in many ways: it is simply rarely released. To make talent happen organizations must give it strategic and holistic attention.

The Genesis of Talent Management

Globalization, the process by which economies, societies, and cultures are fast integrating through a globe-spanning network of communication and trade, drives both collaboration and competition. And so, in an age when those who possess knowledge[1]—not land, labor, or capital goods—own the new means of production, it is no surprise that a contest for talent has been raging since the 1990s. Better talent separates high-performance organizations from the rest. They bet on people, not strategies.

---

[1]In the information era, the value of hard assets has declined compared with the value of an organization's intangible assets, e.g., reputation, name recognition, and intellectual property such as knowledge and know-how. Human capital, also known as talent, is the primary source of the intangible assets in organizations today.

© Asian Development Bank 2017
O. Serrat, *Knowledge Solutions*, DOI 10.1007/978-981-10-0983-9_44

Critical talent is scarce (and about to become scarcer) because of three trends: the ongoing retirement of the "Baby Boom Generation",[2] a widening skills gap,[3] and large-scale social integration[4] (driving rapidly changing lifestyles).

Talent management has become one of the most pressing topics in organizations (even if very few have strategies and operational programs in place with which to identify, recruit, develop, deploy, and retain the best). The competition for talent will define organizational milieus for a couple of decades to come. Springing from the three trends, several drivers fuel the emphasis:

- Workforce demographics are evolving.[5]
- The context in which organizations conduct their operations is increasingly complex and dynamic.[6]
- More efficient capital markets have enabled the rise of small and medium-sized organizations that offer opportunities few large organizations can match, exerting a pull across the talent spectrum.
- In knowledge economies, talent is a rapidly increasing source of value creation.
- A demonstrated correlation between talent and organizational performance exists: talented individuals drive a disproportionate share of organizational effectiveness. (Value creation extends beyond individual performance differentials.)
- Financial markets and boards of directors demand more.
- The mobility of personnel[7] is quickening on a par with changing expectations.[8] If talent is hard to find, it is becoming harder to keep.

---

[2]The "Baby Boom Generation" is a term that portrays those born in Asia, Australia, Europe, and North America after the Second World War, essentially between 1946 and 1955. They are now 55–64 years of age.

[3]A skills gap is a discrepancy between an organization's current capabilities and the human capital it needs to achieve its goals. It is the point at which an organization may no longer grow or remain competitive because it cannot fill critical jobs with personnel that has the right knowledge, skills, and abilities.

[4]The large-scale social integration that constitutes modernity involves (i) faster movement of information, capital, goods, and people among formerly discrete populations, and consequent influence beyond the local area; (ii) sharper specialization of the segments of society, e.g., division of labor; and (iii) tighter formal social organization of mobile populations, development of circuits and networks on which they and their influence travel, and societal standardization conducive to socioeconomic mobility.

[5]For example, on top of the ongoing retirement of the "Baby Boom Generation" and certainly in the West, women are no longer joining the workforce en masse, white-collar productivity improvements have peaked, executives are not extending their careers, and immigration levels are stable (but might decline).

[6]Knowledge economies call for people with global acumen, multicultural ease, technological skills, entrepreneurial mindsets, and the ability to manage organizations that are increasingly delayered and disaggregated.

[7]One should perhaps now say partners and volunteers, not personnel or (even worse) employees.

[8]Rapidly changing lifestyles drive different expectations. Today, staffs are more interested in having meaningful and challenging work. They are therefore more loyal to their profession than to

In 1997, McKinsey and Company studied 77 large organizations from various industries to circumscribe the magnitude of the war for talent (Chambers et al. 1998). They talked to the top 200 executives in each company to appreciate why these executives worked where they did and how they had become the professionals they were. Organizations with winning employee value propositions had a compelling answer to the question, "Why would a talented person want to work here?" To create such a proposition, a great organization tailors its brand and products—that is, the jobs it has to offer—to appeal. It also pays the price it takes to recruit and retain talented people. The overall top 200 population cared deeply about values and culture, freedom and autonomy, challenging jobs, and good management. Differentiation was important to their compensation and lifestyle. In sum, their rewards were psychological, developmental, and financial. In 1973, Drucker (1973) wrote: "Making a living is no longer enough. Work also has to make a life." Abraham Maslow had, 30 years earlier, conceptualized a theory of human motivation.[9]

Discovering Talent Management

My main job was developing talent. I was a gardener providing water and other nourishment to our top 750 people. Of course, I had to pull out some weeds, too.

—Jack Welch

Talent management refers to the additional processes and opportunities that an organization makes available strategically to a pool of people who are deemed to have talent. If talent is not identified and managed by the entire management team, not only the human resource management unit, talent may just as well be defined as a dormant or untapped quality to be accessed in the future, either in an individual or in the collective.

In point of fact, all organizations are equipped with a talent management system, be it by default or design—it is the people side of organizational design, usually

---

(Footnote 8 continued)

the organization. It follows that they are less accommodating of traditional structures and authority and more concerned about work–life balance. Therefore, they are better prepared to take ownership of their careers and development.

[9]As long ago as 1943, Abraham Maslow (1908–1970), an American psychologist, conceptualized a hierarchy of human needs. People have a basic desire to meet physiological needs, e.g., food, clothing, shelter. Next they seek safety, e.g., personal and financial security, and health and well-being. After physiological and safety requirements are fulfilled, they try to meet social needs, e.g., friendship, intimacy, and family. Next, all humans want to be respected and to have self-esteem and self-respect. Finally, at the top of the pyramid, is what Maslow called "self-actualization," the aspiration to fulfill one's self and become all that one is capable of becoming.

entrusted to human resource management units. But a keyword here is "additional": historically, organizations have concerned themselves almost exclusively with top executives, particularly their replacement and succession. (Senior leaders certainly constitute talent even if, more frequently in the public sector, they sometimes owe their jobs to political correctness or tenure.)[10] Another is "pool": talent management demands that organizations move from replacement and succession planning to cater to the entire talent pool[11] with other processes and opportunities.[12] From a richer results chain perspective, talent management is also about recognizing and addressing the constant challenge to have the right people matched to the right jobs at the right time, and doing the right things. That is, talent management is about managing the demand, supply, and flow of talent across the organization through the human capital engine based on organizational strengths, weaknesses, opportunities, and threats. (The Develop-Deploy-Connect model helps generate capability, commitment, and alignment in talent pool segments.) The third related keyword is "strategic": with respect to talent, it intimates that an organization, to maintain a sustainable competitive advantage, may wish to maximize organizational capabilities in certain competencies[13] and deemphasize others. First, this requires that,

---

[10]Patronage is the control of appointments to jobs or the power to grant other political favors and the distribution of favors, jobs, and offices on a political basis. The word suggests the transgression of real or perceived boundaries of legitimate political influence and the violation of principles of merit and competition in recruitment and promotion. In the international public sector, many governments accept that some political appointments are legitimate and can help fashion a circle of managers sharing a common agenda. However, it is a problem when such appointments permeate systems and undermine merit and competition principles to the cost of organizational performance. Performance suffers when unqualified individuals are recruited or promoted into positions for which they are not suited. More detrimentally, morale is damaged as rank-and-file personnel witness their prospects for advancement based on merit and competition dim inexorably.

[11]In any organization, the existing talent pool comprises (i) senior leaders, (ii) those with leadership potential at mid-level, (iii) high performers, (iv) key contributors and technical experts, (v) those in roles critical to delivering the business strategy, (vi) those with skills in short supply and high demand, (vii) the entire workforce, and (viii) those with leadership potential at an entry level. Not surprisingly, given the historical preoccupation with replacement and succession planning, the segments that are viewed as most important to an organization follow the order in which they have just been listed. (Paradoxically, since voluntary resignation at the highest levels is typically low, most organizations do not consider senior leaders a high turnover risk. However, as if to confirm that talent is a critical issue facing organizations today, those with skills in short supply and high demand and high performers usually are, even if little is done about them.) Last but not least, the contents of the talent pools should be reviewed regularly but no finality should be ascribed.

[12]This does not mean that organizations should manage the talent in each person, however appealing the idea might be. That notion provides no guidance to determine what resources should be allocated to unearthing (and then perhaps grooming) individual talent.

[13]The *Knowledge Solutions* series couches a set of competencies in terms of strategy development, management techniques, collaboration mechanisms, knowledge sharing and learning, and knowledge capture and storage.

having understood what motivates and drives talented people, organizations become management innovators and recognize that they do not need the same talent pool segments all the time (with implications for talent pool strategies, talent management systems, and talent management activities); second, it recognizes at long last that talent management can no longer be the province of human resource management units; third, it exposes the shortcomings of forced ranking[14] that many have excoriated as misguided, destructive, and outright antithetical to sound leadership.

Like all new fields, there will be strong returns to research. (Ten years after its birth, confusion or disagreement over the way talent management should be defined, operationalized, or supported are still rife.) Promising areas include the architecture of decisions for talent management,[15] talent pool strategies,[16] and the development of valid and reliable talent management measures.[17] Notwithstanding, the proactive, strategic nature of talent management opens new vistas. Across the world, it is agreed that human resource management can, indeed should, add more value to organizations. The best way to accomplish this is to become a business partner that directly improves organizational effectiveness.[18] Any organization needs a wide range of talents to succeed, not only those associated with senior leaders. If an organization recognizes clearly what work needs to be done and what

---

[14]Forced ranking is a management tool that relies on annual evaluations to locate an organization's best and worst performing personnel, using person-to-person comparisons. To improve the quality of the workforce, managers typically rank personnel against one another into three categories: the top 20% are "A" players who are expected to lead the organization in the future; the middle 70% are "B" players who are encouraged to improve; the bottom 10% are "C" players who are either offered training, encouraged to move elsewhere, or dismissed. Where it works, forced ranking loses its effectiveness after a couple of years because the average quality of personnel increases (else, the exercise is proved a failure) and there are fewer "C" players to identify. Critics have argued that forced ranking engenders a pseudo-competitive environment conducive to patronage and yes-men; limited risk taking, creativity, and teamwork; as well as unethical (if not cutthroat) behavior that destroys trust in the workplace and depletes morale. It can also discourage workers from asking for help for fear they will be identified as low performers. Ironically, it can result in even good performers being cut if used on a yearly basis.

[15]For instance, the initial conditions and decisions that led to the adoption of forced ranking to improve the quality of the workforce are rarely examined. Yet, understanding these is central to interpreting linkages between related human resource management practices and their outcomes.

[16]For example, it might be worthwhile to develop systems-level models that illustrate the multi-pool impacts of talent choices in support of a strategy for sustainable competitive advantage.

[17]To labor the point, very few organizations bother to assess that forced ranking accurately identifies high performers. Elsewhere, there is no evidence that anything but the most cursory metrics, if any, feed the talent decisions managers make.

[18]The times are auspicious: as explained earlier, organizations are more and more dependent on their human capital for their competitive advantage. Since change is a constant, they also need more expertise in change management. Through the talent lens, human resource management can help with change management, influencing strategy and delivering a host of other value-added activities that impact organizational effectiveness.

competencies will deliver its strategy for sustainable competitive advantage, knows from talent mapping how best these can be identified and, where current and future gaps are, how they can be closed, numerous methods for managing talent can then be leveraged in support in more open and forward-looking fashion.[19]

"Undefining Talent"

How talent is defined is specific to an organization. Explanations are highly influenced by markets, industries, organizations, geographies, intellectual disciplines, generations, and of course the nature of talent's work. All are dynamic, and so likely to change over time according to organizational priorities. Rather than accepting universal or prescribed explanations, organizations will find greater value if they formulate their own definitions of what talent and talent management are. It is crucial for the meaning each gives to talent and its management to fit the organization's exogenous and endogenous circumstances and particular needs. A language for talent management activities is a prerequisite to developing a coherent talent management strategy.

Five Elements of a Talent Formula

In 2001, McKinsey and Company revisited their earlier study to structure a successful talent formula (Elizabeth et al. 2001). Taking care to highlight the differences between the old way and the new, they identified that leading organizations execute against five talent management imperatives to

- Instill a talent mindset at all levels of the organization, beginning with senior leaders.
- Create a winning employee value proposition that brings scarce talent through the doors and keeps it there. The components of the proposition are exciting work, a great organization, wealth and reward, and growth and development.
- Recruit talent continuously.
- Grow leaders.
- Differentiate and affirm.

---

[19]In declining (but not necessarily appropriate) frequency of use, formal methods typically include in-house development programs, coaching and mentoring, succession planning, cross-functional project assignments, high-potential development schemes, graduate development programs, courses at external institutions, internal secondments, assessment centers, 360-degree feedback, job rotation and shadowing, development centers, MBAs, action learning sets, and external secondments. Many of these can, and should, be applied to talent groups, not only individuals.

Strategic Perspectives

Given that different organizations aim to achieve different things from their talent management systems, while all seek to achieve some form of talent management, the five elements of a talent formula already look dated. More realistically and usefully, the Chartered Management Institute cautions that strategic perspective shapes the way in which the talent management system is viewed, implemented, and put into operation, such that the same activity can result in a different action or outcome depending on the perspective employed. Crucially, the Chartered Management Institute (Blass 2007) remarks that an organization may shift its perspective over time in accordance with changes in the organization's strategy for sustainable competitive advantage, and indeed the development and embeddedness of the talent management system itself.

Toward Integrated Talent Management?

The value of an integrated model for managing talent that links directly to improved organizational effectiveness is not lost on organizations. However, at this juncture, many note that an integrated approach is one of the most difficult of all talent management activities to implement, sustain, and enhance (Watson 2009). Next in line, in terms of difficulty, is creating more consistency in how talent is identified, developed, and moved throughout the organization. Third is giving senior leaders greater ownership of and accountability for the talent pipeline. Next, in diminishing order of difficulty, is focusing more on key workforce segments; redefining the critical attributes and competencies needed for the next generation of leaders; linking rewards more closely to performance; improving quality and use of analytics to monitor the need for, and supply of, talent and better differentiate performance; and scaling and adapting talent strategies on a global basis. Recognizing that these processes are necessary to succeed in the twenty-first century is the first, essential step.

Leading Mavericks

Inevitably, any discussion of talent management brings a focus to bear on mavericks. They are the handful of very clever, willfully independent, and highly creative individuals, often evangelistic believers, who produce remarkable results on their own.[20] If organizations are finding it difficult to retain top talent, they are finding it

---

[20]Mavericks know their self-worth and will not readily offer thanks for help. They are organizationally astute and well connected, which leads them to downplay hierarchy and demand instant access. Their high creativity is the flipside of their low boredom threshold.

almost impossible to maintain productive relationships with mavericks. But mavericks do not necessarily walk away. Contrary to common belief, they need the organization in the same measure that it needs them. (They cannot operate without the systems and resources it makes available.) Managers should be aware of the attributes that mavericks share. (Their one defining characteristic is that they do not want to be "led".) But the art of leading mavericks can be one of the most rewarding skills one can develop for an organization. A few tips follow:

- Understand the multiple motivations and diverging expectations of mavericks: turn their frustrations into satisfaction by actively enabling their talents to find outlets.
- Do not take mavericks for granted: they do not stand still and it pays to grant them attention with productive talk.[21]
- Inspire talent to stay by being personally courageous.
- Be generous: advertise the talent of mavericks to others.
- Expect that mavericks will outgrow you, and help them to do so.

References

Blass E (2007) Talent management: maximizing talent for business performance. Chartered Management Institute

Chambers E, Foulton M, Helen Handfield-Jones H, Hankin S, Michaels E (1998) The war for talent. McKinsey Quarterly. No 3

Drucker P (1973) Management: tasks, responsibilities, and practices. HarperCollins Publishers, Inc

Elizabeth A, Helen Handfield-Jones H, Welsh T (2001) The war on talent, part two. McKinsey Quarterly. No 2

Thorne K, Pellant A (2007) The essential guide to managing talent: how top companies recruit, train, and retain the best employees. Kogan Page Limited

Watson T (2009) Managing talent in tough times: a tipping point for talent management

Further Reading

Lewis R, Heckman R (2006) Talent management: a critical review. Human Resource Management Review 16(2):139–154

---

[21]Thorne and Pellant (2007) have proposed a useful competency-based development plan for talent: (i) generates novel ideas, avoids early conclusions; (ii) identifies and explores wider, less obvious options in a situation; (iii) is intrigued by new concepts and leverages them to gain business advantage; (iv) develops further, implements, and embeds new ideas, processes, or products; (v) takes calculated risks; (vi) offers independent ideas, challenges the status quo; and (vii) turns creative ideas into effective business solutions.

Proposition 45
Sparking Innovations in Management

In a Word Gary Hamel defines management innovation as a marked departure from traditional management principles, processes, and practices (or a departure from customary organizational forms that significantly alters the way the work of management is performed). He deems it the prime driver of sustainable competitive advantage in the twenty-first century.

© Asian Development Bank 2017
O. Serrat, *Knowledge Solutions*, DOI 10.1007/978-981-10-0983-9_45

Celebrating a Century of Management

The Economist's *Guide to Management Ideas and Gurus* (Hindle 2008) enumerates 103 management concepts that have impacted companies over the past century and the 56 more influential people behind them.[1] The *Guide to the Management Gurus* honors 45 key thinkers (Kennedy 2002). There are many other handbooks on the topic: in *The Handy Guide to the Gurus of Management*, the British Broadcasting Corporation (2010) offers students a pithy and accessible selection of a dozen important figures.

On the other hand, Hamel (2007) argues provocatively in *The Future of Management* that management is a maturing technology that has witnessed few genuine breakthroughs since Frederick Winslow Taylor[2] and Max Weber[3] set the ground rules 100 years ago in the wake of the upheaval caused by the industrial revolution and subsequent need for rationalization. From their work and influence, as well as the innovations of contemporaries such as Henri Fayol,[4] grew standardized job descriptions and work methods, protocols for production planning and scheduling, cost accounting and profit analysis, exception-based reporting and detailed financial controls, incentive-based compensation schemes and personnel divisions, capital budgeting, the fundamental architecture of multidivisional

---

[1]Tim Hindle names Peter Drucker, Douglas McGregor, Michael Porter, Alfred Sloan, and Frederick Winslow Taylor. Peter Drucker invented or prefigured almost all leading management theories of the last half-century (and foresaw most trends, such as the emergence of the knowledge worker), including mission, "structure follows strategy", the role of the chief executive, management by objectives, "sticking to the knitting" (the core business), customer care, marketing, and even privatization. Douglas McGregor formulated "Theory X" and "Theory Y", namely, authoritarian as opposed to participative styles of management based on opposing views of human nature at work. Michael Porter defined competitive strategy and advantage. Under "federal decentralization", as he termed it, Alfred Sloan reorganized General Motors into what became the template for every organization; he also introduced a systemic strategic planning procedure for his company's divisions. Frederick Winslow Taylor pioneered time and motion studies, out of which grew the idea of piece work; he enabled Henry Ford's mass-production revolution.

[2]Frederick Winslow Taylor (1856–1915), an American mechanical engineer, sought to improve industrial efficiency. He was the father of scientific management, a theory of management that analyzes and synthesizes workflows, with the objective of improving labor productivity.

[3]Max Weber (1864–1920), a German lawyer, politician, historian, political economist, and sociologist, is reputed for his study of the bureaucratization of society. He viewed bureaucracy as the pinnacle of social organization, considering it a more rational and efficient form than the arrangements that had preceded it, e.g., charismatic domination and traditional domination. (According to his terminology, bureaucracy is part of legal domination.)

[4]Henri Fayol (1841–1925), a French mining engineer and management theorist, developed a general theory of management independently of Frederick Winslow Taylor. He identified the six primary functions of management to be (i) forecasting, (ii) planning, (iii) organizing, (iv) commanding, (v) coordinating, and (vi) controlling.

organizations, and early principles of brand management. These *Knowledge Solutions* promote Gary Hamel's ideas, researched and promulgated also by the "Management Lab" that he and Julian Birkinshaw founded to accelerate the evolution of management knowledge and practice.

The Poverty of Management

Gary Hamel (2002) is known for his work on core competencies[5] and strategic intent.[6] Yet, his ambitions promise more. Advancing from earlier insights, he concludes in *The Future of Management* that it is innovation in management that is most likely to create sustainable competitive advantage in the twenty-first century.

This is not to say that there have been no original ideas: the evidence in guides to management thinkers refutes that argument. (For example, Michael Mol and Julian Birkinshaw (2008) identify 50 important changes categorized under process, money, people management, internal structures, customer and partner interfaces, innovation and strategy, and information efficiency.) However, most innovations—often formulated in purpose-built research and development departments—have been first and foremost in operations, then in products and services, and to a far lesser extent in strategies; they have rarely been in management itself.[7]

The paucity of significant breakthroughs should not surprise: after all, management was invented 100 years ago to solve the problem of inefficiency in organizations.[8] Therefore, to this day, management operates primarily through routine functions, e.g., planning, organizing, commanding, and controlling. Synthesizing a century of management theory, Gary Hamel suggests that the practice of management continues to entail

> *It ain't what you don't know that gets you into trouble. It's what you know for sure that just ain't so.*
>
> —Mark Twain

---

[5]A core competency is a specific factor that an organization sees as central to the way it works.

[6]Strategic intent intuits that strategy should be more active and interactive, with attributes of direction, discovery, and destiny.

[7]This would become more readily apparent if the history of management were taught in business schools.

[8]Efficiency is the ratio of the output to the input of any system.

- Setting goals and objectives and laying out plans;
- Amassing and allocating resources;
- Identifying, developing, and assigning talent;
- Motivating and aligning effort;
- Coordinating and controlling activities;
- Acquiring, accumulating, and applying knowledge;
- Building and nurturing relationships; and
- Understanding, balancing, and meeting stakeholder demands.

Of course, all these tasks are central to the accomplishment of purpose, hence the common focus of innovation on operations, products and services, and strategies. The typical processes for control, discipline, precision, stability, and especially reliability[9] that claim the lion's share of attention, and were themselves one-time management innovations, are

- Strategic planning,
- Return on investment analysis and capital budgeting,
- Project management,
- Research and development,
- Brand management,
- Leadership development,
- Recruitment and promotion,
- Learning and development,
- Internal communications,
- Knowledge management,
- Periodic business reviews, and
- Employee performance assessment and compensation.

Naturally, the public sector is not exempt. In 2000, a study[10] of public management innovation in the United States and Canada examined (i) the characteristics of public sector innovations, (ii) where in the organization innovations originated, (iii) whether innovations came about as a result of planning or groping, (iv) the obstacles to change innovators faced and how they overcame them, (v) the results

---

[9]Organizations value reliability. It is easier to improve existing processes than to ask effective questions about what change might really be needed. It is also more difficult to prove that something new will pay off than to use traditional logic to vaunt the benefits of a modification. Taken to extremes, fascination with "objective" criteria and highly visible indicators perverts systems and feeds hypocrisy so that the behaviors that are desired are not rewarded at all (Kerr 1975).

[10]The study was based on samples of 217 of the best applications to the Ford Foundation-Kennedy School of Government innovation awards and 33 of the best applications to the Institute of Public Administration of Canada's management innovation awards, both between 1990 and 1994 (Borins 2000).

achieved by these innovations, and (vi) whether these innovations were replicated. The study, from which the following text quotes, found that (i) the dominant characteristic of public management innovations is that they were holistic, e.g., systems approaches to problems, coordinating activities, with second-magnitude characteristics being the use of new information technology as well as and process improvement, e.g., partnerships with the private sector, new management philosophies, and empowerment; (ii) the most frequent initiators of public management innovations were local heroes, visionary middle-level and frontline public servants who took risks despite disincentives; (iii) innovations were a result of both comprehensive planning and incremental groping; (iv) the most frequent obstacles to innovations were internal to the bureaucracy; (v) obstacles to change were most frequently overcome by persuasion or accommodation; (vi) innovative programs produced results such as increased demand, reduced costs, and improved service, morale, and productivity; and (vii) innovative programs received substantial media attention and were widely replicated.

> *My interest is in the future because I am going to spend the rest of my life there.*
> —Charles Kettering

Managing with Imagination

Management innovation would concern itself with changing these processes, which govern daily managerial work. With globalization, the conditions that existed in the past are less likely to lead to successful prediction: resources have been redefined, networks thrive, options abound, opportunity reigns, people want to achieve, adaptation and foresight are a must, and speed is required. In a sense, since change is the order of the day, what is happening is not new but a logical extension of what has happened before. Naturally, there is now much greater appreciation of the impact of uncertainty on models and behaviors.

Yet, as if to prove that Henri Fayol holds sway even now, the primary role of management in most organizations is still to ensure that resources are obtained and used effectively and efficiently in the accomplishment of the organization's objectives. (The perception that good management equates—or is closely linked—to good measurement runs deep.) We desire consistent, replicable outcomes, making perhaps marginal improvements. Cybernetic systems such as thermostats certainly have advantages; but they can also go too far when applied, for example, to individuals and organizations.

> *Innovation is not the product of logical thought, although the result is tied to logical structure.*
>
> —Albert Einstein

Treating organizations as well-oiled machines makes robots out of personnel. At the very least in so-called developed countries but increasingly elsewhere, what among other factors has changed since Frederick Winslow Taylor's days is the rise of the knowledge worker. (We can, and should, learn more about why talent is attracted to start-ups.) A result can be consistent if we obtain from it what we seek, and hope to replicate, but it may not be valid in the sense that it delivers the value we really need. In thinking about organizations, it is enlightening to consult Kenneth Boulding's[11] classification of systems, which permits a possible arrangement of "levels" of theoretical discourse. At the level of social organizations, the complexity is overwhelming.[12] We cannot know what we miss if we do not know what it is that we do not know. However, we will not create it if we cannot imagine it.[13] This calls for abductive logic.[14]

---

[11]Kenneth Boulding (1910–1993), a British (then American) economist, educator, systems scientist, and interdisciplinary philosopher, cofounded the general systems theory with Ludwig von Bertalanffy (1901–1972), an Austrian biologist. That is an interdisciplinary theory about complex systems in nature, society, and science. Kenneth Boulding also founded numerous intellectual projects in economics and social science, notably in psychic capital and evolutionary economics.

[12]Hence, to begin to relax control mechanisms, managers had best visualize systems of interconnected and interdependent relationships radiating through their organization to others in its value chain, informed by feedback processes and characterized by emergence.

[13]Martin (2009) has argued that organizations can successfully adopt the methodologies and perspectives that designers use. By so doing, they can move from being reliability-oriented to become validity-embracing organizations (but must still speak both languages). Managers, and other personnel too, are responsible for this necessary and by now urgent shift toward design thinking. The purpose of design thinking is to achieve balance through generative reasoning. The approach is based on (i) respect for exploitation and exploration, (ii) assimilation of the future with the past, (iii) the design of what should be, and (iv) integration of analysis and judgment.

[14]Abduction is a method of intuitive logical inference introduced by Charles Sanders Peirce (1839–1914), an American philosopher, logician, mathematician, and scientist. The colloquial name of abduction is (to have) a "hunch". Deduction allows deriving b as a consequence of a. Induction allows inferring a entails b from multiple instantiations of a and b at the same time. Abduction allows inferring a as an explanation of b.

Table. General systems theory

Frameworks	The geography and anatomy of the universe: the patterns of electrons around a nucleus, the pattern of atoms in a molecular formula, the arrangement of atoms in a crystal, the anatomy of the gene, the mapping of the earth, the solar system, the astronomical universe, etc.
Clockworks	The solar system or simple machines such as the lever and the pulley, even quite complicated machines like steam engines and dynamos, fall mostly under this category
Thermostats	Control mechanisms or cybernetic systems: the system will move to the maintenance of any given equilibrium, within limits
Cells	Open systems or self-maintaining structures. This is the level at which life begins to differentiate itself from not-life
Plants	The outstanding characteristics of these systems, as studied by botanists, are first, a division of labor with differentiated and mutually dependent parts, e.g., roots, leaves, seeds, etc., and second, a sharp differentiation between the genotype and the phenotype, associated with the phenomenon of equifinal or "blueprinted" growth
Animals	Level characterized by increased mobility, teleological behavior and self-awareness, with the development of specialized information receptors, e.g., eyes, ears, etc., leading to an enormous increase in the intake of information
Human beings	In addition to all, or nearly all, of the characteristics of animal systems man possesses self-consciousness, which is something different from mere awareness
Social organizations	The unit of such systems is not perhaps the person but the "role"—that part of the person which is concerned with the organization or situation in question. Social organizations, or almost any social system, might be defined as a set of roles tied together with channels of communication
Transcendental systems	The ultimates and absolutes and the inescapable unknowables, that also exhibit systematic structure and relationship

Source Author

Sparking Management Innovation

Personnel is more often than not dissatisfied with managers.[15] (Mark the interest in 360-degree feedback to improve their performance.[16]) Functional management is an artifact of the twentieth century. In anachronistic organizations that stick to what they can measure instead of imagining the future, managers plead forgiveness for

---

[15]Typically, one third of promotions ends in failure, one third is passable, and the remainder meets the purpose.

[16]Theodore Zeldin recalled in a 2008 interview with the Financial Times (2010) a conversation with chief executives in London. One of them said: "We can no longer select people, they select us. If we want the best people and we want to attract them, we have to say: What do you want in your job?" It is plain that the power of recruiters no longer holds much weight.

being prisoners of a reality they work to reinforce each day. But frustration about the very roles they play is also growing and signals a future in which management is performed less and less by managers.

> *Just as energy is the basis of life itself, and ideas the source of innovation, so is innovation the vital spark of all human change, improvement, and progress.*
>
> —Theodore Levitt

Gary Hamel defines management innovation as a marked departure from traditional management principles, processes, and practices (or a departure from customary organizational forms that significantly alters the way the work of management is performed). To be clear, that is innovation in management principles and processes that ultimately change the practice of what managers do and how they do it. This distinguishes it from innovation in operations, products and services, and strategies. Hamel (2006) picks out 12 innovations that shaped modern management:

> *Innovation! One cannot be forever innovating. I want to create classics.*
>
> —Coco Chanel

- Scientific management (time and motion studies),
- Cost accounting and variance analysis,
- The commercial research laboratory (the industrialization of science),
- Return on investment analysis and capital budgeting,
- Brand management,
- Large-scale project management,
- Divisionalization,
- Leadership development,
- Industry consortia (multicompany collaborative structures),
- Radical decentralization (self-organization),
- Formalized strategic analysis, and
- Employee-driven problem solving.

The process that drove the 12 innovations listed was dissatisfaction with the status quo (the motivation phase), inspiration from other sources, invention, and internal and external validation—after which the innovations were copied by other organizations and spread across entire industries and countries. High-performance organizations take measures to mainstream ad hoc and incremental management innovation and accelerate its process. According to Birkinshaw and Mol (2006), essential steps are to:

- Become a conscious management innovator, able to examine management innovations from various perspectives, e.g., institutional, fashion, cultural, and rational;
- Create a questioning, problem-solving culture;
- Commit to big problems;
- Search for new principles;
- Deconstruct management orthodoxies;
- Seek analogies and exemplars from different environments;
- Build a capacity for low-risk experimentation;
- Make use of external change agents, e.g., academics, consultants, media organizations, management gurus, and former personnel, to test the organization's new ideas; and
- Become a serial management innovator.

Never before in history has innovation offered promise of so much to so many in so short a time.

—Bill Gates

There are elements of destructive creation to this: for each relevant management process, key questions are:

- Who owns the process?
- Who has the power to change it?
- What are its objectives?
- What are the success metrics?
- Who are the customers of this process?
- Who gets to participate?
- What are the data or information inputs for this process?
- What analytical tools are used?
- What events and milestones drive this process?
- What kind of decisions does this process generate?
- What are the decision-making criteria?
- How are decisions communicated, and to whom?
- How does this process link to other management systems?

Visions of the Present

Three forces should drive management innovation in the 2010s: (i) the unremitting development of the Internet[17] (and the communities and networks of interest and practice it has spawned); (ii) globalization (and the new attitudes toward work and the way it is performed that collaboration and competition, mostly encouraged by the Internet, are engendering); and (iii) workforce demographics (as Generation X[18] then Generation Y[19] come of corporate age). High-performance organizations will push management innovation to meet challenges, rather than having it pulled from them.

In *The Future of Management*, Gary Hamel envisions a time when the goal of management is to build nimble, lattice-based organizations that energize and demand, that may be big yet personal. In nimble organizations, there is more freedom and self-management. Personnel—partners and volunteers all, share a sense of purpose and commitment (not assignment) and have no need for exhortation from senior leaders. There is less hierarchy but plenty of leaders.

In nimble organizations, innovation is everyone's responsibility, especially where it humanizes work. Nimble organizations deploy considerable efforts to ensure that personnel is connected and collective wisdom is harnessed through continuous, companywide conversations that build trust and understanding. Generally unmonitored time as well as "elbow room" in terms of human and other resources enable people to think, take measured risk, and innovate freely through rapid, low-cost experimentation. Personnel operates in small, self-managing teams that senior leaders sponsor and referee, with authority given to the teams to recruit, develop, and dismiss members. Individuals can redesign their jobs or relocate themselves in the organization. Freedom travels hand in hand with accountability: performance is rewarded at all levels, both individual and collective.

---

[17]The Internet permeates our lives. It has changed (and will continue to change) how we find and share information, stay in touch, and do business. Indeed, the Internet may be the best metaphor for management in the twenty-first century. It is creating a democracy of ideas (that gives everyone the chance to opt in), amplifying human imagination, aggregating collective wisdom, dynamically reallocating resources, and minimizing the drag of obsolete mental models.

[18]Generation X is the generation born after the post Second World War Baby Boom ended, with earliest birth dates used by researchers ranging from 1961 to the latest 1981.

[19]Generation Y describes the demographic cohort following Generation X. Its members are often referred to as Echo Boomers or Millennials. As there are no precise dates for when Generation Y starts and ends, commentators have used birth dates ranging from the mid-1970s to the early 2000s.

References

Birkinshaw J, Mol M (2006) How management innovation happens. MIT Sloan Management Review 47(4):80–88

Borins S (2000) What border? Public management innovation in the United States and Canada. Journal of Policy Analysis and Management 19(1):46–74

British Broadcasting Corporation (2010) The handy guide to the gurus of management

Financial Times (2010) Lunch with the FT: Theodore Zeldin

Hamel G (2007) The future of management. Harvard Business School Publishing

Hindle T (2008) Guide to management ideas and gurus. Economist Books

Kennedy C (2002) Guide to the management gurus: the best guide to business thinkers. Business Books. The "Famous Five" feature there too

Kerr S (1975) On the folly of rewarding a while hoping for B. Academy of Management Journal 18:769–783

Martin R (2009) The design of business: Why design thinking is the next competitive advantage. Harvard Business School Publishing

Michael M, Birkinshaw J (2008) Giant steps in management: innovations that change the way you work. Pearson Education Ltd

Further Reading

Hamel G (2002) Leading the revolution. Penguin Books

Hamel G (2006) The why, what, and how of management innovation. Harvard Business Review 2:72–84

Proposition 46
Crafting a Knowledge Management Results Framework

In a Word Managing for results requires a coherent framework for strategic planning, management, and communications based on continuous learning and accountability. Results frameworks improve management effectiveness by defining realistic expected results, monitoring progress toward their achievement, integrating lessons into decisions, and reporting on performance.

Background

On May 4, 2009, at the 42nd Annual Meeting of the Board of Governors of ADB, Haruhiko Kuroda—ADB President and concurrent Chairperson of ADB's Board of Directors—stressed the importance of knowledge to that organization:

> *To be fully effective, we must also consciously and actively blend knowledge with financing. We will focus on developing, capturing, and sharing knowledge in all our work, ensuring that ADB serves an intermediary role for both financing and knowledge.*

© Asian Development Bank 2017
O. Serrat, *Knowledge Solutions*, DOI 10.1007/978-981-10-0983-9_46

Enhancing Knowledge Management Under ADB's Strategy 2020

Bite off more than you can chew, then chew it.

—Ella Williams

When it comes to getting things done, we need fewer architects and more bricklayers.

—Colleen Barrett

On July 31, 2009, President Kuroda then approved *Enhancing Knowledge Management under Strategy 2020: Plan of Action for 2009–2011* (2009) to advance the knowledge management agenda under *Strategy 2020: The Long-Term Strategic Framework of the Asian Development Bank (2008–2020)* (2008). Four pillars support the plan of action: (i) sharpening the knowledge focus in ADB's operations—to add value at regional, country, and project levels, (ii) empowering the communities of practice—to collaborate for knowledge generation and sharing, (iii) strengthening external knowledge partnerships—to align and leverage external knowledge, and (iv) further enhancing staff learning and skills development—to enhance opportunities for staff to learn. The four pillars are closely related: the set of actions/outputs that make up the first focuses on adding value to ADB's operations in its developing member countries; the other three sets deal with how that might be achieved.

ADB's plan of action for knowledge management connotes a pragmatic, step-by-step approach: the initial actions/outputs are for a 3-year time frame; in October 2009, measures for their implementation were incorporated into ADB's Work Program and Budget Framework (2010–2012); and progress is to be monitored and reviewed at the time of ADB's annual budget review by the Regional and Sustainable Development Department in ADB, in consultation with ADB's Budget, Personnel, and Management Systems Department and Strategy and Policy Department.

Crafting a Knowledge Management Results Framework

ADB's plan of action does not discuss but flags aspects that support and facilitate knowledge management practices, viz., budgetary allocations, business process improvements, and information technology. These *Knowledge Solutions* showcase the expected outcomes, useful results indicators, specific activity indicators, targets, and sources of verification that comprise the knowledge management results framework for ADB's plan of action. The framework was prepared after extensive internal consultations. It is an important instrument used to assess and improve performance and help identify problems and their solutions. It is the basis for reporting. (These *Knowledge Solutions* also disclose the approach to progress reporting and what will condition ratings of progress in adoption.) The framework is expected to promote a stronger culture of results and performance for knowledge management in ADB.

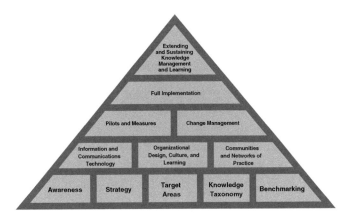

Fig. Building a knowledge-centric organization. *Source* Author

Box 1: Enhancing Knowledge Management under Strategy 2020: Plan of Action for 2009–2011—Knowledge Management Results Framework

Impact: The capacity of ADB and its DMCs to reduce poverty is enhanced			
Outcome	Monitoring indicator	Target[a]	Source of verification
First Pillar Statement: The Knowledge Focus in ADB's Operations is Sharpened			
At the regional level, ADB is increasingly recognized as a lead policy advisor, notably through the knowledge agenda that its TA for research and development advances	**Useful Results Indicators**		
	• Number of staff assessing the commitment and maturity of ADB's knowledge management framework favorably. Baseline year: 2008	10% more every year	• Annual Knowledge Management Survey. RSDD-KM
	• The number and outreach of ADB stand-alone flagship publications, facilitated by enhanced marketing and dissemination efforts. Baseline year: 2008	10% more every year	• DER
	• The number of references to ADB knowledge products in research, press, and policy reports. Baseline year: 2008	5% more every year	• DER
	• Views of web pages and downloads of PDF files from knowledge and operations departments. Baseline year: 2009	10% more every year	• DER
	Specific Activity Indicators		
	• An E-library hosting knowledge products that are indexed and searchable is launched	Done: 2011	• DER
	• TA reports contain information on knowledge management and communication	More, every year	• Special study by national consultant. RSDD-KM
	• Taxonomies, templates, and guidelines for branding and publishing, as well as use of metadata, are prepared or finalized, then disseminated through the knowledge coordinators, for use by authors	Done: 2010	• DER
	• A timetable for digitization of publications, e.g., books, significant papers, from 1966 is established and the process is launched, with care to add metadata to increase searchability, make intellectual patrimony more widely available, and enhance its intellectual equity	Done: 2010	• DER
	• Channels for marketing and distribution of knowledge products are expanded, enhanced, and monitored to build additional relationships and help increase exposure among key stakeholders, opinion makers, and academic institutions	More, every year	• DER
	• A world-class translation system is adopted and introduced with associated training to retool, upgrade, and expand current	Done: 2011	• DER

(continued)

(continued)

Impact: The capacity of ADB and its DMCs to reduce poverty is enhanced			
Outcome	Monitoring indicator	Target[a]	Source of verification
	practices, with emphasis on flow management of journalistically written summaries that where possible coincide with book releases		
At the country level, CPSs guide medium-term operational programming with a focus on results and development effectiveness	**Useful Results Indicators**		
	• Number of instances on record when CPSs led to DMC studies that were used to support policy development and decision-making. Baseline year: 2010	1 more every year	• Annual questionnaire to RMs. RSDD-KM
	Specific Activity Indicators		
	• RRPs contain information on knowledge management and communication	More, every year	• Special study by national consultant. RSDD-KM
	• CPSs contain information on knowledge management and communication	More, every year	• Special study by national consultant. RSDD-KM
	• CPSs state in which sector(s) ADB considers itself a key knowledge partner in the donor community.	More, every year	• Special study by national consultant. RSDD-KM
	• ADB organizes (i) ADB-wide, and (ii) in-country forums, workshops, seminars, conferences, media events, etc. Baseline year: 2010	5 more every year	• Annual questionnaire to RMs. RSDD-KM
At the project or TA level, key documents embody quality, knowledge, and innovation	**Useful Results Indicators**		
	• Downloads of TA reports from internal and external users. Baseline year: 2009	More, every year	• DER, ODs
	• The number of TA consultant reports posted on ADB.org. Baseline year: 2009	More, every year	• DER, ODs
	• The number of books, reports, journals, briefs, working papers, training and instructive materials, and awareness raising and multimedia materials posted on ADB.org. Baseline year: 2009	More, every year	• DER, ODs
	• The number of landing pages on ADB.org for ADB projects and studies. Baseline year: 2009	More, every year	• DER, ODs
	Specific Activity Indicators		
	• TA reports contain information on knowledge management and communication	More, every year	• Offices and departments
	• New sector peer review process implemented in ADB for the preparation of RRPs and TAs	Done: 2010	• SPPI, RSDD
Second Pillar Statement: The Communities of Practice are Empowered			
CoPs become an integral part of ADB's business processes	**Useful Results Indicators**		
	• CoPs are resourced with dedicated staff. Baseline year: 2009	Done: 2010–2011	• BPOD

(continued)

(continued)

Impact: The capacity of ADB and its DMCs to reduce poverty is enhanced

Outcome	Monitoring indicator	Target[a]	Source of verification
	• The number of work plans and PDPs in which participation in CoPs is mentioned. Baseline year: 2009	More, every year	• BPHR
	• The number of meetings and events organized by CoPs. Baseline year: 2010	More, every year	• RSDD-KM, CoPs
	• The number of early informal peer reviews by CoP members, to help staff conceptualize projects and TA. Baseline year: 2010	More, every year	• Annual questionnaire to CoPs. RSDD-KM
	Specific Activity Indicators		
	• The capacity of CoPs in terms of staff positions in direct support of their operational and administrative activities. Baseline year: 2009	Done: 2010–2011	• BPOD
	• CoPs conduct regular self-assessments of effectiveness, including assessments of the CoP convenor, as part of annual sector and thematic reports. Baseline year: 2010	All, every year	• CoPs
	• A *Forum on Learning* and *ADB's CoPs: Learning, Sharing, and Doing Together* is held	Every year	• RSOD, RSDD-KM
	• Sector and thematic websites are revamped and updated with links to relevant information in ADB.	Done: 2010–2011	• RSDD-KM
	• Supervisors are instructed and ensure that institutional initiatives in CoPs are assessed in PDPs and included in work planning.	Every year, at the start	• BPHR
	• Revised *Guidelines for sector and thematic reporting* are prepared and approved	Done: 2009	• RSDD-KM, RSOD
Output-based financing recognizes CoPs that generate and share useful and usable knowledge	**Useful Results Indicators**		
	• The budgets of CoPs support expanding activities and are complemented through TAs	Done: 2010	• BPBM, CoPs
	• Annual CoP work plans are based on triennial sector and thematic reports	80% in 2010, 100% afterwards	• RSDD-KM
	Specific Activity Indicators		
	• Budget allocations are devolved through relevant divisions to heads of CoPs responsible for managing funds.	Done: 2011	• BPBM, CoPs
	• A *CoP Accomplishment Report* is generated.	Every year, in September	• RSDD-KM
The CoPs engage more purposefully in external knowledge partnerships	**Useful Results Indicators**		
	• The number of formal and informal knowledge partnerships with other organizations for knowledge generation and sharing. Baseline year: 2010	More, every year	• Annual questionnaire to CoPs. RSDD-KM
	• Knowledge networking and collaboration is recognized by ADB with mention of this in PDPs	Done: 2010	• Offices and departments, BPHR

(continued)

(continued)

Outcome	Monitoring indicator	Target[a]	Source of verification
Impact: The capacity of ADB and its DMCs to reduce poverty is enhanced			
	Specific Activity Indicators		
	• CoPs engage in formal and informal knowledge partnerships that result in joint activities. Baseline year: 2010		
More, every year	• Annual questionnaire to CoPs. RSDD-KM		
The contributions of the knowledge coordinators in ADB are enhanced	**Useful Results Indicators**		
	• The activities of the knowledge coordinators are reviewed, harmonized, and managed for efficiency and effectiveness	Done: 2010–2011	• RSDD-KM
	Specific Activity Indicators		
	• Meetings, facilitated by RSDD-KM, are held with the knowledge coordinators to structure their contributions and to identify and discuss opportunities to ramp these up. Baseline year: 2010	Every quarter	• RSDD-KM, DER
	• Meetings, facilitated by DER, are held with the knowledge coordinators to identify and discuss marketing and dissemination opportunities to enhance knowledge products and increase their outreach with emphasis on relevance, accuracy, objectivity, and timeliness. Baseline year: 2010	Every quarter	• DER, RSDD-KM
Third Pillar Statement: External Knowledge Partnerships are Strengthened			
The design, implementation, and monitoring of external knowledge partnerships with global, regional, and national institutions are improved	**Useful Results Indicators**		
	• The design, implementation, and monitoring of strategic partnerships in key sectors and themes are informed by the *Guidelines on Designing Knowledge Partnerships* to be finalized in 2010	Done: 2010	• SPPI, RSDD-KM
	• A database of strategic partnerships affords greater transparency and synergies are achieved where institutions are involved in more than one strategic partnership arrangement with ADB	Done: 2010	• SPPI, OIST, RSDD-KM
	Specific Activity Indicators		
	• A resource document, *Guidelines on Designing Knowledge Partnerships*, is drafted that informs the design, implementation, and monitoring of knowledge components in strategic partnerships	Done: 2010	• RSDD-KM, SPPI
	• Midterm review processes for memorandums of understanding with strategic partners are adapted to include review of knowledge generation and sharing components	Done: 2010	• SPPI, RSDD-KM
	• A database of strategic partnerships for use across ADB, including resident missions, is established and managed continuously thereafter.	Done: 2010	• SPPI, OIST, RSDD-KM

(continued)

(continued)

Impact: The capacity of ADB and its DMCs to reduce poverty is enhanced			
Outcome	Monitoring indicator	Target[a]	Source of verification
External knowledge partnerships generate and share knowledge proactively	**Useful Results Indicators**		
	• External stakeholders perceiving ADB as a source of knowledge on development issues. Baseline year: 2006	10% more	• ADB Stakeholder Perceptions Survey, 2009. DER
	Specific Activity Indicators		
	• ADB.org offers improved information on knowledge partnerships and profiles their products and services	Done: 2010	• DER
	• The dissemination and visibility of ADB's knowledge products are expanded and enhanced through ADB's depository library program and multi-donor public information center network	More, every year	• DER
Fourth Pillar Statement: Staff Learning and Skills Development are Enhanced Further			
Staff skills in knowledge management and learning are developed and captured	**Useful Results Indicators**		
	• Staff perceiving that ADB is becoming a learning organization that generates and shares knowledge better. Baseline year: 2008	10% more every year	• Annual KM Survey. RSDD-KM
	• Staff participation in learning and development activities for knowledge management and learning	More, every year	• RSDD-KM, BPDB
	Specific Activity Indicators		
	• A training needs assessment is conducted to identify the learning programs CoPs need and their preferred learning modes, and recommend learning opportunities to support their activities in 2010–2011.	Done: 2010	• RSDD-KM, BPDB
	• RSDD-KM and BPMSD collaborate on the design and conduct of learning and development activities	Done: 2010–2011	• RSDD-KM, BPDB
	• RSDD-KM holds awareness and capacity building sessions on knowledge management and learning. Start in 2010	Continuously, every year	• RSDD-KM, BPDB
	• The awareness, outreach, and impact of the *Knowledge Solutions* and *Knowledge Showcase* series are assessed in the baseline year and annually thereafter.	Done: 2010	• RSDD-KM
	• Expanded staff profile pages are developed in 2010 and made available externally in 2011.	Done: 2010	• OIST[b]
Staff pursue external learning opportunities	**Useful Results Indicators**		
	• The number of staff who express interest in external learning	More, every year	• BPDB

(continued)

Impact: The capacity of ADB and its DMCs to reduce poverty is enhanced			
Outcome	Monitoring indicator	Target[a]	Source of verification
	opportunities and apply for competitive sabbatical leave increases. Baseline year: 2007		
	Specific Activity Indicators		
	• ADB encourages staff exchanges with strategic partners. Baseline year: 2007	Done: 2010	• BPDB
	• The budget for external training expands opportunities. Baseline year: 2007	Done: 2010	• BPDB
Research in priority areas of *Strategy 2020* is boosted	**Useful Results Indicators**		
	• The number of senior researchers invited under the Eminent Speakers' Forum, Distinguished Speakers Program, and Distinguished Speaker Seminar Series. Baseline year: 2009	More, every year	• ADBI, ERD, RSDD-KM
	• Demand-driven studies are undertaken by senior and junior researchers. Baseline year: 2009	More, every year	• Knowledge Departments
	• Knowledge departments produce books, reports, journals, briefs, working papers, training and instructive materials, and awareness raising and multimedia materials. Baseline year: 2009	More, every year	• RSDD, Knowledge Departments
	Specific Activity Indicator		
	• Knowledge departments seize opportunities to research priority areas of *Strategy 2020*. Baseline year: 2009	One per department, every year	• RSDD, Knowledge Departments
The tacit knowledge of departing staff is captured to drive organizational performance improvement	**Useful Results Indicator**		
	• ADB retains critical knowledge from departing staff through exit interview summaries	All departing staff, from 2010	• Offices and departments
	Specific Activity Indicator		
	• Exit interviews, initially for professional staff, are introduced in every department with assistance from RSDD-KM and mainstreamed from 2011	Done: 2010	• RSDD-KM, BPHR, Offices and departments

[a]Baseline values are available in all instances. Their provision, and subsequent reporting on changes, is the responsibility of the source of verification identified
[b]OIST will play supportive roles, as required, in actions toward several other results, including those mentioned herein

Notes
• The impact targeted is that indicated in ADB (2004)
• The primary outcomes, listed in *Knowledge Management in ADB*, that the plan of action supports are (i) an improved management system; (ii) improved business processes and information technology solutions for knowledge capture, enrichment, storage, and retrieval; (iii) improved organizational culture for knowledge sharing; (iv) well-functioning communities of practice; and (v) expanded knowledge sharing, learning, and dissemination through external relations and networking
• From 2010, the annual knowledge management survey will be augmented by an annual survey gauging staff perceptions of competencies to learn for change in ADB
• The annual *Forum on Learning* is expected to focus on CoPs—yet cut across the other three pillars—and focus on what was learned in the preceding year in practical ways with measurable outcomes that leverage multipliers
Source ADB (2009)

Box 2: Enhancing Knowledge Management under Strategy 2020: Plan of Action for 2009–2011—Assumptions and Risks

Pillar Statement	Assumptions and Risks
First pillar: The knowledge focus in ADB's operations is sharpened	(i) Strong commitment by ADB's Senior Management Team; (ii) ADB values adjust in support of knowledge management and learning; (iii) close coordination among offices and departments; and (iv) availability of adequate resources
Second pillar: The communities of practice are empowered	(i) Strong commitment by ADB's Senior Management Team; (ii) availability of staff capabilities (experience, competencies, and technical and professional skills); (iii) staff attitudes (values and beliefs about innovation, commitment, and flexibility) adjust in support of knowledge management and learning; (iv) close coordination among offices and departments; and (v) availability of adequate resources
Third pillar: External knowledge partnerships are strengthened	(i) Strong commitment by ADB's Senior Management Team; (ii) close coordination among offices and departments; and (iii) availability of adequate resources
Fourth pillar: Staff learning and skills development are enhanced further	(i) Strong commitment by ADB's Senior Management Team; (ii) staff attitudes (values and beliefs about innovation, commitment, and flexibility) adjust in support of knowledge management and learning; (iii) staff behaviors (performance, productivity, teamwork, and cooperation) adjust in support of knowledge management and learning; and (iv) availability of adequate resources

Source ADB (2009)

Box 3: Enhancing Knowledge Management under Strategy 2020: Plan of Action for 2009–2011—Progress Reports

Outcome	Target	Specific Activity Indi cator	Rating of Progress in Adoption	RSDD Validation

Notes
- Progress reports on *Enhancing Knowledge Management under Strategy 2020: Plan of Action for 2009–2011* will be drafted in 2010 and 2011
- The following four ratings will present quantitative and qualitative assessments on action: (i) fully adopted; (ii) largely adopted; (iii) partly adopted; and (iv) not adopted

Legend
ADBI Asian Development Bank Institute; *BPBM* Budget and Management Services Division, BPMSD; *BPDB* Staff Development and Benefits Division, BPMSD; *BPHR* Human Resources Division, BPMSD; *BPOD* Office of the Director General, BPMSD; *BPMSD* Budget, Personnel, and Management Systems Department; *CoP* Community of Practice; *CPS* Country Partnership Strategy; *DER* Department of External Relations; *DMC* developing member country; *ERD* Economics and Research Department; *OD* Operations Department; *OIST* Office of Information Systems and Technology; *PDF* Portable Document Format; *PDP* Performance and Development Plan; *RM* Resident Mission; *RRP* Report and Recommendation of the President; *RSDD* Regional and Sustainable Development Department; *RSDD-KM* Knowledge Management Center, RSDD; *RSOD* Office of the Director General, RSDD; *SPD* Strategy and Policy Department; *SPPI* Strategy, Policy, and Interagency Relations Division, SPD; *TA* Technical Assistance
Source ADB (2009)

References

ADB (2004) Knowledge management in ADB. Manila
ADB (2008) Strategy 2020: the long-term strategic framework of the Asian development bank (2008–2020). Manila
ADB (2009) Enhancing knowledge management under strategy 2020: plan of action for 2009–2011. Manila

Proposition 47
Seeding Knowledge Solutions Before, During, and After

In a Word In the age of competence, one must learn before, during, and after the event. Knowledge solutions lie in the areas of strategy development, management techniques, collaboration mechanisms, knowledge sharing and learning, and knowledge capture and storage.

The Age of Competence

Competence is the state or quality of being adequately or well qualified to deliver a specific task, action, or function successfully. It is also a specific range of knowledge, skills, or behaviors utilized to improve performance.

Today, sustainable competitive advantage derives from strenuous efforts to identify, cultivate, and exploit an organization's core competencies,[1] the tangible fruits of which are composite packages of products and services that anticipate and meet demand. (Yesteryear, instead of strengthening the roots of competitiveness, the accent was placed on business units. Innately, given their defining characteristics, business units under-invest in core competencies, incarcerate resources, and bind innovation—when they do not stifle it.)

---

[1]Hamel (1994) is the originator (with Prahalad) of the concept of core competencies.

© Asian Development Bank 2017
O. Serrat, *Knowledge Solutions*, DOI 10.1007/978-981-10-0983-9_47

Core competencies are integrated and harmonized abilities that provide potential access to markets; create and deliver value to audiences, clients, and partners there; and are difficult for competitors to imitate. They depend on relentless design of strategic architecture, deployment of competence carriers, and commitment to collaborate across silos. They are the product of collective learning.

Learning Before, During, and After ...

Knowledge is what you learn from experience before, during, and after the event.[2] Since it is both a thing and a flow, the best way to manage knowledge is to cater at all times to the environment in which it can be identified, created, stored, shared, and used. Leadership, organization, technology, and learning that engender knowledge-enriched solutions are central to that.

... With Knowledge Solutions

Companies should decide what processes and competencies they must excel at and specify measures for each.

—Robert Kaplan and David Norton

But what of tools, methods, and approaches for learning? To drive development forward and enhance its effects, the Asian Development Bank has since 2008 published the *Knowledge Solutions* series. It aims to build competencies in the areas of strategy development, management techniques, collaboration mechanisms, knowledge sharing and learning, and knowledge capture and storage, all of them essential to knowledge management and learning. Because documentation can be cumbersome, these *Knowledge Solutions* offer "cheat sheets" that simplify access and reference to the series.

---

[2]These three phases are concerned with feedforward, concurrent, and feedback control. In each phase, the focus is on inputs, ongoing processes, and outcomes, respectively.

Table. Seeding knowledge solutions before, during, and after

Area of competence	Key for reflection	Knowledge solution
Strategy development	*A strategy is a long-term plan of action designed to achieve a particular goal.*	
	Behavior and change	
	• How can a strategy focus on group relationships with appreciation of their distinctive ideas, beliefs, values, and knowledge? • How can it utilize stories of significant change to monitor and evaluate performance? • How might it shift the focus from changes in state to changes in behaviors, relationships, actions, and activities? • How could you anchor it in understanding of livelihoods and appreciation of the factors that constrain or enhance these as well as their relationships?	• Culture theory • The most significant change technique • Outcome mapping • The sustainable Livelihoods approach
	Emergence and scenario thinking	
	• Is your strategy the outcome of a human-centered, prototype-driven process for the exploration of new ideas? • Does it maintain a balance between strategizing and learning modes of thinking? • How emergent is it? Does it consider other scenarios?	• Design thinking • From strategy to practice • Reading the future
	Institutional capacity and participation	
	• How does a strategy promote participation at requisite levels?	• Building institutional Capacity for development
	Knowledge assets	
	• Is your strategy for knowledge management enriched by regular knowledge audits? • Does its practice integrate the need to systematically review, evaluate, prioritize, sequence, manage, redirect, and if necessary even cancel strategic initiatives? • Is your approach to dissemination underpinned by policy, strategy, planning, and tactics? How can your knowledge products be made available in a flexible range of formats in recognition of the varied needs of consumers?	• Auditing knowledge • Enhancing knowledge management strategies • Linking research to practice
	Marketing	
	• How does a strategy apply a custom blend of the four Ps and other marketing techniques to transform communications with stakeholders and improve performance?	• The future of social marketing • Marketing in the public sector

(continued)

(continued)

Area of competence	Key for reflection	Knowledge solution
	• How might it draw on marketing principles to effect changes in the behavior of individuals or groups?	
	Organizational learning	
	• How can a strategy support and energize organization, people, knowledge, and technology for learning? • How might it integrate evaluation results to support policy, strategy, and operational changes? • How could it distinguish roadblocks to make them part of the solution instead of part of the problem?	• Building a learning organization • Learning lessons with knowledge audits • Overcoming roadblocks to learning
	Partnerships and networks of practice	
	• Does your strategy leverage partnerships and recognize their drivers of success and failure? • How might it make out social networks and analyze the actors and the relationships between them?	• Creating and running Partnerships • Social network analysis
Management techniques	*Leadership is the process of working out the right things to do. Management is the process of doing things right.*	
	Branding and value	
	• How might we embrace branding to drive organizational behavior and behavioral change?	• New-age branding and the public sector
	Complexity and lateral thinking	
	• How might we investigate deeply the cause-and-effect relationships underlying problems? • Do you enable different perspectives to be generated and applied in management processes? • How might one brainstorm to resolve a problem, meet an opportunity, or turn a tired idea into something new and different? • Why should management practices encompass sense and decision making in multiple contexts?	• The five whys technique • The reframing matrix • The SCAMPER technique • Understanding complexity
	Linear thinking	
	• How can we manage for results with a coherent framework for strategic planning, management, and communications? • How does one focus on time, cost, human resources, scope, quality, and actions as common parameters of project performance?	• Crafting a knowledge management results framework • Focusing on project metrics

(continued)

(continued)

Area of competence	Key for reflection	Knowledge solution
	• Do you make use of logic models for objectives-oriented planning that structures the main elements in a project, highlighting linkages between intended inputs, planned activities, and expected results?	• Output accomplishment and the design and monitoring framework
Organizational change		
	• How do organizations overcome resistance to change and secure as much discretionary effort as possible? • How do we get the right knowledge to the right people at the right time, and help them (with incentives) to apply it in ways that strive to improve organizational performance? • How might you prioritize investments in knowledge management? • What are the components of organizational culture and what is the role of organizational learning for change? • How do organizations learn? • How do new knowledge management paradigms compare with the old, and what new structures and managerial attitudes do they require? • Why should we drive management innovation?	• Fast and effective change management • Notions of knowledge management • Picking investments in knowledge management • A Primer on organizational culture • A Primer on organizational learning • The roots of an emerging discipline • Sparking innovations in management
Talent management		
	• Do you manage meetings before, during, and after, with appreciation of their different kinds, to make them productive and fun? • Should one spend more time, integrity, and brainpower on selecting managers than on anything else? • Why should you empower knowledge workers to make the most of their deepest skills and perform best? • How does one manage by walking around to emphasize the importance of interpersonal contact, open appreciation, and recognition and build civility and performance in the workplace? • How can one give talent strategic and holistic attention to make it happen? • Do you have the ability, capacity, skill, or self-perceived ability to identify, assess, and manage the emotions of yourself, of others, and of groups?	• Conducting effective meetings • Growing managers, not bosses • Managing knowledge workers • Managing by walking around • A primer on talent management • Understanding and developing emotional intelligence

(continued)

(continued)

Area of competence	Key for reflection	Knowledge solution
Collaboration mechanisms	*When working with others, efforts sometimes turn out to be less than the sum of the parts. Too often, not enough attention is paid to facilitating effective collaborative practices.*	
	Collaborative tools	
	• How do you harness the power of collaborative minds to innovate faster, cocreate, and cut costs? • How does one represent, link, and arrange concepts, themes, or tasks under a central topic? • How can we actualize the thinking potential of teams?	• Collaborating with wikis • Drawing mind maps • Wearing six thinking hats
	Communities of practice and learning alliances	
	• How do you build a community of like-minded, interacting people to ensure more effective creation and sharing of knowledge in a domain? • How can communities of practice report better? • Why should strategic alliances manage the partnership, not just the agreement, for collaborative advantage?	• Building communities of practice • Improving sector and thematic reporting • Learning in strategic alliances
	Leadership	
	• How should we earn, develop, and retain trust for superior results? • How can one distribute leadership if it is an outcome, not an input to business processes and performance? • Why would you support people who choose to serve first, and then lead, as a way of expanding service to individuals and organizations? • What is the new context for leadership in the public sector?	• Building Trust in the Workplace • Distributing Leadership • Exercising Servant Leadership • Leading in the Workplace
	Social innovations	
	• By what process can one unearth what works to facilitate positive change in organizations? • How can you generate good ideas that meet pressing unmet needs and improve people's lives to foster smart, sustainable globalization?	• Appreciative Inquiry • Sparking Social Innovations
	Teamwork	
	• How do you enable small groups to work regularly and collectively on complicated problems, take action, and learn as individuals and as a team while doing so?	• Action learning • Managing virtual teams • Working in teams

(continued)

(continued)

Area of competence	Key for reflection	Knowledge solution
	• How can we organize and coordinate with effect a group whose members are not in the same location or time zone, and may not even work for the same organization? • How does one develop a successful team?	
Knowledge sharing and learning	*Two-way communications that take place simply and effectively build knowledge.*	
	Creativity, innovation, and learning	
	• What are the forms and functions of networks of practice and how do you monitor and evaluate performance? • How do you harness, individually or in association, useful models of learning and change to reflect on the dimensions of a learning organization? • How can an organization demonstrate commitment to learning, against which provision and practice can be tested and serve as a waymark with which to guide, monitor, and evaluate progress? • What are the stimulants and obstacles to creativity and innovation that drive or impede enterprise in organizations?	• Building networks of practice • Dimensions of the learning organization • Drawing learning charters • Harnessing creativity and innovation in the workplace
	Learning and development	
	• How can we coach and mentor to inspire and empower employees, build commitment, increase productivity, grow talent, and promote success? • What are the five functions of managers toward which learning and development can be extended to improve their insights, attitudes, and skills?	• Coaching and Mentoring • Learning and Development for Management
	Learning lessons	
	• How do you know what question to ask when? • When a critical milestone has been reached, why should we discuss successes and failures in an open and honest fashion? • How does one step back from day-to-day activities to think about the future? • How can individuals come together to share their experiences, insights, and knowledge on an identified challenge or problem? • Is failure a way to an opportunity? • How can one suggest that a process or methodology that has been shown to be effective in one part of an organization and might be effective in another too?	• Asking effective questions • Conducting after-action reviews and retrospects • Conducting successful retreats • Conducting peer assists • Embracing failure • Identifying and sharing good practices • Learning from evaluation • Storytelling

(continued)

(continued)

Area of competence	Key for reflection	Knowledge solution
	• How might evaluation serve as a foundation block in learning organizations? • What is the potential of stories or narratives as a communication tool to value, share, and capitalize on the knowledge of individuals?	
	Dissemination	
	• How can an ordinary presentation become a lively and engaging event? • By what interactive process does one communicate knowledge to target audiences to lead to change? • How do you employ the internet to disseminate research findings? • How do we save time in writing, make writing far easier, and improve understanding?	• Conducting effective presentations • Disseminating knowledge products • Posting research online • Using plain english
Knowledge capture and storage	*Knowledge leaks in various ways at various times.*	
	Knowledge harvesting	
	• How do you garner feedback on why employees leave, what they liked about their job, and where the organization needs improvement? • What, in simple terms, are the most common concepts in knowledge management? • How do you draw out and package tacit knowledge to help others adapt, personalize, and apply it; build organizational capacity; and preserve institutional memory? • Why should one cut information overload and showcase knowledge? • How do we build dynamic, adaptive electronic directories that store information about the knowledge, skills, experience, and interests of people?	• Conducting exit interviews • Glossary of knowledge management • Harvesting knowledge • Showcasing knowledge • Staff profile pages
	Reporting	
	• How can one garner feedback from executing agencies on the effectiveness of assistance in capacity development? • By what simple feedback mechanisms might you promote learning before, during, and after to document accomplishments as well as bottlenecks?	• Assessing the effectiveness of assistance in capacity development • Monthly progress notes
	Technology platforms	
	• How can groups discuss electronically areas of interest and review different opinions and information surrounding a topic?	• Writing weblogs

Note The *Knowledge Solutions* listed were those available as of April 2010
Source Author

Reference

Hamel G, Prahalad CK (1994) Competing for the future. Harvard Business School Press

Further Reading

ADB (2008–) Knowledge solutions. Manila

Proposition 48
The Perils of Performance Measurement

In a Word Interest in performance measurement grows daily but the state of the art leaves much to be desired. To promote performance leadership, one must examine both its shortcomings and its pernicious effects.

The Simple Intent of Performance Measurement

The use of yardsticks to measure performance needs no arguing: one cannot improve what one cannot measure. More emphatically, in the words of Joseph Juran,[1] "Without a standard there is no logical basis for making a decision or taking action."

> *I conceive that the great part of the miseries of mankind are brought upon them by false estimates they have made of the value of things.*
>
> —Benjamin Franklin

---

[1]Joseph Juran (1904–2008), an American electrical engineer and management consultant, was an evangelist of quality and its management.

© Asian Development Bank 2017
O. Serrat, *Knowledge Solutions*, DOI 10.1007/978-981-10-0983-9_48

Performance measurement, a key driver of the Plan–Do–Check–Act iterative cycle that W. Edwards Deming[2] promoted, is the process of gauging achievements against stated goals. A major determinant of sustainable competitive advantage, it hangs on the development of SMART[3] indicators—customarily in a results chain linking activities, inputs, outputs, and outcome to impact—that one should track to reliably verify and promote organizational success. Pre–post comparisons can then be made to assess the relevance, efficiency, effectiveness, sustainability, and impact of endeavors (at least in the case of larger scale ventures).

A Grain of Salt

Today, performance is appraised the world over: in academia, the arts, business, entertainment, government, news, politics, schools, science, sports, and war, among others. In the public sector, the need to sell the idea that management is improving means that indicators proliferate, on the whole, without regard for unintended consequences from the practice. Performance indicators are simultaneously misunderstood, overpromoted, and accordingly misused.

> It is hard to go beyond your public. If they are satisfied with cheap performance, you will not easily arrive at better. If they know what is good, and require it, you will aspire and burn until you achieve it. But from time to time, in history, men are born a whole age too soon.
>
> —Ralph Waldo Emerson

- First, conflicting *definitions* of performance indicators abound. In their shortest yet most stringent expression, they are a numerical measure of the degree to which an objective is being achieved. (From this interpretation, indicators are prone to merge with objectives and effectively become targets.) Others (Bakewell et al. 2004) consider them an observable change or event that provides evidence that something has happened, be that an output delivered, an immediate effect occurred, or a long-term process observed. To such discerning interpreters, indicators do not offer proof so much as reliable clues that the change or event being claimed has actually happened or is happening: rather, evidence from several indicators will make a convincing case for claims being made.

---

[2]William Edwards Deming (1900–1993), an American electrical engineer, statistician, and management consultant, pioneered contemporaneously with Joseph Juran the quality management revolution that took place in postwar Japan.
[3]SMART indicators are specific, measurable, achievable, relevant, and time-bound.

- Second, complex issues of *cause-and-effect* are seldom considered. Obviously, performance indicators can only pertain to matters that an agency controls.[4] But agencies never command much and usually settle for subprime indicators that afford enough control for their purposes. This reality is intrinsic to all human endeavors, especially those that touch political decision-making or aim to spark social change.[5] (Never mind that outcomes will in many cases emerge long after the effort—to which other agencies or even units in the same agency may have been unknown parties—has been deployed.) Consequently, interest has grown in approaches to planning, monitoring, and evaluation of outcomes and their metrics that consider actor-centered development and behavioral change, continuous learning and flexibility, participation and accountability, as well as non-linearity and contribution (not attribution and control).[6]

> *There are two possible outcomes: if the result confirms the hypothesis, then you've made a measurement. If the result is contrary to the hypothesis, then you've made a discovery.*
>
> —Enrico Fermi

- Third, the *dimensions of performance* mentioned earlier—namely, relevance, efficiency, effectiveness, sustainability, and impact—intimate that there can be no single assessment of accomplishments overall. Performance is an amalgam of dimensions, some of which may conflict. Measuring it calls for an appropriate basket of benchmarks developed with full knowledge of their interrelationships.
- Fourth, performance measurement must have a *purpose*—it can never be an end in itself. According to Behn (2003), the separate reasons for engaging in it are to

---

[4]In the real world, where complexity reigns, a myriad factors impact that do not relate to the activities, inputs, and outputs delivered by an agency. And, it is never easy to account for them—in the odd instances where they are discernable—by listing the assumptions and risks that might affect performance. (The imagination and experience of personnel, in any case, limit the consideration of external factors.).

[5]The structure that logical frameworks provide for thinking is helpful. But the failure of linear thinking to cope with unintended consequences makes up one of the most recurrent criticisms of "lock frame" models, especially when they are revisited at evaluation. Logical frameworks patently assume that people have such powers of foresight that neither unforeseen routes nor unanticipated effects are important. In practice, however, their false precision impoverishes the phenomena under scrutiny, going as far as to exclude unanticipated benefits outside the original purview. Sadly, attempts to make logical frameworks flexible have not kept up with changes in the environments in which the tool was planted.

[6]Outcome mapping, developed by the International Development Research Center, is one such approach. The Balanced Scorecard conceptualized by Robert Kaplan and Richard Norton is another: it encompasses client, financial, business process, and learning and growth perspectives.

evaluate,[7] control, budget, motivate, promote, celebrate, learn, and improve. (The list could be shorter or longer: shorter in that the genuine purpose of measuring accomplishments is the last; longer in that the seven others, to which more could be added, can perhaps be considered as some important means for achieving the first.) Manifestly, no single metric is appropriate for all eight objectives. Therefore, practitioners had better consider the managerial purpose (s) to which performance measurement might contribute—these, alas, being ordinarily to control and budget—and how they might best deploy an informative[8] blend of measures anchored in context. Only then will they be able to select valid yardsticks with the characteristics necessary to help meet each purpose, directly and indirectly, concentrating on what matters most.

- Fifth, many *other things* besides performance indicators are needed to ameliorate achievements (after the indicators have been recognized for what they are, namely, individual links in a results chain). The other requisites include Board, Management, and staff who are focused on meeting the explicit and latent needs of client, audiences, and partners; leadership and commitment to developing and extending products and services; and a culture of openness in which personnel are encouraged and willing to question why they do what they do.

... And Some Pernicious Effects

Cynics might argue—thankfully, perhaps, given the state of affairs—that performance measures are seldom used to make decisions.[9] Yet, they do have effects from the suspicion that actions, e.g., sanctions or rewards, might be based on such information. True to form—be they people, rats, or monkeys—organisms compete for scarce resources. They will also naturally search what behaviors and related activities are recompensed and then endeavor to perform these, often to the exclusion of things not rewarded.

In the public sector, but likely elsewhere too, sanctions or rewards can therefore pay off for behaviors other than what they seek. Grizzle (2002) identifies numerous unintended consequences of attempts to measure outcomes, gauge client satisfaction, calculate the quantity of work performed, and introduce efficiency measures. She thinks that, as a general remedy, moral codes and professional standards should

---

[7]That, for example, might cover economic (activity) evaluation, operations evaluation, and/or managerial evaluation.

[8]Performance indicators will not serve if they are brandished to judge performance.

[9]One explanation might be that performance measurement frameworks for understanding and defining metrics, collecting and analyzing data, and prioritizing and tacking action are never spelled out.

normally suffice to prescribe right action.[10] Naturally, specific remedies should be applied to specific problems, most of which ought to be built into the measurement process itself.

Since the principal managerial purposes to which performance measurement contributes are control and budget—control more often than not exercised by means of the budget, it pays to examine the counterproductive effects associated with the crude use of budgets in (much of) the private sector (but in other sectors, too). In Jensen's (2001) opinion, for instance, traditional budgeting processes in corporations waste time, distort decisions, and turn honest managers into schemers. Quoting,

> Corporate budgeting is a joke, and everyone knows it. It consumes a huge amount of executives' time, forcing them into endless rounds of dull meetings and tense negotiations. It encourages managers to lie and cheat, lowballing targets and inflating results, and it penalizes them for telling the truth. It turns business decisions into elaborate exercises in gaming. It sets colleague against colleague, creating distrust and ill will. And it distorts incentives, motivating people to act in ways that run counter to the best interests of their companies.

> *Earnings can be pliable as putty when a charlatan heads the company reporting them.*
>
> —Warren Buffett

To be sure, Michael Jensen agrees that the budget process itself is not the root cause of counterproductive actions; rather, it is the use of budget targets to determine compensation.[11] Comparing traditional,[12] curvilinear,[13] and linear[14] compensation plans, he argues that only by severing the link between budgets and bonuses—in brief, by rewarding people purely for accomplishments, not ability to

---

[10]Needless to say, there must be trust in the workplace that fair use will be made of performance information and that the measurement process should be an empowering, not disempowering, experience. This may require more attention to the design of work environments that promote right action.

[11]Individuals who are short of reaching a goal are more likely to engage in unethical behavior than others who do not have a goal or who exceed a goal. Also, individuals who are close to reaching a goal are more likely to engage in unethical behavior than others who are far from reaching a goal. This happens in all types of organizations.

[12]In a traditional pay-for-performance plan, a manager earns a bonus when performance reaches a certain level. The bonus increases with performance until it hits a maximum cap. When performance hits the cap, the manager has a strong incentive to push revenue and profit into the following year.

[13]Curvilinear pay-for-performance plans encourage managers to increase the variability of year-to-year performance measures.

[14]In a linear pay-for-performance plan, a manager enjoys the same bonus for a particular level of performance whether the budget goal happens to be set beneath the level or above it. This eliminates the incentive to game the process.

hit targets—will organizations remove the incentive to cheat. (Since many public sector organizations now have pay-for-performance plans, seeing how the three types might impact behavior there will not stretch imagination.)

> *Apply yourself. Get all the education you can, but then, by God, do something. Don't just stand there, make something happen.*
>
> —Lee Iacocca

As though the situation was not complicated enough, moving from individual to divisional performance measurement, Jensen (Jensen and Meckling 2009) explains elsewhere that performance indicators should reflect the functions of different business units—that is, most large organizations adopt divisionalized structures, frequently categorized as cost, revenue, profit, investment, and expense[15] centers. Here, an intuitive issue of performance reporting is whether divisional managers should be held accountable for things they cannot influence. Therefore, the manner in which divisional performance is measured, monitored, controlled, and reported on—typically at the behest of, sometimes directly by, higher levels in the hierarchy and often by means of budgets—is particularly important. Should different performance measures and associated decision rights closely relevant to the functions fulfilled not be used more often, certainly in the public sector,[16] to evaluate the performance of divisions? In matters of budgeting, managerial flexibility, decentralization, and devolution would go a long way to offset the perils of performance measurement. As things now stand, the budget too often stands as the de facto strategy.

Transforming Performance Measurement

> *How many cares one loses when one decides not to be something but to be someone.*
>
> —Coco Chanel

---

[15]Expense centers are the private sector equivalent of the classic public sector organization. A division organized as an expense center serves the rest of the organization. (Providers of internal administrative services, such as human resources, information systems and technology, and public relations, are commonly deemed to be expense centers.) However, the receiving units are not charged for the services they consume, hence, the tendency of expense centers to overproduce irrespective of demand, sometimes to maximize their sizes if only because compensation schedules tend to increase rewards for jobs with larger budgets and more personnel. Worse still, the receiving units have no incentives to compare the cost of the services they consume with the value of the services they receive.

[16]In the public sector, personnel must also follow so many processes that fidelity to these supplants devotion to results.

What is important cannot always be measured and what can be measured is not necessarily important. These days, what matters most in organizations are intangible sources of value—such as human and customer capital—and their measurement and management challenge traditional, "technical" approaches. Reverting to Behn (2006), it is therefore a matter of helping managers manage, not making or letting them manage. Good performance cannot be compelled, commanded, or coerced.

It is not so difficult: most professionals are self-motivated but intrinsic drive must be channeled skillfully to excite, engage, and energize. (Therefore, performance measurement must restrain demotivators, such as office politics, and build motivators, such as fairness, that make people strive to do the best they can.) In an environment of positive accountability, collaboration, truth-telling, and learning would be rewarded, not just hitting all-too-often senseless targets.

The better practices that Robert Behn recommends relate to creating the performance framework, driving performance improvement, and learning to enhance performance. Dialogue about measurement is what will turn data and information into knowledge. Right? Only then will you use performance indicators wisely.

References

Bakewell O, Adams J, Pratt B (2004) Sharpening the development process: a practical guide to monitoring and evaluation. International NGO Training and Research Center Praxis Paper Series

Behn R (September–October 2003) Why measure performance? different purposes require different measures. Public Administration Review 63(5):586–606

Behn R (2006) Performance leadership: 11 better practices that can ratchet up performance. IBM Center for the Business of Government

Grizzle G (June 2002) Performance measurement and dysfunction: the dark side of quantifying work. Public Performance and Management Review: 25(4):363–369

Jensen M (2001) Corporate budgeting is broken—let's fix it. Harvard Business Review 11:94–101

Jensen M, Meckling W (2009) Specific knowledge and divisional performance measurement. Journal of Applied Corporate Finance 21(2):49–57

Further Reading

Spitzer D (2007) Transforming performance measurement: rethinking the way we measure and drive organizational success. Amacom Books

Proposition 49
Engaging Staff in the Workplace

In a Word Surveys present clear and mounting evidence that staff engagement correlates closely with individual, collective, and corporate performance. It denotes the extent to which organizations gain commitment from personnel.

Coming of Age

Social exchange theory[1] sheds light on the reciprocal relationship between perceptions of an organization's enabling environment, capacity, and organizational motivation and staff willingness to maximize individual and collective performance.[2]

---

[1]Social exchange theory posits that human relationships—hence, social stability and change—are shaped by negotiated give-and-take. Expressly, they are driven by direct reward, expected gains in influence, anticipated reciprocity, and perceptions of efficacy. (In biology, altruism is explained as an act that may harm an individual but hopefully advances the species or social group. Shockingly, perhaps, to some, social exchange theory suggests that altruism too springs from self-serving motivation—in the sense that it carries psychological rewards.) Everywhere, the theory holds, decisions are made based on the kinds of relationships people think they deserve, the balance between what they put in and what they get out, and the prospects of securing better deals with other parties.
[2]Organizations do not exist in a vacuum: they are open systems. Manifestly, their external environment is of vital consequence. Rules, ethos, and capabilities condition performance within that. Typically, the enabling environment (rules) each builds to operate draws from political, socio-cultural, economic, stakeholder, and administrative ingredients. Its organizational motivation (ethos) is conditioned by history, mission, culture, and incentives and rewards. Its organizational capacity (capabilities) is a function of strategic leadership, human resources, structure, financial management, infrastructure, program management, process management, and intra-organizational linkages. Basically, however, an organization is only as good as the people in it.

© Asian Development Bank 2017

O. Serrat, *Knowledge Solutions*, DOI 10.1007/978-981-10-0983-9_49

Yet, until recently, human resource specialists introduced cleaner, whiter, or more "colory" practices by administrative circular or order, typically after a modicum of consultation. Top-, middle-, and first-level managers would enforce adherence to the line.

Organizations are communities, the members of which want worthwhile jobs that inspire them. Naturally, a committed and willing workforce brings substantial benefits. Some time ago, we recognized that formal relationships cannot by themselves be expected to conduce these entirely: implicit employer–employee exchanges matter.[3] Belatedly, we concede that perceptions of an organization's rules, ethos, and capabilities, not just the experience staff has of human resource practices, drive levels of effort and associated degrees of job satisfaction. More and more, organizations say they are looking for win–win solutions that match their needs with those of personnel: they examine the question of motivation with a fresh sense of purpose and conviction. Better still, high-performance organizations marshal and direct substantial resources to build effective behaviors and relationships, often in concert with human resource divisions.[4] Engaging staff has come of age: in the twenty-first century, the concept affirms the importance of flexibility, change, and unremitting improvement in the workplace.

Defining Engagement (And Its Benefits)

Engagement is a multifaceted construct that has been variously defined.[5] Even so, on the whole, personnel engage when they feel appreciated and involved. In such instances, they are likely to hold a positive attitude vis-à-vis the organization and its

---

[3]Contracts of employment set out responsibilities, duties, and rights in generalized form. As early as 1960, but with little discernible uptake, Argyris (1960) mooted the notion that a "psychological contract" representing unwritten, mutual expectations might set the dynamics of relationships between parties.

[4]Staff engagement is the responsibility of both senior and junior managers. However, human resource divisions have a unique role to play in planning, acting out, reflecting on, and learning from engagement initiatives. This will generally include designing and carrying out surveys, testing findings through focus groups, and advising senior management on their significance. Human resource specialists should also be tasked with helping first-level managers raise their game, and perhaps even select for engagement. (It is often remarked that people join organizations but leave individual managers.) Toward this, they may need to incorporate the findings of surveys in performance management processes, hire managers and other employees who have more potential to drive engagement in the workplace, or liaise with marketing to develop the organization's brand. [From a limited focus on the 4Ps of product (or service), place, price, and promotion, the idea of organizational branding has developed with implications for behavior and behavioral change.]

[5]Most often, it is seen as emotional and intellectual commitment to an organization or the volume of discretionary effort deployed by staff in their work.

corporate values (assuming the latter are enacted, not just espoused). This translates into correct focus and enthusiasm about work as well as mindful proactivity and persistence in the conduct of it.[6] The earlier reference to organizational branding suggests that identity and authenticity are pivots of that.[7]

Engagement is something everyone can offer: but it cannot be forced by terms of reference; hence, early interest in psychological contracts. There are four dimensions to it: (i) cognitive (or intellectual)—thinking hard about one's profession and how one might perform it better; (ii) emotional (or affective)—feeling good about doing a good job; (iii) social—taking opportunities to discuss work-related improvements with others; and, even if the literature rarely mentions it, (iv) physical—mustering the stamina to "go the extra mile".

> *I do not try to dance better than anyone else. I only try to dance better than myself.*
> —Mikhail Baryshnikov

Engagement and enablement through optimized roles and a supportive environment energize people. They develop a stronger sense of personal well-being. They understand the business context and the "bigger picture". They have a desire to work to make things better. They are clear about the desired outcomes of their role. They display consistently superior levels of performance. They behave in ways that support their organization's corporate values. They have a positive impact on services to clients, audiences, and partners. They become willing advocates. They demonstrate higher levels of innovation and drive for efficiency. They keep up to date with developments in their field. They never run out of things to do and

---

[6]Staff engagement goes beyond job satisfaction or even commitment: personnel may be satisfied, yet contribute little; committed people may be fixed on the wrong objectives. Accordingly, a satisfied and committed workforce is a necessary but insufficient precondition to organizational performance.

[7]One of three courses that the Knowledge Management Center in the Asian Development Bank delivered twice in ADB's headquarters in June and September 2010 had to do with Learning in Teams. (The others were connected with Reflective Practice and Learning from Evaluation.) In particular, the course advertised and explored elements of radical collaboration, borne of an intentional attitude that Tamm and Luyet (2005) have described as being in the Green Zone. Interestingly, four groups of participants in eight ranked identity first in a Green Zone diamond ranking of nine preferred attributes including also hospitality, participation, mindfulness, humility, reciprocity, deliberation, appreciation, and authenticity. Three groups of participants ranked authenticity second.

create positive things to act on. They intentionally build supportive relationships and are respectful of, and helpful to, colleagues. They are much more likely to have a productive relationship with their supervisor. They can deal with changes and challenges. They manage stress and enjoy better health and well-being as a result. They have lower rates of sickness or absenteeism. They are less likely to leave. Overall, they derive greater satisfaction in their lives.[8]

Not surprisingly, high levels of engagement and enablement benefit organizations. (Engaged and enabled people generate more revenue.) As expected, the outcome of staff engagement covers a broad range, including increased profitability, higher productivity, contributions to innovation, and lower staff turnover.

Surveying Engagement to Begin

Most, if not all, staff engagement initiatives—that then classify staff as engaged, not engaged,[9] and actively disengaged—begin with the use of surveys to measure attitudes and circumscribe what areas need attention.[10] The common threads relate to organizational advocacy, management styles, decision-making, communications, involvement initiatives, and work–life balance.

---

[8]In truth, however, actively disengaged people proliferate across occupations, industries, and sectors. They do not care about their organizations and probably do not like their jobs: they are blasé, indifferent, or consistently against virtually everything. They curtail efforts to match the limited opportunities they have to succeed. They are busy acting out their unhappiness and have a negative influence on colleagues. They can also drive clients, audiences, and partners away. Some "milk" their host at every opportunity. Still, one is not born disengaged: it is a process that hardens over time as the connectedness of individual and collective expectations breaks. It may also be the product of ingrained barriers to successful staff engagement. Where organizations strain to do more with less, none should reach a situation where it must re-engage deeply frustrated personnel and build back pride and commitment.

[9]Obviously, actively disengaged staff create problems in the workplace. (Thankfully, perhaps, they leave.) But it is even worse to have motivated people who cannot turn their enthusiasm into action. Employees who are not engaged take a wait-and-see attitude toward their employer, job, and coworkers. Typically, in average organizations, individuals who are engaged but not enabled make up half of the workforce. The figure rises to nearly three quarters if one counts personnel who are both not engaged and actively disengaged.

[10]The existence of various conceptualizations of engagement makes the state of knowledge about it difficult to determine, as each survey (or research) is carried out under a different protocol matching different measures to different circumstances. Nevertheless, survey findings can be of considerable value where they support benchmarking of performance, be that over time, between work units, or with comparable organizations.

Box: Barriers to Staff Engagement

Here and there, common barriers hamper the focus, integration, presence, and energy that staff can leverage toward their organization's success. The most frequent relate to

- unimaginative human resource practices, which fail to recognize that certain positions are difficult to fill or have high turnover rates: staff in these areas are likely to disengage if no consideration is given to the need to involve them;
- reactive decision making, which does not pick up problems until it is too late;
- lack of consistency, clarity, timeliness, and fluidity in messages, which stems from rigid communication channels or cultural norms;
- inconsistent management styles on account of the attitudes of individual managers, which lead to perceptions of unfairness;
- poor work–life balance caused by a culture of long working hours; and
- low perceptions of organizational advocacy by senior management, which weaken or shatter trust and respect.

Source Author

However, surveys reveal also that each organization has distinctive issues. Different groups of staff are influenced by different combinations of factors, and organizations need to consider carefully what is most important to them. Hence, there can be no template for deciding which specific policies and practices will have most impact on performance: engagement must be seen in context, which opens rich seams for research.[11] (For instance, research on the predictors[12] of engagement is scant. It is also not known whether or not interventions, such as training managers on how to communicate effectively, actually serve to boost engagement. It might also be necessary to examine individual differences and whether variables, such as personality, impact engagement.)

Surveys also need to be followed by effective action to address issues identified or they will negatively impact on attitudes. Fundamental to managing engagement as a process is ensuring that action is taken on the findings of employee attitude surveys. Failure to follow through generally has a damaging effect on attitudes and

---

[11]However, there is widespread agreement that surveys should measure a number of factors, including staff commitment, organizational citizenship, satisfaction, attitudes to management, teamwork, opportunity to excel, personal and professional growth, rewards and recognition, work–life balance, and intention to leave. Responses can be disaggregated by gender, age, tenure, and staff level.

[12]The spectrum is broad. Predictors can be attitudinal, dispositional, demographic, task-related, leadership-style, or organizational, among others.

on the rate of response to subsequent surveys. Sadly, taking survey data to the next level into something that might—with actionable recommendations and metrics—ultimately renovate business processes and operations remains, unacceptably, largely unexplored territory.[13] The survey event cannot provide all the answers and is still too often isolated from the strategy of the organization.

Driving Engagement

Differences notwithstanding, the key drivers of staff engagement against which actions can be taken are the following[14]:

- feeling valued and well informed about what is happening in the organization,[15]
- having opportunities to feed views upwards, and
- thinking that the immediate supervisor is committed to the organization.

> *You can't cross the sea merely by standing and staring at the water.*
>
> —Rabindranath Tagore

Since groups of employees are influenced by different combinations of factors across occupations, industries, and sectors, managers will need to consider carefully what steps are most relevant to their organization. There is much scope for thoughtful reflection. A possible model, put forward by the Chartered Institute of Personnel and Development (2006), recommends that employers should strengthen links between engagement, performance, and intention to stay through measures that promote

- opportunities for upward feedback,
- feeling informed about what is going on,
- managerial commitment to the organization,
- managerial fairness in dealing with problems, and
- respectful treatment of employees.

---

[13]A useful perspective on this is to appreciate the need for distinct approaches. Senior management should address engagement from a systemic perspective; middle- and first-level managers should tackle it from a one-on-one perspective. Moreover, no single skill or element will suffice.

[14]Various studies have shown that competitive salary levels and other financial rewards are not among the top drivers of staff engagement. Bonuses may not be the answer either: when bonuses are given, expectations are set for the behavior required to continue receiving them in the future; if further bonuses are not forthcoming, staff will scale back efforts.

[15]This may well be the main driver of engagement. Vital components of this are being involved in decision making; feeling enabled to perform well; having opportunities to develop the job; and believing the organization is concerned for staff health and well-being.

That said, embarking on a drive to increase engagement levels should not be taken lightly, bearing in mind the ease with which engagement (much as trust and respect) can be shattered. The Institute for Employment Studies (Robinson et al. 2004), for one, cautions that attempts to raise engagement levels are likely to founder if all the following building blocks are not in place and working well:

- good quality first-level management;
- two-way communications;
- effective internal cooperation;
- a development focus;
- commitment to staff well-being; and
- clear, accessible human resource policies and practices, to which managers at all levels are committed.

Sustaining Workplace Excellence

If your actions inspire others to dream more, learn more, do more and become more, you are a leader.

—John Quincy Adams

If much in organizations can be explained by networks of transactions, treating people as cogs in a machine will impair the potential contribution they might make and engender unpleasant feedback. Organizations that understand the what, why, and how of staff engagement and take continuous actions to overcome generic and more specific barriers to it will unleash performance and well-being in the workplace. Helpfully, Gallup (Wagner and Harter 2006) has defined a practicable number of outcomes the achievement of which would denote that. Stronger from reconciliation, humanized organizations would be able to say they acted on a blindingly obvious but nevertheless often-overlooked rule: Do unto others as you would have them do unto you.

Table. Thoughts on staff engagement

Implications for managers	
Building better organizations	• Management style and leadership are critical to high-performance working • Staff engagement translates into willingness to "go the extra mile", including learning new or better ways of working • Managers should pay more attention to job design, creating more "elbow room" for people to do their jobs • Staffs need to be able to express their opinions upwards to their manager and beyond. • Staff engagement is not simply about the relationship between manager and team members; it is also about organizational culture • The challenge for human resource specialists is to facilitate the building of better organizations
Taking happiness seriously	• Happiness is a serious business issue—feeling good at work is not only a signal of good functioning but will actually enhance the prospect of future resourcefulness • The survey evidence supports the belief that positive emotions are particularly important in relation to several key performance indicators • Organizations are likely to get greater impact by fostering positive emotions rather than simply dealing with problems • Systematically identifying good practice, perhaps through well-being audits, will support organizations to learn from within • Team leaders, line managers, and staff themselves could all promote positive personal and organizational outcomes
Increasing staff engagement	• The top priority for managers who want to increase staff engagement is communication • Staff will be engaged to the extent that their employer meets their needs in terms of benefits, employability, and satisfaction • Managers should offer the package of initiatives that reflects an overall reading of staff engagement and motivation • Staff involvement may reflect deep-seated attitudes that make engagement harder for managers to influence • Managers need to identify staff with a propensity to be engaged, and ensure that they hire the right personnel in the first place
Being sensitive to diversity issues	• One size does not fit all: organizations need to customize their policies and practices to match the needs of different groups in their workforce • Organizations should recognize that older staff are likely to be more engaged and should value their contribution • Organizations need to design approaches to employment that are more attractive to younger people • More needs to be done to make the employment experience of people with disabilities more successful • Stamping out bullying and harassment must become a priority for management attention • Flexible working can leverage staff engagement by facilitating personal choice

(continued)

(continued)

Implications for managers	
Using staff attitude data	• Staff attitude surveys are a fundamental component of sophisticated strategies for managing human capital • Findings on staff engagement can be used to monitor business performance, alongside those on, for example, communication, diversity, leadership, and work–life balance • Combining attitude data with other metrics can provide managers with a greater understanding of the relationship between human resource policies and practices and business performance • Benchmarking detailed results across business units allows managers to compare their results with those of other parts of the organization

Source Author

References

Argyris C (1960) Understanding organizational behavior. The Dorsey Press

Chartered Institute of Personnel and Development (2006) How engaged are British employees?

Robinson D, Perryman S, Hayday S (2004) The drivers of employee engagement. Institute for Employment Studies. Report No 408

Tamm J, Luyet R (2005) Radical collaboration: five essential skills to overcome defensiveness and build successful relationships. HarperCollins Publishers

Wagner R, Harter J (2006) 12: the elements of great managing. Gallup Press

Proposition 50
Leading Top Talent in the Workplace

In a Word Organizations once distinguished themselves by their systems and procedures. They now need distinctive ideas about their objectives, their clients, what their clients value, their results, and their plans. For that, they need top talent.

The Best at Something

In the twenty-first century, certainly in organizations, one has to be the best at something; it is no longer enough to be good—or pretty good—at a number of things. For decades, organizations felt comfortable with policies, strategies, structures, systems, and business processes that kept them in the middle of the road—it made sense: after all, that is where clients stood or sat.

These days, however, the middle of the road is the road to nowhere: there is so much change; there is so much pressure. There are so many different ways of doing everything that business-as-usual is dead. Notions of being an honest broker, a family doctor, or a "Really Useful Engine," pace Thomas and Friends, are antiquated.

It is time to rediscover the power of work and forge better ways to lead or compete—but in both instances succeed—with those who, typically with creativity

© Asian Development Bank 2017

O. Serrat, *Knowledge Solutions*, DOI 10.1007/978-981-10-0983-9_50

and innovation or, some prefer, imagination and invention, do the intellectual work that matters most. Excellence is impossible without top talent, aka chief possibility officers.

Now You See It ...

Talent is a marked innate ability, aptitude, or faculty for achievement.[1] Since there is a myriad of possible productive applications,[2] organizations will find greater value if they formulate their own definitions of what talent and talent management are.[3]

> *Most Americans do not know what their strengths are. When you ask them, they look at you with a blank stare, or they respond in terms of subject knowledge, which is the wrong answer.*
>
> —Peter Drucker

On the other hand, top talent begs no interpretation (even if it too cannot be perfectly identified): it is the natural hallmark of the "clevers," high flyers, mavericks, prima donnas, and superstars whose recurring individuality—honed and fortified by application and practice—infuses performance with a distinctive (and not infrequently disruptive) dimension.[4] Borrowing from Goffee and Jones (2009), top talent is those individuals who have the potential to create and deliver disproportionate amounts of value from the resources made available to them and are therefore of most value to an organization. If intellectual capital drives today's

---

[1]Buckingham and Coffman (1999) define talent as a recurring pattern in thinking, feeling, or behavior that can be productively applied.

[2]A simple taxonomy would list four types, namely, talent to (i) imagine new possibilities, (ii) champion new ideas, (iii) encourage buy-in and commitment, and (iv) make certain that projects and programs are completed.

[3]In the common parlance of talent management, natural abilities and traits are considered together with knowledge, skills, and behaviors. Proponents of talent management take a more inclusive, whole workforce, approach to talent "pools". Whatever the approach, mindful attention to the talent needs of organizations is clearly needed if they are to survive strategic and operational challenges. Conventional organizations have no talent management policies, strategies, or formally developed practices; talent management, if it occurs at all, is informal and incidental. In high-performance organizations, talent management informs and is informed by corporate strategy; individual and pooled talent is understood and considered.

[4]The world of sport appraises talent all the time. When a team manager speaks of a star player, he is talking about who scores the most points, who blocks the other team most often, or who the supporters (and other players) identify as essential to success.

knowledge economies, this brings with it an increased dependence on the highly talented people who generate it.

> *Men of genius do not excel in any profession because they labor in it, but they labor in it because they excel.*
>
> —William Hazlitt

Research shows that superior talent does not just happen ab ovo: it is a combination of our genes and our physical and social development that imposes boundary conditions on what we can do easily or not.[5] Top performers come into being because, to a very high degree, they (i) study and understand what their talents are, this being distinct from what they can learn; (ii) make resolutions and set goals to strengthen themselves; (iii) implement talent development projects and mark out daily, weekly, and monthly indicators of progress; (iv) re-strategize based on emergent learning; and (v) take time to salute their own efforts, steps, and attainments.

... And Understand Its Characteristics

> *Everyone takes the limits of his own vision for the limits of the world.*
>
> —Arthur Schopenhauer

Smart people are the motive power of the knowledge economy and every organization faces challenges in managing[6] and leading them. Most people look up to their leaders; top talent knows its deeply embedded life interests[7] and, through

---

[5]Being exceptionally talented does not negate the requirement for application and practice. They will refine the talent so that it may power the reliably near-perfect concretization of strength. Without application and practice, talent broods; without talent, application and practice do not engender as much benefit. Sad to say, in complicated or complex environments, no amount of hard work or training, nor coaching and mentoring, can ever make up for performance gaps if the talent required is not there in the first place. (But they will unlock or help realize related potential.)

[6]Some say the term "management" is a misnomer—top talent cannot necessarily be managed—and that it is a matter of enablement.

[7]Butler and Waldroop (1999) have identified eight deeply embedded life interests: (i) application of technology, (ii) quantitative analysis, (iii) theory development and conceptual thinking, (iv) creative production, (v) counseling and mentoring, (vi) managing people and relationships, (vii) enterprise control, and (viii) influence through language and ideas. It is common to have more than one; indeed, many exist in pairs.

the organization, focuses on what value it can bring to the equation. Therefore, leading top talent in the workplace begins with the understanding that a rapport with them must be an association of interdependent equals,[8] over whom leaders have limited real authority. It takes relationship, discernment, and deep conversation to get to the heart of top talent and use it organizationally. Why? First, as Salacuse (2006) explains pithily, the talent of mavericks always means that they have options outside the organization; those options give them a strong sense of independence. Second, top talent has a formal or informal proprietary interest in the organization (and may have played a role in selecting its management); in consequence, they can think that the leaders are beholden to them, not the other way around. Third, top talent has its own followers and constituencies, whose loyalties and respect powerfully influence their behavior. Fourth, top talent often has loyalties to institutions outside the organization they work in; the signals they receive from these usually influence them more than anything the leaders can say or do. Fifth, top talent does not conceive of itself as a follower; it sees itself as a leader and wants to be treated as such. Last, because of its special value to the organization, top talent usually feels entitled to special access, benefits, and privileges (and constantly negotiates for that).

Redesigning Work

> *The best way to predict the future is to invent it.*
>
> —Alan Kay

When there is no choice but to explore and exploit opportunity, organizations must unleash their full creative and innovative potential. To imagine without limits answers to the question "What if ...?" they must use tools, methods, and approaches that both empower and nurture possibility and reveal the immediate significance and potentiality of what is then found. Heeding Manu (2007), this is not about how one should fit imagination to business; conversely, it is about how one can fit business to imagination.

---

[8]Effective one-on-one, personal communications that promote interest-based relationships are the fundament of that, masoned by willful skill, not formal authority.

One might think that is easier said than done. But there are good examples of successful renegade thinking to invent the future of management.[9] There is also much open and fertile ground in top talent. Paraphrasing Alexander Manu, they, more than anyone else, intuitively understand that before one learns to manage the "how," the "what" needs to be conceived. What is more, they have the ability to reveal the "why," thereby joining the "how" and the "what," that is, the means and the meaning.[10] To develop distinctive ideas about their objectives, their clients, what their clients value, their results, and their plans, organizations need top talent. To solve wicked problems,[11] they must recreate themselves as organizations of choice for mavericks, not merely make adaptations of no great shakes to existing setups. Albert Einstein said it well: no problem can be solved from the same level of consciousness that created it. And who better to resolve wicked problems than mavericks?

Leading Clever People

Wicked problems in urgent need of solution call for new ways in the workplace. For sure, human resources divisions must shift the focus of what they do, e.g., measuring cost per hire, or the impact of initiatives on skills and attitudes, to the quality of the talent decisions they support.[12] How can you lead people who know their

---

[9]Management 2.0 considers questions such as: What are the design flaws that prevent an organization from changing (until that can only be done by coup) and inspiring the joyful imagination and commitment of their employees? What are the grand challenges that need to be addressed if we are to create organizations that are as adaptable as their environments and as human as the people who work in them? What might answers to these challenges look like, and are there experiments that could help push through the limits of management-as-usual? What can be done to speed up the evolution of management in the future? (Hamel 2008).

[10]Timothy Butler and James Waldroop see that deeply embedded life interests are long-held, emotionally driven passions, intricately linked with personality and thus born of an indeterminate mix of nature and nurture. They propose job sculpting, not standard operating procedure, as a means to better match people to jobs.

[11]The term "wicked problem" was coined to denote a challenge that is difficult or impossible to solve because of incomplete, contradictory, and changing requirements that are often difficult to recognize. (Moreover, because of complex interdependencies, efforts to resolve one aspect of a wicked problem may reveal or create others.)

[12]For sure, talent decisions can be made with the same level of logic and rigor as others. To begin, however, one must understand the psychology of work satisfaction. Wicked problems that top the list include balancing long-term goals with short-term demands, predicting returns on innovative concepts, innovating at the increasing speed of change, winning the war for world-class talent, combining profitability with social responsibility, protecting margins in a commoditizing industry, multiplying success by collaborating across silos, finding unclaimed yet profitable market space, addressing the challenge of eco-sustainability, and aligning strategy with customer experience (Neumeier 2009).

worth, are organizationally savvy, ignore corporate hierarchy, expect instant access, are well connected, have a low boredom threshold, and most likely will not thank you? Above all, since first-level managers (not to excuse top- and middle-level managers) are primordial to engagement, a new type of leader, one that neither lacks self-confidence nor imagination,[13] must emerge. He or she will

- know how to discover and learn, and manage and inspire discovery and learning in others;
- grasp how to identify and validate ideas, and transform them into opportunities; and
- nourish and trigger the imagination of individuals in teams, and translate the results into innovations that benefit organizations and society at large.

Of course, then, one cannot exactly lead top talent hands on. But one can be a guiding force in their lives. Your job is not to be smarter than them, for they will almost always know their specific domains better than you; rather, it is to make sure you provide sociability, infrastructure, credibility, resources, and rewards. Your job is also to remove what obstacles stand in the way of their doing their best. The advice Rob Goffee and Gareth Jones proffer is to lead with a light touch, listen to the silences, tune into leadership, explain and persuade, use expertise, give space and resources, tell them what but not how, provide boundaries, give people time for questioning, offer recognition and amplify achievements, encourage failure to maximize learning, protect clever people from the rain, assign real-world challenges with constraints, talk straight, conduct and connect, and recruit more talent. If, some will say, this should apply to any segment of personnel, the fact that it still does not underscores how far we have to go before we can talk about leading in clever organizations.

References

Buckingham M, Coffman C (1999) First, break all the rules: what the world's greatest managers do differently. Simon and Schuster

Butler T, Waldroop J (September–October 1999) Job sculpting: the art of retaining your best people. Harvard Business Review

Goffee R, Jones G (2009) Clever: leading your smartest, most creative people. Harvard Business School Publishing

Hamel G (2008) Renegade thinking. Labnotes. No 9

Manu A (2007) The imagination challenge: strategic foresight and innovation in the global economy. Peachpit Press

Neumeier M (2009) The designful company: how to build a culture of nonstop innovation. Peachpit Press

Salacuse J (May–June 2006) Leading leaders: how to manage the top talent in your organization. Ivey Business Journal.

---

[13]Insecure or unimaginative managers neither attract nor retain great talent; quite the opposite, they diminish their team's ability to get results.

Proposition 51
Forestalling Change Fatigue

In a Word It is a given that organizational change affects people. It is people, not processes or technology, who embrace or not a situation and carry out or neglect corresponding actions. People will help build what they create.

A Modern Satyricon

Ogburn (1957) recounted his experience as a junior officer during the Second World War: "We trained hard, but it seemed that every time we were beginning to form up into teams we would be reorganized. Presumably the plans for our employment were being changed. I was to learn later in life that, perhaps because we are so good at organizing, we tend as a nation to meet any new situation by reorganizing; and a wonderful method it can be for creating the illusion of progress while producing confusion, inefficiency, and demoralization".

As though it were eternal truth, Charlton Ogburn's quip on change fatigue has since been attributed to sundry sages, most commonly Gaius Petronius (c. 27–66), a Roman courtier and satirist. Is it really the case that "Plus ça change, plus c'est la même chose?" Notwithstanding copious studies and applications of change

© Asian Development Bank 2017
O. Serrat, *Knowledge Solutions*, DOI 10.1007/978-981-10-0983-9_51

management, do we simply—over and over again—lack a unique strategy, candid dialogue, clear roles and accountabilities, and bold action, each powered by visible leadership? Then again, are change and its management both more complex and simpler than that?

On Change and Its Misrepresentation

Because things are the way they are, things will not stay the way they are.

—Bertolt Brecht

Change, that is, the act, process, or result of changing, is the norm. Change alone is unchanging[1]: it works through the coevolving dimensions of economy, environment, polity, society, and technology to make up systems of mutual sustainability or (in opposition) mutual vulnerability. (Since all dimensions are connected, none can change by itself.) On account of that, individually or in groups, we all experience change in our daily professional, personal, social, and civic occupations[2]: change is the law of life. (If anything, the rate of change looks as if it is accelerating. But who are we to speak? Neolithic man probably thought the same.)

Change is also an essential part of the life (and death) of organizations—even when they do not operate in a competitive market.[3] However, purpose-driven organizations with little time for social anthropology or the subtleties of complexity, culture, or social learning theories have customarily misinterpreted developmental, transitional, and transformational change—including its value, and

---

[1]Heraclitus (c. 535–c. 475 BC), a Greek philosopher, wrote in riddles to explain that change is central to the universe: "You cannot step into the same river twice."

[2]Any human being is capable of change. Most individuals do so through the natural process of behavior modification, usually by observing, retaining, and replicating in social learning (provided both motivation and opportunity exist).

[3]Transformative change comes in various shapes for all kinds of reasons. In the private and public sectors, driven by external and internal agents, its "why" might be rationalized by (i) the need to respond creatively to a new climate of public opinion, (ii) the need to speed up decision making, (iii) the need to recapture markets, and (iv) the need to save money. An online McKinsey Quarterly survey (2006) received 1,536 responses from a representative sample of executives at publicly and privately held businesses across a full range of industries, as well as nonprofit and governmental institutions. Cost-cutting was a consistent theme (according to 56% of respondents). Half (50%) said their organization's main objective was to move from good performance to great performance, with 41% observing it was linked to restructuring, e.g., merging, splitting up, or divesting. Only 27% were involved with turning around a crisis situation (on the whole the headline-grabbing context for change).

reduced its elements to processes, technology, and people. In their narrowest and least promising view, the processes they design to meet (when they cannot foresee) complex, rapid, and radical changes in their external environments bank on technology that personnel will be expected to leverage. In a technocratic age[4] with a fondness for performance measurement, aka "doing something,"[5] the means that shareholders or senior management prescribe aim to persuade too: identify, engage, and implement. (Skeptics consider both coercive and participative approaches to change as placebo.[6])

> *No plan survives contact with the enemy.*
>
> —Helmuth von Moltke

With some learning from a poor track record to date, actions along a (typical) three-stage change implementation (or transition) curve depicting take-off (aka ending, losing, and letting go), potential stalling or regression (aka the neutral zone), and success or failure—or somewhere in between (aka the new beginning)[7] have been recommended. The following articulates 10 steps to making it work (if it is going to work) (Floyd 2002):

- Specify the "what"[8] and "why"—set the broad direction, including the rationale and its weight.

---

[4]The term "technocracy" derives from the Greek words *tekhne* (meaning, skill or craft) and *kratos* (power, as in government or rule).

[5]Egged on by inexorable pressure for performance from shareholders or senior management, sometimes both, many organizations adopt lofty targets and embark on flurries of activity with neither well-defined agreements nor routes for achieving them. (Retreats and drop boxes are favorite gimmicks with which to try to bolster team spirit and elicit contributions toward these. Glossy pamphlets, mandatory briefing sessions, and tool kits usually follow.) All too often, it does not matter why the change is needed, who should change, what should change into what, and how the change should take place: the object is to identify key results areas and achieve related milestones. Doing something calms the conscience; it also suggests initiative and can-do qualities in quick-wits and earns them promotion. Corners are cut or taken fast. Pressure builds up on a par with individual and team fears, breeding more initiatives.

[6]A placebo is a tablet, liquid, or other form of medication that has no active ingredients and no intrinsic remedial value but serves to appease or reassure a patient. (In medical research and medicine, simulated interventions can actually produce perceived or actual improvements.)

[7]As though organizations were patients nearing death, some have stretched and applied Kubler-Ross' (1973) five stages of grief, viz., denial, anger, bargaining, depression, and acceptance, to speed recovery.

[8]The "what" of change covers much ground, for instance, an organization's brand; culture; styles of leadership and management; policies; corporate strategy; resources; systems, structure, and business processes; functions; products, programs, and services; communications; degrees of freedom and autonomy afforded to people and operations; and operations and locations.

- Distinguish the "who"—always have individuals at the heart of your change effort and communicate with them.
- Understand the barriers, risks, and issues.
- Identify all the levers, influences, power, and resources at your disposal.
- Formulate the campaign—be clear about the "what" and "how".
- Detail the "how"—think things through as much as possible.
- Launch the campaign—be flexible, adapt, stay cool, persist, and do not give up.
- Define clear measures and establish measurement systems to track progress.
- Sustain, institutionalize, and embed the change.
- Accept that change is a journey—so end, review, and start again.

But it does not help that a strategy that has been decided is frequently overtaken by emerging events or circumstances. This impacts the goal, focus, direction, and perhaps even need for the earlier change; improvisation becomes the order of the day and strategic planners are rued. (Paradoxically, change efforts can, through over-management, reinforce the systemic issues they attempt to address.) As you would expect—given the odds against success only 30% of change efforts succeed —disclaimers precede and follow:

- No amount of advance thinking, planning, and communication guarantees success—change as we think we know it being inherently unpredictable.
- Any change involves a shift of the organization's power structure—that being the greatest causes of passive or open resistance.
- Individuals who support change at the onset can become neutral or even passive or active resisters over time.
- All change efforts run into overt and covert resistance.

Change fatigue pervades organizations that cannot learn for change.[9] (After all, irrespective of the outcome, transformation takes energy that must first be mobilized then sustained.) Tell-tale signs of fatigued organizations are (i) senior management and change sponsors do not attend progress reviews; (ii) there is reluctance to share, perhaps even comment on, information about the change effort; (iii) resources are given over to other strategic initiatives; (iv) clients, audiences, and partners demonstrate impatience with the duration of the change effort or increasingly question its objectives; and (v) change managers, champions, and agents are

---

[9]Peter Senge mooted the idea of the learning organization 20 years ago. But we still have not learned to think less like managers and more like biologists. We still view organizations as rigid hierarchies instead of seeing them as communities and networks of practice. Why then, one might ask, is the static organization not yet extinct? The answer is that it may still have comparative or absolute advantages such as brand identity, technological exclusivity, economies of scale. Else, it may—for a while longer—be operating in slow markets characterized, for instance, by low trading volumes or levels of volatility.

stressed out and the change team considers leaving (not quite, it seems, the hope, sense of focus, enthusiasm, feeling of momentum, or confidence that drive accomplishment). The solution? Forget "heroic" leaders[10]; eschew transformation; focus on continuous (not episodic) developmental (or at most transitional) improvements at the middle or bottom of the organization to maintain long-term organizational health; and, above all, distribute (servant) leadership.

The Social Psychology of Fear

There is nothing wrong with change, if it is in the right direction.

—Winston Churchill

Change is not difficult; couching it in military terminology instills fear and does it a disservice. The central issue is never the "what," "why," "who," and "how" of change: it is always about (triple- or, better still, quadruple-loop) learning,[11] facilitated or hampered by organization, people, knowledge, and technology.

Organizations are human institutions, not machines.[12] Man's fears are of something and for something. People must first understand and buy into the need for change (and use organization, knowledge, and technology in support) if any meaningful progress toward a desired future state is to be made at all. Social neuroscience teaches much: change has significant psychological impacts on the human mind. To the fearful it is threatening (because things may get worse); to the hopeful it is encouraging (because things may get better); to the confident it is inspiring (because the challenge is now to make things better).

In truth, however elaborate they may be, most change management techniques from the mid-twentieth century to date derived from conventional command-and-control mindsets that demotivate knowledge workers. These

---

[10]Transformational leaders infantilize their organizations: they keep personnel at such a low stage of development that they cannot even frame possibilities.

[11]The majority of organizations operate by way of single-loop learning—they spend the bulk of their time detecting and correcting deviations from the "rules". In double-loop learning, they are able to reflect on whether the rules might need to be altered. In triple-loop learning, they deliberate at length on how they think about rules, not just on whether the rules should be changed. Alas, quadruple-loop learning is rarely associated with organizational learning: reflective and comparative, it analyzes systemic options and evaluates the foundational claims of each. This brings it to investigate the deep assumptions of paradigms and the principles they are built on, ethics, horizons, and approaches to knowledge creation. The payoffs are breakthroughs by perpetual practice in humane, built-for-change organizations.

[12]If the success of change efforts were simply a function of resources, or even intelligence, organizations would have found the magic formula by now.

techniques are in point of fact responsible for poor organizational performance and
resistance to change: they threaten status, certainty, autonomy, relatedness, and
fairness—five domains of social experience that are deeply important to the brain.
Consequently, a good number of staff disengage and seek protection in apathy.
(And, in such instances, resistance will not be limited to macro-level changes.)

Co-opting Staff for Self-Led Change

Certainly, it is difficult and ultimately pointless to make people do what they do not
want to do. Nobody likes to be subjected to change. But change that we dream up
and embrace on our own is different—that kind of change staffs undertake and
never tire of. If, instead of forcing personnel to perform this or that somersault, we
found out what they want to do and helped them achieve it—in so doing building
participation and receptivity to change—we would discover that change takes little
suasion to envisage and implement. Redefining a relationship requires openness,
reciprocity, and, especially, an appreciation of one's vulnerability: it does not mean
one must do battle with the old.

According to (2001), Semco SA, a privately held manufacturing and services
company in São Paulo, Brazil that practices "management without control," epit-
omizes the bottom-up approach to change.[13] He reports that (i) staff choose their
jobs, titles, places, hours of work, and even pay; (ii) everyone undergoes a
360-degree evaluation every 6 months, which forms the core of any needed change;
(iii) leaders are picked by staff and almost always come from within Semco SA, so
that no radical changes are imposed by outsiders trying to make a good impression;
(iv) the position of chief executive officer changes regularly: four persons rotate
through the job every year; and (v) the company does not even try to prepare annual
budgets—6 months is as far down the road as it can see. In brief, Semco SA
appears to redefine change: instead of being the work of senior management,
change is the responsibility of "atoms," groups of 8–12 persons who see to the
company's basic processes. As a result, change becomes continual, gradual,
low-level—and virtually unnoticed. How we are conditioned to think determines
how we are conditioned to act.

---

[13]The rules for "management without control" of Ricardo Semler, Semco SA's president, are to
(i) forget about the top line, (ii) never stop being a start-up, (iii) do not be a nanny, (iv) let talent
find its place, (v) make decisions quickly and openly, and (vi) partner promiscuously.

References

Floyd P (2002) Organizational change. Capstone Publishing

Kubler-Ross E (1973) On death and dying. Routledge Publishing

McKinsey Quarterly (July 2006) Organizing for successful change management: a McKinsey global survey

Morgan N (July 2001) How to overcome change fatigue. Harvard Management Communication Letter 4(7)

Ogburn C (January 1957) Merrill's Marauders: the truth about an incredible adventure. Harper's Magazine

Further Reading

ADB (2009) Learning for change in ADB. Manila

Proposition 52
A Primer on Corporate Governance

In a Word Good corporate governance helps an organization achieve its objectives; poor corporate governance can speed its decline or demise. Never before has the glare of the spotlight focused so much on boards of directors. Corporate governance has emerged from obscurity and become a mainstream topic.

Notions of Governance

Direction and control are needed whenever people come together to realize societal and organizational goals. To govern is to do just that, to direct and control, by established laws or—preferably not—by arbitrary will. Its core underlying practices, where the former mode is used, are to specify expectations, delegate authority, and substantiate performance.

> *Different men seek after happiness in different ways and by different means, and so make for themselves different modes of life and forms of government.*
>
> —Aristotle

© Asian Development Bank 2017
O. Serrat, *Knowledge Solutions*, DOI 10.1007/978-981-10-0983-9_52

Complex systems cannot be reduced; however, where society or an organization is multipart or too large for simple management, it usually moves for the creation of entities tasked with guiding related processes and systems in their host's evolving context of society, economy, environment, polity, and technology.

> *You can only govern men by serving them.*
>
> —Victor Cousin

It follows that governance, the activity of governing, is a multifaceted phenomenon; definitions of it can be subtle, challenging, and powerful at once.[1] With frequent overlap and resultant conflict, governance shapes affairs at global, national (including, for instance, state or provincial, municipal, and local), institutional, and community levels by means of the entities that occupy shifting (and frequently permeable) social and economic space there, such as government (including the military), civil society (including the voluntary or not-for-profit sector), and the private sector. (Public and private media play advocacy, entertainment, and advertising roles throughout.) All the same, most definitions of governance rest on three dimensions: (i) authority, (ii) decision-making, and (iii) accountability for conformance (assurance) and performance (value creation and resource utilization). Hence, regimes of governance determine severally who has authority, who makes decisions (and how other stakeholders make their voice heard), and the manner in which account is rendered.

A Short History of Corporate Governance

Until the mid-1990s, the term "corporate governance" meant little to most people except small groups of academics and practitioners.[2] But, with daily mention in the media for the last 10 years, in a globalizing world of organizations, it is now

---

[1]To note, governance is not synonymous with government: the first is a structured process (some say a set of responsibilities and rules about their practices); the second is an agent of that. Governance, then, is about how those tasked with governing exercise political authority and use institutional resources to manage affairs in interaction with stakeholders.

[2]In truth, concern for corporate governance is not totally new; it is as old as enterprise even if the study of the subject can only be traced to the 1930s. Business historians deem the Bubble Act of 1720 an early reaction to abuse of charters in the United Kingdom. (There are no doubt others.) But a milestone was reached in 1932 when, in the aftermath of the Wall Street Crash of 1929, Berle and Means (1991) reflected in *The Modern Corporation and Private Property* on the changing role of the modern corporation in society: through legal and economic lenses, they researched the consequences of separation of ownership and control (primarily stemming from the dispersal of shareholding in large corporations). In *Revolt in the Boardroom*, Murray (2007)

broadly understood as the processes by which the policies, strategies, and operations of organizations are regulated, operated, and controlled by boards of directors[3] to give them overall direction and control, and satisfy reasonable expectations of accountability and performance, including to those outside them.[4] It embraces regulation, structure, best practice, and, increasingly, the ability of boards of directors.

> *Whenever an institution malfunctions as consistently as boards of directors have in nearly every major fiasco of the last forty or fifty years it is futile to blame men. It is the institution that malfunctions.*
>
> —Peter Drucker

Corporate constitutions now owe much to the work of Adrian Cadbury[5]: in 1992, in the wake of corporate catastrophes in the United Kingdom, the Cadbury Report—titled *Financial Aspects of Corporate Governance*—concluded that similar fiascos could be mitigated by way of greater disclosure by management and

---

(Footnote 2 continued)

provides an engaging perspective on American corporations in the twentieth century, covering also the work of Adolf Berle and Gardiner Means and the early travails of crusaders such as Lewis Gilbert, Wilma Soss, Evelyn Davis, and James Peck, and delineates a new world in which the "shoulds" of corporate governance have become "musts"..

[3] A board of directors is a governing body of elected or appointed individuals who jointly oversee an organization's activities for multiple year terms. (Other names for such bodies are board of trustees, board of managers, or executive boards.) The functions of boards of directors are determined by the powers, duties, and responsibilities—typically detailed in the organization's by-laws. (By-laws usually specify how many directors a board will have, how they are to be chosen, and when they are to meet.) To govern the organization, basic functions of boards of directors are to establish vision, mission, and values; set strategy, structure, and objectives; select, appoint, and support the chief executive officer and assess his or her performance; delegate to management; promote effective organizational planning; make available adequate financial and other resources; provide proper financial oversight; ensure legal and ethical integrity; maintain accountability; determine, monitor, and strengthen organizational performance, and give account to shareholders for that; be responsible to relevant stakeholders; enhance the organization's public standing; evaluate the board's own performance; and recruit and orient new board members. These functions are largely discharged through meetings of boards of directors and their committees, during which discussions are conducted and resolutions are passed. (It may also be necessary for board members to consult management, personnel, clients, and other constituents outside of board meetings.)

[4] In a word, corporate governance concerns the way power is exercised over an organization.

[5] The Cadbury Report is the first code on corporate governance. It was followed by codes in Australia (the Hilmer Report, 1993); France (the Viénot Report, 1995); the Netherlands (the Peters Report, 1997); and South Africa (the King Reports, 1994 and 2002), among others.

better oversight by boards of directors. Proclaiming fundamental principles of openness, integrity, and accountability, the Cadbury Report made 19 recommendations addressing the structure, independence, and responsibilities of boards of directors; effective internal financial controls; and the remuneration of board directors and management. In 1999, the Organisation for Economic Co-operation and Development (2004) issued principles of corporate governance, revised in 2004, that made a point of underlining the legitimacy and importance of stakeholders as well as shareholders. (The organization also stated that there is no single model of good corporate governance.) Since 2001, in large part due to the high-profile debacles at Enron Corporation, Tyco, and WorldCom, attention to the governance practices of organizations has run rife. In 2002, the Federal Government of the United States passed the Sarbanes-Oxley Act to set new or enhanced standards for all US public company boards, management, and public accounting firms to restore confidence in corporate governance. Such legislation also marked the start of criminalization of corporate misdemeanors by board directors. In 2009, both the New York Stock Exchange and the NASDAQ Stock Market demanded that companies should have a majority of independent board directors.

> *Transparency is often just as effective as a rigidly applied rule book and is usually more flexible and less expensive to administer.*
>
> —Gary Hamel

In consequence or in parallel, all over the world, "comply or explain" codes on corporate governance emanating from securities commissions, stock exchanges, investors and investor associations, and supranational organizations have grown.[6] They vary in scope and detail but most tackle four fundamental issues: (i) fairness to all shareholders, the "owners," whose rights must be upheld; (ii) clear accountability by the board of directors and management; (iii) transparency, or accurate financial and nonfinancial reporting; and (iv) responsibility for the interests of minority shareholders and other stakeholders and for abiding by the letter and spirit of the law. Some see in current trends to balance the three critical anchors of the corporate balance of powers—shareholders, boards of directors, and management[7]—the

---

[6]A case in point is the code of best practice now adopted in the United Kingdom. First issued in 1998 and updated at regular intervals since then, the UK Corporate Governance Code (formerly the Combined Code) sets out standards of good practice in relation to issues such as board composition and development, remuneration, accountability and audit, and relations with shareholders (Financial Reporting Council 2010).

[7]The basic triad of shareholders, boards of directors, and management reflects the division of ownership, strategic management, and day-to-day operational management of an organization.

general evolution of a democratic model of corporate governance, sped by the revolution in communications (even if boards of directors still seldom appear on an organization chart).[8] Beyond manager-centered, hierarchical attempts to merely redistribute power,[9] recent reforms initiatives aim toward better governed organizations that have more robust, pluralistic, and adaptable decision-making processes.

A Scrapbook Collection of Gremlins

The difficulty lies, not in the new ideas, but in escaping from the old ones, which ramify, for those brought up as most of us have been, into every corner of our minds.

—John Maynard Keynes

Codes on corporate governance can surely help steer organizations but it helps to know where they are currently berthed. Corporate governance malfunctions owe to history and tradition, assumptions and perceptions, people and the values they hold, and an organization's existing governance framework.

---

[8]Notwithstanding trends, differences of opinion will likely continue to polarize debate. Should corporate governance be conceived from the perspective of agency theory or from that of stewardship theory? In addition to owing duty to shareholders, should boards of directors also be responsible to stakeholders? Should corporate governance be driven by principles or by prescriptions? Should the chair of the board of directors and the chief executive officer necessarily be different individuals?

[9]Examples include separating the positions of chair of the board of directors and chief executive officer, conducting (more) formal audits of management performance, appointing lead outside directors, and making the board of directors more accountable to shareholders. Usefully, Pound (1995) differentiates managed-corporation and governed-corporation paradigms. In the managed-corporation paradigm, the role of the board of directors is to hire, monitor, and when necessary replace management; in the governed-corporation paradigm, it is to foster effective decisions and reverse failed policies. The characteristics that conduce governed organizations are (i) expertise sufficient to allow boards of directors to add value to decision-making processes, (ii) incentives to ensure that boards of directors are committed to creating corporate value, and (iii) procedures that foster open debate and keep board members informed and attuned to shareholder concerns.

Table. Governance gremlins

• Cognitive dissonance about the mission of the organization	• Cognitive dissonance about its vision	• High turnover of the board of directors and chief executive officer
• Cognitive dissonance about the role of the board of directors	• Insufficient understanding by board members of duties and liabilities	• Tenuous understanding of financial statements
• Unresolved conflicts between board members or between the board of directors and the chief executive officer	• Insufficient understanding of roles of officers or how one becomes one	• The current practice or structure of the board of directors do not match the by-laws
• Confusion over conflicts of interest	• A superfluous number of committees	• Committees that are not engaged in inconsequential work
• A board of directors that is primarily run by the chief executive officer	• Rubber-stamping by the board of directors	• Micromanagement by the board of directors
• Analysis paralysis	• Insufficient strategic vista and competing priorities for the board of directors	• A board of directors that works well but focuses on unimportant issues
• Lack of unity once board members leave the board room	• Low attendance at board or committee meetings	• Ineffective board or committee meetings
• Information that is inopportunely or inaccurately presented to the board of directors	• Lack of clarity on role of the board of directors vis-à-vis staff	• Poor relationships with shareholders and stakeholders
• Insufficient involvement of or consultation with members of the organization	• Staff burnout or volunteer fatigue	

Source Author

Building Better Governance in the Public Sector

Momentously, more demanding notions of corporate governance—typically drawn from the principles of the Cadbury Report—are spreading to the public sector, arguably with more emphasis on conformance than on performance.[10] (However,

---

[10]In the United Kingdom, the Nolan Report of 1995 later adapted the three principles of the Cadbury Report to the public sector. Its seven principles of public life are selflessness, integrity, objectivity, accountability, openness, honesty, and leadership. These principles were to be reflected in each dimension of governance in the public sector, namely, standards of behavior, organizational structures and processes, and control.

where considerable diversity in governance structures is found,[11] for example, in agencies of the United Nations, the challenge is to devise systems that assure stakeholders services are in capable and honest hands, avoid the negative effects of excessive control and bureaucracy, and enable performance to be achieved and improved.) Naturally, clarity of objectives and identification of and reporting on appropriate performance indicators are vital to this process. (This is easier said than done: by definition, political choice impacts the selection of performance indicators.) Notwithstanding, building on the work of the Organisation for Economic Co-operation and Development, the United Nations Development Programme (1997) articulated in 1997 a set of nine principles of good governance that are somewhat better suited to public organizations than the organization's version and, with slight variations, appear in much subsequent literature. (The need for characterization may be less if one accepts that, in both the private and the public sectors, corporate governance is the application of some external standard to internal management processes; some way of holding management to account for their actions; structures that separate responsibilities, particularly where conflicts of interest might otherwise arise; a means to ensure the identification and safeguarding of the interests of a wider group of stakeholders; and a process to ensure that independent expertise is introduced into decision-taking processes at the very top of the organization (Merson 2010).) In 2003, the Institute on Governance aggregated the principles of the United Nations Development Programme to highlight legitimacy and voice, direction, performance, accountability, and fairness.

---

[11]Differences in governance between the private and public sectors pertain to organizational structure, regulation, agents, objectives, the origin of the governance model, authority, responsibility, independence, accountability, and reporting. Plumptre (2004) distinguishes salient elements of governance at international financial institutions. At the World Bank, for one: (i) the board of directors is chaired by the president (chief executive officer), a member of staff; (ii) the board of directors is subordinate to the board of governors—generally, governors are government officials such as ministers of finance or ministers of development; (iii) both the board of governors and the board of directors are accountable to shareholders; (iv) shareholders are governments, not institutions or individuals; (v) shareholders have very diverse values and objectives; (vi) the board of directors is in more or less permanent session; (vii) directors have weighted votes, unlike directors in the private sector who, by and large, all have an equal voice in decision-making; (viii) directors are selected by member countries based on criteria that may be quite different from those that increasingly apply to directors in the private sector, e.g., expertise, professional knowledge, contacts.

Sourcing and Inducting Directors

Managers may run an organization but the board of directors should make sure that it is run well in the right direction. To curtail corporate governance malfunctions, focus is being brought to bear on the core competencies of directors and their induction into the organization.

- **The core competencies of directors** Concern for both conformance and performance requires, respectively, that directors be equipped with short-term organizational efficiency and long-term organizational effectiveness competencies. The conformance-related functions of boards of directors demand abilities in supervision of management and accountability. Their performance-related functions call for aptitudes in policy formulation and foresight as well as strategic thinking. To help boards of directors become more effective, the Institute of Directors (2002) has suggested what personal attributes directors may need (i) strategic perception, (ii) decision-making, (iii) analyzing and using information, (iv) communication, (v) interacting with others, and (vi) achievement of results. The areas of knowledge it recommends directors be learned in are (i) the role of company director and the board, (ii) strategic business direction, (iii) basic principles and practice of finance and accounting, (iv) effective marketing strategy, (v) human resource direction, (vi) improving business performance, and (vii) organizing for tomorrow.
- **Induction of new directors** New directors must also be given the right preparation to do their job. A principle of the UK Corporate Governance Code is that all directors should receive induction on joining the board. (They should also regularly update and refresh their skills and knowledge). The objective of induction is to inform an individual in such ways that he or she can become as effective as possible in the new role as soon as possible. Obviously, directors vary in the extent of their preparedness. The essential point is that their induction should be planned with care, with a program of site visits and meetings with both major shareholders and management. (The UK Corporate Governance Code gives the chair of the board of directors responsibility for agreeing and reviewing a learning and development plan for each director.) New directors must be thoroughly conversant and competent in their knowledge of the organization, its business, and associated financials.

Evaluating Board Performance

If organizations are to survive and grow, their rate of learning must be equal to or greater than the rate of change in their environment. Comparison, reflection, and action are prerequisites to this. Thus, the ideal of the learning organization is as relevant to boards of directors as to the organizations they direct. To advance organizational efficiency and organizational effectiveness, they must become learning boards that simultaneously balance short-term and long-term, internally and externally oriented thinking. Admitting that the link between the performance of boards of directors and the organization may not always be perfect, boards of directors are ultimately accountable for the performance of an organization and should be judged accordingly. Therefore, there is considerable potential for self- and independent evaluations of boards of directors to improve corporate governance.

Naturally, an evaluation can serve many different purposes; three broad areas where the searchlight of review might be directed are processes and systems, participation, and performance.[12] In 2004, to cater to public sector needs, the Public Services Productivity Panel established in 1998 in the Treasury of the United Kingdom designed a comparable performance evaluation framework to cast light on structures and functions, actions and behaviors, and performance (Barker 2004).

References

Barker L (2004) Building effective boards: enhancing the effectiveness of independent boards in executive non-departmental public bodies. HM Treasury

Berle A, Means G (1991) The modern corporation and private property. Transaction Publishers

Financial Reporting Council (2010) The UK corporate governance code

Institute of Directors (2002) Standards for the board: improving the effectiveness of your board. Kogan Page

Merson R (2010) Rules are not enough: the art of governance in the real world. Profile Books Ltd

Murray (2007) Revolt in the boardroom: the new rules of power in corporate America. HarperCollins Publishers

Organisation for Economic Co-operation and Development (2004) OECD principles of corporate governance

Plumptre T (2004) The new rules of the board game: the changing world of corporate governance and its implications for multilateral development banks. institute on governance.

Plumptre T (2006) "How good is our board?" How board evaluations can improve governance. Institute on Governance

---

[12]Process and system evaluations are concerned with how the board and its committees operate, the role played by the chair, and the support provided to the board by staff. Participation examines the involvement of individual directors. Performance is concerned with the outcomes of board activity—this is where careful judgment must be exercised, as the issues can be complex (Plumptre 2006).

Pound J (March–April 1995) The promise of the governed corporation. Harvard Business Review: 89–98

United Nations Development Programme (1997) Governance for sustainable human development: a UNDP policy document

Further Reading

Garratt B (2003) The fish rots from the head: the crisis in our boardrooms: developing the crucial skills of the competent director. Profile Books Ltd

Proposition 53
The Travails of Micromanagement

In a Word Micromanagement is mismanagement. What is it that one should decide in the higher echelons of an organization that, given the same data and information, personnel in the lower echelons might not run just as well?

Do We Love Our Diseases?

Inevitably perhaps given their subject's compass, publications on management often make recommendations to enrich the discipline and enhance its practice. (Continuing advances in information technology and psychology—that, respectively, enable and accelerate globalization and draw from both social neuroscience and databases on billions of individuals' decisions—will surely broaden the vista.)

Startlingly, however, few articles (even less tomes) ever mention micromanagement as an endemic corporate sickness we ought to cure. Our bodies are, to a

© Asian Development Bank 2017
O. Serrat, *Knowledge Solutions*, DOI 10.1007/978-981-10-0983-9_53

large degree, a reflection of our lives: their physical disorders point to what we should look at, for instance, toxic lifestyles (and their workplaces) to which we may be addicted.[1] But could it be that we learn to love our diseases? Do the belief systems and associated (sub)conscious patterns we fashion shape in turn our lives to such an extent that we eschew common sense and come to "need" what ails us?

A Micromanagement Thesaurus

In a necessarily social context, to micromanage is to direct and control a person, group, or system with excessive or unnecessary oversight or input. (In its mildest form, it translates as setting tasks to "subordinates" but checking on progress frequently, leaving them with the distinct impression that they could do it better and faster.) By doing so, micromanagers take decisions away from those who should be making decisions.

Micromanagers feed on formal authority in personal fiefdoms. The more inveterate among them must know all that is going on. They decide how work gets done. They dictate time and track it. They hold meeting after meeting and meetings before meetings. They demand bullet points, briefing notes, and status reports, preferably in large folders with tagged separators, aka "reportomania". They swear by management information systems and results dashboards. They multiply the levels of approval required and focus on procedural trivia in greater detail than they can actually process. They patrol corridors (but do not manage by walking around). They hover to make sure subordinates do things right. They e-mail at speed messages they asked you to draft. They nitpick and rewrite your correspondence with a red pen, counting salutation and closing. They give tedious advice on minutiae (but do not coach or mentor). They hand out tasks but pull them back at the first sign of trouble, thereby curtailing the reasonable freedom that individuals and teams must have to embrace failure. They rarely entertain proposals for change; when they do it is to deconstruct them. (The only original thinking a micromanager recognizes is his or her own: the fact that he or she was promoted previously is meant to bear that out.) They share responsibility—indeed, magnify that of underlings, but not formal

---

[1]Traditional Chinese medicine—based on Taoist philosophical and religious conceptions of balance and opposites, e.g., Yin-Yang and the Five Elements of fire, earth, metal, water, and wood and other metaphysical belief systems, has for 2,000–3,000 years paid attention to the interrelationships of organs. (Poor health is seen to result from an imbalance between what are believed to be interconnected organ systems, with one organ system weakening or overexciting others.) In the West, Edward Bach (1886–1936), an English physician and homeopath, found that when he treated personalities and feelings the physical distress and unhappiness of patients would be alleviated as the natural healing potential in their bodies was unblocked and allowed to work once more. (He developed the Bach flower remedies, a form of alternative medicine inspired by classical homeopathic traditions.)

authority. They call your home at night from their BlackBerry.[2] They do not like to praise (and therefore go to the boss's office on their own in order not to give credit).

> *Pointy Haired Boss: Build a new server to replace the one with the corrupt operating system.*
>
> *Dilbert: That's what I'm doing right now.*
>
> *Pointy Haired Boss: Recover the data from the bad server and put it on the new one.*
>
> *Dilbert: That's the whole point.*
>
> *Pointy Haired Boss: Then see if you can reinstall the operating system on the old one and redeploy it.*
>
> *Dilbert: Do you have any instructions that are not blindingly obvious?*
>
> *Pointy Haired Boss: This is called managing. The alternative is chaos.*
>
> *Dilbert: How did you just make chaos sound like a good thing?*
>
> *Pointy Haired Boss: You should test the new server.*
>
> *Dilbert: Seriously, can we try the chaos thing?*
>
> —Scott Adams

Obviously, any of these traits can only adversely affect interpersonal communication, feedback, openness, flexibility, vertical and horizontal trust, creativity and innovation, productivity, critical thinking, problem solving, and organizational performance. At worst, "control freaks," aka "dream killers" and "nanomanagers," can make work a wretched experience for personnel (and, of course, their families) with detrimental impacts on work quality and turnover.[3] Intense micromanagement is akin to bullying.

---

[2] The Blackberry is a line of mobile e-mail and smartphone devices introduced in 1999. During meetings, corporate Blackberry owners shuffle the device in and out of their pockets to check for new messages and respond quick-fire amid conversation to affirm their executive status. (In some organizations, trying very hard is more important than delivering useful results: not responding swiftly—even after working hours or over the weekend—might indicate one does not care enough to check.)

[3] It is self-evident that giving people responsibility for making decisions in their jobs generates greater morale, commitment, and productivity. Most of the time, micromanaged personnel become indolent, apprehensive, frustrated, or depressed. They cease being accountable. Since high levels of engagement and enablement clearly benefit organizations, disengagement has commensurately high direct, indirect, and hidden costs, not least of which inhibited staff development. (Micromanagement should also curtail a manager's promotional possibilities: someone who is poor at delegation, or does nothing to develop one or more potential successors, ought not be considered for promotion to a level where delegation takes on even greater importance.)

Why Micromanage?

On the whole, people micromanage to assuage their anxieties about organizational performance: they feel better if they are continuously directing and controlling the actions of others—at heart, this reveals emotional insecurity on their part.[4] It gives micromanagers the illusion of control (or usefulness). Another motive is lack of trust in the abilities of staff—micromanagers do not believe that their colleagues will successfully complete a task or discharge a responsibility even when they say they will.[5] Both explanations owe to poor management (and leadership) skills.

> *The best executive is the one who has sense enough to pick good men to do what he wants done, and self-restraint to keep from meddling with them while they do it.*
>
> —Theodore Roosevelt

To note, although micromanagement is readily distinguished by personnel,[6] micromanagers do not often consider themselves as such: they characterize their working style as structured and organized; if pushed, they will only admit to being perfectionists. But the sum total is that they impose on colleagues conditions that meet their personal needs, not those of the affected parties who may be just as much concerned with, say, application of technical knowledge and skills, client orientation, achieving results, working together, learning and knowledge sharing, managing staff, leadership and strategic thinking, or inspiring trust and integrity as the supervisor (if not more). In such instances, micromanagement gets in the way of organizational performance.

People learn by observing what others do—indeed, the first person everyone examines to determine behavior is one's "superior". To micromanage less and delegate more, supervisors are obliged to embody the right attributes and attitudes. Management is the process of doing things right. (Leadership is the process of working out the right things to do.) Under a manager who dictates all actions and otherwise tries to control every move, individuals and teams will be never be as efficient and effective as they would under servant or distributed leadership. The

---

[4] It can, of course, be the case that the person selected for a job is not a good fit. At the time of appointment, little or no research was done to determine his or her suitability for the demands of the position. Else, the top candidate may have been selected largely based on education, background, experience, and interviews, that is, subjective means, not objective means, e.g., assessment of values, behaviors—including past efforts at delegation since historical performance is a reliable predictor, and personal skills.

[5] In opposition, they may deliberately micromanage staff who have a bigger vision than them.

[6] Hint: epithets people use to describe a micromanager include bothersome, bureaucratic, controlling, critical, dictatorial, judgmental, meddlesome, snooping, suspicious, and toxic.

steps to losing the micromanager label are to (i) admit one's tendencies; (ii) solicit the views of staff (and supervisors)—that is, talking and especially listening to them; (iii) make out the exact cause(s) of one's proclivities[7]; and (iv) ask for advice, guidance, and training.[8] (A key element of learning and development would be experiential exercises that showcase the benefits from delegating and the costs of not doing so.)

Without a doubt, the very structure of an organization can facilitate or hinder delegation: where people have broad purviews, for instance, in flatter, egalitarian organizations, delegation is the norm; hierarchical organizations, on the other hand, can signal the nature and strength of boundaries and favor the emergence of silos, the habitat micromanagers thrive in. Machine, missionary, and political organizations—to name three of Minztberg's (1989) seven configurations—tend to attract people who are by nature autocratic. In time, their management style may sow in inherently fertile ground an organizational mindset that will be difficult to alter if senior management and human resource departments do not pay continuing attention. The entire organization might then develop a culture of micromanagement, whereby the behaviors its structure is prone to encourage become embedded in business processes and serve as the operational model for day-to-day activities. The detrimental effects would then extend beyond the organization's four walls to damage its reputation, as revealed perhaps by external surveys of perceptions, causing insecurity among senior management and prompting further micromanagement.

> *More and more people in the workforce—and most knowledge workers—will have to manage themselves.*
>
> —Peter Drucker

---

[7]Who and what do you micromanage? When and where does the behavior occur? Why do you micromanage?

[8]These *Knowledge Solutions* do not discuss the case of micromanagers who know their shortcomings but still strive to retain direction and control to continue enjoying the status and perquisites of their function. Where micromanagement is consciously carried out, a time-honored sequence runs thus: faced by micromanagement, the more engaged workers that might represent a challenge quickly vote with their feet and move on; since the talent pool shrinks and the micromanager fills vacancies with drones and sycophants, more management "help" becomes necessary. These *Knowledge Solutions* do not purport either to suggest what steps micromanaged persons might take to improve the situation, such as volunteering to take on additional work they are confident in or communicating frequently their progress, lest that exculpate micromanagers for negative behavior.

The Antonym of Micromanagement

Micromanagement is one of the most widely condemned managerial sins yet remains an acceptable way of failing. Culprits should have better things to do with their time[9]: management is not about directing and controlling work; it is about enabling it to be done.

Delegation is the antithesis of micromanagement and a wellspring of organizational performance. Specifically, it is the downward transfer of formal authority, a sure recipe with which to increase empowerment and job satisfaction and more directly meet the needs of clients, audiences, and partners. Currently, four principles underpin measured delegation (and concomitant efforts to build readiness levels): (i) match staff to task, (ii) organize and communicate clearly, (iii) choose the level of delegation carefully, and (iv) transfer formal authority and accountability with the task. However, in the twenty-first century, high-performance organizations might have to go further. They will have to ask: what is it that one should decide in the higher echelons of an organization that, given the same data and information, personnel in the lower echelons might not run just as well? The concept of subsidiarity[10] already exists; with new imperatives and associated belief systems, we can shake the micromanagement disease.

> Surround yourself with the best people you can find, delegate authority, and don't interfere as long as the policy you've decided upon is being carried out.
>
> —Ronald Reagan

Reference

Mintzberg H (1989) Mintzberg on management: inside our strange world of organizations. Simon & Schuster, New York

Further Reading

Chambers H (2004) My way or the highway: the micromanagement survival guide. Berrett-Koehler Publishers, Inc

---

[9]Time and energy spent micromanaging—multiplied across an entire division, office, or even department—amounts to a significant, self-defeating waste of a manager's resources.

[10]The organizing principle of subsidiarity proposes that matters ought to be handled by the smallest, lowest, or least centralized competent authority.

Proposition 54
Managing Corporate Reputation

In a Word Newly minted approaches to corporate reputation are already obsolete. Beyond gaining control of issues, crises, and corporate social responsibility, organizations need to reconceptualize and manage reputation in knowledge-based economies.

At Ev'ry Word a Reputation Dies

Reputation, reputation, reputation! O, I have lost my reputation! I have lost the immortal part of myself, and what remains is bestial, wails Cassio in William Shakespeare's *Othello*. Tongue in cheek, a Chinese proverb enjoins: *Don't consider your reputation and you may do anything you like.* Should we heed that facetious advice?

Reputation is not about likability: it is the aggregate estimation in which a person or entity is held by individuals and the public against a criterion, based on past

© Asian Development Bank 2017
O. Serrat, *Knowledge Solutions*, DOI 10.1007/978-981-10-0983-9_54

actions and perceptual representation of future prospects, when compared to other persons or entities.[1] Since we cannot develop a personal relationship with every entity in the world, the regard in which a party is held is a proxy indicator of predictability and the likelihood the party will meet expectations, a useful earmark that facilitates sense and decision-making against alternatives. Everyday, through what amounts to a distributed means of social control, we assess and judge with effect[2] the competence of individuals and organizations to fulfill expectations based on such social evaluation.

> *I would rather go to any extreme than suffer anything that is unworthy of my reputation, or of that of my crown.*
>
> —Elizabeth I

If individuals have often worried about their reputations to a fault,[3] organizations (as opposed to small businesses) only really began to do so from the 1950s, which saw the materialization of consumer products and growing attempts at product and image differentiation, originally by way of public relations[4] and marketing. These days, however, even successful public relations do not suffice to nurture an

---

[1] The most universally understood measure of corporate reputation is stock price, a prime determinant of which is a company's earnings. Others might include quality of management, quality of products, value for money of products, client orientation, credibility of advertising claims, treatment of employees, dedication to charitable and social issues, and commitment to protection of the environment. Of course, even in the same industry or market, not all stakeholder groups will agree on measures or, if they do, ascribe the same importance to these. (Not to mention the general public, standard stakeholders comprise customers, employees, investors, and suppliers.) The deeper question, therefore, is: do organizations have one reputation or many? (And so, might an alignment process ever reconcile different perceptions to give a more accurate, consensual picture of an organization's corporate reputation than the stock price currently offers for those listed?) The Reputation Institute, for one, works to promote seven dimensions: (i) products and services, (ii) innovation, (iii) workplace, (iv) governance, (v) citizenship, (vi) leadership, and (vii) performance.

[2] Reputation defines the identity—hence, social relationships—of others, sometimes fundamentally. Not surprisingly, many words are synonymous (or antonymous) with it (and not just in the English language).

[3] What people think of an individual conditions, for example, whether they want or not to meet, talk, listen to, or employ him or her.

[4] Public relations—the management function that seeks to establish and maintain a favorable public image for an individual or organization vis-à-vis the clients, audiences, and partners on which success depends—has a long history. Its chief objectives, namely, informing people, persuading people, and integrating people with people, are as old as society. (Of course, the means and methods for crafting related messages have changed as society has changed: early vehicles included art and furnishings, architecture, letters, oratory, poems, and religious texts; of late, they include blogs, broadcast media, celebrity endorsements, exhibitions, media kits, media tours, newsletters, pamphlets, press releases, speaking engagements, special events, sponsorships, social media, and websites.)

organization's reputation.[5] The convergence of globalization and widespread computing since the 1990s,[6] bringing immediate news and online journalism including by the general public, magnify blunders and wrongdoings.[7] Beyond corporate images[8] and efforts to realize value from brand equity, beyond more recent endeavors at differentiation through innovation, operational excellence, or closeness to customers, and beyond even exertions to foster key behaviors for a one-company culture, many organizations now also try to nurture reputational capital, that is, all intangible assets including business processes, patents, and trademarks; repute for ethics and integrity; and quality, safety, security, and sustainability.[9] Put differently, they strive to enhance corporate citizenship in the way

---

[5]If corporate reputation is a consensus of perceptions it cannot change much in the long run owing to public relations. Publicity campaigns may offer short-term solutions but organizations need to convey substance over time: messages must have authentic, candid content backed by real performance; corporate values are the best way to promote that since one must stand for something to be known for something.

[6]In pre-internet days, reputation would travel by word of mouth. In comparison, the evolving and emergent social technologies of Web 2.0 provide rich understanding of the specific organizational contexts that shape and inform practice. They will develop as key applications for managing corporate reputation as organizations move from broadcasting to social casting, paying particular attention to community conversation, participation, and collaboration.

[7]Reputation systems, born of the need for internet users to gain trust in the individuals and organizations they transact with online, are now common. Digg, eBay, and Google, to name but three, are built around feedback from millions of customers to facilitate trust in social news, e-commerce, and web-based search, respectively.

[8]A corporate image is the way in which an organization is perceived by external and internal parties. Put differently, it is the composite psychological impression, of what a corporate entity stands for, that springs up at the mention of a related product or service. (In addition to the psychological perspective, some argue that reputation may be based on the assumption that an organization will behave in a way consistent with social expectations of moral and ethical behaviors. Google's informal corporate motto, "Don't be evil," seems a case in point.) Over and above the latter, it is increasingly recognized to be governed by the visual, verbal, and behavioral elements that make up the organization. The rich concept of the corporate image is important: most people accept there is an a priori link between an individual's image of an organization and that person's behavior toward the organization. Corporate images can be good, bad, (un)deserved, (un)wanted, and out of date. Corporate reputations stand or fall by them, hence the efforts of some to shape unique identities and project a coherent and consistent set of images to their publics.

[9]More simply, reputational capital is the brand an organization carries, the sum total of its good name, good works, and history. A reservoir of goodwill confers clear-cut advantages and privileges: we are loyal to and promote organizations we respect; we are willing to pay a premium for their products and services (believing they are more likely to satisfy our needs than those of lesser-known competitors); and we give them the benefit of the doubt in ambiguous circumstances. Naturally, reputational capital is an overriding concern of knowledge-based organizations: their most valuable assets are what economists term "credence goods," viz., products and services that (unlike "experience goods") are bought on faith. Hence, competition among knowledge-based organizations is at the level of reputation rather than price alone: such organizations actively signal their principal attributes to maximize social status.

they relate to direct clients, audiences, and partners; other stakeholders in society at large; and, more and more, themselves. Are we there yet?

> *It takes 20 years to build a reputation and five minutes to ruin it. If you think about that, you'll do things differently.*
>
> —Warren Buffett

Managing Corporate Reputation 1.0

It is a given that perceptions[10] shape behaviors to drive results. However, nearly all organizations are such complex entities one can hardly expect them to be naturally proficient at gaining and maintaining the trust of sundry clients, audiences, and partners. (Many find it perennially difficult to just build trust in the workplace.) Enter reputation management, the process of tracking an entity's actions and other entities' opinions about these, reporting on those actions and opinions, and reacting to reports through feedback channels to build, maintain, or recover reputation.

> *You can't build a reputation on what you are going to do.*
>
> —Henry Ford

To be sure, much of what passes as reputation management is public relations with a twist. An empirical study of corporate reputation management in 653 major German businesses sheds light on the state of affairs in the private sector in that country (and presumably elsewhere in the West) (Wiedmann and Buxel 2005). From a 20% response rate, the study found that eight times out of 10, responsibility for reputation management is vested in boards of directors and management; elsewhere, it is (as one might have thought) assigned to offices or departments serving corporate communications and marketing functions. Further, the sample showed a differentiated system of objectives. According to 76% of respondents, the primary objective of reputation management is to develop a positive image. This was immediately followed by heightening of customer satisfaction and loyalty

---

[10]These are a function of direct experience, what an organization claims and does, and what others say.

(73%) and improvement of customer relationships (66%). Value was also placed on creating a positive corporate identity (60%), acquiring new customers (57%), and heightening employee motivation (57%) and satisfaction (53%). Predictably, the mix of measures used to achieve reputation objectives was both internal and external: the most important external measures were use of the internet for communication directed outwards (47%), the performance of audits and issuing of certificates of quality (47%), press releases (37%), and company brochures (34%); the most important internal measures were use of the intranet for internal communication and information (44%), encouragement of suggestions for improvement by employees (40%), and a wide range of advanced training and seminars to employees (24%). In a run-of-the-mill way, the controlling instruments favored were measurement of customer satisfaction (55%), classical monetary analysis of financial ratios (55%), and evaluation of customer complaints (48%).

If much of the foregoing is redolent of public relations, self-avowedly full-fledged approaches to corporate reputation management are distinctly risk-based.[11] Griffin (2009), for instance, holds that an organization's reputation is the result of how it manages issues, crises, and corporate social responsibility.[12] (Schwartz and Gibb (1999) wrote an early exposé of the need to reperceive corporate social responsibility in the context of globalization. Good companies must go beyond merely being good, they argued; they must have integrity and a strategy aligned with it.) In the twenty-first century, however, such compartmentalized logic cannot attend to the dynamism of risk in knowledge-based economies: there, it cannot be contained and demands active, "on the go" management. Much as the topic of corporate governance, this makes corporate reputation management (including latter day public relations and reputation risk management) increasingly and inextricably interdependent with other fundamentals of day-to-day management.

Managing Corporate Reputation 2.0

If strengths and weaknesses have always been relative, opportunities and threats in the globalized economy clearly only exist in terms of what knowledge is at hand about them.[13] From this modern perspective, the two main approaches to corporate

---

[11]Hence, and undesirably as we shall see, reputation management is also referred to as reputation risk management. (The term "reputation risk" is commonly used to describe potential threats or actual damage to the standing of an organization from the point of view of what people value.)

[12]Corporate social responsibility, according to the European Commission, is a concept whereby companies integrate social and environmental concerns in their business operations and in their interaction with their stakeholders on a voluntary basis.

[13]The same applies to risk, which can be changed, magnified, dramatized, or minimized within knowledge and is therefore open to social definition and construction, in other words, to processes of chronic revision (Beck 1992).

reputation management can be seen for what they are, viz., static, asset-focused, and reactive (when they are not marginal). If, as Scott and Walsham (2005) recommend, we focus on potential we can shift attention from fixing the present–past to managing the present–future with reputable action. For this, they advise, high-performance organizations need to (i) reconceptualize reputation as a strategic boundary object—which offers a lens through which to analyze tensions between local values, reputation, and the inputs and outputs needed to uphold coherence across intersecting communities; (ii) clarify expectations and conduct ongoing reflective assessments—which help recognize the increased demands placed on strategic reputational boundary objects by changing trust relationships; and (iii) define their stakes—which, by shifting away from fixed notions of stake-holders, makes possible a social constructivist perspective of stake-making and stake-breaking.[14]

More prosaically, but certainly not less usefully, the Reputation Institute has also identified specific forward-looking good practices:

(i) Adopt a common model for reputation management across organizational functions.
(ii) Understand what the seven reputation dimensions and attributes mean to different stakeholders.
(iii) Align corporate messaging and reputing activities with key drivers for their stakeholders.
(iv) Create employee alignment with their reputation platform.
(v) Create a cross-functional reputation committee to ensure coherent actions.
(vi) Monitor reputation with different stakeholders against relevant competitors.
(vii) Integrate reputation management into business processes.

References

Beck U (1992) Risk society: towards a new modernity. Sage Publications
Griffin A (2009) New strategies for reputation management: gaining control of issues, crises, and corporate social responsibility. Kogan Page Limited
Schwartz P, Gibb B (1999) When good companies do bad things. Wiley, Inc
Scott S, Walsham G (2005) Reconceptualizing and managing reputation risk in the knowledge economy: toward reputable action. Organization Science 16(3):308–322
Wiedmann KP, Buxel H (2005) Corporate reputation management in Germany: results of an empirical study. Corporate Reputation Review 8(2):145–163

[14]The longitudinal, contextual analysis this calls for reinforces the conceptual apparatus with which to scrutinize miscellaneous reputation risk claims.

Proposition 55
Moral Courage in Organizations

In a Word Moral courage is the strength to use ethical principles to do what one believes is right even though the result may not be to everyone's liking or could occasion personal loss. In organizations, some of the hardest decisions have ethical stakes: it is everyday moral courage that sets an organization and its members apart.

The Same Thought Each Day

What would life be if we had no courage to attempt anything?, Vincent van Gogh queried. The answer is: nothing; life requires courage—if not, how else can we confront and meet the myriad environmental, economic, social, political, and technological challenges the reality of existence throws at us every day?

Courage[1] is the ability to confront danger, fear, intimidation, pain, or uncertainty. Physical courage is fortitude in the face of death (and its threat), hardship, or physical pain. Moral courage, the form the attribute nowadays refers to, is put simply the ability to act rightly in the face of discouragement or opposition, possibly and knowingly running the risk of adverse personal consequences. Springing

---

[1]The word stems from *cor*, meaning "heart" in Latin. The term "heart" is a widespread metaphor for inner strength.

© Asian Development Bank 2017
O. Serrat, *Knowledge Solutions*, DOI 10.1007/978-981-10-0983-9_55

from ethics[2]—notably integrity, responsibility, compassion, and forgiveness—it is the quality of mind or spirit that enables a person to withstand danger, difficulty, or fear, persevere, and venture. Comprehensively—as said by Rate et al. (2007), it is a willful, intentional act, executed after mindful deliberation, involving objective substantial risk to the bearer, and primarily motivated to bring about a noble good or worthy end despite, perhaps, the presence of the emotion of fear.[3]

> *Courage is the first of human qualities because it is the quality which guarantees the others.*
>
> —Aristotle

Of course, for more than we dare imagine, the solution is unconsciousness; courage is not necessary if one is cocooned, deluded, or enslaved to surroundings.[4] So, what might be the spark of moral courage? Bold enough to differ with Aristotle, Carter (1997) holds that integrity, meaning, steadfast adherence to a strict moral code, comes before anything else. He defines it, operationally, as consisting of three traits: (i) *discerning* what is right or wrong; (ii) *acting on* what one has discerned, even at a personal cost; and (iii) *saying openly* that one is acting on one's understanding of right and wrong.[5] (After reading him, and considering our imperfections, those of us who thought we were living a life of integrity should not lose heart.)[6]

---

[2]Ethics are the principles of conduct individuals or groups rest on to address questions about morality—that is, concepts such as good and evil, right and wrong, virtue and vice, justice, etc. Fundamental principles such as the four mentioned are the same the world over, hence, their espousal by all or most religions. Social neuroscience suggests the universal moral compass these four primary principles and their associated values and beliefs make up is hard-wired in brains as part of Man's approach–avoid response, itself a survival mechanism.

[3]Some propose that moral courage should connote resistance to moral temptations and social pressures in addition to enactment of ethical behavior in pursuit of right over wrong.

[4]This warrants an aside. Anticipating at the international military tribunal in Nuremberg in 1947 the protest of major Nazi war criminals that they were only doing their jobs, the prosecution leveled the charge that "[t]he fact that the defendant acted pursuant to an order of his government or of a superior shall not free him from responsibility." That article stood as a flat rejection, with applications thereafter through international law in other walks of life albeit to date mainly military, of evasion of responsibility. (The salient feature of Nazi crimes in the Second World War was their bureaucratic nature.)

[5]The energy in Stephen Carter's definition derives from the active element that fires it: since ethical judgments only weakly correlate with actual ethical behavior, real integrity requires that one should talk the walk and walk the talk.

[6]Some of these are ethical blindspots, viz., psychological processes, molded by experience and the environment (leadership and context), that distort our behaviors. This said, the conditions upon which integrity depends are usually in our control: where they elude us, the point is not that integrity should be entirely attained but that it should be earnestly sought. Encouragingly, the concept of ethical blindspots suggests that moral courage is not a static trait but, rather, a malleable individual property influenced by situational factors through social learning; therefore, it can be built.

> *Few men are willing to brave the disapproval of their fellows, the censure of their colleagues, the wrath of their society. Moral courage is a rarer commodity than bravery in battle or great intelligence. Yet it is the one essential, vital quality of those who seek to change a world which yields most painfully to change.*
>
> — John F. Kennedy

The Growing Need for Moral Courage

So, what of it? Well, since the age-old practice of organizing[7] calls for organization (s) and organizations have—notwithstanding (as the case may be) the accomplishment of the joint purpose for which they are established—copiously documented shortcomings,[8] both their members and targets obviously stand to gain, *ceteris paribus*, from moral strength and associated ethical and pro-social behavior[9] as both the means and the end of moral agency. Fast-growing interest in corporate governance and corporate reputation bear that out.

At its most basic, moral courage helps cultivate mindful organizational environments that, among others, offset groupthink; mitigate hypocrisy and "nod-and-wink" cultures; educate mechanical conformity and compliance; bridge organizational silos; and check irregularities, misconduct, injustice, and corruption. (Learning organizations put a premium on critical thinking and effective

---

[7]People organize in groups to realize a desired outcome from their activities and outputs in a particular sector. This can happen deliberately or spontaneously, but always with coordinated, sometimes large-scale, effort. Organization—and the coordination it rests on—is a reaction to competition. (If resources were limited, the need to organize would be lesser, perhaps minimal.) What is more, organization breeds specialization. (Specialization, through ensuing efficiencies in production and delivery, increases the quantity, quality, and eventually variety of goods and services.) Through specialization and the interdependences it creates, organizations and their members become differentiated: they draw and depend on different combinations and intensities of capital, knowledge, labor, legitimacy, raw materials, and revenue, all of which "conspire" to shape them; they also evolve distinct assumptions, corporate values, and artifacts, e.g., activities, verbal expressions, and objects.

[8]Much of the literature on organizational failure (or success) still examines that subject through the prism of self-perpetuation, that being the outcome of continuing growth or existence. (From this perspective, challenges pertain, for example, to managing complexity; dealing with multiple clients, audiences, and partners; promoting unremitting entrepreneurship; sustaining in-house diversity; and provisioning human resources.) From the mid-1990s, notions of success (or failure) have been augmented to encompass corporate social responsibility, in which instance organizations voluntarily integrate (or not) social and environmental concerns in their operations and interactions with stakeholders.

[9]Moral courage usually connotes the taking of a stand. Pro-social behavior refers to sundry positive acts, beyond specified role requirements, that promote organizational and peer well-being through respect, helpfulness, and cooperation.

questioning, embrace failure, and generally conduce moral and corporate values[10] to achieve enduring success holding social good.) More profoundly, moral courage consolidates the trust, enshrined in formal contracts, oral contracts, and psychological contracts that organizations depend on.

However, all other things will not be held constant: globalization and the opportunity and competition it stimulates are already heightening tensions.[11] Concurrently, some deficiencies of the free market and the economic models it underpins are more and more manifest, as the global financial crisis of 2007–2008 continues to demonstrate.

There is growing evidence also that organizations, institutions too for that matter,[12] find it hard to respond effectively to the rapidly changing, uncertain environment. (The organizations the world needs in a chaos of change are not those of yesterday, when a tall hierarchy was the organizational model of choice: they are fluid and networked to compete on the edge with distributed leadership, anticipation, and reactivity.)[13] In their understandable bewilderment, they are becoming ever more morally complex environments that impose significant ethical demands and challenges on actors within and outside them.[14] They must renounce ethical mediocrity and transit through minimum ethics to display honesty and authenticity in everyday life, for example, vis-à-vis defensive routines—aka undiscussables—in the workplace.[15] Needless to say, most are not there yet. So, where are they?

---

[10]Corporate values are operating philosophies or principles, to be acted upon, that guide an organization's internal conduct and its relationships with clients, audiences, and partners. To note, since morality and ethics are central to the issue of meaning in corporate values, the latter commonly incorporate related statements.

[11]The *Knowledge Solutions* on sparking social innovations report on the daunting agenda of the twenty-first century.

[12]Many use the terms "organization" and "institution" interchangeably but they are not the same. To sociologists, and by definition, institutions are enduring forms of social life, e.g., customs, norms, positions, roles, and values, including art and culture, education and research, the family and marriage, government, language, medicine, religion, law and legal systems, the military, the police, etc. Unlike organizations, they are instilled with a permanent social purpose aiming to govern cooperative human behavior, thereby transcending individual lives and intentions.

[13]To get there, according to Bryan and Joyce (2005), they (i) streamline and simplify vertical and line-management structures by discarding failed matrix and ad hoc approaches and narrowing the scope of the line manager's role to the creation of current earnings; (ii) deploy off-line teams to discover new wealth-creating opportunities while using a dynamic-management process to resolve short- and long-term trade-offs; (iii) develop knowledge marketplaces, talent marketplaces, and formal networks to stimulate the creation and exchange of intangibles; and (iv) rely on measurements of performance rather than supervision to get the most from self-directed professionals.

[14]The current debate about sustainability, which involves trade-offs between near-term costs and possibly very long-term benefits, is a poignant illustration of how the external environment can throw new challenges to organizations.

[15]Since the list is almost endless, only two other mundane but pervasive issues that call for moral courage need be mentioned. They are (i) decisions should be based on facts, objectively considered; and (ii) people should be engaged, remunerated, and promoted in line with performance, not nationality, seniority, education, personality, or else.

Of Malevolent Bureaucracies, Machines, and Psychic Prisons

An almost universal feature of organizations, both in the private and public sectors, is bureaucracy.[16] The purpose of a bureaucracy is to execute the actions of an organization toward its purpose and mission with the greatest possible efficiency and at the least cost of resources. Defying the edict that organizing is perpetual change, the key characteristics of its "ideal" form remain unchanged since Max Weber outlined them more than a hundred years ago; they are (i) hierarchy, (ii) division of labor, and (iii) departmentalization. Nowadays, however, especially in the public sector, this rational method of organization connotes to many a system of administration marked by officialism, proliferation, and red tape. Worse, the terms "bureaucrat," "bureaucratic," and "bureaucracy" are sometimes used as invectives.

> *You will never understand bureaucracies until you understand that for bureaucrats procedure is everything and outcomes are nothing.*
>
> —Thomas Sowell

In a hard-hitting work, now on its fifth edition, Hummel (2007) takes the position that bureaucracy is malevolent. Fragmentation of knowledge and dilution of individual responsibility are its key features, especially in large organizations including governments, business corporations, professional groups, etc. (In modern society most work is done by organizations.) Paraphrasing at length, this is so because bureaucratic structures force people into behaviors that alter the psyche's processes by which knowledge is acquired and emotions are felt. As a result, individuals no longer retain the right to judge what is right or wrong and are no longer accorded the ability to judge when work is done well or poorly. Above all, bureaucracy determines who or what people are. The individual disappears: his or her personality evanesces to be replaced by a bundle of functions—a role. Ralph Hummel sees that bureaucracy runs roughshod over belief, deliberation, emotion, experience, faith, feeling, judgment, meaning, purpose, and resistance. "Yet, human beings have great difficulty working without a sense of what they are doing (reality), without a sense that what they do affects others for good or for ill (morality), without an inner sense of who they are (personality), and without feelings for the things they belabor or the people they work with or the work itself (intentionality). Imprisoned in reality structures that can enforce such working conditions from without, people in bureaucracy make up their own reality from within. Fantasy comes to dominate." In sum, and all for the sake of efficiency, bureaucrats are asked

---

[16]*Bureau* is the French word for "desk", although it also translates as "office".

to become people without conscience, to abandon any sense of mastery, and to leave their emotions at home.

> *It is ... horrible to think that the world could one day be filled with nothing but those little cogs, little men clinging to little jobs and striving toward bigger ones ... This passion for bureaucracy ... is enough to drive one to despair. It is as if ... we were deliberately to become men who need "order" and nothing but order, who become nervous and cowardly if for one moment this order wavers, and helpless if they are torn away from their total incorporation in it. ... [T]he great question is therefore not how we can promote and hasten it, but what can we oppose to this machinery in order to keep a portion of mankind free from this parceling-out of the soul, from this supreme mastery of the bureaucratic way of life.*
>
> —Max Weber

In like fashion, David Luban, Strudler, and Wasserman (1992) charge that the collectivization of the workplace has wrought a transformation in traditional moral values, replacing individual responsibility and internal norms with group identification and external norms. Bureaucracy makes four knowledge conditions difficult to satisfy, whereby a decision-maker (i) recognizes that he or she has come to a fork in the road; (ii) knows that he or she must make the choice in a fairly short, distinct period; (iii) confronts a small number of well-defined options; and (iv) possesses the information needed to make the decision. Given this predicament, they put forward five obligations arising from the risk that an individual will do or contribute to harm without knowing it. They are obligations of (i) investigation, (ii) communication, (iii) protection, (iv) prevention, and (v) precaution.[17]

Morgan (1986) suggests we should use metaphors to understand and change organizations, with implications for moral courage as we shall see. Specifically, the new ways of thinking metaphors instill facilitate perception from distinct viewpoints to generate both competing and complementary insights and suggest actions that may not have been possible before; they can help improve the design and management of organizations, for instance, to analyze and diagnose problems.

---

[17]What David Luban, Alan Strudler, and David Wasserman suggest amounts to a reconfiguration of the dimensions of individual responsibility and a rework of the structure and culture of bureaucracies. The order may be too tall: so far, elements of the preemptive obligations they advocate are being propounded by means of ombudsmen. (An ombudsman is an official appointed to hear, investigate, report on, and help settle the complaints that individuals may have against maladministration, abuses, or capricious acts, especially that of public authorities. To note, the primary tools that ombudsmen use to resolve disputes are recommendations—binding or not—and mediation.)

Excessive caution, reliance on precedents, and following the beaten path have to give way to innovation and inventiveness and to trying out new methods ... I do believe that the core of the civil services is sound and rooted in values of integrity and fair play ... It is a pity that instances of individual waywardness, of lack of moral courage, and of surrender to pressures and temptations tarnish the image of the civil services and lead to immense criticism and dissatisfaction.

—Manmohan Singh

He makes out eight types of organizations in the public and private sectors: (i) organizations as machines, (ii) organizations as organisms, (iii) organizations as brains, (iv) organizations as cultures, (v) organizations as political systems, (vi) organizations as psychic prisons, (vii) organization as flux and transformation, and (viii) organizations as instruments of domination. (The machine, organism, culture, and psychic prison metaphors resonate most with people. Of course, combinations of the eight types are possible.) Fans claim that the eight perspectives can help us control our destinies and avoid our allotted fate. Humbly, Gareth Morgan advises that, however useful, images must still be used guardedly: by their very nature, they create partial insights that can mislead if relied upon too heavily. Granted that all eight types refer to organizations, the repercussions of which on individual (and collective) responsibility were discussed earlier, an investigation of what light each metaphor throws on the enabling environment for moral courage would seem warranted. In public sector bureaucracies, from among the four readily recognized images, the machine and psychic prison metaphors can explain psychologies of mindless obedience with possible impact on ethical and pro-social behavior. A machine is designed to perform work of a repetitive nature and the machine metaphor promotes the belief that organizations can be engineered. However, even though persons in positions of formal authority may well like to treat their colleagues as though they were cogs in a well-oiled machine, the four primary principles of integrity, responsibility, compassion, and forgiveness require more nuance. Next, to control their impulses and live in harmony with others, individuals go through unconscious psychological mechanisms of denial, displacement, projection, rationalization, regression, and sublimation. Organizations have similar neurotic tendencies leading to debilitating conflict or dysfunctional behavior. But when the collective manifestation of negative psychological states associated with domination press an individual's consciousness, organizations can become psychic prisons. Much as the image of organizations as machines, the dehumanization and exploitation described by that metaphor does not bode well for moral courage.

From Ethical Challenge to Action

People will keep organizing with or without organizations: their survival depends on it. Emergent phenomena, such as civil and nongovernment organizations, and practices, such as outsourcing, are infiltrating or hollowing out once-watertight organizational boundaries. The art and craft of jazz, which distribute leadership, fuel interest in other organizing processes and forms of organization. Notwithstanding, until such new ways of organizing and coordinating develop a critical mass—be that through returning to what worked in the past or pressing into new territory, the bulk of organizing will likely continue to be performed by the routine of bureaucracy, at least in the foreseeable future. And, with that, the need for moral courage will grow unabated.

> A ship in harbor is safe, but that is not what ships are built for.
>
> —John Shedd

Where then might we go from here? Sadly, there is no shortcut. To begin, individuals and organizations should grasp that the development of a desire to act with moral courage is influenced by personal factors in the form of automatic and conscious self-regulation. Personal factors, in turn, are swayed by situational and contextual factors, e.g., organizational directives, rewards, and punishments; social norms; and social pressure. Of equal importance is the notion that moral courage is not automatic behavior per se; it is a practice to which one becomes habituated. Ralph Waldo Emerson thought, rightly, that a great part of courage is the courage of having done the thing before. Marrying cognitive, technical, and emotional intelligence,[18] only by repeatedly going through a process of analysis, interpretation, debate, and judgment enlightened by ethics can people sharpen their skills in moral reasoning and in this manner develop moral intelligence. Beyond statements of corporate values, human resource departments might also need to recruit for values and help spread the message that reinforcing these starts at the top.

References

Bryan L, Joyce C (2005) The twenty-first century organization. McKinsey Quarterly. No 3
Carter S (1997) Integrity. Harper Perennial
Hummel R (2007) The bureaucratic experience: the post-modern challenge. M. E. Sharpe

---

[18]Emotional intelligence is values-free. Without a moral anchor, the skills of emotional intelligence will not necessarily be directed toward doing good.

Luban D, Strudler A, Wasserman D (1992) Moral responsibility in the age of bureaucracy. Michigan Law Review 90(8):2348–2392

Morgan G (1986) Images of organizations. Sage Publications

Rate C, Clarke J, Lindsay D, Sternberg R (2007) Implicit theories of courage. The Journal of Positive Psychology 2(2):80–98

Further Reading

Lennick D, Kiel F (2011) Moral intelligence 2.0: enhancing business performance and leadership success in turbulent times. Prentice Hall

Proposition 56
Business Model Innovation

In a Word Who is your customer? What does the customer value? How do you deliver value to customers at an appropriate cost? Business models that focus on the who, what, and how to clarify managerial choices and their consequences underpin the operations of successful organizations.

Sri Kalika Devi

You may not be interested in strategy, but strategy is interested in you.

—Apocryphal

© Asian Development Bank 2017
O. Serrat, *Knowledge Solutions*, DOI 10.1007/978-981-10-0983-9_56

Almost 80 years ago, Joseph Schumpeter,[1] the prophet of innovation, distinguished five types: (i) a new good, (ii) a new method of production, (iii) a new market, (iv) a new source of supply of raw materials, and (v) (the carrying out of) a new organization of any industry (or market). Regrettably, the body of knowledge he engendered then lays dormant until the end of the twentieth century, with precious few other insights.[2] In modern parlance, the five cases were reinterpreted as product, process, market, input, and organizational innovations; references to a sixth, innovation in services—a sector that did not exist in Joseph Schumpeter's time—began to show up in the mid-1990s.[3]

> *The real voyage of discovery consists not in seeking new landscapes but in having new eyes.*
>
> —Marcel Proust

So far, so (relatively) still: right until the inception of the online era, pretty much everyone played by the same, slowly evolving rules. However, in the wake of the continuing internet revolution—notwithstanding the dot.com fiascos of 1995–2000[4]—

---

[1]Schumpeter (1883–1950), an Austro-American economist and political scientist, held that capitalism can only be understood as an evolutionary process of innovation, the unremitting nature of which wreaks creative destruction in waves favoring those who grasp discontinuities faster. He (1934) hypothesized that instability brought about by entrepreneurs, rather than equilibrium and optimization, is the norm of a healthy economy and the central reality for economic theory and practice. On the process of creative destruction, with which his name is interchangeably associated, he (1942) presciently remarked that "... the problem that is usually being visualized is how capitalism administers existing structures, whereas the relevant problem is how it creates and destroys them."

[2]Notwithstanding, Drucker (1985) was, 50 years later, the first to champion innovation and entrepreneurship as a purposeful and systematic discipline. Helpfully, he identified seven sources of innovation: the first four lie within the enterprise; the others originate outside it. They are (i) the unexpected—the unexpected success, failure, or outside event; (ii) incongruities—discrepancies or dissonance between what is and what is assumed or "ought to be;" (iii) process needs; and (iv) changes in industry (or market) structure that catch everyone unawares; (v) demographics; (vi) changes in perception, mood, and meaning; and (vii) new knowledge, both scientific and nonscientific. Elsewhere, theoretical enhancements cast a barren light on professed levels of innovation intensity: (i) incremental—innovation as improvement, (ii) radical (next generation)—innovation as change, and (iii) systemic (breakthrough)—innovation as revolution.

[3]A familiar definition of innovation transpires from this: innovation is the successful exploitation of new ideas. Then again, if it is deemed a competence and not just a process, innovation is the ability to deliver new value to clients, audiences, and partners.

[4]At the time, the concept of business models was just about synonymous with e-business—the use of information systems and technology to manage administration and financial systems, including human resources, as well as external processes such as marketing and sales, supply of goods and services, and customer relationships. (Successful e-business models introduced novelty, created efficiencies compared with existing ways of doing business, forged complementarities, and enabled the lock-in of customers.) Alas, web-based business models that promised wild profits did

business model innovation is the rage.[5] (This kind of innovation is often more valuable and transformative than the other types: it reduces risks and, conversely, allows more risks to be taken. It has also, perforce, encouraged organizational innovation; for instance, internet-sped innovative processes and structures include peer-to-peer and open-source organization,[6] collaborative mechanisms that would have been inconceivable to our parents, let alone Joseph Schumpeter.) In the globalized economy, not forgetting that about 2.5 billion people live on less than $2 a day, the growing significance of business models is a logical reaction to excessive choices and associated competition from deregulation and technological change.[7] Undeniably, certainly for customers and organizations alike in high-income economies and increasingly elsewhere too, distinguishing between many products and services on a purely functional basis is not easy.[8] In 2005, drawing from a survey of more than 4,000 senior executives and two dozen interviews with corporate decision-makers in 23 countries in Europe, the Asia and Pacific region, and the Americas, the Economist Intelligence Unit (2005) urged organizations to revisit their business models, regularly.[9]

> *If life—the craving for which is the very essence of our being—were possessed of any positive intrinsic value, there would be no such thing as boredom at all: mere existence would satisfy us in itself, and we should want for nothing.*
>
> —Arthur Schopenhauer

(Footnote 4 continued)

much to misrepresent the concept and undermine its intrinsic usefulness. Nevertheless, the experience concentrated attention on (possibly different) ways of doing business and, much as the notion of intellectual capital did from the mid-1990s, on nonfinancial value drivers in organizations.

[5]Tellingly, *The Economist* launched in 2009 a new column titled Schumpeter to champion the role of innovation and entrepreneurship in modern business and management.

[6]The features these working arrangements share are self-governance, adaptive network interaction, and openness to any person who has something to contribute.

[7]The rise of new technology-based and low-cost rivals is challenging established players, reshaping industries (or markets), and redistributing profits. This said, exacerbated by economic stagnation in the West, the pressure to penetrate emerging economies and developing countries is driving business model innovation worldwide.

[8]Of course, products and services matter: however, they are vulnerable to replication and therefore cannot offer durable competitive advantage.

[9]In the private sector, 55% of the executives surveyed declared new business models would be a greater source of competitive advantage than new products and services by 2010. In the public sector, 54% of the executives who responded thought success in 2010 would hinge more on the ability to innovate with delivery channels than with services themselves. (Pursuant to the global financial crisis of 2007–2008, many public sector agencies are in any case cutting services as they struggle to cope with the aftermath of the recession.) In declining order of complexity and degree of change, options for alternative delivery channels include strategic partnerships, joint ventures, outsourcing, shared services, and lead authority models.

The Theory of the Business

The concept of value and the differentiation[10] it rests on are integral to business (and much else). For consumption or use, every organization strives to sell products and services that customers value.[11] To a customer, value added that satisfies tangible needs and intangible wants, and embodies concepts such as brand equity, is what he or she expects from a purchase. The notional value derived from a purchase will abstract what costs—both actual (monetary) and circumstantial (convenience, time, etc.)—a transaction entailed.[12]

> *Price is what you pay. Value is what you get.*
>
> —Warren Buffett

It follows that the notion of value should dominate any discussion of business models; sorry to say, this is not always the case. What is more, as befits a rapidly evolving field, there is no generally accepted definition of what a business model is: literature offers generic, broad, or narrow typologies that singly or jointly provide incomplete and confusing pictures of the perspectives, dimensions, and core issues of the business model concept depending on the lens used. This ought to matter: after all, if having a good business model is an important goal for organizations, they need a simple, logical, measurable, comprehensive, operational, and meaningful definition to plan, monitor, and evaluate deliverables. (However, most organizations can find it difficult to describe their business model in 25 words or less, let alone explain how it is used to reach decisions.)

> *Markets are designed to allow individuals to look after their private needs and to pursue profit. It's really a great invention and I wouldn't underestimate the value of that, but they're not designed to take care of social needs.*
>
> —George Soros

---

[10]Differentiation, the result of efforts to make a product or service stand out as a provider of unique value to customers vis-à-vis competitors, is the wellspring of competitive advantage. Nonperformers focus on obstacles; performers focus on results: the sharper the differentiation, the bigger the advantage. Zook and Allen (2011) mapped three major clusters, all of which wear with age, that high-performance organizations relentlessly build day in day out, usually maximizing customer feedback in virtuous cycles; they are management systems, operating capabilities, and proprietary assets.

[11]Value is created by solving a problem, upgrading performance, or reducing risk and cost.

[12]In short, Value = Benefits − Costs.

A business model is not an explanation of how a company hopes to make money; it is not strategy either.[13] A business model is the core design,[14] the logic, that enables an organization to capture, create, and deliver value to meet explicit or latent needs (and in so doing, of course, derive some form of profit itself).[15] (Most likely, the handiest metaphor would embody characteristics of an organization's way of thinking, operational system, and capacity to generate value.) The best customer value proposition is the viable set of means and ends—at their simplest, resources and processes driven by a formula—that does just that.[16] A proposition that is clear, focused, and consistent—no mean feat—is astonishingly powerful: business model innovation in one or more areas of the customer value proposition can forge a stronger theory of the business to enhance, at least for a while,[17] an archetypal large organization's business structure, organization, supply chain, products and services, customer service, customer experience, and administration.

---

[13]A strategy is a long-term plan of action designed to achieve a particular goal. With respect to business models, it would be the contingent plan to create a unique and valuable position involving a distinctive set of activities, of which business processes and organizational design would be ingredients. (While every organization has some form of business model, not every organization has a strategy.)

[14]Design thinking is a compelling process for exploring new ideas: a good business model will be concise yet complete in every important respect. (Each element or building block will have been carefully thought through and individually crafted, yet with an eye to the sum of synergizing parts.)

[15]More philosophically—but not less pertinently—business models have been described as stories that explain how organizations work, in short, the theory of the business (Drucker 1994). Paraphrasing, a theory of the business has three parts: (i) assumptions about the environment of the organization—society and its structure, the market, the customer, and technology; (ii) assumptions about the specific mission of the organization; and (iii) assumptions about the core competencies needed to accomplish the organization's mission. The specifications for a valid theory of the business are that (i) the assumptions about environment, mission, and core competencies must fit reality; (ii) the assumptions in all three areas have to fit one another; (iii) the theory of the business must be known and understood throughout the organization; and (iv) the theory of the business has to be tested constantly.

[16]Even if it is only implicit, all organizations operate by way of a business model. (The days of those that do not are now short.) For example, government agencies may depend on fees, service revenues, or taxes but they are still held accountable for meeting public needs. Nongovernment organizations may not provide a financial return to investors or owners but they must still deliver value if they are to attract donations, grants, or membership dues. Social enterprises may be mission-driven but must still know how to scale their activities.

[17]Inevitably, every theory of the business—even the soundest—will become obsolete then invalid because the environment of organizations changes constantly. Paraphrasing Peter Drucker further, preventive care, early diagnosis, and cure can help keep to a tolerable level the pain of bringing an organization's behavior in line with the new realities of its environment, with a new definition of its mission, and with new core competencies to be acquired or developed.

> *We don't ask consumers what they want. They don't know. Instead, we apply our*
> *brain power to what they need, and will want, and make sure we're there, ready.*
>
> —Akio Morita

There's a Better Way to Do It—Find It!

> *It is difficult to get a man to understand something, when his salary depends upon*
> *his not understanding it!*
>
> —Upton Sinclair

Competitive advantage can only be achieved by delivering unique products and services for which customers are willing to pay a premium. To be able to perform at a higher level than others in the same industry (or market), organizations must make choices that optimize their business ecosystem. Magretta (2002) thinks their choices must meet two critical tests: the narrative test (the story must make sense), and the numbers test (the profit and loss statement must add up). Across the private and public sectors, there is no single business model as the next figure illustrates. (Organizations that deliver the same product or service can have quite different business models, their relative success hinging on how well they meet customer expectations.) While sundry approaches to fitting systems into a working whole exist, as a select list of currently prominent publications on key elements of a business model demonstrates, most pay attention to five interrelated elements: (i) markets, (ii) products and services, (iii) processes, (iv) people,[18] and (v) economics. Notwithstanding the respective strengths and weaknesses of approaches to the subject, the greatest benefits will be reaped when organizations prepare for a successful business model design project, research and analyze the elements needed for the effort, generate and test viable options and select the best, implement the

---

[18]Most approaches have strengths but most also fall short of a necessary and sufficient accent on people. Configurations of organizations vary—and will undoubtedly change further in the future—but it is generally accepted that an organization's personnel plays a vital role in its business: individually and collectively, what personnel contributes, looks to get in return, and wants to achieve conditions an organization's ability to capture, create, and deliver value. To engage personnel, the business model that an organization uses to describe, reflect on, and enrich its customer value proposition should therefore be used as the basis for communication and motivation.

Fig. 56.1 Examples of business models. *Source* Author

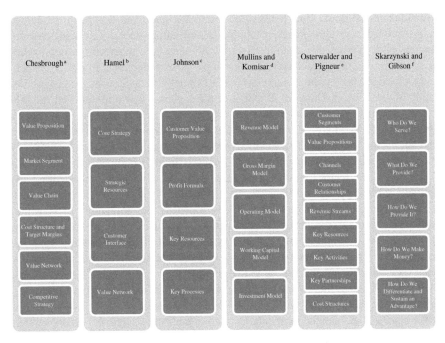

Fig. 56.2 Key elements of a business model. [a]Chesbrough (2003), [b]Hamel (2002), [c]Johnson (2010), [d]Mullins and Komisar (2009), [e]Osterwalder and Pigneur (2010), [f]Skarzynski and Gibson (2008). *Source* Author

prototype in the field, and continually adapt and modify the business model in response to industry (or market) reaction.

> *You can't do today's job with yesterday's methods and be in business tomorrow.*
>
> —Anonymous

If you don't do it excellently, don't do it at all. Because if it's not excellent it won't be profitable or fun, and if you're not in business for fun or profit, what the hell are you doing here?

—Robert Townsend

In the end, an organization is nothing more than the collective capacity of its people to create value.

—Lou Gerstner

To say the least, public sector organizations have their work cut out as well. In the words of Gus O'Donnell, "[they are] ... too inclined to settle for the legacy structures and systems [they] inherit[ed] from the past, and not good enough at going through a design process that selects and tailors delivery systems that are capable of delivering the required outcome, drawing on a repertoire of approaches to structure, incentives, delivery, relationships, governance, and so on ..." (Neely and Delbridge 2007) (The context of Gus O'Donnell's remarks was the program of capability reviews that the Government of the United Kingdom launched in 2006 for all central government departments. To all but the hard of hearing, it rings a familiar bell elsewhere.) Apart from the kind of return—with financial profit making up the larger distinction—there are no reasons public sector organizations should reap smaller rewards from good business models compared to the private sector.[19] Public sector organizations deal with the allocation, production, and delivery of basic public goods and services at the local, national, regional, or global level. For sure, considerable complexity is added by the political context within which they operate, the heterogeneous nature of most of them, and the resulting slower rate of structural change. Therefore, the value of business models would lie particularly in terms of their ability to help these organizations articulate clearly what they will do and, by the same token, what they will not do. Among others, they can also gauge the coherence between an organization's strategic agenda and public needs, help match public needs to an organization's business processes, make obvious the financial implications of an organization's delivery chain, support diagnoses of the need for change and ways that might be achieved, and facilitate communication within an organization and both to and from it.

---

[19]To begin, however, they need to edify their understanding of what a business model constitutes: too often, public sector organizations consider business models merely in terms of resources, key result areas, and outputs.

References

Chesbrough H (2003) Open innovation: the new imperative for creating and profiting from technology. Harvard Business School Press

Drucker P (1985) Innovation and entrepreneurship: practice and principles. HarperCollins Publishers

Drucker P (September–October 1994) The theory of the business. Harvard Business Review: 95–104

Hamel (2002) Leading the revolution: how to thrive in turbulent times by making innovation a way of life. Harvard Business School Press

Johnson M (2010) Seizing the white space: business model innovation for growth and renewal. Harvard Business School Press

Magretta J (May 2002) Why business models matter. Harvard Business Review: 3–8

Mullins J, Komisar R (2009) Getting to plan B: breaking through to a better business model. Harvard Business School Press

Neely A, Delbridge R (2007) Effective business models: what do they mean for whitehall? Sunningdale Institute

Osterwalder A, Pigneur Y (2010) Business model generation: a handbook for visionaries, game changers, and challengers. Wiley

Schumpeter J (1934) The theory of economic development: an inquiry into profits, capital, credit, interest, and the business cycle. Oxford University Press

Schumpeter J (1942) Capitalism, socialism, and democracy. Harper and Brothers

Skarzynski P, Gibson R (2008) Innovation to the core: a blueprint for transforming the way your company innovates. Harvard Business School Press

The Economist (2005) Business 2010: embracing the challenge of change. Economist Intelligence Unit

Zook C, Allen J (November 2011) The great repeatable business model. Harvard Business Review:107–114

Proposition 57
Managing Knowledge in Project Environments

In a Word Projects ought to be vehicles for both practical benefits and organizational learning. However, if an organization is designed for the long term, a project exists only for its duration. Project-based organizations face an awkward dilemma: the project-centric nature of their work makes knowledge management, hence learning, difficult.

Define: Project

In its everyday manifestations, a project[1] is an individual or collaborative endeavor contemplated, formulated, or carried out to achieve something that has not been done before. In the world of organizations, however, a project is often a major, time-bound enterprise requiring concerted inputs, activities, and outputs—that can

---

[1]The word derives from Latin *projectum*, meaning, "something thrown forth," hence, a projectile —another related word.

© Asian Development Bank 2017
O. Serrat, *Knowledge Solutions*, DOI 10.1007/978-981-10-0983-9_57

involve considerable personnel or a single person, data and information, research, services, equipment, goods, materials, and of course finance—toward a unique product, service, or lasting outcome or result. (Indeed, projects are the normal mode of organization for entire industries such as aerospace, architectural practices, construction, design, publishing, research and development, shipbuilding, and software: they live or die by contracts for consulting, goods, works, and related services.)[2] Where a logic model is used to strengthen design and facilitate monitoring and evaluation—for example, in development agencies[3]—a project is framed by deliverables in a results chain specifying performance targets and indicators, data sources and reporting mechanisms, as well as assumptions and risks.

> *My personal philosophy is not to undertake a project unless it is manifestly important and nearly impossible.*
>
> —Edwin Land

> *I am opposed to the laying down of rules or conditions to be observed in the construction of bridges lest the progress of improvement tomorrow might be embarrassed or shackled by recording or registering as law the prejudices or errors of today.*
>
> —Isambard Kingdom Brunel

Large-scale projects from times past have been synonymous with the marshalling and division of labor by master builders and early engineers for the construction of burial mounds and temples then, as populations grew, fortifications, amphitheaters, roads, bridges, aqueducts and other hydraulic applications, cathedrals, harbors, railways, dams, etc. At the beginning of the twentieth century, Henry

---

[2]The value that project-based organization can add draws from (i) unity of command, since the project manager is also the functional manager; and (ii) focus, since everyone on the team only has the project for his/her primary responsibility, supposedly. From clear authority and direction, project-based organization is expected to beget swift decision-making, simple and flexible team structures, shorter lines of communication, high levels of individual and collective engagement, maintenance of a permanent group of experts, and holistic support to project formulation and implementation. Obviously, the challenge is to move from the realm of the possible to the realm of practice: the *Knowledge Solutions* on working in teams list characteristics of successful teams and discuss how they might be developed. (They caution also that teams are not necessarily the best configuration for what an organization sets out to accomplish; hence, the existence of other ways to organize.)

[3]Bilateral and multilateral development agencies are major sources of financial support and professional advice to developing countries, purposely for poverty reduction. Their main devices are loans, grants, policy dialogue, technical assistance, and equity investments, all of them project-centric.

Gantt,[4] a proponent of Frederick Winslow Taylor's theories of workflow efficiency, and Henri Fayol, a pioneer of modern management, synthesized planning and control techniques. Today, engineering continues to make good use of projects but applications cut across pretty much all spheres of human activity, such as business and science.[5]

Projects drive change, and their good organization and coordination are the best way to concretize that. Project management—a discipline that emerged as a profession in the mid-twentieth century and sometimes seems to define working lives —is the application of knowledge, skills, and techniques to realize projects and their intended benefits efficiently and effectively over the period specified within scope, resources, and other limitations. Conventionally, its processes fall into five broad process groups: (i) initiating, (ii) planning, (iii) executing, (iv) monitoring and controlling, and (v) closing.[6] What is more, six parameters are always given weight in its methodologies: (i) time, (ii) cost, (iii) human resources, (iv) scope, (v) quality, and (vi) actions.[7] Project management is here to stay[8]: in fact, a growing number of organizations practice project portfolio management to analyze and collectively administer pools of (ongoing or proposed) projects and their interfaces based on such parameters, aiming to reduce uncertainty while honoring singular constraints imposed by external real-world factors.

To be true to form (and its etymological roots), a project must be a one-off, unique set of activities meant to accomplish a desired outcome by a cut-off date. Crucially, therefore, the temporary nature of a project stands in sharp contrast with

---

[4]Henry Gantt (1861–1919), an American mechanical engineer, developed the eponymous chart in the 1910s to illustrate project schedules by defining and grouping terminal and summary elements in work breakdown structures.

[5]The construction of a bridge, building, or road; the relief effort after a natural disaster; the acquisition or development of a new or modified information system; the introduction of a change in the structure, staffing, or style of an organization; the implementation of an improved business process; the expansion of sales into another market—all are projects.

[6]In project environments characterized by a significant exploratory element, e.g., research and organizational change, these process groups are habitually reinforced by decision points— meaning, go-no-go gates—at which continuation is debated and decided.

[7]Needless to say, other crosscutting parameters lie in project integration, communications, procurement, and risk management.

[8]In a world of relentless change, organizing by project is on the increase: to meet increasingly complex challenges and ferocious competition in the public and private sectors, organizations must formulate innovative solutions. As one would expect, the mustering and concentration of resources that characterize projects as a knowledge-intensive organizational form promotes their burgeoning, even if the boundaries between projects and their permanent hosts in particular and the state of the art of knowledge management in general still constrain what learning has been experienced in one to fully benefit the other. (At the turn of this millennium Peters (1999) affirmed that all work is now project work. Because of demand, the techniques developed for project management are well-nigh innumerable: project management frameworks, scope management, communication, change management, and building support for projects are recurring areas of interest for which miscellaneous tools, methods, and approaches have been devised.

the business as usual, aka operations,[9] it both engenders and relies on. (Temporary means that every project has a definite beginning and a definite end, even though the duration need not be short.) And so, the management of projects and the administration of business as usual should be quite different and as such require discrete competencies in strategy development, management techniques, and collaboration mechanisms, not forgetting—the subject of these *Knowledge Solutions* —knowledge capture and storage and knowledge sharing and learning.

> *Successful Project Management:* "Plan, execute, evaluate" *sounds simple, but most projects aren't well planned nor are they evaluated well. The tendency is to jump right into execution and as soon as execution is completed (which usually isn't soon), move on to the next project without evaluating what happened on the present project and what could have been improved. Successful project management requires more front and back end resources (and less middle) than are usually allocated.*
>
> —Anonymous
>
> *What is actual is actual only for one time. And only for one place.*
>
> —T.S. Eliot

The Knowledge Quandary of Project Settings

In any project-based organization, sound knowledge husbandry is central to the delivery of current and future project performance. Knowledge is a strategic asset and a critical source of competitive advantage. In addition, apart from their innate worth, projects have for long also been a favored, flexible instrument for design thinking and systematizing complex processes of creativity and innovation. For these reasons, it might at first glance be a surprise that only for about 10 years has attention been specifically directed at what strengths, weaknesses, opportunities, or

---

[9]Be they (less and less) face-to-face or (more and more) virtual, project teams regularly include people who do not normally work together. In comparison, business as usual are recurring, permanent, or semipermanent activities for mass production of standard operations, typified by layers of management, sharp divisions of labor, and explicit instructions, manuals, and procedures; witness the numbers of support staff working in, say, administration or information systems and technology in most organizations.

threats may relate to knowledge management in project environments[10]—compared to the more substantive work on organizational learning.[11]

> *If you want things to stay as they are, things will have to change.*
>
> —Giuseppe di Lampedusa

But let us look again: as it happens, knowledge management where learning is project-based confronts tough challenges; the causes are multiple and a short list of the chief extenuating circumstances will suffice. To note first and last, projects are transient: novel (but temporal) associations must be forged then fortified. Yet, pressing matters compete for what time, discipline, and skills ought to be made available for that; all the while, the certainty that team members will go their separate ways to take up other work when the project closes militates against earnest intentions to engage in deep knowledge sharing, never mind debriefings.[12] (Because knowledge is embodied in individuals, processes, and practices, short-lived organizational forms will necessarily operate in distinct circumstances and associated relationships in their respective external environments, thereby conditioning how knowledge might be harvested and shared.)

> *I love deadlines. I like the whooshing sound they make as they fly by.*
>
> —Douglas Adams

Next, no two projects are similar, even when they are framed by comparable historical and organizational environments[13]: in the same industry or market, they will differ markedly from one another. So, the discontinuities in flows of personnel, data and information, research, and other inputs that illustrate such variety make it hard to develop steady-state routines, maximize stocks and flows of knowledge, and seed learning across projects. (It may be tricky in the best of instances if, as purists surmise, information is inseparable from the people who create it, react to it, or pass

---

[10]What progress has been achieved is confined to the use of information and communications technology, largely for codification purposes. However, such technologies do not easily translate the situated nature of tacit knowledge and its embeddedness in social groups and situations.

[11]The *Knowledge Solutions* on overcoming roadblocks to learning spell out what obstacles can exist at the organizational level. They also translate at the project level.

[12]On top of this, team members are often assigned to more than one project at any given moment. And so, they do not readily see what personal gains they might derive from coding their experience.

[13]This is not to say that every project is an island; however, there are close bounds to insights generated by cross-section comparisons over simultaneous projects and historical trajectories over successive projects.

it along.) Additionally, in certain if not most settings, such discontinuities are exacerbated by the fragmentation of project teams in isolated professions: since meaning must be shared if knowledge is to be understood, accepted, and exploited, codification and transfer of knowledge within a pluridisciplinary team—where no one member has ready (if any) access to peers—is complicated.

Moreover, reckoning that the project they are working on is the only one of its kind, as it might well be depending on perspective, project teams are prone to assume that the knowledge they hold is also unique, or at least does not warrant being made explicit and validated for the benefit of a distant hierarchy[14]: this leads to "reinvention of the wheel" and the replication of mistakes. What is more, by their very nature, most projects are designed and implemented in a "hothouse" of planning and control: given the odds stacked against whatever is attempted without previous certainty of success, managers and their supervisors strive to deliver projects on budget and on schedule, with corresponding lack of emphasis on knowledge capture and storage and knowledge sharing and learning, let alone reflective practice or learning in teams. [Witness the millstones (*sic*) of associated business processes even though projects, as temporary organizations, clamor for empowerment and support, not the command and control that permanent organizations thrive on.]

> *It is better to laugh about your problems than to cry about them. It's not that I'm so smart, it's just that I stay with problems longer.*
>
> —Albert Einstein

Last but not least, projects are rich in politics[15]: agitators impact learning within and across them subject to individual authority levels, project sponsor actions, organizational environment influences, organizational arrangements between projects, inter-project assimilation practices, and connections with other projects. Despite their huge variety, project management tools that, notwithstanding their intrinsic usefulness, single-mindedly concentrate on initiating, planning, executing, monitoring and controlling, and closing make no impression when knowledge, not just data and information, must be managed. (At any rate, the attention they bring to

---

[14]To identify, create, store, share, and use knowledge, large organizations favor centralized approaches. Indeed, after concentrating it, they are wont to defer learning to certain points in time: first, specialized offices and departments collect and corroborate "lessons learned" for eventual release in prescribed formats; next, when they deem that a similar problem has emerged, they prescribe that a party should promptly avail of the knowledge.

[15]Quintessentially and incorrigibly, organizations are political structures.

bear on efficiency and effectiveness makes the act of capturing and transmitting knowledge a lesser priority during project design and implementation. This state of affairs is compounded by the fact that the potential knowledge requirements of prospective projects do not lie within the purview of the current project's concerns.) As things too often stand, the end of a project is consequently the end of collective learning and project amnesia sets in: domain, process, institutional, and cultural knowledge fades. Partnerships, communication channels, contacts, and other intangible relational and structural assets evaporate too as intellectual capital dwindles.

Knowledge Management in Project Environments—The Poor State of the Art

Surely, project-based organizations ought to reap hefty benefits—over and above the monetary value of the intrinsically creative and innovative nature of their work. Since projects involve the development of products and services, the prospects for fresh ideas to emerge that might be fructified elsewhere and for cross-functional learning to occur ought to be good. From good practices and lessons, one might also expect such organizations to develop or better utilize core capabilities, build sturdier technological platforms, and reduce project development times, among others.[16]

> *Ideas are like rabbits. You get a couple and learn how to handle them, and pretty soon you have a dozen.*
>
> —John Steinbeck

To date, beyond commonplace statements about the necessity to establish efficient knowledge systems to disseminate knowledge and experience across projects, what approaches have been taken to build organizational capacity with project-based learning have followed "cognitive" and "community" (or "personalization") models of knowledge management. The first, and by far the most common, has relied on

---

[16]In the immediate, systematic retention of project experience would curtail project risks from mistakes, mishaps, and potential pitfalls, all with associated costs, no small benefit.

codification[17] through process-[18] and documentation-based[19] methods for extraction, storage, and reuse of knowledge, more often than not relying on electronic repositories. The common feature and limiting factor of such methods is that contributions come about at the tail end of a project, not during it (when the seams of learning are probably richest).[20] If each project is distinctive, what good practices and lessons have been gleaned can only be nonspecific, meaning that they are of the know-how, not know-why variety. That is fine, since strengths and weaknesses can be generic, but it can only inform so much learning before doing.[21] The second approach, courtesy of the present, welcome vogue for communities of practice and other such social networks, has shone a powerful light on the tacit dimension of knowledge and encouraged dialogue between individuals, not between knowledge objects in a database. However, the embeddedness of tacit knowledge within social groups, promoted by storytelling and joint work, means that shared mental models or

---

[17]Codification follows a "people-to-document" approach: knowledge is harvested from the person who holds it, made independent of him or her, and reused for other purposes.

[18]Here, the primary tools are self- and independent evaluations. The original purpose of these lies in performing a status analysis, which in effect reins in what learning might be collected. The *Knowledge Solutions* on learning from evaluation note shortcomings of evaluations for accountability and suggest how evaluations for learning might be retooled. After-action reviews and retrospects are a less frequently used—if more versatile—approach to learn immediately from successes and errors. The *Knowledge Solutions* on after-action reviews and retrospects elucidate their process. Micro articles are another: spanning at most one page of text, they describe a problem with the aid of a story and a solution to locate context-bound knowledge and document it in a learning diary after project implementation. ADB's (2008a–) *Knowledge Showcase* series follows a similar approach by structuring over two sides the problem or challenge faced, the approach taken to address it, and the outcome or result. (Even then, they are not easy to draft: as Blaise Pascal put it, "I would have written a shorter letter, but I did not have the time.").

[19]Learning histories are a recent, valuable approach to documentation-based learning. The *Knowledge Solutions* on learning histories explain how they can be used to surface the thinking, experiments, and arguments of actors.

[20]The overwhelming emphasis that organizations place on (so it is said) learning after, as opposed to before and during a project, deserves commentary. To be sure, singly or in loud unison, the agents listed in the *Knowledge Solutions* on overcoming roadblocks to learning, e.g., the bias for action, undiscussables, commitment to the cause, advocacy at the expense of inquiry, cultural bias, not practicing what is preached, the funding environment, not thinking strategically about learning, not having strong leadership, inability to unlearn, organizational structures, knowledge inaction, false images, lack of penalties for not learning, exclusion, and complexity, conspire to usher in and implement new projects. Learning takes reflection and means behavioral change; yet, organizationally, behavioral change is daunting. Where glaring gaps in goals, incentives, and processes have been identified and must be closed—no easy task in large organizations as that requires supportive leaders, a culture of continuing improvements, a defined learning structure, and intuitive knowledge processes—it is assuredly easier to assume risks away, rush headlong, and stay the course at (well, nearly) all cost. Hence, the paucity of tools, methods, and approaches for learning before and during, and their infrequent use, since there is little demand.

[21]Peer assists are a rare form of learning before doing. The *Knowledge Solutions* on conducting peer assists publicize their process.

systems of meaning, buttressed by trust and norms, must exist to enable others outside these to understand and accept that knowledge. Both approaches, which call for different sets of incentives, are complementary and necessary but neither has sufficiently lent a hand. In project settings, what good practices and lessons have been extracted and stored in databases are not widely used because they are poorly represented[22] and archived. Conversely, where team members made time to help others cope with similar problems, crystallized their insights, and made them easy to find they are not accepted by reason of the "Not Invented Here," "Proudly Found Elsewhere," or "Invented Here, But Let's Reinvent It Anyway" syndromes. What is more, *pace* the interorganizational contractual obligations that characterize many projects, the temporal, disciplinary, cultural, and spatial differentiation of project teams ineluctably frustrates the efforts of members to understand and apply the insights of other social groups to their own context of practice and gives them no breathing space in which to build their own networks of actors because they are so task focused.[23]

> *Nothing is too small. I counsel you, put down in record even your doubts and surmises. Hereafter it may be of interest to you to see how true you guess. We learn from failure, not from success!*
>
> —Bram Stoker

> *I'm lazy. But it's the lazy people who invented the wheel and the bicycle because they didn't like walking or carrying things.*
>
> —Lech Walesa

Is there a strong, inherent contradiction between organizing in the short term for a long-lasting outcome or result and doing so for long-term, organizational performance improvement? How might a project-based organization be simultaneously oriented to both practical benefits and organizational learning?

---

[22]Here and there, the design of electronic repositories of good practices or lessons is singularly deficient. With applicability during and after a project, a checklist allied to guiding questions might help individuals decide whether they are passing on a noteworthy lesson or not by shining a light on validity and the potential scope of application. Regular contributions might be framed in a project scenario highlighting an originating action, its outcome or result, the good practice or lesson, its applicability, conditions for reuse, and suggestions. Metadata would enable users to find the "right" lessons depending on need. Users would on their part be requested to answer questions, generated by the system, to add relevant context information.

[23]This said, there is no reason why a higher degree of formality than is usually warranted for a community of practice might not connect peers working in dispersed projects with one another. The key, we shall see, is to widen the compass of team activities from peripheral project roles to more central role positions within practice groups.

Managing Knowledge in Project Settings

Projects need to be reconceptualized as knowledge carriers, not end products, bridging to both contemporaneous and yet-to-come projects. How might this be achieved? To learning organizations, these *Knowledge Solutions* recommend three realistic and mutually reinforcing options relating to (i) project typologies, (ii) organizational design, and (iii) strategic planning and operations. Others surely exist and project-based organizations could do worse than research what they might be.

First, if project environments are to be opened up for learning, it is essential to recognize that projects are not all one and the same. Realizing this will help project-based organizations maximize opportunities for knowledge management both within and across projects by applying techniques appropriate to the nature of the projects in question. Conveniently, Turner and Cochrane (1993) have shown that projects fall into four discrete types, which means project managers should use appropriate start-up and implementation methodologies.[24] The following summarizes the spectrum of their goals-and-methods matrix, highlighting the project management approach best suited to the conditions the four types exhibit. Leveraging the knowledge management architecture the author elucidated in *Learning in Development* (2010), it quickly weaves in preferential, exemplar knowledge management approaches[25]:

- **Well-Defined Goal and Methods** Initiatives with well-defined goals and methods are typified by engineering and construction projects. Drawing from rich historical experience and known techniques, team members move swiftly into specialized activity-based planning of what must be done in the milieu of a stable project configuration. In this type of project environment, operative aids to knowledge management include regular, effective meetings and presentations during which team leaders—acting as conductors—lead skilled implementers in well-defined activities set against milestones, communicate experiences and learning, and hold problem-sharing sessions or project clinics. Briefings can also be organized to support knowledge sharing in a structured project environment

---

[24]To note, projects are originally of a particular type but they can in practice morph into another. Naturally, effective tools, methods, and approaches for knowledge management will need to change synchronously.

[25]The *Knowledge Solutions* series aims to build competencies in the areas of strategy development, management techniques, collaboration mechanisms, knowledge sharing and learning, and knowledge capture and storage. In conjunction with the 2 × 2 matrix, but also from a wider perspective, readers are invited to search its articles for (other) tools, methods, and approaches relevant to the four project typologies presented. In no particular order, they would pertain among others to leadership, human resources, project management, routine procedures, organizational practices, knowledge ecologies, internal and external relationships, knowledge partnerships, trust, and information and communications technology (ADB 2008b–).

permitting sequenced communication, connection, collaboration, and capital-ization. (Project management approach: task and activity scheduling. Knowledge management approach: leadership, technology.)

- **Well-Defined Goal, Poorly Defined Methods** Initiatives with well-defined goals but poorly defined methods comprise product development projects. In these instances, while the functionality of the required product is known, how that is to be achieved is not sufficiently clear. In this type of project environ-ment, advisable aids to knowledge management include collaboration mecha-nisms to identify peers who may have encountered and dealt with similar problems in the past; an accent would be placed on the definition of techniques. Ways to brainstorm and stimulate creativity and innovation would also be sought. Technology would play an important role in connecting peers and team members, for example, with wikis, to advance joint work. (Project management approach: milestones for components of product. Knowledge management approach: leadership, learning, technology.)

- **Poorly Defined Goal, Well-Defined Methods** Initiatives with poorly defined goals and well-defined methods include systems development projects. In such cases, in the search for sharper definition of the goal, milestones representing completion of life cycle stages come to the fore but should not blind team members to the complicated and complex and to the need for emergent strate-gies, with willingness to embrace failure on the way. In this type of project environment, useful aids to knowledge management center on people issues and the sponsoring of informed dialogue. Coaching and mentoring, knowledge facilitators, and internet forums would all score highly as team members agree on the goal in close working relationships. (Project management approach: milestones for life cycle stages. Knowledge management approach: learning, organization, technology.)

- **Poorly Defined Goal and Methods** Initiatives with poorly defined goals and methods encompass research and organizational change projects. Here, a chaotic context owes to unclear directional sources. From the onset, team members must define the mission, engage in scenario planning, navigate and practice the strategy, refine the objective, and assiduously cater to team-building and engagement. There is no stable project configuration: inspiration, negotiation, and communication are paramount in a conflict-prone state of affairs. In this type of project environment, valuable aids to knowledge management include (i) harnessing top talent, (ii) being flexible about the procurement of new skill types, (iii) stimulating creative thinking, (iv) identifying peers in and outside the organization, (v) tapping internal knowledge markets, and (vi) managing change. (Project management approach: mission definition, refinement of objective, team building. Knowledge management approach: leadership, learn-ing, organization, technology.)

Method is much, technique is much, but inspiration is even more.

—Benjamin Cardozo

Often people attempt to live their lives backwards: they try to have more things, or more money, in order to do more of what they want so that they will be happier. The way it actually works is the reverse. You must first be who you really are, then, do what you need to do, in order to have what you want.

—Margaret Young

The true method of knowledge is experiment.

—William Blake

Second, and for traditional, project-based organizations, the bad news: the command-and-control hierarchies that configure them may speed the preparation of relatively simple deliverables within pressured deadlines but run counter to the exploitation and exploration of knowledge for learning and organizational performance. Hierarchies cannot straightforwardly, to maximize their organization's knowledge-related effectiveness, conduct any of the following: (i) monitor and facilitate knowledge-related activities; (ii) establish and update knowledge infrastructure; (iii) create, renew, build, and organize knowledge assets; or (iv) distribute and apply knowledge assets effectively. This should matter a lot to project-based organizations. Auspiciously, the resolution is close at hand and they need not despair: if their strength lies in projects, surely, might an organizational configuration parallel to, but integrated with, that of offices and departments not be advantageous?

The rise of communities of practice bodes well but is per se insufficient: the learning infrastructure of knowledge-intensive organizations, that project teams would tap and enrich in chorus, must be enlarged. To help manage knowledge in project settings, Verteramo and Carolis (2009) have made a vital distinction between customary (sector and thematic) communities of practice[26] and (technical) practice groups—the former being in the main dedicated to learning, with

---

[26]There are many different kinds of communities of practice. They may (i) organize and manage information that is worth paying attention to, i.e., filter; (ii) take new, little-known, or little-understood ideas, giving them weight, and making them more widely understood, i.e., amplify; (iii) offer a means to give members the resources they need to carry out their main activities, i.e., invest and provide; (iv) bring together different, distinct people or groups of people, i.e., convene; (v) promote and sustain the values and standards of individuals or organizations, i.e., build community; and/or (vi) help members carry out their activities more efficiently and effectively, i.e., learn and facilitate.

contributions from a swath of disciplines; the latter translating as a project-based organizational structure for experts engaged in subject-specific domains transversal to projects, such as project management, business development, etc. Practice groups, the origin of which lies especially in the legal profession, would represent bodies in which discrete and objective facts as well as practical information can be found; learning loci in which professional competencies can be improved; and social networks in which both exploitation and exploration of knowledge take place. More structured, stable, and formalized than communities of practice, practice groups can be an effective organizational solution for managing knowledge in project-based organizations. Projects nourish practices and are nourished in turn: through projects, personnel acquire or develop competencies and improve practices of interest; through practices, ideas, and innovations that generate other projects are sparked and recognized.

> *Most Japanese companies don't even have a reasonable organization chart. Nobody knows how Honda is organized, except that it uses lots of project teams and is quite flexible.*
>
> —Kenichi Ohmae

Third, to activate the transformation of projects as knowledge carriers to the future, the priority of knowledge management should be reflected in strategy and its operationalization, with inputs at all stages from communities of practice, practice groups, and, of course, offices and departments. In brief, strategic plans should systematically identify the particular instruments needed to enhance the organization's knowledge management capacities at the requisite level, be it the global, regional, national, provincial, commune, or local level, or else the industry, sector, or market level. In terms of operating outputs, the project cycle would need to be retooled to integrate knowledge management throughout project design, implementation, and evaluation, evidently in light of the four discrete types discussed earlier. In both instances—strategic and operational, protocols for identification, creation, storage, sharing, and—yes—actual use of knowledge should be set.

References

ADB (2008–a) Knowledge showcases. Manila
ADB (2008–b) Knowledge solutions. Manila
ADB (2010) Learning in development. Manila
Peters T (1999) The WOW project: in the new economy, all work is project work. Fast Company 24:138–144

Turner R, Cochrane R (1993) Goals-and-methods matrix: coping with projects with ill-defined goals and/or methods of achieving them. International Journal of Project Management 11(2):93–102

Verteramo S, De Carolis M (2009) Balancing learning and efficiency crossing practices and projects in project-based organizations: organizational issues. The case history of "practice groups" in a consulting firm. Electronic Journal of Knowledge Management 7(1):179–190

Proposition 58
Knowledge as Culture

In a Word Culture must not be seen as something that merely reflects an organization's social reality: rather, it is an integral part of the process by which that reality is constructed. Knowledge management initiatives, per se, are not culture change projects; but, if culture stands in the way of what an organization needs to do, they must somehow impact.

Why Culture Defines Knowledge

Broadly speaking, approaches to knowledge management have followed "cognitive" and "community" (or "personalization") models. The former, by far the most common, has relied on codification through process- and documentation-based methods for extraction, storage, and reuse of knowledge, more often than not relying on electronic repositories. The latter, courtesy of the present, welcome vogue for communities of practice and other such social networks, has shone a powerful light on the tacit dimension of knowledge and encouraged dialogue between individuals, the active agents of sense making, not between knowledge objects in a database.

© Asian Development Bank 2017
O. Serrat, *Knowledge Solutions*, DOI 10.1007/978-981-10-0983-9_58

Redolent as they are of the chicken-and-egg dilemma,[1] both approaches, which face different opportunities and constraints and call for distinct systems of incentives, are complementary and necessary but neither has sufficiently helped. Depending on industry, sector, or market, among other determinants, some organizational cultures may be inclined to the community approach; others may be more receptive to the cognitive approach (if the cap doesn't fit, don't wear it). More importantly, irrespective of the approach taken, isolated knowledge management initiatives will not last: like it or not, only embedded, organization-wide activities to identify, create, store, share, and use knowledge can give knowledge management the opening it needs to pay back handsomely.

> *If you see in any given situation only what everybody else can see, you can be said to be so much a representative of your culture that you are a victim of it.*
>
> —Samuel Hayakawa

Organizational culture either bedevils or blesses knowledge management. Sad to say, although it is widely cited as a challenge in knowledge management initiatives, investigations seldom consider its implications for knowledge generation and sharing; fewer still examine how it influences approaches to knowledge management. Culture theory and notions of organizational configuration (Mintzberg 1989) are essential diagnostic lenses through which to contextualize and formulate enterprise. The first aggregates the distinctive ideas, beliefs, values, and knowledge of social beings to make possible a focus on the whole and the parts, on contexts and contents, on values and value systems, and on strategic relationships between key variables. The second draws attention to the main internal and external influencers of an organization to elucidate the basic pulls on it, hence, the strengths and weaknesses of characteristic typologies.

On Organizational Culture

"Organizational culture" is a term whose currency these days rivals that of "organizational learning". Its study is a major constituent of organizational development—that is, the process through which an organization develops the internal

---

[1] Knowledge is no ordinary commodity: it is highly context dependent. If it exists principally in a milieu, when it comes to a sociology of knowledge—"knowledges" might be the better word, the knowledge in question is thus both and concurrently the cause and the effect. It is little wonder, then, that proponents of the two approaches are typically unable to juggle causality in relationships. And yet, they must.

capacity to be the most effective it can be in its work and to sustain itself over the long term. Organizational culture may have been forged by the founder; it may emerge over time as the organization faces challenges and obstacles; or it may be created deliberately by Management. One thing is sure: in the twenty-first century, a vital source of competitive advantage in successful organizations is their culture, a distinctly human product. So, what is it?

> *If we are to achieve a richer culture, rich in contrasting values, we must recognize the whole gamut of human potentialities, and so weave a less arbitrary social fabric, one in which each diverse human gift will find a fitting place.*
>
> —Margaret Mead

Organizational culture comprises the assumptions, values and beliefs, behaviors, artifacts, and measurements and actions of an organization, shaped by social learning, that control the way individuals and groups in the organization interact with one another and with parties outside it. Prosaically, personnel usually explain organizational culture as the way things are done in an organization—what goes and what does not. Even shorter writ might read "know how".[2] (To state the obvious, organizations have subcultures,[3] which much as the overarching philosophy may not be well articulated and communicated.)

A standard typology refers to communal, networked, mercenary, and fragmented cultures.[4] Nevertheless, the indispensable notion to grasp is that organizational

---

[2]Logically, "know why" would equate with purpose; "know what, when, and where" would be defined by strategy. The "know who" linking strategy to purpose, aka execution, would represent the sum of policies, organization, procedures, controls, support systems, incentives, and related measurements and actions, themselves of course influenced by organizational culture.

[3]An organization is a social arrangement to pursue a collective intent. Yet, the well-known metaphor of organizational silos suggests that organizational units—and their management teams—often lack the desire or motivation to coordinate (at worst, even communicate) with other entities in the same organization. This evidences the existence of cultures whereby the incentive is to maximize the performance of the silo, not that of the organization; promoting effective cross-functional teams demands that an enabling environment be built for that.

[4]Numerous other typologies exist. One distinguishes coercive, utilitarian, and normative organizations. (To this, others add another dimension, namely, the professional or collegial organization.) Another focuses on how power and control are delegated, with organizations labeled as autocratic, paternalistic, consultative (else democratic), participative (else power sharing), delegative, or abdicative. A third classifies organizations according to their internal flexibility (viz., clans or hierarchies) and external outlook (viz., adhocracies or markets). The four cultures that Handy (1978) popularized are power cultures (which concentrate power among a few), role cultures (which delegate authority within highly defined structures), task cultures (which form teams to solve particular problems), and people cultures (which allow individuals to think themselves superior to their organization).

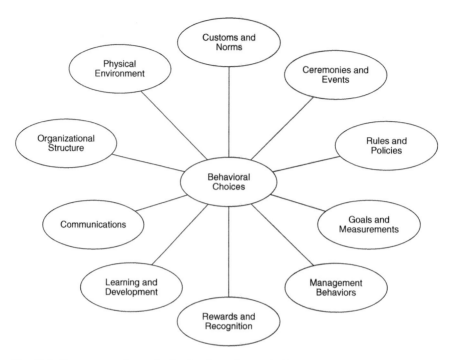

Fig. 58.1 Components of organizational culture. *Source* Author

culture is determined by sundry factors that find expression in organizational structure, making structure itself a chief culture-bearing mechanism.[5]

Figure 58.1 delineates 10 components that, together, influence organizational culture. Importantly, identifying discernible elements of culture allows organizations to determine features that can be managed to help implement and sustain constructive organizational change. But just as none of the 10 components in the figure shapes organizational culture on its own, none can individually support desired improvements. The art is to synergize organization, people, knowledge, and technology (ADB 2009a).

---

[5]Henry Mintzberg saw seven basic configurations: (i) entrepreneurial, (ii) machine, (iii) diversified, (iv) professional, (v) innovative, (vi) missionary, and (vii) political. The truth is that one can find all these forms in any organization. Notwithstanding, approaches to knowledge management had better consider the organization in which they are to be practiced. What configuration does it have and what does that mean? What might one do to enhance the strengths and minimize the weaknesses of the structure?

Organizational culture varies more than any other corporate asset, including large and tangible information and communications technology infrastructure. It is said to be strong when employees respond to stimuli because of their alignment with it. Conversely, it is said to be weak where there is little alignment, and control is exercised with administrative orders.

Regardless, if an organization is to succeed and thrive, a knowledge culture must develop to help it deal with its external environment. But organizational culture is hard to change in the best circumstances. Employees need time to get used to new ways of organizing. Defensive routines pollute the system, more often than not unwittingly—but on occasion quite deliberately, and undermine it. The dynamics of culture change must be considered an evolutionary process at individual, group, organizational, and interorganizational levels, to be facilitated by psychologically attentive leaders who do not underestimate the value of selection, socialization, and leadership. People cannot share knowledge if they do not speak a common language. So there is a serious, oft-ignored need to root learning in human resource policies and strategies.

> *Organizational cultures are created by leaders, and one of the most decisive functions of leadership may well be the creation, the management, and—if and when that may become necessary—the destruction of culture.*
>
> —Edgar Schein

Observers recognize a correlation between the orientation of organizational culture and organizational learning. Indeed, the inability to change behavioral choices is repeatedly cited as the biggest hindrance to knowledge management. For this reason, even if the need to take a hard look at an organization's culture extends the time required to prepare knowledge management initiatives, the benefits from doing so are likely to tell.

Organizations that are more successful in implementing knowledge management initiatives embody both operations- and people-oriented attributes. Typically, a learning culture is an organizational environment that values, enables, rewards, and uses the learning of its members, both individually and collectively. Learning charters may advance it. But many cultural factors inhibit knowledge transfer. The above table lists the most common sources of frictions and suggests ways to overcome them. Most importantly, when generating and sharing knowledge, the method must always suit the culture as that affects how people think, feel, and act.

Table. Highlights of ADB's action plan for knowledge management, 2009–2011

Pillar	Actions/outputs
Sharpen the knowledge focus in ADB's operations	• ADB conducted studies to promote understanding of knowledge management, including (i) *A Survey of Demand for ADB Knowledge Products through Resident and Regional Missions;*[a] (ii) *A Study of ADB's Knowledge Taxonomy;*[b] and (iii) *A Study of Information on Knowledge Management and Communication in CPSs, RRPs, and TA Reports* • The TA Strategic Forum was established in 2008 to set research and knowledge priorities in line with *Strategy 2020* • New peer review procedures were incorporated into ADB's business processes for country partnership strategies and lending and nonlending products. A database of peer reviewers was set up • ADB strengthened the terms of reference of the knowledge management coordinators[d] • Efforts to transform sector- and theme-related information into knowledge were boosted • ADB's drive to broaden understanding of tools, methods, and approaches for knowledge management and learning continued through the (oft-cited) *Knowledge Solutions* and *Knowledge Showcase* series.[e, f] Flash animations of a dozen *Knowledge Solutions* were produced under a new *Handle with Knowledge* series. *Handle with Knowledge* planners showcasing 54 *Knowledge Solutions* each were printed for the years 2011 and 2012. *Knowledge Primers* —briefings on knowledge management and learning applications—were attractively packaged for interactive presentation and self-learning for action • ADB published the *ADB Sustainable Development Timeline*, which catalogs major sector and thematic landmarks in ADB's journey to promote sustainable development.[g] This subsequently led to the construction of an interactive multimedia platform showcasing ADB's accomplishments • Marketing and distribution of knowledge products were expanded via Twitter, Facebook, Scribd, and Google Books • *knowledge@ADB*, a monthly email service, and *Intersections*, a quarterly e-newsletter promoting innovative sector, thematic, and other practices in ADB's operations, were introduced. (Beginning 2012, *Ahead of the Curve* think pieces have been extracted from the *Intersections*.)
Empower the communities of practice	• ADB formulated revised guidelines for sector and thematic reporting[k] • Eight new staff positions were allocated and the budget of the communities of practice increased tenfold in 2010 with additional expense categories • CoPs were mainstreamed into operations via (i) legitimization of their role in the peer review process for country partnership strategies and lending and

(continued)

(continued)

Pillar	Actions/outputs
	nonlending operations, (ii) representation in the in-house panel for recruiting ADB international staff, and (iii) participation in midterm and annual budget review and planning exercises • Participation in CoPs was incorporated in the 2011 performance review process for ADB staff • CoPs conducted self-assessments and customized training programs to bridge knowledge and skills gap • Collaboration mechanisms for cross-departmental and multidisciplinary knowledge sharing were set up, including *i.prompt.u*—a database-driven platform harvesting for wider impact the news, events, and knowledge products that individual CoPs promote—and webpages for CoPs on my ADB, ADB's intranet platform • Performance surveys of ADB-hosted CoPs were conducted[l, m] • A year-end event for networking and knowledge sharing among CoPs was introduced in 2009 and has been held annually thereafter • A select set of resources in the areas of strategy development, management techniques, collaboration mechanisms, knowledge sharing and learning, and knowledge capture and storage was made available to help CoPs create value through knowledge networks[n]
Strengthen external knowledge partnerships	• *Guidelines for Knowledge Partnerships* were formulated and published[o] • A database on strategic partnerships and related agreements was created • Knowledge management perspectives informed midterm reviews of ADB's memorandums of understanding with the United Nations Economic and Social Commission for Asia and the Pacific and Agence Française de Development • Development of a system to facilitate ADB-wide and decentralized management and monitoring of strategic partnerships was initiated • Dissemination and visibility of ADB's knowledge products were expanded through ADB's depository library program and multi-donor public information center network
Further enhance staff learning and skills development	• Six hour-long modules for a new *Learning for Change Primers* series were developed and conducted on the subjects of (i) *Building a Learning Organization*, (ii) *Communities of Practice: Passing the Fitness Test*, (iii) *Designing Knowledge Partnerships Better*, (iv) *Leveraging Knowledge with ICT*, (v) *Managing Knowledge at Work*, and (vi) *Understanding Knowledge Management and Learning Essentials* • Three training programs under a new *Knowledge Management and Learning* series were developed and conducted on the subjects of (i) *Reflective Practice*,

(continued)

(continued)

Pillar	Actions/outputs
	(ii) *Learning in Teams*, and (iii) *Learning from Evaluation*. A fourth module on the subject of *Learning in Partnerships* was developed
	• Two batches of a Narrative Practitioners training program were conducted
	• The budget for external training was expanded
	• Efforts to capture, store, and share the tacit knowledge of past and present staff gave birth to a publication, *ADB: Reflections and Beyond*, and an audio composition, *Beyond: Stories and Sounds from ADB's Region*[p, q]

CoP Community of practice; *CPS* Country partnership strategy; *RRP* Report and recommendation of the President; TA = technical assistance
[a]ADB (2010a)
[b]ADB (2011a)
[c]ADB (2011b)
[d]The terms of reference are reproduced in ADB (2010b)
[e]ADB (2008a–)
[f]ADB (2008b–)
[g]ADB (2011c)
[h]The *Knowledge Solutions* on improving sector and thematic reporting reproduce the guidelines
[i]ADB (2009b)
[j]ADB (2011d)
[k]ADB (2011e)
[l]ADB (2011f)
[m]ADB (2010c)
[n]ADB (2010d)
Source Author

Going over the main points, knowledge management initiatives stand a greater chance of success if they spring from, advance, or at least understand the primordiality of

- flat, decentralized organizational structures that leverage distributed leadership;
- measures of organizational performance;
- information and communications technology that provides quick, unrestricted feedback on the performance of the organization and its components;
- systems of incentives that sponsor organizational learning;
- mechanisms for surfacing and appraising implicit organizational theories of action and for cultivating systematic programs of experimental inquiry; and
- ideologies associated with mindfulness, such as openness, adaptability, flexibility, avoidance of stability traps, boundary crossing, inquiry orientation, propensity to experiment, readiness to rethink means and ends, continuous learning, excellence, total quality, realization of human potential, and creation of organizational settings as contexts for human development.

> *An immense and ever-increasing wealth of knowledge is scattered about the world today; knowledge that would probably suffice to solve all the mighty difficulties of our age, but it is dispersed and unorganized. We need a sort of mental clearinghouse for the mind: a depot where knowledge and ideas are received, sorted, summarized, digested, clarified, and compared.*
>
> —H.G. Wells

The following summarizes what actions ADB took in 2009–2011 to advance its knowledge management agenda. Their rationale owed no small debt to appreciative inquiry of ADB's organizational configuration and culture. Their negotiated definition[6] was helped by insights from psychology, sound understanding of ADB's business processes, and earlier investigations in *Learning for Change in ADB* of 10 challenges that ADB must overcome to develop as a learning organization. To note, both explicitly and implicitly, activities were often driven by the imperative of organizational learning for change. Mixing "cognitive" and "community" tools, methods, and approaches, awareness raising, communities of practice, learning and development, perceptions surveys,[7] reporting, and storytelling were relied upon individually and collectively to foster a stronger and more evident culture of knowledge and knowledge reputation at ADB.[8] For sure, culture must not be seen as something that merely reflects an organization's social reality: rather, it is an integral part of the process by which that reality is constructed. Integrated knowledge enterprise for identification, creation, storage, sharing, and use of knowledge would establish knowledge products and services as a central activity and key basis for ADB's development effectiveness.[9]

---

[6]Key change agents (and thereafter sources of verification) included ADB's Budget, Personnel, and Management Systems Department; Department of External Relations; Regional and Sustainable Development Department, in which the Knowledge Management Center was located; and Strategy and Policy Department.

[7]The point of a survey is to retrieve information about something in order to improve it. Perceptions surveys are important because they express the beliefs of respondents. Surveys were conducted for baselining but also to establish comparability across offices and departments for aggregated ownership through full discloser of findings.

[8]Knowledge management initiatives, per se, are not culture change projects; but if culture stands in the way of what an organization needs to do, they must somehow impact. They can do so by helping reshape assumptions, mediating the relationships between individual and organizational knowledge, fashioning an environment for interactions that enhance the value drawn from knowledge, and refreshing an organization's outlook vis-à-vis new knowledge.

[9]Development effectiveness is about ensuring maximum impact. ADB's corporate results framework has four levels: (i) Asia and the Pacific development outcomes—indicators track the development progress of the region through selected regional outcomes to which ADB contributes, (ii) core outputs and outcomes—indicators assess ADB's contribution to country and regional outcomes by aggregating key outputs delivered to developing member countries through ADB programs and projects, (iii) operational effectiveness—indicators aim to improve the performance of ADB's operational portfolio to increase its contribution to country outcomes and overall development effectiveness, and (iv) organizational effectiveness—indicators aim to capture

Enhancing Knowledge Management Under Strategy 2020: Taking Action in ADB

Five years ago, ADB set a new strategic course to help developing member countries in Asia and the Pacific improve their living conditions and quality of life. It crafted a long-term strategic framework, 2008–2020, referred to as *Strategy 2020* (2008), to serve as ADB's corporate-wide planning document and give ADB a more relevant and innovative role in shaping the region's future. *Strategy 2020* focuses ADB's support on three distinct but complementary development agendas: inclusive economic growth, environmentally sustainable growth, and regional integration.[10] Holding that knowledge is a powerful catalyst for propelling development forward and enhancing its effects, *Strategy 2020* also underlines knowledge solutions as a driver of change, among others.[11]

> *Successful knowledge transfer involves neither computers nor documents but rather interactions between people.*
>
> —Thomas Davenport

- **ADB's Knowledge Strategy and Approach** The generation and sharing of knowledge have always been an essential, catalyzing element of ADB's mandate. Through its long-term strategic framework, 2001–2015, ADB (2001) committed to become a learning institution and a primary source of development knowledge in Asia and the Pacific. *Knowledge Management in ADB* (2004) signaled ADB's intent to become a learning organization. The framework pursues two mutually supportive outcomes: (i) increased assimilation of and dissemination by ADB of relevant, high-quality knowledge to developing member countries and other stakeholders; and (ii) enhanced learning within ADB. In the context of the

---

(Footnote 9 continued)

progress in increasing efficiency in the use of internal resources and implementing reforms necessary to maintain ADB's ability to remain a relevant and results-oriented institution.

[10]It goes without saying that an organization's physical layout can conduce, or conversely discourage, a culture of knowledge. In support of *Strategy 2020*, ADB's Library decided in 2008 to develop a collaborative space for "knowledge accidents". Now branded as the knowledge hub, or kHub, it is a center where ideas are shared and built upon. *Insight Thursday*, a weekly, 30-min seminar open to all ADB staff, has taken place there since 2010. The events bring together different groups of people and promote understanding of, organize, and manage information that is worth paying attention to—from global or regional debates to institutional challenges and more (ADB 2012a).

[11]ADB's proclivity to contribute and apply development knowledge owes to its role in identifying contexts and trends within and across Asia and the Pacific, interdisciplinary and integrated assistance approach, and capacity to implement insight and knowledge via large, attractive financing.

knowledge management framework of 2004, ADB also established a Knowledge Management Center to coordinate and monitor all knowledge initiatives as well as the action plans that constitute it.

> *The store of wisdom does not consist of hard coins which keep their shape as they pass from hand to hand; it consists of ideas and doctrines whose meanings change with the minds that entertain them.*
>
> —John Plamenatz

In 2008, *Strategy 2020* reinforced ADB's commitment to catalyze knowledge for development when it urged the organization to play a bigger role in putting the potential of knowledge solutions to work in the region. That year, given disappointing progress under *Knowledge Management in ADB*, a rapid review of the knowledge management framework generated a wish list of work packages for change. The need to achieve visible gains inspired the Knowledge Management Center to formulate *Enhancing Knowledge Management under Strategy 2020, Plan of Action, 2009– 2011* (2009c), a comprehensive set of actions/outputs—arranged in four clusters— designed to ensure that ADB's knowledge continues to expand, is practical and usable, and remains of the highest quality.[12] The four pillars were closely related for corporate agility: the set of actions/outputs that made up the first focused on adding value to ADB's operations in its developing member countries; the other three sets dealt with how that might be achieved. The unspoken intentions were stirring a desire for knowledge (knowledge pull) and bringing it to bear (knowledge push).

Sharpening the Knowledge Focus in ADB's Operations

ADB's unique abilities to generate, disseminate, and apply knowledge are based on three areas of comparative advantage: ADB's central position in identifying trends within and across the region; its capacity for interdisciplinary and integrated

---

[12]The Knowledge Management Center was tasked with monitoring and reporting on implementation and played the lead role in delivering the actions/outputs. To this intent, it aligned its structure, recruited personnel, and designed work programs in direct relation to the four pillars of the action plan. In synergistic support of these, it also set itself annual deliverables for clarifying knowledge management and learning strategies and promoting knowledge management and learning—they included producing the *Knowledge Solutions* series, which aims to broaden ADB staff's understanding of and support fort knowledge management and learning; managing the *Knowledge Showcase* series, which highlights ground-level innovative ideas; revamping the knowledge management and learning webpages at adb.org; designing and disseminating sundry awareness-raising collaterals; turning out training and instructive materials; extending advice on knowledge sharing and harvesting to offices and departments; and reaching out to external partners who can serve as knowledge resources for ADB.

approaches; and its ability to then blend knowledge and insight with large, concessional financing. Knowledge enriches financing operations and, combined with
ADB's convening power, spurs development effectiveness. Effective knowledge
management can—in fact, must—help identify and put potential knowledge services and knowledge solutions to work through regional and country partnership
strategies, investment programs and projects, and technical assistance and policy
dialogue. Actions/outputs were proposed to sharpen the knowledge focus in ADB's
operations at the regional, country, and project levels.

Empowering the Communities of Practice

Communities of practice are a potential instrument through which knowledge
management is implemented in ADB, ultimately to the benefit of its clients. The
communities of practice keep know-how of a domain alive by sharing what they
know, building on that, and adapting knowledge to specific sector and project
applications. ADB introduced the concept of communities of practice in 2001,
when it planned a reorganization, and refined it in 2005. Actions/outputs were
proposed to ensure that communities of practice become an integral part of ADB's
business processes; increase the budget of the communities of practice, based on a
clear set of objectives, and, most importantly, measurable "outcomes" of improved
knowledge management; require the communities of practice to more purposefully
engage in external partnerships; and review the role of the knowledge management
coordinators in ADB.

Strengthening External Knowledge Partnerships

Knowledge networks facilitate information exchange toward practice-related goals.
ADB will need to further augment internal knowledge sharing through communities
of practice by strengthening its knowledge networking and partnerships with
external institutions within and outside Asia and the Pacific. Through such external
knowledge networking, ADB can share insights from its development financing
practices with external partners and benefit from knowledge generated by others.
Significantly, external knowledge networking enables ADB to serve one of its core
roles as a multilateral development bank—to promote learning and innovation for
the benefit of developing member countries. Actions/outputs were proposed to
develop criteria for the selection of external knowledge networks including non-
regional institutions, ensure that expected outputs and outcomes are strategically
aligned to the priorities of ADB and its developing member countries, make sure
that agreements with knowledge networks spell out the need to conduct proactive
dissemination activities in ADB and its developing member countries, and consider
knowledge partnerships when ADB enters into agreements with other institutions.

Further Enhancing Staff Learning and Skills Development

The ability of ADB and all staff to learn is a precondition to the success of *Strategy 2020*. Engaging all staff in knowledge management is crucial to generating and sharing knowledge. Yet mainstreaming knowledge management takes time and resources. Actions/outputs were proposed to design and implement a focused (and needs-based) knowledge management and learning program for all staff; introduce the concept of a "sabbatical" in the current "Special Leave without Pay" arrangement, according to merit and focused on results to encourage staff to compete for external learning and knowledge-sharing opportunities; invite a number of senior and junior researchers to ADB for short-term assignments in forward-looking studies; increase the budget for external training for administration by Vice-Presidents; and capture the knowledge and experience of departing staff, especially retiring members, through exit debriefings and participation in the staff induction program.

> *I love talking about nothing. It's the only thing I know anything about.*
>
> —Oscar Wilde

- **Some Knowledge Management Initiatives** To articulate and pace the initiatives of the *Action Plan for Knowledge Management, 2009–2011* as well as the Knowledge Management Center's annual deliverables for clarifying knowledge management and learning strategies and promoting knowledge management and learning, the Knowledge Management Center drew the model of a knowledge-centric organization (ADB 2011g). Coincidentally, it reflected the five levels of knowledge management maturity specified by the Most Admired Knowledge Enterprises (MAKE) Knowledge Management Implementation Model in the context of which ADB has conducted annual MAKE surveys since 2005 (ADB 2005–).[13] Details of more prominent knowledge management initiatives at ADB since 2009—in terms of both results and impacts—follow with an accent on those taken to promote a culture of knowledge transfer. Their intent was to help

---

[13]The findings of MAKE surveys are benchmarked against eight knowledge performance dimensions that measure ADB's ability to (i) create and sustain an enterprise knowledge-driven culture; (ii) develop knowledge workers through senior management leadership; (iii) develop and deliver knowledge-based projects and/or services; (iv) manage and maximize the value of an enterprise's intellectual capital; (v) create and sustain an enterprise-wide collaborative knowledge-sharing environment; (vi) create and sustain a learning organization; (vii) manage client knowledge to create value and enterprise intellectual capital; and (viii) transform knowledge to reduce poverty and improve clients' standard of living. Organizations implementing knowledge strategies generally go through five stages, according to the MAKE Knowledge Management Implementation Model: (i) pre-implementation (up to 1 year), (ii) implementation (1–3 years), (iii) reinvigoration (4–6 years), (iv) inculcation (7–9 years), and (v) holistic (10+ years). The process can take anywhere from 12–15 years for nonprofit, public sector organizations (such as ADB).

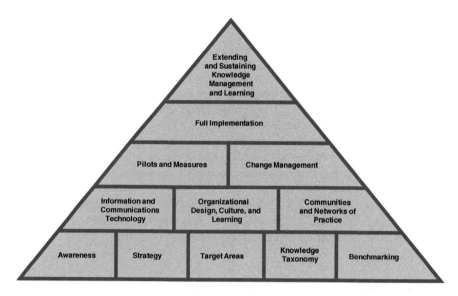

Fig. 58.2 Building a knowledge-centric organization. *Source* Author

reshape assumptions, mediate the relationships between individual and organizational knowledge, fashion an environment for interactions that enhance the value drawn from knowledge, and refresh ADB's outlook vis-à-vis new knowledge (Fig. 58.2).

> *I have always thought that one man of tolerable abilities may work great changes, and accomplish great affairs among mankind, if he first forms a good plan, and, cutting off all amusements or other employments that would divert his attention, make the execution of that same plan his sole study and business.*
>
> —Benjamin Franklin

Delivering a Knowledge Management Action Plan

The *Action Plan for Knowledge Management, 2009–2011* included a knowledge management results framework: it specified expected outcomes, useful results indicators, specific activity indicators, targets, and sources of verification with which to assess and improve performance and help identify problems and their solutions; it also formed the basis for reporting. The framework helped to promote a stronger culture of results and performance for knowledge management in ADB. At quarterly intervals beginning July 2009, ADB (2011h) tracked with ratings the progress of the 37 action points specified in the framework. The plan was successfully completed in July 2011.

> *I have never yet seen any plan which has not been mended by the observations of those who were much inferior in understanding to the person who took the lead in the business.*
>
> —Edmund Burke

Growing Communities of Practice

> *We don't accomplish anything in this world alone ... and whatever happens is the result of the whole tapestry of one's life and all the weavings of individual threads from one to another that creates something.*
>
> —Sandra Day O'Connor

Arguably, ADB (2011i) accomplished most under the second of the four pillars, aimed at empowering the communities of practice. Communities of practice gather people who share a common passion for something they do and who interact regularly to learn how to do it better. They are peer-to-peer collaborative networks driven by the willingness of their members to share work-related knowledge, further develop expertise, and solve problems in a specific domain. They enhance learning and empower people in their work. What is more, the simple act of joining and being regularly involved in organized groups significantly impacts individual health and well-being. The unambiguous "community" dimension of the actions/outputs executed under the *Action Plan for Knowledge Management, 2009– 2011* portends well for ADB's organizational culture. The short-term and long-term value they can add is considerable.[14]

---

[14]The short-term value a community of practice brings to members includes (i) help with challenges, (ii) access to expertise, (iii) confidence, (iv) fun with colleagues, and (v) meaningful work. The short-term value it brings to the organization comprises (i) problem solving, (ii) time saving, (iii) knowledge sharing, (iv) synergies across units, and (v) reuse of resources. The long-term value to members includes (i) personal development, (ii) reputation, (iii) professional identity, (iv) collaborative advantage, and (v) marketability. The long-term value to the organization comprises (i) strategic capabilities, (ii) keeping abreast, (iii) innovation, (iv) retention of talent, and (v) new strategies.

Box 1: Empowering ADB-Hosted Communities of Practice

- Communities of practice are groups of people who share a passion for something they know how to do and who interact regularly to learn how to do it better.
- Appearing in 2002 after a bank-wide reorganization, ADB-hosted CoPs were empowered under the *Action Plan for Knowledge Management, 2009–2011*.
- Interventions ranging from budget increases to integration in ADB operations have helped affirm CoPs as the heart and soul of knowledge generation and sharing in ADB.

Background

Professionals working in a particular field often converge, hoping thereby to both impart and enrich their knowledge. This is also true of ADB staff.

First CoPs Informal peer groups emerged in ADB in the 1990s but only in 2002 did they find their footing in ADB's organizational structure. That year saw the birth of 19 sector and thematic networks intended to promote cross-fertilization of knowledge across departments. However, in the first few years of their existence, the committees and networks were hampered by many factors, which included the following:

- Nonvoluntary membership—departments nominated staff and required them to devote 15% of their time to the networks.
- Mixed responsibilities—the networks not only provided think-tank type services in their respective fields but also performed executive functions such as trust fund management.
- Weak committee chairing—even though they were not recognized champions in their field, staff were sometimes appointed as committee chairs.
- Inadequate resourcing—the networks were not given adequate budgets and the work of members was not recognized in staff performance reviews.

In 2005, the recommendations of an independent panel commissioned to assess the effectiveness of ADB's reorganization prompted a consolidation of the networks. Their number was reduced to 10, and the term "community of practice" or CoP entered the picture.

Reconstituted CoPs The new batch of CoPs fared better. Membership became voluntary, chairing of committees was based on technical expertise, and their functions focused mainly on sector and thematic work. Naturally, the 10 CoPs progressed at different speeds, and the more sophisticated among them began to feed into debates on sector or thematic directions, offer advice on staff skills mix and competencies, and conduct activities on knowledge generation and sharing. The CoPs as a group also started receiving an annual budget of $100,000, shared equally among them and spent on strategy review activities, conference participation, and conduct of studies.

The community stagnates without the impulse of the individual. The impulse dies away without the sympathy of the community.

—William James

A 2008 review of the CoPs revealed that they had traveled far, but not far enough. Clearer roles and responsibilities vis-à-vis ADB's operations were called for. Interchangeable use of the terms "committees," "networks," and "CoPs" had led to considerable confusion about the meaning of each. Resources were still meager. Things turned for the better, and at a much faster rate, when the empowerment of CoPs was specified as a pillar of the *Action Plan for Knowledge Management, 2009–2011*.

Approach

In July 2009, ADB President Haruhiko Kuroda approved the *Action Plan for Knowledge Management, 2009–2011* to ensure that ADB's knowledge remains of the highest quality and relevance. The action plan committed results in four pillars:

- Sharpening the knowledge focus in ADB's operations
- Empowering the communities of practice
- Strengthening external knowledge partnerships
- Further enhancing staff learning and skills development

The second pillar highlighted CoPs as an instrument to promote knowledge generation and sharing in ADB. To set a benchmark for the coming years, ADB surveyed the performance of CoPs in 2009. This first survey revealed that CoPs helped build relationships and benefited daily work. However, they also needed to reach out to all members, especially those in ADB's resident missions and representative offices; align their work programs with *Strategy 2020*, ADB's long-term strategic framework; and concretize their roles in reviewing country partnership strategies and lending and nonlending products.

To address the survey's recommendations, ADB took steps to boost CoP effectiveness. The main interventions were:

- **Higher budgets** In 2010, individual CoP budgets rose from about $10,000 to roughly $100,000. (They would increase further in 2012.)
- **Streamlined guidelines for sector and thematic reporting** Detailed guidelines formalized the feedback process of CoPs to inform ADB's annual *Development Effectiveness Review* and work program and budget frameworks.
- **New peer review guidelines** The guidelines legitimized the CoPs' participation in the peer review process and enabled country partnership

strategies and lending and nonlending products to benefit from the operations-based inputs of CoP members.

- **CoP work in performance reviews** ADB's staff performance review templates were modified to incorporate knowledge work. Beginning 2011, CoPs also have the opportunity to provide performance feedback about a staff as an "input supervisor".
- **CoPs as partners in recruitment** Acknowledging that subject matter experts in CoPs best understand what skills are needed in their field, ADB has, since mid-2010, arranged for CoP chairs, coschairs, and practice leaders to participate in screening and interviewing prospective international staff.

Results

Between 2005 and 2011, four more CoPs were established, bringing the total number of ADB-hosted CoPs to 14. Over the 2 years of action plan implementation, CoPs demonstrated they have become the heart and soul of knowledge generation and sharing in ADB.

Strengthening internal relationships Since late 2009, the number of collaborative initiatives between and among CoPs have been increasing. They include joint knowledge-sharing events and joint knowledge products. At year-end gatherings, begun in 2009, CoPs highlight their accomplishments, exchange lessons, and explore areas of collaboration. (The year-end gathering of 2011 would have them share lessons learned with one another.)

Building knowledge and expertise CoPs now help prepare key ADB documents such as the operational plans for education, food security, transport, and water. In support, regional sector studies build the knowledge and expertise of their members. The CoPs themselves have also taken an active role in developing the technical capacity of members by conducting or arranging training courses tailor-made for them.

Expanding outreach Outreach to stakeholders has greatly improved with CoP members providing advice on projects managed by their peers. CoPs have also forged stronger links with ADB's development partners and stakeholders by acting as technical experts and focal points on key issues. Moreover, they have shared good-practice studies on education, tool kits for urban transport development, e-newsletters and video documentaries on water, and other engaging and creative materials.

Without a sense of caring, there can be no sense of community.

—Anthony Burgess

The second survey of CoPs, undertaken in 2011, revealed considerable improvements across the board. Naturally, challenges persist. For example, CoPs might need to crystallize their functions better around filtering, amplifying, investing and providing, convening, community building, and learning and facilitating. CoPs can carry out several of these functions simultaneously but there are trade-offs: each function requires specific capacities, skills, resources, and systems. Overlooking trade-offs can drive CoPs away from their original role.

A community is like a ship; everyone ought to be prepared to take the helm.

—Henrik Ibsen

Nevertheless, however they develop, CoPs will need ADB's continued support; the potential from their activities is just too great. They can more decidedly

- Promote innovative approaches to address specific development challenges.
- Develop, capture, and transfer good practices on specific topics by stimulating the active generation and sharing of knowledge.
- Link diverse groups of practitioners from different disciplines and be thus intertwined in ADB's organizational structure.
- Serve as an ongoing learning venue for staff (and outside practitioners) who share similar goals, interests, problems, and approaches.
- Respond rapidly to individual inquiries from members and ADB clients, audiences, and partners with specific answers.

Source Extracted from ADB (2011j).

Box 2: ADB-Hosted Communities of Practice—Driving Knowledge Activities

- Communities of practice are a prime tool of organizational development.
- Empowering CoPs was one of the four pillars of *Enhancing Knowledge Management under Strategy 2020: Plan of Action, 2009–2011*.
- Since 2009, fast advances in core knowledge activities instituted ADB-hosted communities of practice as the heart and soul of knowledge generation and sharing in the organization.

Empowering ADB-Hosted Communities of Practice
At the 42nd Annual Meeting of the Board of Governors of ADB held in 2009, President Haruhiko Kuroda stressed the importance of knowledge to the organization: *"To be fully effective, we must also consciously and actively blend knowledge with financing. We will focus on developing, capturing, and sharing knowledge in all our work, ensuring that ADB serves an intermediary role for both financing and knowledge."*

Three months later, President Kuroda approved *Enhancing Knowledge Management under Strategy 2020: Plan of Action, 2009–2011* to advance the knowledge management agenda in ADB. Four pillars framed the plan: (i) sharpening the knowledge focus in ADB's operations, (ii) empowering CoPs,[a] (iii) strengthening external knowledge partnerships, and (iv) further enhancing staff learning and skills development.

Tacit knowledge, specifically how to access and share it, offers a particularly complex challenge in pursuing any knowledge agenda; it needs special methods to transmit it. Therefore, the second pillar of the action plan emphasizes CoPs as a collaboration mechanism to generate and share knowledge.

CoPs were first introduced in 2002 during an ADB-wide reorganization. However, in the years after the action plan was introduced, they have grown swiftly as centers of expertise. Since 2009, they have variously enriched knowledge of sector and thematic issues, informed country partnership strategies and lending and nonlending operations, and contributed to human resource development and management ADB-wide. What is more, CoPs empower people in their work: the simple act of joining and being regularly involved in such organized groups has significantly impacted individual well-being among ADB personnel.

Delivering Core Knowledge Activities

To excel in their respective domains, ADB-hosted CoPs aim to identify, create, store, share, and use knowledge. All these are core knowledge activities that learning organizations align or integrate into business processes and balance according to the specificities of each. Since 2009, annual and triennial reports have helped define work programs and report on accomplishments in these areas.

> *It is vain to talk of the interest of the community, without understanding what is the interest of the individual.*
>
> —Jeremy Bentham

Identifying knowledge Many CoPs now conduct surveys or interviews to help determine the knowledge products and services their members can create or improve on. Examples include the *Water CoP Perceptions* survey and *The Philippines Environment and Natural Resources Country Assessment: "A Call to Action"*. In 2009, ADB's Knowledge Management Center also introduced a biennial survey of ADB-hosted CoPs to help them assess performance and identify means to reach optimal levels.

Creating knowledge Many CoPs have published and produced documentaries to showcase initiatives, programs, and activities. The Water CoP, for instance, has pioneered the *Water for All* series. The Education CoP has launched the *Focus on Education* series. The Environment CoP helped articulate Asia's voice in preparing for the 2012 United Nations Conference on Sustainable Development or Rio + 20 through the report *Green Growth, Resources and Resilience*.

Storing knowledge ADB-hosted CoPs have become ubiquitous, thanks to the myriad means for knowledge capture and storage the digital world now offers. Because perceptions of information overload have less to do with quantity than with the quality by which knowledge is presented, many CoPs craft products that highlight achievements and outcomes. The material is stored for ready access through multiple platforms including the CoP webpages in ADB's internal and external sites. eStar, an electronic storage and retrieval system, is now also used to store publications. Some CoPs, such as that for transport, also use YouTube to upload video footage.

Sharing knowledge ADB-hosted CoPs bring a focus to bear on knowledge sharing through peer reviews, notably of country partnership strategies and lending and nonlending operations;[c] customized in-house and external training of members; regular meetings, seminars, conferences, and forums;[d] external knowledge partnerships; etc. These activities are not just an add-on; they are becoming integral part of daily work.

CoPs extensively use information and communications technology in support of knowledge sharing. Knowledge databases, discussion boards, blogs, and webpages were developed for this. The focus of webpages such as the Energy CoP's *ENERcall* and the Urban CoP's *UrbInfo* remains internal but the applications are mobile and provide cumulative data and information anywhere, anytime.

A monthly internal e-newsletter dedicated to CoPs, *i.prompt.u*, was introduced by the Knowledge Management Center in 2011 to expand knowledge sharing within and outside ADB. It serves to aggregate information from contributors to enhance relationship building and networking. Specifically, *i.prompt.u* highlights knowledge products, events, and news of CoPs; links to individual newsletters[e] of CoPs; showcases annual and triennial reports of CoPs; fosters inter-CoP collaboration and cross-fertilization through rich exchange of information; and advances interest in multiple domains.

Using knowledge ADB-hosted CoPs also draft operational plans in sector and thematic areas to refine the strategic directions that *Strategy 2020* laid out. The purpose of the plans is to review experiences and past practices, assess broader development issues and challenges, and identify short- to medium-term approaches and activities needed to act on ADB's strategic thrusts. In 2009, ADB completed an operational plan for sustainable food security. A year later, ADB approved three more plans for climate change, sustainable transport, and education; another on finance was approved in 2011.

The man who does not take pride in his own performance performs nothing in which to take pride.

—Thomas J. Watson

Achieving Full Potential

ADB recognizes the potential that CoPs hold in support of *Strategy 2020*. To help CoPs reach optimal performance, ADB has since 2009 conducted biennial surveys in eight areas of inquiry:

- The extent of participation in CoPs
- Insights into the clarity of domains
- Perceptions of the value-added by CoPs
- Critical success factors
- Insights into the varying possible functions of CoPs
- Dimensions of participation in CoPs
- Perceptions of ADB's approach to CoPs
- Recommendations to strengthen CoP effectiveness

The results of the *2011 Survey of ADB-Hosted Communities of Practice* suggest that ADB is reaping the benefits of investments and hard work over the last 2 years. With greater cross-fertilization among CoPs, initiated in 2009 with the first year-end gathering of CoPs, the value that this prime tool of organizational development brings to ADB's core business can only increase. CoPs, now considered the "heart and soul" of knowledge sharing in ADB, are gaining vigor.

[a]Following ADB's reorganization in 2001, which introduced the concept of networks, 15 CoPs are now active: Agriculture, Rural Development, and Food Security; Education; Energy; Environment; Financial Sector Development; Gender Equity; Governance and Public Management; Health; Public–Private Partnerships; Regional Cooperation and Integration; Social Development and Poverty; Transport; Urban; and Water. (The latest, a CoP on Operations, was established in 2012 to help address ADB-wide project (2011k) and portfolio management issues.)

[b]Tacit knowledge is personal, context-specific knowledge that is difficult to formalize, record, or articulate: it is stored in the heads of people. It is mainly developed through interaction, debate, and trial and error encountered in practice.

[c]CoPs are now also being requested to provide quality-at-entry and quality-at-exit reviews of key publications of ADB's operations departments.

[d]The CoPs that helped shape knowledge generation and sharing through forums are the Agriculture, Rural Development, and Food Security (2010); Education (2004); Transport (2008, 2010, 2012); Urban (2011); and Water (2006–2011) communities.

eCoPs with individual newsletters include Gender Equity, Health, Social Development and Poverty, Transport, and Water.

Source Extracted from ADB (2011l).

Cultivating Reflective Practice

People are wired to tell and listen to stories. Yet institutions have largely ignored the power of storytelling in favor of official reports, formal speeches, and press releases. In 2008, ADB began to explore storytelling as a medium to capture, store, and share its past and present staff's vast knowledge.

> *Action and faith enslave thought, both of them in order not be troubled or inconvenienced by reflection, criticism, and doubt.*
>
> —Henri-Frédéric Amiel

The first product, the publication *ADB: Reflections and Beyond*, was an introspective look at ADB over four decades of development work, culled from the memories of past and present, senior and junior, and local and international staff. Often called the "Yellow Book," this publication is the result of painstaking efforts —conducting over 40 interviews, trawling through the voluminous materials produced, and transforming the spoken words into written language without losing their spontaneity, essence, or appeal.

Reactions to the Yellow Book were overwhelmingly positive. Contrasting sharply with the dominant tone and style of ADB's usual products, the book adopted an easy-reading approach that made ADB's rich history doubly interesting. Readers pored over their copies and asked when the next volume would be released. The next volume, as it turned out, came in a hugely different format.

Concerned with giving staff a more dynamic walk down "memory lane," ADB designed an interactive multimedia documentary, powered by a Flash-based application, that would allow users to browse through ADB's experiences using various entry points, e.g., subjects, years, decades, ADB presidents, etc. The product, currently nearing completion, is anchored by four timelines: the *ADB Sustainable Development Timeline*, a *World Sustainable Development Timeline*, ADB historical milestones, and a *Timeline of ADB-Hosted Communities of Practice*. The addition to ADB's living archive was launched in December 2011 on the occasion of the organization's 44th anniversary.

Box 3: Building Narrative Capacity at ADB

- ADB makes growing use of knowledge management tools, methods, and approaches but must better capture and store its wealth of tacit knowledge.
- In 2009, the Knowledge Management Center in ADB's Regional and Sustainable Development Department launched an oral history project to help ADB hear itself.
- ADB staff expressed deep appreciation for *ADB: Reflections and Beyond* and its companion audio composition, *Beyond: Stories and Sounds from ADB's Region*—ADB has developed an appetite for storytelling in various contexts and applications.

Origins

ADB has insufficient means of capturing and storing its vast wealth of tacit experience. Coaching and mentoring are somewhat ad hoc; exit interviews are still cursory; the Critical Incident technique finds few applications; structured peer assists have not yet been introduced; knowledge harvesting is not practiced; after-action reviews and retrospects are more or less unheard of; and only a small number of weblogs exists. In short, knowledge sharing is limited to small (but rapidly expanding) communities and networks of practice, meetings over coffee, or occasional exchanges in hallways. A particular concern is that senior staff do not often transfer their experience with audiences outside Management circles.

ADB is both a repository of stories waiting to be told and an audience ready to listen. At the 2007 annual meeting of the Knowledge Management for Development community, Olivier Serrat, the future head of the Knowledge Management Center in ADB, learned of a storytelling project of the Islamic Development Bank conducted in 2006 because many of that organization's staff were about to retire. Upon joining the Knowledge Management Center in September 2008, he formulated an oral history project to create a means by which ADB might hear itself and learn from past and present experience. Storytelling would surely help ADB become a learning organization as envisaged in *Strategy 2020*, ADB's long-term strategic framework.

In October 2008, the Knowledge Management Center decided to test ADB's appetite for storytelling. A scoping exercise soon confirmed that staffs were ready and willing to share their experiences with narrative techniques. According to an early participant, "It's easier to talk about the future if you ground it in the events of the past."

It is not part of a true culture to tame tigers, any more than it is to make sheep ferocious.

—Henry David Thoreau

Listening to ADB Through Stories

In March 2009, long tables covered with blank sheets were laid out in ADB's Library, inviting staff to jot down significant memories and mark out ADB's crossroads over the years. With some difficulty at the start, a timeline of ADB's history, born of staff reminiscences, emerged. It articulated a healthy blend of recollections—some fundamental, others more subtle. It became the basis for the structure of *ADB: Reflections and Beyond*. Accordingly, that would intersperse reminiscences of arrivals and early years, descriptions of ADB projects and day-to-day operations, reports of complex situations and tricky judgment calls, etc., with personal memories of colleagues.

Interviews with alumni, Management, and staff provided the most trying yet fulfilling moments. Storytelling was still new to ADB, even though some had used it in projects. The Knowledge Management Center initially identified over 40 interviewees—a judicious mix of senior and junior international and local staff, alumni, and former members of the Board of Directors and Management. "I heard a story about something you did 15 years ago. Can you tell me more?" Some interviewees declined the invitation to take part. Others said they could only spare 30 min but reminisced for more than 2.5 hours. A few were eager to be interviewed but hesitated—they felt they were not senior enough. Two quickly said that interviews can preserve institutional memory and requested follow-up sessions.

The book *ADB: Reflections and Beyond* is one of many fruits from the interviews. A companion audio composition, *Beyond: Stories and Sounds from ADB's Region*, selects pearls of wisdom, artistically allied to sounds captured in headquarters and the field, in the form of podcasts.

Poring over the material yielded by 33 interviews and making selections for the publication was not easy. But the greater challenge lay in transcribing spoken words into written language without losing vivacity. Dealing with these difficulties occupied the Knowledge Management Center in the second half of 2009.

> *Culture is not made up but something that evolves which is human.*
>
> —Edward T. Hall

ADB: Reflections and Beyond was printed in January 2010. But, there was still a sense of uncertainty stemming from concerns over how the book should be launched, how staff would react to it, and what unintended effects it might have. Eventually, what became known as the "Yellow Book" was released on 2 February 2010, coinciding with ADB President Haruhiko Kuroda's town hall presentation of ADB's *Our People Strategy*, a document that sets out the principles for how the organization will recruit, motivate, and manage its workforce to achieve the operational and institutional goals of *Strategy 2020*. The limited number of copies of the book placed on display at the launch were snapped up by staff as they arrived. Every staff member received a copy of the book the following day.

ADB: Reflections and Beyond is now given to each prospective staff.

Appreciation and Follow-up
Reactions to the book were overwhelmingly positive. During the town hall meeting, staff who held advance copies began to flick through the book. Reactions ranged from surprise to amusement to delight. A department head later asked: "Are you the guys behind the Yellow Book? When is the next volume coming out?"

ADB: Reflections and Beyond and *Beyond: Stories and Sounds from ADB's Region* succeeded in connecting staff with ADB's very rich history. They contrast sharply with the authoritative, yet distant voice of traditional ADB products. The book is refreshingly different, "... a bit on the light side, which is fine, but future stories can go deeper."

There is something to be said for positive deviance. As is the case for many radical innovation projects, starting small and flying below the radar helped get things done. Once personel see, recognize, and understand the benefits of approaches such as storytelling (especially when products begin to take shape), demand for related initiatives typically increases. Other departments are beginning to use the technique for training purposes. For example, storytelling is being used to develop a source book for country directors.

As a postscript, the Knowledge Management Center later asked the interviewees how narrative techniques might be applied elsewhere. One suggested that ADB should consider capturing stories from its audiences, clients, and partners. Their feedback might feature people who helped shape the evolution of ADB's development work across Asia and the Pacific.

Source Extracted from ADB (2010e).

Box 4: Interactive Stories of Sustainable Development

- In early 2009, ADB embarked on a first organization-wide knowledge-harvesting exercise to collect a blend of recollections and reminiscences through storytelling. It gave birth to two much-appreciated contributions that stimulated in-house appetite for use of narrative techniques in various contexts and applications.
- In late 2010, a follow-up interactive, audiovisual project was conceptualized to promulgate further the use of storytelling to elicit, capture, store, and share knowledge.
- The potential of the new multimedia platform to energize staff recruitment, induction, and training; add color to conferences and other events; enrich education; and boost ADB's profile externally was immediately recognized.

Setting

In March 2009, long tables covered with blank sheets were laid out in ADB's library, beckoning staff to record special memories and mark out ADB's crossroads over the years. The intention was to (i) draw out and package tacit knowledge of struggles and triumphs working for development in the Asia and Pacific region, and ADB's evolution as an institution, to help others adapt, personalize, and apply it; (ii) preserve institutional memory; and (iii) build organizational capacity. A blend of staff recollections and reminiscences formed and became the basis for the well-regarded publication titled *ADB: Reflections and Beyond* (also referred to as the "Yellow Book") and its audio companion *Beyond: Stories and Sounds from ADB's Region.* The two products marked ADB's first endeavor at knowledge harvesting through storytelling. ADB took time to listen to itself and staff liked what they heard. In short, the Yellow Book and sound composition whetted ADB's appetite for storytelling in various contexts and applications.

Then, in August 2010, the Knowledge Management Center mapped out sector and thematic milestones in ADB's journey toward sustainable development—the *ADB Sustainable Development Timeline.* The brochure framed a select record of progress by ADB and its member countries across the many dimensions of sustainable development, e.g., social, economic, and environmental. But it was decided from the onset that the timeline should amount to more than just a sheet of paper. In fact, after the success of the preceding knowledge-harvesting exercise, it seemed natural to take things further and represent the timeline in a more versatile medium—an interactive, audiovisual platform that would allow users to browse not just data and information but also, more importantly, evocations of events. In December 2010, the Knowledge Management Center initiated the long and arduous task of morphing the *ADB Sustainable Development Timeline* brochure multidimensionally.

> *A people are as healthy and confident as the stories they tell themselves. Sick storytellers can make nations sick. Without stories we would go mad. Life would lose its moorings or orientation ... Stories can conquer fear, you know. They can make the heart larger.*
>
> —Ben Okri

Approach

Platform The *ADB Sustainable Development Timeline* would host an easy-to-access and organic repository of interviews, short documentaries of projects shot on location, sounds (as in *Beyond: Stories and Sounds from ADB's Region*), B-roll footage, animations, graphics, voice-overs, videos, statistics, photo essays, etc.

Research With the *ADB Sustainable Development Timeline* brochure setting the compass for content, project staff rummaged through ADB reports and publications from 1966, archived films and stills, online research material, and sundry other references to scope the context of milestones. By the time research and writing had ended, the project's reach had grown to four timelines: the existing *ADB Sustainable Development Timeline*, and timelines of world events touching sustainable development since 1948, historical highlights of ADB since its establishment, and ADB-hosted communities of practice from the 1990s. (The *World Sustainable Development Timeline* was subsequently published with an eye to Rio + 20, scheduled on 20–22 June 2012.)

Production Some 72 ADB staff—past and present, senior and junior— were invited to an outside setting and their experiences of particular events or projects mined and preserved through video. This yielded 11 hours and 30 min of film, later categorized and tagged in multiple topics. Location shoots inside ADB premises—both in headquarters and resident missions— followed. Visits to Indonesia and Viet Nam were also made to interface with beneficiaries and put on view associated landmarks and landscapes. The trips delivered high-quality interviews and footage that made for compelling documentaries.

Knowledge Organization The wealth of knowledge generated by the exercise demanded systematic organization. Using Adobe Flash Player to house the structure for the product, project staff arranged the material by year, theme, region, community of practice, ADB president, and more. The effect is a personal experience: each user can click or scroll through videos, pick a story of interest, and probe content in nonlinear fashion.

Challenges A multimedia creation of 300+ videos does not come easily. In the early stages, working through the rigid business processes of ADB slowed progress and caused frustration. Next, staff were sometimes noncommittal— this affected scheduling. Then, after transcription and tagging, hours were spent sifting through collections to showcase stimulating content.

> *Their story, yours and mine—it's what we all carry with us on this trip we take, and we owe it to each other to respect our stories and learn from them.*
>
> —William Carlos Williams

Way Forward

In December 2011, on the occasion of ADB's 44th anniversary, the intro- ductory video of the *ADB Sustainable Development Timeline* was shown to ADB staff who enthused about it. A series of longer demonstrations took place soon after, all generating pleased responses. Many saw the potential of the videos, either used collectively or individually, for learning and development, recognizing firsts, safeguarding institutional memory, and a myriad other uses. ADB's human resources division, for example, suggested that the product be showcased during induction programs for new staff, noting that the story- telling mode eases learning and retention of critical knowledge. Some of ADB's external partners, such as the University of the Philippines in Los

Baños and Bangko Sentral ng Pilipinas (Central Bank of the Philippines), were impressed when elements of the timeline were presented to them during their field trips to ADB, and wanted to see more. More content is being generated to expand the range of the product. Through the briefings, ADB realized that gaps need to be filled, such as deeper coverage of subregions, even greater variety in topics, additional inclusion of women and new staff, etc.

Conclusion

The *ADB Sustainable Development Timeline* video sprang from creativity and innovation, method, and no small amount of work. But collaboration and open-mindedness in the organization powered performance. For ADB to have embarked on such an initiative proves how much it values the knowledge, experience, and insights of its professionals and wants to share those. Through this, ADB hopes to better shape the future, with respect to the past.

Source Extracted from ADB (2012b).

Reporting on Knowledge Management

Between 2005, when ADB first conducted a MAKE survey, and 2011 the increase in the number of respondents jumped a cumulative 1,132%, averaging 162% annually.[15] Without a doubt, more and more ADB staff have become aware of the organization's efforts to improve its knowledge stocks and flows. The highest annual percentage increase, 155%, was recorded in 2009, the year the *Action Plan for Knowledge Management, 2009–2011* was approved. Various factors have contributed to this growing engagement, one of which is the change in the way ADB testifies on knowledge management initiatives at the corporate level. One concrete example is ADB's Annual Report, which showcases ADB's operations, projects, internal administration, financial management, special funds, and more. In 2004, when the knowledge management framework was approved, "knowledge management" merited 350 words in the chapter on institutional effectiveness. The next 2 years saw "knowledge management" shuttled between the chapters on operations and internal initiatives. In 2007, a new chapter on generating and sharing knowledge was introduced: it highlighted ADB's comparative advantages as a knowledge institution and discussed approaches to meeting the needs of external and internal audiences. Somewhat belatedly, given the importance of evaluation-based learning, a new chapter on independent evaluation also appeared. In 2008, a new chapter on sector and thematic highlights underscored quality, knowledge, and innovation for

---

[15]At the end of 2005, ADB had a staff of 2,456. (The total comprised 887 international staff and 1,569 national and administrative staff.) At the end of 2011, it had a staff of 2,958, that is, 6 members of Management and 1,055 international and 1,897 national and administrative staff.

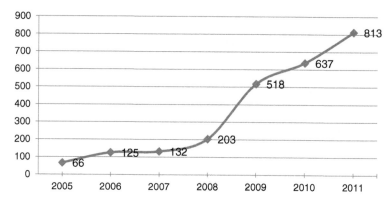

Fig. 58.3 ADB respondents to MAKE surveys. *Source* Author

inclusive and sustainable development. In 2009, ADB once again expanded reporting specific to knowledge management: in addition to the chapter on generating and sharing knowledge, a new chapter on delivering an effective organization carried a section on strengthening learning, which accorded pride of place to implementation of the *Action Plan for Knowledge Management, 2009–2011*. In 2010, three of ADB's five regional departments included sections on knowledge management in their respective chapters; in 2011, all of them did. Another example is ADB's *Development Effectiveness Review*, which reports annually on ADB's corporate results framework and, since its introduction in 2008, uses the annual MAKE survey assessment rating to help gauge ADB's operational effectiveness in managing knowledge better. The Knowledge Management Center instigated all such reporting throughout (Fig. 58.3).

> *As we read the school reports on our children, we realize a sense of relief that can rise to delight that thank Heaven nobody is reporting in this fashion on us.*
>
> —Joseph Priestley

Some Benefits of Pursuing a Culture-Based Knowledge Strategy

An organization can benefit severally from pursuing a knowledge strategy.[16] For ADB, a relative newcomer in the field of knowledge management, the bottom line is:

---

[16]The *Knowledge Solutions* on internal knowledge markets list illustrative motivations behind knowledge management efforts.

> *Change is the end result of all true learning.*
>
> —Leo Buscaglia

Affirming Knowledge as a Strategic Asset and Critical Resource

With Asia experiencing rapid economic growth over the recent decades, ADB recognizes that financial assistance is not always the primary commodity its developing member countries need. In many ways, ADB's knowledge—which benefits from its strategic position to identify trends within and across the region and capacity for interdisciplinary and integrated approaches—has greater pull and push. Pursuing a culture-based knowledge strategy has further promoted the view of knowledge as a strategic asset and a critical source of competitive advantage and highlighted its dual nature as both an input and output. Offices and departments in ADB now pay greater attention to the sourcing, quality, dissemination, and use of the knowledge they husband.

Setting Clearer Directions

> *The learning and knowledge that we have, is, at the most, but little compared with that of which we are ignorant.*
>
> —Plato

Over the last 3 years, ADB has developed a habit of asking if it is managing knowledge better. Now that the *Action Plan for Knowledge Management, 2009–2011* is closed, ADB ought to capture lessons from past successes and shortcomings by raising the following questions: What did ADB set out to do? What worked well, and why? Moving forward, what might ADB do differently next time, and how?

Learnings?

An organization's culture—not forgetting its subcultures—determines assumptions about what knowledge is, hence, what stocks and flows of that may be worth managing. It arbitrates the relationships between individuals, teams, and communities; sets the context for social interaction; and shapes the processes whereby knowledge is identified, created, stored, shared, and used. No two organizations are similar and there are disquieting limits to what learnings can be vulgarized for the benefit of others. If knowledge is the combination of information and human context, there is no easy way from the earth to the stars. "An intelligent hell would be better than a stupid paradise," declared Victor Hugo. Yet, practitioners must have their take-aways. Pending an after-action review of the *Action Plan for Knowledge Management, 2009–2011*, some easy and not-so-easy lessons might be:

Fostering and Sustaining a Culture of Knowledge Transfer

One must, with hard work, offset counterproductive assumptions—"Knowledge is power," "I cannot share without Management approval," "Who am I to teach others?"—with values, beliefs, and behaviors conducive to knowledge generation and sharing. Knowledge management is the responsibility of each member of the organization. To innovate knowledge management and learning holistically, individuals, teams, and communities in organizations must be heartened to continually ask, learn, and share. In ADB, the current popularity and perceived value of communities of practice should not be taken for granted. Of course, communities work best if they are clear about domain, values, membership, norms and rules, structure and process, resources, flow of energy, and results. But, if too much informality can kill a community so can too much attention from Management to what is, in the final analysis, a voluntary way of organizing. One cannot force people to collaborate and a chicken does not get fatter the more you weigh it. Management must learn to cultivate these fertile organizational forms without destroying them; after all, since members select themselves, communities of practice only last for as long as there is interest in joining and maintaining the group. Equally, it should be recognized that action plans, even when they provide impetus, are by nature dysfunctional: an organization that professes to become a knowledge organization should not rely on temporary expedients: knowledge management must be part and parcel of everyday occupation in a culture of knowledge.

Recognizing Different Learning Styles

Personnel—in ADB's case, international staff and national and administrative staff—develop knowledge management capabilities at different rates. It is important that ADB should draw knowledge management initiatives that meet the distinct needs of personnel streams as the MAKE surveys continue to explain.

Culture is the widening of the mind and of the spirit.

—Jawaharlal Nehru

Leveraging off Strengths

The *2010 Learning for Change* survey undertaken by ADB revealed that of the four learning subsystems of organization, people, knowledge, and technology, ADB staff feel most satisfied with technology. There is little surprise here. Taking off from this, ADB rolled out a bevy of integrated and mutually supportive collaboration mechanisms; aggregators of news, events, and knowledge products; and other tools anchored in technology, including social media. A rising tide lifts all ships.

Becoming a Learning Organization

A decided step that ADB took in pursuing its knowledge strategy was to break things into outcome indicators, useful results indicators, specific activity indicators, targets and associated baseline values, sources of verification, and assumptions and risks. This enabled ADB (2010f) to benchmark and subsequently rate and validate progress. Surveys such as the biennial *Learning for Change* survey—developed and conducted by the Knowledge Management Center in 2010—and the well-established MAKE survey have provided insights into ADB's performance and given reason to raise the bar.

Culture is the process by which a person becomes all that they were created capable of being.

—Thomas Carlyle

The 2010 MAKE survey revealed that ADB has successfully transitioned from stage 2 (implementation) to stage 3 (reinvigoration) of the MAKE Knowledge Management Implementation Model. The 2011 MAKE survey confirmed even more progress in ADB's knowledge capabilities across all eight MAKE performance dimensions and its transition from stage 3 (reinvigoration) to stage 4 (inculcation). This view is supported by the fact that the average total score for all staff improved steadily since the 2008 MAKE survey. The 2011 Asian MAKE panel of experts confirmed this by recognizing ADB, for the first time, as a 2011 Asian MAKE Winner at the 12th World Knowledge Forum held in Seoul, Republic of Korea, in October 2011.[17] [To note, it only took 1 year for ADB to transition from stage 3 (reinvigoration), a stage reached in 2010, to stage 4 (inculcation) in 2011.][18] However, stage 4 is perhaps the most critical juncture. Staff complacency must be challenged with a new set of ambitious goals and objectives to inculcate knowledge management and learning into all organizational processes and procedures. Besides improving internal knowledge capabilities and processes, external partners and stakeholders must also become more integrated into the organization's core knowledge activities to create a transparent, "boundary-less" enterprise that sees knowledge as culture. *A posse ad esse.*

References

ADB (2001) Moving the poverty reduction agenda forward in Asia and the Pacific: the long-term strategic framework of the Asian development bank 2001–2015. Manila
ADB (2004) Knowledge management in ADB. Manila
ADB (2005–) Assessment of ADB's knowledge management implementation framework. Manila
ADB (2008) Strategy 2020: the long-term strategic framework of the Asian development bank (2008–2020). Manila
ADB (2008a–) Knowledge solutions. Manila
ADB (2008b–) Knowledge showcases. Manila
ADB (2009a) Learning for change in ADB. Manila
ADB (2009b) Strengthening communities of practice in ADB. Manila
ADB (2009c) Enhancing knowledge management under strategy 2020, plan of action, 2009–2011. Manila
ADB (2010a) A survey of demand for ADB knowledge products through resident and regional missions. Manila
ADB (2010b) Enriching knowledge management coordination. Manila
ADB (2010c) ADB: reflections and beyond. Manila
ADB (2010d) Beyond: stories and sounds from ADB's region. Manila
ADB (2010e) Building narrative capacity at ADB. Manila
ADB (2010f) Learning for change survey. Manila
ADB (2011a) A study of ADB's knowledge taxonomy. Manila
ADB (2011b) A study of information on knowledge management and communication in CPSs, RRPs, and TA reports. Manila
ADB (2011c) ADB sustainable development timeline. Manila
ADB (2011d) Survey of ADB-hosted communities of practice. Manila
ADB (2011e) ADB resources for communities of practice: creating value through knowledge networks. Manila
ADB (2011g) Building a knowledge-centric organization. Manila
ADB (2011f) Guidelines for knowledge partnerships. Manila

[17]The chapter on delivering an effective organization in ADB's annual report for 2011 celebrated the award.

[18]ADB began its transition from stage 2 (implementation) to stage 3 (reinvigoration) in 2009. This coincides with the approval in July of that year of the *Action Plan for Knowledge Management, 2009–2011.*

ADB (2011h) Enhancing knowledge management under strategy 2020: plan of action for 2009–2011—final report as of July 2011. Manila
ADB (2011i) Communities of practice 101. Manila
ADB (2011j) Empowering ADB-hosted communities of practice. Manila
ADB (2011k) Timeline of ADB-hosted communities of practice. Manila
ADB (2011l) ADB-hosted communities of practice—driving knowledge activities
ADB (2012a) Insight thursday—beyond the headline. Manila
ADB (2012b) Interactive stories of sustainable development. Manila
Handy C (1978) Gods of management: the changing work of organizations. Souvenir Press Ltd
Mintzberg H (1989) Mintzberg on management: inside our strange world of organizations. Simon and Schuster

Proposition 59
Innovation in the Public Sector

In a Word Innovation is something that is new, capable of being implemented, and has a beneficial impact. It is not an event or activity; it is a concept, process, practice, and capability that defines successful organizations. Innovation in the public sector can help create value for society.

Why Innovate?

Innovation has a longer history than the tools, methods, and approaches we mechanically associate with it. (The first image that web browsers return is invariably a lightbulb.)[1] At the intersection of nature and culture, spurred by competition, innovation connotes mankind's reaction to incessant change.

---

[1]Thomas Edison (1847–1931), a prolific American inventor and businessman, developed many devices that greatly influenced life around the world, including the electric lightbulb, the phonograph, and the motion picture camera. He applied principles of large-scale teamwork and mass production to the process of invention; because of that, he is credited with the creation at Menlo Park, New Jersey of the first industrial research laboratory.

© Asian Development Bank 2017
O. Serrat, *Knowledge Solutions*, DOI 10.1007/978-981-10-0983-9_59

From the dawn of human organization—after the retreat of continental glaciers opened fertile tracts, especially in the Fertile Crescent, from about 15,000 BC[2]—increasing size and complexity in many societies forced them evermore to capture energy by consuming raw materials, fuel, and food; accumulate data and information in support; and resort to war—itself a mighty spring of innovation—when access to livelihood assets[3] was insecure. Energy drives productivity, wealth, and power, Morris (2010) explains, and innovation serves to satisfy these. The "why," if not the "how," of innovation is thus simple: it is the purpose, reason, or cause behind whatever adaptation, improvement, or invention is needed and successfully applied to beget from scarce resources valuable outcomes that meet explicit or latent needs. Innovation is something that is new, capable of being implemented, and has beneficial impact.[4] Insights from biology, geography, and sociology confirm little distinguishes what impelled our Neolithic ancestors from what drives modern man.[5]

---

[2]A strong correlation exists between the appearance of human settlements and the rate of innovation. Between 60,000–10,000 BC, circumstantial evidence suggests the appearance in turn of boats, bows and arrows, cloth, mining, pottery, ropes, and sewing needles. Agriculture, alcohol, animal husbandry, baskets, irrigation, and metalworking emerged from 10,000 BC. From 5,000–2,000 BC, innovation gathered speed: aqueducts, bread, candles, canals, cement, combs, currency, measuring devices, ploughs, papyrus, paving, protowriting, reservoirs, sailing, sewers, silk, soap, and wheels are examples.

[3]The *Knowledge Solutions* on the sustainable livelihoods approach identify the resources that people make trade-offs and choices about as human, social, natural, physical, and financial capital. Defined in terms of the ability of a social unit to cope with shocks and stresses over time, the approach is used to understand, measure, and analyze poverty and its alleviation. However, there is no reason why it might be not applied to any socioeconomic strata.

[4]Innovation can have loose definitions. This simple one, crafted from sundry others, is on purpose both helpful and taxing. It is helpful because it encompasses a wide range of activities; it is taxing for the same reason. At the conceptual level, consideration of at least five questions conditions deeper understanding of what is a complex notion. What is success? (Time is a crucial factor: innovations that are initially successful may eventually fail—and vice versa.) What does application mean? (An innovation may be put into operations in one part of an organization or it may be disseminated outside among a large group of users.) What about typology overlap? (Innovation occurs in products, services, processes, and methods of delivery; however, what is a product to a person may be a service, process, or method to another.) Are all innovations equal within and across organizations? (An improvement deemed incremental by some may be thought radical by others.) What of the sources of ideas? (Patently, innovations combine existing and new thinking; very little originates *ab ovo*. It may well be that nearly every problem has been solved by somebody, somewhen, somewhere.).

[5]The *Knowledge Solutions* on business model innovation recount the early years of innovation thinking with emphasis on the two main theories, viz., evolutionary economics and dynamic capabilities frameworks for business strategy.

> *[T]he evolution of the human brain not only overshot the needs of prehistoric man, it is also the only example of evolution providing a species with an organ which it does not know how to use; a luxury organ, which will take its owner thousands of years to learn to put to proper use—if he ever does.*
>
> —Arthur Koestler

Still, the environment that most individuals and organizations confront today is not what it was at the recent turn of the century; it is even radically dissimilar from what it was, say, 25, 50, or 100 years ago—market conditions were consistent; assumptions would remain valid for years; decisions would not have to be revisited for some time. This is no longer true: innovations sparked by globalization and, especially, information and communications technology have provoked bewildering change and fuelled globalization and technology to compound intricacy. Goods, ideas, information, money, people, and services flow with growing ease. Massive global competition and cooperation have been enabled; markets have shifted dramatically; and the values, aspirations, motivations, attitudes, and fears of customers and employees everywhere have been altered. In a shrinking world, since the rate of change is exponential, we cannot (yet) live on love alone, and we do not know what the future will bring, one and all must innovate to prepare for and, preferably, fashion change.[6] (Lest we forget, one and all must also, in equal measure and without trade-off, execute in the present. In successful organizations that last, the social architecture of individual behavior, structure, and culture is primed and leveraged for both exploitation and exploration.)[7]

---

[6]In the pre-industrial age that closed in the early 1800s, many organizations could survive if they just provided quality products, with token upgrades to maintain competitiveness. (This method still applies where the lifecycle of market introduction, growth, maturity, and saturation and decline is long; Coca Cola and Pepsi are examples of products that have existed for decades.) But competition now means that most organizations need more than "good products;" they require management innovation that creates value. Higher expectations from clients, audiences, and partners—from better information and wider choice—also drive what innovations markets must shape. (Into the bargain, the twenty-first century has more than its fair share of pressing needs; the *Knowledge Solutions* on sparking social innovations point up the worldwide societal challenges we face.)

[7]The question rattles: why should it be hard to simultaneously perform well and adapt? The answer is that the demands of exploitation set roadblocks to exploration. According to Beinhocker (2006), they are (i) hierarchies—mental models become more rigid, more locked in, and more averse to novelty as, paradoxically, experience is gained; (ii) organizational complexity—highly interdependent systems become so complicated that they go into gridlock and change becomes impossible; and (iii) mismatch of resources—an organization's resources determine what its plans might be, but their execution breeds path dependence and constrains opportunities in a vicious circle. The only way past the roadblocks is to trim hierarchy, sanction autonomy, and encourage diversity.

> *The intuitive mind is a sacred gift and the rational mind is a faithful servant. We have created a society that honors the servant and has forgotten the gift.*
>
> —Albert Einstein

On Yin and Yang

Innovating is interactive, social, and therefore takes time (and effort). Needless to say, some individuals and some forms of organization are more adept at probing possibilities and reaping benefits from the fourfold knowledge-brokering process of idea generation, idea selection, idea implementation (conversion), and idea diffusion—each stage drawing from different values, resources (people, in particular), and processes. Companies live or die by innovation.[8] To respond to relentless market pressures and stay competitive, drawing from many people with complementary resources, skills, and talents, the finest among them take (and find ways to reduce) risks[9]: they invest in organizational, technical, and social novelties and reward handsomely for new or significantly improved products, services, processes, and methods of delivery (or other elements of their business model(s), such as policy and strategy or system interaction). To this intent, along a continuum of internal to external orientation, they cultivate, replicate, partner, network, or procure

---

[8]To note belatedly, this is not to say that there are no unintended, undesirable outcomes from innovation. (The subject does not attract attention mainly due to general pro-innovation bias.) Of course, there will be: marrying Adam Smith and Joseph Schumpeter, why should disruptions not occur if invisible hands promote ends that were not part of original intentions? One man's loss is another man's gain: direct and indirect outcomes will be wanted by some; others will suffer (Sveiby et al. 2009). (Mark, for instance, the Luddite Movement of 1811–1813. The Luddites were English handloom weavers who protested—often by destroying mechanized looms—the social havoc wreaked by the Industrial Revolution. New textile factories were replacing them with less-skilled, low-wage labor, leaving them without work and hurting their way of life.).

[9]Innovators must, for instance, consider the following: (i) demand risk—how big is the market for the new product, service, process, and method of delivery and will competitors emerge?; (ii) business risk—is monetary and physical capital available to meet the costs of innovation and what effect will the innovation have on organizational branding and corporate reputation?; (iii) technological risk—will the new technology work, will it be safe, does it complement other technologies, and will competing technologies emerge?; (iv) organizational risk—is the right structural capital, including organizational culture and structure, available and is the necessary human capital, including the necessary mental abilities and engagement, at hand?; (v) network risk—is the right relational capital, including supply chains, in place and are there gaps?; and (vi) contextual risk—how volatile is the external environment, e.g., the institutional, policy, and regulatory framework, and financial markets?

from open source to generate incremental, radical, or transformative (systemic) improvements that sustain or alter performance trajectories. (From this perspective, innovation is perhaps best explained as change that fashions new dimensions of performance.) *In Search of Excellence* (Peters 1982) praised 43 companies for their long-term profitability and continuing innovation. The fact that many did not hold up only confirms that innovation equates with survival and fitness—this much is generally accepted.

> *Every act of creation is first of all an act of destruction.*
>
> —Picasso

But it is conventional wisdom also that public sector agencies, by contrast, merely hope for incremental improvement. Policy makers have been slow to appreciate that the public sector should build public services around requirements, rather than making them fit existing arrangements with outdated one-size-fits-all approaches. "Business as usual—if possible better" might be the motto of these near-monopolies: it is rare for innovation to be institutionalized in budgets, roles, and processes.[10] Innovation is typically seen as an optional, technological[11] extra or an added burden.

Often made from the same mold,[12] civil servants are also short of the discovery skills—viz., observing, questioning, associating, networking, and experimenting—

---

[10]The media, advocacy groups, and opposition parties, to name a few, have an interest in exposing public sector failures. (Hence, ornate if not tentacular routines have developed around performance management; inspection; anticorruption; and audit—nearly all current models of which are stacked against innovation.) Criticism forms a powerful impediment: when mishap is so much more visible and accountable, innovation is no one's job.

[11]The truth is that innovation belongs in all sectors and is only occasionally driven by technology.

[12]Psychometric tests of personnel in the public sector suggest the best part are Sensing-Judgers, notably ISTJs—Introversion, Sensing, Thinking, Judgment—according to the Myers-Briggs Type Indicator. (ISTJs normally account for about 10–14% of the population.) ISTJs are earnest, logical, organized, and trusty traditionalists who keep their lives and environments well regulated. They may be compared to worker bees that strive toward their goal. Typically reserved and serious, they earn success from thoroughness and reliability: they are detail-oriented and ponder options to decide on the factual and the present, although they generally keep to the conventional. They can shut out distractions and take a logical, practical approach to endeavors. They are able to take tough decisions that other psychological types may shirk. They take joy in upholding institutions and they value loyalty and tradition. Potential shortcomings include not seeing the forest for the trees, looking at ideas and people for the purpose of finding fault, using judgment to dismiss opinions and perspectives without really understanding them (yet rarely judging themselves), not encouraging others to experiment or innovate, having generally self-centered tendencies, and becoming slaves to rules and regulations. The unknown, the future, and the unplanned stress them. Some quip that if anyone actually invented the chain of command it was probably an ISTJ, aka "I Seldom Tell Jokes". The Keirsey Temperament Sorter dubs them "inspectors". ENTP— ·Extroversion, Intuition, Thinking, Perception—the Myers-Briggs Type Indicator associated with

that distinguish innovators from run-of-the-mill administrators. (First and foremost, innovators are good at associating: they make connections between seemingly unrelated problems and solutions, and synthesize ideas.) Immobilized by red tape in functional silos, risk-averse, when innovation happens it is despite rather than because of the way the public sector does things.[13] (Nobody ever talks of entrepreneurship as survival there; what risks are identified are financial, project, and compliance risks, not the risk of missing an opportunity. Put differently, how many senior civil servants—one might ask—reached the top as a reward for their innovations?)[14]

> *I cannot help fearing that men may reach a point where they look on every new theory as a danger, every innovation as a toilsome trouble, every social advance as a first step toward revolution, and that they may absolutely refuse to move at all.*
>
> —Alexis de Tocqueville

Except when people's lives are at stake, agreeing also that the public realm should remain legible and coherent and that the public sector should be a stabilizing force, precautionary mindsets are not an excuse. And to push service-improving and bottom-up creativity, an organization intent on innovating for the future should surely—and undoubtedly can—staff itself with a reasonable variety of personality types; where there is a will, there is a way. So, what real extenuating circumstances might the public sector plead? In the private sector, the prime reason to innovate is to increase—or at least maintain—profits to keep going in a more and more competitive global economy. In contrast, the public sector operates under an exigent set of concerns, demands, interests, pressures, and restrictions that make it a far

---

(Footnote 12 continued)

innovation, displays with one exception, viz., T (Thinking)–F (Feeling), near-opposite attributes. (ENTPs normally account for 2–5% of the population—they are rarities in the public sector.) The Keirsey Temperament Sorter refers to ENTPs as "inventors".

[13]The *Knowledge Solutions* on moral courage in organizations critique the principal features of bureaucracy, reminding us that its raison d'être is—merely if unequivocally—to execute the actions of an organization toward its purpose and mission with the greatest possible efficiency and at the least cost of resources. (Indeed, they are structured to perform their core tasks with consistency and stability and resist change or disruption of these tasks.) Specifying, formalizing, and systematizing make bureaucracies equally poor at changing from within and at learning from outside. Therefore, innovation will be self-defeated when grounded in the classic bureaucratic model of hierarchy, division of labor, and departmentalization.

[14]Innovation is directly proportional to the behavior of senior Management: it must set the context; guide the process; clearly communicate reasons; shield creative teams; appreciate distinctiveness in people and their thinking; and welcome change. The more ambitious the proposed change, the higher the priority senior Management must ascribe to it. (Because corporate governance by way of strategy review, risk management, performance evaluation, auditing, and nomination of chief executive officers can bear on innovation, some contend that boards of directors also have a role to play.)

more open—and therefore complex when not chaotic—system.[15] Not surprisingly, therefore, what innovation does come to pass is politically directed innovation instigated by crisis, organizational turnarounds initiated by agency heads, and a modicum of bottom-up innovation driven by champions.[16] The time horizons are typically short.[17] Irrespective, all endeavors must at some point secure political or bureaucratic support.

> *There is simply no way to keep up with public expectations, to get better value for money, or to solve the deep and wicked problems if you just whip the existing system harder.*
>
> —Geoff Mulgan

And yet, in the public sector too, business as usual has become business at risk: lest they forget, public sector organizations must wait on stakeholders and share-holders—perceptions, never mind evidence, that they do not create public value will dissuade the hand that feeds them and lead to destitution. More with less will not get them there either. One should never let a crisis go to waste: the ongoing global recession of 2008–2012 is putting extreme pressure on public spending as fiscal deficits soar. It is high time to lead innovation in public sector agencies to contain costs and maximize the relevance, efficiency, effectiveness, impact, and sustainability of "personalized" outcomes that address old and new public needs with more coordinated approaches. (Delivery, of course, is a function of policy, practice, and provision; fresh thinking is required there, too.) To finish, one should

---

[15]Three key differences come to mind: (i) decision point—in the private sector the primary decision unit within which innovation is weighed up is the profit center, whereas in the public sector it is more likely to be a loosely specified outcome; (ii) value—in the private sector the wellspring of innovation is ordinarily shareholder value, while in the public sector the intention is to gratify public interest; and (iii) legislation—in the public sector companies are "merely" obliged to abide by the law, but in the public sector legal constraints on organizations impose wider requirements.

[16]Predictably, the resulting approaches often have to do with organizational structure, partnerships, horizontal integration, devolution and decentralization, new business processes, and some customer-centered service improvement. (In contrast, *pace* Steve Jobs and Akio Morita, innovation in the private sector turns on heavy upfront investment in realizing the needs of customers and understanding the experiences of suppliers.)

[17]The organizations of the future, not the eternal present, manage to focus at once on four different horizons of decision making: (i) the short-term horizon of urgent problems and crises, including the pressures of media and politics—the time span of innovative tactics is days, weeks, or months; (ii) the medium-term horizon of existing programs, where implementation is normally the principal concern—the time span of incremental innovation is 1–3 years; (iii) the longer-term horizon in which new policies and strategies become ever more critical to survival and success—the time span of radical innovation is 3–20 years; and (iv) the generational (or legacy) horizon of issues that require the public sector to look far into the future—the time span of very radical innovation is 50 years (Mulgan 2007).

stress an obvious but often overlooked truth: innovation in the public sector is vital, given that it influences the welfare of myriads and is often entrusted with socially important mandates.

Taking Mammon's Goad to the Body Politic

Organizational performance, including good public service, cannot withstand indifference to the need to innovate: in both the private and public sectors, organizations that consistently generate and execute new ideas tend to be more effective at achieving their goals, whatever these may be, and to be leaders in their fields. Innovation is a concept, process, practice, and capability, better, a culture that should be germane to any kind of organization, or at least systematically pursued where it is inhibited by business as usual, aka operations, or inbred short-termism.

How then might the public sector innovate to be competent in the present and be ready for the future? How might innovation be driven more by public needs than by policy or process? Specifically, how might public sector organizations develop explicit systems to eliminate, reduce, raise, and create for value—thereby giving customers less of what they do not want (or use) and more of what they need—that visibly pervade, quicken streams of ideas, and are seen as vital? Bason (2010) sees four action areas: (i) develop innovation consciousness, (ii) build innovation capacity, (iii) leverage the power of cocreation, and (iv) strengthen leadership so there is the courage to innovate at all levels. So far, so good. But how exactly might they create cultures of innovation that wed individual, group, and organizational creativity so that they stop counting on people succeeding despite the odds and instead shift the odds? Fusing individualistic, structuralist, and—especially—interactive process perspectives, there are three inseparable and mutually reinforcing ways to take innovation in the public sector seriously.

> *Innovation is the specific instrument of entrepreneurship. It is the act that endows resources with a new capacity to create wealth.*
>
> —Peter Drucker

- **Values** Barring the odd maverick, personnel will not innovate without license: an innovative culture needs pro-innovation governance and support from the top to make sure ideas take carriage. Policies and behaviors matter: tout innovation in every message. Foster a culture of trust in which innovation is seen as natural, even ordinary, and personnel communicate freely in support: new ideas and new ways of doing things are welcome. Align incentives and rewards, fix disincentives, and recognize innovation in every part of the organization, for example, through awards, pay determination, and storytelling. Grow what works to make innovative culture self-reinforcing.

- **Resources** A resource is a source or supply from which an organization gains profit. Put innovation at the heart of strategy and equip it. Identify priority fields for innovation. Refresh human resource policies to bring out the best from innovators. Build physical surroundings that join people in concert. Exploit differences: engage spirited personnel who think creatively and see new patterns, drawing on new technologies to pull needs and possibilities together. Set up dedicated teams and networks responsible for promoting innovation. Push and pull to create pressure for innovation, also using information and communications technology. Manage stock and flows of knowledge to enrich the raw material of creative thought. Finance innovation to ensure that lack of resources is not a serious constraint. Divert a small proportion of the budget for generating, selecting, implementing, and diffusing innovation, including training. Fund for outcomes achieved, not rules adhered to. Take stock with appreciative inquiry, inspections, and audits of what is working, promising, or emerging.

The greatest mistake you can make in life is to be continually fearing you will make one.

—Elbert Hubbard

- **Processes** A business process is a collection of related, structured activities or tasks that serve a particular goal: it begins with a mission objective and ends with the achievement of that objective.[18] Endow the organization with management, operational, and supporting processes that improve knowledge brokering of ideas from generation to selection, implementation, and diffusion. Make innovation a job prerequisite and define jobs around it. Give time to think. Open up the space for ideas and draw these from people at all levels. Develop a menu of tools, methods, and approaches for trying things out, including incubators, laboratories, pathfinders, pilots, and skunk works. Tinker and try with prototypes and pilots. Evaluate experiments. Emphasize user-pull over technology-push to co-opt consumers in innovation. Collaborate with outsiders

---

[18]An efficient and effective business process has the following characteristics: (i) definability—it has clearly defined boundaries, inputs, and outputs; (ii) order—it consists of activities that are ordered according to their position in time and space; (iii) customer—its outcome has a recipient; (iv) value-adding—it adds value to the customer, either upstream or downstream, through the transformation it impels; (v) embeddedness—it is implanted in an organizational structure; a process cannot exist in itself; and (vi) cross-functionality—it regularly can, but not necessarily must, span several functions.

to help solve problems. Seek also information from the outside, for example, by benchmarking, making site visits, and participating in professional networks. Relax evidence-based procedures. Shape inducements for adoption, scaling, and diffusion by teams and networks. Be smart about risks and how they can be managed.

References

Bason C (2010) Leading public sector innovation: co-creating for a better society. Policy Press
Beinhocker E (2006) The adaptable organization. McKinsey Quarterly No 2
Morris I (2010) Why the west rules—for now: the patterns of history, and what they reveal about the future
Mulgan G (2007) Ready or not? taking innovation seriously in the public sector. NESTA
Peters T, Waterman R (1982) In search of excellence: lessons from Americas best run companies. Warner Books
Sveiby K-E, Gripenberg P, Segercrantz B, Eriksson A, Aminoff A (2009) Unintended and undesirable consequences of innovation. Paper presented at the International Society for Professional Innovation Management Conference on The Future of Innovation in Vienna, 21–24 June

Proposition 60
On Decision-Making

In a Word Decision-making is a stream of inquiry, not an event. Decision-driven organizations design and manage it as such: they match decision-making styles to appropriate techniques and, wherever possible, encourage parties to play roles rife with dissent and debate; decision rights are part of the design.

Decisions, Decisions

A decision is the cognitive process of choosing between possible actions in a situation of uncertainty. By definition, the steps entailed lead to a final choice, that is, the selection of a sequence of activities among several alternative scenarios, based on values and preferences, purportedly resulting in a more optimal outcome.

In view of the resources organizations pool, decision-making permeates all dimensions of corporate life, be they (i) strategic—related to the design of a long-term plan of action to achieve a particular goal, (ii) organizational—related to the way different parts and aspects of a group are arranged to deliver the goal, or (iii) operational—related to the way individuals and groups work on a daily basis to

© Asian Development Bank 2017
O. Serrat, *Knowledge Solutions*, DOI 10.1007/978-981-10-0983-9_60

accomplish specific results toward the goal.[1] It follows that decision-making is a conditioning ingredient of success in any venture. The stakes are high: organizations that make better, faster, and more effective decisions—both small, routine, and big, one-off decisions—will outrun competitors and outshine peers. Therefore, one might expect that organizations would put copious options on the table and invite sufficient evaluation to make certain the best choice emerges.

On Decision-Making Techniques and Styles ...

Inevitably, given the pressing omnipresence of decision situations, the world of organizations is not short of techniques. The main clusters articulate decision-making models, help choose between options, make financial decisions, improve decision-making, organize group decision-making, surface values and preferences, and decide whether to go ahead. Then again, whether the tools at hand are leveraged depends on styles that—born of the typology of the organization and associated configuration[2]—range from autocratic to unanimity-based decision-making, each with its raison d'être and related pros and cons (Figs. 60.1 and 60.2).

... And What Typically Determines Their Use

Ten primary criteria shape decision-making. These comprise the decision environment[3] that may influence the decision style, the complexity of the decision being made, the value of the decision's desired outcome, alternative scenarios that have the potential to lead to the desired outcome, the information available to support the decision-making process and cognitive biases to its selection and interpretation, the quality requirements of the decision, the personalities of those involved in decision-making, the time available to conduct the decision-making process, the

---

[1]It follows that problems from suboptimal decision-making—since no organization is perfect—will occur in the same areas: (i) strategy—for example, where decisions are made with too little regard to those who are affected by them; (ii) organization—for instance, where there are overlapping responsibilities between decision-making groups, leading to lack of direction or duplication of effort; and (iii) operations—such as where implementation can prove difficult due to inconsistent factual analysis.

[2]Mintzberg (1989) circumscribed seven basic types: entrepreneurial, machine, diversified, professional, innovative, missionary, and political. (Undoubtedly, one can find elements of all these forms in any particular organization.)

[3]The decision environment would be a function of an organization's organizational context, organizational knowledge, inter- and intraorganizational relationships, and the external environment.

Using Decision -Making Models
- The Kepner-Tregoe Matrix—making unbiased, risk-assessed decisions
- Observe–Orient–Decide–Act Loops—understanding the decision cycle
- The Recognition-Primed Decision Process—making good decisions under pressure
- The Vroom–Yetton–Jago Decision Model—deciding how to decide

Choosing Between Options
- The Analytic Hierarchy Process—choosing by weighing up many subjective factors
- Conjoint Analysis—measuring buyer preferences
- Decision Trees—choosing by projecting expected outcomes
- The Futures Wheel—identifying future consequences of a change
- Grid Analysis—making a choice balancing many factors
- Paired Comparison Analysis—working out relative importances
- Pareto Analysis—using the 80:20 rule to prioritize
- The Quantitative Strategic Planning Matrix—choosing the best strategic way forward

Making Financial Decisions
- Break-Even Analysis—determining when a product becomes profitable
- Cash Flow Forecasting—testing the viability of a project
- Cost–Benefit Analysis—evaluating quantitatively whether to follow a course of action
- Net Present Value and Internal Rate of Return—deciding whether to invest

Improving Decision Making
- Blindspot Analysis—avoiding common fatal flaws in decision making
- Critical Thinking—developing the skills for successful thinking
- Decision Making: Cautious or Courageous?—understanding risk preference and making better decisions
- Decision Making Under Uncertainty—making the best choice with the information available
- The Ladder of Inference—avoiding jumping to conclusions
- Linear Programming—optimizing limited resources
- Monte Carlo Analysis—bringing uncertainty and risk into forecasting
- Pros and Cons—listing the advantages and disadvantages of each option
- Reactive Decision Making—making good decisions under pressure
- Satisficing—examining alternatives only until an acceptable one is found
- Six Thinking Hats—looking at a decision from all points of view

Organizing Group Decision Making
- Avoiding Groupthink—avoiding fatal flaws in group decision making
- The Delphi Technique—achieving well thought-through consensus among experts
- Hartnett's Consensus-Oriented Decision-Making Model—developing solutions collectively
- Multi-Voting—choosing fairly between many options
- The Nominal Group Technique—prioritizing issues and projects to achieve consensus
- Organizing Team Decision Making—reaching consensus for better decisions
- The Stepladder Technique—making better group decisions

Surfacing Values and Preferences
- The Foursquare Protocol—learning to manage ethical decisions
  What Are Your Values?—deciding what is most important in life
- Spiral Dynamics—understanding how people's values may affect their decision making

Deciding Whether to Go Ahead
- Force Field Analysis—analyzing pressures for and against change
- Go-No-Go Decisions—deciding whether to proceed
- Impact Analysis—identifying the unexpected consequences of a decision
- Plus, Minus, Interesting—weighing the pros and cons of a decision
- Risk Analysis—evaluating and managing risks
- "What If" Analysis—making decisions by exploring scenarios

Fig. 60.1 Decision-making techniques. *Source* Author

Autocratic	• Instantaneous; relied upon in times of crisis • Quality of decision may suffer; less likely to be accepted
Consultative	• Generates more ideas and information • Takes longer; leader still holds final say; fewer chances of acceptance and commitment by others
Minority Rule	• Very fast; decision by "experts" • Alternative points of view not necessarily taken into account; not representative of majority
Majority Rule	• Applicable to any group size; most people are familiar with this procedure • Win-lose mentality; lack of commitment by losers; issues become personalized
Consensus	• Thoroughly critiqued decision based on common principles and values; backed by all members; elicits strong commitment • Time-consuming; requires mature populations; difficult in large groups; can beget lowest common denominator decisions
Unanimity	• Most comfortable; based on common principles and values; elicits strongest commitment • Near-impossible to achieve with more than two persons

Fig. 60.2   Decision-making styles. *Source* Author

necessary level of commitment to or acceptance of the decision, and the impact on valued relationships that the choice of decision style may have.

> *It's not hard to make decisions when you know what your values are.*
>
> —Roy Disney

Sure enough, several of these criteria can hold at the same time and amplify one another. Assuming organizations do not eschew problem analysis to rush decision-making—a big, hairy, and audacious hypothesis,[4] that, four recurring themes regularly conspire to warp decisions. They have to do with bounded rationality, cognitive bias, personality, and free will. First, the information at hand, the information-processing ability of the mind, and what time is available bear strongly on decision-making. (Bounded rationality does not often conduce optimal decisions by "maximizers;" again and again, "satisficers" reach for what solution is

---

[4]Manifestly, a problem should first be analyzed with effective questions so that the data and information gathered can afterward inform a course of action.

good enough.) Second, cognitive biases creep into decision-making processes. (A select list includes anchoring and adjustment, attribution asymmetry, choice-supportive bias, framing bias, groupthink, incremental decision-making and escalating commitment, optimism or wishful thinking, premature termination of search for evidence, inertia, recency, repetition bias, role fulfillment, selective perception, selective search for evidence, source credibility bias, and underestimates of uncertainty and the illusion of control.) Third, personality profiles color cognitive styles. (Psychological traits revealed by the Myers–Briggs Type Indicator along four bipolar dimensions—extroversion and introversion, sensing and intuiting, thinking and feeling, and judging and perceiving—correlate with decision-making styles. In any organization, the predominance of one psychological type will sway approaches to decision-making. What is more, national or cross-cultural peculiarities exist across entire societies.) Fourth, advances in social neuroscience increasingly question whether and in what sense rational agents exercise control over their actions or decisions, thereby testing the easy presumption of free will. What hopes, after that, are there for better decision-making?

Toward Decision-Driven Organizations

"It is hard to imagine a more stupid or more dangerous way of making decisions than by putting those decisions in the hands of people who pay no price for being wrong," Thomas Sowell reasons. Indeed, many organizations treat decision-making as an event, the performance of which is more often than not the prerogative of a few—not necessarily best equipped—where there is obdurate proclivity for formal authority.[5]

---

[5]In the twenty-first century, many still assume the lines and boxes on an organizational chart are a key determinant of performance. Hierarchy is passé: Hayek (1945) understood that as early as 1945. Rather, an organization's structure should be in tune with its decisions with consideration to quality, speed, yield, and effort. Blenko et al. (2010) identify 10 drivers that may undermine or support effective decisions, for assessment using a four-point Likert scale from strongly disagree to strongly agree. They are (i) structure (our structure helps—rather than hinders—the decisions most critical to our success); (ii) roles (individuals understand their responsibilities and accountabilities in our most critical decisions); (iii) processes (our processes are designed to produce effective, timely decisions and action); (iv) information (the people in critical decision roles have the data and information they need when and how they need them); (v) measures and incentives (our measures and incentives focus people on making and executing effective decisions); (vi) priorities (people understand their priorities well enough to be able to make and execute the decisions they face); (vii) decision style (we make decisions in a style that is effective, for example, that appropriately balances inclusiveness with momentum); (viii) people (we put our best people in the jobs where they can have the biggest decision impact); (ix) behaviors (our leaders at all levels consistently demonstrate effective decision behaviors); and (x) culture (our culture reinforces prompt, effective decisions and action throughout the organization).

> *Most discussions of decision making assume that only senior executives make decisions or that only senior executives' decisions matter. This is a dangerous mistake.*
>
> —Peter Drucker

To enrich decisions in the majority of decision-making styles, two related concerns should be concurrently raised and addressed:

- Quoting Isaac Azimov, "It is change, continuing change, inevitable change, that is the dominant factor in society today. No sensible decision can be made any longer without taking into account not only the world as it is, but the world as it will be ..." Too often, decision-making is considered an exercise in advocacy; it is, rather, a process of inquiry. How might decision-making encompass the larger organizational context, organizational knowledge, inter- and intraorganizational relationships, and external environment that ultimately determine the success of a selected course of action?
- Decision rights[6] are a vital but insufficiently understood component of organizational design. Who is empowered to make what types of decisions has profound effects on day-to-day performance; and yet, allocating decision rights to maximize that can be controversial and therefore difficult. To deepen the decision-making process, one should assign single point responsibility and accountability along a more delineated continuum of inputs, outputs, and outcomes. Where should decision rights be lodged in an organization and can one describe and assign more precise decision-making roles?

On Decision-Making as a Process

Decision-making is where thinking and doing overlap. For that to happen profitably in an organization, a decision must be logically consistent with what the parties to it know, want, and agree they can do. Nothing, then, could do decision-making a greater disservice than to treat it as a single, isolated event, not the clearly defined process it inherently is or rather should be.

---

[6]The term is analogous to property right, namely, the exclusive authority to determine how a resource is used. When decision-makers themselves do not feel the true cost of decisions, incremental poor even if small choices can compound into severely negative outcomes. By attributing unequivocal ownership of decision-making privileges, unambiguous responsibility can be ascribed for what decisions are made. This means that decision-makers can both reap the benefits of a good choice and pay the price of a bad one. Allowing a person's decision rights to fructify based on how well he or she exercises them makes better sense than letting privileges accumulate based on rank or seniority. The key notion is that decision rights should be earned, not granted, yet reviewed and updated routinely.

Helpfully, David Garvin and Michael Roberto compare advocacy and inquiry approaches to decision-making. Advocacy tends to push a single solution. To make a compelling case for the proposal they hope to sell, proponents assert positives and downplay negatives; they offer no alternatives—instead, a go-no-go decision on the option is forced. The pitfalls of advocacy are many: reliance on one solution precludes the chance to explore alternatives; personalities come into play and disagreements grow fractious, probably antagonistic; behind-the-scenes maneuvering comes into play; the solution inevitably produces winners and losers— losers, to the extent they can, continue to fight the decision in the execution phase, thereby stretching decision cycle time.[7] In contrast, the goal of inquiry is to reach agreement on a course of action. Because people hold diverse interests, inquiry makes convictions visible for testing; generates multiple alternatives; evaluates feasibility according to well-defined criteria using a range of techniques; fosters collaboration to work through differences of ideas, concepts, and assumptions; and helps arrive at an agreeable solution. Rather than suppress dissent and debate, inquiry encourages constructive conflict, consideration, and closure with perceived fairness; patently, it produces decisions of higher quality—decisions that not only advance an organization's objectives but are also reached in a timely manner and can be implemented effectively.

> *Painting is something that takes place among the colors, and ... one has to leave them alone completely, so that they can settle the matter among themselves. Their intercourse: this is the whole of painting. Whoever meddles, arranges, injects his human deliberation, his wit, his advocacy, his intellectual agility in any way, is already disturbing and clouding their activity.*
>
> —Rainer Maria Rilke

On Decision Rights

Marcia Blenko, Michael Mankins, and Paul Rogers make out six steps in which to (re) organize around decisions. First, organizations should know which decisions have a disproportionate impact on organizational performance—a decision inventory is a prerequisite to that.[8] Second, they should determine where those decisions should happen. Third, they should organize the structure of decision nodes around sources of

---

[7] Decision cycle refers to the continual use of mental and physical processes exercised by an entity to reach and implement decisions.

[8] Obviously, these do not all reside at the top. Offices and departments, teams too for that matter, ought to develop then winnow their own lists of critical decisions to ascertain the value at stake and the degree of attention required.

value. Fourth, they should figure out what level of authority decision-makers need, regardless of status, and give it to them. Fifth, they should align other parts of the organizational system, such as processes, data, and information—including their flows, measures, and incentives—to support decision-making and execution. Sixth, they should help managers develop the skills and behaviors necessary to make decisions and translate them into action quickly and well.

> *The man who is denied the opportunity of taking decisions of importance begins to regard as important the decisions he is allowed to take.*
>
> —C. Northcote Parkinson

   Decision rights are the coin of the realm. In a small organization, an entrepreneur might know all about his or her business and make every decision with minimal supplementary data and information. However, as the scale and scope of operations grow, an entrepreneur will find it more difficult to decide. In a world of large organizations, one solution to this problem is to convey data and information to whoever possesses decision rights; another is to grant decision rights to whoever holds data and information.[9] To strike a balance, modern organizations turn to both solutions[10]: the falling prices of information and communications technology have cut the costs of transmission and the growingly intense use of these technologies in many organizations confirms they convey more data and information to those with decision rights; at the same time, the common reliance on teams and other col-laboration mechanisms implies that organizations are decentralizing decision rights. Naturally, the mix of solutions—and the centralization or decentralization of rela-tionships it implies—is unique to the organization: yet, it is still a rare organization —especially in the public sector—that actually studies the optimal allocation of its stock of decision rights and acts on that knowledge to reap the fullest advantage.

> *If we can agree that the economic problem of society is mainly one of rapid adaptation to changes in the particular circumstances of time and place, it would seem to follow that the ultimate decisions must be left to the people who are familiar with these circumstances, who know directly of the relevant changes and of the*

---

[9]The costs associated with the first approach stem from (possibly inaccurate) transmission of data and information from the source to the decision-maker and what delays the process occasions. Those of the second approach owe to the risk that data and information are not necessarily aligned with the objectives and motivations of the individual to whom the decision rights are now given.

[10]Those in favor of centralization usually contend it ensures uniformity in standards, promotes coherence and coordination, minimizes duplication, builds economies of scale, and reduces inequalities. Champions of decentralization think it enhances autonomy and empowerment, aug-ments participation, and fosters creativity and innovation. It stands to reason that one should even out the two.

> *resources immediately available to meet them. We cannot expect that this problem will be solved by first communicating all this knowledge to a central board which, after integrating all knowledge, issues its orders. We must solve it by some form of decentralization.*
>
> —Friedrich Hayek

There is more: decentralization is one thing; a more differentiated chain of deliverables for decision-making is another. Establishing what helps pinpoint who and demarcate how. Rogers and Blenko (2006) offered early guidance before the last article cited: advertising a tool of Bain & Company, Inc., they further untangle the decision-making process by identifying various activities that must occur for a decision to be made well. The name of the tool is RAPID: each letter in the acronym stands for an activity associated with decision-making. To begin, someone must "recommend" that a decision be made. Next, "input" will likely be required to inform the decision. Down the road, depending on corporate governance arrangements, one or several persons will formally "agree" to a recommendation before one or several persons wield the authority to "decide". Subsequently, someone must, of course, "perform" the decision, meaning, execute it. The acronym does not suggest a strict sequence in which the five activities must occur, certainly in the preparatory stages: reality is iterative and RAPID merely happens to be a handy mnemonic. (This writer, for instance, believes that inputs should precede any recommendation, not just follow it, and may actually be required throughout the process.)[11] In addition, agents may be assigned more than one activity. (The person recommending the decision may eventually be tasked with carrying it out.)

Paraphrasing Albert Camus, an organization's value is the sum of the decisions it makes and executes. For sure, even good decisions such as may have been reached with RAPID occasionally engender bad outcomes. But redistributing decision rights because of a bad outcome—even though they were well allocated in the first place —will not help and could make matters worse. One should not confuse a particular outcome with the process itself.

---

[11]One might say that every decision follows from previous decisions and both enables and prevents other future decisions. Consequently, inputs will be required before, during, and after a decision.

References

Blenko M, Mankins M, Rogers P (June 2010) The decision-driven organization. Harvard Business Review 54–62

Hayek F (1945) The use of knowledge in society. American Economic Review 35(4):519–530

Mintzberg H (1989) Mintzberg on management: inside our strange world of organizations. Simon and Schuster

Rogers P, Blenko M (January 2006) Who has the D? how clear decision roles enhance organizational performance. Harvard Business Review 53–61

Part III
Collaboration Mechanisms

Proposition 61
Building Communities of Practice

In a Word Communities of practice are groups of like-minded, interacting people who filter, amplify, invest and provide, convene, build, and learn and facilitate to ensure more effective creation and sharing of knowledge in their domain.

What are They?

According to Etienne Wenger, communities of practice are groups of people who share a passion for something they do and who interact regularly to learn how to do it better. Communities of practice define themselves along three dimensions: what they are about, how they function, and what capabilities they produce. Table 61.1 summarizes their principal attributes. Each community of practice has a unique domain, community, and practice (and the support it requires).[1] But, in connecting and collecting, communities of practice share the following common characteristics:

---

[1]The *domain* defines the area of shared inquiry. The *community* comprises the relationships among members and the sense of belonging. The *practice* is the body of knowledge, methods, stories, cases, tools, and documents. The goal of community design is to bring out the community's own internal direction, character, and energy.

© Asian Development Bank 2017

O. Serrat, *Knowledge Solutions*, DOI 10.1007/978-981-10-0983-9_61

Table 61.1 Communities of practice: what are they?

What are communities of practice?	What do communities of practice do?	How do communities of practice operate?
• Communities of practice share a domain • They have a desire to share work-related knowledge • They break down communication barriers • They have a passion for learning • They are self-selected and gain value from their membership	• Communities of practice provide a means to exchange data, information, and knowledge freely • They provide an informal, welcoming social environment • They provide a means for relationship building and networking • They populate and reference their knowledge network workspace	• Communities of practice are in continuous communication • They hold annual and quarterly gatherings • They arrange monthly teleconferences • They have daily or weekly informal interaction • They regularly access their communication platform

What is the value of communities of practice?	Community of practice success factors
• Communities of practice identify, create, store, share, and use knowledge • They decrease the learning curve of new employees • They enable professional development • They reduce rework and prevent reinvention of the wheel • They permit faster problem solving and response time to needs and inquiries • They illuminate good practice • They spawn new ideas for products and services • They enable accelerated learning • They connect learning to action • They make for organizational performance improvement	• **Strategic relevance**—the strategic relevance of the domain, which lets the community find a legitimate place in the organization • **Domain**—directly related to real work • **Membership**—experts are involved • **Activities**—relevant to the members and the domain, with the right rhythm and mix • **Governance**—clear roles and expectations • **Facilitation**—a dedicated, passionate, skillful, and well-respected coordinator • **Culture**—a consistent attitude to sharing and collaboration • **Incentives**—a desire to participate • **Reward and recognition**—the organizational environment is adapted to support participation • **Information technology**—an appropriate medium of communication that adds value and helps deliver work programs • **Time**—members are given time and encouraged to participate • **Longevity**—needed both for communication and to build up trust, rapport, and a true sense of community • **Measurement**—how do we know a community of practice is successful?

Source Author

- They are peer-to-peer collaborative networks.
- They are driven by the willing participation of their members.
- They are focused on learning and building capacity.
- They are engaged in sharing knowledge, developing expertise, and solving problems.

Topics, Focal Areas, and Sample Technical Features
of a Hypothetical Community of Practice

Table 61.2 lists the topics for interaction of a hypothetical community of practice in monitoring and evaluation and the areas that it might focus on in each case. On each topic for interaction, the members of a community of practice would ask one another

- What challenges do you face?
- Are the challenges you face the same or different from mine?
- What resources do you have that can be shared?
- What ideas do you have about how to move ahead?
- How can we be mutually supportive?

Table 61.3 is the menu of combinations of some technical features that might support specific goals of that community.

Design and Management

To continuously design and manage a community of practice, members typically follow the 5D model depicted in the below figure (Lave and Wenger 1991). It involves

Table 61.2 A community of practice in monitoring and evaluation—topics and focal areas

	Formulating monitoring and evaluation policy	Putting in place a monitoring and evaluation framework	Planning and designing an evaluation	Conducting an evaluation	Using evaluation findings
Relationship building					
Collaboration mechanisms					
Knowledge sharing and learning					
Knowledge capture and storage					

Source Author

Table 61.3 A community of practice in monitoring and evaluation—sample technical features

Relationship building	Collaboration mechanisms	Knowledge sharing and learning	Knowledge capture and storage
• Partnerships • Member networking profiles • Member directory with "relationship-focused" data fields • Subgroups defined by administrators or that allow members to self-join • Online meetings • Online discussions	• Action learning sets • Project management • Task management • Document collaboration • File version tracking • Instant messaging • Individual and group calendaring • Web conferencing • Online meetings • Online discussions	• Stories • Peer assists • After-action reviews and retrospects • Structured databases • Idea banks • Visiting speakers • Expert database and search tools • Announcements • Web conferencing • Online meetings • Online discussions • Website links	• Exit interviews • Member profiles • How-to guides • Slideshows • E-learning tools • Visiting speakers • Assessments • Web logs • Web conferencing • Online meetings • Online discussions • Website links

Source Author

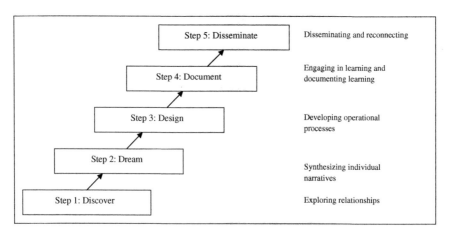

Fig. 5D model for designing and managing sustainable communities of practice. *Source* Author

- **Discovering**—exploring relationships to the community through individual narratives.
- **Dreaming**—synthesizing individual narratives into a community story centered on joint purpose and mutual engagement.
- **Designing**—developing operational processes for the community.
- **Documenting**—engaging in learning and documenting knowledge.
- **Disseminating**—disseminating and reconnecting the community's learning.

Building a Community of Practice

The members of a community of practice will need to plan and ask themselves key questions on *strategy*

- What change(s) in the work we do will take place in the next 3–6 months because of the community of practice?
- Why is the community the best way of bringing about this change?
- What is the one thing that I need to do next week to facilitate the community?

Sample *domain*-related questions will include

- What specific topics do we want to address in the community of practice in the next 3–6 months?
- Why are these topics relevant to our organization?
- What kind of influence do we want to have on our organization?
- Who will assume leadership in promoting our domain?

Sample *community*-related questions will include

- Who will be the members of the community of practice in the next 3–6 months?
- How can ownership and management of the community of practice be fostered?
- How often will the community meet?[2] How will the members connect?
- How can the community balance the needs of various members?
- How will members deal with conflict?
- How will new members be introduced into the community?

Sample *practice*-related questions will include

- How should we identify, create, store, share, and use knowledge?
- How should we evaluate the effectiveness of our community of practice in the next 3–6 months?
- How should we ensure ongoing connection between the members?

---

[2]The initial members could plan an inaugural physical meeting, to be followed by annual meetings. Physical meetings for a virtual platform seem counter-intuitive but the experience of many communities of practice shows that to be a key success factor.

- How should we deal with conflicts between our own work and community work?

  A sample *support*-related question will be

- What support do we need to be successful in achieving changes to our work through the community of practice?

Communication Platforms[3]

An appropriate medium of communication is critical to the success of communities of practice.[4] It should be monitored continuously. The box below suggests what its main attributes might be. Specifically, the communication platform would

- Serve as an ongoing learning venue for practitioners who share similar goals, interests, and concerns.
- Help connect members to the right people and provide a platform for rapid responses to individual inquiries from members.
- Provide news of community activities and events to members.
- Develop, capture, and transfer good practices on specific topics by stimulating active sharing of knowledge.
- Promote partnership arrangements with interested knowledge hubs and other networks.
- Influence development outcomes by promoting greater and better-informed dialogue.
- Promote innovative approaches to address specific challenges.

Box: Communication Platforms for Communities of Practice—Architecture

Contents

- Home page: relevant information and news, latest news on the progress of related activities and projects, ongoing activities and online discussions
- About the community: background information, expected outcomes and impact

---

[3]Before the advent of the internet, the operations of communities of practice were defined by face-to-face meetings in specific locales. Today, they can span a variety of contexts and geographies. With Web 2.0, technology will continue to change what it means to be part of a community. The cost of entry is lower than ever and practitioners often straddle two or three online communities. Yet, to draw value, they must contribute value. From now on, communities of practice will have to pay more attention to harnessing the commitment and energy of members.

[4]Needless to say, the medium of communication must have connectivity. Members should not experience technical difficulties. Queries should be addressed by a secretariat. The communication platform should also provide a simple user manual and other help tools.

- News and announcements: news archives, email newsletter archives
- Library (repository of relevant documents and tools)
- Discussions (online discussions on particular topics of interest)
- Members: list of members with background information and email addresses
- Photo gallery
- Links to other websites
- Help (information on how to use the site and how to get assistance)
- Contact us

Tools

- Search facility
- Email this page/notify members of this page
- Download and print this page
- Optional: online chat facility, an events calendar

Look-and-Feel

- Lively and dynamic
- Friendly and accessible
- Professional and credible

Tagline

- A memorable phrase to brand the communication platform and awareness of it

Optional Orientations

- Rooms for working groups, face-to-face events, or special-interest topics
- Business opportunities and advertisements
- Podcasts/webcasts
- Web logs
- Wikis
- Enhanced member profiles including an individual member's website bookmarks and web log

Source Author

Reference

Lave J, Wenger E (1991) Situated learning: legitimate peripheral participation. Cambridge
    University Press

Proposition 62
Action Learning

In a Word Action learning is a structured method that enables small groups to work regularly and collectively on complicated problems, take action, and learn as individuals and as a team while doing so.

Rationale

Conventional approaches to learning hinge on the presentation of knowledge and skills. Then again, knowledge is revealed through methods of questioning amid risk, confusion, and opportunity. Reginald Revans, the originator of action learning, recommended that one should keep away from experts with prefabricated answers.[1] Rather, people should become aware of their lack of knowledge and be prepared to explore their ignorance with suitable questions and help from others: finding the right questions rather than the right answers is important, and it is one's perception

---

[1]Revans distinguished cleverness, i.e., knowledge, and wisdom. He described the formula $L = P + Q$ where L is learning, P is programmed, i.e., taught or read, knowledge, and Q is questioning to create insight. Q uses four major questions: where? who? when? what?; and three minor questions: why? how many? how much? From this, he demonstrated that powerful learning comes from people learning with and from others.

© Asian Development Bank 2017

O. Serrat, *Knowledge Solutions*, DOI 10.1007/978-981-10-0983-9_62

Fig. 62.1 Learning from experience. *Source* Author

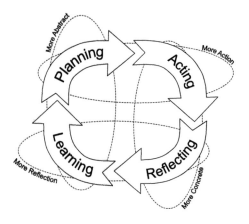

of a problem, one's evaluation of what is to be gained by solving it, and one's estimation of the resources available to solve it that supply the springs of human action.[2] Figure 62.1 depicts the cycle of learning.

Definition

Action learning is an educational process by which a person studies his or her own actions and experience to improve performance. Put simply, it is about solving problems and getting things done. In action learning, a small group of 5–8 persons (called action learning set) meets regularly for a day or half a day over at least 6 months and works collectively on a problem faced in ongoing practice.[3] The action learning set helps a "presenter" work on a problem through supportive but challenging questioning. It encourages a deeper understanding of the issues involved, a reflective reassessment of the problem, and an exploration of ways forward. (Action learning requires that actions be agreed at the end of each meeting.) By so doing, it provides a structured way of working that provide the discipline we often need to learn from what we do and improve practice as a result.

---

[2]High-level questions theorize, reflect, and hypothesize. Low-level questions seek factual answers and tend to converge in that they have correct answers. High-level questions require people to make connections and to engage in application, analysis, interpretation, or evaluation of ideas. Examples include: Are you in agreement with the group's answer? What do you think would happen if …? What is the difference between … and …? How are … and … similar? Why do you believe these differences or similarities occur? Low-level questions require people to recall information that has been presented or to retrieve information from memory.

[3]Revans believed that those best able to help in developing the self are those comrades in adversity who also struggle to understand themselves.

Applications

The most common applications of action learning are in professional and managerial learning and development, namely

- A work-based project or program in which set members are involved and for which they have a level of responsibility and are therefore able to realistically influence by their actions.
- An issue that concerns how set members operate in their work context, and one that they wish to improve and that could benefit from the support and challenge of the other members.

Action learning is not useful if the task that a set member is working on is a technical puzzle with a limited number of correct solutions. In such instances, it is better to tackle that the issue through consultation with experts, research, or training.

Benefits

Action learning sets have been used by civil and nongovernment organizations. They

- Increase awareness and enable individuals to identify personal development challenges.
- Develop self-confidence and readiness to take responsibility and initiative.
- Help people relate to and communicate and network with others more effectively.
- Provide structured peer support.
- Enable more disciplined ways of working in powerful teams.
- Enable individuals and teams to learn while working.[4]
- Build leadership competencies.
- Develop systems thinking, creativity, flexibility, and problem-solving skills.
- Foster the emergence of corporate cultures that can handle change and learn.
- Support innovation.

Still, for organizations to really feel the benefits of action learning there must be will to support participation in sets and respect for their outcomes. The disciplines and behaviors that encourage action learning are those of a learning organization. Peter Senge catalogs the attributes of learning organizations as personal mastery, shared vision, mental models, team learning, and systems thinking (the fifth discipline that integrates the other four).

---

[4]Learning can take place at several levels. They include learning about the wider organization of which the set members are a part, learning about group processes, learning about the issue being presented, learning about oneself, the way one works and interacts with issues and people, and learning how to learn.

Key Principles of Action Learning

The key principles of action learning are that

- Learning begins with not knowing.
- Individuals and groups who assume responsibility stand the best chance of taking actions that will make a difference.
- Learning involves both programmed knowledge and questioning insight. Learning should be greater than the rate of change.

Process

Action learning brings together small groups of participants with the following intentions. Figure 62.2 depicts the action learning process as cyclical: it begins at the top of the diagram and moves round systematically, giving each set member the opportunity to present a problem and comment on others.

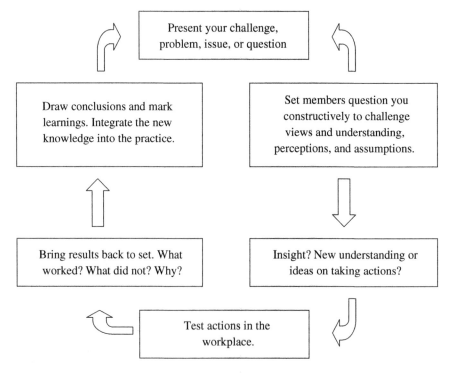

Fig. 62.2 The action learning process. *Source* Author

A typical set meeting might run like this[5]:

- Before the meeting, each set member thinks about the work-based issues he or she wishes to bring to the set.
- Set members agree to set aside the necessary time for the meeting. It should be held where they will be free from distraction.
- The facilitator might remind set members of the ground rules established during the formation of the set and may recap the key principles of the methodology.
- The set members check-in and those who had an opportunity to explore their issue in the previous set report to the others on actions taken since the last meeting.
- One of the set members is given airtime for about 1 hour. This begins with the member taking 5–10 uninterrupted minutes to outline the work-based issue that he or she is bringing to the set members. Then, the other members ask questions of clarification, move into reflective and analytical questions, and towards the end question future action.
- During this process, the facilitator may sometimes "stop" the set to raise awareness on matters of process, for example if set members are giving advice packaged as questions.
- At the end of the airtime, the set member presenting the issue provides feedback on how he or she experienced the process and what learning took place. Set members also offer observations and learnings on both process and content.
- The process of airtime is repeated for as many set members as possible in the time available. (This is normally two members in a half-day or four in a full day meeting).
- The meeting may conclude with the completion of an action review sheet that aims to capture key learnings and action plans from the meeting. The logistics of the next meeting are also agreed.

Facilitation

A significant aspect of action learning is the "unlearning" of all-too-common habits of jumping from problem to solution and offering advice. For this, it is necessary to adhere to a disciplined methodology of good listening and questioning. A skilled and experienced facilitator can help to achieve this. Specifically, a facilitator would help create safe space for honest discussion, remind set members of the methodology, model helpful questioning, ensure that the questioning moves around the action learning cycle at an appropriate pace, draw attention to issues of process, and act as timekeeper.

---

[5]This section draws from BOND Guidance Notes No. 5.1. (Pay 2004).

Tips

Action learning is most effective when the commitment is voluntary. It should also focus on real-life, practice-related problems that are open-ended in nature and do not have a right or wrong answer. Importantly, action learning sets should be clear about the objective; engage the support of management; decide on selection criteria for set members; commit regular time; set dates for meetings and workshops; make sure there is some energy; be honest with themselves and others; respect others and their viewpoint; learn to listen; ask helpful questions[6]; refrain from giving advice; follow the action learning cycle; give individual airtime to others; take responsibility for their actions; and decide early on how the program will be evaluated, who will be involved, and how the results and future actions will be communicated more widely.

Reference

Pay C (2004) Action learning sets (Guidance Notes No. 5.1). BOND, London

---

[6]Examples include: What other questions does this question raise for us? What is it that we do not understand about this situation? What would someone who had a very different set of beliefs than we do say about this situation? Why did you draw those conclusions? How does x affect y? In your opinion, which is best, x or y? And why? What are the strengths and weakness of …?

Proposition 63
Appreciative Inquiry

In a Word Appreciative inquiry is the process of facilitating positive change in organizations. Its basic assumption is uncomplicated: every organization has something that
works well. Appreciative inquiry is therefore an exciting generative approach to
organizational development. At a higher level, it is also a way of being and seeing.

Rationale

Most organizational change processes are based on problem-solving. We ask "what
is the problem?" but in doing so focus energy on what we want less of. We then
work to fix things (and keep finding problems). However, organizations change in
the direction in which they inquire. Appreciative inquiry is based on the following
propositions:

- Organizations are not machines.
- Organizations are a social reality—that reality is co-constructed.
- Important organizational processes, e.g., communicating, decision-making, and
  managing conflict, hinge on how the people involved make meaning out of their
  interactions, not so much on the skillful application of techniques.
- Endeavors to identify or develop the right formula for successful change are
  often misguided—one cannot treat social reality as if it were objective.

© Asian Development Bank 2017

O. Serrat, *Knowledge Solutions*, DOI 10.1007/978-981-10-0983-9_63

Every organization has something that works right, even if only in small quantities. Hence, it might be easier to foster organizational effectiveness by focusing on what one wants more (not what one wants less of). Getting people to inquire into the best examples of what they want more of creates a momentum toward the creation of more positive organizations. Of necessity, such inquiries should be appreciative, applicable, provocative, and collaborative.[1] To sum up, an organization that tries to discover what is best in itself will find more and more that is good: its discoveries will help build a future where the best becomes more common.

Definition

Appreciative inquiry is a relatively new form of action research that originated in the United States in the mid-1980s and is now being used around the world. It studies the positive attributes of organizations to create new conversations among people as they work together for organizational renewal. It involves in its broadest focus, the systematic discovery of what gives life to a human system when it is most alive, most effective, and most capable in environmental, economic, societal, political, and technological terms. It involves, in a central way, the art and practice of asking questions that strengthen a system's capacity to apprehend, anticipate, and heighten positive potential. It is based on two assumptions: first, organizations always move in the direction of the questions their members ask and the things they talk about; second, energy for positive change is created when organizations engage continually in remembering and analyzing circumstances when they were at their best rather than focusing on problems and how they can be solved. The approach invites organizations to spend time creating a common vision for their desired future and developing the images and language to bring that vision to life.

Process

Appreciative inquiry is usually worked out using a 4D Cycle[2]:

- **Discover** People talk to one another, often via structured interviews, to discover the times when their organization is at its best. These stories are told as richly as possible.

---

[1]Appreciation means looking for the positive core of an organization and seeking to use that as a foundation for future growth. Applicability means that inquiry is grounded in stories of what has actually taken place in the past and is therefore essentially practical. Provocation means inviting people to take some risks in the way they imagine the future and to redesign their organization to bring that about. Collaboration means involving the whole organization, or a representative cross-section of it, so that all voices can be heard and everyone's contribution valued.

[2]The 4-D Cycle is not the only way of thinking about the process of appreciative inquiry. Some favor the 4-I Model of initiation, inquiry, imagination, and innovation.

- **Dream** The dream phase is commonly run as a large group conference with the help of facilitators. People are encouraged to envision the organization as though the peak moments identified in the discover phase were the norm rather than the exception.
- **Design** A team is empowered to go away and design ways to create the organization dreamed in the large group conference.
- **Deliver** The final phase delivers the dream and the new design. It is one of experimentation and improvisation. Teams are formed to follow up on the design elements and continue the appreciative process. This phase may itself contain more small-scale appreciative inquiries into specific aspects of organizational life).

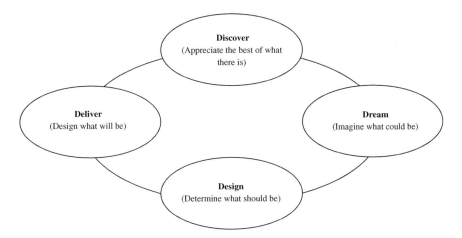

Fig. The 4D cycle of appreciative inquiry. *Source* Author

Table. A generic appreciative interview questionnaire	Think of a peak experience or high point in your work or experience in your organization
	In that experience, think about the things you valued most about (i) yourself, (ii) the nature of your work, and (iii) your organization
	Think about the core factors that give life to your organization, viz., the really positive values it can build upon
	What three wishes would you have that could boost the vitality and health of your organization?
	Source Author

Applications

Appreciative inquiry can help

- Build a common vision where one is lacking.
- Challenge preconceived notions of what might be by locating the best of what already exists.
- Discover, understand, and amplify the positive forces that exist in organizations.
- Create openness and rapport between people and groups where a negative work climate has prevailed.
- Forge new approaches to human resource issues that will be accepted by staff and lead to positive change.
- Provide an alternative to conventional team building processes.
- Demonstrate the power and value of teamwork by highlighting ways in which teams give life to organizations.
- Open up opportunities for continuous organizational improvement by illuminating the principles, core values, and exemplary practices that support successful teams.
- Develop communities in various ways.

Further Reading

Cooperrider D, Whitney D, Stavros J (2007) Appreciative inquiry handbook. Berrett-Koehler, San Francisco

Proposition 64
Working in Teams

In a Word Cooperative work by a team can produce remarkable results. The challenge is to move from the realm of the possible to the realm of practice.

Background

Groups[1] that range from two persons to many are a very big part of social life (indeed, of human experience). They can be significant sites of socialization and learning, places in which beneficial relationships form and grow, and settings where knowledge and wisdom flourish. Because they also offer individuals the opportunity to work together on joint tasks and develop more complex and larger-scale activities (projects), groups can be highly rewarding to their members, organizations, and society at large. On the other hand, the socialization they offer can constrict or even oppress members. Groups can also become environments that

---

[1]Definitions of a group abound but one can identify common attributes. A group is a set of individuals who identify with one another; share beliefs, values, and norms about areas of common practice or interest; define themselves (and are defined by others) as a group; engage in frequent interactions; and come together to work on joint tasks for an agreed common purpose. Importantly, this list suggests that groups are intended and organic—whether they are primary or secondary, or planned or emergent, they are not a random experience. Therefore, there are three crucial characteristics to groups: there are parts, there is relationship between the parts, and there is an organizing principle.

© Asian Development Bank 2017

O. Serrat, *Knowledge Solutions*, DOI 10.1007/978-981-10-0983-9_64

exacerbate interpersonal conflict, for example, if one individual dominates or tries to "score points". In addition, the boundaries that are drawn around them can exclude others—sometimes to their detriment—and create inter-group conflict. What is more, belonging to a group often warps the judgment of members: pressure to conform can lead to "groupthink" or poor decision-making. Other well-nigh mundane shortcomings include diffusion of responsibility; excessive diversity of views, goals, and loyalties; and the tendency to "solve" (but not analyze) problems. These potential strengths, weaknesses, opportunities, and threats make groups an essential focus for research, exploration, and action, for instance, regarding group development (teamwork) in organizations.

Rationale

In our day, most organizations embrace the notion of teamwork. The justification is that teams are better at solving problems and learn more rapidly and with more effect than individuals.[2] (As a minimum, they are meant to help divide work and thereby increase productivity with speed.) Still, if teams are often deemed a necessary component of organizational success, their use does not guarantee it. To tell the truth, many are apprehensive about teams or even pessimistic about their value. Most prefer to deal with individuals. Others are happier still when working on their own. Therefore, to leverage the potential value that teams can add and ensure that they are effective, members must have more than a limited appreciation of what teamwork is and what it entails: they must be competent in using small-group skills. Since these are not innate and collaboration usually stems from a feeling of being "in the same boat," entering teams or forming them and then behaving in such ways that members can interface, take responsibility, and work together effectively on joint tasks can involve quite sophisticated abilities on the part of practitioners. (The challenge augments in the increasingly common case of virtual teams, certainly with regard to spatial distance and the technology needed to bridge data, information, and personal communication needs.)

What Is Teamwork?

From the foregoing, it follows that teamwork is a process whereby a small number of people—commonly 3–10—with complementary skills become committed to a common purpose and reach agreement on specific performance targets and

---

[2]By nature, teams embody wider and deeper knowledge, broader understanding, a greater diversity of problem-solving styles and skills, and firmer commitment.

indicators, a working approach, and mutual accountability. It follows further that teamwork is not a panacea, a management fad, or a way to cut costs: it is a means to an end. A team does not make "things" happen: it enables them by looking to purpose, thinking as a group, and keeping in touch with the identity and integrity of members.

When to Use Teams

Is a team the best organizational structure for what an organization sets out to accomplish? Not necessarily. Given the potential weaknesses and threats associated with teams, they should only be used in situations where the strengths and the opportunities they offer are critical. That is when

- the problem is relatively complex, uncertain, and holds potential for conflict;
- the problem requires inter-group cooperation and coordination;
- the problem and its solution have important organizational consequences;
- deadline are tight but not immediate; and
- widespread acceptance and commitment are critical to successful implementation of a response to a situation, condition, or issue.

The Characteristics of Successful Teams

Successful teams share many characteristics. They tap the diverse knowledge, skills, experience, and interests of members; they generate more creative responses to challenges than individuals; they catalyze fresh ideas for new products and services, better business processes, and profitable strategies; they hone the leadership abilities of members; they carry out their mission with dedication, energy, and efficiency; they engender feelings of satisfaction and pride among members; they channel conflict into productive directions. The enabling environment for such accomplishments rests on positive interdependence, individual accountability, use of emotional intelligence, promotive (face-to-face) interaction, and group processing.[3]

---

[3]In group processing, members reflect on the team's work and their interactions with each other to clarify and improve efforts to achieve the team's purpose and maintain effective working relationships. This involves describing what member actions were helpful and unhelpful, and making decisions about what actions to continue or change.

The Keys to Developing a Successful Team

To develop a successful team

- **Encourage the team leader to follow the manager-as-developer approach** In high-performance, contemporary organizations, team leaders must move beyond the adequate accomplishments their heroic methods have pulled off. Their prime functions are now to help determine and build common purpose, continuously develop individual skills, and groom shared-responsibility teams. These functions require not only technical competence but also problem-solving abilities and interpersonal skills.
- **Clarify the common purpose** The members of the team must understand what the purpose is and believe that it is sufficiently important for them to sublimate their personal concerns.[4] For this, they need to know what outcome they are expected to deliver and understand how they will work together toward it.
- **Build trust** Trust is a fragile thing: it takes time to build and it can be destroyed instantly. It is important to keep all team members in the loop. As attention drifts to new initiatives, team leaders may forget to alert members to opportunities or challenges. Belatedly, members may receive data and information that might have influenced their actions and they may begin to question interest in their efforts. Team leaders should also be candid about their problems and limitations. They should be available and approachable, fair and objective, and consistent and dependable. They should listen with respect to the ideas of members. They should also create a climate of openness in which members can reveal and thrash out difficulties without fear of retaliation.
- **Establish mutual accountability** For a team to qualify as such, all members must feel responsible for both successes and failures. There must be mutual accountability.
- **Deliver quick-wins** Developing a successful team takes time. Its members should put quick-wins under their belts. This can be done by setting achievable targets and spotlighting team progress. Easy accomplishments will drive cohesiveness and confidence.
- **Set up a team-support system** Organizations that pay lip service to the value of staff working together offer little support. However, it is still possible to set ground rules when the team is formed. They might cover issues such as rotation of members and duties, including leadership; announcements about milestones met; rewards for individual efforts; standards by which the team evaluates its own progress; and even the process by which the team will disband if members think it has lost its usefulness.[5] If the success of the team depends critically on

---

[4]Notwithstanding, in a fast-changing environment a team can find itself working on a mission relevant to an obsolete strategy. To avoid this, the team should review its purpose regularly in light of changing organizational priorities.

[5]Regular review of team processes and procedures is necessary, too.

resources from the organization, it is important to ensure those resources will be there.

- **Teach team members new skills** Team members and the team as a group may need to build their knowledge and skills. This may be in the areas of problem solving, communication, negotiation, conflict resolution, group processing, and learning as a team.[6] The opportunity for training can revitalize a team. If a team is charged with and is made responsible for training members in the best possible way to do a job, its chances of success will be higher.

- **Rotate team assignments** Teams are formed as needed. Work, however, may become monotonous over time. Depending on the complexity of assignments, it is possible to rotate functions and jobs, including leadership, sometimes even through drawing. Besides keeping interest and morale high, this approach ensures that members are cross-trained; it acts also as an informal certification system. On occasion, changing the composition of a group (if that is possible) may also be necessary.

- **Reward team members** One of the hardest things for organizations to recognize is that if they install teams, they need to reward based on teams. The team's performance management system should reward interdependence and mutual accountability. Ways to evaluate and reward contributions to collective, not individual, goals can include cash and noncash awards.

The Stages of Team Development

Teams are always work-in-progress. Bradford and Cohen (1997) have described team (group) development in terms of five stages leading from simple membership to shared responsibility.[7] The stages they distinguish also provide a relational model against which to judge progress toward a shared-responsibility team.[8] At that stage, individual uniqueness and collective effort are both valued. The team addresses the issues that are vital to the joint task. Members keep each other informed without wasting time. They trust one another to act, but all fight hard and fair over issue-based disagreements. A team can soar that is truly dedicated to its common

---

[6]Learning as a team is often overlooked. Training in this area can focus on what makes a learning team; creating and maintaining a learning environment in teams; understanding professional mindsets and valuing diversity; harnessing emotional intelligence; understanding learning preferences and how to use them; and avoiding "groupthink" through the use of "devil's advocates".

[7]The (relatively simple) stages of team development identified by Bruce Tuckman in the 1960s (and refined in the 1970s) are (i) forming, (ii) storming, (iii) norming, (iv) performing, and (v) adjourning.

[8]Although not every group (team) progresses in exactly this sequence (and many do not get past subgrouping or confrontation), each stage is common enough and the issues fundamental enough that the model serves as a useful approximation of reality.

purpose, able to move freely between individual and collective effort, willing to confront and support members, committed both to performance and learning, and increasingly eager to take on management functions.

Reference

Bradford D, Cohen A (1997) Managing for excellence: the guide to developing high performance in contemporary organizations. Wiley, New York

Proposition 65
Drawing Mind Maps

In a Word Mind maps are a visual means that represent, link, and arrange concepts, themes, or tasks, with connections usually extending radially from a central topic. They are used by individuals and groups (informally and intuitively) to generate, visualize, structure, and classify these.

Thinking as a Skill

Intelligence is a potential, and thinking is the operating skill through which it acts upon experience. Outside highly technical matters, perception is the most important part of thinking. If most errors of thinking are errors of perception—that are being colored by emotions and values—thinking as a skill can be improved by practice and education. Numerous straightforward yet powerful tools encourage creativity and flexibility, and help optimize different styles of reasoning (including analyzing, integrating, planning, and problem solving). They include APC,[1] OPV,[2] PMI,[3] brainstorming, lateral thinking, and mind maps. After they are mastered, these tools can be applied explicitly.

---

[1]A stands for Alternatives, P stands for Possibilities. C stands for Choices.
[2]This stands for Other People's Views.
[3]P stands for Plus, or the good points. M stands for Minus, or the bad points. I stands for Interesting, or the interesting points.

© Asian Development Bank 2017
O. Serrat, *Knowledge Solutions*, DOI 10.1007/978-981-10-0983-9_65

Definition

We usually write notes as sentences that we break into paragraphs, lists, or bullet points. A mind map is a circular, nonlinear way of organizing information: it shows the connections between a central topic and the relative importance of the concepts, themes, or tasks that one relates to it. It can be applied by individuals and groups to generate, visualize, structure, and classify these whenever clearer thinking and improved learning will enhance performance and effectiveness.

Advantages

Here are a few advantages to using mind maps:

- The process of drawing a mind map is more interesting and entertaining than writing a report, or drafting a standard chart or table.
- The visual quality of mind maps allows users to identify, clarify, classify, summarize, consolidate, highlight, and present the structural elements of a subject more simply than with a standard set of notes. (It also assists review.)
- Mind maps facilitate recall because the clear association and linking of ideas mirrors the way the brain works—keywords and images are remembered with lesser effort than linear notes.[4]
- Mind maps are compact, with no unnecessary words; easy to draw; very flexible; and can summarize pages of information.
- Mind maps help identify gaps in information and shine clarity on important issues.

Process

The process of drawing a mind map can be described in a few steps: (i) start at the center of the page (rather than from the top-left corner),[5] (ii) adopt an open, creative attitude, (iii) associate and link keywords and images freely, (iv) think fast, (v) break black-and-white boundaries with different colors and styles, (vi) do not judge, (vii) keep moving, and (viii) allow gradual organization by adding relationships and connections.

---

[4]Memory is associative, not linear. Any idea probably has thousands of links in one's mind: mind maps allow associations and links to be recorded and reinforced.

[5]Mind maps are usually drawn by hand. But software packages can be used to organize large amounts of information, combining spatial organization, dynamic hierarchical structuring, and node folding.

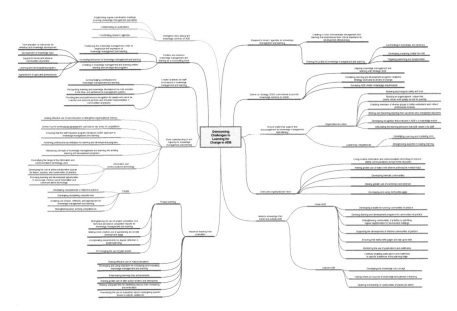

Fig. 65.1 Illustrative mind map. *Source* Author

Further Reading

Buzan T (1995) The mind map book. BBC Books, London
De Bono E (2006) De Bono's thinking course: powerful tools to transform your thinking. BBC Active

Proposition 66
Collaborating with Wikis

By Norman Lu and Olivier Serrat

In a Word Wikis are websites that invite voluntary contributions to organize information. They harness the power of collaborative minds to innovate faster, cocreate, and cut costs. They are now serious business.

Background

As the Internet revolution presses on, computer-mediated communications through social (conversational) technologies[1] also seem to advance every day.[2] (Social sites such as MySpace and Facebook, commercial sites such as Amazon.com and eBay, and media sites such as Flickr and YouTube, to name a few applications, have become very popular.) Given the fast-rising number of these technologies, the confused might recall that people form online communities by combining one-to-one, one-to-many, and many-to-many communication modes. The commonality is that all tap the power of new information and communications

---

[1]Many older media, such as mailing lists and Usenet forums, qualify as "social". These days, however, the term "social technologies" is used to describe Web 2.0 tools that are based on the internet. Typically, they include authoring, extension, link, search, signal, and tag features. (Other equally important tools do not require a web platform, such as mobile telephone communications, radio services, and real-life, face-to-face socializing methods.)

[2]There is little wonder in this as the internet was conceived as a participative, social technology.

O. Serrat, *Knowledge Solutions*, DOI 10.1007/978-981-10-0983-9_66

technology and the resultant interconnectivity to facilitate engagement, collaboration, and sharing of tacit knowledge. Wikis[3] are one such form of social technology, designed to enable anyone with access to contribute or modify content using a simplified markup language. They are used to create and power collaborative websites. Some believe that such open, peering, sharing, and global tools ring the death knell of old-school, inwardly focused, self-contained corporations.[4]

Definition

A wiki is a website—for corporate or personal use—that facilitates interactive,[5] self-referencing, and open-ended collection of definitions, descriptions, and references, viz., articles placed in topics and subtopics, using a simplified markup language. Wikis first appeared in response to the difficulty of using weblogs[6] (blogs) in a collaborative context. They have evolved into an increasingly popular tool for sharing all kinds of information in a browser-independent format, and a growing number of companies offer free and subscription-based applications as well as online storage for wikis.[7]

---

[3]"Wiki" is the abbreviation of WikiWikiWeb, the name that Ward Cunningham gave in 1995 to a code he programmed to facilitate development of collaborative websites, the content of which could be edited by anyone with access to the sites. Wikiwiki means "fast, speedy" in Hawaiian.

[4]According to Tapscott and Williams (2006), this is because (for businesses) they (i) harness external talent, (ii) keep up with users, (iii) boost demand for complementary offerings, (iv) reduce costs, (v) shift the locus of competition, (vi) take the friction out of collaboration, and (vii) develop social capital. To reap these benefits, the "wikinomics" design principles are (i) take cues from your lead users, (ii) build critical mass, (iii) supply an infrastructure for collaboration, (iv) take time to get the structure and governance right, (v) abide by community norms, (vi) let the process evolve, and (vii) hone your collaborative mind.

[5]Since any user has the right to create, edit, and delete content, system abuses are avoided by a revision control system that tracks changes and enables the administrator to revert to previous versions.

[6]Wikis and blogs are websites but the two differ in the publishing processes they follow. Blogs are typically published by a single author, who may have a certain point of view.

[7]The principal advantage of relying on vendors is the low cost for start up: by leveraging a vendor's infrastructure, capital investment is minimized. Also, this hosted model eliminates the need to manage software versions as well as their upgrades and technical environments. The disadvantages of the hosted model are that it requires trust with the vendor, establishes a degree of lock-into the service, and precludes any modification that an organization might like to effect to the original configuration of the application.

Uses

The potential of wikis as open knowledge exchange systems is perhaps best illustrated by the rise of Wikipedia[8] since 2001. Naturally, since contributions are voluntary, the uses of a wiki are limited only by the creativity of the people who access it. Potential uses include

- primary, secondary, and tertiary education;
- corporate knowledge repositories;
- organizational directories;
- network resource databases;
- operations manuals;
- standard operating procedures;
- technical support manuals;
- guides to reordering parts and services;
- user's guides;
- cross-project overviews;
- collaborative workspaces;
- invoice tracking systems;
- logs of client work;
- lists of references;
- lists of contacts;
- to-do lists; and
- frequently asked questions (FAQs).

Features

A Common Scenario In many organizations, exchanging electronic mail among multiple recipients has replaced the shuffling of paper documents. But electronic mail is quite inefficient if it is used to circulate documents for commenting or revision. An author may send a single document to, say, three peers, thereby creating three distinct copies of it. They may, in turn, respond by correcting their copy, blissfully unaware of one another's comments or revisions. The author is then given three new copies of the same document, and burdened with the Sisyphean task of synchronizing the versions.

... No More Wikis address the circulation problems caused by electronic mail by keeping one document, but preserving various states of its evolution by recording the changes made by authorized editors. Hence, what starts as one document ends as one document. Also, by recording the history of changes, editors and authors remain focused on the same copy.

---

[8]Wikipedia is a multilingual project to create a complete and accurate open-content encyclopedia.

Wikis operate on a special type of content management system. Their main features are

- **Authentication and account management** Wiki administrators process users, provide access privileges, and determine an individual's role as reader (permitted to view documents and download content), editor (allowed to update existing content), or author (able to create new content, delete, and reorganize existing content).
- **Content management** Wikis provide authorized users a simple web interface to add, edit, and save content in the system. Many popular content management systems employ WYSIWYG (what you see is what you get) interfaces that resemble those of a word processor. This permits authorized users to adjust elements such as font size, style (bold, underscore, italics), and other textual elements. Wikis also allow multimedia elements such as images and online videos.
- **Revision (change) history** Each change to a wiki document is logged by the system. This function is important for two reasons: it establishes a record of revisions for accountability purposes and it permits administrators to roll back ("undo") changes to an earlier version of the document. Wikis generally support the ability to let readers compare versions based on the revision history.
- **Cross platform compatibility** Wikis rely on standard web-authoring languages to display output.[9] No special brand-specific software is required to read or edit a wiki, other than a standard web browser.
- **Others** Wikipedia, the world's most popular community-edited wiki, introduced a new feature called "Criticism". While anyone can edit a particular entry on Wikipedia, authorized users may publish opinions about a particular update on a document.

Challenges

The principal impediments to wiki usage relate to integration and motivation:

- **Integration** Most organizations operate with bundled, standardized office suites such as Microsoft Office or StarOffice. These suites typically offer powerful and integrated word processing, spreadsheet, database, drawing, and presentation capabilities, and allow users to copy and paste content across these. However, it is not easy for wikis to embed diagrams that users can continue to modify, such as flowcharts, while wiki tables are not as flexible or robust as Microsoft Office

---

[9]That is, HyperText Markup Language (HTML), the predominant markup language for web pages. It provides a means to describe the structure of text-based information in a document by denoting certain text as links, headings, paragraphs, lists, etc., and to supplement that text with interactive forms, embedded images, and other objects.

or StarOffice tables. Also, office applications allow faster copy and paste of images, a process that in a wiki usually requires two steps (uploading the file and linking to it).

- **Motivation** The most active wikis will be those that motivate users to create and update content. Clearly, incentive programs and positive feedback in performance reviews have a role to play. Making wiki contribution part of standard deliverables will also improve its adoption rate.

Caveat

Trust and credibility are a challenge for public wikis because these are very much shaped by the abilities of their authors. Sites such as Wikipedia have been criticized on quality and accuracy (even if founder Jimmy Wales thinks that his product measures up to the Encyclopedia Britannica). Be this as it may, Wikipedia now delivers free knowledge products from purely voluntary contributions while the content of the Encyclopedia Britannica depends on paid subscriptions: the collaborative advantage of this most famous public wiki demands respect.

Reference

Tapscott D, Williams A (2006) Wikinomics: how mass collaboration changes everything. Atlantic Books

Proposition 67
Wearing Six Thinking Hats

In a Word The difference between poor and effective teams lies not so much in their collective mental equipment but in how well they use their abilities to think together. The Six Thinking Hats technique helps actualize the thinking potential of teams.

Introduction

Routinely, many people think from analytical, critical, logical perspectives, and rarely view the world from emotional, intuitive, creative, or even purposely negative viewpoints. As a result, their arguments do not make leaps of imagination, they underestimate resistance to change, or they fail to draw contingency plans.

Lateral thinking[1] is reasoning that offers new ways of looking at problems—coming at them from the side rather than from the front—to foster change,

---

[1]The term was coined by Edward de Bono in 1967.

© Asian Development Bank 2017
O. Serrat, *Knowledge Solutions*, DOI 10.1007/978-981-10-0983-9_67

creativity, and innovation. One tool of lateral thinking, the Six Thinking Hats technique, was devised by Edward de Bono in 1985 to give groups a means to reflect together more effectively, one thing at a time.

Six Hats, Six Colors

The Six Thinking Hats technique involves the use of metaphorical hats in discussions.[2] Participants put on hats in turn, possibly more than once but not necessarily all of them, to indicate directions (not descriptions) of thinking. The color of each is related to a function

- White hat thinking—neutral, objective—focuses on the data and information that are available or needed.
- Red hat thinking—emotional—looks at a topic from the point of view of emotions, feelings, and hunches, without having to qualify or justify them.
- Black hat thinking—somber, serious—uses experience, logic, judgment, and caution to examine the difficulties and problems associated with a topic and the feasibility of ideas.
- Yellow hat thinking—sunny, positive—is concerned with benefits and values.
- Green hat thinking—growth, fertility—intimates creative thinking and movement, not judgment, to generate new ideas and solutions.
- Blue hat thinking—cool, the sky above—concentrates on reflection, metacognition (thinking about the thinking required), and the need to manage the thinking process.[3]

Applications

Pertinent applications for the Six Thinking Hats technique include team productivity and communication; product and process improvement, as well as project management; critical and analytical thinking, problem solving, and decision-making; and creativity training, meeting facilitation, and meeting management.

---

[2]The larger benefits lie in conversations. But the technique can be also used by an individual.

[3]A blue hat should always be used both at the beginning and at the end of a discussion. What follows it depends on the nature of the topic and emotions about it. For instance, wearing a red hat next might defuse strong feelings. Discussions to brainstorm problems might adopt blue, white, green, red, yellow, black, green, and blue hats in sequence. Conversations seeking feedback might follow a blue, black, green, and blue hat pattern.

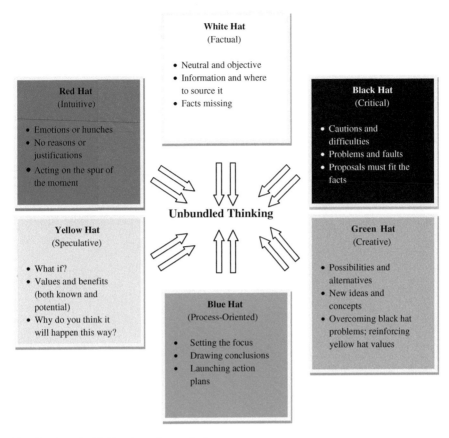

Fig. Wearing six thinking hats. *Source* Author

Benefits

The Six Thinking Hats technique provides a common language that works in different cultures. It promotes collaborative thinking, sharpens focus, facilitates communication, reduces conflict, enables thorough evaluations, improves exploration, fosters creativity and innovation, saves time, and boosts productivity.

Discipline

Discipline is important. The facilitator's role is to define the focus of the thinking, plan the sequence and timing of the thinking, ask for changes in the thinking if needed, handle requests from participants for changes in the thinking, and form periodic or final summaries of the thinking for consideration by participants. Each participant must follow the lead of the facilitator, stick to the hat being used, try to work within time limits, and contribute honestly and fully under each hat.

Further Reading

De Bono E (1999) Six thinking hats. Back Bay Books

Proposition 68
Managing Virtual Teams

In a Word Virtual team management is the ability to organize and coordinate with effect, a group whose members are not in the same location or time zone, and may not even work for the organization. The predictor of success is—as always—clarity of purpose. But group participation in achieving that is more than ever important to compensate for lost context. Virtual team management requires deeper understanding of people, process, and technology, and recognition that trust is a more limiting factor compared with face-to-face interactions.

Background

A team is a cooperative unit of interacting individuals who are committed to a common purpose on tasks; endowed with complementary skills, for instance, in technical competence, problem-solving ability, and emotional intelligence; and who share interdependent performance goals (with indicators and deadlines) as well as an approach to work for which they hold themselves mutually accountable.[1] (People try to accomplish with others what they cannot do alone.) When they are effective, teams are typified by intelligibility of purpose, trust, open communication, clear roles, the right mix of talent and skills, full participation, individual perfor-

---

[1]Some hold that mutual accountability distinguishes a team from a working group.

© Asian Development Bank 2017

O. Serrat, *Knowledge Solutions*, DOI 10.1007/978-981-10-0983-9_68

mance, quality control, risk taking, collective delivery of products and services, an appropriate level of sponsorship and resources, and balanced work-life interactions. Their stages of development are likely universal.[2]

But here commonalities end: thanks to globalization and, chiefly, the advent of the Internet, unusual teams whose members may never meet face to face have come to proliferate.[3] Their distinct configurations raise unique challenges for managers, to which the literature and practice are only just beginning to pay attention.

Rationale

Competitive advantage is derived through cost leadership, differentiation, and focus. Organizations that pool knowledge workers quickly from different functions, locations, and organizations can leverage virtual teams as a factor of competitive advantage. The tools, methods, and approaches that they use to do so with effect spell the difference between success and failure, within and across organizations.

Definition

A virtual team is a group of people who routinely work interdependently for a joint objective across time, distance, and organization. (To these three dimensions some add culture.) There are many types of virtual teams,[4] but probably the most

---

[2]All groups develop in five stages beginning with membership, working through subgrouping, confrontation, and differentiation to the more effective form of shared responsibility.

[3]Real-time remote teaming may be recent but remote coordination has existed for centuries, gaining speed as documentation techniques and communications improved. Nowadays, you work virtually—even internally—if you communicate by electronic mail, share information with colleagues on websites or via social (conversational) technologies, e.g., instant messaging, text chat, Internet forums, web logs, and wikis, or take part in teleconferences. To what extent depends on each and every.

[4]Typologies admit that the nature of a virtual team varies in a continuum determined by the variability of their characteristics. Two extreme cases are the archetype of the virtual team (primarily defined by a short lifespan) and relatively permanent virtual teams (defined by a stable framework). The seven basic types are (i) networked teams—that collaborate for a common purpose with generally diffuse and fluid membership; (ii) parallel teams—that boast distinct membership and work in the short term to carry out special assignments, tasks, or functions; (iii) project or product development teams—that conduct nonroutine tasks for customers or users over a defined period, with specific and measurable results, and wield decision-making authority; (iv) work, functional, or production teams—that deliver regular, ongoing activities with clearly defined membership; (v) service teams—that take turns to meet customer or organizational needs with technical support around the clock; (vi) action teams—that offer rapid responses, often in emergency situations; (vii) offshore information system development outsourcing teams—that deliver portions of subcontracted work to an offshore independent service provider in conjunction

important characteristic is that the members cannot always meet face to face (for one reason or another)[5]: Of necessity, they rely on (an increasingly powerful array of) interactive technologies.[6]

The Pros and Cons of Virtual Teams

The main benefit of virtual teaming is that it allows organizations to be more flexible and procure talent from different functions, locations, and organizations without geographical restrictions.[7] The main drawback owes to lost context,[8] which generates feelings of isolation and undermines trust[9] (especially when members are from different cultures).

> *Coming together is a beginning. Keeping together is progress. Working together is success.*
>
> —Henry Ford

The Challenges of Virtual Teaming

> *The problem with communication...is the illusion that it has been accomplished.*
>
> —George Bernard Shaw

(Footnote 4 continued)

with an onshore team; and (viii) management teams—that act collaboratively in an organization on a daily basis but are dispersed across a country or around the world.

[5] A member of a virtual team is not always a teleworker: teleworkers are individuals who work from home.

[6] These include audio conferencing, videoconferencing, electronic mail, voice/video mail, chat services, news forums, bulletin boards, web logs, and wikis, among others.

[7] Virtual teaming can also cut travel, relocation, real estate, and other business costs. (Virtual teams involved in product development can exploit time difference by sharing a design process around the world. Service teams can reap comparable benefits.).

[8] Communication that is not face-to-face becomes difficult because cues from facial expressions and gestures are lost.

[9] Trust is a means of coping with complexity and uncertainty in contexts where high levels of interdependence and interaction between different actors are necessary. It is a relationship of reliance, and the highest form of human motivation. It is the springboard of high-performance teams. (Indeed, the words "trust" and "team" are well-nigh synonymous.) Trust leads to mutual motivation, enhanced unity, and increased effectiveness and efficiency.

It is of course vital that virtual teams enjoy the same (or higher) critical foundations as effective face-to-face teams. In the absence of the normal give-and-take of face-to-face interaction, they must overcome the obstacles associated with time, distance, organization, and culture. Seven critical success factors can be identified, each calling for dedicated organizational policies, strategies, and partnerships, including their design, implementation, results, and associated business processes:

- **Human Resource Management** Building and maintaining virtual employee identity in modern organizations is a new challenge: human resource management must resonate with virtual knowledge workers, and deal with unique issues such as visibility in the organization, career options, and paths to advancement. Virtual staff needs to feel they are on a par with other workers in the organization and that their different personal and work circumstances are understood. Human resource management must overcome the perceived natural advantage of in-house employees, with possible implications for organizational design. Lack of a sense of belonging can show up in human resource indicators, such as low morale and retention.

- **Learning and Development** Modern organizations must commit to, and make resources available for, training and other ongoing learning development activities focused on working in a virtual environment. They must also educate all employees, not just virtual employees, in virtual team culture.

- **Organizational Culture** Leadership and organizational commitment must recognize that virtual teaming is fast becoming a preferred way of working. Recognition entails promoting virtual teaming and rewarding and recognizing team members who lead and participate in virtual teams.

- **Information Management Systems** New management, measurement, and control systems must be designed. The workload tracking and management systems that are required in a virtual, matrixed world differ from those used in conventional organizations. Details of work assignments must be made available more widely so that data and information gathered in one place for one purpose can be used in another for other purposes as well as up and down the management chain for planning and decision-making. Workload tracking and management systems must evolve to span all the work performed both in and out of a department.

- **Electronic Communication and Collaboration Technologies** For virtual teams to work effectively, members from all geographic and functional areas need access to a standard set of electronic communication and collaboration technologies.

- **Leadership** Senior leadership must recognize that virtual teaming is fast becoming a preferred (and useful) way of working. Cross-functional management teams must be established to handle and resolve the complex,[10] cross-functional, and virtual issues that virtual teams deal with. Management

---

[10]The complexity of the issues that virtual teams deal with is a key variable in their nature that influences and shapes all other criteria.

system flaws in decision-making must be resolved if virtual projects are to succeed. Because problems from one team can pollinate other virtual teams, management must define the escalation path to resolve cross-functional, virtual team issues.

- **Team Leader and Team Member Competencies** Team leaders must see themselves as critical to facilitating the team's success, with a particular role in bringing the team closer together and building the interpersonal relations its members need to succeed.[11] Just as importantly, team members must be proficient in the use of interactive technologies—working across time, distance, organization, and culture with sensitivity to project and time parameters—and able to network.

> *One must be fond of people and trust them if one is not to make a mess of life.*
>
> —E.M. Forster

Building Trust

Trust is easier to destroy than to build. To appear and develop, it requires that certain conditions be met, such as a shared culture, social context, and values; physical proximity; information exchange; and time. Needless to say, most of these conditions are not easily met in the context of virtual teams. In a virtual environment, trust is based more on (ability and) delivery of the task at hand than on interpersonal relationships.[12] Members of virtual teams need to be sure that all others will fulfill their obligations with competence and integrity and behave in a consistent, predictable manner with a concern for the well-being of others. The level of member performance over time builds or denies trust in greater degrees than it does in conventional environments. If trust is a much more limiting factor in virtual teams, compared with face-to-face teams, it is therefore helpful to recognize the types that exist in professional relationships:

---

[11]This goes beyond traditional responsibilities, associated with handing out assignments and coordinating work, to ensuring activities and processes that promote effective team relationships. The team leader is the person who is managing the boundary, feeding the team's accomplishments to the organization and to the individuals' function or line managers. Especially in a virtual environment, lack of recognition can make an individual feel isolated. Better recognition can be achieved though continual feedback and solicitation of the team's opinion. The team leader must also keep the team informed of management and other corporate news or events.

[12]Feelings, engagement, and exchanges are less important than actions.

- **Deterrence-Based Trust** This basic type of trust hinges on adoption of consistent behavior and the threat of punishment if people do not follow through on what they are supposed to do, or committed themselves to doing. It is not well suited to the work of a virtual team.
- **Calculus-Based Trust** This basic type of trust is grounded not only in fear of punishment for violating trust but also in rewards for preserving it. Such trust is based on comparison of the costs and benefits of creating and sustaining a relationship over the costs and benefits of severing it. This level of trust is easily broken by a violation of expectations and cannot meaningfully sustain a virtual team's relationship.
- **Knowledge-Based Trust** This type of trust occurs when an individual has enough information and understanding about another person to predict that person's behavior. Accurate prediction depends on understanding—which develops from repeated interactions, communication, and efforts to build a relationship. Unlike deterrence-based trust and calculus-based trust, this type of trust is founded on information, not control. Parties cultivate knowledge of one another by gathering data and information, meeting in different contexts, and experiencing each other's range. This type of trust is the minimum that virtual teams should aim to establish.
- **Identification-Based Trust** This type of trust develops when parties understand and endorse one another, and can act on behalf of one another in interpersonal transactions. This requires that they fully internalize and harmonize with one another's desires and intentions. Certain activities can enhance identification-based trust. For instance, organizations and individuals can assume a common identity, co-locate, create joint products and goals, and share core values. To succeed, virtual teams should aim to shift up to this level of the trust ladder.

> *Light is the task where many share the toil.*
>
> —Homer

Clearly, the nature and development of trust in virtual teams will vary according to their typology, that is, according to the properties of the team. But to trust and to be trustworthy within the limits of a virtual system means that team members may have to wade in on trust rather than wait for experience to gradually show who can be trusted with what. Trust may have to be conferred presumptively at first, but must develop to the stage that it is grounded in mutual identification. Fundamental determinants of that are open expression, information equity, and performance reliability. Trust is not 1D, but changes as a relationship develops. To build trust in virtual teams, it is essential to ask effective questions; generate clear and concise objectives, including a project implementation plan; talk (and walk) the talk; build tell-and-ask patterns; enable the free flow of data and information for constant, consistent, concerned, and concrete discussion, including the development of communication and meetings protocols; diagnose problems early and act on them; grow the virtual team's own culture and identity, including the promotion of virtual socializing skills; and make, share, and celebrate good news.

Further Reading

Duarte D, Snyder N (2006) Mastering virtual teams: strategies, tools, and techniques that succeed. Wiley, Inc
Lipnack J, Stamps J (2000) Virtual teams: people working across boundaries with technology. Wiley, Inc

Proposition 69
Building Trust in the Workplace

In a Word Workplace dynamics make a significant difference to people and the organizations they sustain. High-performance organizations earn, develop, and retain trust for superior results.

Introduction

Dictionary.com's first definition of trust is "reliance on the integrity, strength, ability, surety, etc., of a person or thing; confidence". The website prompts also that it is "the obligation or responsibility imposed on a person in whom confidence or authority is placed: *a position of trust*". Both definitions imply that trust is a relationship of reliance[1]: indeed, a relationship without trust is no relationship at all.

Trust is therefore both an emotional[2] and a rational[3] (cognitive, calculative, and rational) act. The emotions associated with it include affection, gratitude, security,

---

[1]To be exact, trust is a *prediction* of reliance, derived from what a party knows about another.
[2]The act of trusting exposes one's vulnerabilities to others in the belief that they will not take advantage of these.
[3]The act of trusting involves assessing probabilities of profit and loss, calculating expected utility based on (past, current, and expected) performance, and concluding that the party in question will behave in a predictable manner.

© Asian Development Bank 2017
O. Serrat, *Knowledge Solutions*, DOI 10.1007/978-981-10-0983-9_69

confidence, acceptance, interest, admiration, respect, liking, appreciation, content-
ment, and satisfaction, all of them necessary ingredients of psychological health.
The logic of it is grounded in assessments of a party's dependability, which play a
significant role in decisions to trust. As expected, there are different intensities to
trust, depending on why one grants trust and why it is accepted[4]: knowing the
different types of trust informs decision-making at each level.[5]

Strangely, however, despite instinctive recognition of the importance of trust in
human affairs, its conceptualization in the workplace remains limited in the literature—but grew in the 1990s, while actions to foster it in that environment are still
not readily discernible in practice.

Benefits

In organizations, business processes[6]—be they management, operational, or supporting processes—are conducted via relationships. Since trust among interacting
parties is the foundation of effective relationships, it stands to reason that organizations can reap benefits from strengthening it. As a matter of fact, high-trust
environments correlate positively with high degrees of personnel involvement,
commitment, and organizational success. Decided advantages include increased
value; accelerated growth; market and societal trust; reputation and recognizable

---

[4]Kramer (1999) has identified six kinds of trust. *Dispositional trust* refers to an individual's
predisposition to trust; it is based on experiences with relationships and the outlook on human
nature that then guides decisions. *History-based trust* relies on the build up of interactions over
time; expectations that are met increase trust while those that are unmet decrease it. *Third-party
dependent trust* is a secondhand trust determinant; a large component of it is gossip, which means
that trust is bolstered for some people and degraded for others depending on the subjective view of
the gossiper. *Category-based trust* is anchored in membership of a group or organization; problems arise from blindly trusting members that one does not really know and excluding outsiders
whom it may be more beneficial to trust. *Role-based trust* is founded on knowing that the person
assigned to a job can fulfill its requirements; it owes more to reliance on the business processes that
underpin the job than to trust in the person who performs it. *Rule-based trust* establishes a sense of
normalcy in organization and elicits trust-binding force; it persuades us to take for granted that
people will follow directives and behave in consistent, procedural ways. Other typologies of trust
categorize deterrence-, calculus-, knowledge-, and identification-based trust.

[5]Future research might investigate the ways in which types of trust—including their emotional and
rational elements—combine and evolve. There is fertile ground too in examining the impact of
cultural contexts on trust. From there, one might conceive of trust as a single (but nevertheless still
complex) function, with the amount of trust given or received varying as the result of a combination of (i) characteristic similarity, (ii) experiences of reciprocity, and (iii) embedded predisposition to trust (generated by broad societal norms and expectations).

[6]A business process is a collection of related, structured activities or tasks that produce a specific
service or product for a particular client.

brands; effortless communication; enhanced innovation; positive, transparent relationships with personnel and other stakeholders; improved collaboration and partnering; fully aligned systems and structures; heightened loyalty; powerful contributions of discretionary energy; strong innovation, engagement, confidence, and loyalty; better execution; increased adaptability; and robust retention and replenishment of knowledge workers. Nothing is as relevant as the ubiquitous impact of high trust.[7]

Trust as a Key Leadership Competency

The leaders who work most effectively, it seems to me, never say "I". And that's not because they have trained themselves not to say "I". They don't think "I". They think "we"; they think "team". They understand their job to be to make the team function. They accept responsibility and don't sidestep it, but "we" gets the credit. This is what creates trust, what enables you to get the task done.

—Peter Drucker

In organizations, managers are initiators of trust and must play a central role in determining both its overall level and specific expectations within individual work units.[8] Their ability to establish, grow, extend, and restore trust is a key managerial competency. Some say that extending trust is the first job of any manager, to be conducted in ways that release the talent, creativity, capacity, and contribution of individuals and teams and enable them to give their best in synergy with others. The responsibilities of managers, in support of which they must harness vivid and compelling communications, cover at least five areas:

- **Vision** An organization's vision (and associated mission and strategic direction) is a statement of ambitious and compelling strategic intent that provides the emotional and rational energy for an organization's journey. If staffs are to trust the organization, the vision must be clear and represent an attainable stretch that emphasizes the importance of contributions in achieving it. It cannot be a

---

[7]Conversely, the costs of mistrust include toxic cultures (office politics); dysfunctional working environments; redundant hierarchies (excessive layers of management, overlapping structures); punishing systems (complex and cumbersome policies, rules, regulations, procedures, and processes); poor company loyalty; decreased commitment; disengagement; low productivity; intense micromanagement; militant stakeholders; high employee turnover; and fraud.

[8]Depending on the nature of their role relative to trust, they do so through the organizational form employed, vertical exchanges, the design and application of reward and control systems, and the flow of information, among others.

statement that is devoid of action. The role of managers is to help individuals and teams translate the organization's vision into their own personal vision.

- **Values** Values are beliefs or convictions that guide behavior to achieve the organization's vision.[9] They help define or describe the desired culture. They also convey what is important to the organization as well as what key practices and behaviors will be recognized and rewarded (or sanctioned). Trust pervades when—and only when—managers follow and support the organization's values; by publicizing and modeling these, they provide a benchmark for all staff.

- **Work Environment** The environment in which individuals and teams work contributes significantly to their perceptions of management and the extent they believe it cares about their welfare. Conditions that betray a lack of interest will create feelings of distrust. More important than physical amenities, however, is the atmosphere that exists in an organization: a negative atmosphere sows discontent throughout—personnel should be able to trust that management works to create an enabling environment.

- **Personnel** Some of the more difficult decisions that managers make relate to hiring, firing, appraising, promoting, and transferring staff. If an organization is to build trust, such decisions must be based on factual, objective data. Personnel will scrutinize promotion decisions to determine whether management cares about performance and values. Poor decisions erode trust in management and leads staff to question why they work so hard to meet performance expectations if—it appears—performance does not really matter.

- **Compensation** Few issues create as much argument and suspicion as compensation (and other benefits). For an organization's compensation system to be perceived as fair rather than manipulative, managers need to follow a consistent and honest approach by sharing salary ranges; reaching merit pay decisions based on actual performance; quantifying bonus, severance, and related systems transparently; conducting internal equity comparisons for same or similar jobs; and carrying out external market equity comparisons for critical jobs.

> *Set your expectations high; find men and women whose integrity and values you respect; get their agreement on a course of action; and give them your ultimate trust*
>
> —John Akers
>
> *I'm not upset that you lied to me, I'm upset that from now on I can't believe you*
>
> —Friedrich Nietzsche

---

[9]Typical corporate values emphasize innovation, excellence, service, integrity, respect, bias for action, or teamwork, often in the form of small statements.

Enhancing Personal Credibility

> *There are seven social sins: politics without principles; wealth without work; pleasure without conscience; knowledge without character; commerce without morality; science without humanity; worship without sacrifice.*
>
> —Mohandas K. Gandhi

Notwithstanding the responsibilities of management, earning, developing, and retaining trust in the workplace is an obligation for each member of the organization. The key principle undergirding ability to set and accomplish objectives, keep commitments, and "walk the talk" is credibility, which intimates to others that one is trustworthy. Credibility is made of four attributes of character and competence[10]:

- **Integrity** According to Dictionary.com, integrity is "adherence to moral and ethical principles; soundness of moral character; honesty". Men and women who are imbued with integrity stand for something, make and keep commitments to themselves, and remain open. Time and again, this may require courage.
- **Intent** Intent refers to motives, agendas, and resulting behaviors. Trust grows when all three are candid and based on mutual interest.
- **Capabilities** Capabilities are the talents, attitudes, skills, knowledge, and styles we leverage to deliver results. Capable people know where they are going, run with their strengths (and compensate for weaknesses), and keep themselves relevant.
- **Results** Results crown credibility to offer visible, tangible, and measurable contributions that can be evaluated by others. Results are delivered by performers who expect to win, take responsibility for results, and finish strong.

Reference

Kramer R (1999) Trust and distrust in organizations: emerging perspectives, enduring questions. Annual Review of Psychology 50:569–598

Further Reading

Covey S (2006) The speed of trust: the one thing that changes everything. Free Press

---

[10]Because credibility is the sum of integrity, intent, capabilities, and results, it is possible to score high in some of these foundational elements but low in others.

Proposition 70
Leading in the Workplace

In a Word Theories of leadership are divided: some underscore the primacy of personal qualities; others stress that systems are all-important. Both interpretations are correct: a larger pool of leaders is desirable all the time (and superleaders are necessary on occasion) but its development must be part of systemic invigoration of leadership in organizations.

Introduction

Leadership is a complex and contested subject. But there is no doubt that the consequences of modernity throw up unprecedented challenges that beg better understanding of its nature in organizations.

More and more, contemporary discussions of leadership in organizations run thus

> *Leadership is the key that unlocks (or blocks) performance and change. It is a social process—something that moves people. It is not what leaders do: it is what springs from purposeful relationships. Leadership does not depend on one person but on how groups act together to make collective sense of the situations they confront. From this perspective, leadership in organizations is the process by which individual and team contributions to a shared cause increase (at least) on a par with job-related psychological well-being.*

Source Author

© Asian Development Bank 2017
O. Serrat, *Knowledge Solutions*, DOI 10.1007/978-981-10-0983-9_70

Early Models of Leadership

Indeed. These days, leadership is more and more defined as the means of influence by which a person enlists the help of others to accomplish tasks of common interest. Of course, this definition has not always held and the literature continues to frustrate: until about 20 years ago, the images associated with leadership were rooted in conflict, that is, moments of crisis or decision when the actions of an individual are pivotal.

Early models of leadership—usually Western and borrowed from the military—were wont to examine the circumstances in which leaders emerge, and then search for psychological traits. The definite, often heroic endowments they identified typically embraced vision, ideological orientation, charisma, physical vitality and stamina, courage and resolution, intelligence and action-oriented judgment, decisiveness, self-confidence, assertiveness, a need for achievement, eagerness to accept responsibility, task competence, capacity to motivate people, understanding of followers and their needs, skill in dealing with people, trustworthiness, and adaptability.[1]

> *No institution can possibly survive if it needs geniuses or supermen to manage it. It must be organized in such a way as to be able to get along under a leadership composed of average human beings.*
>
> —Peter Drucker

The archetypal qualities desired from leaders are undoubtedly opportune in dire circumstances. However, "old paradigm" trait approaches[2] and notions of

---

[1]Only quite recently—that is, in the last 10 years—has attention been paid to social distance. What characterizes distant leaders, typically active in politics or the military, is usually quite different from what we identify in the nearby leaders we contact regularly. The latter are frequently perceived as intelligent, original, expert, dynamic, sociable, open, and considerate, for example. This distinction is crucial if we are to realize what is required in "normal" walks of life.

[2]Thankfully, perhaps, the seemingly innumerable traits that leaders are thought to exhibit (admitting also differences by sector) have since been pared into five dispositions: (i) self-confidence, (ii) empathy, (iii) ambition, (iv) curiosity, and (v) self-control. Many organizations still find uses for psychometric assessments inspired by trait approaches, for instance, by means of the Myers-Briggs Type Indicator, even though critiques suggest that such tests construct rather than discover traits, and might encourage surreptitious subordination of individuals to the professed needs of an organization.

situational,[3] contingency,[4] transactional,[5] and even transformational[6] leadership—
all of which smack of command and control more or less overtly—cannot serve the
miscellany of organizations that need leadership in the workplace in the twenty-first
century. Certainly, all over the world, "ordinary" people work with remarkable
success in extraordinarily challenging circumstances yet do not advertise super-
human characteristics in their leadership styles.

The New Context for Leadership in the Public Sector

The challenges that organizations face in their efforts to perform owe to the rapid
spread and connectedness of production, communication, and technologies across
the world, and attendant changes in perceptions, expectations, opportunities,
requirements, and workforces. In response, from the early 1990s, public sector
organizations worldwide launched reforms inspired by President Clinton's National

---

[3]Situational approaches underscore the context in which leadership is exercised and emphasize that
what is needed differs from situation to situation. At one extreme, proponents argue that context
determines everything. At the other, they suggest that leaders are able to work in different ways
depending on the state of affairs, i.e., adapt their style and patterns of behavior to suit circumstances based on (i) their position power, (ii) the structure of the task, and (iii) their relationship
with followers. At heart, both interpretations belittle somewhat the role of followers, who are
shepherded into more or less learned subordinate acceptance through a decision process that can
range from autocratic to democratic. Under the directive leadership style, leaders take decisions for
others and expect instructions to be followed. Under the participative leadership style, leaders
share decision making with others and may encourage them to "buy into" the task, emphasizing
the achievement of concrete objectives.

[4]Contingency approaches are skeptical that a leader can operate successfully in radically different
situations. They suggest that leadership should change when the context changes or that the leader
should change the context to ensure that his or her leadership style remains appropriate.

[5]Transactional approaches involve trading. They recognize what employees seek from work. They
design incentives to accomplish a predetermined goal, make promises, and exchange rewards for
aligned efforts. Power is given to the leader to correct and train subordinates when outcomes are
not those desired. Transactional leaders are more common than other types of leaders.

[6]Transformational approaches are a variant of transactional approaches—some see them as a polar
opposite—that aim to raise levels of awareness about the significance and value of designated
outcomes and arrange ways to reach them, beyond self-interest, for the sake of the organization.
Proponents claim that, unlike transactional approaches, transformational approaches are not based
on "give and take" relationships but on the ability of leaders to redesign perceptions and values
and change the expectations and aspirations of employees. The four elements of transformational
leadership are (i) individual consideration (listening and attending to needs), (ii) intellectual
stimulation (sharing cutting-edge information), (iii) inspirational motivation (framing a vision that
appeals), and (iv) idealized influence (modeling the attitudes and behaviors one wants to see in
others).

Partnership for Reinventing Government, introduced in 1993.[7] They continue unabated to this day.

Leading Change in the Public Sector, released by the Chartered Management Institute (Charlesworth et al. 2003), gave a reality check on the pressures from public reform agendas in the United Kingdom that is quite suggestive of what is still being experienced there as elsewhere.[8] Importantly, the research project also presented a sober assessment of what attributes and skills survey respondents desired from their leaders and saw demonstrated. It revealed a clear perceived cultural shift in terms of the (then) new focus on delivery and working through partnerships. But, it made clear that resources and manpower levels were the greatest hindrance on reform. Clarity of vision was placed firmly at the top of the list of desired leadership attributes, followed by integrity and sound judgment. Yet, the survey respondents reported that the top three qualities their most senior management team demonstrated instead were those of being knowledgeable, strategic, and committed to people. The three top desired public leadership skills were communication, engaging employees with a vision of the organization, and creating an enabling culture. That said, the gap was considerable in all three instances, notably regarding the third.

Where to from There?

Recent developments in theory and practice have emphasized the growing complexity of leadership. Organizations are not machines and should not be treated as such. Since they are communities (of communities), we should want them to share the flexible, resilient, and adaptive attributes that characterize living systems. Learning organizations,[9] much as living systems, are able to self-organize, sustain themselves, and move toward greater complexity and order when needed. They can respond intelligently to the imperatives of change without awaiting directives from the outside.

Despite the abundance of trust, however, the learning organization is not necessarily a comfortable place for conventional leaders: much of the power resides at

---

[7]The mission was to create a government that "works better, costs less, and gets results Americans care about".

[8]The research project surveyed almost 1,900 public sector managers—mostly at middle and junior level—in central government, local government, health, education, the armed forces, the fire service, and the police.

[9]*Learning for Change in ADB* (2009) broadly defines a learning organization as a collective undertaking, rooted in action, that builds and improves its own practice by consciously and continually devising and developing the means to draw learning from its own (and others') experience.

the edges of these organizations, and imposed authority (even when subtly disguised) no longer really works—rather, it must be earned. A learning culture is born of beliefs, values, and principles that are shared by people who are committed to one another and to a common goal.[10] Therefore, running it requires a powerful theory: many suggest that this should be founded on questions, ideas, tests, and reflections in a wheel of learning.

> *The leader is best when people are hardly aware of his existence, not so good when people praise his government, less good when people stand in fear, worst when people are contemptuous. Fail to honor people and they will fail to honor you. But of a good leader who speaks little when his work is done, his aim fulfilled, the people say: "We did it ourselves".*
>
> —Lao Tzu

Still, keeping the wheel of learning in motion—without it stalling for too long in one quadrant—is no easy matter. In twenty-first century organizations, certainly in the public sector, that and not much else may then be considered to be the primary task of a leader and his community of servant-leaders.[11] Each will find different ways of carrying it out, based on the mission of the organization, the distinctive context in which it operates, and the leadership attributes and skills that these demand—preferably to foster vision, give constant encouragement, and put on view personal examples. But all will ensure as they do so that the constituent members of the organization become and remain "change agile". In an uncertain world, high-performance organizations will be those that continuously renew, reinvent, and reinvigorate themselves.[12] To these intents, they will wisely identify, engage, and develop individuals who possess the "learning habit" and delight in the unknown. They will invest immensely in them and trust them in equal proportions. Leadership will be collective, irrespective of hierarchical position or authority: true leaders will be those who build the organization and its capabilities.

---

[10]Such organizations might more appropriately be envisioned as communities of commitment, and certainly not as organizations of command and control.

[11]Servant-leaders are seen as humble stewards of their organization's resources. Servant leadership is a philosophy and practice of leadership, coined and defined by Robert Greenleaf. The general concept is ancient, with roots in China (Lao Tzu) and India (Chanakya). Servant-leaders, said Greenleaf, constantly inquire whether the highest priority needs of others are being served. Do those served grow as persons? Do they, while being served, become healthier, wiser, freer, more autonomous, and more likely themselves to become servants?

[12]Inevitably, heeding Peter Drucker, each will recurrently ask itself: What is our mission? Who are our clients? What do our clients value? What are our results? What is our plan? These five simple —yet complex and compelling—questions are as essential and relevant today as they were yesterday and will be tomorrow.

Table. Toward systemic invigoration of leadership

From	To
Command and control	Cultural coherence
Individual leaders	Leadership institutions
Inherited traits and acquired skills	Developed will
One-dimensional man	Diversity
Private interest	Public service
Reductionism	Complexity
Rules	Principles
Self-isolating individual leaders	Self-supporting leadership teams
Win–lose arguments	Win–win conversations

Source Author

References

ADB (2009) Learning for change in ADB. Manila
Charlesworth K, Cook P Crozier G (2003) Leading change in the public sector: making the
    difference. Chartered Management Institute

Further Reading

Greenleaf R (1977) Servant leadership: a journey into the nature of legitimate power and greatness.
    Paulist Press

Proposition 71
Learning in Strategic Alliances

In a Word Strategic alliances that bring organizations together promise unique opportunities for partners. The reality is often otherwise. Successful strategic alliances manage the partnership, not just the agreement, for collaborative advantage. Above all, they also pay attention to learning priorities in alliance evolution.

Preamble

The resource-based view of the firm that gained currency in the mid-1980s considered that the competitive advantage of an organization rests on the application of the strategic resources[1] at its disposal. These days, orthodoxy recognizes the merits of the dynamic, knowledge-based capabilities[2] underpinning the positions organizations occupy in a sector or market.

---

[1]The resources that the theory deemed of strategic importance were valuable, rare, inimitable, and non-substitutable (leading to charges of tautology). Importantly, the list of what constitutes a resource was expanded in the 1990s with the refinement that the encompassing construct previously called resources should be segregated into resources and capabilities.

[2]Dynamic capability is an organization's ability to integrate, build, and reconfigure internal and external competences to address rapidly changing environments.

© Asian Development Bank 2017
O. Serrat, *Knowledge Solutions*, DOI 10.1007/978-981-10-0983-9_71

Strategic alliances—meaning cooperative agreements between two or more organizations—are a means to enhance strategic resources: self-sufficiency is becoming increasingly difficult in a complex, uncertain, and discontinuous external environment that calls for focus and flexibility in equal measure. Everywhere, organizations are discovering that they cannot "go" it alone and must now often turn to others to survive.[3]

Definition

The greatest change in corporate culture—and in the way business is being conducted—may be the accelerating growth of relationships based not on ownership but on partnership; joint ventures; minority investments cementing a joint marketing agreement or an agreement to do joint research ... alliances of all sorts.

—Peter Drucker

A strategic alliance is a voluntary, formal arrangement between two or more parties to pool resources to achieve a common set of objectives that meet critical needs while remaining independent entities. Strategic alliances involve exchange, sharing, or codevelopment of products, services, procedures, and processes. To these ends, strategic alliances can—in fact, frequently do—call on contributions of organization-specific resources and capabilities (that may involve trade-offs in capital, control, and time). The generic motive, to a greater extent than in the 1990s, is to sustain long-term competitive advantage in a fast-changing world, for example, by reducing costs through economies of scale or more knowledge, boosting research and development efforts, increasing access to new technology, entering new markets, breathing life into slowing or stagnant markets, reducing cycle times,

---

[3]In the twenty-first century, the challenges go beyond facing global competition, meeting client expectations or demands for integrated solutions to their needs, adjusting to shortened product life cycles, coping with increased specialization of skills and capabilities, or adapting to the internet and anytime/anywhere communication technologies, to name five worldwide phenomena. They have to do with the business models that underpin operations in both the private and public sectors, and which now encounter severe social and environmental limits. Henceforth, organizations must proactively work with others to achieve system changes. (In the 1970s, the driver of strategic alliances was the product and its performance: alliances aimed to procure the best raw materials at the lowest prices, deploy the latest technology, and stretch market penetration across borders. In the 1980s, the motive was to strengthen positions in the sector or market of activity, using alliances to develop economies of scale and of scope. In the 1990s, the lifting of barriers to market entry and the opening of borders between sectors brought a focus on capabilities: it was no longer enough to defend one's position—to stay ahead of the competition, innovations that give recurrent competitive advantage had become de rigueur.)

improving quality, or inhibiting competitors.[4] (Doz and Hamel (1998) grouped the primary purposes of an alliance into three: co-option, co-specialization, and learning and internalization.)

Types of Alliances

Strategic alliances between organizations are now ubiquitous.[5] Depending on the objectives or structure of the alliance, they take various configurations along a continuum of cooperative arrangements, e.g., cartels, cooperatives, joint ventures, equity investments, licensing, subcontracting (outsourcing), franchising, distribution relationships, research and development consortiums, industrial standards groups, action sets, innovation networks, clusters, letters of intent, memorandums of understanding, partnership frameworks, etc.[6] Some are short-lived; others are the prelude to a merger. In the public sector, from the 1990s, the formation of partnerships began to sweep through policies, strategies, programs, and projects, including their design, implementation, results, and associated business processes.

---

[4]Several interlinked trends, many of them already dominant, will accelerate the formation of strategic alliances in the near future. They include developments in telecommunications; the convergence of technologies; product, service, and organizational (procedural or process) innovations; decreasing costs in research and development; further shortening of product life cycles; the efforts of governments to attract foreign capital and technologies (sometimes, as in the case of the People's Republic of China, by giving select key investors privileged access); and the growing permeability of borders between sectors and markets, often on account of deregulation and privatization.

[5]Strategic alliances can be struck with a wide variety of players: customers, suppliers, competitors, universities, research institutes, government agencies, nongovernment organizations, etc. Partners may continue to compete elsewhere; some even argue that collaboration in strategic alliances is tantamount to competition in a different form.

[6]The last form of strategic alliance is notably popular in academia, government, and development agencies. A memorandum of understanding describes a bilateral or multilateral agreement. It expresses a convergence of will between parties and records an intended common line of action. It is a more formal alternative to a gentlemen's agreement (but this, by no means, curtails opportunistic behavior). It is used most often where parties do not imply a legal commitment or in situations where the parties cannot draft a legally binding agreement. (In some cases, depending on the wording, memorandums of understanding can have the enforceable power of a contract.) In development agencies, for instance, shared objectives might, for example, include working together to assist developing countries reduce poverty, achieve sustainable development, and realize the United Nations Millennium Development Goals; ensuring the delivery of development assistance in line with the principles of the Paris Declaration on Aid Effectiveness and the Accra Agenda for Action; and building public awareness of the outcomes of the partnership. Sharing of information is usually central to such joint undertakings.

Conventional Approaches to Strategic Alliances ...

The usual steps to forming a strategic alliance, each the subject of learned texts, are[7]:

1. Locate and validate the alliance within the long-term vision, mission, and strategy of the organization.
2. Specify the objectives and scope of the alliance regarding the organization-specific resources and capabilities that are desired, and underscore the importance of these.[8]
3. Question what to offer and what to receive in exchange to highlight interdependence. (Alternatively, what must be retained internally for strategic purposes, what cannot be done internally, and what could be done externally.)
4. Evaluate and select potential partners based on the level of synergy and the ability of the organizations to work together.[9]
5. Identify and mutually recognize the opportunities, including the transparency and receptivity of information they call for.
6. Evaluate negotiation capabilities.
7. Understand joint task requirements and develop and propose a working interface with the prospective partner. (This might necessitate an evaluation of the impact on shareholders and stakeholders.)
8. Negotiate and implement an agreement, anticipating longevity, that defines progress and includes systems to monitor and evaluate performance (while eschewing performance myopia).
9. Define the governance system that will oversee the alliance, enforce its administration, build trust and reciprocity, and curtail opportunistic behavior.
10. Plan the integration and its points of contacts.[10]
11. Create the alliance and catalyze it with leadership commitment.
12. Manage for value identification, creation, storage, sharing, and usage over time, while assessing the alliance's interdependence with other relationships.[11]

---

[7]Succinctly, Steinhilber (2008) identifies three essential building blocks that strategic alliances should set: (i) the right framework, (ii) the right organization, and (iii) the right relationships.

[8]The key questions are: What are the intended uses of the desired resources and capabilities? When would these be used? How would these be used?

[9]The key elements relate to sector and market; products, services, procedures, and processes; culture; compatibility; commitment; and financial positions.

[10]The key questions are: What would be, for instance, the training, equipment, maintenance, and awareness-raising implications of participating in the alliance? Would there be additional requirements? Would financial obligations need to be contemplated?

[11]Alliances should not be viewed in a vacuum: they are elements of strategic portfolios of evolving inter-organizational relationships. Each alliance is embedded in an organizational context that constrains certain developments but enables others in a coevolutionary way.

… And Their Shortcomings

However, strategic alliances and the proverbial win–win situations they promise frequently meet with difficulties (that can result in the termination of the alliance). Typical factors include poor communications, incompatible objectives, inability to share risks, opportunism, (perceived) low performance and flexibility, control and ownership arrangements, lack of trust, and conflict. These rifle across the decision to form an alliance, the selection of the partner, the choice of the governance structure for the alliance, the dynamic evolution of the alliance as the partnership spans time, the performance of the alliance, and the consequences for the partners.[12]

A Starter Kit for Strategic Alliances

Because conventional advice such as that given above has (when followed) still not sufficiently made up for the shortcomings of strategic alliances, Hughes and Weiss (2007) have proposed simple tenets to help the latter work better. The rules are to (i) focus less on defining the business plan and more on how the partners will work together; (ii) develop metrics pegged not only to alliance goals but also to alliance progress; (iii) leverage differences to create value, rather than attempt to eliminate them; (iv) go beyond formal governance structures to encourage collaborative behavior; and (v) spend as much time on managing internal stakeholders as on managing the relationship with the partner.

Promise, Reality, and Promise: Learning in Strategic Alliances

Notwithstanding, time and again, a subtler but far more important rationale behind strategic alliances (even those aimed at co-option or co-specialization) is obscured by their explicit strategic motives. That rationale is the intent to learn—especially

---

[12]Partners may not have the same ability to learn from an alliance and knowledge-related asymmetries will influence respective performances. And yet, learning from partners is of the essence of strategic alliances…

knowledge that is tacit,[13] collective, and imbedded: and it is probably failure in this arena that explains shortcomings.[14]

In brief, strategic alliances open up opportunities for organizations to gain knowledge and leverage strengths with partners.[15] (Indeed, the ability to learn through alliances is often vital to their continued existence.) Building knowledge- and identification-based trust, not just calculus-based trust, is fundamental to this. But strategic alliances also evolve as partners learn (or fail to learn). As competencies change, their goals are redefined. And the potential for learning also changes. However, even though alliance knowledge is tacitly or explicitly deemed useful, organizations will not necessarily actively seek to acquire it. Learning is a difficult, frustrating, and often misunderstood process.

With exceptions, studies of strategic alliances have focused on initial conditions and ignored the dynamic and interactive learning dimensions of strategic alliances.[16] Doz (1996) has explored five areas for learning as strategic alliances evolve in phases: (i) environment, (ii) task, (iii) process, (iv) skills, and (v) goals.[17] Central to each phase are systems, mechanisms, processes, and behaviors that build and improve practice in ongoing fashion by consciously and continually devising

---

[13]Tacit knowledge is the personalized knowledge that people carry in their heads. It is more difficult to formalize and communicate than explicit knowledge, but can be shared through discussion, storytelling, and personal interactions. There are two dimensions to tacit knowledge: (i) a technical dimension, which encompasses the kind of informal personal skills or crafts often referred to as know-how; and (ii) a cognitive dimension, which consists of beliefs, ideals, values, schemata, and mental models that are ingrained in individuals and often taken for granted.

[14]The formation of a strategic alliance is the acknowledgment that a partner has useful knowledge. If it had none there would be no reason to form the alliance.

[15]Organizations do not have brains but they have cognitive systems and memories.

[16]Over the years, strategic alliances have been analyzed from the perspectives of transaction cost economics, game theory, bargaining theory, and resource dependence theory. The social exchange perspective is a recent addition: it explores the circumstances and requirements leading to identification-based trust and the associated belief that an organization will behave with good intentions toward the alliance and its partner.

[17]The environment is both external (e.g., sectors, markets, competition, government, society, culture, etc.) and internal (e.g., the strategic context within each partner operates). The tasks are the (inter)actions, at multiple levels, that the partners must share and perform successfully. The processes encompass the decisions, operations, and associated business processes needed to successfully meet the tasks of the alliance. The skills are the more tacit, collective, and imbedded abilities and related knowledge, germane to the alliance, that must be transferred for the purposes of the alliance. The goals are the motives and agendas that partners bring to the alliance.

and developing the means to draw learning and translate that into evolving action for mutual benefit. Successful strategic alliances are highly evolutionary and grow in interactive cycles of learning, reevaluation, and readjustment. They do so at different levels, e.g., individual, group, and organization. Such are the attributes of learning organizations.[18]

Enhancing Learning Effectiveness in Strategic Alliances

> *We cannot always assure the future of our friends; we have a better chance of assuring our future if we remember who our friends are.*
>
> —Henry Kissinger

Knowledge can only be acquired if it is accessible. But accessibility, though necessary, does not guarantee learning: learning effectiveness is primordial. Much as in the case of individuals, the capacity of organizations to learn may be constrained for miscellaneous reasons. (Absorptive capacity is the ability to recognize the value of new knowledge and to assimilate it.)

Inkpen (1998) identified three integrative dimensions of maximum joint learning that influence learning effectiveness in strategic alliances: (i) the intensity of knowledge connections between partners, which occur through both formal and informal relationships between individuals and groups; (ii) the relatedness of alliance knowledge, nourished by knowledge of the partner and knowledge about alliance management; and (iii) the cultural alignment between alliance managers and their respective organizations. He flagged six objectives that, if met, should enhance learning effectiveness. And, he matched each with a series of questions to stimulate managerial thought and action.

---

[18]Organizational learning occurs when an organization acquires, assimilates, and applies new information, knowledge, and skills that improve its long-run performance and augment its competitive advantage. In a strategic alliance, the behavioral and organizational characteristics of each partner will condition success. Important behavioral characteristics include commitment, coordination, interdependence, and trust; communications; and conflict-resolution techniques. Crucial organizational attributes relate to structure (e.g., formalization, centralization, and complexity) and control (e.g., focus, mechanisms, and extent).

Moreover

Summing up, the success of strategic alliances can be variously attributed to the fit between partners, openness to change, the embedment of alliance management capabilities into the fabric of partner cultures, the strong involvement of leadership, and, above all, alliance learning. The failure of strategic alliances has, somewhat simplistically, been ascribed to a failure to collaborate—a convenient turn of phrase that explains much away.

If, however, learning in alliances can do much to promote success, then it should be predominantly mutual. In this respect, one last barrier must be overcome: asymmetries between firms do exist, which of course explains why they partner in the first place.[19] But if resolving variegated differences will serve alliances well, it follows that knowledge-related asymmetries should be tackled too.

Knowledge-related asymmetries fall naturally in three categories: (i) information, (ii) knowledge, and (iii) learning. Each will have a different effect on the individual performance of partners, the realization of objectives, and the stability of the alliance. The least that partners can do is to be conscious of that.

References

Andrew I (1998) Learning and knowledge acquisition through international strategic alliances. The Academy of Management Executive 12(4):69–80

Doz Y (1996) The evolution of cooperation in strategic alliances: initial conditions or learning processes. Strategic Management Journal 17:55–83

Doz Y, Hamel G (1998) Alliance advantage: the art of creating value through partnering. Harvard Business School Press

Hughes J, Weiss J (November 2007) Simple rules for making alliances work. Harvard Business Review: 122–131

Steinhilber S (2008) Strategic alliances: three ways to make them work. Harvard Business School Press

---

[19]Asymmetries can be eclectic, strategic, competitive, power-related, or network-based.

Proposition 72
Exercising Servant Leadership

In a Word Servant leadership is now in the vocabulary of enlightened leadership. It is a practical, altruistic philosophy that supports people who choose to serve first, and then lead, as a way of expanding service to individuals and organizations. The sense of civil community that it advocates and engenders can facilitate and smooth successful and principled change.

Preamble

On July 1–3, 1863, more than 158,000 soldiers fought near the market town of Gettysburg, Pennsylvania in what proved to be a turning point of the American Civil War (1861–1865). On November 19, 1863, President Abraham Lincoln dedicated the battlefield as a national cemetery. He gave the Gettysburg Address, one of the most quoted speeches in the history of the United States, in 10 sentences and about 2 min. Its last words—... *government of the people, by the people, for the people,* ...—have come to define democracy to many.

© Asian Development Bank 2017

O. Serrat, *Knowledge Solutions*, DOI 10.1007/978-981-10-0983-9_72

Background

Ancient schools of thought about great men[1] and more recent (sometimes over-lapping) explanations form an ever-growing literature on leadership.[2] In modern times, three broad categories have encompassed related theories: approaches have explored the traits (1940s–1950s) then behaviors or styles (1950s–1960s) of successful leaders; examined the contextual nature of leadership and the role of followers (1960s–1970s); and investigated what interactions of traits, behaviors, and situations (as well as group facilitation) might allow people to transact or transform for excellence (1980s).[3] At the risk of simplifying, notwithstanding a few notable exceptions,[4] these perspectives have been hierarchical, linear, male, Newtonian, pragmatic, and, above all, concerned with the leader as an individual.

Leadership and the Challenge of Change[5]

Theory and practice are inexorably intertwined: to understand developments in leadership theory is to fathom the nature of leadership itself. Leadership is difficult because, quintessentially, it must often focus on the challenge of change.[6] Change that is transformational defies easy solutions: it involves value-laden issues; it tests strongly held loyalties; it surfaces deep-seated conflicts. But people do not resist

---

[1]The great man theory (associated with Thomas Carlyle) became popular in the nineteenth and twentieth centuries, with numerous histories of Roman emperors and charismatic leaders such as Napoleon, Gandhi, Winston Churchill, and Franklin Delano Roosevelt, among others. It assumed that the capacity for leadership is inherent—that great leaders are exceptional people, born with innate qualities, destined to lead, and certainly not made. Trait explanations stemmed from it.

[2]Early studies of leadership, preoccupied with power and influence, date back to Sun Tzu, Plato, and Niccolò Machiavelli. In spite of this, leadership only became a focus of academic studies in the last 60 years—particularly more so in the last 20 years.

[3]The problem with leadership theory is that even though no school of thought is completely defensible many explanations offer interesting insights. (None would have achieved prominence if it had no face validity.) However, they are neither comprehensive nor well-tested. Yet, most make arguments that hold true on occasion—the difficulty is that we do not know which are valid in what circumstances.

[4]Selznick (1957), a political sociologist, was initially ignored by the mainstream. As long ago as 1957, he compared leadership to institutionalization, in the sense that leadership is about infusing values and clarifying purpose in an organization. Burns (1978), a biographer, historian, and political scientist, infused his model of transformational leadership with ethical and moral dimensions, and was the first to see the need for leaders to develop a binding and mutually stimulating relationship with followers.

[5]This section draws from Ronald Heifetz ad Marty Linsky. Leadership is 1% Inspiration and 99% Perspiration (Kurtzman et al. 2004).

[6]It is at times of organizational strain that effective leaders can make a significant and visible impact.

change per se; rather, they refuse to accept the losses that it may cause them to incur. To exercise leadership is to invite people to make adaptive change (as distinct from technical change that concerned parties address daily)—for this they must learn new ways and discard old habits against the promise of an uncertain outcome. The process is intrinsically disruptive and therefore induces disequilibrium and stress.

In a globalizing world of organizations, pressures to change will only increase over the next decades. Given the complexity of the subject, new explanations of leadership are bound to arise and should influence how future leaders behave. Since much of leadership is about change, and the problems that leadership endeavors to address lie with people themselves, those in positions of authority are more often than not apt to collude and shy away from challenges. (Authority is a contract for services: for that reason, people in positions of authority are [paradoxically] rarely authorized to exercise transformational leadership, whatever the job description may advertise.) It follows that *leadership of the people, by the people, for the people* could conduce change better, coaxing them to clarify what is vital and what is not.

The Distribution of Leadership

The most valuable "currency" of any organization is the initiative and creativity of its members. Every leader has the solemn moral responsibility to develop these to the maximum in all his people. This is the leader's highest priority.

—W. Edwards Deming

A new moral principle may be emerging which holds that the only authority deserving of one's allegiance is that which is freely and knowingly granted by the led to the leader in response to, and in proportion to, the clearly evident servant stature of the leader. Those who choose to follow this principle will not casually accept the authority of existing institutions. Rather, they will freely respond only to individuals who are chosen as leaders because they are proven and trusted servants. To the extent that this principle prevails, the only truly viable institutions will be those that are predominantly servant led.

—Robert Greenleaf

The idea of the leader may be misplaced, at least in complex, modern organizations. The trends in leadership theory are clear: explanations have moved from heroic leadership to leadership by power and influence, thence to the interactive nature of leadership, and of late to leadership by consent. If leaders (can be made to) exist throughout an organization, the future may witness the spread of leadership groups, not individual leaders. (Katzenbach and Smith (1993) have written about the "following part of leading".)

Since the 1990s, two interrelated schools of thought with foundations in humanistic psychology, philosophy, politics, social psychology, and sociology rather than management science and psychology, have received growing recognition. They promote people-oriented, or servant, leadership and offer promising notions of informal, emergent, dispersed, or distributed leadership.[7] (To some, not this writer, they are reminiscent of the transformational theory.)[8] Paraphrasing Kotter (1996), these relatively new schools of thought may fuel the common and persistent sense of urgency, home-grown vision and strategy, cultural anchorage, ownership, broad-based empowerment of people, delegated management for immediate wins, ambient communications, and powerful guiding coalitions needed to overcome what are often massive forces of inertia. Quoting Warren Bennis: "None of us is as smart as all of us … The Lone Ranger, the incarnation of the individual problem solver, is dead. In his place, we have a new model for creative achievement: The Great Group." (Bennis and Biederman 1997)

Exercising Servant Leadership …

The philosophy and practice of servant leadership was coined and defined by Robert Greenleaf in the 1970s.[9] The general concept is ancient, with roots in China (Lao Tzu) and India (Chanakya). Jesus of Nazareth urged his followers to be servants first, and became a messenger of a great religion. It begins with the natural feeling that one wants to serve, to serve first. Then, conscious choice brings one to aspire to lead. Servant leadership seems to touch an innate need in many and probably harks back to the beginning of time.[10]

---

[7]As for all theories, their explanatory power will need to meet the five criteria set by Kuhn (1962): (i) accurate—empirically adequate with experimentation and observation; (ii) consistent—internally consistent but also externally consistent with other theories; (iii) broad scope—a theory's consequences should extend beyond what it was initially designed to explain; (iv) simple—the simplest explanation, in line with Occam's Razor; and (v) fruitful—a theory should disclose new phenomena or new relationships among phenomena.

[8]The primary difference between the two is the focus of the leader. That of the transformational leader is directed at the organization: his or her behavior builds follower commitment toward organizational objectives. The focus of the servant-leader is on others—including fellow employees, clients, and communities: the achievement of organizational objectives is a subordinate outcome.

[9]Kenneth Blanchard, Stephen Covey, Max DePree, Peter Senge, Margaret Wheatley, and others support it. To Margaret Wheatley, the belief that calls a person to be a servant-leader is the belief of who we are as a species. She thinks that if the real work is to stay together, then we are not only the best resource to move into the future: we are the only resource. We need to learn how to be together—that is the essential work of the servant-leader.

[10]The emphasis on serving a higher purpose has made this model popular in the Church.

- **Definition and Best Test** Servant leadership is about moving people to a higher level of individual and communal self-awareness by leading people at a higher level. Its principal tenet is that it is the duty of a leader to serve followers, his or her key role being to develop, enable, and support team members, helping them fully develop their potential and deliver their best. From this perspective, in a world of organizations, servant-leaders are considered humble stewards of their organization's resources and capabilities. In a 1970 essay, *The Servant as Leader*, Greenleaf explained:

> *The servant-leader **is** servant first ... It begins with the natural feeling that one wants to serve, to serve **first**. Then conscious choice brings one to aspire to lead. That person is sharply different from one who is **leader** first, perhaps because of the need to assuage an unusual power drive or to acquire material possessions ... The leader-first and the servant-first are two extreme types. Between them there are shadings and blends that are part of the infinite variety of human nature.*

This is no pie in the sky: the proof of the pudding is in the eating and the test of a servant-leader is one of pragmatism based on visible outcomes. Greenleaf (1977) continued:

> *The best test, and difficult to administer, is: do those served grow as persons; do they, **while being served**, become healthier, wiser, freer, more autonomous, more likely themselves to become servants? **And**, what is the effect on the least privileged in society; will he benefit, or, at least, will he not be further deprived?*

Importantly, neither Greenleaf's definition of a servant-leader nor its best test requires one to hold a formal leadership position. What matters is what we do in "our little corner of the world" and why we are doing it. Indeed, servant-leaders turn leadership into a territory, a field of endeavor in which people can operate—each leveraging individual abilities and capacities—to serve the mission of the organization and the people who make the organization happen. The objective, to repeat, is to enhance the growth of individuals in organizations and promote teamwork and personal involvement.

- **Servant-Leader Attributes** Spears (1998),[11] who served for 17 years as the head of the Robert K. Greenleaf Center for Servant Leadership, identified in Greenleaf's writings 10 characteristics of servant-leaders. They are by no means exhaustive but he views them as central to the development of servant-leaders. (They are, primarily, behavioral in nature.) The attributes are listening, empathy, healing, awareness, persuasion, conceptualization, foresight, stewardship, commitment to the growth of others, and (a concern for) building community. Unlike the models mentioned earlier, which gaze at leadership through the prism

---

[11]Larry Spears' identification of themes can help operationalize the concept of servant leadership. A few servant leadership assessment instruments have already been formulated; since the concept continues to gain attention in practice, we can expect to see additional research in the area.

of top-down organizational hierarchies, servant leadership emphasizes collaboration, empathy, trust, and the ethical use of power.[12]

- **Caveat** Servant leadership does not pose as an explanatory or quick-fix theory: it cannot be readily instilled in an organization. But it is a long-term, transformational approach to life and work—in short a way of being—that has the potential to generate positive change in its milieu: when followers see evidence that their leaders truly follow the ideals of servant leadership, they are more likely to become servants themselves.

... With Distributed Leadership

The distributed leadership approach views leadership as a social contract. It shifts the emphasis from developing leaders to developing "leaderful" organizations through concurrent, collective, and compassionate leadership with a collective responsibility for the latter. The distributed leadership theory

- Regards leadership as a process of sense making and direction giving—this constitutes a move from individuals to relationships.
- Rejects the notion of heroic leaders and the focus on top management, and submits a less formalized model whereby leadership is dissociated from organizational hierarchies.
- Distinguishes the exercise of leadership and the exercise of authority, and treats leadership as a decentralized activity that is not, unavoidably, the sole responsibility of formally appointed leaders.
- Aims to nurture leadership capacity through the development of leadership processes and skills in others.

References

Bennis W, Biederman P (1997) Organizing genius: the secret of creative collaboration. Perseus Books
Burns JM (1978) Leadership. Harper and Row
Greenleaf R (1977) Servant leadership: a journey into the nature of legitimate power and greatness. Paulist Press
Katzenbach J, Smith D (1993) The wisdom of teams: creating the high-performance organization. Harvard Business School Press
Kotter (1996) Leading change. Harvard Business School Press
Kuhn T (1962) The structure of scientific revolutions. University of Chicago Press

---

[12]Daniel Goleman's model of emotional intelligence is (almost uncannily) applicable to servant leadership.

Kurtzman J, Rifkin G, Griffith V (2004) MBA in a book: mastering business with attitude. Three
    Rivers Press
Selznick (1957) Leadership in administration: a sociological interpretation. Harper and Row
Spears L (ed) (1998) Insights on leadership: service, stewardship, spirit, and servant-leadership.
    Wiley, Inc

Further Reading

Kofman F, Senge P (1995) Communities of commitment: the heart of learning organizations. In:
    Sarita C, John R (eds) Learning organizations: developing cultures for tomorrow's workplace.
    Productivity Press, Inc

Proposition 73
Distributing Leadership

In a Word The prevailing view of leadership is that it is concentrated or focused. In organizations, this makes it an input to business processes and performance—dependent on the attributes, behaviors, experience, knowledge, skills, and potential of the individuals chosen to impact these. The theory of distributed leadership thinks it best considered as an outcome. Leadership is defined by what one does, not who one is. Leadership at all levels matters and must be drawn from, not just be added to, individuals and groups in organizations.

Fossil Fuel

Modern humans (Homo sapiens) evolved in East Africa some 200,000 years ago. They lived in tightly knit nomadic groups of 10–30 individuals, perhaps as large as 30–50. (Seasonally, they may have assembled in social collectives of 100 or more when resources were abundant.) To subsist, they foraged edible plants and sometimes caught wild animals—without much recourse to the domestication of either—in adaptive strategies.

© Asian Development Bank 2017

O. Serrat, *Knowledge Solutions*, DOI 10.1007/978-981-10-0983-9_73

These band societies had nonhierarchical and egalitarian[1] social structures: individuals had no authority over one another and, barring gender, distinctions based on power, prestige, wealth, or rank did not exist. Individuals came forward when their expertise was needed. Elders were looked to for advice but decisions were consensual. There were no written laws and none of the specialized coercive roles played in more complex societies; customs were transmitted orally.

Some nomadic groups began the transition to sedentary life in built-up villages and towns, then in early chiefdoms and embryonic states, about 6,000 years ago—most likely following the appearance of agriculture (and domestication of animals) some 4,000 years before that.[2] Once begun, the process of agriculture-driven social, economic, and technological expansion led to more densely populated and stratified societies and, eventually, the development of Byzantine governments. However, only in the last 100–500 years have there been state-level polities.

Fast Forward

The Neolithic Revolution was, in effect, the first agricultural revolution and the mother of all changes.[3] Other agricultural revolutions followed the early move from hunter-gatherer to agrarian societies, including the Muslim Agricultural Revolution that unfurled from the eighth to the thirteenth century, later manifestations in seventeenth and eighteenth century Europe, and the Green Revolution of the mid-twentieth century. In the eighteenth and nineteenth centuries, an Industrial Revolution in the United Kingdom sparked major transformations in agriculture, manufacturing, mining, and transport, and sped advances in natural, social, and interdisciplinary sciences, e.g., astronomy, biology, chemistry, human anatomy, mathematics, and physics, that had come to light from the sixteenth century. Later

---

[1]The mobility of families on the move demanded that material possessions be minimized. For that reason, single members could not accumulate surpluses of resources.

[2]When the last glacial period ended about 10,000 years ago, much of the earth became subject to drier spells. The new climate favored the emergence of annual plants that die in the dry season, leaving a dormant seed or tuber. It is the availability of readily storable wild grains—especially cereals—and pulses that may have enabled some hunter-gatherers to settle in villages. Evidence points to the Fertile Crescent of the Middle East, viz., the Levant and Mesopotamia, as the site of the earliest planned sowing and harvesting of plants. Development of agriculture also seems to have occurred in northern and southern China (as early as 10,000–11,000 years ago, findings now suggest), the Sahel Belt, the island of New Guinea, and regions of the Americas.

[3]The sedentary societies that the Neolithic Revolution engendered modified their natural environment with specialized cultivation and storage technologies that made surplus production possible. This laid the basis for high population densities; centralized administrations and political structures; hierarchical ideologies; labor diversification; trading economies; the advancement of nonportable art, architecture, and culture; and depersonalized systems of knowledge.

tectonic shifts in human progress included the Commercial Revolution—a period of European economic expansion, colonialism, and mercantilism that lasted from the sixteenth century until the early eighteenth century; and the Digital Revolution— brought about by sweeping changes in computing and communication technology from the 1980s. In all instances, creativity and innovation were born of opportunity and necessity that gradually, then ever more rapidly, transfigured the planet. Their offspring is the phenomenon of globalization.

Organization, Activity, and Knowledge

Individuals group when the perceived benefits from collaboration outstrip those from going it alone.[4] The reverse is that groups act in ways that benefit the group before the individual. Since the Neolithic Period, humans have organized to face a fast-changing environment. Even so, their multifaceted ways have been nothing more (and certainly nothing less) than endeavors to harness and balance innate (self-centered and other-centered) human drives[5] in contexts of scarce resources. From the mid-1990s, to cite an example, the multiplication of communities and networks of practice (not to forget virtual teams)—driven by computing and communication technology as well as globalization—has propagated radically new forms of organization and stimulated thinking about working in groups.[6]

---

[4]People join groups for many reasons. A primary motive is that membership often satisfies basic needs. First, activities that enhance survival, such as hunting and defense against predators, are usually best accomplished collectively rather than on one's own. Second, man has a biological need for social contact. Third, group membership often fills the need for power (which relates to the capacity or potential to influence the behavior of others). Besides gratifying needs, membership can also give a person more opportunity to accomplish goals. A last reason, perhaps related to the third need mentioned earlier, is that being close to others can provide comfort and support. To repeat, individuals do not join groups randomly: they do so for instrumental reasons. Their membership may also serve several purposes simultaneously, while they may belong to several groups at the same time.

[5]The self-centered drives that Ehin (2000) distinguishes are rank, status, discipline, control, territory, possessions, fear, anger, and sex. The other-centered drives are attachment, affiliation, care giving, care receiving, altruism, remorse, shame, and guilt.

[6]The potency of communities and networks of practice, and reason members join them, is that they offer a way to theorize tacit knowledge. By so doing, they decrease the learning curve of new employees, enable professional development, reduce rework and prevent reinvention of the wheel, permit faster problem resolution and response time to needs and inquiries, illuminate good practice, spawn new ideas for products and services, enable accelerated learning, connect learning to action, and make for organizational performance improvement.

> *The strongest human instinct is to impart information, the second strongest is to resist it.*
>
> —Kenneth Grahame

Clearly, learning is in the relationships between people in their environment and the links between organization, activity, and knowledge are intimate. The more successful approaches to organizational structuring have been anthropologically sensitive and recognized that human beings are biological entities that cannot, and therefore should not, be overly controlled. Since knowledge work now demands that we organize better for change, interest has grown in a long-forgotten modus operandi that harks back to the Neolithic Period: it is that of self-organizing teams.

Organizing for Change

In a globalizing world, innovation is more than ever associated with organizational survival. For innovation to thrive, people need to be immersed in flexible social environments, not chained in cause-and-effect constructs. (When it comes to knowledge workers, traditional concepts of management seldom work: knowledge workers carry their means of production—meaning their intelligence—with them.) In self-organizing teams, members eschew reliance on traditional, positional leadership[7] to spontaneously take the lead. If, as evidence shows, most organizations have reached a point in their evolution when they no longer need leaders in front and followers at the back, efforts and money[8] would be better spent on fortifying leadership as a mutual, social phenomenon.

---

[7]The presumption that underpins the near-universal practice of positional leadership is that certain people are eligible or can be groomed for leadership. Indeed, most positions are by appointment. The practice is rooted in the great man model of leadership and more recent, related theories concerned with the traits, behaviors, or styles of successful leaders; the contextual nature of leadership and the role of followers; and the interactions of traits, behaviors, and situations (as well as group facilitation) that empower leaders to transact or transform for excellence. In the twenty-first century, such conceptions of leadership seem more and more outdated.

[8]Executive training is about transfusing leadership into a chosen few, so that they might be transformed and then change their organization. But, even though the anointed may learn, no one else in their organization is likely to by virtue of their nonselection: sending a changed person in an unchanged environment is not necessarily effective.

The Orpheus Chamber Orchestra

The Orpheus Chamber Orchestra was founded in 1972 by cellist Julian Fifer and fellow musicians to bring chamber music's ideals of democracy, personal involvement, and mutual respect into an orchestral setting. It has no conductor.[9] However, being conductorless does not mean that it is leaderless—far from it: the orchestra has developed a system of musical chairs that invites each of the 27 permanent members to assume leadership positions, either by leading the group in rehearsal and performance as concertmaster or by heading one of the orchestra's many different formal or informal teams.

Built on eight supporting principles, the Orpheus process has reportedly unleashed the vision, talent, creativity, innovation, energy, and leadership potential of each member. (The free-spirited energy of its keenly attentive musicians results in an edgy spontaneity, and proves that size is less important than vigor (*The Economist* 2006).) Apparently, the orchestra is also uncommonly responsive to changing conditions in the listening public or in its membership. Finally, although they play in other groups too, the permanent members consider playing in the orchestra their most fulfilling musical experience. According to Eric Bartlett, one of its cellists, "Orpheus has removed a barrier between the audience and the music, the conductor himself."

---

[9]In traditional orchestras, conductors wield unquestioned authority over those who perform under their baton. They select the repertoire, organize rehearsals, and instruct the musicians how to play. In a survey of symphony orchestra musicians and workers in other professions in East Germany, West Germany, the United Kingdom, and the United States, conducted in the late 1980s and early 1990s, orchestra musicians scored the highest in terms of having personal, self-directed internal motivation. However, they ranked seventh out of 13 occupations in terms of job satisfaction, below prison guards and just above industrial production teams. When asked if their job provided for personal growth and development, responses were even more distressing: they ranked ninth. (The occupations surveyed were airline cockpit crews, airline flight attendants, amateur theater companies, beer sales and delivery teams, economic analysts in the government, industrial production teams, mental health treatment teams, operating room nurses, prison guards, professional hockey team, professional string quartets, semiconductor fabrication teams, and symphony orchestra musicians.) (Allmendinger et al. 1996).

Table. The orpheus process

Principle	Rationale
Put power in the hands of the people doing the work	Those closest to the ground are in the best position to know market needs and make decisions that impact these. Organizations that empower personnel with true authority can expect better products and services; more satisfied clients, partners, and audiences; and higher profits
Encourage individual responsibility for product and quality	The converse of giving authority to those closest to the ground is requiring them to be accountable. Personnel who are entrusted to lead must feel a real and personal responsibility for outcomes
Create clarity of roles.	Before personnel can comfortably and effectively take on leadership duties, it must be assigned well-defined roles and know what each one is responsible for. These roles must be communicated widely throughout the organization
Foster horizontal teamwork	No one has all the answers to every question. Horizontal teams—both formal and informal—that are not artificially constrained by the need to focus attention on narrow issues or opportunities can reach and tap expertise across organizational boundaries to obtain inputs, act on opportunities, solve problems, and make decisions
Share and rotate leadership	In most organizations, authority for leadership is vested in certain positions (and not in others): leaders are expected to lead and followers are expected to follow. The higher-up an individual's location on the organizational chart, the more authority his or her position wields. By moving personnel in and out of leadership positions, an organization can tap the leadership potential that exists in individuals and is more often than not ignored or discarded, if not at times punished. Leaders should be selected based on what attributes, behaviors, experience, knowledge, skills, and potential they bring to the table on propitious occasions
Learn to listen, learn to talk	Communications oxygenate the bloodstream of high-performance organizations. Individuals must listen to the views and opinions of others, respect what is said and the person saying it, and know when to talk. Two-way communications must be expected and cultivated constantly
Seek consensus (and build creative systems that favor consensus)	Consensus is built on trust and that is born of participation. Involving personnel in discussions does not take the edge off results; it sharpens them (if participants are willing to listen, be flexible, and compromise on positions). In most organizations, the number of people involved in decisions decreases in direct proportion to the increase in the latter's importance
Dedicate passionately to your mission	Passionate personnel care about their organization; its clients, partners, and audiences; and the way they perform to meet needs

Source Author

Rediscovering Distributed Leadership

> *Grant is the first general I have had. You know how it has been with all the rest. They wanted me to be the general. I am glad to find a man who can go ahead without me.*
>
> —Abraham Lincoln

The widely distributed, interconnected, and virtual forms of organization that have emerged require that organizations unlock the knowledge of their members and empower them to act on their own behalf and on behalf of their organizations.

Positional leadership does not meet the needs of high-performance organizations: when working with knowledge workers, managers can have no direct authority over how their "subordinates" perform; they can at best coax them to do their best.[10] They will deliver more by not clutching the reigns and, instead, entice others to hold them as the situation warrants.

The literature on distributed leadership is young and modest. It rests on a handful of articles written in the 1990s and 2000s, mainly in the field of educational leadership.[11] (Sometimes interchangeable notions of collaborative, delegated, democratic, dispersed, shared, teacher, and thought leadership[12] in these do not make for clarity.) Nonetheless, it constitutes a clear-cut break from the leadership theories that, from the 1980s, examined what combinations of traits, behaviors, and situations (as well as group facilitation) might allow individuals to transact or

---

[10]There may not be much opportunity even there. Much of motivation theory assumes that people are static. They may be from a manager's perspective, but the answer rests with the individual who chooses whether and how to engage. If this argument holds, all that a leader might be able to do is circumscribe the contours of what self-centered and other-centered drives are already at play and help individuals channel these more efficiently and effectively to contribute more.

[11]Peter Gronn has done much to establish its foundations. Notwithstanding, he credits Gibb (1954), an Australian psychologist, with the first use of the term in 1954 in his chapter on leadership in the first edition of the *Handbook of Social Psychology*. According to Gronn (2002), Gibb discerned a crucial distinction between focused and distributed leadership. "Focused" stood for the way leadership can for various reasons be concentrated in or monopolized by one person as the focal point of a group's other members. However, because a group's membership and the patterns of influence across that fluctuate, Gibb intuited that leadership is as likely to be distributed as it is to be concentrated or monopolized. Indeed, the members of a group often develop a history or pattern of working during which different persons emerge as influential on account of their specialist knowledge or expertise. Sadly, Gibb's insights then lay dormant for over three decades.

[12]Proponents of thought leadership press that it must be cultivated as the key form of distributed leadership. The practical implication is that organizations should move beyond simply empowering employees to manage themselves, and start promoting organization-wide leadership conceived as the championing of new ideas.

transform for excellence.[13] Quite simply, it is a different way of thinking about leadership, a new lens through which to view and study leadership as a phenomenon, not just as something that is brought to a team (or organization).

The starting point of distributed leadership is the division of labor that characterizes most organizations[14]: rather than limiting themselves to a binary division of leaders and followers, proponents prefer to examine where organizations manifest leadership in their work practices and, when they do, the various forms that takes. To the extent that leadership is shared or dispersed, Gronn explains that it is likely to be aggregated or holistic.[15]

The basic idea of distributed leadership is not very complicated. In any organized system, people typically specialize, or develop particular competencies, that are related to their predispositions, interests, aptitudes, prior knowledge, skills, and specialized roles. [...] Organizing these diverse competencies into a coherent whole requires understanding how individuals vary, how the particular knowledge and skill of one person can be made to complement that of another, and how the competencies of some can be shared with others. In addition, organizing diverse competencies requires understanding when the knowledge and skill possessed by the people within the organization is [sic] not equal to the problem they are trying to solve, searching outside the organization for new knowledge and skill, and bringing it into the organization. [...] Distributed leadership, then, means multiple sources of guidance and direction, following the contours of expertise in an organization, made coherent through a common culture. It is the "glue" of a common task or goal —improvement of instruction—and a common frame of values for how to approach

---

[13]The unsustainabilibity of a focused model of individual leader omniscience is widely recognized, especially in light of its limitations when dealing with adaptive change. Nevertheless, situational and contingency theories of leadership still shed insight, with a twist: much as situations and cultures, organizations call for different types of leadership and require different skills of that at different moments. The settings that leadership should address can suddenly change and call for norms, authority structures, and adaptive strategies beyond the ken of traditional leadership.

[14]Most theories of leadership only permit a twofold division of labor: people either lead or follow. (The theory of servant leadership is one exception.) Such naive dualism pays no heed to the reality and complexity of business processes and imposes a further layer of involvedness in the form of specialized role titles and job descriptions.

[15]An aggregated pattern is one in which individuals, on different occasions, as part of distinctive activities, for miscellaneous reasons, and for varying periods of time are deemed by their colleagues to exercise leadership. (To note, Gronn's numerical or additive perspective purposely extends no privileges to individuals or groups for providing more leadership than others, makes no assumptions as to what behaviors carry more weight with colleagues, and is prompted by awareness that more than one person counts in contributions to organizational performance.) A holistic pattern is one in which parts combine synergistically to form a new whole. [To note further, Gronn's holistic perspective acknowledges that intuitive working relations emerge when individuals and groups negotiate relationships over time and come to rely on one another. Institutionalized structures and structural relations act as concertive (or conjoint) mechanisms that pool distributed capacity, regularize distributed action, and incorporate these into an organization's governance.]

that task—culture—that keeps distributed leadership from becoming another version of loose coupling (Elmore 2000).

Usefully, a recent study (National College for School Leadership 2004) isolated six ways to distribute leadership: (i) formal, (ii) pragmatic, (iii) strategic, (iv) incremental, (v) opportunistic, and (vi) cultural.[16] The categories are neither fixed nor mutually exclusive: each, be it stand-alone or in combination with others, may be appropriate at a given time depending on circumstances. They can also be considered phases in a development process. To begin, an organization would need to create awareness of distributed leadership. In later phases, work to build trust, confidence, knowledge, and attitudes, enriched by feedback, would move it in increments from formal to cultural distribution.

Three elements distinguish distributed leadership from other theories of leadership (National College for School Leadership 2003). First, it highlights leadership as an emergent property of a group or network of interacting individuals. Second, it suggests openness in the boundaries of leadership. Third, it entails that multiple types of expertise are distributed across the many, not the few. Fundamentally, however, it is the first of the three characteristics, viz., leadership as the product of concertive activity that underscores distributed leadership as an emergent property of a group or network.

Preamble

Distributed leadership is reminiscent of the ideal of the learning organization on account of the importance it ascribes to the collective. (It is also consistent with more familiar precepts of empowerment, such as subsidiarity.) With the burgeoning of communities and networks of practice, there is in modern organizations a sense that it is an idea whose time has come. At the end of the day, all leadership is collective: this underscores, indeed imparts new meaning to, concerns of interdependence and interactions.

Without a doubt, distributing leadership for organizational performance has to do with trust and accountability at individual and group levels. Studying requirements for building these surfaces tensions inherent in processes of consultation, command, and consensus building, but in so doing airs them out. In turn, this bolsters confidence to stop directing and intervening, and stand back. From there, one can initiate, then institutionalize, measures to promote distributed leadership and mitigate the factors that inhibit it.

Once again, trust has primacy among the factors that promote distributed leadership. But acceptance of the leadership potential of others pays too, as does

---

[16]Key concepts in cultural distribution are agency and reciprocity. As organizations mature from individual control to collective activity married to internal accountability, each staff demonstrates respect, personal regard, competence, and integrity.

work to foster shared goals and promote self-esteem. It goes without saying that visionary human resource management can do much to capacitate an organization: good staffing, continuity, and stability do hearten distributed leadership. Besides the absence of the foregoing promoting factors, inhibiting factors tend to be structural, with the exacerbating circumstance of all-too-commonly heavy workloads, as well as lack of time and space for reflection.

References

Allmendinger J, Hackman R, Lehman E (1996) Life and work in symphony orchestras. Musical Quarterly 80:194–219

Ehin C (2000) Unleashing intellectual capital. Butterworth-Heinemann

Elmore R (2000) Building a new structure for school leadership. The Albert Shanker Institute. Washington, DC

Gibb C (1954) Leadership. In Lindzey G (ed) The handbook of social psychology. Addisson-Wesley

Gronn P (2002) Distributed leadership as a unit of analysis. The Leadership Quarterly 13:423–451

National College for School Leadership (2003) Distributed leadership. Nottingham

National College for School Leadership (2004) Distributed leadership in action. Nottingham

The Economist (5 August 2006) Headless—orpheus chamber orchestra. The Economist Newspaper Limited

Further Reading

Spillane J (2006) Distributed leadership. Wiley, Inc

Proposition 74
Improving Sector and Thematic Reporting

In a Word Communities of practice have become an accepted part of organizational development. Learning organizations build and leverage them with effect. To reach their potential, much as other bodies, they stand to gain from healthy reporting. Quality of information and its proper presentation enable stakeholders to make sound and reasonable assessments of performance, and take appropriate action.

Background

On 31 July 2009, Haruhiko Kuroda—ADB President and concurrent Chair of ADB's Board of Directors—approved *Enhancing Knowledge Management Under ADB's Strategy 2020*, a plan of action to advance the knowledge management

© Asian Development Bank 2017
O. Serrat, *Knowledge Solutions*, DOI 10.1007/978-981-10-0983-9_74

agenda under *Strategy 2020: The Long-Term Strategic Framework of the Asian Development Bank (2008–2020).*

> When you wish to instruct, be brief; that men's minds take in quickly what you say, learn its lesson, and retain it faithfully. Every word that is unnecessary only pours over the side of a brimming mind.
>
> —Cicero
>
> The pen is the tongue of the mind.
>
> —Miguel de Cervantes
>
> If you would not be forgotten as soon as you are dead, either write things worth reading or do things worth writing.
>
> —Benjamin Franklin
>
> I believe more in the scissors than I do in the pencil.
>
> —Truman Capote

Four pillars support the plan: (i) sharpening the knowledge focus in ADB's operations, (ii) empowering the communities of practice (CoPs) hosted by ADB, (iii) strengthening external knowledge partnerships, and (iv) further enhancing staff learning and skills development. The four pillars are closely related: the set of actions/outputs that make up the first focuses on adding value to ADB's operations in its developing member countries; the other three sets deal with how that might be achieved.

These *Knowledge Solutions* showcase the revised guidelines for sector and thematic reporting that ADB then approved on 6 October 2009 to empower the CoPs it hosts. ADB, as a learning organization, must build CoPs and leverage them effectively to improve the quality of its operations, eventually in the interest of its developing member countries. A coherent set of directional documents is a prerequisite to this, and the new guidelines constitute a practical, incremental, and forward-looking move in that direction.

Seeking, Giving, and Using Feedback

Feedback is a circular process whereby some portion of a system's output is returned to the input to control dynamic behavior. In ADB, good feedback from CoPs is essential to realize their potential as collaboration mechanisms.

The revised guidelines for sector and thematic reporting by ADB's CoPs forged a new direction. The rationale was to (i) introduce principles of good reporting based on accuracy, transparency, and economy of knowledge sharing; (ii) provide guidance on key elements of reporting for organizational performance, including the use of knowledge management metrics; (iii) present to support coordination, a composite picture of the progress of work on sector and thematic priorities to inform management systems in ADB, including the annual *Development Effectiveness Reviews* and *Work Program and Budget Framework* papers, as well as the *Annual Administrative and Capital Budget* exercises; and (iv) assess the performance of CoPs, without duplicating data reports generated by the operations departments. The guidelines are flexible to the varying needs of each sector and theme.

Box: Guidelines for Sector and Thematic Reporting

Introduction
Sector and thematic reporting is part of a comprehensive monitoring system at regional, country, program, project, sector, thematic, and institutional levels. Over the years, from 2005, the CoPs hosted by ADB have developed to support the sectoral and thematic effectiveness of ADB's operations.

Exhibit: Archetypal Functions of CoPs
Amplifying Taking new, little-known, or little-understood ideas, giving them weight, and making them more widely understood.
Community Building Promoting and sustaining the values and standards of individuals or organizations.
Convening Bringing together different, distinct people or groups of people.
Filtering Organizing and managing information that is worth paying attention to.
Investing and Providing Offering a means to give members the resources they need to carry out their main activities.
Source Author

Enhancing Knowledge Management under Strategy: Proposed Plan of Action (2009–2011), approved on 31 July 2009, emphasizes the need to empower CoPs explaining that ADB, as a learning organization, must build CoPs and leverage them effectively to improve the quality of its operations. Good reporting by CoPs is essential to make the most of their potential as collaboration mechanisms and thereby maximize ADB's development impact, ultimately to the benefit of its clients, partners, and audiences. First, CoPs should be able to clearly present what in their views are key issues that ADB should focus on in terms of strategic studies and new business initiatives. Second, they should be able to distil and synthesize for wider institutional learning what ADB has learned from its sector and thematic operations. Third, flowing from the above, they should be able to demonstrate how ADB's sector and thematic operations have contributed to achieving development effectiveness. In this sense, reporting by CoPs should be seen as integral to overall reporting on that.

To better accomplish their functions under *Strategy 2020: The Long-Term Strategic Framework of the Asian Development Bank (2008–2020)*, the guidelines on sector and thematic level reporting are hereby revised to ensure focus on crucial areas and coverage of assessments and results in high-quality, reader-friendly reports that will inform the annual *Development Effectiveness Reviews* and *Work Program and Budget Framework* papers. The following suggests what sector and thematic level reporting is included, yet acknowledges that it should be adapted to the particular needs of each sector and theme. In the guidelines, CoPs are taken to mean the larger communities of interest and practice of which formal sector and thematic committees are a functional subset.

Strategic Focus of Reports

Sector and thematic reports would track the progress of broader results in terms of outputs and outcomes, and present succinct "value" and "impact" stories that illustrate challenges and accomplishments in the domain of each CoP.[1] Departmental results, aspects of ADB's corporate results framework, and Millennium Development Goals (MDG) results aligning with a particular sector and theme would be considered. Management and staff would use the reports as key internal monitoring and evaluation documents that guide the activities of CoPs to strengthen sector and thematic performance in ADB's operations. They might also be disseminated externally in a form that appeals to the public.

Focal Points for Reports

In consultation with the respective CoP, the lead/principal specialist assigned by the Budget, Personnel, and Management Systems Department (BPMSD) would be responsible for coordinating and preparing triennial (Section I) sector and thematic reports and participating in monitoring and evaluating progress (Section II). A *community convenor*, chosen by CoP members (and who may not necessarily be the lead/principal specialist assigned by BPMSD), would be responsible, working collaboratively with CoP members and the lead/principal sector specialist, for preparing annual reports focusing on the CoP (Section II).[2]

List of Sectors and Themes

The sectors and themes to be monitored and reported on would follow the list in the updated classification system (Appendix 1). Each sector report would include thematic mainstreaming as an important aspect. Likewise, thematic reports would indicate the progress of sector-wise mainstreaming as appropriate.

---

[1]To note, ADB's Managing for Development Results framework requires regional departments to consolidate sector and thematic reporting of outputs and outcomes. However, the executive and operations dashboards allow management and staff access to basic data on performance of sectors/themes by division, country, department, and ADB-wide. Hence, it is no longer necessary to include such data in sector and thematic reports. Notwithstanding, during the preparation process, these sources should be consulted and analyzed to inform content.

[2]Where no CoP exists or functions, the lead/principal specialist prepares both sections. However, Section II would likely be truncated.

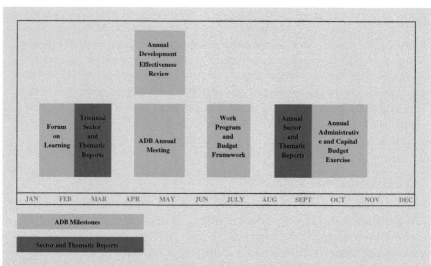

Fig. 74.1 Coincidence of sector and thematic reports with ADB milestones

Period and Periodicity

Full reports would be written every 3 years, with an annual update on the progress, activities, and plans of corresponding CoPs prepared collaboratively by the CoPs. Appendix 1 lists the years of the next reports. Annual reports would be due by the end of the third quarter of each year to feed into the *Annual Administrative and Capital Budget* exercises. Triennial reports would be due at the end of the first quarter to feed the annual *Development Effectiveness Reviews* and *Work Program and Budget Framework* papers.

They might also inform ADB's annual meetings.

Content

Though not prepared together each year, the two sections are mutually supportive. Section I contains priority strategic directions and broad results evaluation, while Section II looks at good practice and lessons more specifically. Planning and budgeting in Section II will be able to draw from analyses and conclusions in Section I.

Section I: Performance of Sector and Theme in ADB's Operations (every 3 years) would be limited to 30 pages of main text. Each report would have a core narrative, as suggested by Section I focusing on strategic directions and results evaluation. It might be usefully informed by discussions at retreats and regular peer gatherings. Apart from this, there could be a focus on special areas of interest that arose during the period reported against, placed in an appendix.

Another appendix could contain brief "value" and "impact" stories illustrating the findings of the report with direct experience. Appendix 2 provides a recommended tool, namely, a scorecard to summarize the performance of a sector and theme in ADB's operations.

Section II: Assessing the Performance of CoPs (annual update) would be limited to 15 pages of main text and aim, principally, to demonstrate the contributions of CoPs with good practices and lessons. This section would include a plan of activities with estimated budget figures. It might be usefully informed by annual surveys of the perceptions of CoP members, themselves informed by or building on the results of the *2009 survey of the CoPs hosted by ADB*, and those of the annual Most Admired Knowledge Enterprise survey that ADB conducts. Appendix 3 provides a recommended tool, namely, a sample scorecard with which to summarize CoP performance. The CoPs must meaningfully adapt the format of Section II and the scorecard tools to ensure that the report is useful to both the CoPs and to management.

Methods

The reporting process would generally begin by consulting CoP members on the task at hand and seeking performance information about both the sector and theme and the CoP. Rather than limiting the information to descriptive data, eliciting "value" and "impact" stories from CoP members and other interested parties would give management and staff a better picture of work in the sector and theme. Reviewing key documents and identifying trends across the sector or theme can be useful. Trends and patterns in the quantitative data on sectors and themes from ADB's information management system can be interpreted at different levels of operation. Informal interviews could be conducted with CoP members and with management. However, the most beneficial approach would be to gather CoP participants together for a planning/evaluation session to interpret findings and discuss lessons around key issues in the sector and theme and what activities the CoP can undertake to support change. This group might also choose a unifying focus for the report as it emerges from deliberation. Many tools and metrics support these processes including Strengths, Weaknesses, Opportunities, and Threats (SWOT), outcome mapping, appreciative inquiry, search conferences, and the like (see scorecards in Appendixes 2 and 3).[3]

---

[3]The *Knowledge Solutions* series offers guidance on many related tools, methods, and approaches. See ADB (2008–b).

Report Recommendations

Reports will often include recommendations to point to a direction in which positive changes can be made. When a recommendation is made, it should be (i) fully supported by and flow from the associated observations and conclusions, (ii) aimed at correcting the underlying causes of the deficiency, and (iii) directed specifically at the entity or entities with the responsibility to act on it. A recommendation should be clearly stated. It should be (i) succinct, straightforward, and contain enough detail to make sense on its own; (ii) broadly stated (stating what needs to be done while leaving the specifics of how to do it to entity officials); and (iii) positive in tone and content. Crucially, a recommendation should also be action-oriented. It should be (i) practical (able to be implemented in a reasonable time frame, taking into account constraints); (ii) cost-effective (the benefits of implementing it will outweigh the costs); (iii) efficient (optimizing the use of resources); (iv) results-oriented (giving some indication of what the intended outcome is, ideally in measurable terms); and (v) able to be followed up (the originating entity will be able to determine whether it has been acted upon).

Management Forum and Responses

Feedback is a circular causal process whereby some portion of a system's output is returned to the input to control dynamic behavior. Good feedback by the CoPs hosted by ADB is essential to make the most of their potential as collaboration mechanisms and thereby maximize ADB's development impact, ultimately to the benefit of its clients, partners, and audiences. Management responses to reports are likewise necessary. Upon release of triennial reports the lead/principal specialist should schedule an informal session with management to discuss the report's findings and recommendations. Members of the relevant CoP should be invited to participate. Such interaction can help clarify understanding and motivate CoP members to move forward with action. Similarly, the annual reports (Section II) should be discussed with relevant managers in a constructive CoP-led open forum upon release. All reports would be coursed to the Vice Presidency for Knowledge Management and Sustainable Development (VP-KM&SD) through the Director General, Regional and Sustainable Development Department (DG, RSDD) or, as the case may be, through Head, Office of Regional Economic Integration. (New CoPs, hosted by other offices and departments, would course their reports to VP-KM&SD through relevant heads.) Management would meet the initiating CoP and/or relevant offices and departments, consider the highlights of reports, and provide guidance on recommendations. Beyond management, the reports should be made available to all staff on the intranet and announced in *ADB Today*. The reports may lead to additional discussions, brownbag seminars, or other interactive means to explore issues raised.

Resource Implications

Resource requirements of up to two-and-a-half (2.5) person-months of professional staff and two-and-a-half (2.5) person-months of consulting services would be required to prepare a full report for each sector and theme, as the guidelines propose, every 3 years. Annual updates could be completed with 2 weeks of consulting services through a facilitated retreat for CoP members, with the results consolidated in a report. Based on these estimates and the current number of sectors and themes, the total revised resource needs for implementing this reporting program is about 22 person-months of professional staff[4] and 22 months of consulting services per year.

Others

Appendix 4 articulates ways to empower the CoPs hosted by ADB for better knowledge generation and sharing.

Sector and Thematic Reports: Suggested[a] Outline of Contents for *Section I: Performance of Sectors and Themes in ADB's Operations* (every 3 years)

Subject and Guiding Questions	Indicator/Method of assessment	Source of data/Method of feedback
Executive summary and key messages to management		
Introduction		
Period covered Relevant background information Target audience Structure of the report	Not applicable	Not applicable
Regional trends in the concerned sector and thematic area		
Status and outlook of the sector and thematic area How has ADB's work in this sector and theme contributed to (i) achieving related MDGs? (where applicable) (ii) achieving Level 1 regional outcomes in ADB's Corporate Results Framework?	CoP deliberations; MDG indicators (as applicable); proxy indicators (for CPSs); RSDD assessments Portfolio analysis for impact and outcome contributions of sector and thematic activities to *Strategy 2020*, particularly on (i) vision (an Asia and Pacific region free of poverty);	Regional MDG reports, Key Indicators for Asia and the Pacific, RCPS documents, reports of bilateral and multilateral agencies, data from country sources, CPSs, etc.

(continued)

---

[4]This level of staff effort may not be uniform. A large CoP, such as the Water Group, may involve many more professional staff hours in participatory consultation than a smaller, less active CoP. This is not a problem if we assume the investment to deliver a commensurately higher benefit in return in terms of ownership and participation in the sector or theme.

(continued)

Subject and Guiding Questions	Indicator/Method of assessment	Source of data/Method of feedback
(iii) supporting *Strategy 2020*?	(ii) strategic agenda (inclusive economic growth, environmentally sustainable growth, regional integration); and (iii) drivers of change (private sector development and private sector operations, good governance and capacity development, gender equity, knowledge solutions, partnerships)	
Contributions to sector and thematic policy and strategy[b]		
Contribution to key elements of sector and thematic policy or strategy (specify examples), action plans and their achievements, and determining whether review is necessary Role of ADB knowledge products in the sector and theme Crosscutting efforts with other sectors and themes Mainstreaming themes in sectors	RSDD/Committee/CoP assessments	ADB strategy and policy updates, TA reports, TCRs, RRPs, PCRs, PERs, CPS completion reports, CAPEs, special evaluation studies, etc.
Contributions to regional and subregional cooperation		
Contribution of sector and theme to RCPS Regional activities conducted per sector and thematic area	CoP deliberations Contribution to RCPS outcomes Assessment of regional activities	Regional MDG reports, Asia Economic Monitor reports, RCPS documents, MIS data, reports from regional departments on regional activities, RSDD, etc.
Contributions to country-level operations (inclusive economic growth, environmentally sustainable growth, regional integration)		
How has ADB's work in this sector and theme contributed to (i) outcomes in ADB's Corporate Results Framework [country outcomes]; (ii) quality of sector and thematic assessments and road maps in CPSs finalized during the review period	CoP deliberations Assessment of CPS documents by RSDD Stories of innovations (particularly in project/program design)	National MDG reports, CPSs, COSO data, MIS data, country performance assessments (poverty, economic, thematic, and sector assessments), RRPs, IED reports, reports from regional departments, etc.

(continued)

(continued)

Subject and Guiding Questions	Indicator/Method of assessment	Source of data/Method of feedback
• conformity with sector and thematic policies; • linkage to CPS outcomes and the three pillars of the PRS; • consistency with sector and thematic assessments; • depth, comprehensiveness, and data quality; • partnerships and work of other stakeholders; (iii) sector and thematic implementation record • contribution to CPS outcomes; • strengthening borrowers capacity in the sector and theme; and • portfolio performance issues, implementation		
Partnerships		
Funding generated, including bilateral funds Participation of NGOs/civil society organizations Harmonization	CoP deliberations Generation of cofinancing Generation of bilateral grants/funds Approval of SWAps Projects with NGO/civil society participation Joint projects/conferences	MIS data, OCO data, PSOD data, reports from regional departments, NGO Center, reports from regional departments
Operational and organizational effectiveness		
How has ADB's work in this sector and theme performed against (i) portfolio performance (ii) ADB's Corporate Results Framework targets for operational effectiveness [Level 3]; and (ii) budgetary resources and business processes (efficiency) [Level 4]	CoP deliberations Specific particular investment tools and modalities that are significantly affecting the sector and theme Strategic alignment of sector and theme in pipelines	ADB Annual Reports, Development Effectiveness Reviews, etc.
Human resources		
Skills mix and adequacy (use competency framework if available) How has ADB's work in this sector and theme performed	CoP deliberations Gaps/surpluses of specialist positions in departments[c] Unfilled vacancies	BPMSD data, CoPs, reports from regional departments, etc.

(continued)

(continued)

Subject and Guiding Questions	Indicator/Method of assessment	Source of data/Method of feedback
against ADB's Corporate Results Framework for use of human resources [Level 4]?	Percentage of specialists who completed training requirements	

Conclusions and recommendations for future activities

What are the conclusions? What changes are required for more effective sector and thematic outcomes in the future, including (i) key issues and considerations? (ii) recommendations about future programs? (iii) suggestions on project quality, and quality of sector and thematic assessments and road maps? (iv) analysis of existing policy and strategy and determining whether review is necessary? (v) human resources and other suggestions?	CoP deliberations Overall RSDD recommendations	Annual and triennial reports from CoPs, consultations with partners, RSDD, etc.

Appendixes: value stories, impact stories, special topics

BPMSD Budget, Personnel, and Management Systems Department; *CAPE* Country assistance program evaluation; *CoP* Community of practice; *COSO* Central Operations Services Office; *CPS* Country partnership strategy; *IED* Independent Evaluation Department; *MIS* Management information system; *MDG* Millennium development goal; *NGO* Nongovernment organization; *OCO* Office of Cofinancing Operations; *PCR* Project completion report; *PER* Project/program evaluation report; *PRS* Poverty reduction strategy; *RCPS* Regional Cooperation Partnership Strategy; *RRP* report and recommendation of the President; *RSDD* Regional and Sustainable Development Department; *SPD* Strategy and Policy Department; *SWAps* Sector-wide approaches; *TA* Technical assistance; *TCR* Technical assistance completion report; *UN* United Nations
Source Author
[a]Both format and content are flexible and need to be adapted (and specified) to each sector or theme
[b]The Independent Evaluation Department has developed a framework for assessing the soundness of a strategy: (i) adequacy of strategic gap analysis through baseline indicators and targets; (ii) quality of sector analysis; (iii) adequacy of option identification; (iv) internal integrity of strategy; (v) partnership and external consistency; (vi) positioning for organizational competence and comparative advantage; (vii) acceptability to key stakeholders; (viii) feasibility of strategy; (ix) basis for strategy selection
[c]Assessment of gaps may require collecting information on the actual number of specialists working in the specialist positions as opposed to the number of specialists recruited

Sector and Thematic Reports: Suggested[a] Outline of Contents for *Section II: Assessing the Performance of CoPs* (annual update)

Subject and Guiding Questions	Indicator/Method of assessment	Source of data/ method of feedback
Executive summary and key messages to management		
Introduction		
Period covered Relevant background information Target audience Structure of the report	Not applicable	Not applicable
Performance score and critical success factors		
Customize indicators and evidence for a scorecard summarizing CoPs' performance (see Appendix 3) (i) Where has your CoP come from? Where is it now? Where would you like to bring it? Illustrate (ii) How does your CoP filter, organize, and manage information? What should the group pay attention to? Illustrate (iii) How does your CoP take new or unfamiliar ideas and help participants understand them? Illustrate (iv) How does your CoP help participants locate or successfully acquire resources to work in their sector and theme more effectively? Illustrate (v) How does your CoP bring together people with different experiences or perspectives to share ideas and practice? Illustrate (vi) How does your CoP build a sense of community based on shared values and professional standards? Illustrate (vii) How does your CoP help participants work better and do things that are more effective? Illustrate	Specific to the plans of the CoP, minutes of meetings, records of activities, CoP deliberations	Projects, knowledge products and services, innovative activities in the sector or thematic area over the past year, surveys of CoPs, etc.

(continued)

(continued)

Subject and Guiding Questions	Indicator/Method of assessment	Source of data/ method of feedback
Knowledge in practice		
How does your CoP engage its members in reflection on practice? Illustrate Do you use any ways of helping staff share their practical tacit knowledge[b] with one another? Illustrate	CoP deliberations, staff interviews	Peer assists, after-action reviews, retrospects, coaching and mentoring, exit interviews, etc.
Contributions to knowledge management and good practices		
Is your CoP contributing to the spread of good practices in its sector and thematic area through (i) knowledge generation? (ii) knowledge sharing? Illustrate.	Assessments of all knowledge products and services including economic and sector work, guidelines, tool kits, etc.	CoP deliberations, brownbag seminars, Knowledge Showcases, K-Hub presentations, Learning Curves, sector and thematic newsletters, etc.
Plans and recommendations for CoP focus and activities		
In light of past performance and based on the analysis of the aspects highlighted above and the assessment framework, what changes are required for more effective sector and thematic CoP outcomes in the future, including (i) recommendations about your CoP's future program? (ii) suggestions regarding knowledge management?	CoP deliberations, guidance of committee and sector and thematic lead/principal specialist	Projects, knowledge products and services, innovative activities in the sector or thematic area over the past year, surveys of CoPs, etc.
Appendix: value stories, impact stories		
Highlight key stories that illustrate the knowledge generation and sharing activities that occurred in your CoP this past year	CoP deliberations, staff interviews	ADB Annual Reports, stories of change, etc.

CoP Community of practice; *RSDD* Regional and Sustainable Development Department
Source Author
[a]Both format and content are flexible and need to be adapted (and specified) to each sector or theme
[b]Tacit knowledge is personalized knowledge that people carry in their heads. It is more difficult to formalize and communicate than explicit knowledge, but can be shared through discussion, storytelling, and personal interactions

Appendix 1: Updated Sector and Theme Classification System

Sector reports, Section I: Sector performance in ADB's operations	Next triennial report (Q1)	Sector reports, Section II (annually Q3): Assessing the performance of CoPs
1. Agriculture and Natural Resources	2009	Agriculture, Rural Development, and Food Security CoP
2. Education	2010	Education CoP
3. Energy	2011	Energy CoP
4. Finance[a]	2009	–
5. Health and Social Protection	2010	Health CoP
6. Industry and Trade[b]	2011	–
7. Public Sector Management	2009	Financial Management CoP
8. Transport and ICT	2010	Transport CoP ICT CoP
9. Water Supply, Sanitation and Waste Management	2011	Water CoP Urban Development CoP

ICT Information and communications technology, *NGO* Nongovernment organization
Source Author
[a]No CoP
[b]No CoP

Thematic reports, section I: Thematic performance in ADB's operations	Next triennial report (Q1)	Thematic reports, Section II (annually Q3): Assessing the performance of CoPs
1. Capacity Development[a]	2009	–
2. Economic Growth	2010	Poverty Reduction and Inclusive Growth CoP
3. Environmental Sustainability	2011	Environment CoP
4. Gender Equity	2009	Gender CoP
5. Governance	2010	Governance CoP NGO and Civil Society CoP
6. Social Development	2011	Social Development CoP Resettlement CoP
7. Private Sector Development[b]	2009	–
8. Regional Cooperation and Integration[c]	2010	–

CoP Community of practice; *NGO* Nongovernment organization
Source Author
[a]Reports only. No CoP or committee
[b]Reports only. No CoP or committee
[c]No CoP

Appendix 2: Summary of Sector and Thematic Performance in ADB's Operations[5]

Criteria	Indicator (illustrative)	Evidence (illustrative)	Score
Asia and the Pacific Development Outcomes (Board of Governors Perspective)	• MDG indicator (s) • Corporate Results Framework and other indicators • Regional cooperation • Policy and strategy	• Sector and theme contribution to the MDGs and poverty reduction in the region and subregions • Strategic objectives, including client and audience, well defined and linked to relevant corporate, country, sector, and thematic strategies, and core business processes. • Clear purpose for programs and activities	G A R G A R G A R G A R
Contribution to Country Development Outcomes (DMC Client Perspective)	• Strategic focus in operations • CPS • By particular subsector and subtheme	• Contributions to country outcomes against stated objectives • By particular subsector and subtheme satisfaction of DMC clients • Harmonization	G A R G A R G A R
Effectiveness of Projects (Beneficiary Perspective)	• Operational quality • Partnership • By particular key activity area of sector and theme • Mainstreaming	• Successful attainment of objectives through tangible "value" and "impact" stories • Jointly funded projects • By particular key activity area of sector and theme • Participation of NGOs and civil society organizations • Satisfaction of project beneficiaries	G A R G A R G A R G A R
Organizational Effectiveness (Management Perspective)	• Human resources • Budget adequacy • Business processes and practices	• Adequate skills mix • Adequate and well-tracked resources for innovation • Quality of support and administrative services	G A R G A R G A R G A R G A R

(continued)

[5]Scorecard categories and content are flexible and must be adapted (and specified) to each sector or theme.

(continued)

Criteria	Indicator (illustrative)	Evidence (illustrative)	Score
	• Portfolio performance • Finance mobilization	• Adequacy of operational tools	
Learning and Growth (Staff Perspective)	• Knowledge management • Professional development • Technology	• Views of staff on knowledge products and services as responsive, state-of-the-art, and future-oriented • Integration of knowledge products and services into staff and client (team) learning activities • Ready access of staff to up-to-date sector and thematic knowledge enabling them to do their jobs • Lessons learned and good practices captured and shared to ADB and clients • Applies appropriate technology	G A R G A R G A R

G Green "On track" (More than 50% of the indicators in the group have shown improvements over baselines or previous periods.)

A Amber "Potential regression" (Results are mixed: equal number of indicators improving or beginning to stagnate or regress.)

R Red "Stagnated or regressed" (More than half of indicators in the group stagnating or regressing over 2 or more years.)

CPS Country partnership strategy; *DMC* Developing member country; *MDG* Millennium development goal; *NGO* Nongovernment organization

Source Author

Appendix 3: Summary of Community of Practice Performance[a]

Criteria	Indicator (Illustrative)	Evidence (Illustrative)	Score
Relevance and Focus	• Programs and activities help strengthen ADB's work in sector and theme advancing	• CoP strategic objectives, including client and audience, well defined and linked to relevant	

(continued)

(continued)

Criteria	Indicator (Illustrative)	Evidence (Illustrative)	Score
	corporate and country priorities • CoP participants are committed to improvement	corporate, country, sector, and thematic strategies, and core business processes • Clear purpose for programs and activities • Level of participation is strong across activities	G A R G A R
Quality and Timeliness of Knowledge Products and Services	• Aggregated knowledge is tailored and timed to needs, and are clearly presented, technically sound, and state of the art • CoP has realistic timetable for delivery	• Demand for knowledge products and services • Staff, CoP member, client, and expert reviews and surveys • ADB/CoP content management processes • Staff view knowledge products and services as responsive and future-oriented	G A R G A R
Access to Practical Knowledge and Reach in ADB	• CoP members demonstrate trust, respect, mutual support • CoP is widely inclusive across departments and seniority • CoP members have ready access to up-to-date knowledge to do their jobs	• Dissemination tracking, usability testing, usage monitoring of published and online knowledge, and information and knowledge services • Staff, CoP member, client, and expert participation in knowledge-sharing events and feedback • CoP application of appropriate technology to support activities and communicate	G A R G A R G A R
Utility	• Shared knowledge are adopted and applied in policies, strategies, partnerships, programs, and projects • Lessons learned and good practices are	• Knowledge management strategy articulated in sector and thematic strategies and sector road maps in country partnership strategies (CPS)	

(continued)

(continued)

Criteria	Indicator (Illustrative)	Evidence (Illustrative)	Score
	captured and shared to ADB and clients • CoP knowledge products and services are part of staff work plans and performance reviews, and supported by management	• Knowledge products and services built into staff and client (team) learning activities • Staff, CoP member, client, and expert surveys and activity self-assessments • Self- and independent assessments of knowledge-sharing process in CPSs, and lending and nonlending services • CoP members actively seeking and giving support	G A R G A R G A R
Likely Impact	• ADB and client knowledge bases and capacities are enhanced. • Improvements are targeted in ADB development results • Staff development is enhanced with greater work engagement	• Ongoing knowledge assessments • Successful attainment of objectives is demonstrated through tangible "value" and "impact" stories • Sector and thematic reports demonstrate improved outcomes against stated objectives	G A R G A R G A R
Cost Effectiveness	• Programs and activities are carried out without the right amount of resources to achieve objectives	• Tracking and benchmarking costs of activities • Resources are adequate for innovation	G A R

[a]Score card categories and content are flexible and must be adapted (and specified) to each sector or theme

G Green "On track" (More than 50% of the indicators in the group have shown improvements over baselines or previous periods.)

A Amber "Potential regression" (Results are mixed: equal number of indicators improving or beginning to stagnate or regress.)

R Red "Stagnated or regressed" (More than half of indicators in the group stagnating or regressing over 2 or more years.)

Source Author

Appendix 4: Empowering Communities of Practice to Generate and Share Knowledge

The communities of practice (CoPs) hosted by ADB encompass both formal sector and thematic committees and what were previously called "informal networks". Any staff can join as a member of one or more CoPs. Each CoP is proposed to have a *community convenor*, chosen by CoP members, normally an expert in the concerned sector and theme, and active in managing funds designated for the CoP, sharing articles and newsletters, driving informal dialogues with other staff to share information, leading annual reporting (including preparation of annual two-pagers for broad circulation specifying the domain, community, and function and achievements of the CoP, as well as its plans for the future, e.g., finance, clients, internal processes, and innovation and learning, and external knowledge partnerships), and updating websites, among other things. The *community convenor* need not be the sector and thematic committee chairs or co-chairs. The duration of any CoP depends on continuing interest from CoP members (but also demand from staff); thus, some may serve their purpose over the span of only a couple years and then choose to disband. He or she would confer with the relevant sector and thematic committee and be responsible to the CoP.

The committees reside within CoP's (where corresponding CoPs exist), each having at least five to eight members holding at least level 5 positions. Committee chairs and co-chairs would be appointed by VP-KM&SD. Chairs and co-chairs would appoint members of their respective committees while keeping DG, RSDD, and VP-KM&SD (through RSDD-KM) informed. The committee chairs or co-chairs have no formal authority over the CoP at-large but function as members of the CoP.

ADB's sector and thematic committees would continue to be tapped as advisors on policies and strategies for sectors and themes. They would (i) provide advice on formulation of sector and thematic policies and strategies; (ii) propose actions to address implementation issues associated with sector and thematic policies and strategies, for instance, through the annual and triennial reports prepared by the lead/principal specialist; (iii) represent the interests of their respective sector and thematic areas at management level at annual meetings with VP-KM&SD; and (iv) act as advocates of CoP operations and achievements. While CoPs are formed at the initiative of staff, *Strategy 2020*, or ADB's current and changing priorities would drive the formation of committees as they are accountable to VP-KM&SD through DG, RSDD.

CoPs can play a critical role in generating and sharing knowledge that enriches ADB's operations. Complementing sector and thematic committees, the typical CoP member may have more current and direct field experience to draw from than those at the director level and above. Their practical knowledge may be tapped as sources of information during preparation of country

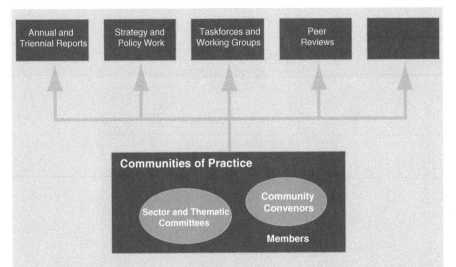

Fig. 74.2 Communities of practice for quality, knowledge, and innovation. *Source* Author

partnership strategies (CPS), project/program design, policy review, operational guidance, or as members of a workgroup or task force on crosscutting issues, e.g., members of energy and transport CoPs collaborating in the area of clean energy. To take advantage of their potential to strengthen ADB, new CoPs would be encouraged and supported as much as possible across diverse areas, not limited to ADB's priority sectors and themes (Fig. 74.2).[6]

The CoPs hosted by ADB would also help drive individual and collective learning and development to improve performance at both levels by providing an environment for continuous learning, solving common problems, pursuing joint solutions, and facilitating decision-making. This environment includes activities to (i) produce and disseminate knowledge, information, and best practices; (ii) facilitate access to community resources, including the latest trends, developments, and innovations related to their areas of expertise; (iii) provide diverse avenues for interaction, dialogue, and collaboration between and among CoP members; and (iv) provide informal learning opportunities to help build the capacity and strengthen the skills of CoP members. The *community convenor* would be accountable to the members of a CoP and to ADB or external donors when a CoP receives grant, technical assistance, or project funds (Fig. 74.3).

From experience to date, a strength of CoPs is likely to be the hosting of learning events, e.g., brown bags, talks, presentations, etc., in collaboration with other CoPs, regional departments, knowledge departments, and relevant

---

[6]A CoP can be formed simply by sending an electronic mail to RSDD-KM indicating the title of the CoP, the name of the *community convenor*, and initial group members.

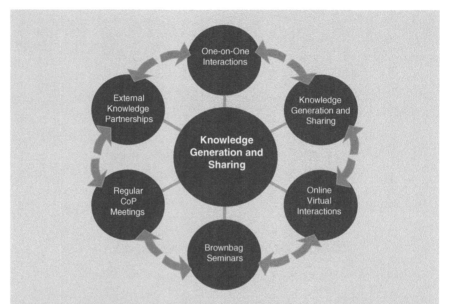

Fig. 74.3 Communities of practice for knowledge generation and sharing. *Source* Author

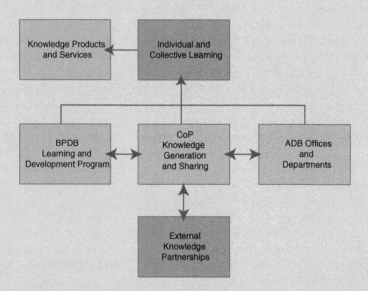

Fig. 74.4 Communities of practice for individual and collective learning. *Source* Author

offices and departments. To ensure the relevance of topics and a high quality of content in learning events, CoPs would be consulted on events organized by offices and departments. All events would support interactive learning toward identified learning outcomes. This means that events would not only entail more than the delivery of a talk or presentation but would also involve specific learning processes that allow discussion on the relevance and applicability of the topic to staff work, issues, and concerns. If necessary, support to apply learning through follow-up activities would be made available. Good collaboration between CoPs and relevant departments would translate key learning into high-quality knowledge products and services that support *Strategy 2020*.

BPMSD and other departments would continue to support training. CoPs would work with the Staff Development and Benefits Division (BPDB) to develop specific learning and development programs, engage speakers, and address opportunities related to staff's professional development. CoPs and relevant departments would collaborate to translate learning into knowledge products and services (Fig. 74.4).

References

ADB (2008a) Strategy 2020: the long-term strategic framework of the Asian development bank (2008–2020). Manila

ADB (2008b) Strategy 2020: the long-term strategic framework of the Asian development bank (2008–2020). Manila

ADB (2008c) Development effectiveness review. Manila

ADB (2008–a) Development effectiveness review. Manila

ADB (2008–b) Knowledge solutions. Manila

ADB (2009a) Enhancing knowledge management under strategy 2020: plan of action for 2009–2011. Manila

ADB (2009b) In focus series: communities of practice. Manila

ADB (2009c) Enhancing knowledge management under strategy 2020: plan of action for 2009–2011. Manila

ADB (2009d) Strengthening communities of practice in ADB. Manila

The opinions expressed in this chapter are those of the author(s) and do not necessarily reflect the views of the Asian Development Bank, its Board of Directors, or the countries they represent.

Proposition 75
Sparking Social Innovations

In a Word Necessity is the mother of invention. The demand for good ideas, put into practice, that meet pressing unmet needs and improve people's lives is growing on a par with the agenda of the twenty-first century. In a shrinking world, social innovation at requisite institutional levels can do much to foster smart, sustainable globalization.

The Agenda of the Twenty-First Century

In consequence of successive scientific revolutions, mankind has changed its conditions and capacities with increasing speed. Globalization is a given: today, mankind's activities are affecting the entire planet—and thereby mankind itself— for good and ill.

A select list of the worldwide challenges we face includes alleviating poverty; mitigating and adapting to climate change; ending abuse of natural resources and the environment; cleaning up environmental pollution; dealing with natural disasters; countering medical challenges, e.g., pandemics; encouraging disarmament; coping with security threats; accommodating non-state power; handling failed states; tapping capacity for social action; allaying frustration among minorities; confronting violence; identifying global rights; building a global rule of law;

© Asian Development Bank 2017
O. Serrat, *Knowledge Solutions*, DOI 10.1007/978-981-10-0983-9_75

evolving regulatory and institutional frameworks to contain global financial and economic crises; optimizing international trade; managing mass migrations; employing human resources better; and optimizing knowledge.[1]

> *Opportunities are usually disguised as hard work, so most people don't recognize them.*
>
> —Ann Landers

The issues our population of 6.9 billion people—projected to reach 7.7 billion in 2020—now meets head-on have causes and effects in communities, villages, towns, provinces, regions, countries, and groups of countries, needless to say in varying degrees of attribution. We must therefore explore human perceptions, relations, and institutions from the perspective of how societies at different scales form, operate, interface, and treat the natural world. Enlightened self-interest intimates that as many actors and agents as possible collaborate in such discussions at the optimum institutional levels to leverage social innovation in support of smart, sustainable globalization.

Innovation,[2] that is, incremental and emergent or radical and revolutionary changes in thinking, products, services, processes, or organizations, has always been a feature of human societies.[3] Typically, but not exclusively, it has since the fifteenth century been spurred by cumulative advances in material civilization, themselves impelled by entrepreneurial then, increasingly, profit-seeking corporate

---

[1]Transformations in the global economy impact at all levels. However, for the more locally minded, examples of challenges in modern cities include unemployment, homelessness, crime, urban decay, pollution, access to health care, sickness and old age, disability, social discrimination, social exclusion, prostitution, drug and alcohol abuse, racism, sexism, domestic violence, teenage pregnancy, abortion, and underage drinking, among many others. For example, the Young Foundation mapped Britain's unmet needs in 2006. It found 40 key needs in six interconnected clusters: (i) poverty of power, money, and place; (ii) new forms of destitution—the results of globalization; (iii) psychic needs; (iv) needs arising from fractured families and weak family substitutes; (v) needs arising from damaging consumption; and (vi) violence and abuse (Mulgan et al. 2006).

[2]Simply put, innovation is the act of introducing something new (or reapplying old ideas in a new way). It is commonly classified along the following dimensions: (i) process versus product, (ii) radical versus incremental, (iii) technological versus organizational, and (iv) science-led versus customer-driven.

[3]Peter Drucker catalogued seven causes for that: (i) unexpected occurrences, (ii) incongruities of various kinds, (iii) process needs, (iv) changes in an industry or market, (v) demographic changes, (vi) changes in perceptions, and (vii) new knowledge.

interests.[4] But the role of corporate innovation can only be limited where social matters press in throngs to the fore and markets imperfectly (if at all) meet demand with supply.[5] Until we expand the reach of markets so that more people can find profit, or at least make a living, from turning their entrepreneurial mindsets to social problems, many will continue to expect that governments or charities should subsidize and fill deficits.

Yet, despite successful attempts at fostering entrepreneurial government from the mid-1990s, efforts still fall short of rising expectations and related social sector institutions continue, unfairly perhaps given the variety of needs, to be viewed as inefficient, ineffective, and unresponsive. (A more pointed observation would be that public sector organizations are just not good at embracing failure and could learn much from design thinking.) Still, government can only provide part of the answer, and for this it would have to better reflect the values of taxpayers (assuming they recognize then care about social problems).[6] Long-term solutions to social

---

[4]From a corporate perspective, innovating is creating value by doing things differently (or doing them in a novel way). Based on this viewpoint, however, the incidence and value of innovation can only be established after the event. Thus, innovating is the process of creative problem solving or solution seeking in response to real problems, needs, or opportunities—designed to produce practical outcomes. Interestingly, some now argue that the private sector has a better chance of making a difference if it knows how its business agenda relates to specific social needs.

[5]Besides, most corporate innovation is no longer born within the walls of an organization. Technologies, for instance, as distinct from their applications, are increasingly being bought and sold. "The cathedral and the bazaar" connotes closed and open models of innovation (and the gradual erosion of the former). At the same time, today's users demand a role in defining and shaping what they need. Traditional concepts of innovation—such as what it is, who does it, where it is conceived, where it comes from, how it is organized, and who it affects, as well as the discovery skills associated with individual "serial innovators", e.g., associating, questioning, observing, experimenting, and networking—provide less and less explanatory traction. This is not to denigrate the crucial role of outstanding individuals, as the accomplishments of William Wilberforce, Robert Owen, Florence Nightingale, Gandhi, Fazle Hasan Abed, and Muhammad Yunus, among others, attest. However, given the barriers that concern for efficiency, vested interests, mindsets, and longstanding relationships pose, it is better not to conceive of social innovation as a discovery: it is rather a continuous, collaborative, and cumulative activity involving many actors and agents in which ideas are shared, tested, refined, developed, and applied, with the occasional leap forward—or across to another sector. A systems approach to innovation would locate actors and agents as well as their interactions at individual, interpersonal, organizational, inter-organizational, and system levels, and pay attention to the norms, regulations, rules of the game, and habits that govern these.

[6]An externality is a consequence of an economic activity that is experienced by unrelated third parties. In imperfect markets, externalities are the rule, not the exception, and their impacts grow in proportion to social inequality. Externalities color value. Measuring and communicating social value is important and can help social enterprise become more competitive. However, social accounting practices are underdeveloped and only rarely codified in legislation. A related concern is that of ethical markets, embodying values of trust, transparency, and contract law, aiming to offset mankind's propensity to barter without concern for the social and environmental consequences of production and exchange, including side- (or frontal) effects on third parties. While the ability of government to allocate resources is limited, its role as norm setter, rule maker, enforcer, and overseer of markets is essential.

inequities must be broad-based and self-sustaining: in imperfect markets, that means finding ways to turn a profit so that social entrepreneurs can keep going.

Daily news provides countless examples of global interdependence and the domino effect of geopolitical settings. (The financial crisis of 2007 to the present is but the most recent.) Social enterprise is needed to cultivate products, services, models, and approaches that address the agenda of the twenty-first century, finding its rightful place in, and certainly informing, the continuum of human affairs that includes mainstream business, socially responsible business, public services, and voluntarism.[7] The qualitative development that it can bring to the table is borne of more engaged, personalized, joined-up, adaptable, and economical services that use fewer resources to deliver better outcomes. Indeed, the agenda of the twenty-first century may be pointing toward a social economy in which social values and mission play stronger roles. In May 2009, President Obama announced that his administration would request a $50 million allocation of the following year's budget to seed a Social Innovation Fund.

Quid Social Innovation?

> *If you have built castles in the air, your work need not be lost; that is where they should be. Now put foundations under them.*
>
> —Henry David Thoreau

First and foremost, social entrepreneurs are exercised by an explicit ethical imperative. Obviously, this conditions how they perceive and assess opportunities. In comparing social and for-profit entrepreneurs, then, the question of what it is that they seek to maximize is paramount. Put simply, social innovation equates with new ideas that successfully meet social goals through mission-related impacts. Mulgan (2007) has defined it as innovative activities and services that are motivated by the goal of meeting a social need and that are predominantly developed and

---

[7]Voluntarism is the sphere of social activity undertaken by organizations that are nonprofit and nongovernmental, e.g., voluntary and community groups, charities, cooperatives, and mutuals. It is sometimes referred to as the third sector in reference to the public and the private sectors. (In the United Kingdom, the Office of the Third Sector in the Cabinet Office, which coordinates policy and strategy across government departments, is tasked with enabling voice and campaigning, strengthening communities, transforming public services, and encouraging social enterprise.) In 1976, Daniel Bell predicted that the third sector would become the predominant sector in larger society, increasingly central to its health and well-being.

diffused through organizations whose primary purposes are social. That is, social innovation from individuals, movements, and organizations tackles pressing social problems or new social issues, with a focus on problem solving and experimentation to formulate new products, services, models, and approaches.[8]

Much as corporate innovation, social innovation can only thrive if it meets a need. And, as might be expected, its stages also involve (i) generating ideas by understanding needs and pressure to change and identifying potential solutions; (ii) designing, developing, prototyping, and piloting ideas; (iii) assessing, then scaling up and diffusing the best ideas; and (iv) learning and evolving.[9] However, there is another side to the coin. The motives that spark social innovation, for instance, are likely to be quite different: they may include material incentives but the principal drivers of accomplishment will habitually range broadly to include such concerns as care, compassion, identity, autonomy, and recognition. Critical resource requirements will also diverge: money is the bottom line in business; however, social innovations often seek out and rest on political support, volunteers, and philanthropic commitment. Patterns of growth are not the same either: social organizations or movements do not in general grow as quickly as corporate interests yet tend to be more resilient. How the success of innovation is judged defers too: scale or market share, for example, matter little when the unmet need is intense but well circumscribed. Lastly, each social field exhibits distinct patterns, drivers, and inhibitors, with implications for short- (days, weeks, months), medium- (1–3 years), and long-term (3–20 years) horizons for decision making.[10] (Some social problems may require generational timescales.)

---

[8]The definition distinguishes social from corporate innovation. To this day, that is generally stimulated by profit maximization. In truth, however, there are many borderline cases. What is more, and is increasingly likely to be so, the products and services that organizations sell can in the final analysis only succeed if they address a fundamental social needs, however that might reveal itself. Therefore, recognizing that innovation is inescapably a public–private undertaking, Rosabeth Moss Kanter presciently envisioned 10 years ago that the social sector might become a learning laboratory for corporate interests. (By the same token, more and more social entrepreneurs use business formats to achieve their objectives.) (Kanter 1999).

[9]The process of social innovation is given a full treatment in Murray et al. (2010).

[10]In social organizations, Geoff Mulgan explains that social innovation is facilitated by practitioner networks, political allies, strong civic institutions, and the support of progressive foundations and philanthropists. For social movements, basic legal protections and status, in addition to open media and the Internet, are key. In politics and government, the conditions are likely to include competing parties, think tanks, innovation funds, contestable markets, and plentiful pilots. In business, social innovation can be driven by competition, open cultures, and accessible capital. In all social fields, global links make it easier to learn lessons and share ideas at an early stage.

Using Emergence to Boost Social Innovation

Notwithstanding the difficulties caused by externalities and the shortage of ethical markets, the paucity of sustained and systematic analysis is hindering the practice of social innovation. This is where innovation accelerators such as the Social Innovation Fund can play a role.[11]

> *We are what we repeatedly do. Excellence, then, is not an act, but a habit.*
>
> —Aristotle

However, rather than worry about critical mass, social entrepreneurs foster critical connections to kindred spirits, strengthen these as communities of practice, and develop those further as systems of influence. Critical to this, from a systems perspective, are what Geoff Mulgan calls connectors, viz., the entrepreneurs, brokers, and institutions that link the demand and supply and the push and pull of people, ideas, and resources. In *Social Innovation: What It Is, Why It Matters, and How It Can Be Accelerated*, from which the following draws extensively, he identifies ready entry points for action:

> *Social entrepreneurs have existed throughout history. St. Francis of Assisi, the founder of the Franciscan Order, would qualify as a social entrepreneur—having built multiple organizations that advanced pattern changes in his "field". Similarly, Florence Nightingale created the first professional school for nurses and established standards for hygiene and hospital care that have shaped norms worldwide. What is different today is that social entrepreneurship is developing into a mainstream vocation, not only in the United States, Canada, and Europe, but increasingly in Asia, Africa, and Latin America. In fact, the rise of social entrepreneurship represents the leading edge of a remarkable development that has occurred across the world over the past three decades: the emergence of millions of new citizen organizations.*
>
> —David Bornstein

- **Leadership and Structures Suited to Innovation** Leaders with the power to act in fields such as health and education can visibly value and reward social entrepreneurs and social innovations. Separate structures, insulated from day-to-day concerns, can also be developed to straddle the boundaries of organizations or systems and combine freshness of perspective with the authority to make things happen.

---

[11]In the United Kingdom, the Young Foundation's Launchpad develops promising ideas into new ventures by providing funding, social capital, and entrepreneurial expertise.

- **Finance Focused on Innovation** It costs to generate, test, and then adapt ideas in the light of experience. Social innovation requires a mix of resources including grants, tax credits, subsidies, and private investment through dedicated vehicles ranging from technology-oriented venture capital to banks.
- **Public Policy Frameworks that Encourage Innovation** Governments can improve the climate for innovation in many ways. To begin, innovativeness can be made a criterion for competitive bidding associated with public procurement. Markets for social solutions can also be developed further to include outcome-based funding models and greater competition and contestability. Decentralization can also give communities greater freedom to shape their own solutions. Innovation units can be set up in government agencies to coordinate pioneers, encourage new ideas, and promote faster learning. Laboratories can test ideas with the close involvement of users. Technology labs can focus specifically on mining mature or near-mature technologies for social potential.
- **Dedicated Social Innovation Accelerators** New ideas must be given time to incubate in a protected environment that provides support, advice, and the freedom to evolve. A related approach is to develop accelerators that emphasize scaleable innovations in particular sectors. These accelerators can provide development funding, rapidly test out new ideas in practice, allow fast learning across a community of social innovators, and establish clear pathways for scaling up the most promising models.
- **National and Cross-National Innovation Pools** Many of the social problems that communities around the world face are not unique. Cross-national innovation pools can gather groups of interested governments or foundations from several countries for an aligned innovation process.
- **Research to Enhance Learning** The world needs much more extensive, rigorous, imaginative, and historically aware research on social innovation. Alongside greater conceptual clarity and common definitions, this calls for more case studies and better analysis of success factors and inhibitors at each stage of the innovation process. Research can also investigate better links with adjacent disciplines working on private sector innovation and science, public sector improvement, and civil society. There are also opportunities for researching some specifics of social innovation, for instance, which styles of philanthropy achieve the greatest long-term impact, how corporate social responsibility systems can best contribute to scalable and replicable models, and where Internet-based business models can address social challenges.

Box: Are We There Yet? Private Financial Organizations Struggle to Find Green Solutions

Presumably, the creation of sustainable livelihoods is a topic that private financial service organizations know something about. So, excitement ran high when the United Nations Environment Programme discussed the environmental implications of globalization with several of them in Frankfurt last November.

To be sure, a few saw that financial service organizations can encourage sustainable development. The market-based opportunities and challenges that one speaker identified include ethical or green funds, green securities, tradable permits, and mixed instruments such as environmental bonds. The knowledge-based openings he made out could be voluntary agreements, certification, reporting, and disclosure of information. Another explained the workings of the Nikko Eco Fund (which invests in companies that excel in environmental conservation). But most highlighted the direct, indirect, and image risks associated with environmentally sensitive projects. Except for one speaker who reminded the audience that 1.3 billion people live on less than $1 a day, they contemplated only emerging markets.

Predictably, then, few new business models were outlined. One participant (from the United Nations Environment Programme) made clear the potential of cleaner production financing in terms of cost reduction (materials, energy, waste treatment), business upgrading (improved quality and competitiveness of green processes, products, services), and risk reduction (inherent to cleaner production). Even so, he recognized constraints, of which the small sizes of investments. (Others are the absence of business incentives, the lack of ability of the private sector to prepare creditworthy proposals, the longer payback period of such investments, undervaluation of environmental risks, and the fact that financial organizations often do not see the technical and financial merits of investment proposals.) One session on environmental management and reporting guidelines for the financial services sector also came unstuck. A panelist explained the endeavors of the Global Reporting Initiative. But subsequent talks described separate attempts to develop a common reporting framework at the national level, and in isolation from the global initiative.

Yet the relationship between companies and the environment in which they operate is more important, and senior managers recognize increasingly that companies have a responsibility not only to shareholders but also to other stakeholders. Environmental (and social) accounting could embed these responsibilities. But despite its topicality, the United Nations Environment Programme's roundtable did little to advance knowledge and much remains to be done before a practical framework for action comes about.

The emphasis that several speakers placed on image risks is not encouraging. So, those who lament aid fatigue will take comfort in the fact that most examples provided on smart environmental lending were drawn from multilateral development banks such as ADB. This suggests that they could help the financial services sector of their developing members to incorporate environmental considerations in their activities, and share their practical experiences of environment-friendly lending. And there surely exists potential for cleaner production financing—the hidden cost of waste is far greater than the cost of its treatment and disposal (counting compliance with regulations, wasteful use of raw materials, energy, and labor, tarnished images, and liability). For this reason, constraints on cleaner production financing ought not to be insurmountable, and development banks could mitigate them by means of credit lines, trust funds, policy dialogue, and training.

But the growing number of initiatives on environmental reporting, which use very different reporting frameworks, is cause for worry. It could set off a race to the top and spawn restrictive trade practices. What is more, the applicability in developing countries of the frameworks advertised is debatable. Should environmental reporting allow for regional variations? If this is not the case, how should the drafting process for global guidelines proceed?

Source Author. 2000. *News from ERO.* Manila

References

Kanter RM (May–June 1999) From spare change to real change: the social sector as a beta site for business innovation. Harvard Business Review: 122–132

Mulgan G (2007) Social innovation: what it is, why it matters, and how it can be accelerated. Skoll Center for Social Entrepreneurship. Working Paper

Mulgan G, Buonfino A, Geissendorfer L (2006) Mapping Britain's unmet needs. The Young Foundation

Murray R, Caulier-Grice J, Mulgan G (2010) The open book of social innovation. The Young Foundation

Further Reading

Gregory Dees J (2001) The meaning of "social entrepreneurship". Center for the Advancement of Social Entrepreneurship

Proposition 76
A Primer on Corporate Values

In a Word Corporate values articulate what guides an organization's behavior and decision making. They can boost innovation, productivity, and credibility, and help deliver thereby sustainable competitive advantage. However, a look at typical statements of corporate values suggests much work remains to be done before organizations draw real benefits from them.

Some Facts on Corporate Guidance Systems

Advertising strong, positive corporate values is à la mode.[1] Why? In a globalizing world, meaningful values can, for example, instill a sense of identity and purpose in organizations; add spirit to the workplace; align and unify people; promote employee ownership; attract newcomers; create consistency; simplify decision

---

[1] The impetus came from *In Search of Excellence*, a book that made out eight common attributes—hands-on, value-driven company philosophies among them, credited with the success (at the time) of the 43 organizations covered (Peters and Waterman 1982).

© Asian Development Bank 2017
O. Serrat, *Knowledge Solutions*, DOI 10.1007/978-981-10-0983-9_76

making; energize endeavors; raise efficiency; hearten client trust, loyalty, and for-giveness for mistakes; build resilience to shocks; and contribute to society at large.[2]

However, corporate values can backfire with glare when management or per-sonnel fail to live up to the messages, a sure recipe for disenchantment or cynicism among clients, audiences, and partners, not to forget personnel itself.[3] In most such cases, the cause of tension is that organizational goals, principally couched in financial terms, often do not reflect (when they do not conflict with) the corporate values propounded and the underlying organizational culture from which such values are supposed to spring. Lest they become debased, corporate values should not be platitudes, orders of preference expressed in operational jargon, or even simple aspirations.[4] They should not be politically correct. To serve as real guid-ance systems, living values that spring from integrity, morality, and ethics must be internalized by personnel[5] and reviewed at intervals to maintain relevance in changing contexts[6]; that rarely happens.

---

[2]As the term should make clear, an organization is both a complex social system and a living community.

[3]Enron Corporation's code of ethics, issued on 1 July 2000, publicized that company's values as respect, integrity, communication, and excellence. In late 2001, it was revealed that Enron's reported financial condition had been sustained by institutionalized, systematic, and creatively planned fraudulent accounting practices. Enron has since become a byword for willful corporate corruption.

[4]A representative smattering of value statements includes words such as teamwork, customers, community, passion, and innovation. All the same, personnel understand what is real about these values not so much from what is written but from what is put into practice.

[5]Corporate values that are drawn by management are not rooted in basic social convictions and cannot be the bedrock of an organizational constitution. They serve only to rally the troops and are therefore manipulative in nature. What is more, advertising corporate values does not necessarily mean they will be practiced: over time, personnel weave their own interpretations and ideologies into organizational behavior; therefore, it is essential that personnel and management share an understanding of what corporate values are (or might be). Obviously, there must be reciprocity of obligation, enshrined in two-way communications.

[6]Some argue that corporate values exist to see an organization through both good and bad times and that they cannot be altered. This may be an excessively uncompromising position: every now and then, even the best business model hits a wall. According to Drucker (1994), business models rest on three legs: assumptions about the environment of the organization, the specific mission of the organization, and the core competencies needed to accomplish that. Without straying from the topic of these *Knowledge Solutions*, in keeping with their focus on improving corporate practices, it is pertinent to note that the assumptions, specific mission, and core competencies of organiza-tions only address the why and what of business. However, relatively new notions of management models are beginning to answer the equally important question of its how. According to Birkinshaw (2010), a management model embodies the choices that the executives of an orga-nization make to define objectives, motivate effort, coordinate activities, and allocate resources—in other words, the choices they make to define how the work of management gets done.

In *The Neuroscience of Leadership*, Rock and Schwartz (2006) share a few home truths on organizational transformation. They bear relevance to the subject of these *Knowledge Solutions* since change is what the introduction of corporate values usually purports, at least from the outset. According then to David Rock and Jeffrey Schwartz:

- **Change is pain** Organizational change is unexpectedly difficult because it provokes sensations of physiological discomfort.
- **Behaviorism does not work** Change efforts based on incentive and threat (the carrot and the stick) rarely succeed in the long run.
- **Humanism is overrated** In practice, the conventional empathic approach of connection and persuasion does not sufficiently engage people.
- **Focus is power** The act of paying attention creates chemical and physical changes in the brain.
- **Expectation shapes reality** The preconceptions of people significant impact what they perceive.
- **Attention density shapes identity** Repeated, purposeful, and focused attention can lead to long-lasting personal evolution.

The Meaning of Corporate Values

People don't resist change. They resist being changed!

—Peter Senge

To note, corporate values do not equate with organizational culture: that describes the attitudes, experiences, beliefs, and values of the organization, acquired through social learning, that control the way individuals and groups in the organization interact with one another and with parties outside it.[7] Corporate values are first-order operating philosophies or principles, to be acted upon, that guide an organization's internal conduct and its relationship with the external world.[8] (To be clear, corporate values do not drive the business; however, if they are imbedded in business

---

[7]A standard typology of this complex subject refers to communal, networked, mercenary, and fragmented cultures.

[8]For reference, at the individual level, values are a small set of key concepts and ideals that guide a person's life and help him or her make important decisions. Evidently, in organizations, matching individual values to corporate values is no easy matter. Still, people are more likely to put effort into living their organization's corporate values if they understand the fit between these and their own.

processes—and made credible to skeptics—they inspire the people who deliver the business, with a healthy balance between work and life and between the short term and the long term.) The ultimate glue that bonds the best organizations, they are usually formalized in explicit—often espoused, not just embedded—mission statements, tag lines, and branding material. Important elements are content and context.[9]

Box 1: The Corporate Values of the United States National Park Service

Shared Stewardship—We share a commitment to resource stewardship with the global preservation community.

Excellence—We strive continually to learn and improve so that we may achieve the highest ideals of public service.

Integrity—We deal honestly and fairly with the public and one another.

Tradition—We are proud of it, we learn from it, we are not bound by it.

Respect—We embrace each other's differences so that we may enrich the well-being of everyone.

Source Author

Drawing Real Value from Corporate Values

The W. Edwards Deming Center for Quality Management has shown that organizations waste up to 50% of productive time through lack of trust (Whitney 1995), a fundamental intangible that corporate values can certainly promote. In view of that, beginning about 10 years ago, some organizations have engaged in values-driven management improvement efforts, including values training, appraising management and personnel on their adherence to corporate values, and employing organizational development specialists to help them understand how their corporate values affect performance. Have any trends emerged from their activities?

Usefully, in 2005, the Aspen Institute and Booz Allen Hamilton executed a major global study of corporate values (Kelly et al. 2005). They surveyed senior management in 365 companies in 30 countries in five regions, almost one-third of whom were chief executive officers or board members.[10] The fundamental findings of the study were the following:

---

[9]Content refers to the meaningfulness of corporate values, characterized for instance by authenticity, specificity, tangibility, and ease of application. Context refers to the degree to which the corporate values can be woven into everyday thinking and behavior: they must pervade the organization, for example, through the ways people are selected, managed, assessed, recognized, promoted, rewarded, etc.

[10]The study invited about 9,500 senior executives from around the world to help understand how companies are dealing with the challenges of managing values: What are the dimensions of

> *How can an enterprise build capabilities, forge empowered teams, develop a deep understanding of customers, and—most importantly—create a sense of community and common purpose unless it has a relationship with its employees based on trust and caring?*
>
> —Robert Waterman

- **Ethical behavior is part of a company's license to operate** Of the 89% of companies that had a written corporate values statement, 90% singled ethical behavior and integrity as an operating philosophy or principle. Further, 81% believed that formal statements of corporate values were important to reinforce these.
- **Most companies believe values influence two important strategic areas— relationships and reputations—but do not see the direct link to growth** Commitment to clients was a value included in corporate statements in 88% of companies. Substantial majorities also categorized employee recruitment and retention and corporate reputation as both important to their business strategy and strongly affected by values. However, although companies said that such values as adaptability, productivity, and product quality and innovation are important to strategy, few thought that these values directly affect revenue and earnings growth.
- **Most companies are not measuring their return on values** In a business environment increasingly dominated by attention to definable returns on specific investments, most senior executives were surprisingly lax in quantifying a return on values. Less than 40% volunteered they can directly link revenue and earnings growth.
- **But financial leaders are approaching values more comprehensively** Companies that reported superior financial results emphasized values such as commitment to employees, drive to succeed, and adaptability far more than their peers. They were also more successful in linking values to the way they run their companies: a significantly greater number reported that their management practices were effective in fostering values that influence growth, and they were more likely to believe that social responsibility and corporate citizenship as well as environmental responsibility have a positive effect on financial performance.
- **Values practices vary significantly by region** Asian and European companies were more likely than North American firms to emphasize values related to the corporation's broader role in society, such as social responsibility and corporate

---

(Footnote 10 continued)

corporate values? What are the factors that enable and hinder executives in making decisions based on their corporate values? What is the value of corporate values? What are the best practices for applying corporate values?

citizenship and environmental responsibility. The manner in which companies reinforced values and aligned them with their strategies also varied by region.

- **The tone of the chief executive officer matters** As many as 85% of the respondents reported their companies relied on explicit chief executive support to reinforce corporate values. And 77% claimed it was the most effective practice for reinforcing the company's ability to act on its values. (Respondents considered it so irrespective of geography, industry, or company size.)

The Strategic Value of Values

Kanter (2009), in a book concerned with the global crisis of business and American-style capitalism, echoes Julian Birkinshaw's view that new business models must arise: specifically, in the corporate sector, these are to be models that serve society in addition to rewarding shareholders and employees. She sees strong potential synergy between financial performance and attention to community and social needs, unique competitive advantage from embracing the values and expectations of a new generation of professionals, and growth opportunities from stressing corporate values and restraining executive egos when seeking strategic alliances and integrating acquisitions. Drawing from her book, the range of advantages that values-based organizations tap through their strategic use of operating philosophies or principles are:

> *It takes 20 years to build a reputation and five minutes to ruin it. If you think about that, you'll do things differently.*
>
> —Warren Buffett

- **Competitive differentiation** An emphasis on corporate values builds specific lines of business and strengthens an organization's brand. Success means that competitors may start emulating particular initiatives but that merely raises the bar: a clear sense of societal purpose provides a wellspring that can produce the next wave of activity. Competitors who attempt to copy initiatives without underlying corporate values will always be behind the vanguard.
- **Public accountability via end-to-end responsibility** Corporate values help meet the public's request that organizations should know, care, and communicate about all aspects of their products and services—from sources to

applications to ultimate disposal. Greater contact with stakeholders across the value chain builds an organization's brand and triggers opportunities for innovation.

- **Rationale for long-term thinking** Corporate values that include operating philosophies or principles of sustainability help organizations create continuity. They become values-based organizations that have meaning[11] beyond their current bundle of assets or lines of business. Such values help them avoid "short-termism" and make choices with an eye on the future.
- **Common vocabulary and guidance for consistent decisions** Corporate values are an essential guide to organizations that need to make fast decisions and take quick action in far-flung or differentiated operations. Their clear articulation helps personnel select among alternatives in a consistent manner.
- **Talent magnets and motivation machines** Talented people are mobile but, essentially, they are attracted (and faithful) to organizations whose corporate values match their key concepts and ideals. (An organization's brand and reputation affect its ability to attract the right people.) If organizations are networks of people working toward the same end, corporate values should help ensure that personnel are proud of what they are doing and are motivated by that.
- **"Human" control systems—peer review and a self-control system** Belief in corporate values strengthens peer responsibility for keeping one another aligned; it also generates self-guidance and self-policing. Such human control systems do not work perfectly but they reduce the need for rules and help make people feel free and autonomous[12]: personnel become willful actors who make their own choices based on values they support.

---

[11]Intuitively, a clear link appears between personnel experiencing meaning and an organization's ability to manage change effectively, attract and retain talent, and engage personnel for high performance.

[12]Over the last 10 years, high-performance organizations have dismantled many stultifying human resource policies and procedures that, borne of old-style command-and-control management systems and enforced through endless orientation sessions, had seemed aimed only at making life harder. (In a globalizing world that demands speed and agility, the near-constant fine-tuning of thick volumes of administrative orders and administrative circulars had become a burden they could no longer afford.) Human resource departments are now expected to contribute to the accomplishment of organizational goals, not just busy themselves with personnel administration. Therefore, it is often the case that they have inspired attempts to articulate corporate values: after all, organizations must still have a behavioral bedrock lest chaos, confusion, and parochialism rule. Some human resource specialists may well feel they have jumped from the frying pan into the fire: if, as the earlier arguments suggest, much work remains to be done before organizations draw real benefits from corporate values, human resource departments must for their part reexamine human resource policies and procedures against the corporate values they (or other units) have helped promote. A checklist against which they must do so includes relevance, strategy, adaptability, applicability, familiarity, clarity, boundaries, and commitment.

Box 2: A Corporate Values Start-Up Kit

- Do you know what your organization's corporate values are? Is the potential tension between multiple aims explicitly acknowledged? Is the language original or reworded from elsewhere? Is it memorable? Are appropriate meanings clear, without restricting the scope of the values? Does a psychological contract suggest an unwritten set of mutual expectations between the organization and its personnel? Has psychological safety been created?
- How did your organization identify its corporate values? Which office or department developed them? Was a formal audit of existing values conducted?
- What difference would it make if your organization really practiced its corporate values? Would you be happier at work?
- How do your organization's corporate values show up in its operations? How are they communicated? How does your organization distinguish between its corporate values and its policies, strategies, structures, systems, and business processes? Has it drawn a learning charter citing commitment to corporate and individual actions?
- What is challenging about practicing, promoting, and living your organization's corporate values? What are the obstacles?
- Is the behavior of your organization's personnel measured against its corporate values through the performance management system? How are new alignments created? How are misalignments identified and corrected?
- What do your organization's corporate values mean to you? How do they fit with your individual values? How do you express these?
- How are you practicing, promoting, and living your organization's corporate values? How do they show up in your daily working life? In which parts are they weak or missing? What can you do differently to start living them, even when it is hard?
- What are you doing to bring your organization's corporate values to your team?
- What support would be helpful to you and your team so that you may better practice your organization's corporate values? To whom can you talk?

Source Author

References

Birkinshaw J (2010) Reinventing management: smarter choices for getting work done. Jossey-Bass

Drucker P (September 1994) Theory of the business. Harvard Business Review: 95–104

Kanter RM (2009) Super corp: how vanguard companies create innovation, profits, growth, and social good. Crown Business

Kelly C, Kocourek P, McGaw N, Samuelson J (2005) Deriving value from corporate values. The Aspen Institute and Booz Allen Hamilton

Peters T, Waterman R (1982) In search of excellence: lessons from America's best-run companies. Harper & Row

Rock D, Schwartz J (2006) The neuroscience of leadership. Strategy + business. 43

Whitney J (1995) The economics of trust: liberating profits and restoring corporate vitality. McGraw-Hill

Further Reading

ADB (2010) Our people strategy. Manila

Proposition 77
Bridging Organizational Silos

In a Word To develop and deliver products and services, large organizations rely on teams. Yet, the defining characteristics of these often hamper collaboration among different parts of the organization. The root cause is conflict: it must be accepted then actively managed. Promoting effective cross-functional teams demands that an enabling environment be built for that.

What's in a Word?

A silo is a tall, self-contained cylindrical structure that is used to store commodities such as grain after a harvest. It is also a figure of speech for organizational entities—and their management teams—that lack the desire or motivation to coordinate (at worst, even communicate) with other entities in the same organization. Wide recognition of the metaphor intimates that structural barriers in sizable organizations

© Asian Development Bank 2017

O. Serrat, *Knowledge Solutions*, DOI 10.1007/978-981-10-0983-9_77

often cause units to work against one another[1]: silos, politics, and turf wars are often mentioned in the same breath.

An organization is a social arrangement to pursue a collective intent.[2] Coordination, and the requisite communication it implies, is fundamental to organizational performance toward that. Yet, many organizations grapple with the challenge of connecting the subsystems they have devised to enhance specific contributing functions. Here and there, organizational, spatial, and social boundaries impede—when they do not block—the flows of knowledge needed to make full use of capabilities. High costs are borne from duplication of effort, inconsistencies, and inefficiencies. Everywhere, large organizations must move from managing silos to managing systems.

Enter the Matrix

It's not enough that we win; everyone else must lose.

—Larry Ellison

For 100 years, (fully or semi-) autonomous organizational arrangements have been designed to manage complexity, keep products and services close to clients, and hold managers accountable. (In the 1970s and 1980s, interest in matrix

---

[1]Specifically, three types of boundaries can be distinguished: (i) organizational, e.g., business units, functional memberships; (ii) spatial, e.g., office locations, inter-office distances; and (iii) social, e.g., gender, tenure (pay grades, job ranks). Of the three, the most widespread are termed product silos—that is, business units defined by product or service offering—and country silos, meaning, geographic silos demarcated by, say, country or region. In 2006, a study of a large structurally, functionally, geographically, and strategically diverse company that analyzed more than 100 million electronic mail messages and over 60 million electronic calendar entries for a sample of more than 30,000 employees over a 3-month period revealed surprisingly little interaction across the three boundaries. Communication patterns were extremely hierarchical: in short, most people tended to communicate with others in their group or with peers. (Women were the exception: they played key "boundary spanning" roles.) (Kleinbaum et al. 2008).

[2]It helps to think of organizations as systems. A system is a group of interacting, interrelated, or interdependent elements that form a complex whole. In an organization, inputs are processed to produce outputs toward outcomes that, in combination, deliver the impact the organization desires. Obviously, rapport among the subsystems, e.g., departments, divisions, offices, teams, programs, etc., involving feedback, insight, and disclosure is essential to ensure they synergize. The processes that link the subsystems are typically defined by corporate values, policies, procedures, and rules.

structures, be they in functional, balanced, or project form, mushroomed.)[3] To this day, multiple command structures are found in most large organizations, even where traditional departmental structures—themselves tall chimneys—hold sway. This is testimony to the perceived effectiveness of such arrangements (even if few organizations track matrix structure performance and fewer still examine the human dimensions of operating and managing in the matrix).[4] Still, silo power misaligns goals, dilutes roles and responsibilities, makes for ambiguous authority, leads to resource misallocation, breeds defensive personnel, and fosters a culture whereby the incentive is to maximize the performance of the silo, not that of the organization. Given frequent emphasis on silo-level metrics, monitoring, and management; the use of independent insights and toolsets across individual silos supporting a product or service; lack of shared understanding of service typologies; and the absence of coherent end-to-end views, silos cannot easily recognize corporate-level opportunities. (Indeed, they may even stand in the way of leveraging success where it occurs.)

We have met the enemy and he is us.

—Pogo

In spite of that, the objective should not be to tear down silos by centralizing and standardizing—even though some of that may be part of the solution.[5] In the name of performance improvements, the organizational designs that engender silos are usually the result of earnest attempts to identify the right business issues, pinpoint

---

[3]The matrix is a grid-like, multiple command structure that, in theory, allows organizations to target multiple business goals; leverage large resources while staying small and task-focused; enable quick transfer of inputs; facilitate the management of information through lateral communication channels; develop economies of scale; encourage creativity and innovation; and speed responses to changes in the external environment. In opposition, the matrix violates the principles that authority should equal responsibility and that personnel should report to a single manager; can create ambiguity and conflict; increases management and administrative costs; and raises the likelihood of resistance to change as personnel can associate the matrix with loss of status, authority, and control over their traditional domains. Notwithstanding, organizations continue to adopt the matrix because they believe its strengths outweigh its weaknesses (Sy and D'Annunzio 2005).

[4]Without specific, measurable, achievable, relevant, and time-bound performance indicators, it will not be easy for managers to recognize problems and take necessary remedial actions. Arguably, there probably also is a need for a matrix guardian tasked, for instance, with monitoring and evaluation of matrix performance as well as identification of good practices for dissemination and uptake across an organization.

[5]Gone are the days when simple hierarchical structures could serve the needs of organizations. Complexity thinking must now help deal with complexity and personnel should be equipped for that. From this perspective, operating and managing in the matrix ceases to be a structural constraint to become a frame of mind.

the right underlying obstacles, adopt the right design characteristics, and implement change the right way. And so, in general, silos do not exist because something was intentionally done: they come about because something was left undone, that is, the provision of compelling motives, means, and opportunities for personnel to come together. The idea, then, should be to replace competition with collaboration. Successful matrix (but also traditional) organizations take care to communicate a clear, consistent corporate vision and to define expectations; work to expand individual perspectives to co-opt ambitions, energies, and skills into the broader organizational agenda[6]; increase congruence with corporate values through training that reinforces desired attitudes and behaviors; evaluate personnel for work across functions; and help build relationships. (More and more, communities and networks of practice are empowered to accomplish the latter end.)

Lights to Go: From Red to Green

Collaboration begins with individuals (although organizations can do much to foster it).[7] It is born of an intentional attitude that Tamm and Luyet (2005) have described as being in the Green Zone.[8] Green Zone environments are marled by high trust, dialogue, excitement, honesty, friendship, laughter, mutual support, sincerity, optimism, cooperation, friendly competition, shared vision, flexibility, risk taking, a tendency to learn from mistakes, the ability to face difficult truths, the taking of broad perspectives, openness to feedback, a sense of contribution, the experience of work as pleasure, internal motivation, and ethical behavior.[9]

The outer and inner selves of individuals in the Green Zone are congruent. They seek connection according to deeply held values and character, rather than tactical or strategic thinking. Therefore, they convey an authentic, nondefensive presence. Their actions in a relationship are not driven by fearful motives, nor are they determined by

---

[6]After all, it stands to reason that the interaction of a broad range of types of jobs—and people—is required to make the whole greater than the sum of its parts.

[7]Attitudes are impacted by biological and cultural factors, as well as personal history. But overcoming defensiveness to build successful relationships, both personal and professional, is still a choice that individuals make.

[8]FIRO, the theory of fundamental interpersonal relations orientation, lies at the heart of the book. William Schutz (1925–2002), an American psychologist, is credited with its development. The theory explains human interaction by means of three primary dimensions: (i) inclusion, (ii) control, and (iii) affection. (The dimensions can be used to assess group dynamics.).

[9]In opposition, Red Zone environments are marled by low trust, high blame, alienation, undertones of threats and fear, anxiety, guardedness, hyper rivalry, hostility, withholding, denial, hostile arguments, risk avoidance, cheating, greed, an attitude of entitlement, deadness, cynicism, suspicion, sarcasm, a tendency for people to hide mistakes, work experienced as painful, and dependence on external motivation. For individuals, the consequences of Red Zone behavior include loneliness, depression, anxiety, emptiness, self-centeredness, lack of intimacy, codependency, aggression, and the absence of enjoyment.

an unconscious competitive spirit. When conflict arises, they seek to understand and to grow because they desire mutual gains rather than victory. They can do so because they have tools, methods, and approaches to cope in less reactive ways.

The Green Zone is a catalyst for creativity and innovation and for high levels of problem solving. It allows individuals to focus their ambitions, energies, and skills. In an atmosphere that is free of intrigue, mistrust, and betrayal, they have greater opportunities to realize the potential of their circumstances. They dream, believe, dare, and do. Until individuals operate in the Green Zone, organizations will not be able to tap the excitement, aliveness, and productive power of collaborative relationships.

On the contrary, silos are Red Zone environments ruled by fear and defensiveness. (A parallel can be drawn to the notion of the passive-aggressive organization that Booz Allen Hamilton diagnose with inability to execute, ineffective decision making, information disconnect, and inconsistent or conflicting motivators.) Developing four introspective skills can help staff and management there cultivate mindsets and enhance organizational cultures to conduce and sustain high-performing, long-term, collaborative relationships. The skills are (i) collaborative intention, (ii) truthfulness. (ii) self-accountability, and (iv) self-awareness and awareness of others.[10]

From Silos to Systems

It follows that bridging organizational silos calls for collaboration, coordination, capability, and connection. This is easier said than done: practically, how can one aim at silo-driven problems? Usefully, Lencioni (2006) has proposed a model for combating silos, against which actions to build collaboration, coordination, capability, and connection can be framed. It is, of course, reminiscent of the logic models used to design and monitor projects or programs; the breakthrough lies in the proposed application at the corporate level of a system to overcome the barriers that turn colleagues into competitors. The model comprises four components:

- **Establish a Thematic Goal** A thematic goal is a single, qualitative, and time-bound focus that is shared by the entire organization irrespective of area of interest, expertise, gender, or title. It is a rallying cry for personnel to work together for the common good. It is not a long-term vision or a measurable objective.
- **Articulate Defining Objectives for the Thematic Goal** The defining objectives provide actionable context so that personnel knows what must be done to accomplish the thematic goal. They too must be qualitative, time-bound, and shared.
- **Specify a Set of Ongoing Standard Operating Objectives** The thematic goal and defining objectives only exist for a specified period of time. Standard

---

[10]Fortunately, modern organizations now also offer learning and development to promote emotional intelligence in the workplace. Importantly, many recognize too the need to identify and recruit personnel for collaborative intent. (The use of psychometric tests to that effect is growing.).

operating objectives never change, no matter what the short-term focus is. They may include client satisfaction, productivity, market share, quality, etc. Of course, they must be consistent with the thematic goal.

- **Select Metrics** Metrics are selected after the thematic goal has been established, the defining objectives for the goal have been articulated, and the standard operating objectives have been specified. They are necessary to manage and monitor the accomplishment of the thematic goal and defining objectives. Color schemes can be used to represent progress, e.g., Green = Made progress, Yellow = Progress beginning to stall or regress, and Red = Progress stalled or regressed.

References

Kleinbaum A, Stuart T, Tushman M (2008) Communication (and Coordination?) in a modern, complex organization. Harvard Business School. Working Paper No. 009–004

Lencioni P (2006) Silos, politics and turf wars: a leadership fable about destroying the barriers that turn colleagues into competitors. Jossey-Bass

Sy T, D'Annunzio L (2005) Challenges and strategies of matrix organizations: top-level and mid-level managers' perspectives. Human Resource Planning 28(1):39–48

Tamm J, Luyet R (2005) Radical collaboration: five essential skills to overcome defensiveness and build successful relationships. HarperCollins Publishers

Proposition 78
A Primer on Social Neuroscience

In a Word The human mind is driven by an emergent array of biological, cognitive, and social properties. Unconscious processes perform feats we thought required intention, deliberation, and conscious awareness. The breakthroughs of social neuroscience are fostering more comprehensive theories of the mechanisms that underlie human behavior.

Aristotle's Social Animal …

Aristotle[1] saw the city—what we now call the state—as a natural community.[2] Since the whole must necessarily precede the parts—for if you take away the man, you cannot say that a foot or hand remains—the city comes before the family that,

---

[1]Aristotle (384–322 BC), a Greek philosopher and scientist, investigated an extraordinary range of subjects including agriculture, biology, botany, chemistry, dance, ethics, government, history, literary theory, logic, mathematics, medicine, metaphysics, music, poetry, physics, politics, psychology, rhetoric, theater, and zoology. A highly original and prolific writer, he radically transformed most, if not all, the areas of knowledge he touched. More than 2,300 years after his death, despite the unavoidable shortcomings of his wide-ranging, original thinking, he counts as one of the most influential scholars who ever lived.

[2]Formed initially for the satisfaction of natural wants, according to him, the state exists thereafter for moral ends and the promotion of higher life.

© Asian Development Bank 2017

O. Serrat, *Knowledge Solutions*, DOI 10.1007/978-981-10-0983-9_78

logically, heralds the individual. And so, the city is last in the order of becoming but first in the order of being.

Aristotle, a forward-looking naturalist who relentlessly sought the reality behind appearances and all the time expected that it might be different from what it seemed, thought it obvious that man is by nature a social animal (and that whosoever is naturally and not accidentally unfit for society must be either inferior or superior to man). In his *Politics* and elsewhere—for example, in *The History of Animals, Metaphysics, On Memory and Reminiscence,* and *On the Soul*—he stressed the logic of relations between parts and wholes. Had later thinkers such as René Descartes[3] followed Aristotle in conceptualizing the mind as an array of powers or potentialities (rather than as a separate entity), attributing thereby physiological or psychological capacities to the whole organism, they would have edged closer to the truth; they would not have become ensnared in intractable problems of inter-action between the mind and the body. (Dualism is the condition of being double. In psychology, it is the view that the mind and body function separately, without interchange; Cartesian dualism is summed up in the philosophical statement "Cogito, ergo sum". ["I think, therefore I am."]) In the twenty-first century, it is belatedly recognized that human beings are natural: they are part of nature and they are evolving naturally[4]; human thinking too is natural.[5]

---

[3]René Descartes (1596–1650), a French philosopher, mathematician, and physicist, insisted that mental reality must be exactly as it seems.

[4]Human institutions and related artifacts are the offspring of thought, skill, and social interaction. In the form of dyads, families, and groups, to cities, civilizations, and cultures, Homo sapiens has created emergent, constantly evolving and complex adaptive social structures that extend far beyond the individual. Over time, these have coevolved with the neural and hormonal mechanisms that support them because the allied social behaviors and processes have helped individuals stay alive, reproduce, and care for children sufficiently long that they too might survive to procreate and contribute adaptive socio-neural mechanisms to the gene pool. In so doing and as a result of doing so, Homo sapiens has evolved a brain and biology whose functions include formation and maintenance of social recognition, attachments, collectives, and alliances; and development of communication, oftentimes deception, as well as reasoning about the mental states of others (Cacioppo et al. 2005).

[5]In comments on memory and learning phenomena, Aristotle distinguished between recalling information to mind and storing information—or, as he put it, between remembering (the rein-statement in consciousness of something that was there before) and memory (the existence, potentially, in the mind of an earlier perception or conception). In his opinion, the main difficulties were to explain (i) how the perception of a state of affairs can be stored; (ii) how it can later be brought to mind; (iii) how it happens that, when the perception of a state of affairs is brought to mind, the relation between the representation and the original state of affairs, now absent, is such that the first is a memory of the second and is known to be such. In modern parlance, these problems relate to storage of information, retrieval of information, and the question of how representations represent.

... Meets Social Neuroscience ...

Human history is not only social history but also neurobiological history. Throughout most of the twentieth century, social and biological explanations were widely viewed as incompatible. However, from the 1990s, the emergence of social neuroscience[6] vindicates Aristotle's pioneering deductions. The young science accepts that the brain is a single, pivotal component of an undeniably social species and that it is orderly in its complexity. It treats the human brain as a social organ, whose physiological and neurological reactions are directly and profoundly shaped by social interaction. (To a mammal, being socially connected to caregivers is indispensable for survival: this, incidentally, suggests that Abraham Maslow's hierarchy of needs might need to be revised to ascribe more weight to social needs, e.g., love and belonging, and esteem, in relation to self-actualization.)

Nondualistic and nonreductionistic, social neuroscience, through a multilevel and integrative approach, aims to understand the role of the central nervous system in the formation and maintenance of social behaviors and processes. Spanning the social and biological domains, e.g., molecular, cellular, system, person, relational, collective, and societal, it exploits biological concepts and neurobiological techniques such as functional magnetic resonance imaging[7]—which measures patterns of blood oxygenation responses in the brain as a subject engages in a particular task, to inform and refine theories of social behavior. In short, it focuses on how the brain mediates social interaction.[8] (Brain scans captured through functional magnetic resonance imaging show that the same areas are associated with distress, be that caused by social rejection or by physical pain.)

Arguably, the potential benefits of social neuroscience are that it can inform debates in social psychology, provide tools for measuring brain–body activity directly and unobtrusively and provide information that would be impossible to assess using other techniques, and permit the examination of social processes by pointing to the importance of social variables (from context to culture) in altering processes within the brain and body.

---

[6]Traditional neuroscience has treated the nervous system as an isolated entity and has largely ignored the influences of the social environments in which human beings live. We now recognize the considerable impact that social structures have on the operations of the mind and body.

[7]Magnetic resonance imaging is a relatively new technology: the first image was published in 1973. (In comparison, the first human X-ray was taken in 1895.) Unlike regular magnetic resonance imaging, functional magnetic resonance imaging captures a sequence of activity while it is in progress. The other techniques of neuroscience include positron emission tomography, event-related potentials, magnetoencephalography, transcranial magnetic stimulation, electrocardiograms, electromyograms, endocrinology, galvanic skin response, and studies of focal brain lesion patients.

[8]In the last decade, social neuroscience has shed light on aspects of social life as diverse as social regulation; social rejection; impression formation; self-awareness; emotion regulation; and attitudes, beliefs, and memory involving social groups.

... Through the Doors of Perception

Everything has beauty, but not everyone sees it.

—Confucius

Perception is the process of acquiring, interpreting, selecting, and organizing sensory information to attain awareness. It involves cognitive and affective interaction between an organism and the external world. (In the case of people, what someone perceives is a result of interplay between the perceiver,[9] the situation, and the perceived.) Hence, perception is not a passive reaction to, say, events or circumstances: it is an active, pervasive, and significant process through which the structure and function of the sense organs and nervous system form a vital link between the organism and the external world. In society, perception is all-important because people's attitudes and behaviors are based on their discernment of what reality is, not on reality itself. The world as it is perceived is the world that is behaviorally important: perception is projection—we all have individual assumptions and theories that help guide us through life.[10]

Relating Human Nature to Organizational Context

It is a pleasure to give advice, humiliating to need it, normal to ignore it.

—Anonymous

By bringing together biological and psychological models of the brain, social neuroscience confirms that much of human life revolves around pain and pleasure.

---

[9]The components of a person's perceptive makeup that, in combination with the situation and the perceived, will determine behavior, are physical, social, and personal. They can be influenced by culture, religion, values, ethics, emotions, authority, rapport, attitude, persuasion, coercion, hypnosis, and genetics. Combinations of these drive, in turn, cognition and affect.

[10]For a taxonomy of perception, see Moore (1970).The paper identifies (i) sensation—behavior that indicates awareness of the qualities (informational aspects) of a stimulus (or of material) as perceived by the senses; (ii) figure perception—behavior that suggests awareness of an entity; (iii) symbol perception—behavior that reveals awareness of figures in the form of denotative signs (when associated meanings are not considered); (iv) perception of meaning—behavior that displays awareness of the significance commonly associated with forms and patterns and events and the ability to assign personal significance to them; interpretive ability; and (v) perceptive performance—behavior that evidences sensitive and accurate observation, ability to make complex decisions where many factors are involved, and ability to change ongoing behavior in response to its effectiveness.

It should come as no surprise that social behavior is governed by an overarching organizing principle of minimizing threat and maximizing reward, informed by brain networks used for primary survival needs.[11] Depending on the environment, these trigger different innate human drives vis-à-vis scarce resources, to which access may be shared or controlled, that Ehin (2000) terms self-centered or other-centered. (More common usage refers to selfishness or altruism.)

Charles Ehin offers a comprehensive framework to understand how human nature can support (or undermine) voluntary workplace collaboration and innovation. He suggests that for these to thrive, organizations must develop an organizational "sweet spot". To that intent, Rock and Schwartz (Rock 2008) have put forward a brain-based model—reminiscent of Charles Ehin's innate human drives —that caters to the primary reward or primary threat circuitry (and associated networks) of the brain.[12] The model, which defines five domains of social experience deeply important to the brain—status, certainty, autonomy, relatedness, and fairness[13]—allows exploration of what nuanced actions to reduce threats and increase rewards might be taken in each domain to support the expansion of Charles Ehin's organizational sweet spots (Rock 2009). (Supportive measures lie in the areas of managing oneself,[14] coaching and mentoring,[15] training, leadership development, and organizational systems.) Usefully, David Rock also makes suggestions for further research, which serve to underscore the potential of the approach. Questions that beg answers—and the potential of social neuroscience is such that the list could be endless—include the following:

---

[11]Brains are built to detect perceived changes in the environment. Error detection signals are generated by the orbital cortex, which is closely connected to the fear circuitry in the two amygdalae. (The amygdalae perform a primary role in the processing and memory of emotional reactions.) Next, the orbital cortex and the amygdalae compete with and pull brain resources away from the prefrontal cortex, which promotes and supports higher intellectual functions, e.g., learning and comprehension. Animal instincts take over, with fight-or-flight responses.

[12]The approach–avoid response is a survival mechanism intended and designed to help people stay alive by quickly and easily remembering what is good or bad in the external environment. Not surprisingly, responses to threats tend to last longer than responses to rewards (Gordon 2000).

[13]As defined by David Rock and Jeffrey Schwartz, status is relative importance to others; certainty is the ability to predict the future; autonomy affords a sense of control over events; relatedness is the sense that one is safe with others, that they are friends rather than foes; and fairness is the perception that exchanges between people are evenhanded.

[14]Thanks to the physiological perspective, we can now understand that individuals need to generate their own answers and, accordingly, that a solutions-focus is more advantageous than dwelling on problems. The power is in the focus.

[15]Learning new skills takes time because old patterns are hard-wired. Therefore, coaches and mentors—managers too—should refrain from giving advice: if they do, they should be unattached to the recommendations they make and flag these as options (certainly not as orders); advice puts people on the defensive because they perceive the person extending it as claiming superiority. They also need to focus on solutions with concentration and serenity. (In a threatened state, people are more likely to be "mindless".) According to David Rock, the science of attention is a cornerstone of coaching: the elements of his ARIA model are (i) awareness of dilemma, (ii) reflection, (iii) insight, and (iv) action (Rock and Schwartz 2006).

> *Nature is trying very hard to make us succeed, but nature does not depend on us. We are not the only experiment.*
>
> —Buckminster Fuller

- Which of the domains in the SCARF model generate the strongest threats or rewards given different types of organization?
- What are the links between the five domains?
- What are the best techniques for minimizing threats and maximizing rewards in each domain?
- Does the relative importance of each domain vary across, say, individuals, gender, or tenure?
- What are the implications of the model for organizational design?

Live Wires

Astonishingly, the study of the brain and nervous system is starting to allow direct measurement of thoughts and feelings. Inevitably, from applications in psychology, social neuroscience will foray into other fields.[16]

Organizational behavior, for one, draws considerably on social psychology and psychoanalysis. (Theories of motivation and personality are rooted in these social sciences.) There, brain-based approaches will help study the building blocks of what professionals do, such as solving complex problems, negotiating transactions, trying to persuade others, promoting change, making decisions under pressure, and sparking creativity and innovation. They can also shed light on the critical matter of giving feedback, which most persons perceive as an attack on their status.[17]

Because of its very breadth, social neuroscience will bring new tools, methods, and approaches to the challenges people and their institutions face. It will, for

---

[16]Neuroeconomics, for one, is already born. Adding observation of the nervous system to the set of explanatory variables, it enriches analyses of social, cognitive, and emotional factors (that behavioral economics concentrates on) to better interpret the economic decisions of individuals as they interact, categorize threats and rewards, and evaluate decisions. Neuromarketing, a distinct discipline related to neuroeconomics, studies the brain activity of potential consumers to marketing stimuli.

[17]From the foregoing, one can be forgiven for concluding that traditional management techniques owe more to animal training than human psychology. If constant, disruptive change is the necessary, often painful, condition of mankind, the benefits of carrot-and-stick or command-and-control approaches can only be temporary (if they arise at all). Social neuroscience explains why people find change so disconcerting: therefore, it is best, with effective questions, to help people derive their own conclusions and develop homemade resolutions.

instance, test orthodox thinking about responsibility and blame and will impact social policies. Notwithstanding, if the journey has begun, much work remains to be done before the revolution in neuroscience applies with effect new knowledge to real-world settings.

References

Cacioppo J, Visser P, Pickett C (eds) (2005) Social neuroscience: people thinking about thinking people. MIT Press

Ehin C (2000) Unleashing intellectual capital. Butterworth-Heinemann

Gordon E (ed) (2000) Integrative neuroscience: bringing together biological, psychological, and clinical models of the human brain. Overseas Publishers Association

Moore MR (1970) The perceptual-motor domain and a proposed taxonomy of perception. Educational Technology Research and Development 18(4):379–413

Rock D (2008) SCARF: a brain-based model for collaborating with and influencing others. NeuroLeadership Journal 8(1):1–9

Rock D (2009) Managing with the brain in mind. Strategy + business 56

Rock D, Schwartz J (2006) A brain-based approach to coaching. International Journal of Coaching in Organizations 4(2):32–44

Further Reading

ADB (2009) Learning for change in ADB. Manila

Harmon-Jones E, Winkielman P (eds) (2007) Social neuroscience: integrating biological and psychological explanations of social behavior. The Guildford Press

Proposition 79
Informal Authority in the Workplace

In a Word In most types of organizations, formal authority is located at the top as part of an exchange against fairly explicit expectations. In networked, pluralistic organizations that must rapidly formulate adaptive solutions in an increasingly complex world, its power is eroding as its functions become less clear. In the twenty-first century, the requirements of organizational speed demand investments in informal authority.

The Insufficient Returns from Formal Authority in Organizations

Formal authority—the power to influence or command thought, opinion, or behavior—is the defining characteristic of societal and organizational hierarchy.[1] Ideally, after Heifetz (1994), it is expected to serve five functions that most will agree are indispensable to social life. They are to (i) provide direction, (ii) offer protection, (iii) orientate roles, (iv) control conflict, and (v) maintain norms. Then

---

[1]Formal authority, in management, is the legitimate right, specified in job descriptions and terms of reference, that gives an individual the license and associated responsibilities to decide on behalf of an organization (or in the name of its sponsoring executive).

© Asian Development Bank 2017
O. Serrat, *Knowledge Solutions*, DOI 10.1007/978-981-10-0983-9_79

again, in practice, there is a darker side to what formal authority can do on any given day: for instance, a boss can restrict a subordinate's actions, invalidate his or her decisions, or move for dismissal.

Charting a chain of command up a hierarchy, one will eventually locate someone (or some group) who administers the organization's collective decision rights (and enjoys the perquisites ascribed to the function). With power comes a set of resources with which to manage the holding environment of the organization and marshal attention. Yet, if formal authority resides at the top in most types of organizations to this day, it is located there as part of an exchange against overt expectations in a specific context.[2] Therefore, it can be taken away. Commonly, it is also lent on to lower level managers according to the relevance and importance of their positions (with which special rights and privileges are in turn associated). Paradoxically, in all cases, managers can be made responsible for getting things done but are not given the requisite authority—certainly not over their own bosses or peers.

> *I would rather try to persuade a man to go along, because once I have persuaded him, he will stick. If I scare him, he will stay just as long as he is scared, and then he is gone.*
>
> —Dwight Eisenhower

Formal authority cuts less and less ice: in networked, pluralistic organizations that have no choice but to rapidly devise adaptive, not just technical,[3] solutions in a composite world, the power of formal authority is eroding as its utility becomes less clear. (As a result, many managers often feel they have traded their erstwhile, relative freedom against a chimera.) At the same time, since many organizations are discarding command-and-control hierarchies in favor of flatter management structures, and essential expertise and decision-making ability is ever more widely dispersed in organizations,[4] it is necessary to excel at persuasion to move people in the right direction and get work done through others under new conditions. Therefore, all things considered, formal authority is best understood as the potential for power, the total amount of which twenty-first century organizations should aim to expand by leveraging mutual influence among personnel.

---

[2]Typically, job descriptions and terms of reference are accompanied by stipulations of education and experience requirements and specifications of desired competencies. Reporting relationships are made clear, too.

[3]More often than not, individuals advance to managerial positions because of their track record in resolving technical problems, chiefly through individual contributions; however, meeting adaptive challenges also necessitates human and conceptual skills in the realm of social learning.

[4]Education levels have risen and information and communications technology makes more knowledge accessible to many more than in the past. Moreover, creativity and innovation are now seen as central to organizational performance: management cannot be expected to be their sole source but must certainly manage for them.

The Challenge of New Age Leadership

Leadership is a process of social influence by which a person enlists the aid and support of others in accomplishing a common task. Having a positive leadership effect does not depend on formal authority; indeed, some of the best leadership comes from people who purposely eschew that. Conversely, many persons in positions of authority do not exercise leadership: to (endeavor to) fulfill the five basic social functions enumerated above, they navigate warily between Charybdis and Scylla, keen to avoid the troubles that arise when one asks people to confront problems; they are quite happy to simply preserve equilibrium. Extreme responses are to become overly directive or too collaborative.

Clearly then, there is a difference between what returns can be expected from formal authority on one side and from leadership on the other. Hence, clarion calls for more informal authority in organizations. Unlike the former, which relies on conformity without acceptance (Kelman 1958), the power of informal authority to influence attitudes and behaviors rests on admiration, credibility, respect, and trust, which conduce conformity coupled with acceptance. Notions of distributed leadership and management by persuasion appeal: by their means, organizations can become sophisticated and versatile, listening to and utilizing the expertise of many to intensify mutual influence and make vision real and central.

Defining Influence

Character may almost be called the most effective means of persuasion.

—Aristotle

The record of mankind's attempts to define (then refine) the principles of successful social influence is long.[5] In the sphere of interpersonal relationships, influence is having a vision of the optimum outcome for events or circumstances and then motivating people to work together to make the vision authentic.

Herbert Kelman has identified three broad varieties of social influence—namely, compliance, identification, and internalization—that represent three qualitatively different ways of accepting influence. Paraphrasing, compliance takes place when an individual accepts influence because he or she hopes to achieve a favorable reaction from another person or group. That is, the individual adopts the induced attitude or behavior because he or she expects to gain specific rewards or approval

---

[5]Aristotle's *Rhetoric* dates from the fourth century BC. It gives a working definition of rhetoric, namely, the ability, in each particular case, to see the available means of persuasion; investigates the three means of persuasion that an orator must draw on, that is, ethos, logos, and pathos; and introduces the elements of style (word choice, metaphor, and sentence structure) and arrangement (organization).

and avoid specific punishments or disapproval by conforming. Identification occurs when an individual accepts influence because he or she wants to establish or maintain a satisfying self-defining relationship with another person or group. He or she adopts the induced behavior or attitude because it is associated with the desired relationship. Internalization happens when an individual accepts influence because the contents of the induced behavior or attitude—the ideas and actions that compose it—are intrinsically rewarding. He or she adopts it because of congruence with his or her value system. From a social psychology perspective, the determinants of conformity are normative[6] and informational.[7]

Enter the Law of Reciprocity

> *I don't know the rules of grammar. If you're trying to persuade people to do something, or buy something, it seems to me you should use their language.*
>
> —David Ogilvy

In truth, irrespective of whether authority is formal or informal, the force that drives attitudes and behaviors, and therefore influence, is the near-universal belief that people should (in one form or another) be paid back for what they do, be that good or bad. Individuals and groups will respond to one another in similar ways: they will react to kindnesses and gifts with benevolence; conversely, they will respond to hurtful acts with some form of retaliation (or at least indifference). Their methods can be crude and mechanical, such as a literal execution of the principle of "an eye for an eye" ("tit for tat"); or they can be complex and sophisticated, e.g., one-to-one, one-to-many, many-to-one, and generalized reciprocity. (Parallels exist in the animal world.)

> *"I" cannot reach fulfillment without "thou". The self cannot be self without other selves. Self-concern without other-concern is like a tributary that has no outward flow to the ocean.*
>
> —Martin Luther King

Connection promotes collaborative intent and multiplies the chances of collaboration. Usefully, Cohen and Bradford (2005) have framed an influence model

---

[6]Normative social influence happens when one conforms to be liked or accepted by the members of a group.

[7]Informational social influence takes place when one turns to the members of a group to obtain and accept information as evidence about reality.

based on reciprocity[8]; it brings the metaphor of currencies into play to describe the process of influence as exchange. They contend that effective managers attempt to build collaborative arrangements with potential allies, even when the latter seem at first adversaries, by discerning what currencies they might have to offer. (Sources of currencies are, broadly, organizationally, job-, and personally determined.) In other words, a manager will exercise influence only insofar as he or she can offer something that others value. (The model needs not be restricted to management; it applies to other walks of life too.)

At least five types of currencies are at work in various organizational settings: (i) inspiration-related, (ii) task-related, (iii) position-related, (iv) relationship-related, and (v) person-related.[9] Many require no permission to spend, e.g., expressing gratitude, showing appreciation, paying respect, making the attainments of others visible, enhancing someone else's reputation, and extending one's personal help on tasks.[10] Unsurprisingly, the use of each is context-specific and hinges on the availability of capital. However, almost everyone has a portfolio of currencies, even though some are more highly valued than others, trade-offs are often possible—granting that some people may have such fundamental differences in what they hold dear that joint understanding is on occasion difficult to reach[11]: The key is to identify one's resources relative to a potential ally's wants without underestimating what one has to offer. The Cohen–Bradford model of influence rests on a long-established feature of human nature as it relates to organizational context. (The recent breakthroughs of social neuroscience are fostering other comprehensive theories of the mechanisms that underlie human behavior.) At both individual and organizational levels, also in the case of formal authority, and enriched or not by Robert Cialdini's five other principles of persuasion, the model illuminates the necessary practice of persuading in the workplace. It does well to expose the fallacies of gratuitous guidelines for mastering the art of persuasion and the pseudoscientific injunctions of persuasion campaigns.[12]

---

[8]Cialdini (1984) lists reciprocity—people repay in kind—as one of six principles of (ethical) persuasion. The others he cites are (i) consistency—people align with their clear commitments, (ii) social proof—people follow the lead of similar others, (iii) liking—people like those who like them, (iv) authority—people defer to experts, and (v) scarcity—people want more of what they can have less of.

[9]One can also, by the same token, identify negative currencies. These come in two forms: (i) withholding payment of a known valuable currency, and (ii) using directly undesirable currencies. Common examples of the former include not giving recognition, not offering support, not providing challenge, and threatening to quit a particular situation. Directly undesirable currencies include raising one's voice, shouting, refusing to cooperate when asked, escalating issues to a common supervisor, going public with a contentious issue, making lack of cooperation visible, and attacking a person's reputation or integrity.

[10]We are, sages say, better defined by what we share than by what we own.

[11]This is more likely where societal cultural values and individual social beliefs conflict.

[12]An example of the former typically runs as follows: (i) connect emotionally, (ii) find the common ground, (iii) establish your credibility, and (iv) become an effective team builder. In the phases of change management campaigns, the persuasion process would typically ask change

References

Cialdini R (1984) Influence: the psychology of persuasion. William Morrow and Company, Inc
Cohen A, Bradford D (2005) The influence model: using reciprocity and exchange to get what you
    need. Journal of Organizational Excellence 25(1):57–80
Heifetz R (1994) Leadership without easy answers. Harvard University Press
Kelman H (1958) Compliance, identification, and internalization: three processes of attitude
    change. Journal of Conflict Resolution 2(1):51–60

Further Reading

Cohen A, Bradford D (1989) Influence without authority. Wiley, Inc

(Footnote 12 continued)
agents to (i) convince personnel that radical change is imperative and demonstrate why a new
direction is the right one; (ii) position and frame the preliminary plan, gather feedback, and
announce the final plan; (iii) manage the mood of personnel through constant communication; and
(iv) reinforce behavioral guidelines to avoid backsliding.

Chapter 80
Enriching Knowledge Management Coordination

In a Word With decreasing bureaucracy and decentralization of operations, the span of knowledge coordination should be as close as possible to relevant knowledge domains. Coordinating mediums, or knowledge managers, have key roles to play.

Distributing Knowledge Coordination for Organizational Problem Solving

To manage knowledge—in the sense of making explicit and systematic efforts to enable vital individual and collective knowledge resources to be identified, created, stored, shared, and used for benefit—learning organizations build adaptive and generative institutions, systems and processes, and functions across leadership, organization, technology, and learning dimensions. Only by doing so can they, irrespective of configuration, hope to enjoy the capacity to act effectively to achieve shared vision.

© Asian Development Bank 2017
731
O. Serrat, *Knowledge Solutions*, DOI 10.1007/978-981-10-0983-9_80

Concern for sound management of stocks and, increasingly, flows of knowledge is not a fad.[1] To accomplish their missions, organizations must continually refresh their stocks of knowledge by being part of relevant flows of new knowledge. To this intent, communities (and networks) of practice have, since the mid-1990s, become an accepted part of organizational development. (In a mobile workforce, people are more likely to be aligned to their professional identity than to their organizational affiliation.) They are groups of like-minded, interacting people who filter, amplify, invest and provide, convene, build, and learn and facilitate to ensure more effective creation and sharing of knowledge in their domain. It is also recognized that a coordinating medium, or knowledge manager,[2] is a key factor for managing knowledge in organizations, be that with reference to well-structured, ill-structured, or wicked problem solving.[3] With decreasing bureaucracy and decentralization of operations, it makes sense to distribute leadership for organizational problem solving: the span of knowledge coordination should be as close as possible to relevant knowledge domains.

Knowledge Coordination Under ADB's Knowledge Management Framework

ADB (2004) formulated a framework to guide its work on managing knowledge. The framework pursues two mutually supportive outcomes: (i) increased assimilation of and dissemination by ADB of relevant and high-quality knowledge to developing member countries and other stakeholders, and (ii) enhanced learning in ADB. Its outputs are intended to be an improved organizational culture for knowledge sharing; better management system; more efficient business processes and information technology solutions for knowledge capture, enrichment, storage, and retrieval; well-functioning communities of practice; and expanded knowledge sharing, learning, and dissemination through external relations and networking. Since 2004, the Knowledge Management Center in the Regional and Sustainable Development Department is responsible for coordinating and monitoring

---

[1]Put simply, a stock of knowledge is the level of knowledge, skills, and competencies of a person or organization. A flow of knowledge is the amount of such human capital that is transferred between people; in an organization, it is the use of knowledge in organizing activities to create intellectual (or structural and relational) capital.

[2]A knowledge manager has operational and developmental responsibility for knowledge management principles and practices. He or she often acts as central owner of taxonomies and content standards and knowledge processes. He or she also works to promote access to information, intelligence support, expertise, and good practices.

[3]For well-structured problems, knowledge managers would focus on the division of labor across the various units within their organizational boundaries. For ill-structured problems, they would endeavor to leverage networks of influence outside these. For wicked problems, they would ask webs of experts across the latter to act as a conduit to influential managers and decision-makers on their behalf.

knowledge initiatives in ADB, and the action plans of the knowledge management framework. It plays a critical role in introducing new knowledge management approaches and reporting to ADB Management. In each office and department, a knowledge management coordinator is tasked with helping mainstream knowledge management in ADB.

ADB (2008, 2009) approved *Enhancing Knowledge Management under Strategy 2020: Plan of Action for 2009–2011* to advance the knowledge management agenda under *Strategy 2020: The Long-Term Strategic Framework of the Asian Development Bank (2008–2020)*. Four pillars support the plan of action: (i) sharpening the knowledge focus in ADB's operations, (ii) empowering the communities of practice, (iii) strengthening external knowledge partnerships, and (iv) further enhancing staff learning and skills development.

> *When we seek to discover the best in others, we somehow bring out the best in ourselves*
>
> —William Arthur Ward

In 2010, the Knowledge Management Center reexamined the roles and functions of ADB's knowledge management coordinators—who currently number 45 staff members—and discussed opportunities to enrich these with them.[4] It then recommended a rationalized framework to align their roles and functions with *Enhancing Knowledge Management under Strategy 2020: Plan of Action for 2009–2011* and the corresponding Knowledge Management Results Framework. The new roles and functions for the knowledge management coordinators would

- Gather the functions of point persons for knowledge management, information technology, web development, and publishing, most of which are related and frequently overlap.
- Validate the need for full-time work on knowledge management and learning.
- Enhance the visibility of knowledge management functions in ADB.
- Provide a common language enabling structured activities, inputs, outputs, and outcomes; interdepartmental complementarity and partnerships; cross-referencing of ADB-wide initiatives; mutual learning; critical mass; and wider outreach and impact.
- Inspire other staff to engage in knowledge management and learning.
- Drive *Enhancing Knowledge Management under Strategy 2020: Plan of Action for 2009–2011* and the corresponding Knowledge Management Results Framework.

---

[4]Some offices and departments have nominated stand-alone point persons for information technology, web development, and publishing. Under the current arrangements are unclear divisions of labor and potential gaps in coordination among the point persons.

These *Knowledge Solutions* showcase the new terms of reference for knowledge management coordinators in ADB.

Box: Roles and Functions for Knowledge Management Coordination

In July 2009, ADB approved *Enhancing Knowledge Management Under Strategy 2020: Plan of Action for 2009–2011*[a] to advance *Knowledge Management in ADB.*[b] In March 2010, it finalized *Enhancing Knowledge Management under Strategy 2020: Plan of Action for 2009–2011* to specify the expected outcomes, useful results indicators, specific activity indicators, targets, and sources of verification that will operationalize ADB's plan of action.

Notwithstanding the distinct mandates, systems, and resources of ADB's offices and departments[c] and the job descriptions of their staff, the knowledge management coordinators can advance ADB's knowledge management agenda by selectively and progressively facilitating the following range of roles and functions. Their focus, approach, and involvement will depend on the primary responsibility of their respective office or department.[d]

Sharpening the Knowledge Focus in ADB's Operations The knowledge management coordinators would

- Develop a knowledge management work plan for the office or department, aligned with ADB's plan of action for 2009–2011, and advise its head of progress.
- Recognize good practice approaches, methods, and tools to enhance the identification, creation, storage, sharing, and use of knowledge from the operations cycle in ways consistent with the needs and systems of the office or department and developing member countries directly supported.
- Promote the use of knowledge management principles in preparing country partnership studies, reports and recommendations of the President, and technical assistance reports.
- Distinguish opportunities for the generation and sharing of knowledge from both lending and nonlending products and services throughout the project cycle and encourage related actions.
- Help boost research and analytical work relevant to the role of the office or department in priority areas of Strategy 2020 and the needs of unit clients, with attention to aligning with stages of the project cycle.

Empowering the Communities of Practice The knowledge management coordinators would

- Enhance interactions between the office or department and communities of practice to identify, create, store, share, and use knowledge and extend related products and services.

- Promote awareness, understanding, and use of sector and thematic work and research between communities of practice and the office or department.
- Facilitate feedback to communities of practice on the perceived relevance and effectiveness of their activities in the office or department's sector divisions and resident and regional missions.
- Identify opportunities for knowledge generation and sharing at community of practice events.

Strengthening External Knowledge Partnerships The knowledge management coordinators would

- Identify and share good practices from lending and nonlending products and services (including those sourced from outside ADB) to promote uptake.
- Explore opportunities to generate and share knowledge solutions with decision-makers in developing member countries before, during, and after interventions.
- Integrate knowledge components in external partnerships.

Further Enhancing Staff Learning and Skills Development The knowledge management coordinators would

- Raise awareness of learning and development opportunities in knowledge management and learning in the office or department and provide feedback to learning program providers on their effectiveness.
- Help capture the tacit knowledge of departing staff to drive organizational performance improvement.

Promoting Knowledge Management and Learning The knowledge management coordinators would

- Take part in, or keep aware of, the development and implementation of information technology solutions that facilitate knowledge generation and sharing in the office and department and developing member countries directly supported.
- Link with the Information Resources and Services Unit to optimize use of the Library's information resources and the library and records resources in the office or department and facilitate access in resident and regional missions and representative offices.[e]
- Launch or support knowledge transfer initiatives through web development, storytelling, e-marketing, media promotion, and multilingual outreach.

[a]ADB (2009). The paper articulates four pillars to (i) sharpen the knowledge focus in ADB's operations, (ii) empower the communities of practice, (iii) strengthen external knowledge partnerships, and (iv) further enhance staff learning and skills development.

[b]ADB (2004).

[c]Where feasible, deploying a single coordinator for knowledge management, publishing, and the web is likely more efficient and effective than having separate liaisons for these roles and functions. Nonetheless, a knowledge coordination approach can also be taken that mainstreams these through wider office or department systems and resources.

[d]The Knowledge Management Results Framework lists opportunities for action across the four pillars.

[e]This would enable the Information Resources and Services Unit to optimize the complementarity of its three functions, namely information research and coordination, library, and records and archive management for the benefit of ADB as a whole.

Source Author

References

ADB (2004) Knowledge management in ADB. Manila
ADB (2008) Strategy 2020: the long-term strategic framework of the Asian development bank (2008–2020). Manila
ADB (2009) Enhancing knowledge management under strategy 2020: plan of action for 2009–2011. Manila

Proposition 81
Delegating in the Workplace

In a Word The act of delegating calls for and rests on trust. In organizations, delegation had better be understood as a web of tacit governance arrangements across quasi-boundaries rather than the execution of tasks with definable boundaries.

Delegation Rules

No man is an island, entire of itself; …, meditated John Donne. In more ways than one, too: cooperation, especially the trust and graduated delegation of authority it usually implies when people come together to realize societal and organizational goals, determines how we live, learn, work, and play.

Because the perceived benefits from cooperation normally outstrip those from going it alone—for instance, by reducing transaction costs, collaboration mechanisms are integral to necessary management of (scarce) natural, human, tangible, and intangible resources—we delegate (and pay for), say, procurement of foodstuff, health care, education, entertainment, and protection to supermarkets, doctors, schools, the film industry, and armed forces. We do so by framing obligations for exchange of valuable things in marketplaces. Most exchanges are straightforward, self-executing matters giving satisfaction, e.g., the sale and purchase of a soft drink

© Asian Development Bank 2017

O. Serrat, *Knowledge Solutions*, DOI 10.1007/978-981-10-0983-9_81

—if this were not so, controversy and dispute would soon suffocate society at large and the commerce that nurtures it; however, others are not.[1]

A Diversion on Contract Law, Oral Contracts, and Psychological Contracts

Without contract law, agreements would immediately become impractical at many levels, even in the simplest of cases. Contract law is based on the principle that what has been agreed upon must be kept. In this respect, a formal contract is a voluntary, binding promise between two or more persons or entities to produce or undertake in good faith works or services in relation to a particular subject. To be enforceable, certainly by law, it must include certain factual elements: (i) an offer; (ii) an acceptance of the offer; (iii) a promise to perform; (iv) a valuable consideration, which can be a promise or payment in some form; (v) a time or event when performance must be made; (vi) terms and conditions for performance, which includes the fulfillment of promises; and (vii) performance. (Nonviolation of public policy is, of course, expected.) The remedy at law for breach of contract to produce or undertake is "damages" or monetary compensation. Contracts can be written or oral.

> *An oral contract isn't worth the paper it's written on.*
>
> —Samuel Goldwyn

Oral contracts are ordinarily valid and therefore legally binding if their terms can be proved or are admitted by contracting parties. However, in the absence of proof of the terms of an oral contract, the parties may be unable to enforce the agreement or may be forced to settle for less than the original bargain. Therefore, in most jurisdictions, certain types of contracts must be reduced to writing to be enforceable (and prevent frauds and perjuries).

---

[1] In addition to its palpably omnipresent role in daily life, delegation is a central feature of government and governance. Representative democracy can be considered a chain of delegated power: to simplify, in a parliamentary democracy, voters assign authority to representatives in parliament; the parliamentarians entrust power to act to a prime minister and cabinet who later deputize that to ministers heading government departments; in turn, the ministers task civil servants in the departments with related roles and responsibilities (as well as accountability). Without a doubt, the modern nation-state could not exist without delegation: lawmakers would have to personally enforce every law they pass. Nowadays, many use the language of agency theory to describe the logic of delegation.

The best way to appreciate your job is to imagine yourself without one, quipped Oscar Wilde. Since most of us work for a living, formal contracts of employment[2] are a familiar cornerstone of cooperation in the workplace, thereby embedding contract law in the heart of legal systems. For this reason, formal contracts serve as the foundation of entire societies and their economies. To be sure, Argyris (1960)[3] coined the notion of the "psychological contract" 50 years ago to refer also to the quid-pro-quo expectations that exist between employers and employees, namely, aspirations, diligence, loyalty, mutual obligations, and corporate values. These operate over and above formal contracts of employment to impact behavior over time. His delineation of implicit understandings was and certainly remains of strategic significance. Even so, the erosion of corporate career structures in the last 20 years and far-reaching changes in society and the global economy have since emphasized, beyond individuals and their career niches, how organizations can leverage psychological contracts to sustain performance.[4] In *The Individualized Corporation*, Ghoshal and Bartlett (1997)[5] promoted the idea of a new "moral contract" whereby organizations and senior management respect the individual as a value creator and bear a responsibility to help him or her develop to full potential.

---

[2]The features of a contract of employment, specifically, its conditions, detail in labor law the terms to which an employer and an employee agree. They include the start and end dates. Specifics on the services to be rendered are detailed therein, including the general tasks or functions of the position filled, key roles and responsibilities, location of work performance, reporting requirements, evaluation metrics, etc. Of course, the contract specifies what compensation and other rights an employee will receive in exchange for the work delivered. (If the contract is eligible for renewal, the method and circumstances for that might also be listed.)

[3]The Dorsey Press. If the term is new, the notion of mutual expectations goes back thousands of years; social exchange theory posits that human relationships are shaped by negotiated give-and-take. While Chris Argyris originally referred to a specific understanding between a work group and their foreman or team leader, Schein (1965) later focused on the high-level collective relationship between individuals and senior management of the organization on the other. (He is credited with inventing the term "corporate culture".).

[4]Boundary-less organizations that emphasize knowledge work are typified by horizontal career moves and a diversity of employer–employee relations. Wellin (2007) sees that, in support, they also operate a range of psychological contracts, a summary of which would read: (i) the organization and its personnel are both "adult," (ii) staff define their own worth and identity, (iii) a regular flow of people in and out of the organization is healthy, (iv) long-term employment is unlikely—one should expect and prepare for multiple employments, and (v) growth is through personal accomplishment.

[5]In that book, and in three admirable articles published in 1994–1995, Ghoshal and Bartlett (1994, 1995a, b) explained that great organizations are defined by purpose, processes, and people, not outmoded concerns for strategy, structure, and systems. Managers should focus on leveraging the individual's unique talents and skills, an organization's most important source of sustainable competitive advantage.

Defining Delegation

> *The finest plans are always ruined by the littleness of those who ought to carry them*
> *out, for the Emperors can actually do nothing.*
>
> —Bertolt Brecht

In broad terms, delegation is the grant of authority by one party to another for an agreed purpose. In the language of agency theory, it is the transfer to an agent of the right to act for a principal that can take place only with the acquiescence of the principal, where it is customary or where it is necessary for the performance of the entrusted duty. From a management perspective, it is the sharing or transfer of authority and associated responsibility from an employer or "superior" having the right to delegate to an employee or "subordinate".

The Relevance of Contracts to Delegation

To delegate well in the workplace and help transform that into a place that works for all, it is important to appreciate contract law, oral contracts, and psychological contracts as well as the transactional, implicit, and inferred deals they severally promulgate. Why? Because the act of delegating, meaning, empowering, calls for and rests on trust.[6] However, the sociality of work and the complex actions and interactions in social networks that characterize workflows can never be accurately codified (even if software applications sometimes model workflows in particular domains). If trust, the fundamental basis of all value, does not come easily in traditional exchange agreements over price and quantity, it is even more difficult to build and maintain when it must also embody elements of responsiveness, creativity, innovation, quality, and reliability in fleeting interpersonal relationships.[7]

---

[6]Delegation entails a transfer of power and the danger is that trust will be abused. This can only be avoided if the principal and the agent share interests and if the principal is knowledgeable about the activities of the agent as well as their possible consequences.

[7]Again, agency theory provides valuable insights. In delegation, an agent is granted freedom to make decisions subject to constraints that the principal may have specified. Full delegation can only come about if information and preferences are fully congruent or, more usually, the principal feels secure about an uncertain situation.

> *Only free men can negotiate; prisoners cannot enter into contracts. Your freedom and mine cannot be separated.*
>
> —Nelson Mandela

Delegation is a fundamental, win–win management process that cannot be readily contracted in the hustle and bustle of the workplace.[8] Hence, within organizations, it had better be understood as a web of tacit governance arrangements across quasi-boundaries rather than the execution of tasks with definable boundaries. To a much greater extent than contract-based forms of transaction, disaggregated structures require high-powered incentives along a continuum of "boss"-centered and distributed leadership. The predictors of delegation along that continuum would be distinctions based on the characteristics of supervisors, the (real or perceived) characteristics of their subordinates, and situational factors.

Of Continuums, Predictors, and Consequences

Forces in the supervisor, in the subordinate, and in the situation drive delegation in the workplace. The continuum that depicts the locus of authority in decision making is typically anchored at one end by completely autocratic decision making and at the other by a delegation process that permits maximum influence by subordinates.[9] Participation is the midpoint between autocratic and delegative arrangements.

> *You must trust and believe in people or life becomes impossible.*
>
> —Anton Chekhov

The Tannenbaum and Schmidt Continuum is the best known model of areas of freedom for supervisors and subordinates (Tannenbaum and Warren 1958). In the range of behaviors the model depicts, a supervisor makes the decision and announces

---

[8] Of course, SMART delegation rules are supposedly at hand to help formalize the process. [The acronym stands for Specific, Measurable, Agreed, Realistic, and Time-bound. SMARTER rules are also Ethical (to which Enjoyable or Exciting are sometimes substituted) and Recorded.] In truth, not all delegated work can ever be subject to such precision (let alone be enjoyable or exciting).

[9] Many argue that, however he or she may vest others with authority, a supervisor can never entirely delegate final accountability for results. The only resort is to make sure things go right through executive participation.

it; sells the decision; presents his ideas and invites questions; presents a tentative decision subject to change; presents the problem, gets suggestions, and then makes the decision; defines the limits and requests the subordinate to make a decision; or permits the subordinate to make decisions within prescribed limits. We are all familiar with the subtle nuances between telling, selling, checking, including, involving, and empowering.

Leana (1986)[10] has conducted useful work on delegation as a distinct management practice that complements better known investigations of delegation as one point in a continuum of involvement in (un)participative decision making. She hypothesized sensibly and then demonstrated that the perceptions that supervisors have of subordinates, e.g., capability, responsibility, and trustworthiness, as well as situational characteristics, such as the importance of the decision to make and the supervisor's workload, are significant predictors of delegation. To boot, the actual job competence of subordinates and the degree of congruence in the goals of supervisors and subordinates moderate the effects of delegation on the performance of subordinates. Interestingly, neither the characteristics of supervisors nor the satisfaction of subordinates were found to be significantly related to delegation.[11]

Spieglein, Spieglein an der Wand …

Literature offers many tips on how one should delegate; linear advice commonly runs thus: (i) define the task, (ii) assess ability and training needs, (iii) explain the reasons, (iv) state the results required, (v) consider the resources needed, (vi) agree on deadline, (vii) support and communicate, and (viii) feedback on results. A little more introspection would certainly help if, as argued earlier, it is more sagacious to frame delegation as a web of inferred governance arrangements.

> She generally gave herself very good advice, (though she very seldom followed it).
> —Lewis Carroll

Following a modicum of soul-searching supervisors might even say mea culpa. From the health sector, where professionals and patients alike need clear knowledge

---

[10]The survey that underpinned research covered 19 branch offices of a large national insurance company in the United States, or 198 claims adjusters reporting to 44 supervisors. Research in other sectors, professions, and disciplines might reveal different weights in the predictors and consequences.

[11]Those who see job enrichment as a basic function of delegation, besides efficient completion of assigned work and enhanced effectiveness of a supervisor's performance—these, habitually, being deemed the higher benefits from delegation—might be troubled by that last finding.

for decision-making and so much rests on nurses, comes pithy advice on delegation from the receiving end. In the United States, the following principles guide delegation of nursing activities, for which nurses must ultimately bear accountability for. The five "rights" of delegation are (i) the right task (one that is delegable); (ii) the right circumstances (appropriate setting, available resources, and other relevant factors considered); (iii) the right person (the right person is delegating the right task to the right person); (iv) the right direction and communication (clear, concise description of the task, including its objective, limits, and expectations); and (v) the right supervision (appropriate monitoring, evaluation, intervention as needed, and feedback).[12]

References

Argyris C (1960) Understanding organizational behavior. The Dorsey Press

Ghoshal S, Bartlett C (November–December 1994) Changing the role of top management: beyond strategy to purpose. Harvard Business Review

Ghoshal S, Bartlett C (January–February 1995a) Changing the role of top management: beyond structure to processes. Harvard Business Review

Ghoshal S, Bartlett C (May–June 1995b) Changing the role of top management: beyond systems to people. Harvard Business Review

Ghoshal S, Bartlett C (1997) The individualized corporation: a fundamentally new approach to management. Harper Paperbacks

Leana C (1986) Predictors and consequences of delegation. Academy of Management Journal 29 (4):754–774

Schein E (1965) Organizational psychology. Prentice Hall

Tannenbaum R, Warren (March–April 1958) How to choose a leadership pattern. In: Harvard Business Review

Wellin M (2007) Managing the psychological contract: using the personal deal to increase performance. Gower Publishing Ltd

---

[12]These parallel the five rights of medication safety: (i) the right patient, (ii) the right drug, (iii) the right dose, (iv) the right route, and (v) the right time.

Proposition 82
Surveying Communities of Practice

In a Word Surveys are used to find promising opportunities for improvement; identify, create a consensus about, and act on issues to be addressed; record a baseline from which progress can be measured; motivate change efforts; and provide two-way communication between stakeholders. Healthy communities of practice leverage survey instruments to mature into influence structures that demand or are asked to assume influential roles in their host organizations.

Define: Communities of Practice

If you have an apple and I have an apple and we exchange these apples then you and I will still each have one apple. But if you have an idea and I have an idea and we exchange these ideas, then each of us will have two ideas.

—George Bernard Shaw

Communities of practice (CoPs or communities) are groups of like-minded, interacting people who filter, amplify, invest and provide, convene, build, and learn and facilitate to ensure more effective creation and sharing of knowledge in their

© Asian Development Bank 2017
O. Serrat, *Knowledge Solutions*, DOI 10.1007/978-981-10-0983-9_82

domain. They define themselves according to their focus, how they function, and what capabilities they produce.

There are six key dimensions to a CoP: (i) domain, (ii) community, (iii) practice, (iv) motivation, (v) structure, and (vi) mandate. A domain is a defined area of shared inquiry (often with a sector or thematic focus) and a community refers to the relationships among active members and the sense of belonging and identity that membership provides. Practice refers to the body of knowledge and information used by the CoP; each member has expertise in the domain and this is recognized by other members. Motivation refers to the personal interest and priority that members are willing to commit to the CoP in their work plans and work activities. Structure describes the balance of formal and informal relationships and ways of working. (Hierarchy is not an important characteristic of CoPs: the status of the members is measured by the value of the contributions they make to the community.) Finally, mandate refers to the priority that management of the host organization, where there is one, ascribing to the CoP and the resource implications they are willing to commit; it defines the sector or thematic focus and the expected results of the community and helps generate the space for individual commitment by the members.

Typically, CoPs comprise a core group, an inner circle, and an outer circle. The core group manages the CoP based on an agreed coordination mandate. It provides secretarial support as necessary. The inner circle serves as a steering committee with an informal structure, meeting once or twice a year. Together, the core group and the inner circle form the "active group" of the community—its source of energy and direction. The outer circle embraces interested members, contributors, and readers in a loose network.

On ADB's Communities of Practice

I offer you peace. I offer you love. I offer you friendship. I see your beauty. I hear your need. I feel your feelings. My wisdom flows from the Highest Source. I salute that Source in you. Let us work together for unity and love.

—Mohandas K. Gandhi

In light of their potential contribution to organizational development, ADB decided to promote well-functioning CoPs in 2002, from the time of ADB's reorganization. ADB's (2008) long-term strategic framework cited them as a powerful collaboration mechanism for internal learning. Their mandate is to contribute or advise on (i) general strategic directions in priority sectors and themes of ADB; (ii) ADB-wide sector and thematic work, including inputs to related sector and thematic reports; (iii) ADB-wide knowledge products and services, including good practices, and technical and flagship publications; and (iv) staffing issues, including the skills mix in ADB and staff participation in external learning events.

"Unless ... commitment is made, there are only promises and hopes, but no plan," said Peter Drucker. However, committing is contingent on knowing the state of affairs. A first-ever survey of ADB-hosted CoPs (2009a) conducted by ADB's Knowledge Management Center revealed that

- CoPs represent areas of common interest, usually (but not always) have clear domains, provide a welcome social environment and give staff members a sense of belonging, help build relationships, and benefit daily work.
- CoPs are driven by willingness to participate, motivate members to share work-related knowledge, but do not always build up communal resources.
- CoPs break down communication barriers among staff members but communication platforms are not very user-friendly.
- CoPs do not leverage knowledge management tools particularly well.
- The contribution of CoPs to accomplish better results in projects and economic and sector work can be improved.
- Linkages to country partnership strategies and policy work are weak.
- CoPs deliver unevenly on knowledge management–related functions, viz., strategy development, management techniques, collaboration mechanisms, knowledge capture and storage, and knowledge sharing and learning.
- A dedicated and passionate facilitator is considered most important to success, together with building trust, rapport, and a sense of community.
- Opinions diverge widely regarding the six functions of CoPs, but convening and learning and facilitating are deemed to be what the CoPs hosted by ADB are best at.
- Participation is severely limited by lack of time and incentives.
- The motivation to participate calls for a wide mix of incentives, with an accent on opportunities for learning and development and staying currently in one's sector or theme.
- Involving external partners would help generate and share knowledge.
- ADB's approach (business processes) to CoPs is flexible.

The 2009 survey concluded that, notwithstanding their good work, (i) CoPs had limited outreach to all staff, especially those in ADB's resident missions and representative offices; (ii) the budget for staff development and knowledge sharing was limited; and (iii) there was a need to realign the work and mandates of CoPs with Strategy 2020.

The great end of knowledge is not knowledge, but action.

—Thomas Henry Huxley

On 31 July 2009, Haruhiko Kuroda—ADB President and concurrent Chairperson of ADB's Board of Directors (2009b)—approved *Enhancing Knowledge Management under Strategy 2020: Plan of Action for 2009–2011*, detailing actions/outputs to advance the knowledge management agenda under Strategy 2020 (ADB 2004). Of particular interest is the second pillar of the action plan, which supports initiatives that promote and empower CoPs to act as drivers of change, promote exchange of ideas and good practices, and upgrade technical skills among peers.

The 2009 review of CoPs triggered four key proposals to empower the communities under the action plan

1. Ensure that CoPs become an integral part of ADB's business processes. Supervisors should fully support both professional and national staff (including those in resident missions and representative offices) to participate in the communities, with the staff's contributions recognized more vigorously in the Performance and Development Plan exercise. Management will provide sufficient time for the chairs of the committees to perform their functions for the CoPs.

> *Teamwork is the ability to work together toward a common vision; the ability to direct individual accomplishment toward organizational objectives. It is the fuel that allows common people to attain uncommon results.*
> —Andrew Carnegie

2. Increase the budget of the CoPs, based on a clear set of objectives, and, most importantly, measurable "outcomes" of improved knowledge management. Increased budgets will be allocated clearly, directly, and explicitly in proportion to how practical and tangible knowledge management occurs. This will be a case of "output-based financing," rewarding those who generate and share useful and usable knowledge. CoPs with vague or input- and/or process-focused proposals will not be funded. This will entail revising the current purpose and structure of the biannual sector and thematic reports.
3. Require the CoPs to more purposefully engage in external partnerships including especially the regional knowledge hubs that ADB finances. (Engaging non-regional knowledge hubs is to be considered as well.)
4. The role of the knowledge management coordinators in ADB will be reviewed and ways to harness their knowledge, skills, experience, and interests in the form of a CoP in knowledge management will be proposed.

In the wake of the 2009 survey, ADB's support to communities improved as evidenced by increased budgets, streamlined sector, and thematic reporting, improved participation in peer reviews of country partnership strategies and lending products, strengthened collaboration between and among CoPs, increased recognition of staff knowledge and expertise, and expanded outreach to stakeholders. Considering these milestones, a follow-up review of the performance of CoPs was

Table 82.1 Membership of ADB-hosted CoPs, March 2011

Agriculture, rural development, and food security	75
Education	41
Energy	171
Environment	110
Financial sector development	196
Gender equity	100
Social development and poverty	246
Governance and public management	93
Health	24
Regional cooperation and integration	26
Transport	147
Urban	115
Water	214
Total CoP membership	**1,558**

Source ADB (2011)

Note Some individuals were members of more than one community so the number does not represent the number of individuals involved in CoPs

needed to identify ways to further improve performance, as well as challenges and opportunities ahead.[1] ADB (2011) launched a second survey of ADB-hosted CoPs. (The total membership had by then reached 1,558.) A total of 207 CoP members and 68 non-CoP members completed the survey out of a total staff complement of 2,705 as of 30 June 2010. (In 2009, the number of responses for CoP members was 77 and for non-CoP members, 30. This shows a significant growth rate in responses between 2009 and 2011 of 268% for CoP members, and 226% for non-CoP members (Table 82.1).

[1]Two other important initiatives also examined knowledge management more widely in ADB (2010a, b), with implications for CoPs. First, the sixth in a series of Most Admired Knowledge Enterprise (MAKE) surveys, conducted in 2010, confirmed positive trends in knowledge management in ADB. Survey findings were benchmarked against the eight recognized MAKE knowledge performance dimensions. To note, Dimension 5 refers to developing CoPs as one of eight drivers for "Creating an environment for collaborative knowledge sharing". Dimension 6 refers to developing CoPs as one of nine drivers for "Creating a learning organization". Second, the results of the new Learning for Change survey, introduced in 2010, also bore implications for understanding CoPs in ADB. The survey examined characteristics of the four main subsystems of knowledge management, namely, organization, people, knowledge, and technology, but from the perspective of organizational learning. CoPs span all four subsystems in ADB: they form part of the organizational infrastructure for learning and knowledge management; they engage people in learning communities; they provide a space for members to identify, create, store, share, and use knowledge; and finally, they harness information and communications technology for the purposes of learning and improving organizational effectiveness.

The 2011 Survey of ADB-Hosted Communities of Practice: Survey Design

At the time of the 2011 survey, ADB had 13 CoPs[2] in key sector and thematic areas (domains). The survey design reproduced, with minor amendments, the survey of CoPs conducted in 2009. This was done to facilitate the comparison of responses across the two surveys.

Separate online questionnaires were used to elicit responses from those who participate as members of CoPs and those who do not. The questionnaire for CoP members comprised three sections. Section I (questions 1–24) examined the respondents' view of the purpose and utility of CoP activities. Section II (question 25) elicited recommendations for strengthening CoP effectiveness, and Section III (questions 28–31) was used to develop a profile of CoP members. The questionnaire for non-CoP members comprised nine questions. Using similar wording for most of the questions made it possible to compare the views of members and non-members.

The 2011 Survey of ADB-Hosted Communities of Practice: Methodology

Data the survey was collected on 4–25 February 2011 using a web-based questionnaire. The survey was widely advertised on *ADB Today*, ADB's daily e-newsletter. Data analysis was conducted in March–April 2011. During the data analysis, comparisons were made between the 2009 and 2011 survey results and between the 2011 responses from CoP members and non-CoP members. The quantitative data generated by the questions was plotted on bar charts that used percentage response rates to facilitate comparison between the 2009 and 2011 surveys. The responses to free form questions provide a rich source of views and ideas. Because qualitative data is more challenging to analyze, particular efforts were made to interpret this data. Responses to free form questions were clustered under headings generated by close examination of the responses. The headings were developed by first examining the responses of CoP members then applying the same headings to cluster the responses of the non-CoP members. In this way, direct comparisons could be made between the two groups.

---

[2]This has now increased to 14 CoPs with the recent addition of a community on public–private partnerships.

The 2011 Survey of ADB-Hosted Communities of Practice: Analytical Framework

Three "lenses" were used to analyze and interpret the data collected in the survey. These were areas of inquiry, critical success factors, and the "CoP Fitness Test".

The survey was designed to address eight areas of inquiry as follows:

- the extent of participation in CoPs
- insights into the clarity of domains
- perceptions of the value added by CoPs
- success factors
- insights into the varying possible functions of CoPs
- dimensions of participation in CoPs
- perceptions of ADB's approach to CoPs
- recommendations to strengthen CoP effectiveness.

The areas of inquiry formed the main headings for examining the survey findings. They were enhanced by references to critical success factors and "CoP Fitness Test" headings and questions.

Research on CoPs has identified a number of factors critical to their success. The analysis of survey findings clustered these under three headings: (i) community, (ii) organization, and (iii) functions (Table 82.2).

In a valuable contribution to the field of study of CoPs, the Knowledge Management Center introduced the idea of communities passing a fitness test. The test refers to a series of questions under eight headings: (i) domain, (ii) membership, (iii) norms and rules, (iv) structure and process, (v) flow of energy, (vi) results, (vii) resources, and (viii) values. Although the survey was not designed to explicitly answer all fitness test questions, these questions provided a useful analytical framework and were used to structure some of the concluding remarks in the report (Table 82.3).

Table 82.2 Critical success factors for communities of practice

Community	Organization	Functions
• A domain that energizes the core group and inner circle • Skillful and reputable managers and facilitators • Clearly defined roles, particularly in the core group and inner circle • Involvement of members • The details of practice are addressed • Regularity and mix of activities	• Strategic relevance of the domain • Management sponsorship (without micromanagement) • Integration of CoP with organization's business processes • Judicious mix of formal and informal structures • Adequate resources • Consistent attitude	• Clearly delineated functions • Capacities, skills, resources, and systems match functions • Recognition given for achievement of functions

Source Author

Table 82.3 The "CoP Fitness Test" headings and questions

Domain	• Are the area of shared inquiry, the key issues that relate to it, and the function(s) of the CoP strategically relevant to ADB? • Are the topics of interest to all members? • Do all members have their own practice in the domain?
Membership	• Is the relevant experience on board? • Is the heterogeneity of the members assured? • Is the CoP open to new members and advertised as such?
Norms and rules	• Are roles and accountabilities defined in a common agreement? • Are both distant contacts and face-to-face meetings possible? • What is the balance between giving and taking among members?
Structure and process	• Is the chosen structure clear and flexible enough? • Are key roles in the core group defined, e.g., manager, facilitator, and back-stopper? • Is the step-by-step work planning process open and transparent?
Flow of energy	• Do members care about common interests, commitment, and trust? • Are there regular face-to-face events? Are social moments celebrated? • Is the history of the CoP alive and shared with new members?
Results	• Is delivering and reporting on tangible results a common concern? • Do members draw direct and practical benefits from their involvement? • Are results officially recognized by ADB?
Resources	• Do members have sufficient time for the CoP? • Is ADB willing to provide time, space, and incentives? • Is CoP facilitation attractive and stimulating?
Values	• Is listening to others a cardinal virtue? • Are members willing to give without immediate return? • Is diversity in thinking and practice validated?

Source Author

The 2011 Survey of ADB-Hosted Communities of Practice: Observations on Survey Design

The survey provided a valuable overview of the operation of CoPs in ADB. However, the survey design limits the opportunities to examine and understand the work of individual communities in-depth. This is because the responses of some respondents who belong to more than one community refer to all the CoPs to which they belong. So, for example, it is not possible to identify how respondents involved as members of particular CoPs scored those communities on the questions with five-point scales. The benefits of using a consistent survey are considerable as this enables year-on-year comparisons. One way of gaining a more in-depth insight into the communities without sacrificing the ability to make year-on-year comparisons would be to use the same survey questions but ask the respondents to specify which CoP they will be using when considering their answers.

The 2011 Survey of ADB-Hosted Communities of Practice: Observations on In-Depth Understanding

> *It is said that if you know your enemies and know yourself, you will not be imperiled in a hundred battles; if you do not know your enemies but do know yourself, you will win one and lose one; if you do not know your enemies nor yourself, you will be imperiled in every single battle.*
>
> —Sun Tzu

Fortunately, the annual reports of individual CoPs provide in-depth under-standing of their ways of working, achievements, and overall effectiveness. CoPs have been encouraged to produce annual and triennial reports on their work since December 2009. To date, not all communities have produced both sets of reports, but those that have provided valuable data and detailed analyses of the CoP's modus operandi. An analysis of the annual and triennial reports of individual communities was beyond the scope of survey but a brief examination of a sample revealed some useful insights about how communities operate in the pursuit of ADB's mission and objectives. A systematic examination of CoP reports would enable benchmarking and would ensure that some comparability (using, for example, critical success factors) between CoP outcomes exists.

The 2011 Survey of ADB-Hosted Communities of Practice: Observations on Benchmarking and Peer Learning

Given the ability of some communities to create the success factors critical for effective working, a valuable body of experience can clearly provide benchmarks for all CoPs in ADB. This is not to say that those CoPs working successfully should be used as role models for all communities. Domain, context, and other factors should be taken into account when designing and running a CoP. However, in the spirit of a learning organization, ADB's home-grown CoP expertise can provide a unique source of knowledge about how best to leverage value from its communi-ties. This expertise could undoubtedly be more widely applied across all CoPs through more focused benchmarking process. One way of doing this might be to establish an annual "forum on learning" in which CoPs would share their success stories, identify how best to implement success factors, and celebrate achievements.

Did ADB-Hosted Communities of Practice Pass the Fitness Test?

You would fain be victor at the Olympic games, you say. Yes, but weigh the conditions, weigh the consequences; then and then only, lay to your hand—if it be for your profit. You must live by rule, submit to diet, abstain from dainty meats, exercise your body perforce at stated hours, in heat or in cold; drink no cold water, nor, it may be, wine. In a word, you must surrender yourself wholly to your trainer, as though to a physician.

—Epictetus

- **Domain** The areas of shared inquiry and the function of CoPs have varying degrees of relevance to ADB's strategic priorities. The topics of some communities are of undoubted interest to their members. Other CoPs are less able to inspire interest though this may be due to issues of weak community leadership or being unable or unwilling to prioritize time for participation rather than an inherently uninteresting topic. It was not possible to ascertain from the survey whether all the members have their own practice in the respective domains.
- **Membership** It is difficult to ascertain from the 2011 survey if all the necessary relevant experience is available to all the CoPs. However, as this was not raised as a concern by any respondents, it is reasonable to assume that all communities have access to the relevant experience they need. Broadening the diversity of membership by including ADB's partners is worthy of further consideration as is the need to improve staff awareness of communities, and thereby extending access to CoPs.
- **Norms and Rules** The conduct of some communities seems to be very well organized but this does not appear to be true of all CoPs. Some respondents expressed satisfaction about the nature and frequency of contact in their CoPs whereas others, particularly those members based in resident missions, would welcome more opportunities to participate. It is difficult to ascertain the balance between giving to and taking from CoPs but active membership of a community suggests that members receive enough from their involvement to justify their participation. There are enough positive comments about membership to suggest that this is the case for many communities.
- **Structure and Process** Each community has the flexibility to choose and modify its own structure. Some CoP members referred to weak leadership or overly controlling leadership while others praised the work of their core groups. Members described the planning process for some communities as weak or, in some cases, nonexistent.
- **Flow of Energy** The responses to the 2011 survey demonstrated that 207 people care enough about their communities and their evolution in the future to have

completed an online questionnaire. According to some members, face-to-face events do not happen regularly enough in their CoPs and, by definition, such events are not accessible to those who are located away from head office. Some communities need to be more creative about ways of engaging members in shared activity by learning from the experience of those that have successfully achieved the involvement of remote members.

- **Results** Respondents had very different ideas about what results their CoPs were aiming to achieve. Some viewed these mainly in organizational terms while others explained results more in terms of professional and career development. The two are, of course, not mutually exclusive; indeed one of the strengths of CoPs should be their ability to deliver different types of results. The responses to questions 13–15 suggest that communities are under-functioning in their ability to help individuals achieve better results. Nevertheless, members who responded to the survey report tangible benefits of their involvement in CoPs. To understand the detailed results of specific communities, it is necessary to examine their annual reports.

- **Resources** Many members identified time as the main obstacle to their involvement in CoPs. In the view of many respondents, ADB appears to give mixed messages about the use of their time in communities. While officially sanctioned and even encouraged, the experience reported by some respondents was that their managers appeared lukewarm in their support of time spent on CoPs. At the time of the survey, this tension was exacerbated because some of ADB's human resource systems seemed to be misaligned with ADB's official commitment to CoPs. However, with the recent introduction of the new Time Management System, time spent on CoP activity (such as management and peer review) is now officially recognized. CoP facilitation varies from stimulating to being in need of injection of fresh ideas. The potential for peer learning here is considerable.

- **Values** Because the absence of evidence is not the same as the evidence of absence, it was not possible to comment on the "CoP Fitness Test" questions concerning CoP values.

Conclusions

ADB's investment in CoPs, particularly since 2009, has brought about a positive change in the way they are perceived by both members and non-members. The 2011 survey of ADB-hosted CoPs shows ample evidence that ADB is reaping the benefits of its investment. With greater sharing of experience between communities, the value they bring to ADB's core business is likely to increase. CoPs have been characterized as the "heart and soul" of knowledge sharing in ADB. The results of the survey showed that both heart and soul are gaining in vigor.

Box 1: 2011 Survey of ADB's Communities of Practice: Survey Questionnaire for CoP Members

Which CoPs are you most active in?

- ☐ Agriculture, Rural Development, and Food Security
- ☐ Education
- ☐ Energy
- ☐ Environment
- ☐ Evaluation Cooperation Group
- ☐ Financial Sector Development
- ☐ Gender Equity
- ☐ Health

- ☐ Managing for Development Results
- ☐ Monitoring and Evaluation
- ☐ Public Management and Governance
- ☐ Regional Cooperation and Integration
- ☐ Social Development and Poverty
- ☐ Transport
- ☐ Urban
- ☐ Water
- ☐ Others, please specify: [＿＿＿＿＿＿]

My CoPs ...

1. represent an area of common interest for a number of ADB staff/clients/partners.
   ○ strongly agree   ○ agree   ○ neutral   ○ disagree   ○ strongly disagree

2. currently have a clear focus in their sectors or themes.
   ○ strongly agree   ○ agree   ○ neutral   ○ disagree   ○ strongly disagree

3. give me a sense of belonging.
   ○ strongly agree   ○ agree   ○ neutral   ○ disagree   ○ strongly disagree

4. help me build relationships and network with others.
   ○ strongly agree   ○ agree   ○ neutral   ○ disagree   ○ strongly disagree

5. benefit my daily work from the relationships established.
   ○ strongly agree   ○ agree   ○ neutral   ○ disagree   ○ strongly disagree

My CoPs ...

6. are mainly driven by the willingness of members to participate.
   ○ strongly agree   ○ agree   ○ neutral   ○ disagree   ○ strongly disagree

7. motivate me to share work-related knowledge.
   ○ strongly agree   ○ agree   ○ neutral   ○ disagree   ○ strongly disagree

8. build up an agreed set of communal resources over time.
   ○ strongly agree   ○ agree   ○ neutral   ○ disagree   ○ strongly disagree

9. break down communication barriers among members.
   ○ strongly agree   ○ agree   ○ neutral   ○ disagree   ○ strongly disagree

10. provide an informal, welcoming social environment.
    ○ strongly agree   ○ agree   ○ neutral   ○ disagree   ○ strongly disagree

My CoPs ...

11. have a user-friendly communication platform.
    ○ strongly agree   ○ agree   ○ neutral   ○ disagree   ○ strongly disagree

12. leverage a variety of knowledge management tools (appreciative inquiry, exit interviews, identifying and sharing good practices, knowledge harvesting, peer assists, storytelling, etc.).
    ○ strongly agree   ○ agree   ○ neutral   ○ disagree   ○ strongly disagree

13. help me achieve better results (quality, productivity, stakeholder satisfaction) in projects and programs.
    ○ strongly agree   ○ agree   ○ neutral   ○ disagree   ○ strongly disagree

14. help me achieve better results in economic, sector, and thematic work.
    ○ strongly agree   ○ agree   ○ neutral   ○ disagree   ○ strongly disagree

15. help me achieve better results in country partnership strategy and policy work.
    ○ strongly agree   ○ agree   ○ neutral   ○ disagree   ○ strongly disagree

CoPs help ADB to ...

16. capture and store tacit and explicit knowledge so it can be easily accessed and applied.
    ○ strongly agree   ○ agree   ○ neutral   ○ disagree   ○ strongly disagree

17. build knowledge sharing and learning into work life.
    ○ strongly agree   ○ agree   ○ neutral   ○ disagree   ○ strongly disagree

18. strengthen collaboration across departments, offices, and units.
    ○ strongly agree   ○ agree   ○ neutral   ○ disagree   ○ strongly disagree

19. leverage management techniques to improve performance.
    ○ strongly agree   ○ agree   ○ neutral   ○ disagree   ○ strongly disagree

20. become more adept at strategy development in sectors and themes.
    ○ strongly agree   ○ agree   ○ neutral   ○ disagree   ○ strongly disagree

21. The value of CoPs is that they ...

- ☐ identify, create, store, share, and use knowledge.
- ☐ reduce the learning curve for new employees.
- ☐ enable professional development.
- ☐ reduce duplication and prevent reinvention of the wheel.
- ☐ permit faster problem solving and better response times.
- ☐ showcase good practices.
- ☐ spawn new ideas for products and services.
- ☐ enable accelerated learning.
- ☐ connect learning to action.
- ☐ enhance organizational competencies.

22. The success my CoPs have depends on ...

- ☐ raising the strategic relevance of their sectors or themes in ADB.
- ☐ involving experts in their sectors or themes.
- ☐ specifying their members' roles and expectations.
- ☐ being inspired by a dedicated and passionate coordinator.
- ☐ adopting a consistent attitude to collaboration and knowledge sharing.
- ☐ encouraging new members to participate.
- ☐ recognizing and rewarding members.
- ☐ using staff time wisely.
- ☐ building trust, rapport, and a sense of community.
- ☐ measuring their success and effectiveness.

23. My CoPs are best at ...

- ☐ filtering (organizing and managing important information).
- ☐ amplifying (helping to understand important but little known information).
- ☐ investing and providing (offering a means to give members the resources they need).
- ☐ convening (bringing together different individuals or groups).
- ☐ community-building (promoting and sustaining values and standards).
- ☐ learning and facilitating (helping work more efficiently and effectively).

24. Participation

a. What *strongly* limits your ability to participate in your CoPs?

- ☐ Time
- ☐ Lack of management support
- ☐ Low awareness of activities
- ☐ Lack of incentives
- ☐ Communication barriers/jargon
- ☐ Groups appear to be exclusive

b. What would *strongly* motivate you to participate in CoPs?

- ☐ Meeting work goals
- ☐ Staying current in the sector or theme
- ☐ Career development
- ☐ Solutions to work challenges
- ☐ Learning and development
- ☐ Expanding personal network
- ☐ Support for daily activities

c. What might be done to attract new members?

```



```

25. Recommendations for strengthening CoP effectiveness
   a. How might my CoPs become better at identifying, creating, storing, sharing, and using knowledge?

   ☐ Involve external partners.
   ☐ Customize learning and development programs at headquarters and in the field.
   ☐ Offer professional development opportunities (outside headquarters).
   ☐ Organize conferences, meetings, and workshops.
   ☐ Link more to other CoPs (across sectors and themes).
   ☐ Sponsor more brief seminars.
   ☐ Provide direct support to project and country teams.
   ☐ Use information, communication, and technology more actively and innovatively.
   ☐ Systematically review work with peers before, during, and after.
   ☐ Develop mechanisms for sharing ideas with management.

   b. How might ADB better support CoPs to identify, create, store, share, and use knowledge?

   ☐ Systematize management encouragement to participate more actively in CoP activities.
   ☐ Provide learning and development opportunities in running CoPs.
   ☐ Allow more time for those who take a leadership role to work with their CoPs.
   ☐ Provide effective information, communication, and technology tools.
   ☐ Assign time for knowledge sharing in members workplans.
   ☐ Provide incentives and rewards for significant work in a CoP.
   ☐ Increase guidance from management.
   ☐ Reduce guidance from management.
   ☐ Help CoPs access funding (internal/external).

   c. To achieve my CoPs' purposes, ADB's approach (business processes) to CoPs is:

-2	-1	0	1	2
○	○	○	○	○
too loose		optimal flexibility / structure		too structured

   d. Please suggest ways to marry formality and informality in CoPs.

   e. Please suggest ways in which ADB's Knowledge Management Center might assist your CoPs?

   f. What other recommendations do you have to strengthen your CoPs' effectiveness?

26. What is the relationship between your CoPs and any of the regional knowledge hubs?

○ None

○ Occasional communication

○ Regular communication

○ The activities of my CoPs are well-integrated with a regional knowledge hub

○ Unknown

27. What describes you best?

○ I have a particular role or function in a CoP in ADB.

○ My primary role is as a participant in activities and events organized by CoPs.

28. How long have you been involved in your CoPs?

○ Less than 1 year   ○ 1 - 2 years

○ 2 - 5 years   ○ Over 5 years

29. How often are you involved in face-to-face CoP activity?

○ Daily   ○ Weekly

○ Monthly   ○ Quarterly

○ Yearly   ○ Never

30. How often are you involved in internet-based CoP activity?

○ Daily   ○ Weekly

○ Monthly   ○ Quarterly

○ Yearly   ○ Never

31. How many years of experience do you have that relate to your CoPs?

○ Less than 1 year   ○ 1 - 2 years

○ 2 - 5 years   ○ 5 - 10 years

○ Over 10 years

Please select 1 item you would like to receive :

◉ The final report on the survey of the CoPs hosted by ADB

○ The *Compendium of Knowledge Solutions*

○ The *Learning in Development* publication

○ **No, thanks. Don't send me anything.**

In order to receive the item, please enter your email address: [   ] .

Box 2: 2011 Survey of ADB's Communities of Practice: Survey Questionnaire for Non-CoP Members

CoPs help ADB to ...

1. capture and store tacit and explicit knowledge so it can be easily accessed and applied.
   ○ strongly agree   ○ agree   ○ neutral   ○ disagree   ○ strongly disagree

2. build knowledge sharing and learning into work life.
   ○ strongly agree   ○ agree   ○ neutral   ○ disagree   ○ strongly disagree

3. strengthen collaboration across offices, departments, and units.
   ○ strongly agree   ○ agree   ○ neutral   ○ disagree   ○ strongly disagree

4. leverage knowledge management to improve performance.
   ○ strongly agree   ○ agree   ○ neutral   ○ disagree   ○ strongly disagree

5. become more adept at strategy development.
   ○ strongly agree   ○ agree   ○ neutral   ○ disagree   ○ strongly disagree

6. The value of CoPs is that they ...
   ☐ identify, create, store, share, and use knowledge.
   ☐ reduce the learning curve for new employees.
   ☐ enable professional development.
   ☐ reduce duplication and prevent reinvention of the wheel.
   ☐ permit faster problem solving and better response times.
   ☐ showcase good practices.
   ☐ spawn new ideas for products and services.
   ☐ enable accelerated learning.
   ☐ connect learning to action.
   ☐ enhance organizational competencies.

7. Participation
   a. What *strongly* limits your ability to participate in your CoPs?
      ☐ Time   ☐ Lack of incentives
      ☐ Lack of management support   ☐ Communication barriers/jargon
      ☐ Low awareness of activities   ☐ Groups appear to be exclusive

   b. What would *strongly* motivate you to participate?
      ☐ Meeting work goals   ☐ Learning and development
      ☐ Staying current in the sector or theme ☐ Expanding personal network
      ☐ Career development   ☐ Support for daily activities
      ☐ Solutions to work challenges

   c. What might be done to attract new participants?

8. Recommendations for Strengthening CoP effectiveness
    a. How might my CoPs become better at identifying, creating, storing, sharing, and using knowledge?

    ☐ Involve external partners.
    ☐ Customize learning and development programs at headquarters and in the field.
    ☐ Offer professional development opportunities (outside headquarters).
    ☐ Organize conferences, meetings, and workshops.
    ☐ Link more to other CoPs (across sector and theme).
    ☐ Sponsor more brief seminars.
    ☐ Provide direct support to project and country teams.
    ☐ Use information communication technology more actively and innovatively.
    ☐ Systematically review work with peers before, during, and after.
    ☐ Develop mechanisms for sharing ideas with management.

    b. How might ADB better support CoPs to identify, create, store, share, and use knowledge?

    ☐ Systematize management encouragement to participate more actively in CoP activities.
    ☐ Provide learning and development opportunities in running CoPs.
    ☐ Allow more time for those who take a leadership role to work with their CoPs.
    ☐ Provide effective information, communication, and technology tools.
    ☐ Assign time for knowledge sharing in members workplans.
    ☐ Provide incentives and rewards for significant work in a CoP.
    ☐ Increase guidance from management.
    ☐ Reduce guidance from management.
    ☐ Help CoPs access funding (internal/external).

    c. To achieve my CoPs' purposes, ADB's approach (business processes) to CoPs is:

-2	-1	0	1	2
○	○	○	○	○
too loose		optimal flexibility / structure		too structured

    d. Please suggest ways to marry formality and informality in CoPs.

    e. Please suggest ways ADB's Knowledge Management Center might assist your CoPs.

    f. What other recommendations do you have to strengthen your CoPs effectiveness?

9. How many years of experience do you have that relate to your CoPs?
    ○ Less than 1 year
    ○ 1 - 2 years
    ○ 2 - 5 years
    ○ Over 5 years

Please select 1 item you would like to receive :

⊙ The final report on the survey of the CoPs hosted by ADB

○ The *Compendium of Knowledge Solutions*

○ The *Learning in Development* publication

○ **No, thanks. Don't send me anything.**

In order to receive the item, please enter your email address: [   ] .

References

ADB (2004) Knowledge management in ADB. Manila

ADB (2008) Strategy 2020: the long-term strategic framework of the Asian development bank (2008–2020). Manila

ADB (2009a) Strengthening communities of practice in ADB. Manila

ADB (2009b) Enhancing knowledge management strategies under strategy 2020: plan of action for 2009–2011. Manila

ADB (2010a) Assessment of ADB's knowledge management implementation framework. Manila

ADB (2010b) Learning for change survey. Manila

ADB (2011) Survey of ADB-hosted communities of practice. Manila

Proposition 83
Conflict in Organizations

In a Word Complex adaptive systems are the source of much intra-organizational conflict that will not be managed, let alone resolved. To foster learning, adaptation, and evolution in the workplace, organizations should capitalize on its functions and dysfunctions with mindfulness, improvisation, and reconfiguration.

Why Men Fight

War, the state of (usually open and declared) armed, hostile conflict between communities, has been conducted by most societies since at least the Bronze Age—that is, from about 4,000–3,000 BC.[1] Its perdurance suggests adaptive attributes; might it serve some deeper level of rationality?

---

[1]Before nomadic groups settled for sedentary life in villages and towns that grew into early chiefdoms and then embryonic states, war likely amounted to small-scale raiding. (There is no convincing evidence of collective intergroup hostility before 10,000 years ago and in many isolated parts of the world much more recently than that.) But the invention and spread of agriculture, allied to the domestication of animals, circa 5,000 BC, set the stage for the emergence of complex urban societies. The aggregation of large populations required that people refocus their allegiances away from the extended family, clan, and tribe toward a larger social entity, the state. Then, warfare was made possible by the development of articulated social structures—of which standing armies surfaced as permanent parts—providing legitimacy and stability to new social roles and behaviors.

© Asian Development Bank 2017
O. Serrat, *Knowledge Solutions*, DOI 10.1007/978-981-10-0983-9_83

Ethnographic literature on war is sparse but demonstrates that contention is a cultural phenomenon, that is to say, institutionalized behavior framed by consensus. The justification is that actual or potential warfare promotes solidarity among social groups, consolidating relationship by polarizing differences. By means of contest, the subjugated are made to assimilate; for this reason, *ceteris paribus*, social groups have enlarged steadily over the course of history.[2] Another—probably complementary—perspective argues that war is a product of natural human belligerence as individuals and groups struggle to maximize benefits.[3] (The fact that warfare has also stimulated technological progress[4] cannot be considered a driver of war even if men—and women, albeit to a lesser degree—seem enamored with new tools, methods, and approaches.) In modern times, ancient hatreds, identity politics, manipulative elites, political and economic systems, and contention for power have, singly or in combination, fuelled violence and fed from it.[5]

A reading of Donkin's (2010) *History of Work* intimates it may be a short step from the field of battle to that of organizations. Situations of feud and acts of negative reciprocity in the corporate world, if thankfully bloodless, are an obdurate truth: everywhere, there is much talk of "winning," as if the term had ageless definition. Surely, however, what it means to win should be seen as culturally and socially situated. In general, instead of prevailing over another party, one might more beneficially recognize and promote consciousness of a shared concern and common interests in facing it.

Satisficing at Work

Paraphrasing John Rambo, if war is normal and peace an accident, one could at least expect collaboration *within* organizations.[6] Yet, even there, particularly in public and illegitimate organizations, the quasi-resolution of conflicts is the norm (Cyert and March 1963).

---

[2] It is as if cultural representations, to survive, must propagate and durably invade entire populations. In the process, of course, people, their environment, and the ideas themselves are transformed (Sperber 1996).

[3] Thankfully, Fry (2005) posits that along with the capacity for aggression humans also possess a strong ability to prevent, limit, and resolve conflicts without mayhem.

[4] For example, the Bronze Age saw the development of offensive weapons, e.g., axes, composite bows, daggers, spears, and swords; protective gear, e.g., armor, shields, and helmets; and tactical innovations, e.g., battle plans, chariotry, (counter)intelligence and communications, mobility, patrolling techniques, phalanx formations, rank structures, and staffs.

[5] Conflict theory, which deduces civilization as a fight for power and authority between groups that struggle over limited means, offers a handy lens through which to analyze society. Notions of political economy are likewise relevant.

[6] Simon (1956) coined the word "satisfice"—a portmanteau combining "satisfy" with "suffice"—in 1956 to characterize approaches to information processing and decision making based on bounded rationality. With implications for human beings, he argued that the psychological environment of

Cohen et al. (1972) have developed an influential, agent-based representation of organizational decision-making processes. They submit that organizations are—at least in part and part of the time—distinguished by three general properties: (i) problematic preferences, (ii) unclear technology, and (iii) fluid participation. Citing, "Although organizations can often be viewed conveniently as vehicles for solving well-defined problems or structures within which conflict is resolved through bargaining, they also provide sets of procedures through which participants arrive at an interpretation of what they are doing and what they have done while in the process of doing it. From this point of view, an organization is a collection of choices looking for problems, issues and feelings looking for decision situations in which they might be aired, solutions looking for issues to which they might be the answer, and decision makers looking for work." Decision opportunities characterized by problematic preferences, unclear technology, and fluid participation, viz., ambiguous stimuli, generate three possible outcomes, each driven by the energy it requires within the confines of organizational structure.[7] These outcomes, whose meaning changes over time, are resolution, oversight, and flight.[8] Significantly, resolution of problems as a style for making decisions is not the most common; in its place, decision-making by flight or oversight is the feature. Is it any wonder then that the relatively complicated intermeshing of elements does not enable organizations to resolve problems as often as their mandates demand?

A problem is a chance for you to do your best.

—Duke Ellington

A major feature of the Garbage Can Model is the partial uncoupling of problems and choices. Decision-making is usually thought of as a process for solving the former but that is often not what happens. Quoting further from Michael Cohen, James March, and Johan Olsen, "Problems are worked upon in the context of some choice, but choices are made only when the shifting combinations of problems,

---

(Footnote 6 continued)

organisms limits the cognitive resources they have to maximize. In other words, because they lack complete information, they choose what might not be optimal but will make them happy enough.

[7]Four factors have substantial effects on organizational choice. They are an organization's net energy load, problem access structure, decision structure, and energy distribution. As expected, inherent and contextual risks are higher in structurally complex organizations.

[8]Decisions by resolution can only come to pass if the participants to the decision process are suitably able, a sufficiently good solution is available to them, and the problem they are called to solve is relatively simple. Decisions by oversight are routines that confirm the legitimacy of an organization but cannot solve problems. Flight is no decision but may allow reexamination of the choice after the trickiest issue has been set aside.

solutions, and decision makers happen to make action possible. Quite commonly this is after problems have left a given choice arena or before they have discovered it (decisions by flight or oversight)." One device for quasi-resolution of conflicts is local rationality; since each division or department within an organization only deals with a narrow range of problems, each can at least pretend to be rational in addressing local concerns. (Of course, as a general rule, local rationalities are mutually inconsistent and so will not build synergy. The metaphor of organizational silos begs no explanation.) A second device is acceptable-level decision rules; where they are met, the level of consistency between one decision and another is low enough for the divergence to be tolerable. A third is sequential attention to goals; this allows consideration to be given first to one goal and then to another. Obviously, surface, latent, or open conflicts run through all organizational choices even if satisficing exists to maintain them at levels that are not unacceptably detrimental. Concluding, contemporary views of conflict think it endemic, inevitable, and often legitimate.

Decision is a risk rooted in the courage of being free.

—Paul Tillich

A Précis on Organizational Conflict

Heterogeneity in values and ideas is a profound reality that organizations (and societies at large, as we saw) have to deal with; it can—and usually does—breed conflict, that is, an interactive process or state in which the interests of individuals or groups in an organization appear divergent or incompatible,[9] often resulting in overt or covert attempts to block or thwart the other party's attempts to satisfy these for preferred outcomes.[10] In addition to miscommunication, large bones of contention are freedom, goals, positions, rewards and recognition, resources, and task

---

[9]When all is said and done, a shocking number of conflicts owe to miscommunication, that is, semantic sources. Increased self-knowledge and mutual understanding will promote cohesion. Even then, communication distortions can have structural origins: as information is passed up or down a hierarchy, it is susceptible to ambiguity and breakdown.

[10]Recurrently, the process that unfolds will have a group tell stories about its views and misrepresent (if they are understood at all) those of the other party. What it perceives as "good" in its position will be underscored and what is "bad" will be ignored. The position of the other party will be assessed as "bad" with little "good," if any. As a result, the objectivity and judgment of both parties will be impaired and discussions of differences will not exhibit rational or constructive behavior. Each party will phrase questions and answers in such ways that strengthen its position and disparage the other's.

interdependences.[11] (Low formalization of rules and regulations may also exacerbate jurisdictional misunderstanding.) Conflict is also an inevitable part of dynamic growth (or decline) (Fig. 83.1).

> *If civilization is to survive, we must cultivate the science of human relationships—the ability of all peoples, of all kinds, to live together, in the same world at peace.*
>
> —Franklin Delano Roosevelt

"A strange justice that is bounded by a river! Truth on this side of the Pyrenees, error on the other side," Blaise Pascal reflected. One school of thought holds that effective management should conduce such a healthy environment that conflicts do not arise; a larger body of opinion believes that conflict must be, reluctantly, accepted as a fact of life but that it should be avoided and suppressed rather than understood and cured[12]; a third group of advocates, often encamped in the private sector, argues that not letting the lions in can actually be ruinous because conflict engages—it leads to deeper understanding, more comprehensive choice, and better contingency planning. For sure, if faced well, conflict can lead to positive change; unresolved, it can take on a life of its own and become the center of all thought and action—it might then hurt people, ruin reputations, inhibit relationships, and fragment organizations causing a downward spiral in organizational health.[13]

---

[11]Individuals and groups who value autonomy resist calls for conformity. Due to their respective functions and responsibilities, members of organizations frequently pursue goals that are somewhat (when not entirely) different from one another. Those who seek power tussle with others for status. Everywhere, rewards, recognition, and resources are thought insufficient and improperly distributed, driving competition for such prizes. What is more, the assistance, information, compliance, or co-coordinative activities that a group needs to accomplish its tasks may not be forthcoming. A six-point checklist covering corporate values, strategy, organization, people, business processes, and rewards and recognition provides a ready framework for diagnosing in-house conflict.

[12]Human resource divisions typically view conflict as the failure to develop appropriate congenial social norms for groups; organizations should be ordered, smooth-running, and harmonious.

[13]This is an understatement. Win–lose conflicts among individuals and groups delay decisions, create deadlocks, divert energy and time from the main concern, obstruct exploration of alternatives, interfere with listening, decrease or destroy sensitivity, and cause general defensiveness. All too commonly, they also interfere with empathy, arouse anger, provoke personal abuse, cause members to withdraw from task forces or committees, relegate resentful or now-indifferent losers to the sidelines, and incline underdogs to sabotage.

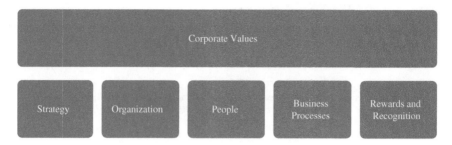

Fig. 83.1 Diagnosing organizational conflict. *Source* Author

In short, organizational conflict can be (i) intrapersonal,[14] (ii) interpersonal, (iii) intragroup, and (iv) intergroup.[15] The strategies for managing the last three structural types, each revealing different levels of concern for self and others are (i) integrating—resolving problems to reach an effective solution acceptable to all disputants; (ii) obliging—satisfying the concerns of the other party to preserve a relationship and perhaps obtain something in exchange; (iii) dominating—achieving a win–lose resolution that is in the best interest of one group and at the expense of the other; (iv) avoiding—sidestepping situations; and (v) compromising—seeking a resolution that satisfies at least part of each party's demands.[16] Interest-based relational approaches to integrating urge protagonists to make mutual respect and good relationships the first priority, keep people and problems separate, listen very carefully (before talking) to the grievances presented, set out what verifiable specifics give reasons for the conflict, and explore options together. To note, most diagnoses and treatments of organizational conflict ignore the issue of authority to settle, meaning, the obligation of parties to report to or obtain consent from supervisors who were not involved in discussions or may not be familiar with

---

[14]Conflict within individuals refers to a person's inner workings and personality problems. Related difficulties are the province of professional counselors but there are surely aspects of intrapersonal conflict that managers should understand and possibly help remedy. With due respect to Maslow's (1943) hierarchy, these might be explored in relation to the need that humans have for esteem and self-actualization.

[15]As recognized earlier, conflicts can be constructive too, although the art of sparking that remains esoteric outside sports. Some individuals and groups use conflict as a motivating force toward innovation and change.

[16]Thomas and Kilmann's (1997) taxonomy of conflict styles classifies such responses as competitive (assertive, uncooperative); collaborative (assertive, cooperative); compromising (intermediate assertiveness and cooperativeness); accommodating (unassertive, cooperative); and avoiding (unassertive, uncooperative). Surprisingly, the framework has also found application in an area that one might have assumed directly opposite to conflict management, that is, collective knowledge development in strategic alliances (Larsson et al. 1998). This goes to show that organizations are likely to eschew internecine conflict, or learn most together, when they choose collaborative strategies of high transparency and receptivity.

the dilemmas.[17] (This is a widespread difficulty in hierarchical organizations where attempts at resolution, oversight, or even flight can necessitate approval by several echelons.) What is more, most aim to resolve or manage organizational conflict through technocratic approaches that pay little heed to learning—always necessary to enhance individual, group, and organizational effectiveness.

A Complexity View of Organizational Conflict

Approaches that reduce complexity make sense in low-context situations[18] but do not in the sphere of multiple, interacting phenomena. The social context of conflicts is evolutionary, meaning that causes and effects are not always directly linked, proportionate, or predictable: complex adaptive systems such as conflicts are better understood through requisite variety—this means having at least as much complexity as the issue being discussed.

> *Some problems are so complex that you have to be highly intelligent and well informed just to be undecided about them.*
>
> —Laurence Peter

Basic concepts of complexity science—the study of dynamic relationships in complex adaptive systems rather than the isolated properties of their agents—have entered everyday language. (Foremost among them is the notion of emergence, which connotes unpredictability. Others include connectivity, interdependency, nonlinearity, sensitivity to initial conditions, feedback processes, bifurcation, phase space, chaos and edge of chaos, adaptive agents, self-organization, and co-evolution.)

Applied to organizations, now perhaps best described as collectives of human activity, complexity thinking puts a damper on naive hopes of an ordered and controllable existence. Instead, it helps explain change through learning, adaptation, and evolution, often by means of competition and cooperation and usually in the interest of survival. It does so by acknowledging that people are intelligent, dynamic, self-organizing, and emergent beings who are capable of discerning thoughtfulness and innovative reactions to conflict. Indeed, when cause-and-effect

---

[17]The conflicting parties may wish to adjust their respective positions as they learn together but they are under the influence of remote, sometimes even unknown, decision makers who have the ability to influence mediation and its outcome.

[18]For instance, in low-context communications the mass of information is vested in the explicit message; in high-context communications it is either in the physical context or initialized in the person.

relationships between people, experiences, and contexts can only be perceived in retrospect, not in advance through deliberate strategy, the wiser approach is to probe, sense, and respond rather than be deceived by the empty promise of command and control. Reinterpreted as pattern fluctuation—not breakdown, noise, or error—conflict should more usefully be seen as the product of perpetual surprise, itself generated by ongoing nonlinear interactions. Andrade et al. (2008)[19] propose that mindfulness,[20] improvisation, and reconfiguration—no small order, if trust is added—will then help fructify that for organizational growth and renewal.

References

Andrade L, Plowman DA, Duchon D (2008) Getting past conflict resolution: a complexity view of conflict. Emergence: Complexity and Organization 10(1):23–38

Cohen M, March J, Olsen J (1972) A garbage can model of organizational choice. Administrative Science Quarterly 17(1):1–25

Cyert R, March J (1963) A behavioral theory of the firm. Prentice Hall

Donkin R (2010) The history of work. Palgrave Macmillan

Fry D (2005) The human potential for peace: an anthropological challenge to assumptions about war and violence. Oxford University Press

Larsson R, Bengtsson L, Henriksson H, Sparks J (1998) The interorganizational learning dilemma: collective knowledge development in strategic alliances. Organization Science 9(5):285–305

Maslow A (1943) A theory of human motivation. Psychological Review 50(4):370–396

Simon H (1956) Rational choice and the structure of the environment. Psychological Review 63 (2):129–138

Sperber D (1996) Explaining culture: a naturalistic approach. Blackwell Publishers

---

[19]Quoting, "When organizations improvise, they test competing interpretations and experiment with alternative notions of what might work. When organizations develop the capacity for mindfulness, they highlight differences and let the differences inform organizational members and offer opportunities to learn. When organizations reconfigure themselves and function more like a federation of patches, each of which is trying to find success, the whole system is capable of learning from its patches and find successful co-evolutionary adaptations."

[20]Mindfulness is the state of active, open attention to the present. It involves continuing scrutiny of expectations, their unremitting refinement and differentiation based on experience, and willingness and ability to define new prospects that make sense of unprecedented events or circumstances. In organizations, it is responsible for elevating collective intelligence and nurturing a mindful culture.

Proposition 84
On Organizational Configurations

In a Word To manage organizations in ways that will make us society manageable, we need to spark innovations in management. Consider the organization in which you work. What configuration does it have and what does that tell you? What might you do to enhance the strengths and minimize the weaknesses of its structure?

Of Human Hives …

In the quickening process of globalization, ours has become a society of large, often machine-like, organizations. In many parts of the world, human beings now live in an organizational world from birth and depend on centralized hierarchies as infants, children, youth, students, citizens, consumers, clients, employers, and employees. A convergence of technological and economic factors is reinventing the organizations

These *Knowledge Solutions* celebrate the work of Henry Mintzberg (1989) on the subject.

© Asian Development Bank 2017
O. Serrat, *Knowledge Solutions*, DOI 10.1007/978-981-10-0983-9_84

of the twenty-first century[1]; but until they take more recognizable shapes, since most people spend much of their waking hours in formal organizations, it makes sense to circumscribe the main typologies of those of the nineteenth and twentieth centuries. With newfound understanding, we may then, among countless opportunities for improvement, moderate the organizational conflict they fan, bridge the organizational silos they make happen, appreciate the informal authority they write off, revive the moral courage they dampen, and by so doing—perhaps—help rationalize and fructify our lives.

... And Their Configurations

> *We do as much harm holding onto programs and people past their natural life span as we do when we employ massive organizational air strikes. However, destroying comes at the end of life's cycle, not as a first response.*
>
> —Margaret Wheatley

Historically, models for organizational rationality and efficiency echoed religious or military forms. At the turn of the twentieth century, Taylorism[2] (aka scientific management) guided industrial and commercial organizations. Today, most organizations are designed as bureaucracies in which authority and responsibility are arranged in hierarchy.[3] Yet the joint purpose for which a group exists should be the foundation for everything its members do. The idea is to organize in a way that best suits that, and, increasingly, the attention has turned to classifying different forms of organizational structure and exploring their implications. However, instead of form (structure) following function (work tasks), bureaucracies normally fill positions.[4]

---

[1]To wit, Thomas Malone foresees that loose hierarchies, democracies, and markets will—along a continuum of increasing decentralization—move management styles for organizational structures from command-and-control to coordinate-and-cultivate (Malone 2004).

[2]A precedent to industrial engineering, scientific management sought to optimize workflow processes thereby improving labor productivity. Contemporary management thinking critiques Taylorism as deskilling and dehumanizing personnel.

[3]Rules, policies, and procedures are applied across the hierarchy to dictate behavior. Activity is organized in subunits (working groups, offices, or departments) where people perform specialized functions. Those who carry out similar tasks are often clustered together.

[4]Bureaucratic ways of organizing limit or work against learning. Groups can possibly "learn their way out" toward more effective work relationships—those in which responsibility and arrangements for work rest primarily with those who actually deliver it. However, although the principle is simple, unlearning bureaucratic behavior can be extremely difficult.

> *A corporation doesn't have a culture. A corporation is a culture. That's why they're so horribly difficult to change.*
>
> —Karl Weick

At the heart of any organization are the persons who produce its products and deliver its services. They are its operating core. Next, all but the simplest organization require at least one full-time manager,[5] who occupies what might be called the strategic apex—from where the organization is overseen. Then, typically, as organizations grow, they add more managers who manage operators and their managers, forming a middle line between the operating core and the apex position. As it grows ever more complex, the organization includes a technostructure of analysts; like managers, they perform administrative duties—specifically, they will plan and coordinate the work of others. Most organizations will also have support staff who provide diverse internal services, for instance regarding travel, information systems and technology, or external relations. Finally, every organization has an ideology—a culture that infuses the structure and sets it apart from others, sometimes a little, sometimes very much. The following figure depicts how these six basic parts may be thought as influencers; it suggests also that entities outside the organization exert influence to affect the decisions and actions it takes. The role of this task environment is crucial but often poorly understood.

> *It would be difficult to exaggerate the degree to which we are influenced by those we influence.*
>
> —Eric Hoffer

The members of the operating core will pull to professionalize to minimize the influence others may have over their work. Naturally, the strategic apex will exert its pull to lead, if only to retain control over decision-making by direct supervision. In their search for autonomy, the middle line will balkanize the structure and concentrate power through vertical decentralization to themselves. The technostructure will

---

[5]Whether this manager functions primarily as a supervisor ordering the work of subordinates or as a leader undertaking strategic high-level support roles for the group depends on the organizational culture. Without mindfulness, most organizations create complex, inefficient hierarchies of command.

endeavor to rationalize by standardizing business processes. Support staff will collaborate to involve themselves in the central activity of the organization. Ideology, where it exists as a force in organizations, encourages members to pull together. Politics may also exist in certain types of organizations—especially when no part dominates—and cause people to pull apart. Together, these configurations and the pulls and needs represented by each seem to encompass and integrate a good deal of what is known about organizations. The next figure shows all basic pulls on an organization. When conditions favor one of these pulls, the organization will be drawn to design itself in a particular configuration.

> *The only things that evolve by themselves in an organization are disorder, friction, and malperformance.*
>
> —Peter Drucker

> *I won't belong to any organization that would have me as a member.*
>
> —Groucho Marx

Henry Mintzberg saw seven basic configurations. The "entrepreneurial organization" is a centralized—perhaps autocratic—arrangement typified by a small hierarchy, with power in the hands of a chief executive, often the founder. Simplicity, flexibility, informality, and a sense of mission promote loyalty. The "machine organization" gains strength from its technostructure; it is best at mass production and is characterized by layers of management, formal procedures, sharp divisions of labor, and a large number of routine operations. The "diversified organization" is borne of mergers made to combine businesses into larger entities under the label of vertical integration, aiming to exploit synergies. The "professional organization" is built less on hierarchy than on shared experience, be it a practice, a school, or a hospital; it is more democratic and highly motivated than the "machine organization," with lines of authority less clearly set out. The "innovative organization" that burgeoned after the Second World War is often found in new technology industries, which need to innovate constantly and respond quickly to changing markets. In the "missionary organization" that spread from the mid-1970s on, ideology can be so strong that the entire structure is sometimes built around it, that is, coordinated through the standardization of norms and reinforced by selection, socialization, and indoctrination. To finish, the "political organization" expresses itself in political games, with conventional notions of concentrated coordination and influence replaced by the play of informal power. However, the truth is that one can find all these forms in all organizations. Only truly creative organizations dedicated to continuous improvement and evolution model unique configurations. Drawing from the respective strengths of the seven types of organizations, these configurations would integrate forces of direction, efficiency, concentration, proficiency, learning, cooperation, effectiveness, and competition.[6] Differences would often be detected across working groups, offices, or departments as these units create their own configurations.

Ushering Organizations of the Future

> *Leaders must encourage their organizations to dance to forms of music yet to be heard.*
>
> —Warren Bennis

Yogi Berra would and did say: "It's déjà vu all over again." If people establish and maintain organizations to do things that are not already being done, it follows that organizations will die and materialize in new forms when the joint purpose that engendered their birth is no longer being satisfactorily served.[7] Form follows function to a certain point; it follows failure when function hiccups, gags, or ceases. However, we still think of organizations in mechanistic terms as collections of replaceable parts, including staff, capable of being reengineered. And so, the reason the great majority of our organizations misses the future is that we overinvest in what is at the expense of what could be. To manage organizations in ways that will make our society manageable, we need to spark innovations in management.

---

[6]Organizations can decide to move toward a particular type or types. The decision requires an articulated vision with action to adjust the structure, business processes, and norms resulting in a modified culture. If one wishes to reinforce professional, innovative, or entrepreneurial types, the actions should come from personnel with management support rather than control. While workers obviously understand their work best, they rarely control the design of structures and business processes to guide it. Contemporary organizational development research and practice proves that employee-driven approaches are the only way toward sustainable improvements in quality, productivity, and staff engagement.

[7]Organizing in myriad purposeful ways is the fundamental characteristic of mankind: from the simple to the complex; people constantly strive to perform in groups what they cannot accomplish individually.

References

Malone T (2004) The future of work: how the new order of business will shape your organization, your management style, and your life. Harvard Business School Press
Mintzberg H (1989) Mintzberg on management: inside our strange world of organizations. Simon and Schuster

Further Reading

ADB (2009) Learning for change in ADB. Manila

Proposition 85
On Networked Organizations

In a Word Hierarchy, market, and network forms of organization are not mutually exclusive: in the twenty-first century, the need for resilience, intelligence, speed, and flexibility demands that each organizational form finds requisite expression in individual organizations.

The Shape of Things to Come

Taking off the past, the future always starts today. Right now, three interrelated variables stand out from a wide array of forces shaping—with bewildering dynamism and complexity—human aspirations in the twenty-first century: separately

© Asian Development Bank 2017
O. Serrat, *Knowledge Solutions*, DOI 10.1007/978-981-10-0983-9_85

and in confluence, they have to do with demography,[1] science and technology,[2] and globalization.[3]

In the Anthropocene, a term coined to mark the impact that human population and economic growth are having on the Earth's ecosystems, risks and opportunities are more pronounced and entangled than ever before. Sustainable development is of the essence but we cannot grasp its multitudinous dimensions.[4] Additionally, at the same time as we are annexing nature in ways that have no precedent, we are also invading human nature in unprecedented ways.

Table. Stylized features of organization

Key feature	Hierarchy	Market	Network
• Purpose	• Realize the mission of a central executive	• Provide a forum for transactions	• Advance the interests of a cooperative
• Agent of governance	• Authority	• Prices	• Trust
• Locus of decision-making	• Top–down	• Relatively autonomous	• Joint or negotiated
• Type of product and service	• Mass-produced from economies of scale	• Highly varied by virtue of spot contracts	• Customized from economies of scale and scope
• Basis of control	• Status and rules-based	• Price-based	• Expertise- and reputation-based
• Basis of relations	• Employment	• Contracts and property rights	• Exchange of resources

(continued)

[1]Notwithstanding the growing global population, predicted to swell over 10 years from about 6.9 billion in 2010 to approximately 7.6 billion in 2020, the pool of (skilled) workers is in fact shrinking. Labor force contraction is no longer the preserve of advanced, aging countries, e.g., Germany, Italy, or Japan: the People's Republic of China and the Russian Federation—two large emerging markets, are feeling a demographic pinch too, with more people retiring than are entering their workforces. In short, extraordinary shifts in the balance of populations are in motion that will factor themselves into economic, political, and social systems.

[2]The pace of progress in science and technology—whether through developments in additive manufacturing (or 3D printing), biotechnology, information and communications technology (and the digital networks it enable around image, text, and voice), nanotechnology, neuroscience, or stem cell technology—will accelerate over the next 10–15 years. On top, synergies across science and technology and other areas of human endeavor will presently lead to auxiliary manifestations in research and development, production processes, and the nature of products and services; their corollaries are expected to continue to inflate demand for a (highly) skilled workforce, raise productivity, and transform employment relationships, among others.

[3]The effects of globalization—marked as yet by mounting trade in intermediate and final products and services, expanding capital flows, quicker transfer of knowledge and technologies, and precipitously mobile populations—will further impact every diverse reach.

[4]The burning issues or wicked problems that confront mankind—in arenas like climate change, conflict, energy, health, hunger, pandemics, security, urbanization, and water—are born of intertwined webs of cause and effect.

(continued)

Key feature	Hierarchy	Market	Network
• Basis of transactions	• Routines	• Prices	• Relations
• Nature of transactions	• Long-term	• Short-term	• Medium- to long-term
• Basis of tasks	• Function	• Unitary	• Project
• Degree of dependence among parties	• Dependent	• Independent	• Interdependent
• Degree of vertical integration	• High and centralized	• Low and decentralized	• Variable
• Degree of commitment of parties	• Low	• High	• Moderate to high
• Assets and resources	• Highly specific, largely tangible, and not easily traded	• Moderately specific, tangible and intangible, and easily traded	• Highly specific, largely intangible, and shared
• Nature of organizational boundaries	• Fixed and rigid	• Flexible and permeable	• Discrete and atomic
• Approach to conflict resolution	• Administrative fiat	• Negotiation and legal systems	• Diplomacy and reciprocity
• Culture	• Subordination	• Competition	• Reciprocity
• Tone	• Formal	• Precise and suspicious	• Friendly and open-ended
• Nature of incentives	• Pre-specified	• High-powered	• Reputational
• Approach to information gathering	• Cursory, through specialized offices	• Information conveyed by prices	• Distributed

Source Author

Note Describing the open source phenomenon in the software industry, with perhaps limited applications outside it with the growing exception of information goods incorporating codified knowledge, some add bazaar governance to evolving forms of organization. Hierarchical, market, and network forms of organization are discrete structural alternatives for any transaction: in comparison, bazaar governance blossoms in conditions of open license and anonymity

It is not just the velocity of change but the snowballing multiplicity of inter-connected actors that typifies our world. What traditional institutions have been in place since the end of the Second World War, including their guiding rules of engagement, seem less and less fit for purpose. In their guise, we increasingly make out intersecting megacommunities of hyperconnected individuals and (local, national, regional, international, and global) organizations in the public, private, and civil (or plural) sectors.[5]

> *I think the next century will be the century of complexity.*
>
> —Stephen Hawking

Velocity, multiplicity, and interconnectivity make for complexity and unpredictable, sudden, and drastic changes. This much we know: the higher the complexity, the higher the risk of collapse. Hence, in converse of (habitually reductive) scenario planning, we will before long have to learn to backcast[6] rather than forecast. Proximately, it is through intense intra- and inter-organizational learning—akin to swarm intelligence—that, having discovered and studied the principles that govern complexity, we can hope to confront the challenges of the twenty-first century.

> *The crisis that the world finds itself in as it swings on the hinge of a new millennium is located in something deeper than particular ways of organizing political systems and economies.*
>
> —Huston Smith

Managing for change is not just smart: more often than not, it is to boot a matter of survival. "Whosoever desires constant success must change his conduct with the times," advised Niccolò Machiavelli. And so, because organizing is the process of arranging into structured wholes and organization is the concrete outcome of that, it is worth reviewing past and prevailing models of organization and what forms are emerging on account of the three variables flagged above—demography, science and technology, and globalization.

---

[5]Much as the steel fulcrum that Max Couper displayed in Dusseldorf in 1997 and at the European Parliament in Brussels in 1998 to symbolize good governance, a balanced society rests on three legs: a public sector of political forces, a private sector of economic forces, and a civil sector of social forces.

[6]Forecasting is the process of predicting the future based on current trend analysis. Backcasting is the process of defining a desirable future and then working in reverse to make out policies, strategies, and programs that will connect the future to the present. Future Search conferencing is a methodology that enables diverse and potentially antagonistic groups to find common ground for constructive action.

Organizing to the Twentieth Century

Organizing is a key activity in life and organizations are its most visible manifestation. An organization happens when people come together and match up with commitment and trust.[7] So, why exactly do people form groups? Apart from the anticipated social, political, economic, and cultural benefits of cooperation,[8] a principal stimulus of organization is competition; after all, if resources were unlimited the need to organize would be minimal.

> *In the business world, the rearview mirror is always clearer than the windshield.*
>
> —Warren Buffett

The coordination of human interests and related activities can range from the innate, e.g., the breastfeeding of a child, to the very demanding, e.g., climate change mitigation. Where it requires unremitting, calculated attention, organization design refers to precisely how a collective entity—compromising between acceptability, economy, flexibility, reliability, and simplicity—seeks (and all being well achieves) the right combination of differentiation and integration of its operations given the level of uncertainty in the external environment. Conventional management theory tells us that combination is achieved by alignment of vision and mission, values and operating principles, strategies, objectives, systems, structure, people, processes, culture, and performance measures.

By and large, the early nomadic,[9] next, agricultural forms of organization structured work to secure the generic requirements of food, shelter, and clothing.

---

[7]This is what "organization" means, at heart, usually in the form of a relatively durable, reliable, and accountable social structure with an identifiable label, say, General Motors. At sophisticated levels, it forms around shared purpose and principles that shape relationships, decisions, and human behavior. In 2012, the world's 10 largest public and private organizations by number of employees were, in descending order, the United States Department of Defense, People's Liberation Army, Walmart, McDonald's, National Health Service, People's Republic of China National Petroleum Corporation, State Grid Corporation of China, Indian Railways, Indian Armed Forces, and Hon Hai Precision Industry.

[8]Strictly speaking, cooperation and collaboration are not the same: to cooperate is to pool resources, as in an agricultural cooperative; to collaborate is to labor together. Cooperation and collaboration carry connotations that become important in the management context: unassumingly, these *Knowledge Solutions* use the latter terminology in what follows.

[9]In the wake of band society, beginning thousands of years ago, the tribe was the first form of organization to come into existence. Its core operating principle was kinship through ties of descent from a common ancestor, community of customs and traditions, adherence to the same leaders, etc.: it gave members a sense of identity and belonging. Today, tribalism still exists in certain regions but also, more prevalently, in such social expressions as civic interest groups, cultural festivities, fan clubs, sports, and nationalism. Some hold kinship to be so fundamental to human nature that tribalism is the primary fallback option when other forms of organization fail.

Nevertheless, in the busyness of time, work and its organization soon came to mean more than the orderly use of tools and techniques: in successive waves, beginning unambiguously with the multiplicative aftermath of the division (and coordination) of labor, industrialization,[10] and scientific management, consecutive technological improvements helped stretch the reach of the hand, magnify the power of muscle, intensify the senses, and fructify the capacities of the mind. From the mid-twentieth century, the computer and ensuing Digital Revolution in particular propelled social transformation: indeed, hitherto unimaginable changes are ongoing.[11]

> *That men do not learn very much from the lessons of history is the most important of all the lessons that history has to teach.*
>
> —Aldous Huxley

In spite of that, organizingand managing are still mentioned in the same automatic breath. If, as some contend, management is a maturing technology that has delivered few authentic breakthroughs since Frederick Winslow Taylor and Max Weber outlined its rudiments 100 years ago, the same can with like deduction be said of organizationalforms in the late twentieth century,[12] redolent as they were of eighteenth and nineteenth century command-and-control designs. Manifestly, if the marshaling of activities to achieve objectives is a function of the configuration of the host, the paucity of innovations in management is attributable to the lingering orthodoxy of organization design. To wit, forged by the experience of the Industrial Revolution and its long-lasting, life-changing consequences, the worldview that conditioned mechanistic perspectives to organizing throughout the twentieth century—aka the factory system—continued to be that (i) hierarchy maintains productivity and performance, (ii) specialization and division of labor maximize the quality and quantity of goods and services, (iii) every organization has an optimal

---

[10]To note, cities grew spectacularly as industrialization concentrated populations in the nineteenth century and engendered service economies. Accordingly, the modern business enterprise took shape circa 1870 and pioneering theories of business administration and organizational behavior surfaced shortly after courtesy, respectively, of Henri Fayol and Mary Parker Follett.

[11]To generalize, science and technology are putting astonishing knowledge and ability in the hands of people who have the same basic mental faculties as humans born, say, 10,000–15,000 years ago. Since their dispositions have not varied and are not expected to alter in the coming millennia —evolution works more leisurely than that, progress in the twenty-first century can only come from institutional and cultural development.

[12]Combining variously—subject to internal and external influencers—the six basic parts and people of any organization, e.g., operating core, strategic apex, middle line, technostructure, support staff, and ideology, Mintzberg (1989) drew in the 1980s seven broad configurations— entrepreneurial, machine, professional, diversified, innovative, missionary, and political—that for ease of reference others segregate simply into hierarchies and markets.

structure, and (iv) fine-tuning the organizational structure suffices to tackle emerging problems.

> *Leaders must encourage their organizations to dance to forms of music yet to be heard.*
>
> —Warren Bennis
>
> *A system is a network of interdependent components that work together to try to accomplish the aim of the system. A system must have an aim. Without the aim, there is no system.*
>
> —W. Edwards Deming

The Once and Future World

If, supposedly, the outcome of organizing is superior to the sum of its parts, why is it the case here and there that twenty-first century individuals fight twentieth century organizations? Why is it that consistency is still the predominant principle of organization design? To recap, the select list of issues cited earlier—to which the after-effects of the financial crisis of 2007–2008, code-named the Great Recession, can be added—is proof-incarnate that the operating system of organizations is less and less compatible with many aspects of society in the twenty-first century. And yet, scientific management works for detailed, prescribed, and regular procedures—meaning, routine work—and will indubitably go on encompassing much of our lives.[13] For this reason alone, organizations are still regarded as corporeal and constant despite quickening tremors from demography, science and technology, and globalization. Where complexity perturbs the strategic, organizational, and operational dimensions of organizations, managers use techniques and styles that wish it away.[14] (What with bounded rationality, cognitive bias, personality, and free will, it is easier to make decisions with fewer variables and a partial understanding of cause and effect.) And, given that it is (in the short to medium term) safer to be wrong with the majority than to be right alone, managers likewise prefer to direct their efforts at strategy, structure, and systems, parameters that lie mainly within an organization's boundaries. Therefore, personnel are forever devising workarounds

---

[13]Without doubt, formalization, goal orientation, order, rationality, regularity, size, and—most definitely—standardization matter to the delivery of many goods and services. Notwithstanding, even for simple tasks, personnel craves motivation more than the carrot, never mind the stick.

[14]Indeed, it is testimony to the pervasiveness of scientific management that rules-based work is so deeply ingrained in our psyches that most of us take it as a given.

because machine organizations, what with restructuring, downsizing, and re-engineering, continue to rule the roost by force of inertia.[15]

> We are caught in an inescapable network of mutuality, tied in a single garment of destiny. Whatever affects one directly, affects all indirectly.
>
> —Martin Luther King, Jr.
>
> Purpose and principles, clearly understood and articulated, and commonly shared, are the genetic code of any healthy organization. To the degree that you hold purpose and principles in common among you, you can dispense with command and control. People will know how to behave in accordance with them, and they'll do it in thousands of unimaginable, creative ways. The organization will become a vital, living set of beliefs.
>
> —Dee Hock

Even so, in today's dynamic and complex environment, enduring success in the public, private, and civil sectors[16] requires organizational agility across boundaries, not merely within them. In the century of complexity, organizations must be "in the making" and the locus of attention should become purpose, processes, and people. So, if intra- and inter-organizational boundaries need not be barriers, and may even be unavoidable even with permeability, how does an organization—on average hierarchical and at best collegial—that is explicitly or implicitly built for linear performance develop agility and resilience for iterative, decided change? In other words, how can it with fluidity—and without losing as a result the raison d'être of what act of organizingestablished it in the first place—both generate goods and services (that meet unequivocal or latent needs) in the present, and concurrently design for the future? In a

---

[15]The time lag should not surprise: what mix of organizational forms exists at any moment is the upshot of innovative responses to earlier environmental conditions. All the same, and in a show of unexpected resilience, some features of bureaucracy may just be naturally selected for survival simply because they promote efficiency more effectively while others pragmatically adapt to the imperatives of the "Age of Knowledge" in the form of professional organizations. (Pell-mell, topical notions of creative destruction, environmental imprinting, and organizational speciation come to mind.) More prosaically, bureaucracy also enables those in power to maintain control. Last but not least, if not first of all, vertical structure appears to be hard-wired in human nature, beginning with the family.

[16]The civil sector, the weakest of the three constituencies so far, may yet find it must lead forcefully to provoke reforms in the well-established institutions of government and business. Significantly, to this day, most organizations are either publically or private owned, meaning, not-for-profit or for-profit. (Public–private partnerships are funded and operated under contracts between public sector authorities and private sector companies but the distinction remains.) In April 2008, the State of Vermont in the United States allowed a form of low-profit limited liability company (L3C) to exist legally. An L3C is to operate as a for-profit corporation that generates at least modest profits even if its chief objective is to offer social benefits. (A dozen other states now authorize L3Cs and legislation has been drafted in many others).

blast from the past, some realize—since they cannot recall[17]—that collaborative (intra- and inter-organizational) networks[18] are the organization.

The (Not So) New Social Operating System

> ... a living system continually re-creates itself. But how this occurs in social systems such as global institutions depends on both our individual and collective level of awareness ... As long as our thinking is governed by habit—notably by industrial, "machine age" concepts such as control, predictability, standardization, and "faster is better"—we will continue to re-create institutions as they have been, despite their disharmony with the larger world, and the need of all living systems to evolve.
>
> —Peter Senge, C. Otto Scharmer, Joseph Jaworski, and Betty Sue Flowers

Bill Gates was not wrong when he trumpeted business at the speed of thought at the turn of this century: brought into organizations, information and communications technology open up possibilities for re-punctuating operations throughout. In their more and more temporal environments—even if all too commonly after the fact due to the (heretofore) slow tempo of social consensus, along the lifecycle of formation, development, maturity, decline, and (perhaps) renewal, all organizations must refrain from future-proofing and strive for better fit in the coevolving realms of environment, economy, society, polity, and technology. In the digital economy, therefore, organizations must network to relentlessly gather, manage, and use data, information, and knowledge to try to make the grade (or last for more than a few years).

---

[17]The *Knowledge Solutions* on distributing leadership remind us that the original Homo sapiens enjoyed nonhierarchical and egalitarian social structures: individuals led when their know-how was needed.

[18]In a social setting, a network is an organic pattern of nonlinear, nonhierarchical relationships—characterized by nodes, ties, and patterns of connection among individuals and organizations—instigated by agency, opportunity, and exogenous or random factors. Its dynamics are framed by such influencers as brokerage, closure, heterophily, homophily, or prominence attraction, which in turn mold network architecture in terms of structure, e.g., assortativity, clustering, connectivity, density, and distribution, as well as content, e.g., numbers and types of flows. This four-fold analytical framework of components, drivers, dynamics, and dimensions, elucidated by Ahuja et al. (2012), helps understand how networks emerge, evolve, and change. Social network analysis seeks to understand networks and their participants and has two main emphases: (i) the actors, and (ii) the relationships between them in a social context.

> *Relationships are all there is. Everything in the universe only exists because it is in relationship to everything else.*
>
> —Margaret Wheatley

In the twenty-first century, the seven configurations of Henry Mintzberg are still readily recognizable but this may not hold much longer.[19] (At any rate, pure examples will become elusive.) A tipping point, or critical threshold, is reached when inertia cannot resist pressure from without or within: for at least a generation, frequent daily crossings of geographical and organizational boundaries by means of the internet have been commonplace; social media tipped the scales of electronic transactivity pronouncedly circa 2004 when Web 2.0 enabled many-to-many connections in numerous domains of practice and interest. The tools of social media are evolving fast and spatial proximity is no longer integral to information, communication, and decision-making processes.[20] Sped by the Internet and by ubiquitous mobile computing[21] quite recently, networks[22] are once again—but more extensively and multifariously than in the past—becoming the new social operating system: information and communications technology affords vastly expanded opportunities, away from the logic of efficiency that defined the Industrial Revolution and its aftermath, toward rapid mediation of decisions over production and consumption and the collaboration each usually entails. These days, a myriad of dense or loose networks geared varyingly for flexibility and responsiveness defines the social, political, economic, and cultural landscape[23]: even when piecemeal and transient, they are sources of value, usually intangible,[24] that imparts

---

[19]Not so long ago, for example, employees fretted about jobs being outsourced overseas. Today, virtual teams gather "in the cloud" to conduct research, offer services to clients, and perform many other tasks, a form of organization that could not have been foreseen in the 1980s.

[20]At first, the use of blogs, wikis, and other applications was understandably piecemeal: organizations selected one tool or cobbled a few together. Currently, many social media applications are moving toward the suite approach and tools are interoperable.

[21]From notebook computers to personal digital assistants, e.g., the BlackBerry and iPhone, to standard cell phones, mobile computing embraces a host of portable technologies that makes internet access on the go not only possible but, with portability, social interactivity, connectivity, and individuality, rapidly integral to everyday life.

[22]Alliances, communities of practice, joint ventures, partnerships, and face-to-face or virtual teams —among other forms of networks—have been around for a while. Of course, care must be taken to distinguish informal groups from, say, flat organizations operating on decentralized principles or temporary electronically sustained alliances. Critically, the normative, legal, or institutional embeddedness of networks can—and does—differ considerably.

[23]For sure, hierarchies and markets in industries such as aerospace, architectural practices, construction, design, publishing, research and development, shipbuilding, and software have for some time used temporary, team-based arrangements, aka projects, to accomplish their purposes.

[24]Intellectual capital is central to any discussion of networks: it comprises human capital, relational (or customer) capital, and structural (or organizational) capital.

competitive advantage to their members. Amplified individuals—newly equipped by science and technology and galvanized by the collective intelligence of their networks—can do things that only big organizations or no organizations at all could do heretofore. While organizingremains, formal organization wanes: it is no longer the defining feature of modernity. Had we not better, then, discuss business models rather than organizational models?

> ... there's no real evidence that one can become expert in something as broad as "decision making" or "policy" or "strategy". Auto repair, piloting, skiing, perhaps even management: these are skills that yield to application, hard work, and native talent. But forecasting an uncertain future and deciding the best course of action in the face of that future are much less likely to do so. And much of what we've seen so far suggests that a large group of diverse individuals will come up with better and more robust forecasts and make more intelligent decisions than even the most skilled "decision maker".
>
> —James Surowiecki

Are Organizations Networks?

Our organizations are us: they reflect the way we see the world; they are representations to which people are drawn, hoping to benefit by association. The more dynamic the environment, the more fluid organizations must become. No form of present-day organization can solve the momentous issues facing society because none has the resources, talent, or time to do so on its own, or even in collaboration: their dense social spaces cannot handle complexity. Conversely, networksgarner micro-contributions from scores of people to deliver large impacts.

> I must create a system, or be enslaved by another man's; I will not reason and compare: my business is to create.
>
> —William Blake

Even as (slow-moving) hierarchies and (creative but volatile) markets are being complemented, not replaced, by networks, a "living systems" perspective on organizingis enriching the previously dominant "engineering" model. This said, the greater the capacity to identify, create, store, share, and use data, information, and knowledge, the more complex the organization. In view of that, attempts to deal with complexity will not succeed if they aspire to simplify or assert control: one had better harness the creative energies of complex situations and encourage the emergence of innovative solutions by probing, sensing, and responding. By opening themselves to stakeholders and communities—thereby displaying corporate social responsibility—and becoming networks of networks, organizations can step up and extend their core expertise to raise their game with economies of scale and scope that better meet needs. Thus, organizations should at the outset, not as an afterthought, weigh up what relationships and reciprocities make the most sense, bearing in mind that collaboration taxes partners as interdependence intensifies.[25] Internally too, organizations should not be so fixated by formal structures that they discount informal ones.[26]

Building the Networked Organization[27]

In the language of organizations, a network is a set of connections that allows interactions to form and influences to flow among people. Networksfavor linking over leading, convincing over controlling, and dealing over doing: what typically ties a group together are social relations, viz., affective, cognitive, kinship, and other relations, as well as similarities, viz., attribute, location, and membership. (Not to forget, networks both include and, we shall see, exclude people.) If this sounds otherworldly, a network can be considered a collective of individuals and entities that, by stimulating know-how and know-who, hone capabilities and leverage resources across a domain, community, and practice to achieve a specific

---

[25]The *Knowledge Solutions* on learning in strategic alliances note that partners consistently crack down on initial conditions and ignore the dynamic and interactive learning dimensions of strategic alliances. Successful strategic alliances are highly evolutionary and grow in interactive cycles of learning, reevaluation, and readjustment.

[26]Organizational silos appropriate and sequester resources: personnel who want to collaborate must shin up the organization before they can cross it. Sadly, organizations that cannot pull expertise together because of silos—or, say, lack of brokers, talent pools, or knowledge markets—are often reduced to contract or procure from the outside what already exists inside. In the same vein, the contemporary necessity for organizational speed prompts greater acknowledgment of informal authority.

[27]Other overlapping definitions are ambidextrous, boundaryless, flexible, hybrid, knowledge-creating, network-centric, post-bureaucratic, post-entrepreneurial, postmodern, reengineered, and virtual. (Most of these formulations, which hark back to the 1990s, sometimes the 1980s, derive from case studies of organizational innovations: some captured the paradigms of embryonic forms of organization; others focused on aspects.) Drawing insights from institutional economics, new institutionalism, organizational ecology, and strategic management, to name a few instrumental disciplines, recurrent themes are disembodiment, information intensity, interdependence, and velocity. The question of engagement, which denotes the extent to which organizations gain commitment from personnel, is raised repeatedly. How can networks that thrive on impersonal transactions enlist engagement? Will psychological contracts gain in importance?

outcome.[28] Collective intelligence, the quantity and quality of intellectual collaboration, is well-managed freedom.[29]

> *One of the advantages of being disorderly is that one is constantly making exciting discoveries.*
>
> —A.A. Milne

In no order of importance, let alone means and ends, claims for networks include cultural diversity, flexibility, innovation, learning, problem-solving, high-trustrelationships, constructive synergies, reduced uncertainty, re-configuration and regeneration, reach, resource-richness, and self-activation; not coincidentally, such are the attributes of the internet, which acts both as conceptual model and practical enabler of networking. However, one must for good measure point out some drawbacks of networks: chiefly, they can relate to (diffuse) accountability, (the difficulty of determining) effectiveness, (the intricacy of) governance arrangements, (the loose steerage of) gestation, leadership, and upkeep, and (the imponderables of) sustainability. Others cite cliquishness, (the suppressing of) dissent, and exclusivity but this may have been more prevalent in pre-internet days.

> *Nature is a collective idea, and, though its essence exists in each individual of the species, can never in its perfection inhabit a single object.*
>
> —Henri Fuseli

From the drawbacks alluded to, aside from their advantages, networks are demonstrably not a panacea: more pragmatically, depending on the emergent property of the choices of agents in an organizational ecology, the core operating principle of trust that is the hallmark of networks should round out authority (hierarchies) or price (markets) in the world of organizational forms, on a case-by-case basis and with much local selection and interpretation. Trust, prices, and authority are now inexorably intertwined: only in rare cases does one form of organization triumph over others. The "Age of Knowledge" means that widespread hybridization is coming in the public, private, and civil sectors. Therefore, in all likelihood, pure networks—meaning, entirely free associations of people interacting for reciprocal interest—will often coexist on the margins of a much larger number of managed networks established to accomplish express corporate or institutional tasks.

---

[28]In 1998, the Health Promotion Glossary of the World Health Organization defined a network, straightforwardly, as a grouping of individuals, organizations, and agencies organized on a non-hierarchical basis around common issues or concerns, which are pursued proactively and systematically based on commitment and trust.

[29]Evidently, collective intelligence is founded on three values: sharing, responsibility, and respect.

Fig. The hybridization of
organizational governance.
Source Author

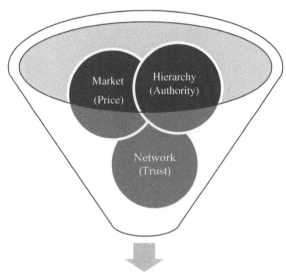

Hybrid Organization

> *Society is joint action and cooperation in which each participant sees the other
> partner's success as a means for the attainment of his own.*
>
> —Ludwig von Mises

The exercise of effective networking constitutes a daunting challenge in both hierarchiesand markets, but especially so in the first organizational form. The biggest obstacle that must be overcome is the difficulty of evaluating individual merit in enhanced collective enterprise; put differently, how can value be ascribed to enhanced collective enterprise when compensation and other benefits still connect to individuals, this insufficiently so on the word of top talent? To leverage networks that fuel individual and organizational performance in synergistic tandem, organizations need to look at personnel from synchronized perspectives of individual and network effectiveness, foster talent management practices that account for and strengthen networks, and devise mechanisms that replicate the types of networksthat high performers have (Schweer 2012). From the foregoing, essential design principles that should serve would-be networked organizations follow:

> *The greater the loyalty of a group toward the group, the greater is the motivation
> among the members to achieve the goals of the group, and the greater the proba-
> bility that the group will achieve its goals.*
>
> —Rensis Likert

- In a social context,[30] individuals and collective entities collaborate in networks when the benefits they leverage are greater than the time and effort it takes to act jointly.
- Networks are innovations in organization design that, drawing from computer science, economics, and sociology, intuit and pend on willingness to innovate in management.
- Networks must be fit for purpose, in other words, good enough to do the job they were designed for. Critically, the purpose defines the processes that drive the network, that is to say, how attention is focused and how resources are directed.
- The governance of networks calls for behavioral components, necessary to organize individual and collective work. Trustis the crucial ingredient: to share, you have to be able to trust;[31] there are interpersonal, group, intra-organizational, and inter-organizational dimensions to this and trade-offs among them.
- Every network must have at least one knowledge broker,[32] an individual who unifies the network and assumes responsibility for advancing its interests.

References

Ahuja G, Soda G, Zaheer A (2012) The genesis and dynamics or organizational networks. Organization Science 23(2):434–448

Mintzberg H (1989) Mintzberg on management: inside our strange world of organizations. Simon and Schuster

Schweer M, Assimakopoulos D, Cross R, Thomas R (2012) Building a well-networked organization. MIT Sloan Management Review 53(2):34–42

---

[30]The backdrop comprises the organizational context, organizational knowledge, and intra- and inter-organizational relationships within the external environment.

[31]The *Knowledge Solutions* on managing virtual teams labor the point that trust is a far more limiting factor where communication is not face-to-face.

[32]Organizational silos open structural holes and consequently weaken ties. A knowledge broker is an intermediary who facilitates identification, creation, storage, sharing, and use of knowledge by linking supply and demand. (In many cases, given their frequent interactions between parties, knowledge brokersare well-placed to generate knowledge itself.) In networks, the ability of knowledge brokers to knit interests together in a high-touch way can add substantial value. On top, knowledge brokers tend to have a good perspective on what can work across functions, locations, and occupations—they can boost the odds of fast and effective organizational change. Besides knowledge brokering, the other skills called for by networking are diplomacy, facilitation, learning, and trading.

Proposition 86
Fighting Corruption with ICT: Strengthening Civil Society's Role

by Haidy Ear-Dupuy and Olivier Serrat

In a Word With information and communication technology, civil society plays an increasing role in governance, promoting transparency and accountability to tackle corruption. Development agencies can strengthen civil society-led, ICT-driven anticorruption initiatives by funding projects and programs that foster institutional environments conducive to participation in public affairs, promote cooperation and mobilization, and develop capacities.

Realizing the Asian Century

The force and magnitude of Asia's economic performance from the 1980s, compared to that of other regions of the world, make perhaps the strongest case yet for the possibility of an "Asian Century".[1] According to *Asia 2050: Realizing the Asian Century*, a 2011 study financed by the Asian Development Bank (2011), Asia will

---

[1]This echoes the characterization of the nineteenth century as the British Century and the twentieth century as the American Century. Then again, some believe that the twenty-first century will be multipolar due to liberalization and globalization and that no country will monopolize influence even if the world's two most populous countries—the People's Republic of China and India, are in Asia.

© Asian Development Bank 2017
O. Serrat, *Knowledge Solutions*, DOI 10.1007/978-981-10-0983-9_86

likely account for half of global output, trade, and investment by 2050. On account of nearly doubling its share of global gross domestic product (at market exchange rates) from 27 to 51% over the period 2010–2050, the region would regain the economic position it held before the Industrial Revolution. Consequently, three billion Asians could in 40 years' time enjoy living standards similar to those of populations in the West.

However, an Asian Century is not preordained. In the immediate, the region remains home to two-thirds of the world's poor, with over 800 million people living below \$1.25 a day and 1.7 billion surviving below \$2 a day. What is more, progress toward the Millennium Development Goals has been lopsided across subregions and Asia as a whole still faces moderate to high levels of hunger and maternal mortality and lack of productive and decent employment. In the medium to long term, as the region endeavors to cement gains from a decades-long economic boom and sustain its growth momentum, governments will need to take bold action across the board. Threats have to do with (i) increasing inequality within countries, which could undermine social cohesion and stability[2]; (ii) the risk, for some countries and for a host of domestic economic, social, and political reasons, of getting caught in the "middle-income trap"[3]; (iii) intense competition for finite natural resources as newly affluent Asians aspire to higher standards of living; (iv) rising income disparities across countries, which could destabilize the region; (v) global warming and climate change, which could impact agricultural production, coastal populations, and major urban areas; and (vi) poor governance and weak institutional capacity, faced by almost all countries. Meeting any one of these hazards in a shifting global environment while continually recreating comparative advantages is not a given. What is more, the risks are not mutually exclusive: they can exacerbate one another to jeopardize growth, stability, and security.

---

[2]For instance, the 6 January 2014 edition of the *Japan Times* (2014) reported that a survey of elites by the World Economic Forum identified rising income disparities as the second top global trend for 2014, with 64 % of Asian respondents saying the economic system in their countries favors the wealthy. Despite the fact that substantial wealth was produced before, and even after, the Great Recession that began in late 2007, returns have it seems been monopolized by a small and shrinking portion of the population. The article makes the point that concentration of wealth slows growth, weakens demand, and contributes to financial crises. More ominously still, it may erode the legitimacy of governmen.

[3]Poor countries tend to grow faster than rich ones, largely because imitation is easier than invention. The middle-income trap is a situation whereby a country that has attained a certain income from given advantages—such as cheap labor—remains stuck at the same level.

This is the moment when we must build on the wealth that open markets have created, and share its benefits more equitably. Trade has been a cornerstone of our growth and global development. But we will not be able to sustain this growth if it favors the few, and not the many.

—Barack Obama

The investor of today does not profit from yesterday's growth.

—Warren Buffett

Asia's governments come in two broad varieties: young, fragile democracies—and older, fragile authoritarian regimes.

—Paul Samuelson

Prominent among the above-mentioned challenges to the Asian Century is rising corruption, which has widened the governance deficit in government, businesses, and institutions.[4] Although corruption is not a new phenomenon, and is certainly not confined to the region, it could if left unchecked weaken institutions, corrode the fabric of governance, and unravel hard-won gains. In any event, changes in demographics, galloping urbanization, and an expanding middle class will precipitate pressures to drive the transformation of governance and institutions in Asia over the next 40 years. Failure to deal with corruption would create a binding constraint to efforts to maintain social and political stability and to fortify the legitimacy of government.[5]

The next 40 years are expected to see major changes in Asians' needs, expectations, and demands for governance reforms. All trends suggest the emergence of a more empowered citizenry with sharper claims from the state in terms of greater transparency and accountability[6] and more efficient service delivery. All being well, these aspirations will make for demand-led reform for genuine transformation of

---

[4]Governance refers to all processes of governing. Applied to a country's economic and social resources, the exercise of authority is reflected in policy, institutional and regulatory frameworks, incentive structures, capacity, and transparency and accountability dimensions. Institutions, the vehicles through which the processes of governing are conducted, are any structure or mechanism of social order governing behavior, e.g., laws, systems, and procedures, including the organizational entities that exercise the "rules of the game".

[5]Transparency International's Corruption Perceptions Index 2013 serves as a reminder that abuse of power, secret dealings, and bribery continue to ravage societies around the world. Sixty four percent and 95% of countries in Asia-Pacific and Eastern Europe and Central Asia, respectively, scored below 50, indicating a serious corruption problem. (For comparison purposes, only 23% of countries in the European Union and Western Europe scored below 50.)

[6]Accountability can be determined after the fact. But, it must also be galvanized before the fact by making the rules of the game transparent in advance of their application.

governance across the region. Prescriptions for good governance already abound and will intensify; all the same, progress will have to come from within the region.

Power does not corrupt. Fear corrupts ... perhaps the fear of a loss of power.

—John Steinbeck

Governance and Institutions

Every day, and not just in Asia, we are reminded of the changes needed for economic and social progress, but not that institutions are the channels through which change happens. To promote good governance, we would do well to consider what is meant by (and can be accomplished through) participation, how participation grows out of democratic processes, how these processes depend on the structure of institutions, and how institutions originate from (and are supported by) human resources. Only then will we understand better what determines progress and picture more accurately the necessarily diverse levels of the institutional set-ups on which it depends.

The rights and responsibilities of people are central to progress. Participation is essential since privileged minorities seldom approve of reform: concentration of economic, social, and political power in their hands has retarded progress. Therefore, five questions must be asked: Who initiates? Who participates? Who decides? Who controls? Who benefits? If it is the people,[7] then development activities will most likely succeed (bearing in mind that the chance to take part hinges in turn on access to information, freedom of association to hold discussions, and arrangement of regular meetings at which officials and representatives can listen and respond to communities and be held accountable for carrying out their duties and responsibilities.)

Elections belong to the people. It's their decision. If they decide to turn their back on the fire and burn their behinds, then they will just have to sit on their blisters.

—Abraham Lincoln

---

[7]Thomas Jefferson, the third President of the United States, held that: "The basis of our governments being the opinion of the people, the very first object should be to keep that right; and were it left to me to decide whether we should have a government without newspapers, or newspapers without a government, I should not hesitate a moment to prefer the latter".

However, democracy is more than multi-partyism or the granting of concessions by authorities. Civil society needs to be fortified at all levels in agreement with the customary checks and balances of cultures. One should also ask what kinds of institutions and what manner of democratic processes are necessary to release the productive energies of people, and what conditions are required to make these institutions and processes work. The answer is that democracy must start from where people are and that—for democratic processes to unfold—transparency and accountability as well as the participation they hang on are essential. It follows that institutions (and their democratic processes) should be at three levels

- At the *community* level, a viable institution reflects the ideas, interests, and needs of communities. It has their confidence and the strength to communicate their views to higher authorities. Naturally, this assumes a degree of decentralization of decision-making. It presupposes too a capacity to act on rights and responsibilities. Above all, perhaps, the right to organize must exist.
- At the *regional* level, a viable institution possesses a mix of technical, managerial, and information-handling skills. It has also the ability to interpret communities to the nation (and vice versa). Most of all, it has a reasonable measure of autonomy (including independent revenues).
- At the *national* level, a viable institution has competence in policy-making, in socioeconomic analysis, and in technical research. It has negotiating parity with international bilateral and multilateral agencies. It provides inputs to national policy-making without relying on external advice. And it assists in the identification of linkages between the national, regional, and community levels.

A tall order? Yes, on which economic and social progress in Asia (as elsewhere) depends—even more so if one also integrates the *global* level.

Transforming Governance and Institutions in Asia

Even over the uncertainties of a 40-year horizon, governance and institutions are a good foundation from which to discuss the broad direction of Asia. Whereas regulations can be changed relatively quickly, e.g., 1–3 years, institutions need to be assessed over the long term, e.g., 10–15 years. Governance evolves incrementally over a longer time horizon, unless it is exposed to sudden and fundamental disruptions such as armed conflict or revolutions.[8] An analytical framework to stimulate governance and institutions would continuously examine the following issues: Who leads the public sector? How are policies applied? How are policies

---

[8]When citizens think that the economic system itself favors a certain class, and that class is shrinking, then the political system is under assault. Democracies are intended to represent the interests of all citizens and a healthy democracy must give hope to all citizens, especially those at the bottom.

implemented? How are resources allocated? How are public oversight functions carried out? Are there redress mechanisms?

> *Courage is what it takes to stand up and speak, Courage is also what it takes to sit down and listen.*
>
> —Winston Churchill
>
> *A "no" uttered from deepest conviction is better and greater than a 'yes' merely uttered to please, or what is worse, to avoid trouble.*
>
> —Mohandas K. Gandhi

Thankfully, there is no shortage of indicators with which to track the governance and institutional evolution of countries over time. The Worldwide Governance Indicators published by the World Bank Institute measure six core dimensions: voice and accountability, political stability and the absence of violence, government effectiveness, regulatory quality, rule of law, and control of corruption. From 2010 data, weighting country scores by gross domestic product, it appears that between 1998 and 2009 (i) Asia worsened in voice and accountability as well as political stability and the absence of violence, but improved in other areas; (ii) Asia-7[9] outperformed the rest of Asia in all six core dimensions of governance, also if weighted by population; (iii) Asia-7 lagged behind the rest of the world in governance; (iv) northeast Asia outperformed other subregions of Asia in control of corruption; and (v) Asia, including Asia-7, underperformed the rest of the world.

> *The one good thing about repeating your mistakes is that you know when to cringe.*
>
> —Aleksandr Solzhenitsyn

Corruption affects the quality and composition of public investment, thereby restricting access to essential goods, services, assets, and opportunities and ultimately undermining efforts at poverty reduction and human development. In a world characterized by macroeconomic uncertainty, rapid social change, and technological innovation, citizens' expectations of what government ought to deliver are rising. It is essential that all Asian countries should focus on improving governance and transforming institutions to meet the challenges of the coming decades. Deterioration in the quality and credibility of national political and economic institutions in many Asian countries, evidenced early, among others, by the

---

[9]Asia-7 are the People's Republic of China, India, Indonesia, Japan, Republic of Korea, Malaysia, and Thailand.

1997 Asian financial crisis, is a daunting concern and a reason why Asia's rise should not be considered preordained. Against this background, governments must do more with less, and they must do so in much more visible ways, if they are to retain (or regain) the faith of their constituents. Eight principles and priorities deserve special attention: (i) focus on building strong and transparent institutions—they define success; (ii) grasp that corruption cannot be left unchecked; failing this, it will eventually suffocate rule-of-law institutions; (iii) devise participatory approaches to policy-making and reinforce accountability mechanisms; (iv) appreciate that designing policies is only a start; implementation is what matters; (v) ensure that the rule of law applies equally to everyone; (vi) institute a civil service that is based on merit; (vii) understand that a healthy relationship between authority and citizens is a function of trust; and (viii) recognize that "best-practice" approaches will not suffice: countries have to adapt to "best-fit".

> *The government has a responsibility to protect society, to help maintain society. That's why we have laws ... The rule of law creates a set of standards for our behavior.*
>
> —Vint Cerf

The Reach of ICT

Information and communication technology—meaning technologies that facilitate by electronic means the processing, transmission, and display of information—is one of the forces shaping the twenty-first century. Through faster and cheaper communication, ICT provides the means for sweeping reorganization of business; boosts efficiency and productivity; reduces transaction costs and barriers to entry; allows people to seek, acquire, and share expertise, ideas, services, and technologies locally, nationally, regionally, and across the world; and generally makes markets more efficient. Globalization is its most pronounced outcome.

> *You affect the world by what you browse.*
>
> —Tim Berners-Lee

Bearing in mind that almost half the world—over three billion people—live on less than $2.50 a day, developing countries that harness ICT for Internet and mobile phone connectivity can leapfrog stages of development. This said, ICT can serve goals other than sustainable economic growth and public welfare: given the primacy of governance in underpinning development effectiveness, one of ICT's most important applications is in e-government.[10]

Fighting Corruption with ICT

ICT has great potential[11] to act as democratic media and the use of ICT in e-government is a major focus. [Motives and incentives owe severally to (i) interest in the promise of e-government and open data to improve government; (ii) interest in the potential of open data as a resource for growth and innovation; (iii) a desire to use ICT to address particular principal–agent problems; (iv) outside or competitive pressure; (v) bottom-up pressure from citizens; or (vi) a desire to domesticate otherwise disruptive technologies.] Its appeal owes to the enormous potential to improve public service delivery by making services more citizen-centric, soliciting citizen input to improve public services, and tapping citizens to help deliver better services at a lower cost; raise the level of participation available to citizens in the processes of governing; and increase transparency and accountability in government agencies.

> *Sunlight is the best disinfectant.*
>
> —William O. Douglas

> *It is to be regretted that the rich and powerful too often bend the acts of government to their selfish purposes. Distinctions in society will always exist under every just government. Equality of talents, of education, or of wealth cannot be produced by human institutions. In the full enjoyment of the gifts of Heaven and the fruits of superior industry, economy, and virtue, every man is equally entitled to protection by law; but when the laws undertake to add to these natural and just advantages artificial distinctions, to grant titles, gratuities, and exclusive privileges, to make the rich richer and the potent more powerful, the humble members of society—the farmers, mechanics, and laborers—who have neither the time nor the means of securing like favors to themselves, have a right to complain of the injustice of their Government.*
>
> —Andrew Jackson

---

[10]E-government (short for electronic government) refers to the use of ICT to enhance service delivery in the public sector, allow greater public access to information, and make government more accountable to citizens. It encompasses digital interactions between a government and citizens, government and business, government and employees, and government and governments.

[11]This potential springs from scalability, itself conditioned by the ability to reach citizens directly; data mashing; and sheer efficiency improvements over static technology and traditional project management tools.

Corruption is the abuse of public office for private gain. Whether grand or petty,[12] it can occur at all levels of society: in local and national government, in the judiciary, in large and small businesses, in the police and military, etc. Regardless of where it takes place, it tends to affect the poorest sectors of society the most in the competition for scarce resources and inadequately funded services.

Helpfully, Tim Davies and Silvana Fumega identify eight kinds of ICT interventions that hold potential for preventing, detecting, analyzing, and addressing corruption:

- *Transparency portals*—platforms that offer timely publication of key government documents online.
- *Open data portals*—platforms that provide free access to data sets in machine-readable formats.
- *Service automation*—platforms that replace discretionary decision-making by public officials with auditable software processes.
- *Online services*—platforms that allow citizens to self-serve for public service access.
- *Online right-to-information requests*—platforms that allow citizens to file right-to-information requests.
- *Crowdsourced reporting*—platforms that allow citizens to report corruption or grievances and publicly share data on reports and trends.
- *Online corruption reporting*—platforms that allow citizens to report corruption or grievances.
- *Issue reporting*—platforms that allow citizens to report problems with public services.

The first four ICT interventions are usually government-led. (Interventions 1 and 2 seek primarily transparency reforms; interventions 3 and 4 aim at automating transaction with government reforms.) The other four are generally civil society-led. (Interventions 5 and 6 seek transparency reforms; interventions 7 and 8 aim at transaction reforms.) Civil society also plays an important role in anticorruption theories of change around many government-led ICT interventions (Figs. 86.1 and 86.2).

---

[12]In transition economies, the spotlight has been shone more intently on a different type of grand corruption, namely state capture. The term refers to oligarchic interests that manipulate policy formulation for their own substantial but narrow interest.

Fig. 86.1 I paid a bribe. *Note* The I paid a bribe website asks users if they had ever paid a bribe to get their work done at a government office, to whom the bribe was paid, why, and when. *Source* www.ipaidabribe.com/

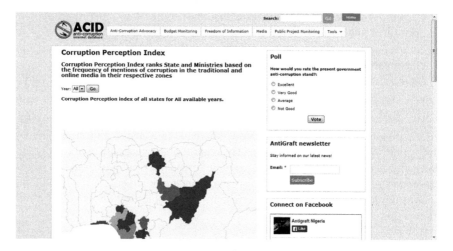

Fig. 86.2 The anti-corruption internet database. *Note* The anti-corruption internet database, or ACID, is a multifunctional web repository for all corruption related issues. It provides a collaborative platform for information on anticorruption and good governance initiatives undertaken by civil society organizations, media agencies, and organizations; and tools to facilitate civic engagement and public advocacy. *Source* Anti-corruption internet database. 2014

Strengthening Civil Society-Led Anticorruption ICT Initiatives

The majority of ICT-enabled anticorruption initiatives originate from civil society.[13] For sure, there are instances of refreshed political administrations—not discussed here—that deliver change through well-resourced line agencies, and governments remain the largest provider of information and services that are important for all, but especially the poor as a 2013 policy report of ADB (2013) makes clear. But, even where governments adopt ICT innovations for their anticorruption potential, civil society action can boost uses of the technology, under its own steam or—preferably—in partnership with the public and private sectors, including development agencies.[14]

> *Justice and power must be brought together, so that whatever is just may be powerful, and whatever is powerful may be just.*
>
> —Blaise Pascal

Civil society-led interventions have been of two kinds: push and pull. In the former, citizens speak up and communicate their experience of an issue; in the latter, they draw information from available sources and use that to act in some way. Evidently, the two approaches are not incompatible: considerations of drivers of success commonly focus on either push or pull but advocates increasingly argue for synergy-based approaches that cater also to the mechanisms of interaction between the two; such approaches recognize that state–society factors do not exist in isolation from one another but are interdependent—in any case, all the time more, ICT blurs the lines between the two to inform theories of change.

Civil society organizations that enjoy a trusted relationship with their members (or the constituencies they represent) can channel information between these and government. Where they have avoided questionable allegiances they can also serve as watchdogs. In addition, if they are well-developed, they can represent a wide variety of interests and bring diverse perspectives to design strategy and increase chances of success. Of course, not all civil society organizations display these ideal

---

[13]Here, civil society refers to groups other than government and business that operate around shared interests, purposes, and values. They include nongovernment organizations and such groups as trade unions, faith-based groups, and professional organizations.

[14]For example, governments may set up open data portals primarily for economic benefit but civil society can campaign for related interventions to include important information on budgets and spending, and can use that to hold governments to account (provided, that is, it has the awareness and technical skills needed to do this).

attributes: limits may be imposed by government, resources, or citizens themselves (who may not be sufficiently aware of the costs of corruption).

In poorer nations, development agencies are well placed to stimulate outreach activities that augment civil society's contribution to the fight against corruption. Expressly, through the second set of civil society-led ICT interventions that Davies et al. circumscribe,[15] they can on advice of the Organisation for Economic Co-operation and Development (2003) (i) foster institutional environments conducive to the development of civil society and its participation in public affairs; (ii) promote the cooperation of public and civil society actors in anticorruption efforts; (iii) encourage a broad mobilization against corruption; and (iv) develop the capacities of civil society organizations that fight corruption, including technical capacity.

> *To give real service you must add something which cannot be bought or measured with money, and that is sincerity and integrity.*
>
> —Douglas Adams
>
> *One hand washes the other.*
>
> —Seneca

- To foster *institutional environments*, they can fund projects and programs that (i) advance basic civil liberties for active public participation in anticorruption activities and other public affairs; (ii) promulgate legislation that facilitates the establishment of civil society organizations; (iii) stimulate the development of independent media, able to scrutinize government operations freely; and (iv) contribute to increase government's transparency and accountability as well as cooperation with civil society organizations.[16]
- To promote *cooperation*, they can boost outreach initiatives such as the ADB/OECD Anti-Corruption Initiative for Asia and the Pacific.
- To encourage a broad *mobilization*, they can (i) strengthen citizen support for existing civil society organizations that fight corruption; and (ii) equally, increase the participation of organizations whose primary interest is not to fight corruption.
- To develop *capacities*, they can (i) provide civil society organizations with information and expertise; (ii) sponsor training programs; (iii) contribute funds; and (iv) nurture partnerships between civil society actors.

---

[15]Obviously, they can also associate directly with governments to advance the second set.

[16]In the Philippines, for example, ADB (2008) has promoted citizen involvement in mitigating governance risks in local government units.

Transparency and accountability are central to the fight against corruption. Corruption's most pernicious effect is that it undermines faith in public institutions. Because corruption is a function of the opportunity to abuse public office and the risk of detection, ICT is an invaluable tool with which to swell both the demand and supply sides of good governance, that is, the willingness and capacity to demand as well as the willingness and capacity to account. Working with civil society to fight corruption, development agencies can integrate ICT interventions for online right-to-information requests, crowdsourced reporting, online corruption reporting, and issue reporting across a broad spectrum of outreach activities that foster institutional environments, promote cooperation, encourage a broad mobilization, and develop capacities.

> *But what is government itself, but the greatest of all reflections on human nature? If men were angels, no government would be necessary. If angels were to govern men, neither external nor internal controls on government would be necessary. In framing a government which is to be administered by men over men, the great difficulty lies in this: you must first enable the government to control the governed; and in the next place oblige it to control itself. A dependence on the people is, no doubt, the primary control on the government; but experience has taught mankind the necessity of auxiliary precautions.*
>
> —James Madison

> *There is always time to make right what is wrong.*
>
> —Susan Griffin

Opportunities for Learning

The scope of ICT-enabled anticorruption initiatives is large, irrespective of whether they are government- or civil society-led. In parallel with Davies et al., Åke Grönlund typifies eight kinds of actions that combat monopoly and discretion: they involve (i) automation—to remove human agents and hence opportunities for corruption in repetitive operations; (ii) transparency—to reduce the room for discretion; (iii) detection in operations—to make out anomalies and unexpected performance; (iv) preventive detection—to detect preparations for corrupt action by online social networks and individuals; (v) awareness raising—to inform citizens of the rules of the game so they may resist arbitrary treatment; (vi) reporting—to mobilize users to report cases that will make it easier to take corrective action and reorganize systems to avoid "loopholes"; (vii) deterrence—to dissuade individuals from engaging in corruption by publishing information about reported cases, as well as indicators; and (viii) promoting ethical attitudes—to engage citizens by pursuing discussions in various (online) forums.

ICT for transparency and accountability is a burgeoning field. In Asia as elsewhere, at community, national, and regional levels, the largest agenda for future work touches on untested assumptions and unarticulated theories of change. Here and there, what, exactly, would be the conditions under which ICT can deploy innate synergies between transparency, accountability, and participation? Drawing from political economy analysis,[17] practitioners must at a minimum, for each ICT intervention for transparency and accountability, diagnose in each different situation a theory of change laying out (i) the initial assessment of the milieu, (ii) what information each ICT intervention will provide and who will provide it, (iii) who will use the information and why, and (iv) how the use of the information will deliver tangible outcomes for transparency and accountability.

$1 + 1 + 1 = \infty$

ICT-driven initiatives play an increasing role in good governance. In Asia (as elsewhere), development agencies can work with civil society to fight corruption with ICT interventions for online right-to-information requests, crowdsourced reporting, online corruption reporting, and issue reporting across a broad spectrum of outreach activities that foster institutional environments, promote cooperation, encourage a broad mobilization, and develop capacities. Of course, the functionality, accessibility, and usability of the ICT in the prevailing context of technological literacy lie at the heart of all this.

> *If the misery of our poor be caused not by the laws of nature, but by our institutions, great is our sin.*
>
> —Charles Darwin

References

ADB (2008) Technical assistance for support for implementation of the second governance and anticorruption action plan. Manila

ADB (2011) Asia 2050: realizing the Asian century. Manila

ADB (2013) Empowerment and public services delivery in developing Asia and the Pacific. Manila

---

[17]Political economy analysis investigates the interaction of politics and economics: this entails comprehending (i) the power and authority of groups in society, counting the interests they hold and the incentives that drive them, in conducing particular outcomes; (ii) the role that formal and informal institutions play in allocating scarce resources; and (iii) the influence that values and ideas —including culture, ideologies, and religion—have on shaping relations and interaction.

Japan Times (6 January 2014) Rising tides and drowning citizens
Organisation for economic co-operation and development (2003) Fighting corruption: what role for civil society? The Experience of the OECD, Paris

Further Reading

Davies T, Fumega S (2013) Mixed incentives: adopting ICT innovation in the fight against corruption. Practical Participation. Draft working paper for U4 Anti-Corruption Resource Centre
Grönlund Å (2010) Using ICT to Combat Corruption. In: Grönlund Å et al. Increasing transparency and fighting corruption through ICT: empowering people and communities. SPIDER ICT4D Series No. 3

Part IV
Knowledge Sharing and Learning

Proposition 87
Conducting Peer Assists

In a Word Peer assists are events that bring individuals together to share their experiences, insights, and knowledge on an identified challenge or problem. They also promote collective learning and develop networks among those invited.

Rationale

The experience that an organization has gained is its most important asset. Exit interviews are a way of capturing knowledge from leavers, but can only be relied upon once. Peer assists capture knowledge before employees leave, and in such ways that can repeatedly apply and strengthen good practice as well as consistency across an organization.

Definition

The formal use of peer assists as a management tool was pioneered by British Petroleum to help staff learn from the experiences of others before they embark on an activity or project. Put simply, a peer assist is the process whereby a team working on an activity or project calls a meeting or workshop to seek knowledge

© Asian Development Bank 2017
O. Serrat, *Knowledge Solutions*, DOI 10.1007/978-981-10-0983-9_87

Table 87.1 How does a peer assist differ from a peer review?

	Peer review	Peer assist
Goal	To judge the work of others	To transfer knowledge to others
Purpose	The purpose of a peer review is evaluative	The purpose of a peer assist is collaborative
Task	The core task of a peer review is to critique the activity or project	The core task of a peer assist is to learn with and through the team that calls the assist
Participants	Peer reviewers are selected by others	The team that calls the peer assist selects the assisters, i.e., those whom they think could be of help to them
Nature	Peer reviews can be a "dog-and-pony" show aimed at receiving a good evaluation	A peer assist is a problem-solving, working session
Roles	Some people are always peer reviewers. Others are always receivers	The role of participants to a peer assist is reciprocal. Members of the team calling the assist may themselves assist others
Reporting	The peer review report is sent to management	The peer assist report is sent only to the team requesting the peer assist

Source Author

and insights from a good mix of people in other teams. From the onset, the distinction between a peer assist and a peer review should be made explicit: without it, participants will fall into the familiar patterns of peer reviews and little knowledge will be transferred. Table 87.1 explains the principal differences between the two.

Benefits

Peer assists are part of the process of "learning before doing". They are about gathering knowledge from knowledge brokers before embarking on an activity or project, or when facing a difficulty in the course of related events. The benefits of peer assists are quickly realized: learning is focused directly on a specific issue and can therefore be applied immediately. A peer assist allows the team involved to gain input and insightsfrom people outside the team, and to identify possible new lines of enquiry or approach—in short, reusing existing knowledge and experience rather than having to reinvent the wheel. Peer assists also have wider benefits: they promote sharing of learning between teams, and help develop strong networks among people. They are relatively simple and inexpensive to organize: they do not require special resources or new, unfamiliar processes. It is worth using a peer assist when a team is facing a challenge, where the knowledge of others will really help, and when the potential benefits outweigh the costs of travel.

Process

There is no single way to hold a peer assist. Box outlines the method that has worked for British Petroleum. Table 87.2 shows what a meeting agenda for a peer assist might look like.

Box: Fundamentals of Peer Assists

Clarify the Purpose of the Peer Assist Peer assists work well when their purpose is clear and you communicate that purpose to participants. Define the specific problem you are seeking help with, and be sure that your aim in calling a peer assist is to learn something (rather than seeking endorsement for a decision you have already made).

Has the Problem Already Been Solved? Do some research to find out who else has already solved or tackled a similar problem. Also, share your peer assist plans with others, as there may be other teams who are currently tackling a similar problem who could also benefit from participating in the peer assist.

Enlist the Help of a Facilitator You will need a facilitator from outside the team to make sure participants to the meeting reach the desired outcome. The facilitator also may or may not record the event: be sure to agree on that before the meeting.

Pay Attention to Timing Ensure that you plan a date for the peer assist that is early enough in your project to make use of the input you receive and to do something different on the basis of what you have learned. A frequent mistake is to hold the meeting too close to the decision date to make a real impact. Consider that you might get a different response to the one you expect: will you have time to do anything about it? The length of a peer assist depends on the complexity of the problem and tends to be somewhere between half a day and two days.

Select the Participants Once you are clear on your purpose, select participants who have the diversity of knowledge, skills, and experiences needed for the peer assist. Four to five people are a good number.[1] Look "across" the organization rather than "up" it—hierarchies can hamper the free exchange of knowledge whereas peers tend to be much more open with each other and can challenge without feeling threatened. Avoid the temptation to select "the usual suspects". If the same experts are selected for peer assists again and again, you may be limiting the number of fresh ideas and perspectives available to you. Similarly, seek to select people who will challenge your

---

[1]Having more than five participants makes it difficult to have an in-depth discussion.

ways of thinking and working and perhaps offer a different angle, rather than looking for people who will validate your current approach. You might consider inviting people from outside your organization. The major criteria is to invite participants who have knowledge of the type of situation being faced.

Be Clear about Deliverables Be clear about what you hope to achieve during the peer assist and then plan the time to achieve that. The deliverables should comprise options and insightsrather than providing an answer. It is up to the person or team who called the peer assist to then make the relevant decisions, based on what is learned. Provide the participants with any briefing materials in advance so that they have adequate time to prepare.

Allow Time for Socializing Allow time in your agenda for the teams to get to know one another; this might be a dinner the night before or time for coffee at the start of the day. It is important to build rapport so that the group can work openly together.

Describe the Purpose and Set the Ground Rules At the start of the meeting, ensure that everyone is clear about the purpose of the peer assist and their roles within it. The role of the host team is to listen in order to understand and learn. The role of the visiting team is to share knowledgeand experience to help resolve the challenge without adding to the workload. Agree that where there are areas of contention, you will focus on the activity or project rather than on the individual people involved.

Share Information and Context Divide the meeting time roughly into four equal parts. During the first quarter, the host team will present the context, history, and their future plans regarding the problem or challenge in question. Keep this part short and sharp—you only want to say enough to get the visiting team started in the right direction. Remember that the purpose of the peer assist is to learn rather than tell. When communicating the problem or challenge about which you are seeking input, be prepared for it to be redefined as part of the peer assist process. It may be that the problem you have identified is in fact the symptom of a further problem and the peer assist will help you identify the root cause.

Encourage the Participants to Ask Questions and Give Feedback In the second quarter, the participants consider what they have heard, and then begin by discussing what they have heard that has surprised them, and what they expected to hear but have not. The host team should take a back seat at this stage and simply listen; in some cases they may even opt to leave the room. The participants then consider what else they need to know to address the problem and where might they find that knowledge. It may be that they want to make some telephone calls and talk to some other people, or request some data or reports. Remember, they are not seeking to solve the problem but to offer some options and insightsbased on their own knowledge and experience.

Analyze What You Have Heard The third quarter of the meeting is for the visiting team to then analyze and reflect on what they have learned and to examine options. Again, the home team remains largely in the back seat; it might be appropriate to involve one or two of them, provided that they continue to listen and learn rather than closing off options or seeking to draw conclusions too early.

Present Feedback and Agree on Actions In the fourth and final quarter of the meeting, the visiting team presents their feedback to the host team and answers any questions. The presentation will be along the lines of "what we have learned, what options we see, and what has worked elsewhere". As with all feedback, this should start with the positive—what has been done well, and then what options there are to do things differently. When presenting what has worked elsewhere, participants should simply tell the story rather than prescribing "you should…" In closing, the person who called the peer assist should acknowledge the contribution of the visiting team, and also commit to when he or she will get back with an action list of what the team are going to do differently. Finally, invite the visiting team to reflect on what they have learned and what they will take away and apply. Learning is never one-way.

Source Author

Table 87.2 Meeting agenda for peer assists[a]

Item	Time allotted
1. The participants introduce themselves. The activity or project leader presents the context, history, and ideas regarding the activity or project at hand. He or she states the objective of the peer assist and enables possible redefinition of the session	
2. The participants consider the problem or challenge the activity or project team faces. They present or discuss what has been covered and whatever information was not included in the pre-documents[b]	
3. The peer assisters consider what the activity or project team might need to know to address the problem or challenge it faces	
4. The peer assisters are given time to reflect on what has been learned and to examine options[c]	
5. The peer assisters provide non-prescriptive recommendations to the activity or project team.[d] They respond to specific questions	

(continued)

Table 87.2 (continued)

Item	Time allotted
6. The activity or project team acknowledges the contributions of participants. It responds to the peer assisters, noting what it found particularly useful. It may commit to a timeline for delivery of an action list, emphasizing the different things that it will do as a result of the peer assist.[e] Follow-up interviews may be considered	

[a]Complex problems or challenges may require time for the peer assisters and the activity or project team to socialize outside of meeting times. The establishment of good rapports is fundamental to the learning process
[b]Participants should be given material in advance so that they may prepare for the peer assist
[c]This may require that the activity or project team leave the premises
[d]Participants share knowledge to help resolve the problem or challenge without adding to the workload
[e]This is not the time for decisions. The team will make these on a separate, team-held occasion
Source Author

Others

An important consideration is that of evidence-based practice. When conducting peer assists, staff will need to ensure that lessons learned are based on a combination of both on-the-job experience and evidence. They might wish to carry out an after-action review[2] following the peer assist to look at whether the process went according to plan, what was different and why, and what can one learn from that for the next time. While the peer assist process is designed to provide input for a specific purpose or project, they should consider who else might benefit from the lessons learned.

---

[2]After-action reviews are a tool pioneered by the United States army, now widely used in a range of organizations to capture lessons learned both during and after an activity or project.

Proposition 88
Conducting After-Action Reviews and Retrospects

In a Word Organizational learning calls for nonstop assessment of performance—its successes and failures. This makes sure that learning takes place and supports continuous improvement. After-action reviews and retrospects are a tool that facilitates assessments; they enable this by bringing together a team to discuss an activity or project openly and honestly.

Rationale

Exit interviews are a way to capture knowledge from leavers. Peer assists are about teams asking for help for the benefit of their members. They are about "learning before doing". But continuously assessing organizational performance to meet or exceed expectations requires also that one obtain feedback and understand what happened (or did not happen) during an activity or project, or soon after completion. After-action reviews are about "learning while doing:" they identify how to correct shortcomings and sustain accomplishments. Retrospects are about "learning after doing:" they capture the new knowledge acquired after the fact.[1] In both

---

[1]After-action reviews and retrospects are not audits. The latter are often evaluative or conducted for purposes of accountability. The former aim to turn knowledge into action, not make judgments.

© Asian Development Bank 2017

O. Serrat, *Knowledge Solutions*, DOI 10.1007/978-981-10-0983-9_88

instances, knowledge gleaned from and compiled by those closest to the review can be used to improve results and can be shared with others who are planning, developing, implementing, and evaluating similar efforts.

Definition

After-action reviews are a leadership and knowledge-sharing tool which bring together the team that is closest to the activity or project, when a critical milestone has been reached, to discuss successes and failures in an open and honest fashion. The purpose is to learn from the experience and take the lessons learned into the next phase of the activity or project, or to accomplish related tasks more effectively the next time a similar activity or project is conducted. After-action reviews and retrospects are linked conceptually. The difference lies in the degree of detail and the formality applied to the process of conducting them.

Benefits

When administered in a climate of openness, candid discussion, clarity, and commitment to identifying and recommending solutions, after-action reviews and retrospects yield many benefits. The participants in the review, e.g., managers, leaders, and those planning to pursue a similar activity or project in the future, will understand more clearly what was originally intended, what transpired and why, as well as what might be done better and how. The number of subsequent repeats of mistakes or missteps will decrease. Furthermore, reports from after-action reviews and retrospects that make concrete and actionable recommendations will increase the chances of success of similar activities or projects. Finally, the promotion of open and frequent communication and sharing and the institutionalization of regularly held meetings that examine strengths to sustain and shortcomings to remedy will also improve morale.

Process

The focus of an after-action review is to answer three broad questions: What did we set out to do? What worked well, and why? What might we do differently next time, and how? However, there are many ways to tackle these questions: the desired simplicity at the heart of after-action reviews and retrospects means that there is potential to experiment and find ways that will work best with the activity or project examined and the team involved in these. Be it for after-action reviews or retrospects, the process should be kept simple and easy to remember. To note, the questions posed for a retrospect follow the after-action review format but involve asking the following more detailed questions:

- What did you set out to achieve?
- What was your plan to achieve this?
- How did this change as you progressed?
- What went well and why?
- What could have gone better?
- What advice would you give yourself if you were to go back to where you were at the start of the activity or project?
- What were the two or three key lessons you would share with others?
- What's next for you in terms of this project?
- Can you think of a story that summarizes your experience of work on this activity or project?
- What should we have learned from this activity or project a year from now?
- Are there any lessons for you personally?

Others

After-action reviews and retrospects are not critique or complaint sessions. They are intended to maximize experience by allowing everyone to learn from each other. They are not a full-scale evaluation. And, they are not a cure for all problems. After-action reviews are successful when leaders support them, they are done immediately—by the team and for the team, and participants agree to be honest.

Proposition 89
Using Plain English

In a Word Many people write too much, bureaucratically, and obscurely. Using plain English will save time in writing, make writing far easier, and improve understanding.

Purpose

Reports are a visible part of work. They remain and are used long after it is done. Work is advanced by readable[1] reports that give the target audience a good chance of understanding the document at first reading, and in the sense that the writers meant them to be.

---

[1]Merriam-Webster's defines "readable" as pleasing, interesting, or offering no great difficulty to the reader.

© Asian Development Bank 2017
O. Serrat, *Knowledge Solutions*, DOI 10.1007/978-981-10-0983-9_89

What Is Plain English?

Plain English—or plain language—is a message written for the reader in a style that is clear and concise. It is quicker to write, faster to read, and puts messages across more often, more easily, and in friendlier ways. Using plain English, writers should

- Select simple words.
- Make lists.
- Keep sentences short.
- Refrain from giving unnecessary details.
- Cut down on jargon and use defined terms sparingly.
- Discard superfluous words.
- Reduce nominalizations.[2]
- Avoid weak verbs.
- Use the active voice with strong verbs.
- Be specific rather than general.
- Write personally, as if you were talking to the reader.

Knowing the Audience

Knowing the target audience is the most important step in assuring that a document is understandable. One can create a profile of individual target audiences based on the following questions:

- What are the demographics of the audience, e.g., age, education, and work experience?
- How familiar is the audience with technical terminology?
- What concepts can one safely assume the audience understands?
- How will the audience read the document for the first time? Will they read it straight through or will they skip to sections of particular interest? What data and information will they look for, and is it easy to find?
- How will the audience use the document?

Knowing the Information to Disclose

The following steps can be taken to ascertain that a document written in plain English is readable:

---

[2]A nominalization is a noun derived from a verb. It usually ends in -tion. To make writing more vigorous and less abstract, writers should find the noun and try to make it the main verb of the sentence. For example, "We made an application" becomes "We applied".

- Read and outline the current document.

  – Read the table of contents to see if there is an obvious logical flow to the argument.
  – Read the entire document without taking notes to gain a general understanding of the information presented.
  – Read the entire document a second time, taking notes on what information is covered and what questions the target audience might have. The notes will show if the information flows through the document in logical order.
  – As you read, consider the following: Will the audience understand the language? Does the document emphasize information of importance to the audience? Is any important information missing? Does the document include information that is not required and will not help the audience make informed decisions?

- Eliminate redundant information.

  – Question the need for repeating any information. Reading similar material more than once bores—perhaps even troubles—readers.
  – Readers skip over paragraphs they think they have read before.

- Discuss the executive summary.

  – An executive summary is an inviting entryway to a document. It should orient the reader, highlighting the most important points that are presented in detail in the document.
  – Many executive summaries seem as long as the document itself and all-too-often consist of paragraphs copied from the main text.

Applying the Rule of 15

A rule of thumb for preparing plain English reports is to use the "rule of 15":

- Not more than 15% of sentences should be longer than 15 words.
- Not more than 15% of sentences should be written in the passive voice.
- Not more than 15% of words should be longer than three syllables.

Editing the Document

When it is time to edit the document, it is best to work in the following order:

- Edit for overall structure.
- Edit for sequencing and logical flow within subsections.

- Edit for plain English.
- Edit for style conventions.
- Edit for typographical errors and punctuation.

Checking Microsoft Word's Readability Statistics

Microsoft Word allows users to check how difficult text is to read. Aim for

- Flesch Reading Ease score > 50 (higher scores are easier to read).
- Flesch-Kincaid Grade Level score < 12 (lower scores are easier to read).

Using Readability Formulas and Style Checkers

Readability formulas establish how difficult a document is to read. Several websites offer free readability services online.[3] They include

- Gunning Fog Index
- Juicy Studio
- Online-Utility

Box: "Brevity"—Memo to the War Cabinet from Winston Churchill, 9 August 1940

To do our work, we all have to read a mass of papers. Nearly all of them are far too long. This wastes time, while energy has to be spent in looking for the essential points.

I ask my colleagues and their staff to see to it that their reports are shorter. The aim should be reports which set out the main points in a series of short, crisp paragraphs.

If a report relies on detailed analysis of some complicated factors, or on statistics, these should be set out in an appendix.

Often the occasion is best met by submitting not a full-dress report, but an aide-memoire consisting of headings only, which can be expanded orally if needed.

---

[3]Caution: no formula examines the content of the document being evaluated, and none can tell if the information is being conveyed clearly. Most formulas only count the numbers of syllables and words in a sentence and the number of sentences in the sample document.

Let us have an end of such phrases as these:

"It is also of importance to bear in mind the following considerations," or "consideration should be given to the possibility of carrying into effect". Most of these woolly phrases are mere padding, which can be left out altogether, or replaced by a single word. Let us not shrink from using the short expressive phrase, even if it is conversational.

Reports drawn up on the lines I propose may first seem rough as compared with the flat surface of "officialese" jargon. But the saving in time will be great, while the discipline of setting out the real points concisely will prove an aid to clearer thinking.

Source The National Archives. 2016.

Further Reading

ADB (2002) Handbook on correspondence and writing. Manila
ADB (2011) Handbook of style and usage. Manila

Proposition 90
Posting Research Online

In a Word Dissemination is an indispensable means of maximizing the impact of research. It is an intrinsic element of all good research practice that promotes the profile of research institutions and strengthens their capacities. The challenge is to ensure the physical availability of research material and to make it intelligible to those who access it.

Yesterday's Town Square of Tomorrow Today

Knowledge and information often stay where they are generated. For that reason, the performance of research institutions hangs on the ability to disseminate research findings to different audiences.[1] For each research agenda, this calls for a dissemination policy, a dissemination plan, a dissemination strategy, and dissemination tactics.

Over the past 10 years, the world has witnessed the amazingly rapid development of the Internet as a worldwide communications network linking millions of

---

[1]Dissemination is the process of sharing knowledge and information. The challenge is to improve accessibility to audiences. This means making research findings physically accessible in comprehensible ways to as many audiences as possible.

© Asian Development Bank 2017
O. Serrat, *Knowledge Solutions*, DOI 10.1007/978-981-10-0983-9_90

computers. Not surprisingly, the internet is now the primary means of disseminating research findings, such as through digital libraries containing electronic journals, electronic print archives, and conference proceedings. It is now possible for all researchers to use the Internet to promote research online so that it may be invoked by peers, educators, students, journalists, customers for research expertise, and the general public. Research institutions ignore the Internet at their peril.

Posting Research Online

There are powerful arguments for using the Internet to disseminate research findings:

- **Outlay** Posting is almost free of charge. The main cost is associated with compiling, designing, and producing material. Once material is online, hundreds, thousands, or even hundreds of thousands of people can access it at no additional cost to the supplier.
- **Speed and Flexibility** The Internet is very fast compared to most print media. It also enables hypertext-specific and interactive actions, such as linking to full journals or conference papers from publication lists or summaries (if copyright permits it). Posting takes minutes, unlike printing, and helps material to be opportune and fresh. (Furthermore, updating material does not require a new print run.)
- **Synergies** Posting enhances and sponsors other dissemination methods by allowing people to see the quality of work. Making material available online means that audiences are more likely to buy, subscribe to, or request other products.
- **Audiences** The internet exposes work to new audiences. Although not everyone has access to it, more people will be able to find and access materials if they are available online as well as in print.
- **Monitoring and Evaluation** Internet publication facilitates online impact assessment.[2]
- **Fund-raising** The investors that fund research know that the Internet links research to practice. Increasingly, Internet publication is a requirement of research funding. Dissemination raises the profile of an organization and builds its capacity. Investors are more likely to be attracted to research institutions that are demonstrably committed to disseminating research findings to many end users.
- **Others** The Internet limits the need for gatekeepers, offers greater control over intellectual property, and eliminates the constraints posed by lack of space.

---

[2]Conversely, it also draws broad-based feedback on the quality of work, which is an intrinsic element of all good research practice.

Communicating Online

Successful online communication means actively encouraging end users to read and absorb material. Simple operating principles can be drawn from an understanding of how people use the web:

- **Reading Online** How do people behave online? End users are impatient. They are typically short of time and may be paying for the connection. They want immediate gratification. They want to see the value of a page instantly. They are also active, not passive. They have the power to move from page to page and they want to exercise it. Research shows too that reading from a computer screen is tiring and takes about 25% longer than reading from paper. Therefore, end users are less willing to invest time and they make on-the-spot judgments about the value of the knowledge and information presented. Further, about 80% of end users do not actually read but scan for knowledge and information. They will not scroll down a page if they are not convinced upfront that it contains useful data. And they do not like self-serving publicity. The implication for Internet publication is simple: the challenge for disseminating the full content of research findings online is to convince end users to print the documents in which they are found.
- **Disseminating Successfully Online** Building on this understanding of how people use the web, the operating principles are that websites must be scannable (because end users do not read),[3] concise (because end users do not scroll),[4] and objective (because end users do not like self-serving publicity).[5]

Posting Research in a Web-Friendly Way

Paradoxically, however, researchers are probably most averse to posting research online. The Internet is a relatively new method of disseminating research findings that can upset long-standing conventions within research institutions. Despite persuasive, common-sense arguments to the contrary, some researchers are still not convinced of its usefulness. Others fret that their work will be pirated or that they

---

[3]This means using headings, breaking text into short sections, marking key knowledge and information-carrying words in bold, limiting each paragraph to one idea and stating what that is in the first sentence, using bullets and numbered lists, and splitting long text into multiple pages according to subject.

[4]This entails keeping to the subject; giving background information with hyperlinks to other pages; eschewing repetition, adjectives, and metaphors; using simple sentence structures; and writing in the active, not the passive.

[5]This requires composing for the audience, reining in superlatives and vague statements, presenting nothing as fact without providing evidence, avoiding exaggerations or self-congratulations, curbing promotional talk, and giving facts and letting end users decide what is relevant.

will lose their status. To make matters worse, research writing is inherently not web-friendly.[6] All the more cause, then, to make a special effort:

- **Assisting End Users to Find Research** Researchers can help end users find research findings without difficulty if they display prominent links to the materials in the website; advertise examples of latest research with short, informative descriptions; make the work discernible to search engines with compelling page and section headings, page descriptions, and meta tags;[7] and advise audiences, notably by electronic mail but also through other various marketing techniques, that research findings are available on the website.
- **Organizing Links to Documents** Researchers must think outside the box. What is the perspective of outsiders who know little about a research institution? A helpful logic is to categorize materials by type, e.g., working paper, discussion paper, et cetera; year of publication; and research theme. This logic must then be made obvious to end users by providing a menu at the top of the page enabling direct access to the section of interest. It is also helpful to make explicit that a document is downloadable or not. A customized search engine should be built if numerous documents are hosted on the website.
- **Selecting a Digital Format** Documents featured on the website must be in a format that will enable end users to both open and print them. Documents should not be split or zipped.

Building on Commitment

Successful websites are not constructed in a corporate vacuum. They have a reason for being and a mission statement. They light the way and make navigation easy. They have ever-changing, targeted, and credible content. They load very quickly. They are consistent in look, feel, and design. They are interactive. They are marketed. They are measured. They understand search engines. They are built for growth and look to the future.

---

[6]The full-text version of research findings appears on a computer screen as a mass of text. Research papers are also commonly written in what is known as the pyramid style: starting with a foundation and gradually building to a conclusion. And the need to convey depth of knowledge and information is such that research writing can be wordy. And so research papers are not scannable or concise, nor do they satisfy the desire that most web users have for immediate gratification. In contrast, the Internet has its own writing style, which serves to convey knowledge and information directly. It is akin to the journalistic style, which inverts the pyramid: starting with a conclusion, laying out essential information, and developing the background.

[7]Meta tags are used to store information that is normally relevant to search engines. An example is a tag instructing the browser to load a specific address of documents after a number of seconds.

Proposition 91
Storytelling

In a Word Storytelling is the use of stories or narratives as a communication tool to value, share, and capitalize on the knowledge of individuals.

Definition

Storytelling is the vivid description of ideas, beliefs, personal experiences, and life-lessons through stories or narratives that evoke powerful emotions and insights.

Advantages

Storytelling has advantages over the communication techniques commonly used in organizations, be they electronic mail, reports, or formal speeches. First, it enables articulation of emotional aspects as well as factual content, allowing expression of tacit knowledge (that is always difficult to convey). Second, by providing the broader context in which knowledge arises, it increases the potential for meaningful knowledge-sharing. Third, by grounding facts in a narrative structure, it augments the likelihood that learning will take place and be passed on. Purposeful storytelling

© Asian Development Bank 2017
O. Serrat, *Knowledge Solutions*, DOI 10.1007/978-981-10-0983-9_91

can deliver results that conventional, abstract modes of communications such as those mentioned earlier cannot. Anyone can use it and become better at using it to reach many rapidly.

Communicating Naturally

The age-old practice of storytelling is one of the most effective tools that people can use. Storytellers communicate naturally: analysis might excite the mind but it does not offer an easy route to the heart, which is where one must go to motivate people. Working with stories is one of the best ways to

- Communicate complex messages simply
- Help connect people and ideas
- Create sense, coherence, and meaning
- Operate effectively in networks
- Develop valuable descriptions of situations in which knowledge is applied and solutions are found
- Examine organizational values and culture
- Give breathing space and allow different perspectives to emerge
- Inspire imagination and motivate action
- Drive change

Table. Storytelling template for use in workshops

The Title of the Story: **The Name of the Storyteller**: **The Name of the Listener**:	
Place: The precise location where the action occurred	
Context: The scene in time (year) and space (country)	
Characters: The actors, their attributes, and roles in the story	
Challenge: The problem or task that triggered the action	
Action: The sequence of events before, during, and after the turning point	
The Turning Point: The moment the change happened	
Conclusion: The ending including the moral, lesson learned, or message	
Mementos: Mnemonics to help partners re-tell the story	

Source Author

Applications

Storytelling is used to identify and exchange learning episodes, explore values, and inspire people toward the possibility of change, enrich quantitative information with qualitative evidence, make out connections and create common purpose, and improve the effectiveness of strategic decisions.

Potential applications of stories include

- Oral histories
- Team or community-building exercises
- Workshop warm-ups
- Back-to-office reports
- Activity or project reviews
- Monitoring and evaluation systems
- Recreation

Elements of a Good Story

Good stories are generally interesting, unusual, provocative, serious, controversial, surprising, intriguing, or inspiring. They

- Respond to demand.
- Exploit a specific opportunity.
- Include personal and human elements of experience.
- Present the point of view of someone who has been directly involved.
- Use a variety of narrative patterns for different aims.
- Achieve a balance between words from persons and statements from organizations.
- Recount a successful intervention.
- Describe an unsuccessful intervention.
- Provide a solution to both immediate and broader problems.
- Play to what is already in people's minds.
- Target people with the authority to make decisions and change things.

Caveats

Storytelling is not suitable for every situation and there may be instances when they are not the right choice. That is when the audience does not want one, when analysis would be better, when the story is not ready, or when a story would be deceptive. In some working contexts, they will also need patience and management backing for a long time.

Proposition 92
Identifying and Sharing Good Practices

In a Word Good practice is a process or methodology that has been shown to be effective in one part of the organization and might be effective in another too.

Rationale

Most organizations know that learning from the past increases the chances of success in the future—finding ways to do so can also link staff with the resources they need to complete tasks faster, better, and more cheaply. Frequently, this is done by means of instruction manuals or "how-to" guides—which typically provide information or advice on a particular topic, or with taxonomies—which are a common way to organize content logically. Leading organizations maximize opportunities across all core knowledge activities to identify, create, store, share, and use better.

A good practice is defined as anything that has been tried and shown to work in some way—whether fully or in part but with at least some evidence of effectiveness—and that may have implications for practice at any level elsewhere. Three possible levels of good practice flow from this: promising practices, demonstrated practices, and replicated practices.[1] Since knowledge is both explicit and tacit, good

---

[1]Some prefer to use the term "best practice" but it is debatable whether there is a single "best" approach and approaches are constantly evolving and being updated.

O. Serrat, *Knowledge Solutions*, DOI 10.1007/978-981-10-0983-9_92

practice programs should comprise two elements: good practices databases that connect people with information, and collaboration or knowledge sharing and learning mechanisms, such as communities of practice or peer assists that connect people with people.

Benefits

The benefits from identifying and sharing good practice are that doing so will

- Identify and replace poor practices
- Raise the performance of poor performers closer to that of the best
- Decrease the learning curve of new employees
- Reduce rework and prevent "reinvention of the wheel"
- Cut costs through better productivity and efficiency
- Improve services
- Minimize organizational knowledge loss (both tacit and explicit)

Needless to say, good practice programs give the highest returns where business processes are already quite developed and where knowledge and experience has already accumulated. They will also be useful where several units perform similar tasks but are dispersed and cannot easily learn from one another through day-to-day contact.

Process

Skyrme Associates (2002) suggest a six-step approach to identifying and sharing good practice:

- **Identify Users' Requirements** Although this step seems obvious it is not uncommon to start by designing a database. This is a case of putting the cart before the horse. One should start by considering where one can really add value, looking at what areas of the organization need attention. Who will benefit most from better knowledge and understanding of good practices? How will they access and use these?
- **Discover Good Practices** There are several ways to identify good practices. One is to examine individuals and groups that deliver excellent results and are therefore likely to be using good practices. Having discovered these, one will then need to discern what parts of their overall approach or methodology represent good practice. This is likely to be done best by people knowledge of the relevant practice. But other approaches exist too: they include communities of practice, after-action reviews and retrospects, and exit interviews. Also, much

can be learned from the practices of other organizations in the same field, or even from organizations in others.

- **Document Good Practices** Good practice descriptions are commonly kept in a database in standard format. A typical template might include the following:

  - **Title** A short descriptive title that can be accompanied by a short abstract.
  - **Profile** Several short sections outlining processes, function, author, keywords, etc.
  - **Context** Where is this applicable? What problems does it solve?
  - **Resources** What resources and skills are needed to carry out the good practice?
  - **Description** What are the processes and steps involved? Are performance measures associated with the good practice?
  - **Lessons Learned** What proves difficult? What would the originators of the practice do differently if they were to do it again?
  - **Links to Resources** Expert contact details, workbooks, video clips, articles, transcripts of review meetings, etc.
  - **Tools and Techniques** A description of the approach and methodology used in developing the good practice.

- **Validate Good Practices** A practice is only good if there is a demonstrable link between what is practiced and the end result. Still, in most cases judgment is needed as to what constitutes good practice. A frequent approach is to have a panel of peer reviewers evaluate a potential good practice. It is better to seek input and feedback from clients too.

- **Disseminate and Apply** Databases of good practices are a useful starting point but most organizations find it necessary to complement these with face-to-face knowledge sharing. This is where true value is added for the process can also generate two-way benefits. Mechanisms include communities of practice, quality circles, visits to individuals and groups displaying high performance, organized learning events, secondments, and exchanges.

- **Develop a Supporting Infrastructure** To successfully implement a good practice program, you need to ensure you have the required infrastructure in place. This infrastructure is often developed as part of a wider knowledge management strategy. Typically, several generic aspects need attention. The people to facilitate and drive the process through its initial stages, until it becomes embedded in the organization's ways of working, e.g., a good practice team or a network of good practice coordinators. The technical infrastructure for document sharing and databases. The content management infrastructure to ensure that good practices are documented and classified electronically in a way that makes them easy to find.

Caution

Here are a few Do's and Don'ts to identifying and sharing good practice

- Good practices are not a quick-fix solution and setting up the required processes and infrastructure can be resource intensive.
- Good practice evolves constantly.
- Do not underestimate the importance of organizational culture.
- Resist the temptation to focus on explicit knowledge: it is through people that deep knowledge is transferred.
- Do not be too prescriptive about good practices and focus instead on encouraging people to identify and share them voluntarily.
- Tie good practices to business drivers, focus on those that add value, demonstrate benefits, and give evidence.
- Recognize the individuals and groups who submit good practices.
- Promote the good practice resource actively.
- Monitor usage of the good practice resource.
- Make contact to the provider of the good practice easy.

Reference

David Skyrme Associates (2002) Best practices in best practices

Proposition 93
Conducting Successful Retreats

by Peter Malvicini and Olivier Serrat

In a Word A retreat is a meeting designed and organized to facilitate the ability of a group to step back from day-to-day activities for a period of concentrated discussion, dialogue, and strategic thinking about their organization's future or specific issues. Organizations will reap full benefits if they follow basic rules.

Rationale

People look forward to retreats (or workshops) with excitement or dread. At best, it is a time for renewal, team building, and focusing work. At worst, it is a dull 2 days of lectures or extended meetings. A good retreat works in three dimensions—the practical, the ideal, and the political—ignore any one and you are headed for trouble.

Applications

There are as many reasons for conducting a retreat as there are issues and challenges facing an organization. Among the most common uses of retreats are

© Asian Development Bank 2017
O. Serrat, *Knowledge Solutions*, DOI 10.1007/978-981-10-0983-9_93

- Helping set or change strategic direction.
- Fostering a collective vision.
- Creating a common framework and point of reference.
- Developing annual goals, objectives, and budgets.
- Discussing specific issues or challenges facing the organization.
- Dealing with sources of conflict and confusion.
- Generating creative solutions for entrenched problems.
- Improving working relationships and increasing trust.
- Encouraging honest and enlightened conversations.
- Letting people be heard on issues that are important to them.
- Orienting new staff.

Tips for Effective Retreats

Here is a dozen tips to make retreats more effective:

- **Start at the End** Know what you want from your retreat, "your intended outcomes," and how you will follow up the event. Work with a Strategic planning group in your unit and be clear about these outcomes from the beginning. Be careful not to define predetermined results: instead choose a focus to guide your work: "a plan to implement x," "a new strategy for y," "actions to strengthen workflows and business processes," etc.
- **Get Away** Allow some physical or psychological distance from the office and see what happens. If you are on-site, distractions can undermine work and preserve the formality one is trying to break down.[1] Crossing the street is better than going nowhere. If working for a couple of days try something further afield —the cost is small compared with the gain from the energy and continuity you create. The intensive effort and concentrated time staff can give to an effort normally pays off. The work and fun had in two 10h days off-site gains more than two six hour days on-site and much more than weekly committee meetings for a year.
- **Suspend the Rules** The workplace carries sets of unspoken rules and implied norms of behavior, especially when dealing with people of different position and status within the hierarchy. At least during your retreat, remove these boundaries and create broad ownership of the task as a team. During introductions make this clear. Rein in any dominant senior personnel and let participants see how

---

[1]The reasons for this are straightforward: (i) retreats require long periods of intense, uninterrupted discussion; (ii) participants are less likely to be interrupted by phone calls and other staff if they are away from the office; (iii) participants can better focus on the topics under discussion; (iv) participants are more like to stay for the entire time; and (v) being "away on retreat" creates an atmosphere that is more conducive to teamwork, creative thinking, and consensus building.

important it is that all have a voice. And please leave formal business dress behind.

- **Work as a Team** Retreats are special. So do not organize them like a two-day staff meeting or a symposium. If participants are passive, they will lose interest even in the most captivating speakers. Information sharing is more effective by print through a briefing pack for the event. Short briefings are useful as background for an activity, but spend most of your time in deliberation, preferably in smaller groups, and large group discussion of those ideas.

- **Discuss the "Undiscussable"** All units have concerns not normally put on the table (but everyone is aware of them)—typically these issues are a barrier to productive work. A retreat can be a time to work on these areas positively and productively. Discussions in smaller groups can help staff vent any frustrations and then return to the larger group with practical solutions. Do not miss a chance to do important work and break through a serious bottleneck to effectiveness.

- **Keep it Real** Do real work. As much as possible, avoid simulations, abstract discussions, and lectures from experts. Real tasks energize participants, combined with challenging matters that concern them most, and a process that lets them question, deliberate, and refine their ideas and actions. "Experts" can be useful as resource persons to serve the task, but many find the combined expertise of their staff to be more than adequate for the job.

- **Do Not Play Games (Just Have Fun)** By design, a retreat is less formal than the workplace. That informality is one way of engaging people and creating a safe environment. Game-playing may send mixed signals, especially when the organization's culture views them as silly. Creative ways of working with small groups or teams and creative ways of presenting ongoing work will allow the humor of participants to break through spontaneously—this can be useful especially when dealing with difficult topics and concerns. This is also an effective way of indirect teambuilding.

- **Mix it Up** Variety will hold the interest of participants. Try different size discussion groups, different small group processes, and different ways of sharing group outputs. Avoid organizing things the same way you would back at the workplace. People learn and plan differently—create opportunities for all participants.

- **Think Big** By stepping away from work routine, participants have a chance to rediscover the meaning and motivation for their daily work. Whenever possible, allow all staff to envision the future of the organization—they can build a shared understanding, and this is powerful. Staff then move swiftly from a "bird's eye view" of desired outcomes and goals, translating them into concrete results.

- **Think Small** Staff and management want concrete results. Discussing the "nuts and bolts" of implementation means the difference between real follow-up and good intentions. There will not be time to consider all details. But, draft basic timetables and share responsibility for follow-up tasks before you leave the retreat.

- **Just Do It** Deliberation is great. Deliberative action is better. The climax of a good retreat should be decisions for new action. A poorly planned retreat will not leave enough time for this and the lack of follow-up will be obvious.
- **Get Professional Help** Planning your retreat need not drive you insane. Most organizations can benefit from using a facilitator with expertise in group dynamics, group processes, team building, decision making, and consensus building. He or she will help plan the retreat, develop the agenda, and set realistic goals and expectations. During the retreat the facilitator will manage or facilitate group discussions.[2] The facilitator should have no particular stake or interest in the issues being discussed. His or her sole interest should be in helping the group have a successful retreat. During the retreat, the facilitator will also function as a recorder for the group by capturing the key points on a flip chart or on computer. After the retreat, the facilitator will generally provide the group with a written report summarizing the discussions, any decisions that were made, and action steps to be taken. If no professional facilitators is available, consider training members of your unit or borrow (or swap) experienced facilitators from other units.

Table. Retreat planning checklist

Purpose	*Location*
• What is the purpose of the retreat? • What criteria will we use to determine that the retreat was successful? • Who supports the idea of holding a retreat? • Who is opposed to the idea? • Who needs to attend the retreat? • Who will participate? • Will all the key participants be able to attend? • How much time will they be willing to spend at the retreat?	• Where will the retreat be held? • Are the rules governing the use of the space acceptable? • Can the room be arranged as we want it? • Are the chairs comfortable? • Is there good control over lighting and air conditioning? • Can we have food, snacks, and refreshments in the room? • Who will provide food, snacks, and refreshments? • Can we hang flip chart paper on the walls? • How will breaks and meals be handled? • Will overnight accommodation be needed?
Equipment	*Facilitator*
• What equipment will be needed? • Who will provide it? • Who will operate it?	• Do we need an outside facilitator? • Who will facilitate? • How much experience does the facilitator have with groups like ours?
Recording and reporting	
• Do we want to record the meeting? • What kind of a retreat report do we need?	

Source Author

---

[2]This will involve tracking three levels of activity—the substance of the work, the process, and the relationships (psychosocial environment).

Reasons Not to Hold a Retreat

Retreats will not help if the organizer has no intention (or ability) to follow through
or act on the suggestions of participants or if the intention is to

- Fulfill a covert agenda.
- Make an individual's problem the group's problem.
- Talk at participants instead of with them.
- Improve morale.
- Treat the retreat as a reward.

Proposition 94
Conducting Effective Presentations

by Peter Malvicini and Albert Dean Atkinson

In a Word Simple planning and a little discipline can turn an ordinary presentation into a lively and engaging event.

From interviews and our own observations, this scenario is too common: the speaker at a seminar shares about thirty slides, skipping over many. Time goes on … and on. Some participants lose interest; others are distracted. Some even slip out. Finally, the sponsor says, "Time has run out, but maybe we can have one or two questions." It looked as though the speaker had just reached the heart of the matter and it was over. What happened?

In most organizations, staff are busy and they vote with their feet. If they are bored or not actively engaged, many find excuses to leave the room. Some never return to seminars sponsored by the same staff member. The good news is that guidelines for effective seminars and brown bags are simple and do not depend on the speaking ability of the person sharing the message.

© Asian Development Bank 2017
O. Serrat, *Knowledge Solutions*, DOI 10.1007/978-981-10-0983-9_94

Not, "How Should I Talk?" but "How Do They Learn?"

Most speakers ask the wrong questions. Their efforts are dedicated to the substantive preparation of content ("What should I say?") while paying too little attention to the most important questions: "Who are my audience, and *how will they learn best?*" Years of research on adult learning tell us *adults learn best when*:

- The learning purpose and boundaries are clear. The invitation, welcome, and introduction of the topic all orient participants to why they are there and what to expect.
- They first establish common ground by sharing experiences or perspectives. People need to connect to the topic right away. Participants should relate the content meaningfully to prior knowledge or experience Knowledge sharing and learning.
- Ideas can be shared freely in open environments. Setting an informal collegial tone helps establish trust.
- Ideas are heard before they are critiqued. Encourage participants to listen to what people have to say and not jump to conclusions—this is essential for innovation to take root.
- They question assumptions driving their behavior and consider alternatives. Does the presentation challenge existing practice or frameworks?
- The learning is based on experience, the person's own, a simulation, or a real "case". Statistics can be powerful, but participants will also want to know what the reality looks like, what the implications are in a country or project.
- They engage actively, rather than receive information passively. Questions, discussion, and analysis all draw people into content.
- Working with a variety of methods (and senses)—different from typical daily routines. Be creative and do not be afraid to involve participants.
- The focus is future oriented—on actions for the future, instead of problem-solving.[1] This creates anticipation as people begin to consider the implications for changes in practice.
- Topics apply directly to their professional work and participants decide next steps to follow up learning before they leave the room.

---

[1]There is nothing wrong with *problem-solving*, but it often traps energy. A strategic approach only addresses problems as they are barriers to critical action. According to psychologist Carl Jung—problems tend to resolve or "fall off the radar" naturally: "All the greatest and most important problems of life are fundamentally insoluble ... They can never be solved, but only outgrown. This 'outgrowth' proved on further investigation to require a new level of consciousness. Some higher or wider interest appeared on the patient's horizon, and through this broadening of his or her outlook the insoluble problem lost its urgency. It was not solved logically in its own terms but faded when confronted with a new and stronger life urge."

Full Disclosure

Let staff know what the seminar is about and who will be sharing. The opportunities include:

- A visitor from a partner agency sharing experience.
- The release of a study, report, or evaluation.
- A case study of a particular project.
- A new technology, tool, or concept.
- A perspective or inspirational talk from a leader or respected expert.

If the seminar is given primarily by a consultant marketing a tool or expertise the announcement will need to make that clear (or participants will feel that they were invited under false pretenses).

Share Expectations

Without being condescending, ask the speaker what his or her approach will be and whether you can see their slides. A complex game plan or an unrealistic number of slides are good warning signs. Share these *Knowledge Solutions* with them in advance as another way to encourage good preparation.

Agree on a Length of Time in Advance

If the event is a 1h seminar, the time will pass quickly. One approach is to take (i) 20 min for a formal presentation; (ii) move to a question and answer session and, if time permits; (iii) a constructive group discussion. Better still, if possible, integrate brief questions after slides or sections of the presentation instead of saving them all for last.

Twenty-Minute Attention Span

Even if your speaker is spellbinding, research shows most people lose interest after 20 min. If you must share longer, break it up with questions and answers or open discussion. Also, try "saving some of your thunder" in the form of an extra slide or couple stories to answer questions. Better to leave the group wanting more, than wishing you had given less.

Tell Your Story

Illustrations and anecdotes are key to making points effectively and relating to the participants.

Takeaways

Supplement the presentation with a brief handout (not merely a copy of the slides)—takeaways add value and catalyze follow through.

Discussion Questions

Ask your speaker to craft several discussion questions in advance. Questions drawing experience work best first, then analytic questions, and then a question on applying ideas. Sample: (i) What is *your* experience in this area?; (ii) Why do you think it worked that way?; and (iii) What can be done differently in the future?

Organizing a Presentation

In the introduction to the movie, *The Prestige,* the magician explains there are three parts to every illusion. The first part is the *pledge* where the audience is told what they will see, capturing their attention. The second is the *turn* where the trick is done. Third, in the *prestige*, the magician restores what he disappeared—it is a moment of awe and appreciation, "ta da". Though not magic, research in communication and adult learning shows even a brief presentation should follow a similar rhythm. For this we can use *hook-look-took*:

- **Hook** The very start of any presentation should answer the participants' question, "What's in it for me?" This effectively draws people in, helping them quickly relate the topic to their experience (past, present, or future). You establish relevance. An effective hook can be a question or a brief story. Do not wait until the end of a presentation to show the relevance of the message. Even before the presentation begins, have your presentation's title page displayed on the screen as participants are seated. This allows participants to focus and prepare themselves for the topic. Better yet, if you have a pre-presentation show that automatically loops slides relevant to the topic you will present, this can provide informative background information wisely using their time while they wait for the presentation to begin.

- **Look** This is the heart of the presentation, where the concepts and experiences are explained, illustrated, and examined. A seminar is different from a workshop—the presenter must be selective and synthetic. In many cases, introducing a topic and piquing participant interest is all you can reasonably expected in the timeframe. Here is where a few well-placed illustrations or stories can pull together a presentation nicely.
- **Took** Most speakers would like participants to apply or use what they learn in their professional work. Ask, "Should participants do anything with knowledge gained from the seminar?" If the answer is yes, *they are unlikely to do anything they do not begin to discuss at the seminar*. Application is not automatic—even the best seminars are quickly forgotten. If there is a specific opportunity to follow up or take a next step, try to "close the deal" at the seminar.

Death by Slide is slow and painful, but avoidable. The Rule of 7 (or 777) recommends

- *A Maximum 7 lines of text on any slide*. On a slide, less really is more—more impact and more focus.
- *A Maximum of 7 words on any one line*. Otherwise the text will be crammed and too small to read.
- *A Maximum of 7 slides in a 20-min talk* (not counting "Title" and "Thank You" slides).

Other Slide Maxims

- *Please don't read your slides*—most participants can read well. Paraphrasing the content works, as does illustrating it.
- *Fonts help (or hurt)*. Sans-serif fonts (such as Arial) are best used for titles, while serif fonts (such as Times New Roman) make text of the main body easier to read.[2]
- *Dizzying effects*. Avoid elaborate fade-ins and fade-outs changing with every slide. Similarly, be consistent with fonts and graphics so they are easy to follow.
- *Don't skip slides*. Edit the presentation in advance based on the time given. "Recycled" talks need to be adapted to the particular group.
- *A picture is worth a thousand words*. Full slide photographs or clearly illustrated diagrams can be inserted every three to five slides to provide visual learners with a medium that will appeal to their senses. Similarly, short audio bits reinforce concepts for auditory learners, while short video clips meet the needs of both audio and visual learners.
- *Do you really need slides?* It sounds like heresy but not every seminar benefits from a slide presentation. In some cases, a handout, with informal sharing of experience or "stories" is more effective. Try it for a change.

---

[2]And you can read them up to 20% faster, as the curly serifs help the eye tie letters together.

On the Day of the Presentation

If possible, arrive at the venue at least 15 min in advance to check the sound system, projector, computer connection, and Internet connection. If using a remote control for slide advancement or laser pointer, familiarize yourself with how they work. Nothing is more frustrating to participants than to sit and watch a presenter attempt to get a laptop connected and displayed on a projector, and then have them fumble with a remote control or laser pointer while they speak.

Preparation

A little preparation, when it comes to the process of a seminar, is much better than none. Do not try to apply all the ideas in these *Knowledge Solutions* at once. Choose a few points to try at your next seminar and see what happens.

Proposition 95
Building Networks of Practice

In a Word Organizational boundaries have been stretched, morphed, and redesigned to a degree unimaginable 10 years ago. Networks of practice have come of age. The learning organization pays attention to their forms and functions, evolves principles of engagement, circumscribes and promotes success factors, and monitors and evaluates performance with knowledge performance metrics.

Background

Extensive media coverage of applications such as Facebook, MySpace, and LinkedIn suggests that networks are a new phenomenon. They are not: the first network was born the day people decided to create organizational structures to serve common interests—that is, at the dawn of mankind. However, the last 10–20 years have witnessed rapid intensification and evolution of networking activities, driven of course by information and communications technology as well as globalization. These make it possible for individuals to exchange data, information, and knowledge; work collaboratively; and share their views much more quickly and widely than ever before. Thus, less and less of an organization's knowledge resides within its formal boundaries or communities of practice.

© Asian Development Bank 2017
O. Serrat, *Knowledge Solutions*, DOI 10.1007/978-981-10-0983-9_95

Rationale

Knowledge cannot be separated from the networks that create, use, and transform it. In parallel, networks now play significant roles in how individuals, groups, organizations, and related systems operate. They will be even more important tomorrow. Since we can no longer assume that closely knit groups are the building blocks of human activity—or treat these as discrete units of analysis—we need to recognize and interface with less-bounded organizations, from nonlocal communities to links among websites. We should make certain that knowledge harvested in the external environment is integrated with what exists within, especially in dynamic fields where innovation stems from interorganizational knowledge sharing and learning. Therefore, the structure and composition of nodes and ties,[1] and how these affect norms and determine usefulness, must become key concerns. This makes the study of networks of practice a prime interest for both researchers and practitioners.

Networks of Practice

Brown and Duguid (2000) originated the concept of networks of practice. The notion is related to the work on communities of practice of Jean Lave and Etienne Wenger, and refers to the overall set of informal, emergent networks that facilitate information exchange toward practice-related goals. These networks range from communities of practice where learning occurs to electronic networks of practice (often referred to as virtual or electronic communities).[2] They differ from work groups created through formal organizational mandate with regard to control mechanisms,[3] composition and participation,[4] and expectations about

---

[1]Nodes are individuals, groups, or organizations within networks. Ties are the relationships between them.

[2]Clearly, the distinction between formality and informality can be tenuous. Some organizations have cultivated communities of practice to integrate them into their strategies (which might test the loyalties of members). If communities of practice are a localized and specialized subset of networks of practice, typically consisting of like-minded individuals who coordinate, communicate, and reciprocate in a shared domain in face-to-face situations and to a high degree on implicit knowledge, they can be considered to lie at one end of a continuum of network forms. At the other lie electronic networks of practice, the members of which may never know one another or meet face-to-face and display relatively little reciprocity (they generally communicate through electronic mailing lists, bulletin boards, newsletters, or web logs).

[3]In formal work groups such as project teams, control mechanisms customarily involve organizational hierarchies, mandated rules, contractual obligations, and both cash and noncash awards.

[4]The composition of networks of practice may range from a few individuals to very large, open electronic communities numbering thousands of participants. In the latter case, no formal restrictions are placed on membership. In contrast, the members of work groups are formally designated and assigned.

participation.[5] The underlying implication is that, to be competitive, organizations should promote participation in both traditional communities of practice and networks of practice and stimulate interactions between the two.

Building Networks of Practice for Collaborative Advantage

Networks are ordinarily founded on the hypothesis that we can accomplish more by working together than by working alone. Successful networking delivers collaborative advantage, viz., something that could not have been achieved without the collaboration. In other words, if the underlying premise is that the whole is greater than the sum of the parts, a significant benefit of participating in a knowledge network is that each of the parts also becomes stronger. The rewards can include (i) a better sense of belonging, ownership, and understanding; (ii) improved outcomes that would not otherwise be attained; and (iii) higher performance and productivity. To draw such benefits, the learning organization pays attention to the forms and functions of networks, evolves principles of engagement, circumscribes and promotes success factors, and monitors and evaluates operations with knowledge performance metrics.

- **The Forms of Networks** Understanding what knowledge products and services a network offers does not necessarily shed light on how or why it does it. These questions have more to do with its structure. The principal features of a network's internal and external environment relate to function, governance, localization and scope, membership, capacities and skills, resources, communications, and strategic and adaptive capacity.
- **The Functions of Networks** Networks bring together individual and organizational entities that remain geographically separated and institutionally distinct. Driven by technological innovation and globalization, the last ten years have seen a profound transformation in the wide-ranging functions they play. Yet, surprisingly little attention has been paid to what these are, and to the strategic development and management implications from that. Networks can fulfill six,

---

[5]In work groups, participation is determined jointly. Members are expected to commit to a common purpose and reach agreement on specific performance targets and indicators, a working approach, and mutual accountability. In communities of practice, participation is also determined jointly but individuals seek knowledge from identified experts. In electronic networks of practice, participation is determined individually; knowledge seekers have no control over who responds to their queries. In turn, knowledge contributors have no assurances that the knowledge seekers will understand the answers they gave or reciprocate the favor.

nonexclusive functions.[6] (The six can be further segregated into supra-functions, namely, agency or support.)[7] They are: (i) amplifying; (ii) community-building; (iii) convening; (iv) filtering, (v) investing, and (vi) learning and facilitating.

- **Steps to Applying the Network Functions Approach** The six functions of networks can be examined in a structured, step-by-step process to confirm, rethink, or reshape the work of an existing network. The process would entail analyzing the relevance of the network's vision and mission, mapping existing and planned activities against the six functions, identifying the current and planned balance of effort across the six functions, confirming for each function how the network's role is balanced between "agency" or "support", rating efficiency and effectiveness, and reflecting on vision and mission. These steps can clarify thinking, hone strategies, sharpen activities, and ultimately improve performance, thus delivering greater value. (The approach can also be used to guide the design of a new network.)
- **Principles of Engagement** Networks are not magic bullets. They can do what they were designed to do, but to adopt new functions they need long-term investments. It serves to appreciate that (i) there are no templates for success and one should expect setbacks; networks are complex; (ii) one should work with networks to agree on their functional balance and to support that balance; (iii) interventions to develop a network cannot be conceptualized as projects driven by a "logical framework"; other approaches such as outcome mapping offer better alternatives; (iv) networks should be helped to function as networks —with and through their members—and should not be tasked to deliver specific services that can be delivered by other forms of organizations; (v) one should not treat networks as traditional nongovernment or civil society organizations nor allow funds to undermine community-building functions; (vi) when networks carry out a funding role, one should ensure they have the necessary skills and that their other functions are not affected; (vii) network support timeframes should consider the different stages of network development; (viii) appropriate support for networks and their members is needed to develop the right competencies and skills to collaborate; (ix) a culture of knowledge and learning is a cornerstone of network development; an (x) sustainability should be judged against the needs of the members of a network. Toward this, it helps to have clear governance arrangements, strength in numbers as well as authoritative members, representativeness, well-leveraged informal links, good quality and packaging of evidence, information and communications technology that

---

[6]Networks can carry out one or more of these functions simultaneously—and many activities would fall under more than one category—but one must also recognize that there are important trade-offs between them. Each function requires specific capacities and skills, resources, and systems: overlooking trade-offs can drive networks away from their original roles.

[7]An agency bears responsibility for pursuing a particular change in policy or practice. A supporting role is one in which agency itself remains with the members: the organization exists to support them. In reality, of course, networks endeavor to conduct both functions to some degree.

multiplies networking opportunities, complementing official structures, and persistence.

- **Tools for Monitoring and Evaluation** Just like any other system, networks stand to benefit from feedback. Put simply, they need to be evaluated from two perspectives: the effectiveness of the network (doing the right thing) and the efficiency of the network (doing things right). Techniques that lend themselves to monitoring and evaluation of networks include SWOT analysis (strengths, weaknesses, opportunities, threats); results-based management; logical framework analysis; outcome mapping; and appreciative inquiry. Since networks are about relationships, it is also pertinent to leverage evaluation methods from the human resources field.

Summing Up

Networks are an important alternative for individuals, groups, and organizations trying to influence practice. (Indeed, some prophesy that they will become the preeminent collaboration mechanism. Certainly, information and communications technology is well suited to support, develop, and even strengthen them.) However, surprisingly little has been written on their strategic development and management, and even less is known about how capacity can be built. Still, rich seams of investigation relate to their forms and functions, key elements of which relate to the external context in which networks are set out and the interests of their members. Work in these areas provides a natural entry point for thinking about the resources, capacities, and skills that networks can offer or might need to develop. Moreover, since networks exist for a purpose, there surely is interest also in their use of evidence to influence practice, and ways to improve that. Finally, more research is needed on simple but effective means to evaluate performance.

Reference

Brown JS, Duguid P (2000) The social life of information. Harvard Business School Press, Boston, MA

Further Reading

Court J, Mendizabal E (2005) Networks and policy influence in international development. Euforic E-newsletter
International Institute for Sustainable Development (2004) Knowledge networks: guidelines for assessment. Canada
Ramalingam B, Mendizabal E, van Mierop S (2008) Strengthening humanitarian networks: applying the network functions approach. ODI Background Note. Overseas Development Institute

Proposition 96
Dimensions of the Learning Organization

In a Word Organizational learning is still seeking a theory and there can be no (and perhaps cannot be) agreement on the dimensions of the learning organization. However, useful models associated with learning and change can be leveraged individually or in association to reflect on the overall system of an organization.

Background

If organizational learning is still seeking a theory, there can be no (and perhaps cannot be) agreement on the dimensions of the learning organization. Even if the dimensions were understood, the connection between learning (or lack thereof) and performance remains unclear.[1] However, regardless of the disputed state of the art, a multilevel, practical but necessarily exploratory and simple framework of common and individual variables associated with learning and change follows. Here as

---

[1]Most organizations know little about where they lose knowledge, so the costs of lost knowledge are largely hidden. As a result, there is no clear ownership of the problem and little value is given to knowledge-sharing activities.

© Asian Development Bank 2017
O. Serrat, *Knowledge Solutions*, DOI 10.1007/978-981-10-0983-9_96

Fig. 96.1 Dimensions of the learning organization. *Source* Author

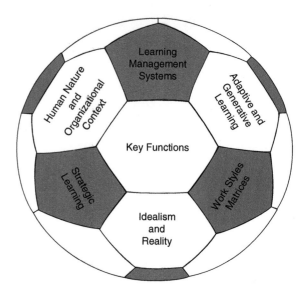

elsewhere, experimentation has an important role to play. Individual and collective learning are not about finding out what others already know, even if that is a useful first stage—it is about solving problems[2] by doing, reflecting, connecting, and testing until a solution forms part of organizational life. There is no stock answer nor is there a single best approach.[3] Figure 96.1 suggests concepts that can be used individually or in association to reflect on the overall system.

> *The purpose of science is not to analyze or describe but to make useful models of the world. A model is useful if it allows us to get use out of it.*
>
> —Edward de Bono

---

[2]Some streams of open systems theory reject problem solving as unproductive, instead preferring to work on desirable futures and necessary actions (only "solving problems" as they become barriers to a goal). The difference in the outlooks is significant.

[3]A parallel can be found in the disparity of systems models for organizational design. Those used often in the last 20–30 years have included McKinsey's 7-S Model, Galbraith's Star Model, Weisbord's Six Box Model, Nadler and Tushman's Congruence Model, and Burke-Litwin's Causal Model. Each of these shines a particular light on an organizational system, in the way perhaps that astronomers standing on different planets would examine different configurations of the universe. No one perspective is correct. The choice of model depends also on how complex its user wishes it to be. In recent years, less inward-looking (closed system) models have been developed.

Learning Management Systems

At the simplest level, one might consider the critical applications that would allow an organization to recognize its learning orientations and, from there, mark out the structures that affect how easy or hard it is for learning to occur. Figure 96.2 isolates 12 key learning systems from a managerial, somewhat top-down, perspective.

Key Functions

The literature on learning organizations suggests that certain key tasks must be undertaken for an organization to learn effectively. A set of competencies that might need to be developed to support learning, largely from a functional perspective, would include gathering internal evidence; accessing external learning; priming communication systems; drawing conclusions; developing organizational memory; and integrating learning into policy, strategy, and operations.

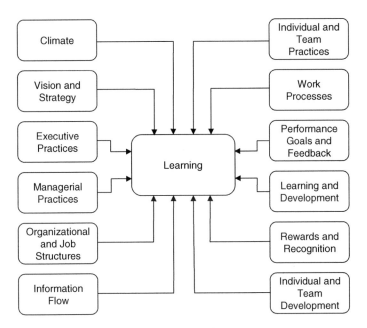

Fig. 96.2 Learning management systems. *Source* Author

Adaptive and Generative Learning

It is also helpful to demarcate some dimensions of the learning organization in terms of adaptive and generative learning, the two most commonly cited distinguishing characteristics of organizational learning.

Relating Human Nature to Organizational Context

Social capital is the stock of active connections among people, that is, the mutual understanding, shared values and behaviors, and trust that bind members of networks and communities, making cooperative action possible. The social cohesion that results is critical for societies to prosper and for development to be sustainable. The literature on social capital is vast but the idea of looking at social capital in organizations, not society, is relatively new. Here, the argument is that social capital makes an organization more than a collection of individuals. Ehin (2000) offered a comprehensive framework to understand how human nature supports or undermines voluntary workplace collaboration and innovation.

Strategic Learning

Organizational learning must be understood as a pattern in a stream of decisions. How does strategy form in organizations? The various types of strategies uncovered in research can be located somewhere between the ends of a continuum along which real-world strategies lay. The most common might be labeled "planned," "entrepreneurial," "ideological," "umbrella," "process," "unconnected," "consensus," and "imposed". The results will either be intended or realized. More interestingly, Henry Mintzberg distinguished deliberate strategies—realized as intended —from emergent strategies—patterns or consistencies realized despite, or in the absence of, intentions.[4]

---

[4]Still, notwithstanding the intuitive sense of Mintzberg's approach to strategy learning, failing to grasp thoroughly the influence of power on the strategy-making process can severely inhibit the potential of strategy making as a vehicle of organizational learning. Views of organizations as cohesive entities are unrealistic and unhelpful, and it is vital to recognize the plethora of interest groups that inevitably compete to shape an organization's direction.

Work Styles Matrices

Ultimately, learning must be customized to the circumstances of an organization and the work it conducts. Each organization is different, but the work styles of any organization fall under four models: process, systems, network, and competence. In brief, the process and systems models correspond to work settings that are routine and require little interpretation. What is needed to perform tasks is know-how; learning takes place through generalized learning and development training with the help of how-to guides. Evaluation and other reports can help as well. However, the network and competence models call for much higher levels of judgment and depend on deeper understanding and insight as well as an ability to improvise. Work on policies, strategies, programs, and projects fits in these domains.

Idealism and Reality

Without denigrating concepts of systemic thinking—since a better appreciation of the whole and the interrelationship between the parts will lead to more pertinent action—certain types of organizations of machine, missionary, or political configurations have a long way to go before they reach the ideal of learning organizations.

Reference

Ehin C (2000) Unleashing intellectual capital. Butterworth-Heinemann, Boston

Further Reading

ADB (2008) Auditing the lessons architecture. Manila
ADB (2009) Learning for change in ADB. Manila

Proposition 97
Disseminating Knowledge Products

By Muriel Ordoñez and Olivier Serrat

In a Word Dissemination is the interactive process of communicating knowledge to target audiences so that it may be used to lead to change. The challenge is to improve the accessibility of desired knowledge products by those they are intended to reach. This means ensuring physical availability of the product to as large a proportion of the target audience as possible and making the product comprehensible to those who receive it.

Rationale

The production of knowledge,[1] much of which represents invaluable intellectual capital, lies at the heart of modern organizations. However, the value of any knowledge product hangs on its effective dissemination to present and future

---

[1]E.g., know-how, good practices, and intellectual property.

audiences: without outreach the efforts of knowledge workers are wasted.[2] For this reason, dissemination is a core responsibility of any organization tasked with generating and sharing knowledge products, especially of new kinds of unique (and uniquely valuable) content[3] that are as usable and accessible as possible. Dissemination of knowledge is just as important as its production.[4]

Definition

At the simplest level, dissemination is best described as the delivery and receipt of a message, the engagement of an individual in a process, or the transfer of a process or product. Dissemination serves three broadly different purposes: awareness, understanding, and action.[5] Indeed, effective dissemination of a knowledge product will most likely require that it satisfies all three in turn: utilization is the goal.

Barriers to Dissemination

Most barriers to dissemination are psychological or social from the onset.[6] But where efforts to disseminate knowledge products are earnest, low impact[7] is mainly attributable to poor planning and the absence of a dissemination strategy (Central to

---

[2]Poor dissemination explains much of the gap between knowledge and practice. Enormous amounts of knowledge are never communicated beyond their immediate circles of interest and remain unused. Diffusion of innovation in health care, for example, is a considerable challenge (In this complex case, dissemination dictates that particularly close attention be paid to perceptions of the innovation, the characteristics of the people who adopt the innovation or fail to do so, and contextual factors such as communication, incentives, leadership, and management.).

[3]Traditional dissemination practices have on the whole relied on production of print artifacts through established publishing routes (even though print-based distribution systems retard and limit the development of ideas). Research data, audio, video, and multimedia works, as well as new forms of digital works and scholarly resources, are instances of nontraditional content that must be actively managed for dissemination purposes in a networked environment.

[4]Taken to its logical conclusion, this means that high-performance organizations must employ all existing infrastructure and continue to invest in policy work as well as in organizational and technological strategies to build capability to disseminate.

[5]Awareness may foster interest in greater understanding that may in turn provide the basis for action.

[6]In an organization, psychological barriers relate to reciprocity, repute, and altruism. Social barriers relate to organizational culture and the social networks that frame it. Social factors are the most frequently cited roadblock to knowledge management success.

[7]Intended impacts are not necessarily the same. Specific objectives might be to influence policy, change practice, contribute to an evidence base, and/or inform target audiences of progress. Obviously, the nature of intended impacts has implications for approaches to dissemination of related knowledge products.

that is recognition that the dissemination process should be interactive, allowing feedback from audiences according to a cyclical model of communications flow.).

Fig. Relationship of key elements of dissemination leading to knowledge utilization. *Source* Author

Key Steps

High-performance organizations (i) adopt a strategic approach to dissemination, (ii) know their target audiences, (iii) formulate generic, viable dissemination strategies that can be amended to suit different purposes, (iv) hit the target, and (v) monitor and evaluate their accomplishments. They do so because they can answer the following questions:

- **What do we want to disseminate?** Dissemination is only achievable and successful if, from the outset, there is a shared vision and common under-standing of what one wants to disseminate, together with a way of describing that to those who stand to benefit from it.
- **Who is the target audience and what are we offering it?** It is important to clearly identify who the target audience is to map it to one of the categories in the awareness, understanding, and action model. Since target audiences tend to be many, it is best to concentrate on who, at the very least, needs to be informed, and then prioritize for awareness, understanding, and action. Next, it is essential to think about what benefits the knowledge product will offer. A user is most interested in a potential solution to his or her particular problem: successful dissemination strategies are those that actively engage target audiences and deliver what they both need and want. One must then examine the knowledge product and think of how it might be presented as a benefit and solution to users.

- **When do we disseminate?** Dissemination exercises have milestones that must be identified and set early. They must also be realistic.
- **What are the most effective ways of disseminating?** Reports are concrete outputs that can be easily evidenced as solid methods of dissemination. But it is important to explore and evaluate what vehicles meet the needs of target audiences most effectively and appropriately. Varying them will also increase the chances of success.
- **Who might help us disseminate?** Target audiences already have journals, events, professional bodies, and subject associations they engage with. Dissemination will stand a greater chance of success if one can work through existing channels. Collaborating probably improves the impact of dissemination and reduces costs.
- **How do we prepare our strategy?** The strategy flows from the above to cover (i) the objective of dissemination, (ii) what knowledge product one proposes to disseminate, (iii) target audiences, (iv) benefits to users, (v) dissemination methods and related activities, (vi) timescales and responsibilities, (vii) targets, (viii) costs, and (ix) evaluation and criteria for success.
- **How do we turn our strategy into a dissemination plan?** Producing a coherent dissemination strategy does not necessarily result in effective implementation. A clear set of actions must be articulated covering (i) objective, (ii) target audiences, (iii) methods, (iv) vehicles, (v) timing, and (vi) responsibility.
- **How do we cost our dissemination activities?** Having developed the dissemination strategy and turned it into a dissemination plan, one needs to make sure that each dissemination activity has been carefully costed. It is always possible to obtain estimates of costs for all aspects of dissemination. The different aspects for consideration when running a workshop, for example, will relate among others to venue or room hire; equipment, e.g., overhead projectors, laptops; refreshments; lunch; travel to and from the workshop; publicity materials; and subsidies for participants.
- **How will we know we have been successful?** An effective dissemination strategy will only continue to be effective if it is viewed as an evolving and constantly developing process. The context in which we work changes over the course of our activities and the contexts in which users work are likely to change, too.[8] Therefore, it is important to put in place mechanisms for reviewing progress. However, one can only do so if clear targets are established at the outset. One of the most effective ways of establishing targets is to link them to the broad purposes of dissemination: (i) awareness, (ii) support and favorability, (iii) understanding, (iv) involvement, and (v) commitment. In each instance, it will be useful to identify beforehand (i) the target group, (ii) the target, (iii) the timescale, (iv) the reasons for selection, and (v) the criteria for success.

---

[8]The conventional model of knowledge transfer is linear: information flows from a provider to a user via a certain medium. In reality, knowledge transfer is an interactive, multidirectional exchange of know-how, good practices, or intellectual property.

Table. Relative merits of development research dissemination pathways

Dissemination pathway	Advantage	Disadvantage
Working document	• May target research findings to particular groups	• Limited access
Research report	• Provides a single reference point for all aspects of the research	• Assumes the report is read by a single audience group • May be written in an inaccessible manner
Academic, refereed journal	• Informs the scientific community of findings • Citations lead to wider impacts on intellectual networks	• Limited audience • May be written in an inaccessible manner • Lacks a practical orientation
Professional journal	• Reaches a wide practitioner community	• Academic rigor may be lower than that in a referred journal
Stand-alone textbook	• Potential for impact on wide audiences • Potential to influence development professionals	• Difficulty in accessing key texts in developing countries • Not practice oriented
Conference, workshop, seminar	• May allow professionals to learn more • Potential for networking	• Expense
Training manual	• Helps translate information into knowledge that can be applied	• Limited audience • Expense
Networking	• Reaches members who share common interests • Reduces "reinvention of the wheel" • Potential for interaction, discussion, and review of findings	• Typically low levels of active participation • Requires strong incentives for participation • Time consuming to operate and manage
Internet, electronic mail	• Immediate, convenient • Wide interest in electronic media	• Access to hardware may be limited in developing countries • Potential may be or is temporarily underdeveloped • Expense
Intermediaries	• Ensures that knowledge is translatable based on local norms	• Problems may arise if research agenda of intermediaries is not consistent with the knowledge product
Popularization, promotional artifact	• Reaches wide audiences	• Core message may be diluted or misinterpreted during the process of popularization
Publicizing	• Reaches wide audiences at relatively low cost	• No control over interpretation of message
Participatory concept	• Translates research results into practical guidance at the community level	• Time consuming
Policy briefs	• Potential to influence the decision-making process	• Difficulty in gaining access to decision makers
Interactive computer presentation	• High impact	• Difficulty in gaining access to decision makers • Limited access to hardware • Expense
Demonstration	• High impact	• Limited audience

Source Author

Box: Characteristics of a Successful Dissemination Plan

The dissemination plan reflects the needs of the target audiences. It relies on appropriate form, language, and information content levels.

The plan incorporates various dissemination techniques such as written, graphical, electronic, print, broadcast, and verbal media. The methods include summary documents; electronic dissemination within the organization and to key informants outside it; cross-postings on webpages; press releases; media coverage; flyers, posters, and brochures; letters of thanks to study participants; newsletters to study participants; events and conferences; and seminars. Each method calls for its own format and means of dissemination and includes both proactive and reactive channels—that is, it includes information content that the target audiences have identified as important and information content that the audiences may not know to request but is likely to be of interest. The dissemination techniques are more likely to succeed when their packaging and information content has been influenced by inputs from the target audiences.

The dissemination plan draws on existing capabilities, resources, relationships, and networks to the maximum extent possible. It also builds the new capabilities, resources, relationships, and networks that the target audience needs.

The dissemination plan includes effective quality control mechanisms to ensure that the information content is accurate, relevant, representative, and timely.

The plan identifies the resources required for implementation.

The plan provides a framework for monitoring and evaluation. It explains how one will know that dissemination activities have been successful. If data is to be gathered, it describes how this will be achieved, when, and who will gather it.

Lessons Learned

In their review of organizational experience in improving the impact of knowledge and research, Fisher et al. (2003) drew five sets of lessons:

Table. Spreading the word further

Area	Key lesson
Dissemination strategy	• A generic, organizational strategy that can be amended to suit different purposes is the most effective mechanism • Dissemination planning is best informed by carrying out a use needs' assessment of the target audiences whom one seeks to influence • Using the experience of all individuals involved in dissemination in an organization leads to a comprehensive strategy • Internal dissemination is a necessary element of a dissemination strategy as it strengthens overall capacity in this area

(continued)

(continued)

Area	Key lesson
Target audience	• A formal target audience information needs assessment (including an understanding of sociocultural factors) generates information on what information (content, style, resource requirements, and language) should be provided and the way in which it should be delivered • Ensuring local relevance of information results in increased receptiveness by audiences • Different local versions of information can be produced based on user needs analysis data
Dissemination pathways	• A multiple-channel dissemination approach reaches the broadest audience • The mass media can be a useful mass dissemination pathway, if a corresponding information culture prevails in which research and information are distributed in this way • The potential of electronic information is recognized but this should be supplemented by other dissemination approaches • Dissemination methods found to be successful in the South but used less frequently by the Northern researchers can provide valuable opportunities to reach target audiences • A useful route of access to target audiences is through infomediaries although careful selection is important
Viability and funding issues	• Insufficient funding is the main barrier to a viable dissemination strategy and accurate costs associations attached to the issue of paying for information • Use of networks provides a means of strengthening the viability of a dissemination strategy for the chosen period
Impact issues	• The various dissemination monitoring and evaluation techniques should be pre-tested before use • Indicators of successful uptake of the message are often perceived to be indicators of successful dissemination practice. A combination of direct and proxy indicators can provide an acceptable measure of how well we have reached our audience

Source Author

Reference

Fisher J, Odhiambo F, Cotton A (2003) Spreading the word further: guidelines for disseminating development research. Water, Engineering, and Development Center, Loughborough University

Proposition 98
Learning from Evaluation

In a Word Evaluation serves two main purposes: accountability and learning. Development agencies have tended to prioritize the first, and given responsibility for that to centralized units. But evaluation for learning is the area where observers find the greatest need today and tomorrow.

Redirecting Division-of-Labor Approaches

Because the range of types (not to mention levels) of learning is broad, organizations have, from the early days, followed a division-of-labor approach to ascribing responsibility for learning. Typically, responsibility is vested in a policy (or research) unit to allow managers to focus on decision-making while other organizational constituents generate information and execute plans. Without doubt, this has encouraged compartmentalization of whatever learning is generated. What is more, since organizational constituents operate in different cultures to meet different priorities, each questions the value added by the arrangement.

© Asian Development Bank 2017
O. Serrat, *Knowledge Solutions*, DOI 10.1007/978-981-10-0983-9_98

> *Give me a fruitful error any time, full of seeds, bursting with its own corrections.*
> *You can keep your sterile truth for yourself.*
>
> —Vilfredo Pareto

Increasing Value Added from Independent Operations Evaluation

In many development agencies, independent evaluation contributes to decision-making throughout the project cycle and in the agencies as a whole, covering all aspects of sovereign and sovereign-guaranteed operations (public sector operations); nonsovereign operations; and the policies, strategies, practices, and procedures that govern them. The changing scope of evaluations and fast-rising expectations in relation to their use are welcome. However, the broad spectrum of independent evaluation demands that evaluation units strengthen and monitor the results focus of their operations. This means that the relevance and usefulness of evaluation findings to core audiences should be enhanced. Recurrent requests are that evaluation units should improve the timeliness of their evaluations, strengthen the operational bearing of the findings, and increase access to and exchange of the lessons. Minimum steps to increase value added from independent evaluation involve (i) adhering to strategic principles, (ii) sharpening evaluation strategies, (iii) distinguishing recommendation typologies, (iv) making recommendations better, (v) reporting evaluation findings, and (vi) tracking action on recommendations (ADB 2007). Here, performance management tools such as the balanced scorecard system might enable them to measure nonfinancial and financial results, covering soft but essential areas as client satisfaction, quality and product cycle times, effectiveness of new product development, and the building of organizational and staff skills.

Even so, the problématique of independent evaluation is still more complex. At the request of shareholders tasked with reporting to political leadership, taxpayers, and citizens, feedback from evaluation studies has often tended to support accountability (and hence provide for control), not serve as an important foundation block of a learning organization. Some now argue for a reinterpretation of the notion of accountability. Others cite lack of utility; the perverse, unintended consequences of evaluation for accountability, such as diversion of resources; emphasis on justification rather than improvement; distortion of program activities; incentive to lie, cheat, and distort; and misplaced accent on control (Bemelmans-Videc et al. 2007).

The tension between the two functions of evaluation demands also that evaluation agencies distinguish primary audiences more clearly. Barring some overlap, these are audiences for accountability or learning. Obviously, this has implications for the knowledge products and services that evaluation units should deploy to reach different target groups, including the dissemination tactics associated with each, and underlines the message that one approach cannot be expected to suit all audiences. The key ingredients of the distinct reports that would have to be tailored for each pertain to evidence (by means of persuasive argument and authority), context (by means of audience context specificity and actionable recommendations), and engagement (by means of presentation of evidence-informed opinions, clear language and writing style, and appearance and design). Naturally, several knowledge management tools mentioned earlier would be leveraged to quicken the learning cycle of practice, experience, synthesis and innovation, dissemination, and uptake with one-time, near-term, and continuous efforts.

This is not to say that evaluation units face an either-or situation. Both accountability and learning are important goals for evaluation feedback. One challenge is to make accountability accountable. In essence, evaluation units are placing increased emphasis on results orientation while maintaining traditional checks on use of inputs and compliance with procedures. Lack of clarity on why evaluations for accountability are carried out, and what purpose they are expected to serve, contributes to their frequent lack of utility. Moreover, if evaluations for accountability add only limited value, resources devoted to documenting accountability can have a negative effect, perversely enough. However, evaluation for learning is the area where observers find the greatest need today and tomorrow, and evaluation units should be retooled to meet it. The table below suggests how work programs for evaluation might be reinterpreted to emphasize organizational learning.

Table. Programming work for organizational learning

Organizational level	Strategic driver[a]	Reporting mechanism	Content/focus	Responsibility	Primary user and uses	Timing
Corporate						
Policy						
Strategy						
Operations						

[a]The strategic drivers might be (i) developing evaluation capacity, (ii) informing corporate risk assessments by offices and departments, (iii) conducting evaluations in anticipation of known upcoming reviews, (iv) monitoring and evaluating performance, (v) critiquing conventional wisdom about development practice, and (vi) responding to requests from offices and departments
Source ADB (2007)

Evaluation capacity development promises much to the learning organization, and should be an activity in which centralized evaluation units have a comparative advantage. Capacity is the ability of people, organizations, and society as a whole to manage their affairs successfully; and capacity to undertake effective monitoring and evaluation is a determining factor of aid effectiveness. Evaluation capacity development is the process of reinforcing or establishing the skills, resources, structures, and commitment to conduct and use monitoring and evaluation over time. Many key decisions must be made when starting to develop evaluation capacity internally in a strategic way.[1] Among the most important are

- **Architecture** Locating and structuring evaluation functions and their coordination.
- **Strengthening evaluation demand** Ensuring that there is an effective and well-managed demand for evaluations.
- **Strengthening evaluation supply** Making certain that the skills and competencies are in place with appropriate organizational support.
- **Institutionalizing evaluations** Building evaluation into policy-making systems.

Why development agencies should want to develop in-house, self-evaluation capacity is patently clear. Stronger evaluation capacity will help them

- Develop as a learning organization.
- Take ownership of their visions for poverty reduction, if the evaluation vision is aligned with that.
- Profit more effectively from formal evaluations.
- Make self-evaluations an important part of their activities.
- Focus quality improvement efforts.
- Increase the benefits and decrease the costs associated with their operations.
- Augment their ability to change programming midstream and adapt in a dynamic, unpredictable environment.
- Build evaluation equity, if they are then better able to conduct more of their own self-evaluation, instead of hiring them out.
- Shorten the learning cycle.

The below figure poses key questions concerning how an organization may learn from evaluation, combining the two elements of learning by involvement and learning by communication. It provides the context within which to visualize continuing efforts to increase value added from independent evaluation, and underscores the role in internal evaluation capacity development. It also makes a strong case for more research into how development agencies learn how to learn.

---

[1] A discussion of the benefits of external evaluation capacity development is in Serrat (2008).

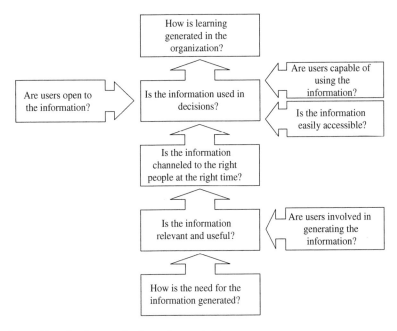

Fig. Internal learning from evaluations. *Source* Author

References

ADB (2007) Acting on recommendations and learning from lessons in 2007. Manila
Bemelmans-Videc ML, Lonsdale J, Perrin B (eds) (2007) Making accountability work: dilemmas
    for evaluation and for audit. Transaction Publishers, New Brunswick, New Jersey
Serrat O (2008) Increasing value added from operations evaluation. ADB, Manila (unpublished)

Further Reading

ADB (2009) Learning for change in ADB. Manila, ADB

Proposition 99
Learning and Development
for Management

In a Word The insights, attitudes, and skills that equip managers for their various responsibilities come from many sources outside formal education or training. To identify areas for improvement, it is first necessary to identify what these responsibilities are.

Background

To improve the performance of development agencies, international assistance has traditionally employed three approaches. They are

- **Improving technologies** This approach has centered on deploying electronic platforms and databases to managers, thereby enabling them to use resources more efficiently and to make their performance more effective. Transfers of technology have centered on tools for budgeting, accounting, and expenditure control; the speed and accuracy of information flows, particularly through computers; and more rational methods of scheduling, monitoring, and implementing projects and programs.
- **Rationalizing organization and procedures and adjusting structures and methods** This approach has sought to enhance management control, save resources, increase efficiency, and speed the delivery of services. Basically, it

© Asian Development Bank 2017

O. Serrat, *Knowledge Solutions*, DOI 10.1007/978-981-10-0983-9_99

has entailed applying to government operations the prescriptions and experiences of the scientific management movement.

- **Strengthening bureaucracies as social institutions** This approach has focused on building institutions in ways that enhance their internal capabilities and improve their ability to interact productively with their external environment and thus sustain the activities for which they are responsible.

All three approaches are fairly technocratic, however, and have not always been fully adapted to the uncertainties, complexities, and societal pluralism that characterize the environments in which development agencies operate. Hence new methods have been developed to complement them. They have to do with

- **Reforming structures** Structural approaches have been concerned with administrative deconcentration, institutional devolution, the organization of work to relax the rigidities of conventional bureaucratic structures, and the use of paraprofessionals from local communities and associations to implement projects and programs.
- **Reinventing operational procedures** The reform of operational procedures has been concerned with information management to maintain the integrity of information in bureaucratic structures, and social marketing to determine what society wants, and what methods of supplying services it would prefer.
- **Motivating** Motivational approaches relate to rewards and punishments, working conditions, participatory management, and compensation.
- **Strengthening accountability** More recently, we have also seen greater attention to responsiveness and accountability, and a desire on the part of the public sector to resist political pressures at the level of project and program implementation.
- **Eradicating corruption** We are also witnessing renewed efforts to minimize corruption, negligence, and arbitrary behavior in the public sector.

The Importance of Learning and Development for Management

International assistance to improve the organizational performance of development agencies may have underestimated the value of enhancing managerial skills by learning and development, and by establishing and strengthening training institutions and programs. Management capacities can improve. This is necessary because the insights, attitudes, and skills that equip managers for their various responsibilities come from many sources outside formal education or training. To identify the areas for improvement, however, it is first necessary to identify what these responsibilities are. Five functions or roles can be identified for managers and, for each, targeted management learning and development is required.

(i) **Instrumental functions** For the instrumental functions of managers, learning and development might enhance

- Generic management techniques, e.g., financial, personnel and human relations, informational, supervisory, structural, and procedural.
- Project and program management skills, e.g., the processes of design, implementation, and evaluation of individual service, regulatory, enterprise, and promotional activities sponsored by governments.

(ii) **Political functions** For the political functions of managers, learning and development might reinforce

- Skills in policy analysis, both generic and as they apply to the substantive sectors in which managers are expected to achieve specialized competence.
- Sensitivity to methods for coping with inter-bureaucratic influences, societal forces, and political interventions that impinge on projects and programs.
- Appreciation of the differential benefits and costs of policy and program outputs on the publics they affect.

(iii) **Entrepreneurial functions** For the entrepreneurial functions of managers, learning and development might improve

- Appreciation of the opportunities and limitations of proactive management styles outside normal operating routines. These include management interventions that attempt to modify policies, invigorate operations, recombine resources in fresh patterns, and enhance both staff and public participation in projects and programs.

(iv) **Inter-organizational functions** For the inter-organizational functions of managers, learning and development might build

- Analytical insights, such as linkage management.
- Operating skills, such as environmental mapping, required for policy and program implementation that involve two or more government agencies and multi-institutional service networks.

(v) **Public Interest functions** For the public interest functions of managers, learning and development might strengthen

- Skills in identifying and articulating long-term societal goals and in shaping policies and projects and programs that implement these goals.
- Criteria and methods of dealing with the ethical dilemmas that inevitably confront managers.

... and Performance Evaluation. Although the specific functions and roles of managers vary, the criteria by which their performance should be evaluated can be grouped under five headings. The common management goals of effectiveness, e.g., achieving intended outputs, and of efficiency, e.g., the economical employment of resources, of course, remain necessary. They are not, however, sufficient guides for managers. Accordingly, management performance must also be oriented toward, and assessed by, three other interconnected values. These are responsiveness, e.g., success in meeting actual demand and the needs of society while heeding its preferences and convenience; outreach, e.g., success in promoting participation and resource contributions from society; and sustainability, e.g., success in insuring the continuity of services by innovating and adapting to new circumstances, maintaining support from society, and garnering the required resources. These are the demanding but nevertheless attainable criteria by which managers should expect to be evaluated.

Proposition 100
Asking Effective Questions

In a Word Questioning is a vital tool of human thought and interactional life. Since questions serve a range of functions, depending on the context of the interaction, the art and science of questioning lies in knowing what question to ask when.

Background

Seeking information is a vital human activity that contributes to learning, problem solving, and decision-making. Questioning[1] is a vital tool of human thought and social interaction[2] with which to open doors to data, information, knowledge, and

---

[1]A question is any statement—even nonverbal, e.g., hmmm?—that invites an answer. Of course, most questions are verbal in nature (even if nonverbal signs often accompany them).
[2]Social interaction is a dynamic, changing sequence of social actions that take into account the actions and reactions of other individuals (or groups) and are modified based on them. Put differently, they are events in which people attach meaning to a situation, interpret what others are meaning, and respond accordingly.

© Asian Development Bank 2017
O. Serrat, *Knowledge Solutions*, DOI 10.1007/978-981-10-0983-9_100

wisdom. Questions serve a range of functions,[3] depending on the context of the interaction. Therefore, the art and science of questioning lies in knowing what question to ask when.[4] A question is only as good as the answer it evokes, and questions thus contribute to success or failure across different contexts.[5]

Typologies of Questions

Derived from the context of social interaction, different classifications of questions have been proposed. The most common refers to the degree of freedom, or scope, given to the respondent. Those that leave the respondent free to select any one of several ways in which to answer are termed open questions; those that require a short response of a specific nature are labeled closed questions. Other types include recall and process questions, affective questions, leading questions, probing questions, rhetorical questions, and multiple questions (Fig. 100.1).

> *I keep six honest serving-men,*
>
> *(They taught me all I knew);*
>
> *Their names are What and Why and When,*
>
> *And How and Where and Who.*
>
> —Rudyard Kipling

---

[3]For example, questions can be used to (i) obtain information; (ii) maintain control; (iii) express interest; (iv) stimulate interest and curiosity; (v) sustain attention; (vi) diagnose difficulties; (vii) ascertain attitudes, feelings, and opinions; (viii) communicate that participation is expected and valued; (ix) foster participation; (x) assess the extent of a respondent's knowledge; (xi) encourage comments on the responses of others; and (xii) prompt critical thinking and evaluation.

[4]In Western thought, investigation of knowledge owes much to Socrates (469–399 BC), an Athenian moral philosopher concerned with the conduct of virtuous human life through critical reasoning. The Socratic method requires participants to clarify their beliefs and understanding through questioning and dialogue.

[5]In 1956, Benjamin Bloom proposed a taxonomy of the different educational objectives that teachers set for students, encompassing psychomotor (manual or physical skills), affective (growth in feelings or emotional areas), and cognitive (mental skills) domains. Like most taxonomies, Bloom's cognitive domain is hierarchical—meaning that learning at the higher levels is dependent on having attained prerequisite knowledge and skills at lower levels. The six levels, moving through the lowest order processes to the highest, are knowledge, comprehension, application, analysis, synthesis, and evaluation. In 2001, Lorin Anderson and David Krathwohl revised the taxonomy and its verbiage.

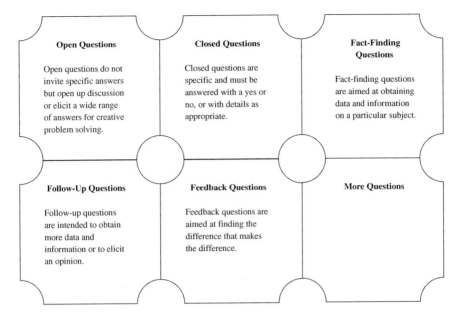

Fig. 100.1 A basic typology of questions. *Source* Author

The Art and Science of Powerful Questions[6]

Questions are a prerequisite to learning. They are a window into creativity and insight. They motivate fresh thinking. They challenge outdated assumptions. They lead us into the future. A powerful question

- generates curiosity in participants;
- stimulates reflective thinking and conversation;
- surfaces and challenges assumptions;
- is thought-provoking;
- channels attention, focuses inquiry, and promises insight;
- invites creativity and new possibilities;
- generates energy, a vector to explore, and forward movement;
- is broad, enduring, and stays with participants;
- touches a deep meaning; and
- evokes more questions.

---

[6]This section and the next draw heavily from Vogt et al. (2003).

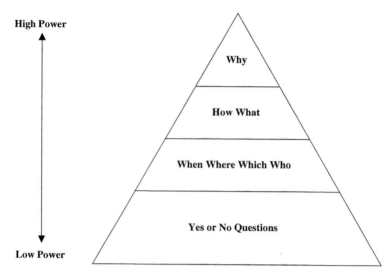

Fig. 100.2 The architecture of a question. *Source* Author

Powerful questions have three dimensions: (i) architecture; (ii) scope; and (iii) assumptions (context, meaning). Most work on the first dimension, *architecture*, produces a variant of the general hierarchy illustrated below—the hypothesis is that any question can be transformed into a more powerful question by moving up the pyramid (Fig. 100.2).

In other words, the linguistic construction of a question can make a critical difference in either opening our minds or narrowing the possibilities we can consider. Is it a yes or no question? Is it an either/or question? Does it open with an interrogative, such as when, where, who, how, what, or why?

- If a question asks "when", it is inquiring about time or duration.
- If a question asks "where", it is looking for a location.
- If a question asks "who", it is soliciting identification.
- If a question asks "how", it is requesting an instruction or procedure.
- If a question asks "what", it is inviting a description.
- If a question asks "why", it is calling for an explanation.

> *The unexamined life is not worth living.*
>
> —Socrates

Next, it is important to know that, besides the words we choose, the *scope* of a question affects the effectiveness of a query. Powerful questions, typically beginning with how or why, encompass more people, more resources, more volume, more time, and more concerns. Obviously, the scope of a question must be tailored and kept within realistic boundaries and the needs of an investigation if an answer is to emerge at all, at least in the short term.[7]

> *A prudent question is one-half of wisdom.*
>
> —Francis Bacon

Lastly, the *assumptions* that underlie a question comprise a more complex, subtle axis. All questions are nourished by explicit or implicit assumptions that may not be shared by the individuals (or groups) taking part in the discussion. These presuppositions and axioms are taken for granted but have implications and consequences that will flow logically as effects. Assumptions must be surfaced if the question being raised is to display the powerful characteristics mentioned earlier.

> *It is error only, and not truth, that shrinks from inquiry.*
>
> —Thomas Paine
>
> *The trouble with the world is that the stupid are cocksure and the intelligent are full of doubt.*
>
> —Bertrand Russell

Fostering Strategic Inquiry

In *The Art of Powerful Questions*, Eric Vogt, Juanita Brown, and David Isaacs outlined the steps of a game plan that organizations might follow to use query to catalyze insight, innovation, and action. The game plan involves (i) assessing the current situation, (ii) discovering the big questions, (iii) creating images of possibilities, and (iv) evolving workable strategies. In support, they devised a questionnaire to help judge the degree to which an organization is an inquiring system. (Only when an answer generates further questions does thought continue as inquiry that stimulates new ways to think and new paths to follow.) They also formulated sample questions to focus collective attention on a situation, connect ideas and find deeper insight, and create forward movement. Focusing on effective questioning,

---

[7]The domains that might be embedded in a complex question include mathematics and quantitative disciplines, physical and life sciences, arts and humanities, and social disciplines.

they identified the roles that leaders might play to design inquiring systems that coevolve the future.[8] They are

- Engage in shared conversation,
- Convene and host learning conversations,
- Include diverse perspectives,
- Support appreciative inquiry,[9]
- Foster shared meaning,
- Nurture communities of practice, and
- Use collaborative technologies.

Reference

Vogt E, Brown J, Isaacs D (2003) The art of powerful questions: catalyzing insight, innovation, and action. Whole Systems Associates

Further Reading

Browne N, Keeley S (2009) Asking the right questions: a guide to critical thinking. Allyn & Bacon
Paul R, Elder L (2002) Critical thinking: tools for taking charge of your professional and personal life. Prentice Hall

---

[8] It is not possible to be a good thinker and a poor questioner. With a nod to critical thinking, the intellectual standards that leaders might apply to assess reasoning are (i) clarity, (ii) accuracy, (iii) precision, (iv) relevance, (v) depth, (vi) breadth, (vii) logic, (viii) significance, and (ix) fairness. As they help their organization focus on asking effective questions, the elements of thought that will be implied are (i) what is our fundamental purpose?, (ii) what is the key question we are trying to answer?, (iii) what information do we need to answer our question?, (iv) what is the most basic concept in our question?, (v) what assumptions are we using in our reasoning?, (vi) what is our point of view with respect to the issue?, (vii) what are our most fundamental inferences or conclusions?, and (viii) what are the implications of our reasoning (if we are correct)?

[9] Appreciative inquiry is the process of facilitating positive change in organizations. Its basic assumption is uncomplicated: every organization has something that works well. Appreciative inquiry is usually worked out using a 4-D Cycle of discovery, dream, design, and delivery.

Proposition 101
Coaching and Mentoring

In a Word Coaching and mentoring can inspire and empower employees, build commitment, increase productivity, grow talent, and promote success. They are now essential elements of modern managerial practice. However, many companies still have not established related schemes. By not doing so, they also fail to capitalize on the experience and knowledge seasoned personnel can pass on.

Rationale

High-performance, contemporary organizations know that a company is only as good as its employees. They place strong emphasis on personal attributes in selecting and developing staff. However, this does not come without challenges, not least of which may be (significant) gaps in the experience, knowledge, attitudes, skills, aspirations, behaviors, or leadership required to perform demanding jobs. Formal training courses may vaunt wholesale transfer of these; but employees will not likely stretch to their full potential without dedicated guidance that inspires, energizes, and facilitates. In the new millennium,[1] good coaching and mentoring

---

[1]The 1990s saw the rapid emergence of coaching as an identifiable industry.

© Asian Development Bank 2017

O. Serrat, *Knowledge Solutions*, DOI 10.1007/978-981-10-0983-9_101

schemes are deemed a highly effective way to help people, through talking, increase self-direction, self-esteem, efficacy, and accomplishments.

Definition

Both coaching and mentoring are an approach to management and a set of skills to nurture staff and deliver results. They are, fundamentally, learning and development activities that share similar roots despite lively debate among academics and practitioners as to the meaning (and implications) of each word.[2] A good coach will also mentor and a good mentor will coach too, as appropriate to the situation and the relationship. Hence, these *Knowledge Solutions* treat the two terms interchangeably: both are related processes for analysis, reflection, and action, intended to enable employees achieve their full potential with a focus on skills, performance, and "life" (personal) coaching and mentoring.[3] (A substantial side effect of investments to bring out potential is that organizations will enable seasoned personnel to delegate more and supervise less.)[4] Unlike conventional training, coaching and mentoring focus on the person, not the subject; they draw out rather than put in; they develop rather than impose; they reflect rather than direct; they are continuous—not one-time—events. In brief, they are a form of change facilitation.

---

[2]Differences of opinion have been fueled by the wide range of contexts in which coaching and mentoring take place; by the perceptions of stakeholders as to the purpose of related conversations; by resulting variations in the application of coaching and mentoring activities; and by not counting commercial, practical, and ethical considerations. Somewhat elitist definitions have it that coaching means encouraging employees to do their jobs well, while mentoring is about helping top performers excel. (The people performance potential model that categorizes teams and organizations, not individuals, as icebergs, problem children, backbone, and stars is an accepted extension of this approach.) From there, the two camps specify that the attributes of each activity can be distinguished according to focus, role, relationship, source of influence, personal returns, and arena. The psychologically minded, on the other hand, have viewed coaching and mentoring as adjuncts to therapy. (Attempting to fix poor performance is termed counseling.) Possibly, the main distinction one might make in differentiating coaching from mentoring is that the former does not necessarily rely on the specific experience and knowledge of the coach being greater than that of the client, and may emphasize cross-disciplinary skills. Also, mentoring usually refers to one-on-one relationships, whereas coaching can target both individuals and teams.

[3]The moral is that it is essential to first determine exactly what the needs are to make sure that the mentor coach can supply the type and level of service required, whatever that service might be. Clearly, one size does not fit all: to profile needs (without being distracted by details), it is important to look at demographic, motivating, and learning factors; the subject's background; and his or her availability.

[4]Mentor coaches draw benefits too. Coaching and mentoring help develop leadership and communications skills, and learn new perspectives and ways of thinking. Significantly, good mentor coaches are never motivated entirely by money: personal development is a very important aspect of this two-way process.

> *To live is to change, and to be perfect is to have changed often.*
>
> —John Henry Newman

Applications

Coaching and mentoring can be used whenever performance or motivation levels must be increased. There are many applications, each to be looked at from as many points of view as possible. Recurring opportunities relate to developing careers, solving problems, overcoming conflicts, and remotivating staff. In all instances, feedback should be specific, factual, and objective. (Ideally, the final stage of a coaching and mentoring cycle should form a platform from which to initiate another, with a view to long-term learning and development.)

Process

For any single coaching and mentoring goal, there is a cycle of six basic stages, each of which hinges on effective questioning, active listening, clear feedback, and well-organized sessions. First, the mentor coach and the client get to know one another to establish clarity and rapport, engage, and agree what the goal is[5]; second, they discuss the current reality, to which the mentor coach will adapt the coaching and mentoring style[6]; third, they explore available options; fourth, they identify and commit to a course of action (at a pace the client is comfortable with) in line with shared expectations (that might involve training); fifth, the client implements the agreed actions with the support of and clear (meaning constructive and positive) feedback from the coach; sixth, the mentor coach and the client consider what has

---

[5]Goal setting forms the crux of coaching and mentoring, springing from a sound diagnosis of the capabilities and attitudes of the client. The smart goals agreed from there are specific, measurable, achievable, relevant, and timed.

[6]Coaching and mentoring styles typically lie within a skill–will matrix. Skill depends on experience, training, understanding, and role perception. Will depends on desire to achieve, incentives, security, and confidence. Coaching and mentoring styles should vary according to a client's endowment of each.

been learned and how they might build on that knowledge, possibly by initiating a new coaching and mentoring cycle. All the while, the mentor coach should, with empathy and sensitivity, encourage the client to come to his or her own conclusions. Mentor coaches must have a high degree of emotional intelligence, viz., self-awareness, self-regulation, self-motivation, social awareness, and social skills.[7] This is essential to achieving a good relationship that combines autonomy and shared responsibility toward accomplishment of the performance goal. Last but not least, everything that is said must remain confidential.

> *I don't know any other way to lead but by example.*
>
> —Don Shula

Appraising

The purpose of appraisal is to identify accomplishments and make sure new performance goals are realistic. Appraisal will call for a joint review and a development plan. The joint review should cover (i) the last period's objectives, (ii) examples of achievements, (iii) the client's self-rating, (iv) the mentor coach's appreciation, (v) the next period's objectives, and (vi) the client's comments on these. The development plan should specify (i) the long-term objectives, (ii) immediate objectives, (iii) the competencies required, (iv) training needs (if any), (v) the actions agreed, and (vi) the review date agreed.

---

[7]Not everyone can be a mentor coach. Even if emotional intelligence skills can be learned, some are more naturally gifted with "people" skills than others. Before committing, would-be practitioners should ask themselves: Do I enjoy encouraging and motivating others? Do I want to contribute to the growth and success of others? Do I want to share my experience and knowledge with others? What specific expertise can I claim and offer? In what areas am I willing to help? Am I comfortable with posing challenging questions? Am I prepared to regularly invest time and energy in coaching and mentoring? What is my preferred duration for a partnership? What is my preferred frequency and method of contact? What type of client would I prefer to coach and mentor? Can I describe the professional and personal qualities of that client? Do I want to coach and mentor someone from the same profession or the same career path? How would coaching and mentoring add to my sense of contribution and community? How would coaching and mentoring contribute to my own goals? Are there any areas that I do not want to visit?

Evaluating

Evaluation determines merit or worth, assesses impact, identifies improvements, and provides accountability. When assessing coaching and mentoring programs, five critical levels of performance, for which data and information must be gathered and analyzed, apply:

- Level 1: reaction (did the clients like the interventions?)
- Level 2: learning and development (did the clients benefit as planned?)
- Level 3: organizational support (did the clients receive the institutional support needed?)
- Level 4: behavior (do the clients apply their learning and new competencies in the workplace)
- Level 5: results (what is the impact on the organization?)

> *The miracle, or the power, that elevates the few is to be found in their industry, application, and perseverance under the prompting of a brave, determined spirit.*
>
> —Mark Twain

Afterword

All development is self-development. One cannot force employees to develop: they must want that themselves.[8] Nonetheless, what an organization can do is to help set an environment that makes it more likely its staff will want to learn, grow, and succeed.

> *Yet when asked to spend time with an unknown and unproven young man seeking his way in the world, Drucker freely gave the better part of a day to mentor and give guidance. I had the honor of writing about that day in the foreword to "The Daily Drucker," wherein I recount how Drucker altered the trajectory of my life by framing our discussion around one simple question: "What do you want to contribute?"*
>
> *Source* Excerpted from Collins (2005)

---

[8]The conscious competence learning model, for instance, takes a learner from stage 1 (unconscious incompetence) to stage 4 (unconscious competence), having passed through stage 2 (conscious incompetence) and stage 3 (conscious competence). Yet, some will resist progression even to stage 2 because they refuse to acknowledge or accept the relevance and benefit of a particular skill or ability.

Reference

Collins J (28 November 2005) Lessons from a student of life. Business Week

Further Reading

Eaton J, Johnson R (2001) Coaching successfully. Dorling Kindersley Limited

Proposition 102
Harnessing Creativity and Innovation in the Workplace

In a Word Creativity plays a critical role in the innovation process, and innovation that markets value is a creator and sustainer of performance and change. In organizations, stimulants and obstacles to creativity drive or impede enterprise.

Introduction

> *There is no doubt that creativity is the most important human resource of all. Without creativity, there would be no progress, and we would be forever repeating the same patterns.*
>
> —Edward de Bono

These *Knowledge Solutions* do not discuss intellectual property, the new knowledge that arises out of the innovation process, nor the management systems that identify, protect, value, manage, and audit an organization's intellectual property, e.g., copyrights, trademarks, patents, etc.

© Asian Development Bank 2017
O. Serrat, *Knowledge Solutions*, DOI 10.1007/978-981-10-0983-9_102

Creativity has always been at the heart of human endeavor. Allied to innovation, which creates unexpected value, it is now recognized as central to organizational performance. (Some hold that the capacity to harness intellectual and social capital —and to convert that into novel and appropriate things—has become the critical organizational requirement of the age.) The shift to knowledge economies has been abrupt and there is a flurry of interest in creativity and innovation in the workplace. Innovation is considered, quite simply, an imperative for organizational survival. It may even be the key to some of the biggest challenges facing the world, such as global warming and sustainable development. Notwithstanding, we are still far from a theory of organizational creativity: the avenues for promising research that might contribute to its emergence are innumerable because of the increasing use of systems approaches and the growing number of agents involved in knowledge flows.[1]

Definitions

Creativity[2] is the mental and social process—fueled by conscious or unconscious insight—of generating ideas, concepts, and associations.[3] Innovation[4] is the successful[5] exploitation of new ideas: it is a profitable outcome of the creative process, which involves generating and applying in a specific context products, services, procedures, and processes that are desirable and viable. Naturally, people who create and people who innovate can have different attributes and perspectives.

---

[1] Usefully, given the plethora of opportunities, systemized research might cover four distinct stages: (i) ideas capture, (ii) growth and development, (iii) demonstration, and (iv) application. In general, little work has been done on what types of innovation have the biggest or most significant impact, and in what contexts.

[2] www.Dictionary.com defines creativity as "the ability to transcend traditional ideas, rules, patterns, relationships, or the like, and to create meaningful new ideas, forms, methods, interpretations, etc.; originality, progressiveness, or imagination".

[3] Creativity was once considered the province of artists, scientists, and writers. But the creative urge can express itself elsewhere and need not be limited by the job description. There is variety in typologies of creative people too: they can be quick and dramatic, or careful and quiet. It is also true that most new ideas are not flashes of inspiration in an inventor's head; they come from how people identify, create, store, share, and use knowledge. According to the Snowflake Model of Creativity of David Perkins, developed in the 1980s, the six common traits of creative people are (i) a strong commitment to a personal esthetic, (ii) the ability to excel in finding solutions, (iii) mental mobility, (iv) a willingness to take risks (and the ability to accept failure), (v) objectivity, and (vi) inner motivation. The first three traits are largely cognitive; the last three are dispositional attributes. Because none of the six is thought to be genetic, Perkins argued that creativity can be taught, or at least encouraged.

[4] Dictionary.com defines innovation as "the act of innovating; [the] introduction of new things or methods".

[5] Success, of course, should be defined by quantitative and qualitative indicators. In addition to market share and reduced costs, for instance, scale and permanence can serve among others.

The Challenge

The key question isn't "What fosters creativity?" but it is why in God's name isn't everyone creative? Where was the human potential lost? How was it crippled? I think therefore a good question might be not why do people create? But why do people not create or innovate? We have got to abandon that sense of amazement in the face of creativity, as if it were a miracle if anybody created anything.

—Abraham Maslow

It follows, then, that innovation begins with creativity. In the world of organizations, be they private or public, lack of either leads to stagnation, and leaves an organization unable to perform or meet change.[6] However, creative thinking cannot be turned on and off at the flick of a switch. And innovation does not occur in a vacuum; it requires effective strategies and frameworks, among which incentives are paramount. Creativity flourishes in organizations that support open ideas:[7] these organizations create environments that inspire personnel and maintain innovative workplaces; those that fail are large organizations that stifle creativity with rules and provide no slack for change. There is a role for management in the creative process: but it is not to manage it; it is to manage for it. Why? Because creativity does not happen exclusively and tacitly in a person's head but in interaction with a social context wherein it may be codified. For any organization, operating in an external environment, an interactionist model of creativity and innovation needs to encompass organizational context, organizational knowledge, and inter- and intra-organizational relationships, not forgetting the (increasingly multicultural) creative makeup of the individuals (antecedent conditions, cognitive style, ability,

---

[6]This is not to say that private and public sector organizations have the same reasons to innovate. In the private sector, the imperative owes primarily to economic contexts and concerns, e.g., reducing costs and raising productivity, maintaining competitiveness, breathing life into slowing or stagnant markets (or, alternatively, facilitating entry into new markets), adapting to changing environments. In the public sector, motivation can be political (and therefore less amenable to rational planning and analysis). For instance, innovation has often been exploited to enhance reputation and image. But innovation is also becoming crucial to the design and delivery of public services in a dynamic society. In the twenty-first century, it is only through innovation, including at policy level, that public sector organizations will shift out of mass provision to efficient, personalized modes of service provision: society is becoming increasingly diverse, and individuals now demand more from public services too—innovations are the product of the creative interaction of supply and demand, for example, in the areas of broad areas of shared services, procurement, efficiency, and joined-up services.

[7]Peter Drucker maintained that creativity is rarely a limiting factor. He argued that there are more ideas in any organization than can possibly be put to use. The issue was how to create value out of them.

intrinsic motivation, knowledge, personality), and teams (group composition, characteristics, and processes) who operate in it.[8]

Types and Sources of Innovation

The main types of innovation are divided into product innovations, service innovations, and organizational (procedural or process) innovations.[9] The most common are market-led or market-push innovation; others are technology-led innovations (for which markets must be developed). All can be classified depending on the degree of their impact, viz., incremental, radical, or systemic. Drucker (1985) identified seven sources of innovation: (i) unexpected occurrences, (ii) incongruities of various kinds, (iii) process needs, (iv) changes in an industry or market, (v) demographic changes, (vi) changes in perceptions, and (vii) new knowledge. (These seven sources overlap, and the potential for innovation may lie in more than one area at a time.) He explained that purposeful, systematic innovation begins with the analysis of the sources of new opportunities. However, he emphasized that in seeking opportunities, innovative organizations need to look for simple, focused solutions to real problems. That takes diligence, persistence, ingenuity, and knowledge.

Leveraging Enterprise

Creativity in products, services, procedures, and processes is now more important than ever. It is needed equally in the established enterprise, the public sector organization, and the new venture. Why is it then that many organizations unwittingly carry out managerial practices that destroy it? With exceptions, most managers do not stifle creativity on purpose.[10] Yet, in the pursuit of productivity,

---

[8]Put simply, drawing from Van de Ven (1986), the model articulates four basic factors: new ideas, people, interactions, and institutional context. This means that managers seeking to harness creativity and innovation confront four basic problems: (i) a human problem related to managing attention, (ii) a process problem related to managing new ideas into good currency, (iii) a structural problem related to managing part-whole relationships, and (iv) a strategic problem related to institutional leadership.

[9]More recently, ancillary innovations in the form of changes in the boundary relationships of an organization have also appeared. These lead an organization to work with new partners outside previously existing areas and require close cooperation and collaboration in strategic alliances. Knowledge-sharing partnerships may qualify as such. Some have expanded the three conventional categories further, citing organizational innovations.

[10]Still, preventing innovation can secure control over a workforce, be it by centralizing authority in a particular department or person, limiting possibilities for action, or reducing the need for human capital. A further explanation for aversion to risk in the public sector might be that the costs of failure remain so high—both politically and professionally—that managers shy away from

efficiency, and control, they often undermine it. Creative-thinking skills are one part of creativity, but expertise and motivation are also essential. Managers can influence the first two, but doing so is costly and takes time.[11] They can make a more effective difference by boosting the intrinsic motivation of personnel. To manage for creativity and innovation in ways that keep clients, audiences, and partners satisfied, they have five levers: (i) the amount of challenge they give to personnel to stimulate minds, (ii) the degree of freedom they grant around procedures and processes to minimize hassle, (iii) the way they design work groups to tap ideas from all ranks, (iv) the encouragement and incentives they give, which should include rewards and recognition, and (v) the nature of organizational support. Needless to say, managers must themselves be motivated.

Opening Doors to Diverse Perspectives

If you want to make an apple pie from scratch, you must first create the universe.
—Carl Sagan

Before World War II, closed innovation was the operating paradigm for most companies.[12] Innovating enterprises kept their discoveries secret and made no attempt to assimilate information from outside their own research and development laboratories. Collaboration need not be bounded by the wall of the organization. In

---

(Footnote 10 continued)

innovation as a feature of everyday practice. Another might be that there are few financial or career incentives to think outside the box. Monopolistic structures, "adhocism," tight budgets, and heavy workloads can also hinder the long-term investment and commitment that is needed to truly embed a culture of innovation. Paradoxically, the need to keep up sometimes also means that new technologies or ways of working are adopted before a prior innovation takes root.

[11]Hiring the right person is the single, biggest, most important decision an organization makes. Obviously, success or failure flow from understanding (or not) the need to recruit. Having a talent management strategy gives managers guidance about what they should do more or less of. It also helps to ensure that everyone is familiar with the priorities of the organization and how recruitment can impact it. The steps are to (i) specify what kind of talent the organization needs, (ii) identify what and where the gaps are, (iii) identify high potentials, (iv) assess readiness for leadership transitions, (v) accelerate development, and (vi) focus and drive performance. (Personnel should play an active role in the management of their own talent too.)

[12]In the past, innovation was considered a simple process of investment in fundamental research leading to commercialization of new products by farsighted management, usually in the "traditional" high-technology and manufacturing sectors. (However, knowledge-intensive services such as finance, business services, and engineering have formed important and successful elements of a trend of innovations in service and organizational, not product, innovations. Silicon Valley has been the world's most prolific laboratory for information technology innovation for more than 40 years.).

recent years, the world has seen major advances in technology and organization assisting the diffusion of information. Not least of these are electronic communication systems, including the internet. Today, data and information can be transferred so swiftly that it seems impossible to prevent movement (should one want to). Since organizations cannot stop this phenomenon, they must learn to take advantage of it.[13] Communities and networks of practice are fertile venues that provide intellectual challenge, allow people to pursue their passions, foster mutual trust, organize a setting for "noble" work, and gather appreciative audiences. The above table underscores that open innovation requires mindsets and organizational cultures different from those of traditional (closed) innovation.

Table. Closed and open innovation

Closed innovation principles	Open innovation principles
• The smart people in our field work for us	• Not all the smart people work for us. We need to work with smart people inside and outside our company
• To profit from research and development, we must discover it, develop it, and ship it ourselves	• External research and development can create significant value; internal research and development is needed to claim some portion of that value
• If we discover it ourselves, we will get it to market first	• We do not have to originate the research to profit from it
• The company that gets an innovation to market first will win	• Building a better business model is better than getting to market first
• If we create the most and the best ideas in the industry, we will win	• If we make the best use of internal and external ideas, we will win
• We should control our innovation process, so that our competitors do not profit from our ideas	• We should profit from others' use of our innovation process, and we should buy others' intellectual property whenever it advances our own business model

Source Author

Components of Innovation Systems

To turn really interesting ideas and fledgling technologies into a company that can continue to innovate for years, it requires a lot of disciplines.

—Steve Jobs

---

[13]Famously, Albert Einstein suggested that problems cannot be solved at the same level of awareness that created them. This means that novel answers often lie outside the current system. Therefore, individuals who search widely for innovations are crucial to a positive future. Organizations that mean to foster performance and change should identify and value scouts and give them the leeway and resources to search in distant places.

There is no simple universal formula for successful innovation: it is nonlinear, works at many levels, and is too complex to be pinned down in that way. It is uniquely human and cannot be done by machines. Nevertheless, innovations are not random: they occur in relation to the past, present, and future conditions of an organization. The characteristics of innovation systems are that they recruit and retain highly skilled and trained personnel, give them access to knowledge, and then encourage and enable them to think and act innovatively. Components of an effective innovation system include:

- Clarity in *mission statements and goals*, which invariably feature a commitment from senior managers to assume responsibility for the risk of failure.
- An *organizational culture* that values innovation, where there is encouragement for personnel to think differently, take calculated risks, and challenge the status quo. Major forces such as leadership, attitudes to risk, budgeting, audit, performance measurement, recruitment, and open innovation are aligned in support.
- A *systems approach* to management that understands innovation as one part of a wider context, appreciates interconnections, and can conduct systematic analyses of how a problem interacts with other problems, parts of the organization, projects, etc. Management fosters coordination across these interconnections and stresses integration rather than compartmentalization.
- The adequate *resourcing* of innovation in line with strategy.
- The placing of *responsibility* for innovation on all staff.
- Understanding that *creativity* is desirable but insufficient. Innovation ambassadors must still take responsibility for follow-through.
- An enriched *physical workplace* that enhances creativity by providing accessible, casual meeting spots; physical stimuli; space for quiet reflection; a variety of communication tools, e.g., white boards, bulletin boards; contact space for clients, audiences, and partners; and room for individual expression, among others.
- Human resource systems that ensure *staff* have diverse thinking (or learning) styles, giving them a variety of perspectives on single problems.
- Team set-ups that avoid *groupthink* and balance the beginner's mind with experience, freedom with discipline, play with professionalism, and improvisation with planning. Teams embody divergent and convergent thinking, diverse thinking styles, and diversity of skills; and handle conflict.
- High levels of *decentralization* and *functional differentiation* and a range of *specialized areas* within the organization.
- Honed *knowledge management* systems and processes that constantly bring new ideas, concepts, data, information, and knowledge into the organization.
- Numerous and empowered members of relevant *communities and networks* of practice.
- Processes and methodologies that identify and share *good practice*.
- A *performance measurement* system that measures the innovative pulse of the organization; ensures monitoring and evaluation of inputs, activities, outputs, outcomes, and impacts; and feeds lessons back to the system.
- The instigation of *incentives* and *rewards* for innovative individuals and teams.

- Plentiful *space* for creative thinking and reflective practice, e.g., away-days, brainstorming sessions, peer assists, after action reviews and retrospects, problem-solving groups, discussion groups and forums.[14]
- Linkages with the *marketing* function, in ways that involve stakeholders and seek regular feedback.
- Effective *dissemination* systems.
- Dedication *information systems* that ensure positive coverage and publicize success.
- Structured *intellectual property management* systems that identify, protect, value, manage, and audit the organization's intellectual property.

References

Drucker P (1985) Innovation and entrepreneurship. HarperCollins, New York
Van de Ven A (1986) Central problems in the management of innovation. Management Science 32 (5):590–607

Further Reading

Woodman R, Sawyer J, Griffin R (1993) Toward a theory of organizational creativity. Academy of Management Review 18(2):293–321

---

[14]All Google engineers are encouraged to spend 20% of their work time, i.e., one-day per week, to pursue independent projects that interest them. At 3 M, it is 15%.

Proposition 103
Drawing Learning Charters

In a Word Despite competing demands, modern organizations should not forget that learning is the best way to meet the challenges of the time. Learning charters demonstrate commitment: they are a touchstone against which provision and practice can be tested and a waymark with which to guide, monitor, and evaluate progress. It is difficult to argue that what learning charters advocate is not worth striving for.

Communicating for Change

Often, strategic reversals in organizational change are failures of execution. Poor communications explain much. That is because the real power of the vision that underpins change can only be unleashed if institutional commitment is verbalized to frame a desirable future; share core beliefs, common values, and understandings; and help motivate and coordinate the actions that drive transformation.

To spark action, credible, focused, jargon-free, on-time, liberal, face-to-face, and two-way communication[1] in the right context is necessary. Effective visions cannot be imposed on people: they must be set in motion by way of persuasion.

---

[1]The pillars of effective communication are (i) simplicity; (ii) metaphor, analogy, and illustration; (iii) multiple forums; (iv) repetition; (v) leadership by example; (vi) explanation of apparent inconsistencies; and (vii) give-and-take.

© Asian Development Bank 2017

O. Serrat, *Knowledge Solutions*, DOI 10.1007/978-981-10-0983-9_103

Progressively then, communication for change (i) raises awareness and informs stakeholders of vision, progress, and outcomes; (ii) edifies stakeholders regarding their active involvement in the change process and imparts skills, knowledge, and appreciation; and (iii) generates buy-in and a sense of excitement about the transformation.[2] Personnel who communicate well incorporate each day, at every conceivable opportunity, messages that update, educate, and commit. They preach a vision through conversation and storytelling. They continually reaffirm it. The best visions call on the past, relate to the present, and link to the future.

Drawing Learning Charters

> *He that gives good advice, builds with one hand; he that gives good counsel and example, builds with both; but he that gives good admonition and bad example, builds with one hand and pulls down with the other.*
>
> —Francis Bacon

A charter is a written instrument given as evidence of agreement.[3] It can also be a document setting forth the aims and principles of a united group to inform stakeholders in an endeavor and serve as a reference of authority for the future. A clear, concise statement of the direction of an organization that outlines purposes and results is a useful tool with which to stimulate enthusiasm.

For example, the Learning Declaration Group (Cunningham 2006) has promoted learning and development for many years. The 13 signatories[4] to its Declaration on Learning, people who have researched and written extensively about effective learning[5], have isolated the benefits for society, organizations, and individuals. The declaration spells out what these are and invites responses from policy makers;

---

[2]Depending on the organization, audiences, and the nature of the change, these must be aligned along a commitment curve of contact, awareness, understanding, positive perception, adoption, institutionalization, and internalization.

[3]In numerous instances, that can be a document issued by a sovereign, legislature, or other authority to create a public or private corporation, e.g., a city, college, or bank, and define its privileges and purposes.

[4]They are Margaret Attwood, Tom Boydell, John Burgoyne, David Clutterbuck, Ian Cunningham, Bob Garratt, Peter Honey, Andrew Mayo, David Megginson, Alan Mumford, Michael Pearn, Mike Pedler, and Robin Wood.

[5]The characteristics of effective learning are reflectiveness, resourcefulness, reciprocity, and resilience.

leaders in organizations; teachers, trainers, and developers; and individual learners. The notable tenets of the declaration include:

- Learning reinforces the informed, conscious, and discriminating choices that underpin democracy.
- Learning is the only source of sustainable development.
- Learning to learn is the most fundamental learning of all.
- Learning is the key to developing your identity and potential.
- Society, and the communities of which it is comprised, survives, adapts, and thrives through developing and sharing learning.
- Regular and rigorous use of learning processes increases everyone's capacity to contribute to the success of organizations by challenging, reshaping, and meeting its goals.
- Learning expands the horizons of who we are and what we can become.

Since the first version of the declaration was launched in 1998, the group has received reactions ranging from "It's not very radical" to "It's too radical for us to implement". More critically, others have decried the communication mode of the declaration—which mixes principles, analyses, and plans of action somewhat indigestibly—or demonstrated its dominant discourses and assumptions.[6] Yet, its avowed intention is only to promote dialogue on learning in organizations, and its originality lies in the fact that very few organizations practice what is suggested in the paper. It poses fascinating questions: specifically, how can policy makers; leaders in organizations; teachers, trainers, and developers; and individual learners maximize the learning ability of people by encouraging and supporting individual and collective learning that enables society, organizations, and individuals to change and adapt more effectively?

Learning for Change in ADB

A publication of the Asian Development Bank (2009a) examined what that organization might say, to what purposes and results, and through what commitments to corporate action, if it were to make a statement of intent on learning for change in ADB. If its staff members were to pledge themselves to individual actions, what

---

[6]The authors would be pleased to see what progress the National College for School Leadership and National Education Trust in the United Kingdom are making in encouraging schools to create charters for learning in primary schools.

Table 103.1 A learning charter for ADB

Statement of Intent
• ADB embraces the concepts of the learning organization to work better with its developing member countries and cultivate the talent of its staff members.
Purposes and Results
• To take concrete actions to transform ADB into a learning organization in its policies, strategies, programs, and projects, as well as the business processes and partnerships associated with these, to meet the challenges of the time.
• To support lifelong learning and development by staff members to ensure that ADB is able to attract, retain, and develop the talent it needs in support of its mission.
Commitments to Corporate Action
• Hold a regular caucus on learning (such as a forum on "Learning in Action").
• Clarify, simplify, and drive governance for human resources management, including learning and development.
• Make clear the roles and responsibilities for learning and development so that there is clear accountability for results.
• Develop learning and development plans in every department and office, and track and evaluate results.
• Establish a minimum annual commitment of funds or time for learning for employees.
Commitments to Individual Action
• Be open to different ideas and ways of doing things.
• Build (and model) an environment where discussion, debate, and questioning are encouraged.
• Look out for good practices and capture and share them as appropriate.
• Investigate and master tools, methods, and approaches that might enrich team discussions.
• Seek regular inputs from clients, and benchmark the services provided against the best in ADB and comparable aid agencies.
• Hold regular team meetings to examine what could be done differently, capture lessons learned, and share lessons with others.
• Participate in communities of practice and other value networks, and encourage staff members to do the same.
• Volunteer to coach and mentor younger or new staff members, and build requisite skills continuously.
• Prepare an individual learning and development plan that incorporates my needs and demonstrates what I will do to support those of others.
• Work with my teams to develop team learning and development plans.
• Cooperate with staff members under my supervision to develop individual learning and development plans that reflect a balance of organizational and personal learning and development needs.
• Provide time and resources necessary to live up to the learning and development needs determined and agreed upon.
• Monitor and evaluate the learning and development activities of staff members under my supervision.
• Take care that I have a diversity of talents, skills, and perspectives represented on teams.
• Ensure that staff members in my unit have the chance to share learning and development experiences with others.
• Resist the temptation to divert learning and development funds to other uses or to use operational requirements as an excuse to delay learning.

Source ADB (2009a)

might these be? The learning charter that the document champions is not prescriptive, nor is it exhaustive. But it is assuredly specific, measurable, achievable, realistic, and timely (Table 103.1).

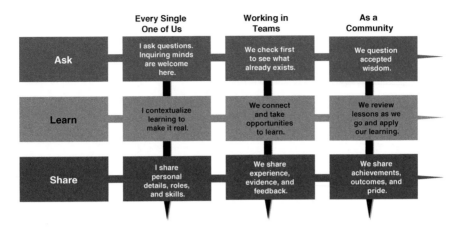

Fig. 103.1 Knowledge behaviors. *Source* Author

ADB offers other recent examples of statements on learning. On 31 July 2009, Haruhiko Kuroda—ADB President and concurrent Chairperson of ADB's Board of Directors (2008, 2009b)—approved *Enhancing Knowledge Management Under Strategy 2020* to advance the knowledge management agenda under *Strategy 2020: The Long-Term Strategic Framework of the Asian Development Bank (2008–2020)*. Four pillars will support the plan of action: (i) sharpening the knowledge focus in all ADB operations, (ii) promoting and empowering communities of practice for knowledge capture and sharing, (iii) strengthening external knowledge partnerships to develop and disseminate knowledge, and (iv) scaling-up staff development programs to improve technical skills and manage knowledge. In relation to the second, ADB's Knowledge Management Center proposed for adoption by ADB's communities of practice a dynamic, interactive, and organic framework that articulates the need to ask, learn, and share at individual, team, and community levels. From a knowledge sharing and learning perspective, translating the framework into inputs, activities, and outputs for key outcomes will help maintain focus on the things that matter to communities of practice and serve the needs and aspirations of their members (Fig. 103.1).

References

ADB (2008) Strategy 2020: the long-term strategic framework of the Asian development bank (2008–2020). Manila
ADB (2009a) Learning for change in ADB. Manila
ADB (2009b) Enhancing knowledge management under strategy 2020: plan of action for 2009–2011. Manila
Cunningham I (2006) A declaration on learning: how do you respond? Development and Learning in Organizations 20(6)18–23

Proposition 104
Embracing Failure

In a Word Success is a process and failure on the way is an opportunity. Successful individuals and organizations fail well.

Living on the Edge

Infinite complexity, endless possibilities, and resulting constant change characterize the twenty-first century. More intimately and faster than ever before, the realms of environment, economy, society, polity, and technology coevolve in adaptive systems. The times demand the ability to take risks, embrace failure, and move on.

Developing a culture of intelligent experimentation and failure analysis is no longer an option. Individuals, groups, and organizations must create, innovate, and reflect to generate the radical solutions they need to tackle challenges in markets, industries, organizations, geographies, intellectual disciplines, and generations. To accomplish this, they must learn to learn and learn to unlearn before, during, and after.[1]

---

[1] For most of the twenty-first century, learning was about acquiring skills, usually through knowledge transfer. It was about learning to be. In a world of flux, it must develop as a theory of how one becomes time and again.

© Asian Development Bank 2017
O. Serrat, *Knowledge Solutions*, DOI 10.1007/978-981-10-0983-9_104

Learning from Children

I didn't see it then, but it turned out that getting fired from Apple was the best thing that could have ever happened to me. The heaviness of being successful was replaced by the lightness of being a beginner again, less sure about everything. It freed me to enter one of the most creative periods of my life.

—Steve Jobs

Success and failure are borne of the same mother. Children are not afraid to fall short. They fail countless times at standing, walking, talking, riding a bicycle, tying shoelaces, and other important tasks. But they are resilient and never give up. They embrace failure and adapt until they achieve the desired result. Playing is a vital part of their lives.[2] It leads to making (constructing) in a social world that values participation and that leads to knowing. Is it because they no longer play that adults are afraid to fail? After all, is play not the opposite of work?

Allaying Adult Fears

Failure is something organizations shy away from. Instead of learning from failure in detail, adults profess they will never repeat that mistake again. Their fear is understandable: they are paid to succeed, not fail.[3] Hence, errors can only reflect negatively on their intelligence, chipping away at self-confidence and self-esteem. And so, despite the occasional exhortation inviting mistakes—"If you're not making mistakes, you're not trying hard enough"—personnel knows that mistakes are more often punished than rewarded. As a result, many are reluctant to admit inadequacies, weaknesses, mistakes, and their distinct needs (everyone has different talents and learning styles) and take as few chances as possible. This inhibits individual and collective growth and leads to paralysis, procrastination, and purposelessness.

Organizations cannot promote a passion for learning and pursue courses of action that frustrate it. In a learning culture or learning organization, failures are considered opportunities to learn, not recrimination—worse still in instances, point scoring. (To this effect, some draw learning charters.) If failure is branded as unacceptable, learning is made impossible—with the paradoxical result that failure will inevitably recur, if not prevail. The key to establishing learning systems is

---

[2]Play provides the opportunity to experiment and fail—to fail yet continue to play with different outcomes. Playing is always about becoming, not being.

[3]It follows that compensation is based on tasks well done, not spectacular (and sometimes costly) failures that might eventually produce breakthroughs.

tolerance of failure, continuous feedback on effectiveness,[4] and willingness to foster creativity and innovation. Psychological safety, appreciation of differences, receptiveness to new ideas, and time for reflection are prerequisites to this.

The Attributes of Failure

If success and failure are relatives, failure is not inherently bad. Indeed, it has many advantages. Failure softens hearts, develops maturity, broadens thinking, offers insights, prompts innovation, reveals ability, inspires, reinforces the need for risk, builds courage, fortifies, opens other opportunities, brings unexpected benefits, pushes the envelope of future performance, liberates, makes success sweeter, and is preferable to bitterness and regret. However, to better grasp the attributes of failure and treat it as a friend, we should not define them (nor those of success) narrowly. Failure is best conceptualized as deviation from expected and desired results.[5]

Failing Well

Successful individuals, groups, and organizations fail much more than they succeed. However, their larger success derives from the fact that they fail well. The difference lies in their perception of and their response to failure.[6] In a word, they treat it as a process. They

---

[4]Over the years, independent and self-evaluations have rightly found a role in discovering what results are being achieved, what improvements should be considered, and what is being learned. However, evaluation is still something of a niche occupation and the value it adds is conditioned by the objective specified. There are two competing, often mutually exclusive, purposes to evaluation. Evaluation for accountability centers on the past. Evaluation for learning seeks to improve future performance. Accordingly, there are differences in basic aim, emphasis, audiences, selection of topics, the status of evaluation, the status of evaluators, the significance of data from evaluations, and the importance ascribed to and the manner of feedback. What is more, even organizations that profess to evaluate for learning still lean heavily on evaluation for accountability in their methodologies and practices.

[5]This includes both avoidable errors and unavoidable negative outcomes of experimentation and risk taking. It also includes interpersonal failures arising from misunderstanding and conflict.

[6]Many individuals deemed highly successful, including some Nobel prize winners, set great store by their mistakes. This impacts every aspect of their lives. They appreciate that success is a process and that failure on the way is an opportunity. They concentrate on engaging, not just achieving. Struggles, periods of confusion, wrong turns, and dead ends are not cause for alarm; they are expected—indeed inevitable—parts of the journey. (Knowledge is much more than a stock. It is deeply contextual and sparked by circumstance. Hence, there is a natural flow to its creation, disruption, and use. The context can be simple, complicated, complex, or chaotic and related decisions must try to match the context's characteristics.) Highly successful individuals have a high tolerance for failure because they have developed the skill of learning to fail.

- appreciate that failure is not avoidable, objective, a single event, a stigma, the enemy, or final;
- understand why they made the decision they took based on the information they had;
- assess their decisions based on what they knew at the time;
- judge the systemic errors they committed in under- or overestimating difficulties, costs, timelines, abilities, etc.;
- examine whether they had all the information they needed;
- investigate what successes are contained in the failure and draw dividends;
- plan to obtain more and better information to underpin future decisions;
- use the experience to build and work from strengths; and
- set a new goal, order their plan, take action, reevaluate progress, and adjust continually.

Literature has not yet clearly described the process of learning from failure in organizations. (For individuals, it is in any event shaped by individual experience, knowledge, attitudes, skills, aspirations, and behaviors.)[7] Moreover, the significance of learning is not necessarily proportional to the scope of failure. Simply put, however, the process of embracing failure must involve identifying mishaps; discussing and analyzing them in a spirit of inquiry and openness; and dealing with controversy and disagreement productively. Needless to say, progress will hinge on the existence of shared, constructive beliefs, for instance, vis-à-vis performance outcomes. These will in turn depend on effective coaching and mentoring, clear direction, and a supportive and enabling workplace environment and culture.[8] The barriers to this lie at individual, group, and organizational levels.

Embracing Failure

In the modern world, a mind shift we need is realization that failure is the rule rather than the exception. This begs intellectual honesty. Failure is a promising area of investigation because it is such a common experience. Yet, it is a secret that is never spoken out loud. One hundred years ago, Vilfredo Pareto (1848–1923), an Italian engineer, economist, sociologist, and philosopher, demanded: "Give me a fruitful error any time, full of seeds, bursting with its own corrections. You can keep your sterile truth for yourself." Failing well breeds success. It is not difficult to be definitely tentative, turn means into ends, be less prejudiced but more discriminatory, transform work into play, and celebrate mistakes. Why wait?

---

[7]Stating the obvious, individuals display more differences in perception, sense making, estimation, and attribution than groups or organizations do.

[8]Next, tools and techniques can be applied to enhance recognition of the value of knowledge developed from experience and enrich sense making. They include action learning sets, after-action reviews and retrospects, the Five Whys technique, mind maps, the Most Significant Change technique, peer assists, the Reframing Matrix, the SCAMPER technique, the Six Thinking Hats technique, social network analysis, and storytelling, among others.

Box 1: Are You Ready To Embrace Failure?

1. Do you keep your mistakes to yourself?
2. Do you try new things only if you are sure you can succeed?
3. Do you become very cautious after something does not work out?
4. Do you try to immediately forget your failures?
5. Do you think failure is shameful?

If you have answered "Yes" to one or more of these questions, you are probably not ready to embrace failure. To fail successfully, you must take every aspect of failure to heart and learn to the full.

Source Author

Box 2: Inspirations for Embracing Failure

Truth will sooner come out of error than from confusion.

—Francis Bacon

Failure is the condiment that gives success its flavor.

—Truman Capote

'Tis the maddest trick a man can ever play in his whole life, to let his breath sneak out of his body without any more ado, and without so much as a rap o'er the pate, or a kick of the guts; to go out like the snuff of a farthing candle, and die merely of the mulligrubs, or the sullens.

—Miguel de Cervantes

Success consists of going from failure to failure without loss of enthusiasm.

—Winston Churchill

You will do foolish things, but do them with enthusiasm.

—Colette

Mistakes are almost always of a sacred nature. Never try to correct them. On the contrary: rationalize them, understand them thoroughly. After that, it will be possible for you to sublimate them.

—Salvador Dali

Box 3: More Inspirations for Embracing Failure

I have not failed. I've just found 10,000 ways that won't work.

—Thomas Edison

Even a mistake may turn out to be the one thing necessary to a worthwhile achievement.

—Henry Ford

A man's errors are his portals of discovery.

—James Joyce

Don't be afraid to make a mistake. But make sure you don't make the same mistake twice.

—Akio Morita

It is not the critic who counts, not the man who points out how the strong man stumbled, or where the doer of deeds could have done better. The credit belongs to the man who is actually in the arena, whose face is marred by dust and sweat and blood, who strives valiantly, who errs and comes short again and again, who knows the great enthusiasms, the great devotions, and spends himself in a worthy cause, who at best knows achievement and who at the worst if he fails at least fails while daring greatly so that his place shall never be with those cold and timid souls who know neither victory nor defeat.

—Theodore Roosevelt

Would you like me to give you a formula for... success? It's quite simple, really. Double your rate of failure. You're thinking of failure as the enemy of success. But it isn't at all... you can be discouraged by failure—or you can learn from it. So go ahead and make mistakes. Make all you can. Because, remember that's where you'll find success. On the far side.

—Thomas J. Watson

Further Reading

Heath R (2009) Celebrating failure: the power of taking risks, making mistakes and thinking big. The Career Press

Maxwell J (2000) Failing forward: turning mistakes into stepping stones for success. Thomas Nelson, Inc

Proposition 105
Social Media and the Public Sector

In a Word Social media is revolutionizing the way we live, learn, work, and play. Elements of the private sector have begun to thrive on opportunities to forge, build, and deepen relationships. Some are transforming their organizational structures and opening their corporate ecosystems in consequence. The public sector is a relative newcomer. It too can drive stakeholder involvement and satisfaction.

R.I.P. Web 1.0

Global conversations, especially among Generation Y,[1] were born circa 2004. Beginning 1995 until then, the Internet had hosted static, one-way websites. These were places to visit passively, retrieve information from, and perhaps post comments about by electronic mail.

---

[1]Generation Y (also known as the Millennial Generation, Generation Next, or the Net Generation) describes the demographic group born between the mid-1970s and the early 2000s, with ages ranging 10–35 years. It is characterized by growing familiarity with communications, media, and digital technologies.

© Asian Development Bank 2017
O. Serrat, *Knowledge Solutions*, DOI 10.1007/978-981-10-0983-9_105

> *The loss of control you fear is already in the past.*
>
> —Clay Shirky

Sixteen years later, Web 2.0^2 enabled many-to-many connections in numerous domains of interest and practice, powered by the increasing use of blogs, image and video sharing, mashups, podcasts, ratings, Really Simple Syndication, social bookmarking, tweets, widgets, and wikis, among others. Today, people expect the Internet to be user-centric. Web 1.0 was about getting people connected, even though its applications were largely proprietary and only displayed information their owners wished to publish. More advanced (and cheap or free) software can now assume, correctly, that people stand ready to connect; it is therefore far more interactive and people-aware. Users generate content (e.g., blogs, Flickr, wikis), business intelligence (e.g., FreshBooks, Prosper), reviews, and opinions (e.g., TripAdvisor), products (e.g., eBay), networks of contacts (e.g., Facebook, MySpace), statements on the value of web pages (e.g., Google PageRank), distributed storage and server capacity (e.g., Peer-to-Peer networks), connectivity (e.g., mesh networks, Wi-Fi sharing), and expressions of taste and emotion (e.g., Delicious, Last.fm) that search engines, not portals, fetch. Since traffic equals money, simple online economics drive uninterrupted change in the way we live, learn, work, and play.

> *As far as the customer is concerned, the interface is the product.*
>
> —Jef Raskin

The form that communications take is collectively dubbed as "social media".^{3} Where that is enriched by high levels of user interactions, the contents of the platforms promoting it across connected devices are in near-permanent "beta" stages of development, being and becoming at the same time, both As-Is and To-Be. In all instances, success hinges on a plausible promise, effective Web 2.0 applications, and an acceptable bargain with users (Shirky 2008). Meaning is the new message.

---

^{2}The term "Web 2.0" refers to applications that facilitate interactive information sharing, interoperability, user-centered design, and collaboration on the Internet. These are the result of cumulative changes in the ways software developers and users employ the Internet as an information transport mechanism. Typical features and techniques include search, links, authoring, tags, extensions, and signals.

^{3}Social media is an umbrella term. At its simplest, it is the integration of technology with social interaction to create value. It rests on internet tools that enable shared community experiences through multidirectional conversations that create, organize, edit, combine, and share content.

The world may not yet be flat but technology is most assuredly leveling organizations and the silos in them: users have been given the tools to do things together in networks and no longer rely exclusively on the traditional structures, viz., functional, geographical, product, customer/market, or matrix organizations, that up to this time had enabled them to collaborate and contribute to serve common aims in (the lower echelons of) the hierarchy of needs.[4] They are newly empowered and emboldened. Specifically, with positive (and, to the unprepared, negative) ramifications, information is far more transparent than in the past; users can access up-to-date information instantly on any topic; there are few barriers to involvement; and online communities therefore coalesce all of a sudden.

Table. Short glossary of web 2.0 terminology[a]

Form	Description
Blog	Short for web log, an editor-less, chronologically ordered journal of commentary and descriptions of events, written in a conversational tone, sometimes accompanied by other materials such as graphics or video, that is frequently updated with permanent links to other sources and contains entries inviting comments
Chat	Interaction on a website with users adding text items in sequence into the same space at almost the same time
Crowdsourcing	A compound of crowd and outsourcing, the broadcast by an initiating agent of problems in need of solutions to a group of solvers, with convergent interests and behaviors, in the form of an open call
Folksonomy	A system of classification, sometimes visualized as word clouds, derived from the method and practice of collaboratively creating and managing user-defined labels or tags to annotate and categorize content
Image and video sharing site	A user-generated website that allows users to upload pictures or videos and view and comment on those of others
Internet forum	Also called a message board, a discussion area on a website where users can discuss issues with asynchronous posts
Mashup	An application combining data from two or more external sources into a single integrated tool that performs a new service
Metadata	Structured information that describes—and allows users to find, manage, control, and understand—other information
Microblogging	A web service that allows users to write tweets and publish them to be viewed and commented upon by their network

(continued)

---

[4]The phenomenon of Web 2.0 jives with other societal trends. They include demographic changes, the consumerization of information and communications technology, the empowerment of consumers, the gradual move from hierarchical to network-based forms of organizations, the rise of the knowledge worker, the accent on creativity and innovation, and the growing importance of informal learning.

(continued)

Form	Description
Mobile text messaging	Short messages of text exchanged between mobile devices
Mobile web	A mobile device incorporating a web browser to access the Internet
Podcast	Audio or video "show" made available on the Internet, usually through a subscription, for downloading to personal computers or mobile devices
Really simple syndication feed	A file that contains regularly updated information such as news headlines or blog posts and can be subscribed to using aggregators or newsreaders
Social bookmarking	A method enabling users to store, organize, search, and manage bookmarks of websites
Social media	Online technologies and practices that users leverage to share concepts, experiences, insights, opinions, and perspectives in social interface
Social networking	The process of engaging in online communities, typically through "groups" and "friends lists," that allows users to connect and interact with like-minded parties
Tweet	A single message or status update of up to 140 characters that can be read by users following individuals on Twitter, a microblogging service, or the act of posting it
Virtual world	A computer-based simulated game environment in which users interact with one another via avatars, viz., virtual representations of themselves, typically in the form of two- or three-dimensional cartoonish representations of humanoids
Widget	Also called a gadget, badge, or applet, a piece of self-contained, transportable code, often displayed in a small box, that can be embedded into a website or program to perform a specific function, such as providing weather forecasts or news
Wiki	Collaborative publishing technology, often taken to mean a collection of webpages that allows users to work on and modify content online with appropriate version control

Source Author

[a]Social media builds on existing platforms for communication and collaboration. They include face-to-face meetings, telephone calls, paper mail, fax, and so on. Those where information and communications technology comes to the fore include electronic mail, instant messaging, desktop sharing, person availability, video conferencing, Voice over Internet Protocol, and web conferencing

Box: Examples of Social Media Sites[5]

Craigslist—classified ads.
Delicious—social bookmarking.
Digg—social news.
Engadget—gadget news and reviews.
Facebook—social networking.
Flickr—photo sharing.
Flixster—movie reviews and ratings.
LinkedIn—professional networking.
MyBlogLog—blog networking.
MySpace Music—music sharing.
Netvibes—information aggregator.
Ning—social network space.
NutshellMail—social network aggregation.
Second Life—virtual worlds.
Slideshare—presentation sharing.
Twitter—microblogging.
Wikipedia—web-based encyclopedia.
WordPress—open source blog publishing application.
Yahoo! Answers—community answers.
YouTube—video sharing.

Source Author

Creating Value in Communities

Social communities now exist in almost every conceivable domain. However, four broad types of online communities have morphed into Web. 2.0 entities in a new, horizontal architecture of participation and connection that prizes credibility.[6] They are relationship-, interest-, transaction-, and fantasy-oriented. Communities of the first type organize around (usually) intense life experiences that lead to personal bonding between members. In the second type, interactions center on topics of common interest. The third type of community revolves around facilitated buying

---

[5]All industries and technologies experience consolidation, and social media is no exception. Many Web 2.0 applications are absorbed by others. Facebook, for instance, grew after its acquisition of FriendFeed in 2009. New entrants will continue to challenge incumbents because Web 2.0 applications allow for rapid prototyping, failure, and adaptation.

[6]For bloggers, for example, endorsement value is a function of their authority on a given topic, their network's interest in and authority on the topic, and the trust level among the network on the topic.

and selling of products and services and the delivery of information that supports transactions.[7] The fourth type plays roles in simulated environments.

These four types of online communities hold significant value-creation potential for users, public sector agencies, nongovernment organizations, and the private sector. Opportunities to add value through new channels lie pell-mell in content addition; subscription revenues; closer understanding of explicit or latent needs; product or service ideation or creation; and better targeting of market segments. Naturally, the scope for value-creation hinges on the particulars of a community and who organizes its space. Nonetheless, well-designed and well-implemented social media brings with it the power of every user on the planet: its influence can only grow because, unlike in the past, control is shared with the crowd and very real feedback is fast. Users generate content and voice their feelings far and wide. From "wisdom of the crowd"[8] reactions, organizations can collect detailed information on users, build valuable relationships through conversations about people's experiences, deploy higher levels of engagement, and refine offerings and related messages to better match needs. The uses of social media are boundless: Web 2.0, a.k.a the Social or Relationship Web, amounts to nothing less than a massive social experiment.

Growing Web 2.0 Organizations ...

Many individuals already use Web 2.0 applications every day and consider life without these applications unimaginable. As time flies, a greater percentage of the population will feel the same. Already, younger personnel expect to work in organizations where Web 2.0 is the norm and are dismayed to discover that many of the applications they use in their personal lives are not available professionally. What is more, today's teenagers will soon enter the workforce.

This groundswell invites public sector agencies, nongovernment organizations, and the private sector to engage, innovate, and create relevance according to the types of relationships they want. Organizations and Web 2.0 are not the easiest fit: sometimes, a cultural shift must happen for technology to make a difference. But all must learn how to stay nimble and flexible in an ever-changing digital environment.

---

[7]The chief attraction here is that social media eliminates inefficient middlemen and lowers the cost of products and services.

[8]Borrowing a leaf from Surowiecki (2004), judicious use of Web 2.0 applications can promote the diversity of opinion, independence, decentralization, and aggregation needed to form a wise crowd.

> *Decision by democratic majority vote is a fine form of government, but it's a stinking way to create.*
>
> —Lillian Hellman

Elements of the private sector have begun to thrive on opportunities to forge, build, and deepen relationships with people, both internally and externally. From the early adoption of Web 2.0 applications such as blogs and wikis, they are expanding the mix of tools and shifting from using them experimentally to embedding them in their business processes.[9] Some are transforming their organizational structures and opening their corporate ecosystems in consequence, for example, by encouraging clients, audiences, and partners to join them in developing products. They can now reach mass audiences, target niche markets, craft messages, and create great client experiences, cost-effectively, in ways they only dreamed about before. To build Web 2.0-friendly cultures that are transparent, agile, creative, user-centric, and empowering these high-performance organizations at once asked themselves:

- How can we use Web 2.0 applications to be more successful?
- How can we leverage them to fuse the knowledge, skills, and resources of clients, audiences, and partners?
- How will they change the way we operate?
- How can they help us protect and nurture our brand and reputation?
- How can we use them to identify, recruit, develop, deploy, and retain talent?
- How can we ensure that the information we do not want to share stays in-house?

... In the Public Sector ...

> *If your target audience isn't listening, it's not their fault, it's yours.*
>
> —Seth Godin

Driven by internally focused objectives rather than a service-delivery mentality, bureaucratic in decision-making, traditionally slow to change, saddled with

---

[9]Internally, in declining order of incidence, the primary purposes of Web 2.0 applications are to manage knowledge, foster collaboration across the organization, enhance corporate culture, conduct training, and develop products and services. When interfacing with clients, audiences, and partners, again in declining order of incidence, the main objectives are to improve customer service, acquire new customers in existing markets, invite customer contributions to product development, and enable customers to interact (McKinsey & Co. 2008).

top-down hierarchical structures in which positional authority no longer compels, the public sector is a relative newcomer to social media. On the social technographics ladder, most public sector organizations are inactives (Li and Bernoff 2008)[10] that continue to rely on yesterday's technology to address tomorrow's problems.[11] They must change their world or the world will change them. Accepting that the Internet is increasing the economic and social value of the information they hold, they must stretch mindsets to understand emerging mental models and equip themselves with the right policies, strategies, resources, delivery mechanisms, and management skills to take part in collaborative relationships in the digital economy. Why should they do so? First, the public sector bears social responsibility for embracing change—else, it faces reputational risk. Second, the social media will soon play a major role in defining how public sector organizations are considered: their accomplishments are measured not just by what they do but also, more and more, by perceptions of that.[12] Third, and most important, Web 2.0 applications offer unprecedented opportunities to achieve more simple, user-oriented, transparent, accountable, participative, inclusive, responsive, joined-up, networked, and efficient government.[13] To reap these, public sector organizations must meet people where they are. Increasingly, that is online. All the time more, they will need to be aided by third parties acting as intermediaries in providing more granular, or component-based, content and services, with implications for the design of these.

For Web 2.0 applications, the most favorable context is high trust, collaborative, and knowledge intensive. Three aspects, all having to do with management

---

[10]At the top of the ladder are creators (who publish and upload). They are followed in turn by critics (who post ratings and reviews, comment, and contribute to Internet forums and wikis); collectors (who organize content using RSS feeds, tags, and voting sites); joiners (who connect in social networks such as Facebook and MySpace); spectators (who read blogs, watch videos, listen to podcasts, and read online forums and ratings and reviews); and inactives (who neither create nor consume social content of any kind).

[11]In some of them, to break the fetters of command-and-control, communities and networks of practice spontaneously come together using team collaboration and content-sharing software such as Lotus Quickr.

[12]Every organization has a brand and that is constantly under threat. Clients, audiences, and partners have always had an idea about what brands signify, and their ideas may vary from the images organizations are trying to project. Web 2.0 applications elicit opinions in real time.

[13]Social media can (i) amplify access to clients, audiences, and partners and improve the accessibility of the public sector's communications; (ii) enable the public sector to be more active in its relationships; (iii) offer greater scope to adjust or refocus communications quickly, where necessary; (iv) improve the long-term cost effectiveness of communications; (v) benefit from the credibility of nongovernment channels; (vi) speed feedback and input; (vii) reach market segments on specific issues; and (vii) reduce the public sector's dependence on traditional media channels and counter inaccurate press coverage.

(including that of human resources), favor success on the Social Web: a lack of internal barriers to Web 2.0,[14] a culture that favors cooperation, and early adoption of Web 2.0 applications for communication, interaction, and service. (Web 2.0, as much else, is about people, not technology.) For this, public sector organizations must develop social media strategies across multiple networks, both internally and externally focused: from how their personnel should conduct themselves as employees[15] to what is considered competition. The transition they must accomplish requires strong leadership for engagement by senior managers (whom most surveys discover cannot easily grasp the potential returns from Web 2.0); competency in forging, building, and deepening relationships on the Internet; policies to both protect organizational assets and ensure appropriate personnel behavior;[16] and, finally, training so that everyone understands Web. 2.0 applications, how to use them in the context of the organization, and their respective roles.

... In Quick Steps

You can never cross the ocean unless you have the courage to lose sight of the shore.

—Christopher Columbus

In the twenty-first century, three broad challenges are plain to see: emerging global issues, rising citizen expectations, and aging populations. In the age of the Internet, Web 2.0 applications dictate how responsive the public sector must be.[17] A

---

[14]Potential barriers stem from demographics, reliance on outdated hardware or software that cannot access or use Web 2.0 applications, and institutional blockers from various units. In the public sector, blockers typically include offices of information systems and technology, external relations, and the general counsel as well as line managers. Tools of control cannot be condoned but legitimate concerns over legal, privacy, and information technology issues; media and communications; and security should be addressed through policy, process, education, and training.

[15]See, for instance, IBM (2010). The guidelines give advice for appropriate behavior by personnel when they interface on blogs, wikis, social networks, and virtual worlds. Personnel are expected to act professionally, respectfully, and responsibly. The guidelines are measured and balance the need to protect the company while encouraging collaboration, creativity, and innovation. They recognize that personnel need to make their own decisions about the extent of their contributions.

[16]The key is risk management, not risk avoidance. The spectrum of activities of a public servant on the Social Web, for example, ranges from the individual to the professional to the official. As an individual, he or she might express private views and take part in social networks in both private and professional capacities. As a professional, he or she might explore alternatives or present authoritative views. As an official, he or she might discuss the organization's policies or represent them.

[17]Usefully, the Organisation for Economic Co-operation and Development has articulated 13 principles to provide a general framework for the wider and more effective use of public sector

shared vision for the journey necessarily encompasses stakeholders (who to engage with), reason (rationale for acting), activity (what to do), and tools (how to do it). In quick steps, public sector organizations can start with the following:[18]

- Edify the organization by helping personnel at all levels realize what Web 2.0 applications are and how they can help it recognize and manage fast-evolving explicit or latent needs.
- Craft social media policies that capitalize on the benefits of adopting Web 2.0 applications in the organization, including policies for individual departments.
- Formulate social media strategies that delineate clear priorities and determine the opportunity or requirement for online collaboration aligned to evolving organizational mandates.
- Evaluate existing technologies to determine their compatibility with morphing Web 2.0 applications.
- Launch internal and external pilots that, with an eye to authenticity as well as risk and governance frameworks, identify and act on specific opportunities to drive early success and enable departments to familiarize themselves with Web 2.0 applications, understand the management required, and refine their objectives for subsequent initiatives.
- Define broader scopes for online engagement as a new way of working through the lifecycle of listen and identify, inform, consult and involve, and collaborate and empower.
- Measure engagement by focusing on the usability of Web 2.0 applications and the extent of engagement as a result of their use.
- Gauge effectiveness by examining the degree to which Web 2.0 applications help create new relevant knowledge and solve cases.
- Inculcate a culture of collaboration by relentlessly progressing how interactions with clients, audiences, and partners take place inside and outside of the organization.
- Foster organizational learning from pilots and regular initiatives based on measurements of engagement and effectiveness and comments from clients, audiences, and partners.

(Footnote 17 continued)

information and content and the generation of new uses from it. They relate to openness, access and transparent conditions for reuse, asset lists, quality, integrity, new technologies and long-term preservation, copyright, pricing, competition, redress mechanisms, public–private partnerships, international access and use, and best practices. Some would argue that timeliness and metadata should have been given more prominence in the list (OECD 2008).

[18]Wider scope can be found in (i) identifying problems, opportunities, or future issues; (ii) policy consultations; (iii) service and service-delivery; and (iv) promotion and communication.

References

IBM (2010) IBM social computing guidelines

Li C, Bernoff J (2008) Groundswell: winning in a world transformed by social technologies. Harvard Business School Publishing

McKinsey & Co (July 2008) Building the web 2.0 enterprise. McKinsey Quarterly

OECD (2008) OECD recommendation of the council for enhanced access and more effective use of public sector information

Shirky C (2008) Here comes everybody: the power of organizing without organizations. The Penguin Press

Surowiecki J (2004) The wisdom of crowds: why the many are smarter than the few and how collective wisdom shapes business, economies, societies, and nations. Doubleday

Further Reading

Government 2.0 Taskforce (2009) Engage: getting on with government 2.0: report of the government 2.0 taskforce

Tapscott D, Williams A (2006) Wikinomics: how mass collaboration changes everything. Atlantic Books

Proposition 106
Enriching Policy with Research

By Arnaldo Pellini and Olivier Serrat

In a Word The failure of researchers to link evidence to policy and practice produces evidence that no one uses, impedes innovation, and leads to mediocre or even detrimental development policies. To help improve the definition, design, and implementation of policy research, researchers should adopt a strategic outcome-oriented approach.

The Promise of Research in Development

In the 2010s, global, regional, and national challenges and their local effects will impact all and the poorest most.[1] In the development sector, research in science, technologies, and ideas can make a difference if they identify what tools, methods, and approaches no longer work; test new ways of doing things; and link knowledge

---

[1] In aid agencies, the short list includes climate and environment, food and agriculture, health, education, governance and social development, growth and investment, and trade. The *Knowledge Solutions* on sparking social innovations paint a fuller (and darker) picture.

© Asian Development Bank 2017
O. Serrat, *Knowledge Solutions*, DOI 10.1007/978-981-10-0983-9_106

of that in ways that inform policy and practice. (Here, policy is taken to mean a deliberate course of action to guide decisions and achieve outcomes.)[2]

Research, the systematic effort to increase the stock of knowledge, has innumerable applications. For this reason, educational institutions, governments, and philanthropic organizations—the three major purveyors of money—spend billions of dollars on research every year. A propos developing country, where utilitarian science policy[3] is favored, proponents contend persuasively that it can help save lives, reduce poverty, and improve the quality of human existence.[4] (Utilitarian research is more likely to be funded as it costs less and pledges more.)

Even so, if most people agree that science and research deserve support, consensus about their benefits quickly breaks down beyond that. In truth, researchers routinely miss opportunities to turn their inquiries into lasting change. The cause of this is the weak rapport between their investigations and recommendations and the real world of policy making. (In the meantime, practitioners just get on with it.) A nonlinear analytical and practical framework to enrich policy with research is missing.[5] These *Knowledge Solutions* showcase (and draw liberally from) the work

---

[2]Policy change can be (i) discursive—involving new concepts and terminology, (ii) procedural—altering the way policy makers do things, (iii) content-oriented—inducing modifications in strategy or policy documents, or (iv) behavioral—transforming attitudes.

[3]Utilitarian science prioritizes projects that can reduce large amounts of suffering for many people. Basic science, on the other hand, tries to stimulate breakthroughs. Scholastic conservation, the third kind of science policy, aims to efficiently impart all available knowledge to whoever can use it. Monumental science sponsors science for the sake of science, often through large projects. Technology development, the fifth branch of science policy, advances the application of science mainly through engineering.

[4]The Department for International Development of the United Kingdom, for one, announced in 2008 that it would double its commitment and invest up to £1 billion in development research over the next 5 years. (It will channel that to six priority areas: growth; sustainable agriculture, particularly in Africa; climate change; health; governance in challenging environments; and future challenges and opportunities.)

[5]Policy processes are complex and rarely linear or logical: simply presenting information to policy makers and expecting them to act upon it is not likely to work. Summarizing the gap, researchers typically propound "scientific" (objective) evidence that is proven empirically and theoretically driven, even if it is conducted over as long as it takes and is then offered with caveats and qualifications. However, policy makers need evidence that is "colloquial" (linked to context); seems policy relevant, reasonable, and timely; and delivers a clear message. Put differently, in a chaos of purposes and accidents, policy makers do not—certainly, not often—identify the problem, commission research, analyze the results, choose the best option, establish the policy, implement the policy, and monitor evaluate the policy. They are not at all preoccupied with the rational implementation of so-called "decisions" through selected strategies. Source: Davies (2005).

that the Overseas Development Institute[6] conducts to bridge research and policy, and help thereby improve practice for better outcomes.

Bridging Research and Policy

Theory would have decision makers know what kinds of research—that have already delivered results—can help them make the right choices. It would have them base these on the best experience and knowledge available. Yet, reality begs to differ: poor research circulates and is acted upon while good research is ignored and disappears. Why?

> *The important thing in science is not so much to obtain new facts as to discover new ways of thinking about them.*
>
> —Lawrence Bragg

The question is potent. One cannot just transport research to the policy sphere. In a world shaped by complexity, policy makers have to deal with the pros and cons of policy decisions daily. Various interrelated factors interact dynamically to determine what sort of evidence, namely, information indicating whether a belief or assertion is true or valid, is likely to be adopted by policy makers who some see are driven by the Five S's of speed, superficiality, spin, secrecy, and scientific ignorance.[7]

> *In science the credit goes to the man who convinces the world, not the man to whom the idea first occurs.*
>
> —Francis Darwin

According to the Overseas Development Institute, the factors that define courses of action fall into three overlapping areas: (i) the political context, (ii) the evidence, and (iii) the links between policy and research communities, within a fourth set of

---

[6]The Overseas Development Institute is the United Kingdom's leading independent think tank on international development and humanitarian issues. Thanks to its Research and Policy in Development program, the institute works with partners in developing and developed countries at the intersection of research, policy, and practice to promote better outcomes for the poor. The program seeks to clarify (i) the role of knowledge in policy and practice, and (ii) the skills and capacities needed for researchers and organizations to effectively translate knowledge into action.

[7]This indictment needs moderation. Factors other than the Five S's and evidence condition uptake: they are experience and expertise, judgment, values and policy context, pragmatics and contingencies, resources, habits and tradition, and lobbyists and pressure groups. Source: Cable (2003).

factors: external influences. Admittedly, this framework is a generic, perhaps ideal, explanatory model: in instances, there will not be much overlap between the different spheres; in others the overlap may vary considerably. Notwithstanding, the framework holds explanatory power. It provides clear (yet flexible) guidance as to what researchers need to know, what they need to do, and how they should go about it. It suggests that research-based and other forms of evidence is more likely to enrich policy and thence (hopefully) practice if:

- It fits within the political and institutional limits and pressures of policy makers, and resonates with their assumptions, or sufficient pressure is exerted to challenge them.
- The evidence is credible and convincing, provides practical solutions to pressing policy problems, and is packaged to attract the interest of policy makers.
- Researchers and policy makers share common networks, trust one another, and communicate effectively.

In brief, by making more informed, strategic choices, researchers can maximize the chances that evidence will impact policy and practice.

Grooming Policy Entrepreneurs

> *As for the future, your task is not to foresee it but to enable it.*
>
> —Antoine de Saint-Exupéry

Researchers live in a competitive environment. To remain competitive, they must become entrepreneurs who (i) operate effectively in highly political environments; (ii) distill powerful policy messages from the results of research; (iii) use networks, hubs, and partnerships and build coalitions to work effectively with all stakeholders; and (iv) maintain long-term programs that pull all of these together. If they have clear intent,[8] they should equip themselves with skills: they need to be fixers, storytellers, networkers, and engineers. This means that they probably need to work in multidisciplinary teams with others who possess such skills.

> *That theory is worthless. It isn't even wrong!*
>
> —Wolfgang Pauli

---

[8]To have intent, one needs to know what one wants to do and really want to do it. This demands that research institutes (or departments) have a clear policy objective; focused research; more communications that include simple, unexpected, concrete, credible, and emotional stories; the right incentives; the right systems; and that they engage.

None of this is easy. The Overseas Development Institute (Young and Mendizabal 2009) cautions that grooming policy entrepreneurs (or turning research institutes or departments into policy-focused think tanks) involves a fundamental reorientation from academic achievement to policy engagement. This entails grappling with the policy community, developing a research agenda focusing on policy issues rather than academic interests, acquiring new skills or building multidisciplinary teams, establishing new internal systems and incentives, spending much more on communications, producing a different range of outputs, and working in partnerships and networks. It may even call for radically different funding models.

Box: Strengthening Research Communication at the Viet Nam Academy of Social Sciences

The Support for Effective Policy Making Through the Development of Scientific Evidence-Based Research project will last until mid-2011 and has been implemented since 2008 by the Viet Nam Academy of Social Sciences. Funding is provided by the United Nations Development Programme through three mutually reinforcing streams of work: (i) strengthening research management capacity, (ii) carrying out research using the human development paradigm, and (iii) supporting researchers in linking their research with policy processes. The Overseas Development Institute is responsible for the third stream.

The Viet Nam Academy of Social Sciences hosts 30 institutes and about 1,500 researchers. A needs assessment conducted in June 2009 showed that since 2005 demand on the academy for policy research has increased. The demand is greater when policy windows open due to important policy events, such as the National Congress of the Communist Party (every 5 years) or when the National Assembly convenes (twice a year).

Not surprisingly, the results of the assessment showed that the academy's researchers are perceived to have a good competency with research methods. Moreover, several institute directors mentioned that they are involved in policy making or policy discussions through their personal networks and linkages with policy makers. The results showed also an awareness of the meaning of "evidence-based policy". However, only 11% (out of a total of 700) of the respondents to the survey put policy influencing as the key focus of their research. The majority of the academy's researchers do not adopt a specific strategy to reach a policy audience with the results of their research.

As the main channel to reach policy makers are institute directors, the capacity building conducted in the academy so far focuses on planning and producing research communication outputs such as policy briefs, research briefs, and stories of change. These will help researchers and directors synthesize research results and provide policy recommendations that are then to be communicated to policy makers. Information and communications technology is also being introduced as a way for researchers to better collaborate in research projects as well as in sharing research results.

During the needs assessment conducted in the academy, one respondent recognized that "researchers have a habit of making things complicated and bore the audience". There is therefore a growing need for researchers to be equipped with knowledge about "ways to simplify messages for different audiences". In other words, as mentioned by one institute director, there is a need for researchers "to learn about simplicity". This is what the Support for Effective Policy Making Through the Development of Scientific Evidence Based Research project aims to achieve.

Source Arnaldo Pellini

The RAPID Outcome Mapping Approach

The relationship between research, policy, and practice is complex, multi-factoral, nonlinear, and highly context-specific—what works in a situation may not in another. What is more, traditional project management tools such as cost–benefit analysis and logical frameworks fail to account for complexity.

The Overseas Development Institute's RAPID Outcome Mapping Approach draws on concepts of complexity, outcome mapping tools developed by the International Development Research Center, and other tools for policy engagement to provide policy entrepreneurs with more information about the context they are operating in and enable them to make better strategic choices (and be better placed to take advantage of unexpected policy windows and opportunities). The approach comprises distinct steps, although not all will be needed in all situations:

- **Define a clear, overarching policy objective** Influencing objectives need not be limited to facilitating changes in the written content of government policies. The agenda may also include discursive, procedural, attitudinal, and behavioral changes.
- **Map the policy context** Mapping the policy context around the issue means identifying key factors that may influence the policy process. How do policies influence the local political context? Is there political interest in change in the country? How do policy makers perceive the problem? Is there enough of the right sort of evidence to convince them of the need for change? How is it presented? Who are the key organizations and individuals with access to policy makers? What is the donor's agenda where external actors are involved? Are there existing networks to use?
- **Identify the key stakeholders** Identifying the key influential stakeholders and target audiences involves determining what are their positions and interests in

relation to the policy objective. Some can be very interested and aligned and can be considered natural allies for change. Other can be interested, though not yet aligned, and can yet be brought into the fold of reformers so they do not present obstacles.

- **Identify desired behavioral changes** Developing a theory of change entails describing precisely the current behavior and the behavior that is needed, if the key influential stakeholders are to contribute to the achievement of the desired policy objective. It also calls for short- and medium-term step-changes that can be monitored to ensure that the priority stakeholders are moving in the right direction and responding to the efforts of the change program.
- **Develop a strategy** Developing a strategy entails spelling out milestone changes in the policy change process. Force field analysis is a flexible tool that can be used to further understand the forces supporting and opposing the desired policy change and suggest concrete responses.
- **Analyze internal capacity to effect change** To operationalize a strategy, one must ensure the engagement team has the competencies required. In other words, the team must have the set of systems, processes, and skills that can help inform or involve policy makers in research. The information gathered should prove useful in starting tangible actions to meet the desired policy objective. The information gathered up to this point can then be used to establish an action plan.
- **Establish a monitoring and learning framework** The final step is to develop a monitoring and learning system not only to track progress, make necessary adjustments, and assess the effectiveness of the approach, but also to learn lessons for the future. Crucial to the collection of knowledge is sharing it and using it.

References

Cable V (7 May 2003) Does evidence matter? meeting series. Overseas Development Institute, London

Davies P (October 17 2005) Evidence-based policy at the cabinet office. Impact and insight workshops. Overseas Development Institute, London

Young J, Mendizabal E (2009) Helping researchers become policy entrepreneurs. Overseas Development Institute. Briefing Paper

Further Reading

Jones H, Hearn S (2009) Outcome mapping: a realistic alternative for planning, monitoring, and evaluation. Overseas Development Institute. Background Note

Overseas Development Institute (2004) Bridging research and policy in international development. Briefing Paper

Proposition 107
E-learning and the Workplace

In a Word Many work arrangements discourage learning. In organizations, classroom instruction is obviously not the most efficient method. However, if e-learning is to justify the publicity that surrounds it, there is a great need to understand its organizational environment and to evolve design principles.

Geneses of Lifelong Learning

The Talmud enjoins well: Do not confine your children to your own learning, for they were born of another time. Then again, the flipside these days is that parents themselves must cross the generational divide and embark on lifelong learning.[1] It

---

[1]With the development of self-conscious adult education from the late 1920s, courtesy of Basil Yeaxlee, came the view that education should be lifelong. In 1972, to promote the vision of a learning society, the United Nations Educational, Scientific and Cultural Organization affirmed that society at large should become a learning resource for each individual; the emphasis should be on learning to learn (and not on matching schooling to the needs of the labor market) (Faure et al. 1972). Lifelong learning is now considered the continuous, voluntary, and self-motivated use of formal, nonformal, and informal learning opportunities throughout people's lives to develop and improve the knowledge, skills, and competencies they need for professional, personal, social, or civic reasons. (In reality, the boundaries or relationships between formal, nonformal, and informal learning can only be understood within particular historical, social, political, and economic contexts; the three frequently overlap. The same applies to terms such as "learner" and "learning," which mean different things in different contexts. Certainly, learning is a process, not a product; more precisely, it is the dialectical interplay of process and product.)

© Asian Development Bank 2017
O. Serrat, *Knowledge Solutions*, DOI 10.1007/978-981-10-0983-9_107

is not news that Information Age, digital technology now pervades our lives and occupations; but it is less often remarked that it has also begun to change the ways we (must) learn from the cradle to the grave.

> *Learning is not a product of schooling but the lifelong attempt to acquire it.*
>
> —Albert Einstein

E-learning,[2] taken to mean all forms of electronically supported learning and teaching, entered formal higher education in the mid- to late 1990s, riding on the wave of interest in the knowledge economy (and thereafter the learning organization).[3] (This is not to say that the experience has been an unqualified success: early attempts in universities, up to the mid-2000s, miscarried because e-learning ventures somehow failed to appreciate that education is not just a business, students are not mere consumers, and obtaining a degree is not quite the same as shopping online.)[4] Currently, because the delivery of content through electronic information and communications technology expands the realm of how, where, and when learners can engage, e-learning is also being mooted as a cheap and effective (just-in-time) way to provide private and public sector organizations the everyday learning opportunities they need to improve organizational outcomes.

> *We now accept the fact that learning is a lifelong process of keeping abreast of change. And the most pressing task is to teach people how to learn.*
>
> —Peter Drucker

Organizations have a vested interest in attracting, engaging, and retaining talent; but they also need to help personnel perform at the top of their game after they are hired. What is more, because the shelf life of information is shorter and forces each one to constantly take on new roles, the rules of the game change daily. When it comes to learning, what is good for personnel is good for their organization.

---

[2]Synonyms include computer-, internet-, and web-based training.

[3]Learning, the cognitive process of coming to understand things and developing increased capacities to do what one wants or needs to do, is obviously as old as mankind. It is equally evident, however, that the advent of e-learning owes to the ubiquity of the Internet and related technologies as well as computer hardware from the mid-1990s.

[4]The main reason for unsuccessful e-learning initiatives has been poor learner-orientation, as evidenced by lack of personalization, collaboration, and interactivity. Reiterating John Naisbitt's nearly 30-year old advice, one of the keys to the success of technology is to marry "high tech" with "high touch".

Training programs that are well managed can have a measurable effect.[5] (That might be gauged at several levels, namely, reaction and satisfaction, learning results, on-the-job application, business impact, intangible benefits, and return on investment.)[6] Since the need and associated rhetoric of flexible learning has been strongest in adult and continuous education, and explains in large part the attention given to communities and networks of practice in recent years, e-learning at the workplace augurs well.[7]

The New Learning Paradigm

Certainly, many work arrangements discourage learning—never mind lifelong learning—and any attempt to overcome roadblocks is welcome. Many organizations have a habit of herding learners, but not senior management, in a room—sometimes for 8 hours a day, 5 days a week, and instructing the same generic, standardized training programs—as if each had identical prior knowledge, learning styles, and knowledge needs.[8] This does little to encourage indispensable interactivity, taken to be the active involvement, participation, and engagement of an individual in the learning process. (Good interaction and the motivation it sparks do not just happen—these have to be designed.)[9]

---

[5]The challenge is that, much as regular deposits and the power of interest will only yield a major change in a bank account over time, positive results hinge on permanent investment and support.

[6]Return on investment is the holy grail of e-learning analytics. It depends on business needs, shaped by problems and opportunities, which differ greatly among organizations. If a business need is quantifiable, then the rate of return will be a function of the net benefits from the learning solution over its costs. (Note that calculating return on investment may not be appropriate for all learning solutions.)

[7]Some see the day, glimmers of which are already apparent, when (i) the responsibility for e-learning development will decentralize across the organization, (ii) e-learning will shift from instructivism to constructivism and connectivism, (iii) staff will collaborate and share knowledge, (iv) learning will be fully networked, (v) m-learning, that is, any sort of learning that happens when the learner takes advantage of opportunities offered by mobile technologies, will be popular; and (vi) e-learning will be smart (Tracey 2010). Others suspect that the *e* will eventually disappear.

[8]This practice owes to the still dominant view that learning is a product. Being a learner in organizations where this paradigm has adherents can be tricky: there, a learner is someone who has yet to acquire the requisite knowledge, skills, and competencies for carrying out the work he or she was recruited to perform; a learner in such a workplace has a deficit and consequently has less authority and influence. (He or she must therefore stop being a "learner" as quickly as possible.) This pervasive view of learning makes two debilitating assumptions: first, that the products of learning must be stable over time; second, that the learning of different learners is identical. Rather, learning is a process that changes both the learner and the environment.

[9]For reference, a taxonomy of levels of interactivity identifies three, ranging from reactive to coactive to proactive. Another gauges interaction from passive, limited, complex, and real-time.

> *An organization's ability to learn, and translate that learning into action rapidly, is the ultimate competitive advantage.*
>
> —Jack Welch

Classroom training is no longer the most efficient training method. (It definitely cannot be when increasingly dispersed personnel must be brought out of their offices from multiple locations, at high direct and indirect costs, to attend classes.) No one claims that corporate universities[10] are the be-all and end-all of training. (They are better described as a state of mind or, if that is deemed too ambitious, a system of interest.) To begin, they demand e-literacy.[11] But, given that, they can build in learning organizations what Meister (1998) calls the 3 C's of Corporate Citizenship, Contextual Framework, and Core Workplace Competencies. The new learning paradigm emphasizes the following critical issues:

- a shift from training to self-responsible learning;
- self-organized learning, based on metacognitive learning strategies for the development of lifelong learning skills;
- process-oriented learning, focusing on learning to learn, not product-oriented learning;
- highly flexible, personalized, and individualized learning based on different learning types and personal preferences); and

---

[10]A corporate university is any centralized educational entity or initiative that aims, frequently under the purview of a human resource division, to assist a parent organization achieve its goals by conducting activities that foster individual and organizational learning. In both large and small organizations, the usual business advantages vaunted (via learning management systems) are (i) easy accessibility 24 hours a day, 7 days a week; (ii) just-in-time training that is personalized, modular, collaborative, measured, and within reach across multiple channels; (iii) reduced time away from the job, (iv) built-in participant enrollment and course management; (v) consistent and accurate messages; (vi) centralized knowledge management; and (vii) significant cost savings. To be sure, corporate universities are not entirely new: General Motors founded the General Motors Institute as long ago as 1926, renaming it from a 1919 venture. In the late 1950s, General Electric established the Management Development Institute and Walt Disney opened Disney University. Some surmise that, if growth keeps, corporate universities will soon outnumber traditional universities. Most organizations do not at the start set out to form a corporate university: the fact is that they often originally intend to become a learning organization; only later—never for some— do they enter the critical stage of repositioning their development in a more specifically strategic context, namely, that of a corporate university.

[11]E-literacy is the ability to use information and communications technology, in this particular instance, to learn and transfer knowledge.

- individual- and team-oriented methods of collaborative learning based on constructive and connective learning theories using communities of learners, experts, facilitators, coaches.[12]

Notwithstanding, the lessons of past experience in e-learning—at least in higher education since documented studies of the labor market are still sparse—must be heeded: to create sustainable enterprise, corporate universities (and learning and development units in human resource divisions) must eschew quick-fix e-learning solutions, commonly masquerading as technology-driven learning management systems[13] that automate the administration, tracking, and reporting of training events but ignore the organizational learning environment.

For effective structuring and administration of e-learning solutions, organizations must develop vibrant and committed formal learning organizational cultures and supporting virtual and traditional infrastructure that grow customized training programs, flexibly tailored to the needs of personnel, using good practices from both inside and outside. (Increasingly, such responsibilities are ascribed to chief learning officers.)[14] To note, given the evolutionary nature of e-learning and its innate diversity, articulating a viable one-dimensional universal solution is impossible. E-learning is an immature but quite dynamic enterprise characterized by established brand names, continuing convergence, market consolidation, and requirements for scalable business models on the one hand and modularization and standardization, demand for one-stop shopping and added-value services, the establishment of e-learning partnerships and strategic alliances, and the emergence

---

[12]Viewing learning as a process has intuitive advantages: after all, work practices are processes, the features of which are better captured by constructive and connective, rather than by acquisition (or even participation), metaphors.

[13]Learning management systems are software applications for administration, documentation, tracking, and reporting of training programs, including training material and classroom and online events. Robust systems (i) centralize and automate administration, (ii) create and deliver content quickly, (iii) bring training initiatives together on a scalable web-based platform, (iv) support standards, (v) offer self-guided services, (vi) help learners personalize content and enable knowledge reuse, and (vii) display software portability. (Most are web based and rely on a database as back-end.) Examples of large-scale software vendors are Oracle and SAP.

[14]In the era of talent management, as the value of traditional learning diminishes and personnel relies ever more on learning through online references, communities, and networks of practice, and online performance support tools, the position of chief learning officer has been introduced in organizations. It continues to evolve and expand to make continuous learning a driver of sustainable competitive advantage through enhanced relationships with functions and departments associated with strategic planning, human resource management, knowledge and information management, and corporate communications. The ambitious terms of reference of a chief learning officer can be to (i) facilitate learning and change, which involves establishing learning governance structures and managing cultural transformation and maintenance; (ii) improve individual, team, and organizational effectiveness through integrated use of better training programs (including e-learning), talent development, knowledge generation and sharing practices, business processes, internal and external communications, enterprise-wide learning and collaboration platforms, branding, decentralized capabilities to create and transfer knowledge, and performance-raising interventions; and (iii) support corporate strategy through research and experimentation.

of new learning models that involve communities and networks of practice on the other. If most agree that e-learning should not be seen as isolated events taking place in parallel to an organization's practice but, instead, as an integrated part of the organization's environment, context, relationships, and knowledge, it is assuredly neither easy nor cheap.[15] However, design principles can help.

Organizational Learning Environments

An organizational learning environment is conditioned by the external environment, within which organizational context, inter- and intra-organizational relationships, and organizational knowledge interact. Usefully, Dealtry (2005) has itemized the individual elements that, across functions and departments, constitute an intervention platform for strategic management of e-learning. The following draws from his work to share them.

> *In this age, which believes that there is a shortcut to everything, the greatest lesson to be learned is that the most difficult way is, in the long run, the easiest.*
>
> —Henry Miller

- **Corporate strategy** The formulation of corporate strategy must elevate adult and continuous education as a foremost input to the development of organizational capability. Interpreting the organization's vision, mission, and goals in terms of learning needs across all major functions and departments has a strong bearing on sustainable competitive advantage and provides the foundation for detailed planning of and funding for learning.
- **Learning policy** The provision of quality learning on demand drives organic individual and collective development. A learning policy would specify the goal to build a learning organization as well as the core values and objectives for that. The core values might, for instance, state that (i) an investment in staff learning is an investment in high organizational performance; (ii) learning, coaching, and mentoring are shared responsibilities; and (iii) equitable access to training opportunities is critical for renewal. The objectives could, for example, include (i) the creation of a learning culture that encourages learning, creativity and innovation, and the acquisition, transfer, and use of knowledge; and (ii) training programs that meet the needs of personnel. A learning charter would demonstrate commitment: learning charters are a touchstone against which provision and practice can be tested and a

---

[15]The primary determinants of cost are the size of the content; level of interactivity; use of multimedia to combine different content forms, e.g., text, audio, still images, animation, video, and interactivity content forms; and tracking requirements.

waymark with which to guide, monitor, and evaluate progress. First-level managers must participate in learning policy development: they should therefore be able to distinguish learning needs from current business-as-usual realities; they should have the skills to plan performance development in relation to the learning policy as it affects their activities. Moreover, learning performance management should play a greater role in direct reporting relationships.

- **Funding for learning** The approach to funding for learning must move the financing of interventions out of the annual budgeting process and affirm learning as a major component of investment for organizational development. (This involves rigorous formulation of the business case for investments in human capital, the scheduling of resourcing, monitoring, and evaluation.) It must be based on a clear understanding of the relationship between an organization's intellectual capital[16] and its place in the market.

- **Learning portfolio** The learning portfolio must define the provision of internal and external, formal and informal training for technical, supervisory, and managerial development strands. Program curriculum development, timing, on-call infrastructure support, and the provision of distributed e-learning solutions must meet changing needs flexibly with quality content.

- **Personnel development** The overt introduction of a learning component in the work of individuals injects a very different perspective on professional occupations. Changing psychological contracts in a positive way cannot be achieved simply by introducing an e-learning system. Hence, the alignment between an individual's desire to learn and an organization's learning requirements needs careful balancing.

- **Knowledge, skills, and competencies** Most organizations have developed specifications of desired knowledge, skills, and competencies. Knowledge is a most critical organizational resource: making sure that knowledge workers have both the capability and the maximum number of opportunities to release their potential is a key objective of strategic learning management.

- **Talent development** In a learning organization, the meaningful joint exploration of interest-based relationships, mutual learning needs, expectations, and working objectives is fundamental to the nurturing of talent once it is onboard. Personnel, especially top talent, quickly become actively disengaged, or at least not engaged, if they are not allowed to achieve.

- **Performance management** Learning performance management has many different strands, involving monitoring and evaluation at individual and organizational levels. Learning about the dynamics of the external and internal organizational contexts and ensuring that first-level managers and personnel have the decisional power and related capability to sustain high performance is a strategic imperative for success, if not survival, that senior and middle management must seek to act on.

---

[16]An organization's intellectual capital is human capital—the knowledge, skills, and competencies of personnel; structural capital—knowledge that has been transformed into strategies, structures, or routines; and relational capital—the relationships that an organization has with its clients, audiences, and partners and external environment.

Design Principles for E-learning

For sure, e-learning is not the key to organizational nirvana. The generative learning perspectives that must accompany its introduction—and with which training programs must converse—include continuous improvement strategies and methodologies; business process design and implementation; business process improvement tools; community and network of practice models; knowledge management systems and tools; specific training provisions; physical and virtual learning spaces and delivery channels; branding; cadres of skilled facilitators, process builders, and implementers; and recognition and rewards programs (Campbell and Dealtry 2003).

E-learning per se is not without challenges: it is a costly and time-consuming enterprise. Organizations must overcome three generic impediments to its introduction and continuing use: (i) the cost of developing (or purchasing) software applications at the onset, compounded by running costs once e-learning interventions are under way; (ii) (perceived) lack of time to devote to workplace learning and to formulate and maintain e-learning solutions; and (iii) content issues—quality content is not available on the market or is not suited for e-learning and must therefore be developed. Extensive research and careful planning will help circumscribe requirements and surmount these barriers.

To kick-start effective e-learning design, the simple questions that beg answers are: What objectives must the training satisfy? What is the audience for which the training is intended? Does the content already exist or must it be created? What technical limitations exist, if any? What data must be tracked to a learning management system? What interactivity level is applicable? What type of training is required? Is the e-learning solution part of a blended solution?[17] How long should the training be?

Usefully, Brown and Voltz (2005) have determined that six elements, combining skills and tasks associated with lesson planning, instructional design, creative writing, and software specification, lie at the heart of e-learning design itself. They pertain to (i) activity—paying attention to the provision of a rich learning activity;[18] (ii) scenario—situating this activity within an interesting story line; (iii) feedback—providing meaningful opportunities for student reflection and

---

[17]Blended learning refers to the mixing of different learning environments. In the context of e-learning, it combines face-to-face classroom facilitation with remote, usually computer-mediated, activities and shorter classroom contact hours (reduced seat time).

[18]Among others, a rich learning activity would support both individual reflection and collaborative knowledge building. It would integrate theoretical knowledge with the practical experience of participants to lead them, in real dialogue, collaboration, and knowledge exchange with different groups of people, to examine their work in the light of the conceptual tools provided and explain implicit knowledge. The orientation to problem solving would be progressive and integrate different forms of representation and different forms of learning activities, e.g., reading, writing, discussing, using metaphors, audio, visual, etc., with structured support and guidance at all phases of the learning process.

third-party criticism; (iv) delivery—considering appropriate technologies for delivery; (v) context—ensuring that the design is suitable for the context in which it will be used; and (vi) impact—bearing in mind the personal, social, and environmental impact of the designed activity. If e-learning is to justify the publicity that now surrounds it, more efforts need to be devoted to explicating these.

References

Brown A, Voltz B (2005) Elements of effective e-learning design. The International Review of Research in Open and Distance Learning 6(1)

Campbell I, Dealtry R (2003) The new generation of corporate universities—co-creating sustainable enterprise and business development solutions. Journal of Workplace Learning 15 (7/8):368–381

Dealtry R (2005) Configuring the structure and administration of learning management. Journal of Workplace Learning 17(7):467–477

Faure E et al (1972) Learning to be. UNESCO

Meister J (1998) Corporate universities: lessons in building a world-class workforce. McGraw-Hill

Tracey R (2010) Learning in the corporate sector

Proposition 108
Learning Histories

In a Word How can we gauge the successes and failures of collective learning? How can the rest of the organization benefit from the experience? Learning histories surface the thinking, experiments, and arguments of actors who engaged in organizational change.

All Aboard

In the corporate world, the precedence ascribed to individual learning can run counter to organizational learning, the process by which an organization and its people develop their capabilities to create a desired future. Without doubt, developing capabilities is a precondition of a desired future; however, if the essence of a learning organization is that it actively identifies, creates, stores, shares, and uses knowledge[1] to anticipate, adapt to, and maybe even shape a changing environment, the driving concern must be reflection, communication, and collective sense making for action across its personnel.[2] (Proponents of organizational learning grumble that people in organizations perform collectively yet still learn individually from incomplete, heterogeneous information to which they ascribe different meaning.)[3] Intra-organizational interaction for learning cannot depend on serendipity:[4] it must be encouraged, facilitated, recognized, and rewarded. Increasingly, narration is deemed a good vessel for bridging knowledge and action in the workplace.

---

[1]Knowledge management activities begin with identifying what core tacit and explicit knowledge should be at hand, including its sources. Knowledge creation is the process of making tacit knowledge explicit. Knowledge storage sees that routines are applied to retain essential knowledge. Knowledge sharing involves the dissemination to others of what has been generated in usable forms. Knowledge utilization entails integrating what knowledge has been identified, created, stored, and shared so that it can be assimilated and generalized to new situations.

[2]Knowledge per se is not of much consequence; its value resides in application. Hence, knowledge is better understood as the potential for effective action.

[3]*Pace* self- and independent evaluation, there are still few tools, methods, and approaches with which to capture institutional experience and broadcast with effect to clearly identified users what practicable lessons well up from that. (All attempts to enhance organizational performance must ultimately prove their own value: why should one create knowledge that does not respond to needs nor gets absorbed by those parts of a system that invite it most? Two problems continue to limit self- and independent evaluation: (i) the "lessons learned"—that should more accurately be termed "lessons to be learned"—are not often well formulated; and (ii) processes to promote ownership and uptake of lessons are rarely fully fledged.) Conversely, where appreciative inquiry informs generative approaches to organizational development, write-ups of good practices that were shown to be effective in one part of the organization and might be in another habitually count out the false starts and failures one could learn from as well as the hidden logic and toil that made the breakthroughs possible. The case study method—synonymous with education for management since the early twentieth century—ignores the rich context of organizational challenge: in the real world, for example, problems are not clean, clear, or discrete; information is seldom of the quality or quantity required; and both stakeholder consultation and decision rights constrain progress toward resolution of complex issues. In a different genre, data from in-house and external surveys will not mean much if the latter are not well designed and would still need to be acted upon if it does. And what of strategic reviews by high-level panels assembled to promote new thinking, possibly even jump-start reform? As it happens, the eminent persons who comprise them are pragmatic: by and large, their reports are tailored to please those who hired them—not critique arrangements with evidence from the frontline—and only rarely better the workings of an organization.

[4]In organizations where knowledge is dominant, daily operations should be designed to raise its productivity.

Storytelling in Organizations

A story is a narrative of events or circumstances, or a series of them, designed to draw attention, amuse, or instruct. Organizations have a renewed interest in this ancient yet powerful form of sense making to exchange and consolidate sometimes complex knowledge:[5] potentially, storytelling can, for example, convey values and associated norms; prompt emotional connection; share the tacit knowledge in peoples' heads; build trust, engagement, and collaboration; facilitate unlearning; and spark action. Individually and collectively, by opening perspective, stories help us fathom times past and understand possible futures.[6]

Stimulating Reflection in Action

> *I am always ready to learn although I do not always like being taught.*
>
> —Winston Churchill

Too often, slip-ups happen again: the intellect, relationships, and routines that set them in motion have not been examined—if they have been discussed—and spawn further mishap. Basically, many efforts to foster organizational learningfall short because reflective practice is not easy to master; neither—in the rare cases when senior management introduces and backs tools, methods, and approaches for that— is it seen to provide immediate solutions to pressing business problems. *Perhaps there is only one cardinal sin: impatience. Because of impatience we were driven out of Paradise, because of impatience we cannot return*, thought W.H. Auden. In the meantime, surely, the continuing development of research methods and measures of knowledge management and learning remains a priority. The questions that should direct investigations in actionable knowledge transfer are: What types of organizational learning work effectively and what types do not? Why?

---

[5]Much knowledge can be codified in formal, systematic language and shared in discussion or writing. But much also cannot be easily abstracted and conveyed explicitly and requires communicative forms that synthesize rather than explicate—stories are such a form, with undoubted use to share multi-dimensional information and emotion in various domains if they are well designed and well told. A useful way to characterize explicit and tacit knowledge is to consider each type, respectively, as the core and the context.

[6]For sure, not all narratives are good stories: as a minimum, one must be clear about why they are being told, keep them simple and accessible, use more than one medium if possible, monitor and evaluate how the accounts are received, and continuously hone storytelling (and story-listening) skills.

> *Each year has been so robust with problems and successes and learning experiences and human experiences that a year is a lifetime at Apple. So this has been ten lifetimes.*
>
> —Steve Jobs

Of some cheer is that a relatively recent, qualitative action research[7] methodology, the learning history,[8] can help an organization become more collectively aware of learning and change efforts within its boundaries—even when these have not been adequately documented in advance. The fresh, new medium is a document (or series of documents)[9] presented in a two-column format 25–100 pages long that captures retrospectively perceptions of critical events or circumstances, insights of actors[10] regarding notable hard and soft[11] results from these, and objective analyses to build capacity for reflectionand communication. Hence, it can be employed to deliberate, assess, and evaluate any learning opportunity. (That might be an organizational change, initiative, innovation, product launch, etc.) Of course, the value of a learning historydoes not lie in the document produced: it stems from the consultation processthat engendered it.

Noteworthy characteristics of a learning history are that: (i) it takes a systems view of organizations; (ii) it makes extensive use of narrativeand cuts back and forth between different recollections to generate multiple stories; (iii) it brings assumptions, reactions, and implications to light; (iv) it helps people tell stories without fear of being judged, measured, and evaluated—assessment is not emotionally neutral territory; (v) it dissolves hierarchical privileges and makes for conversations among equals; (vi) it does not directly explicit the knowledge embodied, unlike "lessons learned" and good practices: rather, the actors must construct and surface tacit knowledge from the events or circumstances and their own experiences and discussions of them; (vii) it helps learn from both the good

---

[7]Action research is a reflective, constructively self-critical process of progressive problem solving aimed to enhance the performance of individuals, groups, and organizations in their working environment.

[8]Kleiner and Roth (1997) are the co-developers of this new form of corporate oral history. The Critical Incident technique is another, related tool for identifying, describing, and enhancing learning processes that focuses on specific events or circumstances.

[9]In the age of the internet, the possibility also exists to include multimedia products.

[10]They are the persons who initiated, implemented, or participated in the event or circumstance; they include champions, skeptics, people who benefitted or were affected, and close observers.

[11]Many results that cannot be measured must still be managed. An interview protocol based on notable results might ask: Which results from this project or program do you think are significant? What else can you tell us about them?

and the not-so-good;[12] and (viii) it catalyzes double-loop thinking and reconsideration of values, reasoning, impulses, or practices to achieve a desired future.

The audiences of a learning history are the actors, looking for perspective on what they accomplished so they may move forward without having to reinvent what has already discovered; newcomers, who might need to be informed; the organization they belong to, which usually knows what it wants to hear but may lack the capacity to listen to what it is trying to tell itself; and, possibly, interested parties outside the organization.

Documenting Organizational Learning

We now accept the fact that learning is a lifelong process of keeping abreast of change. And the most pressing task is to teach people how to learn.

—Peter Drucker

The two-column format of a learning history keeps the commentaries of the research team separate from the reminiscences of the actors. The right-hand column is a jointly told tale that presents a deliberately emotional story of events or circumstances through interwoven quotations[13] of actors; the individual, free-flowing, audio-recorded and transcribed retrospective interviews that generate them last about 1 hour.[14] The left-hand column contains analytical comments by a research team,[15] which distill key recurring themes in the narrative; query assumptions, reactions, and implications; raise undiscussable subjects; and make recommendations. Full column text at the top sets the context and background of each thematic section. Once it has been written, the learning historyis validated by the actors and disseminated for group discussion in workshops seeking shared understanding and

---

[12]The not-so-good represents the gap between aspiration and reality: where a learning history acts as a mirror to an organization is where it brings most value.

[13]Each person is identified only by title but quoted directly. As actors review the learning history and find that their points of view are represented fairly, they come to appreciate the perspectives of others (and may even recognize their own blinders).

[14]Principal actors may need to be interviewed several times: they understand things more clearly on the second (or third) time.

[15]The research team had best combine (concerned and knowledgeable) insiders and (trained) outsiders: almost inevitably, an organization's personnel finds it difficult to reflect objectively on events or circumstances because it has ongoing relationships and is swayed by corporate culture; outsiders, on the other hand, can feel pressured to take on routine note-taking work, which drains the time available for critical thinking.

responses to two questions: So what? What's next?[16] Re-experiencing the event or circumstance, the group learns collectively and its members make meaning together.

Reference

Kleiner A, Roth G (1997) How to make experience your company's best teacher. Harvard Business Review: 172–177

Further Reading

Roth G, Kleiner A (1998) Developing organizational memory through learning histories. Organizational Dynamics 27(2):43–60

---

[16]The development of a learning history often follows six stages: planning, reflective interviews, distillation, writing, validation, and dissemination.

Proposition 109
Learning in Conferences

In a Word The true value of a conference lies in its effects on participants. Conferences are to generate and share knowledge that impacts behavior and links to results: this will not happen if the state of the art of conference evaluation remains immature and event planners do not shine a light on the conditions for learning outcomes.

No Loose Change

Lest we forget, a conference is a purposeful gathering of people aiming to pool ideas on at least one topic of joint interest or needing to achieve a common goal through interaction (and, naturally, relation). They are face-to-face, sometimes virtual,[1] venues for situated learning dedicated to the generation and sharing of knowledge, usually to reach agreement, in formal or informal (yet planned) settings.

---

[1]Conferences ordinarily occur face-to-face but information and communications technology now also enables virtual mediation—through telephone and, increasingly, video—between people who are geographically separated.

© Asian Development Bank 2017
O. Serrat, *Knowledge Solutions*, DOI 10.1007/978-981-10-0983-9_109

> *Minds that have nothing to confer find little to perceive.*
>
> —William Wordsworth

Conferencing, then, is an age-old technique for reasoning and problem solving, aka sense making, the process by which people give meaning to experience through spoken and written narratives. Certainly, the Socratic Method—a debate between individuals with opposing views that used effective questions to stimulate critical thinking—was a form of it (and the oldest known way of teaching).

> *Meetings are a great trap. Soon you find yourself trying to get agreement and then the people who disagree come to think they have a right to be persuaded. However, they are indispensable when you don't want to do anything.*
>
> —John Kenneth Galbraith

Nowadays, new modes of transport and communication mean that conferences can take many forms including (i) conventions—large meetings of delegates, industries, members, professions, representatives, or societies seeking concurrence on certain attitudes or routines, such as processes, procedures, and practices; (ii) forums—broad occasions for open discussion, as a rule among experts but now and then involving audiences; (iii) seminars—prolonged and sometimes repeated meets for exchange of results and interaction among a limited number of professionals or advanced students engaged in intensive study or original research; (iv) workshops—brief educational programs for small groups of peers focusing on techniques and skills in a particular field; (v) retreats—periods of group withdrawal from regular activities for development of closer relationships, instruction, or self-reflection; and (vi) meetings[2]—sundry instances of coming together for business, civic, courtship, educational, government, health and wellness, leisure, religious, social, sports, and other functions.

Conventions, forums, seminars, workshops, retreats, and meetings—to which the emerging practice of "unconferencing"[3] should hereafter be added—are a pervasive form of interaction. The resources allocated to their organization, conduct, and

---

[2] In the workplace, one-time, recurring, or series of meetings that regularly draw on the services of a chairperson include briefings, advisory meetings, committee meetings, council meetings, and negotiations. Other types are ad hoc, investigative, one-on-one, team, and work meetings.

[3] Unconferences are participant-driven meetings. The label has been ascribed to a wide range of gatherings—made possible by the spread of personal computers and the internet over the last 25 years—based on the premise that in any professional gathering the people in the audience, not just those who speak on stage, also have know-what, know-how, and know-why to communicate. The tools, methods, and approaches of unconferences include Barcamp, Birds of a Feather, Conferences That Work, Everyday Democracy, Fishbowl Conversation, Future Search,

attendance—of which the opportunity cost incurred from taking part is no loose change—must surely be astronomical. Even so, we seldom assess their relative value to either participants or event planners. (Run-of-the-mill, end-of-session surveys requesting participants to jot down what they enjoyed or disliked—namely, to log reactions—will no longer do.) Granted that conferences serve different purposes, these *Knowledge Solutions* concentrate on gatherings that are ostensibly designed to generate and share (relevant, effective, and therefore valued) knowledge[4] and leverage related networking in support, such as forumsand seminars. [That said, given the claims that other meetingsmake about knowledge generation and sharing —*pace* the disconnect between their means and ends, it stands to reason (and would indeed be logical) that these *Knowledge Solutions* also apply there.]

The Poverty of Conference Evaluations

> *True genius resides in the capacity for evaluation of uncertain, hazardous, and conflicting information.*
>
> —Winston Churchill

Questionnaires are synonymous with conference evaluation. (Indeed, few other tools seem to be used.) In all probability, the language that event planners employ to allegedly gauge conference satisfaction—they hardly ever dare establish outcome and impact—will read: "Thank you for taking time to complete this survey. Your opinion is important: it will inform plans for the next event." All too predictably when some pretense at conference evaluation is in fact made, the following "key" questions will be posed: Did the event lead to its goal?[5] What

---

(Footnote 3 continued)

Knowledge (or World) Café, Lightning Talks, Open Space Technology, Pecha Kucha, Speed Geeking, and TeachMeet.

[4]Here, it may be pertinent to distinguish two types of knowledge: instrumental (or procedural) knowledge that can be exploited in a reasonably well defined and specific way; and conceptual knowledge that shapes the way people consider issues but that may not have an obvious, direct impact.

[5]It goes without saying that the absence of a clearly stated goal and related objective(s) complicates evaluation. (From the onset, it also makes it well-nigh impossible to decide on the best learning strategy, resources, and logistics.)

were its main strengths and weaknesses? What did you value in the event?[6] Were the sessions[7] relevant to the subject matter? How well did they align with your expectations? Can you rate the quality of the presenters? Has your knowledge of the subject matter increased as a result of the event? Will the event set in motion changes in the way you work in the future?[8] What undertakings can you now initiate? How might the event be improved? (For sure, there will also be open fields inviting further suggestions for improvement.) Be these as they may, the politically incorrect question must be asked: What might data compiled from chiefly formative, not summative, quizzes possibly help validate or change in any meaningful way?[9] Stating the obvious, feedback that cannot be used should not be sought. Ironically, since a dog's tail should not wag its owner, what practical recommendations for improvement are proposed will probably be turned down, with thanks, as great but simply not possible given this or that constraint.

There has, of course, been much debate over the near-universal reliance on questionnaires for conference evaluation. Detractors wonder if they really provide worthwhile information[10]; adherents research how to obtain a representative cross-section of attendants since, more often than not, there is no strong motivation to respond—they remark that surveys can (at low cost) ensure at least summarily uniform coverage of all information areas deemed essential; provide an opportunity to triangulate resultsusing different techniques; and allow the same questions to be submitted in the same way year after year so that evaluation results can be

---

[6]As you would expect, since surveys more often than not deliberately require that names and professional titles be recorded—not counting demographic and other information captured during the registration process or before that through short surveys to gather baseline data and perhaps help shape the event—positive responses to this question will help craft testimonials that, with social proof, are intended to lend credence to the marketing campaign for the next event.

[7]This is shorthand: conferences can bring into play a mix of keynote addresses, presentations, panel discussions, roundtable discussions, breakout sessions, workshops, hands-on labs, and luncheons.

[8]The selection of the conference goal and its objective(s) should permit event planners to identify the terminal, applied behavior of participants by name, viz., the kind of behavior that would be accepted as evidence that the conference has achieved its objective(s). Therefore, the definition of the desired behavior should describe the important conditions under which it would be presumed to occur. Criteria of acceptable performance should also be specified.

[9]The areas that would stand to benefit from evaluation are the event planner's operations and conference programs. The first includes aspects such as planning processes, decision-making procedures, personnel, physical facilities, public relations, and administration and management. The second would include objectives, clientele, methodsand techniques, materials, and quality of learning outcomes.

[10]Questionnaires are complicated instruments: when well designed, a repeated mistake is to try to read too much into responses; when badly designed, they mislead. If the response rate is high they can describe the broad characteristics of a large population but, all in all, the quality of data is not as high as with alternative methods of data collection such as structured and semi-structured individuals and focus group interviews. Certainly, they are an unsuitable means of evaluation in complex and chaotic contexts where probing and sensing are required—there is no real possibility to follow up on the responses they elicit.

compared against a baseline. Innovators advocate "recent life histories" that high-light the event's influence on selected individuals, for example in terms of edu-cation, networking, professional development, and application of knowledge gained; or "roving reporters" who would converse with participantsthroughout the event with a mix of demographic, short-answer, and open-ended questions.[11]

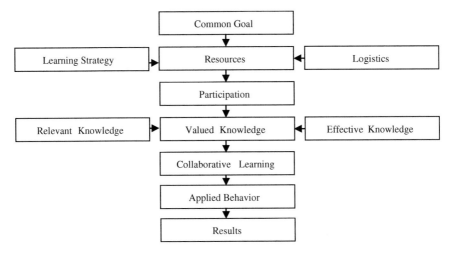

Fig. Linking conferences to results. *Source* Author

> *One test of the correctness of educational procedure is the happiness of the child.*
> —Maria Montessori

Put bluntly, the valuethat conference evaluationsadd is incongruously scant. In declining order of interest—with variations depending on the sector, theme, and discipline addressed, evaluations home in on (i) the overall reactionsof participants, (ii) conference strengths and weaknesses, (iii) ratings of sessions and presentations, (iv) ratings of the extent to which the needs of participants were met, (v) areas for

---

[11]In addition to questionnaires, quantitative and qualitative methods of data collection for con-ference evaluation can—yet too infrequently—include (i) individual face-to-face or telephone interviews; (ii) focus group interviews; (iii) online surveys; (iv) printed surveys; (v) structured observations of conference sessions and areas; (vi) examination of conference programs and online resources; (vii) review of statistical data on conference registration, abstracts, etc.; (viii) review of statistical data and evaluation findings from previous events; (ix) rapporteurs; (x) "instant" feed-back systems; (xi) social network analysis; (xii) analysis of media coverage; and, more recently, (xiii) scrutiny of posts left by participants on conference display boards, web logs, Facebook pages, and Twitter accounts.

improvement, (vi) financial return on investment, (vii) participant learning in the short term, and (viii) new behaviors in the medium term. The case must be made that the last two areas demand more attention. And, there surely is scope for Donald Kirkpatrick's four levels of learning evaluation, even if they were developed in 1959 for the evaluation of training programs (Kirkpatrick D and Kirkpatrick J 2006). With minor modifications to adapt them to the context of conferences, the levels are as follows:

- Reaction—To what degree do participants react favorably to an event?
- Learning—To what extent do participants acquire the intended knowledge, skills, attitudes, confidence, and commitment based on their participation in the event?
- Behavior—To what degree do participants apply what they learned during the event when they return to their job?
- Results—To what extent do targeted outcomes occur as a result of the event and subsequent interaction and relation?

The Poverty of Learning in Conferences

> *No grand idea was ever born in a conference, but a lot of foolish ideas have died there.*
>
> —F. Scott Fitzgerald

Most conferences are called to achieve a shared goal—that, ultimately, being collaborative learning that links to results—yet dispense at best information; they do not generate knowledge. Participantsdepart with their own learning[12]—that, as noted above, is rarely evaluated and, in the first instance, not necessarily shared. This is because most conferences funnel programmed information; they do not know-what potential collaborative learning, if any transpired, could enrich theory, research, and practice in their domain as a whole. Why? Chapman et al. (2006) remark that event planners assert they want to create spaces for learning but do not evaluate if that, and the changes in behavior linking to results it should conduce, actually did occur. Rather they aggregate individual responses, thereby missing opportunities for subtler analyses of more diverse inputs. Helpfully, Chapman et al.

---

[12]The world over, people attend conferences, take notes, and hardly ever (if at all) study them again. (Back-to-office reports are another ineffective receptacle of findings and conclusions.) Never mind collaborative learning: to boost their individual learning, participants might, for example (i) draw 2–3 objectives, personal or organizational; (ii) listen actively; (iii) ask questions; (iv) plan a networking strategy; (v) tap by design the ideas of fellow participants; and (vi) take time to reflect and innovate, away from the rigors of daily schedules.

remind us that, from an etymological perspective, to evaluate is to ascertain or fix the value of something; more profoundly, and typically after careful appraisal and study, evaluation helps establish its significance, worth, or *condition*. The first definition suggests determination of positive or negative effects; the second embraces the idea of determination of condition, which removes the requirement to assign worth. Evaluation techniques that rest on the first definition serve accountability; those that spring from the second propel learning. Chapman et al. posit a three-pronged "New Learning" conceptual framework integrating notions of learning organizations, communities of practice, and knowledge creation[13] to facilitate learning in conferences—not forgetting their evaluation—which uncovers fertile ground for research and practice.

> *I believe we are going to move into a situation where the more effective conferences will be smaller, more specialized, more focused, with occasional large gatherings to get the attention of the larger world.*
>
> —Maurice Strong

The nascent practice of unconferencing, cited earlier, bodes well too. Summarizing, the shortcomings of conferences are that: (i) conference programs are set by event planners and do not predict well what sessions are actually wanted; (ii) a distinction is made between presenters (teachers) and participants (learners); (iii) sessions are dominated by presenters; participants receive predetermined information passively; (iv) logistics revolve around general and breakout sessions; (v) content is broadcast in long, uninterrupted sessions; and (vi) chances to network are restricted to meals and social gatherings outside sessions. In contrast, some characteristics of unconferences are that: (i) the culture of unconferences is participatory, not passive; (ii) the intellectual capital of participants, not presenters, is harnessed; (iii) unconferences give time for individualized knowledge sharing and learning: the intent is not just to work toward the goal of the event; (iv) knowledge sharing and learning happen in small groups rather than in sessions; (v) interaction is put center stage; (vi) participants have greater input and control over sessions and are thus more apt to engage in knowledge sharing and learning that help realize the goal of the event; (vii) teaching and learning roles are not fixed; and (viii) sessions can be created on the spot. To note, however, event planners still do not take advantage of unconferencing despite improved connectivity; the chief explanation

---

[13]Nonaka's (1974) SECI Approach, for one, is relevant: it isolates four processes through which tacit and explicit knowledge interact: (i) socialization, (ii) externalization, (iii) combination, and (iv) internalization. The *Knowledge Solutions* on intellectual capital enumerate tools, methods, and approaches for value creation besides others for value extraction and value reporting.

is fear that unconferences will not work, fuelled by understandable concern over loss of control over one's event and general unfamiliarity with associated facilitation requirements, technical and logistical considerations, and revenue models.

References

Chapman D, Wiessner CA, Storberg-Walker J, Hatcher T (2006) New learning: the next generation of evaluation? North Carolina State University, pp 1–8
Kirkpatrick D, Kirkpatrick J (2006) Evaluating training programs: the four levels. Berrett-Koehler Publishers
Nonaka I (1974) A dynamic theory of organizational knowledge creation. Organization Science 5 (1):14–37

Further Reading

Hameister D (1974) Conference evaluation: pro or con. Pennsylvania State University, pp 1–20

Proposition 110
On Internal Knowledge Markets

In a Word In large organizations, knowledge can move rapidly or slowly, usefully or unproductively. Those who place faith in internal knowledge markets and online platforms to promote knowledge stocks and flows should understand how extrinsic incentives can crowd out intrinsic motivation.

From Possibility to Reality

There is no disputing the obvious: for organizations, ability and, of course, willingness to generate and share knowledge, especially tacit, internally across professions and disciplines—and the corporate silos that constrict them—are an essential source of competitive advantage. In the workplace, remarkable things can happen when people marry creativity and innovation with communication and cooperation. Sorry to say, mainstream organizations still make heavy weather of it. But the competition most face in the globalized economy, compounding the twenty-first century challenges we all face, compels them to move from possibility to reality if they are to raise productivity and endure. Why? Because data and information (and the contacts they can engender) have never been so cheap, so readily shared, and consequently so ubiquitous. Consequently, societies are experiencing unprecedented rates of change and organizational performance is

© Asian Development Bank 2017
O. Serrat, *Knowledge Solutions*, DOI 10.1007/978-981-10-0983-9_110

increasingly defined by the capacity to capture, create, and deliver value to meet explicit or latent needs. And so, in the interest of their clients, audiences, and partners—therefore in their self-interest, organizations must put their houses in order so they may improve organizational effectiveness with knowledge solutions that scale scope. All the time more, they look to internal knowledge markets for help, hence the rise of communities of practice and other such networks.

Technology Impels Nations

> *Man often becomes what he believes himself to be. If I keep on saying to myself that I cannot do a certain thing, it is possible that I may end by really becoming incapable of doing it. On the contrary, if I have the belief that I can do it, I shall surely acquire the capacity to do it even if I may not have it at the beginning.*
>
> —Mohandas K. Gandhi

In progressive organizations that strive beyond adaptive learning to realize generative, better, radical learning, the objectives of knowledge management are to make the enterprise operate as intelligently as it might to get the most out of knowledge assets and so promote success and viability.[1] To these ends, as the discipline matures, theory and practice have been enriched by techno-centric—and alas, to a much lesser degree, organizational and ecological—perspectives, with the internet revolution supplying constant technological impetus.[2]

> *Biological systems are adaptable, resilient, and capable of generating perpetual novelty. That's not a bad list of attributes for a company of the future.*
>
> —Margaret Wheatley

---

[1]To this intent, in no order, illustrative motivations behind knowledge management efforts up until now have been (i) increasing the knowledge content of products and services to fit an ever-sharper characterization of customer needs and wants; (ii) harnessing creativity and innovation for product and service leadership; (iii) achieving shorter product development cycles; (iv) storing information about the knowledge, skills, experience, and interests of personnel in dynamic, adaptive electronic directories; (v) intensifying network connectivity between individuals; (vi) building enabling environments that allow personnel to access insights and ideas appropriate to their work; (vii) maximizing intellectual—more often than not human—capital; and (viii) solving "wicked" problems.

[2]The first perspective focuses on information and communications technology, ideally that which enhances knowledge generation and sharing. The second examines how an organization can best be designed to encourage and facilitate core knowledge activities, e.g., identifying, creating, storing, sharing, and using knowledge. The third directs attention to the behaviors, relationships, and interactions of people within environmental borders—subject to external influencers—that may or may not conduce a collaborative learning ecosystem.

For sure, learning together is an important part of working together: sharing is an integral part of core knowledge activities that include identification, creation, storage, and use. In fact, how can know-how be brought into play if it has not been made available in one form or another? (Knowledge that does not flow cannot grow; in opposition, know-how that is exchanged sparks ideas and prompts new knowledge.) For that reason, in quick-thinking organizations, search parties for the Holy Grail of intrafirm knowledge transfer set off a long time ago. (Uncovering and transferring tacit knowledge were an early goal of knowledge management when that discipline emerged in the 1980s following the groundbreaking work of Peter Drucker, Dorothy Leonard-Barton, and Peter Senge in the 1970s.) In short, learning organizations have put great store in sharing across their entire body (preferably proprietary, in the private sector) insights into clients, audiences, and partners; innovations, and good practices that enhance the products and services developed and extended to cater to them; lessons from planning, acting, reflecting (both on and in action), and learning, as well as emerging research; etc.[3]

> Discontent is the first step in the progress of a man or a nation.
>
> —Oscar Wilde
>
> New technology is common, new thinking is rare.
>
> —Peter Blake

Still, it is a reality that in large twentieth century organizations, finding people with the experiences, insights, knowledge, and skills one needs on a specific topic remains difficult. The division of labor, standardization of procedures, formal hierarchy, and impersonal relationships that allegedly help large organizations achieve maximum efficiency draw boundaries within which knowledge can be combined and applied; they also hamper knowledge flows internally. (Incompleteness, asymmetry, and localness of knowledge are the outcome.) Peer assists, events that bring individuals together to magnify collective learning and develop networks among those invited, were introduced for the very purpose; they remain a rare occurrence. Inevitably, perhaps, knowledge management has relied on information and communications technology for sharing.[4] To simplify, for instance,

---

[3]With the help of narrative techniques such as learning histories, social reminiscing, and story-telling, the more discerning among them build and maintain corporate memories to augment their future with their past and eschew corporate amnesia when staff leave.

[4]Arguments about the role of information and communications technology in knowledge management are pointless. De facto, such technologies are already in pervasive use and qualify as natural media with which to amplify and drive stocks and flows of knowledge. Yet, some fear that affiliated outlays can come at the expense of investments in, say, human capital or that they might objectify then calcify knowledge into inert information, thus debasing the importance of tacit knowledge and collaboration mechanisms for its socialization. Practicable truth lies somewhere in

an early knowledge management prop involved online staff profile pages, aka Yellow Pages, as locators of in-house expertise. In the mid-1990s, forays deepened with the introduction of collaborative technologies such as Lotus Notes, a client–server platform. In the 2000s, organizations aimed to leverage semantic technologies for search and retrieval and to develop e-learning tools for communities of practice. From the mid-2000s, Web 2.0 "social technologies" based on the internet —e.g., blogs, bookmarks, tweets, and wikis—began to facilitate unstructured, self-governing, or ecosystem approaches that engage clients, audiences, and partners; let them have their say; and thereby build synergies through crowdsourcing.[5] Nowadays, advocates of knowledge markets[6] campaign for enterprise-wide electronic marketplaces and push to stipulate associated tasks (routines).

Out of Many, Many

> *This city has many public squares, in which are situated the markets and other places for buying and selling.*
>
> —Hernán Cortés

The vision is of a forum within an organization that matches knowledge seekers with knowledge providers. An explanation of what that might be would first define markets as actual or nominal places where the forces of demand and supply meet and where buyers and sellers trade goods and services, directly or via

---

(Footnote 4 continued)

the middle: these *Knowledge Solutions* assert that information and communications technology can for sure help collect and connect knowledge but that deployment will only achieve that if they are expressly designed for knowledge management and accompanied by a cultural change toward knowledge values. *Learning Lessons in ADB* (2007)underscores that leadership, organization, and learning are—in addition to technology—the three other pillars of an architecture for lesson learning.

[5]Crowdsourcing taps collective intelligence to execute business-related tasks that an organization would normally either perform itself or outsource to a third party. In no small addition to expanding the size of the talent pool at its disposal, the organization gains deeper insights into what stakeholders and shareholders really want.

[6]With their penchant for equilibrium and optimization, economists would contend such markets can ensure that the scarce resource—in this instance, knowledge—is used efficiently. By addressing the inefficiency of the underuse and "undersharing" of large amounts of data and information, they would boost knowledge creation and development and help capture returns on that knowledge. Of course, this transactional way of thinking assumes clients actively pursue explicit knowledge now exactly available from others for trading and that the market can readily connect parties. And yet, knowledge is no ordinary commodity: it is highly context dependent and explicit representation by sellers will inevitably decontextualize it.

intermediaries.[7] It follows that knowledge marketplaces would then be (broadly) defined as (real or virtual) environments, (formal or informal) community contexts, or (online) platforms for facilitating, aggregating, organizing, coordinating, brokering, and communicating flows and exchanges of data, information, and knowledge between seekers and providers, for free or against payment.[8] (To note, knowledge markets already exist in intellectual property trading, recruitment, management consultancies, research and development, etc. The pervasiveness of the internet is simply moving the organizations involved more decidedly into the web. Helpfully, Kostas Kafentzis et al. make clear that the direction and speed at which they can forge ahead in the knowledge trading framework are conditioned by their strategic orientation, community, implementation processes, transactions and services, information and communications technology infrastructure, and knowledge assets.) The resources traded would be those parts of an organization's intellectual capital that relate specifically to human, relational (or customer), and structural (or organizational) assets that are embedded in intellect, relationships, and routines. (They would be in explicit forms such as questions and answers, copyrights, databases, designs, documents, guides, good practices, information systems and technology, manuals, patents, procedures, project libraries, research and development, software code, etc.)[9] The figure below illustrates the four basic types of marketplaces that organizations can operate in and indeed straddle based on their outlook and capabilities along two dimensions, namely, the openness of the community and the extent of commercialization of its knowledge products and services.[10] Hereafter, these *Knowledge Solutions* refer exclusively to intrafirm knowledge transfer by means of online platforms.[11]

---

[7]Businesses are no more and no less than customer-satisfying processes. However, because external orientation ultimately depends for implementation on the responsiveness, motivation, and behavior of personnel, particularly in the services sector, resource-based views of organizations rightly dictate that internal aspects be treated on an equal footing.

[8]Kafentzis et al. (2004) write down that, where the business model rests on revenue, sources may include advertising fees, event fees, fees for value-added services, membership fees, sales fees, subscription fees, and transaction fees. Prices may be fixed or set by direct negotiation, auction, or reverse auction. Payment mechanisms include credit card charges, wire transfers, offline payments, and micropayments.

[9]The *Knowledge Solutions* on intellectual capital list sundry other knowledge assets.

[10]The boundaries between the four basic types of knowledge marketplaces are not hermetic. Inter-organizational learning networks such as professional associations are closed, almost by definition, but may have for-profit or not-for-profit orientations.

[11]Physical spaces dedicated to knowledge sharing exist in most organizations. They include brown bag seminars, venues for distinguished speakers, knowledge fairs, talk rooms, etc. Knowledge is seldom received in the passive way that electronic communications encourage: face-to-face exchanges serve to weigh up the worth of experience for later testing and validation in action.

Fig. A typology of knowledge marketplaces. *Source* Author

Let the Buyer Beware

There seems to be some perverse human characteristic that likes to make easy things difficult.

—Warren Buffett

"Rarely do we find men who willingly engage in hard, solid thinking. There is an almost universal quest for easy answers and half-baked solutions. Nothing pains some people more than having to think," reckoned Martin Luther King. The search for the Holy Grail of intrafirm knowledge transfer has often led corporate knights-errant to worship iconic knowledge platforms in internal knowledge markets. Spellbound by technical genuflections, they cannot see that to democratize knowledge an organization must let personnel concurrently reflect, debate, cast votes, contend, and work in partnerships. What is more, democratizing knowledge opens organizations to new forms of corporate governance as well as new roles and functions for those who would help manage know-how, standing tall on the two legs of integrity and psychology.[12]

Characteristically, and in contrast to a social network that connects members to people they already know, intrafirm knowledge transfer is to be achieved by an information and communications technology–supported platform whose value would grow as more users join into share information, propagate good practices and impact stories, and fire off real-time responses to what questions personnel may have—all of this regardless of knowledge use. Paraphrasing Bryan's (2004) critique

---

[12]Motivation can be intrinsic as well as extrinsic. The former is essential when tacit knowledge must be transferred. Personnel are extrinsically motivated when they can satisfy their needs indirectly, conspicuously through monetary compensation that provides satisfaction independent of the activities they undertake. Motivation is intrinsic if an activity is inherently fulfilling.

of misguided management: Take it from the top, build it and they will use it, and let a thousand websites bloom![13]

Were it that easy … At the simplest level, in organizations, people search for knowledge (and knowledgeable people) to find solutions to pressing challenges or simply to do better in their work: they derive utility from what they find in the open, barter for, or buy. Naturally, knowledge providers expect a fair return, at least through reciprocity.[14] Markets for tangible goods and services have a price system so that exchanges can be rendered efficiently and recorded; however, money is hardly ever the form of payment in the case of intrafirm knowledge transfer even though a scarce resource has been exchanged. (Even then, factors such as consistency, quality, repute, and timeliness weigh more heavily still in the expectations of knowledge seekers, who might treat online knowledge with suspicion if it has not been evaluated and edited by a dependable broker. The result? More browsing than buying on the part of those in need, which devalues what knowledge might have been painstakingly imparted by the provider.) Therein lies the crux of the matter, the reason why internal knowledge markets time and again fall short. Hence, the critical issue is to build trust in the workplace as demand for highly specific knowledge products and services is bound to intensify and spread.

From False Principles

The first rule of any technology used in a business is that automation applied to an efficient operation will magnify the efficiency. The second is that automation applied to an inefficient operation will magnify the inefficiency.

—Bill Gates

---

[13]A disconcerting aside is warranted since the theme of intrafirm knowledge transfer is unapologetically internal. Tanya Menon and Jeffrey Pfeffer have found that, although many hypothesize in-group favoritism, cases of preference for knowledge obtained from outsiders are prevalent. The grass is greener on the other side because of (i) the innate motivation to learn from competitors, not "ordinary" colleagues; and (ii) the proximity of internal knowledge—the relative availability of which subjects it to greater scrutiny then devaluation, compared to external knowledge, the scarcity of which makes it appear special. *Nul n'est prophète en son pays.* Hence, Menon and Pfeffer (2003) infer, organizational practices that give credit for internal knowledge transfers and recognize the biases that arise from close oversight will curb dysfunctional search and energize internally generated competitive advantage.

[14]This said, altruism is real and can be encouraged. However, it is limited by the time, energy, and opportunity costs of benefactors when it is not constrained by cultural factors. Furthermore, it makes little sense for an organization to depend on goodwill to power something as important as knowledge transfer.

The technology-efficiency argument is deceptive: technology per se will not entice someone to share experiences, insights, and knowledge with others; technology alone will not make a disinterested party search or browse; and the mere availability of information and communications technology will not usher in a meritocracy, a knowledge-creating company, or a learning organization.

Management should not tout the virtues of knowledge sharing without substantively committing to change. Knowledge management initiatives such as internal knowledge markets—including online platforms—that do not consider the motivations of individuals are likely to fail, depressing morale and galvanizing resistance against future endeavors. Without a shred of doubt, where creativity and innovation are required, success and viability spring from intrinsic incentives. There must be social inducements to information sharing:[15] devising them requires deeper thinking about human systems,[16] some enabling information and communications technology, and much more dedicated leadership in this area than organizations commonly deploy. Integrating these requirements, Hind Benbya and Marshall Van Alstyne offer advice on how to design effective internal knowledge platforms. Key recommendations are to (i) seed the internal knowledge market with key content and then subsidize the development of additional solutions; (ii) let prices float in the market; and (iii) manage the market like a market maker, not a central planner.

References

ADB (2007) Learning Lessons in ADB. Manila
Bryan L (2004) Making a market in knowledge. McKinsey Quarterly. No 3
Kafentzis K, Mentzas G, Apostolou D, Georgolios P (2004) Knowledge marketplaces: strategic issues and business models. Journal of Knowledge Management 8(1):130–146
Menon T, Pfeffer J (2003) Valuing internal versus external knowledge: explaining the preference for outsiders. Management Science 49(4):497–513

[15]Extrinsic motivation has patent disadvantages where knowledge must be leveraged for competitive advantage: the pressure of sanctions it is built on leads to lower levels of learning and conceptual understanding; the work performed is more superficial and people tend to produce stereotyped repetitions of what already works; and (not a few) individuals treat knowledge as a means to achieve upward mobility and seek information rather than share. With intrinsic motivation, personnel put more effort into seeding knowledge beyond their immediate work group. (There are implications for organizational culture too: people are less motivated to both share and seek knowledge beyond their unit, office, or department if reciprocity norms do not govern exchange with other work groups or if they identify more with theirs than with the organization.)

[16]Organizations come about to achieve a certain purpose in an external environment. Therefore, one had better also examine closely what configuration an organization displays to appreciate better any cultural or behavioral dysfunctionality it may have. It is important to get beyond organizational charts—which reflect formal authority, not stocks and flows of knowledge—and process maps to understand how a system works in real life before attempting to make any meaningful change. Currently, one of the best ways to do that is through social network analysis.

Further Reading

Davenport T, Prusak L (2000) Working knowledge: how organizations manage what they know. Harvard Business School Press

Proposition 111
On Knowledge Behaviors

In a Word Where large organizations make an effort to boost knowledge sharing, the solutions they fabricate can aggravate problems. Designing jobs for knowledge behaviors and recruiting people who are positive about sharing to start with will boost knowledge stocks and flows at low cost.

Is the Chief Cause of Problems Solutions?

"If I had an hour to solve a problem and my life depended on the solution, I would spend the first 55 min determining the proper question to ask, for once I know the proper question, I could solve the problem in less than 5 min," Albert Einstein is alleged to have said. Another apocrypha imparts that "Problems cannot be solved at the same level of awareness that created them." Famous remarks are seldom cited correctly but what becomes folklore is somehow imbued with wisdom: the first quote intimates that the quality of a solution is in direct proportion to that of the description of what one thinks must be solved; the second, that answers often lie outside the system.

© Asian Development Bank 2017

O. Serrat, *Knowledge Solutions*, DOI 10.1007/978-981-10-0983-9_111

> *Good management is the art of making problems so interesting and their solutions so constructive that everyone wants to get to work and deal with them.*
>
> —Paul Hawken

> *A lot of people in our industry haven't had very diverse experiences. So they don't have enough dots to connect, and they end up with very linear solutions without a broad perspective on the problem. The broader one's understanding of the human experience, the better design we will have.*
>
> —Steve Jobs

Irrespectively, what with globalization, man devises and applies in ever-growing numbers a myriad tools, methods, and approaches to speed the business of mankind.[1] These days, competitive advantage in the corporate world is often considered to spring from knowledge management for organizational learning. (In *The Future of Management*, Hamel (2007) calls for nimble, lattice-based organizations where innovation, modern management's new panacea, is everybody's business. The work of management will be less and less the responsibility of managers: distributed leadership will come of age.) Yet, well into the twenty-first century, organizations that profess to manage for knowledge generation and sharing in the current competitive reality eschew the effective questions of critical thinking. Hackneyed solutions to misalignment of strategy, structure, and systems still proliferate—and spawn further problems—even though alternative organizational forms, characteristically flexible and open, have come into sight at business, corporate, and inter-organizational levels.[2] (In contrast, in high-performance organizations, the locus of interest has for some time been purpose, processes, and people.) Since the great accomplishments of man result from ideas of enthusiasm, habits of mind and knowledge behaviors can help root out dogma—e.g., strategy, structure, and systems; imagine or invent futures; and refute Eric Sevareid's assertion that "The chief cause of problems is solutions."

Habits of Mind

By definition, a problem is any situation or matter involving uncertainty, the response to which involves perplexity or difficulty and is not immediately known. Complex problems demand craftsmanship, creativity, insightfulness, perseverance,

---

[1] To date, processes for control, discipline, precision, stability, and above all reliability have claimed the lion's share of attention.

[2] The common, contemporary paradigm is that all consider themselves bundles of knowledge-enriched products and services aiming to meet expressed or latent needs of customers. Regardless of form, all configurations have implications for knowledge management and learning; information and communications technology; human resource management; and roles, competencies, and careers in management.

and strategic reasoning. However, mindsets[3] borne of our education, experience, or (especially) environment instruct us to see things in ways that do not necessarily conduce efficient or effective problem solving, when they do not perpetuate or inflame the problem. (What is more, taking a reflective stance in the midst of active problem solving is admittedly not easy.) Exercising mindfulness, the psychological quality of self-regulation of attention coupled with curiosity and openness, can help individuals recognize and rework habitual patterns of mind. Since excellence is not an act but a practice, each of us can develop composite habits of mind that attend to value, inclination, sensitivity, capability, and commitment—all defined toward behaving intelligently when confronted with problems. These are the transcending characteristics of peak performers (Fig. 111.1).

On Knowledge Behaviors

Without a doubt, knowledge management has much to do with behavioral change. For that reason, high-performance organizations seek to minimize the drag of old mental models and help embed knowledge behaviors. What might these be? From the 16 desirable habits of mind, a practical, multiagent operating model would see that individuals, groups, and organizations consciously ask, learn, and share before, during, and after an activity.[4] A high-end inventory of knowledge behaviors—that together would enrich a knowledge culture—reads as follows:

- Ask—asking questions; checking first to see what already exists; questioning accepted wisdom.
- Learn—contextualizing learning to make it real; connecting and taking opportunities to learn; reviewing lessons as one goes and applying learning.
- Share—conveying personal details, roles, and skills; imparting experience, evidence, and feedback; communicating achievements, outcomes, and pride (Fig. 111.2).

Put differently, knowledge behaviors anchored in the 16 habits of mind require that every person, team, and community should make decided inquiries before taking action, harvest knowledge during its execution, and share the fruits of experience—however bitter—later. This is nothing new: all are fundamentally social behaviors. The difficulty, we shall see, is to do so in concert.

---

[3]A mindset is a set of assumptions—held by one or more persons or groups of people—that is so ingrained it acts as a strong incentive to continue to adopt or accept prior behaviors, choices, or techniques. The cognitive biases it cultivates beget mental inertia and "groupthink" and impact decision-making.

[4]The *Knowledge Solutions* on drawing learning charters illustrate what commitments to action organizations and the individuals within them might make.

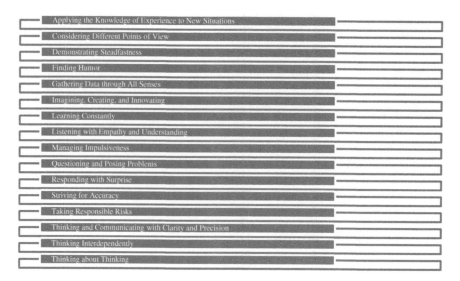

Fig. 111.1 Habits of mind. *Source* Author

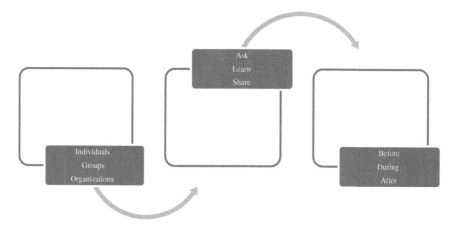

Fig. 111.2 Fueling knowledge behaviors. *Source* Author

The Bottlenecks of Behavior

"You can lead a horse to water, but you can't make it drink" is an adage of
universal application. It signifies that you can give someone means and opportunity
but cannot force that person to avail of them. The relationship between motive,
means (or ability), and opportunity—and what happens where it is not close—
explains much human behavior by dint of reasoned action. Beyond means and
opportunity, the theory of planned behavior posits an obvious argument: intention,

which is assumed to capture intrinsic and extrinsic motivational factors,[5] determines behavior, hence action.

The theory of planned behavior has had large application, for instance, in health, nutrition, and environmental psychology.[6] In respect of knowledge sharing, however, Siemsen et al. (2007) have concluded that the three variables are neither linear not multiplicative: a bottleneck—or constraining factor—in any one of them will determine what knowledge sharing may occur[7]; also, the variables should not be addressed independently but in a dynamic and coordinated manner. Having said this, motivation is pivotal. Surely, investigations about motive, means, and opportunity can help organizations determine better where to invest resources productively across the knowledge sharing landscape.[8]

Staffing Matters

What we need to do is learn to work in the system, by which I mean that everybody, every team, every platform, every division, every component is there not for individual competitive profit or recognition, but for contribution to the system as a whole on a win-win basis.

—W. Edward Deming

In the all-too-rare instances where large organizations make a dedicated effort at boosting knowledge sharing, endeavors generally target job design,[9] performance

---

[5]In brief, the theory submits that human behavior is governed not only by personal attitudes toward the behavior but also by social norms regarding that and beliefs about one's control over the behavior.

[6]For example, these days, environment-friendly actions are widely promoted as positive behaviors. In spite of that, their application can be thwarted by the belief that one's behavior will have no significant impact. Here, the theory elucidates contradictions between sustainable attitudes and unsustainable behavior.

[7]A concrete example suffices: if personnel lacks time to share knowledge—that is, if opportunity is the bottleneck—motivation and means will be blocked from having an impact on knowledge sharing behavior. If time is the constraining factor it will make no difference how motivated personnel are or what means they have at their disposal; they simply will not engage in knowledge sharing.

[8]Detecting and widening bottlenecks are essential for two reasons. In the presence of a bottleneck, resources allocated to enhancing other variables are not likely to be productive. Also, the constraining-factor model throws up insights into what metrics might be used to compare the relative costs and benefits of knowledge sharing initiatives and gauge their progress.

[9]The importance of job design owes to the impact it has on staff engagement. Job descriptions usually place cognitive factors center stage. However, job design matters for fundamentally motivational reasons. Variables such as autonomy, task identity, and feedback bear on intrinsic and extrinsic motivation to share knowledge, purposely in different ways, to cheer organization-wide knowledge behaviors, boost knowledge stocks and (particularly) flows, and nurture social capital: these variables are indispensable part of job descriptions.

appraisal, compensation and rewards, managerial styles, information and communications technoloy, and training as important predictors of motivation. These
organizations should also consider recruiting personnel who already display
knowledge behaviors: surely, considering person–environment fit to ensure congruence of individual and organizational values and goals is the easiest way to
facilitate knowledge sharing among personnel. Evidently, an organization that
values knowledge sharing and selects personnel who swear by this value will equip
itself with staff who are positive about sharing to start with; investments elsewhere
may no longer be so urgent because the likelihood that the organization's human
resource management practices fulfill needs will accordingly be higher. Time spent
on hiring is time well spent. "Hire peoplewho are better than you are, then leave
them to get on with it. Look for people who will aim for the remarkable, who will
not settle for the routine," David Ogilvy advised.

References

Hamel G (2007) The future of management. Harvard Business School Publishing
Siemsen E, Roth A, Balasubramanian S (2007) How motivation, opportunity, and ability drive
    knowledge sharing: the constraining-factor model. Journal of Operations Management 26:
    426–445

Proposition 112
Communications for Development Outcomes

In a Word Communication is the process through which relationships are instituted, sustained, altered, or ended by increases or reductions in meaning. Belatedly, as the field of development englobes ever-wider realms, it is finally recognized as a driver of change. Sped by the internet, strategic communications can explain activity and connect to purpose in more instrumental ways than have been considered so far.

Communication Matters

Communication is the process by which information[1] is conveyed through a common system of symbols, signs, or behaviors. This is as pithy a definition as one is likely to read: and yet, it barely scratches the surface of a complex subject. Still, it is convenient that understatements, especially when they masquerade as exactitudes, give imagination the latitude it needs to elaborate: in actual fact, communicating occupies such a large part—if not the totality—of human interaction that it is well-nigh integral to our existence.

---

[1]Over the past 3–4 decades, a General Definition of Information in terms of *data + meaning* has become an operational standard. The life cycle of information typically includes the following phases: (i) occurrence, (ii) transmission, (iii) processing and management, and (iv) usage.

© Asian Development Bank 2017
O. Serrat, *Knowledge Solutions*, DOI 10.1007/978-981-10-0983-9_112

> *The void created by the failure to communicate is soon filled with poison, drivel, and misrepresentation.*
>
> —C. Northcote Parkinson

Basically, people communicate to help themselves, particularly where resources—controlled or shared—are scarce.[2] From this optic, our definition rudely relegates communication to a supporting role, as if it were merely something that transpires between agents: it does not pay necessary and sufficient regard to communication as a defining state of affairs, intrinsic to organizing. More usefully, then, communication should be recognized as the process through which relationships are instituted, sustained, altered, or ended by increases or reductions in meaning.

> *To make our communications more effective, we need to shift our thinking from "What information do I need to convey?" to "What questions do I want my audience to ask?"*
>
> —Chip Heath

The utter pervasiveness of communication as a part of everything so numbs our senses we forget its primordial function and think little of its value: this probably explains why we are not better at it, with telling results across the ages, aka miscommunication (and its quick antagonistic offsprings). Simply put, miscommunication owes to divergence between what a party wants to say to another, what it actually says, what the other party hears, what it understands, what it wants to say in response, and what it actually says if it responds at all. Even if facial expressions, tone of voice (including volume), and body language (including appearance) evidently impact more than words in oral communication, the same disconnects affect

---

[2]"In the beginning was the Word, and the Word was with God, and the Word was God," the Gospel of John asserts in the New Testament. More down-to-earth, sociobiologists track the origin of language to the turning point when, from about 1 million years ago, groups of Homo erectus and later Homo neanderthalensis and Homo sapiens established home bases at which they raised their young and from which they foraged and scavenged for food; once they had instituted nests (campfires), environmental pressures began to select for traits that drew group members into ever more collaborative interaction. For in-group cooperation to ensue between humans, added mental capacity was needed—and grew—to let them construe one another's intentions and work together on what would otherwise be impossible tasks. Eventually, the added mental capacity developed into the ability to grasp abstraction and draw symbols for communication, thus leading to language. (Writing came to light in Mesopotamia much later, circa 3,500 BC.) Language made inferential communication—encoded or not—much more effective than mimicry. Oral and written expression of language is considered the most important dividing line between humans and animals. In our time, most humans can talk fluently by age four; by age six or seven, most can read and write with ease.

written forms of communication. In both instances, failure to relate effectively generally owes to emotional, cultural, organizational, personal, and situational filters—hardened by stress when information is transmitted *viva voce*—that only empathy and active listening can mitigate.

> *"Why?" is always the most difficult question to answer. You know where you are when someone asks you "What's the time?" or "When was the battle of 1066?" or "How do these seatbelts work that go tight when you slam the brakes on, Daddy?" The answers are easy and are, respectively, "Seven-thirty-five in the evening," "Ten-fifteen in the morning," and "Don't ask stupid questions."*
>
> —Douglas Adams

"The single biggest problem in communication is the illusion that it has taken place," George Bernard Shaw contended. To which Peter Drucker added that miscommunication intuits we do not know what to say, when to say it, how to say it, or to whom to say it.[3] Therefore, in any definition of communication, "commonality" is the operative word: communication does not just require a sender, a message and its conducive channel(s), as well as a recipient, preferably with means to feed back; it must also be intelligible and make agreeable mutual sense.[4] Therein lies the why of it.

If only it were that simple … Over the past half century, information and communication technologies have revolutionized the world. They have evolved from recording systems (writing and manuscript production) to communications systems (the printing press) to processing and producing systems (the computer), conspicuously in the latter case by way of Web 2.0[5] applications. Nowadays, almost all ("advanced") societies depend absolutely on information-based assets for the provision of information-intensive and information-oriented products and services, a verity that underscores the essential need to comprehend the life cycle of

---

[3]There is more: all too often, the attempt to communicate is intentionally disingenuous and favors certain aspects of an argument. In worst-case scenarios, disinformation equates with propaganda, that is, the manipulation of information to influence public opinion. "Spin" is not the subject of these *Knowledge Solutions*.

[4]To note, the receiver need not be present or aware of the sender's intent to communicate at the time of communication. (Thus, communication can occur across vast distances, even ages.) Still, communication requires that the parties to it share an area of communicative commonality; the process can only be complete after the receiver has understood the message of the sender.

[5]Hyperlinks between web pages—some with downloadable files—appeared less than 20 years ago with the advent of the World Wide Web in 1993. What is now known as Web 1.0 was the first stage in the evolution of the Web, driven at first by a top-down approach to posting and retrieving information in a set user interface. The early versions of organizational websites were de facto virtual brochures: unlike Web 2.0, which emerged 10 years later, information was closed to external editing.

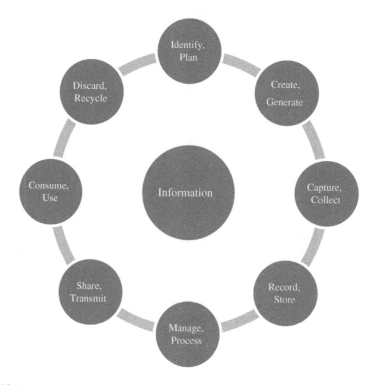

Fig. 112.1 A typical information life cycle. *Source* Author

information and what core knowledge activities can bear on that. Today, social media[6] that magnetize participation introduce substantial and pervasive changes to communication between individuals, communities, and organizations.[7] For sure, however, the newfangled web- and mobile-based technologies that fuel them are but tools. In view of that, what is their end? It helps to restate the obvious: communication is about people (Fig. 112.1).

---

[6]Social media technologies take on many different forms, such as internet forums, magazines, microblogging, pictures, podcasts, ratings, social blogs, social bookmarking, social networks, videos, weblogs, and wikis.

[7]For example, social media became in 2012 one of the most powerful sources of news updates through platforms such as Facebook, Google+, Twitter, and YouTube. (And, it is no overstatement to say that news—the communication of selected information on current events—have always played a vital role in human affairs.)

Communication for Development 1.0

> *If you make customers unhappy in the physical world, they might each tell six friends. If you make customers unhappy on the internet, they can each tell 6,000 friends with one message to a newsgroup.*
>
> —Jeff Bezos

In development aid, which is also unequivocally about people, communication is essential to human, social, and economic progress, the purpose of which is the improvement of well-being and the betterment of the quality of life. And yet, it was never conspicuous—if at all present—in the prevailing bilateral and multilateral development agenda of the 1960s (industrialization), 1970s (basic needs), 1980s (neoliberalism and structural adjustment), 1990s (good governance), and 2000s (the Millennium Development Goals, aid effectiveness, new philanthropy and social impact investors).[8] Belatedly,[9] as the field of development englobes ever-wider

---

[8]Since 2000, emerging and developing countries have driven global economic growth, new sources of development finance have mushroomed, and the number of actors, instruments, and delivery mechanisms has continued to diversify. The emerging development agenda of the 2010s may be characterized by public–private partnerships, climate change finance, South–South styles of cooperation, evidence-based solutions, and what some term "Finance ++". (The first "plus" represents leverage; the second is knowledge.) In higher parallel, in increasingly felt kickbacks, the compass of development encircles eclectic interests in social change—applicable to any group regardless of geographical setting or material base—informed by a more fluid sense of transnational collectivities and agencies. (Spaceship Earth was a worldview, sponsored in the mid-1960s by Kenneth Boulding, Buckminster Fuller, and Barbara Ward, that expressed disquiet about mankind's frenetic use of vulnerable resources and invited everyone to band and work toward the greater, common good by making responsible choices in areas of ecology, economics, and ethics. In the 1980s and 1990s, post-development theory began to question the purpose of "developmentalism" and assailed its patronizing ideology of modernization, notably through the works of Arturo Escobar and Wolfgang Sachs. This critique underlies recent calls to drop the notion of development in favor of social change and social justice.)

[9]This is not to say nothing happened. The seminal and controversial MacBride Report of the United Nations Educational, Scientific, and Cultural Organization, *Many Voices One World*, appeared in 1980. It invited nations to make communications central to the diagnosis of needs and the design and implementation of resulting development strategies. But it took another 10 years for declarations and statements on communication for development to gather steam—never mind being acted upon in ways that promote change. And, a further 15 years went by before the first World Congress on Communication for Development was held in Rome on 25–27 October 2006 to position and promote the field of communication for development in the overall agenda of development and international cooperation (London 2007). Historically, communication for development owes much to Paulo Freire's work on participatory communications with landless Brazilian peasants from the 1950s: he believed education to be a political act that could not be divorced from pedagogy. From the outset, the focus of participatory communication was on dialogical communication for agriculture and rural development, this in opposition to what were felt to be acontextual, ethnocentric, hierarchical, and linear Western concepts and mediated technologies, e.g., radio, television, for modernization. Communities were to be the protagonists of

realms, there are indications that communication is finally deemed a key factor of development and a driver of change even if here and there it is still unavoidably colored by changing theories (and associated paraphernalia) of that, the only constant being the modes of persuasion—if not the mix—employed in support.[10]

> *When we change the way we communicate, we change society.*
>
> —Clay Shirky
>
> *The beauty of social media is that it will point out your company's flaws; the key question is how quickly you address these flaws.*
>
> —Erik Qualman

Communication for development is not public relations or corporate communication[11]: communication for development is a process of strategic, imbedded interventions[12]—initiated by individuals, communities, and organizations—designed to advance the public good. Beyond mere telling, using a wider range of tools, methods, and approaches than heretofore courtesy of social media, it is about listening, respecting, suspending, and voicing to build organizational and system capacity at different levels. With social media, which demonstrates that more value can be extracted from voluntary participation than anyone ever imagined until now, dialogical communication can contribute to sustainable individual, communal, and organizational development outcomes. With a click, stakeholders can now make their realities count. Now positioned as real-time discourse, especially if it appreciates political economy to better circumscribe the geometry of development and take on the goal of empowerment, communication for development can create awareness, foster norms, influence policy makers, mobilize support, encourage

---

(Footnote 9 continued)

social change, not the passive beneficiaries of decisions made by foreign experts who know better. Paulo Freire's *Pedagogy of the Oppressed* was translated and published in English in 1970. Robert Chambers, a leading figure of the participatory tradition thereafter, framed the argument well when he inquired about whose reality counts.

[10]Aristotle's *On Rhetoric*, written circa 350 BC, identified three modes of persuasion: ethos (an appeal to the authority or honesty of the presenter), logos (an appeal to logic), and pathos (an appeal to the audience's emotions).

[11]For the sake of completeness, one should add advocacy, participatory communication, policy communication, and technology (or educational) transfer to the list. The point is that they are not the same: each function has its own rationale; each brings into play different tools, methods, and approaches.

[12]Social marketing remains a frequently employed approach, particularly in health, nutrition, and population projects. (It bodes well for environmental conservation too.) Radio and television, now used to emphasize access and dialogue, are still popular. Telecenters, community theater, and development journalism, to name a few, are relatively recent additions.

change, and even shift the frames of social issues. On account of the internet, the formerly reactionary conceptualizations and justifications that advocates of participatory development promulgated in the mid-1970s have come of age: the greatest accolade is that they are now taken for granted in the broader framework of strategic communications that inform and inspire clients, audiences, and partners and just as importantly help the initiating parties learn. In the 2010s, with the added realization that we need better communication of evidence,[13] no development agency can afford the business-as-usual of old-fashioned, reactive external communications.[14]

> *It may be hard for an egg to turn into a bird: it would be a jolly sight harder for it to learn to fly while remaining an egg. We are like eggs at present. And you cannot go on indefinitely being just an ordinary, decent egg. We must be hatched or go bad.*
>
> —C.S. Lewis

Communication for Development 2.0

In a globalizing world of mobile money, new institutions, business models, and practices are challenging long-established development agencies.[15] Yet, the majority of the latter still fail to see communication as a systemic issue, meaning, something linked to political economy and what institutions (or forces) and processes shape that. Not surprisingly, the run-of-the-mill recommendations they make to improve communication for development offer options at the project level, rarely

---

[13]Witness, for instance, the accent that is now placed on conducting impact evaluations and linking research to practice. Central to corporate governance, both sets of activities aim to bridge the evidence gap to help actors invest responsibly: both inform policy by spreading lessons of what works in development, including how and under what circumstances. Toward this, prerequisites are improving the quality of research; promoting communication, dissemination, and marketing of research; investing in translational research; and building capacity for evidence-based policy—all necessarily at the same time. To note, from the mid-2000s, development agencies have also sought to enhance the internal and external effectiveness of their operations with tools, methods, and approaches of knowledge management.

[14]It is easy to confirm the commitment of development agencies to communication for development: (i) has the organization formulated a communication policy and a strategy for its implementation? (ii) have senior positions been created for communication strategists and have specialized staff been recruited? (iii) is there a specific budget allocation to communication for development, e.g., 10%, distinct from information dissemination?

[15]Shocking though it may be, it helps to envisage development agencies as just another industry, one that is admittedly undergoing creative destruction as the emerging agenda of the 2010s, delineated earlier, intimates.

anything else, and even then as afterthoughts.[16] (Lest we forget, such communication support can in any event only be as effective as the project itself.)[17]

> *You can have brilliant ideas, but if you can't get them across, your ideas won't get you anywhere.*
>
> —Lee Iacocca

Under pressure to change, development agencies must with strategic communications emulate the disruptors of the 2010s or face irrelevance. Communication for Development 2.0 can help them ramp up dialogue with engagement by beneficiaries and stakeholders to make their realities count; build partnerships and support for the work they conduct; and transparently demonstrate impact.[18] In a virtuous circle counting on knowledge products and services, Communication for Development 2.0 can also boost staff commitment, team collaboration, and business agility, and thereby help development agencies deliver more with less.

Of Strategic Communications

> *Think like a wise man but communicate in the language of the people.*
>
> —William Butler Yeats

---

[16]At best, Communication for Development 1.0 aimed to maximize direct impact through content-based change. It was rarely exploited to induce discursive change in the way we see the world and the concepts we use to understand it, in other words, double-loop learning. To Waisbord (2008), the potential contributions of Communication for Development 1.0 were cut in three ways. First, bureaucratic needs for messaging favored informational models over participatory approaches. Second, the weak status of communication as an autonomous field of study and practice in development agencies undermined prospects for expanding understanding where the discipline did not fit prevalent institutional expectations. Third, the predominance of technical mindsets that held out solutions to political problems limited participation thinking. (Many will say this situation holds in our day.).

[17]Even then, as the *Knowledge Solutions* on value cycles for development outcomes describe, opportunities to communicate, connect, collaborate, capitalize, and communicate further occur variously at distinct stages of the project cycle.

[18]Compare this with the following statement: "The overall goal of the communication strategy is to demonstrate to key stakeholders and the general public that [*name of the organization*] should be seen as the premier development finance institution in [*name of the region*]." Clearly, Communication for Development 2.0 cannot be a one-way process whereby narratives flow from the core for unquestionable application by agents. In any case, cyberspace now lets clients, audiences, and partners wield the swift rod of critical feedback.

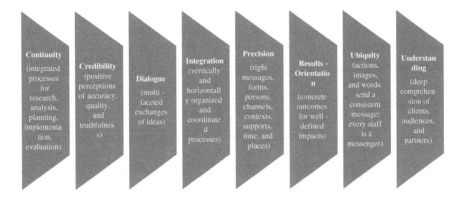

Fig. 112.2 Principles of strategic communications. *Source* Author

Strategic communications consider the what, why, where, and how of comprehensive engagement at international, national, sector, and theme as well as project levels. Based on what values they espouse, principles of continuity, credibility, dialogue, integration, precision, results-orientation, ubiquity, and understanding can underpin their communications for development outcomes.

Specifically, in an ensuing collection of ideas, preferences, and methods, strategic communications combine multimedia, multi-outlet, and multiparty outreach with face-to-face efforts, including storytelling, to explain activity and connect to purpose. Sure enough, they must be designed for adaptive and generative learning in a complex and fast-changing environment. Plainly, that cannot be achieved by fixed, central structures: instead, what is needed is a shared strategic communications mindset, integral to every office and department in an organization; it is the fostering of such culture in the immediacy of social media that will promote the necessary changes in current practice. In short, strategic communications are not a component of an organization's long-term strategic framework but an enabler that both delivers and conditions it, this in more instrumental ways than have been considered so far (Fig. 112.2).

Crafting a communication strategy is more of an art than a science but the steps are not foreign. Irrespective of level, e.g., national or project, a communication strategy should establish the objectives and policy context—the latter subject to external influences; audiences; desired changes;[19] messages; tools and activities; capacities and resources; timescales; and, vitally, provide for monitoring and evaluation and subsequent amendment. Being strategic means consistently making what core directional choices will best move an organization toward its hoped-for future. In communications as elsewhere, it depends on having vision; building

---

[19]Change expresses itself in five ways: (i) discursive, (ii) procedural, (iii) content-based, (iv) attitudinal, and (v) behavioral.

alliances; setting priorities; adopting goal- and action-oriented approaches; applying logical consistency but also adaptability in unfolding elements of the strategy; and managing resources systematically.

References

London P (2007) Mapping declarations and statements on communication for development. Panos Publications Ltd
Waisbord S (2008) The institutional challenge of participatory communication in international aid. Social Identities 14(4):505–522

Proposition 113
Learning in a Flash

In a Word Text is no longer the primary means of learning transfer. Character-based simulation, in which animated characters provide a social context that motivates learners, can improve cognition and recall and bodes well for high-impact e-learning.

Slowly, E-Learning Comes of Age

In business, community, educational, and governmental organizations it has for some time been an article of faith that the delivery of content through information and communications technology can—through democratization of and access to knowledge—greatly expand the realm of how, when, and where increasingly mobile learners can engage.[1] The world over, e-learning—viz, all forms of electronically supported learning and development—is mooted as a cheap and effective

---

[1]E-learning intersects numerous fields of thought and practice. These *Knowledge Solutions* do not take up "higher-end" matters such as the role of e-learning in knowledge management, organizational performance—both individual and collective, or organizational change.

© Asian Development Bank 2017
O. Serrat, *Knowledge Solutions*, DOI 10.1007/978-981-10-0983-9_113

way to provide people the everyday learning opportunities required, cradle to grave, to improve organizational outcomes in the modern labor market.[2]

> *Education is not the filling of a pail, but the lighting of a fire.*
>
> —William Butler Yeats

Notwithstanding, 20-odd years after the World Wide Web was launched in 1991, it must be admitted that key concepts and understandings of e-learning are still emerging. In brief, most of the difficulties that have beleaguered attempts to transfer knowledge electronically owe, so far, to exaggerated weight on specific technologies—typically to transmit for easy (re)use much smaller units of content than traditional educational and other learning and development settings do—at the expense of a commitment to improving the experience and outcome of learning.[3] (Easy things first, one might argue.)

> *The function of education is to teach one to think intensively and to think critically. Intelligence plus character—that is the goal of true education.*
>
> —Martin Luther King, Jr.

---

[2]Take the education sector. As you would expect, e-learning is suited to flexible, distance learning. Because knowledge is no longer tethered to lecterns or a teacher's desk tertiary and secondary education is seen prone to technological disruption just as encyclopedias, journals and magazines, movies, music, newspapers, and television, to name a few other information-centric industries, became from the early 2000s. (Certainly, brick-and-mortar institutions of higher learning are growingly challenged by commercial providers of lecture series; for-profit universities; nonprofit learning organizations, e.g., the Khan Academy; online services, e.g., iTunes U; and specialized training centers that issue instruction and credentials in sundry trades and professions—all of whom can easily scale delivery of online instruction.) But, there is more: e-learning can also be used in conjunction with face-to-face teaching in blended learning mode, be that synchronous or asynchronous. Therefore, some think that the traditional model of instruction in universities—the main societal hub for higher education since the end of the eleventh century—will soon be inverted: instead of attending lectures on campus and after that heading off to work on assignments students will first scrutinize online material and then gather in hybrid learning spaces to explore a subject in rich conversations (or laboratory exercises) with professors and fellow students. Proponents of blended learning reckon that the Flipped Classroom model may even enhance critical thinking. (Paradoxically, since economic reasons determine much in higher education, traditional but exclusive face-to-face tuition may become the privilege of a few while demand for global standardization in some fields may lower the level in many cases. In reality, consolidation and diversification are not mutually exclusive.).

[3]In the education sector, to use our example, most internet classes have consisted largely of videotaped lectures, sometimes broken into brief segments and punctuated by on-screen exercises and quizzes. Elsewhere, automated Powerpoint presentations are still a staple.

The point is that digital media alone does not guarantee message uptake: like any learning process, e-learning depends on effective communication of human knowledge in social context.[4] Still, even if one-way communication attenuates the learning experience, the technical affordances[5] of the Internet mean that such communication is for sure here to stay (and hopefully improve). Therefore, especially in the ever more common mode of self-paced, solitary learning, the greatest challenge of e-learning is to make training programs a dynamic, immersive experience akin, to the extent possible, to the learner engagement that occurs in a lecture hall or classroom.

Making E-Learning Come Alive

> *I would rather entertain and hope that people learned something than educate people and hope they were entertained.*
>
> —Walt Disney

In the digital world of the twenty-first century, text is no longer the primary means of learning transfer: people, certainly those in the workforce who have grown up with computer games, are more and more drawn to multimedia. Flash animations[6] that skillfully entice[7] people to construct their own meaning from content and apply instruction to their lives after program completion are a working example.

---

[4] The *Knowledge Solutions* on e-learning and the workplace contend that if e-learning is to justify the publicity that surrounds it proponents should understand its organizational environment and evolve design principles. And, for sure, learners learn in different ways: some learn best by engaging in dialogue; others do so by reading text, watching a demonstration, or playing a game—each takes a different path. Through large-scale data processing and machine learning, information and communications technology may in the not-too-distant future incorporate adaptive learning routines that help tailor a learning environment to the needs and learning styles of individuals—at any rate where a body of knowledge can be made explicit. A far cry from what is currently at hand, such technologies would measure meaning, promote learning, and evaluate new understandings and capabilities. But, we are not there yet. What is more, pace the availability of technology, purveyors of e-learning must also be equipped with systems and competences for content creation and management, learning activity delivery, and learning management.

[5] These include cloud-based computing, digital textbooks, high-quality streaming video, just-in-time information gathering, and mobile connectivity.

[6] A Flash animation is a film created with Adobe Flash or similar software. Such software manipulates vector and raster graphics to animate drawings, still images, and text.

[7] Media psychologists say the "e" in e-learning should be understood to mean exciting, energetic, engaging, and extended, not just electronic.

> *In all aspects of life, we take on a part and an appearance to seem to be what we wish to be—and thus the world is merely composed of actors.*
>
> —François de La Rochefoucauld

Character-based simulation, for one, bodes well for high-impact e-learning. Animation is the act, process, or result of imparting life, hence, activity, interest, motion, spirit, or vigor. (Else, it is the quality or condition of being lively.) Animated characters[8] that in well-designed social roles speak, interact, and guide the learning experience can through storytelling[9] enhance e-learning by providing a "real world" social context, e.g., a case study, that motivates learners, thereby improving cognition and recall for learning outcomes. Reeves (2004) recognizes that human-media interactions are intrinsically social: therefore, character interfaces bring much-needed social intelligence to e-learning. Specifically, from a teaching perspective, the 10 benefits of character interfaces Reeves identifies derive from the fact that

- Characters make explicit the social responses that are inevitable (in human-computer interaction).
- Interactive characters are perceived as real social actors.
- Interactivity increases the perceived realism and effectiveness of characters.
- Interactive characters increase trust in information sources.
- Characters have personalities that can represent brands.
- Characters can communicate social roles.
- Characters can effectively express and regulate emotions.
- Characters can effectively display important social manners.
- Characters can make interfaces easier to use.
- Characters are well liked.

> *Don't lies eventually lead to the truth? And don't all my stories, true or false, tend toward the same conclusion? Don't they all have the same meaning? So what does it matter whether they are true or false if, in both cases, they are significant of what I*

---

[8]Avatars, especially, but also actors, pedagogical characters, and personas are four terms for objects that represent (or stand in for) humans in virtual environments. In the context of e-learning, they are most commonly used as instructors but are also used to represent learners.

[9]Organizations are rediscovering the significance of the primeval skill of storytelling. In a globalizing world, this owes to quickening realization that technology, more precisely for information and communications, is but a reproducible tool. Tools are designed for functionality and assessed against utility and reliability; but they can neither create complex meaning and understanding nor help frame common values and beliefs, essential to resilient human organization in conditions of uncertainty; on the other hand, stories do just that, not least of all by disclosing and leveraging tacit knowledge, meaning, human capital. Resilience is the capacity to undergo deep change without or prior to a crisis; here, tools are not enough.

> *have been and what I am? Sometimes it is easier to see clearly into the liar than into*
> *the man who tells the truth. Truth, like light, blinds. Falsehood, on the contrary, is a*
> *beautiful twilight that enhances every object.*
>
> —Albert Camus

Designing Character-Based Simulations

Characters never tire and are always available; all the more reason, then, to design them well with emphasis on interactions between actors in the interface, not technology. To enhance learning comprehension, characters usually assume one or more of four roles to guide learners through a training program: (i) authority figure, (ii) cooperative co-learner, (iii) expert instructor, and (iv) peer instructor. Notwithstanding, in any case, the characters must exude authenticity,[10] entertain, and demonstrate soft skills through voice, first and foremost, as well as body language.

De Vries (2004) offers helpful tips for designing character-based simulations:

- **Create Life-Like Characters** Be purposeful about seemingly trivial and non-instructional characteristics such as body language, clothing, hairstyle, speech and idiom, and, especially, voice.
- **Plan the Scenes Before Development** Plan scenes with storyboarding techniques and pace them for learners.
- **Check for Understanding** Ensure that characters interact with learners in common situations and verify with questions that learning objectives are being met.
- **Focus on Learning Objectives** Get to the point: character development can be distracting.
- **Use Text to Speech before Recording the Final Script** Draft the script first and use plain text on screen until it is finalized and recorded in audio with real voices.

---

[10]Does the design tell a story with a human element? Are the characters likeable? Do they have feelings? Where do they exist, live, or work? What contextual background can one give to make them more realistic? What tone of voice might best reinforce content?

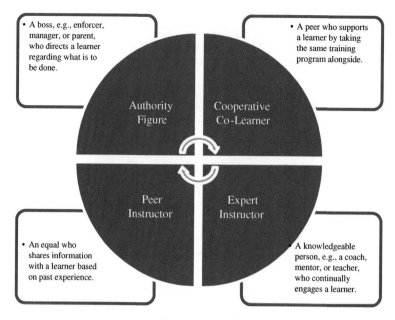

Fig. Social roles for characters. *Note* Of course, even if this is less frequent, a fifth role for a character might also be that of a learner, e.g., a professional or student, who develops a skill, gains knowledge, takes up beliefs, or acquires a behavioral tendency. *Source* Author

> *Never in the history of cinema has a medium entertained an audience. It's what you do with the medium.*
>
> —John Lasseter

- **Consider a Multi-Skilled Team** Engage a script writer to craft the storyboard and draft text; a graphic artist to draw the characters, backgrounds, and other artwork; and a web developer to integrate Flash, wave, graphic, and other files.
- **Run a Pilot** Pilot test to gather what normal questions learners may have, that should reasonably be addressed by the characters.

> *There have been great societies that did not use the wheel, but there have been no societies that did not tell stories.*
>
> —Ursula K. Le Guin

Screenshot 1: Building trust in the workplace	Screenshot 2: Conducting peer assists

Learning Objective: High-performance organizations earn, develop, and retain trust for superior results	Learning Objective: Peer assists let individuals share experiences, insights, and knowledge to promote collective learning
Description: Workplace dynamics make a significant difference to people and the organizations they sustain. High-performance organizations earn, develop, and retain trust for superior results	Description: Peer assists are events that bring individuals together to share their experiences, insights, and knowledge on an identified challenge or problem. They also promote collective learning and develop networks among those invited
Area of Competence: Collaboration Mechanisms	Area of Competence: Knowledge Sharing and Learning
Uploaded on 14 November 2012. Duration: 4:57 mns	Uploaded on 14 November 2012. Duration: 4:15 mns
Source: ADB. 2017. *ADB Knowledge*. In *Facebook*	Source: ADB. 2017. *ADB Knowledge*. In *Facebook*
Further Information: ADB. 2009. *Building Trust in the Workplace* Manila	Further Information: ADB. 2008. *Conducting Peer Assists*. Manila
Source Author	*Source* Author

Screenshot 3: Creating and running partnerships	Screenshot 4: The critical incident technique

Learning Objective: To create and run partnerships, one must understand the drivers of success and failure	Learning Objective: The Critical Incident technique offers a starting point and a process to identify and resolve workplace problems
Description: Partnerships have a crucial role to play in the development agenda. To reach the critical mass required to reduce poverty, there must be more concerted effort, greater collaboration, alignment of inputs, and a leveraging of resources and effort. Understanding the drivers of success and the drivers of failure helps efforts to create and run them	Description: Organizations are often challenged to identify and resolve workplace problems. The Critical Incident technique gives them a starting point and a process for advancing organizational development through learning experiences. It helps them study "what people do" in various situations

(continued)

(continued)

Screenshot 3: Creating and running partnerships	Screenshot 4: The critical incident technique
Area of Competence: Strategy Development	Area of Competence: Knowledge Capture and Storage
Uploaded on 15 November 2012. Duration: 6:58 mns	Uploaded on 14 November 2012. Duration: 5:27 mns
Source: ADB. 2017. *ADB Knowledge*. In *Facebook*	Source: ADB. 2017. *ADB Knowledge*. In *Facebook*
Further Information: ADB. 2008. *Creating and Running Partnerships*. Manila	Further Information: ADB. 2010. *The Critical Incident Technique*. Manila
Source Author	*Source* Author

Screenshot 5: Distributing leadership	Screenshot 6: The five whys technique
Learning Objective: Leadership is best considered as an outcome. It is defined by what one does, not who one is	Learning Objective: The Five Whys is a question-asking technique that explores the cause-and-effect relationships underlying problems
Description: The prevailing view of leadership is that it is concentrated or focused. In organizations, this makes it an input to business processes and performance—dependent on the attributes, behaviors, experience, knowledge, skills, and potential of the individuals chosen to impact these. The theory of distributed leadership thinks it best considered as an outcome. Leadership is defined by what one does, not who one is. Leadership at all levels matters and must be drawn from, not just be added to, individuals and groups in organizations	Description: When confronted with a problem, have you ever stopped and asked "why" five times? If you do not ask the right question, you will not get the right answer. The Five Whys is a simple question-asking technique that explores the cause-and-effect relationships underlying problems
Area of Competence: Collaboration Mechanisms	Area of Competence: Management Techniques
Uploaded on 14 November 2012. Duration: 4:26 mns	Uploaded on 14 November 2012. Duration: 4:58 mns
Source: ADB. 2017. *ADB Knowledge*. In *Facebook*	Source: ADB. 2017. *ADB Knowledge*. In *Facebook*
Further Information: ADB. 2009. *Distributing Leadership*. Manila	Further Information: ADB. 2009. *The Five Whys Technique*. Manila
Source Author	*Source* Author

Screenshot 7: Harvesting knowledge	Screenshot 8: The reframing matrix
Learning Objective: Knowledge harvesting can enrich group know-how, build organizational capacity, and preserve institutional memory	Learning Objective: The reframing matrix enables different views to be generated and used to solve problems
Description: If 80% of knowledge is unwritten and largely unspoken, we first need to elicit that before we can articulate, share, and make wider use of it. Knowledge harvesting is one way to draw out and package tacit knowledge to help others adapt, personalize, and apply it; build organizational capacity; and preserve institutional memory	Description: Everyone sees things differently —knowledge often lies in the eye of the beholder. The reframing matrix enables different perspectives to be generated and used in management processes. It expands the number of options for solving a problem
Area of Competence: Knowledge Capture and Storage	Area of Competence: Management Techniques
Uploaded on 14 November 2012. Duration: 4:25 mns	Uploaded on 15 November 2012. Duration: 3:17 mns
Source: ADB. 2017. *ADB Knowledge.* In *Facebook*	Source: ADB. 2017. *ADB Knowledge.* In *Facebook*
Further Information: ADB. 2010. *Harvesting Knowledge.* Manila	Further Information: ADB. 2008. *The Reframing Matrix.* Manila
Source Author	*Source* Author

Screenshot 9: Showcasing knowledge	Screenshot 10: Working in teams
Learning Objective: Information overload has less to do with quantity than with the qualities by which knowledge is presented	Learning Objective: Cooperative work by a team can produce remarkable results
Description: Information has become ubiquitous because producing, manipulating, and disseminating it is now cheap and easy. But perceptions of information overload have less to do with quantity than with the qualities by which knowledge is presented	Description: Cooperative work by a team can produce remarkable results. The challenge is to move from the realm of the possible to the realm of practice
Area of Competence: Knowledge Capture and Storage	Area of Competence: Collaboration Mechanisms

(continued)

(continued)

Screenshot 9: Showcasing knowledge	Screenshot 10: Working in teams
Uploaded on 14 November 2012. Duration: 5:18 mns	Uploaded on 15 November 2012. Duration: 4:04 mns
Source: ADB. 2017. *ADB Knowledge*. In *Facebook*	Source: ADB. 2017. *ADB Knowledge*. In *Facebook*
Further Reading: ADB. 2010. *Showcasing Knowledge*. Manila	Further Reading: ADB. 2009. *Working in Teams*. Manila
Source Author	*Source* Author

References

De Vries J (2004) Character-based simulations: what works™—the use of character-based simulations in e-learning. Bersin & Associates

Reeves B (2004) The benefits of interactive online characters. Center for the Study of Language and Information. Stanford University

Proposition 114
Toward a Library Renaissance

In a Word In the age of the internet, many think libraries are being destroyed. One need not yield to pessimism: identifiable trends point to a promising future. In light of these, one should be able to circumscribe plausible scenarios. Approaches to strategic planning that count on ownership should make a big difference and point to desirable skills for librarians. If they also invest in resilience and give unequivocal attention to branding, libraries can enjoy a renaissance.

On Alexandria and the Name of the Rose

To ask why we need libraries at all, when there is so much information available elsewhere, is about as sensible as asking if roadmaps are necessary now that there are so very many roads.

—Jon Bing

These *Knowledge Solutions* reproduce a paper presented at a Satellite Meeting on Knowledge Management as a Vital Tool for Change Management held on 15 August 2014 in Lyon, France in advance of the 2014 IFLA World Library and Information Congress.

© Asian Development Bank 2017
O. Serrat, *Knowledge Solutions*, DOI 10.1007/978-981-10-0983-9_114

For centuries, librarians have tried to safeguard information, sometimes in the face of destruction. Think of the great Library of Alexandria,[1] the burning of which symbolizes the irretrievable loss of knowledge. Think also of Umberto Eco's novel, *The Name of the Rose*, and the (fictitious) fourteenth century story about the search for a "lost" volume of Aristotle that no one is allowed to read—but yet must be preserved—because it might reveal that Jesus could and did laugh, contrary to the death-obsessed zeitgeist of the time. Fast- forward to the age of the internet, when some fear libraries are again being destroyed[2] and many ask: "Who wants libraries when you have Google?"[3] This is not an easy question to address but one need not yield to pessimism.[4] These *Knowledge Solutions* argue that identifiable trends direct to a promising future: in light of these, one should be able to circumscribe plausible scenarios. Approaches to strategic planning that count on ownership should make a big difference and point to desirable skills for librarians. If they also invest in resilience and give unequivocal attention to branding, libraries can enjoy a renaissance.[5]

---

[1]Founded by Ptolemy I Soter (367–283 BC), this library was said to have amassed an estimated 400,000 manuscripts. With collections of works, lecture halls, meeting rooms, and gardens, it was considered as the leading intellectual metropolis of the Hellenistic world.

[2]For sure, the internet is not the only driver of change. Indubitably, the logarithmic growth of the internet has given libraries a rival as a provider of information and leisure; but, certainly in the West, many libraries have also become geographically isolated from urban centers, while a changing cultural landscape has fashioned different user profiles and expectations. All the while, budgetary cuts compel libraries to challenge, compare, consult, and compete, to use the 4Cs of commitment to "Best Value" that, from the late 1990s, government policy in the United Kingdom stipulated for provision of public services.

[3]An apple should not be faulted for not being an orange. In the "Age of Knowledge," libraries are too easily judged by the standards of (highly innovative) companies such as Amazon, Apple, and Google.

[4]A majority of libraries operate from a distinctive—sometimes wondrous—physical infrastructure based on a particular "theory of the business". Then again, the media, music, and publishing industries too face disintermediation, meaning, the elimination of intermediaries in transactions between parties. To this list, some would add universities: instead of attending lectures on campus and after that heading off to work on assignments students will first scrutinize online material and then gather in hybrid learning spaces to explore a subject in rich conversations (or laboratory exercises) with professors and fellow students. Proponents of blended learning reckon that the Flipped Classroom model may even enhance critical thinking. (Paradoxically, since economic reasons determine much in higher education, traditional but exclusive face-to-face tuition may become the privilege of a few while demand for global standardization in some fields may lower the level in many cases. In reality, consolidation and diversification are not mutually exclusive.)

[5]The Renaissance was a cultural movement that spanned the fourteenth to seventeenth centuries, spreading across Europe from its birthplace in Italy, especially Florence, in the Late Middle Ages. A time of great cultural and social change, the period was characterized by astonishing creativity and innovation in the fields of art and architecture, literature, philosophy, and science. Propelled by bustling trade, humanism and renewed interest in Classical learning and values led to seismic realization after the "Dark Ages"—viz., the entire period after the decline of the Roman Empire in the fourth to fifth centuries—that things might be different.

Wanted: Information Overload—Better, Knowledge Management—Specialists

> *We all would like to know more and, at the same time, to receive less information. In fact, the problem of a worker in today's knowledge industry is not the scarcity of information but its excess. The same holds for professionals: just think of a physician or an executive, constantly bombarded by information that is at best irrelevant. In order to learn anything we need time. And to make time we must use information filters allowing us to ignore most of the information aimed at us. We must ignore much to learn a little.*
>
> — Mario Augusto Bunge

From our contemporary vantage point, it is well-nigh impossible to imagine how we could exist without the internet: we can—and are not to—work, study, shop, and play from a laptop or smartphone. On the other hand, since freelancing "seeders" proactively generate and share data and information, we are now awash in it. Google, for one, has greatly helped to organize the world's information and make it universally accessible and useful, its mission statement.

Information is ubiquitous because producing, manipulating, and disseminating it has become cheap and easy. The digital world provides a myriad means: distance no longer matters. We generate (create), collect (capture), store (record), process (manage), transmit (share), use (consume), recycle (discard), and plan (identify) information throughout the day. By means of the internet, electronic mail remains the communication channel of choice but instant messaging and social media are two technologies that increasingly challenge its preeminence.

Data smog, infobesity, infoxication, and—more frequently—information glut are fitting metaphors that describe the deluge of information we are experiencing. Information overload occurs when the amount of input to a system exceeds its processing capacity. Where content abounds, cognitive and perceptual factors constrain consumption; Davenport and Beck (2001) define attention as focused mental engagement on a particular item of information. They coin the term "attention economy" to describe an environment where the scarcest resource is not ideas or even talent but attention itself. In the attention economy, channels of information constantly compete to attract the largest share of attention, leading to information overload. According to Simon (1971), "In a knowledge-rich world, progress does not lie in the direction of reading and writing information faster or storing more of it. Progress lies in the direction of extracting and exploiting the patterns of the world so that far less information needs to be read, written, or stored."

> *... a wealth of information creates a poverty of attention ...*
>
> —Herbert Simon

In the twenty-first century, exploring the distinction between information and knowledge is a primary area of inquiry. Lest we forget, the time-honored function of librarians was precisely that: to curate[6] knowledge, which entails pulling together, sifting through, selecting, and interpreting content. Today, by filtering the wealth of information into meaningful insights, they can find the signal in the noise and both energize and synchronize communities and networks of interest and practice. Working across contents, structures, and stakeholders, librarians can turn disruptive chaos into creative clusters. To maximize outreach, librarians must in the "Age of Knowledge" consider what transformations challenge the value of libraries to clients, audiences, and partners recognize opportunities to engage with design thinking[7] in new forms and functions of "knowledge work".[8] Storage aside, what are the most valuable products and services that they can deliver?

Key Trends Affecting Libraries

Doubtlessly, many librarians would welcome a vision of the future that foresees a growing need for libraries because of recent advances in social media, mobile computing, and open data. But, there is danger in counting on such trends if libraries fail in any case to demonstrate the value of the products and services they must now provide in both physical and virtual[9] settings and in a variety of formats.

---

[6]It ought not surprise that this verb derives from Medieval Latin *curatus*, from *cura* meaning "care," with first-known use also in the fourteenth century. A curate was, and, however, archaically remains, any ecclesiastic entrusted with the care or cure of souls, such as a parish priest.

[7]That is a human-centered, prototype-driven process for the exploration of new ideas that can be applied to operations, products, services, strategies, and even management.

[8]Exhaustively, the International Federation of Library Associations and Institutions classifies a dozen different types: academic and research libraries, art libraries, government libraries, health and biosciences libraries, law libraries, libraries serving persons with print disabilities, library and research services for parliaments, metropolitan libraries, national libraries, public libraries, school libraries, science and technology libraries, and social science libraries. More prosaic typologies refer to academic libraries, public libraries, school libraries, and special libraries.

[9]For many people, a library remains a bricks-and-mortar building that stocks paper books. But a library does not have to be a physical entity: at a more intellectual level, it is a repository of information in various formats. As likely as not, Wikipedia too is a library. This does not imply that the library of the future is inevitably digital: what with nearly half of the world's population— more than 3 billion people—living on less than $2.50 a day, there is no need to explain that not everybody can afford a laptop and home connection to the internet.

Thomas Frey (n.d.) of the DaVinci Institute identifies 10 trends. Paraphrasing and reordering:

> *I tell this story to illustrate the truth of the statement I heard long ago in the Army: Plans are worthless, but planning is everything. There is a very great distinction because when you are planning for an emergency you must start with this one thing: the very definition of "emergency" is that it is unexpected, therefore it is not going to happen the way you are planning.*
>
> —Dwight D. Eisenhower

- Trend No. 1—The demand for information is growing very rapidly.
- Trend No. 2—The stage is being set for global cultural, economic, political, social, and technological systems.
- Trend No. 3—Information and communications technology is constantly shaping the way people tap information.
- Trend No. 4—We have not reached the smallest particle for storage capacity but may soon.
- Trend No. 5—Search technology is becoming increasingly complex.
- Trend No. 6—Busyness is driving the lifestyles of library users.
- Trend No. 7—We are transitioning to a verbal society, less reliant on the keyboard.
- Trend No. 8—We are shifting from product to experience-based lifestyles.
- Trend No. 9—Many libraries are morphing into centers of culture.
- Trend No. 10—The information and communications technology we currently depend on will ineluctably become obsolete.

Pure Scenarios for Future Libraries

Libraries are fundamental to teaching and learning: one might think that this is enough to endear them to us. However, the world is and will continue to be an ever-changing place. Based on a horizon scan and a political, economic, social, technological, legal, and environmental (PESTLE) analysis of the environment for higher education and libraries, the Academic Libraries of the Future project[10]

---

[10]The Academic Libraries of the Future project spanned 2010–2011. In the United Kingdom, it aimed to generate scenarios of how libraries might be by 2050 have evolved in light of long-term uncertainties. The uncertainties included how higher education will be funded and operated; how information will be created, discovered, accessed, and managed; how learning, teaching, and research will evolve to take best advantage of improvements in information and communications technology; and what will be the information needs of users for learning, teaching, and research,

fleshed out three (somewhat exaggerated) scenarios for libraries, positioned along open–closed and market–state axes:

- **The Wild West Scenario**—Under this scenario, private providers compete with one another and with governments to offer consumers information services and learning material. The power lies in the hands of the consumers, who are able to pick and choose from materials to create a personal experience.
- **The Beehive Scenario**—Under this scenario, for instance in the education sector, governments remain the primary funder and controller of information services and learning material. The overarching goal is to produce a skilled workforce, created mostly by largely homogenous higher education systems for the masses while allowing elites to attend private institutions. A limited market is used to provide competition in higher education and drive up quality.
- **The Walled Garden Scenario**—Under this scenario, for instance in the education sector, the closed nature of society makes higher education systems insular and inward-looking, isolated from other institutions by competing value systems. Here, the provision of information services is as much concerned with protecting own materials as it is with enabling access.

Enter Future Search Conferencing

Optimism is a strategy for making a better future. Because unless you believe that the future can be better, you are unlikely to step up and take responsibility for making it so.

—Noam Chomsky

Fatigue pervades organizations that cannot learn to change. Tell-tale signs are (i) senior management and change sponsors do not attend progress reviews; (ii) there is reluctance to share, perhaps even comment on, information about the change effort; (iii) resources are given over to other strategic initiatives; (iv) clients, audiences, and partners demonstrate impatience with the duration of the change effort or increasingly question its objectives; and (v) managers, champions, and agents are stressed out and the change team considers leaving. We should not forget that organizations are human institutions, not machines: people must understand and buy into the need for change if any meaningful progress toward a desired future

---

(Footnote 10 continued)

the knowledge economy, and students and researchers as "consumers". The project was sponsored by the British Library, the Joint Information Systems Committee, the Research Information Network, Research Libraries UK, and the Society of College, National, and University Libraries. Its final report is dated 18 May 2011.

is to be made at all. It is difficult and ultimately pointless to make people do what they do not want to do.

> For millions of years, mankind lived just like the animals. Then something happened which unleashed the power of our imagination. We learned to talk and we learned to listen. Speech has allowed the communication of ideas, enabling human beings to work together to build the impossible. Mankind's greatest achievements have come about by talking, and its greatest failures by not talking. It doesn't have to be like this. Our greatest hopes could become reality in the future. With the technology at our disposal, the possibilities are unbounded. All we need to do is make sure we keep talking.
>
> —Stephen Hawking

Futurists deal with probable, possible, preferable, and prospective futures.[11] Trend analysis, one of their tools, is valuable because moving with trends, not against them, is a logical undertaking. However, the patterns that trend analysis identifies can lead to organizational lock-in of the either–or, black-and-white variety the three outright scenarios may conduce; conversely, they may open too many unrealizable vistas. Trends analysis works best when accompanied by other techniques. Future Search conferencing has emerged as a system-wide strategic planning tool that enables diverse and potentially conflicting groups to find common ground for constructive action. After all, it stands to reason that, where the stakes are communal, people should work as a group to bring common sense to bear on organizational change.

Future Search conferencing was conceptualized to help organizations create shared visions and plot organizational directions linked to results over a 5–20-year horizon.[12] It is a three-day event structured to:

---

[11]These futures are all subject to cultural, psychological, and sociological influences but cannot be explored in the same way: the first (one future) entails trend analysis; the second (many futures) calls for imagination and flexibility; the third (an "other" future) springs from value positions, both critical and ideological; the fourth (futuring) hinges on preparedness to act, rooted in self-reliance and solidarity. The research methods associated with each orientation differ too.

[12]Not all topics invite the same time span. The maximum horizon should lie beyond the normal planning vista, but not stretch so far away as to seem irrelevant; one should still be able to make an impression with today's decisions. The factors that help define the perspective of a Future Search exercise are (i) the inertia or volatility of the system; (ii) the schedule of decisions to be made, the authority to make them, and the means to be used; and (iii) the degree of rigidity or motivation of participants. The horizon an organization selects has a serious effect on results—a narrow timeframe lowers the net present value of an endeavor by overlooking future benefits; an unduly long vista overestimates them. Organizations should plump for a horizon that encompasses all conceivable benefits and costs likely to ensue from an endeavor, but they must also consider how far they can reasonably predict effects.

- Represent the system in one room;
- Explore the whole in context before seeking to act on parts, focusing on common ground and desired futures, and treating problems as information; and
- Self-manage work and take responsibility for action.

Future Search conferencing links inputs, activities, and outputs to result in a vision built on

- Appreciation of an organization's history;
- Acknowledgment of present-day strengths and weaknesses; and
- Considered opinion about major opportunities in the future.

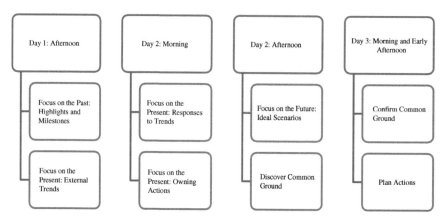

Fig. A typical future search agenda. *Source* Author

Not a free-floating brainstorming exercise, Future Search conferencing is a carefully designed methodology linking inputs, activities, and outputs. In four or five sessions each lasting half a day, participants keep to the following in small groups or plenary sessions[13]:

> *Human relationships always help us to carry on because they always presuppose further developments, a future—and also because we live as if our only task was precisely to have relationships with other people.*
>
> —Albert Camus

---

[13]In the United States, libraries that report having used Future Search conferencing include, for instance, Drexel University Libraries, Durham County Library, Monroe County Public Library, and Nebraska Library Services. For an informative account of the experience of Drexel University Libraries see Nitecki et al. (2013).

- **Focus on the Past: Highlights and Milestones**—In the first half-day, prefer-ably after a warm-up allowing participants to converse with one another, the Future Search gets underway with a look at the past. The eight groups contribute historical information and compose timelines of key events in the world, their personal lives, and the history of the Future Search topic. The groups tell stories about each timeline and what implications the stories have for the work they have come to do. No items are too trivial and no individual dominates: for-bearance on the beliefs and positions of others deepens comprehension and acceptance. This process creates a shared, global context for the Future Search.
- **Focus on the Present: External Trends**—Later, the entire assembly draws a mind map, ranks ongoing trends affecting the system the participants operate or exist in, and identifies which are most important in relation to the topic. This process clarifies what is impacting the organization.
- **Focus on the Present: Responses to Trends**—In the morning of the second day, the groups describe what they are doing about the key trends identified and explain what they plan to do in the future. This process helps assess current actions.
- **Focus on the Present: Owning Actions**—Later, the groups report on what they are proud of and sorry about in the way they are dealing with the Future Search topic. This process surfaces strengths and weaknesses in the organization and affords psychological safety for admission of errors.
- **Focus on the Future: Ideal Scenarios**—In the afternoon of the second day, the groups project themselves into the future and describe their preferred vision10 of the future as though it had already come about. This process generates a clear and powerful image of a healthy organization—and its values—through which the participants would like to advance their joint purpose, to be made real over the selected horizon.
- **Discover Common Ground**—Later, the groups post which they believe hold common—but not necessarily easy—ground for all participants. Disagreements are acknowledged without auxiliary discussion. This process enables partici-pants to locate springboards for action, having elucidated what assumptions—e.g., the nature of society, the means of social change, and the attributes and roles of knowledge—underpin each.
- **Confirm Common Ground**—In the morning of the third day, the entire assembly dialogues to agree on common ground. This process helps participants conceptualize behaviors for cooperative ventures.
- **Plan Actions**—In the afternoon of the third day, champions throughout the organization sign up to implement action plans. Of course, authority, resources, and arrangements for action are confirmed by reality checks. Participants walk out of the assembly room committed and ready to accomplish the envisioned future based on a more cogent framework that connects values and actions in

new relationships and real time. This process formulates mutually supportive,
practicable sets of rapid undertakings for individuals, groups, and the organization they are members of, close follow-up which will determine whether
change has occurred.

Here too, Thomas Frey's recommendations for libraries deserve mention, if only
because many of them have to do with the sort of conversations that Future Search
conferencing engenders. Paraphrasing and expanding, he advises them to:

> *The art challenges the technology, and the technology inspires the art.*
>
> —John Lasseter

- **Evaluate the Library Experience**—Libraries can survey the opinions and
  suggestions of clients, audiences, and partners to grasp what matters most to
  them. The patrons are the community at large and the people who walk through
  the library doors.
- **Embrace New Information and Communications Technology**—Information
  and communications technology is being introduced on a daily basis and most
  people are at a loss when it comes to deciding what to use or what to stay away
  from. Because no organization has taken the lead in helping the general public
  to understand new technology where there are opportunities for libraries to
  become centers of digital learning and points of reference—culture (including
  recreation), research, innovation, etc.—for local communities: they can, for
  instance, create technology advisory boards; enroll technology-savvy members
  of the community to hold monthly discussions that the community at large
  would be invited to join; and organize guest lecture series on technology—this
  is quite converse to the idea that the internet will make them superfluous or
  irrelevant.[14]

---

[14]As early as 1999, Basefsky envisioned libraries as agents of change. Beyond collecting, organizing, and assisting, he made the case they needed to (i) inform patrons about the material being
collected, presumably on their behalf; (ii) discuss the issues that the curated material was to
provide background and enlightenment on; (iii) solicit end user buy-in through extensive
demonstration programs of how to best use the information collected, and for what purposes;
(iv) ascribe key individuals in libraries to special services so they might convey the value of the
information to patrons; (v) team with management in libraries to bring the perspectives of
knowledge and information providers (librarians) to the table; and (vi) stretch the job description
of librarians or the organizational role of libraries to better fit the needs of the organizations they
serve. Toward these, he argued (1999) that they had to act as facilitators, consultants, trainers, and
journalists/reporters.

- **Preserve the Memories of Their Own Communities**—The historical memories of a community amount to much, much more than a few documents: they embody many forms that should not disappear and libraries have a quintessential role to play.[15]
- **Experiment with Creative Spaces so the Future Role of the Library Can Define Itself**—Because the role of libraries, 20 years hence have changed and will likely embrace multiple new forms and functions, libraries can design creative spaces to enable clients, audiences, and partners, not forgetting staff, to experiment and determine what ideas draw attention and get traction. With social innovation, possible uses for creative spaces include art studios; band practice rooms; blogger stations; cybercafés; daycare facilities; drama studios; exercise bicycles and treadmills; gamer stations; imagination rooms; mini-theaters; podcast studios; recording studios; video studios; and virtual world stations.

> *Imagination is the beginning of creation. You imagine what you desire, you will what you imagine, and at last you create what you will.*
>
> —George Bernard Shaw

Since, they juxtapose also the Wild West, Beehive, and Walled Garden scenarios described earlier, it is relevant to note Thomas Frey's three configurations for libraries. He calls them the Time Capsule Room (n.d.), the Search Command Center (n.d.), and the Electronic Outpost (n.d.). Not an "official story," the Time Capsule Room would preserve and make accessible sensory information about the essence of community in audio, video, and image forms (Over time, new technologies may capture frequencies, pressures, smells, tastes, textures, vibrations, and other situational attributes.) To establish a library as a center of gravity for exploration, the Search Command Center would draw attention to databases, specialized search engines, and other available resources; provide expert, hands-on assistance in finding and using databases; and teach patrons how to access information remotely. To extend the digital world to efficiently run community gathering places, the Electronic Outpost would in different shapes and sizes, and for varying purposes,

---

[15]For example, the role of Library and Archives Canada, established in 2004, is to preserve Canada's documentary heritage and make it accessible. Its products comprise databases, digitized microforms, an electronic collection, open data, research aids, thematic guides, and virtual exhibitions.

serve as the satellite branch of a central library; some outposts would offer selections of digital tablets and book readers; others would feature daycare centers, gamer stations, mini-theaters, working studios, etc., perhaps also a Search Command Center.

> *It's easy to run to others. It's so hard to stand on one's own record. You can fake virtue for an audience. You can't fake it in your own eyes. Your ego is your strictest judge. They run from it. They spend their lives running. It's easier to donate a few thousand to charity and think oneself noble than to base self-respect on personal standards of personal achievement. It's simple to seek substitutes for competence— such easy substitutes: love, charm, kindness, charity. But there is no substitute for competence.*
>
> —Ayn Rand

A Skills Framework for Librarians

Creating a shared vision and plotting organizational directions is one thing but delivering the dream is another. At a time when increasingly advanced skills are required for success in life and work, all libraries must retool. Competence is the state or quality of being adequately or well qualified to deliver a specific task, action, or function successfully. It is also a specific range of knowledge, skills, or behaviors utilized to improve performance. Today, sustainable competitive advantage derives from strenuous efforts to identify, cultivate, and exploit an organization's core competencies, the tangible fruits of which are products and services that anticipate and meet demand. (Yesteryear, instead of strengthening the roots of competitiveness, the accent was placed on business units. Innately, given their defining characteristics, business units under invest in core competencies, incarcerate resources, and bind innovation—when they do not stifle it.)

Core competencies are integrated and harmonized abilities that provide potential access to markets; create and deliver value to audiences, clients, and partners there; and are difficult for competitors to imitate. They depend on relentless design of strategic architecture, deployment of competence carriers, and commitment to collaborate across silos. They are the product of collective learning. The Five Competencies Framework that ADB's (2008–) Knowledge Solutions series promotes and aims to build strengths in the areas of strategy development, management techniques, collaboration mechanisms, knowledge sharing and learning, and knowledge capture and storage. Over the medium- to long-term, libraries may need to build competencies in the first two areas, and unremittingly strengthen abilities in the other three.

More immediately, citing the Institute of Museum and Library Services (2009),[16] a skills framework (particularized to the configuration of each library) would likely comprise:

> *You have no idea how eager I am to ensure that the notion of library does not disappear – it's too important. But the thing is, it's going to have to curate an extremely broad range of materials, and increasingly digital content.*
>
> —Vint Cerf

- **Learning and Innovation Skills**, e.g., critical thinking and problem solving; creativity and innovation; communication and collaboration; visual literacy; scientific and numerical literacy; cross-disciplinary thinking; and basic literacy.
- **Information, Media, and Technology Skills**, e.g., information literacy; media literacy; and information, communications, and technology literacy.
- **Life and Career Skills**, e.g., flexibility and adaptability; initiative and self-direction; social and cross-cultural skills; productivity and accountability; and leadership and responsibility.
- **Twenty-First Century Themes**, e.g., global awareness; financial, economic, business, and entrepreneurial literacy; civic literacy; health literacy; and environmental literacy.

Toward Resilience, Not just Sustainability

Organizations must be resilient if they are to survive and thrive in turbulent times: it is no longer sufficient to throw efforts at strategy, structure, and systems, parameters that lie mainly within an organization's boundaries. In today's dynamic and complex environment, enduring success requires organizational agility across boundaries. In the century of complexity, organizations must be "in the making" and the locus of attention must become purpose, processes, and people, the vital factors that Future Search conferencing investigates.

Libraries must accommodate environmental turbulence and effectively manage disruptive change and its pace to engage, adapt, and recover; to capture or realize opportunity; and in some cases to actually morph to become stronger on account of

---

[16]With attention to institutional assets (human capital, physical infrastructure, information technology, collections, programs), leadership and management (vision and planning, access, resource allocation and sustainability), partnering (business partners, community partners, education partners), and accountability (goal setting, metric development, continuous improvement), the Institute of Museum and Library Services also provides a self-assessment tool to helps libraries (and museums) scan the organization and focus planning efforts around core areas of operations.

the experience. With newfound purpose from Future Search conferencing, investments in three areas would assuredly move libraries from passivity to action[17]:

- **Leadership and Culture**—which define the adaptive capacity of the
  organization.
- **Networks**—which amount to the internal and external relationships fostered and
  developed for the organization to leverage when needed.
- **Change Readiness**—which signifies the planning undertaken and direction
  established to enable the organization to be change-ready.

Investments in leadership and culture relate to leadership, staff engagement,
situation awareness, decision making, and creativity and innovation. Investments in
networks relate to effective partnerships, leveraging knowledge, breaking silos, and
internal resources. Investments in change readiness relate to unity of purpose,
proactive posture, planning strategies, and stress-testing plans.

A Postscript on Branding

I have always imagined that Paradise will be a kind of library.

—Jorge Luis Borges

Irrespective of configuration, libraries must in addition do more about branding.
Branding is a means to identify an organization's products or services, differentiate
them from others, and create and maintain an image that encourages confidence
among clients, audiences, and partners. Until the mid-1990s, brand management—
based on the 4Ps of product (or service), place, price, and promotion—aimed to
engineer additional value from single brands. The idea of organizational branding
has since matured to embrace relational capital, with implications for behavior, and
is making inroads in the public sector too. Marketers have come to agree that the
parties to a transaction are in fact exchanging one behavior with another as individuals or communities: they do not just "transact". And so, if relationships—in
other words, supply chains—are crucial to marketing and marketing is not an act
but a habit, libraries should do the following:

- Think in terms of social capital and relationships, which requires that they plan
  for the long-term and build brand equity accordingly.

---

[17]Work in this area owes much to Resilient Organizations. On top, Resilient Organizations has
devised a resilience benchmark tool and associated questionnaire to gauge the resilience of an
organization, monitor progress over time, and compare resilience strengths and weaknesses against
other organizations in the sector of interest or of a similar size. See Resilient Organizations. 2015.

- Consider what deep-seated values relate to the behaviors of targeted end users and ascertain better what value and motivational attributes products and services have from the perspective of end users.
- Focus, simplify, and organize products and services by emphasizing and facilitating and understanding of unique selling propositions, which demands that for all products and services they look at the why, what, how, when, where, and who of end user behaviors.
- Bring more and different partners together to initiate and deploy synergies.
- Constantly, monitor and evaluate efforts by surveying the perceptions of end users.
- Visualize marketing as change management, the success of which hinges on explicit consideration of relevant determinants of intraorganizational behaviors throughout marketing activities, institutions, and processes.
- Accept that organizational behavior is central to marketing and branding: it is a management philosophy for organizational practice; a strategy that relates to end users; an organizational tool for structuring and infusing teams; a tactic with which to drive inputs; and a measurement of the relevance, efficiency, efficacy, impact, and sustainability of activities, outputs, and outcomes.

References

ADB (2008–) Knowledge solutions. Manila

Basefsky S (1999) The library as an agent of change: pushing the client institution forward. Information Outlook 3(8):37–40

Davenport T, Beck J (2001) The attention economy: understanding the new currency of business. Harvard Business School Press

Frey T (n.d.) The future of libraries

Frey T (n.d.) The future of library series: part 1—the time capsule room

Frey T (n.d.) The future of library series: part 2—the search command center

Frey T (n.d.) The future of library series: part 3—the electronic outpost

Institute of Museum and Library Services (2009) Museums, libraries, and twenty-first century skills

Nitecki D, Livingston J, Gorelick G, Noll S (2013) Evaluating a future search conference for an academic library's strategic planning. Library Leadership and Management 27(3):1–21

Simon H (1971) Designing organizations for an information-rich world. In: Greenberger M (ed) Computers, communications, and the public interest. The Johns Hopkins University Press

Part V
Knowledge Capture and Storage

Proposition 115
Conducting Exit Interviews

In a Word Exit interviews provide feedback on why employees leave, what they liked about their job, and where the organization needs improvement. They are most effective when data is compiled and tracked over time. The concept has been revisited as a tool to capture knowledge from leavers. Exit interviews can be a win–win situation: the organization retains a portion of the leaver's knowledge and shares it; the departing employee articulates unique contributions and leaves a mark.

Rationale

Together with staff engagement surveys, exit interviews are one of the most widely used methods of gathering employee feedback. The less tacit and explicit knowledge an organization captures from staff on a regular basis, the more it needs to capture when they exit. Exit interviews are a unique chance to survey and analyze the opinions of departing employees, who are generally more forthcoming and objective on such occasions.

From an employer's perspective, the purpose is to learn from the employee's departure on the basis that feedback is a helpful driver of organizational performance improvement.

© Asian Development Bank 2017
O. Serrat, *Knowledge Solutions*, DOI 10.1007/978-981-10-0983-9_115

More recently, the practice of exit interviews has been revisited as a knowledge management tool to capture and store knowledge from departing employees and minimize loss through staff turnover. This is especially relevant in roles where the employee embodies significant human capital that may be passed to appropriate employees remaining in the organization. Most departing employees are pleased to share knowledge, help a successor, or brief management, in so doing yield information that may be used to enhance all aspects of an organization's working environment including culture, management, business processes, and intra- as well as inter-organizational relationships. Notwithstanding, participation in exit interviews and responses to exit interview questionnaires must be voluntary.

Benefits

At negligible cost, the benefits of learning-based exit interviews are that they

- Help to retain vital knowledge in the organization.
- Shorten the learning curve of new employees or successors to the departing employee.
- Catalyze identification of specific mistakes and improvement opportunities.
- Enhance the understanding and experience that managers have of managing people and organizations.
- Inform management succession planning.
- Support an organization's human resource practices.
- Provide direct indications on how to improve staff retention.
- Generate useful information for training needs analysis and training planning processes.
- Result in the departing employee having a more positive view of the organization and its culture.

Preparation

Face-to-face interactions are central to exit interviews. The management of the exit interview process must be initiated as early as possible after it is known that the employee is leaving. In preparation, it is important to

- Consider who currently accesses the departing employee's knowledge and what they need to know from the replacement staff. It is useful in this respect to think about documented explicit knowledge (in files, documents, and electronic mails) as well as tacit knowledge (know-how) that need to be explained.
- Develop a plan in a participatory way to ensure that knowledge can be captured and stored during the departing employee's notice period. This requires a review

of key tasks, drawing from the original terms of reference of the departing employee. For explicit knowledge, the departing employee should move relevant files into shared folders or a document library. Ideally, they should organize all files and draw up a related set of notes for the successor. For important tacit knowledge, activity-based knowledge mapping could prove useful, providing a framework for conversations about how key activities are undertaken, what inputs and outputs are involved, or what obstacles and bottlenecks might exist. Internal and external networks and other sources of knowledge could also be discussed.

Last Words

The last words of departing employees can provide valuable insights into corporate culture, dysfunctions, and opportunities to do better. It is important to listen carefully during an exit interview, track answers, and look for long-term trends. But it is even more important to act on the information received to correct mistakes or improve further in areas of success.

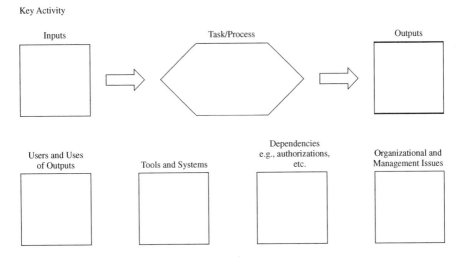

Fig. Activity-based mapping template. *Source* Author

Table. Exit interview questionnaire[a]

Details (to be completed by the unit but checked by the departing employee)	
Name:	
Gender:	
Nationality:	
Position:	
Level:	
Type of contract:	
Start and finish date:	
What Next	
What are you going to do?	
If employment, who will be your new employer?	
If employment, what sort of job and at what level?	
If employment, what attracted you to your new job?	
If employment, how will your new job differ from your current one?	
About the Unit	
Do you feel the description of your job in the engagement process was accurate?	
Were the purpose and expected results of your position clear throughout your work in the unit?	
Could your qualifications, experience, and skills have been used to better advantage?	
Do you feel you received appropriate support to enable you to do your job?	
Was the training you received in the unit adequate to enable you to accomplish your job?	
Are there further training opportunities you think the unit should be offering?	
What did you see as your promotion and career prospects in the unit?	
How might those prospects have been improved?	
How was your working environment generally?	
Can you list the three most important things that should be done to make the unit more effective in terms of influencing decisions in the organization?	
Can you list the three most important things that should be done to make the unit a better place to work?	
Are there any other issues you wish to raise?	
Others	
Can you suggest ways to improve this questionnaire?	
Signed:	Date:

Source Author

[a]Please return to the head of the unit (or office, division, or department as appropriate) with copy to designated supervising staff

Box: Sample Exit Interview Questions

The following questions can be used in face-to-face exit interviews to complement or deepen, on a case-by-case basis, the responses made to the exit interview questionnaire.

General

- What was satisfying during your time in the unit? What was frustrating?
- What could you have done better or more?
- What extra responsibility would you have welcomed?

Induction

- Were you inducted adequately for your role(s)?
- What improvement could be made to the way you were inducted for your role(s)?

Training and Development

- How well do you think your training and development needs were assessed and met?
- What training and development did you find helpful and enjoyable?
- What training and development would you have liked or needed that you did not receive and what effect would that have had?

Performance Evaluation

- What can you say about the way your performance was measured and the feedback on your performance results?
- How well do you think the performance and development plan worked for you?
- How would you have changed the expectations (or absence of) that were placed on you? And why?

Communications

- What can you say about communications in the unit? How could these be improved?
- What could you say about communications between the unit and other departments and offices? How could these be improved?

Working Conditions

- How would you describe the culture of the unit?
- What suggestion would you make to improve working conditions?
- What examples of inefficiencies in business processes and procedures in the unit could you point to?
- How could the unit reduce stress levels among employees where stress is an issue?

Management

- What can you say about the way you were managed? On a day-to-day basis? On a month-to-month basis?

- What things did the unit and its management do to make your job more difficult?
- What would you say about how you were motivated and how could that have been improved?
- How could the unit have enabled you to have made better use of your time?

Knowledge Transfer

- What would you consider to be your foremost knowledge assets?
- How might your explicit and tacit knowledge be transferred prior to your departure?
- Would you be happy to take part in a briefing meeting with managers, replacements, successor, and/or colleagues so that we can benefit further from your knowledge prior to your departure?
- What can the unit do to enable you to pass on as much of your knowledge as possible to your replacement or successor prior to your departure?
- How and when would you prefer to pass on your knowledge to your successor?
- Could you introduce (name of successor) to your key contacts before you go?
- How can the unit gather and make better use of the knowledge of employees?

Source Author.

Proposition 116
Monthly Progress Notes

In a Word feedback is the dynamic process of presenting and disseminating information to improve performance. Feedback mechanisms are increasingly being recognized as key elements of learning before, during, and after. Monthly progress notes on project administration, in which document accomplishments as well as bottlenecks, are prominent among these.

Rationale

Feedback is a circular causal process whereby some portion of a system's output is returned to the input to control the dynamic behavior of the system. In organizations, feedback is the process of sharing observations, concerns, and suggestions to improve performance. In work that seeks to address the increasingly complex challenges of development, often with limited resources, feedback is essential to maximize development impact.[1] Examples of feedback include audits, performance appraisals, monitoring and evaluation, shareholders' meetings, surveys, and 360° assessments.

---

[1]Typically, feedback mechanisms on development activities seek to (i) improve future policies, strategies, programs, and projects, including their design, implementation, and results, through feedback of lessons learned; (ii) provide a basis for accountability, including the provision of information to the public; and (iii) facilitate the updating or reformulation of current project design to increase the implementability and sustainability of the project.

© Asian Development Bank 2017
O. Serrat, *Knowledge Solutions*, DOI 10.1007/978-981-10-0983-9_116

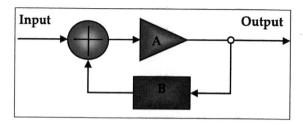

Fig. The feedback mechanism. *Source* Author

Monitoring and Evaluation

The essential first steps of feedback are the processes of monitoring and evaluation. Monitoring[2] provides senior management with information about current and emerging problems and data to assess if objectives are being met and remain valid. Monitoring reports should be based on a set of simple indicators that can be collected and processed in time for senior management to take the necessary actions. Evaluation,[3] in the context of project implementation, is an ongoing activity used to reassess components necessary to meet objectives in the light of experience as implementation proceeds. Evaluation draws on information supplied through monitoring, as well as special studies to reconsider and adjust project components as required through such mechanisms as reformulation. As a tool, evaluation can be applied at different points in the project cycle to elicit information for project identification and, subsequently, project design; for ongoing management (monitoring and reviews); or for future development activities (post-evaluation studies). Monitoring and evaluation mechanisms should be timely, accessible, simple, ongoing, and systematic. They should also offer a variety of approaches and promote follow-up.

The Challenge

The challenge of feedback is to develop ways for the results of monitoring and evaluation to be disseminated and returned through the system to relevant individuals and groups. Thus, feedback mechanisms require information dissemination

---

[2]The primary questions of monitoring are: (i) Are the right inputs being supplied or delivered at the right time? (ii) Are the planned inputs producing the planned outputs? (iii) Are the outputs leading to the achievement of the desired outcome? (iv) Is the policy environment consistent with the design assumptions? (v) Are the project or program's objectives still valid?

[3]The primary questions of evaluation are: (i) Were the commitments honored from all sides? Did the planned activities actually occur? (ii) What should have been planned (rather than what was actually planned) to reach the project's objectives more effectively and efficiently? (iii) What could have been achieved with the same resources and in the same time if the project or program had been managed more effectively and efficiently?

strategies and formal mechanisms that ensure integration of findings into the project cycle. Institutionalization of the feedback loop facilitates this process. This involves establishing a variety of formal and less formal means that can be used to ensure that findings are considered during project or program implementation and in the development of new projects or programs. Typically, these include linkages to

- senior management,
- policy development,
- program management,
- agency procedures, and
- training.

Common Constraints

Constraints on feedback mechanisms are many. They include

- poor appreciation of the benefits from feedback, and thus poor cooperation in its conduct;
- insufficient clarity and precision in performance indicators;
- shortages of personnel with skills in performance evaluation and confidence in its effectiveness;
- overemphasis on official or regulatory procedural aspects, which often means that more attention is given to accomplishing a necessary task than to looking beyond immediate requirements to the needs of current and future projects and programs;
- inadequate financial resources;
- the poor quality of information generated;
- the absence of well-established management information systems; and
- lack of a truthful environment in certain political cultures.

Monthly Progress Notes

Monthly progress notes on project administration should be considered an essential feedback mechanism. They document accomplishments as well as the problems or bottlenecks encountered during project or program preparation and implementation, and assess alternate means of replicating or dealing with them, respectively. They are also a means of establishing accountability for various actions at various stages of the project cycle, and assessing the budgetary implications of improving development effectiveness. Yet, the submission of monthly progress notes on activities and accomplishments is too infrequently provided in the scope of projects and programs.

Template

The text and tables below provide guidance on the preparation by consultants of monthly progress notes in the form of a recommended format and a description of the contents required. Naturally, flexibility in the interpretation and use of the instructions should be exercised as they are intended to introduce approximate conformance in the more obvious components of reporting. The monthly progress notes, completed at the end of each month or partial month, should be submitted by consultants to their direct supervisor(s), e.g., the project implementation office head, department director, and project director, and entered into the central files of executing and implementing agencies.

Consultants may wish to copy other personnel as well (Tables 116.1 and 116.2).

The monthly progress notes should serve the function of monitoring and evaluation and purport to inform others in the interest of coordination. They should be concise statements of work accomplished or shortcomings during the preceding month. They should consist of a few pages of text followed by attachments including (i) details of daily work output in a calendar format, and (ii) a summary of output against terms of reference. Other attachments may be added to clarify aspects of activities.

Table 116.1 Schedule of daily activities—[Month, Year]

Sun	Mon	Tue	Wed	Thu	Fri	Sat
A form such as this can be used to show daily activities. It should be filled out each day of the month	Type in the day's activities, e.g., "Met with PIO Head. Prepared monthly progress note," etc.	1	2	3	4	5
6	7	8	9	10	11	12
13	14	15	16	17	18	19
20	21	22	23	24	25	26
27	28	29	30	31		

Table 116.2 Terms of reference and monthly summary of activities—[Month, Year]

Item	Terms of reference	Summary of monthly activities
1.	[List items in terms of reference here.]	[Describe activities undertaken during the month against items in the consultant's terms of reference]
2.		
3.		
4.		
5.		
6.		
7.		
8.		
9.		
10.		

Note Variations on the style and layout of this table are acceptable
Source Author

Needless to say, the body text of the monthly progress note should vary depending on the amount of information that needs to be reported. It may consist of a few paragraphs that summarize the work output or may include separate sections that provide additional information on activities undertaken. In either case the note should contain a section that summarizes the actions taken during the month on the previous month's recommendations. Any other information should be shown as additional attachments.

Text: Monthly Progress Note

[Month] [Year]

To:	[Primary recipients—LIST]
From:	[Name], [Position]
Copy:	[Secondary Recipients—LIST]

Introduction

The opening paragraph should describe the period covered by the note, and indicate whether the consultant was present on the project full or part time. It should also reference any attachments to the progress note that are used to provide additional details on the consultant's work. There are generally two: the first attachment provides a calendar review of activities for the month; the second provides a brief synopsis of activities against the consultant's terms of reference. Other attachments, added as necessary, should be referenced here.

General

This should be a brief summary list of the major categories of work over the past month. Further details on these topics should be provided in later sections.

Actions Taken in Response to the Recommendations of the Previous Monthly Progress Note

Recommendations from the previous Monthly Progress Note should be presented in italics, followed by a summary of actions taken over the past month to address the recommendations.

[Summary of First Recommendation in italics.]

[Summary of actions taken]

[Summary of Second Recommendation, etc.]

[Summary of actions taken against second recommendation, etc.]

[Activity Category 1]

These sections (as many as needed) should address in some detail individual categories of activity as identified in the section labeled "General," above. A description of the activities and their importance can be described in one or more paragraphs here. Examples of categories include "Purchasing," "Work Planning," "Project Coordination," and "Meetings and Reports".

Any recommendations for future redirection of activity can be provided here.

[Activity Category 2—N]

This paragraph addresses in the same fashion the second category. Additional sections should be added as needed (up to "N").

Recommendation: This paragraph provides any relevant recommendations for the second category.

[Overarching Category]

For most consultants there may be one category that overarches all others, and is the primary focus of the consultant's work. If so, activities under this category can be described here and used to sum up and integrate all the consultant's activities for the month.

Recommendation: General, overarching recommendations may be offered here.

Signed:

[The note should be signed, at least in hard copy]

_____
[Name], [Title]

Proposition 117
Assessing the Effectiveness of Assistance in Capacity Development

In a Word Feedback is the dynamic process of presenting and disseminating information to improve performance. Feedback mechanisms are increasingly being recognized as key elements of learning before, during, and after. Assessments by executing agencies of the effectiveness of assistance in capacity development are prominent among these.

Rationale

Feedback is a circular causal process whereby some portion of a system's output is returned to the input to control the dynamic behavior of the system. In organizations, feedback is the process of sharing observations, concerns, and suggestions to improve performance. In work that seeks to address the increasingly complex challenges of development, often with limited resources, feedback is essential to maximize development impact. The *Knowledge Solutions* on monthly progress notes assert that the essential first steps of feedback are the processes of monitoring and evaluation. They identify challenges, recognize common constraints, and note that the submission of monthly progress notes on activities and accomplishments is too infrequently provided in the scope of projects and programs. There are

© Asian Development Bank 2017
O. Serrat, *Knowledge Solutions*, DOI 10.1007/978-981-10-0983-9_117

opportunities too for more systematic capture and storage of feedback from executing agencies on the effectiveness of assistance in capacity development, prior to knowledge sharing and learning.

Assessing the Effectiveness of Assistance in Capacity Development

Capacity development is the process whereby people, organizations, and society as a whole unleash, strengthen, create, adapt, and maintain capacity over time. In 2005, the Paris Declaration on Aid Effectiveness called for capacity development to be an explicit objective of the national development and poverty reduction strategies of partner countries. Bilateral and multilateral agencies, among others, have responded by elevating capacity development in their operations, and given attention to factors that drive success and factors that deter from it.

A special evaluation study of the Independent Evaluation Department in ADB on the effectiveness of ADB's (2008) capacity development assistance classified these positive and negative factors into four categories: (i) design and quality-at-entry factors within ADB's control, (ii) design and quality-at-entry beyond ADB's control, (iii) implementation factors within ADB's control, and (iv) implementation factors beyond ADB's control. Since the success drivers in categories (i) and (iii) are design and quality-at-entry factors as well as implementation factors within ADB's control, they can be achieved through improvement in ADB's design and implementation practices for capacity development interventions. Since the success drivers in categories (ii) and (iv) are design and quality-at-entry factors as well as implementation factors beyond ADB's control, which are contextual or external level factors by nature, they tend to act as incentives (*opportunities*) to capacity development performance. However, the negative side of these factors will tend to act as risks or constraints (*threats*) to capacity development performance. The study noted that although ADB has no direct control over these risks, some of them should be identified and mitigation mechanisms formulated during the design stage with good diagnostics. In more challenging environments, it may be necessary to be more realistic by developing a phased approach to capacity development interventions, or deferring them until some of these risks are addressed.

Presumably, the findings of the study are relevant elsewhere. Further, much remains to be done to put the preconditions for such good practices in place. This does not necessarily call for reinvention of the wheel. Development agencies can, by doing less and doing it well, do better for capacity development. Simple knowledge management tools that harvest experience for subsequent sharing and use are at hand. With regard to the technical assistance modality that donors often use, that described below shows how to invites feedback on preparation, design, and implementation; the performance of consultants; the contribution to change management, policy development, and capacity building; and constraints to implementation.

Template

The questionnaire[1] laid out below provides guidance on the preparation by executing agencies of assessments of the effectiveness of capacity development in the form of a recommended format and a description of the contents required. Naturally, flexibility in the use of the questionnaire should be exercised as it is intended to introduce approximate conformance in the more obvious components of monitoring and evaluation. The assessment, completed at the end of a technical assistance, should be submitted by the executing agency to the donor concerned, and inform both the preparation of technical assistance completion reports and the formulation of next steps.

Table. Assessing the effectiveness of assistance in capacity development: a questionnaire for executing agencies

Technical Assistance Data			
TA Title			
TA Number			
Executing Agency			
TA Amount			
Date Approved			
TA Objective			
Technical Assistance Preparation			
1. How high was the TA's objective in the Government's overall priorities at the time, as indicated, for instance in the Five-Year Development Plan at the time or later?	High	Medium	Low	Do Not Know
2. Was the TA's objective a high priority of the executing agency at that time?	Yes	No		Do Not Know
3. Who was the principal player in identifying the need for the TA?	ADB	Government	Executing Agency	Do Not Know
4. How satisfactory was the process of developing the terms of reference for the TA in terms of adequate consultation with the staff of the executing agency?	Very Satisfactory	Satisfactory	Not Satisfactory	Do Not Know
4a. *If not satisfactory:* please cite the major reasons.			
5. Was a satisfactory process for institutional strengthening (i.e.,	Yes	No		Do Not Know

---

[1]The questionnaire is adapted from ADB (1996).

	enabling the executing agency itself to build on the outputs of the TA) developed before the TA was accepted by the executing agency (e.g., starting with a diagnostic analysis)?				
6.	Before the start of the TA, did the executing agency realistically consider that by the end of the TA, it would gain the technical expertise to do the desired work itself?	Yes	No		Do Not Know
7.	Were the major constraints, both inside and outside the executing agency, which could prevent the effective completion of the TA satisfactorily addressed prior to the terms of reference being finalized?	Yes	No		Do Not Know
7a.	*If yes*: please indicate whether the constraints were	Internal		External	
7b.	*If no*: please list the major constraints not addressed. (See Annex for a sample of constraints and problems.)				
Technical Assistance Design					
8.	How satisfactory was the design of the TA to achieve its objective?	Very Satisfactory	Satisfactory	Not Satisfactory	Do Not Know
8a.	*If satisfactory*: please list strengths.	*If not satisfactory*: please list weaknesses.			
9.	How important was the TA's objective to the work of the executing agency?	Very Important	Important	Not Very Important	No Opinion
9a.	In what way were they important? • From a technical point of view • From an institutional strengthening point of view				
10.	Did the design seek to transfer skills to the executing agency by the end of the TA?	Yes	No		Do Not Know
10a.	*If yes*: how satisfactory was the approach to technology and skills transfer?[a]	Very Satisfactory	Satisfactory	Not Satisfactory	Do Not Know
10b.	*If not satisfactory*: please state in what way.				
11.	Did the senior management of the executing agency play a major role in the design of the TA?	Yes	No		Do Not Know
Technical Assistance Implementation					
12.	Were appropriate counterpart staff available to participate in the TA and benefit from it?[b]	Yes	No		Do Not Know
12a.	*If yes*: were the counterpart staff and trainees released as required without jeopardizing other high priorities of the executing agency?	Yes	No		Do Not Know

12b. When were counterpart staff made available for the TA?	From The Outset	Shortly After The Beginning	Late In The Project	Not At All
12c. Was the counterpart approach to skills transfer effective?	Yes	No		Do Not Know
12d. *If no*: please cite the major reasons.				
13. Were recommendations made under the TA to improve the functioning of the executing agency?	Yes	No		Do Not Know
13a. *If yes*: were the recommendations appropriate?	Yes	No		Do Not Know
13b. *If yes*: were the recommendations accepted?	Yes	No		Do Not Know
13c. *If yes*: how substantially were the recommendations acted upon?	Significantly	Partially		Not At All
14. Did the TA do any staff training?	Yes	No		Do Not Know
14a. *If yes*: approximately how many staff were planned to be trained and how many were actually trained?	Planned To Be Trained		Actually Trained	
14b. What level of long-term improvement in staff performance did the training produce?	Marked Improvement	Some Improvement	No Improvement	Do Not Know
15. Were the trainers	Very Competent	Competent	Not Very Competent	Do Not Know
16. Was the training	Just Long Enough	Slightly Too Short	Too Short	Do Not Know
17. At the end of the TA, how well could the counterparts and trainees, without further technical assistance, perform the tasks they were supposed to perform?	Very Satisfactory	Satisfactory	Not Satisfactory	Do Not Know
17a. *If not satisfactory*: please cite the major reasons.				
18. How satisfactorily was the TA's objective achieved?	Very Satisfactory	Satisfactory	Not Satisfactory	Do Not Know
18a. Please identify one significant and enduring outcome directly resulting from the implementation of the TA's objective.				
19. Did the senior management of the executing agency play a major role in the implementation and general guidance of the TA?	Yes	No		Do Not Know
19a. *If no*: did the lack of involvement have an adverse effect on the outcomes of the TA?	Yes	No		Do Not Know
20. Would the TA have been more effective if staff in central agencies had been more involved?	Yes	No		Do Not Know
20a. *If yes*: please explain in what way.				
21. Did women working in the executing agency benefit from the TA?	Yes	No		Do Not Know

21a.	*If yes*: please indicate approximately how many and in what way.				
22.	Please list the major problems with TA implementation. (See Annex for a sample of constraints and problems.)				
Performance of Consultants					
23.	Please rate the overall performance of the consultants.	Very Satisfactory	Satisfactory	Not Satisfactory	Do Not Know
23a.	In terms of technical competence.	Very Satisfactory	Satisfactory	Not Satisfactory	Do Not Know
23b.	In terms of training and skills transfer.	Very Satisfactory	Satisfactory	Not Satisfactory	Do Not Know
24.	How well did the consultants understand the needs of the executing agency?	Very Satisfactory	Satisfactory	Not Satisfactory	Do Not Know
25.	Please rate how well the consultants adapted their technical competencies to the needs and competencies of the executing agency.	Very Satisfactory	Satisfactory	Not Satisfactory	Do Not Know
26.	How culturally sensitive was the work of the consultants?	Very Satisfactory	Satisfactory	Not Satisfactory	Do Not Know
27.	How well did the consultants understand the professional needs of the people working in the executing agency?	Very Satisfactory	Satisfactory	Not Satisfactory	Do Not Know
28.	Did the consultants pay any special attention to the needs of the women working in the executing agency?	Yes	No		Do Not Know
29.	Did the consultants	Help The Executing Agency To Do Things	Do Things For The Agency		Do Not Know
30.	Would you employ the consultants again?	Yes	No		Do Not Know
30a.	*If no*: please explain why.				
Institutional Development					
31.	Please rate the contribution of the TA in the improvement of the following:	Major	Minor	None At All	Do Not Know
31a.	Management competencies of the executing agency (i.e., is the executing agency better managed as a result of the TA?).	Major	Minor	None At All	Do Not Know
31b.	Policy capacity of the executing agency.	Major	Minor	None At All	Do Not Know
31c.	Operating systems of the executing agency (i.e., did the TA improve budget, planning, information systems, and procedures on a sustainable basis?).	Major	Minor	None At All	Do Not Know
31d.	Organizational efficiency of the executing agency (i.e., has productivity of the executing agency increased as a direct result of the TA?).	Major	Minor	None At All	Do Not Know

31e.	Technical competencies of staff working in the executing agency.	Major	Minor	None At All	Do Not Know
31f.	Operational effectiveness of the executing agency (i.e., does the executing agency provide a better quality of service for the Government?).	Major	Minor	None At All	Do Not Know
31g.	Planning, monitoring and control of the executing agency.	Major	Minor	None At All	Do Not Know
32.	Did the TA result in the development of any performance indicators?	Yes	No		Do Not Know
32a.	*If yes*: are those performance indicators still being used?	Yes	No		Do Not Know
32b.	*If no*: can you suggest performance indicators to assess the long-term effectiveness of the TA?				
32c.	Over time, has the performance rating on the basis of these indicators	Improved	Remained The Same	Declined	Do Not Know
General					
33.	To achieve the best sustainable results for the executing agency, was the length of time for the TA	Just Right	Slightly Too Short	Far Too Short	Do Not Know
33a.	*If too short*: please explain why it was too short.				
34.	Do the majority of the counterparts still work in the executing agency?	Yes	No		Do Not Know
34a.	*If no*: do they still work in the public sector?	Yes	No		Do Not Know
34b.	*If no*: broadly, why did they leave the executing agency and the public sector?				
35.	Do the majority of trainees still work in the public sector?	Yes	No		Do Not Know
35a.	*If no*: broadly, why did they leave the executing agency and the public sector?				
36.	Have the facilities created under the TA continued to receive funding even after TA completion?	Yes	No		Do Not Know
37.	Did public service rules and procedures constrain the full effectiveness of the TA?	Yes	No		Do Not Know
37a.	*If yes*: please explain in what way.				
38.	Were there any incentives to encourage executing agency officers to participate in training provided under the TA?	Yes	No		Do Not Know
38a.	*If yes*: please describe the incentives.				
39.	How could TA implementation be improved?				
40.	Would earlier reform of central agencies and their rules and procedures have improved the effectiveness of the TA?	Yes	No		Do Not Know

40a.	*If yes*: please explain in what way.				
41.	Have the benefits of the TA been sustainable?	Yes	No		Do Not Know
41a.	*If no*: please cite the major reasons.				
42.	Please rate the performance of the ADB in TA preparation, administration, and supervision.	Very Satisfactory	Satisfactory	Not Satisfactory	Do Not Know
42a.	*If not satisfactory*: please explain in what way.				
42b.	Please rate the ADB's responsiveness and flexibility.	Very Satisfactory	Satisfactory	Not Satisfactory	Do Not Know
42c.	*If not satisfactory*: please explain in what way.				
43.	In retrospect, please rate the long-term effectiveness of the TA on the executing agency.	Successful	Partly Successful	Unsuccessful	Do Not Know

Annex: Sample of Constraints and Problems in Implementation		
	Question 7b	Question 22
1. Shortage of counterpart staff and trainees/staff had no time.		
2. Lack of managerial skills/inadequate technical know-how.		
3. Management/financial/organizational problems within the executing agency and within the Government itself.		
4. Sociopolitical/cultural/geographic and demographic factors.		
5. Unclear or absent policy/legislation/guidelines/control mechanisms.		
6. Inadequate database/inaccurate data generated/ineffective or poor management information system.		
7. Lack of incentives, support services, infrastructure, and facilities.		
8. Lack of coordination/communication/overlapping functions/disputes among concerned implementing agencies/task network.		
9. Lack of capital/funds/delay in release of Government counterpart funds.		
10. Delay in recruitment of consultants/poor performance of consultants		
11. Training		
11a. Was too difficult or too short.		
11b. Was not relevant to work/did not provide skills usable in the prevailing circumstances.		
11c. Did not interest the trainees/did not offer incentives.		

Source Author

[a]Refers to transfer of technology and skills to counterparts and to the executing agency as distinct from trainees

[b]Staff nominated to facilitate the consultants' work and sometimes assist it. Counterparts are not trainees

References

ADB (1996) Special study on assessment of the effectiveness of bank technical assistance for capacity building in Indonesia. Manila

ADB (2008) Special evaluation study on effectiveness of ADB's capacity development assistance: how to get institutions right. Manila

Proposition 118
Staff Profile Pages

In a Word Staff profile pages are dynamic, adaptive electronic directories that store information about the knowledge, skills, experience, and interests of people. They are a cornerstone of successful knowledge management and learning initiatives.

Rationale

A determinant of organizational performance is the ability to leverage expert knowledge. Much of that is tacit and therefore difficult to capture, codify, and make available through search engines and database technologies. And so, when looking we usually turn to people we know for quick, reliable information. (Chance conversations can help too.) However, in the globalized economy, personal networks are no longer sufficiently diverse to identify all the right persons, much as reliance on random connections is a thing of the past. Staff directories are no longer adequate to the task[1]: learning organizations thrive on rich and fluid linkages and need expertise location capabilities to put people in contact with one another.

---

[1]Staff directories list names, job titles, departments, and contact details. Typically, they are NOT: linked to knowledge resources, connected to sector or thematic communities, searchable, attractive, lively, or championed by managers. What is worse, their more advanced versions are often mistakenly linked to skills assessment and evaluative systems: consequently, they encourage people to overstate their skills or conversely discourage them from populating the database.

© Asian Development Bank 2017
O. Serrat, *Knowledge Solutions*, DOI 10.1007/978-981-10-0983-9_118

Definition

Staff profile pages[2] are electronic tools that locate knowledge and expertise in an organization. Their purpose is to enable conversations that facilitate the emergence of rich communities of practice (or interest) in and across sector or thematic groups. In the process, especially if they can be linked with the knowledge resources that an individual has contributed, they create context-rich knowledge assets.

Benefits

Staff profile pages are technologically simple and quite effective in helping organizations know what they know. They allow people to find the tacit knowledge they need by making it easy to find those who hold it, and can also underpin corporate initiatives for collaboration, knowledge sharing and learning, and knowledge capture and storage. Naturally, they are particularly beneficial to large organizations that have offices in different locations.

Building Dynamic Pages

Staff profile pages that connect people to generate conversations can only be voluntary and must therefore encourage personal ownership and maintenance. To build dynamic pages:

• Preserve a balance between the discipline of restrictive formats and the chaos of not having a format. This calls for a delicate mix of formal and informal content,[3] and templates that individuals can use to customize, create, and update their entries are popular. Fixed terms or options for some fields may be appropriate. Multiple versions of uploaded biodata should be allowed.

---

[2]The term is taken here to equate with "white pages," experts' directories, expertise directories, skills directories, and capabilities catalogues.

[3]Staff profile pages will help people find others but the chances that they will actually act on the information and contact a person will be greater if they feel they "know" them. Familiarity can be promoted by including some personal information, e.g., hobbies, interests, holidays, etc., and avoiding sterile passport-style photographs in people's entries.

Box: Staff Profile Page Template

Photograph:
Name:
Job Title:
Department and Division:
Contact Details:
Expertise: Fast facts (2 paragraphs) covering

- Areas of Knowledge or Expertise (selected from a pre-defined list of themes; staff should record extensive knowledge only)
- Sectors and Countries of Experience (selected from a pre-defined list of sectors; staff should record extensive experience only)

Education and Professional Qualifications:

Biography: Fast facts (2–3 paragraphs) covering

- Work Experience (employment history)
- Current Job Description
- Main Areas of Interest (memberships in communities of practice, working groups, knowledge networks, etc.)
- Languages Spoken (staff should rank their ability, e.g., "good", "fair", "slight")

Recent Work: (listed)

- Current Studies
- Previous Involvements

Publications: (listed)

- Books
- Monographs, Journal Articles
- Magazine, Newspaper, and Selected Less Formal Publications
- Selected Unpublished Items
- Selected Speeches

Biodata:

- Biodata in HTML and PDF (staff should prepare both short and long versions, preferably)

Staff Profile—Keyword Search:

Source Author

- Ensure that the design is inclusive, embedded in people processes, and connects to sector and thematic networks in the organization. By helping forge communities of interest or practice it is possible to identify champions and promote use.
- Maximize the attractiveness of the platform with multimedia that relates to the expertise advertised.
- Turn the pages into an evolving or smart system: however, powerful staff profile pages are in themselves, they still force staff to seek answers. But, staff have no means to know if someone else is investigating the same subject, thereby missing the opportunity to pool resources and avoid duplication of effort: adaptive staff profile pages that learn as they are used enhance an organization's ability to identify, create, store, share, and use knowledge.
- Add further value to the staff profile pages by linking them to the other knowledge management tools that might be available on an intranet or internet, such as good practice notes, and vice versa.

Others

Of course, any electronic directory must be marketed internally to encourage participation and senior staff should sponsor the rollout. Guidelines and training to encourage staff to use the pages and add entries are necessary too. Last, it is also necessary to track use and measure that effectively to continuously promote staff profile pages across the organization.

Proposition 119
Writing Weblogs

By Norman Lu and Olivier Serrat

In a Word A weblog, in its various forms, is a web-based application on which dated entries of commentary, descriptions of events, or other material such as graphics or video are posted. A weblog enables groups of people to discuss electronically areas of interest and to review different opinions and information surrounding a topic.

Background

Electronic communications were one of the first expressions of networked computing.[1] They were developed to enable individuals, groups, organizations, and related systems to collaborate on documents, regardless of their respective physical locations.

However, until recent times, posting content on networks was a task that only technology savvy persons could perform. It required skills in navigating directories

---

[1]Others are electronic mail, bulletin board systems, message boards, and hypertext.

© Asian Development Bank 2017

O. Serrat, *Knowledge Solutions*, DOI 10.1007/978-981-10-0983-9_119

and coding HyperText Markup Language (HTML). But, weblogs (blogs)[2] of various types are now relatively easy to set up and maintain and have become a ubiquitous feature of the Internet.[3] As a result, they are redefining collaboration and knowledge capture and storage among digital communities to great effect. Increasingly, they allow the creation of networks of practice (or communities of interest) based on the particular topic discussed.[4]

Definition

Blogs are websites. Typically, they are written, edited, and maintained by individuals acting in their own capacity, as subject-matter specialists, or on behalf of organizations. (Some are written by multiple contributors after editor approval.) They share common features with journals: they are published regularly, e.g., daily, weekly, or monthly; they have subscription mechanisms;[5] and they undergo review.[6] Elsewhere, they differ substantially too: unlike journals, blogs can evolve in a matter of seconds—authors have the means to respond to reader comments and update entries as required; while journals are typically produced by scientific or academic communities, blogs do not have clear-cut parameters; also there are no set criteria for writing blogs as they are considered a vehicle for personal expression. (Increasingly, however, they are also being used to break, shape, and spin news stories.)

---

[2]The term "weblog" was coined by Jorn Barger in 1997 to describe the process of logging the web. The short form, "blog," was coined by Peter Merholz in 1999.

[3]Many portals offer free tools for bloggers and space to host blogs.

[4]Not surprisingly, given their use for social networking, research reveals that blogs become popular through citation and affiliation.

[5]Unlike journals, they rely on Really Simple Syndication (RSS) to push new content to subscribers.

[6]Unlike journals, which are reviewed by peers or external referees, blogs do not have formal review process. But, they receive critical inputs through the feedback (comments) feature most incorporate (but can still be vetted).

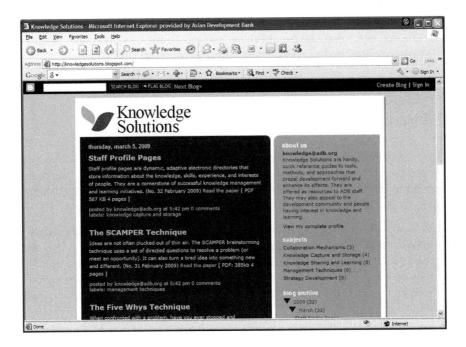

Source Author

Features

Needless to say, the format of a blog should match the purpose for which it is intended. This has implications for the features it should rest on, or advertise. Even so, the common features of blogs are:

- Text—Most blogs are primarily textual, although some focus on art, sketches, photographs, video clips, music, and podcasts.
- Tags—Posts are classified into subject areas and subtopics.
- Reverse chronological order—New posts are found at the top of the page.
- Comments—Readers can react to a post, and discuss it with the author and other interested parties.
- Links—A typical blog offers links to other blogs, web pages, and other media related to its primary topic.
- Archives—A searchable database of previous posts.
- RSS feed—RSS enables visitors to subscribe a blog and know what is new without having to visit the site itself.

- Permalinks—It is important that links not be lost. Many sites archive older entries and generate a permalink for individual entries.[7] Permalinks also allow an entire blog to be transferred to a new server without changing the link structure.

Writing a Blog

In the age of "push-button publishing" (a term used to denote the ease with which one can create, write, and maintain a blog) anybody can have a fully functional platform in 30 min or less. While there are no hard-and-fast rules, authors should observe a few basic guidelines:

- Write as you talk. Blogging is a conversation. The message should be clear and easy to understand. Use plain English to start a discussion and engage readers. They will respond if they are interested. This is an opportunity for mutual enrichment.
- Stay on topic. The majority of readers are interested in content that centers on a specific theme. If the content of all posts relate to it, authors will create a loyal following.
- Label posts. Each post must be filed under a specific category or subject. This makes it easier for readers to find related posts.
- Use keywords. If the goal of the blog is to increase visibility the title of the blog should include related keywords. The title should be no longer than half a dozen words.
- RSS. RSS will increase readership and distribution and extend a blog's reach.
- Old news is not news. Blogging each day can be a drain but it is important that the information presented be current, informative, and accurate.
- Adhere to a schedule. Blogs and RSS feeds are created on a daily basis. Realizing that blogging requires time and effort, authors should not create unrealistic expectations. Still, search engines spider pages at regular intervals and frequent update of blog content will raise profile.
- Create links. Linking to other blogs also raises profile. (These should relate to similar subject areas.) Search engines use links as a means to validate blogs, which raises their profiles in search results.[8]
- Use media whenever appropriate. Many blogs offer capabilities to add photographs and video clips. However, if several media files relate to a post,

---

[7]A permalink is a Uniform Resource Locator designed to refer to a specific information item and to remain unchanged permanently (or at least for a lengthy period of time).

[8]Aside from metadata, search engines use the number of referencing links to weigh up a site's relevance to search terms. For instance, if several websites link to a particular blog on aquaculture, search engines will accept that as a validation of the blog's content and assign to it a higher rating in search results for queries on aquaculture.

consider placing them elsewhere, for example on media sharing sites such as Flickr. Blogs that are saddled with large files rapidly become unusable.
- Look up to peers and readers. Bloggers are Internet users. Paying respect to their views will enhance the relevance and credibility of posts. Blogs are easy to set up but they can take down with speed if authors do not treat their audiences well.
- Recognize intellectual property. On the Internet, citing sources is easier, especially if these are already available online. An embedded reference that provides a hyperlink is usually sufficient for citation purposes.

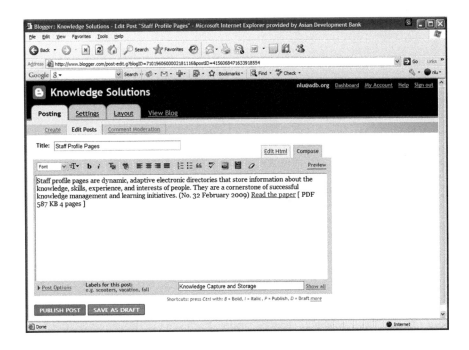

Source Author

Proposition 120
Glossary of Knowledge Management

In a Word The knowledge management discipline can be cryptic. These *Knowledge Solutions* define its most common concepts in simple terms.

Communities of Practice

Networks of people who work on similar processes or in similar disciplines and who come together to develop and share their knowledge in that field for the benefit of both themselves and their organization. Communities of practice may be created formally or informally, and members can interact online or in person.

Core Knowledge Activities

Knowledge activities that have been identified as most widely used by an organization, often also called the knowledge life cycle or the knowledge value chain. They are to identify, create, store, share, and use knowledge, often in a two-way exchange. Two important requirements have to be fulfilled to achieve improvements from these activities: (i) the activities should be aligned or integrated into business processes; and (ii) the activities should be balanced in accordance with the

O. Serrat, *Knowledge Solutions*, DOI 10.1007/978-981-10-0983-9_120

specificities of each process and organization. A knowledge management solution should not focus only on one or two activities in isolation.

Data

Discrete and objective facts, measurements, or observations that can be analyzed to generate information.

Explicit Knowledge

Knowledge that can be codified in formal, systematic language, and shared in discussion or writing. Examples include a telephone directory, an instruction manual, or a report of research findings.

Information

Data that have been categorized, analyzed, summarized, and placed in context in a form that has structure and meaning.

Information Management

The management of an organization's information resources to improve performance. Information management underpins knowledge management, as people derive knowledge from information.

Information Technology

A term that encompasses the physical elements of computing including servers, networks, and desktop computing, that enable digital information to be identified, created, stored, shared, and used.

Intellectual Capital

The value, or potential value, of an organization's intellectual assets (or knowledge products and services). Attempts to place a financial value on knowledge often define intellectual capital as the combination of human, structural, and technological capital.

Know-How

Skill or capability derived from knowledge and experience.

Knowledge

A combination of data and information, to which is added expert opinion, skills, and experience, resulting in a valuable asset that aids decision making. In organizational terms, knowledge is generally thought of as being know-how, applied information, information with judgment, or the capacity for effective action. Knowledge may be tacit, explicit, individual, and/or collective. It is intrinsically linked to people.

Knowledge Assets

The parts of an organization's intangible assets that relate specifically to knowledge such as know-how, good practices, and intellectual property. Knowledge assets (or products and services) are categorized as human (people, teams, networks, and communities), structural (the codified knowledge that can be found in business processes), and technological (the technologies that support knowledge sharing such as databases and intranets). By understanding the knowledge assets it possesses, an organization can use them to better effect and identify what gaps may exist.

Knowledge Audit

Systematic identification and analysis of an organization's knowledge needs, resources, flows, gaps, uses, and users. A knowledge audit usually includes a review of people-based knowledge, capability, and skills as well as information. It also examines critically an organization's values, vision, culture, and skills from the perspective of its knowledge needs.

Knowledge Base

An organized structure that facilitates the storage of data, information, and knowledge to be retrieved in support of a knowledge management process.

Knowledge Economy

An economy in which knowledge plays a dominant part in the creation of wealth. The four pillars of a knowledge economy framework are: (i) an economic incentive and institutional regime that provides good economic policies and institutions that permit efficient mobilization and allocation of resources and stimulate creativity and incentives for the efficient creation, dissemination, and use of existing knowledge, (ii) educated and skilled workers who can continuously upgrade and adapt their skills to efficiently create and use knowledge, (iii) an effective innovation system of firms, research centers, universities, consultants, and other organizations that can keep up with the knowledge revolution and tap into the growing stock of global knowledge and assimilate and adapt it to local needs, and (iv) a modern and adequate information infrastructure that can facilitate the effective communication, dissemination, and processing of information and knowledge.

Knowledge Flows

The ways in which knowledge moves around, and into and out of, an organization.

Knowledge Harvesting

A set of methods and techniques for making tacit knowledge more explicit so that it can be shared more easily.

Knowledge Management

The explicit and systematic management of processes enabling vital individual and collective knowledge resources to be identified, created, stored, shared, and used for benefit. Its practical expression is the fusion of information management and organizational learning.

Knowledge Management Tools

The methods and techniques that are used to support or deliver practical knowledge management. These can be either information technology systems, e.g., databases, intranets, extranets, and portals; methodologies; or human networks, e.g., communities of practice.

Knowledge Management Strategy

A detailed plan that outlines how an organization intends to implement knowledge management principles and practices to achieve organizational objectives.

Knowledge Manager

A role with operational and developmental responsibility for implementing and reinforcing knowledge management principles and practices. Often acts as central owner of taxonomies and content standards and knowledge processes. Works to promote access to information, intelligence support, expertise, and good practices.

Knowledge Worker

A staff member whose role relies on his or her ability to find, synthesize, communicate, and apply knowledge.

Learning Organization

An organization skilled at identifying, creating, storing, sharing, and using knowledge; and then modifying its behavior to reflect new knowledge.

Lessons Learned

Concise descriptions of knowledge derived from experience that can be communicated through methods and techniques such as storytelling and debriefing or summarized in databases. These lessons often reflect on what was done right, what one might do differently, and how one might improve processes to be more effective in the future.

Mentoring

A one-to-one learning relationship in which a senior staff member of an organization is assigned to support the development of a newer or more junior staff member by sharing his or her knowledge and wisdom.

Organizational Culture

The specific collection of values and norms that are shared by individuals and groups in an organization and control the way they interact with one another and with people outside the organization.

Storytelling

The use of stories as a way of sharing knowledge and helping to learn in an organization. Stories can describe complicated issues, explain events, communicate lessons, and/or bring about cultural change.

Tacit Knowledge

The personalized knowledge that people carry in their heads. Tacit knowledge is more difficult to formalize and communicate than explicit knowledge. It can be shared through discussion, storytelling, and personal interactions. There are two dimensions to tacit knowledge: (i) a technical dimension, which encompasses the kind of informal personal skills of crafts often referred to as know-how, and (ii) a cognitive dimension, which consists of beliefs, ideals, values, schemata, and mental models that are ingrained in individuals and often taken for granted.

Proposition 121
Showcasing Knowledge

In a Word Information has become ubiquitous because producing, manipulating, and disseminating it is now cheap and easy. But, perceptions of information overload have less to do with quantity than with the qualities by which knowledge is presented.

The Great Information Glut

In the twenty-first century, the digital world provides a myriad means of communication. Distance, speed, and time no longer hold the importance they once did. Each day and night feed a growing flow.[1] Are today's (and tomorrow's) technologies

---

[1]Electronic mail is a major source, as people struggle to keep up with the rate of incoming messages, including unsolicited commercial mail. Users must also contend with the growing use of e-mail attachments. (And it does take time to return to work after an e-mail interruption.) In addition, the internet provided access to billions of pages of information: search engines help find information quickly but users must often cross-check what they read before using it for decision making, which takes up more time. More recent, social media such as Facebook and Twitter has grown at an unbelievable rate. (At work, other channels of information include the telephone, of course, instant messaging, and Really Simple Syndication.).

© Asian Development Bank 2017
O. Serrat, *Knowledge Solutions*, DOI 10.1007/978-981-10-0983-9_121

leading to information overload[2] in a variety of formats? Information has become ubiquitous because producing, manipulating, and disseminating it is now cheap and easy.

But is more information necessarily good? A few responses follow. First, although we may be becoming better at capturing and storing information, there are processing limitations. (Observation suggests that "attention economy" emerges naturally from information overload.) Second, in reaction to the overabundance of views, we may avoid drawing conclusions. Third, with the increase in channels of information, people seem to have abandoned storytelling, that age-old technique that every society used to educate, entertain, and preserve culture; and to instill moral values. Fourth, without knowing the validity of content, we run the risk of misinformation. Fifth, are important discoveries, accomplishments, or initiatives being missed because vital papers are buried among others?

> *As long as the centuries continue to unfold, the number of books will grow continually, and one can predict that a time will come when it will be almost as difficult to learn anything from books as from the direct study of the whole universe. It will be almost as convenient to search for some bit of truth concealed in nature as it will be to find it hidden away in an immense multitude of bound volumes.*
>
> —Denis Diderot

Denis Diderot (1713–1784), a French philosopher, art critic, and writer, mused about the information explosion in 1775.[3] Inevitably, the difficult concept of information overload will continuously rewrite its history. But some things will never change: in the twenty-first century, much as in the years that followed the invention of the mechanical printing press,[4] exploring the critical distinction between information and knowledge remains the most important thing anyone must do.[5]

---

[2]Forty years ago, Toffler (1970) conjectured that the human brain can only absorb and process so much information. Past that theoretical limit, it becomes overloaded: thinking and reasoning become dulled; decision making becomes flawed and, in some instances impossible. He suggested that this could lead to widespread physical and mental disturbances.

[3]Denis Diderot was a prominent figure of the Enlightenment. He is best known for serving as chief editor of and contributor to the Encyclopédie, which he helped create.

[4]Johann Gutenberg (c. 1398–1468), a German goldsmith and businessman, invented a mechanical printing press with movable type in 1436 (completed by 1440). This revolutionized the production of books and fostered rapid development in the sciences, arts, and religion through the transmission of texts.

[5]Data are discrete and objective facts, measurements, or observations that can be analyzed to generate information. Information is data that have been categorized, analyzed, summarized, and placed in context in a form that has structure and meaning. Knowledge is a combination of data and information, to which is added expert opinion, skills, and experience, resulting in a valuable asset that aids decision making.

Cutting "Info-Pollution"

Modern organizations are breeding grounds for information overload. (Sometimes, even trivial matters are packaged and marketed as important.) Long messages, especially in writing, overwhelm. Communicators of all types develop armor-piercing measures to attract attention (if not make a lasting impression).

Accountability for cutting "info-pollution" starts at the individual level. We can be smart agents and there are ways to manage our individual signal-to-noise ratios, for example, by not carbon-copying electronic mail to all. But, as primary sources of information smog, organizations should explore ways to contribute too.[6] They might formulate strategies to eliminate duplication or exchange of unnecessary information. (Some argue that the issue is not information overload but filter failure. Others see information overload as organization underload.) Technological solutions that organizations might introduce promise relief. For instance, software can automatically sort and prioritize incoming electronic mail to regulate or divert the deluge. Importantly, nontechnological solutions may need to help people change the way they think and behave when communicating.

Showcasing Knowledge

Then again, given our propensity for attention economy, is it possible that perceptions of information overload have less to do with the quantity of information in production or circulation at any time than with the qualities by which knowledge is presented? Might the biggest drain on our time simply be ineffective communication? For sure, there will always be demand for good knowledge products. Yet, paradoxically, authors often do not begin to understand how to disseminate these well.

Dissemination of knowledge is just as important as its production. High-performance organizations (i) adopt a strategic approach to dissemination; (ii) know their target audiences; (iii) formulate generic, viable dissemination strategies that can be amended to suit different purposes; (iv) hit the target; and (v) monitor and evaluate their accomplishments. Good marketing is essential to this and information sheets are a key element of effective outreach. In a crowded marketplace, a concise, well-written summary and its calibrated dissemination will allow readers to easily gain information and understanding that is found more deeply in the document summarized. Knowledge that is available but not summarized might just as well be lost.

Each organization needs to come up with a solution that works within its own culture. These *Knowledge Solutions* advertise a series of one-pagers, the *Knowledge Showcase*, that the Asian Development Bank (2008–) introduced to record, store,

---

[6]The Information Overload Research Group works to understand, publicize, and solve the information overload problem.

and share cornerstone information about the success of specific tools, methods, and approaches to problems and challenges; cut "info-pollution"; and generate and share knowledge.

Box: Guidelines for Drafting Knowledge Showcases

Purpose The *Knowledge Showcase* series highlights innovative ideas from ADB technical assistance and other knowledge products. It seeks to foster discussion and research, perhaps even encourage replication. Rather than summaries of ADB (and other) reports, a *Knowledge Showcase* focuses on the crux of a discussion and refers readers to other sources, whenever possible, to deepen understanding.

Audiences Target audiences include the governments of ADB's developing member countries; its Board of Directors, Management, senior staff, staff in headquarters, resident missions, and representative offices; knowledge management centers in developing member countries, such as universities and research institutes, local stakeholders, nongovernment organizations, and other development agencies.

Writers for the *Knowledge Showcase* should consider the following questions:

- Who are my readers? What unites them?
- Why should they care about what I am writing?
- What reaction am I looking to provoke in my readers?
- How might my readers change their behavior based on what I have written?

Source Material *Knowledge Showcases* may be prepared for strategic knowledge products generated under technical assistance and nontechnical assistance–funded means, such as staff work and staff consultancies.

It is with words as with sunbeams. The more they are condensed, the deeper they burn.

—Robert Southey

Contents *Knowledge Showcases* present the "essence of the solution" to problems or challenges addressed by the technical assistance, project, or study. They emphasize tools, methods, and approaches used to resolve these. The topics may include the project design, assistance mode, consultation with stakeholders, reliance on indigenous skills, and other aspects that made the technical assistance, project, or study unique. Solutions to problems or challenges must be evident in the content.

Format The format of the outreach is readily available multimedia (online and hard copy). Soft copies will be available online on ADB's website and departmental intranets. Hard copies can be made available to target audiences as needed.

Title Contributors should select succinct, catchy titles that attract readers' attention without revealing too much of the main message. The shorter the title, the better.

Text The main text should be 500–800 words couched in two columns over two pages. Graphs, tables, or photographs should be included. A graphic should occupy not more than 20 lines of one column. The one-pager will also contain standard language about ADB, the purpose of the *Knowledge Showcase* series, the author, contact information, and links to cited materials on ADB's website.

Structure The main text should be structured as follows:

- Main points—up to four bullet points that summarize key messages;
- Introduction or background—a paragraph or two describing the basis, rationale, stakeholders, and beneficiaries of the technical assistance, project, or study;
- Problems or challenges—a discussion of the obstacles experienced by the stakeholders and/or project implementers, which may include feelings associated with these obstacles;
- Analysis—arguments and/or key findings that discuss the actions taken; the time and place markers related to the actions taken; the main turning points, outcomes, and impacts as supported by facts, figures, images, and vivid language; and
- Conclusions or recommendations—a summary of how things turned out; the endings; the learning that outcomes and impacts presented; and/or recommendations for replication of the tools, methods, and approaches used to resolve the problems or challenges.

Beginning the text with bullets on main points (matched to color-coded sentences in the main text) helps the reader navigate from principal arguments to details. The first sentence of key paragraphs is in bold (color-coded to the bullet points at the top). A note at the end of the first page refers readers to the Uniform Resource Locator (web link) of the source document, where available, and the e-mail address of the author of the *Knowledge Showcase*. Technical notes for information that cannot be accommodated on the first page can be included on the second page. Standard information about ADB is presented at the bottom of the second page.

Style Writers should (i) start and finish strong, i.e., attract and maintain the attention of readers and generate interest in the knowledge product associated with the *Knowledge Showcase*; (ii) keep sentences short; (iii) avoid unnecessary words; (iv) select active verbs; and (v) use concrete language. The use of hyperlinks, which can connect documents (or elements thereof) to others, is recommended. Hyperlinks are an essential ingredient of all hypertext systems, including the internet.

References The *Knowledge Showcase* can include bibliographic references, for which URLs should be provided.

A sentence should contain no unnecessary words, a paragraph no unnecessary sentences, for the same reason that a drawing should have no unnecessary lines and a machine no unnecessary parts.

—William Strunk

Approval In consultation with the office or department's Knowledge Management Unit (or designated equivalent), the proponent should submit the draft *Knowledge Showcase* to his/her supervisor for approval following intradepartmental and, as necessary, interdepartmental peer review with other relevant knowledge departments. Following approval, the draft and associated metadata should be submitted to the Sustainable Development and Climate Change Department (focal point Olivier Serrat) for review. The Department of External Relations will copyedit and lay out the draft and return it to the author for final approval.

Dissemination ADB's website and *ADB Today* are the primary dissemination tools. A dedicated external *Knowledge Showcases* blogsite and website also exist. Printed copies can be circulated to the targeted audiences on a selective basis.

Source Author

References

ADB (2008–) Knowledge showcases. Manila
Toffler A (1970) Future shock. Random House

Proposition 122
Harvesting Knowledge

In a Word If 80% of knowledge is unwritten and largely unspoken, we first need to elicit that before we can articulate, share, and make wider use of it. Knowledge harvesting is one way to draw out and package tacit knowledge to help others adapt, personalize, and apply it; build organizational capacity; and preserve institutional memory.

The Know-Do Gap

The so-called know-do gap is one outcome of poor knowledge translation[1] and organizational forgetting. In decreasing order of incidence, that is commonly attributed to (i) shortage of resources, e.g., skills, time, and finance, (ii) lack of buy-in at all levels within and across organizations, and (iii) information overload. Shortage of resources affects policy makers, researchers, and practitioners equally. Practitioners commonly think insufficient buy-in to be the greatest challenge.

Except when messages are complex, the three most desirable knowledge translation strategies advocated in response are stakeholder engagement, dedicated knowledge brokers, and effective communications (with commensurate recognition,

---

[1]Knowledge translation is emerging as a paradigm to learn and act to close the know-do gap. It has been characterized as the synthesis, exchange, and application of knowledge.

© Asian Development Bank 2017
O. Serrat, *Knowledge Solutions*, DOI 10.1007/978-981-10-0983-9_122

support, and funding in all three cases). Sure enough, the "wisdom of the crowd" element in the three responses emphasizes the importance of paying due attention to the "who," "what," and "how" of knowledge translation.

It is indeed vital to get the right knowledge to the right people at the right time, and help them apply it, if we are to do something better everytime we do it again.[2] However, if 80% of knowledge resides in the minds of people, both as a thing and as a flow, it is now recognized, we first need to elicit that before we can articulate, share, and make use of it.[3] (Certainly, in most fields of human endeavor, current levels of explicit knowledge only reveal a fraction of what must be known to produce results.)[4]

In the twenty-first century, intra-organizational flows of knowledge have become as important the resource itself.[5] And so, managing both stocks and flows has

---

[2]Little used databases of "lessons learned" from self and independent evaluations are all-too-familiar artifacts of failed approaches.

[3]Michael Polanyi (1891–1976), a Hungarian–British polymath whose work spanned physical chemistry, economics, and philosophy, held that all knowledge is either tacit or rooted in tacit knowledge. Using a mutually agreed language, much (but probably not all) can be communicated between individuals (even though we can never quite know what is implied by what we say because of the tacit nature of meaning.). However, paraphrasing Snowden (2002), we can probably convey more by storytelling than we can write. (This probably explains why apprenticeship was the dominant form of knowledge transfer until it succumbed to scientific management and other instruments of modernity.) From there, the following types of knowledge emerge: (i) knowledge that cannot be communicated; (ii) knowledge that can be communicated but cannot be expressed in documents; and (iii) knowledge that can be made explicit and shared through written language, often embedded in documents.

[4]Even then, the documents available on servers are not necessarily being exploited to potential. Most of us are merely more knowledgeable about their existence. Technologies remain to be developed and deployed, and much associated work conducted, before we can profit fully from the knowledge contained in such records. For instance, even simple memoranda contain valuable information such as tribal knowledge in a small group, opinions, and decision drivers. Yet, such knowledge is not codified. Where metadata has been inserted—incredibly, a rare occurrence— there are no set standards: it is therefore difficult to satisfy a particular query. Still, XML (Extensible Markup Language) topic maps, intended to convey knowledge of sets of resources, promise much. Three building blocks of topics, associations, and occurrences can be superimposed over the documents to describe them and enable that knowledge to be managed separately from what the documents describe.

[5]Until the mid-1990s, knowledge management was synonymous with process reengineering and underpinned by the computerization of business applications. Thereafter, excessive distinction between the tacit and explicit nature of knowledge encouraged useful but limiting attempts to build stocks. (The fabrication of repositories—platforms containing sets of guidance or support information—was integral to this.) The accent is now put on content, narrative, and context management to encourage the emergence of new meaning through the interactions of the formal and informal. Notions of complexity offer a wealth of insights and guidance with which to do so.

become an imperative rather than an alternative for most organizations. Knowledge harvesting is a means[6] to draw out, express, and package tacit knowledge to help others adapt, personalize, and apply it; build organizational capacity; and preserve institutional memory.[7] In addition to context and complexity, the concepts that relate to it are tacit knowledge stocks, tacit knowledge flows, and enablers and inhibitors of tacit knowledge work.[8]

> *If nature has made any one thing less susceptible than all others of exclusive property, it is the action of the thinking power called an idea, which an individual may exclusively possess as long as he keeps it to himself; but the moment it is divulged, it forces itself into the possession of every one, and the receiver cannot dispossess himself of it. Its peculiar character, too, is that no one possesses the less, because every other possesses the whole of it. He who receives an idea from me, receives instruction himself without lessening mine; as he who lights his taper at mine, receives light without darkening me.*
>
> —Thomas Jefferson

Harvesting Knowledge …

Knowledge harvesting is not a catch-all solution. It hinges on trust and that is engendered by shared context.[9] It cannot succeed in adversarial environments, where potential knowledge contributors think they will jeopardize their status or job security if they share their know-how. However, in learning organizations, it can be leveraged judiciously to codify some human expertise in such ways that others can

[6]Other techniques for knowledge capture and storage before, during, or after include peer assists, after action reviews and retrospects, storytelling, staff profile pages, and exit interviews (This said, knowledge harvesting is less about capture and decidedly much more about connection and conversation.).

[7]Institutional memory is the interrelated framework of an organization's concepts, rationales, policies, procedures, experiences, decisions, know-how, good practices, and facts that exists independently of the tenure of the individuals who contribute to it. Organizational forgetting is accidental but can also be purposeful. By accident, the dominant mode of organizational forgetting, new knowledge can fail to consolidate, and thereby dissipates while established knowledge is not maintained and degrades. But innovations can also be abandoned or suspended on purpose while established knowledge may be purged under managed unlearning. Much as knowledge, organizational forgetting is context-dependent.

[8]Tacit knowledge enablers and inhibitors include an organization's culture, policies, structures, processes, technologies, working arrangements, and activities, not forgetting individuals that can potentially influence knowledge flows and consequently impact knowledge stocks.

[9]Knowledge is the emergent, transient, active process of experiencing, often in communities. Accordingly, knowledge harvesting stands to thrive in communities of practice that encourage informal and social learning, where narrative is primordial.

make use of it, for instance during staff induction or through learning and development programs, good practices, and how-to guides.[10] Numerous benefits can flow from enabling the movement of knowledge stocks between entities: (i) the knowledge of individuals (but also groups) is made available to who might need it independently of human memory, (ii) a wide range of solutions to organizational issues is produced, (iii) the ability to manage change is increased, (iv) the likelihood of repeated mistakes is reduced, (v) the learning curve of new personnel is shortened, (vi) precious knowledge is not lost when personnel leaves, and (vii) the tangible knowledge assets of the organization can be increased to create organizational value.

With care, knowledge harvesting can be applied to any field of human activity. In organizations, ready opportunities lie in operations, products, services, strategies, and even management. In association with other techniques for knowledge capture and storage, it might one day inform organization-wide Total Quality Management systems that deliberately elicit, organize, package, and share know-how. Several intra-organizational factors drive its design: the principal are (i) tacit knowledge enablers and inhibitors, (ii) the criticality of the knowledge to the organization, (iii) the need for immediate transfer, (iv) the complexity of the knowledge topic, (v) the qualities of knowledge contributors, (vi) the characteristics of knowledge seekers, (vii) the dispersion of knowledge contributors and knowledge seekers, (viii) the type of facilitation required, and (ix) the need for external review and validation.[11]

... In Steps

Approaches to knowledge harvesting typically follow seven steps, the intricacies and resource requirements of which necessarily depend on the object and scale of the exercise:

- **Focus** It is impossible to collect and transmit everything that individuals know. An organization should determine what critical knowledge it wishes to connect more intimately with, and be clear about the benefits from that. Where does it expend the bulk of its resources? What does it need to do better or continue doing well to accomplish its objectives? What role does tacit knowledge play in

---

[10]Expert systems, that is, software that attempts to provide an answer to a problem or clarify uncertainties where normally one or more human experts would need to be consulted, were quickly proposed as tools with which to harvest knowledge. The experience has not been fully satisfactory. Expert systems require well-bounded, static domains, and do not easily incorporate learning: they are most useful in narrow problem domains.

[11]High-performance organizations harness the intellectual capital of retirees. They enable them to deploy needed skills and experience on specific projects or programs, mentor junior personnel, and participate in storytelling and learning and development activities. In the same spirit, they can also help review and validate harvested knowledge.

helping it achieve that? It is crucial to focus: only individuals who are likely to contribute critical knowledge that can be profitably transferred can justify the investment of time and talent that knowledge harvesting requires. Obviously, an inseparable issue relates to the knowledge seekers: who are they, what are their specific needs, and how will they use the information generated? The organization can then harvest mindfully, with reuse and learning, and development in sight.

- **Find** Next, the organization should locate the critical positions where knowledge harvesting stands to generate most benefits, or where knowledge loss is the greatest threat, and identify and prioritize the know-how at risk. (Logically, this also calls for an examination of existing, useful documents.) Planning at this stage relates to identification and logistics. First, it should be understood that the holders of the critical knowledge are not necessarily the most senior. Second, some effort should be devoted to circumscribing their qualities and identifying gaps and overlaps with the knowledge of others. Relevant biodata information can be collated including languages and degrees of proficiency, education and training, countries of work experience, job descriptions, roles and responsibilities, details of work experience, etc.

- **Elicit** To elicit is to generate, obtain, or provoke a response or answer. Here, this entails effectively guiding a person through the process of expressing what he or she feels or knows about a particular topic or theme, preferably using one-on-one, face-to-face interviews supported by video and audio recording.[12] (In addition, transcribing the audio into text will enable tagging, distillation, and conversion to other formats, to name a few possible enhancements that will make the information more visible to and accessible by others.) Interviews can be structured, semi-structured, or (preferably) unstructured.[13] They must be well-prepared. The lists of questions or topic and thematic guides developed should be shared in advance, aiming to provoke reflection and draw out details. Effective harvesting persuades participants to speak concretely, shun blame, temper judgment, and anchor assumptions in shared meaning. Some advocate a

---

[12]Other methods exist, including laddering and concept mapping, process modeling, commentating, observation, constrained tasks, concept sorting, and repertory grids. Like expert systems, however, these are bounded in ways that constrain learning.

[13]In structured interviews, questions are preset, ordered, and closed, and enable replication with other knowledge contributors. The questions (and responses) can be coded to collect quantitative data. In semi-structured interviews, harvesters also use preset questions but can make spontaneous investigations. Quantitative data can still be collected and some coding used. In unstructured interviews, harvesters do not use preset questions but must still have a topic and some idea of the depth of information needed. Unstructured interviews allow harvesters to be responsive to the knowledge contributor and are probably better instruments to deal with multiple simple, complicated, complex, and chaotic contexts, all of which are apt to provoke emotions. (Knowledge harvesting is not so much about what the knowledge harvester wants to hear but rather what the knowledge contributor thinks is important for others to know.) However, the harvester's control of the process can be limited, the data produced is qualitative and therefore more difficult to cross-reference, and interviews can take time. There is also potential for interviewer bias.

process under which the knowledge harvester conducts a preliminary interview with knowledge contributors, and then presents the results to representatives of the knowledge seekers. Gaps in what the latter need to know or in their understanding of what has been communicated can then inform a second interview. (Knowledge seekers have a natural, vested interest in the outcome of interviews and, presumably, a clear and practical understanding of what they want to know.) Cycling between knowledge contributors and seekers can promote a good fit between what is desired and what is imparted, propitious also to later brokering by the knowledge seekers. Of course, effective knowledge harvesters are a key to success: they must have strong communication, interpersonal, and interviewing skills coupled with high emotional intelligence.

- **Organize** The knowledge elicited must be examined for sense, recurrent patterns, as well as gaps and inconsistencies, and then arranged in coherent and systematic forms for ease of access. By and large, the materials can be ordered and structured into logical groups comprising signals that provide context, guidance that enhances action, and support information that develops understanding.

- **Package** After they have been organized, insights must be packaged into deliverable knowledge assets and made available through media that are tightly integrated with the original purpose of knowledge harvesting. Again, it is essential to consider knowledge seekers and their needs. What formats will best serve them? For effect, this stage must include individuals from other functions and disciplines, including methodology keepers, learning and development specialists, and marketing experts. The miscellaneous outcomes may include manuals, checklists, guidelines, collections of reminiscences on topics and themes,[14] films, etc.

- **Evaluate** Based on feedback from knowledge seekers, and further enrichment from continual harvesting, the relevance, efficiency, effectiveness, sustainability, and impact of outreach should be monitored and evaluated. Organizations should also consider the value of know-how over time: knowledge that is codified in static documents can quickly date.

- **Adapt** To adapt means to make fit for, or change to suit, a new purpose. As knowledge assets are shared and applied, new requirements will inevitably emerge. Organizations must facilitate, empower, and document instances of learning so that critical knowledge assets incessantly evolve.

---

[14]Stories are a good vehicle for capturing and storing tacit knowledge. An organizational story is a detailed narrative of management actions, personnel interactions, and significant intra-organizational events that are communicated informally in an organization. It provides very rich cultural context, so that the story remains in the conscious memory longer and leaves more trace. Organizational stories impart common values and rule sets and boost organizational learning.

Reference

Snowden D (2002) Complex acts of knowing: paradox and descriptive self-awareness. Journal of Knowledge Management 6(2):100–111

Further Reading

ADB (2010) ADB: reflections and beyond. Manila

Proposition 123
The Critical Incident Technique

In a Word Organizations are often challenged to identify and resolve workplace problems. The Critical Incident technique gives them a starting point and a process for advancing organizational development through learning experiences. It helps them study "what people do" in various situations.

Tales of the Unexpected

One might think there are no answers to the following questions: How fast can you think on your feet? How do you react in the face of the unexpected? How can you prepare if you cannot predict? And yet, there are.

Evidently, some behaviors contribute to the success or failure of individuals—and organizations—in specific situations. And so, responses to the unforeseen lie in identifying before the fact events or circumstances, or series of them, that are outside the range of ordinary human experiences.

© Asian Development Bank 2017
O. Serrat, *Knowledge Solutions*, DOI 10.1007/978-981-10-0983-9_123

The questions posed earlier are as old as mankind; but our ability to address them owes largely to the relatively recent work of John Flanagan.[1] These days critical incidents can be harvested to provide a rich, personal perspective of life that facilitates understanding of the issues and obstacles people face every now and then and illuminates avenues for improvement (or replication if outcomes are effective) —avenues that may not be apparent through purely quantitative methods of data collection. This should matter to high-performance organizations.

> *If history repeats itself, and the unexpected always happens, how incapable must Man be of learning from experience.*
>
> —George Bernard Shaw

Of Critical Incidents, Their Analysis ...

A critical incident[2] need not be spectacular: it suffices that it should hold significance. As such, at the individual level, it can be events or circumstances that made one stop and think, perhaps revisit one's assumptions, or impacted one's personal and professional learning. At the collective level, it can be a systemic problem from organizational maladaptation, or an issue arising from differences among stakeholders. In short, an incident may be defined as critical when the action(s) taken contributed to an effective or an ineffective outcome. At heart, all incidents pertain to matters such as culture, knowledge, competence, relationships, beliefs, emotions, communication, or treatment.

---

[1] John Flanagan (1906–1996), an American psychologist, devised aptitude tests for the selection of aircrews during the Second World War. To identify the skills service members needed, trainees and their observers were asked to recount incidents when a subject had succeeded or failed. John Flanagan's team then characterized common threads in the aptitude, proficiency, and temperament underlying success or failure. After identifying the critical requirements of a good pilot, copilot, navigator, and bombardier, he formulated tests that looked for those qualities. John Flanagan later adapted the technique to education. He questioned high-school students to discover what they liked, what they were able to do, and how much instruction and career counseling they were receiving. Follow-up research 1, 5, and 11 years after their graduation revealed that schools had frustrated some of the best students. John Flanagan then framed systems for individualized study plans. The Critical Incident technique has since then been used in management—more specifically human resource management, for example, to establish performance requirements for positions; customer service; education; health; information systems development; operation of complex devices; surgery; and industry.

[2] An incident is an occurrence or condition, contingent on or related to something else, that interrupts normal procedure.

Relaxing eligibility criteria lets stakeholders select incidents for a range of purposes (by and large categorized under planning and exploration, evaluation, and empowerment and animation). This is assuredly what Flanagan (1954) must have intended: in his seminal article, written 10 years after the Second World War, he described the Critical Incident technique as "a set of procedures for collecting direct observations of human behavior in such a way as to facilitate their potential use-fulness in solving practical problems and developing broad psychological princi-ples". To wit, the technique seeks, largely through qualitative processes of exploration and investigation, to identify actions associated with effective or acceptable performance in defined situations.[3] Hence, the analysis of a critical incident describes the setting in which an incident occurred, the behavior (including the attitudes, emotions, skills, knowledge, and resources) of the people involved, and the outcome or result of the behavior. The analysis brings cognitive, affective, and behavioral dimensions together, touching both the content of what is learned and the process of learning.

To expect the unexpected shows a thoroughly modern intellect.

—Oscar Wilde

... And the Outline of a Process to Map Them[4]

When analyzing a critical incident, reflective individuals ask: Why did I view the original situation in that way? What assumptions about it did I make? How else could I have interpreted it? What other action(s) might I have taken that could have been more helpful? What will I do if I am faced again with a similar situation?

Organizations find this much more difficult to do, the degree of complication depending on their type, e.g., entrepreneurial, machine, diversified, professional, innovative, missionary, or political. Fortunately, the Critical Incident technique structures such queries with a versatile, open-ended method of data collection for improving organizational performance that can be applied effectively in varied situ-ations. This makes it a much-awaited addition to organizational tool kits.

---

[3]Critical incidents can thereby be used to identify the learning needs of personnel.

[4]The versatility of the Critical Incident technique is demonstrated by the variety of its possible applications across the sectors, professions, and disciplines in which it has found favor. They include, for instance, observing effective or ineffective ways of doing something; identifying conducive or limiting factors; collecting behavioral descriptions of problems; and determining functional characteristics that are critical to certain aspects of a situation. Hence, the technique should be applied through flexible steps: it cannot follow a single, rigid set of rules.

(Kolb's 1984) learning cycle, which emerged later, is reminiscent of it.) Additionally, by managing the issue internally, organizations are given the opportunity to collaboratively resolve problems without all-too-frequent reliance on consultants.[5]

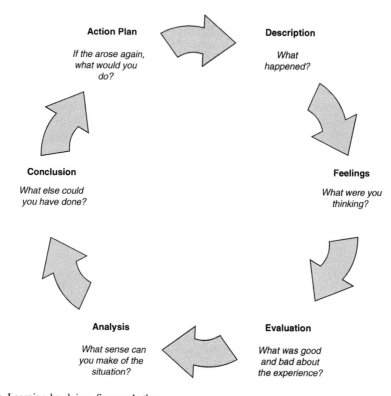

Action Plan

If the arose again, what would you do?

Description

What happened?

Conclusion

What else could you have done?

Feelings

What were you thinking?

Analysis

What sense can you make of the situation?

Evaluation

What was good and bad about the experience?

Fig. Learning by doing. *Source* Author

---

[5]The rationale for not relying too much on consulting services is well argued in Parcell and Collison (2009). Without straying from the topic of these *Knowledge Solutions*, in keeping with their focus on reflective practice, it is instructive to ponder the five key questions Geoff Parcell and Chris Collison invite an organization to pose: Can we identify the issue? Do we know our internal capability? Does anyone do this well internally? Do we know who is good at it externally? Having identified who does it well, are they available to help us, either by sharing what they know or by implementing it? Their book then marks out a workable framework for an organization to ascertain when and why it should rely on the expertise and experience of its own people. (Regrettably, the authors make no reference to the Critical Incident technique.)

Under the technique, critical incidents are generated by asking individuals, usually subject-matter experts, to describe through interviews[6] incidents they (or someone else) handled well or poorly. (Where the critical incident is a spectacular success, the Critical Incident technique complements the process of appreciative inquiry. However, organizations tend to ignore great achievements, in a technical sense; this means that the technique's value is more commonly seen to lie in helping them fix problems and eradicate causes of failure.)

To kick off a Critical Incident technique intervention, it is essential to agree on whether the issue meets established critical incident criteria and then prepare a clear, concise statement of the purpose of the intervention.[7] (Obviously, the amplitude of consequences should define criticality.) If the issue meets the criteria, can the agency secure stakeholder support and capacities for an intervention? Next, one must understand what core questions need to be addressed,[8] especially as this helps prioritize the intervention and its expected impact against other priorities. Specifically,

- What were the events or circumstances that led to the critical incident?
- What were the behaviors of the agents that made these (events or circumstances) a critical incident?
- What were the outcomes of the critical incident?
- What are the possible future outcomes if behaviors remain unchanged?
- What are the possible future outcomes if behaviors change based on lessons learned?

One should then decide on the investigative method and the population to be tapped in the context of the intervention. The subsequent steps rest on more familiar tools, methods, and approaches for project management, entailing as they do actual collection and analysis of data; the design and review of strategies and plans for problem solving; implementation and monitoring; evaluation; and requisite adjustments.[9]

---

[6]To clarify, information about critical incidents in an organization can be collected through numerous vehicles other than interviews. They include focus groups, surveys, performance records, and work diaries. In focus groups, a facilitator leads a small number of people to identify and describe in structured discussion specific examples of, say, past performance. Surveys can be administered in print or online. (The individuals completing the surveys may be assembled in a room, or may complete the survey on their own.) Examination of performance records might, for example, focus on leadership and personnel satisfaction. Another method of investigation is work diaries that can be drawn to record incidents of successes or failures as they occur during the working day or working week.

[7]This may require that guidelines for selecting, observing, interpreting, and classifying critical incidents be drawn beforehand.

[8]People are more likely to give candid accounts of their experiences if they are assured of anonymity. This is especially important if they belong to communities that share strong bonds.

[9]For a methodological guide on key steps of the Critical Incident technique, see Hettlage and Steinlin (2006).

> *If you do not expect the unexpected, you will not find it; for it is hard to be sought out, and difficult.*
>
> —Heraclitus

Advantages and Limitations

The Critical Incident technique shows promise, but is still establishing itself as a qualitative research tool. Since it focuses on behavior, it can be leveraged in numerous events or circumstances as long as the inherent bias of retrospective judgment is understood. Some advantages are the following:

- The Critical Incident technique helps identify and analyze rare events or circumstances that might not be picked up by methods of investigation dealing with everyday episodes. Its focus on critical issues can bring major benefits.
- The Critical Incident technique maximizes the positive and minimizes the negative attributes of anecdotes, turning complex experiences into rich data and information. Most people enjoy telling stories: they like to be listened to and are glad that their experiences are thought important. Especially when data and information are collected anonymously, investigators can obtain deep information about the emotions, feelings, and actions of individuals, and find new meaning. (As you would expect, the technique is therefore especially useful where hazard, security, or privacy confuse a situation.)
- Critical incidents provide dramatic demonstrations of the impact of behavior, whose cause and severity may not have been known. With real-life examples, they tell the human story behind action(s) and their outcomes and spark interest in associated reports and presentations.
- Critical incidents help gauge abstract constructs such as motivation through their demonstration in reported behavior. (These are more difficult to assess with other tools, methods, and approaches.)
- Critical incidents provide in-depth information at a much lower cost and with much greater ease than observation.

Some limitations are that the following:

- Critical incidents cast a personal perspective on organizational issues. (Reports of behavior are filtered through the lens of individual perceptions, memory, honesty, and bias: for that reason, they may not be entirely accurate.) Therefore, the Critical Incident technique may need to be combined with other methods of data collection, analysis, and interpretation before an organization can obtain a comprehensive understanding of a situation.

- Similarly, it cannot be assumed that people can and will provide incidents that are critical to success in their particular jobs—hence the need to select critical incidents carefully—nor that qualitative analysis alone is enough to clearly identify the aptitudes, proficiencies, and temperaments underlying success or failure.
- Some applications of the Critical Incident technique take time: investigation of data and information can be laborious.
- It may not be easy to convince people to share critical incidents if the investigative approach requires them to write their own stories.

References

Flanagan J (1954) The critical incident technique. Psychological Bulletin 51(4):327–358
Hettlage R, Steinlin M (2006) The critical incident technique in knowledge management-related contexts. Swiss Association for International Cooperation
Kolb D (1984) Experiential learning: experience as the source of learning and development. Prentice Hall
Parcell G, Collison C (2009) No more consultants: we know more than we think. Wiley

Proposition 124
Taxonomies for Development

In a Word Organizations spend millions of dollars on management systems without commensurate investments in the categorization needed to organize the information they rest on. Taxonomy work is strategic work: it enables efficient and interoperable retrieval and sharing of data, information, and knowledge by building needs and natural workflows in intuitive structures.

Taxis

Bible readers think that taxonomy[1] is the world's oldest profession. Whatever the case, the word is now synonymous with any hierarchical system of classification that orders domains of inquiry into groups and signifies natural relationships among these. (A taxonomic scheme is often depicted as a "tree" and individual taxonomic units as "branches" in the tree.) Almost anything can be classified according to some taxonomic scheme. Resulting catalogs provide conceptual frameworks for miscellaneous purposes including knowledge identification, creation, storage, sharing, and use, including related decision making.

---

[1]The word "taxonomy" derives from the Greek *taxis* (signifying order or arrangement, from the verb *tassein*, meaning, to classify) and *nomos* (that is, law or science).

© Asian Development Bank 2017
O. Serrat, *Knowledge Solutions*, DOI 10.1007/978-981-10-0983-9_124

> *And out of the ground the LORD God formed every beast of the field, and every fowl of the air; and brought them to Adam to see what he would call them: and whatever Adam called every living creature, that was the name thereof.*
>
> —Genesis 2:19

In their simplest expression, taxonomies are but systems for naming and organizing things. Not surprisingly, early conceptions applied to the living planet: Aristotle's animal classification, the first comprehensive attempt to compartmentalize that, divided organisms into two groups—plants and animals, the latter into blood and bloodless and then according to how they moved. Barring minor improvements, his system held well into the eighteenth century, when it was superseded by Linnaean taxonomy.[2] Librarians have coded and organized "books"—for example, in the form of blocks of wood, tablets, papyri, parchments, and papers—for a long time, too.[3]

The idea that information can be depicted as a tree is an old chestnut.[4] With the advent of the internet, however, the need to classify and categorize it has become even more urgent: beyond parent–child hierarchies, taxonomic schemes can now depict networks of relationships as well as the intensity of these.[5] Taxonomies will always matter because they help categorize information. In the digital age, however, information proliferates at a rate that far surpasses (traditional) institutional frameworks and controls. What is more, it can be classified with ease in myriad categories. (A book can only be placed in one place on a shelf.) Hence,

---

[2]Carl Linnaeus (1707–1778), a Swedish botanist, physician, and zoologist, laid the foundations for the modern scheme of nomenclature. He elaborated principles for defining genera and species of organisms and a uniform system for naming them: binomial (two-name) nomenclature—the first part is the genus, followed by the species. He is considered one of the fathers of modern ecology.

[3]Of course, almost anything—animate objects, concepts, events, inanimate objects, places, properties, and relationships—can be classified according to some taxonomic scheme. Some have explained that the human mind naturally organizes its knowledge of the world with such constructs, themselves shaped by local cultural and social systems.

[4]The proverbial tree of knowledge bore many fruits: from hierarchies of organisms to offices and departments, we have fashioned life in tree-like ways, expediently forgetting that classification systems are neither value-free nor objectively true.

[5]In Web 2.0 applications, tag (or word) clouds lead to collections of items that are associated with a particular tag. (Here, the notion of folksonomy is important: a folksonomy is a type of distributed system of categorization for ascribing and managing tags to online items such as images, videos, bookmarks, and text. Typically, users freely select tags from a chosen set of keywords, category names, or metadata. Examples of folksonomy systems are Delicious and Flickr.) Admittedly, low-quality tags are no replacement for formal systems: however, it may well be their emergent quality and openness that makes folksonomy tagging so useful; the tags that users select and attach can always be refined. There is also scope for improving tag literacy; the community would need to set rules and agree on standards for tags.

organizations must move from nurturing trees to managing windswept piles of leaves under the watchful eye of the Semantic Web.[6] (Tags mean that users regulate information. Much as search engines do, this provides clues about what content has been deemed useful.) They must now work with taxonomies[7] every day to maximize the value and capability of their business, or function unsustainably under par for lack of ability to index, retrieve, organize, and help navigate knowledge assets. Taxonomy work is strategic work.

> *Taxonomy (the science of classification) is often undervalued as a glorified form of filing—with each species in its folder, like a stamp in its prescribed place in an album; but taxonomy is a fundamental and dynamic science, dedicated to exploring the causes of relationships and similarities among organisms. Classifications are theories about the basis of natural order, not dull catalogues compiled only to avoid chaos.*
>
> —Stephen Jay Gould

It's All About Context and Sense Making

Taxonomies are not artifacts for safekeeping: they adapt and change in coevolution with the efforts of users to make sense of ambiguity, emergence, and uncertainty in their environment.[8] (Therefore, effective taxonomies are extensible over time.) To begin, however, context drives information needs, which in turn spur the identification, creation, storage, sharing, and use of content. Logically, then, the availability of (or need for) content coupled with the information-seeking behaviors of users should influence the design and upkeep of taxonomies. Next, values or terms

---

[6]Rendering taxonomy web-based is inevitable and desirable in equal measure. The Semantic Web is a group of methods and technologies that would allow machines to understand the meaning, or "semantics", of information on the internet. Beyond Web 2.0's participatory technologies and social networks, the vision of the Semantic Web, aka Web 3.0, is to link metadata in such ways that it can easily be processed by machines on a global scale. It lies where computers, not humans, generate new information.

[7]These *Knowledge Solutions* use the term "taxonomy" inclusively to refer to any classified collection of elements, be it descriptive—meaning labeled or tagged, or navigational—that is, aimed at facilitating the discovery of information through browsing. (Ontologies, which are used to reason about the properties of a domain and may be used to describe it, and mind maps, which involve considerable human interpretation, lie at the polar extremes of formality and potential for inference.)

[8]That is a function of the organizational context, organizational knowledge, inter- and intra-organizational relationships, and the external environment. Taxonomy must be structured around people (both at the individual and at the community levels), their ideas and activities, and the information systems and technologies that are available to them.

from the taxonomies must be applied to content.[9] (Logically, values or terms from the taxonomies should also be applied to staff profile pages.) And, as knowledge of information-seeking behaviors is garnered and staff profile pages expand, it becomes possible to both refine taxonomies and tag knowledge workers with metadata to identify them to other users and "push" what data, information, and knowledge will help them create situational awareness and understanding in complicated or complex situations so that they may make decisions.[10]

Table. Essential steps to taxonomy design

Assign roles and associated responsibilities
• The role of a governance board is to define strategy and appropriate types of content
• The function of a taxonomy team, comprising 6–12 members, is to ensure the value of content placement and metadata
• Content owners prepare content and apply metadata
• Content managers edit and approve content

Know your content
• Clean out obsolete content
• Strive for topical taxonomy, with attention to scope, use, complexity, and scalability
• Give every item one correct categorization
• Accept that items can be organized in multiple categories
• Minimize the number of "clicks"
• Build in flexibility and redundancy
• Understand that it takes time to tag (or re-tag) content

Before getting started, understand your
• Business context and priorities
• Knowledge workers
• Content
• Clients, audiences, and partners
• Information systems and technologies
• Limitations

Get started
• Seek inspiration from existing taxonomic schemes: much taxonomy, unitary or not, already resides on the internet
• Focus on primary, top-level concepts
• Keep the taxonomy broad, simple, shallow, and elegant

(continued)

---

[9]In most instances, one can directly apply values or terms from taxonomies through metadata tags or by adding properties to files. One can also apply metadata tags indirectly by storing values or terms separately from content but by providing a pointer to that. (Content registries, metadata registries, and library catalogs are examples of indirect application.).

[10]Key applications, among many others, would include indexing, searching, and retrieval of project and program information and profiles of staff expertise on the internet, intranets, or shared drives.

(continued)

• Decide on standards values or terms that can be applied logically and consistently across different types of items. (Link synonyms and related terms.)
• Identify a general, intuitive category for the area of work being addressed
• Define 6–12 top-level subcategories that are consistent with user expectations
• Drill 2–3 levels deep
• Repeat the process of division, based on the planned application of the taxonomy and the users concerned
• Establish and share simple rules to encourage consistent practice and provide guidance on how to use different taxonomies
• Review the draft taxonomy with users and subject matter experts
• Test for user satisfaction from information-seeking tasks using the taxonomy
• Refine and maintain the taxonomy, using it to the fullest

Source *Author*

Prologue

Drucker (1998) declared that the next information revolution would be in concepts, not technology, machinery, techniques, software, or speed. It would ask: What is the meaning of information, and what is its purpose? That would lead rapidly to redefining the tasks to be done with the help of information and, with it, to redefining the institutions that perform these tasks. For learning organizations that leverage organization, people, knowledge, and technology, including the power of taxonomies, the revolution has already begun.

Box: A Study of ADB's Knowledge Taxonomy[11]

Effective use of data, information, and knowledge is essential to the development effectiveness of the Asian Development Bank. Even so, how knowledge is identified, created, stored, and shared is as important as the use it is put to. A vital ingredient of that is a taxonomy with which to classify data, information, and knowledge in an ordered system that indicates natural relationships. In 2004, *Knowledge Management in ADB*[b] characterized the variety of knowledge products and services that ADB provides to its

---

[11]Excerpted from ADB (2010)

developing member countries and other stakeholders as (i) formal knowledge products and services, that are programmed as such and targeted at clients, audiences, and partners; and (ii) knowledge by-products derived from delivering loans or other activities.[c] To note, the framework document did not consider what data, information, and knowledge—including their flows—ADB rests on, that must be continuously enriched and facilitated to operate ADB itself as a learning organization.

> *Ancient traditions, when tested by the severe processes of modern investigation, commonly enough fade away into mere dreams: but it is singular how often the dream turns out to have been a half-waking one, presaging a reality.*
>
> —Thomas Huxley

More recent documents, expressly, *Enhancing Knowledge Management under Strategy 2020: Plan of Action for 2009–2011*[d] and the attendant Knowledge Management Results Framework are testimony to the fact that ADB feels it can manage knowledge better, ultimately to the benefit of its developing member countries. However, in spite of noteworthy recent accomplishments, a sense of dissatisfaction remains due to the drive for unremitting improvement that is inherent to any knowledge strategy. One area of concern is ADB's knowledge taxonomy, which many if not all consider unrepresentative, unwieldy, and, frankly, uninformative.[e] With rapid changes in the demand for ADB's knowledge products and services in countries such as the People's Republic of China and India but elsewhere in general, ADB must think hard about how best to classify, describe, and map its most precious resource. (ADB's core assets might be described as financing, knowledge, and convening power.) Fast-transforming information systems and technologies, including the advent of Web. 2.0 and the Semantic Web, leave it no choice.

In 2010, the Knowledge Management Center in the Regional and Sustainable Development Department in ADB brainstormed on a possible classification of knowledge. It intuited that ADB's knowledge falls into four categories that marry tacit and explicit forms:

- **Lending and Nonlending Operations Knowledge** This is largely tacit, even if official knowledge products are strictly codified and there is much potential to better learn before, during, and after implementation in more explicit ways.
- **Sector and Thematic Knowledge** This is largely tacit, but communities and networks of practice increasingly offer ways to make that know-how explicit. More and more, strategic partnerships include knowledge components too.

- **Research Knowledge** This is primarily explicit. However, staff also hold a wealth of tacit research know-how in their subject areas and research methods, as well as insights about how their work fits into the wider development context.
- **Business and Corporate Knowledge** This is primarily explicit know-how about the corporate framework, for example, operational policies, operational procedures, project administration instructions, and business processes. Much codified project-management knowledge lies in databases. Tacit "street-wise" knowledge also exists.

The study of ADB's knowledge taxonomy purports to explore, recommend, and draw implications from a classification of knowledge products and services that improves ADB's organizational efficiency from internal and external perspectives. The classification contained in *Knowledge Management in ADB* and the possible taxonomy outlined by the Knowledge Management Center will be subjected to validation. The knowledge audit methodology described in *Auditing the Lessons Architecture*[f] may serve as reference.

- **Define the Scope, Purpose, and Types of Content Formats** This entails also identifying the target audiences the taxonomy will serve, both internally and externally.[g] Sample questions to be addressed include: What objective does the proposed taxonomy hope to meet? What are the problems that staff in ADB are trying to solve and what concepts are important to them? What do they spend most of their time searching for? What are the existing sources for categorizing information? What are current, typical (or desired) information flows?[h] Are there technology constraints that might impact the development of the proposed taxonomy? What are the implications for ADB's external audiences? Accepting that knowledge is an asset while learning is a practice, what is the demand and supply for both tacit and explicit forms of knowledge, including the time dimensions of these?
- **Identify Concepts within the Proposed Taxonomy** This entails discovering where and what the needed contents are, performing a content inventory, and conducting user and subject-matter expert interviews.[i]
- **Develop a Draft Taxonomy Organized Around Major Domains** This entails establishing common rules for the format, relationships, and structure of taxonomy values or terms.
- **Review and Refine the Draft Taxonomy with Users and Subject-Matter Experts** Sample questions to be addressed include: Are the users and subject-matter experts able to validate the taxonomy? Does the structure make sense to them? What are their thought processes and expectations? Are all major concepts included in the taxonomy? Does the taxonomy go too deep in any place? Are there any gaps?[j]

Supported by a review of the literature and using best practices from other agencies as comparators, the approach to the study will focus on a series of interviews that will address the challenge from two angles:

- Using a typical decision as a starting point, tracking back to the factors that influence it to understand where ADB's knowledge products and services fit.
- Using ADB's knowledge products and services as starting points, tracking forward to understand the ways in which these are used and influence the work of ADB staff and other users of the said knowledge products and services.

Within the context of assessing the influence of knowledge on policy and practice, these methods tend to underestimate and overestimate, respectively, the state of affairs. Hence, by approaching the topic from both perspectives, it will be possible to work toward a balanced understanding based on triangulation of findings from interviewees (as well as between interviewees).

To cover the first angle, questions will draw on good practice for understanding real-world decision making, as seen in works such as those of Cynthia Kurtz and David Snowden and Gary Klein,[1] as well as a decision-making typology recently developed for a study of how the United Kingdom's Department for International Development learns from research and evaluations. Questions will be fairly open to delve into how interviewees typically approach decisions in a real-world context, in order to draw out the ways in which they use different knowledge products and services in their everyday work. The interviews will be sensitive to a number of theoretical issues in this area that should aid the analysis, for example: different phases of policy decision-making (e.g., agenda formulation, implementation, and evaluation); decision regimes (e.g., routine, incremental, fundamental, and emergent); and learning styles (e.g., activist, theorist, reflector, and pragmatist).

To cover the second angle, questions will be developed around a "theory of change" concerning how knowledge is used in ADB. This approach is suitable for understanding complex issues and involves identifying expectations about how ADB's knowledge products and services are expected to contribute to lesson learning and, eventually, better policy making; through what processes and mechanisms; and with what intermediate outcomes. Analyzing whether these processes are functioning, or whether different intermediate outcomes are occurring, will help analyze the relevance and usefulness of the current knowledge taxonomy and will provide crucial insights into how that could be improved—or how the current taxonomy might be better employed.

Where possible, the interviews will identify a few examples of ADB knowledge products and services, or particular policy processes, and delve into these in slightly more depth to provide examples in the final report. This approach will help deliver some components of a knowledge audit, viz., knowledge needs analysis and knowledge flow analysis—but not knowledge mapping nor a knowledge inventory. The knowledge inventory and mapping will need to be taken from the literature and provided by ADB. It is this inventory (and its knowledge taxonomy) that will be under review during the study.

[a]Applications are well-nigh innumerable. They include policy and strategy formulation, strategic communication, business process formulation and implementation, corporate reporting, managing for results, staff learning and development, country partnership strategy formulation, policy dialogue, lending and nonlending activities, partnership building, effective knowledge management, project administration, and monitoring and evaluation for learning and accountability.

[b]ADB (2004).

[c]ADB's classification echoes a tendency to prioritize value-generating types of knowledge, specifically, the expertise that enables an organization to achieve its goals.

[d]ADB (2009).

[e]If taxonomies classify, describe, and map knowledge domains, taxonomy work is what one must do to achieve that outcome. The list of activities includes listing, creating and modifying categories, standardizing, mapping, representing, discovering native vocabularies and categories, and negotiating common terms. From this perspective, the classification proposed in *Knowledge Management in ADB* is unsophisticated. The application of taxonomies to organizations is more than the mere cataloging or indexing of documents. This is evident from the distinction between information management—which is the collection and management of information from one or more sources and the distribution of that information to one or more audiences—and knowledge management—which comprises a range of strategies and practices to identify, create, store, share, and use knowledge to support decisions and related tasks. From this, Lambe (2007) distinguishes three kinds of taxonomies: (i) objective taxonomies, usually of physical things, e.g., biological species, books; (ii) "embedded" taxonomies of how an organization has always done things (and often taken that for granted); and (iii) negotiated taxonomies based on stakeholder agreement or social negotiation. He sees that different kinds of taxonomies can (i) structure and organize (both things and processes), (ii) establish common ground, (iii) span boundaries between groups, (iv) help in sense making, and (v) aid in the discovery of risk and opportunity.

[f]ADB (2008).

[g]A sample question to be addressed is: Can a picture of client demand be drawn, based on the inquiries sent by external "consumers" of ADB's knowledge, as expressed, for example, by hit and download trends through ADB.org?

^hSample questions to be addressed include the following: What type of knowledge is needed? Who provides it and how does it arrive? How is it improved and reused? What happens to new knowledge that is created? What hinders ADB from doing more, better, faster? How can knowledge flows (therefore) be improved?

ⁱSince staff numbers and the range of subject matters in ADB are high, the approach to the conduct of interviews will involve a mix of representative interviews and the use of an online questionnaire.

^jGaps in the suggested categories can be elicited through the online questionnaire.

^kKurtz and Snowden (2003).

^lKlein (2001).

References

ADB (2004) Knowledge management in ADB. Manila

ADB (2008) Auditing the lessons architecture. Manila

ADB (2009) Enhancing knowledge management under strategy 2020: plan of action for 2009–2011. Manila

ADB (2010) Terms of reference for a study of ADB's knowledge taxonomy. Manila

Drucker P (24 August 1998) The next information revolution. Forbes 46–58

Klein G (2001) Sources of power: how people make decisions. MIT Press

Kurtz C, Snowden D (2003) The new dynamics of strategy: sense-making in a complex and complicated world. IBM Systems Journal 42(3)

Lambe P (2007) Organizing knowledge taxonomies, knowledge, and organizational effectiveness. Chandos Publishing

Proposition 125
Critical Thinking

In a Word The quality of our lives depends on the quality of our thoughts. Critical thinking is the art of analyzing and evaluating thinking with a view to improving it. Excellence in thought can be cultivated and fertilized with creativity.

Polar Opposites on a Cartesian Circle

Blaise Pascal[1] felt that "Man is obviously made for thinking. Therein lies all his dignity and his merit; and his whole duty is to think as he ought." A contemporary of René Descartes,[2] Pascal is however best remembered for resisting rationalism, which he thought could not determine major truths: "The heart has its reasons, which reason does not know." Blaise Pascal and René Descartes are reference points for two major

---

[1]Blaise Pascal (1623–1662), a French mathematician, physicist, inventor, theologian, and man-of-letters, is deemed one of the great minds in Western intellectual history. Best known as a scientist, he dedicated the latter half of his life to religious study. He prefigured existentialism.

[2]René Descartes (1596–1650), a French mathematician and natural philosopher, helped establish the scientific method (that being a body of techniques for investigating phenomena, acquiring new knowledge, or correcting and integrating previous knowledge). His required (i) accepting as "truth" only clear, distinct ideas that could not be doubted; (ii) breaking a problem down into parts; (iii) deducing one conclusion from another; and (iv) conducting a systematic synthesis of all things.

© Asian Development Bank 2017
O. Serrat, *Knowledge Solutions*, DOI 10.1007/978-981-10-0983-9_125

attitudes to conscious representation of the world: although both saw reason as the primary source of knowledge, they disagreed profoundly over the competence of Man—the truth, as always, lies between faith and radical doubt.

> *I cannot teach anybody anything; I can only make them think.*
>
> —Socrates

The Idea of Critical Thinking ...

For sure, *pace* the propensity of intellectuals to promulgate eternal truths, or at least make a lasting impression, the idea of critical thinking neither begins nor ends with Pascal or Descartes. Socrates set the agenda nearly 2,500 years ago when the "Socratic Method" established the need to seek evidence, analyze basic concepts, scrutinize reasoning and assumptions, and trace the implications not only of what is said but of what is done as well: "Knowledge will not come from teaching but from questioning."[3] Thereafter, within the overall framework of skepticism, numerous scholars raised awareness of the potential power of reasoning and of the need for that to be systematically cultivated and cross-examined.[4]

> *Read not to contradict and confute; nor to believe and take for granted; nor to find talk and discourse; but to weigh and consider.*
>
> —Francis Bacon

Critical thinking, by its very nature, demands recognition that all questioning stems from a point of view and occurs within a frame of reference; proceeds from

---

[3]Different kinds of thinking underpin dogmatic and critical approaches. The former is, fundamentally, a matter of evaluative judgment: it is the usual way of thinking or, to be precise, not thinking; the second suspends explanatory (or value) schemes to examine what might be found in the subject of study. This is not to disparage dogmatism: for sure, it serves many basic purposes of mankind and makes life simple. However, the more prevalent change is, the greater the need for critical thinking, which enhances the process of learning.

[4]Plato, the Greek skeptics, Thomas Aquinas, John Colet, Erasmus, Niccolò Machiavelli, Thomas More, and Francis Bacon, for example, built on Socratic questioning. Thomas Hobbes was a contemporary of Blaise Pascal and René Descartes. John Locke, Pierre Bayle, Isaac Newton, Montesquieu, Voltaire, Jean-Jacques Rousseau, Adam Smith, Immanuel Kant, Auguste Comte, John Stuart Mill, Charles Darwin, Karl Marx, Herbert Spencer, Charles Sanders Peirce, Sigmund Freud, William Graham Sumner, and John Dewey, among others, made significant contributions to the history of critical thought in many domains.

some purpose—presumably, to answer a question or solve a problem; relies on concepts and ideas that rest in turn on assumptions; has an informational base that must be interpreted; and draws on basic inferences to make conclusions that have implications and consequences. To note, each dimension of reasoning is linked simultaneously with the other; problems of thinking in any of them will impact others and should be monitored.[5] Hence, effective, full-spectrum questioning[6] that connects from multiple perspectives must illuminate each element of thought so it may permeate the model.

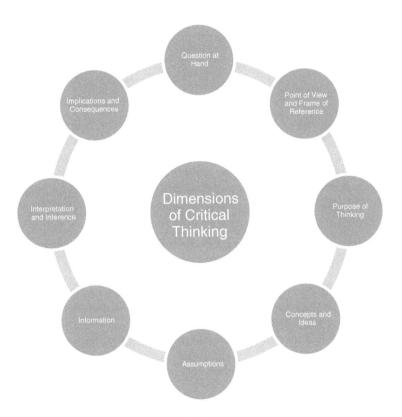

Fig. Dimensions of critical thinking. *Source* Author

---

[5]For example, interpretation and inference may change as new information becomes available. Changes in information may generate new questions, bear on the point of view and frame of reference, and require new concepts and ideas. Elsewhere, changes in assumptions may affect interpretation and inference.

[6]A question is only as good as the answer it evokes, and questions thus contribute to success or failure across different contexts. Good questions query responses to "so what?"; elucidate meaning or conceptual vocabulary; investigate rationale, assumptions, and sources; endeavor to identify causes and effects or outcomes; and deliberate on appropriate action. Much as the problems they intend to address, questions are not always simple.

... And Some Definitions

Critical thinking is discerning judgment. It is the art of analyzing and evaluating thinking with the intention of improving it. It is the purposeful, reflective, reasonable, and self-regulatory process of thinking out possible explanations for findings and outcomes and determining how compatible the explanations are with these, with attention to the evidential, conceptual, methodological, "criteriological," and contextual considerations upon which judgment is based.

> *Men become civilized, not in proportion to their willingness to believe, but in their readiness to doubt.*
>
> —H.L. Mencken

Else, it is an attitude of mind for analyzing and evaluating data and information gathered from observation, experience, reasoning, or communication with clarity, accuracy, precision, relevance, depth, breadth, logic, significance, and fairness.[7] It rests on (i) a set of cognitive, reflective skills in interpretation, analysis, evaluation, inference, explanation, and self-regulation; and (ii) the ability and disposition to use these skills to guide behavior. According to Paul and Elder (2002), a well-cultivated critical thinker

- raises vital questions and problems, formulating them clearly and precisely;
- gathers and assesses relevant information, using abstract ideas to interpret it effectively;
- thinks open-mindedly within alternative systems of thought, recognizing and assessing as need be assumptions as well as implications and consequences from interpretations and inferences;
- comes to well-reasoned conclusions and solutions, testing them against relevant criteria and standards; and
- communicates effectively with others to figure out solutions to problems.

---

[7]These are tough intellectual standards. They spring from, and call for the development of, intellectual traits (or virtues) of humility, autonomy, integrity, courage, perseverance, confidence in reasons, empathy, and fair-mindedness (Paul and Elder 2002). By its very nature, learning is a tense endeavor that requires effort. Learners must recognize and resolve conflicts between observation and action and between experience and abstraction: in so doing, they must accommodate the external environment and assimilate experience. Put simply, learning involves thinking, perceiving, feeling, and behaving, all of them foundational elements of human adaptation. Conversely, hindrances to critical thinking and learning include basic human limitations, use of language, faulty logic or perception, and psychological or sociological pitfalls.

Reconciling Pascal and Descartes

Critical thinking underpins the scientific method: that is an organized, systematic, and cognitive process used by scientists in particular (but generally anyone wishing to answer a question or solve a problem) to search for cause-and-effect relationships. Its essential steps, each subject to peer review for possible mistakes, are to

  (i)   Define the question or problem[8];
 (ii)   Conduct background research, including data and information gathering and the literature review;
(iii)   Form hypotheses ("educated guesses");
 (iv)   Test the hypotheses through experimentation;
  (v)   Analyze and interpret data and information to draw a conclusion; and
 (vi)   Verify and re-verify the conclusion (and then communicate results).[9]

> *The definition of insanity is doing the same thing over and over and expecting different results.*
>
> —Benjamin Franklin

Critical thinking, then, is analytical, judgmental, and selective. (When you are thinking critically, you are making choices.) But what of creative (or lateral) thinking? That is generative, nonjudgmental, and expansive. (Creative thinking has to do with change, especially when that involves escaping from a pattern. When you are thinking creatively, you are generating ideas that are unique and effective.) Sadly, even if critical thinking and creative thinking are both crucial for solving problems and discovering new knowledge, they are often treated separately. (Critical thinking is typically thought of as a left-brain activity and creative thinking as a right-brain activity.)[10] Yet, they both involve "thinking". (Some have spoken of critico-creative thinking to emphasize the positive, imaginative aspects of critical thinking; however, this ungainly expression has not caught on.)

Culturally, we need to discard the belief that critical thinking is sufficient: it is a quite valuable part of thinking but it is totally inadequate in the absence of the possibility systems that the generative, productive, creative, and design aspects of creative thinking throw up. For superior outcomes, since nature has equipped us

---

[8]Since definition sets the stage, the scientific method depends on characterizations of the subjects of investigation.

[9]Retesting may be done by others. (Indeed, this is frequent in the case of scientists).

[10]The right hemisphere controls the left side of the body and the left brain controls its right side. Experiments have also shown that the two hemispheres are responsible for different manners of thinking: activities that stimulate the left brain use logic; those that stimulate the right brain use feeling.

with complementary ways of processing information, whole-brain thinking is needed. To this intent, thankfully, Howard Gardner's notion of multiple intelligences refreshes and expands traditional views of human potential.[11]

References

Gardner H (2008) Five minds for the future. Harvard Business Press
Paul R, Elder L (2002) Critical thinking: tools for taking charge of your professional and personal life. Financial Times Prentice Hall

---

[11]Gardner (2008) has delineated five kinds of mental abilities that will be critical to success in a twenty-first century landscape of accelerating change. His disciplined, synthesizing, creating, respectful, and ethical minds are not presented as personality types but as ways of thinking available to anyone who invests the time and effort to cultivate them.

Proposition 126
On Second Thought

In a Word Remembering times past stimulates the mind and helps give perspective and a sense of who we are. Social reminiscence is a gain in performance without practice.

Of Family Albums

Reminiscing, be it simple, informative, or of the life review, therapeutic variety—different but overlapping types exist—is a unique human activity that plays a vital role. By recalling the past, celebrating accomplishments and—as necessary—coming to terms with disappointments, individuals can achieve a heightened sense

© Asian Development Bank 2017

O. Serrat, *Knowledge Solutions*, DOI 10.1007/978-981-10-0983-9_126

of personal identity and self-continuity, notably in their social relationships. At the confluence of voluntary memory[1] and events, circumstances, and experience, they can find meaning and coherence in life and work.[2]

Interestingly, beyond the self-positive and self-negative functions of reminiscence,[3] a wide variety of disciplines now also finds benefits, however indirect, to social functions through simple and informative reminiscing on behalf of user groups. For example, instrumental reminiscence would look to past experience to solve problems in the present; transmissive reminiscence would communicate cultural and personal knowledge of earlier times; narrative reminiscence would use storytelling, with conversational and interactional properties, to convey anecdotal evidence of (usually) positive stories and positive emotions.[4] (Obviously, information and communications technology can now be leveraged to help people

---

[1]In psychology, memory refers to the processes used to acquire, store, retain, and later retrieve information. Voluntary memory, the deliberate effort to remember things past, is the binary opposite of involuntary memory, aka flashback, about which little research has been done except in the clinical field where it is identified as a symptom of mental disorders. (No method of studying reminiscence is as yet entirely satisfactory; rather than differentiating sharply between cognitive and clinical psychology, it would help to explore common ground.) Hermann Ebbinghaus (1850–1909), a German psychologist, pioneered theories and research on both processes, which function independently of one another. (Specifically, he classified three distinct classes of memory: sensory, short term, and long term.) He was the first to describe the learning curve—the changing rate of learning after initial attempts; the forgetting curve—the decline of memory retention in time; and the spacing effect—the ability to learn items in a list when they are studied a few times over a long period rather than studied repeatedly over a short period.

[2]Even if man is by nature a social animal, we see ourselves as unique individuals. Hence, the recollection of experience through storytelling satisfies our lifelong need to also be recognized as such by others. Consider what happens when you make friends or engage in a community: you spend time sharing life histories. (To note, reminiscence by means of autobiographical material, e.g., artifacts, family scrapbooks, photographs, and video footage, has become an increasingly widespread approach to promoting older people's mental health in gerontology. Indeed, literature on reminiscence work is rarely published outside medicine, psychology, and social care.)

[3]Identity exploration, problem solving, and death preparation are served by the first. Bitterness revival, boredom reduction, and intimacy maintenance are served by the second (Webster 1993). These overlap somewhat with the (more frequently cited) six types of reminiscence identified by Wong and Watt (1991), namely, integrative, instrumental, transmissive, narrative, escapist, and obsessive. To note, some of these types are not mutually exclusive: reminiscence can serve different purposes all at once.

[4]The importance of the time-honored practice of storytelling needs no emphasis: it performs irreplaceable identity, emotional, and social functions across life spans. First, the stories we tell about ourselves, not to mention their selection and emotional content, go beyond mere recounting of defining episodes to contribute to the development and maintenance of individual identity, e.g., self-presentation and self-image. Second, stories help process stress by allowing us to reflect on what happened. Third, they enable us to connect with one another and shape the world in which we live: reminiscing as a social activity that engages both storytellers and story listeners makes them part of a collective story or history—this is important for dealing with events of cultural significance.

reminisce.) Moreover, reminiscing need not be confined to older people,[5] thereby opening possibilities for change and development in groups and organizations, notably through social reminiscence.[6]

Stimulating the Future by Reminiscing the Past

Reminiscence is the volitional or nonvolitional act or process of evoking and reconstructing memories, typically but not necessarily of one's self in the past, sometimes for the purpose of sharing.

> *You are today where your thoughts have brought you; you will be tomorrow where your thoughts take you.*
>
> —James Allen

Especially in the latter instance, instrumental, transmissive, and narrative reminiscence might be considered a gain in performance without practice. The premise is that memory in general is created and recreated in social interactions in which moments and, above all, their interpretations at multiple levels of individual and cultural analysis are highlighted, shared, contested, negotiated, enriched, and

---

[5]To state the obvious, every person reminisces: we are all constantly reading our lives. That said, derived from age group and lifestyle, there are differences in the function, frequency, and amount of reminiscing. The elderly and the young reminisce more than middle-aged people, which stands to reason since the majority of people in midlife have little time to spare from the demands of work and family. Simplifying greatly, young adults try to keep boredom at bay; older adults aim to solve problems; and people in later life are concerned with maintaining the family relationships and friendships on which they increasingly depend (Cohen and Taylor 1998). Much of this is work in progress: given that gender, health, and personality—all of them understudied thus far—may also exert powerful effects on reminiscence, Gillian Cohen and Stephanie Taylor caution that the role of aging can only be seen as one of several factors; what is more, as Paul Wong and Lisa Watt point out, "successful agers" in terms of mental and physical health and adjustment spend more time on positive, e.g., integrative and instrumental, and less on negative, e.g., obsessive, reminiscence. (And yet, for what we know, successful adjustment may be the cause, not the consequence, of these types of reminiscing.).

[6]However, the triggers of reminiscence would differ. Unlike private reminiscence, which may occur involuntarily or be evoked by contextual cues, preceding trains of thought, moods, and emotional states, or in response to current problems, social reminiscence is more likely to be elicited by prompts and questions in conversation or by shared activities and settings, with implications for spontaneity. (Knowledge harvesting in organizations comes to mind; its techniques aim to draw out and package tacit knowledge to help staff adapt, personalize, and apply it; build organizational capacity; and preserve institutional memory.) To note further, the preoccupations of age groups—as should be expected—drive the functions of both private and social reminiscence.

confirmed, leading to dynamic, fluid, and historical representations and evaluations that define selves, others, and the world. If reminiscing is both shaped by and shapes our understanding of history, and if meaning is created by how we link choices, achievements, and challenges in our lives, stories (such as those told below)[7] can help readers discover, dream, design, and deliver.

Box 1: A Young Person's Guide to Economic Policy in Developing Countries

Economic policy, like other policy, is not just shaped by events: the prevailing intellectual environment matters. Following the reconstruction of Western Europe, after the Second World War, hopes for rapid development in the "Third World" were extravagantly high: political leaders and development economists saw "underdevelopment" as a temporary and primary material problem to be solved by industrial investment. They also believed that welfare would spread automatically through the trickle-down effect and, accordingly, need not be considered. And so, economic growth was the sole aim of economic policy until the late 1960s. An important factor in this endeavor was development assistance.

Economic growth did improve the lot of the poor in many developing countries and was still favorable throughout the 1970s, despite a mounting debt burden and the first oil crisis (1973–1974), which saw the price of raw materials fall. However, skepticism in developed countries about the adequacy of economic growth as the sole measure of development mounted because of growing poverty, unemployment, and income inequality in developing countries. (The distribution of welfare depends more on the structure of the economy, which does not necessarily change as a result of economic growth.) Consequently, the growth objective was supplemented by concern for increased employment, redistribution of welfare, and the satisfaction of basic needs. These ideas, however, were not received with enthusiasm in developing countries because they threatened to divert attention from the perceived need to reduce inequalities between countries, and from the developed countries' joint responsibility in this enterprise. Notwithstanding, at the end of the decade, the second oil crisis (1979–1980) provoked a deep economic recession in developed countries and a further drop in the demand for raw materials, which had already been in structural decline as a result of technological advances (stemming from greater efficiency and recovery of used products and the emergence of substitutes). Many countries experienced swingeing adjustment programs. More people than perhaps ever before suffered falling standards of living because of forced

---

[7]The analyses, observations, and interpretations the four stories relay prefigured the third Asian agricultural survey commissioned by ADB in 1997 to explore opportunities and challenges facing rural society in Asia. The author worked to conceptualize and initiate that in 1996 and 1997 (ADB 2000–2001).

reductions in government spending, elimination of food subsidies, devaluations, and privatizations.

If economists could manage to get themselves thought of as humble, competent people on a level with dentists, that would be splendid.

—John Maynard Keynes

The 1980s were overshadowed by the debt crisis and structural adjustments but witnessed also a reassessment of the market mechanism and the role of the private sector, as well as important steps toward the liberalization of the world economy. East and Southeast Asian countries were the only developing countries able to achieve more rapid economic growth than that experienced in the 1960s, largely because they managed to stabilize their economies (via low inflation, realistic exchange rates, and control of government spending), implemented adjustment programs, and therefore attracted more development assistance. Because of the retreat of central planning in the 1980s and the apparent success of East Asian countries, there is now a desire for less government control, finance sector liberalization, more private enterprise, more autonomy for government-owned enterprises, and more reliance on competition.

Signs of a world order geared to economic performance, and of a division splitting the South and the East into front-runners, those of intermediate pace, and stragglers appeared in the 1990s. Front-runners are countries whose economies feature high levels of technical innovation in products and production processes, and in methods of organizing production, distribution, and marketing. Countries of intermediate pace have economies that will certainly not lead the field but which will have sufficient comparative advantages in certain sectors to derive a measure of benefit from their activities. The stragglers are those whose economies do not have enough inherent vitality to stay the pace. With the end of the Cold War, symbolized by the breaching of the Berlin Wall on 9 November 1989, the political relevance of the latter has waned and they are being left more to their own devices.

To complicate the situation, however, there is ample evidence to suggest that development does not work when attention is focused exclusively, or even primarily, on economies. Until the 1990s, the reigning worldview that economic growth deserves highest priority went almost entirely unchallenged. Not only was it assumed that the development of economies should be the central preoccupation of public policy, but most corporations, governments, and international institutions exerted all their efforts to this end: societal goals became synonymous with economic goals, e.g., material production and consumption, investment, productivity, growth, and profit. Those favoring societal goals now contend that culture, defined as the total way of life of a people or society, should be the focus of future developmental activity because it is concerned with the entire spectrum of human needs, as well as mankind's relationship with the environment.

Economic advance is not the same thing as human progress.

—John Clapham

Increasingly, some of the less appealing consequences of the Western economic miracle are condemned. They include pollution and destruction of the global ecosystem; heavy exploitation and exhaustion, respectively, of renewable and nonrenewable resources; and satisfaction of the materialistic demands of the few at the expense of the many. Not only is the environment more and more polluted and incapable of generating the resources required to support a rapidly expanding population, but the economic system as a whole fosters the interests of a small group of countries to the detriment of others. Thus, despite the appreciable gains that have been achieved in industry, agriculture, commerce, health, education, and technology as a result of placing economics and economies at the center of economic policy, these accomplishments have been offset by the numerous inequalities, inequities, and injustices which exist in income distribution, as well as by the colossal damage being inflicted on the environment.

Source Author. 1996. Unpublished.

Box 2: A Young Person's Guide to Environmental Economics

Until quite recently, it was thought that developing countries could postpone environmental improvements while awaiting economic growth. But better understanding of the links between the environment and economic growth now stress the need to devise approaches for dealing with the former to not derail the latter. This need has been intensified by ever-greater environmental degradation in even the wealthiest of these countries and by the realization that the well-being of developed countries can be drastically affected by activities in the developing world. The fear is that continued population expansion and economic growth, along with the energy- and materials-intensive consumption patterns that they bring, will aggravate environmental degradation in developing countries and hurt one and all.

There is a basis for such fear, even if environmental problems should not be viewed solely through the lens of the affluent. The Asia and Pacific region, for example, contains the world's fastest-growing and most dynamic economies. Their unprecedented development is expected to carry on.

However, growth rates—though high—are derived from low levels of per capita income, so that demand for goods and services will continue to swell. At the same time, continuing high population growth rates are exerting pressure and more than two-thirds of the world's 1.2 billion people living in poverty reside in that region (which now contains 12 of the world's 21 megacities). Policy and market failures are many. Institutions are weak and their absorptive capacities are uncertain.

Behold, my brothers, the spring has come. The earth has received the embraces of the sun and we shall soon see the results of that love! Every seed is awakened and so has all animal life. It is through this mysterious power that we too have our being and we therefore yield to our neighbors, even our animal neighbors, the same right as ourselves to inhabit this land. My love of our native soil is wholly mystical.

—Sitting Bull

Naturally, the relative importance that governments in that region assign to resource and environmental issues is changing. Although environmental problems were once considered limited to those resulting from urbanization and industrialization, they now include air and water pollution, land degradation, soil erosion, desertification, deforestation, loss of biological diversity, greenhouse gas emissions, acid rain, urban pollution, and toxic and hazardous wastes.

Interactions between the environment, population growth, and economies have continual, complex, and multiple feedback mechanisms that are difficult to understand. This has implications for the balance of actions to resolve problems. In brief, uncertainty centers on how physical processes will respond to human intervention, how people will react, and how institutions will echo policy initiatives. Because the environment can no longer be looked upon as an area of marginal concern that is best addressed by natural scientists, social scientists are more and more called upon to provide both analysis and prescription for environmental problems. And economists, once again, make strong claims about their ability to contribute to the debate.

From an economic perspective, nature performs three main functions. First, the environment is a resource base comprising renewable and nonrenewable resources: it provides economies with both raw materials, which are transformed into consumer products by the production process, and energy, which fuels this transformation. Ultimately, all these raw materials and energy are discharged into the environment as waste products. From this, it follows that the environment also acts as a waste sink (which refers to its regulating or stabilizing function, including its capacity to process waste products). Last, the environment also serves as an amenity base whose services, e.g., recreational facilities, flow to individuals without the intermediation of productive activity.

Based on this model, economics promises and often delivers predictions to policy makers aimed at environmental management. However, it ignores the environment's primary function as a life support system; ascribes little or no value to the three economic functions that it does recognize; allows substitution between natural and produced capital even though the former is multifunctional and sometimes irreplaceable; provides no guidelines for approaches to environmental uncertainty; and cannot answer questions regarding the equity of resource use across people and through time (intragenerational and intergenerational equity objectives). If, as generally agreed, sustainable development is economic development that endures over the long run, economics must resolve these issues before it can really help society attain the goal of sustainability.

To waste, to destroy, our natural resources, to skin and exhaust the land instead of using it so as to increase its usefulness, will result in undermining in the days of our children the very prosperity which we ought by right to hand down to them amplified and developed.

—Theodore Roosevelt

Economic frameworks and methods, however, are founded on an a priori commitment to a particular model of human nature and social behavior, namely, the traditional growth ethos that inspired and sustained developed countries for centuries, and which most developing countries still seek to emulate. This model has become counter-productive and the planet's physical endowment can no longer accommodate such an expansionist worldview. The planet is experiencing negative growth, resource domination, environmental degradation, and species elimination. It is time to examine the underlying social commitments that determine the way we use the environment and the cumulative social impacts of our individual choices.

Source Author. 1996. Unpublished.

Box 3: A Young Person's Guide to the Green Revolution

In the 1950s and the 1960s, excessive interest in industry worked against agriculture in developing countries. Even though agriculture was often their mainstay, accounted for the major share of their national product, and employed the bulk of their population, rural areas were considered to be little more than sources of labor and primary products or markets for industrial goods. Was underdevelopment not a temporary and primarily material problem to be solved by increasing investment in capital goods to promote industrial development? And so, the few government funds earmarked for agriculture went primarily to parastatal enterprises; foreign currency earnings from the export of agricultural products served to finance industrial investment in and around towns; excessive duties on exports of agricultural products made reinvestment in agriculture unattractive; and overvalued exchange rates made the import of agricultural products financially attractive. Having once exported food, many developing countries became net importers. By the mid-1960s, famine loomed in India and Pakistan.

When we try to pick out anything by itself, we find it hitched to everything else in the universe.

—John Muir

Toward the end of the 1960s, development planners thought that they had found the Holy Grail: they began to encourage cultivation of higher-yielding varieties of wheat and rice. Yet, two key components of what came to be known as the Green Revolution reflected the industrial model favored earlier. They were the priority given to increasing production and a belief in the neutrality of technology. The dominant assumption underlying the first component was that increases in production are the best way to solve the problems of hunger. The dominant assumption underlying the second was that the high-yielding varieties developed were economically, socially, and politically neutral. For these reasons, the Green Revolution embodied technocracy and its proponents never intended to modify the economic, social, and political structures that maintain inequality of incomes and access to resources.

The impact of the Green Revolution is well documented. Agriculture became increasingly productive in many developing countries, with crop yields increasing as much as threefold. These increases were attained through the use of large amounts of inorganic fertilizers and pesticides. However, they were often accompanied by environmental degradation (soil erosion, pollution by pesticides, salinization); social problems (elimination of the family farm, concentration of land, resources and production, growth of agribusiness and its domination over farm production, change in rural and/or urban migration patterns); and by excessive use of natural resources. They also led to a shrinking farm population, much larger farms and fields, and the production of a very restricted number of crops, often grown in monoculture or biculture. Moreover, the transfer-of-technology approach embodied in the Green Revolution did not work well outside irrigated areas: it was confined to about one-fifth of all farmland in the Asia and Pacific region. The remaining areas are mainly rainfed, undulating areas found in hinterlands, mountains, hills, wetlands and the semiarid, subhumid, and humid tropics. These areas have a deepening crisis, with populations rising, landholdings becoming smaller, environments degrading, and per capita food production remaining static or declining. In the Asia and Pacific region, about 1 billion people depend on such agriculture.

To a large extent, rural life was also rearranged to suit the new technology. While the Green Revolution was under way, every aspect of agriculture and rural life was reassessed. Social institutions in rural areas were assessed in terms of their presumed contribution to agricultural productivity. At best, agricultural development occurred in spite of these social institutions; at worst, agricultural development required changes in these institutions since they were commonly considered to hold back development. Also, a panoply of modern rural institutions was created to provide technological packages; these institutions were chiefly concerned with marketing, credit, the supply of agricultural inputs (seed and fertilizer), and extension advice. And the small farmers who failed to take advantage of these institutions were characterized as resistant to agricultural change.

Hopefully, it is now finally realized that one of the most important areas of difference between agriculture and the industrial model lies in the great contextual variability of agriculture (where climate, weather, soil, topography, resources, cultural, social, and institutional variations all profoundly affect its viability) as opposed to industry (where the universalism and rationalism of modern science and technology encourage blueprint approaches whereby local variation can be fitted, although not easily, to the design). It is, belatedly, accepted that the contemporary challenges of agriculture in developing countries are not technical since development projects emphasizing capital-intensive, high-input technologies (mechanization, agrochemicals, imported seeds) are in many instances proving ecologically unsound and socially inequitable by mostly benefiting a small portion of the local populations. The questions are, increasingly, socioeconomic and environmental. And so, in the new century, rural development includes two new but crucial dimensions: the ecological management of agricultural resources and the empowerment of rural communities into actors of their own development.

What is a weed? A plant whose virtues have not yet been discovered.

—Ralph Waldo Emerson

Source Author. 1996. Unpublished.

Box 4: A Young Person's Guide to Population Growth

Mortality started to decline in Europe and North America about 200 years ago. In the developing countries, enormous reductions in child mortality occurred between 1960 and 1990, mainly through the prevention of infectious diseases and through improved nutrition. The factors that have been important in the decline of mortality are income growth, improvements in medical technology, and public health programs combined with the spread of knowledge about health. However, death control without birth control has sparked a population explosion.

The problem is no longer that with every pair of hands that comes into the world there comes a hungry stomach. Rather it is that, attached to those hands are sharp elbows.

—Paul Samuelson

Two hundred years ago, there were about 1 billion people on earth. The second billion was added over the next 130 years; the third in 35 years; the fourth in 15 years; and the fifth in just 10 years. The population of the world is now close to 6.3 billion. Each year, it increases by almost 100 million. It was once forecast that the world population would settle at about 10.2 billion by 2100; this estimate has now been revised to 12 billion. More than 90% of this growth is occurring in developing countries, where death rates have been falling without commensurate declines in birth rates, and much of the population increase will be in cities, as it has been in the past.

The age structure of population in developing countries also gives ground for deep concern. This population contains more children who have yet to reproduce than it does adults (the mean proportion of the population under 16 years of age in developing countries ranges from 40–50%). With age structures so heavily skewed toward the young, the obvious conclusion would be that, when these children reach reproductive age, the population will grow rapidly. Without birth control and with low death rates for children, this will be true. Moreover, the age structure of the population provides a measure of the economic impact of the population. The dependency ratio, the ratio of people over 65 and under 15 years of age to the rest of the population, indicates the proportion of the population that contributes little to the economy and must be supported. A high dependency ratio is a fearful burden on the economy; it is now increasing in most countries.

The worldwide economic slowdown experienced since the late 1970s and population growth mean that incomes have declined in many countries. More than 1 billion people, or one-fifth of the world's population, live in poverty. Between 700 and 800 million are in Asia and about 500 million of these live in absolute poverty. It is now accepted (if not acted upon) that economic growth is by itself not enough to reduce poverty. Governments must also promote employment and offer poor people the opportunity to acquire skills, health, and the information they require to improve their lives. The proportion of people living in poverty can be reduced if there is, at least, broad-based economic growth; a firm government commitment to reduce poverty; an institutional capacity to design and follow through on appropriate policies and programs; good public sector management that minimizes unproductive expenditures; and a strengthening of essential services such as primary education and vocational training, preventive health care, family planning, nutrition, clean water, sanitation, and rural infrastructure. None of these are easy to achieve.

Population growth adds to the need for employment and livelihoods, which exerts additional direct pressure on the environment. It also increases the demand for food, drinking water, and sewage and solid waste disposal, as well as for energy-intensive products and services such as transportation. To the extent that per capita incomes rise and practices remain unchanged, such demand will be exacerbated. Excessive demand for natural resources from a rapidly increasing population leads directly to environmental degradation as economic, social, and political systems fail to keep pace with demands. In rural areas, inequitable land distribution obliges the poor live off marginal lands, causing erosion and other environmental problems. To survive, they then tend to use the resource base to derive the quickest benefit: this is an action forced on them by poverty.

Man will survive as a species for one reason: he can adapt to the destructive effects of our power-intoxicated technology and of our ungoverned population growth, to the dirt, pollution, and noise of a New York or Tokyo. And that is the tragedy. It is not man the ecological crisis threatens to destroy but the quality of human life.

—René Dubos

One way or the other, population growth will slow down because many developing countries simply cannot sustain their escalating numbers. It will happen through family planning and development, or by famine, disease, and war brought about by collapsing economies. The risk to future generations would be less and the options would be richer if population growth were to cease sooner rather than later. The longer population growth continues, the more committed all countries become to a particular set of problems: more rapid depletion of resources; greater pressures on the environment; more dependence on continued rapid technological development to solve these problems; fewer options; and perhaps continued postponement of the resolution of other problems, including those resulting from past growth. The sooner population increase slows, the more time humanity has to redress the mistakes of past growth, the more resources it has to implement solutions, and the more options it has to decide how it wants to live in the future.

Source Author. 1996. Unpublished.

References

ADB (2000–2001) A study of rural Asia. Manila
Cohen G, Taylor S (1998) Reminiscence and ageing. Ageing and Society 18(5):601–610
Webster J (1993) Construction and validation of the reminiscence functions scale. Journal of
    Gerontology 48(5):256–262
Wong P, Watt L (1991) What types of reminiscence are associated with successful aging?
    Psychology and Aging 6(2):272–279

Further Reading

ADB (2010a) ADB: reflections and beyond. Manila
ADB (2010b) Building narrative capacity at ADB. Manila
ADB (2012) Interactive stories of sustainable development. Manila

Appendix A
Cheat Sheet—A Competency-Based Approach to Managing

- **Strategy Development**

  1. Behavior and Change

     - How can a strategy focus on group relationships with appreciation of their distinctive ideas, beliefs, values, and knowledge? *Culture Theory*
     - How can it utilize stories of significant change to monitor and evaluate performance? *The Most Significant Change Technique*
     - How might it shift the focus from changes in state to changes in behaviors, relationships, actions, and activities? *Outcome Mapping*
     - Why should it embrace the complex political nature of decision-making to investigate how power and authority affect economic choices in a society? *Political Economy Analysis for Development Effectiveness*
     - How could you anchor it in understanding of livelihoods and appreciation of the factors that constrain or enhance these as well as their relationships? *The Sustainable Livelihoods Approach*

  2. Emergence and Scenario Thinking

     - How might futurizing enable diverse and potentially conflicting groups find a common ground for constructive action? *Future Search Conferencing*
     - Is your strategy the outcome of a human-centered, prototype-driven process for the exploration of new ideas? *Design Thinking*
     - Does it maintain a balance between strategizing and learning modes of thinking? *From Strategy to Practice*
     - How can one formulate strategic efforts to effect change when they are constantly challenged by emerging forces? *Past Visions of Rural Asia's Future*
     - Working backward, does it integrate alternatives that emerge from the perspective of future failure? *The Premortem Technique*
     - How emergent is it? Does it consider other scenarios? *Reading the Future*
     - How can one navigate the complexity of social change to intended results? *Theories of Change*

© Asian Development Bank 2017
O. Serrat, *Knowledge Solutions*, DOI 10.1007/978-981-10-0983-9

3. Institutional Capacity and Participation

- How does a strategy promote participation at requisite levels? *Building Institutional Capacity for Development*
- How might investments in leadership and culture, networks, and change readiness build resilience to survive and thrive in turbulent times? *On Resilient Organizations*

4. Knowledge Assets

- Is your strategy for knowledge management enriched by regular knowledge audits? *Auditing Knowledge*
- Does its practice integrate the need to systematically review, evaluate, prioritize, sequence, manage, redirect, and if necessary even cancel strategic initiatives? *Enhancing Knowledge Management Strategies*
- Is your approach to dissemination underpinned by policy, strategy, planning, and tactics? How can your knowledge products be made available in a flexible range of formats in recognition of the varied needs of consumers? *Linking Research to Practice*
- How might you realize your organization's true value? *A Primer on Intellectual Capital*

5. Marketing

- How does a strategy apply a custom blend of the four Ps and other marketing techniques to transform communications with stakeholders and improve performance? *The Future of Social Marketing*
- How might it draw on marketing principles to effect changes in the behavior of individuals or groups? *Marketing in the Public Sector*

6. Organizational Learning

- How can a strategy support and energize organization, people, knowledge, and technology for learning? *Building a Learning Organization*
- How might it integrate evaluation results to support policy, strategy, and operational changes? *Learning Lessons with Knowledge Audits*
- How could it distinguish roadblocks to make them part of the solution instead of part of the problem? *Overcoming Roadblocks to Learning*
- How would you gauge perceptions of competencies to learn for change? *Seeking Feedback on Learning for Change*

7. Partnerships and Networks of Practice

- Does your strategy leverage partnerships and recognize their drivers of success and failure? *Creating and Running Partnerships*
- How might it make out social networks and analyze the actors and the relationships between them? *Social Network Analysis*

- **Management Techniques**

  1. Branding and Value

     - Why, in knowledge-based economies, should high-performance organizations reconceptualize the notions of corporate reputation? *Managing Corporate Reputation*
     - How might we embrace branding to drive organizational behavior and behavioral change? *New-Age Branding and the Public Sector*

  2. Complexity and Lateral Thinking

     - How might we investigate deeply the cause-and-effect relationships underlying problems? *The Five Whys Technique*
     - If decision-making is a stream of inquiry, not an event, how might one move toward decision-driven organizations? *On Decision Making*
     - Do you enable different perspectives to be generated and applied in management processes? *The Reframing Matrix*
     - How might one brainstorm to resolve a problem, meet an opportunity, or turn a tired idea into something new and different? *The SCAMPER Technique*
     - By what effective questioning might you reap insights into strategy development, management techniques, collaboration mechanisms, knowledge sharing and learning, and knowledge capture and storage? *Seeding Knowledge Solutions Before, During, and After*
     - Why should management practices encompass sense and decision-making in multiple contexts? *Understanding Complexity*

  3. Linear Thinking

     - How can we manage for results with a coherent framework for strategic planning, management, and communications? *Crafting a Knowledge Management Results Framework*
     - How does one focus on time, cost, human resources, scope, quality, and actions as common parameters of project performance? *Focusing on Project Metrics*
     - Do you make use of logic models for objectives-oriented planning that structures the main elements in a project, highlighting linkages between intended inputs, planned activities, and expected results? *Output Accomplishment and the Design and Monitoring Framework*
     - What are some pernicious effects of performance measurement and how might one improve the state of the art? *The Perils of Performance Measurement*

  4. Organizational Change

     - What are business models and how might they enable organizations to capture, create, and deliver value to meet explicit or latent needs? *Business Model Innovation*

- In what ways do organizations benefit from staff engagement and how might that be driven? *Engaging Staff in the Workplace*
- How do organizations overcome resistance to change and secure as much discretionary effort as possible? *Fast and Effective Change Management*
- If transformation change rarely succeeds, what rationale is there for bottom-up approaches? *Forestalling Change Fatigue*
- How might the public sector innovate to be competent in the present and ready for the future? *Innovation in the Public Sector*
- How might knowledge management initiatives impact an organization's social reality to drive change? *Knowledge as Culture*
- If a project exists only for its duration, how might project-based organizations reconcile the project-centric nature of their work to also promote organizational learning? *Managing Knowledge in Project Environments*
- What is moral courage and why is it so often constrained in organizations? *Moral Courage in Organizations*
- How do we get the right knowledge to the right people at the right time, and help them (with incentives) to apply it in ways that strive to improve organizational performance? *Notions of Knowledge Management*
- Why do organizations need direction and control and based on what principles and practices might boards of directors better provide that? *A Primer on Corporate Governance*
- What are the components of organizational culture and what is the role of organizational learning for change? *A Primer on Organizational Culture*
- How do organizations learn? *A Primer on Organizational Learning*
- How do new knowledge management paradigms compare with the old, and what new structures and managerial attitudes do they require? *The Roots of an Emerging Discipline*
- Why should we drive management innovation? *Sparking Innovations in Management*
- Why is micromanagement mismanagement? *The Travails of Micromanagement*

5. Talent Management

- Do you manage meetings before, during, and after, with appreciation of their different kinds, to make them productive and fun? *Conducting Effective Meetings*
- Should one spend more time, integrity, and brainpower on selecting managers than on anything else? *Growing Managers, Not Bosses*
- Is your organization attractive to people who already know how valuable they are? *Leading Top Talent in the Workplace*
- Why should you empower knowledge workers to make the most of their deepest skills and perform best? *Managing Knowledge Workers*
- How does one manage by walking around to emphasize the importance of interpersonal contact, open appreciation, and recognition and build

civility and performance in the workplace? *Managing by Walking Around*

- How can one give talent strategic and holistic attention to make it happen? *A Primer on Talent Management*
- Do you have the ability, capacity, skill, or self-perceived ability to identify, assess, and manage the emotions of yourself, of others, and of groups? *Understanding and Developing Emotional Intelligence*

- **Collaboration Mechanisms**

  1. Collaborative Tools

     - How do you harness the power of collaborative minds to innovate faster, cocreate, and cut costs? *Collaborating with Wikis*
     - How does one represent, link, and arrange concepts, themes, or tasks under a central topic? *Drawing Mind Maps*
     - How can we actualize the thinking potential of teams? *Wearing Six Thinking Hats*

  2. Communities of Practice and Learning Alliances

     - How do you build a community of like-minded, interacting people to ensure more effective creation and sharing of knowledge in a domain? *Building Communities of Practice*
     - Through what collaboration mechanisms can one decentralize the span of knowledge coordination? *Enriching Knowledge Management Coordination*
     - How can communities of practice report better? *Improving Sector and Thematic Reporting*
     - Why should strategic alliances manage the partnership, not just the agreement, for collaborative advantage? *Learning in Strategic Alliances*
     - Why are hierarchy, market, and network forms of organization not mutually exclusive? *On Networked Organizations*
     - How does social neuroscience foster more comprehensive theories of the mechanisms that underlie human behavior? *A Primer on Social Neuroscience*
     - How might one design and analyze a survey of communities of practice? *Surveying Communities of Practice*

  3. Leadership

     - How should we earn, develop, and retain trust for superior results? *Building Trust in the Workplace*
     - How can one distribute leadership if it is an outcome, not an input to business processes and performance? *Distributing Leadership*
     - Why would you support people who choose to serve first, and then lead, as a way of expanding service to individuals and organizations? *Exercising Servant Leadership*

- What is the new context for leadership in the public sector? *Leading in the Workplace*

4. Social Innovations

- By what process can one unearth what works to facilitate positive change in organizations? *Appreciative Inquiry*
- How might development agencies strengthen civil society-led, ICT-driven anticorruption initiatives? *Fighting Corruption with ICT: Strengthening Civil Society's Role*
- How can you generate good ideas that meet pressing unmet needs and improve people's lives to foster smart, sustainable globalization? *Sparking Social Innovations*

5. Teamwork

- How do you enable small groups to work regularly and collectively on complicated problems, take action, and learn as individuals and as a team while doing so? *Action Learning*
- How might one bridge silos to promote effective cross-functional teams? *Bridging Organizational Silos*
- What are the roots of organizational conflict and how might complexity thinking help capitalize on its functions and dysfunctions? *Conflict in Organizations*
- Why, in organizations, is it better to understand delegation as a web of tacit governance arrangements? *Delegating in the Workplace*
- How can reciprocity intensify mutual influence in organizations? *Informal Authority in the Workplace*
- How can we organize and coordinate with effect a group whose members are not in the same location or time zone, and may not even work for the same organization? *Managing Virtual Teams*
- What configuration does your organization have and what does that tell you? What might you do to enhance the strengths and minimize the weaknesses of its structure? *On Organizational Configurations*
- What role can corporate values play in guiding behavior and decision-making? *A Primer on Corporate Values*
- How does one develop a successful team? *Working in Teams*

- **Knowledge Sharing and Learning**

  1. Creativity, Innovation, and Learning

     - What are the forms and functions of networks of practice and how do you monitor and evaluate performance? *Building Networks of Practice*
     - How do you harness, individually or in association, useful models of learning and change to reflect on the dimensions of a learning organization? *Dimensions of the Learning Organization*

- How can an organization demonstrate commitment to learning, against which provision and practice can be tested and serve as a waymark with which to guide, monitor, and evaluate progress? *Drawing Learning Charters*
- What are the stimulants and obstacles to creativity and innovation that drive or impede enterprise in organizations? *Harnessing Creativity and Innovation in the Workplace*
- How might event planners shine a light on learning outcomes? *Learning in Conferences*
- Why is intrinsic motivation necessary to drive internal knowledge markets? *On Internal Knowledge Markets*
- Why must motive, means, and opportunity be aligned to invest resources productively across the knowledge-sharing landscape? *On Knowledge Behaviors*
- How can the public sector use Web 2.0 applications to forge, build, and deepen relationships? *Social Media and the Public Sector*
- Challenged by the Internet, how might libraries worldwide reconsider the products and services they offer? *Toward a Library Renaissance*

2. Learning and Development

- How can we coach and mentor to inspire and empower employees, build commitment, increase productivity, grow talent, and promote success? *Coaching and Mentoring*
- Can better understanding of organizational environments and design principles improve e-learning interventions? *E-Learning and the Workplace*
- What are the five functions of managers toward which learning and development can be extended to improve their insights, attitudes, and skills? *Learning and Development for Management*
- How can we provide a social context to motivate learners and improve cognition and recall? *Learning in a Flash*

3. Learning Lessons

- How do you know what question to ask when? *Asking Effective Questions*
- When a critical milestone has been reached, why should we discuss successes and failures in an open and honest fashion? *Conducting After-Action Reviews and Retrospects*
- How does one step back from day-to-day activities to think about the future? *Conducting Successful Retreats*
- How can individuals come together to share their experiences, insights, and knowledge on an identified challenge or problem? *Conducting Peer Assists*
- Is failure a way to an opportunity? *Embracing Failure*
- How can one suggest that a process or methodology that has been shown to be effective in one part of an organization and might be effective in another too? *Identifying and Sharing Good Practices*

- How might evaluation serve as a foundation block in learning organizations? *Learning from Evaluation*
- How might one surface the thinking, experiments, and arguments of actors who engaged in organizational change? *Learning Histories*
- What is the potential of stories or narratives as a communication tool to value, share, and capitalize on the knowledge of individuals? *Storytelling*

4. Dissemination

- How can strategic communications explain activity and connect to purpose in more instrumental ways? *Communications for Development Outcomes*
- How can an ordinary presentation become a lively and engaging event? *Conducting Effective Seminars*
- By what interactive process does one communicate knowledge to target audiences to lead to change? *Disseminating Knowledge Products*
- How can we enrich the definition, design, and implementation of policy research? *Enriching Policy with Research*
- How do you employ the Internet to disseminate research findings? *Posting Research Online*
- How do we save time in writing, make writing far easier, and improve understanding? *Using Plain English*

- **Knowledge Capture and Storage**

1. Knowledge Harvesting

- How do you garner feedback on why employees leave, what they liked about their job, and where the organization needs improvement? *Conducting Exit Interviews*
- How can the study of critical incidents help solve practical problems? *The Critical Incident Technique*
- By what process can one analyze and evaluate thinking to improve it? *Critical Thinking*
- What, in simple terms, are the most common concepts in knowledge management? *Glossary of Knowledge Management*
- How do you draw out and package tacit knowledge to help others adapt, personalize, and apply it; build organizational capacity; and preserve institutional memory? *Harvesting Knowledge*
- Why might groups and organizations benefit from social reminiscing? *On Second Thought*
- Why should one cut information overload and showcase knowledge? *Showcasing Knowledge*
- How do we build dynamic, adaptive electronic directories that store information about the knowledge, skills, experience, and interests of people? *Staff Profile Pages*

- How might taxonomy work become strategic work? *Taxonomies for Development*

2. Reporting

   - How can one garner feedback from executing agencies on the effectiveness of assistance in capacity development? *Assessing the Effectiveness of Assistance in Capacity Development*
   - By what simple feedback mechanisms might you promote learning before, during, and after to document accomplishments as well as bottlenecks? *Monthly Progress Notes*

3. Technology Platforms

   - How can groups discuss electronically areas of interest and review different opinions and information surrounding a topic? *Writing Weblogs*

Appendix B
Cheat Sheet—Recurring Themes in Management

- **Corporate Creativity and Innovation**

  1. *Business Model Innovation*
  2. *Design Thinking*
  3. *Harnessing Creativity and Innovation in the Workplace*
  4. *Innovation in the Public Sector*
  5. *On Knowledge Behaviors*
  6. *Sparking Innovations in Management*
  7. *Sparking Social Innovations*

- **Creating Teams with an Edge**

  1. *Building Communities of Practice*
  2. *Managing Knowledge in Project Environments*
  3. *Managing Virtual Teams*
  4. *Surveying Communities of Practice*
  5. *Working in Teams*

- **How-To Guides**

  1. *Asking Effective Questions*
  2. *Coaching and Mentoring*
  3. *Collaborating with Wikis*
  4. *Conducting After-Action Reviews and Retrospects*
  5. *Conducting Effective Meetings*
  6. *Conducting Effective Seminars*
  7. *Conducting Exit Interviews*
  8. *Conducting Peer Assists*

- **Knowledge Management Techniques**

  1. *Appreciative Inquiry*
  2. *The Critical Incident Technique*
  3. *The Five Whys Technique*
  4. *The Most Significant Change Technique*

© Asian Development Bank 2017
O. Serrat, *Knowledge Solutions*, DOI 10.1007/978-981-10-0983-9

5. *The Premortem Technique*
6. *The SCAMPER Technique*
7. *Wearing Six Thinking Hats*

- **Leading in Organizations**

  1. *Distributing Leadership*
  2. *Exercising Servant Leadership*
  3. *Leading in the Workplace*
  4. *Leading Top Talent in the Workplace*

- **Making Partnerships Work**

  1. *Building Networks of Practice*
  2. *Creating and Running Partnerships*
  3. *Learning in Strategic Alliances*

- **Nurturing Knowledge Ecologies**

  1. *Harvesting Knowledge*
  2. *Knowledge as Culture*
  3. *Learning Histories*
  4. *On Internal Knowledge Markets*
  5. *On Second Thought*
  6. *Storytelling*

- **Priming the Public Sector**

  1. *Marketing in the Public Sector*
  2. *New-Age Branding and the Public Sector*
  3. *Social Media and the Public Sector*

- **Research in Development**

  1. *Enriching Policy with Research*
  2. *Linking Research to Practice*
  3. *Posting Research Online*

- **Simple Guides to Difficult Subjects**

  1. *A Primer on Corporate Governance*
  2. *A Primer on Corporate Values*
  3. *A Primer on Intellectual Capital*
  4. *A Primer on Organizational Culture*
  5. *A Primer on Organizational Learning*
  6. *A Primer on Social Neuroscience*
  7. *A Primer on Talent Management*

- **Workplaces That Work**

  1. *Building Trust in the Workplace*
  2. *Conflict in Organizations*

3. *Delegating in the Workplace*
4. *E-Learning and the Workplace*
5. *Engaging Staff in the Workplace*
6. *Informal Authority in the Workplace*
7. *On Networked Organizations*
8. *On Organizational Configurations*
9. *The Travails of Micromanagement*
10. *Understanding and Developing Emotional Intelligence*

Index